LPI LINUX
CERTIFICATION

IN A NUTSHELL

D0937557

Other Linux resources from O'Reilly

Related titles

Linux in a Nutshell
Linux Network
   Administrator's Guide
Running Linux
Linux Device Drivers
Understanding the Linux
   Kernel
Building Secure Servers
   with Linux

Learning Red Hat Linux
Linux Server Hacks
Linux Security Cookbook
Managing RAID on Linux
Linux Web Server CD
   Bookshelf
Building Embedded Linux
   Systems

**Linux Books
Resource Center**

linux.oreilly.com is a complete catalog of O'Reilly's books on Linux and Unix and related technologies, including sample chapters and code examples.

ONLamp.com is the premier site for the open source web platform: Linux, Apache, MySQL, and either Perl, Python, or PHP.

Conferences

O'Reilly brings diverse innovators together to nurture the ideas that spark revolutionary industries. We specialize in documenting the latest tools and systems, translating the innovator's knowledge into useful skills for those in the trenches. Visit *conferences.oreilly.com* for our upcoming events.

Safari Bookshelf (*safari.oreilly.com*) is the premier online reference library for programmers and IT professionals. Conduct searches across more than 1,000 books. Subscribers can zero in on answers to time-critical questions in a matter of seconds. Read the books on your Bookshelf from cover to cover or simply flip to the page you need. Try it today for free!

LPI LINUX
CERTIFICATION

IN A NUTSHELL

Second Edition

Steven Pritchard, Bruno Gomes Pessanha,
Nicolai Langfeldt, James Stanger, and Jeff Dean

O'REILLY®

Beijing • Cambridge • Farnham • Köln • Paris • Sebastopol • Taipei • Tokyo

LPI Linux Certification in a Nutshell, Second Edition
by Steven Pritchard, Bruno Gomes Pessanha, Nicolai Langfeldt, James Stanger, and Jeff Dean

Copyright © 2006 O'Reilly Media, Inc. All rights reserved.
Printed in the United States of America.

Published by O'Reilly Media, Inc., 1005 Gravenstein Highway North, Sebastopol, CA 95472.

O'Reilly books may be purchased for educational, business, or sales promotional use. Online editions are also available for most titles (*safari.oreilly.com*). For more information, contact our corporate/institutional sales department: (800) 998-9938 or *corporate@oreilly.com*.

Editor: Tim O'Reilly	**Indexer:** Ellen Troutman
Developmental Editor: Andy Oram	**Cover Designer:** Karen Montgomery
Production Editor: Philip Dangler	**Interior Designer:** David Futato
Copyeditor: Norma Emory	**Illustrators:** Robert Romano and Jessamyn Read

Printing History:

June 2001:	First Edition.
July 2006:	Second Edition.

 This book uses RepKover™, a durable and flexible lay-flat binding.

ISBN: 0-596-00528-8
[C]

Table of Contents

Part I. General Linux Exam 101

Part III. General Linux Exam 201

Part IV. General Linux Exam 202

Preface

Certification of professionals is a time-honored tradition in many fields, including medicine and law. As small computer systems and networks proliferated over the last decade, Novell and Microsoft produced extremely popular technical certification products for their respective operating system and network technologies. These two programs are often cited as having popularized a certification market for products that had previously been highly specialized and relatively rare. These programs have become so popular that a huge training and preparation industry has formed to service a constant stream of new certification candidates.

Certification programs, offered by vendors such as Sun and Hewlett-Packard, have existed in the Unix world for some time. However, since Solaris and HP-UX aren't commodity products, those programs don't draw the crowds that the PC platform does. Linux, however, is different. Linux is both a commodity operating system and is PC- based, and its popularity continues to grow at a rapid pace. As Linux deployment increases, so too does the demand for qualified and certified Linux system administrators.

A number of programs such as the Linux Professional Institute (LPI), the Red Hat Certified Engineer (RHCE) program, and CompTIA's Linux+ have formed over the last few years to service this new market. Each of these programs seek to provide objective measurements of a Linux administrator's skills, but they approach the problem in different ways.

The RHCE program requires that candidates pass multiple exam modules, including two hands-on and one written, whose goals are to certify individuals to use their brand of products. The Linux+ program requires a single exam and is focused at entry-level candidates with six months' experience. LPI's program is a job-based certification and currently consists of two levels that focus on two-year (Level 1) and four-year (Level 2) experienced candidates.

The Linux Professional Institute

The Linux Professional Institute (*http://www.lpi.org*) is a nonprofit organization formed with the single goal of providing a standard for vendor-neutral certification. This goal is being achieved by certifying Linux administrators through a modified open source development process. LPI seeks input from the public for its exam Objectives and questions, and anyone is welcome to participate. It has both paid and volunteer staff and receives funding from some major names in the computer industry. The result is a vendor-neutral, publicly developed program that is offered at a reasonable price.

LPI currently organizes its Linux Professional Institute Certification (LPIC) series in two levels: LPIC Levels 1 and 2. Each level consists of two exams that are priced at about U.S. $100 each (prices vary by continent). This book covers the LPIC Level 1 Exams 101 and 102 in Parts I and II, while LPIC Level 2 Exams, 201 and 202 are covered in Parts III and IV.

LPI is in the process of building a third level of exams, which will focus on specialty fields. It is also working with other organizations to start building certification modules based on the LPI standard.

Level 1 is aimed at junior to midlevel Linux administrators with about two years of practical system administration experience. The Level 1 candidate should be comfortable with Linux at the command line as well as capable of performing simple tasks, including system installation and troubleshooting. Level 1 certification is required prior to obtaining Level 2 certification status.

Level 2 is for senior Linux system administrators and team leaders. A Level 2 administrator is likely to have four or more years of practical administration experience. Beyond the ability to work effectively with native tools on standard Linux distributions, Level 2 covers customizing all aspects of your Linux systems, from the kernel to its filesystems, as well as implementing a number of network applications for Linux servers. At a glance, Level 2 Objectives may appear to overlap several areas of content with Level 1; however, the depth and expertise level required is much higher. Often, a Level 2 candidate is expected to be the individual that a Level 1 candidate would refer to for higher-level projects or problems within a production environment.

Level 2 certification will be required prior to obtaining the future Level 3 certification status.

All of LPI's exams are based on a published set of technical Objectives. These technical Objectives are posted on LPI's web site and for your convenience printed at the beginning of each chapter within this book. Each Objective set forth by LPI is assigned a numeric weight, which acts as an indicator of the importance of the Objective. Weights run between 1 and 8, with higher numbers indicating more importance. An Objective carrying a weight of 1 can be considered relatively unimportant and isn't likely to be covered in much depth on the exam. Objectives with larger weights are sure to be covered on the exam, so you should study these closely. The weights of the Objectives are provided at the beginning of each chapter.

Audience for This Book

The primary audience for this book is, of course, candidates seeking the LPIC certification. These may range from administrators of other operating systems looking for a Linux certification to complement an MSCE certification to Unix administrators wary of a growing pool of Linux-certified job applicants. In any case, this book will help you with the specific information you require to be successful with both the Level 1 and Level 2 Exams. Don't be fooled, however, as book study will not be enough to pass your exams. Remember, practice makes perfect!

Due to the breadth of knowledge required by the LPI Objectives and the book's one-to-one coverage, it also makes an excellent reference for skills and methods required for the day-to-day use of Linux. If you have a basic working understanding of Linux administration, the material in this book will help fill gaps in your knowledge while at the same time preparing you for the LPI Exams, should you choose to take them.

This book should also prove to be a valuable introduction for new Linux users and administrators looking for a broad, detailed introduction to Linux. Part of the LPI exam-creation process includes a survey of Linux professionals in the field. The survey results drive much of the content found on the exams. Therefore, unlike general-purpose introductory Linux books, all of the information in this book applies directly to running Linux in the real world.

Organization

This book is designed to exactly follow the Topics and Objectives established by LPI for Levels 1 and 2. That means that the presentation doesn't look like any other Linux book you've read. Instead, you can directly track the LPI Objectives and easily measure your progress as you prepare.

The book is presented in four parts. Part I covers Exam 101 and Part II covers Exam 102. New for the second edition, we have added Parts III and IV to cover Exams 201 and 202 for LPI's Level 2 Exams. Each part contains chapters dedicated to the LPI Topics, and each of those sections contains information on all of the Objectives set forth for the Topic. In addition, each part contains a practice exam (with answers), review questions and exercises, and a handy highlighter's index that can help you review important details.

Book Chapters

Each part of this book contains some combination of the following materials:

Exam overview
> Here you find an introduction to the exam along with details about the format of the questions.

Study guide
> This chapter offers a few tips to prepare for the LPI Exams and introduces the Objectives contained in the Topic chapters that follow.

Topic chapters

A separate chapter covers each of the Topic areas on the exam. These chapters provide background information and in-depth coverage for each Objective, with On the Exam tips dispersed throughout.

Review questions and exercises

This chapter reinforces important study areas with review questions. The purpose of this section is to provide you with a series of exercises that can be used on a running Linux system to give you valuable hands-on experience before you take the exams.

Practice test

The practice test is designed to be similar in format and content to the actual LPI Exams. You should be able to attain at least an 80% score on the sample test before attempting the live exam.

Highlighter's index

This unique chapter contains highlights and important facts culled from the Topic chapters. You can use this as review and reference material prior to taking the actual exams. This chapter was omitted from parts II and IV due to the variety and complexity of topics disscussed in those sections.

There is also a glossary at the back of the book, which you can use to help familiarize yourself with different Linux-related terms.

Conventions Used in This Book

This book follows certain typographical conventions:

Italic

Italic is used to indicate URLs, filenames, directories, commands, options, system components (such as usernames), and to highlight comments in examples.

`Constant Width`

Used to show the contents of files or the output from commands.

`Constant Width Bold`

Used in examples and tables to show commands or other text that should be typed literally by the user.

`Constant Width Italic`

Used to show arguments and variables that should be replaced with user-supplied values.

#, $

Used in some examples as the root shell prompt (#) and as the user prompt ($) under the Bourne or Bash shell.

> ## On the Exam
>
> Provides information about areas you should focus on when studying for the exam.

 Indicates a tip, suggestion, or general note.

 Indicates a warning or caution.

A final word about syntax: in many cases, the space between an option and its argument can be omitted. In other cases, the spacing (or lack of spacing) must be followed strictly. For example, -wn (no intervening space) might be interpreted differently from -w n. It's important to notice the spacing used in option syntax.

Using Code Examples

This book is here to help you get your job done. In general, you may use the code in this book in your programs and documentation. You do not need to contact us for permission unless you're reproducing a significant portion of the code. For example, writing a program that uses several chunks of code from this book does not require permission. Selling or distributing a CD-ROM of examples from O'Reilly books *does* require permission. Answering a question by citing this book and quoting example code does not require permission. Incorporating a significant amount of example code from this book into your product's documentation *does* require permission.

We appreciate, but do not require, attribution. An attribution usually includes the title, author, publisher, and ISBN. For example: "*LPI Linux Certification in a Nutshell* by Steven Pritchard et al. Copyright 2006 O'Reilly Media, Inc., 0-596-00528-8."

If you feel your use of code examples falls outside fair use or the permission given above, feel free to contact us at *permissions@oreilly.com*.

Safari Enabled

 When you see a Safari® Enabled icon on the cover of your favorite technology book, that means the book is available online through the O'Reilly Network Safari Bookshelf.

Safari offers a solution that's better than e-books. It's a virtual library that lets you easily search thousands of top tech books, cut and paste code samples, download chapters, and find quick answers when you need the most accurate, current information. Try it free at *http://safari.oreilly.com.*

How to Contact Us

We have tested and verified the information in this book to the best of our ability, but you may find that features have changed (or even that we have made mistakes!). As a reader of this book and as an LPI examinee, you can help us to improve future editions. Please let us know about any errors you find, as well as your suggestions for future editions, by writing to:

O'Reilly Media, Inc.
1005 Gravenstein Highway North
Sebastopol, CA 95472
800-998-9938 (in the U.S. or Canada)
707-829-0515 (international/local)
707-829-0104 (fax)

There is a web page for this book where you can find errata, examples, and any additional information. You can access this page at:

http://www.oreilly.com/catalog/lpicertnut2

To comment or ask technical questions about this book, email:

bookquestions@oreilly.com

For more information about our books, conferences, Resource Centers, and the O'Reilly Network, see our web site:

http://www.oreilly.com

If you have taken one or all of the LPIC Exams after preparing with this book and find that parts of this book could better address your exam experience, we'd like to hear about it. Of course, you are under obligation to LPI not to disclose specific exam details, but comments regarding the coverage of the LPI Objectives, level of detail, and relevance to the exam will be most helpful. We take your comments seriously and will do whatever we can to make this book as useful as it can be.

Acknowledgments

The size and complexity of the LPI tests required the collaboration of numerous authors and reviewers to get this edition done. Material was contributed by Bjørn Ruberg (Sendmail, DNS, networking, printing), Adam Haeder (file and service sharing, web services), and Faber Fedor (troubleshooting).

For the second edition, we thank reviewers Keith Burgess, Donald L. Corbet, Chander Kant, and Rick Rezinas.

Bruno dedicates his work to his grandfather, Oswaldo Cabral Pessanha, in memorium.

General Linux Exam 101

Part I covers the Topics and Objectives for the LPI's General Linux Certification for Exam 101 and includes the following sections:

Chapter 1, *LPI Exams*

Chapter 2, *Exam 101 Study Guide*

Chapter 3, *Hardware and Architecture (Topic 1.101)*

Chapter 4, *Linux Installation and Package Management (Topic 1. 102)*

Chapter 5, *GNU and Unix Commands (Topic 1.103)*

Chapter 6, *Devices, Linux Filesystems, and the Filesystem Hierarchy Standard (Topic 1.104)*

Chapter 7, *The X Window System (Topic 1.1.10)*

Chapter 8, *Exam 101 Review Questions and Exercises*

Chapter 9, *Exam 101 Practice Test*

Chapter 10, *Exam 101 Highlighter's Index*

LPI Exams

LPI offers its exams through Pearson VUE (*http://www.vue.com*), Thomson Prometric (*http://www.prometric.com*), and at on-site locations at special Linux events, such as tradeshows. Before registering for any of these testing methods, you need to obtain an LPI ID number by registering directly with LPI. To obtain your LPI ID, visit *http://www.lpi.org/en/register.html*. Once you've received your LPI ID, you may continue your registration by registering with a testing center or special event. You can link to any of these registration options through LPI's registration web site.

In testing centers, the exams are delivered using a PC-based automated examination program. As of this writing, the exams are available in both English and Japanese. Exam questions are presented in multiple-choice single-answer, multiple-choice multiple-answer, and fill-in-the-blank styles. However, the majority of the questions on the exams are multiple-choice single-answer.

For security purposes, multiple forms of each exam are available at testing centers to help minimize memorization and brain dumps of exams if candidates take them multiple times. Due to this, actual question numbers may vary slightly. LPI's psychometric team develops these forms and adjusts the scoring appropriately so all forms are equally difficult.

Exam 101 Overview

LPI Exam 101 is one of two exams required for the LPIC Level 1 certification. In total, 14 major Topic areas are specified for Level 1; this exam tests your knowledge on 5 of them.

Exam Topics are numbered using a *level.topic* notation (e.g., 1.101, 1.102, 1.113). In LPI's early stages of development, Topics were assigned to exams based on a different scheme than we see today. When the scheme changed, the Topics were redistributed to Exams 101 and 102, but the pairing of Topic numbers to exams was dropped. As a result, LPI has 1.*x* and 2.*x* Topics in both Level 1 Exams. In the 2002 revision of the Objectives, LPI decided to reformat the numbering scheme to be more scalable for its multiple levels of certifications. Therefore, the exams now use an *x.y.z* numbering scheme where *x* equals the LPIC level (e.g., 1 or 2), *y* equals the Objective Topic (e.g., 101, 102, 201, 202, etc.) which are unique to all levels of LPI exams, and *z* equals the Objective number within the Topic area (e.g., 1, 2, 3, 4, and so on).

The Level 1 Topics are distributed between the two exams to create tests of similar length and difficulty without subject matter overlap. As a result, there's no requirement for or advantage to taking them in sequence.

Each Topic contains a series of Objectives covering specific areas of expertise. Each of these Objectives is assigned a numeric weight, which acts as an indicator of the importance of the Objective. Weights typically run between 1 and 8, with higher numbers indicating more importance. An Objective carrying a weight of 1 can be considered relatively unimportant and isn't likely to be covered in much depth on the exam. Objectives with larger weights are sure to be covered more heavily on the exam, so you should study these Topics closely. The weights of the Objectives are provided at the beginning of each Topic section.

The Topics for Exam 101 are listed in Table 1-1.

Table 1-1. LPI Topics for Exam 101

Name	Number of objectives	Description
Hardware and Architecture	4	These Objectives cover all the fundamentals of working with common types of hardware on Linux. The Objectives included configuring PC system BIOS and IDE hard drives, installing plug-and-play–based modems and sound cards, setting up SCSI-based devices, and configuring USB hardware.
Linux Installation and Package Management	6	Objectives for this Topic include the basics of getting any LSB-compliant Linux distribution installed and installing applications. Some of the basics include partitioning hard drives, installing your choice of boot managers, installing programs from source, managing shared libraries, and using package management systems such as Debian and Red Hat (RPM).
GNU and Unix Commands	8	This heavily weighted Topic addresses the most utilized command-line tools used on standard Linux systems as well as most commercial Unix systems. The Objectives detail working on a command line, processing text streams using command-line tools, managing files, manipulating text with pipes and redirects, monitoring system processes, managing task priorities, using regular expressions, and editing files with vi. lilo, syslog, runlevels, shutdown, and reboot.
Devices, Linux Filesystems, and the Filesystem Hierarchy Standard	8	Objectives for this Topic include the creation of partitions and file-systems, filesystem integrity, mounting, quotas, permissions, ownership, links, and file location tasks.
The X Window System	3	The X-based Objectives cover only subjects that every Level 1 sysadmin are expected to encounter. Some of these tasks include installing and configuring XFree86, setting up a display manager such as XDM, GDM, or KDM, and installing and customizing Window Manager Environments.

As you can see from Table 1-1, the Topic numbers assigned by the LPI are not necessarily sequential. This is due to various modifications made by the LPI to its exam program as it developed. The Topic numbers serve only as reference and are not used on the exam.

Exam 101 lasts a maximum of 90 minutes and contains approximately 65 questions. The exam is administered using a custom application on a PC in a private room with no notes or other reference material. The majority of the exam is made up of multiple-choice single-answer questions. These questions have only one correct answer and are answered using radio buttons. Some of them present a scenario needing administrative action. Others seek appropriate commands for a particular task or proof of understanding of a particular concept.

About 10 percent of the exam questions are multiple-choice multiple-answer questions, which are answered using checkboxes. These questions specify that they have multiple correct responses, each of which must be checked to get the item correct. There is no partial credit for partially answered items. This is probably the most difficult question style because the multiple answers increase the likelihood of mistakes. But they also are a good test of your knowledge of Unix commands, since an incorrect response on any one of the possible answers causes you to miss the entire question.

The exam also has fill-in-the-blank questions. These questions provide a one-line text area input box for you to fill in your answer. These questions check your knowledge of concepts such as important files and commands, plus common facts that you are expected to be aware of. The second release of the LPI Level 1 exams included more of these types of items since the psychometric evaluation LPI uses for exam development determined that the fill-in-the-blank type of questions were the best indicators for truly competant administrators. Don't let this scare you, however, since most of these items accept multiple answers. Unless specified otherwise they are not case-sensitive and do not require full paths in your answers.

2

Exam 101 Study Guide

Part I of this book contains a section for each of the five Topics found on LPI Exam 101. Each section details certain Objectives, which are described here and on the LPI web site, *http://www.lpi.org/p-obj-101rel2.html*.

Exam Preparation

LPI Exam 101 is thorough, but you should find it fairly straightforward if you have a solid foundation in Linux concepts. You won't come across questions that intend to trick you, and you're unlikely to find ambiguous questions.

Exam 101 mainly tests your knowledge of facts, including commands and their common options, important file locations, configuration syntax, and common procedures. Your recollection of these details, regardless of your level of Linux administration experience, will directly influence your results.

For clarity, the material in the following sections is presented in the same order as the LPI Topics and Objectives. However, you may choose to study the Topics in any order you wish. To assist you with your preparation, Tables 2-1 through 2-5 list the Topics and Objectives found on Exam 101. Objectives within each Topic occupy rows of the corresponding table, including the Objective's number, description, and weight. The LPI assigns a *weight* for each Objective to indicate the relative importance of that Objective on the exam on a scale of 1 to 8. We recommend that you use the weights to prioritize what you decide to study in preparation for the exams. After you complete your study of each Objective, simply check it off here to measure and organize your progress.

Table 2-1. Hardware and architecture (Topic 1.101)

Objective	Weight	Description
1	1	Configure Fundamental BIOS Settings
3	1	Configure Modem and Sound Cards

Table 2-1. Hardware and architecture (Topic 1.101) (continued)

Objective	Weight	Description
4	1	Set Up Non-IDE Devices
5	3	Set Up Different PC Expansion Cards
6	1	Configure Communication Devices
7	1	Configure USB Devices

Table 2-2. Linux installation and package management (Topic 1.102)

Objective	Weight	Description
1	5	Design Hard Disk Layout
2	1	Install a Boot Manager
3	5	Make and Install Programs from Source
4	3	Manage Shared Libraries
5	8	Use Debian Package Management
6	8	Use Red Hat Package Manager

Table 2-3. GNU and Unix commands (Topic 1.103)

Objective	Weight	Description
1	5	Work on the Command Line
2	6	Process Text Streams Using Filters
3	5	Perform Basic File Management
4	5	Using Streams, Pipes, and Redirects
5	5	Create, Monitor, and Kill Processes
6	3	Modify Process Execution Priorities
7	3	Search Text Files Using Regular Expressions
8	1	Perform Basic File Editing Operations Using vi

Table 2-4. Devices, Linux filesystems, and the Filesystem Hierarchy Standard (Topic 1.104)

Objective	Weight	Description
1	3	Create Partitions and Filesystems
2	3	Maintain the Integrity of Filesystems
3	3	Control Mounting and Unmounting Filesystems
4	3	Managing Disk Quota
5	5	Use File Permissions to Control Access to Files
6	1	Manage File Ownership
7	1	Create and Change Hard and Symbolic Links
8	5	Find System Files and Place Files in the Correct Location

Table 2-5. The X Window System (Topic 1.110)

Objective	Weight	Description
1	5	Install and Configure X11
2	3	Set Up a Display Manager
4	5	Install and Customize a Window Manager Environment

3

Hardware and Architecture (Topic 1.101)

This Topic requires general knowledge of fundamental PC architecture facts that you must know before attempting any operating system installation. It includes these Objectives:

Objective 1: Configure Fundamental BIOS Settings
This Objective states that candidates should be able to configure fundamental system hardware by making the correct settings in the system BIOS. This Objective includes a proper understanding of BIOS configuration issues such as the use of LBA on integrated device electronics (IDE) hard disks larger than 1024 cylinders, enabling or disabling integrated peripherals, and configuring systems with (or without) external peripherals such as keyboards. It also includes the correct setting for IRQs, DMAs, and I/O addresses for all BIOS administrated ports and settings for error handling. Weight: 1.

Objective 3: Configure Modem and Sound Cards
An LPI 101 Candidate must ensure devices meet compatibility requirements (particularly that the modem is *not* a winmodem). The candidate should also verify that both the modem and sound card are using unique and correct IRQs, DMAs, and I/O addresses; if the sound card is plug-and-play (PnP), install and run sndconfig and isapnp; configure the modem for outbound PPP, SLIP, and CSLIP connections; and set the serial port speeds. Weight: 1.

Objective 4: Set Up Non-IDE Devices
This Objective states that the candidate should be able to configure SCSI (pronounced "scuzzy") devices using the SCSI BIOS as well as the necessary Linux tools. He should also be able to differentiate between the various types of SCSI. This Objective includes manipulating the SCSI BIOS to detect used and available SCSI IDs and setting the correct ID number for different devices, especially the boot device. It also includes managing the settings in the computer's BIOS to determine the desired boot sequence if both SCSI and IDE drives are used. Weight: 1.

Objective 5: Set Up Different PC Expansion Cards

This Objective states that a candidate should be able to configure various cards for the various expansion slots. She should know the differences between ISA and PCI cards with respect to configuration issues. This Objective includes the correct settings of IRQs, DMAs, and I/O ports of the cards, especially to avoid conflicts between devices. It also includes using isapnp if the card is an ISA PnP device. Weight: 3.

Objective 6: Configure Communication Devices

The candidate should be able to install and configure different internal and external communication devices such as modems, ISDN adapters, and DSL switches. This Objective includes verification of compatibility requirements (especially important if that modem is a winmodem), necessary hardware settings for internal devices (IRQs, DMAs, and I/O ports), and loading and configuring suitable device drivers. It also includes communication device and interface configuration requirements, such as the right serial port for 115.2 Kbps and the correct modem settings for outbound PPP connections. Weight: 1.

Objective 7: Configure USB Devices

Candidates should be able to activate USB support, use and configure different USB devices. This Objective includes the correct selection of the USB chipset and corresponding module. It also includes knowledge of the basic architecture of the layer model of USB as well as the different modules used in the different layers. Weight: 1.

Objective 1: Configure Fundamental BIOS Settings

Setting up a PC for Linux (or any other operating system) requires some familiarity with the devices installed in the system and their configuration. Items to be aware of include modems, serial and parallel ports, network adapters, SCSI adapters, hard drives, USB controllers, and sound cards. Many of these devices, particularly older ones, require manual configuration of some kind to avoid conflicting resources. The rest of the configuration for the system hardware is done in the PC's firmware, or Basic Input/Output System (BIOS).

BIOS

The firmware located in a PC, commonly called the BIOS, is responsible for bringing all of the system hardware to a state at which it is ready to boot an operating system. Systems vary, but this process usually includes system initialization, the testing of memory and other devices, and ultimately locating an operating system from among several storage devices. In addition, the BIOS provides a low-level system configuration interface, allowing the user to choose such things as boot devices and resource assignments. Quite a few BIOS firmware vendors provide customized versions of their products for various PC system architectures. Exams do require an understanding of the basics. For example, a laptop BIOS may differ significantly from a desktop system of similar capability from the same manufacturer. Due to these variations, it's impossible to test specifics, but the LPIC Level 1 exams do require an understanding of the basics

At boot time, most PCs display a method of entering the BIOS configuration utility, usually by entering a specific keystroke during startup. Once the utility is started, a menu-based screen in which system settings can be configured appears. Depending on the BIOS vendor, these will include settings for disks, memory behavior, on-board ports (such as serial and parallel ports), the clock, as well as many others.

Date and time

One of the basic functions of the BIOS is to manage the on-board hardware clock. This clock is initially set in the BIOS configuration by entering the date and time in the appropriate fields. Once set, the internal clock keeps track of time and makes the time available to the operating system. The operating system can also set the hardware clock, which is often useful if an accurate external time reference, such as an NTPD server (see Chapter 18), is available on the network while the system is running.

Disks and boot devices

Another fundamental configuration item required in BIOS settings is the selection of storage devices. Modern PCs can contain a variety of removable and fixed media, including floppy disks, hard disks, CD-ROMs, CD-RWs, DVD-ROMs, and Zip and/or Jaz drives. Newer systems are able to detect and properly configure much of this hardware automatically. However, older BIOS versions require manual configuration. This may include the selection of floppy disk sizes and disk drive parameters.

Most PCs have at least three bootable media types: an internal hard disk (IDE or SCSI, or perhaps both), a CD-ROM drive (again IDE or SCSI), and a floppy disk. After initialization, the BIOS seeks an operating system (or an operating system loader, such as the Linux Loader [LILO]) on one or more of these media. By default, many BIOS configurations enable booting from the floppy or CD-ROM first, then the hard disk, but the order is configurable in the BIOS settings.

In addition to these default media types, many server motherboard BIOS (as well as high-end system motherboards) support booting from a network device such as a NIC with a bootable ROM. This is often used when booting diskless workstations such as Linux-based terminals.

On the Exam

You should be familiar with the general configuration requirements and layout of the BIOS configuration screens for a typical PC.

Resource Assignments

Some of the details in the BIOS configuration pertain to the internal resources of the PC architecture, including selections for *interrupts* (also called IRQs), I/O addresses, and Direct Memory Access (DMA) channels. Interrupts are electrical signals sent to the PC's microprocessor, instructing it to stop its current activity and respond to an asynchronous event (a keystroke, for example). Modern devices in PCs often share interrupts, but older hardware requires manual verification that interrupt settings are unique to avoid conflicts with other devices.

I/O addresses are locations in the microprocessor's *memory map* (a list of defined memory addresses) reserved for input/output devices such as network interfaces. The microprocessor can write to the devices in the same way it writes to memory, which simplifies the device interface. If multiple devices inadvertently share the same I/O address, the system might behave oddly or crash.

DMA allows some devices to work directly with memory through a DMA channel, freeing the microprocessor for other tasks. Without DMA, data must be read from I/O ports for a device and stored in memory, all by the microprocessor. A device that has DMA capabilities has direct access to memory and writes its own data there when the microprocessor is busy with computation. This can improve performance.

These are all finite resources, and it is important to avoid conflicting settings. Common devices such as serial and parallel ports have standard assignments, as shown in Table 3-1.

Table 3-1. Common device settings

Device	I/O address	IRQ	DMA
ttyS0 (COM1)	3f8	4	NA[a]
ttyS1 (COM2)	2f8	3	NA
ttyS2 (COM3)	3e8	4	NA
ttyS3 (COM4)	2e8	3	NA
lp0 (LPT1)	378-37f	7	NA
lp1 (LPT2)[b]	278-27f	5	NA
fd0, fd1 (floppies 1 and 2)	3f0-3f7	6	2
fd2, fd3 (floppies 3 and 4)	370-377	10	3

[a] NA: not applicable.
[b] *lp1* uses IRQ 5. Some older PC audio devices commonly use this interrupt, which could be a problem if two parallel ports are required.

Most PCs don't contain all of these devices. For example, a typical configuration includes two serial ports, *ttyS0* and *ttyS1*. These two ports can be used to attach external modems or terminals and occupy interrupts 4 and 3, respectively. For systems with additional serial ports installed, *ttyS0* and *ttyS2* share interrupt 4, and *ttyS1* and *ttyS3* share interrupt 3. However, the system design does not allow these ports to concurrently share the interrupt and exchange serial data. Otherwise, communications would fail if both ports from either pair were used together.

1024-Cylinder Limit

With most PC operating systems, data loaded by the BIOS to boot the operating system is found at the beginning of the disk in the Master Boot Record (MBR). Windows users rarely have to think about the MBR because there is no alternate location for the boot record. With Linux, however, the user can place the boot loader (LILO or GRUB) into either the MBR or the root partition. This flexibility can lead to a problem for the BIOS and boot loader, and it can cause a failure at boot time. The failure can occur because the BIOS must load the boot loader into memory and start it, but the BIOS can't always access portions of the disk beyond the 1024th cylinder. If the BIOS can't read all of the boot loader, the boot fails. Also, older versions of LILO must have a kernel image located within the first 1024 cylinders for similar reasons. These limitations aren't significant, but do require planning during the partitioning of disks at installation time. This Topic is discussed further in Objective 2 of Chapter 14.

Objective 3: Configure Modems and Sound Cards

Modems and sound cards, while non-essential, are two of the most common pieces of hardware installed in a Linux system; unfortunately, they are also two of the most problematic to configure. This Objective covers the tasks required to complete modem and sound card configuration.

Modems

A modem (a word derived from *mo*dulate and *de*modulate) is that familiar device that modulates a digital signal into an analog signal for transmitting information via telephone lines. A modem on the other end of the connection demodulates the signal back into its digital form. Modems can also add digital compression and error correction capabilities to increase speed and reliability.

Modem types

Modems are serial devices, where data enters and exits one bit at a time. Traditionally, modems were external devices attached via cable to industry standard RS-232 serial ports, such as those still found on most PCs. This arrangement continues to work well, because the data rates of telephone connections are still below the maximum rate of the serial ports. As a result, external devices yield solid performance. Internal modems (ISA or PCI bus cards that reside inside a PC) were developed to reduce costs associated with external modems (namely, the case, power supply, and shipping charges) and offer the same functionality as an external modem.

Most internal modems present themselves to the PC as a standard serial port. In a typical PC with the first two serial ports built in (*/dev/ttyS0* and */dev/ttyS1*), an internal modem will appear as the third port (*/dev/ttys2*). This means that from a programming point of view, internal modems are indistinguishable from external modems. While there is some variation in modem configuration across manufacturers, the differences are small, and most serial-port-style modems will work with Linux. One exception is a modem designed specifically to work with the Windows operating system. These so-called *winmodems* rely on the CPU and a special software driver to handle some of the communications processing, and thus lack the full hardware capabilities of standard modems. As such, winmodems are not compatible with Linux unless a Linux-specific driver is available. Information on such support is available from *http://www.linmodems.org*.

Modem hardware resources

As with any add-on card, particularly cards configured manually, the user must be careful to avoid resource conflicts. Modems shouldn't cause much difficulty since they're simple serial ports. However, you should confirm that the correct interrupt and I/O addresses are set on your modem. If the modem shares an interrupt with another serial port, that port cannot be used at the same time as the modem.

Sound Devices

Nearly every laptop and desktop PC shipped today includes a sound device. Fortunately, Linux sound drivers are available for most sound chipsets, including the old industry standard chipset defined by Creative Labs with its SoundBlaster series. Today's PC is typically built with AC97 chipset sound devices built in or include a PCI device with similar chipset. For cards that don't work with the native kernel modules, you may have to use a tool such as *sndconfig* or for more ancient ISA hardware, *isapnp*. In either case, part of the configuration for a sound card involves correctly specifying the sound card's resources to the sound driver.

On the Exam

Be aware that the sound driver is a kernel module that has its settings stored in */etc/modules.conf*.

---

sndconfig

Syntax

    sndconfig [options]

Description

sndconfig is a text-based tool used to configure a sound card for your Linux kernel. When executed, it will probe your system for PnP-based devices. If none are found, you are probed to select your card and appropriate I/O settings. If you must use this tool, be careful. It is your responsibility to ensure you don't have conflicting devices since *sndconfig* won't detect the problem.

Frequently used options

--help
> Prints help information and exits.

--noprobe
> Tells *sndconfig* not to probe for PnP devices.

--noautoconfig
> Tells *sndconfig* not to autoconfigure any PnP devices.

isapnp

Syntax

    isapnp [options] conffile

Description

The *isapnp* tool is used to configure ISA-based PnP devices. The configuration file (`conffile`) can be either a text file or a hyphen (-), which indicates the configuration file should be read from STDIN.

Frequently used options

-h
> Prints help information and exits.

-v
> Prints the *isapnptools* version.

Objective 4: Set Up Non-IDE Devices

SCSI

SCSI is an interface for streaming devices and block storage devices such as tape drives, hard disks, CD-ROMs, and other peripheral instruments. SCSI is the standard interface on server-style PCs, Unix workstations, and many older Apple models (mostly 604 and earlier systems). Desktop PCs and newer Apple systems (G3 and above) usually opt for the IDE (ATA)-style disk interfaces because they are less expensive. The advantage that SCSI has over IDE is that it offers much more flexibility and expandability, as well as faster throughput.

SCSI defines a *bus* to which multiple devices are connected. The medium is a high-quality cable or a series of cables connected to daisy-chained devices in series. One of the devices in the chain is the *SCSI controller*, which is the host interface to the other connected SCSI devices. The controller and each of the other devices on the bus is assigned a permanent *SCSI address*, also known as the *SCSI ID*, which defines each SCSI device uniquely on the bus. The controller can access devices individually by using the unique SCSI address to access a specific device.

SCSI types

The world of SCSI can be a little confusing, despite the standards set by ANSI. The original SCSI-1 interface is a 5 MBps 8-bit interface. It uses a 50-pin Centronics connector, similar to but larger than those found on most printers. This interface is still in popular use today, although the connector is usually replaced by a 50-pin Micro-D connector. (This connector is similar to the DB-25 used for serial ports but has a much higher pin density.) As performance demands have escalated, manufacturers have begun offering enhanced products with faster data transfer rates. Current interfaces include:

SCSI-1
> The original: 8-bit, 5 MBps Centronics 50-pin connector.

SCSI-2
> 8-bit, 5 MBps Micro-D 50-pin connector. Interchangeable with SCSI-1. This interface is still adequate for low-end to midrange tape drives but is too slow for current technology disks.

Wide SCSI
> 16-bit, 10 MBps, Micro-D 68-pin connector. This standard uses a wider cable to support 16-bit transfers, obtaining faster throughput using the same clock rate.

Fast SCSI
> 8-bit, 10 MBps, Micro-D 50-pin connector. Higher throughput is obtained by doubling the original clock rate.

Fast Wide SCSI
> 16-bit, 20 MBps, Micro-D 68-pin connector. This interface combines both the higher clock rate and the wider bus.

Ultra SCSI
> 8-bit, 20 MBps, Micro-D 50-pin connector. Additional changes to clocking yield still better performance.

Ultra Wide SCSI (also known as SCSI-3)
> 16-bit, 40 MBps.

Ultra2
> 8-bit, 40 MBps.

Wide Ultra2
> 16-bit, 80 MBps.

Recent developments have yielded additional SCSI interface types with up to 160 MBps throughput, and efforts continue to keep SCSI competitive with other technologies. As performance increases, however, constraints on cabling and connectors become more significant. Such constraints are a major factor in deploying large SCSI-based systems. Also, with the variety of connectors, cables, and transfer rates available in the SCSI standards, it's important to plan carefully. The other inhibiting factor, at least on the consumer level, is that SCSI hard drives tend to cost two to three times the amount of similar-sized IDE drives.

SCSI IDs

Each device on a SCSI bus, including the controller, has an address based on a binary reading of the address lines. The 8-bit SCSI buses have three address lines and thus will accommodate $2^3=8$ devices, including the controller. For the 16-bit buses, there are four address lines resulting in a possible $2^4=16$ devices. This results in a maximum of 7 and 15 devices, respectively. These addresses can be configured using jumpers (typical for disk drives) or switches. SCSI addresses run from 0 to 7 for 8-bit buses and from 0 to 15 for 16-bit buses. It is customary for the controller to occupy address 7 for both bus widths. Disks and other devices must be assigned a unique address on the bus, and they must be provided with proper *termination*, which is discussed later in this section.

SCSI logical unit numbers

Some SCSI devices, such as RAID controllers, appear to the SCSI controller as a disk drive with a single SCSI address. For the controller to access multiple logical devices using a single SCSI address, an accompanying *logical unit number* (LUN), is reported to the controller. Single disks and tape drives usually only report LUN zero, but sometimes they report the same on all LUNs, and this must be coped with.

Linux SCSI disk device files

On Linux systems, IDE disk devices are known as */dev/hda*, */dev/hdb*, */dev/hdc*, and */dev/hdd*. For SCSI, a similar pattern emerges, with */dev/sda*, */dev/sdb*, and so on. The first partition on disk */dev/sda* will be */dev/sda1*—but remember that the partition number has nothing to do with the SCSI ID. Instead, the letter names of the Linux SCSI devices start with *sda* and proceed across all SCSI IDs and LUNs. The numbers are sequentially assigned to partitions on a single ID/LUN combination.

For example, a SCSI-2 bus with two disks, a tape drive, a RAID controller with two LUNs, and the SCSI controller might be assigned addresses as shown in Table 3-2.

Table 3-2. Sample SCSI configuration

Device	SCSI address	LUN	Linux device
Disk 0	0	-	/dev/sda
Disk 1	1	-	/dev/sdb
Tape drive	5	-	/dev/st0
RAID controller device 0	6	0	/dev/sdc

Table 3-2. Sample SCSI configuration (continued)

Device	SCSI address	LUN	Linux device
RAID controller device 1	6	1	/dev/sdd
Controller	7	-	-

If a disk on the SCSI bus is to be bootable, you may need to configure the SCSI controller's BIOS with the disk's address. By default, address 0 is expected to be a bootable disk.

Termination

Another facet of SCSI that can be confusing is termination. A SCSI bus can be considered a cable with devices connected along its length, but not at the ends. Instead of devices, the ends of the SCSI bus have *terminators*, which are simple electrical devices that condition the signal and reduce electrical noise on the bus. Termination can be particularly problematic if you attempt to mix 8- and 16-bit devices on a single bus and use an 8-bit terminator, leaving half of the 16-bit SCSI bus unterminated.

Termination devices aren't always separate pieces of equipment. In fact, most device manufacturers include termination circuitry on their devices, so the application of an external terminator device is not necessary. SCSI controllers can terminate one end of the SCSI bus while an external terminator or a disk's internal terminator is used on the other end. Whichever type of terminator is being used, you must be sure that exactly one terminator is placed at each end of the SCSI bus (for a total of exactly two terminators), otherwise the bus may fail.

SCSI controllers on PCs

Most PCs don't come with integrated SCSI controllers, but a number of add-on cards are available. SCSI controllers have their own firmware installed along with an accompanying BIOS, which has its own configuration menus. If you're using SCSI on a PC, it's important to be able to manipulate these settings appropriately.

Like the BIOS, a SCSI controller BIOS usually has a keyboard combination, announced at boot time, to enter the setup utility. Once the utility is launched, you can control a number of aspects of the controller, including:

Controller SCSI address
  The default controller address is usually 7, but you may use any address.

Default boot device
  Typically this is set to address 0 for a hard disk.

Onboard termination
  Depending on how a controller is utilized (internal or external bus, or both) you may elect to turn on the controller's terminator.

SCSI bus speed
  Most SCSI adapters that are capable of higher speeds (Ultra SCSI, for example) can be manually set to lower speeds to accommodate older devices or longer cable lengths.

Objective 5: Set Up Different PC Expansion Cards

As described in Objective 1, when you add hardware to a PC you must accommodate the resource requirements of all installed devices. Your requirements will depend on the type of card, such as whether it is Industry Standard Architecture (ISA) or PCI. This Objective covers the technical details you are required to understand when configuring these types of devices.

Plug and Play

Older hardware, particularly ISA bus hardware, requires manual configuration. Exam 102 requires familiarity with these configuration problems.

Generally speaking, we may think about device configuration methodologies from one of three general eras:

Jumper era
> This hardware was constructed in such a way that settings were controlled by changing the position of shorting jumpers on terminal strips. This method is inconvenient in that it requires internal access to the PC as well as available documentation on the jumper locations. On the other hand, it is a hardware-only solution, and the settings are obvious to the observer. Many such devices are still in service on older PCs.

Nonvolatile era
> These more recent hardware designs abandoned jumpers in favor of settings that, while still manually set, are stored in a nonvolatile memory space. This design eliminated the physical access problem with jumpered hardware, but introduced a requirement that custom configuration programs be written, supported, and provided to consumers by hardware vendors. This software was almost always based on MS-DOS. Using these configuration tools to program a card for use under Linux may require a working MS-DOS machine to provide initial configuration.

Modern era
> Most recent cards work with the PCI bus to automatically configure themselves. The settings are done during system initialization, prior to loading the operating system. This automation eliminates manual configuration and frees the user from worrying about device conflicts.

To configure an older device, you may need to set jumpers or possibly run MS-DOS and a proprietary configuration utility. More often than not, factory default settings can be used with the Linux networking drivers. However, once manual configuration is accomplished, you'll need to be sure that you don't have conflicts with IRQs, I/O addresses, and possibly DMA channel assignments.

Using the /proc filesystem

When adding new hardware to an existing Linux system, you may wish to verify which resources the existing devices are using. The *proc* filesystem, the kernel's status repository, contains this information. The *proc* files, *interrupts*, *dma*, and *ioports*, show how system resources are currently utilized. (These files may not show devices unless their device files/drivers are open/active. This may make the problem harder to find if you're experiencing resource conflicts.) The following is an example of */proc/interrupts* from a dual-CPU system with an Adaptec dual-AIC7895 SCSI controller:

```
# cat /proc/interrupts
          CPU0        CPU1
   0:  98663989           0        XT-PIC  timer
   1:     34698       34858    IO-APIC-edge  keyboard
   2:         0           0        XT-PIC  cascade
   5:      7141        7908    IO-APIC-edge  MS Sound System
   6:         6           7    IO-APIC-edge  floppy
   8:  18098274    18140354    IO-APIC-edge  rtc
  10:   3234867     3237313   IO-APIC-level  aic7xxx, eth0
  11:        36          35   IO-APIC-level  aic7xxx
  12:    233140      216205    IO-APIC-edge  PS/2 Mouse
  13:         1           0        XT-PIC  fpu
  15:     44118       43935    IO-APIC-edge  ide1
 NMI:         0
 ERR:         0
```

In this example, you can see that interrupt 5 is used for the sound system, so it isn't available for a second parallel port. The two SCSI controllers are using interrupts 10 and 11, respectively, while the Ethernet controller shares interrupt 10. You may also notice that only one of the two standard IDE interfaces is enabled in the system BIOS, freeing interrupt 14 use for another device.

Here are the */proc/dma* and */proc/ioports* files from the same system:

```
# cat /proc/dma
0: MS Sound System
1: MS Sound System
2: floppy
4: cascade
# cat /proc/ioports
0000-001f : dma1
0020-003f : pic1
0040-005f : timer
0060-006f : keyboard
0070-007f : rtc
0080-008f : dma page reg
00a0-00bf : pic2
00c0-00df : dma2
00f0-00ff : fpu
0170-0177 : ide1
02f8-02ff : serial(auto)
0370-0371 : OPL3-SAx
0376-0376 : ide1
0388-0389 : mpu401
```

```
03c0-03df : vga+
03f0-03f5 : floppy
03f7-03f7 : floppy DIR
03f8-03ff : serial(auto)
0530-0533 : WSS config
0534-0537 : MS Sound System
e800-e8be : aic7xxx
ec00-ecbe : aic7xxx
ef00-ef3f : eth0
ffa0-ffa7 : ide0
ffa8-ffaf : ide1
```

On the Exam

You should be aware of the default resource assignments listed in Table 3-1.
You should also know how to examine a running Linux system's resource
assignments using the /proc filesystem.

Objective 6: Configure Communications Devices

In today's world of electronic communications, it's rare to find a computer that
isn't connected to the Internet in some form, either on a local network or via a
direct connection such as a modem, DSL, or even telephony-based circuits such as
ISDN or T1. This Objective covers the same details as Objective 4, but applies it
to network connectivity.

Objective 7: Configure USB Devices

Universal Serial Bus (USB) is a type of interface used to connect various types of
peripherals, ranging from keyboards and mice, to hard drives, scanners, digital
cameras, and printers. The USB Objective covers the general architecture of USB,
USB modules, and configuring USB devices.

USB Topology

USB devices are attached to a host in a tree through some number of hub devices.
The *lsusb* command can be used to see how devices are physically attached to a
Linux system.

```
# lsusb -t
Bus# 4
`-Dev#   1 Vendor 0x0000 Product 0x0000
Bus# 3
`-Dev#   1 Vendor 0x0000 Product 0x0000
  |-Dev#   2 Vendor 0x046d Product 0xc501
  `-Dev#   3 Vendor 0x0781 Product 0x0002
Bus# 2
`-Dev#   1 Vendor 0x0000 Product 0x0000
```

```
|-Dev#    2 Vendor 0x0451 Product 0x2036
| |-Dev#   5 Vendor 0x04b8 Product 0x0005
| `-Dev#   6 Vendor 0x04b8 Product 0x0602
`-Dev#    3 Vendor 0x0451 Product 0x2046
  `-Dev#   4 Vendor 0x056a Product 0x0011
Bus#  1
`-Dev#    1 Vendor 0x0000 Product 0x0000
```

USB Controllers

There are three types of USB host controllers:

- Open Host Controller Interface (OHCI)
- Universal Host Controller Interface (UHCI)
- Enhanced Host Controller Interface (EHCI)

OHCI and UHCI controllers are both USB 1.1 controllers, which are capable of a maximum of 12 Mbps. EHCI controllers are USB 2.0 controllers, which are capable of a theoretical maximum of 480 Mbps. To get greater than USB 1.1 speeds, you must have a USB 2.0 controller, as well as USB 2.0 devices, hubs, and cables. A USB 2.0 device attached to a USB 1.1 hub will only be able to run at USB 1.1 speeds.

USB Devices

There are several classes of USB devices, including the following:

Human Interface Device (HID)
 Input devices (mice, keyboards, etc.)

Communications device
 Modems

Mass storage device
 Disk devices, flash readers, etc.

Audio
 Sound devices

IrDA
 Infrared devices

Printer
 Printers and USB-to-parallel cables

USB Drivers

USB support was added to the Linux kernel in the 2.3.x development kernel series, then back-ported to 2.2.x, minus support for USB mass storage devices (due to SCSI changes in 2.3.x). The back-port was included in the 2.2.18 kernel release.

 There is *no* kernel USB support in 2.0.x and earlier.

The Linux kernel USB drivers fall into three categories:

Host controller drivers
> The USB host controller drivers include *usb-ohci.o* (OHCI driver), *usb-uhci.o* (UHCI driver), *uhci.o* (old "alternate" UHCI driver), and *ehci-hcd.o* (EHCI driver).

Class drivers
> The USB class drivers include *hid.o*, *usb-storage.o* (mass storage driver), *acm.o* (Automated Control Model [ACM] communications class driver, which deals with modems that emulate the standard serial modem AT command interface), *printer.o*, and *audio.o*.

Other device drivers
> There are many drivers for devices that either don't fit into one of the standard USB classes or don't work with one of the standard class drivers. Examples include *rio500.o* (the driver for the Diamond Rio 500 MP3 player) and *pwc.o* (the driver for various Philips webcams).

The Linux drivers implement USB support in layers. At the bottom is *usbcore.o*, which provides all of the generic USB support for the higher-level drivers as well as USB hub support. The host controller drivers load in the middle of the stack. On top are the device and class drivers and any modules they require.

The following is an example of what you might see in */proc/modules* (or from the output of *lsmod*) on a system with several USB devices:

```
Module          Size   Used by
usb-storage     68628  0
scsi_mod       106168  2 [usb-storage]
evdev            5696  0 (unused)
printer          8832  0
wacom            7896  0 (unused)
keybdev          2912  0 (unused)
mousedev         5428  1
hid             21700  0 (unused)
input            5824  0 [evdev wacom keybdev mousedev hid]
ehci-hcd        19432  0 (unused)
usb-uhci        25964  0 (unused)
usbcore         77760  1 [usb-storage printer wacom hid ehci-hcd \
                          usb-uhci]
```

USB Hotplug

Modularized USB drivers are loaded by the generic */sbin/hotplug* support in the kernel, which is also used for other hotplug devices such as CardBus cards.

 While not covered on the LPI exams, the Linux IEEE 1394 (also known as FireWire or i.Link) drivers have a similar design. If you understand how to set up USB devices, setting up IEEE 1394 devices should be easy.

4

Linux Installation and Package Management (Topic 1.102)

Many resources, such as the book *Running Linux* (O'Reilly) describe Linux installation. Despite its title, this section's Topic and Objectives do not provide an overview for the installation of any particular Linux distribution. Rather, they focus on four installation Topics and packaging tools as required for LPI Exam 101.

As of the Release 2 LPI Exams, knowlege of both Debian (Objective 5) and RPM Package Managers (Objective 6) are no longer required. Instead, you are given a choice of which package manager you wish to be tested on.

Objective 1: Design Hard Disk Layout

This Objective covers the ability to design a disk partitioning scheme for a Linux system. The Objective includes allocating filesystems or swap space to separate partitions or disks and tailoring the design to the intended use of the system. It also includes placing */boot* on a partition that conforms with the BIOS's requirements for booting. Weight: 5.

Objective 2: Install a Boot Manager

An LPIC 1 candidate should be able to select, install, and configure a boot manager. This Objective includes providing alternative boot locations and backup boot options using either LILO or GRUB. Weight: 1.

Objective 3: Make and Install Programs from Source

This Objective states that you should be able to build and install an executable program from source. This includes being able to unpack a source file. Candidates should be able to make simple customizations to the *Makefile* such as changing paths or adding extra include directories. Weight: 5.

Objective 4: Manage Shared Libraries

This Objective includes being able to determine the shared libraries that executable programs depend on and install them when necessary. The Objective also includes stating where system libraries are kept. Weight: 3.

Objective 5: Use Debian Package Management

This Objective indicates that candidates should be able to perform package management on Debian-based systems. This indication includes using both command-line and interactive tools to install, upgrade, or uninstall packages, as well as find packages containing specific files or software. Also included is obtaining package information such as version, content, dependencies, package integrity, and installation status. Weight: 8.

Objective 6: Use Red Hat Package Manager (RPM)

An LPIC 1 candidate should be able to use package management systems based on RPM. This Objective includes being able to install, reinstall, upgrade, and remove packages as well as obtain status and version information on packages. Also included is obtaining package version, status, dependencies, integrity, and signatures. Candidates should be able to determine what files a package provides as well as find which package a specific file comes from. Weight: 8.

Objective 1: Design a Hard Disk Layout

Part of the installation process for Linux is the design of the hard disk partitioning scheme. If you're used to systems that reside on a single partition, this step may seem to complicate the installation. However, there are advantages to splitting the filesystem into multiple partitions and even onto multiple disks.

You can find more details about disks, partitions, and Linux filesystem top-level directories in Chapter 6. This Topic covers considerations for implementing Linux disk layouts.

System Considerations

A variety of factors influence the choice of a disk layout plan for Linux, including:

- The amount of disk space
- The size of the system
- What the system will be used for
- How and where backups will be performed

Limited disk space

Except for read-only filesystems (such as CD-ROMs or a shared */usr* partition), most Linux filesystems should have some free space available. Filesystems holding user data should be maintained with a maximum amount of free space to accommodate user activity. When considering the physical amount of disk space available, you may be forced to make a trade-off between the number of filesystems in use and the availability of free disk space. Finding the right configuration depends on system requirements and available disk resources.

When disk space is limited, you may opt to reduce the number of filesystems, thereby combining free space into a single contiguous pool. For example, installing Linux on a PC with only 1 GB of available disk space might best be implemented using only a few partitions:

/boot
> 50 MB. A small /boot filesystem in the first partition ensures that all kernels are below the 1024-cylinder limit.

/
> 850 MB. A large root partition holds everything on the system that's not in /boot.

swap
> 100 MB.

The /boot partition could be combined with the root partition as long as the entire root partition fits within the 1024-cylinder limit (see Chapter 3).

Larger systems

On larger platforms, functional issues such as backup strategies and required filesystem sizes can dictate disk layout. For example, suppose a file server is to be constructed serving 100 GB of executable data files to end users via NFS. Such a system will need enough resources to compartmentalize various parts of the directory tree into separate filesystems and might look like this:

/boot
> 100 MB. Keep kernels under the 1024-cylinder limit.

swap
> 1 GB.

/
> 500 MB (minimum).

/usr
> 4 GB. All of the executables in /usr are shared to workstations via read-only NFS.

/var
> 2 GB. Since log files are in their own partition, they won't threaten system stability if the filesystem is full.

/tmp
> 500 MB. Since temporary files are in their own partition, they won't threaten system stability if the filesystem is full.

/home
> 90 GB. This is the big filesystem, offered to users for their home directories.

On production servers, much of the system is often placed on redundant media, such as mirrored disks. Large filesystems, such as /home, may be stored on some form of disk array using a hardware controller.

System role

The role of the system also can dictate disk layout. In a traditional Unix-style network with NFS file servers, most of the workstations won't necessarily need all of their own executable files. In the days when disk space was at a premium, this represented a significant savings in disk space. While space on workstation disks isn't the problem it once was, keeping executables on a server still eliminates the administrative headache of distributing updates to workstations.

Backup

Some backup schemes use disk partitions as the basic unit of system backup. In such a scenario, each of the filesystems listed in */etc/fstab* is backed up separately, and they are arranged so that each filesystem fits within the size of the backup media. For this reason, the available backup device capabilities can play a role in determining the ultimate size of partitions.

Swap Space

When you install Linux, you're asked to configure a *swap*, or *virtual memory*, *partition*. This special disk space is used to temporarily store portions of main memory containing programs or program data that is not needed constantly, allowing more processes to execute concurrently. An old rule of thumb for Linux is to set the size of the system's swap space to be double the amount of physical RAM in the machine. For example, if your system has 512 MB of RAM, it would be reasonable to set your swap size to at least 1 GB. These are just guidelines of course. A system's utilization of virtual memory depends on what the system does and the number and size of processes it runs. As hard disk and memory gets cheaper and Linux application footprints grow, the guidelines for determining swap sizes become more and more about personal preference. However, when in doubt, using twice the amount of main memory is a good starting point.

General Guidelines

Here are some guidelines for partitioning a Linux system:

- Keep the root filesystem (/) simple by distributing larger portions of the directory tree to other partitions. A simplified root filesystem is less likely to be corrupted.

- Separate a small */boot* partition below cylinder 1024 for installed kernels used by the system boot loader.

- Separate */var*. Make certain it is big enough to handle your logs and their rotation scheme.

- Separate */tmp*. Its size depends on the demands of the applications you run. It should be large enough to handle temporary files for all of your users simultaneously.

- Separate */usr* and make it big enough to accommodate kernel building. Making it standalone allows you to share it read-only via NFS.

- Separate */home* for machines with multiple users or any machine where you don't want to affect data during distribution software upgrades. For even better performance (for multi-user environments) put */home* on a disk array.

- Set swap space to at least the same size (double preferred) as the main memory.

On the Exam

Since a disk layout is the product of both system requirements and available resources, no single example can represent the best configuration. Factors to remember include placing the kernel below cylinder 1024, effectively utilizing multiple disks, sizing partitions to hold various directories such as */var* and */usr*, and the importance of the root filesystem and swap space size.

Objective 2: Install a Boot Manager

While it is possible to boot Linux from a floppy disk, most Linux installations boot from the computer's hard disk. This is a two-step process that begins after the system BIOS is initialized and ready to run an operating system. Starting Linux consists of the following two basic phases:

Run the boot loader from the boot device
> It is LILO's job to find the selected kernel and get it loaded into memory, including any user-supplied options.

Launch the Linux kernel and start processes
> Your boot loader starts the specified kernel. The boot loader's job at this point is complete and the hardware is placed under the control of the running kernel, which sets up shop and begins running processes.

All Linux systems require some sort of boot loader, whether it's simply bootstrap code on a floppy disk or an application such as LILO or GRUB. Because the popularity of GRUB has grown, LPI has added it to the second release of the 101 exams.

LILO

The LILO is a small utility designed to load the Linux kernel (or the boot sector of another operating system) into memory and start it. A program that performs this function is commonly called a boot loader. While other boot loaders exist, LILO is the most popular and is installed as the default boot loader on most Linux distributions. LILO consists of two parts:

The boot loader
> This part of LILO is a two-stage program intended to find and load a kernel. It's a two-stage operation because the boot sector of the disk is too small to hold the entire boot loader program. The code located in the boot sector is compact because its only function is to launch the second stage, which is the

interactive portion. The first stage of LILO usually resides in the MBR of the hard disk. This is the code that is started at boot time by the system BIOS. It locates and launches a second, larger stage of the boot loader that resides elsewhere on disk. The second stage offers a user prompt to allow boot-time and kernel image selection options, finds the kernel, loads it into memory, and launches it.

The lilo command

Also called the *map installer*, *lilo* is used to install and configure the LILO boot loader. The *lilo* command reads a configuration file, which describes where to find kernel images, video information, the default boot disk, and so on. It encodes this information along with physical disk information and writes it in files for use by the boot loader.

The boot loader

When the system BIOS launches, LILO presents you with the following prompt:

```
LILO:
```

The LILO prompt is designed to allow you to select from multiple kernels or operating systems installed on the computer and to pass parameters to the kernel when it is loaded. Pressing the Tab key at the LILO prompt yields a list of available kernel images. One of the listed images will be the default as designated by an asterisk next to the name:

```
LILO: <TAB>
linux*    linux_586_smp    experimental
```

Under many circumstances, you won't need to select a kernel at boot time because LILO will boot the kernel configured as the default during the install process. However, if you later create a new kernel, have special hardware issues, or are operating your system in a dual-boot configuration, you may need to use some of LILO's options to load the kernel or operating system you desire.

The LILO map installer and its configuration file

Before any boot sequence can complete from your hard disk, the boot loader and associated information must be installed by the LILO map installer utility. The *lilo* command writes the portion of LILO that resides in the MBR, customized for your particular system. Your installation program will do it, then you'll repeat it manually if you build a new kernel yourself.

lilo

Syntax

```
lilo [options]
```

The *lilo* map installer reads a configuration file and writes a map file, which contains information needed by the boot loader to locate and launch Linux kernels or other operating systems.

Frequently used options

-C config_file
> Read the *config_file* file instead of the default */etc/lilo.conf*.

-m map_file
> Write *map_file* in place of the default as specified in the configuration file.

-q
> Query the current configuration.

-v
> Increase verbosity.

LILO's configuration file contains options and kernel image information. An array of options is available. Some are global, affecting LILO overall, while others are specific to a particular listed kernel image. Most basic Linux installations use only a few of the configuration options. Example 4-1 shows a simple LILO configuration file.

Example 4-1. Sample /etc/lilo.conf file

```
boot = /dev/hda
timeout = 50
prompt
read-only
map = /boot/map
install = /boot/boot.b
image = /boot/vmlinuz-2.2.5-15
  label = linux
  root = /dev/hda1
```

Each of these lines is described in the following list:

boot
> Sets the name of the hard disk partition device that contains the boot sector. For PCs with IDE disk drives, the devices will be */dev/hda*, */dev/hdb*, and so on.

timeout
> Sets the timeout in tenths of a second (deciseconds) for any user input from the keyboard. To enable an unattended reboot, this parameter is required if the prompt directive is used.

prompt
> Sets the boot loader to prompt the user. This behavior can be stimulated without the prompt directive if the user holds down the Shift, Ctrl, or Alt key when LILO starts.

read-only
> Sets the root filesystem to initially be mounted read-only. Typically, the system startup procedure will remount it later as read/write.

map
> Sets the location of the map file, which defaults to */boot/map*.

install
> Sets the file to install as the new boot sector, which defaults to */boot/boot.b*.

image
> Sets the kernel image to offer for boot. It points to a specific kernel file. Multiple image lines may be used to configure LILO to boot multiple kernels and operating systems.

label
>Sets the optional label parameter to be used after an image line and offers a label for that image. This label can be anything and generally describes the kernel image. Examples include linux and smp for a multiprocessing kernel.

root
>Sets the devices to be mounted as root for specified image (used after each image line).

There is more to configuring and setting up LILO, but a detailed knowledge of LILO is not required for this LPI Objective. It is important to review one or two sample LILO configurations to make sense of the boot process. A discussion on using LILO to boot multiple kernels is presented in Chapter 13.

LILO locations

During installation, LILO can be placed either in the boot sector of the disk or in your root partition. If the system is intended as a Linux-only system, you won't need to worry about other boot loaders, and LILO can safely be placed into the boot sector. However, if you're running another operating system you should place its boot loader in the boot sector. Multiple-boot and multiple-OS configurations are beyond the scope of the LPIC Level 1 exams.

On the Exam

It is important to understand the distinction between *lilo*, the map installer utility run interactively by the system administrator, and the boot loader, which is launched by the system BIOS at boot time. Both are parts of the LILO package.

GRUB

GRUB is a multistage boot loader, much like LILO. Unlike LILO, GRUB is very flexible, including support for booting arbitrary kernels on various filesystem types and support for booting several different operating systems.

GRUB device naming

GRUB refers to disk devices as follows:

    (xdn[,m])

The xd above will either be fd or hd for *floppy disk* or *hard disk* respectively. The *n* refers to the number of the disk as seen by the BIOS, starting at 0. The optional *,m* denotes the partition number, also starting at 0.

The following are examples of valid GRUB device names:

    (fd0)
>The first floppy disk.

(hd0)
> The first hard disk.

(hd0,1)
> The second partition on the first hard disk.

Note that GRUB does not distinguish between IDE and SCSI disks. It only refers to the order of the disks as seen by the BIOS, which means that the device number that GRUB uses for a given disk will change on a system with both IDE and SCSI if the boot order is changed in the BIOS.

Installing GRUB

The simplest way to install GRUB is to use the `grub-install` script.

For example, to install GRUB on the master boot record of the first hard drive in a system, invoke *grub-install* as follows:

```
# grub-install '(hd0)'
```

grub-install looks for a device map file (*/boot/grub/device.map* by default) to determine the mapping from BIOS drives to Linux devices. If this file does not exist, it will attempt to guess what devices exist on the system and how they should be mapped to BIOS drives. If *grub-install* guesses incorrectly, just edit */boot/grub/device.map* and re-run *grub-install*.

The device map file contains any number of lines in this format:

```
(disk) /dev/device
```

So, for example, on a system with a floppy and a single SCSI disk, the file would look like this:

```
(fd0)    /dev/fd0
(hd0)    /dev/sda
```

GRUB can also be installed using the *grub* command. The *grub-install* example above could also have been done as follows, assuming */boot* is on the first partition of the first hard disk:

```
# grub
grub> root (hd0,0)
grub> setup (hd0)
```

Booting GRUB

If there is no *configuration file* (or the configuration file does not specify a kernel to load), when GRUB loads it will display a prompt that looks like this:

```
grub>
```

GRUB expects a certain sequence of commands to boot a Linux kernel. They are as follows:

1. root *device*

2. kernel *filename* [*options*]

3. *(optional)* initrd *filename*

4. boot

For example, the following sequence would boot a stock Red Hat 8.0 system with */boot* on */dev/hda1* and / on */dev/hda2*:

```
grub> root (hd0,0)
grub> kernel /vmlinuz-2.4.18-14 ro root=/dev/hda2
grub> initrd /initrd-2.4.18-14.img
grub> boot
```

The GRUB configuration file

GRUB can be configured to boot into a graphical menu, allowing the user to bypass the GRUB shell entirely. To display this menu, GRUB needs a specific configuration file, */boot/grub/menu.lst*.

 The location of this file may be different on your system. For example, on Red Hat systems the default configuration file is */boot/grub/ grub.conf*.

The configuration file defines various menu options along with the commands required to boot each option. The earlier example of booting a stock Red Hat 8.0 system could have been accomplished with the following configuration file:

```
default=0
timeout=3
title Red Hat Linux (2.4.18-14)
        root (hd0,0)
        kernel /vmlinuz-2.4.18-14 ro root=/dev/hda2
        initrd /initrd-2.4.18-14.img
```

GRUB has many more features, including serial console support, support for booting other operating systems, and so on. For more information about GRUB, see the info documentation (*info grub* or *pinfo grub*) or the online documentation at *http://www.gnu.org/manual/grub*.

Objective 3: Make and Install Programs from Source

Open source software is credited with offering value that rivals or even exceeds that of proprietary vendors' products. While binary distributions make installation simple, you sometimes won't have access to a binary package. In these cases, you'll have to compile the program from scratch.

Getting Open Source and Free Software

Source code for the software that makes up a Linux distribution is available from a variety of sources. Your distribution media contain both source code and compiled binary forms of many software projects. Since much of the code that comes with Linux originates from the Free Software Foundation (FSF), the GNU web site contains a huge array of software. Not just for Linux, either. Although Linux distributions are largely made up of GNU software, that software runs on many other Unix and Unix-like operating systems, including the various flavors of BSD (e.g., FreeBSD, NetBSD, and OpenBSD). Major projects, such as Apache (*http://www.apache.org*), distribute their own code. Whatever outlet you choose, the source code must be packaged for your use, and among the most popular packaging methods for source code is the tarball.

What's a tarball?

Code for a significant project that a software developer wishes to distribute is originally stored in a hierarchical tree of directories. Included are the source code (in the C language), a *Makefile*, and some documentation. To share the code, the entire tree must be encapsulated in a way that is efficient and easy to send and store electronically. A common method of doing this is to use *tar* to create a single *tarfile* containing the directory's contents, and then use *gzip* or *bzip2* to compress it for efficiency. The resulting compressed file is referred to as a *tarball*. This method of distribution is popular because both *tar* and *gzip* are widely available and understood, ensuring a wide audience. A tarball is usually indicated by the use of the multiple extensions *.tar* and *.gz*, put together into *.tar.gz*. A combined single extension of *.tgz* is also popular. (*bzip2* offers significantly smaller compressed files at a cost of additional CPU overhead. Files compressed with *bzip2* usually use the extension *.bz2*.)

Opening a tarball

The contents of a tarball are obtained through a two-step process. The file is first uncompressed with *gzip* and then extracted with *tar*. The following is an example, starting with *tarball.tar.gz*:

```
$ gzip -d tarball.tar.gz
$ tar xvf tarball.tar
```

The *-d* option to *gzip* indicates "decompress mode." If you prefer, you can use *gunzip* in place of *gzip -d* to do the same thing:

```
$ gunzip tarball.tar.gz
$ tar xvf tarball.tar
```

You can also skip the intermediate unzipped file by piping the output of *gzip* straight into *tar*:

```
$ gzip -dc tarball.tar.gz | tar xv
```

In this case, the *-c* option to *gzip* tells it to keep the compressed file in place. This saves disk space. For even more convenience, avoid using *gzip* entirely and use the decompression capability in *tar* (GNU *tar* offers compression; older *tar* programs don't):

```
$ tar zxvf tarball.tar.gz
```

Files compressed with *bzip2* can be opened with exactly the same options that *gzip* uses.

```
$ bzip2 -dc tarball.tar.bz2 | tar xv
```

Recent versions of GNU tar also support the *j* option to run *bzip2* directly.

```
$ tar jxvf tarball.tar.bz2
```

Compiling Open Source Software

Once you've extracted the source code, you're ready to compile it. You'll need to have the appropriate tools available on your system, such as gcc and make.

configure

Most larger source code packages include a *configure* script located at the top of the source code tree. *configure* is produced for you by the programmer using the *autoconf* utility. *autoconf* is beyond the scope LPIC Level 1 exams. This script needs no modification or configuration from the user. When it executes, it examines your system to verify the existence of a compiler, libraries, utilities, and other items necessary for a successful compile. It uses the information it finds to produce a custom *Makefile* for the software package on your particular system. If *configure* finds that something is missing, it fails and gives you a terse but descriptive message. *configure* succeeds in most cases, leaving you ready to begin the actual compile process.

make

make is a utility for controlling and scripting software compilation. When multiple source code files are used in a project, it is rarely necessary to compile all of them for every build of the executable. Instead, only the source files that have changed since the last compilation really need to be compiled again.

make works by defining *targets* and their *dependencies* as specified in the *Makefile*. The ultimate target in a software build is the executable file or files. They depend on object files, which in turn depend on source code files. When a source file is edited, its date is more recent than that of the last compiled object. *make* is designed to automatically handle these dependencies and do the right thing.

Typical usage for make is:

```
make [-f makefile ] [ option [...] ] [ target ]
```

Commonly used options include:

-f *filename*
> Use *filename* as a *Makefile*.

-j number_of_jobs
> Tells *make* how many processes to run simultaneously.

Linux
Installation

Installing the compiled software

Most mature source code projects come with a predetermined location in the filesystem for the executable files created by compilation. In many cases, they're expected to go to */usr/local/bin*. To facilitate installation to these default locations, many *Makefiles* contain a special target called *install*. By executing the *make install* command, files are copied and set with the appropriate attributes.

 The default installation directory included in a project's *Makefile* may differ from that defined by your Linux distribution. If you upgrade software you are already using, this could lead to confusion over versions.

Example: Compiling bash

GNU's bash shell is presented here as an example of the process of compiling. You can find a compressed tarball of the bash source at the GNU FTP site, *ftp://ftp.gnu.org/gnu/bash/*. Multiple versions might be available. Version 2.03 is used in this example (you will find more recent versions). The compressed tarball is *bash-2.03.tar.gz*. As you can see by its name, it is a *tar* file that has been compressed with *gzip*. To uncompress the contents, use the compression option in *tar*:

```
# tar zxvf bash-2.03.tar.gz
bash-2.03/
bash-2.03/CWRU/
bash-2.03/CWRU/misc/
bash-2.03/CWRU/misc/open-files.c
bash-2.03/CWRU/misc/sigs.c
bash-2.03/CWRU/misc/pid.c
... (extraction continues) ...
```

Next move into the new directory, take a look around, and read some basic documentation:

```
# cd bash-2.03
# ls
AUTHORS      NEWS
CHANGES      NOTES
COMPAT       README
COPYING      Y2K
CWRU         aclocal.m4
```

```
INSTALL       alias.c
MANIFEST      alias.h
Makefile.in   ansi_stdlib.h
... (listing continues) ...
# less README
```

The build process for bash is started by using the *dot-slash* prefix to launch *configure*:

```
# ./configure
creating cache ./config.cache
checking host system type... i686-pc-linux-gnu
Beginning configuration for bash-2.03 for i686-pc-linux-gnu
checking for gcc... gcc
checking whether the C compiler (gcc  ) works... yes
checking whether the C compiler (gcc  ) is a
  cross-compiler... no
checking whether we are using GNU C... yes
checking whether gcc accepts -g... yes
checking whether large file support needs explicit
  enabling... yes
checking for POSIXized ISC... no
checking how to run the C preprocessor... gcc -E # make
... (configure continues) ...
```

Next, compile:

```
# make
/bin/sh ./support/mkversion.sh -b -s release -d 2.03 \
  -p 0 -o newversion.h && mv newversion.h version.h
***********************************************************
*                                                         *
* Making Bash-2.03.0-release for a i686 running linux-gnu
*                                                         *
***********************************************************
rm -f shell.o
gcc  -DPROGRAM='"bash"' -DCONF_HOSTTYPE='"i686"' \
  -DCONF_OSTYPE='"linux-gnu"' -DCONF_MACHTYPE='"i686
-pc-linux-gnu"' -DCONF_VENDOR='"pc"' -DSHELL \
  -DHAVE_CONFIG_H  -D_FILE_OFFSET_BITS=64  -I.  -I. -I./
lib -I/usr/local/include -g -O2 -c shell.c
rm -f eval.o
... (compile continues) ...
```

If the compile yields fatal errors, *make* terminates and the errors must be addressed before installation. Errors might include problems with the source code (unlikely), missing header files or libraries, and other problems. Error messages will usually be descriptive enough to lead you to the source of the problem.

The final step of installation requires that you are logged in as *root* to copy the files to the system directories:

```
# make install
/usr/bin/install -c -m 0755 bash /usr/local/bin/bash
/usr/bin/install -c -m 0755 bashbug /usr/local/bin/bashbug
( cd ./doc ; make  \
```

```
            man1dir=/usr/local/man/man1 man1ext=1 \
            man3dir=/usr/local/man/man3 man3ext=3 \
            infodir=/usr/local/info install )
make[1]: Entering directory `/home/ftp/bash-2.03/doc'
test -d /usr/local/man/man1 || /bin/sh ../support/mkdirs /usr/local/man/man1
test -d /usr/local/info || /bin/sh ../support/mkdirs
  /usr/local/info
/usr/bin/install -c -m 644 ./bash.1
  /usr/local/man/man1/bash.1
/usr/bin/install -c -m 644 ./bashbug.1
  /usr/local/man/man1/bashbug.1
/usr/bin/install -c -m 644 ./bashref.info
  /usr/local/info/bash.info
if /bin/sh -c 'install-info --version'
  >/dev/null 2>&1; then \
  install-info --dir-file=/usr/local/info/dir
  /usr/local/info/bash.info; \
else true; fi
make[1]: Leaving directory `/home/ftp/bash-2.03/doc'
```

The installation places the new version of bash in */usr/local/bin*. Now, two working versions of bash are available on the system:

```
# which bash
/bin/bash
# /bin/bash -version
GNU bash, version 1.14.7(1)
# /usr/local/bin/bash -version
GNU bash, version 2.03.0(1)-release (i686-pc-linux-gnu)
Copyright 1998 Free Software Foundation, Inc.
```

On the Exam

Familiarize yourself with the acquisition, configuration, compilation, and installation of software from source. Be prepared to answer questions on *make* and *Makefile*, the function of the *configure* script, *gzip*, and *tar*.

Objective 4: Manage Shared Libraries

When a program is compiled under Linux, many of the functions required by the program are linked from system *libraries* that handle disks, memory, and other functions. For example, when printf( ) is used in a program, the programmer doesn't provide the printf( ) source code, but instead expects that the system already has a library containing such functions. When the compiler needs to link the code for printf( ), it can be found in a system library and copied into the executable. A program that contains executable code from these libraries is said to be *statically linked* because it stands alone, requiring no additional code at runtime.

Statically linked programs can have a few liabilities. First, they tend to get large because they include executables for all of the library functions linked into them. Also, memory is wasted when many different programs running concurrently contain the same library functions. To avoid these problems, many programs are *dynamically linked*. Such programs utilize the same routines but don't contain the library code. Instead, they are linked into the executable at runtime. This dynamic linking process allows multiple programs to use the same library code in memory and makes executable files smaller. Dynamically linked libraries are shared among many applications and are thus called *shared libraries*. A full discussion of libraries is beyond the scope of the LPIC Level 1 exams. However, a general understanding of some configuration techniques is required.

Shared Library Dependencies

Any program that is dynamically linked will require at least a few shared libraries. If the required libraries don't exist or can't be found, the program will fail to run. This could happen, for example, if you attempt to run an application written for the GNOME graphical environment but haven't installed the required GTK+ libraries. Simply installing the correct libraries should eliminate such problems. The ldd utility can be used to determine which libraries are necessary for a particular executable.

---

ldd

Syntax
> ldd *programs*

Description
Display shared libraries required by each of the *programs* listed on the command line. The results indicate the name of the library and where the library is expected to be in the filesystem.

Example
The *bash* shell requires three shared libraries:

```
# ldd /bin/bash
/bin/bash:
     libtermcap.so.2 => /lib/libtermcap.so.2 (0x40018000)
     libc.so.6 => /lib/libc.so.6 (0x4001c000)
     /lib/ld-linux.so.2 => /lib/ld-linux.so.2 (0x40000000)
```

Linking Shared Libraries

Dynamically linked executables are examined at runtime by the shared object dynamic linker, *ld.so*. This program looks for dependencies in the executable being loaded and attempts to satisfy any unresolved links to system-shared libraries. If *ld.so* can't find a specified library, it fails, and the executable won't run.

To find a new library, *ld.so* must be instructed to look in */usr/local/lib*. There are a few ways to do this. One simple way is to add a colon-separated list of directories to the shell environment variable LD_LIBRARY_PATH, which will prompt *ld.so* to look in any directories it finds there. However, this method may not be appropriate for system libraries, because users might not set their LD_LIBRARY_PATH correctly.

To make the search of */usr/local/lib* part of the default behavior for *ld.so*, files in the new directory must be included in an index of library names and locations. This index is */etc/ld.so.cache*. It's a binary file, which means it can be read quickly by *ld.so*. To add the new library entry to the cache, first add its directory to the *ld.so.conf* file, which contains directories to be indexed by the ldconfig utility.

ldconfig

Syntax

```
ldconfig [options] lib_dirs
```

Description

Update the *ld.so* cache file with shared libraries specified on the command line in *lib_dirs*, in trusted directories */usr/lib* and */lib*, and in the directories found in */etc/ld.so.conf*.

Frequently used options

-p

    Display the contents of the current cache instead of recreating it.

-v

    Verbose mode. Display progress during execution.

Example 1

Examine the contents of the *ld.so* library cache:

```
# ldconfig -p
144 libs found in cache `/etc/ld.so.cache'
        libz.so.1 (libc6) => /usr/lib/libz.so.1
        libuuid.so.1 (libc6) => /lib/libuuid.so.1
        libutil.so.1 (libc6, OS ABI: Linux 2.2.5) => /lib/libutil.so.1
        libutil.so (libc6, OS ABI: Linux 2.2.5) => /usr/lib/libutil.so
        libthread_db.so.1 (libc6, OS ABI: Linux 2.2.5) => /lib/libthread_db.so.1
        libthread_db.so (libc6, OS ABI: Linux 2.2.5) => /usr/lib/libthread_db.so
            libtermcap.so.2 (libc6) => /lib/libtermcap.so.2
(... listing continues ...)
```

Example 2

Look for a specific library entry in the cache:

```
# ldconfig -p | grep ncurses
        libncurses.so.5 (libc6) => /usr/lib/libncurses.so.5
```

Example 3

Rebuild the cache:

```
# ldconfig
```

After *usr/local/lib* is added, *ld.so.conf* might look like this:

```
/usr/lib
/usr/i486-linux-libc5/lib
/usr/X11R6/lib
/usr/local/lib
```

Next, *ldconfig* is run to include libraries found in *usr/local/lib* in */etc/ld.so.cache*. It is important to run *ldconfig* after any changes in system libraries to be sure that the cache is up-to-date.

Objective 5: Use Debian Package Management

The Debian package management system is a versatile and automated suite of tools used to acquire and manage software packages for Debian Linux. The system automatically handles many of the management details associated with interdependent software running on your system.

Debian Package Management Overview

Each Debian package contains program and configuration files, documentation, and noted dependencies on other packages. The names of Debian packages have three common elements, including:

Package name
> A Debian package name is short and descriptive. When multiple words are used in the name, they are separated by hyphens. Typical names include *binutils*, *kernel-source*, and *telnet*.

Version number
> Each package has a version. Most package versions are the same as that of the software they contain. The format of package versions varies from package to package, but most are numeric (`major.minor.patchlevel`).

A file extension
> By default, all Debian packages end with *.deb* file extension.

Figure 4-1 illustrates a Debian package name.

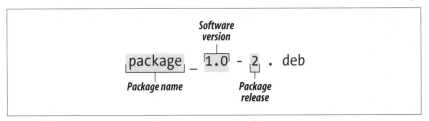

Figure 4-1. The structure of a Debian GNU/Linux package name

Managing Debian Packages

The original Debian package management tool is *dpkg*, which operates directly on *.deb* package files and can be used to automate the installation and maintenance of software packages. The alternative *apt-get* tool operates using package names, obtaining them from a predefined source (such as CD-ROMs, FTP sites, etc.). Both tools work from the command line.

The *dselect* command offers an interactive menu that allows the administrator to select from a list of available packages and mark them for subsequent installation. The *alien* command allows the use of non-Debian packages, such as the Red Hat RPM format.

For complete information on Debian package management commands, see details in their respective manpages.

dpkg

Syntax

```
dpkg [options] action
```

Description

The Debian package manager command, *dpkg*, consists of an *action* that specifies a major mode of operation as well as zero or more *options*, which modify the action's behavior.

The dpkg command maintains package information in */var/lib/dpkg*. There are two files that are of particular interest:

available
    The list of all available packages.

status
    Contains package attributes, such as whether it is installed or marked for removal.

These files are modified by *dpkg*, *dselect*, and *apt-get*, and it is unlikely that they will ever need to be edited.

Frequently used options

-E
    Do not overwrite a previously installed package of the same version.

-G
    Do not overwrite a previously installed package with an older version of that same package.

-R (also --recursive)
    Recursively process package files in specified subdirectories. Works with *-i*, *--install*, *--unpack*, and so on.

Frequently used options

--configure package
    Configure an unpacked package. This involves setup of configuration files.

-i package_file (also --install package_file)
    Install the package contained in *package_file*. This involves backing up old files, unpacking and installation of new files, and configuration.

-l [pattern] (also --list [pattern])
    Display information for installed package names that match *pattern*.

-L package (also --listfiles package)
    List files installed from *package*.

--print-avail package
    Display details found in */var/lib/dpkg/available* about *package*.

--purge package
    Remove everything for *package*.

-r package (also --remove package)
    Remove everything except configuration files for *package*.

-s package (also --status package)
    Report the status of *package*.

-S search_pattern (also --search search_pattern)
    Search for a filename matching *search_pattern* from installed packages.

--unpack package_file
    Unpack *package_file*, but don't install the package it contains.

Example 1

Install a package using *dpkg -i* with the name of an available package file:

```
# dpkg -i ./hdparm_3.3-3.deb
(Reading database ... 54816 files and directories
  currently installed.)
Preparing to replace hdparm 3.3-3 (using hdparm_3.3-3.deb)
Unpacking replacement hdparm ...
Setting up hdparm (3.3-3) ...
```

Alternatively, use *apt-get install* with the name of the package. In this case, the package comes from the location or locations configured in */etc/apt/sources.list*. For this example, the location is *http://http.us.debian.org*:

```
# apt-get install elvis
Reading Package Lists... Done
Building Dependency Tree... Done
The following extra packages will be installed:
  libncurses4 xlib6g
The following NEW packages will be installed:
  elvis
2 packages upgraded, 1 newly installed, 0 to remove
  and 376 not upgraded.
Need to get 1678kB of archives. After unpacking 2544kB
  will be used.
Do you want to continue? [Y/n] y
Get:1 http://http.us.debian.org stable/main
  libncurses4 4.2-9 [180kB]
Get:2 http://http.us.debian.org stable/main
  xlib6g 3.3.6-11 [993kB]
Get:3 http://http.us.debian.org stable/main
  elvis 2.1.4-1 [505kB]
Fetched 1678kB in 4m11s (6663B/s)
(Reading database ... 54730 files and directories
```

```
    currently installed.)
Preparing to replace libncurses4 4.2-3 (using
    .../libncurses4_4.2-9_i386.deb) ...
Unpacking replacement libncurses4 ...
(installation continues...)
```

Example 2

Upgrading a package is no different from installing one. However, you should use
the *-G* option when upgrading with *dpkg* to ensure that the installation won't
proceed if a newer version of the same package is already installed.

Example 3

Use *dpkg -r* or *dpkg --purge* to remove a package:

```
# dpkg --purge elvis
(Reading database ... 54816 files and directories
    currently installed.)
Removing elvis ...
(purge continues...)
```

Example 4

Use the *dpkg -S* command to find a package containing specific files. In this
example, *apt-get* is contained in the *apt* package:

```
# dpkg -S apt-get
apt: /usr/share/man/man8/apt-get.8.gz
apt: /usr/bin/apt-get
```

Example 5

Obtain package status information, such as version, content, dependencies, integrity, and installation status, using *dpkg -s*:

```
# dpkg -s apt
Package: apt
Status: install ok installed
Priority: optional
Section: admin
Installed-Size: 1388
(listing continues...)
```

Example 6

List the files in a package using *dpkg -L* and process the output using *grep* or *less*:

```
# dpkg -L apt | grep '^/usr/bin'
/usr/bin
/usr/bin/apt-cache
/usr/bin/apt-cdrom
/usr/bin/apt-config
/usr/bin/apt-get
```

Example 7

List the installed packages using *dpkg -l*; if you don't specify a pattern, all packages will be listed:

```
# dpkg -l xdm
ii  xdm             3.3.2.3a-11    X display manager
```

Example 8

Use *dpkg -S* to determine the package from which a particular file was installed with the filename:

```
# dpkg -S /usr/bin/nl
textutils: /usr/bin/nl
```

---

apt-get

Syntax

```
apt-get [options] [command] [package_name ...]
```

Description

The *apt-get* command is part of the Advanced Package Tool (APT) management system. It does not work directly with *.deb* files like *dpkg*, but uses package names instead. *apt-get* maintains a database of package information that enables the tool to automatically upgrade packages and their dependencies as new package releases become available.

Frequently used options

-*d*

Download files, but do not install. This is useful when you wish to get a large number of package files but delay their installation to prevent installation errors from stopping the download process.

-*s*

Simulate the steps in a package change, but do not actually change the system.

-*y*

Automatically respond "yes" to all prompts, instead of prompting you for a response during package installation/removal.

Frequently used commands

dist-upgrade

Upgrade automatically to new versions of Debian Linux.

install

Install or upgrade one or more packages by name.

remove

Remove specified packages.

update

Fetch a list of currently available packages. This is typically done before any changes are made to existing packages.

upgrade

> Upgrade a system's complete set of packages to current versions safely. This command is conservative and will not process upgrades that could cause a conflict or break an existing configuration; it also will not remove packages.

Additional commands and options are available. See the *apt-get* manpage for more information.

apt-get uses */etc/apt/sources.list* to determine where packages should be obtained. The file should contain one or more lines that look something like this:

```
deb http://http.us.debian.org/debian stable main contrib non-free
```

Example

Remove the *elvis* package using *apt-get*.

```
# apt-get remove elvis
Reading Package Lists... Done
Building Dependency Tree... Done
The following packages will be REMOVED:
  elvis
0 packages upgraded, 0 newly installed, 1 to remove
  and 376 not upgraded.
Need to get 0B of archives. After unpacking 1363kB
  will be freed.
Do you want to continue? [Y/n] y
(Reading database ... 54816 files and directories
  currently installed.)
Removing elvis ...
(removal continues...)
```

In this example, the user is required to respond with **y** when prompted to continue. Using the *-y* option to *apt-get* would eliminate this interaction.

dselect

Syntax

```
dselect
```

Description

dselect is an interactive, menu-driven, frontend tool for *dpkg* and is usually invoked without parameters. The *dselect* command lets you interactively manage packages by selecting them for installation, removal, configuration, and so forth. Selections are made from a locally stored list of available packages, which may be updated while running *dselect*. Package actions initiated by *dselect* are carried out using *dpkg*.

alien

Syntax

```
alien [--to-deb] [--patch=patchfile] [options] file
```

Description

Convert to or install a non-Debian (or "alien") package. Supported package types include Red Hat *.rpm*, Stampede *.slp*, Slackware *.tgz*, and generic *.tar.gz* files. rpm must also be installed on the system to convert an RPM package into a *.deb* package. The *alien* command produces an *output package* in Debian format by default after conversion.

Frequently used options

-i

Automatically install the output package and remove the converted package file.

-r

Convert package to RPM format.

-t

Convert package to a gzip tar archive.

Example

Install a non-Debian package on Debian system using *alien* with the *-i* option:

```
alien -i package.rpm
```

On the Exam

dselect, *apt-get*, and *alien* are important parts of Debian package management, but detailed knowledge of *dpkg* is of primary importance for Exam 101.

Objective 6: Use Red Hat Package Manager (RPM)

The Red Hat Package Manager is among the most popular methods for the distribution of software for Linux and is installed by default on most distributions. It automatically handles many of the management details associated with interdependent software running on your system.

RPM Overview

RPM automates the installation and maintenance of software packages. Built into each package are program files, configuration files, documentation, and dependencies on other packages. Package files are manipulated using the *rpm* command, which maintains a database of all installed packages and their files. Information from new packages is added to this database, and the database is consulted on a file-by-file basis for dependencies when packages are removed, queried, and installed. As with Debian packages, RPM packages have four common elements:

Name

An RPM package name is short and descriptive. If multiple words are used, they are separated by hyphens (not underscores, as you might expect). Typical names include *binutils*, *caching-nameserver*, *cvs*, *gmc*, *kernel-source*, and *telnet*.

Version

Each package has a version. Most package versions are the same as that of the software they contain. The format of package versions varies from package to package, but most are numeric (`major.minor.patchlevel`).

Revision

The revision tag is simply a release number for the package. It has no significance except to determine if one package is newer than another when the version number does not change.

Architecture

Packages containing binary (compiled) files are by their nature specific to a particular type of system. For PCs, the RPM architecture designation is *i386*, meaning the Intel 80386 and subsequent line of microprocessors and compatibles.

Packages optimized for later x86 CPUs will have an architecture tag appropriate for the specific CPU the code is compiled for, such as *i586* for Intel Pentium (and compatible) processors, *i686* for Intel Pentium Pro and later processors (Pentium II, Celeron, Pentium III, and Pentium 4), or *athlon* for AMD Athlon.

Other possible architecture tags include *alpha*, *ia64*, *ppc*, and *sparc* (for the Alpha, Itanium, PowerPC, and SPARC, respectively). Another arch tag, *noarch*, is used to indicate packages that can install on any architecture.

While the filename of an RPM package is not significant, Red Hat does have a standard naming scheme for its packages that most of the other RPM-based distributions also follow. It is constructed by tying these elements together in one long string.

Running rpm

The *rpm* command provides for the installation, removal, upgrade, verification, and other management of RPM packages. *rpm* has a bewildering array of options, including the traditional single-letter style (*-i*), and the double-dash full word style (*--install*). In most cases, both styles exist and are interchangeable.

Although configuring *rpm* may appear to be a bit daunting, its operation is simplified by being segmented into *modes*. *rpm* modes are enabled using one (and only one) of the *mode options*. Within a mode, additional mode-specific options become available to modify the behavior of *rpm*. The major modes of rpm and some of the most frequently used mode-specific options follow. For complete information on how to use and manage RPM packages, see the *rpm* manpage or the synopsis offered by *rpm --help*.

rpm

Syntax

```
rpm -i [options] (also rpm --install)
rpm -U [options] (also rpm --upgrade)
rpm -e [options] (also rpm --uninstall)
rpm -q [options] (also rpm --query)
rpm -V [options] (also rpm --verify)
```

Install/upgrade mode

The *install mode* (*rpm -i*) is used to install new packages. A variant of install mode is the *upgrade mode* (*rpm -U*), where an installed package is upgraded to a more recent version. Another variant is the *freshen mode* (*rpm -F*), which only upgrades packages where an older version is already installed on the system. *rpm*'s *-F* option has historically been of limited usefulness since it doesn't handle dependency changes at all. In other words, if a new version of a package requires that another package be installed, *-F* won't automatically install the new package, even if it is listed on the command line.

Frequently used install and upgrade options

--force
> Allows the replacement of existing packages and of files from previously installed packages; for upgrades, it allows the replacement of a newer package with an older one. (Literally, it is equivalent to setting all of the options *--replacepkgs*, *--replacefiles*, and *--oldpackage*. *Use this option with caution.*

-h (also --hash)
> Prints a string of 50 hash marks (#) during installation as a progress indicator.

--nodeps
> Allows you to install a package without checking for dependencies. *This command should be avoided, since it makes the dependency database inconsistent.*

--test
> Runs through all the motions except for actually writing files; it's useful to verify that a package will install correctly prior to making the attempt. Note that verbose and hash options cannot be used with *--test*, but *-vv* can.

-v
> Sets verbose mode. (Package names are displayed as the packages are being installed.)

-vv
> Sets really verbose mode. The manpage describes this as "print lots of ugly debugging information."

Example 1

To install a new package, simply use the *rpm -i* command with the name of a package file. If the new package depends upon another package, the install fails, like this:

```
# rpm -i gcc-2.96-113.i386.rpm
error: failed dependencies:
        binutils >= 2.11.93.0.2-6 is needed by gcc-2.96-113
        cpp = 2.96-113 is needed by gcc-2.96-113
        glibc-devel is needed by gcc-2.96-113
```

To correct the problem, the dependency must first be satisfied. In this example, *gcc* is dependent on *binutils*, *cpp*, and *glibc-devel*, which all must be installed first (or at the same time, as in this example):

```
# rpm -i binutils-2.11.93.0.2-11.i386.rpm cpp-2.96-113.i386.rpm \
  glibc-devel-2.2.5-44.i386.rpm gcc-2.96-113.i386.rpm
```

Example 2

Upgrading an existing package to a newer version can be done with the *-U* option. Upgrade mode is really a special case of the install mode, where existing packages can be superseded by newer versions. Using *-U*, a package can be installed even if it doesn't already exist, in which case it behaves just like *-i*:

```
# rpm -U gcc-2.96-113.i386.rpm
```

Uninstall mode

This mode is used to remove installed packages from the system. By default, *rpm* uninstalls a package only if no other packages are dependent on it.

Frequently used uninstall options

--nodeps

> *rpm* skips dependency checking with this option enabled. *This command should be avoided, since it makes the dependency database inconsistent.*

--test

> This option runs through all the motions except for actually uninstalling things; it's useful to verify that a package can be uninstalled correctly without breaking other dependencies prior to making the attempt. Note that verbose and hash options cannot be used with *--test*, but *-vv* can.

Example

Package removal is the opposite of installation and has the same dependency constraints:

```
# rpm -e glibc-devel
error: removing these packages would break dependencies:
        glibc-devel is needed by gcc-2.96-113
```

Query mode

Installed packages and raw package files can be queried using the *rpm -q* command. Query-mode options exist for package and information selection.

Frequently used query package selection options

-a (also --all)

> Display a list of all packages installed on the system. This is particularly useful when piped to *grep* if you're not sure of the name of a package or when you want to look for packages that share a common attribute.

-f filename (also --file)

> Display the package that contains a particular file.

-p package_filename

> Query a package file. Most useful with *-i*, described next.

Frequently used query information selection options

-c (also --configfiles)
> List only configuration files.

-d (also --docfiles)
> List only documentation files.

-i package
> Not to be confused with the *install mode*. Display information about an installed package, or when combined with -p, about a package file. In the latter case, *package* is a filename.

-l package (also --list)
> List all of the files contained in *package*. When used with -p, the *package* is a filename.

-R (also --requires)
> List packages on which this package depends.

Example 1

To determine the version of the software contained in an RPM file, use the query and package information options:

```
# rpm -qpi openssh-3.4p1-2.i386.rpm | grep Version
Version     : 3.4p1          Vendor: Red Hat, Inc.
```

For installed packages, omit the *-p* option and specify a package name instead of a package filename. Notice if you have multiple versions of the same package installed, you will get output for all of the packages:

```
# rpm -qi kernel-source | grep Version
Version     : 2.4.9          Vendor: Red Hat, Inc.
Version     : 2.4.18         Vendor: Red Hat, Inc.
Version     : 2.4.18         Vendor: Red Hat, Inc.
```

Example 2

List the files contained in a package:

```
# rpm -qlp gnucash-1.3.0-1.i386.rpm
/usr/bin/gnc-prices
/usr/bin/gnucash
/usr/bin/gnucash.gnome
/usr/doc/gnucash
/usr/doc/gnucash/CHANGES
   (...output continues ...)
```

For an installed package, enter query mode and use the *-l* option along with the package name:

```
# rpm -ql kernel-source
/usr/src/linux-2.4.18-14
/usr/src/linux-2.4.18-14/COPYING
/usr/src/linux-2.4.18-14/CREDITS
/usr/src/linux-2.4.18-14/Documentation
/usr/src/linux-2.4.18-14/Documentation/00-INDEX
/usr/src/linux-2.4.18-14/Documentation/BUG-HUNTING
/usr/src/linux-2.4.18-14/Documentation/Changes
   (...output continues ...)
```

Example 3

List the documentation files in a package:

```
# rpm -qd at
/usr/doc/at-3.1.7/ChangeLog
/usr/doc/at-3.1.7/Copyright
/usr/doc/at-3.1.7/Problems
/usr/doc/at-3.1.7/README
/usr/doc/at-3.1.7/timespec
/usr/man/man1/at.1
/usr/man/man1/atq.1
/usr/man/man1/atrm.1
/usr/man/man1/batch.1
/usr/man/man8/atd.8
/usr/man/man8/atrun.8
```

Use *-p* for package filenames.

Example 4

List configuration files or scripts in a package:

```
# rpm -qc at
/etc/at.deny
/etc/rc.d/init.d/atd
```

Example 5

Determine what package a particular file was installed from. Of course, not all files originate from packages:

```
# rpm -qf /etc/fstab
file /etc/fstab is not owned by any package
```

Those that are package members look like this:

```
# rpm -qf /etc/aliases
sendmail-8.11.6-15
```

Example 6

List the packages that have been installed on the system.

```
# rpm -qa
```
(... hundreds of packages are listed ...)

To search for a subset with kernel in the name, pipe the previous command to grep:

```
# rpm -qa | grep kernel
kernel-source-2.4.18-24.7.x
kernel-pcmcia-cs-3.1.27-18
kernel-utils-2.4-7.4
kernel-doc-2.4.18-24.7.x
kernel-2.4.18-24.7.x
```

Verify mode

Files from installed packages can be compared against their expected configuration from the RPM database by using *rpm -V*. The output is described under Objective 1 in Chapter 21.

Frequently used verify options

--nofiles
> Ignores missing files.

--nomd5
> Ignores MD5 checksum errors.

--nopgp
> Ignores PGP checking errors.

On the Exam

Make certain that you are aware of *rpm*'s major operational modes and their commonly used mode-specific options. Knowledge of specific options will be necessary. Read through the *rpm* manpage at least once.

5

GNU and Unix Commands (Topic 1.103)

This Topic covers the essential aspect of working interactively with Linux command-line utilities. While it's true that GUI tools are available to manage just about everything on a Linux system, a firm understanding of command-line utilities is required to better prepare you to work on any LSB-compliant Linux distribution.

The family of commands that are part of Linux and Unix systems has a long history. Individuals or groups that needed specific tools contributed many of the commands in the early days of Unix development. Those that were popular became part of the system and accepted as default tools under the Unix umbrella. Today, Linux systems carry new, often more powerful *GNU* versions of these historical commands, which are covered in LPI Topic 1.103.

This LPI Topic has eight Objectives:

Objective 1: Work on the Command Line
This Objective states that a candidate should be able to interact with shells and commands using the command line. This includes typing valid commands and command sequences, defining, referencing and exporting environment variables, using command history and editing facilities, invoking commands in the path and outside the path, using command substitution, applying commands recursively through a directory tree and using man to find out about commands. Weight: 5.

Objective 2: Process Text Streams Using Filters
This Objective states that a candidate should be able to apply filters to text streams. Tasks include sending text files and output streams through text utility filters to modify the output, and using standard Unix commands found in the GNU textutils package. Weight: 6.

Objective 3: Perform Basic File Management

This Objective states that candidates should be able to use the basic Unix commands to copy, move, and remove files and directories. Tasks include advanced file management operations such as copying multiple files recursively, removing directories recursively, and moving files that meet a wildcard pattern. This includes using simple and advanced wildcard specifications to refer to files, as well as using *find* to locate and act on files based on type, size, or time. Weight: 5.

Objective 4: Use Unix Streams, Pipes, and Redirects

This Objective describes that a candidate should be able to redirect streams and connect them to efficiently process textual data. Tasks include redirecting standard input, standard output, and standard error. Also included is piping the output of one command to the input of another, using the output of one command as arguments to another command, and sending output to both stdout and a file. Weight: 5.

Objective 5: Create, Monitor, and Kill Processes

An LPI 101 candidate should be able to manage processes. This includes knowing how to run jobs in the foreground and background, bring a job from the background to the foreground and vice versa, start a process that will run without being connected to a terminal, and signal a program to continue running after logout. Tasks also include monitoring active processes, selecting and sorting processes for display, sending signals to processes, killing processes and identifying and killing X applications that did not terminate after the X sessions were closed. Weight: 5.

Objective 6: Modify Process Execution Priorities

This Objective states that a candidate should be able to manage process execution priorities. The tasks include running a program with higher or lower priority, determining the priority of a process and changing the priority of a running process. Weight: 3.

Objective 7: Search Text Files Using Regular Expressions

This Objective states you should be able to manipulate files and text data using *regular expressions*. This Objective includes creating simple regular expressions containing several notational elements. It also includes using regular expression tools to perform searches through a filesystem or file content. Weight: 3.

Objective 8: Perform Basic File Editing Operations Using vi

This Objective states a candidate should be able to edit files using *vi*. This Objective includes *vi* navigation, basic *vi* nodes, inserting, editing, deleting, copying, and finding text. Weight: 1.

The tools and concepts discussed here represent important and fundamental aspects of working with Linux and are essential for your success on Exam 101.

Objective 1: Work on the Command Line

Every computer system requires a human interface component. For Linux system administration, a text interface is typically used. The system presents the administrator with a *prompt*, which at its simplest is a single character such as $ or #. The prompt signifies that the system is ready to accept typed commands, which usually occupy one or more lines of text. This interface is generically called the *command line*.

It is the job of a program called a *shell* to provide the command prompt and to interpret commands. The shell provides an interface layer between the Linux kernel and the human user, which is how it gets its name. The original shell for Unix systems was written by Steve Bourne and was called simply *sh*. The default Linux shell is *bash*, the *Bourne-Again Shell*, which is a GNU variant of *sh*. The *bash* shell is the subject of an entire LPI Topic, covered in Chapter 17. At this point, we are primarily concerned with our interaction with *bash* and the effective use of commands.

The Interactive Shell

The shell is a powerful programming environment, capable of automating nearly anything you can imagine on your Linux system. The shell is also your interactive interface to your system. When you first start a shell, it does some automated housekeeping to get ready for your use, and then presents a command prompt. The command prompt tells you that the shell is ready to accept commands from its *standard input* device, which is usually the keyboard. Shells can run standalone, as on a physical terminal, or within a window in a GUI environment. Whichever the case, their use is the same.

Shell variable basics

During execution, *bash* maintains a set of *shell variables* that contain information important to the execution of *bash*. Most of these variables are set when *bash* starts, but they can be set manually at any time.

The first shell variable of interest in this Topic is called PS1 (which simply stands for *Prompt String 1*). This special variable holds the contents of the command prompt that are displayed when *bash* is ready to accept commands (there is also a PS2 variable, used when *bash* needs multiple-line input to complete a command). You can easily display the contents of PS1, or any other shell variable, by using the echo command with the variable name preceded by the $ symbol:

```
$ echo $PS1
\$
```

The \$ output tells us that PS1 contains the two characters \ and $. The backslash character tells the shell not to interpret the dollar symbol in any special way (that is, as a *metacharacter*, described later in this section). A simple dollar sign was the default prompt for *sh*, but *bash* offers options to make the prompt much more informative. On your system, the default prompt stored in PS1 is probably something like:

```
[\u@\h \W]\$
```

Each of the characters preceded by backslashes have a special meaning to *bash*, while those without backslashes are interpreted literally. In this example, \u is replaced by the username, \h is replaced by the system's hostname, \W is replaced by the unqualified path (or basename) of the current working directory, and \$ is replaced by a $ character. (Unless you are root, in which case \$ is replaced by #.) This yields a prompt of the form:

```
[jdean@linuxpc jdean]$
```

How your prompt is formulated is really just a convenience and does not affect how the shell interprets your commands. However, adding information to the prompt, particularly regarding system, user, and directory location, can make life easier when hopping from system to system and logging in as multiple users (as yourself and *root*, for example). See the online documentation on *bash* for more information on customizing prompts.

Another shell variable that is extremely important during interactive use is PATH, which contains a list of all the directories that hold commands or other programs you are likely to execute. A default path is set up for you when *bash* starts. You may wish to modify the default to add other directories that hold programs you need to run.

> Every file in the Linux filesystem can be specified in terms of its location. The *less* program, for example, is located in the directory */usr/bin*. Placing */usr/bin* in your PATH enables you to execute *less* by simply typing less rather than the explicit /usr/bin/less.
>
> Also be aware that . (the current directory) is not included in the PATH either implicitly (as it is in DOS) or explicitly for security reasons. To execute a program named *foo* in the current directory, simply run ./foo.

For *bash* to find and execute the command you enter at the prompt, the command must be one of the following:

- A bash *built-in* command that is part of *bash* itself
- An executable program located in a directory listed in the PATH variable
- Explicitly defined

The shell holds PATH and other variables for its own use. However, many of the shell's variables are needed during the execution of programs launched from the shell (including other shells). For these variables to be available, they must be *exported*, at which time they become *environment variables*. Environment variables are passed on to programs and other shells, and together they are said to form the *environment* in which the programs execute. PATH is always made into an environment variable. Exporting a shell variable to turn it into an environment variable is done using the export command:

```
$ export MYVAR
```

When a variable is exported to the environment, it is passed into the environment of all child processes. That is, it will be available to all programs run by your shell.

Entering commands at the command prompt

Commands issued to the shell on a Linux system generally consist of four components:

- A valid command (a shell built-in, program, or script found among directories listed in the PATH, or an explicitly defined program)
- Command options, usually preceded by a dash
- Arguments
- Line acceptance (i.e., pressing the Enter key), which we assume in the examples

Each command has its own unique syntax, although most follow a fairly standard form. At minimum, a *command* is necessary:

```
$ ls
```

This simple command lists files in the current working directory. It requires neither options nor arguments. Generally, *options* are letters or words preceded by a single or double dash and are added after the command and separated from it by a space:

```
$ ls -l
```

The -*l* option modifies the behavior of *ls* by listing files in a longer, more detailed format. In most cases, single-dash options can be either combined or specified separately. To illustrate this, consider these two equivalent commands:

```
$ ls -l -a
$ ls -la
```

By adding the -*a* option, *ls* displays files beginning with a dot (which it hides by default). Adding that option by specifying -*la* yields the same result. Some commands offer alternative forms for the same option. In the preceding example, the -*a* option can be replaced with --*all*:

```
$ ls -l --all
```

These double-dash full-word options are frequently found in programs from the GNU project. They cannot be combined like the single-dash options can. Both types of options can be freely intermixed. Although the longer GNU-style options require more typing, they are easier to remember and easier to read in scripts than the single-letter options.

Adding an *argument* further refines the command's behavior:

```
$ ls -l *.c
```

Now the command will give a detailed listing only of C program source files, if any exist in the current working directory.

 Using the asterisk in ***.c** allows any file to match as long as it ends with a *.c* extension. More information on file globbing and using wildcards will be discussed later in this chapter.

Sometimes, options and arguments can be mixed in any order:

```
$ ls --all *.c -l
```

In this case, *ls* was able to determine that *-l* is an option and not another file descriptor.

Some commands, such as *tar* and *ps*, don't require the dash preceding an option because at least one option is expected or required. To be specific, *ps* doesn't require a dash when it is working like BSD ps. Since the Linux version of *ps* is designed to be as compatible as possible with various other versions of *ps*, it sometimes does need a dash to distinguish between conflicting options. (As an example, try *ps -e* and *ps e*.)

Also, an option often instructs the command that the subsequent item on the command line is a specific argument. For example:

```
$ tar cf mytarfile file1 file2 file3
$ tar -cf mytarfile file1 file2 file3
```

These equivalent commands use *tar* to create an archive file named *mytarfile* and put three files (*file1*, *file2*, and *file3*) into it. In this case, the *f* option tells *tar* that archive filename *mytarfile* follows immediately after the option.

Just as any natural language contains exceptions and variations, so does the syntax used for GNU and Unix commands. You should have no trouble learning the essential syntax for the commands you need to use often. The capabilities of the command set offered on Linux are extensive, making it highly unlikely that you'll memorize all of the command syntax you need. Most systems administrators are constantly learning about features they've never used in commands they use regularly. It is standard practice to regularly refer to manpages or infopages and other documentation on commands you're using, so feel free to explore and learn as you go.

Entering commands not in the PATH

Occasionally, you will need to execute a command that is not in your path and not built into your shell. If this need arises often, it may be best to simply add the directory that contains the command to your path. However, there's nothing wrong with explicitly specifying a command's location and name completely. For example, the *ls* command is located in */bin*. This directory is most certainly in your PATH variable (if not, it should be!), which allows you to enter the *ls* command by itself on the command line:

```
$ ls
```

The shell will look for an executable file named *ls* in each successive directory listed in your PATH variable and will execute the first one it finds. Specifying the *fully qualified filename* for the command eliminates the directory search and yields identical results:

```
$ /bin/ls
```

Any executable file on your system may be started in this way. However, it is important to remember that some programs may have requirements during execution about what is listed in your PATH. A program can be launched normally but may fail if it is unable to find a required resource due to an incomplete PATH.

Entering multiple-line commands interactively

In addition to its interactive capabilities, the shell also has a complete programming language of its own. Many programming features can be very handy at the interactive command line as well. Looping constructs, including for, until, and while are often used this way. (Shell syntax is covered in more detail in Chapter 17.) When you begin a command such as these, which normally spans multiple lines, *bash* prompts you for the subsequent lines until a valid command has been completed. The prompt you receive in this case is stored in shell variable PS2, which by default is >. For example, if you wanted to repetitively execute a series of commands each time with a different argument from a known series, you could enter the following:

```
$ ...series of commands on arg1...
command output
$ ...series of commands on arg2...
command output
$ ...series of commands on arg2...
command output
```

Rather than entering each command manually, you can interactively use *bash*'s for loop construct to do the work for you. Note that indented style, such as what you might use in traditional programming, isn't necessary when working interactively with the shell:

```
$ for var in arg1 arg2 arg3
> do
> echo $var
> ...series of commands...
> done
arg1
command output
arg2
command output
arg3
command output
```

Entering command sequences

There may be times when it is convenient to place multiple commands on a single line. Normally, *bash* assumes you have reached the end of a command (or the end of the first line of a multiple-line command) when you press Return. To add more than one command to a single line, separate the commands and enter them sequentially with the *command separator*, a semicolon. Using this syntax, the following commands:

```
$ ls
$ ps
```

are, in essence, identical to and will yield the same result as the following single-line command that employs the command separator:

```
$ ls ; ps
```

Command History and Editing

If you consider interaction with the shell as a kind of conversation, it's a natural extension to refer back to things "mentioned" previously. You may type a long and complex command that you want to repeat, or perhaps you need to execute a command multiple times with slight variation.

If you work interactively with the original Bourne shell, maintaining such a "conversation" can be a bit difficult. Each repetitive command must be entered explicitly, each mistake must be retyped, and if your commands scroll off the top of your screen, you have to recall them from memory. Modern shells such as *bash* include a significant feature set called *command history*, *expansion*, and *editing*. Using these capabilities, referring back to previous commands is painless and your interactive shell session becomes much simpler and more effective.

The first part of this feature set is command history. When *bash* is run interactively, it provides access to a list of commands previously typed. The commands are stored in the history list *prior* to any interpretation by the shell. That is, they are stored before wildcards are expanded or command substitutions are made. The history list is controlled by the HISTSIZE shell variable. By default, HISTSIZE is set to 500 lines, but you can control that number by simply adjusting HISTSIZE's value. In addition to commands entered in your current bash session, commands from previous bash sessions are stored by default in a file called ~/.bash_history (or the file named in shell variable HISTFILE).

If you use multiple shells in a windowed environment (as just about everyone does), the last shell to exit will write its history to ~/.bash_history. For this reason you may wish to use one shell invocation for most of your work.

To view your command history, use the *bash* built-in *history* command. A line number will precede each command. This line number may be used in subsequent *history expansion*. History expansion uses either a line number from the history or a portion of a previous command to re-execute that command. History expansion also allows a fair degree of command editing using syntax you'll find in the *bash* documentation. Table 5-1 lists the basic history expansion designators. In each case, using the designator as a command causes a command from the history to be executed again.

Table 5-1. Command history expansion designators

Designator	Description
!!	Spoken as *bang-bang*, this command refers to the most recent command. The exclamation point is often called *bang* on Linux and Unix systems.
!*n*	Refer to command *n* from the history. Use the *history* command to display these numbers.
!-*n*	Refer to the current command minus *n* from the history.
!string	Refer to the most recent command starting with string.
!?string	Refer to the most recent command containing string.
^string1^string2	Quick substitution. Repeat the last command, replacing the first occurrence of string1 with string2.

While using history substitution can be useful for executing repetitive commands, command history editing is much more interactive. To envision the concept of command history editing, think of your entire *bash* history (including that obtained from your *~/.bash_history* file) as the contents of an editor's buffer. In this scenario, the current command prompt is the last line in an editing buffer, and all of the previous commands in your history lie above it. All of the typical editing features are available with command history editing, including movement within the "buffer," searching, cutting, pasting, and so on. Once you're used to using the command history in an editing style, everything you've done on the command line becomes available as retrievable, reusable text for subsequent commands. The more familiar you become with this concept, the more useful it can be.

By default, *bash* uses *key bindings* like those found in the Emacs editor for command history editing. (An editing style similar to the *vi* editor is also available.) If you're familiar with Emacs, moving around in the command history will be familiar and very similar to working in an Emacs buffer. For example, the key command Ctrl-p (depicted as C-p) will move up one line in your command history, displaying your previous command and placing the cursor at the end of it. This same function is also bound to the up arrow key. The opposite function is bound to C-n (and the down arrow). Together, these two key bindings allow you to examine your history line by line. You may re-execute any of the commands shown simply by pressing Return when it is displayed. For the purposes of Exam 101, you'll need to be familiar with this editing capability, but detailed knowledge is not required. Table 5-2 lists some of the common Emacs key bindings you may find useful in *bash*. Note that C- indicates the Ctrl key, while M- indicates the Meta key, which is usually Alt on PC keyboards (since PC keyboards do not actually have a Meta key).

In circumstances where the Alt key is not available, such as on a terminal, using the Meta key means pressing the Escape (Esc) key, releasing it, and then pressing the defined key. The Esc key is not a modifier, but applications will accept the Esc key sequence as equivalent to Meta key.

Table 5-2. Basic command history editing Emacs key bindings

Key	Description
C-p	Previous line (also up arrow)
C-n	Next line (also down arrow)
C-b	Back one character (also left arrow)
C-f	Forward one character (also right arrow)
C-a	Beginning of line
C-e	End of line
C-l	Clear the screen, leaving the current line at the top of the screen
M-<	Top of history
M->	Bottom of history
C-d	Delete character from right
C-k	Delete (kill) text from cursor to end of line
C-y	Paste (yank) text previously cut (killed)
M-d	Delete (kill) word
C-r*text*	Reverse search for *text*
C-s*text*	Forward search for *text*

Command substitution

bash offers a handy ability to do *command substitution*. This feature allows you to replace the result of a command with a script. For example, wherever $(*command*) is found, its output will be substituted. This output could be assigned to a variable, as in the number of lines in the *.bashrc* file:

```
$ RCSIZE=$(wc -l ~/.bashrc)
```

Another form of command substitution is `command`. The result is the same, except that the *back quote* syntax has some special rules regarding metacharacters that the $(*command*) syntax avoids.

Applying commands recursively through a directory tree

There are many times when it is necessary to execute commands *recursively*. That is, you may need to repeat a command throughout all the branches of a directory tree. Recursive execution is very useful but also can be dangerous. It gives a single interactive command the power to operate over a much broader range of your system than your current directory, and the appropriate caution is necessary. Think twice before using these capabilities, particularly when operating as the superuser.

Some of the GNU commands on Linux systems have built-in recursive capabilities as an option. For example, *chmod* modifies permissions on files in the current directory:

```
$ chmod g+w *.c
```

In this example, all files with the *.c* extension in the current directory are modified with the group-write permission. However, there may be a number of directories and files in hierarchies that require this change. *chmod* contains the *-R* option (note the uppercase option letter; you may also use *--recursive*), which instructs the command to operate not only on files and directories specified on the command line, but also on all files and directories contained *under* the specified directories. For example, this command gives the group-write permission to all files in a source-code tree named *src*:

```
$ chmod -R g+w src
```

Provided you have the correct privileges, this command will descend into each subdirectory in the *src* directory and add the requested permission to each file and directory it finds. Other example commands with this ability include *cp* (copy), *ls* (list files), and *rm* (remove files).

A more general approach to recursive execution through a directory is available by using the *find* command. *find* is inherently recursive and is intended to descend through directories looking for files with certain attributes or executing commands. At its simplest, *find* displays an entire directory hierarchy when you simply enter the command with a target directory. (If no *action* arguments are given to *find*, it prints each file it finds, as if the option *-print* were specified.):

```
$ find src
...files and directories are listed recursively...
```

As an example of a more specific use, add the *-name* option to search the same directories for C files (this can be done recursively with the *ls* command as well):

```
$ find src -name "*.c"
....c files are listed recursively...
```

find can also be used to execute commands against specific files by using the *-exec* option. The arguments following *-exec* are taken as a command to run on each *find* match. They must be terminated with a semicolon (;), which needs to be escaped (\;, for example) since it is a shell metacharacter. The string { } is replaced with the filename of the current match anywhere it is found in the command.

To take the previous example a little further, rather than execute *chmod* recursively against all files in the *src* directory, *find* can execute it against the C files only, like this:

```
$ find src -name "*.c" -exec chmod g+w { } \;
```

The *find* command is capable of much more than this simple example and can locate files with particular attributes such as dates, protections, file types, access times, and others. While the syntax can be confusing, the results are worth some study of *find*.

Objective 2: Process Text Streams Using Filters

Many of the commands on Linux systems are intended to be used as *filters*, which modify text in helpful ways. Text fed into the command's standard input or read from files is modified in some useful way and sent to standard output or to a new file leaving the original source file unmodified. Multiple commands can be combined to produce *text streams*, which are modified at each step in a pipeline formation. This section describes basic use and syntax for the filtering commands important for Exam 101. Refer to a Linux command reference for full details on each command and the many other available commands.

cut

Syntax
```
cut options [files]
```

Description
Cut out (that is, print) selected columns or fields from one or more *files*. The source file is not changed. This is useful if you need quick access to a vertical slice of a file. By default, the slices are delimited by a tab character.

Frequently used options
-b list
> Print bytes in *list* positions.

-c list
> Print characters in *list* columns.

-d delim
> Set field delimiter for *-f*.

-f list
> Print *list* fields.

Example
Show usernames (in the first colon-delimited field) from */etc/passwd*:
```
$ cut -d: -f1 /etc/passwd
```

expand

Syntax
```
expand [options] [files]
```

Description
Convert tabs to spaces. Sometimes the use of tab characters can make output that is attractive on one output device look bad on another. This command eliminates tabs and replaces them with the equivalent number of spaces. By default, tabs are assumed to be eight spaces apart.

Frequently used options

-t number

> Specify tab stops, in place of default 8.

-i

> Initial; convert only at start of lines.

---

fmt

Syntax

```
fmt [options] [files]
```

Description

Format text to a specified width by filling lines and removing newline characters. Multiple *files* from the command line are concatenated.

Frequently used options

-u

> Use uniform spacing: one space between words and two spaces between sentences.

-w width

> Set line width to *width*. The default is 75 characters.

---

head

Syntax

```
head [options] [files]
```

Description

Print the first few lines of one or more files (the "head" of the file or files). When more than one file is specified, a header is printed at the beginning of each file, and each is listed in succession.

Frequently used options

-c n

> Print the first *n* bytes, or if *n* is followed by k or m, print the first *n* kilobytes or megabytes, respectively.

-n n

> Print the first *n* lines. The default is 10.

---

join

Syntax

```
join [options] file1 file2
```

Description

Print a line for each pair of input lines, one each from *file1* and *file2*, that have identical *join fields*. This function could be thought of as a very simple database table join, where the two files share a common index just as two tables in a database would.

Frequently used options

-j1 field
> Join on *field* of *file1*.

-j2 field
> Join on *field* of *file2*.

-j field
> Join on *field* of both *file1* and *file2*.

Example

Suppose *file1* contains the following:

```
1 one
2 two
3 three
```

and *file2* contains:

```
1 11
2 22
3 33
```

Issuing the command:

```
$ join -j 1 file1 file2
```

yields the following output:

```
1 one 11
2 two 22
3 three 33
```

nl

Syntax

```
nl [options] [files]
```

Description

Number the lines of *files*, which are concatenated in the output. This command is used for numbering lines in the body of text, including special header and footer options normally excluded from the line numbering. The numbering is done for each *logical page*, which is defined as having a header, a body, and a footer. These are delimited by the special strings \:\:\:, \:\:, and \:, respectively.

Frequently used options

-b style
> Set body numbering style to *style*, t by default.

-f style
> Set footer number style to *style*, n by default.

-h style
> Set header numbering style to *style*, n by default.

Styles can be in these forms:

A
> Number all lines.

t
> Only number non-empty lines.

n
> Do not number lines.

pREGEXP
> Only number lines that contain a match for regular expression *REGEXP*.

Example

Suppose file *file1* contains the following text:

```
\:\:\:
header
\:\:
line1
line2
line3
\:
footer
\:\:\:
header
\:\:
line1
line2
line3
\:
footer
```

If the following command is given:

```
$ nl -h a file1
```

the output would yield numbered headers and body lines but no numbering on footer lines. Each new header represents the beginning of a new logical page and thus a restart of the numbering sequence:

```
     1  header
     2  line1
     3  line2
     4  line3
footer
     1  header
     2  line1
     3  line2
     4  line3
footer
```

od

Syntax

```
od [options] [files]
```

Description

Dump files in octal and other formats. This program prints a listing of a file's contents in a variety of formats. It is often used to examine the byte codes of binary files but can be used on any file or input stream. Each line of output consists of an octal byte offset from the start of the file followed by a series of tokens indicating the contents of the file. Depending on the options specified, these tokens can be ASCII, decimal, hexadecimal, or octal representations of the contents.

Frequently used options

-t type
> Specify the *type* of output. Typical types include:

A
> Named character

c
> ASCII character or backslash escape

O
> Octal (the default)

x
> Hexadecimal

Example

If *file1* contains:

```
a1\n
A1\n
```

where \n stands for the newline character. The *od* command specifying named characters yields the following output:

```
$ od -t a file1
00000000   a   1  nl   A   1  nl
00000006
```

A slight nuance is the ASCII character mode. This *od* command specifying named characters yields the following output with backslash-escaped characters rather than named characters:

```
$ od -t c file1
00000000   a   1  \n   A   1  \n
00000006
```

With numeric output formats, you can instruct *od* on how many bytes to use in interpreting each number in the data. To do this, follow the type specification by a decimal integer. This *od* command specifying single-byte hex results yields the following output:

```
$ od -t x1 file1
00000000  61 31 0a 41 31 0a
00000006
```

Doing the same thing in octal notation yields:

```
$ od -t o1 file1
00000000   141 061 012 101 061 012
00000006
```

If you examine an ASCII chart with hex and octal representations, you'll see that these results match those tables.

paste

Syntax

```
paste [options] [files]
```

Description

Paste together corresponding lines of one or more *files* into vertical columns.

Frequently used options

-dn

    Separate columns with character *n* in place of the default tab.

-s

    Merge lines from one file into a single line. When multiple files are specified, their contents are placed on individual lines of output, one per file.

For the following three examples, *file1* contains:

```
1
2
3
```

and *file2* contains:

```
A
B
C
```

Example 1

A simple paste creates columns from each file in standard output:

```
$ paste file1 file2
1    A
2    B
3    C
```

Example 2

The column separator option yields columns separated by the specified character:

```
$ paste -d'@' file1 file2
1@A
2@B
3@C
```

Example 3

The single-line option (-s) yields a line for each file:

```
$ paste -s file1 file2
1    2    3
A    B    C
```

pr

Syntax

```
pr [options] [file]
```

Description

Convert a text file into a paginated, columnar version, with headers and page fills. This command is convenient for yielding nice output, such as for a line printer from raw uninteresting text files. The header will consist of the date and time, the filename, and a page number.

Frequently used options

-d
> Double space.

-h header
> Use *header* in place of the filename in the header.

-l lines
> Set page length to *lines*. The default is 66.

-o width
> Set the left margin to *width*.

sort

Syntax

```
sort [options] [files]
```

Description

Write input to *stdout*, sorted alphabetically.

Frequently used options

-f
> Case-insensitive sort.

-k POS1[,POS2]
> Sort on the key starting at *POS1* and (optionally) ending at *POS2*.

-n
> Sort numerically.

-r
> Sort in reverse order.

-t SEP
> Use *SEP* as the key separator. The default is to use whitespace as the key separator.

Example

Sort all processes on the system by resident size (RSS in ps):

```
$ ps aux | sort -k 6 -n
USER    PID  %CPU %MEM VSZ    RSS   TTY     STAT START  TIME  COMMAND
root    2    0.0  0.0  0      0     ?       SW   Feb08  0:00  [keventd]
root    3    0.0  0.0  0      0     ?       SWN  Feb08  0:00  [ksoftirqd_CPU0]
root    4    0.0  0.0  0      0     ?       SW   Feb08  0:01  [kswapd]
root    5    0.0  0.0  0      0     ?       SW   Feb08  0:00  [bdflush]
root    6    0.0  0.0  0      0     ?       SW   Feb08  0:00  [kupdated]
root    7    0.0  0.0  0      0     ?       SW   Feb08  0:00  [kjournald]
root    520  0.0  0.3  1340   392   tty0    S    Feb08  0:00  /sbin/mingetty tt
root    335  0.0  0.3  1360   436   ?       S    Feb08  0:00  klogd -x
root    1    0.0  0.3  1372   480   ?       S    Feb08  0:18  init
daemon  468  0.0  0.3  1404   492   ?       S    Feb08  0:00  /usr/sbin/atd
root    330  0.0  0.4  1424   560   ?       S    Feb08  0:01  syslogd -m 0
root    454  0.0  0.4  1540   600   ?       S    Feb08  0:01  crond
root    3130 0.0  0.5  2584   664   pts/0   R    13:24  0:00  ps aux
root    402  0.0  0.6  2096   856   ?       S    Feb08  0:00  xinetd -stayalive
root    385  0.0  0.9  2624   1244  ?       S    Feb08  0:00  /usr/sbin/sshd
root    530  0.0  0.9  2248   1244  pts/0   S    Feb08  0:01  -bash
root    3131 0.0  0.9  2248   1244  pts/0   R    13:24  0:00  -bash
root    420  0.0  1.3  4620   1648  ?       S    Feb08  0:51  sendmail: accepti
root    529  0.0  1.5  3624   1976  ?       S    Feb08  0:06  /usr/sbin/sshd
```

split

Syntax

```
split [option] [infile] [outfile]
```

Description

Split *infile* into a specified number of line groups, with output going into a succession of files, *outfile*aa, *outfile*ab, and so on (the default is *xaa*, *xab*, etc.). The *infile* remains unchanged. This command is handy if you have a very long text file that needs to be reduced to a succession of smaller files. This was often done to email large files in smaller chunks, because at one time it was considered bad practice to a send single large email message.

Frequently used option

-n

    Split the *infile* into *n*-line segments. The default is 1,000.

Example

Suppose *file1* contains:

```
1  one
2  two
3  three
4  four
5  five
6  six
```

Then the command:

```
$ split -2 file1 splitout_
```

yields as output three new files, *splitout_aa, splitout_ab,* and *splitout_ac.* The file *splitout_aa* contains:

```
1  one
2  two
```

splitout_ab contains:

```
3  three
4  four
```

and *splitout_ac* contains:

```
5  five
6  six
```

tac

Syntax

```
tac [file]
```

Description

This command is named as an opposite for the *cat* command, which simply prints text files to standard output. In this case, *tac* prints the text files to standard output with lines in reverse order.

Example

Suppose *file1* contains:

```
1  one
2  two
3  three
```

Then the command:

```
$ tac file1
```

yields as output:

```
3  three
2  two
1  one
```

tail

Syntax

```
tail [options] [files]
```

Description

Print the last few lines of one or more *files* (the "tail" of the file or files). When more than one file is specified, a header is printed at the beginning of each file, and each is listed in succession.

Frequently used options

-c n

This option prints the last *n* bytes, or if *n* is followed by k or m, the last *n* kilobytes or megabytes, respectively.

-n m

Prints the last *m* lines. The default is 10.

-f

Continuously display a file as it is actively written by another process. This is useful for watching log files as the system runs.

---

tr

Syntax

    tr [options] [string1 [string2]]

Description

Translate characters from *string1* to the corresponding characters in *string2*. tr does *not* have file arguments and therefore must use standard input and output.

Note that *string1* and *string2* should contain the same number of characters since the first character in *string1* will be replaced with the first character in *string2* and so on.

Either *string1* or *string2* can contain several types of special characters. Some examples follow, although a full list can be found in the tr manpage.

a-z

All characters from *a* to *z*.

\\

A backslash (\) character.

\nnn

The ASCII character with the octal value *nnn*.

\x

Various control characters:

\a	bell
\b	backspace
\f	form feed
\n	newline
\r	carriage return
\t	horizontal tab
\v	vertical tab

[:class:]

A POSIX character class:

[:alnum:]	alphanumeric characters (letters and digits)
[:aplha:]	alpha (letter) characters
[:blank:]	horizontal whitespace (space or tab)
[:cntrl:]	control characters

[:digit:]	numeric (digit) characters
[:graph:]	printable characters, not including space
[:lower:]	lower case alpha characters
[:print:]	all printable characters
[:punct:]	punctuation characters
[:space:]	all whitespace, horizontal, or vertical (space,tab, newline, etc.)
[:upper:]	upper case alpha characters
[:xdigit:]	hexadecimal digits

 The actual contents of the POSIX character classes varies based on locale.

Frequently used options

-c

Use the complement of (or all characters *not* in) *string1*.

-d

Delete characters in *string1* from the output.

-s

Squeeze out repeated output characters in *string1*.

Example 1

To change all lowercase characters in *file1* to uppercase, use:

```
$ cat file1 | tr a-z A-Z
```

or:

```
$ cat file1 | tr '[:lower:]' '[:upper:]'
```

Example 2

To suppress repeated whitespace characters from *file1*:

```
$ cat file1 | tr -s '[:blank:]'
```

Example 3

To remove all non-printable characters from *file1* (except the newline character):

```
$ cat file1 | tr -dc '[:print:]\n'
```

unexpand

Syntax

```
unexpand [options] [files]
```

Description

Convert spaces to tabs. This command performs the opposite action of *expand*. By default, tab stops are assumed to be every eight spaces.

Frequently used options

-a

Convert all spaces, not just leading spaces. Normally *unexpand* will only work on spaces at the beginning of each line of input. Using the *-a* option causes it to replace spaces anywhere in the input.

 This behavior of *unexpand* differs from *expand*. By default, *expand* converts all tabs to spaces. It requires the *-i* option to convert only leading spaces.

-t *number*

Specify tab stops, in place of default 8.

---

uniq

Syntax

    uniq [options] [input [output]]

Description

Writes *input* (or *stdin*) to *output* (or *stdout*), eliminating adjacent duplicate lines.

Since *uniq* works only on adjacent lines of its input, it is most often used in conjunction with *sort*.

Frequently used options

-d

Print only non-unique (repeating) lines.

-u

Print only unique (non-repeating) lines.

Example

Suppose *file* containts the following:

    b
    b
    a
    a
    c
    d
    c

Issuing the command uniq with no options:

    $ uniq file

yields the following output:

    b
    a
    c
    d
    c

Notice that the line with c is repeated, since the duplicate lines were not adjacent in the input file. To eliminate duplicate lines regardless of where they appear in the input, use sort on the input first:

```
$ sort file | uniq
a
b
c
d
```

To print only lines that never repeat in the input, use the *-u* option:

```
$ sort file | uniq -u
d
```

To print only lines that *do* repeat in the input, use the *-d* option:

```
$ sort file | uniq -d
a
b
c
```

wc

Syntax

```
wc [options] [files]
```

Description

Print counts of characters, words, and lines for *files*. When multiple files are listed, statistics for each file output on a separate line with a cumulative total output last.

Frequently used options

-c

　Print the character count only.

-l

　Print the line count only.

-w

　Print the word count only.

Example 1

Show all counts and totals for *file1*, *file2*, and *file3*:

```
$ wc file[123]
```

Example 2

Count the number of lines in *file1*:

```
$ wc -l file1
```

xargs

Syntax

```
xargs [options] [command] [initial-arguments]
```

Description

Execute *command* followed by its optional *initial-arguments* and append additional arguments found on standard input. Typically, the additional arguments are filenames in quantities too large for a single command line. xargs runs *command* multiple times to exhaust all arguments on standard input.

Frequently used options

-n maxargs

Limit the number of additional arguments to *maxargs* for each invocation of *command*.

-p

Interactive mode. Prompt the user for each execution of *command*.

Example

Use *grep* to search a long list of files, one by one, for the word "linux":

```
$ find / -type f | xargs -n 1 grep -H linux
```

find searches for normal files (*-type f*) starting at the root directory. *xargs* executes *grep* once for each of them due to the *-n 1* option. *grep* will print the matching line preceded by the filename where the match occurred (due to the *-H* option).

Objective 3: Perform Basic File Management

This section covers basic file and directory management, including filesystems, files and directories, standard file management commands, their recursive capabilities (where applicable), and wildcard patterns.

Filesystem Objects

Nearly every operating system that has ever been devised structures its collection of stored objects in a *hierarchy*, which is a tree of objects containing other objects. This hierarchy allows a sane organization of objects and allows identically named objects to appear in multiple locations—this is essential for multiuser systems like Linux. Information about each object in the filesystem is stored in a table (which itself is part of the filesystem), and each object is numbered uniquely within that table. Although there are a few special object types on Linux systems, the two most common are *directories* and *files*.

Directories and files

A directory is a container intended to hold objects such as files and other directories. A directory's purpose is primarily for organization. A file, on the other hand, exists within the directory and its purpose is to be responsible for raw data storage. At the top of all Linux filesystem hierarchies is a directory depicted simply by /; this is known as the *root* directory. Beneath / are named directories and files in an organized and well-defined tree. To describe these objects, you simply refer to them by name separated by the / character. For example, the object *ls* is an executable program stored in a directory called */bin* under the root directory; it is depicted simply as */bin/ls*.

 Don't confuse *root* directory with the username *root*, which is separate and distinct. There's also often a directory named */root* for the root user. Keeping /, */root*, and the *root* user straight in a conversation can be a challenge.

Inodes

The identification information for a filesystem object is known as its *inode*. Inodes carry information about objects, such as where they are located on disk, their modification time, security settings, and so forth. Each Linux *ext2* filesystem is created with a finite number of inodes that is calculated based on the size of the filesystem and other options that are given to *mke2fs*. Multiple objects in the filesystem can share the same inode; this concept is called *linking*.

File and directory management commands

Once a hierarchy is defined, there is a constant need to manage the objects in the filesystem. Objects are constantly created, read, modified, copied, moved, and deleted, so wisely managing the filesystem is one of the most important tasks of a system administrator. In this section, we discuss the basic command-line utilities used for file and directory management. While there are GUI tools for this task, the LPI Level 1 exams only test on command-line tools.

cp

Syntax

```
cp [options] file1 file2
cp [options] files directory
```

Description

In the first command form, copy *file1* to *file2*. If *file2* exists and you have appropriate privileges, it will be overwritten without warning (unless you use the *-i* option). Both *file1* and *file2* can be any valid filename, either fully qualified or in the local directory. In the second command form, copy *files* to *directory*. Note that the presence of multiple files implies that you wish to copy the files to a directory. If *directory* doesn't exist, an error message will be printed. This command form can get you in trouble if you attempt to copy a single file into a directory that doesn't exist, as the command will be interpreted as the first form and you'll end up with *file2* instead of *directory*.

Frequently used options

-*f*

Force an overwrite of existing files in the destination.

-*i*

Prompt *interactively* before overwriting destination files. It is common practice (and advised) to alias the *cp* command to *cp -i* to prevent accidental overwrites. You may find that this is already done for you for *root* on your Linux system.

-*p*

Preserve all information, including owner, group, permissions, and timestamps. Without this option, the copied file or files will have the present date and time, default permissions, owner, and group.

-*r*, -*R*

Recursively copy directories. You may use either upper or lowercase for this option. If *file1* is actually a directory instead of a file and the recursive option is specified, *file2* will be a copy of the entire hierarchy under directory *file1*.

-*v*

Display the name of each file verbosely before copying.

Example 1

Copy the messages file to the local directory (specified by .):

```
$ cp /var/log/messages .
```

Example 2

Make an identical copy, including preservation of file attributes, of directory *src* in new directory *src2*:

```
$ cp -Rp src src2
```

Copy *file1*, *file2*, *file5*, *file6*, and *file7* from the local directory into your home directory (in bash):

```
$ cp file1 file2 file[567] ~
```

On the Exam

Be sure to know the difference between a file destination and a directory destination and how to force an overwrite of existing objects.

---

mkdir

Syntax

```
mkdir [options] directories
```

Description

Create one or more *directories*. You must have write permission in the directory where *directories* are to be created.

Frequently used options

-m mode
> Set the access *mode* for *directories*.

-p

> Create intervening parent directories if they don't exist.

Examples

Create a read-only directory named *personal*:

> `$ mkdir -m 444 personal`

Create a directory tree in your home directory, as indicated with a leading tilde (~), using a single command:

> `$ mkdir -p ~/dir1/dir2/dir3`

In this case, all three directories are created. This is faster than creating each directory individually.

On the Exam

Verify your understanding of the tilde (~) shortcut for the home directory.

---

mv

Syntax

> mv [*options*] *source target*

Description

Move or rename files and directories. For *targets* on the same filesystem (partition), moving a file doesn't relocate the contents of the file itself. Rather, the directory entry for the target is updated with the new location. For *targets* on different filesystems, such a change can't be made, so files are copied to the target location and the original sources are deleted.

If a target file or directory does not exist, *source* is renamed to *target*. If a *target* file already exists, it is overwritten with *source*. If *target* is an existing directory, *source* is moved into that directory. If *source* is one or more files and *target* is a directory, the files are moved into the directory.

Frequently used options

-f

> Force the move even if *target* exists, suppressing warning messages.

-i

> Query interactively before moving files.

rm

Syntax

```
rm [options] files
```

Description

Delete one or more files from the filesystem. To remove a file, you must have write permission in the directory that contains the file, but you do not need write permission on the file itself. The *rm* command also removes directories when the *-d*, *-r*, or *-R* option is used.

Frequently used options

-d

Remove directories even if they are not empty. This option is reserved for privileged users.

-f

Force removal of write-protected files without prompting.

-i

Query interactively before removing files.

-r, -R

If the file is a directory, recursively remove the entire directory and all of its contents, including subdirectories.

rmdir

Syntax

```
rmdir [option] directories
```

Description

Delete *directories*, which must be empty.

Frequently used option

-p

Remove *directories* and any intervening parent directories that become empty as a result. This is useful for removing subdirectory trees.

On the Exam

Remember that recursive remove using *rm -R* removes directories too, even if they're not empty.

---

touch

Syntax

    touch [options] files

Description

Change the access and/or modification times of *files*. This command is used to refresh timestamps on files. Doing so may be necessary, for example, to cause a program to be recompiled using the date-dependant *make* utility.

Frequently used options

-a

Change only the access time.

-m

Change only the modification time.

-t timestamp

Instead of the current time, use *timestamp* in the form of [[CC]YY]MMDDhhmm[.ss]. For example, the timestamp for January 12, 2001, at 6:45 p.m. is 200101121845.

File-Naming Wildcards

When working with files on the command line, you'll often run into situations in which you need to perform operations on many files at once. For example, if you are developing a C program, you may want to *touch* all of your *.c* files in order to be sure to recompile them the next time you issue the *make* utility to build your program. There will also be times when you need to move or delete all the files in a directory or at least a selected group of files. At other times, filenames may be long or difficult to type, and you'll want to find an abbreviated alternative to typing the filenames for each command you issue (see Table 5-3).

To make these operations simpler, all shells on Linux offer *file-naming wildcards* ( ).

 Wildcards are expanded by the shell, not by commands. When a command is entered with wildcards included, the shell first expands all the wildcards (and other types of expansion) and passes the full result on to the command. This process is invisible to you.

Rather than explicitly specifying every file or typing long filenames, you can use *wildcard characters* in place of portions of the filenames can usually do the work for you. For example, the shell expands things like **.txt* to a list of all the files that end in *.txt*. File wildcard constructs like this are called *file globs*, and their use is awkwardly called *globbing*. Using file globs to specify multiple files is certainly a convenience, and in many cases is required to get anything useful accomplished. Wildcards for shell globbing are listed in Table 5-3.

Table 5-3. Common file-naming wildcards

Wildcard	Description
*	Commonly thought to "match anything," it actually will match zero or more characters (which includes "nothing"!). For example, x* matches files or directories *x*, *xy*, *xyz*, *x.txt*, *xy.txt*, *xyz.c*, and so on.
?	Match exactly one character. For example, x? matches files or directories *xx, xy, xz*, but not *x* and not *xyz*. The specification x?? matches *xyz*, but not *x* and *xy*.
[*characters*]	Match any single character from among *characters* listed between the brackets. For example, x[yz] matches *xy* and *xz*.
[!*characters*]	Match any single character other than *characters* listed between the brackets. For example, x[!yz] matches *xa* and *x1* but does not match *xy* or *xz*.
[*a-z*]	Match any single character from among the range of characters listed between the brackets and indicated by the dash (the dash character is not matched). For example, x[0-9] matches *x0* and *x1*, but does not match *xx*. Note that to match both upper- and lowercase letters (Linux filenames are case-sensitive), you specify [a-zA-Z]. Using x[a-zA-Z] matches *xa* and *xA*.
[!*a-z*]	Match any single character from among the characters not in the range listed between the brackets.

{*frag1,frag2,frag3,...*}	Create strings *frag1, frag2, frag3*, etc. For example, file_{one,two,three} yields the strings *file_one, file_two,* and *file_three*. This is a special operator named *brace expansion* that can be used to match filenames but isn't specifically a file wildcard operator and does not examine directories for existing files to match. Instead, it will expand *any* string.
	
	For example, it can be used with echo to yield strings totally unrelated to existing filenames:
	`$ echo string_{a,b,c}`
	`string_a string_b string_c`

The following are a few common applications for wildcards:

- If you remember part of a filename but not the whole thing, use wildcards with the portion you remember to help find the file. For example, if you're working in a directory with a large number of files and you know you're looking for a file named for Linux, you may enter a command like this:

  ```
  $ ls -l *inux*
  ```

- When working with groups of related files, wildcards can be used to help separate the groups. For example, suppose you have a directory full of scripts you've written. Some are Perl scripts, for which you've used an extension of *.pl*, and some are Python, with a *.py* extension. You may wish to separate them into new separate directories for the two languages like this:

  ```
  $ mkdir perl python
  $ mv *.pl perl
  $ mv *.py python
  ```

- Wildcards match directory names as well. Suppose you have a tree of directories starting with *contracting*, where you've created a directory for each month (that is, *contracting/january, contracting/february,* through *contracting/december*). In each of these directories are stored invoices, named simply *invoice_custa_01.txt, invoice_custa_02.txt, invoice_custb_01.txt*, and so on, where *custa* and *custb* are customer names of some form. To display all of the invoices, wildcards can be used:

```
$ ls con*/*/inv*.txt
```

The con* matches *contracting*. The second matches all directories under the *contracting* directory (*january* through *december*). The last matches all the customers and each invoice number for each customer.

See the *bash* manpages or info page for additional information on how *bash* handles expansions and on other expansion forms.

Objective 4: Use Streams, Pipes, and Redirects

Among the many beauties of Linux and Unix systems is the notion that *everything is a file*. Things such as disk drives and their partitions, tape drives, terminals, serial ports, the mouse, and even audio are mapped into the filesystem. This mapping allows programs to interact with many different devices and files in the same way, simplifying their interfaces. Each device that uses the file metaphor is given a *device file*, which is a special object in the filesystem that provides an interface to the device. The kernel associates device drivers with various device files, which is how the system manages the illusion that devices can be accessed as if they were files. Using a terminal as an example, a program reading from the terminal's device file will receive characters typed at the keyboard. Writing to the terminal causes characters to appear on the screen. While it may seem odd to think of your terminal as a file, the concept provides a unifying simplicity to Linux and Linux programming.

Standard I/O and Default File Descriptors

Standard I/O is a capability of the shell, used with all text-based Linux utilities to control and direct program input, output, and error information. When a program is launched, it is automatically provided with three *file descriptors*. File descriptors are regularly used in programming and serve as a "handle" of sorts to another file. Standard I/O creates the following file descriptors:

Standard input (abbreviated stdin)
> This file descriptor is a text input stream. By default it is attached to your keyboard. When you type characters into an interactive text program, you are feeding them to standard input. As you've seen, some programs take one or more filenames as command-line arguments and ignore standard input. Standard input is also known as *file descriptor 0*.

Standard output (abbreviated stdout)
> This file descriptor is a text output stream for normal program output. By default it is attached to your terminal (or terminal window). Output generated by commands is written to standard output for display. Standard output is also known as *file descriptor 1*.

Standard error (abbreviated stderr)
> This file descriptor is also a text output stream, but it is used exclusively for errors or other information unrelated to the successful results of your

command. By default, standard error is attached to your terminal just like standard output. This means that standard output and standard error are commingled in your display, which can be confusing. You'll see ways to handle this later. Standard error is also known as *file descriptor 2*.

Standard output and standard error are separated because it is often useful to process normal program output differently than errors.

The standard I/O file descriptors are used in the same way as those created during program execution to read and write disk files. They enable you to tie commands together with files and devices, managing command input and output in exactly the way you desire. The difference is they are provided to the program by the shell by default and do not need to be explicitly created.

Pipes

From a program's point of view there is no difference between reading text data from a file and reading it from your keyboard. Similarly, writing text to a file and writing text to a display are equivalent operations. As an extension of this idea, it is also possible to tie the output of one program to the input of another. This is accomplished using a *pipe* (|) to join two or more commands together. For example:

```
$ grep "01523" order* | less
```

This command searches through all files whose names begin with order to find lines containing the word 01523. By creating this pipe, the standard output of *grep* is sent to the standard input of *less*. The mechanics of this operation are handled by the shell and are invisible to the user. Pipes can be used in a series of many commands. When more than two commands are put together, the resulting operation is known as a *pipeline* or *text stream*, implying the flow of text from one command to the next.

As you get used to the idea, you'll find yourself building pipelines naturally to extract specific information from text data sources. For example, suppose you wish to view a sorted list of inode numbers from among the files in your current directory. There are many ways you could achieve this. One way would be to use *awk* in a pipeline to extract the inode number from the output of *ls*, then send it on to the sort command and finally to a pager for viewing (don't worry about the syntax or function of these commands at this point):

```
$ ls -i * | awk '{print $1}' | sort -nu | less
```

The pipeline concept in particular is a feature of Linux and Unix that draws on the fact that your system contains a diverse set of tools for operating on text. Combining their capabilities can yield quick and easy ways to extract otherwise hard to handle information.

Redirection

Each pipe symbol in the previous pipeline example instructs the shell to feed output from one command into the input of another. This action is a special form of *redirection*, which allows you to manage the origin of input streams and the destination of output streams. In the previous example, individual programs are unaware that their output is being handed off to or from another program because the shell takes care of the redirection on their behalf.

Redirection can also occur to and from files. For example, rather than sending the output of an inode list to the pager *less*, it could easily be sent directly to a file with the > redirection operator:

```
$ ls -i * | awk '{print $1}' | sort -nu > in.txt
```

When you change the last redirection operator, the shell creates an empty file (*in. txt*), opens it for writing, and the standard output of *sort* places the results in the file instead of on the screen. Note that, in this example, anything sent to standard error is still displayed on the screen. In addition, if your specified file, *in.txt*, already existed in your current directory it would be overwritten.

Since the > redirection operator *creates* files, the >> redirection operator can be used to append to existing files. For example, you could use the following command to append a one-line footnote to *in.txt*:

```
$ echo "end of list" >> in.txt
```

Since *in.txt* already exists, the quote will be appended to the bottom of the existing file. If the file didn't exist, the >> operator would create the file and insert the text "end of list" as its contents.

It is important to note that when creating files, the output redirection operators are interpreted by the shell *before* the commands are executed. This means that any output files created through redirection are opened first. For this reason you cannot modify a file in place, like this:

```
$ grep "stuff" file1 > file1    don't do it!
```

If *file1* contains something of importance, this command would be a disaster because an empty *file1* would overwrite the original. The *grep* command would be last to execute, resulting in a complete data loss from the original *file1* file because the file that replaced it was empty. To avoid this problem, simply use an intermediate file and *then* rename it:

```
$ grep "stuff" file1 > file2
$ mv file2 file1
```

Standard input can also be redirected. The input redirection operator is <. Using a source other than the keyboard for a program's input may seem odd at first, but since text programs don't care about where their standard input streams originate, you can easily redirect input. For example, the following command will send a mail message with the contents of the file *in.txt* to user *jdean*:

```
$ mail -s "inode list" jdean < in.txt
```

Normally, the *mail* program prompts the user for input at the terminal. However, with standard input redirected *from* the file *in.txt*, no user input is needed and the command executes silently. Table 5-4 lists the common standard I/O redirections for the *bash* shell, specified in the LPI Objectives.

GNU and Unix
Commands

Table 5-4. Standard I/O redirections for the bash shell

Redirection function	Syntax for bash
Send *stdout* to *file*.	`$ cmd > file` `$ cmd 1> file`
Send *stderr* to *file*.	`$ cmd 2> file`
Send both *stdout* and *stderr* to *file*.	`$ cmd > file 2>&1`
Send *stdout* to *file1* and *stderr* to *file2*.	`$ cmd > file1 2> file2`
Receive *stdin* from *file*.	`$ cmd < file`
Append *stdout* to *file*.	`$ cmd >> file` `$ cmd 1>> file`
Append *stderr* to *file*.	`$ cmd 2>> file`
Append both *stdout* and *stderr* to *file*.	`$ cmd >> file 2>&1`
Pipe *stdout* from *cmd1* to *cmd2*.	`$ cmd1	cmd2`
Pipe *stdout* and *stderr* from *cmd1* to *cmd2*.	`$ cmd1 2>&1	cmd2`

On the Exam

Be prepared to demonstrate the difference between filenames and command names in commands using redirection operators. Also, check the syntax on commands in redirection questions to be sure about which command or file is a data source and which is a destination.

Using the tee Command

Sometimes you'll want to run a program and send its output to a file while at the same time viewing the output on the screen. The tee utility is helpful in this situation.

---

tee

Syntax

```
tee [options] files
```

Description

Read from standard input and write both to one or more *files* and to standard output (analogous to a tee junction in a pipe).

Option

-a

Append to *files* rather than overwriting them.

Example

Suppose you're running a pipeline of commands *cmd1*, *cmd2*, and *cmd3*:

```
$ cmd1 | cmd2 | cmd3 > file1
```

This sequence puts the ultimate output of the pipeline into *file1*. However, you may also be interested in the intermediate result of *cmd1*. To create a new *file_cmd1* containing those results, use *tee*:

```
$ cmd1 | tee file_cmd1 | cmd2 | cmd3 > file1
```

The results in *file1* will be the same as in the original example, and the intermediate results of *cmd1* will be placed in *file_cmd1*.

Objective 5: Create, Monitor, and Kill Processes

This Objective looks at the management of *processes*. Just as file management is a fundamental system administrator's function, the management and control of processes is also essential for smooth system operation. In most cases, processes will live, execute, and die without intervention from the user because they are automatically managed by the kernel. However, there are times that a process will die for some unknown reason and need to be restarted. Or, some process may "run wild" and consume system resources, requiring that it be terminated. You will also need to instruct running processes to perform operations, such as rereading a configuration file.

Processes

Every program, whether it's a command, application, or script, that runs on your system is a *process*. Your shell is a process, and every command you execute from the shell starts one or more processes of its own (referred to as *child processes*). Attributes and concepts associated with these processes include:

Lifetime
> A process lifetime is defined by the length of time it takes to execute (it's "life"). Commands with a short lifetime such as *ls* will execute for a very short time, generate results, and terminate when complete. User programs such as web browsers have a longer lifetime, running for unlimited periods of time until terminated manually. Long lifetime processes include server daemons that run continuously from system boot to shutdown. When a process terminates, it is said to *die* (which is why the program used to manually signal a process to stop execution is called *kill*; succinct, though admittedly morbid).

Process ID (PID)
> Every process has a number assigned to it when it starts. PIDs are integer numbers unique among all running processes.

User ID (UID) and Group ID (GID)
> Processes must have associated privileges, and a process's UID and GID are associated with the user who started the process. This limits the process's access to objects in the filesystem.

Parent process

The first process started by the kernel at system start time is a program called *init*. This process has PID 1 and is the ultimate parent of all other processes on the system. Your shell is a descendant of *init* and the parent process to commands started by the shell, which are its *child* processes, or *subprocesses*.

Parent process ID (parent PID)

This is the PID of the process that created the process in question. If that parent process has vanished, the parent PID will be 1, which is the PID of *init*.

Environment

Each process holds a list of variables and their associated values. Collectively, this list is known as the *environment* of the process, and the variables are called *environment variables*. Child processes inherit their environment settings from the parent process unless an alternative environment is specified when the program is executed.

Current working directory

The default directory associated with each process. The process will read and write files in this directory unless they are explicitly specified to be elsewhere in the filesystem.

On the Exam

The parent/child relationship of the processes on a Linux system is important. Be sure to understand how these relationships work and how to view them. Note that the *init* process always has PID 1 and is the ultimate ancestor of all system processes.

Process Monitoring

At any time, there could be tens or even hundreds of processes running together on your Linux system. Monitoring these processes is done using three convenient utilities: *ps*, *pstree*, and *top*.

---

ps

Syntax

ps [*options*]

Description

This command generates a one-time snapshot of the current processes on standard output.

Frequently used options

-a

Show processes that are owned by other users and attached to a terminal. Normally, only the current user's processes are shown.

-f

"Forest" mode, which is used to display process family trees. For example, using this option will display all running child web servers (*httpd*) in a hierarchical diagram under the parent web server. (There is also a separate command called *pstree* that does this nicely.)

-l

Long format, which includes priority, parent PID, and other information.

-u

User format, which includes usernames and the start time of processes.

-w

Wide output format, used to eliminate the default output line truncation. Useful for the *-f* option.

-x

Include processes without controlling terminals. Often needed to see daemon processes and others not started from a terminal session.

-C *cmd*
Display instances of command name *cmd*.

-U *user*
Display processes owned by username *user*.

Examples

Simply entering the *ps* command with no options will yield a brief list of processes owned by you and attached to your terminal:

    $ ps

Use the *-a*, *-u*, and *-x* options to include processes owned by others and not attached to terminals as well as to display them in the "user" mode. The command is valid with or without the dash:

    $ ps -aux
    $ ps aux

In this case, the dash is optional. However, certain *ps* options require the dash. (See the manpage for details.)

If you are interested in finding process information on a particular command, use the -C option. This command displays all web server processes:

    $ ps u -C httpd

You'll note that the -C option *requires* the dash, but the *u* option won't work with it if a dash is included. This confusion exists because the *ps* command as implemented on Linux understands options in three differing forms:

Unix98 options
These may be grouped and must be preceded by a dash.

BSD options
These may be grouped and must *not* be used with a dash.

GNU long options
These options are preceded by two dashes.

The Linux *ps* tries to be compatible with *ps* from various other systems. How it interprets various command-line options, which determines how compatible it is with other versions of *ps*, can be controlled by setting I_WANT_A_BROKEN_PS, PS_PERSONALITY, and various other environment variables. See the *ps* manpage for details.

All of these option types may be freely intermixed. Instead of the -C option, you may wish to use *ps* with other options that you usually use and pipe the output to *grep*, searching for process names, PIDs, or anything else you know about the process:

```
$ ps aux | grep httpd
```

In this case, the result would be the same list of *httpd* servers, as well as the *grep* command itself.

pstree

Syntax

```
pstree [options] [pid|user]
```

Description

The *pstree* command is similar to the "forest" mode of *ps -f*. This command displays a hierarchical list of processes in a tree format. *pstree* is very handy for understanding how parent/child process relationships are set up.

If the PID is specified, the displayed tree is rooted at that process. Otherwise, it is rooted at the *init* process, which has PID 1. If *user* (a valid username) is specified, trees for all processes owned by *user* are shown. The tree is represented using characters that appear as lines, such as | for vertical lines and + for intersections (VT100 line-drawing characters, displayed as solid lines by most terminals, are optional). The output looks similar to this:

```
httpd-+-httpd
      |-httpd
      |-httpd
      |-httpd
      `-httpd
```

By default, visually identical branches of the tree are merged to reduce output. Merged lines are preceded by a count indicating the actual number of similar processes. The preceding example is normally displayed on a single line:

```
httpd---5*[httpd]
```

This behavior can be turned off with the -c option.

Frequently used options

-a

Display command-line arguments used to launch processes.

-c

Disable the compaction of identical subtrees.

-G

Use the VT100 line-drawing characters instead of plain characters to display the tree. This yields a much more pleasing display but may not be appropriate for printing or paging programs.

-h

Highlight the ancestry of the current process (usually the shell). The terminal must support highlighting for this option to be meaningful.

-n

The default sort order for processes with the same parent is alphanumerically by name. This option changes this behavior to a numeric sort by PID.

-p

Include PIDs in the output.

Example

Display a process tree including PIDs:

```
# pstree -p
init(1)-+-atd(468)
        |-bdflush(5)
        |-crond(454)
        |-httpd(440)-+-httpd(450)
        |            |-httpd(451)
        |            |-httpd(452)
        |            |-httpd(453)
        |            |-httpd(455)
        |            |-httpd(456)
        |            |-httpd(457)
        |            `-httpd(458)
        |-keventd(2)
        |-kjournald(7)
        |-klogd(335)
        |-ksoftirqd_CPU0(3)
        |-kswapd(4)
        |-kupdated(6)
        |-login(475)---bash(478)---pstree(518)
        |-sendmail(420)
        |-sshd(385)
        |-syslogd(330)
        `-xinetd(402)
```

top

Syntax

```
top [options]
```

Description

The *top* command also offers output similar to *ps*, but in a continuously updated display. This is useful in situations in which you need to watch the status of one or more processes or to see how they are using your system.

In addition, a header of useful uptime, load, CPU status, and memory information is displayed. By default, the process status output is generated with the most CPU-intensive processes at the top of the listing (and is named for the "top" processes). To format the screen, *top* must understand how to control the terminal display. The type of terminal (or terminal window) in use is stored in the environment variable TERM. If this variable is not set or contains an unknown terminal type, *top* may not execute.

Popular command-line options

Dashes are optional in *top* options:

-b

> Run in batch mode. This is useful for sending output from *top* to other programs or to a file. It executes the number of iterations specified with the *-n* option and terminate. This option is also useful if *top* cannot display on the terminal type you are using.

-d delay

> Specify the *delay* in seconds between screen updates. The default is five seconds.

-i

> Ignore idle processes, listing only the "interesting" ones taking system resources.

-n num

> Display *num* iterations and then exit, instead of running indefinitely.

-q

> Run with no delay. If the user is the superuser, run with highest possible priority. This option causes *top* to update continuously and will probably consume any idle time your CPU had. Running *top -q* as superuser will seriously affect system performance and is not recommended.

-s

> Run in secure mode. Some of *top*'s interactive commands can be dangerous if running as the superuser. This option disables them.

Frequently used interactive options

Once *top* is running interactively, it can be given a number of commands via the keyboard to change its behavior. These commands are single-key commands, some of which cause top to prompt for input:

Ctrl-L

> Refresh the screen.

h

> Generate a help screen.

k

> Kill a process. You will be prompted for the PID of the process and the signal to send it. (The default signal is 15, *SIGTERM*.) See the later section "Terminating Processes."

n

> Change the number of processes to show. You will be prompted to enter an integer number. The default is 0, which indicates that the screen should be filled.

q

> Quit the program.

r

Change the priority of a process (*renice*). You will be prompted for the PID of the process and the value to nice it to (see *nice* and *renice* later in this chapter in "Objective 6: Modify Process Execution Priorities"). Entering a positive value causes a process to lose priority. If the superuser is running top, a negative value may be entered, causing a process to get a higher than normal priority. This command is not available in secure mode.

s

Change the delay in seconds between updates. You will be prompted for the delay value, which may include fractions of seconds (i.e., 0.5).

Example 1

Simply executing *top* without options gives a full status display updated every five seconds:

```
$ top
```

Use the q command to quit.

Example 2

To run *top* with a faster refresh rate, use the interval option, specified here with a one-second refresh:

```
$ top -d 1
```

Example 3

To have *top* update constantly, you could specify *-d 0*, or use the *-q* option. Here, this feature is used to watch only non-idle processes, which will include *top* itself:

```
$ top -qi
```

Example 4

You may wish to use *top* to log its output to a file. Use the *-b* (batch) option for this purpose. In this batch example, the *-i* option eliminates idle processes, the *-n* option, with its argument, indicates five iterations, and the *-d* option indicates a one-second interval. Results will be redirected to *file1*. This command will take five seconds to execute and does not use the optional dashes:

```
$ top bin 5 d 1 > file1
```

The single-key interactive commands can be used when *top* is running interactively. For example, if you type the h command, *top* displays a help screen. If you enter the *n* command, top prompts you for the number of lines you wish to display.

Using *top* to change the *nice* (priority modifier) value for a process is discussed in "Objective 6: Modify Process Execution Priorities" later in this chapter.

Signaling Active Processes

Each process running on your system listens for *signals*, simple messages sent to the process either by the kernel or by a user. The messages are sent through inter-process communication. They are single-valued, in that they don't contain strings or command-like constructs. Instead, signals are numeric integer messages, predefined and known by processes. Most have an implied action for the process to take. When a process receives a signal, it can (or may be forced) to take action.

For example, if you are executing a program from the command line that appears to hang, you may elect to type Ctrl-C to abort the program. This action actually sends an *SIGINT* (interrupt signal) to the process, telling it to stop running.

There are more than 32 signals defined for normal process use in Linux. Each signal has a name and a number (the number is sent to the process, the name is only for our convenience). Many signals are used by the kernel, and some are useful for users. Table 5-5 lists popular signals for interactive use.

Table 5-5. Frequently used interactive signals

Signal name[a]	Number	Meaning and use
HUP	1	Hang up. This signal is sent automatically when you log out or disconnect a modem. It is also used by many daemons to cause the configuration file to be reread.
INT	2	Interrupt; stop running. This signal is sent when you type Ctrl-C.
KILL	9	Kill; stop unconditionally and immediately. Sending this signal is a drastic measure, as it cannot be ignored by the process. This is the "emergency kill" signal.
TERM	15	Terminate, nicely if possible. This signal is used to ask a process to exit gracefully.
TSTP	20	Stop executing, ready to continue. This signal is sent when you type Ctrl-Z. (See the later section "Shell Job Control" for more information.)
CONT	18	Continue execution. This signal is sent to start a process stopped by SIGTSTP or SIGSTOP. (The shell sends this signal when you use the *fg* or *bg* commands after stopping a process with Ctrl-Z.)

[a] Signal names will often be specified with a SIG prefix. That is, signal HUP is the same as signal SIGHUP.

As you can see from Table 5-5, some signals are invoked by pressing well-known key combinations such as Ctrl-C and Ctrl-Z. You can also use the *kill* command to send any message. The *kill* command is implemented both as a shell built-in command and as a standalone binary command.

kill

Syntax

```
kill [-s sigspec | -sigspec] [pids]
kill -l [signum]
```

Description

In the first form, *kill* is used with an optional *sigspec*. This is a signal value, specified as either an integer or the signal name (such as *SIGHUP*, or simply *HUP*). The *sigspec* is case-insensitive but is usually specified with uppercase letters. The *bash* built-in *kill* is case-insensitive both when using the *-s sigspec* and the *-sigspec* forms, but the standalone *kill* is only case-insensitive in the *-s sigspec* form. For this reason, it is best to use uppercase signal names. You may use *-s sigspec* or simply *-sigspec* to make up the signal value or name. If a *sigspec* is not given, then *SIGTERM* (signal 15, "exit gracefully") is assumed. The *sigspec* is followed by one or more PIDS to which the signal is to be sent. In the second form with the *-l* option, *kill* lists the valid signal names. If *signum* (an integer) is present, only the signal name for that number will be displayed.

Examples

This command displays the signal name *SIGTERM*, the name of signal 15, and the default when kill is used to signal processes:

```
$ kill -l 15
TERM
```

All of these commands will send *SIGTERM* to the processes with PIDs 1000 and 1001:

```
$ kill 1000 1001
$ kill -15 1000 1001
$ kill -SIGTERM 1000 1001
$ kill -sigterm 1000 1001
$ kill -TERM 1000 1001
$ kill -s 15 1000 1001
$ kill -s SIGTERM 1000 1001
```

If those two processes are playing nicely on your system, they'll comply with the *SIGTERM* signal and terminate when they're ready (after they clean up whatever they're doing). Not all processes will comply, however. A process may be hung in such a way that it cannot respond, or it may have *signal handling* code written to trap the signal you're trying to send. To force a process to die, use the strongest *kill*:

```
$ kill -9 1000 1001
$ kill -KILL 1000 1001
```

These equivalent commands send the *KILL* signal to the process, which the process cannot ignore. The process will terminate immediately without closing files or performing any other cleanup. Because this may leave the program's data in an inconsistent state, using the *KILL* signal should be a last resort. When a process is blocked waiting for I/O, such as trying to write to an unavailable NFS server or waiting for a tape device to complete rewinding, the *KILL* signal may not work. See the "Terminating Processes" section.

The *httpd* daemon will respond to the *HUP* signal by rereading its configuration files. If you've made changes and want *httpd* to reconfigure itself, send it the *HUP* signal:

```
$ kill -HUP `cat /var/run/httpd.pid`
```

Many other daemons respond to *SIGHUP* this way.

The back quotes are replaced by the shell with the contents of the file *httpd.pid*, which *httpd* creates when it starts.

GNU and Unix
Commands

On the Exam

Note that *kill* is used for sending all kinds of signals, not just termination signals. Also, be aware of the difference between the PID you intend to kill and the signal you wish to send it. Since they're both integers, they can sometimes be confused.

Terminating Processes

Occasionally, you'll find a system showing symptoms of high CPU load or run out of memory for no obvious reason. This often means an application has gone out

kill | 97

of control on your system. You can use *ps* or *top* to identify processes that may be having a problem. Once you know the PID for the process, you can use the *kill* command to stop the process nicely with *SIGTERM* (kill -15 *PID*), escalating the signal to higher strengths if necessary until the process terminates.

 Occasionally you may see a process displayed by *ps* or *top* that is listed as a *zombie*. These are processes that are stuck while trying to terminate and are appropriately said to be in the *zombie state*. Just as in the cult classic film *Night of the Living Dead*, you can't kill zombies, because they're already dead!

If you have a recurring problem with zombies, there may be a bug in your system software or in an application.

Killing a process may also kill all of its child processes. For example, killing a shell may kill all the processes initiated from that shell, including other shells.

Shell Job Control

Linux and most modern Unix systems offer *job control*, which is the ability of your shell (with support of the kernel) to stop and restart executing commands, as well as place them in the *background* where they can be executed. A program is said to be in the *foreground* when it is attached to your terminal. When executing in the background, you have no input to the process other than sending it signals. When a process is put in the background, you create a *job*. Each job is assigned a job number, starting at 1 and numbering sequentially.

The basic reason to create a background process is to keep your shell session free. There are many instances when a long-running program will never produce a result from standard output or standard error, and your shell will simply sit idle waiting for the program to finish. Noninteractive programs can be placed in the *background* by adding a & character to the command. For example, if you start mozilla from the command line, you don't want the shell to sit and wait for it to terminate. The shell will respond by starting the browser in the background and will give you a new command prompt. It will also issue the job number, denoted in square brackets, along with the PID. For example:

```
$ mozilla &
[1]  1748
```

Here, Mozilla is started as a background process. Mozilla is assigned to job 1 (as denoted by [1]), and is assigned PID 1748. If you start a program and forget the & character, you can still put it in the background by first stopping it by typing Ctrl-Z:

```
^Z
[1]+  Stopped         mozilla
```

Then issue the *bg* command to restart the job in the background:

```
$ bg
[1]+ mozilla &
```

When you exit from a shell with jobs in the background, those processes may die. The utility *nohup* can be used to protect the background processes from the hangup signal (*SIGHUP*) that it might otherwise receive when the shell dies. This can be used to simulate the detached behavior of a system daemon.

Putting interactive programs in the background can be quite useful. Suppose you're logged into a remote Linux system, running Emacs in text mode. Rather than exit from the editor when you need to drop back to the shell, you can simply press Ctrl-Z. This stops Emacs, puts it in the background, and returns you a command prompt.* When you are finished, you resume your Emacs session with the *fg* command, which puts your stopped job back into the foreground.

Background jobs and their status can be listed by issuing the *jobs* command. Stopped jobs can be brought to the foreground with the *fg* command and optionally placed into the background with the Ctrl-Z and bg sequence.

bg

Syntax
    bg [jobspec]

Description
Place *jobspec* in the background, as if it had been started with &. If *jobspec* is not present, then the shell's notion of the *current job* is used, as indicated by the plus sign (+) in output from the *jobs* command. Using this command on a job that is stopped will allow it to run in the background.

fg

Syntax
    fg [jobspec]

Description
This command places the specified job in the foreground, making it the current job. If *jobspec* is not present, the shell's notion of the current job is used.

jobs

Syntax
    jobs [options] [jobspecs]

---

* This example ignores the fact that Emacs is capable of hosting a shell itself, which would probably eliminate your need to use job control to get to the command line.

Description

List the active jobs. The optional *jobspecs* argument restricts output to information about those jobs.

Frequently used option

-*l*

    Also list PIDs.

On the Exam

Be sure to know how to display background jobs and how to switch among them.

Objective 6: Modify Process Execution Priorities

One of the features of Linux is that the administrator has the ability to prioritize process execution. This feature is handy when you have a high load machine and want to make sure special processes (like yours!) get more rights to use system resources than others. It also is useful if you have a process that's gone haywire and you want to debug the problem prior to killing it. On the flip side, you can bury non-essential processes giving them the lowest priority so they don't ever conflict with other processes. (Particularly useful when participating in experiments to search for extraterrestrial intelligence with SETI@home.)

Generally, on a day-to-day basis, you don't need to worry about execution priority because the kernel handles it automatically. Each process's priority level is constantly and dynamically raised and lowered by the kernel according to a number of parameters, such as how much system time it has already consumed and its status (perhaps waiting for I/O—such processes are favored by the kernel). Linux gives you the ability to bias the kernel's priority algorithm, favoring certain processes over others.

The priority of a process can be determined by examining the PRI column in the results produced from issuing either the *top* or *ps -l* commands. The values displayed are relative; the higher the priority number, the more CPU time the kernel offers to the process. The kernel does this by managing a queue of processes. Those with high priority are given more time, and those with low priority are given less time. On a heavily loaded system, a process with a very low priority may appear stalled.

nice

One of the parameters used by the kernel to assign process priority is supplied by the user and is called a *nice number*. The *nice* command[*] is used to assign a

---

[*] Some shells, not including *bash*, have a built-in *nice* command.

---

priority number to the process. It is so named because it normally causes programs to execute with lower priority levels than with their default. Thus, the process is being "nice" to other processes on the system by yielding CPU time. With this scheme, more "niceness" implies a lower priority, and less niceness implies a higher priority.

By default, user processes are created with a *nice number* of zero. Positive numbers lower the priority relative to other processes, and negative numbers raise it. For example, if you have a long-running utility and don't want to impact interactive performance, a positive nice number will lower the job's priority and improve interactive performance.

Nice numbers range from -20 to +19. Any user can start a process with a positive nice number, but only the superuser (*root*) can lower a process's nice number and thus raise its priority.

nice

Syntax
```
nice [-n adjustment] [command ]
nice [-adjustment] [command ]
```

Description
The *nice* command is used to alter another command's nice number at start time. For normal users, *adjustment* is an integer from 1 to 19. If you're the superuser, the *adjustment* range is from -20 to 19. If an *adjustment* number is not specified, the process's nice number defaults to 10. The *command* consists of any command that you might enter on the command line, including all options, arguments, redirections, and the background character &.

If both *adjustment* and *command* are omitted, *nice* displays the current scheduling priority, which is inherited.

Example 1
The following command starts a program in the background with reduced priority, using the default nice number of 10:
```
$ nice somecmd -opt1 -opt2 arg1 arg2 &
```

Example 2
As superuser, you can start programs with elevated priority. These equivalent commands start the *vi* editor with a higher priority, which may be necessary for administrative purposes if the system is exceptionally slow:
```
# nice --10 vi /etc/hosts.deny
# nice -n -10 vi /etc/hosts.deny
```
Note the double dash (--10) in the first form. The first dash indicates that an option follows, while the second dash indicates a negative number.

Be careful when using *nice* on interactive programs such as editors, word processors, or browsers. Assigning a program a positive nice number will most likely result in sluggish performance. Remember, the higher the positive number, the lower the resulting priority level.

For that reason, you should try not to assign positive nice numbers to foreground jobs on your terminal. If the system gets busy, your terminal could hang awaiting CPU time, which has been sacrificed by *nice*.

Changing nice numbers on running processes

The *nice* command works to change the nice number for new processes only at the time that they're started. To modify a running program, use the *renice* command.

renice

Syntax

```
renice [+|-]nicenumber [option] targets
```

Description

Alter the *nicenumber* to set the scheduling priority of one or more running *target* processes. By default, *renice* assumes that the *targets* are numeric PIDs. One or more *option*s may also be used to interpret *targets* as processes owned by specific users.

Frequently used options

-u
   Interpret *targets* as usernames, affecting all processes owned by those users.

-p
   Interpret *targets* as PIDs (the default).

Examples

This command will lower the priority of the process with PID 501 by increasing its nice number to the maximum:

```
$ renice 20 501
```

The following command can be used to increase the priority of all of user *jdean*'s processes as well as the process with PID 501:

```
# renice -10 -u jdean -p 501
```

In this command, -10 indicates a nice value of negative 10, thus giving PID 501 a higher priority on the system. A dash isn't used for the nice value because the dash could be confused for an option, such as -*u*.

On the Exam

Be sure to know the range and meaning of nice numbers and how to change them for new and existing processes. Also note that *nice* and *renice* specify their numbers differently. With *nice*, a leading dash can indicate a nice number (e.g., -10), including a negative one with a second dash (e.g., --10). On the other hand, *renice* does not need the dash.

You can renice processes interactively using top's text interface by using the single-keystroke r command. You will be prompted for the PID of the process whose nice number you wish to change and for the new nice number. If you are the superuser, you can enter negative values. The new nice number will be displayed by top in the column labeled NI for the process you specify.

Objective 7: Search Text Files Using Regular Expressions

Linux offers many tools for system administrators to use for processing text. Many, such as *sed*, *awk*, and *perl*, are capable of automatically editing multiple files, providing you with a wide range of text-processing capability. To harness that capability, you need to be able to define and delineate specific text segments from within files, text streams, and string variables. Once the text you're after is identified, you can use one of these tools or languages to do useful things to it.

These tools and others understand a loosely defined pattern language. The language and the patterns themselves are collectively called regular expressions (often abbreviated just *regexp* or *regex*). While regular expressions are similar in concept to file globs, many more special characters exist for regular expressions, extending the utility and capability of tools that understand them.

Two tools that are important for the LPIC Level 1 exams and that make use of regular expressions are *grep* and *sed*. These tools are useful for text searches. There are many other tools that make use of regular expressions, including the *awk*, Perl, and Python languages and other utilities, but you don't need to be concerned with them for the purpose of the LPIC Level 1 exams.

Regular expressions are the topic of entire books, such as *Mastering Regular Expressions* (O'Reilly). Exam 101 requires the use of simple regular expressions and related tools, specifically to perform searches from text sources. This section covers only the basics of regular expressions, but it goes without saying that their power warrants a full understanding. Digging deeper into the regular expression world is highly recommended when you have the chance.

Regular Expression Syntax

It would not be unreasonable to assume that some specification defines how regular expressions are constructed. Unfortunately, there isn't one. Regular expressions have been incorporated as a feature in a number of tools over the years, with varying degrees of consistency and completeness. The result is a cart-before-the-horse scenario, in which utilities and languages have defined their own flavor of regular expression syntax, each with its own extensions and idiosyncrasies. Formally defining the regular expression syntax came later, as did efforts to make it more consistent. Regular expressions are defined by arranging strings of text, or *patterns*. Those patterns are composed of two types of characters, *literals* (plain text or literal text) and *metacharacters*.

Like the special file *globbing* characters, regular expression metacharacters take on a special meaning in the context of the tool in which they're used. There are a few metacharacters that are generally thought of to be among the "extended set" of metacharacters, specifically those introduced into *egrep* after *grep* was created.

The *egrep* command on Linux systems is simply a wrapper that runs *grep -E*. Examples of metacharacters include the ^ symbol, which means "the beginning of a line," and the $ symbol, which means "the end of a line." A complete listing of metacharacters follows in Tables 5-6, 5-7, and 5-8.

 The backslash character (\) turns off (escapes) the special meaning of the character that follows, turning metacharacters into literals. For non-metacharacters, it often turns on some special meaning.

Table 5-6. Regular expression position anchors

Regular expression	Description
^	Match at the beginning of a line. This interpretation makes sense only when the ^ character is at the left-hand side of the *regex*.
$	Match at the end of a line. This interpretation makes sense only when the $ character is at the right-hand side of the *regex*.
\< \>	Match word boundaries. Word boundaries are defined as whitespace, the start of line, the end of line, or punctuation marks. The backslashes are required and enable this interpretation of < and >.

Table 5-7. Regular expression character sets

Regular expression	Description
[abc] [a-z]	Single-character groups and ranges. In the first form, match any single character from among the enclosed characters a, b, or c. In the second form, match any single character from among the range of characters bounded by a and z (POSIX character classes can also be used, so [a-z] can be replaced with [[:lower:]]). The brackets are for grouping only and are not matched themselves.
[^abc] [^a-z]	Inverse match. Match any single character not among the enclosed characters a, b, and c or in the range a-z. Be careful not to confuse this inversion with the anchor character ^, described earlier.
.	Match any single character except a newline.

Table 5-8. Regular expression modifiers

Basic regular expression	Extended regular expression (egrep)	Description
*	*	Match an unknown number (zero or more) of the single character (or single-character *regex*) that precedes it.
\?	?	Match zero or one instance of the preceding *regex*.
\+	+	Match one or more instances of the preceding *regex*.
\{*n*,*m*\}	{*n*,*m*}	Match a range of occurrences of the single character or *regex* that precedes this construct. \{*n*\} matches *n* occurrences, \{*n*,\} matches at least *n* occurrences, and \{*n*,*m*\} matches any number of occurrences from *n* to *m*, inclusively.
|			Alternation. Match either the *regex* specified before or after the vertical bar.
\(*regex*\)	(*regex*)	Grouping. Matches *regex*, but it can be modified as a whole and used in back-references. (\1 expands to the contents of the first \(\) and so on up to \9.)

It is often helpful to consider regular expressions as their own language, where literal text acts as words and phrases. The "grammar" of the language is defined by the use of metacharacters. The two are combined according to specific rules (which, as mentioned earlier, may differ slightly among various tools) to communicate ideas and get real work done. When you construct regular expressions, you use metacharacters and literals to specify three basic ideas about your input text:

Position anchors
> A position anchor is used to specify the position of one or more character sets in relation to the entire line of text (such as the beginning of a line).

Character sets
> A character set matches text. It could be a series of literals, metacharacters that match individual or multiple characters, or combinations of these.

Quantity modifiers
> Quantity modifiers follow a character set and indicate the number of times the set should be repeated.

Using grep

A long time ago, as the idea of regular expressions was catching on, the line editor ed contained a command to display lines of a file being edited that matched a given regular expression. The command is:

```
g/regular expression/p
```

That is, "on a global basis, print the current line when a match for *regular expression* is found," or more simply, "global *regular expression* print." This function was so useful that it was made into a standalone utility named, appropriately, *grep*. Later, the regular expression grammar of *grep* was expanded in a new command called *egrep* (for "extended *grep*"). You'll find both commands on your Linux system today, and they differ slightly in the way they handle regular expressions. For the purposes of Exam 101, we'll stick with *grep*, which can also make use of the "extended" regular expressions when used with the -E option. You will find some form of *grep* on just about every Unix or Unix-like system available.

---

grep

Syntax
```
grep [options] regex [files]
```

Description
Search *files* or standard input for lines containing a match to regular expression *regex*. By default, matching lines will be displayed and nonmatching lines will not be displayed. When multiple files are specified, *grep* displays the filename as a prefix to the output lines (use the -h option to suppress filename prefixes).

Frequently used options
-c
> Display only a count of matched lines, but not the lines themselves.

-h

Display matched lines, but do not include filenames for multiple file input.

-i

Ignore uppercase and lowercase distinctions, allowing abc to match both abc and ABC.

-n

Display matched lines prefixed with their line numbers. When used with multiple files, *both* the filename and line number are prefixed.

-v

Print all lines that *do not* match *regex*. This is an important and useful option. You'll want to use regular expressions, not only to *select* information but also to *eliminate* information. Using -v inverts the output this way.

-E

Interpret *regex* as an extended regular expression. This makes *grep* behave as if it were *egrep*.

Examples

Since regular expressions can contain both metacharacters and literals, *grep* can be used with an entirely literal *regex*. For example, to find all lines in *file1* that contain either *Linux* or *linux*, you could use *grep* like this:

```
$ grep -i linux file1
```

In this example, the *regex* is simply linux. The uppercase L in Linux will match since the command-line option -i was specified. This is fine for literal expressions that are common. However, in situations in which *regex* includes regular expression metacharacters that are also shell special characters (such as $ or *), the *regex* must be quoted to prevent shell expansion and pass the metacharacters on to *grep*.

As a simplistic example of this, suppose you have files in your local directory named *abc*, *abc1*, and *abc2*. When combined with *bash*'s *echo* built-in command, the abc* wildcard expression lists all files that begin with abc, as follows:

```
$ echo abc*
abc abc1 abc2
```

Now, suppose that these files contain lines with the strings abc, abcc, abccc, and so on, and you wish to use *grep* to find them. You can use the shell wildcard expression abc* to expand to all the files that start with abc as displayed with echo above, and you'd use an identical regular expression abc* to find all occurrences of lines containing abc, abcc, abccc, etc. Without using quotes to prevent shell expansion, the command would be:

```
$ grep abc* abc*
```

After shell expansion, this yields:

grep abc abc1 abc2 abc abc1 abc2   *no!*

This is *not* what you intended! *grep* would search for the literal expression abc, because it appears as the first command argument. Instead, quote the regular expression with single or double quotes to protect it (the difference between single quotes and double quotes on the command line is subtle and is explained later in this section):

```
$ grep 'abc*' abc*
```

or:

```
$ grep "abc*" abc*
```

After expansion, both examples yield the same results:

```
grep abc* abc abc1 abc2
```

Now this is what you're after. The three files *abc*, *abc1*, and *abc2* will be searched for the regular expression abc*. It is good to stay in the habit of quoting regular expressions on the command line to avoid these problems—they won't be at all obvious because the shell expansion is invisible to you unless you use the *echo* command.

On the Exam

The use of *grep* and its options is common. You should be familiar with what each option does, as well as the concept of piping the results of other commands into grep for matching.

Using sed

sed, the *stream editor*, is a powerful filtering program found on nearly every Unix system. The *sed* utility is usually used either to automate repetitive editing tasks or to process text in pipes of Unix commands (see "Objective 4: Use Streams, Pipes, and Redirects," earlier in this chapter). The scripts that *sed* executes can be single commands or more complex lists of editing instructions.

---

sed

Syntax

```
sed [options] 'command1' [files]
sed [options] -e 'command1' [-e 'command2'...] [files]
sed [options] -f script [files]
```

Description

The first form invokes *sed* with a one-line *command1*. The second form invokes *sed* with two (or more) commands. Note that in this case the *-e* parameter is required for each command specified. The commands are specified in quotes to prevent the shell from interpreting and expanding them. The last form instructs *sed* to take editing commands from file *script* (which does not need to be executable). In all cases, if *files* are not specified, input is taken from standard input. If multiple *files* are specified, the edited output of each successive file is concatenated.

Frequently used options

-e cmd
> The *-e* option specifies that the next argument (*cmd*) is a *sed* command (or a series of commands). When specifying only one string of commands, the *-e* is optional.

-f file
> *file* is a *sed* script.

-g
>Treat all substitutions as global.

The *sed* utility operates on text through the use of *addresses* and *editing commands*. The address is used to locate lines of text to be operated on, and editing commands modify text. During operation, each line (that is, text separated by newline characters) of input to *sed* is processed individually and without regard to adjacent lines. If multiple editing commands are to be used (through the use of a script file or multiple *-e* options), they are all applied in order to each line before moving on to the next line.

Addressing

Addresses in *sed* locate lines of text to which commands will be applied. The addresses can be:

- A line number (note that *sed* counts lines continuously across multiple input files). The symbol $ can be used to indicate the last line of input. A range of line numbers can be given by separating the starting and ending lines with a comma (*start,end*), so for example the address for all input would be 1,$.

- A regular expression delimited by forward slashes (/*regex*/).

- A line number with an interval. The form is *n~s*, where *n* is the starting line number and *s* is the step, or interval, to apply. For example, to match every odd line in the input, the address specification would be 1~2 (start at line 1 and match every two lines thereafter). This feature is a GNU extension to *sed*.

If no address is given, commands are applied to all input lines by default. Any address may be followed by the ! character, and commands are applied to lines that *do not match* the address.

Commands

The *sed* command immediately follows the address specification if present. Commands generally consist of a single letter or symbol, unless they have arguments. Following are some basic sed editing commands to get you started.

d
>Delete lines.

s
>Make substitutions. This is a very popular *sed* command. The syntax is as follows:
>```
>s/pattern/replacement/[flags]
>```

The following *flags* can be specified for the s command:

g
>Replace all instances of *pattern*, not just the first.

n
>Replace *n*th instance of *pattern*; the default is 1.

p
>Print the line if a successful substitution is done. Generally used with the *-n* command-line option.

w *file*
>Print the line to *file* if a successful substitution is done.

y
>Translate characters. This command works in a fashion similar to the *tr* command, described earlier.

Example 1

Delete lines 3 through 5 of *file1*:

```
$ sed '3,5d' file1
```

Example 2

Delete lines of *file1* that contain a # at the beginning of the line:

```
$ sed '/^#/d' file1
```

Example 3

Translate characters:

```
y/abc/xyz/
```

Every instance of a is translated to x, b to y, and c to z.

Example 4

Write the @ symbol for all empty lines in *file1* (that is, lines with only a newline character but nothing more):

```
$ sed 's/^$/@/' file1
```

Example 5

Remove all double quotation marks from all lines in *file1*:

```
$ sed 's/"//g' file1
```

Example 6

Using *sed* commands from external file *sedcmds*, replace the third and fourth double quotation marks with (and) on lines 1 through 10 in *file1*. Make no changes from line 11 to the end of the file. Script file *sedcmds* contains:

```
1,10{
s/"/(/3
s/")/4
}
```

The command is executed using the *-f* option:

```
$ sed -f sedcmds file1
```

This example employs the positional flag for the s (substitute) command. The first of the two commands substitutes (for the third double-quote character. The next command substitutes) for the fourth double-quote character. Note, however, that the position count is interpreted *independently* for each subsequent command in the script. This is important because each command operates on the results of the commands preceding it. In this example, since the third double quote has been replaced with (, it is no longer counted as a double quote by the second command. Thus, the second command will operate on the *fifth* double quote character in the original *file1*. If the input line starts out with the following:

```
""""""
```

after the first command, which operates on the third double quote, the result is this:

```
""(""""
```

At this point, the numbering of the double-quote characters has changed, and the fourth double quote in the line is now the fifth character. Thus, after the second command executes, the output is as follows:

```
""(")"
```

As you can see, creating scripts with sed requires that the sequential nature of the command execution be kept in mind.

If you find yourself making repetitive changes to many files on a regular basis, a sed script is probably warranted. Many more commands are available in sed than are listed here.

Examples

Now that the gory details are out of the way, here are some examples of simple regular expression usage that you may find useful.

Anchors

Anchors are used to describe position information. Table 5-6 lists anchor characters.

Example 1

Display all lines from *file1* where the string Linux appears at the start of the line:

```
$ grep '^Linux' file1
```

Example 2

Display lines in *file1* where the last character is an x:

```
$ grep 'x$' file1
```

Display the number of empty lines in *file1* by finding lines with nothing between the beginning and the end:

```
$ grep -c '^$' file1
```

Display all lines from *file1* containing only the word null by itself:

```
$ grep '^null$' file1
```

Groups and ranges

Characters can be placed into groups and ranges to make regular expressions more efficient, as shown in Table 5-7.

Example 1

Display all lines from *file1* containing Linux, linux, TurboLinux, and so on:

```
$ grep '[Ll]inux' file1
```

Example 2

Display all lines from *file1* which contain three adjacent digits:

```
$ grep '[0-9][0-9][0-9]' file1
```

Example 3

Display all lines from *file1* beginning with any single character other than a digit:

```
$ grep '^[^0-9]' file1
```

Example 4

Display all lines from *file1* that contain the whole word Linux or linux, but not LinuxOS or TurboLinux:

```
$ grep '\<[Ll]inux\>' file1
```

Example 5

Display all lines from *file1* with five or more characters on a line (excluding the newline character):

```
$ grep '.....' file1
```

Example 6

Display all nonblank lines from *file1* (i.e., that have at least one character):

```
$ grep '.' file1
```

Example 7

Display all lines from *file1* that contain a period (normally a metacharacter) using an escape:

```
$ grep '\.' file1
```

Modifiers

Modifiers change the meaning of other characters in a regular expression. Table 5-8 lists these modifiers.

Example 1

Display all lines from *file1* that contain ab, abc, abcc, abccc, and so on:

```
$ grep 'abc*' file1
```

Example 2

Display all lines from *file1* that contain abc, abcc, abccc, and so on, but not ab:

```
$ grep 'abcc*' file1
```

Example 3

Display all lines from *file1* that contain two or more adjacent digits:

```
$ grep '[0-9][0-9][0-9]*' file1
```

or:

```
$ grep '[0-9]\{2,\}' file1
```

Example 4

Display lines from *file1* that contain file (because ? can match zero occurrences), file1, or file2:

```
$ grep 'file[12]\?' file1
```

Example 5

Display all lines from *file1* containing at least one digit:

```
$ grep '[0-9]\+' file1
```

Example 6

Display all lines from *file1* that contain 111, 1111, or 11111 on a line by itself:

```
$ grep '^1\{3,5\}$' file1
```

Example 7

Display all lines from *file1* that contain any three-, four-, or five-digit number:

```
$ grep '\<[0-9]\{3,5\}\>' file1
```

Example 8

Display all lines from *file1* that contain Happy, happy, Sad, sad, Angry, or angry:

```
$ grep -E '[Hh]appy|[Ss]ad|[Aa]ngry' file1
```

Example 9

Display all lines of *file* that contain any repeated sequence of abc (abcabc, abcabcabc, and so on):

```
$ grep '\(abc\)\{2,\}' file
```

Basic regular expression patterns

Example 1

Match any letter:

```
[A-Za-z]
```

Example 2

Match any symbol (not a letter or digit):

```
[^0-9A-Za-z]
```

Example 3

Match an uppercase letter, followed by zero or more lowercase letters:

```
[A-Z][a-z]*
```

Example 4

Match a U.S. Social Security Number (123-45-6789) by specifying groups of three, two, and four digits separated by dashes:

```
[0-9]\{3\}-[0-9]\{2\}-[0-9]\{4\}
```

Example 5

Match a dollar amount, using an escaped dollar sign, zero or more spaces or digits, an escaped period, and two more digits:

```
\$[ 0-9]*\.[0-9]\{2\}
```

Example 6

Match the month of June and its abbreviation, Jun. The question mark matches zero or one instance of the e :

```
June\?
```

On the Exam

Make certain you are clear about the difference between *file globbing* and the use of regular expressions.

Using regular expressions as addresses in sed

These examples are commands you would issue to *sed*. For example, the commands could take the place of *command1* in this usage:

```
$ sed [options] 'command1' [files]
```

These commands could also appear in a standalone sed script.

Example 1

Delete blank lines:

```
/^$/d
```

Example 2

Delete any line that doesn't contain #keepme::

```
/#keepme/!d
```

Example 3

Delete lines containing only whitespace (spaces or tabs). In this example, Tab means the single tab character and is preceded by a single space:

```
/^[ Tab]*$/d
```

Because GNU *sed* also supports character classes, this example could be written as follows:

```
/^[[:blank:]]*$/d
```

Example 4

Delete lines beginning with periods or pound signs:

```
/^[\.#]/d
```

Example 5

Substitute a single space for any number of spaces wherever they occur on the line:

```
s/  */ /g
```

or

```
s/ \{2,\}/ /g
```

Example 6

Substitute def for abc from line 11 to 20, wherever it occurs on the line:

```
11,20s/abc/def/g
```

Example 7

Translate the characters *a*, *b*, and *c* to the @ character from line 11 to 20, wherever they occur on the line:

```
11,20y/abc/@@@/
```

Objective 8: Perform Basic File Editing Operations Using vi

vi is perhaps the most ubiquitous text editor available on Linux systems. Since most system administration tasks eventually require editing text files, being able to work effectively in *vi* essential.

This Objective concentrates on a subset of *vi* functionality. *Learning the vi Editor* (O'Reilly) is an indispensable reference for anyone interested in learning more about *vi* and the enhancements available in the various implementations of *vi*. There is also a large amount of documentation available at *http://vimdoc. sourceforge.net* and *http://www.vim.org* for the popular *vi* implementation Vim, most of which is applicable to any version of *vi*.

Invoking vi

To start *vi*, simply execute it. You will be editing a temporary file. To directly edit one or more files, give the names of the files on the command line:

```
$ vi file1.txt file2.txt
```

You are presented with a main window showing the contents of *file1.txt*, or if the specified files don't already exist, a blank screen with tilde (~) characters running the length of the left column (they indicate areas of the screen containing no text, not even blank lines).

vi Basics

The *vi* editor has two modes of operation: *command* or *insert*. In command mode, *vi* allows you to navigate around your file and enter commands. To enter new text, put *vi* into insert mode. In command mode, the keyboard keys are interpreted as *vi* commands instead of text. The convenience of being able to manipulate the editor without moving your hands from the keyboard is considered one of *vi*'s strengths.

Commands are brief, case-sensitive combinations of one or more letters. For example, to switch from command to insert mode, press the i key. To terminate insert mode, press the Escape key (Esc), which puts you back in command mode.

Almost any command can be prefixed with a number to repeat the command that number of times. For example, r will replace the character at the current cursor position. To replace exactly 10 characters, use 10r.

Table 5-9. vi commands

Key command	Description
h	Move left one character.
j	Move down one line.
k	Move up one line.
l	Move right one character.
H	Move to the top of the screen.
L	Move to the bottom of the screen.
G	Move to the end of the file.
w	Move forward one word.
b	Move backward one word.
0 (zero)	Move to the beginning of the current line.
^	Move to the first non-whitespace character on the current line.
$	Move to the end of the current line.
Ctrl-B	Move up (back) one screen.
Ctrl-F	Move down (forward) one screen.
i	Insert at the current cursor position.
I	Insert at the beginning of the current line.
a	Append after the current cursor position.
A	Append to the end of the current line.
o	Start a new line after the current line.
O	Start a new line before the current line.
r	Replace the character at the current cursor position.
R	Start replacing (overwriting) at the current cursor position.
x	Delete the character at the current cursor position.
X	Delete the character immediately before (to the left) of the current cursor position.
s	Delete the character at the current cursor position and go into insert mode. (This is the equivalent of the combination xi.)
S	Delete the contents of the current line and go into insert mode.
dX	Given a movement command X, cut (delete) the appropriate number of characters, words, or lines from the current cursor position.
dd	Cut the entire current line.
D	Cut from the current cursor position to the end of the line. (This is equivalent to d$.)
cX	Given a movement command X, cut the appropriate number of characters, words, or lines from the current cursor position and go into insert mode.
cc	Cut the entire current line and go into insert mode.
C	Cut from the current cursor position to the end of the line and enter insert mode. (This is equivalent to c$.)
yX	Given a movement command X, copy (yank[a]) the appropriate number of characters, words, or lines from the current cursor position.
yy or Y	Copy the entire current line.
p	Paste after the current cursor position.
P	Paste before the current cursor position.
.	Repeat the last command.

Table 5-9. vi commands (continued)

Key command	Description
u	Undo the last command.[b]
/regex	Search forward for regex.
?regex	Search backward for regex.
n	Find the next match.
N	Find the previous match. (In other words, repeat the last search in the opposite direction.)
:n	Next file; when multiple files are specified for editing, this command loads the next file. Force this action (if the current file has unsaved changes) with :n!.
:e file	Load file in place of the current file. Force this action with :e! file.
:r file	Insert the contents of file after the current cursor position.
:q	Quit without saving changes. Force this action with :q!.
:w file	Write the current buffer to file. To append to an existing file, use :w >>file. Force the write (when possible, such as when running as root) with :w! file.
:wq	Write the file contents and quit. Force this action with :wq!.
:x	Write the file contents (if changed) and quit (the ex equivalent of ZZ).
ZZ	Write the file contents (if changed) and quit.
:! command	Execute command in a subshell.

[a] Emacs users should be careful not to confuse the vi definition of yank (copy) with that of Emacs (paste).

[b] Many of the popular vi implementations support multi-level undo. Vim breaks compatibility with traditional vi by making a repeated u perform another level of undo. Nvi uses . after u to do multi-level undo, and, like traditional vi, uses a repeated u to redo (undo the undo, so to speak). This can cause some confusion when moving between Linux distributions that have different default implementations of vi.

Keep in mind that this is *not* a complete list, but it is not necessary to know every *vi* command to use it effectively. In fact, even after using *vi* as your only editor for years, you may find yourself only using a small subset of the available commands.

There is a pattern in *vi*'s keyboard commands that makes them easier to remember. For every lowercase character that has some action assigned to it, the same uppercase character *usually* has some related action assigned to it. As an example, i and I both put *vi* in insert mode, at the current cursor position and at the beginning of the line respectively.

On the Exam

You'll need to be familiar with *vi*'s command and insert modes, how to switch between them, and how to perform basic navigation and editing tasks.

Devices, Linux Filesystems, and the Filesystem Hierarchy Standard (Topic 1.104)

Filesystem management is among the most critical activities that you must perform to maintain a stable Linux system. In simple situations, after a successful installation, you may never have a problem or need to manage filesystem specifics. However, understanding how to configure and maintain Linux filesystems is essential to safely manage your system and to pass Exam 101. This section contains the following Objectives:

Objective 1: Create Partitions and Filesystems
This Objective states that an LPIC 1 candidate should be able to configure disk partitions and create filesystems on media such as hard disks. It also includes using various *mkfs* commands to set up partitions to filesystems such as *ext2*, *ext3*, *reiserfs*, *vfat*, and *xfs*. Weight: 3.

Objective 2: Maintain the Integrity of Filesystems
A candidate should be able to verify the intergrity of filesystems, monitor free space and inodes, and repair simple filesystem problems. This Objective includes the commands required to maintain a standard filesystem as well as the extra data associated with a *journaling* filesystem. Weight: 3.

Objective 3: Control Filesystem Mounting and Unmounting
Candidates should be able to manually mount and unmount filesystems, configure filesystem mounting on system boot, and configure user mountable removeable filesystems such as tape drives, floppies, and CDs. Weight: 3.

Objective 4: Managing Disk Quotas
This Objective includes managing disk quotas for system users. You should be able to set up a disk quota for a filesystem, edit, check, and generate user quota reports. Weight: 3.

Objective 5: Use File Permissions to Control Access to Files
Candidates should be able to control file access through file permissions. This Objective includes access permissions on regular and special files as well as directories. Also included are access modes such as *suid*, *sgid*, and the

sticky bit. You should also be aware of the use of the group field to grant file access to workgroups, the *immutable flag*, and the default file creation mode. Weight: 5.

Objective 6: Manage File Ownership
An LPIC 1 candidate should be able to control user and group ownership of files. This Objective includes the ability to change the user and group owner of a file as well as the default group owner for new files. Weight: 1.

Objective 7: Create and Change Hard and Symbolic Links
Candidates should be able to create and manage hard and symbolic links to a file. This Objective includes the ability to create and identify links, copy files through links, and use linked files to support system administration tasks. Weight: 1.

Objective 8: Find System Files and Place Files in the Correct Location
This Objective states that candidates should be thoroughly familiar with the FHS, including typical file locations and directory classifications. This includes the ability to find files and commands on a Linux System. Weight: 5.

Objective 1: Create Partitions and Filesystems

The term *filesystem* refers to two different things. First, it can mean the way files and directories are physically structured on a disk or other storage medium. Linux supports many different filesystems (in this sense of the word), including ext2 and ext3, the non-journalled and journalled (respectively) native filesystems; msdos or vfat, the native MS-DOS and Windows (respectively) filesystems; JFS, a filesystem used on OS/2 and AIX; XFS, the native IRIX filesystem; and many, many others.

In the second sense of the word, it refers to the structure and contents of some storage medium. To view the contents of a filesystem (in this sense of the word) on a Linux system, the device must be *mounted*, or attached to the hierarchical directory structure on the system. Much of the strength and flexibility of Linux (and Unix) comes from the ability to mount any filesystem that it supports, whether that filesystem is somewhere remote on the network or on a locally-attached disk, anywhere in its directory structure, in a way that is completely transparent to users. For example, the files under /usr will work equally well whether they are on a disk attached to the system or mounted from a master server. Even the / (root) filesystem can be located on a distant server if the system is properly configured.

Disk Drives Under Linux

Linux supports many types of disk devices and formats. Any SCSI or IDE hard disk will work with Linux, as will floppy disks, CD-ROMs, CD-Rs, Zip and Jaz disks, and other types of removable media. These media can contain the standard Linux *ext2* filesystem, FAT, FAT32, NTFS, as well as other filesystem types. This flexibility makes Linux coexist nicely with other operating systems on multiboot systems.

The most commonly found hard disks on PCs are IDE drives. These disks feature a relatively simple system interface, and most of the "smarts" of the disk are onboard the disk itself. The IDE standard allows disk manufacturers to sell their product at a very competitive price, expanding their markets to more consumers and limited budget commercial customers.

A single IDE interface is capable of attaching two disk drives to a system. One device is named *master* and the other is the *slave*. Most PCs have a *primary* and *secondary* IDE interface. Together, these interfaces allow up to four devices (primary master, primary slave, secondary master, and secondary slave).

Also used on PCs are SCSI drives. SCSI is an older standard for connecting peripherals; however, modern SCSI versions are quite fast and flexible. Typically, SCSI devices are used for their increased speed and reliability in large-scale and high-end server environments. With the increased speeds, however, come increased prices—often two to five times the price of their IDE counterparts.

Compared to IDE, SCSI offers excellent performance, lower CPU utilization, and a much more flexible connection scheme capable of handling up to 15 devices on a single bus. These conveniences allow SCSI systems to grow as space requirements increase without major hardware reconfiguration.

Hard disk devices

By default, Linux defines IDE device files as follows:

/dev/hda
    Primary master IDE (often the hard disk)

/dev/hdb
    Primary slave IDE

/dev/hdc
    Secondary master IDE (often a CD-ROM)

/dev/hdd
    Secondary slave IDE

SCSI device files are similar, except that there is no four-device limitation:

/dev/sda
    First SCSI drive

/dev/sdb
    Second SCSI drive

/dev/sdc
    Third SCSI drive (and so on)

Under Linux, a typical PC with a single hard disk on the primary IDE interface and a single CD-ROM on the secondary IDE interface would have disk drive */dev/hda* and CD-ROM */dev/hdc*.

Disk partitions

Almost every operating system supports a system for dividing a disk into logical devices, called *partitions*. Other terms for the same basic concept are *slices* and *logical volumes*, although logical volumes generally also imply the ability to span physical disks. Linux supports several different partitioning formats, but by default it uses the MS-DOS format. The MS-DOS partition table allows for up to four *primary partitions*. One of these four primary partitions can be replaced with an *extended partition*, which can contain up to 12 *logical partitions*, for a total of 15 possible usable partitions (16 if you count the extended partition "container," but it is not usable for data).

The type of partition (as well as the type of device) affects the name of the device Linux uses to access the partition.

Primary partitions
> This type of partition contains a filesystem. If all four primary partitions exist on an IDE drive, they are numbered as follows:
>
> * */dev/hda1*
> * */dev/hda2*
> * */dev/hda3*
> * */dev/hda4*
>
> One of these primary partitions may be marked *active*, in which case the PC BIOS will be able to select it for boot.

Extended partitions
> An extended partition is a variant of the primary partition but cannot contain a filesystem. Instead, it contains *logical partitions*. Only one extended partition may exist on a single physical disk. For example, the partitions on a disk with one primary partition and the sole extended partition might be numbered as follows:
>
> * */dev/hda1* (primary)
> * */dev/hda2* (extended)

Logical partitions
> Logical partitions exist *within* the extended partition. Logical partitions are numbered from 5 to 16. The partitions on a disk with one primary partition, one extended partition, and four logical partitions might be numbered as follows:
>
> * */dev/hda1* (primary)
> * */dev/hda2* (extended)

- */dev/hda5* (logical)
- */dev/hda6* (logical)
- */dev/hda7* (logical)
- */dev/hda8* (logical)

If the above partitions were made on a SCSI drive, the hda would be replaced by sda such as */dev/sda2*.

On the Exam

Be sure that you understand how partition numbering works. In particular, pay attention to the differences in numbering between primary, extended, and logical partitions.

The root filesystem and mount points

As a Linux system boots, the first filesystem that becomes available is the top level, or *root* filesystem, denoted with a single forward slash. The root filesystem /, also known as *root directory*, shouldn't be confused with the *root* superuser account or the superuser's home directory, */root*. The distinct directories / and */root* are unrelated and are not required to share the same filesystem. In a simple installation, the root filesystem could contain nearly everything on the system. However, such an arrangement could lead to system failure if the root filesystem fills to capacity. Instead, multiple partitions are typically defined, each containing one of the directories under /. As the Linux kernel boots, the partitions are *mounted* to the root filesystem, and together create a single unified filesystem (see "Objective 3: Control Filesystem Mounting and Unmounting" later in this chapter for a discussion about mounting). Everything on the system that is not stored in a mounted partition is stored locally in the / (root) partition. The mounted filesystems are placed on separate partitions and possibly multiple disk drives.

The choice of which directories are placed into separate partitions is both a personal and technical decision. Here are some guidelines for individual partitions:

/ (the root directory)
> Since the only filesystem mounted at the start of the boot process is /, certain directories must be part of it to be available for the boot process. These include:

/bin and /sbin
> Contains required system binary programs

/dev
> Contains device files

/etc
> Contains configuration information used on boot

/lib
> Contains shared libraries

These directories are always part of the single / partition. See the description of the FHS in "Objective 8: Find System Files and Place Files in the Correct Location" for more on the requirements for the root filesystem.

/boot

This directory holds static files used by the boot loader, including kernel images. On systems where kernel development activity occurs regularly, making */boot* a separate partition eliminates the possibility that / will fill with kernel images and associated files during development.

/home

User files are usually placed in a separate partition. This is often the largest partition on the system and may be located on a separate physical disk or disk array.

/tmp

This directory is often a separate partition used to prevent temporary files from filling the root filesystem.

/var

Log files are stored here. This is similar to the situation with */tmp*, where user files can fill any available space if something goes wrong or if the files are not cleaned periodically.

/usr

This directory holds a hierarchy of directories containing user commands, source code, and documentation. It is often quite large, making it a good candidate for its own partition. Because much of the information stored under */usr* is static, some users prefer that it be mounted as read-only, making it impossible to corrupt.

In addition to the preceding six partitions listed, a *swap* partition is also necessary for a Linux system to enable virtual memory. For information on determining the size of a swap partition, see Chapter 4.

Using these guidelines at installation time, the disk partitions for an IDE-based system with two physical disks on the primary IDE controller might look as described in Table 6-1.

Table 6-1. An example partitioning scheme

Partition	Type	Mounted filesystem	Size
/dev/hda1	Primary	/boot	100 MB
/dev/hda2	Primary	/	500 MB
/dev/hda3	Extended	-	-
/dev/hda5	Logical	/usr	4 GB
/dev/hda6	Logical	/var	2 GB
/dev/hda7	Logical	/opt	1 GB
/dev/hda8	Logical	/tmp	500 MB
/dev/hda4	Primary	(*swap* partition)	1 GB
/dev/hdb1	Primary	/home	60 GB

Once a disk is partitioned, it can be difficult or risky to change the partition sizes. Commercial and open source tools are available for this task, but a full backup is recommended prior to their use.

 If you are resizing your partitions, you may want to investigate setting up your system using *Logical Volume Manager* (LVM). LVM is currently not covered on the LPI exams, but its use is quickly growing. For more information read the LVM-HOWTO at the Linux Documentation Project (*http://www.tldp.org*).

Managing partitions

Linux has two basic options for partitioning disk drives. The *fdisk* command is a text-based program that is easy to use and exists on every Linux distribution. It is also required for Exam 101. Another option you may wish to explore after mastering *fdisk* is *cfdisk*, which is still a text-mode program but which uses the *curses* system to produce a GUI-style display.

---

fdisk

Syntax
```
fdisk [device]
```

Description
Manipulate or display the partition table for *device* using a command-driven interactive text interface. *device* is a physical disk such as */dev/hda*, not a partition such as */dev/hda1*. If omitted, *device* defaults to */dev/hda*. Interactive commands to *fdisk* are a single letter followed by a carriage return. The commands do not take arguments, but start an interactive dialog. Commands that operate on a partition will request the partition number, which is an integer. For primary and extended partitions, the partition number is from 1 to 4. For logical partitions, which are available only if the extended partition already exists to contain them, the partition number is from 5 to 16.

When making changes to the partition table, *fdisk* accumulates changes without writing them to the disk, until it receives the write command.

Frequently used commands

a

Toggle the *bootable* flag on/off for a primary partition.

d

Delete a partition. You are prompted for the partition number to delete. If you delete a logical partition when higher numbered logical partitions exist, the partition numbers are decremented to keep logical partition numbers contiguous.

l

List the known partition types. A table of partition types is printed.

m

Display the brief help menu for these commands.

n

Add a new partition. You are prompted for the partition type (primary, extended, or logical). For primary and extended partitions, you are asked for the partition number (1-4). For logical partitions, the next logical partition number is selected automatically. You are then prompted for the starting disk cylinder for the partition and are offered the next free cylinder as a default. Finally, you are prompted for the last cylinder or a size, such as +300M. By default, new partitions are assigned as Linux ext2, type 83. To create another partition type, such as a swap partition, first create the partition with the n command, then change the type with the t command.

 Note that *fdisk* displays options for extended and primary partition types if an extended partition does not yet exist. If the extended partition already exists, *fdisk* displays options for logical and primary partition types.

p

Display the partition table as it exists in memory. This depiction will differ from the actual partition table on disk if changes have not been saved.

q

Quit without saving changes.

t

Change a partition's system ID. This is a hex number that indicates the type of filesystem the partition is to contain. Linux ext2 partitions are type 83, and Linux swap partitions are type 82.

w

Write (save) the partition table to disk and exit. No changes are saved until the w command is issued.

Example 1

Display the existing partition table on */dev/hda* without making any changes:

```
# fdisk /dev/hda
Command (m for help): p
Disk /dev/hda: 255 heads, 63 sectors, 1027 cylinders
Units = cylinders of 16065 * 512 bytes
   Device Boot    Start      End    Blocks   Id  System
/dev/hda1    *        1      250   2008093+   83  Linux
/dev/hda2            251      280    240975   82  Linux swap
/dev/hda3            281     1027   6000277+    5  Extended
/dev/hda5            281      293    104391   83  Linux
/dev/hda6            294      306    104391   83  Linux
/dev/hda7            307      319    104391   83  Linux
Command (m for help): q
#
```

In this configuration, */dev/hda* has two primary partitions, */dev/hda1*, which is bootable, and */dev/hda2*, which is the swap partition. The disk also has an extended partition */dev/hda3*, which contains three logical partitions, */dev/hda5*, */dev/hda6*, and */dev/hda7*. All other primary and logical partitions are Linux *ext2* partitions.

Example 2

Starting with a blank partition table, create a bootable primary partition of 300 MB on
/dev/hda1, the extended partition on */dev/hda2* containing the remainder of the disk, a
logical partition of 200 MB on */dev/hda5*, a logical swap partition of 128 MB on */dev/
hda6*, and a logical partition on */dev/hda7* occupying the remainder of the extended
partition:

```
# fdisk /dev/hda
Command (m for help): n
Command action
   e   extended
   p   primary partition (1-4)
p
Partition number (1-4): 1
First cylinder (1-1027, default 1): Enter
Using default value 1
Last cylinder or +size or +sizeM or +sizeK (1-1027, default 1027): +300M
Command (m for help): a
Partition number (1-4): 1
Command (m for help): n
Command action
   e   extended
   p   primary partition (1-4)
e
Partition number (1-4): 2
First cylinder (40-1027, default 40): Enter
Using default value 40
Last cylinder or +size or +sizeM or +sizeK (40-1027, default 1027): Enter
Using default value 1027
Command (m for help): n
Command action
   l   logical (5 or over)
   p   primary partition (1-4)
l
First cylinder (40-1027, default 40): Enter
Using default value 40
Last cylinder or +size or +sizeM or +sizeK (40-1027, default 1027): +200M
Command (m for help): n
Command action
   l   logical (5 or over)
   p   primary partition (1-4)
l
First cylinder (79-1027, default 79): Enter
Using default value 79
Last cylinder or +size or +sizeM or +sizeK (79-1027, default 1027): +128M
Command (m for help): t
Partition number (1-6): 6
Hex code (type L to list codes): 82
Changed system type of partition 6 to 82 (Linux swap)
Command (m for help): n
Command action
   l   logical (5 or over)
   p   primary partition (1-4)
l
```

```
First cylinder (118-1027, default 118): Enter
Using default value 118
Last cylinder or +size or +sizeM or +sizeK (118-1027, default 1027): Enter
Using default value 1027
Command (m for help): p
Disk /dev/hda: 255 heads, 63 sectors, 1027 cylinders
Units = cylinders of 16065 * 512 bytes
      Device Boot   Start      End     Blocks    Id  System
   /dev/hda1     *      1       39     313236    83  Linux
   /dev/hda2            40     1027   7936110     5  Extended
   /dev/hda5            40       65    208813+   82  Linux swap
   /dev/hda6            66       82    136521    83  Linux
   /dev/hda7            83     1027   7590681    83  Linux
Command (m for help): w
The partition table has been altered!
Calling ioctl( ) to re-read partition table.
Syncing disks.
#
```

Note the use of defaults for the partition start cylinders and for end cylinder selections, indicated by *Enter* in this example. Other partition sizes are specified in megabytes using responses such as +128M .

If you are attempting to create partitions for other operating systems with the Linux *fdisk* utility, you could run into a few problems. As a rule, it is safest to prepare the partitions for an operating system using the native tools of that operating system.

As you might expect, using *fdisk* on a working system can be dangerous, because one errant *w* command can render your disk useless. Use extreme caution when working with the partition table of a working system, and be sure you know exactly what you intend to do and how to do it.

On the Exam

You should understand disk partitions and the process of creating them using *fdisk*.

Creating filesystems

Once a disk is partitioned, filesystems may be created in those partitions using the *mkfs* utility. *mkfs* is a front-end program for filesystem-specific creation tools such as *mkfs.ext2* and *mkfs.msdos*, which are in turn linked to *mke2fs* and *mkdosfs*, respectively. *mkfs* offers a unified front-end, while the links provide convenient names. The choice of which executable to call is up to you.

mkfs

Syntax

mkfs [-t *fstype*] [*fs_options*] *device*

Description

Make a filesystem of type *fstype* on *device*. If *fstype* is omitted, *ext2* is used by default. When called by *mkfs*, these programs are passed any *fs_options* included on the command line. See the manpages for the various filesystem-specific *mkfs* commands, such as *mke2fs* and *mkdosfs*, for full details on their individual options.

Frequently used options

-*c*
> Check *device* for bad blocks (*mke2fs* and *mkdosfs*).

-*L label*
> Set the volume label for the filesystem (*mke2fs* only).

-*n label*
> Set the 11-character volume label for the filesystem (*mkdosfs* only).

-*q*
> Uses mkfs in quiet mode, resulting in very little output (*mke2fs* only).

-*v*
> Used to enter verbose mode (*mke2fs* and *mkdosfs*).

-*j*
> Create an *ext3* journal file (*mke2fs* only). Using -*t ext3* or running *mkfs.ext3* has the same effect as using the -*j* option.

Example 1

Using defaults, quietly create an *ext2* partition on */dev/hda3*:

```
# mkfs -q /dev/hda3
mke2fs 1.14, 9-Jan-1999 for EXT2 FS 0.5b, 95/08/09
#
```

Example 2

Create an *ext2* filesystem labeled *rootfs* on existing partition */dev/hda3*, checking for bad blocks and with full verbose output:

```
# mkfs -t ext2 -L rootfs -cv /dev/hda3
mke2fs 1.27 (8-Mar-2002)
Filesystem label=rootfs
OS type: Linux
Block size=1024 (log=0)
Fragment size=1024 (log=0)
26208 inodes, 104422 blocks
5221 blocks (5.00%) reserved for the super user
First data block=1
13 block groups
8192 blocks per group, 8192 fragments per group
2016 inodes per group
```

```
Superblock backups stored on blocks:
        8193, 16385, 24577, 32769, 40961, 49153,
        57345, 65537, 73729, 81921, 90113, 98305
Running command: badblocks -b 1024 -s /dev/hda3 104422
Checking for bad blocks (read-only test): done
Writing inode tables: done
Writing superblocks and filesystem accounting information: done
This filesystem will be automatically checked every 28 mounts or
180 days, whichever comes first.  Use tune2fs -c or -i to override.
```

Additional options are available in the *mke2fs* and *mkdosfs* programs, which may be needed to fine-tune specific filesystem parameters for special situations. In most cases, the default parameters are appropriate and adequate.

Creating swap partitions

An additional command not specifically cited in the LPI Objectives for this Topic is *mkswap*. This command prepares a partition for use as Linux swap space and is needed if you plan to fully configure a disk from scratch. It is also needed if you need to add an additional swap partition.

---

mkswap

Syntax

```
mkswap device
```

Description

Prepare a partition for use as swap space. This command can also set up swap space in a file on another filesystem.

Example

On an existing partition, which should be set to type 82 (Linux swap), ready swap space:

```
# mkswap /dev/hda5
Setting up swapspace version 1, size = 139792384 bytes
#
```

 Running any of the filesystem creation programs is, like *fdisk*, potentially dangerous. All data in any previously existing filesystems in the specified partition will be deleted. Since *mkfs* does not warn you prior to creating the filesystem, be certain that you are operating on the correct partition.

On the Exam

The exam is likely to contain general questions about using *mkfs*, though details such as inode allocation are beyond the scope of the LPIC Level 1 exams.

Objective 2: Maintain the Integrity of Filesystems

Over the course of time, active filesystems can develop problems, such as:

- A filesystem fills to capacity, causing programs or perhaps the entire system to fail.
- A filesystem is corrupted, perhaps due to a power failure or system crash.
- A filesystem runs out of inodes, meaning that new filesystem objects cannot be created.

Carefully monitoring and checking Linux filesystems on a regular basis can help prevent and correct these types of problems.

Monitoring Free Disk Space and Inodes

A read/write filesystem isn't much good if it grows to the point that it won't accept any more files. This could happen if the filesystem fills to capacity or runs out of *inodes*.

Inodes are the data structures within filesystems that describe files on disk. Every filesystem contains a finite number of inodes, set when the filesystem is created. This number is also the maximum number of files that the filesystem can accommodate. Because filesystems are created with a huge number of inodes, you'll probably never create as many files as it would take to run out of inodes. However, it is possible to run out of inodes if a partition contains many small files.

It is important to prevent space and inode shortages from occurring on system partitions. The *df* command gives you the information you need on the status of both disk space utilization and inode utilization.

---

df

Syntax
    df [options] [file [file...]]

Description
Display overall disk utilization information for mounted filesystems on *file*. Usually, *file* is a device file for a partition, such as */dev/hda1*. The *file* may also be the mount point or any file beneath the mount point. If *file* is omitted, information for mounted filesystems on all devices in */etc/fstab* are displayed.

Frequently used options
-h

   Displays results in a human-readable format, including suffixes such as M (megabytes) and G (gigabytes).

-i

   Displays information on remaining inodes rather than the default disk space information.

Example 1

Check disk space utilization on all filesystems:

```
# df -h
Filesystem       Size  Used Avail Use% Mounted on
/dev/sda1        387M   56M  311M  15% /
/dev/sda5        296M  5.2M  276M   2% /boot
/dev/sda9        1.9G  406M  1.4G  22% /home
/dev/sda6         53M   12M   39M  23% /root
/dev/sda10        99M  104k   93M   0% /tmp
/dev/sda8        972M  507M  414M  55% /usr
/dev/sda7        296M  9.3M  272M   3% /var
```

This example shows that of the seven filesystems mounted by default, none exceeds 55 percent capacity.

Example 2

Check the same filesystems for inode utilization:

```
# df -i
Filesystem      Inodes   IUsed   IFree IUse% Mounted on
/dev/sda1       102800    7062   95738   7% /
/dev/sda5        78312      29   78283   0% /boot
/dev/sda9       514000     934  513066   0% /home
/dev/sda6        14056     641   13415   5% /root
/dev/sda10       26104      60   26044   0% /tmp
/dev/sda8       257040   36700  220340  14% /usr
/dev/sda7        78312     269   78043   0% /var
```

Among these partitions, the largest consumption of inodes is a mere 14 percent. It is clear that none of the filesystems is anywhere near consuming the maximum number of inodes available. Note that the */usr* partition (with 14 percent of inodes used) has used 55 percent of the disk space. With utilization like this, the */usr* volume will most likely fill to capacity long before the inodes are exhausted.

Example 3

Quickly determine which partition the current working directory (represented simply by a single dot) is located:

```
# df .
Filesystem       1k-blocks     Used Available Use% Mounted on
/dev/sda1           102800     7062     95738   7% /
```

When a filesystem is nearing capacity, files may simply be deleted to make additional space available. However, in the rare case in which an inode shortage occurs, the filesystem must be recreated with a larger number of inodes unless a significant number of files can be deleted.

Monitoring Disk Usage

Have you ever found yourself wondering, "Where did all the disk space go?" Some operating systems make answering this question surprisingly difficult using only native tools. On Linux, the *du* command can help display disk utilization information on a per-directory basis and perhaps answer that question. *du* recursively examines directories and reports detailed or summarized information on the amount of space consumed.

du

Syntax

du [options] [directories]

Description

Display disk utilization information for *directories*. If *directories* are omitted, the current working directory is searched.

Frequently used options

-a

    Shows all files, not just directories.

-c

    Produces a grand total for all listed items.

-h

    Displays results in a human-readable format, including suffixes such as M (megabytes) and G (gigabytes).

-s

    Prints a summary for each of the *directories* specified, instead of totals for each subdirectory found recursively.

-S

    Excludes subdirectories from counts and totals, limiting totals to *directories*.

Example 1

Examine disk utilization in */etc/rc.d*:

```
# du /etc/rc.d
882      /etc/rc.d/init.d
1        /etc/rc.d/rc0.d
1        /etc/rc.d/rc1.d
1        /etc/rc.d/rc2.d
1        /etc/rc.d/rc3.d
1        /etc/rc.d/rc4.d
1        /etc/rc.d/rc5.d
1        /etc/rc.d/rc6.d
904      /etc/rc.d
```

Example 2

Display utilization by files in */etc*, including subdirectories beneath it:

```
# du -s /etc
13002    /etc
```

Example 3

Display utilization by files in */etc*, but not in subdirectories beneath it:

```
# du -Ss /etc
1732     /etc
```

Example 4

Show a summary of all subdirectories under /home, with human-readable output:

```
# du -csh /home/*
42k      /home/bsmith
1.5M     /home/httpd
9.5M     /home/jdean
42k      /home/jdoe
12k      /home/lost+found
1.0k     /home/samba
11M      total
```

This result shows that 11 MB of total disk space is used.

Example 5

Show the same summary, but sort the results to display in order of largest to smallest disk utilization:

```
# du -cs /home/* | sort -nr
11386    total
9772     jdean
1517     httpd
42       jdoe
42       bsmith
12       lost+found
1        samba
```

This result shows that user *jdean* is consuming the largest amount of space. Note that the human-readable format does not sort in this way, since *sort* is unaware of the human-readable size specifications.

Modifying a Filesystem

There are many cases where an administrator might want to make changes to an existing filesystem. For example, if the purpose of a particular filesystem changes, the volume label should be changed to match. This and many other *ext2* filesystem settings can be viewed and modified using the *tune2fs* command.

---

tune2fs

Syntax

```
tune2fs [options] device
```

Description

Modify tunable parameters on the ext2 or ext3 filesystem on *device*.

Frequently used options

-l device

    List the tunable parameters on *device*.

-c n

    Set the maximum mount count to *n*. When the filesystem has been mounted this many times, the kernel will warn that the filesystem has exceeded the maximum

---

mount count when the filesystem is mounted, and *e2fsck* will automatically check the filesystem when run with the *-p* option (as it usually run at every system boot).

Setting this value to 0 tells the kernel and *e2fsck* to ignore the mount count.

-i n

> Set the maximum time between two filesystem checks to *n*. If *n* is a number or is followed by d, the value is in days. A value followed by w specifies weeks. A value followed by m specifies months.

> The time since the last filesystem check is compared to this value by the kernel and *e2fsck -p*, much like the maximum mount count. A value of 0 disables this check.

-L label

> Sets the volume label of the filesystem to *label*. The volume label can also be set with the *e2label* command.

-j

> Adds an *ext3* journal file to the filesystem and sets the has_journal feature flag.

-m n

> Sets the reserved block percentage to *n*. By default, ext2 filesystems reserve 5% of the total number of available blocks for *root*. This means that if a filesystem is more than 95% full, only root can write to it. (It also means that *df* will report the filesystem as 100% full when it is really only 95% full.)

> On very large filesystems, or filesystems where only user data will be written, the reserved block percentage can be safely reduced to make more of the filesystem available for writing by regular users.

-r n

> Sets the number of reserved blocks to *n*. This is similar to the *-m* option, except it specifies a number instead of a percentage.

Example 1

List the contents of the superblock on */dev/sda7*:

```
# tune2fs -l /dev/sda7
tune2fs 1.26 (3-Feb-2002)
Filesystem volume name:   /var/log
Last mounted on:          <not available>
Filesystem UUID:          83efa5c0-063a-11d5-9c6c-c2d9509d12e5
Filesystem magic number:  0xEF53
Filesystem revision #:    1 (dynamic)
Filesystem features:      has_journal filetype needs_recovery sparse_super
Filesystem state:         clean
Errors behavior:          Continue
Filesystem OS type:       Linux
Inode count:              647680
Block count:              1295232
Reserved block count:     64761
Free blocks:              1227593
Free inodes:              647542
First block:              0
Block size:               4096
Fragment size:            4096
Blocks per group:         32768
Fragments per group:      32768
```

```
Inodes per group:          16192
Inode blocks per group:    506
Last mount time:           Sat Jan 25 18:59:05 2003
Last write time:           Sat Jan 25 18:59:05 2003
Mount count:               11
Maximum mount count:       20
Last checked:              Mon Nov 11 20:44:53 2002
Check interval:            31536000 (12 months, 5 days)
Next check after:          Tue Nov 11 20:44:53 2003
Reserved blocks uid:       0 (user root)
Reserved blocks gid:       0 (group root)
First inode:               11
Inode size:                128
Journal UUID:              <none>
Journal inode:             8
Journal device:            0x0000
First orphan inode:        0
```

Example 2

Turn off the maximum mount count and check interval tests on */dev/sda7*:

```
# tune2fs -i 0 -c 0 /dev/sda7
tune2fs 1.26 (3-Feb-2002)
Setting maximal mount count to -1
Setting interval between check 0 seconds
```

Checking and Repairing Filesystems

No matter how stable, computers do fail, even due to something as simple as a power cable being accidentally unplugged. Unfortunately, such an interruption can make a mess of a filesystem. If a disk write operation is aborted before it completes, the data in transit could be lost, and the portions of the disk that were allocated for it are left marked as used. In addition, filesystem writes are cached in memory, and a power loss or other crash prevents the kernel from synchronizing the cache with the disk. Both of these scenarios lead to inconsistencies in the filesystem and must be corrected to ensure reliable operation.

Filesystems are checked with *fsck*. Like *mkfs*, *fsck* is a front-end to filesystem-specific utilities, including *fsck.ext2*, which is a link to the *e2fsck* program. (See its manpage for detailed information.)

 e2fsck can also check *ext3* filesystems. When it finds an *ext3* filesystem that was not cleanly unmounted, it first commits the journal, then checks the filesystem as it normally would with *ext2*.

Part of the information written on disk to describe a filesystem is known as the *superblock*, written in block 1 of the partition. If this area of the disk is corrupted, the filesystem is inaccessible. Because the superblock is so important, copies of it are made in the filesystem at regular intervals, by default every 8192 blocks. The first superblock copy is located at block 8193, the second copy is at block 16385, and so on. As you'll see, *fsck* can use the information in the superblock copies to restore the main superblock.

fsck

Syntax

```
fsck [options] [-t type] [fs-options] filesystems
```

Description

Check *filesystems* for errors and optionally correct them. By default, *fsck* assumes the *ext2* filesystem type and runs interactively, pausing to ask for permission before applying fixes.

Frequently used options for fsck

-A
> Run checks on all filesystems specified in */etc/fstab*. This option is intended for use at boot time, before filesystems are mounted.

-N
> Don't execute, but show what would be done.

-t *type*
> Specify the type of filesystem to check; the default is *ext2*. The value of *type* determines which filesystem-specific checker is called.

Frequently used options for e2fsck

-b *superblock*
> Use an alternative copy of the superblock. In interactive mode, *e2fsck* automatically uses alternative superblocks. Typically, you'll try *-b 8193* in non-interactive mode to restore a bad superblock.

-c
> Check for bad blocks.

-f
> Force a check, even if the filesystem looks clean.

-p
> Automatically repair the filesystem without prompting.

-y
> Answers "yes" to all interactive prompts, allowing *e2fsck* to be used noninteractively.

Example 1

Check the ext2 filesystem on */dev/hda5*, which is not mounted:

```
# fsck /dev/hda5
fsck 1.27 (8-Mar-2002)
e2fsck 1.27 (8-Mar-2002)
/dev/hda5: clean, 1011/34136 files, 4360/136521 blocks
```

The partition was clean, so *fsck* didn't really check it.

Example 2

Force a check:

```
# fsck -f /dev/hda5
fsck 1.27 (8-Mar-2002)
e2fsck 1.27 (8-Mar-2002)
```

```
Pass 1: Checking inodes, blocks, and sizes
Pass 2: Checking directory structure
Pass 3: Checking directory connectivity
Pass 4: Checking reference counts
Pass 5: Checking group summary information
/dev/hda5: 1011/34136 files (0.1% non-contiguous), 4360/136521 blocks
```

Example 3

Force another check, this time with verbose output:

```
# fsck -fv /dev/hda5
fsck 1.27 (8-Mar-2002)
e2fsck 1.27 (8-Mar-2002)
Pass 1: Checking inodes, blocks, and sizes
Pass 2: Checking directory structure
Pass 3: Checking directory connectivity
Pass 4: Checking reference counts
Pass 5: Checking group summary information
        1011 inodes used (2%)
           1 non-contiguous inodes (0.1%)
             # of inodes with ind/dind/tind blocks: 0/0/0
        4360 blocks used (3%)
           0 bad blocks
           0 large files
        1000 regular files
           2 directories
           0 character device files
           0 block device files
           0 fifos
           0 links
           0 symbolic links (0 fast symbolic links)
           0 sockets
--------
        1002 files
```

Example 4

Allow *fsck* to automatically perform all repairs on a damaged filesystem by specifying
the -*y* option to run the command automatically:

```
# fsck -y /dev/hda5
fsck 1.27 (8-Mar-2002)
e2fsck 1.27 (8-Mar-2002)
Couldn't find ext2 superblock, trying backup blocks...
/dev/hda5 was not cleanly unmounted, check forced.
Pass 1: Checking inodes, blocks, and sizes
Pass 2: Checking directory structure
Pass 3: Checking directory connectivity
Pass 4: Checking reference counts
Pass 5: Checking group summary information
Block bitmap differences:  +1 +2 +3 +4
Fix? yes
Inode bitmap differences:  +1 +2 +3 +4 +5 +6
Fix? yes
/dev/hda5: ***** FILE SYSTEM WAS MODIFIED *****
/dev/hda5: 1011/34136 files (0.1% non-contiguous), 4360/136521 blocks
```

When Linux boots, the kernel performs a check of all filesystems in */etc/fstab* using the *-A* option to *fsck*. (Unless the */etc/fstab* entry contains the *noauto* option.) Any filesystems that were not cleanly unmounted are checked. If that check finds any significant errors, the system drops into single-user mode so you can run *fsck* manually. Unfortunately, unless you have detailed knowledge of the inner workings of the filesystem, there's little you can do other than to have *fsck* do all of the repairs. As a result, it is common to use the *-y* option and hope for the best.

In some cases, a filesystem may be beyond repair or may even trigger a bug in *e2fsck*. In these (thankfully *very* rare) situations, there are a few commands that can help an *ext2* filesystem wizard debug the problem. These commands are *e2image*, *dumpe2fs*, and *debugfs*. For more information on these tools, read their appropriate manpages.

On the Exam

Familiarity with *du*, *df*, and *fsck* is important. Be sure you understand the differences between the commands and when each is used.

Objective 3: Control Filesystem Mounting and Unmounting

As discussed in "Objective 1: Create Partitions and Filesystems," the Linux directory hierarchy is usually made up of multiple partitions, each joined to the root filesystem. Filesystems on removable media, such as CD-ROMs, Zip disks, and floppy disks, are joined in the same way, but usually on a temporary basis. Each of these separate filesystems is *mounted* to the parent filesystem as a directory (or *mount point*) in the unified hierarchy.

Directories intended as mount points usually don't contain files or other directories. Instead, they're just empty directories created solely to mount a filesystem. If a directory that already contains files is used as a mount point, its files are obscured and unavailable until the filesystem is unmounted. Typical mount points include the directories */usr*, */home*, */var*, and others.

Managing the Filesystem Table

Since the Linux filesystem hierarchy is spread across separate partitions and/or multiple drives, it is necessary to automatically mount those filesystems at boot time. In addition, removable media and filesystems on remote NFS servers may be used regularly with recurring mount properties. All of this information is recorded in the */etc/fstab* file. Filesystems defined in this file are checked and mounted when the system boots. Entries in this file are consulted for default information when users wish to mount removable media.

The *etc/fstab* file (see Example 6-1) is plain text and consists of lines with six fields:

Device
>This field specifies the device file of the partition holding the filesystem (for example */dev/hda1*).

Mount point
>This field specifies the directory on which the filesystem is to be mounted. For example, if */dev/hda1* contains the root filesystem, it is mounted at */*. The root filesystem will contain additional directories intended as mount points for other filesystems. For example, */boot* may be an empty directory intended to mount the filesystem that contains kernel images and other information required at boot time.

Filesystem type
>Next, the type of filesystem is specified. These may include *ext2* filesystems, *swap*, *iso9660* (CD-ROM), and others.

Mount options
>This field contains a comma-separated list of options. Some options are specific to particular filesystem types. Options are described later in this Objective.

Dump frequency
>The dump program, a standard Unix backup utility, will consult */etc/fstab* for information on how often to dump each filesystem. This field holds an integer, usually set to 1 for native Linux filesystems such as *ext2* and to 0 for others.

Pass number for fsck
>This field is used by the *fsck* utility when the -A option is specified, usually at boot time. It is a flag that may contain only the values 0, 1, or 2.

>- A 1 should be entered for the root filesystem and instructs *fsck* to check that filesystem first.

>- A 2 instructs *fsck* to check corresponding filesystems after those with a 1.

>- A 0 instructs *fsck* not to check the filesystem.

Example 6-1. Sample /etc/fstab File

```
/dev/sda1    /            ext2     defaults           1 1
/dev/sda5    /boot        ext2     defaults           1 2
/dev/sda9    /home        ext2     defaults           1 2
/dev/sda6    /root        ext2     defaults           1 2
/dev/sda10   /tmp         ext2     defaults           1 2
/dev/sda8    /usr         ext2     defaults           1 2
/dev/sda7    /var         ext2     defaults           1 2
/dev/sda11   swap         swap     defaults           0 0
/dev/fd0     /mnt/floppy  ext2     noauto,users       0 0
/dev/hdc     /mnt/cdrom   iso9660  noauto,ro,users    0 0
/dev/hdd     /mnt/zip     vfat     noauto,users       0 0
fs1:/share   /fs1         nfs      defaults           0 0
```

The *fstab* in Example 6-1 depicts a system with a single SCSI disk, */dev/sda*. The first partition, */dev/sda1*, contains an *ext2* root filesystem. Partition */dev/sda11* is swap. Partitions */dev/sda5* through */dev/sda10* contain *ext2* filesystems for */boot*, */home*, */root*, */tmp*, */usr*, and */var*, respectively. All of the local *ext2* partitions are to be checked by *fsck* and dumped. Entries for the floppy disk (*/dev/fd0*), CD-ROM (*/dev/hdc*), and IDE Zip drive (*/dev/hdd*) hold appropriate mount properties, making manual mounting of these devices simple. Finally, this example shows a remote NFS mount of directory */share* of system *fs1*. It is mounted locally at */fs1*.

The */etc/fstab* file is automatically created when Linux is installed and is based on the partitioning and mount point configuration specified. This file can be changed at any time to add devices and options, tailoring the filesystem to meet your specific needs.

On the Exam

You should memorize the functions of each column in */etc/fstab* and be prepared to answer questions on each.

Mounting Filesystems

Filesystems are mounted using the *mount* command. At boot time, those filesystems with a nonzero pass number in */etc/fstab* are checked and automatically mounted. Later, you can run *mount* manually to add other filesystems to the filesystem hierarchy.

---

mount

Syntax

```
mount [command_line_options] device
mount [command_line_options] directory
mount [command_line_options] device directory
```

Description

Used to mount filesystems onto the filesystem hierarchy. The first and second forms consult */etc/fstab* and mount the filesystem located on *device* or intended to be attached to *directory*, respectively. In both cases, information necessary to complete the mount operation is taken from */etc/fstab*. The third form is independent of */etc/fstab* and mounts the filesystem on *device* at mount point *directory*.

The *mount* command accepts two kinds of options: *command-line* and *mount*. The command-line options provide general direction for the *mount* command. The mount options are used to specify additional information about the device being mounted.

Command-line options

-*a*

> Mounts all of the partitions specified in */etc/fstab*, except those with the noauto option.

-*h*

> Displays help on the mount command.

-*o mount_options*

> Specifies mount options on the command line.

-*r*

> Mounts the filesystem as read-only.

-*t fstype*

> Specifies that the filesystem to be mounted is of type *fstype*. This option is typically used interactively when no entry for the mount exists in */etc/fstab*.

-*v*

> Sets verbose mode.

-*w*

> Mounts the filesystem read/write mode.

Mount options

A number of parameters are available as options for mounting filesystems. These options may be specified in */etc/fstab* or as arguments of the -*o* command-line mount argument. These options modify the way mount configures the mounted filesystem. Some of the options can provide added security by controlling some operations on the filesystem. Others protect the filesystem from damage. Here is a partial list:

async

> Establishes asynchronous I/O to the mounted filesystem. The opposite is *sync*.

auto

> Enables a mount specification in */etc/fstab* to be processed with the -*a* command-line option, as needed at boot time. The opposite is *noauto*.

defaults

> Implies *rw*, *suid*, *dev*, *exec*, *auto*, *nouser*, and *async*. It is commonly found on */etc/fstab* entries for *ext2* and *ext3* mount points.

dev

> Interprets character or block special devices on the filesystem.

exec

> Enables the execution of programs contained on the mounted partition. The opposite is *noexec*.

noauto

> Prohibits automatic mounting with the -*a* option. This is usually specified for removable media.

noexec

> Prohibits the execution of executable programs, a potential security measure.

nosuid

> Disables the effect of suid or sgid bits on executable files.

nouser

Forbids non-root users from mounting and unmounting the filesystem. See *user* and *users* for the opposite effect.

ro

Equivalent to specifying the command-line option -*r*.

rw

Equivalent to specifying the command-line option -*w*.

suid

Enables the effect of suid and sgid bits on executable files.

sync

Establishes synchronous I/O to the mounted filesystem. The opposite is *async*.

user

Allows an ordinary user to mount the filesystem but prohibits other ordinary users from unmounting it. This is useful for removable media that an individual requires control over. See also *users*.

users

Allows any user to mount and unmount the filesystem.

Note that the *user* and *users* options make the *mount* and *umount* commands available to non-root users. This may be important for some systems where end users must have the ability to mount removable media.

Filesystem types

When mounting a filesystem, the *filesystem type* should be specified either by using the -*t* option to mount or in the third field in */etc/fstab*. (If -*t* is omitted or auto is specified, the kernel will attempt to probe for the filesystem type. This can be convenient for removable media, where the filesystem type may not always be the same or even known.) Linux can mount a variety of filesystems. The following are some of the more popular ones:

ext2

The standard Linux filesystem.

ext3

A journalling filesystem that is backwards-compatible with *ext2*.

msdos

The MS-DOS FAT filesystem, limited to "8.3" filenames (eight characters, a dot, and a three-character extension).

vfat

Virtual FAT, used instead of *msdos* when long filenames must be preserved. For example, you may wish to have access to Windows partitions on systems configured to boot both Linux and Windows.

iso9660

The CD-ROM format, also the default type.

nfs

Remote servers.

swap

Swap partitions.

proc

This type represents the *proc* filesystem, which is not really a filesystem at all. The virtual files found in this virtual filesystem provide a window into the kernel. It is usually mounted on */proc*.

Example 1

Display filesystems currently mounted on the system:

```
# mount
/dev/sda1 on / type ext2 (rw)
none on /proc type proc (rw)
/dev/sda5 on /boot type ext2 (rw)
/dev/sda9 on /home type ext2 (rw)
/dev/sda6 on /root type ext2 (rw)
/dev/sda10 on /tmp type ext2 (rw)
/dev/sda8 on /usr type ext2 (rw)
/dev/sda7 on /var type ext2 (rw)
none on /dev/pts type devpts (rw,mode=0622)
/dev/hdd on /mnt/zip type vfat (rw,noexec,nosuid,nodev)
```

In this example, you can see that most of the filesystems specified in the */etc/fstab* from Example 6-1 are already mounted.

Example 2

Mount the IDE CD-ROM device found on */dev/hdc* to the existing directory */mnt/cdrom*, read-only of course:

```
# mount -rt iso9660 /dev/hdc /mnt/cdrom
```

Note that without the *-r* option, you will receive a warning but still get appropriate results:

```
# mount -t iso9660 /dev/hdc /mnt/cdrom
mount: block device /dev/hdc is write-protected,
mounting read-only
```

Another option would be to add the following to */etc/fstab*:

```
/dev/hdc  /mnt/cdrom  iso9660  ro  0 0
```

Then the device can be mounted with just mount /mnt/cdrom.

Example 3

Mount an MS-DOS floppy in the first floppy disk drive */dev/fd0* (A: in MS-DOS) to the existing directory */mnt/floppy*:

```
# mount -t msdos /dev/fd0 /mnt/floppy
```

Example 4

The filesystems mounted at */home* and */opt* have been unmounted for some kind of maintenance and are now remounted using the *-a* option:

```
# mount -av
mount: /dev/hda5 already mounted on /root
mount: /dev/hda9 already mounted on /usr
mount: /dev/hda7 already mounted on /var
mount: none already mounted on /proc
mount: none already mounted on /dev/pts
mount: 192.168.0.2:/ already mounted on /smp
```

```
/dev/hda10 on /home type ext2 (rw)
/dev/hda8 on /opt type ext2 (rw)
```

Note that mount should work silently without the *-v* option. It also safely skips filesystems that have been previously mounted.

Unmounting Filesystems

Filesystems can be unmounted using the umount command. When a filesystem is unmounted, the buffers of the filesystem are synchronized with the actual contents on disk and the filesystem is made unavailable, freeing the mount point. If the filesystem is busy, *umount* yields an error. This will happen, for example, when the filesystem contains open files or when a process has a working directory within the filesystem. Other less obvious errors can occur when removable media are exchanged without being unmounted first.

---

umount

Syntax

```
umount [options] device
umount [options] directory
```

Description

Unmount the filesystem on *device* or mounted on *directory*.

-a

   Unmounts all of the filesystems described in */etc/mtab*. This file is maintained by the *mount* and *umount* commands and contains an up-to-date list of mounted filesystems. This option is typically used at shutdown time.

-t fstype
   Unmounts only filesystems of type *fstype*.

Example 1

Unmount the CD-ROM mounted on */dev/hdc* at */mnt/cdrom*:

```
# umount /mnt/cdrom
```

or:

```
# umount /dev/hdc
```

Example 2

Unmount all NFS filesystems:

```
# umount -at nfs
```

On the Exam

Be sure that you understand how to use mount and mount points and how */etc/fstab* is used when mounting files.

Objective 4: Set and View Disk Quotas

Managing disk space can be a difficult problem. The available space is a finite resource and is often consumed at an alarming rate, turning today's carefully sized filesystem into tomorrow's expansion requirement. On multiuser systems—no matter how big the filesystem—users will find a way to fill it. The last thing you want is for a filesystem to fill to capacity too early. One way to prevent that from happening is to enforce *disk quotas*, which allow you assign a limit to the amount of space individual users or groups have on a filesystem.

A typical quota size is usually much smaller than the filesystem it is configured on, thus preventing the user or group from consuming too much space. Quotas can be configured for each filesystem mentioned in */etc/fstab*, though they are usually applied only where multiple end users store files (i.e., */home/username*). There is no need for a quota on */usr*, for example, since end users cannot store files there. Quotas may be configured for individual users listed in */etc/passwd* and for groups listed in */etc/group*.

Quota Limits

Each filesystem has up to five types of quota limits that can be enforced on it. These limits are specified in disk *blocks*, usually 1,024 bytes each:

Per-user hard limit
> The *hard limit* is the maximum amount of space an individual user can have on the system. Once the user reaches his quota limit, he won't be allowed to write files to the disk.

Per-user soft limit
> Each user is free to store data on the filesystem until reaching her *soft limit*. The soft limit implements a sort of warning zone, instructing the user to clean up while still allowing her to work. When the amount of data exceeds this limit but does not exceed the hard limit, a message is printed on the user's terminal, indicating that her quota has been exceeded; however, the write operation will succeed.

Per-group hard limit
> This is the final limit set for a group by the quota system. Once this limit has been reached, none of the users within that group will be allowed to write files to the disk—even if the user's individual limits are not exceeded.

Per-group soft limit
> This limit behaves in the same way as a user's soft limit but is enforced based on group ownership instead of individual ownership.

Grace period
> Once a soft limit is reached, the user or group enters the *grace period*. After the grace period expires, the soft limit becomes a hard limit until enough files are deleted to eliminate the over-quota situation. The grace period may be specified for any number of months, weeks, days, hours, minutes, or seconds. A typical value is seven days.

These limits are set using the *edquota* command, detailed in the next section.

When a disk write exceeds a hard limit or an expired soft limit, only part of the write operation will complete, leaving a truncated and probably useless file. The messages reported to the user when a quota is exceeded may be lost if the shell he is using is hidden. This could confuse the user, because the error message generated by the application indicates that the disk is full or write-protected.

Quota Commands

Linux offers a host of commands to manage, display, and report on filesystem quotas. Some of the setup required to initially enable quotas is done manually and without specific quota commands, a process that is covered in the next section.

quota

Syntax

```
quota [-u] [options] user
quota -g [options] group
```

Description

Displays quota limits on *user* or *group*. The *-u* option is the default. Only the superuser may use the *-u* flag and *user* to view the limits of other users. Other users can use the *-g* flag and *group* to view only the limits of groups of which they are members, provided that the *quota.group* files are readable by them.

Frequently used options

-q

Sets quiet mode, which shows only over-quota situations.

-v

Enables verbose mode to display quotas even if no storage space is allocated.

Example 1

As *root*, examine all quotas for user *jdoe*:

```
# quota -uv jdoe
Disk quotas for user jdoe (uid 500):
Filesystem blks  quota limit grace  files quota limit grace
/dev/sda9  9456  10000 10200          32    0     0
/dev/hda1    23     0     0            17    0     0
```

This example shows that *jdoe* is barely within her soft limit of 10,000 blocks, with a corresponding hard limit of 10,200 blocks on */dev/sda9*, and has no quota on */dev/hda1*. The entry for */dev/hda1* is displayed in response to the *-v* option. No values are shown for the grace periods, because the soft limit has not been exceeded.

Example 2

As user *jdoe*, examine quotas for the *finance* group, of which he is a member:

```
$ quota -gv finance
Disk quotas for group finance (gid 501):
```

```
Filesystem  blks  quota  limit grace  files quota limit grace
/dev/sda9   1000*  990    1000 6days    34  3980  4000
/dev/hda1      0     0       0           0     0     0
```

Here, the *finance* group has exceeded its meager soft limit of 990 blocks and has come up against its hard limit of 1,000 blocks. (The write operation that wrote the 1,000th block was probably incomplete.) The original grace period in this example was set to seven days and has six days remaining, meaning that one day has elapsed since the soft limit was exceeded.

quotaon

Syntax

```
quotaon [options] [filesystems]
quotaon [options] -a
```

Description

Enable previously configured disk quotas on one or more *filesystems*.

Frequently used options

-a

> Turns quotas on for all filesystems in */etc/fstab* that are marked read-write with quotas. This is normally used automatically at boot time to enable quotas.

-g

> Turns on group quotas. This option is not necessary when using the *-a* option, which includes both user and group quotas.

-u

> Turns on user quotas; this is the default.

-v

> Enables verbose mode to display a message for each filesystem where quotas are turned on.

Example 1

Turn on all quotas as defined in */etc/fstab*:

```
# quotaon -av
/dev/sda9: group quotas turned on
/dev/sda9: user quotas turned on
/dev/hda1: group quotas turned on
/dev/hda1: user quotas turned on
```

Example 2

Turn on user quotas only on the */home* filesystem:

```
# quotaon -gv /home
/dev/sda9: group quotas turned on
```

quotaoff

Syntax

```
quotaoff [options] [filesystems]
quotaoff [options] -a
```

Description

Disables disk quotas on one or more *filesystems*.

Frequently used options

-a

Turns quotas off for all filesystems in */etc/fstab*.

-g

Turns off group quotas. This option is not necessary when using the *-a* option, which includes both user and group quotas.

-u

Turns off user quotas; this is the default.

-v

Enables verbose mode to display a message for each filesystem where quotas are turned off.

Example

Turn off all quotas:

```
# quotaoff -av
/dev/sda9: group quotas turned off
/dev/sda9: user quotas turned off
/dev/hda1: group quotas turned off
/dev/hda1: user quotas turned off
```

quotacheck

Syntax

```
quotacheck [options] filesystems
quotacheck [options] -a
```

Description

Examine filesystems and compile quota databases. This command is not specifically called out in the LPI Objectives for Exam 101, but is an important component of the Linux quota system. You should run the *quotacheck -a* command on a regular basis (perhaps weekly) via *cron*.

Frequently used options

-a

Checks all of the quotas for the filesystems mentioned in */etc/fstab*. Both user and group quotas are checked as indicated by the usrquota and grpquota options.

-g group

Compiles information only on *group*.

-u user

Compiles information only on *user*; this is the default action. However, if the *-g* option is specified, then this option should also be specified when both group and user quotas are to be processed.

-v

Enables verbose mode to display information about what the program is doing. This option shows activity by displaying a spinning character in the terminal. This is nice but could be a problem if you are logged in over a slow modem link.

Example 1

Initialize all quota files:

```
# quotaoff -a
# quotacheck -aguv
Scanning /dev/sda9 [/home] done
Checked 237 directories and 714 files
Using quotafile /home/quota.user
Using quotafile /home/quota.group
Scanning /dev/hda1 [/mnt/hd] done
Checked 3534 directories and 72673 files
Using quotafile /mnt/hd/quota.user
Using quotafile /mnt/hd/quota.group
# quotaon -a
```

By turning off quotas during the update, the quota database files are updated.

Example 2

With quotas active, update the user quotas in memory for */home*:

```
# quotacheck -v /home
Scanning /dev/sda9 [/home] done
Checked 237 directories and 714 files
Using quotafile /home/quota.user
Updating in-core user quotas
```

edquota

Syntax

```
edquota [-p proto-user] [options] names
edquota [options] -t
```

Description

Modify user or group quotas. This interactive command uses a text editor to configure quota parameters for users or groups. The *vi* editor is used by default unless either the EDITOR or VISUAL environment variables are set to another editor, such as Emacs. When the command is issued, the *vi* editor is launched with a temporary file containing quota settings. When the temporary file is saved and the editor is terminated, the changes are saved in the quota databases.

In the first form, a space-separated list of users or groups specified in *names* is modified. If *proto-user* is specified with the *-p* option, quotas of that user or group are copied and used for *names* and no editor is launched. In the second form with the *-t* option, the soft limit settings are edited interactively for each filesystem.

Frequently used options

-g

Modify group quotas. If *-g* is specified, all *names* are assumed to be groups and not users, even if *-u* is also specified.

-p *proto-user*

Duplicate the quotas of the prototypical user or group *proto-user* for each user or group specified. This is the normal mechanism used to initialize quotas for multiple users or groups at the same time.

-t

Modify soft limits. Time units of *sec*(onds), *min*(utes), *hour*(s), *day*(s), *week*(s), and *month*(s) are understood.

-u

Modify user quotas. This is the default action. This option is ignored if *-g* is also specified.

 The following examples use the *vi* editor. The contents of the edit buffer, not program output, are shown after each example.

Example 1

Modify the user quotas for *jdoe*:

```
# edquota -u jdoe
Quotas for user jdoe:
/dev/sda9: blocks in use: 87, limits (soft = 99900, hard = 100000)
        inodes in use: 84, limits (soft = 0, hard = 0)
/dev/hda1: blocks in use: 0, limits (soft = 0, hard = 0)
        inodes in use: 0, limits (soft = 0, hard = 0)
~
~
"/tmp/EdP.auHTZJ0" 5 lines, 241 characters
```

Here, *jdoe* has been allocated a soft limit of 99,900 blocks (which on a default Linux ext2 or ext3 fileystem with a 4k block size means 390 MB), a hard limit of 100,000 blocks (only 400 KB higher than the soft limit), and no limit on the number of files on */dev/sda9*. She has no limits on */dev/hda1*.

Example 2

Modify soft limits for users on all filesystems:

```
# edquota -tu
Time units may be: days, hours, minutes, or seconds
Grace period before enforcing soft limits for users:
/dev/sda9: block grace period: 7 days,
    file grace period: 3 days
/dev/hda1: block grace period: 7 days,
    file grace period: 3 days
~
~
"/tmp/EdP.aiTShJB" 5 lines, 249 characters
```

Here, the user grace periods have been set to seven days for blocks (disk space) and three days for files (inodes).

repquota

Syntax

```
repquota [options] filesystems
repquota -a [options]
```

Description

Used to report on the status of quotas. In the first form, repquota displays a summary report on the quotas for the given *filesystems* on a per-user or per-group basis. In the second form, the *-a* option causes a summary for all filesystems with quotas to be displayed. This command fails for non-root users unless the quota database files are world-readable. The current number of files and the amount of space utilized are printed for each user, along with any quotas created with *edquota*.

Frequently used options

-a

Report on all of the quotas for the read-write filesystems mentioned in */etc/fstab*. Both user and group quotas are reported as indicated by the *usrquota* and *grpquota* options.

-g

Report quotas for groups.

-u

Report quotas for users; this is the default action.

-v

Enable verbose mode, which adds a descriptive header to the output.

Example

Report user quotas for */home*:

```
# repquota -v /home
*** Report for user quotas on /dev/sda9 (/home)
                        Block limits        File limits
User            used  soft    hard grace used soft hard grace
root      --  418941     0       0       269    0    0
328       --    1411     0       0        20    0    0
jdean     --    9818 99900  100000       334    0    0
u1        --      44     0       0        43    0    0
u2        --      44     0       0        43    0    0
u3        --     127   155     300       124    0    0
jdoe      --      87 99900  100000        84    0    0
bsmith    --      42  1990    2000        41    0    0
```

Enabling Quotas

To use quotas, they must first be enabled. Quota support must also be compiled into the kernel. In the unlikely event that your kernel does not contain quota support, you will need to recompile the kernel (see Chapter 13 for more details on how to compile a kernel). This is not a difficult process, but unfortunately it is not completely straightforward either. To clarify the procedure, this section provides a brief tutorial on how to enable user and group quotas for a filesystem on */dev/sda9* mounted under */home*. Note that you may enable user quotas only, group quotas only, or both, as your needs dictate.

1. Set options in */etc/fstab*. On the line containing the */home* filesystem, add the usrquota and grpquota options to the existing default option, like this:

   ```
   /dev/sda9   /home   ext2   defaults,usrquota,grpquota 1  2
   ```

   These options tell quota configuration utilities which partitions should be managed when the utilities reference */etc/fstab*.

2. Create the *quota.user* and *quota.group* files at the top of the */home* filesystem and set their protection bits for root access only:

   ```
   # touch /home/quota.user /home/quota.group
   # chmod 600 /home/quota.user /home/quota.group
   ```

   These two files are the databases for user and group quotas. Each filesystem with quotas uses its own quota databases. When quotas are enabled, these files will contain binary data (that is, they're not text files). Note that if you want end users to be able to examine quotas on groups to which they belong, *quota.group* will need a protection mode of 644 instead of 600.

3. Run *quotacheck* to initialize the databases:

   ```
   # quotacheck -avug
   Scanning /dev/sda9 [/home] done
   Checked 236 directories and 695 files
   Using quotafile /home/quota.user
   Using quotafile /home/quota.group
   ```

4. Then verify that your quota database files have been initialized by noting that they are no longer of size zero (here they are 16,192 bytes each):

   ```
   # ls -al /home/quota.*
   -rw-------  1 root  root 16192 Dec 27 19:53 /home/quota.group
   -rw-------  1 root  root 16192 Dec 27 19:53 /home/quota.user
   ```

5. Run *quotaon* to enable the quota system:

   ```
   # quotaon -a
   ```

6. Verify that your system's initialization script (*/etc/rc.d/rc.sysinit* or similar) will turn on quotas when your system boots. Something along these lines is appropriate, although your system may be very different:

   ```
   if [ -x /sbin/quotacheck ]; then
       echo "Checking quotas."
       /sbin/quotacheck -avug
       echo " Done."
   fi
   if [ -x /sbin/quotaon ]; then
       echo "Turning on quotas."
       /sbin/quotaon -avug
   fi
   ```

7. Add a command script to a system *crontab* directory (such as the directory */etc/crontab.weekly*) to execute *quotacheck* on a routine basis. An executable script file like the following will work:

   ```
   #!/bin/bash
   exec /sbin/quotacheck -avug
   ```

If you prefer, you could instead put */sbin/quotacheck* in *root*'s *crontab* file (using the *crontab -e* command) for weekly execution, like this:

```
# run quotacheck weekly
0 3 * * 0   /sbin/quotacheck -avug
```

At this point, the */home* filesystem is ready to accept quotas on a per-user and per-group basis, enforce them, and report on them.

On the Exam

A general understanding of quotas is necessary for the exam. In particular, you should know the function of each command. Also remember that quotas are set on a per-filesystem basis.

Objective 5: Use File Permissions to Control Access to Files

Filesystem security is a fundamental requirement for any multiuser operating system. The system's files, such as the kernel, configuration files, and programs, must be protected from accidents and tampering by unauthorized people. Users' files must be protected from modification by other users and sometimes must be kept completely private. In general, a form of *access control* must be implemented to allow secure operations.

Linux Access Control

Native Linux filesystem access control is implemented using a set of properties, maintained separately for each file. These properties are collectively called the *access mode*, or simply the *mode*, of the file. The mode is a part of the file's inode, the information retained in the filesystem that describes the file. A file's mode controls access by these three classes of users:

User
> The user that owns the file.

Group
> The group that owns the file.

Other
> All other users on the system.

Like the mode, user and group ownership properties are a part of the inode, and both are assigned when a file is created. Usually, the owner is the user who created the file. The file's group is usually set to its creator's default group. Group ownership adds flexibility in situations in which a team shares files. The "other" users are those who aren't members of the file's group and are not the file's owner. For each of these three user classes, the access mode defines three types of permissions, which apply differently for files and directories. The permissions are listed in Table 6-2.

Table 6-2. File permissions

Permission	Mnemonic	File permission	Directory permission
Read	r	Examine the contents of the file.	List directory contents.
Write	w	Write to or change the file.	Create and remove files in the directory.
Execute	x	Run the file as a program.	Access (cd into) the directory.

These three permissions apply to the three different classes of users: *user, group,* and *other*. Each has *read, write,* and *execute* permissions, as shown in Figure 6-1.

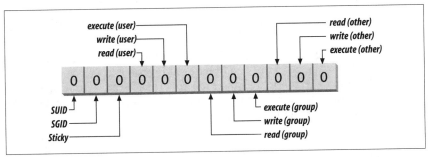

Figure 6-1. Access mode bits

All of the permissions are binary (either granted or not granted) and are thought of as single binary bits in the access mode. When displayed by commands such as ls, the permissions use the mnemonic in Table 6-2 for the true state and a hyphen for the false state. To represent only the read permission, for example, r-- would be used. Read and execute together, typical for directories, would be denoted r-x. These notations are usually offered in sets of three, such as:

    rw-rw-r--

A file with this setting would give read/write permission to the user and group, and read-only permission to everyone else.

In addition to the nine bits for user, group, and other, the access mode contains three more bits, which control special attributes for executable files and directories:

SUID

The SUID property is for executable files only and has no effect on directories. Normally the user who launches a program owns the resulting process. However, if an executable file has its SUID bit set, the file's owner owns the resulting process, no matter who launched it. When SUID is used, the file's owner is usually root. This offers anyone temporary root access for the duration of the command. An example of an SUID program is *passwd*. This command needs special access to manipulate the shadow password file (*/etc/shadow*), and runs as user *root*.

Using the SUID bit in cases like *passwd* enhances security by allowing access to secure functions without giving away the root password. On the other hand, SUID can be a security risk if access is granted unwisely.

SGID

The SGID property works the same way as SUID for executable files, setting the process group owner to the file's group. In addition, the SGID property has a special effect on directories. When SGID is set on a directory, new files created within that directory are assigned the same group ownership as the directory itself. For example, if directory */home/fin* has the group *finance* and has SGID enabled, then all files under */home/fin* are created with group ownership of *finance*, regardless of the creator's group. This is an important attribute for teams, ensuring that shared files all have the same group ownership.

Sticky

At one time, the *sticky bit* applied to executable programs, flagging the system to keep an image of the program in memory after the program finished running. This capability increased performance for subsequent uses by eliminating the programs' load phase, and was applied to programs that were large or were run frequently. Modern virtual memory techniques have made this use unnecessary, and under Linux there is no need to use the sticky bit on executable programs.

When applied to a directory, the sticky bit offers additional security for files within the directory. Regardless of file permissions, the only users who can rename or delete the files from a directory with the sticky bit set are the file owner, the directory owner, and *root*. When used in a team environment, the sticky bit allows groups to create and modify files but allows only file owners the privilege of deleting or renaming them.

Like the other access controls, these special properties are binary and are considered bits in the access mode.

The mode bits

The *special*, *user*, *group*, and *other* permissions can be represented in a string of 12 binary bits, as shown in Figure 6-2.

It is common to refer to these bits in four sets of three, translated into four octal (base-8) digits. The first octal digit represents the special permissions SUID, SGID, and sticky. The other three represent the read, write, and execute permissions, respectively, in each of the user, group, and other user classes. Octal notation is used as shorthand for binary strings like the access mode, and each group of three bits has $2^3 = 8$ possible values, listed in Table 6-3.

The read permission by itself is r--, which can be thought of as binary 100, or octal 4. Adding the write permission yields rw-, or binary 110, which is octal 6. Figure 6-2 shows how to total bit values into the octal equivalents. Memorizing, or even writing, the binary-to-octal equivalents may be easier on the exam than adding bit values. Use the technique that works best for you.

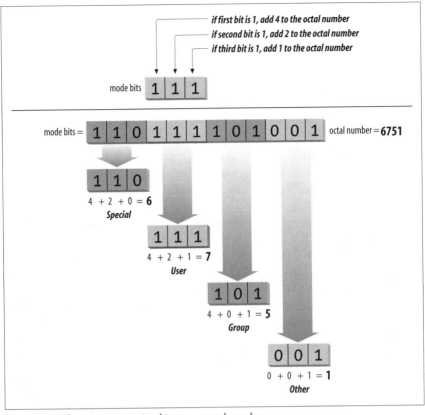

Figure 6-2. Changing permission bits to an octal number

Table 6-3. Octal numbers

Octal value	Binary equivalent
0	000
1	001
2	010
3	011
4	100
5	101
6	110
7	111

To turn the mode bits 110111101001 into an octal representation, first separate them into chunks of three bits: 110, 111, 101, and 001. The first group, representing the special permissions, is 110. This can be thought of as 4 + 2 + 0 = 6. The second group, representing user permissions, is 111, or 4 + 2 + 1 = 7. The third group, representing group permissions, is 101, or 4 + 0 + 1 = 5. The last group, representing other permissions, is 001, or 0 + 0 + 1 = 1. The mode string for this example can then be written as the octal 6751.

This is the form used to display the file mode in the output from the stat command. Here, the octal access mode for the mount command is 4755:

```
# stat /bin/mount
  File: "/bin/mount"
  Size: 53620      Filetype: Regular File
  Mode: (4755/-rwsr-xr-x) Uid: ( 0/ root) Gid: ( 0/  root)
Device:  3,2   Inode: 20335    Links: 1
Access: Tue Aug 10 23:57:11 1999(00144.11:34:49)
Modify: Tue Aug 10 23:57:11 1999(00144.11:34:49)
Change: Wed Dec  8 20:59:02 1999(00024.13:32:58)
```

The special permissions are represented in this example by octal 4, or binary 100, indicating that the SUID permission is set (-rws). The user permission is octal 7, or binary 111, indicating read, write, and execute for the file's owner (in this case, *root*). Both the group and other permissions are set to octal 5, or binary 101, indicating read and execute, but not write.

The mode string

As mentioned earlier, the user, group, and other permissions are often spelled out in symbolic mode descriptions such as rwxr-xr-x. This notation is found in the output of the *ls -l* and *stat* commands. As you can see in the access mode for *mount*, this scheme is modified slightly in the presence of special permissions. Instead of adding three more bits to the left of rwxr-xr-x, the SUID permission is indicated in the string by changing the user execute position from x to s. SGID permission is handled the same way. The sticky permission is indicated by replacing x in the other execute position with T. For example, an executable program with mode 6755 would have the following equivalent symbolic mode:

rwsr-sr-x

A directory with mode 1774 would have this equivalent string:

rwxr-xr-T

While this layering of special permissions may appear to obscure the underlying execute permissions, it makes sense. The special permissions are relatively rare in the filesystem, so depicting the three extra bits would waste space on your terminal or terminal window. When the executable bits are set, the setuid and setgid bits are represented with s. When the executable bits are not set, the setuid and setgid bits are represented with S. Similarly, the sticky bit is represented with either t or T.

Setting Access Modes

New files are created with a default access mode to automatically set the permission levels. Regardless of your default umask, access modes on existing files can be changed or modified at will.

New files

When new files are created, the protection bits are set according to the user's default setting. That default is established using the *umask* command, probably in a startup script. This command accepts only one argument, which is a three-digit octal string that masks the user, group, and other permission bits for newly created files and directories. Without a value, *umask* reports the current value:

```
$ umask
0022
```

When provided with an integer, *umask* sets the value for the current shell:

```
$ umask 2
$ umask
0002
```

A *umask* of 22 can be rewritten as 022, or as 000010010 in binary.

The process of creating the initial mode for newly created files begins with a raw initial mode string, as defined in Table 6-4.

Table 6-4. Initial access modes

Form	For files	For directories
Symbolic	rw-rw-rw-	rwxrwxrwx
Binary	110110110	111111111
Octal	6 6 6	7 7 7

The special bits are always turned off and are not masked by the *umask*. When a file is created, the *umask* is subtracted from 666; for directories, it is subtracted from 777. This calculation yields the effective protection mode for the file or directory. For example, a *umask* of 22 (022) is applied to a new file, masking the write permission for group and other user classes:

```
  110 110 110
- 000 010 010
-------------
  110 100 100
```

This is the same as mode 644, or rw-r--r--.

Using the same mask on a directory yields a similar result:

```
  111 111 111
- 000 010 010
-------------
  111 101 101
```

This is the same as mode 755 or rwxr-xr-x, which is appropriate for directories. A umask of 002 or 022 is typical, although if you wish to ensure maximum privacy, a umask of 077 blocks all access except for the superuser. To set a custom umask, enter the *umask* command in a startup script, such as *.bash_profile*. Here's an example of the *umask* in action:

```
$ umask 27
$ touch afile
```

```
$ mkdir adir
$ ls -ld adir afile
drwxr-x---   2 jdean    jdean        1024 Jan  2 20:31 adir
-rw-r-----   1 jdean    jdean           0 Jan  2 20:31 afile
```

In this case, the *umask* of 27 makes the file *afile* read-only to members of the group and disallows access to the file to all others.

As you can see in the output of the previous example, *ls* adds an extra letter at the beginning of the mode string for the *adir* directory. This symbol indicates the type of file being listed and is not part of the access mode. The letter d indicates a directory, a - indicates a file, the letter l indicates a symbolic link, a b indicates a block device (such as a disk), and a c indicates a character device (such as a terminal).

Changing access modes

Access modes can be changed with the *chmod* command, which accepts either *octal* or *symbolic* access mode specifications. Octal bits, as shown in the previous section, are specified explicitly. However, some people prefer to use symbolic forms because they usually modify an existing mode instead of completely replacing it. Symbolic mode specifications have three parts, made up of individual characters, as shown in Table 6-5.

Table 6-5. Symbolic modes for the chmod command

Category	Mode	Description
User class	u	User
	g	Group
	o	Other
	a	All classes
Operation	-	Take away permission
	+	Add permission
	=	Set permission exactly
Permissions	r	Read permission
	w	Write permission
	x	Execute permission
	X	Execute permission for directories and files with another execute permission, but not plain files
	s	SUID or SGID permissions
	t	Sticky bit

The individual user class characters and permissions characters may be grouped to form compound expressions, such as ug for user and group combined or rw for read and write. Here are some examples of symbolic mode specifications:

u+x

   Add execute permission for the user.

go-w

   Remove write permission from group and other classes.

---

o+t

> Set the sticky bit.

a=rw

> Set read and write, but not execute, permissions for everyone.

a+X

> Give everyone execute permission for directories and for those files with any existing execute permission.

The *chmod* command is used to modify the mode.

---

chmod

Syntax

```
chmod [options] symbolic_mode[,symbolic_mode]... files
chmod [options] octal_mode files
chmod [options] --reference=rfile files
```

Description

Modify the access mode on *files*. In the first form, use one or more comma-separated *symbolic_mode* specifications to modify *files*. In the second form, use an *octal_mode* to modify *files*. In the third form, use the mode of *rfile* as a template to be applied to *files*.

Frequently used options

-c

> Like verbose mode, but report only changes.

-R

> Use recursive mode, descending through directory hierarchies under *files* and making modifications throughout.

-v

> Use verbose behavior, reporting actions for all *files*.

Example 1

Set the mode for a file to rw-r--r--, using an octal specification:

```
$ chmod 644 afile
$ ls -l afile
-rw-r--r--  1 jdean    jdean         0 Jan  2 20:31 afile
```

Example 2

Set the same permission using a symbolic specification, using the verbose option:

```
$ chmod -v u=rw,go=r afile
mode of afile retained as 0644 (rw-r--r--)
```

Example 3

Recursively remove all permissions for *other* on a directory:

```
$ chmod -R -v o-rwx adir
mode of adir retained as 0770 (rwxrwx---)
```

```
mode of adir/file1 changed to 0660 (rw-rw----)
mode of adir/file2 changed to 0660 (rw-rw----)
mode of adir/file3 changed to 0660 (rw-rw----)
mode of adir/file4 changed to 0660 (rw-rw----)
mode of adir/dir1 changed to 0770 (rwxrwx---)
mode of adir/dir1/file6 changed to 0660 (rw-rw----)
mode of adir/dir1/file5 changed to 0660 (rw-rw----)
mode of adir/dir2 changed to 0770 (rwxrwx---)
```

Example 4

Set the sticky bit on a directory:

```
$ chmod -v +t adir
mode of adir changed to 1770 (rwxrwx--T)
```

Setting Up a Workgroup Directory

The steps you may use to create a useful workgroup directory for a small team of people are briefly described here. The goals of the directory are as follows:

- The workgroup is to be called *sales* and has members *jdoe*, *bsmith*, and *jbrown*.
- The directory is */home/sales*.
- Only the creators of files in */home/sales* should be able to delete them.
- Members shouldn't worry about file ownership, and all group members require full access to files.
- Nonmembers should have no access to any of the files.

The following steps will satisfy the goals:

1. Create the new group:

   ```
   # groupadd sales
   ```

2. Add the existing users to the group:

   ```
   # usermod -G sales jdoe
   # usermod -G sales bsmith
   # usermod -G sales jbrown
   ```

3. Create a directory for the group:

   ```
   # mkdir /home/sales
   ```

4. Set the ownership of the new directory:

   ```
   # chgrp sales /home/sales
   ```

5. Protect the directory from others:

   ```
   # chmod 770 /home/sales
   ```

6. Set the SGID bit to ensure that the *sales* group will own all new files. Also set the sticky bit to protect files from deletion by non-owners:

   ```
   # chmod g+s,o+t /home/sales
   ```

7. Test it:

   ```
   # su - jdoe
   $ cd /home/sales
   $ touch afile
   ```

```
$ ls -l afile
-rw-rw-r--   1 jdoe      sales      0 Jan  3 02:44 afile
$ exit
# su - bsmith
# cd /home/sales
# rm afile
rm: cannot unlink `afile': Operation not permitted
```

After the *ls* command, we see that the group ownership is correctly set to *sales*. After the *rm* command, we see that *bsmith* cannot delete *afile*, which was created by *jdoe*. We also note that although *afile* has mode 664, the directory containing it has mode 770, preventing other users from reading the file.

On the Exam

For the exam, you should be prepared to answer questions on file and directory permissions in both symbolic and numeric (octal) forms. You should also be able to translate between the two forms given an example.

Objective 6: Manage File Ownership

Modification of ownership parameters may become necessary when moving files, setting up workgroups, or working in a user's directory as *root*. This is accomplished using the *chown* command, which can change user and group ownership, and the *chgrp* command for modifying group ownership.

chown

Syntax

```
chown [options] user-owner files
chown [options] user-owner. files
chown [options] user-owner.group-owner files
chown [options] .group-owner files
chown [options] --reference=rfile files
```

Description

Used to change the owner and/or group of *files* to *user-owner* and/or *group-owner*. In the first form, *user-owner* is made the owner of *files* and the group is not affected. In the second form (note the trailing dot on *user-owner*), the *user-owner* is made the owner of *files* and the group of the files is changed to *user-owner*'s default group. In the third form, both *user-owner* and *group-owner* are assigned to *files*. In the fourth form, only the *group-owner* is assigned to *files*, and the user is not affected. In the fifth form, the owner and group of *rfile* is used as a template and applied to *files*. Only the superuser may change file ownership, but group ownership may be set by anyone belonging to the target *group-owner*.

Note that historically BSD systems have used the *user.group* syntax, but SysV-based systems have used *user:group* (: instead of .). Older versions of GNU *chown* only accepted the BSD syntax, but recent versions support both.

Frequently used options

-c

> Like verbose mode, but report only changes.

-R

> Use recursive mode, descending through directory hierarchies under *files* and making modifications throughout.

-v

> Use verbose behavior, reporting actions for all *files*.

Example 1

As root, set the user owner of a file:

```
# chown -v jdoe afile
owner of afile changed to jdoe
```

Example 2

As root, set the user and group owner of a file:

```
# chown -v jdoe.sales afile
owner of afile changed to jdoe.sales
```

chgrp

Syntax

```
chgrp [options] group-owner files
chgrp [options] --reference=rfile files
```

Description

Change the group owner of *files* to *group-owner*. In the first form, set the *group-owner* of *files*. In the second form, the group of *rfile* is used as a template and applied to *files*. Options and usage are the same as that of chown.

Example 1

Recursively change the group owner of the entire *sales* directory:

```
# chgrp -Rv sales sales
changed group of `sales' to sales
changed group of `sales/file1' to sales
changed group of `sales/file2' to sales
...
```

Objective 7: Create and Change Hard and Symbolic Links

Often it is useful to have access to a file in multiple locations in a filesystem. To avoid creating multiple copies of the file, use a *link*. Links don't take up very much space, as they only add a bit of metadata to the filesystem, so they're much more efficient than using separate copies.

There are two types of links used on Linux:

Symbolic links

A symbolic link is simply a pointer to another filename. When Linux opens a symbolic link, it reads the pointer and then finds the intended file that contains the actual data. Symbolic links can point to other filesystems, both local and remote, and they can point to directories. They are clearly listed as being a link with the *ls -l* command by displaying a special "l" (a lowercase L) in column one, and they have no file protections of their own (the actual file's permissions are used instead).

A symbolic link can point to a filename that does not actually exist. Such a symbolic link is said to be *broken* or *stale*.

Hard links

A hard link is not really a link at all. It is simply another directory entry for an existing file. The two directory entries have different names but point to the same inode and thus to the same actual data, ownership, permissions, and so on. In fact, when you delete a file, you are only removing a directory entry (in other words, one hard link to the file). As long as any directory entries remain, the file's inode is not actually deleted. In fact, a file is not deleted until its *link count* drops to zero (and the file is no longer open for reading or writing).

Hard links have two important limitations. First, because all of the links to a file point to the same inode, any hard links must by definition reside on the same filesystem. Second, hard links cannot point to directories. However, hard links take no disk space beyond an additional directory entry.

Why Links?

To see an example of the use of links in practice, consider the directories in */etc/rc.d* on a typical Red Hat system:

```
drwxr-xr-x   2 root     root     1024 Dec 15 23:05 init.d
-rwxr-xr-x   1 root     root     2722 Apr 15  1999 rc
-rwxr-xr-x   1 root     root      693 Aug 17  1998 rc.local
-rwxr-xr-x   1 root     root     9822 Apr 13  1999 rc.sysinit
drwxr-xr-x   2 root     root     1024 Dec  2 09:41 rc0.d
drwxr-xr-x   2 root     root     1024 Dec  2 09:41 rc1.d
drwxr-xr-x   2 root     root     1024 Dec 24 15:15 rc2.d
drwxr-xr-x   2 root     root     1024 Dec 24 15:15 rc3.d
drwxr-xr-x   2 root     root     1024 Dec 24 15:16 rc4.d
drwxr-xr-x   2 root     root     1024 Dec 24 15:16 rc5.d
drwxr-xr-x   2 root     root     1024 Dec 14 23:37 rc6.d
```

Devices and
Filesystems

Inside *init.d* are scripts to start and stop many of the services on your system, such as *httpd*, *crond*, and *syslogd*. Some of these files are to be executed with a start argument, while others are run with a stop argument, depending on the *runlevel* of your system. To determine just which files are run and what argument they receive, a scheme of additional directories has been devised. These directories are named *rc0.d* through *rc6.d*, one for each runlevel (see Chapter 14), for a complete description of this scheme). Each of the runlevel-specific directories contains several links, each with a name that helps determine the configuration of services on your system. For example, *rc3.d* contains the following links, among many others:

```
S30syslog -> ../init.d/syslog
S40crond -> ../init.d/crond
S85httpd -> ../init.d/httpd
```

All of these links point back to the scripts in *init.d* as indicated by the arrows (->) after the script name. If these links were copies of the scripts, editing would be required for all of the runlevel-specific versions of the same script just to make a single change. Instead, links allow us to:

- Make changes to the original file once. References to the links will yield the updated contents as long as the filename doesn't change.
- Avoid wasting disk space by having multiple copies of the same file in different places for "convenience."

As another example, consider the directory for the kernel source, */lib/modules/kernel_version/build*:

```
build -> /usr/src/linux-2.4.18
```

Makefiles and other automated tools for building third-party kernel modules can refer to */lib/modules/`uname -r`/build*, but in reality they reference */usr/src/linux-2.4.18*. If a new kernel is added, say version 2.4.20, its source would be placed into an appropriately named directory and the *build* link in the new modules directory would be set, as follows:

```
build -> /usr/src/linux-2.4.20
```

Now the appropriate directory can be selected simply by changing the link. No files need to be moved or deleted. Once created, links are normal directory entries, which may be copied, renamed, deleted, and backed up.

Symbolic and hard links are created with the *ln* command.

---

ln

Syntax

```
ln [options] file link
ln [options] files directory
```

Description

Create links between files. In the first form, a new *link* is created to point to *file*, which must already exist. In the second form, links are created in *directory* for all *files* specified.

Hard links are created unless the *-s* option is specified.

Frequently used options

-f

   Overwrite (force) existing links, or existing files in the destination *directory*.

-i

   Prompt interactively before overwriting destination files.

-s

   Create a symbolic link rather than a hard link.

Example 1

Note that the Bourne shell *sh* on a Linux system is a symbolic link to *bash*:

```
$ ls -l /bin/bash /bin/sh
-rwxr-xr-x   1 root    root      626028 Feb 11 07:34 /bin/bash
lrwxrwxrwx   1 root    root           4 Feb 23 10:24 /bin/sh -> bash
```

Example 2

Create a file named *myfile*, a symbolic link to that file named *myslink*, and a hard link to that file named *myhlink*, then examine them:

```
$ touch myfile
$ ln -s myfile myslink
$ ln myfile myhlink
$ ls -l my*
-rw-r--r--   2 jdoe  jdoe  0 Jan  3 13:21 myfile
-rw-r--r--   2 jdoe  jdoe  0 Jan  3 13:21 myhlink
lrwxrwxrwx   1 jdoe  jdoe  6 Jan  3 13:21 myslink -> myfile
```

Using the stat command on my* demonstrates that *myfile* and *myhlink* both ultimately reference the same inode (the inode numbers are the same) and indicates the number of hard links to the file:

```
# stat my*
  File: `myfile'
  Size: 0             Blocks: 0        IO Block: 4096   Regular File
Device: 3a05h/14853d   Inode: 1212467   Links: 2
Access: (0644/-rw-r--r--) Uid: (    0/    root) Gid: (    0/    root)
Access: 2003-03-15 21:36:33.000000000 -0600
Modify: 2003-03-15 21:36:33.000000000 -0600
Change: 2003-03-15 21:36:33.000000000 -0600
  File: `myhlink'
  Size: 0             Blocks: 0        IO Block: 4096   Regular File
Device: 3a05h/14853d   Inode: 1212467   Links: 2
Access: (0644/-rw-r--r--) Uid: (    0/    root) Gid: (    0/    root)
Access: 2003-03-15 21:36:33.000000000 -0600
Modify: 2003-03-15 21:36:33.000000000 -0600
Change: 2003-03-15 21:36:33.000000000 -0600
  File: `myslink' -> `myfile'
  Size: 6             Blocks: 0        IO Block: 4096   Symbolic Link
```

Devices and Filesystems

```
Device: 3a05h/14853d    Inode: 1213365    Links: 1
Access: (0777/lrwxrwxrwx)  Uid: (    0/    root)  Gid: (    0/    root)
Access: 2003-03-15 21:36:33.000000000 -0600
Modify: 2003-03-15 21:36:33.000000000 -0600
Change: 2003-03-15 21:36:33.000000000 -0600
```

Note that the symbolic link has an inode of its own, which can also be displayed using the -*i* option to *ls*:

```
# ls -li my*
1212467 -rw-r--r--  2 root  root  0 Mar 15 21:36 myfile
1212467 -rw-r--r--  2 root  root  0 Mar 15 21:36 myhlink
1213365 lrwxrwxrwx  1 root  root  6 Mar 15 21:36 myslink -> myfile
```

Here you can see that the directory entries for *myfile* and *myhlink* both point to inode 1212467, while the directory entry for *myslink* points to inode 1213365. That inode contains the symbolic link to *myfile*.

As another example, consider the two filesystems in Figure 6-3. The root partition on */dev/sda1* holds a file intended as an example *bash* startup file, located in */etc/bashrc_user*. On the same filesystem, the *root* user has elected to use */etc/bashrc_user*. Not wanting to maintain both files individually, *root* has created a hard link, */root/.bashrc*, to the example file.

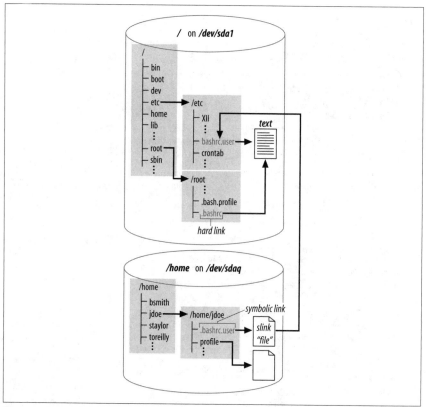

Figure 6-3. Hard and symbolic links

Both of the directory entries, /etc/bashrc_user and /root/.bashrc, point to the same text data in the same file, described by the same inode, on /dev/sda1. User *jdoe* has also elected to link to the example file. However, since his home directory is located in / *home* on /dev/sda9, *jdoe* cannot use a hard link to the file on /dev/sda1. Instead, he created a symbolic link, /home/jdoe/.bashrc, which points to a small file on /dev/sda9. This contains the pointer to directory entry /etc/bashrc_user, which finally points at the text. The result for *root* and *jdoe* is identical, though the two styles of links implement the reference in completely different ways.

Preserving links

Programs such as *tar* and *cp* contain options that control whether symbolic links are followed during operation. In the case of a *tar* backup, this may be important if you have multiple links to large files, because you would get many redundant backups of the same data.

When a symbolic link is encountered with *cp*, the contents of the file to which the link points are copied unless the *-d* option is specified. This "no dereference" operator causes *cp* to copy the links themselves instead. For example, consider a directory *dir1* containing a symbolic link, which is recursively copied to other directories with and without the *-d* option:

```
# ls -l dir1
total 13
lrwxrwxrwx 1 root root       19 Jan  4 02:43 file1 -> /file1
-rw-r--r-- 1 root root    10240 Dec 12 17:12 file2
# cp -r dir1 dir2
# ls -l dir2
total 3117
-rw-r--r-- 1 root root 3164160 Jan  4 02:43 file1
-rw-r--r-- 1 root root   10240 Jan  4 02:43 file2
# cp -rd dir1 dir3
# ls -l dir3
total 13
lrwxrwxrwx 1 root root       19 Jan  4 02:43 file1 -> /file1
-rw-r--r-- 1 root root   10240 Jan  4 02:43 file2
```

Directory *dir2* has a copy of the entire *file1*, which is large, probably wasting disk space. Directory *dir3*, created with *cp -rd*, is the same as *dir1* (including the symbolic link) and takes very little space.

Finding links to a file

Finding the file pointed to by a symbolic link is simple. The *ls -l* command displays a convenient pointer notation, indicating just where links are pointing:

```
lrwxrwxrwx 1 root root       19 Jan  4 02:43 file1 -> /file1
```

Going the other way and finding symbolic links to a file is less obvious but is still relatively easy. The *-lname* option to the *find* utility locates them for you by searching for symbolic links containing the original filename. Here, the entire local filesystem is searched for *myfile*, turning up three symbolic links:

```
# find / -lname myfile
/home/world/rootsfile
```

```
/home/finance/hisfile
/root/myslink
```

Remember that symbolic links could be anywhere, including being located on a remote system (if you're sharing files), so you may not be able to locate them all. (See "Objective 3: Perform Basic File Management in Chapter 5 for additional information on the *find* command).

Since hard links aren't really links but duplicate directory entries, you can locate them by searching directory entries for the inode, which is identical in all the links. Unlike symbolic links, you are guaranteed to find all of the links since hard links cannot cross filesystem boundaries. First, identify the inode you're interested in, as well as the filesystem that contains the links:

```
# df file1
Filesystem     1k-blocks     Used Available Use% Mounted on
/dev/sda9       1981000    451115   1427473  24% /home
# ls -i file
90469 file1
```

Here, *file1* is on the */home* filesystem, and its inode number is 90469. Next, *find* is used with the *-inum* option to locate all instances of inode 90469:

```
# find /home -inum 90469
/home/world/file1
/home/finance/file1
/home/jdoe/private/.myfile1
```

This example turns up three links to *file1*, including one that user *jdoe* appears to be hiding!

On the Exam

You should be prepared to identify the differences between hard and symbolic links, when each is used, and their limitations.

Objective 8: Find System Files and Place Files in the Correct Location

In 1993, the Linux community formed a project to provide a standardized filesystem layout for all general-purpose distributions of Linux. The intent of this standardization was to provide advice on how to reduce the proliferation of proprietary Linux filesystem layouts and their possible contribution to market fragmentation.

The project released a document describing the Linux Filesystem Standard, usually abbreviated FSSTND, in 1994. The following year, the group began to reduce Linux-specific content and to refine the standard to include other Unix or Unix-like operating systems. As the FSSTND attracted broader appeal, it was renamed the *Filesystem Hierarchy Standard*. Although the FHS is not a

---

requirement of Linux developers and distributors, the Linux community under-stands the importance of standards, and all major distributions support the standard.

 The full FHS specification is available at *http://www.pathname.com/ fhs/*. The information in this chapter is consistent with version 2.2 of the specification.

Data Types

To frame its recommendations, the FHS defines two categories of data use, each with two opposing subtypes:

Data sharing
 This category defines the scope of data use in a networked environment:

 Sharable
  Sharable data can be used by multiple host systems on a network. Shar-able files contain general-purpose information, without ties to any specific host. Examples include user datafiles, executable program files, and system documentation.

 Non-sharable
  Data is not sharable when linked to a specific host, such as a unique configuration file.

Data modification
 This category specifies how data changes:

 Variable
  Data is considered variable when changed by natural, frequent processes. Examples include user files and system log files, such as */var/log/ messages*.

 Static
  Static data is left alone for the most part, remaining the same from day to day or even year to year. Examples include binary programs such as ls and bash, which change only when the system administrator performs an upgrade.

Some directories in the Linux filesystem are intended to hold specific types of data. For example, the executable files in */usr* are rarely changed, and thus could be defined as *static* because they are needed by all users on a network. Before disks were as large as they are today, the files commonly found in */usr* were often mounted from remote servers to preserve local disk space. Thus, in addition to being static, */usr* is said to be *sharable*. Keeping files organized with respect to these attributes can simplify file sharing, system administration, and backup complexity, as well as reduce storage requirements. The FHS arranges the preceding data categories into a 2×2 matrix, as shown with a few example direc-tories in Table 6-6.

Table 6-6. FHS data types

	Sharable	Non-sharable
Static	*/usr*	*/etc*
	/usr/local	*/boot*
Variable	*/var/mail*	*/var/log*
	/home	*/proc*

On many networks, */usr* and */usr/local* are mounted by individual workstations from an NFS server. This can save a considerable amount of local storage on the workstations. More important, placing these directories on another system can make upgrades and additions much simpler. These directories are usually shared as read-only filesystems because they are never modified by most end users. The */var/mail* and */home* directories, on the other hand, are shared but must be changed regularly by users. The */etc* and */boot* directories contain files that are static in the sense that only the administrator changes them, but sharing them is not necessary or advised, since they are local configuration files. The */var/log* and */proc* directories are very dynamic but also of local interest only.

The root Filesystem

The FHS offers a significant level of detail describing the exact locations of files, using rationale derived from the static/variable and sharable/nonsharable definitions. However, knowledge of the location of every file is not necessary or required for Exam 101. This section discusses the major portions of the FHS directory hierarchy overall, with specific example files offered as illustrations.

 While the FHS is a defining document for the Linux filesystem, it does not follow that all directories described in the FHS will be present in all Linux installations. Some directory locations cited in the FHS are package-dependent or open to customization by the vendor.

The root filesystem is located at the top of the entire directory hierarchy. The FHS defines these goals for the root filesystem:

- It must contain utilities and files sufficient to boot the operating system, including the ability to mount other filesystems. This includes utilities, device files, configuration, boot loader information, and other essential start-up data.

- It should contain the utilities needed by the system administrator to repair or restore a damaged system.

- It should be relatively small. Small partitions are less likely to be corrupted due to a system crash or power failure than large ones are. In addition, the root partition should contain non-sharable data to maximize the remaining disk space for sharable data.

- Software should not create files or directories in the root filesystem.

While a Linux system with everything in a single root partition may be created, doing so would not meet these goals. Instead, the root filesystem should contain only essential system directories, along with mount points for other filesystems. Essential root filesystem directories include:

/bin

> The */bin* directory contains executable system commands such as *cp, date, ln, ls, mkdir,* and *more*. These commands are deemed essential to system administration in case of a problem.

/dev

> Device files, necessary for accessing disks and other devices, are stored in */dev*. Examples include disk partitions, such as *hda1*, and terminals, such as *tty1*. Devices must be present at boot time for proper mounting and configuration. The exception to this rule is systems using *devfs*, which is a relatively recent addition to the Linux kernel that makes */dev* a virtual filesystem, much like */proc*, where device special files are created by the kernel when drivers register devices. Use of *devfs* is currently not covered by the Level 1 Objectives.

/etc

> The */etc* directory contains configuration information unique to the system and is required for boot time. No binary executable programs are stored here. Prior practice in various versions of Unix had administrative executable programs stored in */etc*. These have been moved to */sbin* under the FHS. Example files include *passwd, hosts,* and *login.defs*.

/lib

> The */lib* directory contains shared libraries and kernel modules, both essential for system initialization.

/mnt

> This directory is provided for the local system administrator's use. Generally, it is empty except for some mount points for temporary partitions, including *cdrom* and *floppy*.

/root

> The recommended default (but optional) home directory for the superuser is */root*. While it is not absolutely essential for */root* to be on the root filesystem, it is customary and convenient, because doing so keeps root's configuration files available for system maintenance or recovery.

/sbin

> Essential utilities used for system administration are stored in */sbin*. Examples include *fdisk, fsck,* and *mkfs*.

The remaining top-level directories in the root filesystem are considered nonessential for emergency procedures:

/boot

> The */boot* directory contains files for the boot loader (such as LILO or GRUB). Because it is typically small, it can be left in the root filesystem. However, it is often separated to keep the boot loader files within the first 1024 cylinders of a physical disk.

/home

The */home* filesystem contains home directories for system users. This is usually a separate filesystem and is often the largest variable filesystem in the hierarchy.

/opt

The */opt* directory is intended for the installation of software other than that packaged with the operating system. This is often the location selected by third-party software vendors for their products.

/tmp

The */tmp* directory is for the storage of temporary files. The FHS recommends (but does not require) that its contents are deleted upon every system boot.

/usr

The */usr* filesystem contains a significant hierarchy of executable programs deemed nonessential for emergency procedures. It is usually contained in a separate partition. It contains sharable, read-only data, and is often mounted locally read-only and shared via NFS read-only. */usr* is described in detail in the next section.

/var

Like */usr*, the */var* filesystem contains a large hierarchy and is usually contained in a separate partition. It holds data that varies over time, such as logs, mail, and spools.

The /usr filesystem

The */usr* filesystem hierarchy contains system utilities and programs that do not appear in the root partition. For example, user programs such as *less* and *tail* are found in */usr/bin*. */usr/sbin* contains system administration commands such as *adduser* and *traceroute*, and a number of daemons needed only on a normally operating system. No host-specific or variable data is stored in */usr*. Also disallowed is the placement of directories directly under */usr* for large software packages. An exception to this rule is made for X11, which has a strong precedent for this location.

The following subdirectories can be found under */usr*:

/usr/X11R6

This directory contains files for XFree86. Because X is deployed directly under */usr* on many Unix systems, X breaks the rule that usually prohibits a custom */usr* directory for a software package.

/usr/bin

The */usr/bin* directory is the primary location for user commands that are not considered essential for emergency system maintenance (and thus are stored here rather than in */bin*).

/usr/include

/usr/include is the standard location for *include* or *header* files, used for C and C++ programming.

/usr/lib

> This directory contains shared libraries that support various programs. FHS also allows the creation of software-specific directories here. For example, */usr/lib/perl5* contains the standard library of Perl modules that implement programming functions in that language.

/usr/local

> */usr/local* is the top level of another hierarchy of binary files, intended for use by the system administrator. It contains subdirectories much like */usr* itself, such as */bin*, */include*, */lib*, and */sbin*. After a fresh Linux installation, this directory contains no files but may contain an empty directory hierarchy. Example items that may be found here are locally created documents in */usr/local/doc* or */usr/local/man*, and executable scripts and binary utilities provided by the system administrator in */usr/local/bin*.

/usr/sbin

> The */usr/sbin* directory is the primary location for system administration commands that are not considered essential for emergency system maintenance (and thus are stored here rather than in */sbin*).

/usr/share

> */usr/share* contains a hierarchy of datafiles that are independent of, and thus can be shared among, various hardware architectures and operating system versions. This is in sharp contrast to architecture-dependant files such as those in */usr/bin*. For example, in an enterprise that uses both i386- and Alpha-based Linux systems, */usr/share* could be offered to all systems via NFS. However, since the two processors are not binary-compatible, */usr/bin* would have two NFS shares, one for each architecture.

> The information stored in */usr/share* is static data, such as the GNU info system files, dictionary files, and support files for software packages.

/usr/src

> */usr/src* is an optional directory on all modern glibc-based systems. On older libc4 and libc5-based systems, */usr/src/linux* was expected to contain a copy of the kernel source, or at least the directories *include/asm* and *include/linux* for kernel header files.

> On glibc-based systems, nothing should refer to the */usr/src/linux* directory. In fact, leaving kernel source at that location is generally regarded as a bad practice, since it has the potential to confuse old software.

The /var filesystem

The */var* filesystem contains data such as printer spools and log files that vary over time. Since variable data is always changing and growing, */var* is usually contained in a separate partition to prevent the root partition from filling. The following subdirectories can be found under */var*:

/var/account

> Some systems maintain process accounting data in this directory.

/var/cache

> */var/cache* is intended for use by programs for the temporary storage of inter-mediate data, such as the results of lengthy computations. Programs using this directory must be capable of regenerating the cached information at any time, which allows the system administrator to delete files as needed. Because it holds transient data, */var/cache* never has to be backed up.

/var/crash

> This optional directory holds crash dumps for systems that support that feature.

/var/games

> This optional directory is used to store state information, user score data, and other transient items.

/var/lock

> Lock files, used by applications to signal their existence to other processes, are stored here. Lock files usually contain no data.

/var/log

> The */var/log* directory is the main repository for system log files, such as those created by the syslog system. For example, the default system log file is */var/log/messages*.

/var/mail

> This is the system mailbox, with mail files for each user. */var/mail* is a replacement for */var/spool/mail* and aligns FHS with many other Unix imple-mentations. You may find that your Linux distribution still uses */var/spool/mail*.

/var/opt

> This directory is defined as a location for temporary files of programs stored in */opt*.

/var/run

> */var/run* contains various files describing the present state of the system. All such files may be deleted at system boot time. This is the default location for PID files, which contain the PIDs of the processes for which they are named. For example, if the Apache web server, httpd, is running as process number 534, */var/run/httpd.pid* will contain that number:
>
> ```
> # cat /var/run/httpd.pid
> 534
> ```
>
> Such files are needed by utilities that must be able to find a PID for a running process. Also located here is the *utmp* file, used by commands such as *who* to display logged-in users.

/var/spool

> The */var/spool* directory contains information that is queued for processing. Examples include print queues, outgoing mail, and *crontab* files.

/var/state

> The */var/state* directory is intended to contain information that helps applica-tions preserve state across multiple invocations or multiple instances.

/var/tmp

As with */tmp* in the root filesystem, */var/tmp* is used for storage of temporary files. Unlike */tmp*, the files in */var/tmp* are expected to survive across multiple system boots. The information found in */var/tmp* could be considered more persistent than information in */tmp*.

Although it is not specified this way in the FHS, some distributions use */var/tmp* as a more secure temporary directory for use by *root*.

/var/yp

This optional directory contains the database files of the Network Information Service (NIS), if implemented. NIS was formerly known as *yellow pages* (not to be confused with the big yellow book).

This directory shouldn't be confused with */var/nis*, which is used by NIS+. Oddly, */var/nis* is mentioned in a footnote in FHS 2.2, but it does not have an entry in the specification.

Linux annex

Since FHS migrated away from being a Linux-only document and expanded to cover other operating systems, information specific to any one operating system was moved to an *annex*. The only annex listed in v2.0 of FHS is the Linux annex, which mentions a few guidelines and makes allowances for the placement of additional program files in */sbin*. The Linux annex also mentions and supports the use of the */proc* filesystem for the processing of kernel, memory, and process information.

Where's that binary?

Compiled executable files, called *binary files*, or just *binaries*, can be located in a number of places in an FHS-compliant filesystem. However, it's easy to become a little confused over why a particular executable file is placed where it is in the FHS. This is particularly true for *bin* and *sbin* directories, which appear in multiple locations. Table 6-7 lists these directories and shows how each is used.

Table 6-7. Binary file locations

Type of file	User commands	System admininistration commands
Vendor-supplied, essential (root filesystem)	*/bin*	*/sbin*
Vendor-supplied, nonessential (*/usr* filesystem)	*/usr/bin*	*/usr/sbin*
Locally supplied, nonessential (*/usr* filesystem)	*/usr/local/bin*	*/usr/local/sbin*

Locating Files

FHS offers the Linux community an excellent resource that assures consistency across distributions and other operating systems. In practice, however, file location problems can be frustrating, and the need arises to find files in the system quickly. These file location tools are required for Exam 101: *which, find, locate, updatedb, whatis,* and *apropos*.

which uses the PATH variable to locate executable files. find searches specified areas in the filesystem. *updatedb*, *whatis*, and *apropos* utilize databases to do quick searches to identify and locate files. *locate* offers a quick alternative to find for file-name searches and is suited for locating files that are not moved around in the filesystem. Without a fresh database to search, *locate* is not suitable for files recently created or renamed.

whatis and *apropos* work similarly to *locate* but use a different database. The *whatis* database is a set of files containing short descriptions of system commands, created by *makewhatis*. Note that these commands are not specifically mentioned in this Objective but may appear on Exam 101.

---

which

Syntax

```
which command
```

Description

Determine the location of *command* and display the full pathname of the executable program that the shell would launch to execute it. which searches only the user's path.

Example

Determine the shell that would be started by entering the *tcsh* command:

```
# which tcsh
/bin/tcsh
```

which is small and does only one thing: determines what executable program will be found and called by the shell. Such a search is particularly useful if you're having trouble with the setup of your PATH environment variable or if you are creating a new version of an existing utility and want to be certain you're executing the experimental version.

---

find

Syntax

```
find paths expression
```

Description

Locate files that match an *expression* starting at *paths* and continuing recursively. The find command has a rich set of *expression* directives for locating just about anything in the filesystem.

Example

To find files by name located in the */usr* directory hierarchy that might have something to do with the *csh* shell or its variants, you might use the *-name filename* directive:

```
# find /usr -name "*csh*"
/usr/bin/sun-message.csh
```

```
/usr/doc/tcsh-6.08.00
/usr/doc/tcsh-6.08.00/complete.tcsh
/usr/doc/vim-common-5.3/syntax/csh.vim
/usr/man/man1/tcsh.1
/usr/share/apps/ktop/pics/csh.xpm
/usr/share/apps/ktop/pics/tcsh.xpm
/usr/share/emacs/20.3/etc/emacs.csh
/usr/share/vim/syntax/csh.vim
/usr/src/linux-2.2.5/fs/lockd/svcshare.c
```

Some of these results are clearly related to *csh* or to *tcsh*, while others are questionable. In addition, this command may take a while because find must traverse the entire */usr* hierarchy, examining each filename for a match. This example demonstrates that if filename wildcards are used, the entire string must be quoted to prevent expansion by the shell prior to launching *find*.

find is among the most useful commands in the Linux administrator's toolkit and has a variety of useful options. *find* is handy in certain cases. For example:

- You need to limit a search to a particular location in the filesystem.
- You must search for an attribute other than the filename.
- Files you are searching for were recently created or renamed, in which case locate may not be appropriate.

Refer to Chapter 5 for additional information on the find command.

On the Exam

You should have a general understanding of *find*. Remember that by default, *find* prints matching directory entries to the screen. However, detailed knowledge of *find* options and usage are beyond the scope of LPIC Level 1 exams.

---

locate

Syntax

```
locate patterns
```

Description

Locate files whose names match one or more *patterns* by searching an index of files previously created.

Example

Locate files by name in the entire directory hierarchy that might have something to do with the *csh* shell or its variants:

```
# locate csh
/home/jdean/.tcshrc
/root/.cshrc
/root/.tcshrc
/usr/bin/sun-message.csh
```

```
/usr/doc/tcsh-6.08.00
/usr/doc/tcsh-6.08.00/FAQ
/usr/doc/tcsh-6.08.00/NewThings
/usr/doc/tcsh-6.08.00/complete.tcsh
/usr/doc/tcsh-6.08.00/eight-bit.txt
/usr/doc/vim-common-5.3/syntax/csh.vim
/usr/man/man1/tcsh.1
/usr/share/apps/ktop/pics/csh.xpm
/usr/share/apps/ktop/pics/tcsh.xpm
/usr/share/emacs/20.3/etc/emacs.csh
/usr/share/vim/syntax/csh.vim
/usr/src/linux-2.2.5/fs/lockd/svcshare.c
/etc/csh.cshrc
/etc/profile.d/kde.csh
/etc/profile.d/mc.csh
/bin/csh
/bin/tcsh
```

The *locate* command must have a recent database to search, and that database must be updated periodically to incorporate changes in the filesystem. If the database is stale, using *locate* yields a warning:

```
# locate tcsh
locate: warning: database /var/lib/slocate/slocate.db' is more than 8 days
old
```

updatedb

Syntax

```
updatedb [options]
```

Description

Refresh (or create) the *slocate* database in */var/lib/slocate/slocate.db*.

Option

-e directories
   Exclude a comma-separated list of *directories* from the database.

Example

Refresh the *slocate* database, excluding files in temporary locations:

```
# updatedb -e "/tmp,/var/tmp,/usr/tmp,/afs,/net,/proc"
```

updatedb is typically executed periodically via *cron*.

Some Linux distributions (Debian, for example) come with a version of *updatedb* that accepts additional options that can be specified on the command line:

Additional options

--netpaths='path1 path2 ...'
   Add network *paths* to the search list.

--prunepaths='path1 path2 ...'
   Eliminate *paths* from the search list.

--prunefs='filesystems ...'

Eliminate entire types of *filesystems*, such as NFS.

These options modify the behavior of *updatedb* on some Linux systems by prohibiting the parsing of certain filesystem locations and by adding others. There are a few more of these options than those listed here, but these three are special in that they can also be specified through the use of environment variables set prior to *updatedb* execution. The variables are NETPATHS, PRUNEPATHS, and PRUNEFS. These variables and the options to *updatedb* are discussed here because this Objective makes specific mention of *updatedb.conf*, a sort of control file for *updatedb*. Despite its name, *updatedb.conf* isn't really a configuration file, but rather a fragment of a Bourne shell script that sets these environment variables. Example 6-2 shows a sample *updatedb.conf* file.

Example 6-2. Sample updatedb.conf file

```
# This file sets environment variables used by updatedb
# filesystems which are pruned from updatedb database:
PRUNEFS="NFS nfs afs proc smbfs autofs auto iso9660"
export PRUNEFS
# paths which are pruned from updatedb database:
PRUNEPATHS="/tmp /usr/tmp /var/tmp /afs /amd /alex"
export PRUNEPATHS
# netpaths which are added:
NETPATHS="/mnt/fs3"
export NETPATHS
```

In this example, the PRUNEFS and PRUNEPATHS variables cause *updatedb* to ignore types of filesystems and particular paths, respectively. NETPATHS is used to add network paths from remote directory */mnt/fs3*.

updatedb.conf doesn't directly control *updatedb*, but eliminates the need for lengthy options on the *updatedb* command line, which can make *crontab* files a bit cleaner.

On the Exam

Remember that *updatedb* does not require configuration to execute. On systems that provide for configuration, *updatedb.conf* can specify a few extra options to *updatedb* by way of environment variables.

---

whatis

Syntax

whatis *keywords*

Description

Search the *whatis* database for exact matches to *keywords* and display results.

Example

```
# whatis mksw
mksw: nothing appropriate
```

apropos

Syntax

```
apropos keywords
```

Description

Search the *whatis* database for partial word matches to *keywords* and display results.

Example

```
# apropos mksw
mkswap (8)          - set up a Linux swap area
```

On the Exam

You must be familiar with the FHS concept and the contents of its major directories. Be careful about the differences between (and reasons for) */bin* and */sbin*, root filesystem and */usr* filesystem, and locally supplied commands. Also practice with various file locations techniques and be able to differentiate among them.

The X Window System (Topic 1.1.10)

Unix has a long history that predates the popular demand for a graphical user interface (GUI). However, a GUI is an essential part of running desktop systems today, and the standard GUI on Linux systems is the X Window System, or more simply, X. Originally developed at MIT and Digital Equipment Corporation, X's Version 11 Release 6 is the version most commonly seen in Linux distributions. This version is more commonly referred to as *X11R6*, or just *X11*. X is a complete windowing GUI and is distributable under license without cost. The implementation of X for Linux is *XFree86* (*http://www.xfree86.org*), which is available for multiple computer architectures and is released under the GNU Public License. This section covers the following three Objectives on XFree86 for LPI Exam 101:

Objective 1: Install and Configure X11
An LPIC 1 candidate should be able to configure and install X and an X font server. This Objective includes verifying that the video card and monitor are supported by an X server as well as customizing and tuning X for the video card and monitor. It also includes installing an X font server, installing fonts, and configuring X to use the font server (which may require manually editing */etc/X11/XF86Config*). Weight: 5.

Objective 2: Setup a Display Manager
This Objective states a candidate should be able to setup and customize a display manager. This includes turning the display manager on or off and changing the display manager greetings. It also includes changing default bitplanes for the display manager and configuring display managers for use by X stations. This Objective covers the display managers *xdm* (X Display Manager), *gdm* (Gnome Display Manager), and *kdm* (KDE Display Manager). Weight: 3.

Objective 4: Install and Customize a Window Manager Environment
LPIC candidates should be able to customize a system-wide desktop environment and/or window manager to demonstrate an understanding of customization procedures for window manager menus and/or desktop panel

menus. This Objective includes selecting and configuring the desired X terminal (*xterm*, *rxvt*, *aterm*, etc.), verifying and resolving library dependency issues for X applications, and exporting X display to client workstations. Weight: 5.

An Overview of X

X is implemented using a client/server model. X servers and clients can be located on the same computer or separated across a network, so that computation is handled separately from display rendering. While X servers manage hardware, they do not define the look of the display and they offer no tools to manipulate clients. The X server is responsible for rendering various shapes and colors on screen. Examples of X Servers include:

- Software from XFree86, which controls your Linux PC's video card.
- XFree86 software on a separate networked system, displaying output from a program running on your system.
- Other networked Unix systems running their own X server software.
- X implementations for other operating systems, such as Microsoft Windows.
- An *X Terminal*, which is a hardware device with no computational ability of its own, built solely for display purposes.

X clients are user programs, such as spreadsheets or CAD tools, which display graphical output. Examples of X clients are:

- A browser, such as Mozilla or Konqueror.
- A mail program, such as Evolution or Kmail.
- Office applications, such as OpenOffice, Gnumeric, or AbiWord.
- A terminal emulator, such as xterm, running within an X window.

A special client program called a *window manager* is responsible for these functions and provides windows, window sizing, open and close buttons, and so forth. The window manager controls the other clients running under an X server. Multiple window managers are available for XFree86, allowing you to choose an interface style that suits your needs and personal taste.

A few complete graphical *desktop environments* are also available. These packages can include a window manager and additional applications that work together to create a complete, unified working environment. Most Linux distributions ship with either the KDE or GNOME, or both, along with a number of standalone window managers. There is no standard window manager or environment for Linux. The selection is entirely up to the user.

Objective 1: Install and Configure X11

Most Linux distributions install and automatically configure XFree86, freeing users from much of its installation and configuration. However, Exam 101 requires specific knowledge of some of the underpinnings of X configuration.

Be careful about installing an X server on a system that already has X installed. A backup should be made prior to the installation.

Selecting and Configuring an X Server

The XFree86 project provides support for an amazing array of graphics hardware. This outcome is possible partly due to cooperation by manufacturers through public release of graphics device documentation and driver software, and partly due to the tenacity of the XFree86 developers. Fortunately, many manufacturers who were historically uninterested in offering technical information to the XFree86 project have become cooperative. The result is that most recent video hardware is well-supported by XFree86.

Supported video hardware

To avoid problems, it is important to verify XFree86 compatibility with your hardware prior to installation. At the very least, you should be aware of these items:

Your XFree86 version
   As with any software, improvements in XFree86 are made over time, particularly in support for hardware devices. You should choose a version of XFree86 that offers a good balance between the video support and stability you require. To determine the version of X you're running, simply issue the following command:

```
$ /usr/X11R6/bin/X -version
XFree86 Version 4.0.1a / X Window System
```

The video chipset
   XFree86 video drivers are written for graphics chipsets, not the video cards they're installed on. Multiple video cards from a variety of manufacturers can carry the same chipset, making those cards nearly identical in function. You must verify that the chipset on your video card is supported by XFree86 to use advanced graphics features.

Monitor type
   XFree86 can be configured to handle just about any monitor, particularly the newer and very flexible multisync monitors sold today, which can handle preset configurations provided in the XFree86 configuration utilities. However, if you have a nonstandard monitor, you need to know some parameters describing its capabilities before configuring X, including your monitor's horizontal sync frequency (in kHz), vertical refresh frequency (in Hz), and resolution (in pixels). These items can usually be found in your monitor's documentation, but since most monitors conform to standard display settings such as *XGA* (1024×768 pixels at 60 Hz vertical refresh), you should be able to use a preset configuration.

Installing XFree86

The procedures for installation vary depending on the release of X you're using. For example, with versions prior to 4.0, a specific X server is required to match your chipset to use modes other than standard VGA. For versions after 4.0, a newer modular design allows a single server program to manage all supported chipsets by calling driver modules. In addition, the type of XFree86 distribution you're using affects installation. XFree86 is available as source code, in precompiled binary form, or as an RPM or Debian package.

It is rare that you'll actually need to install XFree86 by hand, as XFree86 is typically installed during initial system installation for systems that plan to use X. Most Linux distributions include XFree86 packages on the installation media so you can install them from there using your distribution's choice of package managers.

Some applications might require that you install a new release or development version of XFree86 that is not available as a package. In these cases, you can download the source files or precompiled binaries from XFree86's mirror web sites, listed at *http://www.xfree86.org*. Refer to Chapter 4 for more information on installing applications from packages or source.

Configuring an X server and the XF86Config file

XFree86 configuration differs slightly among versions and among Linux distributions, but essentially involves the creation of the *XF86Config* file customized for your system. The X server uses this configuration file as it starts to set such things as keyboard and mouse selections, installed fonts, and screen resolutions.

XF86Config contains technical details concerning the capabilities of system hardware, which can be intimidating for some users. For this reason, automated configuration tools are available that will generate the file for you:

xf86config
> This program is distributed with XFree86. It is a simple text-mode program that requests information about the system from the user and then writes a corresponding *XF86Config* file. This utility does not use information stored in an existing configuration file, so its utility is limited. (Remember that *xf86config* is a binary program that writes the *XF86Config* text file.)

XF86Setup
> This program was distributed with XFree86, though some distributions, such as Red Hat, have deprecated the tool. *XF86Setup* is a graphical program that starts a VGA X server, which should run on most PC hardware. It allows you to select the graphics chipset, monitor, mouse, and keyboard device types and writes the appropriate configuration file for you. As of XFree86 4.3.0, *XF86Setup* hasn't been updated for the new 4.x configuration. XFree86 plans to make it available again in a future version.

xvidtune
> This program is used to fine-tune video settings, adjusting your video display to your monitor. *xvidtune* allows you to move your display up and down, left and right, similar to your monitor controls but with a command-line

interface. Depending on your video chipset, *xvidtune* may also support a number of other options including invert states and screen wrapping.

xf86cfg

This program is distributed with XFree86 v4.0. Like *XF86Setup*, it is a graphical tool; however, *xf86cfg*'s interface is slightly different. Whereas other tools offer a menu-based approach, *xf86cfg* offers a block diagram of the system, including a monitor, video device, keyboard, and mouse. The user configures each element by manipulating its properties. When the user is happy with the configuration, the tool writes the *XF86Config* file.

Distribution-specific tools

Various Linux distributors provide their own configuration utilities. For example, *redhat-config-xfree86* is distributed by Red Hat Software. It is an X based GUI tool that can probe graphics chipsets and features. Older Red Hat systems (7.x and older) used a menu-based system called *Xconfigurator*.

Example 7-1 contains an abbreviated *XF86Config* file created using the Red Hat Xconfigurator tool for XFree86 v3.3.3. (The XF86Config files shown here are examples and are not intended for use on your system.)

Example 7-1. A sample XF86Config file for XFree86 v3.3.3

```
# File generated by XConfigurator.
Section "Files"
        RgbPath     "/usr/X11R6/lib/X11/rgb"
        FontPath    "unix/:-1"
EndSection

Section "ServerFlags"
EndSection

Section "Keyboard"
        Protocol    "Standard"
        AutoRepeat  500 5
        LeftAlt     Meta
        RightAlt    Meta
        ScrollLock  Compose
        RightCtl    Control
        XkbDisable
        XkbKeycodes    "xfree86"
        XkbTypes       "default"
        XkbCompat      "default"
        XkbSymbols     "us(pc101)"
        XkbGeometry    "pc"
        XkbRules       "xfree86"
        XkbModel       "pc101"
        XkbLayout      "us"
EndSection

Section "Pointer"
        Protocol    "PS/2"
        Device      "/dev/mouse"
        Emulate3Buttons
```

Example 7-1. A sample XF86Config file for XFree86 v3.3.3 (continued)

```
        Emulate3Timeout    50
EndSection

Section "Monitor"
        Identifier   "My Monitor"
        VendorName   "Unknown"
        ModelName    "Unknown"
        HorizSync    31.5 - 64.3
        VertRefresh 50-90
        # 1280x1024 @ 61 Hz, 64.2 kHz hsync
        Mode "1280x1024"
                DotClock    110
                Htimings    1280 1328 1512 1712
                Vtimings    1024 1025 1028 1054
        EndMode
EndSection

Section "Device"
        Identifier   "My Video Card"
        VendorName   "Unknown"
        BoardName    "Unknown"
        VideoRam     16256
EndSection

Section "Screen"
        Driver       "svga"
        Device       "My Video Card"
        Monitor      "My Monitor"
        Subsection "Display"
                Depth        32
                Modes        "1280x1024"
                ViewPort     0 0
        EndSubsection
EndSection
```

Under v3.3.3, the default location for the *XF86Config* file is in */usr/X11R6/lib/ X11*, though many distributions use */etc/X11*. The file contains the following sections:

Files

This section is used to specify the default font path and the path to the RGB database. Using the FontPath "*path*" directive multiple times creates a list of directories that the X server will search for fonts. The RGB database is an equivalence table of numeric red/green/blue color values with names. Here's a short excerpt of the RGB database:

```
    255 228 196          bisque
    255 218 185          peach puff
    255 218 185          PeachPuff
    255 222 173          navajo white
```

Hundreds of these names are defined and may be used in the configuration of X applications where color names are required.

ServerFlags

This section allows customization of X server options such as the handling of hotkeys.

Keyboard

This section is used to specify the keyboard input device, its parameters, and default keyboard-mapping options.

Pointer

This section is used to define the pointing device (mouse).

Monitor

Multiple Monitor sections are used to define the specifications of monitors and a list of video modes they can handle.

Device

Multiple Device sections are used to define video hardware (cards) installed.

Screen

The Screen section ties together a Device with a corresponding Monitor and includes some configuration settings for them.

On the Exam

You don't need to memorize details about *XF86Config*, but it is an important file, and your familiarity with it will be tested. In particular, be aware of what each of the sections does for the X server, and remember that the Screen section ties together a Device and a Monitor.

The *XF86Config* file format was modified slightly for XFree86 v4.0. In particular, a new ServerLayout section has been added; it ties the Screen, Pointer, and Keyboard sections together. Example 7-2 contains an abbreviated *XF86Config* file created using the bundled xf86cfg tool from the XFree86 project.

Example 7-2. A Sample XF86Config file for XFree86 v4.0.1

```
Section "ServerLayout"
        Identifier    "XFree86 Configured"
        Screen      0 "Screen0" 0 0
        InputDevice   "Mouse0" "CorePointer"
        InputDevice   "Keyboard0" "CoreKeyboard"
EndSection

Section "Files"
EndSection

Section "InputDevice"
        Identifier   "Keyboard0"
        Driver       "keyboard"
EndSection
```

Example 7-2. A Sample XF86Config file for XFree86 v4.0.1 (continued)

```
Section "InputDevice"
        Identifier  "Mouse0"
        Driver      "mouse"
        Option      "Protocol" "PS/2"
        Option      "Device" "/dev/mouse"
EndSection

Section "Monitor"
        Identifier   "Monitor0"
        VendorName   "Monitor Vendor"
        ModelName    "Monitor Model"
        HorizSync    31.5 - 64.3
        VertRefresh  50.0 - 90.0
EndSection

Section "Device"
        Identifier  "Card0"
        Driver      "nv"
        VendorName  "NVidia"
        BoardName   "Riva TNT"
        ChipSet     "RIVATNT"
        BusID       "PCI:1:0:0"
EndSection

Section "Screen"
        Identifier   "Screen0"
        Device       "Card0"
        Monitor      "Monitor0"
        DefaultDepth 24
        SubSection "Display"
                Depth    24
        EndSubSection
EndSection
```

Under v4.0, the default location for the *XF86Config* file is in */etc/X11*. The file contains the following sections:

ServerLayout

> This section ties together Screen with one or more InputDevices. Multiple ServerLayout sections may be used for multiheaded configurations (i.e., systems with more than one monitor).

Files

> This section is used to add paths to fonts and color information, just as it is in XFree86 v3.3.3.

InputDevice

> Multiple InputDevice sections should be used to include at least a keyboard and mouse. Subsections within InputDevice in v4.0 replace the Pointer and Keyboard sections for XFree86 v3.3.3.

Monitor

This section is similar to the Monitor section for XFree86 v3.3.3, except that mode specifications are not usually necessary. The X server is already aware of standard VESA video modes and chooses the best mode based on the horizontal sync and vertical refresh rates.

Device

This section specifies the modular driver for the X server. Multiple Device sections can be included to handle multiple graphics devices.

Screen

This section ties together a Monitor with a Device and is specified in the ServerLayout. Multiple Screen sections can be included to handle multiple monitor/device pairs.

On the Exam

As already mentioned, you don't need to worry about details in *XF86Config*. However, you should be aware of the major differences in the configuration files for XFree86 Versions 3.3 and 4.0.

X Fonts

XFree86 is distributed with a collection of fonts for most basic purposes, including text displays in terminal windows and browsers. For many users, the default fonts are adequate, but others may prefer to add additional fonts to their system. A variety of fonts are available, both free and commercially, from many sources, such as Adobe. Some very creative fonts are created by individuals and distributed on the Internet (a search should return some useful links to a query such as *XFree86 fonts*).

XFree86 makes fonts that it finds in the *font path* available to client programs. A basic font path is compiled into the X server, but you can specify your own font path using the FontPath directive in the Files section of *XF86Config*. The simple syntax is:

```
FontPath "path"
```

For example:

```
Section "Files"
        RgbPath    "/usr/X11R6/lib/X11/rgb"
        FontPath   "/usr/X11R6/lib/X11/fonts/misc"
        FontPath   "/usr/X11R6/lib/X11/fonts/Type1"
        FontPath   "/usr/X11R6/lib/X11/fonts/Speedo"
        FontPath   "/usr/X11R6/lib/X11/fonts/100dpi"
        FontPath   "/usr/X11R6/lib/X11/fonts/75dpi"
        FontPath   "/usr/X11R6/lib/X11/fonts/local"
EndSection
```

This group of FontPath directives creates a font path consisting of six directories, all under */usr/X11R6/lib/X11/fonts*. When XFree86 starts, it parses these font directories and includes their contents in the list of fonts available during the X session.

Installing fonts

Adding new fonts is straightforward. (For this brief discussion, we assume that we're working with Type 1 fonts. Other types, such as TrueType fonts, may require additional configuration depending on your version of XFree86.) First, a suitable directory should be created for the new fonts, such as */usr/X11R6/lib/ X11/local* or */usr/local/fonts*. You may wish to separate your own fonts from the default XFree86 directories to protect them during upgrades. After the fonts are installed in the new directory, the *mkfontdir* utility is run to catalog the new fonts in the new directory. New entries are added to the *XF86Config* file to include the path for new fonts. For example:

```
FontPath    "/usr/local/fonts"
```

At this point, the X server can be restarted to recognize the new fonts, or the fonts can be dynamically added using the *xset* command:

```
# xset fp+ /usr/local/fonts
```

xset is beyond the scope of the LPIC Level 1 exams.

On the Exam

Be sure you understand how the X font path is created and how to extend it to include additional directories. Knowledge of the internal details of font files is not necessary.

The X font server

On a network with multiple workstations, managing fonts manually for each system can be time consuming. To simplify this problem, the administrator can install all of the desired fonts on a single system and then run *xfs*, the X fonts server, on that system. On a local system, *xfs* off-loads the work of rendering fonts from the X server, which means the X server can do other tasks while fonts are being rendered. This is especially noticeable on slower systems or systems without an FPU.

The X font server is a small daemon that sends fonts to clients on both local and remote systems. Some Linux distributions use *xfs* exclusively, without a list of directories in the manually created font path. To include *xfs* in your system's font path, add a FontPath directive like this:

```
Section "Files"
        RgbPath     "/usr/X11R6/lib/X11/rgb"
        FontPath    "unix/:-1"
EndSection
```

If you install *xfs* from a package from your distribution, it is probably automatically configured to start at boot time and run continually, serving fonts to local and remote client programs. To start *xfs* manually, simply enter the *xfs* command. For security purposes, you may wish to run *xfs* as a non-root user. *xfs* is configured using its configuration file, */etc/X11/fs/config*. Example 7-3 contains an example *config* file for *xfs*.

Example 7-3. Sample configuration file for xfs

```
# Allow a max of four clients to connect to this font server
client-limit = 4

# When a font server reaches its limit, start up a new one
clone-self = on
catalogue = /usr/X11R6/lib/X11/fonts/misc:unscaled,
            /usr/X11R6/lib/X11/fonts/75dpi:unscaled,
            /usr/X11R6/lib/X11/fonts/100dpi:unscaled,
            /usr/X11R6/lib/X11/fonts/misc,
            /usr/X11R6/lib/X11/fonts/Type1,
            /usr/X11R6/lib/X11/fonts/Speedo,
            /usr/X11R6/lib/X11/fonts/75dpi,
            /usr/X11R6/lib/X11/fonts/100dpi,
            /usr/share/fonts/ISO8859-2/100dpi,
            /usr/share/fonts/ISO8859-9/100dpi,
            /usr/X11R6/lib/X11/fonts/local

# In 12 points, decipoints
default-point-size = 120

# 100 x 100 and 75 x 75
default-resolutions = 75,75,100,100

# How to log errors
use-syslog = on
```

As you can see, the *config* file contains the following *keyword=value* pairs:

catalogue
> This keyword holds a comma-separated list of directories containing fonts to be served by *xfs*. This is where new font directories are added.

alternate-servers (*strings*)
> This section contains a listing of alternate font servers that can be found on the local machine or on other machines.

client-limit
> This shows the maximum number of client requests to be served.

clone-self
> When on, the font server makes copies of itself if it reaches the `client-limit`.

You don't need to remember details about the contents of the xfs configuration file (*config*), but be aware of the use and general contents of the file. In particular, remember that the catalogue keyword is used similarly to `FontPath` in *XF86Config*.

Controlling X Applications with .Xresources

The X Window System also has many built-in customization features. Many X applications are programmed with a variety of *resources*, which are configuration settings that can be externally manipulated. Rather than have a configuration utility built into each application, applications can be written to examine the contents of a file in the user's home directory. The *.Xresources* file contains a line for each configured resource in the following form:

```
program*resource: value
```

This line can be translated as follows:

- *program* is the name of a configurable program, such as emacs or xterm.
- *resource* is one of the configurable settings allowed by the program, such as colors.
- *value* is the setting to apply to the resource.

For example, the following is an excerpt from *.Xresources* that configures colors for an xterm:

```
xterm*background: Black
xterm*foreground: Wheat
xterm*cursorColor: Orchid
xterm*reverseVideo: false
```

Objective 2: Set Up a Display Manager

The display manager is the tool to manage X sessions on physical displays both locally and across the network. Part of its job is to handle user authentication through a graphical login screen, which replaces the familiar text-mode login.

Configuring xdm

xdm is distributed as part of XFree86 and is configured by a series of files located in */etc/X11/xdm*. These files include:

Xaccess
> This file controls inbound requests from remote hosts.

Xresources
> This file is similar to *.Xresources*, discussed earlier. It holds configuration information for some *xdm* resources, including the graphical login screen. This file can be edited to modify the appearance of the *xdm* login screen.

Xservers
> This file associates the X display names (:0, :1, ...) with either the local X server software or a foreign display such as an X terminal.

Xsession
> This file contains the script *xdm* launches after a successful login. It usually looks for *.xsession* in the user's home directory and executes the commands found there. If such a file doesn't exist, *Xsession* starts a default window manager (or environment) and applications.

Xsetup_0
> This file is a script started before the graphical login screen. It often includes commands to set colors, display graphics, or run other programs. This script is executed as *root*.

xdm-config
> This file associates *xdm* configuration resources with the other files in this list. It usually isn't necessary to make changes in this file unless an expert administrator plans to customize *xdm* configuration.

Running xdm manually

xdm uses the X server to run on your local display. Therefore, you must have a working X configuration prior to using a display manager. Then, to start *xdm*, simply enter it as *root*:

```
# xdm
```

xdm launches the X server and display the graphical login, and you can log in as usual. xdm then starts your graphical environment. After you log out, *xdm* resets and again displays the login screen.

Most Linux distributions enable virtual consoles. You can switch among them using the key combinations Ctrl-Alt-F1, Ctrl-Alt-F2, and so on. (The Ctrl is only required while switching from an X console to a text or other X console.) Typically, the first six consoles are set up as text-mode screens, and X launches on console 7 (Ctrl-Alt-F7), or the first tty not running *mingetty* or some other *getty* process. This means that, as with *startx*, your original text-mode console remains unchanged after you manually start *xdm*. Therefore, you must log out of your text-mode console if you plan to leave the system unattended with *xdm* running manually.

If you want to stop *xdm*, you first must be sure that all of the X sessions under its management are logged out. Otherwise, they'll die when *xdm* exits and you could lose data. Then simply stop the *xdm* process using *kill* or *killall* from a text console:

```
# killall xdm
```

Of course, *xdm* isn't very useful for your local system if you must always start it manually. That's why most Linux distributions include a boot-time option to start *xdm* for you, eliminating the text-mode login completely.

Running xdm automatically

For Linux systems using the System-V-style initialization, a runlevel is usually reserved for login under *xdm*. This line at the bottom of */etc/inittab* instructs *init* to start *xdm* for runlevel 5:

```
# Run xdm in runlevel 5
x:5:respawn:/usr/X11R6/bin/xdm -nodaemon
```

Using this configuration, when the system enters runlevel 5, *xdm* starts and presents the graphical login as before. See Chapter 14 for more information on runlevels.

It's also possible to automatically start *xdm* simply by adding it to the end of an initialization script, such as *rc.local*. This method offers less control over *xdm* but may be adequate for some situations and for Linux distributions that don't offer runlevels.

Basic xdm customization

You may wish to personalize the look of *xdm* for your system. The look of the graphical login screen can be altered by manipulating the resources in */etc/X11/ xdm/Xresources*. (Note that *Xresources* uses ! to start comments.) For example, the following excerpt shows settings to control the greeting (*Welcome to Linux on smp-pc*), other prompts, and colors:

```
! Xresources file
xlogin*borderWidth: 10
xlogin*greeting: Welcome to Linux on CLIENTHOST
xlogin*namePrompt: Login:\040
xlogin*fail: Login incorrect - try again!
xlogin*failColor: red
xlogin*Foreground: Yellow
xlogin*Background: MidnightBlue
```

You can also include command-line options to the X server in */etc/X11/xdm/ Xservers* if you wish to override those found in *XF86Config*. For example, to change the default color depth, add the *-bpp* (bits per pixel) option for the local display:

```
# Xservers file
:0 local /usr/X11R6/bin/X -bpp 24
```

To include additional X programs or settings on the graphical login screen, put them in */etc/X11/xdm/Xsetup_0*. In this example, the background color of the X

---

display is set to a solid color (in hexadecimal form), and a clock is added at the lower righthand corner of the screen:

```
#!/bin/sh
# Xsetup
/usr/X11R6/bin/xsetroot -solid "#356390"
/usr/X11R6/bin/xclock -digital -update 1 -geometry -5-5 &
```

Note that in this example, *xsetroot* exits immediately after it sets the color, allowing the *Xsetup_0* script to continue. *xclock*, however, does not exit and must be put into the background using an & at the end of the command line. If such commands are not placed into the background, the *Xsetup_0* script hangs, and the login display does not appear.

X Terminals

X terminals are a breed of low-cost display devices for X. They are usually diskless systems that implement an X server and drive a monitor. Such devices can be configured to access a remote host to find an *xdm* daemon or will broadcast to the entire network looking for a "willing host" to offer *xdm* services. The selected system will run an X session across the network with the X terminal as the target display. With this setup, a large number of relatively inexpensive X terminals can make use of a few high-powered host systems to run graphical clients.

xdm for X terminals

To use an X terminal with your host, *xdm* must first be running on the host machine. The host listens for inbound connections from the X terminals using XDMCP, the *xdm* Control Protocol (the default port for *xdmcp* is 177). When a request is received, *xdm* responds with the same graphical login screen that's used on the local system. The difference is that the X server is implemented in the X terminal hardware, not in the XFree86 software on the *xdm* host, and all of the graphics information is transmitted over the network.

On the Exam

You should be aware of the configuration files for *xdm*, how they are used, and where they are located. In particular, remember that the *Xresources* file controls graphical login properties. Also remember that *xdm* can be started using a special runlevel and that *xdm* must be running for X terminals to connect via XDMCP.

You can configure access to your system's *xdm* daemon in the */etc/X11/xdm/Xaccess* file. This file is a simple list of hosts that are to be restricted or enabled. To enable a host, simply enter its name. To restrict a host, enter its name with an exclamation point (!) before it. The * wildcard is also allowed to handle groups of devices.

The following example allows access to all X terminals on the local domain but prohibits access from *xterm1* on an outside domain:

```
*.example.com
!xterm1.anotherexample.com
```

Objective 4: Install and Customize a Window Manager Environment

The selection of a desktop environment for X is a personal decision. At a minimum, you need a window manager such as *twm* to provide basic window frames, menus, and controls. On the more elaborate side, an integrated working environment such as KDE or GNOME offers a rich set of applications. Regardless of how you configure your desktop, it's important to understand some basic customization techniques.

Starting X and a Default Window Manager

Starting XFree86 can be as simple as issuing the X command as *root*. However, X alone doesn't give you a working environment. At the very least, you also need to start a window manager and an application and set up basic X access authority. (X authority configuration is beyond the scope of the LPIC Level 1 certification and is not covered in this book.) You may also wish to choose from among multiple desktop environments and window managers installed on your system.

The XFree86 start up process

Assuming for the moment that we're not using *xdm*, the process of starting X goes like this:

1. The user issues the *startx* command. This is a script provided by XFree86 and often modified by distributors and administrators. *startx* is intended as a frontend to *xinit*.

2. *startx* calls *xinit* with two main arguments:

   a. An *Xinitrc* script, which contains X programs to run. This script could be *.xinitrc* from the user's home directory, or if that doesn't exist, a system-wide default found in */etc/X11/xinit/xinitrc*.

   b. Server options, such as X authority information.

3. *xinit* launches XFree86 and the chosen *Xinitrc* script.

4. XFree86 starts. Note that X itself does not provide any applications. They appear only as the result of the commands found in the *Xinitrc* script.

5. Client programs and a window manager found in the *Xinitrc* script start.

The contents of *startx* and the system default */etc/X11/xinit/xinitrc* can vary from distribution to distribution and can be changed by administrators to suit local needs. They may also reference additional files, such as */etc/X11/xinit/Xclients*, to determine which programs and window manager to run. Example 7-4 shows the contents of */etc/X11/xinit/xinitrc*, a modified version of the original distributed with XFree86.

Example 7-4. A System default xinitrc

```
#!/bin/sh
# $XConsortium: xinitrc.cpp,v 1.4 91/08/22 rws Exp $

userresources=$HOME/.Xresources
usermodmap=$HOME/.Xmodmap

sysresources=/usr/X11R6/lib/X11/xinit/.Xresources
sysmodmap=/usr/X11R6/lib/X11/xinit/.Xmodmap

# merge in defaults and keymaps
if [ -f $sysresources ]; then
    xrdb -merge $sysresources
fi

if [ -f $sysmodmap ]; then
    xmodmap $sysmodmap
fi

if [ -f $userresources ]; then
    xrdb -merge $userresources
fi

if [ -f $usermodmap ]; then
    xmodmap $usermodmap
fi

# start some nice programs
(sleep 1; xclock -geometry 50x50-1+1) &
(sleep 1; xterm -geometry 80x50+494+51) &
(sleep 1; xterm -geometry 80x20+494-0) &
exec twm
```

In this example, resource and keyboard mappings are set, a few applications are launched, and the *twm* window manager is started. *twm* is installed as a basic default window manager on most distributions.

xterm et al.

One of the most important applications available to a system administrator working in a graphical environment is a *terminal emulator*. The standard terminal emulator distributed with X is *xterm*, which understands DEC VT and Tektronix graphics terminal protocols. The VT behavior that is emulated includes cursor positioning, character effects, and reverse video, among others. In essence, an *xterm* is a direct replacement for a hardware terminal.

xterm has a large resource configuration file located in */usr/lib/X11/app-defaults/XTerm* that contains configurable menus, fonts, colors, and actions. You may customize this file to alter the default behavior of *xterm* on your system. These settings can also be overridden by resource settings contained in your own *.Xdefaults* file, located in your home directory.

There are numerous xterm replacements, such as *rxvt*, *aterm*, *eterm*, *gnome-terminal*, and *konsole*. Configuring these programs is well beyond the scope of the LPI Level 1 Objectives. See the documentation packages for more information.

On the Exam

You should be familiar with at least one of the popular X terminal programs available on your Linux system. Remember that some programs have system-wide configuration files that can be used to fine-tune their behavior and appearance.

X Libraries

Just as many executable programs are dependent on shared system libraries for their execution, most X applications require a number of X-specific libraries. XFree86 comes bundled with the necessary set of libraries for traditional X applications. However, many graphical programming projects are created using toolkits whose libraries are not included in the XFree86 distribution. In these cases, you need to install the required libraries before programs requiring them will compile or execute.

For example, the GIMP Toolkit (GTK) is used to build much of the GNOME desktop environment. This means that GTK must be installed on the system in order to run GNOME applications, including The GIMP (*http://www.gimp.org*).

Library dependency issues typically occur when you try new software. Either the compiler fails as you attempt to build the program, or the loader fails when you try to run a precompiled dynamic binary. In either case, you need to locate the correct version of the libraries and install them. It should be relatively easy to find recent versions of the popular libraries in your distribution's package format by visiting web sites of the library distributor or your Linux distribution.

To manually check for library dependencies, you may use the *ldd* utility, described fully in Chapter 4.

Remote X Clients

One of the fundamental design elements of the X Window System is that it is a network protocol, which allows for displays to occur remotely across a network. Many sites employ high-powered systems for computation and use desktop X servers (X terminals or Linux systems, for example) for display rendering.

To send the output from an X application to a remote machine, you need to set the DISPLAY environment variable. (Many X programs also include a command-line option to select the display.) This variable contains a description of the output destination and has three components:

    [host]:display[.screen]

host
> This part of the description specifies the remote hostname on the network. It can be any valid hostname, fully qualified domain name, or IP address. host is optional; the local system is used if the host is not specified.

display
> This specifies which display the output should be directed toward. A single system can manage many displays. Note that the colon is required even if the host is omitted.

screen
> This optional parameter is used for multiheaded systems (i.e., systems with more than one monitor) and specifies on which output screen the application will appear.

Setting DISPLAY to "point to" a remote host display causes all subsequent X applications to be displayed there. For example:

```
# export DISPLAY=yourhost:0.0
# xterm
```

In this example, the *xterm* is displayed on the first display on yourhost. (This example ignores X authentication issues.)

Examples

The default display on the local host:

```
:0
```

The default display on a remote host:

```
yourhost:0
```

Display programs on the first screen of the second display found on the machine located at 192.168.1.2:

```
192.168.1.2:1.0
```

Display programs on the first screen of the third display on *yourhost*:

```
yourhost:2.0
```

On the Exam

You must be familiar with the DISPLAY environment variable and how to use it to direct X client applications to remote X servers.

X Security

Allowing untrusted applications to connect to your X display is a very bad idea. Rogue applications can snoop traffic between X applications and the X server (capturing keystrokes, for example), crash the X server, and do other bad things. There are two commonly-used ways to control access to the X server on Linux systems, host-based access control and MIT-MAGIC-COOKIE-1 authentication.

Host access control

When using host-based access control, the X server will allow connections only from hosts in the list. When this is the only form of access control in use, connections are typically allowed from *localhost*. Unfortunately, allowing connections from *localhost* means allowing connections from *any user* on the local system.

Hosts can be added to the list of allowed hosts by adding them to the file */etc/Xn.hosts* (although this file is only scanned when the X server starts) or by using the *xhost* command.

---

xhost

Syntax

```
xhost [[+-]hostname] [...]
```

Description

xhost is used to add hosts to or remove hosts from the X server's list of hosts that are allowed to connect.

xhost lists the current state of the host access control list when run with no options.

Frequently used options

+

> Turn off access control. Access is granted to all hosts whether they are on the list or not.

-

> Turn on access control. Access is granted only to hosts on the list.

[+]hostname
> Add *hostname* to the list of hosts allowed to connect to the X server. (The + is optional.)

-hostname
> Remove *hostname* from the list of hosts allowed to connect to the X server.

MIT-MAGIC-COOKIE-1 Authentication

The MIT-MAGIC-COOKIE-1 form of authentication is much more secure than host-based access control. In this authentication scheme, *xdm* creates a 128-bit key, or cookie, which is stored in the user's home directory in the file *.Xauthority* at login. When a client connects to the X server, it has to pass the cookie to be allowed to connect.

Since connections to the X server are not encrypted, this authentication method is most secure when used on local connections. Non-local connections should be tunnelled over *ssh* if they are not made over a secure (IPsec or other VPN) connection.

This is the most commonly used method of controlling access to the X server on modern Linux systems, but it is not covered in the LPI Level 1 Objectives.

 This Topic is discussed in-depth in the *Xsecurity* manpage.

8

Exam 101 Review Questions and Exercises

This section presents review questions to highlight important concepts and hands-on exercises that you can use to gain experience with the topics covered on the LPI Exam 101. The exercises can be particularly useful if you're not accustomed to routine Linux administration and should help you better prepare for the exam. To complete the exercises, you'll need a working Linux system that is not in production use. You might also find it useful to have a pen and paper handy to write down your responses as you work your way through the review questions and exercises.

Hardware and Architecture (Topic 1.101)

Review questions

1. Describe the general functions of the PC BIOS and how its embedded routines are used by your boot loader.

2. What is the significance of the 1024 hard disk cylinder to Linux boot loaders?

3. Name three files in the */proc* filesystem that contain information on system resource allocations.

4. Which of the following SCSI interfaces has the fastest data transfer rates: SCSI-1, SCSI-2, Ultra SCSI, or Fast-Wide SCSI?

5. What command is used to obtain serial port information on a Linux system?

6. What driver is used for USB hard drives?

Exercises

1. Boot your PC and enter the BIOS configuration utility. Review settings for correct hardware date and time.

2. Examine the enabled serial and parallel ports. Can you manually configure the interrupts and I/O ports assigned to them?

3. Review the options available for system boot. Does the system support booting from a CD-ROM? Change the default boot order.

4. Examine your modem and sound external interfaces on your PC. Are the devices built into your motherboard or independent expansion cards? If it is a card, identify if it is ISA or PCI.

5. Determine if your installed modem is a software modem.

6. If you have a SCSI controller, reboot your PC and enter the SCSI BIOS. What device number is selected, if any, for boot? How are the controller's onboard terminators configured? What data rate is the controller configured for?

7. Examine the kernel's interrupt assignments by executing *cat /proc/interrupts*. Are your devices reported correctly? Are there any suprises?

8. Review output from *cat /proc/dma* and *cat /proc/ioports* (discussed in the section "Using the /proc filesystem" in Chapter 3).

9. Create a list of all installed PCI devices using *lspci*. Note the devices built into your motherboard.

10. Use *minicom* to attach to your modem. For example:

```
# minicom /dev/modem
Welcome to minicom 1.82
OPTIONS: History Buffer, F-key Macros,
Search History Buffer, I18n
Compiled on Mar 21 1999, 21:10:56.
Press CTRL-A Z for help on special keys
AT S7=45 S0=0 L1 V1 X4 &c1 E1 Q0
OK
AT
OK
```

Does the modem respond to the AT command with OK? Try manually dialing your ISP and watch the output of the modem.

11. Connect a USB device (mouse, printer, etc.) to your system. Run *lsmod* to verify that the appropriate driver loaded.

Linux Installation and Package Management (Topic 1.102)

Review Questions

1. Why is the */var* directory usually located in a partition of its own?

2. As a system administrator for a network with many workstations and a central NFS file server, how can you safely share */usr* with your users while still maintaining control of its contents?

3. Describe how to create a *tar* archive and how its contents are extracted.

4. In general terms, describe the procedure used to compile and install free or open source software from source code.

5. What is a shared library? How can you determine what library dependencies exist in a compiled executable?

6. Briefly describe the major functional modes of *rpm*.

7. Why might a Debian Linux administrator use *dpkg -iG* instead of simply *dpkg -i* to install a package?

Exercises

1. In a shell, examine your disk layout using *cfdisk* or *fdisk*. For example:

```
# fdisk
Command (m for help): p
Disk /dev/sda: 255 heads, 63 sectors, 1109 cylinders
Units = cylinders of 16065 * 512 bytes
   Device Boot    Start      End    Blocks   Id  System
/dev/sda1            1        51    409626    83  Linux
/dev/sda2           52      1109   8498385     5  Extended
/dev/sda5           52        90    313236    83  Linux
/dev/sda6           91        97     56196    83  Linux
/dev/sda7           98       136    313236    83  Linux
/dev/sda8          137       264  1028128+   83  Linux
/dev/sda9          265       519  2048256    83  Linux
/dev/sda10         520       532    104391    83  Linux
/dev/sda11         533       545    104391    82  Linux swap
/dev/sda12         546      1109  4530298+   83  Linux
```

   Is the entire disk consumed by the existing filesystems?

2. Examine how system directories are mapped to disk partitions on your system. Are */var* and */tmp* in their own partitions? Is */boot* in its own partition within cylinder 1024? Is the root filesystem relatively small?

3. Where is LILO installed on your system? If it is installed in the boot sector, does your configuration allow for multiple boot scenarios? If it is installed in the root partition, is it within the first 1024 cylinders?

4. Locate a tarball (from *freshmeat.net*, for example), and install it on your system with the following steps:

   a. Unpack it using *tar xzvf file*.

   b. Configure with *./configure*.

   c. Build the software using *make* as directed in the documentation.

   d. Install the software using the instructions provided.

   Were there any difficulties with this procedure?

5. Use *ldd* to examine library dependencies of executable programs on your system. For example:

```
# ldd `which xterm`
    libXaw.so.7 => /usr/X11R6/lib/libXaw.so.7 (0x40019000)
    libXmu.so.6 => /usr/X11R6/lib/libXmu.so.6 (0x4006a000)
    libXt.so.6 => /usr/X11R6/lib/libXt.so.6 (0x4007e000)
    libSM.so.6 => /usr/X11R6/lib/libSM.so.6 (0x400c7000)
    libICE.so.6 => /usr/X11R6/lib/libICE.so.6 (0x400d0000)
    libXpm.so.4 => /usr/X11R6/lib/libXpm.so.4 (0x400e6000)
```

```
libXext.so.6 => /usr/X11R6/lib/libXext.so.6 (0x400f4000)
libX11.so.6 => /usr/X11R6/lib/libX11.so.6 (0x40101000)
libncurses.so.4 => /usr/lib/libncurses.so.4 (0x401c4000)
libc.so.6 => /lib/libc.so.6 (0x40201000)
/lib/ld-linux.so.2 => /lib/ld-linux.so.2 (0x40000000)
```

6. Using a system that utilizes *dpkg*, obtain a list of all packages installed under *dpkg* management with *dpkg -l | less*. Find a package in the list that looks unfamiliar, and query information about the package using *dpkg -s pkg_name*.

7. Using a system that utilizes RPM, obtain a list of all packages installed under RPM management with *rpm -qa | less*. Find a package in the list that looks unfamiliar, and query information about the package using *rpm -qi pkg_name*.

GNU and Unix Commands (Topic 1.103)

Review Questions

1. Describe the difference between shell variables and environment variables.

2. Compare and contrast built-in and explicitly defined commands and those found in PATH.

3. After a lengthy session of file manipulation on the command line, what will *!ls* produce?

4. What program was the source for the default history editing key bindings in bash?

5. Explain the notion of *pipes* as they refer to shell capabilities, and illustrate using an example of two or more filter programs.

6. Explain the -*p* option to *cp* and give an example of why it is necessary.

7. Give two examples of files matched by the wildcard ??[!1-5].

8. Name the three standard I/O streams and their functions.

9. Give an example of the redirection operator, >, and describe how the outcome would be different using the >> operator.

10. What process is the ultimate ancestor of all system processes? Give both the PID and the program name.

11. Name three common utilities used for process monitoring.

12. What happens to a typical daemon when it receives SIGHUP? How would the behavior be different if it received SIGKILL?

13. Compare and contrast background and foreground jobs, and state the syntax to put a command in the background on the command line.

14. Explain the relationship between a process's *nice number* and its execution priority.

15. What two classifications of characters make up regular expressions?

16. How are the regular expressions [A-Z]* and ^[A-Z]*$ different?

17. What is the difference between executing :q versus :q! in *vi*?

18. What does it mean to put *vi* into *command mode*?

Exercises

1. Start a *bash* shell in a console or terminal window and enter the following commands:

   ```
   $ MYVAR1="Happy"
   $ MYVAR2="Birthday"
   $ export MYVAR1
   $ bash
   $ echo $MYVAR1 $MYVAR2
   $ exit
   $ echo $MYVAR1 $MYVAR2
   ```

   a. Was the behavior of the two *echo* commands identical?

   b. If so, why? If not, why not?

   c. What happened immediately after the *bash* command?

   d. Which variable is an environment variable?

2. Continuing the previous exercise, enter Ctrl-P until you see the last *echo* command. Enter Ctrl-P again.

   a. What do you see?

   b. Why wasn't it the *exit* command?

   c. Enter Ctrl-P again so that the export command is displayed. Add a space and MYVAR2 so that the line now looks like this:

   ```
   $ export MYVAR1 MYVAR2
   ```

   What happens when you enter this command?

3. Still continuing the previous exercise, enter the command !echo. Does anything change as a result of the revised *export* command?

4. The *file* command is used to examine a file's contents and displays the file type. Explain the result of using *file* as follows:

   ```
   $ cd / ; file $(ls | head -10)
   ```

5. Execute this command on your system:

   ```
   $ cut -d: -f1 /etc/passwd | fmt -w 20 | head -1
   ```

   a. What was displayed?

   b. How many lines of output did you see? Why?

   c. What was the width of the output? Why?

6. Execute the following *sed* substitution command and explain why it might be used on */etc/passwd*:

   ```
   $ sed 's/:[^:]*:/:---:/' /etc/passwd | less
   ```

7. Execute this command:

   ```
   $ cd /sbin ; ls -li e2fsck fsck.ext2
   ```

   a. What is the significance of the first field of the output?

   b. Why is it identical for both listings?

   c. Why are the file sizes identical?

8. Execute the following command sequence and explain the result at each step (this example assumes that *cp* is not aliased to *cp -i*, which is a common default alias):

```
$ cd
$ cp /etc/skel .
$ cp -r /etc/skel .
$ cp -rfv /etc/skel .
$ cp -rfvp /etc/skel .
```

9. Remove the directory created in the previous exercise, using *rmdir* and/or *rm*. Which command can complete the task in a single step?

10. Explain when the wildcard {htm,html} might be useful.

11. Give an example of how the wildcard *.[Tt][Xx][Tt] could be used with directory listings.

12. What can be said about filenames matched by the *.? wildcard?

13. Experiment with redirecting the output of *ls* as follows:

```
$ cp /etc/skel . 2> info.txt
```

a. How is the terminal output different than that observed in Exercise 8?

b. What is written to *info.txt*?

14. Experiment with *ps*, *pstree*, and *top* to monitor active processes on your system. Include *top*'s interactive commands.

15. If you have Apache running, use *ps* (and perhaps *grep*) to identify the *httpd* process and its PID, which is owned by root. Send that process the HUP signal as follows:

```
$ kill -SIGHUP pid
```

Using *tail*, examine the Apache error log (the location of your log file may differ):

```
$ tail /var/log/httpd/error_log
```

What was the effect of HUP on Apache?

16. While running X, start some interactive processes in the background and experiment with using *jobs*, *bg*, and *fg*. For example:

```
$ netscape &
$ xterm &
$ emacs &
$ jobs
$ fg 1
$ fg 2
...
```

Were you able to bring each of the jobs to the foreground successfully?

17. This exercise starts a process, using various methods to view and modify the process execution priority:

a. Start an editing session in the background using *nice*:

```
$ nice vi &
```

b. Observe that the process was *nice*'d using *ps*:

```
$ ps -u
```

c. Check it again using *top*:

```
$ top -i
```

d. Within *top*, *renice* the *vi* process using the r command and observe the effect on priority.

e. Exit *top* and use *renice* to set the nice value back to zero.

18. Use a simple regular expression with *grep* to find *sh* and *bash* users in */etc/passwd*.

19. Determine the number of empty lines in */etc/inittab*.

20. Use *vi* to create a text file. Enter *insert mode* with i and insert text. Quit insert mode with Esc and move around using h, j, k, and l, then re-enter insert mode and add more text. End the session with ZZ. *cat* the file. Is it as expected?

Devices, Linux Filesystems, and the Filesystem Hierarchy Standard (Topic 1.104)

Review Questions

1. What are the three types of disk partitions found on a Linux system? Which type can contain other partitions and which type does it contain?

2. Name the directories that must be within the root partition.

3. Describe the differences between physical disks, partitions, and filesystems.

4. What is a *swap* partition used for? Why not just use swap files?

5. What kind of output will *df -h* yield?

6. Describe a common situation that is likely to cause the automatic use of *fsck* on the next system boot.

7. Name the fields in */etc/fstab*.

8. Give the command to mount a CD-ROM drive on the secondary master IDE device, assuming that */etc/fstab* does not contain a line for the device.

9. If the ro option is used in */etc/fstab* for */usr*, what limitation is placed on that filesystem?

10. Compare and contrast hard and soft quota limits.

11. What three types of users can be granted or denied access to filesystem objects and how do they apply to files and directories?

12. Name the symbolic permission that is equivalent to 0754.

13. Describe a situation that requires the SUID permission. What ramifications does this permission imply?

14. Compare and contrast the differences between hard and symbolic links.

15. Name the document to which Linux directory assignments should conform.

16. Compare and contrast the differences between the *locate* and *find* commands.

Exercises

1. As root, run *fdisk* and enter the p command to print the partition table. Examine your system's configuration and make sure you understand everything you see. Enter the l command and review the many partition types Linux can accommodate. Enter the q command to quit without saving changes.

2. If you have available disk space, use *fdisk* to create a new *ext2* partition, then format it with *mkfs*. Pay close attention to the output from *mkfs*.

3. Use a pager to examine */var/log/messages* and search for entries made by *fsck*. Did it find any problems?

4. If you created a new partition in the previous exercises, check it with *fsck* and observe the output:

   ```
   $ fsck -f /dev/partition
   ```

5. Check on the status of filesystems using *df*:

   ```
   $ df -h
   ```

   a. How does the *-h* flag assist you with interpreting the results?

   b. Are any of your filesystems nearly full?

   c. Which are underutilized?

6. As root, get a top-level view of disk usage by user using *du*:

   ```
   $ du -s /home/*
   ```

   a. Are there any surprises?

7. How could you use *sort* to make this output more useful?

8. Review */etc/fstab*. Be sure you can name all six fields and their order as well as describe their function.

9. Examine the output of the mount command without options. Compare the output with the contents of */etc/fstab*.

10. If you created a new partition in the previous exercises, mount it on */mnt/new* or some other location of your choosing:

    ```
    $ mkdir /mnt/new
    $ mount /dev/partition /mnt/new
    $ df /mnt/new
    ```

    a. Did the filesystem mount correctly? Can you store files on it?

    b. Next, unmount it:

       ```
       $ umount /dev/partition /mnt/new
       ```

    c. Add a line to */etc/fstab* for the new partition:

       ```
       /dev/partition  /mnt/new  ext2  defaults  1 2
       ```

11. Test the quotas by setting them low for a particular user, then start adding files as that user until the quota is exceeded. What is the observable consequence of exceeding the quota?

12. Practice converting these file modes from octal to symbolic form:

    a. 0777

    b. 0754

c. 0666

d. 1700

e. 7777

13. Practice converting these file modes from symbolic to octal form. You can assume that x bits are set under SUID, SGID, and sticky bits:

a. -rwxr-xr-x

b. -r--r--r--

c. -rwsrwsrwx

d. -rw-rw---t

e. -rws-w--w-

14. Create temporary files and use *chmod* with both symbolic and numeric mode modifications. Include SUID, SGID, and sticky bits.

15. As *root*, create temporary files and use *chown* to modify user ownership and group ownership.

16. Use *chgrp* to modify group ownership on the temporary files created in the previous exercise.

17. Create a temporary file and links as follows:

```
$ touch a_file
$ ln -s a_file an_slink
$ ln a_file an_hlink
```

18. Now verify that the file and the hard link indeed share an inode and that the symbolic link points to the original file:

```
$ ls -li a_file an_slink an_hlink
```

19. Read the latest version of the FHS (it's not very long).

20. Examine your filesystem. Does it match the FHS? If you find discrepancies, is it clear why they don't?

21. Use *which* to check on the location of executable files.

22. Use *find* to search for *bash*:

```
$ find / -name bash
```

Now use *locate* for the same file:

```
$ locate bash
```

How are the results different? Describe a context in which each command would be useful.

23. Update your *locate* database using *updatedb*. Note the amount of time this command takes and the resources it consumes on your system.

The X Window System (Topic 1.110)

Review Questions

1. When using XFree86 v3.3.x, what software installation may be required when changing to a different video chipset, and why?

2. Describe how the location of fonts is conveyed to the XFree86 X server.

3. How is the use of a font server different from the use of a font path?

4. Which file controls access to *xdm* by remote X terminals?

5. Describe the function of *xinit*.

6. Compare and contrast a window manager, a desktop environment, and an X server.

7. Name the three components of the DISPLAY environment variable.

Exercises

1. From *http://www.xfree86.org/*, obtain XFree86 in the precompiled binary form for your system using the instructions found in Chapter 7. Start with the *Xinstall.sh* script and run it with *./Xinstall.sh -check* to determine which package to get.

2. Back up your old installation (*/etc/X11* and */usr/X11R6*). Install the new version using *Xinstall.sh* as directed in the instructions accompanying the package.

3. Use *xf86config* to configure the new X server. Are you able to get an X display? Is the resolution correct?

4. Try generating the X configuration using *XF86Setup* or *xf86cfg* (depending on the X version). Is the program successful? Does it yield a working X configuration?

5. Obtain a new Type 1 font (or TrueType font, if you are using XFree86 4.x) from the Internet (try a search at *http://www.google.com* or your favorite search engine). Add the font to */usr/X11R6/lib/fonts/local* and use the *mkfontdir* utility on that directory. Add the directory to your font path (with *xset fp+ /usr/X11R6/lib/fonts/local*). Use *xfontsel* to view the new font. Was the font added correctly?

6. Configure *xfs* as described in Chapter 7, and remove the FontPath statements from *XF86Config*, substituting unix/:-1. Start the font server and restart the X server. Using *xfontsel*, are you able to verify the availability of the same fonts as were available before?

7. Start *xdm* on your system, and note that the system starts the X server and presents a login prompt. If all works correctly, change the default runlevel to that which starts *xdm* and reboot. Does the system now present a graphical login screen?

8. Examine the scripts and programs used on your system for starting X, beginning with *startx*. Look for how the system uses files in the user's home directory to control GUI startup.

9. Examine your window manager configuration. Which window manager are you using? Is it part of a desktop environment, such as KDE or GNOME? Determine where its menus are configured and add an item or two to the menus.

9

Exam 101 Practice Test

Exam 101 consists approximately of 65 questions. Most are multiple-choice single-answer, a few are multiple-choice multiple-answer, and the remainder are fill-in the blank questions. No notes or other materials are permitted, and you have 90 minutes to complete this exam. You can check your answers at the end of this chapter.

Questions

1. What two commands display the status of processes on a Linux system?

   a. *ls* and *df*

   b. *ps* and *top*

   c. *ps* and *df*

   d. *df* and *top*

   e. *du* and *df*

2. What does the device file */dev/hdb6* represent?

   a. An extended partition on a SCSI disk drive

   b. A logical partition on a SCSI disk drive

   c. An extended partition on an IDE disk drive

   d. A primary partition on an IDE disk drive

   e. A logical partition on an IDE disk drive

3. Which command will display the last lines of the text file *file1*?

   a. *head -b file1*

   b. *head --bottom file1*

   c. *head -v file1*

   d. *tail file1*

   e. *tail -n 1 file1*

4. In the Bash shell, entering !! has the same effect as which one of the following?

    a. Ctrl-P and Enter

    b. Ctrl-N and Enter

    c. Ctrl-U and Enter

    d. !-2

    e. !2

5. Which of the following commands can be used to check an *ext2* filesystem? Select *three* that apply.

    a. *fsck -ext2 /dev/hda5*

    b. *fsck /dev/hda5*

    c. *e2fsck /dev/hda5*

    d. *fsck.ext2 /dev/hda5*

    e. *fsck.linux /dev/hda5*

6. In response to the *df* command, the system reports a Use% of 98% for the filesystem mounted on */home*. Which one of the following best describes the significance of this information?

    a. Files on */home* are consuming 98% of the physical disk.

    b. File read/write activity on */home* is consuming 98% of system I/O capacity.

    c. Files on */home* are consuming 98% of the */home* filesystem.

    d. Inodes on */home* are nearly exhausted.

    e. Inodes on */home* are 98% free.

7. Of the following directories, which one is the most important to back up on a routine basis?

    a. */var*

    b. */tmp*

    c. */usr*

    d. */root*

    e. */etc*

8. Carolyn has a text file named *guest_list* containing 12 lines. She executes the following command. What is the result?

```
# split -4 guest_list gl
```

    a. The first four columns in the text are written to new files *glaa*, *glab*, *glac*, and *glad*.

    b. The first four columns in the text are written to new files *aagl*, *abgl*, *acgl*, and *adgl*.

    c. The lines of *guest_list* are evenly divided among new files *glaa*, *glab*, *glac*, and *glad*.

    d. The lines of *guest_list* are evenly divided among new files *glaa*, *glab*, and *glac*.

    e. The lines of *guest_list* are evenly divided among new files *aagl*, *abgl*, and *acgl*.

9. Which one of the following commands would be best suited to mount a CD-ROM containing a Linux distribution, without depending on any configuration files?

   a. *mount /dev/cdrom /dev/hdc*

   b. *mount -f linux /dev/hdc /mnt/cdrom*

   c. *mount -t iso9660 /dev/cdrom /mnt/cdrom*

   d. *mount -t linux /dev/cdrom /mnt/cdrom*

   e. *mount -t iso9660 /mnt/cdrom /dev/cdrom*

10. An *ext2* filesystem is configured with user quotas enabled. The soft limit is set at 100 MB per user, the hard limit is set at 110 MB per user, and the grace period is seven days. User *bsmith* already owns 90 MB of the data stored on the filesystem. What happens when *bsmith* writes a new file of size 30 MB? Select one.

    a. The write will fail, but the superuser can recover the entire file within seven days.

    b. The write will fail, and the file will be truncated permanently.

    c. The write will succeed, but the file will be truncated permanently.

    d. The write will succeed, but the file will be available for only seven days.

    e. The write will succeed, but the file will be truncated in seven days.

11. Which of the following commands displays the comments from a bash script? Select all that apply.

    a. *find "^#" /etc/rc.d/rc.local*

    b. *sed '/^#/ !d' /etc/rc.d/init.d/httpd*

    c. *grep ^# /etc/rc.d/init.d/httpd*

    d. *grep ^# /etc/passwd*

    e. *locate "^#" /etc/skel/.bashrc*

12. State the syntax to direct the standard output of cmd1 directly into the standard input of *cmd2*.

13. Which one of the following answers creates an environment variable VAR1, present in the environment of a bash child process?

    a. *VAR1="fail" ; export VAR1*

    b. *VAR1="fail" \ export VAR1*

    c. *VAR1="fail"*

    d. *set VAR1="fail" ; enable VAR1*

    e. *export VAR1 \ VAR1="fail"*

14. Which of the following directories *must* be part of the root filesystem? Select *two* of the following that apply.

    a. */etc*

    b. */home*

    c. */lib*

    d. */usr*

    e. */root*

15. Alex is currently working in a directory containing only one file, *Afile1*. What is displayed after the following commands are entered in bash?

```
# MYVAR=ls
# echo $MYVAR "$MYVAR" '$MYVAR' `$MYVAR`
```

  a. `ls Afile1 Afile1 Afile1`

  b. `ls Afile1 Afile1 Afile1`

  c. `ls ls Afile1 Afile1`

  d. `ls ls $MYVAR Afile1`

  e. `ls ls ls $MYVAR`

16. What does the & character do when placed at the end of a command?

  a. It allows another command to be entered on the same line.

  b. It causes the process to be stopped.

  c. It restarts a stopped process.

  d. It causes the process to be placed into the foreground.

  e. It causes the process to be placed into the background.

17. Which one of the following commands could be used to change all uppercase characters to lowercase in the middle of a pipe?

  a. *grep*

  b. *egrep*

  c. *wc*

  d. *tr*

  e. *pr*

18. What is the PID of *init*? Select one.

  a. 0

  b. 1

  c. 2

  d. undefined

  e. unknown

19. Which one of the following outcomes results from the following command?

```
# chmod g+s /home/software
```

  a. The SUID bit will be set for */home/software*.

  b. The SGID bit will be set for */home/software*, preventing access by those not a member of the *software* group.

  c. The SGID bit will be set for */home/software*, in order to keep group membership of the directory consistent for all files created.

  d. The sticky bit will be set for */home/software*.

  e. The sticky bit will be applied to all files in */home/software*.

20. Which one of the following commands is equivalent to the following command for user *jdoe* whose home directory is */home/jdoe*?

    # chmod 754 ~/file1

    a. *chmod u=rwx,g=rx,o=r /home/jdoe/file1*

    b. *chmod ugo=rwx ~/file1*

    c. *chmod u=7,g=5,o=4 ~/file1*

    d. *chmod 754 \home\jdoe\file1*

    e. *chmod 754 /usr/jdoe/file1*

21. What command and single required option creates a symbolic link in a Linux filesystem?

22. What command can display the contents of a binary file in a readable hexadecimal form? Select one.

    a. *xd*

    b. *hd*

    c. *od*

    d. *Xd*

    e. *dump*

23. Which one of the following commands copies files with the *.txt* extension from */dir1* into */dir2*, while preserving file attributes such as dates?

    a. *mv --copy /dir1/*.txt /dir2*

    b. *mv /dir1/*.txt /dir2*

    c. *cp -k /dir1/*.txt /dir2*

    d. *cp -p /dir1/*.txt /dir2*

    e. *cp -p /dir2 < /dir1/*.txt*

24. Which one of the following file globs matches "Linux" and "linux," but not "linux.com" and not "TurboLinux"?

    a. `[L/linux]`

    b. `?inux`

    c. `\L\linux`

    d. `[Ll]inux`

    e. `[Ll]inux?`

25. A process with PID 4077 is misbehaving on your system. As superuser, you enter the following command:

    # kill 4077

    However, nothing changes as a result. What can you do to terminate the process? Select one.

    a. *kill -9 4077*

    b. *kill -1 4077*

    c. *kill +9 4077*

    d. *kill 4078*

    e. *kill --die 4077*

26. Which one of the following key sequences is used to put a noninteractive text-mode program that is attached to the terminal into the background to allow it to continue processing?

   a. Ctrl-C

   b. Ctrl-B

   c. Ctrl-B and then enter the *bg* command

   d. Ctrl-Z

   e. Ctrl-Z and then enter the *bg* command

27. What basic command is used to create hard disk partitions?

28. With a umask of 027, how is the initial mode set for a newly created file?

   a. 0750

   b. 0640

   c. 0027

   d. 1027

   e. 1640

29. Which one of the following commands verbosely extracts files from a *tar* archive on a magnetic tape device?

   a. *tar cvf /dev/st0*

   b. *tar cvf /dev/ttyS0*

   c. *tar xvf /dev/st0*

   d. *tar xvf /dev/ttyS0*

   e. *tar rvf /dev/st0*

30. Alex wants to protect himself from inadvertently overwriting files when copying them with *cp*. How should he go about this?

   a. Put alias cp='cp -i' in *~/.bashrc*.

   b. Put alias cp='cp -i' in *~/.bash_profile*.

   c. Put alias cp='cp -p' in *~/.bashrc*.

   d. Put alias cp='cp -p' in *~/.bash_profile*.

   e. Put alias cp='cp -I' in *~/.bashrc*.

31. Which one of the following utilities outputs a text file with line numbers along the left margin?

   a. *tar*

   b. *wc*

   c. *tr*

   d. *nl*

   e. *ln*

32. The following line comes from /etc/fstab Which of the statements is accurate given the contents of this line? Choose *two* that apply.

```
/dev/fd0    /mnt/fd0    vfat    noauto,users  0 0
```

   a. Users are prohibited from mounting and unmounting the filesystem.

   b. Users are permitted to mount and unmount the filesystem.

   c. The filesystem will be mounted on mount point /dev/fd0.

   d. The filesystem is expected to be a Linux native filesystem.

   e. The filesystem is on a floppy disk.

33. Which one of the following is an accurate statement regarding this regular expression?

```
[^1-8A-Za-z]
```

   a. It matches all letters and numbers.

   b. It matches all letters and numbers except 9.

   c. It matches all letters and numbers except 9 and 0, but only at the beginning of a line.

   d. It matches 9, 0, and other nonletter and nonnumber characters.

   e. It matches characters other than letters or numbers.

34. Monica consults the /etc/passwd file expecting to find encrypted passwords for all of the users on her system. She sees the following:

```
jdoe:x:500:500::/home/jdoe:/bin/bash
bsmith:x:501:501::/home/bsmith:/bin/tcsh
```

Which of the following is true? Select one.

   a. Accounts *jdoe* and *bsmith* have no passwords.

   b. Accounts *jdoe* and *bsmith* are disabled.

   c. The passwords are in /etc/passwd-

   d. The passwords are in /etc/shadow

   e. The passwords are in /etc/shadow-

35. What command (include applicable options) is used to initiate a change to runlevel 5?

36. What does the "sticky bit" do? Select one.

   a. It prevents files from being deleted by anyone.

   b. It marks files for deletion.

   c. It prevents files from being deleted by nonowners except *root*.

   d. It prevents files from being deleted by nonowners including *root*.

   e. It marks files for archive.

37. Dave has a Linux system with an interrupt conflict caused by his 3c509 network card. Dave's kernel is fully modular. How could Dave instruct the system to use IRQ 11 for his network adapter?

   a. Enter `linux eth0=irq11` at the LILO boot loader prompt.

   b. Enter `linux 3c509=irq11` at the LILO boot loader prompt.

c. Add options 3c509 irq=11 to */etc/conf.modules.*

d. Add options irq=11 3c509 to */etc/conf.modules.*

e. Add ifup -irq 11 eth0 to */etc/rc.d/rc.sysinit.*

38. What is contained in directory */sbin*? Select the single best answer.

    a. Commands needed in the event of a system emergency of interest to all system users.

    b. Commands of interest to all system users.

    c. Commands needed in the event of a system emergency of interest mainly to the administrator.

    d. Commands of interest mainly to the administrator.

    e. Libraries needed in the event of an emergency.

39. What *ext2* filesystem attribute allows a process to take on the ownership of the executable file's owner?

40. What is appended to the beginning of a command line in order to modify the execution priority of the resulting process?

41. How are the *cat* and *tac* commands related? Select one.

    a. *cat* displays files and *tac* does the same but in reverse order.

    b. *cat* concatenates files while *tac* splits a file into pieces.

    c. *cat* creates file catalogs while *tac* displays the catalogs.

    d. The two commands are links to the same executable.

    e. There is no relation or similarity between *cat* and *tac*.

42. With regard to the use of regular expressions to match text in a file, describe a metacharacter. Select one.

    a. They are standard text characters used in the regular expression.

    b. They are special control characters used in the regular expression.

    c. They are used to display results after using a regular expression.

    d. They are used by the shell to display graphics.

    e. Metacharacters aren't used in regular expressions.

43. How many IDE devices can be installed and simultaneously used in a typical Intel-based system? Select one.

    a. 1

    b. 2

    c. 3

    d. 4

    e. 5

44. Which one of the following would be a consequence of a filesystem running out of inodes?

    a. More inodes would be automatically created in the filesystem.

    b. Quotas would become disabled on the filesystem.

    c. The filesystem would be corrupted.

d. The filesystem would be marked read-only.

e. No writes would be possible on the filesystem until existing files were deleted.

45. Consider the following line of console output, excerpted from among other lines of output. Which one of the commands produced it?

    /dev/hda8   1.9G 559M 1.2G 30% /home

    a. *du -s*

    b. *du -k*

    c. *df -h*

    d. *df -k*

    e. *df -m*

46. Which one of the following is true about the LILO boot loader?

    a. It can start the Windows NT Loader.

    b. It is started using the *lilo* command.

    c. It is the only boot loader available for Linux.

    d. It can start multiple Linux kernels, but no foreign operating systems.

    e. It resides entirely in the boot sector.

47. Which one of the following statements correctly describes the > and >> symbols in the context of the bash shell?

    a. > appends standard output to an existing file, and >> writes standard output to a new file.

    b. > writes standard output to a new file, and >> appends standard output to an existing file.

    c. > writes standard error to a new file, and >> appends standard error to an existing file.

    d. > pipes standard output to a new file, and >> pipes standard output to an existing file.

    e. > pipes standard output to an existing file and >> pipes standard error to a new file.

48. What is the correct syntax to remove *mypkg* entirely from a Debian GNU/ Linux system, including configuration files? Select one.

    a. *dpkg -r mypkg*

    b. *dpkg --remove mypkg*

    c. *dpkg --kill mypkg*

    d. *dpkg -R mypkg*

    e. *dpkg --purge mypkg*

49. Your system's FontPath directives include only one entry:

    unix/:-1

    Which of the following is true? Select one.

    a. Error -1 has occurred during X startup

    b. Only the default font will be available to applications

c. An X font server is to be used

d. An X font server failed to initialize

e. No fonts were found by XFree86 or by a font server

50. How do you use *dpkg* to verify the status of an installed package *mypkg*? Select one.

    a. *dpkg -s mypkg*

    b. *dpkg -S mypkg*

    c. *dpkg -stat mypkg*

    d. *dpkg --stat mypkg*

    e. *dpkg --Status mypkg*

51. Which of the following statements is true about an X server? Select one.

    a. An X server is a high-performance system offering graphical programs over a network.

    b. An X server sends its graphical output to a window manager.

    c. An X server is under the control of a window manager.

    d. A window manager is under the control of an X server.

    e. A window manager is also known as an X server.

52. What are the two interrupts usually associated with a PC's onboard serial interface?

53. How can you query the RPM database for a list of all installed RPM packages? Select one.

    a. *rpm -q*

    b. *rpm -qa*

    c. *rpm -a*

    d. *rpm -al*

    e. *rpm -qal*

54. Which pair of *dpkg* options are equivalent and what do they do? Select one.

    a. *-C* and *--configure*; they reconfigure an unpackaged package.

    b. *-C* and *--clear-avail*; they erase existing information about what packages are available.

    c. *-A* and *--audit*; they update information about what packages are available.

    d. *-C* and *--audit*; they provide resource consumption information on installed packages.

    e. *-C* and *--audit*; they search for partially installed packages.

55. What will happen when *rpm* is launched as follows?

```
rpm -Uvh file
```

    a. The RPM file will be verified.

    b. An installed package may be upgraded with the version in file, with verbose output.

c. An installed package may be upgraded with the version in file, with verbose output and hash marks indicating progress.

d. An error will occur because a major mode is not specified.

e. An error will occur because no file options were specified.

56. How are changes to the system BIOS made? Select one.

a. Using *linuxconf*.

b. By manually editing text files.

c. Using the *lilo* command.

d. At boot time using system-specific menus.

e. At boot time using LILO commands.

57. When using *xdm*, which of the following files can be used to start a window manager? Select one.

a. *Xservers*

b. *Xaccess*

c. *xdm-config*

d. *Xsession*

e. *Xsetup_0*

58. When partitioning a disk with more than 1024 cylinders, which of the following could affect the system's ability to boot? Select all that apply.

a. Location of LILO on disk.

b. Location of */boot* on disk.

c. Location of */var* on disk.

d. Disk transfer rate.

e. Disk seek time.

59. Which of the following is a reasonable size for a swap partition for a Linux workstation with 128 MB RAM? Select one.

a. 1 KB

b. 0.5 MB

c. 100 MB

d. 5 GB

e. 10 GB

60. What is XDMCP, and how is it used? Select one.

a. An X utility, used to copy files between a host and an X terminal.

b. An X utility, used to configure XDM.

c. An X utility, used to configure IP addresses on X terminals on the network.

d. An X protocol, used to discover/listen for X terminals on the network.

e. An X protocol, used to exchange graphics information between X clients and X servers over the network.

61. How many target devices can be added to an 8-bit SCSI-2 bus? Select one.

    a. 6

    b. 7

    c. 8

    d. 15

    e. 16

62. What is the *startx* command? Select one.

    a. A script included with XFree86 to make startup user friendly.

    b. A script used to start *xdm*.

    c. A compiled binary program that directly launches the X server.

    d. A configuration file created by X configuration tools such as *XF86Config*.

    e. A script originated by Linux distributors to tailor X startup to their particular X implementation.

63. How can you obtain a list of files contained in an *.rpm* file? Select one.

    a. *rpm -q file*

    b. *rpm -i file*

    c. *rpm -ql file*

    d. *rpm -qlp file*

    e. *rpm -qal file*

64. Which of the following accurately describes the contents of the xdisp:1.0 DISPLAY environment variable? Select one.

    a. System *xdisp* is to send X programs to the first display of the local X server.

    b. System *xdisp* is to receive X programs on the first display of its X server.

    c. System *xdisp* is to receive X programs on the second display of its X server.

    d. Local program *xdisp* is to use the second display of the local X server.

    e. Local program *xdisp* is to use the second display of any available X terminal.

65. Which file contains information on the I/O port assignments in use? Select one.

    a. */dev/ioports*

    b. */etc/ioports*

    c. */etc/sysconfig/ioports*

    d. */etc/proc/ioports*

    e. */proc/ioports*

66. Why might an administrator use the *--force* option for *rpm*?

    a. To overwrite a previously installed package.

    b. To overwrite a Debian package.

    c. To prevent confirmation messages.

d. To force the deletion of installed packages.

e. To force the deletion of package dependencies.

67. Which of the following commands cannot be used to exit from *vi* when in command mode? Select one.

a. ZZ

b. :x

c. :q

d. :q!

e. :bye

68. Which is not a valid *dpkg* installation command? Select one.

a. *dpkg -i package_file*

b. *dpkg -iL package_file*

c. *dpkg -iR package_dir*

d. *dpkg -iG package_file*

e. *dpkg -iE package_file*

69. Which of the following is the text file that contains directories where the dynamic linker should look for libraries? Select one.

a. *ld.so.conf*

b. *conf.ld.so*

c. *ld.so.cache*

d. *so.config*

e. *configld*

Answers

1. b. Both *ps* and *top* yield process status. None of the other listed commands are related to processes.

2. e. IDE disk drives are referred to as */dev/hdx*, where *x* is a, b, c, or d. Partitions are numbered from 1 through 4 for primary and extended partitions and 5 through 16 for logical partitions.

3. d. The *tail* command is used for checking the last lines of a text file. By default, it displays 10 lines.

4. a. The !! command history expansion executes the previous command. Entering the Ctrl-P keystroke uses the Emacs key-binding bash to move up one line in the history; pressing Enter executes that command.

5. b, c, and d. *fsck* is a frontend for the programs that actually do the checking. *e2fsck* and *fsck.ext2* are links to the program that checks native Linux ext2 filesystems.

6. c. *df* reports disk information, including a percentage of the filesystems used. Answer a is incorrect because */home* may not be the only partition on the physical disk.

7. e. /var and /tmp are mainly transient, /usr is typically static (and should be easy to reinstall from the original OS media), /root is simply a home directory for root, but /etc contains system configuration information that frequently changes.

8. d. *split -n* outfile separates a file into multiple output files, each with *n* lines, and names them *outfileaa*, *outfileab*, and so on. Since the original file had 12 lines and Carolyn split it into sets of 4 lines, the result is three files named *glaa*, *glab*, and *glac*, each containing 4 lines.

9. c. CD-ROMs use the *iso9660* filesystem, which is the default for mount, but also indicated using -t. Without the assistance of an entry in /etc/fstab, both the mount device (/dev/cdrom) and the mount point (/mnt/cdrom) must be provided.

10. b. The write will continue until the hard limit of 110 MB is reached, after which the write fails and data is lost.

11. b and c. *find* and *locate* do not search the contents of files. /etc/passwd is not a script.

12. *cmd1 | cmd2*

13. a. The variable must be set and exported. The semicolon separates the two commands.

14. a and c. /etc, /lib, /bin, /sbin, and /dev must be in the / filesystem.

15. d. The first *echo* argument is unquoted and thus returns its contents, ls. The second is quoted with double quotes, which do not preserve the $, so it too returns ls. The third is quoted with single quotes, which do preserve the $, so it returns the string $MYVAR. The last argument is backquoted, which means that it returns the result of the command stored in $MYVAR. The command is *ls*, which displays the only file in the directory, *Afile1*.

16. e. Using the & character puts a program in the background.

17. d. The *tr* program translates characters from one group into another, including case.

18. b. *init*, the grandfather of all processes, always has PID 1.

19. c. The g indicates that we're operating on the group privilege, and the +s indicates that we should add the "set id" bit, which means that the SGID property will be applied.

20. a. User mode 7 is the same as u=rwx, group mode 5 is the same as g=rx, and other mode 4 is the same as o=r. The ~/ syntax implies the user's home directory.

21. *ln -s*

22. c. The octal dump program, when used with the *-t x* option, will output in hexadecimal notation.

23. d. The *-p*, or preserve, option is required to retain dates.

24. d. The [Ll] matches both letters.

25. a. *kill -9* is drastic but necessary for processes unable to respond to other signals.

26. e. Ctrl-Z stops the job and gives control back to the terminal. *bg* places the job into the background and restarts it.

27. *fdisk*.

28. b. By default, files do not have the execute privilege, which rules out all responses containing odd numbers in the mode. They also do not by default have the sticky bit set, which eliminates response e. Response b is the result of masking initial bits 666 with *umask 027*, leaving 640, which is the same as 0640.

29. c. *tar* should be used with the extraction option *x* and a tape device, such as SCSI tape */dev/st0*.

30. a or b. *cp* should be aliased to the interactive mode with the *-i* option in *.bashrc*. *.bash_profile* normally doesn't include aliases, but it will also work.

31. d. The *nl* command numbers lines.

32. b and e. The users option grants nonprivileged users the right to mount and unmount the filesystem. */dev/fd0* is a floppy device.

33. d. Brackets ([ ]) are used to group a character set consisting of numbers 1-8 and characters A-Z and a-z. The ^ just inside the opening bracket negates the whole string, such that the string matches numbers 0, 9, and symbols.

34. d. The shadow password system has been implemented, placing all passwords in */etc/shadow* as denoted by the x following the username.

35. *init 5*. *telinit 5* would also work, as they are both links to the same file.

36. c. The sticky bit in the mode prevents deletion by non-owners, but *root* can still delete the file.

37. c. Since Dave is using a modular kernel, the network driver *3c509.o* is a kernel module. LILO can send kernel parameters but not module parameters. These are stored in */etc/conf.modules*.

38. c. While answers b and d are technically correct, answer c best describes */sbin*.

39. SUID.

40. *nice*.

41. a. *cat* concatenates files, and as a subset, will list one or more files to standard output. *tac* lists files in reverse order.

42. b. A metacharacter is a special character that is used to modify and control the interpretation of literals. File globbing is generally considered distinct but very similar to the use of regular expressions.

43. d. PCs usually have two IDE interfaces, each capable of handling two devices.

44. e. A filesystem without free inodes cannot create new objects until existing objects are removed.

45. c. This is an example line from the output of *df -h*, the "human-readable" mode of *df*.

46. a. LILO can start the Windows NT boot loader and many other operating systems.

47. b. The > character opens and writes to a new file, while >> appends to an existing file, unless that file doesn't exist, in which case it is opened first.

48. e. The --*purge* option is a variant of -*r*, remove.

49. c. The directive indicates that a font server should listen on its default port.

50. a. The appropriate option is either -*s* or --*status*.

51. d. A window manager is a client, controlled by the X server. Answers a and b are incorrect because they imply that the X server originates the graphical output. Answers c and e are common misconceptions.

52. 3 and 4.

53. b. The query mode is required, which implies -*q*. The -*a* option in query mode yields all packages.

54. e.

55. c. Provided that *file* is an RPM file, the -*U* indicates that an upgrade should occur. -*h* turns on hash marks.

56. d. Linux has no control over the BIOS settings.

57. d. Xsession is the system-wide default application startup file.

58. a and b. Both the second stage of LILO and the kernel should be kept within the 1024-cylinder boundary.

59. c.

60. d. X terminals use XDMCP to attach to xdm daemons.

61. b. An 8-bit SCSI bus has three address lines, thus providing 2^3 or 8 addresses. Setting aside one for the controller, there are 7 addresses for devices.

62. a. *startx* is included with XFree86 as a suggestion, and customization is encouraged.

63. d. *rpm -qlp* queries and *l*ists files in the *p*ackage.

64. c. The system, *xdisp*, will display programs on the second display of its X server.

65. e.

66. d.

67. e. :bye is not a valid command in *vi*.

68. b. Options -*i* (install) and -*L* (list installed files) are incompatible and don't make sense together.

69. a. *ld.so.conf* is the text file in which you add library directories. *ld.so.cache* is the binary index resulting from *ldconfig*.

10

Exam 101 Highlighter's Index

Hardware and Architecture

Objective 1: Configure Fundamental BIOS Settings

PC BIOS

- The BIOS is the PC's firmware.
- The BIOS sets date and time for on-board clock, storage device configuration, and so on via menus.

Resource assignments

- Interrupts (IRQs) allow peripherals to interrupt the CPU.
- I/O addresses are locations in the processor's memory map for hardware devices.
- DMA allows certain devices to work directly with memory, freeing the processor (see Table 10-1).

Table 10-1. Common device settings

Device	I/O address	IRQ	DMA
ttyS0 (COM1)	3f8	4	NA
ttyS1 (COM2)	2f8	3	NA
ttyS2 (COM3)	3e8	4	NA
ttyS3 (COM4)	2e8	3	NA
lp0 (LPT1)	378-37f	7	NA
lp1 (LPT2)	278-27f	5	NA
fd0, fd1 (floppies 1 and 2)	3f0-3f7	6	2
fd2, fd3 (floppies 3 and 4)	370-377	10	3

1024-cylinder limit

- LILO and the kernel image should be kept within the first 1024 cylinders on hard disks.

Objective 3: Configure Modems and Sound Cards

Modems

- Modems are serial devices. Some are external and are attached to a serial port. Others are installed in a computer and include serial port electronics on-board.
- Some modems are produced at reduced cost by implementing portions of their functionality in Windows software libraries. These so-called "winmodems" aren't compatible with Linux without add-on drivers.

Sound devices

- PCI sound cards and most ISA PnP cards under 2.4.x kernels are automatically configured when the card's driver is loaded.
- When the old userspace ISA PnP tools are used, *pnpdump* output is stored for use at boot time by isapnp, which does plug-n-play configuration.

Objective 4: Set Up Non-IDE Devices

SCSI

- The SCSI defines a bus for multiple storage devices.
- SCSI capabilities range from 5 MBps to 80 MBps and higher for the newest types.
- 8-bit SCSI offers up to seven devices plus the controller on a single bus.
- 16-bit SCSI offers up to 15 devices plus the controller on a single bus.
- Each device on the bus has a unique SCSI ID, 0-7 or 0-15. Controllers often default to address 7.
- Linux device files for SCSI disks are typically */dev/sda*, */dev/sdb*, and so forth.
- Linux device files for SCSI tape drives are typically */dev/st0*, */dev/st1*, and so on.
- SCSI buses must be terminated on both ends. Many SCSI devices include internal terminators to eliminate the need for external terminators.
- PC SCSI adapters have their own BIOS, where the default boot device, bus speed, and on-board termination settings can be made.

Objective 5: Set Up PC Different Expansion Cards

/proc

- The */proc* filesystem includes information on interrupts, I/O ports, and DMA in */proc/interrupts*, */proc/ioports*, and */proc/dma*.

Commands

- On 2.2.x and earlier kernels (or 2.4.x kernels configured without kernel ISA PnP support), use *isapnp* to configure ISA cards and *pnpdump* for a report of ISA PnP resource information.
- On 2.4.x and higher kernels, use */proc/isapnp* to view and set the configuration of ISA PnP cards.
- For a listing of installed PCI devices, use `lspci`.

Objective 6: Configure Communication Devices

Concepts

- Internal communication devices are configured the same as other PC expansion cards.
- Most broadband communication devices connect to your PC via USB or ethernet interfaces.

Commands

- *setserial* is used to set serial port information.

Objective 7: Configure USB Devices

Host Controllers

- Open Host Controller Interface (OHCI), USB 1.1
- Universal Host Controller Interface (UHCI), USB 1.1
- Enhanced Host Controller Interface (EHCI), USB 2.0

Devices

- HID devices include USB peripherals such as keyboards, mice, and tablets.
- Communication devices include modems and broadband adapters.
- Mass storage devices include hard drives, tape drives, and flash readers.

Drivers

- Host Controller Drivers include *usb-ohci.o*, *usb-uhci.o*, *uhci.o*, and *ehci-hcd.o*.
- Class drivers include *hid.o*, *usb-storage.o*, *acm.o*, *printer.o*, and *audio.o*.

Commands

- *hotplug* is used to automatically load and unload USB modules when devices are plugged in or removed while a system is running.

Linux Installation and Package Management

Objective 1: Design a Hard Disk Layout

Guidelines

- Keep / small by distributing larger parts of the directory tree to other filesystems.
- Separate a small */boot* partition below cylinder 1024 for kernels.
- Separate */var* into its own partition to prevent runaway logs from filling /.
- Separate */tmp*.
- Separate */usr* if it is to be shared read-only among other systems via NFS.
- Set swap size to be somewhere between one and two times the size of main memory.

Objective 2: Install a Boot Manager

LILO

- LILO has historically been the default Linux boot loader.
- LILO consists of the *lilo* command, which installs the boot loader, and the boot loader itself.
- LILO is configured using */etc/lilo.conf*.

GRUB

- GRUB can boot Linux as well as most other PC-based operating systems.
- GRUB relies on various files in the */boot/grub* directory to support reading from various types of filesystems.
- GRUB is configured using */boot/grub/menu.lst* (or */boot/grub/grub.conf* on some distributions).
- GRUB can be configured to present a text or graphical menu interface and also has a command-line interface.

Objective 3: Make and Install Programs from Source

Source Files

- Software often comes in a compressed *tar* archive file.
- Larger source code packages include a *configure* script to verify that everything is in order to compile the software.

make

- *make* is then used to build the software.
- *make* is also often used to install the software into directories such as */usr/local/bin*.

Objective 4: Manage Shared Libraries

Concepts

- System libraries provide many of the functions required by a program.
- A program that contains executable code from libraries is *statically linked* because it stands alone and contains all necessary code to execute.
- Since static linking leads to larger executable files and more resource consumption, system libraries can be shared among many executing programs at the same time.

Commands

- A program that contains references to external, shared libraries is *dynamically linked* at runtime by the dynamic linker, *ld.so*.
- New locations for shared libraries can be added to the LD_LIBRARY_PATH variable. As an alternative, the locations can be added to */etc/ld.so.conf*, which lists library file directories. After this, you must run ldconfig to translate this file into the binary index */etc/ld.so.cache*.

Objective 5: Use Debian Package Management

Commands

- *dpkg* automates the installation and maintenance of software packages and offers a number of options.
- *dselect* uses a text based interactive menu to select (or deselect) packages for installation.
- *alien* can install RPM packages on Debian-based systems.
- *apt-get* is a powerful tool that interfaces with online repositories of Debian packages to install and upgrade Debian packages by package name and resolves each package's dependencies automatically.

Objective 6: Use Red Hat Package Manager (RPM)

Concepts

- RPM automates the installation and maintenance of software packages.
- Package dependencies are defined but not resolved automatically.
- *-i, -e, -U, -v, -h, --nodeps*, and *--force* are common options.

GNU and Unix Commands

Objective 1: Work Effectively on the Command Line

The interactive shell and shell variables

- A *shell* provides the command prompt and interprets commands.
- A *shell variable* holds a value that is accessible to shell programs.
- PATH is a shell variable that contains a listing of directories that hold executable programs.
- Commands must be bash built-ins, found in the PATH, or explicitly defined in order to succeed.
- When shell variables are *exported*, they become part of the *environment*.

Entering commands

- Commands are comprised of a valid command, with or without one or more options and arguments, followed by a carriage return.
- Interactive commands can include looping structures more often used in shell scripts.

Command history, editing, and substitution

- Shell sessions can be viewed as a conversation. History, expansion, and editing make that dialog more productive.
- Commands can be reissued, modified, and edited. Examples are shown in Table 10-2.
- Command substitution allows the *result* of a command to be placed into a shell variable.

Table 10-2. Shell expansion, editing, and substitution examples

History type	Examples
Expansion	!! !n ^string1^string2
Editing	Ctrl-P, previous line Ctrl-K, kill to end of line Ctrl-Y, paste (yank) text
Substitution	VAR=$(command)

Recursive execution

- Many commands contain either a *-r* or *-R* option for recursive execution through a directory hierarchy.
- The *find* command is inherently recursive, and is intended to descend through directories looking for files with certain attributes or executing commands.

Objective 2: Process Text Streams Using Filters

The Commands

The following programs modify or manipulate text from files and standard input:

cut [files]
> Cut out selected columns or fields from one or more *files*.

expand files
> Convert tabs to spaces in *files*.

fmt [files]
> Format text in *files* to a specified width by filling lines and removing newline characters.

head [files]
> Print the first few lines of *files*.

join file1 file2
> Print a line for each pair of input lines, one each from *file1* and *file2*, that have identical join fields.

nl [files]
> Number the lines of *files*, which are concatenated in the output.

od [files]
> Dump *files* in octal, hexadecimal, ASCII, and other formats.

paste files
> Paste together corresponding lines of one or more files into vertical columns.

pr [file]
> Convert a text file into a paginated, columnar version, with headers and page fills.

split [infile] [outfile]
> Split *infile* into a specified number of line groups; the output will go into a succession of files of *outfile*a, *outfile*b, and so on.

tac [file]
> Print *file* to standard output in reverse line order.

tail [files]
> Print the last few lines of one or more files.

tr [string1 [string2]]
> Translate characters by mapping from *string1* to the corresponding character in *string2*.

wc [files]
> Print counts of characters, words, and lines for *files*.

The stream editor, sed

sed is a popular text-filtering program found on every Unix system; it has the following syntax:

sed command [files]
sed -e command1 [-e command2] [files]
sed -f script [files]
> Execute *sed commands*, or those found in *script*, on standard input or *files*.

Objective 3: Perform Basic File Management

Concepts

- Filesystem creation prepares a disk device (or partition) for use. Linux usually uses the native *ext2* (second extended) filesystem or the journalled *ext3* filesystem, but it supports many other filesystem types.

- The Linux filesystem is arranged into a hierarchical structure anchored at the *root directory*, or /. Beneath this is a tree of directories and files.

- Identification information for a filesystem object is stored in its *inode*, which holds location, modification, and security information. Filesystems are created with a finite number of inodes.

File and directory management commands

The following commands are essential for the management of files and directories:

cp file1 file2
cp files directory
> Copy *file1* to *file2*, or copy *files* to *directory*.

mkdir directories
> Create one or more *directories*.

mv source target
> Move or rename files and directories.

rm files
> Delete one or more *files* from the filesystem. When used recursively (with the *-r* option), *rm* also removes directories.

rmdir directories
> Delete *directories*, which must be empty.

touch files
> Change the access and/or modification times of *files* by default to the present time.

File-naming wildcards

Wildcards (also called *file globs*) allow the specification of many files at once. A list of commonly used wildcards can be found in Table 10-3.

Table 10-3. File-naming wildcards

Wildcard	Function
*	Match zero or more characters.
?	Match exactly one character.
[*characters*]	Match any single character from among *characters* listed between brackets.
[!*characters*]	Match any single character other than *characters* listed between brackets.
[*a-z*]	Match any single character from among the range of characters listed between brackets.
[!*a-z*]	Match any single character from among the characters not in the range listed between brackets.
{*frag1,frag2,f rag3*,...}	Brace expansion: create strings *frag1*, *frag2*, and *frag3*, etc., such that file_{one,two,three} yields file_one, file_two, and file_three.

Objective 4: Use Unix Streams, Pipes, and Redirects

Concepts

- A central concept for Linux and Unix systems is that *everything is a file*.
- Many system devices are represented in the filesystem using a *device file*, such as */dev/ttyS0* for a serial port.

Standard I/O

- The shell provides the *standard I/O* capability, offering three default file descriptors to running programs.
- *Standard input* (*stdin*) is a text input stream, by default attached to the keyboard.
- *Standard output* (*stdout*) is an output stream for normal program output.
- *Standard error* (*stderr*) is an additional output stream meant for error messages.

Pipes and redirection

- It is possible to tie the output of one program to the input of another. This is known as a *pipe* and is created by joining commands using the pipe symbol (|).
- Pipes are a special form of *redirection*, which allows you to manage the origin of input streams and the destination of output streams. Redirection syntax for various shells differs slightly. See Table 10-4 for examples of common redirection operators.

Table 10-4. Common redirection operators

Redirection function	Syntax for bash
Send *stdout* to *file*.	`$ cmd > file` `$ cmd 1> file`
Send *stderr* to *file*.	`$ cmd 2> file`
Send both *stdout* and *stderr* to *file*.	`$ cmd > file 2>&1`

Table 10-4. Common redirection operators (continued)

Redirection function	Syntax for bash
Receive *stdin* from *file*.	`$ cmd < file`
Append *stdout* to *file*.	`$ cmd >> file` `$ cmd 1>> file`
Append *stderr* to *file*.	`$ cmd 2>> file`
Append both *stdout* and *stderr* to *file*.	`$ cmd >> file 2>&1`
Pipe *stdout* from *cmd1* to *cmd2*.	`$ cmd1	cmd2`
Pipe *stdout* and *stderr* from *cmd1* to *cmd2*.	`$ cmd1 2>&1	cmd2`
Pipe *stdout* from *cmd1* to *cmd2* while simultaneously writing it to *file1* using *tee*.	`$ cmd1	tee file1	cmd2`

Objective 5: Create, Monitor, and Kill Processes

Concepts

- Processes have:
    - A lifetime.
    - A PID.
    - A UID.
    - A GID.
    - A parent process.
    - An environment.
    - A current working directory.

Monitoring commands

ps
> Generate a one-time snapshot of the current processes on standard output.

pstree
> Display a hierarchical list of processes in a tree format.

top
> Generate a continuous, formatted, real-time process activity display on a terminal or in a terminal window.

Signaling processes

- Processes listen for *signals* sent by the kernel or users using the *kill* command:

    kill *-sigspec* [*pids*]
    Send *sigspec* to *pids*.

- Common *kill* signals are listed in Table 10-5.

Table 10-5. Common signals

Signal	Number	Meaning
HUP	1	Hangup, reread configuration.
INT	2	Interrupt, stop running.
KILL	9	Exit immediately.
TERM	15	Terminate nicely.
TSTP	18	Stop executing.

Shell job control

Shells can run processes in the *background*, where they execute on their own, or in the *foreground*, attached to a terminal. Each process handled in this way is known as a *job*. Jobs are manipulated using job control commands:

bg [jobspec]
> Place *jobspec* in the background as if it had been started with &.

fg [jobspec]
> Place *jobspec* in the foreground, making it the current job.

jobs [jobspecs]
> List *jobspecs* on standard output.

Objective 6: Modify Process Execution Priorities

Concepts

- A process's *execution priority* is managed by the kernel.
- You can bias the execution priority by specifying a *nice number* in the range of -20 to +19 (default is 0).
- Positive nice numbers reduce priority; negative nice numbers increase priority and are reserved for the superuser.

Commands

nice -adjustment [command]
> Apply nice number *adjustment* to the process created to run *command*.

renice [+|-]nicenumber targets
> Alter the *nicenumber*, and thus the scheduling priority, of one or more running *target* processes.

Objective 7: Search Text Files Using Regular Expressions

Concepts

- *Regular expressions* are used to match text. The term is used to describe the loosely defined text-matching language as well as the patterns themselves. A regular expression is often called a *regex* or a *regexp*.
- Regular expressions are made up of *metacharacters* (with special meaning) and *literals* (everything that is not a metacharacter).
- The backslash character (\) turns off (escapes) the special meaning of the character that follows, turning metacharacters into literals. For non-meta-characters, it often turns on some special meaning.

Position anchors

The operators in Table 10-6 match line position.

Table 10-6. Regular expression position anchors

Regular expression	Description
^	Match the beginning of a line.
$	Match the end of a line.
\< \>	Match word boundaries. Word boundaries are defined as whitespace, the start of line, the end of line, or punctuation marks. The backslashes are required and enable this interpretation of < and >.

Character sets

The operators in Table 10-7 match text.

Table 10-7. Regular expression character sets

Regular expression	Description
[abc] [a-z]	Match any single character from among listed characters (abc) or from among the characters comprising a range (a-z).
[^abc] [^a-z]	Match any single character not among listed characters or ranges.
.	Match any single character except a newline.

Modifiers

The operators in Table 10-8 modify the way other operators are interpreted.

Table 10-8. Regular expression modifiers

Basic regular expression	Extended regular expression	Description
*	*	Match zero or more of the character that precedes it.
\?	?	Match zero or one instance of the preceding *regex*.

Table 10-8. Regular expression modifiers (continued)

Basic regular expression	Extended regular expression	Description
\+	+	Match one or more instances of the preceding *regex*.
\{*n*,*m*\}	{*n*,*m*}	Match a range of occurrences of the single character or regex that precedes this construct. \{*n*\} matches *n* occurrences, \{*n*,\} matches at least *n* occurrences, and \{*n*,*m*\} matches any number of occurrences between *n* and *m*, inclusively.
|	|	Match the character or expression to the left or right of the vertical bar.
\(*regex*\)	(*regex*)	Matches *regex*, but it can be modified as a whole and used in back-references. (\1 expands to the contents of the first \(\) and so on up to \9.)

Objective 8: Using vi

Subcommands

- Start *vi* with *vi file1* [*file2* [...]]. See Table 10-9.

Table 10-9. Basic vi editing commands

Command	Description
Esc	Exit insert mode and put the editor back into command mode.
h	Move left one character.
j	Move down one line.
k	Move up one line.
l	Move right one character.
H	Move to the top of the screen.
L	Move to the bottom of the screen.
G	Move to the end of the file.
w	Move forward one word.
b	Move backward one word.
0 (zero)	Move to the beginning of the current line.
^	Move to the first nonwhitespace character on the current line.
$	Move to the end of the current line.
Ctrl-B	Move up (back) one screen.
Ctrl-F	Move down (forward) one screen.
i	Insert at the current cursor position.
I	Insert at the beginning of the current line.
a	Append after the current cursor position.
A	Append to the end of the current line.
o	Start a new line after the current line.
O	Start a new line before the current line.
r	Replace the character at the current cursor position.

Table 10-9. Basic vi editing commands (continued)

Command	Description
R	Start replacing (overwriting) at the current cursor position.
x	Delete the character at the current cursor position.
X	Delete the character immediately before (to the left) of the current cursor position.
s	Delete the character at the current cursor position and go into insert mode. (This is the equivalent of the combination xi.)
S	Delete the contents of the current line and go into insert mode.
d*X*	Given a movement command *X*, cut (delete) the appropriate number of characters, words, or lines from the current cursor position.
dd	Cut the entire current line.
D	Cut from the current cursor position to the end of the line. (This is equivalent to d$.)
c*X*	Given a movement command *X*, cut the appropriate number of characters, words, or lines from the current cursor position and go into insert mode.
cc	Cut the entire current line and go into insert mode.
C	Cut from the current cursor position to the end of the line and enter insert mode. (This is equivalent to c$.)
y*X*	Given a movement command *X*, copy (yank[a]) the appropriate number of characters, words, or lines from the current cursor position.
yy or Y	Copy the entire current line.
p	Paste after the current cursor position.
P	Paste before the current cursor position.
.	Repeat the last command.
u	Undo the last command.[b]
/*regex*	Search forward for *regex*.
?*regex*	Search backward for *regex*.
n	Find the next match.
N	Find the previous match. (In other words, repeat the last search in the opposite direction.)
:n	Next file; when multiple files are specified for editing, this command loads the next file. Force this action (if the current file has unsaved changes) with :n!.
:e *file*	Load *file* in place of the current file. Force this action with :e! *file*.
:r *file*	Insert the contents of *file* after the current cursor position.
:q	Quit without saving changes. Force this action with :q!.
:w *file*	Write the current buffer to *file*. To append to an existing file, use :w >>*file*. Force the write (when possible, such as when running as root) with :w! *file*.
:wq	Write the file contents and quit. Force this action with :wq!.
:x	Write the file contents (if changed) and quit (the ex equivalent of ZZ).
ZZ	Write the file contents (if changed) and quit.
:! *command*	Execute *command* in a subshell.

[a] Emacs users should be careful not to confuse the *vi* definition of *yank* (copy) with that of Emacs (paste).
[b] Many of the popular *vi* implementations support multi-level undo. Vim breaks compatibility with traditional *vi* by making a repeated u perform another level of undo. Nvi uses . after u to do multi-level undo, and, like traditional *vi*, uses a repeated u to redo (undo the undo, so to speak). This can cause some confusion when moving between Linux distributions that have different default implementations of *vi*.

Devices, Linux Filesystems, and the Filesystem Hierarchy Standard

Objective 1: Create Partitions and Filesystems

Disk drives and partitions

- IDE disks are known as */dev/hda*, */dev/hdb*, */dev/hdc*, */dev/hdd*, and so on.
- SCSI disks are known as */dev/sda*, */dev/sdb*, */dev/sdc*, and so on.
- Three types of partitions:

  Primary
  > Filesystem container. At least one must exist, and up to four can exist on a single physical disk. They are identified with numbers 1 to 4, such as */dev/hda1*, */dev/hda2*, and so on.

  Extended
  > A variant of a primary partition, but it cannot contain a filesystem. Instead, it contains one or more *logical partitions*. Only one extended partition may exist, and it takes one of the four possible spots for primary partitions.

  Logical
  > Created *within* the extended partition. From 1 to 12 logical partitions may be created. They are numbered from 5 to 16, such as */dev/hda5*, */dev/hda6*, and so on.

- Up to 15 partitions with filesystems may exist on a single physical disk.

The root filesystem and mount points

- The top of the filesystem tree is occupied by the *root filesystem*. Other filesystems are mounted under it, creating a unified filesystem.
- */etc*, */lib*, */bin*, */sbin*, and */dev* must be part of the root filesystem.

Partition and filesystem management commands

The following commands are commonly used to repair and manage filesystems:

fdisk [device]
> Manipulate or display the partition table for *device* using a command-driven interactive text interface. *device* is a physical disk such as */dev/hda*, not a partition such as */dev/hda1*.

mkfs device
> Make a filesystem on *device*.

mkswap device
> Prepare a partition for use as swap space.

Objective 2: Maintain the Integrity of Filesystems

Filesystem Commands

df [directories]
> Display overall disk utilization information for mounted filesystems on *directories*.

du [directories]
> Display disk utilization information for *directories*.

fsck filesystems
> Check *filesystems* for errors and optionally correct them.

Objective 3: Control Filesystem Mounting and Unmounting

Managing the filesystem table

- */etc/fstab* contains mount information for filesystems. Each line contains a single filesystem entry made up of six fields, shown in Table 10-10.

Table 10-10. Fields found in the /etc/fstab file

Entry	Description
Device	The device file for the partition holding the filesystem.
Mount point	The directory upon which the filesystem is to be mounted.
Filesystem type	A filesystem type, such as *ext2*.
Mount options	A comma-separated list.
Dump frequency	For use with *dump*.
Pass number for fsck	Used at boot time.

Mounting and unmounting

The following commands are used to mount and unmount filesystems:

mount device
mount directory
mount device directory
> Mount filesystems onto the hierarchy. The first and second forms consult */etc/fstab* for additional information.

umount device
umount directory
> Unmount the filesystem on *device* or mount it on *directory*.

Filesystem types

Common filesystem types compatible with Linux include:

ext2
> The standard Linux filesystem.

ext3
> A journalling filesystem that is backwards-compatible with ext2.

iso9660
> The standard CD-ROM format.

vfat
> The Windows FAT filesystem.

nfs
> Remote servers.

proc
> A system abstraction for access to kernel parameters.

swap
> Swap partitions.

Objective 4: Managing Disk Quota

Quota Types

Per-user hard
> The maximum size for an individual.

Per-user soft
> A warning threshold.

Per-group hard
> The maximum size for a group.

Per-group soft
> A warning threshold.

Grace period
> A time restriction on the soft limit.

Commands

quota user

> *quota -g group*
>> Display quota limits on *user* or *group*.

> *quotaon [filesystems]*
>> Enable previously configured disk quotas on one or more *filesystems*.

> *quotaoff [filesystems]*
>> Disable disk quotas on one or more *filesystems*.

quotacheck [filesystems]
Examine filesystems and compile quota databases. Usually run via cron.

edquota names
Modify user or group quotas by spawning a text editor.

repquota filesystems
Display a summary report of quota status for *filesystems*, or use *-a* for all filesystems:

Enabling quotas requires usrquota and/or grpquota options in */etc/ fstab*, creation of *quota.user* and *quota.group* files at the top of the filesystem, a *quotacheck*, and a *quotaon*.

Objective 5: Use File Permissions to Control Access to Files

Access control

- Access control is implemented using a set of properties called the *access mode*, stored in the inode. Three classes of user are defined:

User
The user that owns the file.

Group
The group that owns the file.

Other
All other users on the system.

- Three permissions are either granted or not granted to each class of user:

Read (r)
Allows access to file contents and listing of directory contents.

Write (w)
Allows writing a file or creating files in a directory.

Execute (x)
Allows execution of a file and read/write files in a directory.

- These comprise nine bits in the mode User rwx, Group rwx, and Other rwx.
- Three additional mode bits are defined:

SUID
To grant processes the rights of an executable file's owner.

SGID
To grant processes the rights of an executable file's group.

Sticky bit
Prohibits file deletion by non-owners.

- These 12-mode bits are often referred to in octal notation as well as with mnemonic constructs.
- Mode bits are displayed using such commands as *ls* and *stat*.

Setting access modes

- New files receive initial access mode as described by the *umask*.
- The *umask* strips specified bits from the initial mode settings. Typical umasks are 002 and 022.
- Existing file modes are changed using *chmod* with either symbolic or octal mode specifications:
    - Symbolic:

        ```
        [ugoa][-+=][rwxXst]
        ```
    - Octal bits:

        ```
        user r, w, x, group r, w, x, other r, w, x
        rwxrwxrwx = 111111111 = 777
        rwxr-xr-- = 111101100 = 751
        ```

chmod uses the following syntax:

chmod mode files
> Modify the access mode on *files* using a symbolic or octal *mode*.

Objective 6: Manage File Ownership

Concepts

- Access modes are tied to file ownership.
- Files have both individual and group ownership.

Commands

chown user-owner.group-owner files
> Change the owner and/or group of *files* to *user-owner* and/or *group-owner*.

chgrp group-owner files
> Change the group ownership of *files* to *group-owner*.
>
> *chgrp* functionality is included in *chown*.

Objective 7: Create and Change Hard and Symbolic Links

Concepts

- A link is a pseudonym for another file.
- Links take very little space in the filesystem.
- A *symbolic link* is a tiny file that contains a pointer to another file. Symbolic links can span filesystems.
- A *hard link* is a copy of a file's directory entry. Both directory entries point to the same inode and thus the same data, ownership, and permissions.

ln has the following syntax:

```
ln file link
ln files directory
```

Create *link* to *file* or in *directory* for all *files*. Symbolic links are created with the *-s* option.

Objective 8: Find System Files and Place Files in the Correct Location

File Hierarchy Standard (FHS)

- The FHS is used by Linux distributions to standardize filesystem layout. It defines two categories of data use, each with opposing subtypes:

  Data sharing
  > Sharable data can be used by multiple host systems on a network. Non-sharable data is unique to one particular host system.

  Data modification
  > Variable data is changed continually by naturally occurring (i.e., frequent) processes. Static data is left alone, remaining unchanged over extended periods of time.

- The FHS seeks to define the filesystem contents in these terms and locate information accordingly.

The directory hierarchy

- The root filesystem:
  - Must contain utilities and files sufficient to boot the operating system, including the ability to mount other filesystems.
  - Should contain the utilities needed by the system administrator to repair or restore a damaged system.
  - Should be relatively small.
- */usr* contains system utilities and programs that do not appear in the / (root) filesystem. It includes directories such as *bin*, *lib*, *local*, and *src*.
- */var* contains varying data such as printer spools and log files, including directories such as *log*, *mail*, and *spool*.

Locating files

- Various methods can be used to locate files in the filesystem:

  which command
  > Determine the location of *command* and display the full pathname of the executable program that the shell would launch to execute it.

  find paths expression
  > Search for files that match *expression* starting at *paths* and continuing recursively.

locate patterns

    Locate files whose names match one or more *patterns* by searching an index of files previously created.

updatedb

    Refresh (or create) the *slocate* database, usually via *cron*.

whatis keywords

apropos keywords

    Search the *whatis* database for *keywords*. *whatis* finds only exact matches, while *apropos* finds partial word matches.

The X Window System

- X is a client-server GUI system. XFree86 is the X implementation used on Linux.
- An X server is software or hardware that renders graphical output on a display device.
- An X client is software whose output is displayed by an X server and is usually managed by a window manager.
- An X window manager is a client that applies frames and controls to other client windows.

Objective 1: Install and Configure X11

Selecting and configuring an X server

- XFree86 configuration depends on the software version, the video chipset in use, and the monitor's capabilities.
- XFree86 can be installed from Linux distribution packages (*.rpm*, *.deb*), precompiled binaries, or compiled from source.
- Configuration of XFree86 is done in the *XF86Config* file.
- *XF86Config* contains sections that define input devices, monitors, graphics modes, and so on.
- *XF86Config* files differ between XFree86 Versions 3.x and 4.x.

X fonts

- The X server uses X fonts to satisfy font requests from X clients.
- Fonts are enumerated either through a static list presented in */etc/X11/XF86Config* or through a *font server* such as *xfs*.
- *xfs* is configured using its configuration file, */etc/X11/fs/config*.

.Xresources

- X resource settings in the *.Xresources* file control client program parameters. For example, this line defines a black background for an *xterm*:

  ```
  xterm*background: Black
  ```

Objective 2: Setup A Display Manager

xdm

- *xdm*, the X Display Manager, handles X sessions on physical displays both locally and across the network.
- *xdm* handles authentication.
- *xdm* is configured by a series of files in */etc/X11/xdm*.
- *xdm* is typically started automatically in runlevel 5 by making the appropriate settings in */etc/inittab*.
- *xdm* may be personalized by changing the resources in */etc/X11/xdm/ Xresources*.
- Command-line options for the X server can be added to the */etc/X11/xdm/ Xservers* file.

X terminals

- X terminals, are low-cost hardware systems that implement an X server and display.
- *xdm* can listen for inbound connection requests from X terminals using the *xdmcp* protocol.
- Specific access rules for X terminals to the *xdm* daemon can be configured in */etc/X11/xdm/Xaccess*.

Objective 4: Install and Customize a Window Manager Environment

Concepts

- An X server doesn't supply a working user environment.
- Starting X usually involves launching not only the X server but also a window manager and other clients.
- A default window manager, such as the basic *twm*, is started by a combination of the *startx* script and *xinit*.
- *xinit* also calls scripts that include a window manager and default clients.
- Default system X configuration can be overridden by files in the user's home directory.

Window managers

- Each window manager and desktop environment has its own style of configuration.
- *twm* uses *.twmrc* in the user's home directory. If that file doesn't exist, it uses the system-wide */etc/X11/twm/system.twmrc*.
- Window manager configuration files can contain font and color selections, bindings between actions (such as mouse clicks) and responses, and menu definitions.

xterm

- A *terminal emulator* is a program that offers a command-line interface in a GUI window.
- *xterm* is the standard terminal emulator; there are many others.
- *xterm* can be configured in */usr/lib/X11/app-defaults/XTerm*.

X libraries

- X applications are dependent upon shared X libraries.
- Various graphical toolkits such as GTK or Qt can be used to develop X client applications.
- Software that depends on a particular library will not run unless that library is installed.
- You can determine which libraries an executable requires with ldd.

Remote X clients

- X clients can be displayed on remote X servers.
- The DISPLAY environment variable is used to indicate the destination for X client displays.
- DISPLAY has the format [*host*]:*display*[.*screen*] where *host* is a remote hostname or IP address, *display* is the display target (starting with 0), and *screen* is the screen to use on multiheaded displays.
- DISPLAY must be exported.

II

General Linux Exam 102

Part 2 covers the Topics and Objectives for the LPI's General Linux Certification for Exam 102 and includes the following sections:

11

Exam 102 Overview

LPI Exam 102 is the second of two exams required for the LPI's Level 1 certification. This exam tests your knowledge on 9 of the 14 major Topic areas specified for LPIC Level 1.

Each Topic contains a series of Objectives covering specific areas of expertise. Each of these Objectives is assigned a numeric weight, which acts as an indicator of the importance of the Objective. Weights run between 1 and 8, with higher numbers indicating more importance. An Objective carrying a weight of 1 can be considered relatively unimportant and isn't likely to be covered in much depth on the exam. Objectives with larger weights are sure to be covered on the exam, so you should study these Topics closely. The weights of the Objectives are provided at the beginning of each Topic section.

Exam Topics are numbered using a *level.topic* notation (e.g., 1.101, 1.102, 1.113). In LPI's early stages of development, Topics were assigned to exams based on a different scheme from what we see today. When the scheme changed, the Topics were redistributed to Exams 101 and 102, but the pairing of Topic numbers to exams was dropped. As a result, 1.x and 2.x Topics appeared in both Level 1 exams. In the 2002 revision of the Objectives, LPI decided to reformat the numbering scheme to be more scalable for its multiple levels of certifications. Therefore, the exams now use an *x.y.z* numbering scheme where *x* equals the LPIC level (e.g., 1 or 2), *y* equals the Objective Topic (e.g., 101, 102, 201, 202) which are unique to all levels of LPI exams, and *z* equals the Objective number within the Topic area (e.g., 1, 2, 3, 4, and so on).

The Level 1 Topics are distributed between the two exams to create tests of similar length and difficulty without subject matter overlap. As a result, there's no requirement or advantage to taking the exams in sequence.

The Topics for Exam 102 are listed in Table 11-1.

Table 11-1. LPI Topics for Exam 102

Name	Number of objectives	Description
Kernel	2	Covers kernel module management, as well as building and installing a custom kernel.
Boot, Initialization, Shut-down, and Runlevels	2	Covers details for when you boot, reboot, or change runlevels on a Linux system.
Printing	3	Covers all aspects of printing, including configuring local and remote printers, managing the print queues, and printing files.
Documentation	3	Covers documentation including using local system docu-mentation, using online documentation, and using docu-mentation to work with system users.
Shells, Scripting, Program-ming, and Compiling	2	Covers the shell and its startup files and writing bash scripts. Despite the name, compiling programs from source is not included (it's covered in Topic 1.102).
Administrative Tasks	6	Covers all of the basic administrative tasks done by a junior level Linux sysadmin, including managing users and groups, user and system environment variables, system logs, job scheduling, data backup, and system time.
Networking Fundamentals	3	Explores TCP/IP, network interfaces, DHCP, and PPP; includes troubleshooting commands.
Networking Services	6	Covers network-related applications and services such as inetd as well as basic Sendmail, Apache, NFS, Samba, DNS, and OpenSSH configuration.
Security	3	Covers security issues such as package verification, SUID issues, shadow passwords, iptables, and user limits.

Exam 102 lasts a maximum of 90 minutes and contains approximately 73 ques-tions. The exam is administered using a custom application on a PC in a private room with no notes or other reference material. The majority of the exam is made up of multiple-choice single-answer questions. These questions have only one correct answer and are answered using radio buttons. A few of the questions present a scenario needing administrative action. Others seek the appropriate commands for performing a particular task or for proof of understanding of a particular concept.

The exam also includes a few multiple-choice multiple-answer questions, which are answered using checkboxes. These questions can have multiple correct responses, each of which must be checked. These are probably the most difficult type of question to answer because the possibility of multiple answers increases the likelihood of mistakes. An incorrect response on any one of the possible answers causes you to miss the entire question.

The exam also has some fill-in-the-blank questions. These questions provide a one-line text area input box for you to fill in your answer. These questions check your knowledge of concepts such as important files, commands, or well-known facts that you are expected to know.

12

Exam 102 Study Guide

Part II of this book contains a section for each of the nine Topics found on Exam 102 for LPIC Level 1 certification. Each of the following nine chapters details the Objectives described for the corresponding Topic on the LPI web site, *http://www.lpi.org/en/obj_102.html*.

Exam Preparation

LPI Exam 102 is thorough, but if you have a solid foundation in Linux concepts as described here, you should find it straightforward. If you've already taken Exam 101, you'll find that 102 covers a broader range of Linux administration skills. Included are kernel tasks, boot and system initialization, printing, documentation, shells and scripting, administrative tasks, networking fundamentals, networking services, and security. Exam 102 is quite specific on some Topics, such as network applications like Apache and Sendmail, but you won't come across questions intended to trick you, and you're unlikely to find questions that you feel are ambiguous.

For clarity, this material is presented in the same order as the LPI Topics and Objectives. To assist you with your preparation, Tables 12-1 through 12-9 provide a complete listing of the Topics and Objectives for Exam 102. Because of changes made during test development, the final Objectives are not always in exact numberical order. After you complete your study of each Objective, simply check it off here to measure and organize your progress.

Table 12-1. Kernel (Topic 1.105)

Objective	Weight	Description
1	4	Manage/Query Kernel and Kernel Modules at Runtime
2	3	Reconfigure, Build, and Install a Custom Kernel and Kernel Modules

Table 12-2. Boot, Initialization, Shutdown, and Runlevels (Topic 1.106)

Objective	Weight	Description
1	3	Boot the System
2	3	Change Runlevels and Shut Down or Reboot System

Table 12-3. Printing (Topic 1.107)

Objective	Weight	Description
2	1	Manage Printers and Print Queues
3	1	Print Files
4	1	Install and Configure Local and Remote Printers

Table 12-4. Documentation (Topic 1.108)

Objective	Weight	Description
1	4	Use and Manage Local System Documentation
2	3	Find Linux Documentation on the Internet
5	1	Notify Users on System-related Issues

Table 12-5. Shells, Scripting, Programming, and Compiling (Topic 1.109)

Objective	Weight	Description
1	5	Customize and Use the Shell Environment
2	3	Customize or Write Simple Scripts

Table 12-6. Administrative Tasks (Topic 1.111)

Objective	Weight	Description
1	4	Manage Users and Group Accounts and Related System Files
2	3	Tune the User Environment and System Environment Variables
3	3	Configure and Use System Log Files to Meet Administrative and Security Needs
4	4	Automate System Administration Tasks by Scheduling Jobs to Run in the Future
5	3	Maintain an Effective Data Backup Strategy
6	4	Maintain System Time

Table 12-7. Networking Fundamentals (Topic 1.112)

Objective	Weight	Description
1	4	Fundamentals of TCP/IP
3	7	TCP/IP Configuration and Troubleshooting
4	3	Configure Linux as a PPP Client

Table 12-8. Networking Services (Topic 1.113)

Objective	Weight	Description
1	4	Configure and Manage `inetd`, `xinetd`, and Related Services
2	4	Operate and Perform Basic Configuration of Mail Transfer Agent (MTA)
3	4	Operate and Perform Basic Configuration of Apache
4	4	Properly Manage the NFS, and Samba Daemons
5	4	Set Up and Configure Basic DNS Services
7	4	Set Up Secure Shell (OpenSSH)

Table 12-9. Security (Topic 1.114)

Objective	Weight	Description
1	4	Perform Security Administration Tasks
2	3	Set Up Host Security
3	1	Set Up User-level Security

13

Kernel (Topic 1.105)

In the early days of personal computing, operating systems were simple interfaces, designed to provide access to a rudimentary filesystem and to launch programs. Once a program was running, it had full control of the system. This made the system simple but also contributed to instability, because a single program failure could cause the entire system to crash. To run a computer in an organized and reliable fashion, it is important to isolate physical hardware resources from the software running on the system. In Linux, the *kernel* is the core software that owns and manages your system. It controls hardware, memory, and process scheduling and provides an interface for programs to indirectly access hardware resources.

This Topic on the Linux kernel has two Objectives:

Objective 1: Manage/Query Kernel and Kernel Modules at Runtime
This Objectives states that candidates should be able to manage and query a kernel and its loadable modules. This Objective includes using command-line utilities to get information about a running kernel and kernel modules. It also includes manually loading and unloading modules as appropriate. In addition, a candidate should be able to determine what parameters a module accepts. Weight: 4.

Objective 2: Reconfigure, Build, and Install a Custom Kernel and Kernel Modules
A candidate should be able to customize, build, and install a kernel and kernel modules from source. This Objective includes customizing the current kernel configuration, building a new kernel, and building kernel modules as appropriate. It also includes installing the new kernel and modules and ensuring that the boot manager can locate the new kernel and associated files. Weight: 3.

Objective 1: Manage/Query Kernel and Kernel Modules at Runtime

With Linux, code for system devices can be compiled into the kernel. Because the kernel already has built-in support for most devices, it is said to be *monolithic*, since the kernel manages all system hardware by itself. Monolithic kernels aren't very flexible because a new kernel build is necessary for new peripheral devices to be added to the system. Monolithic kernels also have the potential to become "bloated" by drivers for hardware that aren't physically installed. Instead, most users run *modular* kernels, in which device drivers are inserted into the running kernel as needed. Modular configurations can adapt to changes in the hardware and provide a convenient way of upgrading driver software while a system is running.

Module Files

Linux kernel modules are object files (*.o*) produced by the C compiler but not linked into a completed executable (in this case, the kernel executable file). Most modules are distributed with the kernel and compiled along with it. Because they are so closely related to the kernel, separate sets of modules are installed when multiple kernels are installed. This reduces the likelihood that a kernel module will be inserted into the wrong kernel version.

Modules are stored in */lib/modules/kernel-version*, where `kernel-version` is the string reported by *uname -r*, such as `2.4.18-10`. In this example, the modules directory would be */lib/modules/2.4.18-10*. Multiple module hierarchies may be available under */lib/modules* if multiple kernels are installed. Within each *kernel-version* hierarchy is a *kernel* subdirectory that contains the kernel modules, sorted into additional subdirectories by category.

 The path to these additional *category subdirectories* changed for the 2.4 kernel series to include a *kernel* subdirectory to contain all the categories. Prior to 2.4, all of the category subdirectories were located directly under */lib/modules/kernel-version*.

Some of the categories are:

block
> Modules for a few block-specific devices such as RAID controllers or IDE tape drives.

cdrom
> Device driver modules for nonstandard CD-ROM devices.

fs

> Device drivers for filesystems such as MS-DOS (the *msdos.o* module).

ipv4
> Kernel features having to do with TCP/IP networking, such as the Netfilter firewall modules.

misc

Anything that doesn't fit into one of the other subdirectories ends up here. Note that no modules are stored at the top of this tree.

net

Network interface driver modules.

scsi

Driver modules for the SCSI controller.

video

Driver modules for video adapters.

Manipulating Modules

A module is dynamically linked into the running kernel when it is loaded. Much of Linux kernel module handling is done automatically. However, there may be times when it is necessary for you to manipulate the modules yourself, and you may come across the manipulation commands in scripts. For example, if you're having difficulty with a particular driver, you may need to get the source code for a newer version of the driver, compile it, and insert the new module in the running kernel. The commands listed in this section can be used to list, insert, remove, and query modules.

lsmod

Syntax

```
lsmod
```

Description

For each kernel module loaded, display its name, size, use count, and a list of other referring modules. This command yields the same information as is available in */proc/modules*.

Example

Here, *lsmod* shows that quite a few kernel modules are loaded, including filesystem (*vfat*, *fat*), networking (*3c59x*), and sound (*soundcore*, *mpu401*, etc.) modules, among others:

```
# lsmod
Module            Size  Used by
radeon          112996  24
agpgart          45824  3
parport_pc       18756  1 (autoclean)
lp                8868  0 (autoclean)
parport          36480  1 (autoclean) [parport_pc lp]
e100             59428  1
ohci1394         19976  0 (unused)
ieee1394         48300  0 [ohci1394]
scsi_mod        106168  0
evdev             5696  0 (unused)
```

```
printer           8832   0
wacom             7896   0 (unused)
emu10k1          68104   1
ac97_codec       13512   0 [emu10k1]
sound            73044   0 [emu10k1]
soundcore         6276   7 [emu10k1 sound]
keybdev           2912   0 (unused)
mousedev          5428   1
hid              21700   0 (unused)
input             5824   0 [evdev wacom keybdev mousedev hid]
ehci-hcd         19432   0 (unused)
usb-uhci         25964   0 (unused)
usbcore          77760   1 [printer wacom hid ehci-hcd usb-uhci]
ext3             87240   3
jbd              51156   3 [ext3]
```

insmod

Syntax

insmod [*options*] *module*

Description

Insert a module into the running kernel. The module is located automatically and inserted. You must be logged in as the superuser to insert modules.

Frequently used options

-*s*

Direct output to syslog instead of stdout.

-*v*

Set verbose mode.

Example

The *msdos* filesystem module is installed into the running kernel. In this example, the kernel was compiled with modular support for the *msdos* filesystem type, a typical configuration for a Linux distribution for i386 hardware. To verify that you have this module, check for the existence of */lib/modules/kernel-version/fs/msdos.o*:

```
# insmod msdos
/lib/modules/2.2.5-15smp/fs/msdos.o: unresolved symbol fat_add_cluster_Rsmp_
eb84f594
/lib/modules/2.2.5-15smp/fs/msdos.o: unresolved symbol fat_cache_inval_
inode_Rsmp_6da1654e
/lib/modules/2.2.5-15smp/fs/msdos.o: unresolved symbol fat_scan_Rsmp_
d61c58c7
   ( ... additional errors omitted ... )
/lib/modules/2.2.5-15smp/fs/msdos.o: unresolved symbol fat_date_unix2dos_
Rsmp_83fb36a1
# echo $?
1
```

This *insmod msdos* command yields a series of unresolved symbol messages and an exit status of 1, indicating an error. This is the same sort of message that might be seen when attempting to link a program that referenced variables or functions unavailable to the linker. In the context of a module insertion, such messages indicate that the functions are not available in the kernel. From the names of the missing symbols, you can see that the *fat* module is required to support the *msdos* module, so it is inserted first:

```
# insmod fat
```

Now the *msdos* module can be loaded:

```
# insmod msdos
```

Use the *modprobe* command to automatically determine these dependencies and install prerequisite modules first.

rmmod

Syntax

```
rmmod [options] modules
```

Description

The *rmmod* command is used to remove modules from the running kernel. You must be logged in as the superuser to remove modules, and the command will fail if the module is in use or being referred to by another module.

Frequently used options

-a

Remove all unused modules.

-s

Direct output to syslog instead of stdout.

Example

Starting with both the *fat* and *msdos* modules loaded, remove the *fat* module (which is used by the *msdos* module):

```
# lsmod
Module                  Size   Used by
msdos                   8348   0  (unused)
fat                    25856   0  [msdos]
# rmmod fat
rmmod: fat is in use
```

In this example, the *lsmod* command fails because the *msdos* module is dependent on the *fat* module. So, to unload the *fat* module, the *msdos* module must be unloaded first:

```
# rmmod msdos
# rmmod fat
```

The *modprobe -r* command can be used to automatically determine these dependencies and remove modules and their prerequisites.

modinfo

Syntax

modinfo [*options*] *module_object_file*

Description

Display information about a module from its *module_object_file*. Some modules contain no information at all, some have a short one-line description, and others have a fairly descriptive message.

Options

-a

Display the module's author.

-d

Display the module's description.

-p

Display the typed parameters that a module supports.

Examples

In these examples, *modinfo* is run using modules compiled for a multiprocessing (SMP) kernel Version 2.2.5. Your kernel version, and thus the directory hierarchy containing modules, will be different.

```
# modinfo -d /lib/modules/2.2.5-15smp/misc/zftape.o
zftape for ftape v3.04d 25/11/97 - VFS interface for the
        Linux floppy tape driver. Support for QIC-113
        compatible volume table and builtin compression
        (lzrw3 algorithm)
# modinfo -a /lib/modules/2.2.5-15smp/misc/zftape.o
(c) 1996, 1997 Claus-Justus Heine
        (claus@momo.math.rwth-aachen.de)
# modinfo -p /lib/modules/2.2.5-15smp/misc/ftape.o
ft_fdc_base int, description "Base address of FDC
        controller."
Ft_fdc_irq int, description "IRQ (interrupt channel)
        to use."
ft_fdc_dma int, description "DMA channel to use."
ft_fdc_threshold int, description "Threshold of the FDC
        Fifo."
Ft_fdc_rate_limit int, description "Maximal data rate
        for FDC."
ft_probe_fc10 int, description "If non-zero, probe for a
        Colorado FC-10/FC-20 controller."
ft_mach2 int, description "If non-zero, probe for a
        Mountain MACH-2 controller."
ft_tracing int, description "Amount of debugging output,
        0 <= tracing <= 8, default 3."
```

Kernel

modprobe

Syntax

```
modprobe [options] module [symbol=value ...]
```

Description

Like *insmod*, *modprobe* is used to insert modules. In fact, *modprobe* is a wrapper around *insmod* and provides additional functionality. In addition to loading single modules, *modprobe* has the ability to load modules along with their prerequisites or all modules stored in a specific directory. The *modprobe* command can also remove modules when combined with the *-r* option.

A module is inserted with optional `symbol=value` parameters (see "Configuring Modules" in the next section for more on parameters). If the module is dependent upon other modules, they will be loaded first. The *modprobe* command determines prerequisite relationships between modules by reading *modules.dep* at the top of the module directory hierarchy (i.e., */lib/modules/2.2.5-15smp/modules.dep*).

You must be logged in as the superuser to insert modules.

Frequently used options

-a

> Load all modules. When used with the *-t moduletype*, *all* is restricted to modules in the *moduletype* directory. This action probes hardware by successive module-insertion attempts for a single type of hardware, such as a network adapter (in which case the *moduletype* would be net, representing */lib/modules/kernel-version/kernel/net*). This may be necessary, for example, to probe for more than one kind of network interface.

-c

> Display a complete module configuration, including defaults and directives found in */etc/modules.conf* (or */etc/conf.modules* on older systems). The -c option is not used with any other options.

-l

> List modules. When used with the *-t moduletype*, list only modules in directory *moduletype*. For example, if *moduletype* is net, then modules in */lib/modules/kernel-version/net* are displayed.

-r

> Remove *module*, similar to *rmmod*. Multiple modules may be specified.

-s

> Direct output to syslog instead of stdout.

-t moduletype

> Attempt to load multiple modules found in the directory *moduletype* until a module succeeds or all modules in *moduletype* are exhausted. This action "probes" hardware by successive module-insertion attempts for a single type of hardware, such as a network adapter (in which case *moduletype* would be net, representing */lib/modules/kernel-version/kernel/net*).

-v

> Set verbose mode.

Example 1

Install the *msdos* filesystem module into the running kernel:

```
# modprobe msdos
```

Module *msdos* and its dependency, *fat*, will be loaded. *modprobe* determines that *fat* is needed by *msdos* when it looks through *modules.dep*. You can see the dependency listing using grep:

```
# grep /msdos.o: /lib/modules/2.2.5-15smp/modules.dep
/lib/modules/2.2.5-15smp/fs/msdos.o:
        /lib/modules/2.2.5-15smp/fs/fat.o
```

Example 2

Remove *fat* and *msdos* modules from the running kernel, assuming *msdos* is not in use:

```
# modprobe -r fat msdos
```

Example 3

Attempt to load available network modules until one succeeds:

```
# modprobe -t net
```

Example 4

Attempt to load all available network modules:

```
# modprobe -at net
```

Example 5

List all modules available for use:

```
# modprobe -l
/lib/modules/2.2.5-15smp/fs/vfat.o
/lib/modules/2.2.5-15smp/fs/umsdos.o
/lib/modules/2.2.5-15smp/fs/ufs.o
...
```

Example 6

List all modules in the *net* directory for 3Com network interfaces:

```
# modprobe -lt net | grep 3c
/lib/modules/2.2.5-15smp/net/3c59x.o
/lib/modules/2.2.5-15smp/net/3c515.o
/lib/modules/2.2.5-15smp/net/3c509.o
/lib/modules/2.2.5-15smp/net/3c507.o
/lib/modules/2.2.5-15smp/net/3c505.o
/lib/modules/2.2.5-15smp/net/3c503.o
/lib/modules/2.2.5-15smp/net/3c501.o
```

Configuring Modules

You may sometimes need to control elements of a module such as hardware interrupt assignments or Direct Memory Access (DMA) channel selections. Other situations may dictate special procedures to prepare for, or clean up after, a module insertion or removal. This special control of modules is implemented in the configuration file */etc/modules.conf*, which controls the behavior of *modprobe*. The */etc/modules.conf* file can contain the following information:

Comments
> Blank lines and lines beginning with # are ignored.

keep
> The keep parameter, when found before any path directives, causes the default paths to be retained and added to any paths specified.

depfile=*full_path*
> This directive overrides the default location for the module dependency file, *modules.dep* (described in the next section). For example:
>
>   depfile=/lib/modules/2.2.14/modules.dep

path=*path_directory*
> This directive specifies a directory to search for modules.

options *module opt1=val1 opt2=val2 ...*
> Options for modules can be specified using the options configuration line in *modules.conf* or on the *modprobe* command line. The command line overrides configurations in the file. *module* is the name of a single module without the *.so* extension. Options are specified as *name=value* pairs, where the *name* is understood by the module and reported using *modinfo -p*. For example:
>
>   options opl3 io=0x388

alias
> Aliases can be used to associate a generic name with a specific module. For example:
>
>   alias scsi_hostadapter aic7xxx
>   alias eth0 3c59x
>   alias parport_lowlevel parport_pc

pre-install *module command*
> This directive causes some shell *command* to be executed prior to insertion of *module*. For example, PCMCIA services need to be started prior to installing the *pcmcia_core* module:
>
>   pre-install pcmcia_core /etc/rc.d/init.d/pcmcia start

install *module command*
> This directive allows a specific shell *command* to override the default module-insertion command.

post-install *module*
> This directive causes some shell *command* to be executed after insertion of *module*.

pre-remove *module*

    This directive causes some shell *command* to be executed prior to removal of *module*.

remove *module*

    This directive allows a specific shell *command* to override the default module-removal command.

post-remove *module*

    This directive causes some shell *command* to be executed after removal of *module*.

The following is an example of the */etc/modules.conf* file:

```
alias scsi_hostadapter aic7xxx
alias eth0 3c59x
alias parport_lowlevel parport_pc
pre-install pcmcia_core /etc/rc.d/init.d/pcmcia start
alias sound opl3sa2
pre-install sound insmod sound dmabuf=1
alias midi opl3
options opl3 io=0x388
options opl3sa2 mss_io=0x530 irq=5 dma=0 dma2=1
        mpu_io=0x388 io=0x370
```

Kernel

On the Exam

While it is important for you to understand the configuration lines in */etc/modules.conf*, detailed module configuration is beyond the scope of the LPIC Level 1 Exams.

Module Dependency File

modprobe can determine module dependencies and install prerequisite modules automatically. To do this, *modprobe* scans the first column of */lib/modules/kernel-version/modules.dep* to find the module it is to install. Lines in *modules.dep* are in the following form:

```
module_name.o: dependency1 dependency2 ...
```

A typical dependency looks like this:

```
/lib/modules/2.2.5-15smp/fs/msdos.o:
        /lib/modules/2.2.5-15smp/fs/fat.o
```

Here, the *msdos* module is dependent upon *fat*.

All of the modules available on the system are listed in the *modules.dep* file and are referred to with their full path and filenames, including their *.o* extension. Those that are not dependent on other modules are also listed, but without dependencies. Dependencies that are listed are inserted into the kernel by *modprobe* first, and when all of them are successfully inserted, the subject module itself can be loaded.

The *modules.dep* file must be kept current to ensure the correct operation of *modprobe*. If module dependencies were to change without a corresponding modification to *modules.dep*, then *modprobe* may fail, because a dependency could be missed. As a result, *modules.dep* is created each time the system is booted. On most distributions, the *depmod -a* command is called during *rc.sysinit*:

```
echo "Finding module dependencies"
/sbin/depmod -a
```

The *depmod -a* command re-creates and overwrites *modules.dep* each time the system is booted. This procedure is also necessary after any change in module dependencies. (The *depmod* command is actually a link to the same executable as *modprobe*. The functionality of the command differs depending on which name is used to call it.)

On the Exam

Be sure you know what is in *modules.dep*, as well as what the file is used for, how it is created, and when it is created. Be prepared to cite the consequences of a missing or obsolete *modules.dep* file.

Objective 2: Reconfigure, Build, and Install a Custom Kernel and Kernel Modules

Because Linux is an open source operating system, you are free to create a customized Linux kernel that suits your specific needs and hardware. For example, you may wish to create a kernel for your system if your distribution installed a generic kernel that was compiled using the 80386 instruction set. Such a kernel will run on any compatible processor but may not utilize some of the capabilities of newer processors. Running a kernel optimized for your particular CPU can enhance its performance.

You can also install new kernels to add features, fix bugs, or experiment with kernels still under development. While the compilation of such kernels isn't much of a leap beyond recompiling your existing version, it's beyond the scope of the LPIC Level 1 Exams.

Kernel Background

If you are new to the idea of building a custom kernel, don't feel intimidated. Linux developers have created a simple and reliable process that you can follow, and everything you need is available in your Linux distribution.

Kernel versions

Nearly all software projects, even small ones, use a numerical version scheme to describe each successive release. Kernel versions are numbered using the following convention:

`major.minor.patchlevel`

Major release

Increments in the major release indicate major developmental milestones in the kernel. The present release is 2.6.13 (don't let the low major release number fool you—there have been plenty of developmental milestones in the Linux kernel's history).

Minor release

The minor release indicates significant changes and additions, which taken together will culminate in a new major release. The Linux kernel minor release numbers used to fall into one of the following categories:

Even-numbered releases

Kernels with even-numbered kernel versions (2.0, 2.2, 2.4, and so on) were considered stable.

Odd-numbered releases

Kernels with odd-numbered minor release versions (2.1, 2.3, 2.5, and so on) were in development and were primarily used by kernel developers. Currently, however, development continues on 2.6 and there is no 2.7.

Patch level

As bugs are found and corrected or as planned features are added, the kernel patch level is incremented (2.2.15, 2.3.38, 2.4.18, and so on). Generally speaking, it is safest to run the latest patch level of the kernel to be assured of having the most current bug fixes. In reality, it is more important to track kernel development and upgrade your kernel only if your existing version is found to have a serious problem or if you are already experiencing difficulty.

Required tools and software

To compile a custom kernel, you need development tools including a C compiler, assembler, linker, and the *make* utility. If you selected a kernel development option when you installed Linux, you should already have these tools on your system. The C compiler is the program that translates C source code into the binary form used by your system. The standard compiler on most Linux systems is the GNU C Compiler, *gcc*. The assembler and linker are needed for some portions of the kernel compilation.

The compilation process is controlled by *make*, a utility that executes commands such as *gcc* as directed by a list of dependency rules. These rules are stored in the *Makefile*. A brief introduction to *make* was provided in Chapter 4.

Of course, you also need the kernel source code. The stock kernel source can be found at *ftp://ftp.kernel.org/pub/linux/kernel*. In addition, most distributions come with a kernel source package (usually named *kernel-source* or something similarly descriptive).

The kernel's source code can be found in */usr/src/linux-kernel-version* on most systems. For example, here is the */usr/src* directory for a system with several kernel versions:

```
# ls -l /usr/src
drwxr-xr-x 15 root  root    1024  Jan 29 01:13 linux-2.2.14
drwxr-xr-x 17 root  root    1024  Feb 16 03:00 linux-2.2.5
drwxr-xr-x 14 root  root    1024  Feb 16 04:35 linux-2.3.45
```

On the Exam

Explore the kernel source tree to familiarize yourself with its contents. Pay particular attention to *.config* and the *Makefile*.

Compiling a Custom Kernel

This section provides an overview of kernel compilation and installation by way of example. This example uses kernel Version 2.2.5, and our objective is to create a single-processor kernel for a Pentium system with IDE disks to replace a generic kernel that came with the distribution. (A system that boots from a SCSI disk and has the SCSI driver compiled as a module requires the use of an *initrd* [initial RAM disk], which is not covered here.)

Assume that the development environment—including compiler, *make*, kernel source code, and kernel headers—is installed. The *root* user will be used to create and install the kernel, although any user can compile a kernel; however, like most tasks on a Linux system, it is best to avoid doing things as *root*.

Creating a kernel configuration

The first step in creating a kernel is configuration. There are more than 500 options for the kernel, such as filesystem, SCSI, and networking support. Many of the options list kernel features that can be either compiled directly into the kernel or compiled as modules. During configuration, you indicate for each option whether you:

- Want that feature compiled into the kernel (yes response)
- Want that feature compiled as a module (module response)
- Don't want the feature at all (no response)

Some selections imply a group of other selections. For example, when you indicate that you wish to include SCSI support, additional options become available for specific SCSI drivers and features. The results from all of these choices are stored in the kernel configuration file *.config*, which is a plain text file that lists the options as shell variables set to y, m, or n in accordance with your response for each item.

There are several ways to set up *.config*. Although you can do so, you should not edit the file manually. Instead, you may select from three interactive approaches.

An additional option is available to construct a default configuration. Each is started using *make*. The options presented in each case are the same, as is the outcome.

make config

Syntax

```
make config
```

Description

Running *make config* is the most rudimentary of the automated kernel configuration methods and does not depend on any form of display capability on your terminal. In response to *make config*, the system presents you with a question in your console or window for each kernel option. You respond to the questions with y, m, or n for yes, module, or no, respectively. This method can admittedly get a bit tedious and has the liability that you must answer all the questions before being asked if you wish to save your *.config* file and exit. However, it is helpful if you do not have sufficient capability to use one of the menu-based methods. A *make config* session looks like this:

```
# make config
rm -f include/asm
( cd include ; ln -sf asm-i386 asm)
/bin/sh scripts/Configure arch/i386/config.in
#
# Using defaults found in arch/i386/defconfig
#
*
* Code maturity level options
*
Prompt for development and/or incomplete code/drivers
(CONFIG_EXPERIMENTAL) [Y/n/?]Y
```

Each option is offered in this manner.

make menuconfig

Syntax

```
make menuconfig
```

Description

This configuration method is more intuitive and can be used as an alternative to *make config*. It creates a text mode windowed environment where you may use cursor keys and other keys to configure the kernel. The menu depends on the ability of your terminal or terminal window to use *curses*, a standard library of terminal cursor manipulation instructions. If your terminal does not support curses (although most do), you must select another method. The *make menuconfig* window is illustrated in Figure 13-1 in an *xterm*.

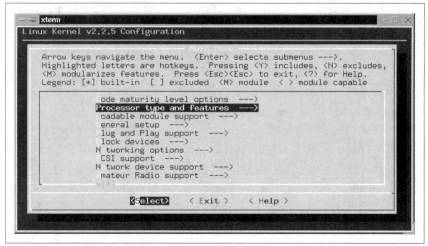

Figure 13-1. The make menuconfig menu display

make xconfig

Syntax

```
make xconfig
```

Description

If you are running the X Window System, the *make xconfig* configuration method presents a GUI menu with radio buttons to make the selections. It is the most appealing visually but requires a graphical console or X display. Figure 13-2 shows the top-level *make xconfig* window.

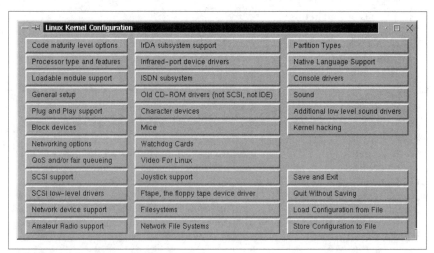

Figure 13-2. The make xconfig menu display

make oldconfig

Syntax

```
make oldconfig
```

Description

make oldconfig creates a new kernel configuration using *.config* as a base. User interaction is required only for options that were not previously configured (such as new options). This is convenient if you have patched your kernel with code that adds a new configuration option and want to be prompted only for configuration choices related to the new configuration option.

In the absence of user responses, *menuconfig* and *xconfig* will create a default *.config* file.

Example

To create the *.config* file for this example, the target processor is set as Pentium. Using *make xconfig*, the selection looks like the window shown in Figure 13-3.

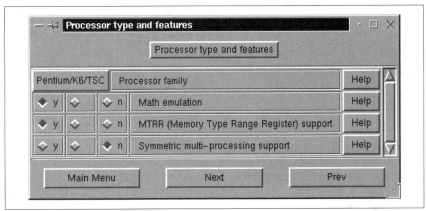

Figure 13-3. The make xconfig processor-selection window

By setting the Processor family parameter to Pentium/K6/TSC and saving the configuration, you cause the following revised configuration lines to be written in *.config*:

```
# Processor type and features
#
# CONFIG_M386 is not set
# CONFIG_M486 is not set
# CONFIG_M586 is not set
CONFIG_M586TSC=y
# CONFIG_M686 is not set
CONFIG_X86_WP_WORKS_OK=y
CONFIG_X86_INVLPG=y
CONFIG_X86_BSWAP=y
CONFIG_X86_POPAD_OK=y
CONFIG_X86_TSC=y
CONFIG_MATH_EMULATION=y
CONFIG_MTRR=y
# CONFIG_SMP is not set
```

The complete *.config* file will contain approximately 800 lines. You should look through the other kernel options with one of the windowed selectors first to familiarize yourself with what is available before making your selections.

Now that *.config* is created, one small change is made to the file *Makefile* in the top level of the kernel source tree to differentiate our new custom kernel from the generic one. The first four lines look like this:

```
VERSION = 2
PATCHLEVEL = 2
SUBLEVEL = 5
EXTRAVERSION = -15
```

You can see that the kernel version is 2.2.5 and that an additional version number is available. In this case, the generic kernel had the extra version suffix of -15, yielding a complete kernel version number 2.2.5-15. This EXTRAVERSION parameter can be used to indicate just about anything. In this example, it denotes the 15th build of kernel 2.2.5, but -pentium is added to the end for our custom version. Edit *Makefile* and change EXTRAVERSION as follows:

```
EXTRAVERSION = -15-pentium
```

This change completes the configuration for this example.

Compiling the kernel

Once the *.config* and *Makefile* files are customized, the new kernel can be compiled by running the following commands:

1. *make dep*

   In this step, source files (*.c*) are examined for dependencies on header files. A file called *.depend* is created in each directory containing source files to hold the resulting list, with a line for each compiled object file (*.o*). The *.depend* files are automatically included in subsequent *make* operations to be sure that changes in header files are compiled into new objects. Since kernel code isn't being developed here, no header file changes are needed. Nevertheless, make dep is an essential first step in the compilation process.

2. *make clean*

   The "clean" operation removes old output files that may exist from previous kernel builds. These include core files, system map files, and others. They must be removed to compile a new, clean kernel.

3. *make bzImage*

   The *bzImage* file is the ultimate goal: a bootable kernel image file, compressed using the *gzip* utility. It is created in this step along with some additional support files needed for boot time. (It is important to remember that the *b* in *bzImage* does not refer to being compressed with *bzip2*. The *bzImage* kernel format allows for a larger image than the old *zImage* format, so *bzImage* just means big *zImage*.)

4. *make modules*

Device drivers and other items that were configured as modules are compiled in this step.

5. *make modules_install*

All of the modules compiled during *make modules* are installed under */lib/ modules/kernel-version* in this step. A directory is created there for each kernel version, including various extra versions.

The *bzImage* and *modules* portions of the kernel-compilation process will take the most time. Overall, the time required to build a kernel depends on your system's capabilities.

After completing this series of *make* processes, compilation is complete. The new kernel image is now located in *arch/i386/boot/bzImage* in the kernel source tree.

Installing the new kernel and configuring LILO

Now that the new kernel has been compiled, the system can be configured to boot it:

1. The first step is to put a copy of our new *bzImage* on the boot partition so it can be booted by LILO. The copy is named just as it was named during compilation, including the extra version:

   ```
   # cp -p arch/i386/boot/bzImage
        /boot/vmlinuz-2.2.5-15-pentium
   ```

2. Now, a listing of kernels should show at least your default kernel and your new one, *vmlinuz-2.2.5-15-pentium*:

   ```
   # ls -1 /boot/vmlinuz*
   /boot/vmlinuz
   /boot/vmlinuz-2.2.14
   /boot/vmlinuz-2.2.5-15
   /boot/vmlinuz-2.2.5-15-pentium
   /boot/vmlinuz-2.2.5-15smp
   /boot/vmlinuz-2.3.45
   ```

3. Next, add a new image section to the bottom of */etc/lilo.conf*:

   ```
   image=/boot/vmlinuz-2.2.5-15-pentium
        label=linux-pentium
        root=/dev/sda1
        read-only
   ```

4. If you're using LILO for your boot loader, you must execute *lilo* (the map installer) to see the new kernel:

   ```
   # lilo
   Added linux-smp *
   Added linux-up
   Added latest
   Added linux-pentium
   ```

It's not uncommon to forget the execution of LILO. If you do forget, LILO won't know about the new kernel you've installed despite the fact that it's listed in the *lilo.conf* file. This is because *lilo.conf* is not consulted at boot time. If you're using

GRUB for your boot loader, editing its configuration file is sufficient. No extra steps are required.

If everything has gone according to plan, it's time to reboot and attempt to load the new kernel.

 As you review the *README* file that comes with the kernel source, you may see suggestions for overwriting your existing kernel, perhaps with a generic name such as *vmlinuz* and reusing your existing LILO configuration unaltered (i.e., without changing *lilo.conf*). Unless you're absolutely sure about what you are doing, overwriting a known good kernel is a bad idea. Instead, keep the working kernel around as a fallback position in case there's a problem with your new one.

Examine the new modules

Now that the new kernel is installed, you should take a look at */lib/modules*, which now has a new directory for the new kernel:

```
# ls -1 /lib/modules
2.2.14
2.2.5-15
2.2.5-15-pentium
2.2.5-15smp
2.3.45
```

On the Exam

Remember the series of make steps required to build the kernel: *config* (or *menuconfig* or *xconfig*), *dep*, *clean*, *bzImage*, *modules*, and *modules-install*. Be aware of where the kernel source code is installed. Also, note that you need to copy the kernel image file (*bzImage*) to the boot filesystem and that you must rerun `lilo` before you can boot it. By all means, practice compiling and installing a kernel at least once before taking Exam 102.

14

Boot, Initialization, Shutdown, and Runlevels (Topic 1.106)

Even the most inexpensive PC has a fairly complex series of steps to execute on its way from idle hardware to productive system. When a system is powered on, a computer's electronics are in a random state and must be reset to a known condition. After this occurs, the CPU in the system begins processing instructions at a specific, hardcoded memory location in ROM. For PCs, the ROM is usually called the BIOS. The startup instructions stored in the BIOS perform basic initialization chores to discover and configure peripheral hardware. When the system is initialized and ready, it begins looking in known locations for an operating system (or operating system loader software). This could be stored on fixed or removable disk media or even placed in memory during initialization. Once an operating system is launched, it begins an initialization sequence of its own.

This chapter covers the latter portions of the boot process, from the point when the BIOS looks for an operating system, as required for Exam 102. (The BIOS is covered in Chapter 3.) This Topic has two Objectives:

Objective 1: Boot the System
    Candidates should be able to understand the system booting process. This includes giving commands to the boot loader and giving options to the kernel at boot time and checking events in the log files. Weight: 3.

Objective 2: Change Runlevels and Shut Down or Reboot System
    This Objective states that a candidate should be able to manage the *runlevel* of the system. This includes changing the system to single-user mode, shutting it down, or rebooting it. Candidates must also be able to alert users and terminate system processes when changing system runlevels. Weight: 3.

Objective 1: Boot the System

It is the job of a boot loader, such as LILO or GRUB, to launch the Linux kernel at boot time. In some cases, the boot loader has to deliver information to the

Linux kernel that may be required to configure peripherals or control other behavior. This information is called a *kernel parameter*.

Boot-time Kernel Parameters

By default, your system's kernel parameters are set in your boot loader's configuration file (*/etc/lilo.conf* or */boot/grub/menu.lst,* and *boot/grub/grub.conf* on Red Hat and some other distributions). However, the Linux kernel also has the capability to accept information at boot time from a kernel command-line interface. You access the kernel command line through your installed boot loader. When your system boots, you can interrupt the "default" boot process when the boot loader displays and specify your desired kernel parameters. The kernel parameters on the command line look similar to giving arguments or options to a program during command-line execution.

For an example, let's say you wanted to boot with a root partition other than your default, */dev/hda1*. Using LILO, you could enter the following at the LILO prompt:

```
LILO: linux root=/dev/hda9
```

This command boots the kernel whose label is linux and overrides the default value of */dev/hda1* to */dev/hda9* for the root filesystem.

On the Exam

There are far too many kernel parameters to list in this book. Consequently, you must familiarize yourself with them in general terms so that you can answer questions on their form. Remember that they are specified to your boot loader as either a single item, such as ro, or *name=value* options such as root=/dev/hda2. Multiple parameters are always separated by a space.

Introduction to Kernel Module Configuration

Modern Linux kernels are *modular*, in that modules of code traditionally compiled into the kernel (say, a sound driver) are loaded as needed. The modules are separate from the kernel and can be inserted and removed by the superuser if necessary. While parameters in the boot loader's configuration file and the kernel command line affect the kernel, they do not control kernel modules.

To send parameters to a kernel module, they are inserted into the file */etc/modules. conf* as text (in the past this configuration file was */etc/conf.modules*). Common module options you may find in your module configuration file are I/O address, interrupt, and DMA channel settings for your sound device. This file will also probably carry PCMCIA driver information when installed on laptops. Module configuration will probably be handled by your distribution's installation procedure but may require modifications if hardware is added or changed later. Example 14-1 shows a typical */etc/modules.conf* file.

Example 14-1. A typical /etc/modules.conf file

```
alias parport_lowlevel parport_pc
alias eth0 8139too
alias sound-slot-0 via82cxxx_audio
post-install sound-slot-0 /bin/aumix-minimal \
    -f /etc/.aumixrc -L >/dev/null 2>&1 || :
pre-remove sound-slot-0 /bin/aumix-minimal \
    -f /etc/.aumixrc -S >/dev/null 2>&1 || :
alias usb-controller usb-uhci
```

On the Exam

Read questions that ask about kernel or module parameters carefully. Kernel options can be passed on the kernel command line; module options are specified in *modules.conf*.

In this example, note that an alias named sound-slot-0 is created for the audio driver via82cxxx_audio. Most devices won't need any additional configuration, but systems with older ISA cards may still need to pass options for I/O port, IRQ, and DMA channel settings. In addition, some drivers may need options to specify nonstandard settings. For example, an ISDN board used in North America will need to specify NI1 signaling to the driver.

```
options hisax protocol=4 type=40
```

Kernel boot-time messages

As the Linux kernel boots, it gives detailed status of its progress in the form of console messages. Modules that are loaded also yield status messages. These messages contain important information regarding the health and configuration of your hardware. Generally, the kinds of messages you will see are:

- Kernel identification
- Memory and CPU information
- Information on detected hardware, such as pointers (mice), serial ports, and disks
- Partition information and checks
- Network initialization
- Kernel module output for modules that load at boot time

These messages are displayed on the system console at boot time but often scroll off the screen too fast to be read. The messages are also logged to disk. They can easily be viewed using the *dmesg* command, which displays messages logged at the last system boot. For example, to view messages from the last boot sequence, simply pipe the output of *dmesg* to *less*:

```
# dmesg | less
```

It is also common to use *dmesg* to dump boot messages to a file for later inspection or archive, by simply redirecting the output:

```
# dmesg > bootmsg.txt
```

 The kernel buffer used for log messages that *dmesg* displays is a fixed size, so it may lose some (or all) of the boot-time messages as the kernel writes runtime messages.

Reviewing system logs

In addition to kernel messages, many other boot-time messages will be logged using the syslog system. Such messages will be found in the system log files such as */var/log/messages*. For example, *dmesg* displays information on your network adapter when it was initialized. However, the configuration and status of that adapter is logged in */var/log/messages* as a result of the network startup. When examining and debugging boot activity on your system, you need to review both kinds of information. syslogd, its configuration, and log file examination are covered in the section "Objective 3: Configure and Use System Log Files to Meet Administrative and Security Needs" in Chapter 18.

Objective 2: Change Runlevels and Shut Down or Reboot System

As mentioned in the introduction, Linux and many Unix systems share the concept of *runlevels*. This concept specifies different ways a system can be used by controlling which services are running. For example, a system that operates a web server program is configured to boot and initiate processing in a runlevel designated for sharing data, at which point the web server is started. However, the same system would not run the web server in a runlevel used for emergency administration, when all but the most basic services are shut down.

Runlevels are specified by the integers through 6 as well as a few single characters. Runlevels 0 and 6 are unusual in that they specify the transitional states of shutdown and reboot, respectively. By instructing Linux to enter runlevel 0, it begins a clean shutdown procedure. Similarly, the use of runlevel 6 begins a reboot. The remaining runlevels differ in meaning slightly among Linux distributions and other Unix systems.

When a Linux system boots, the *init* process is responsible for taking the system to the default runlevel, which is usually either 2, 3, or 5 depending on the distribution and the use for the machine. Typical runlevel meanings are listed in Table 14-1.

Table 14-1. Typical runlevels

Runlevel	Description
0	Halt the system; runlevel 0 is a special transitional device used by administrators to shut down the system quickly. This, of course, shouldn't be a default runlevel, because the system would never come up—it would shut down immediately when the kernel launches the *init* process. See also runlevel 6.
1, s, S	Single-user mode, sometimes called maintenance mode. In this mode, system services such as network interfaces, web servers, and file sharing are not started. This mode is usually used for interactive file-system maintenance.
2	Multiuser. On Debian this is the default runlevel. On Red Hat it is multiuser without NFS file sharing.
3	On Red Hat the default full multiuser mode. This and levels 4 and 5 are not usually used on Debian.
4	Typically unused.
5	On Red Hat: full multiuser mode with GUI login. Runlevel 5 is like runlevel 3 but X11 is started in addition and a GUI login is available. If your X11 cannot start for some reason, you should avoid this runlevel.
6	Reboot the system; used by system administrators. Just like runlevel 0, this is a transitional device for administrators. It shouldn't be a default runlevel because the system would eternally reboot.

Single-User Mode

Runlevel 1, the *single-user* runlevel, is a bare-bones operating environment intended for system maintenance. In single-user mode, remote logins are disabled, networking is disabled, and most daemons are shut down. Single-user mode is used for system configuration tasks that must be performed with no user activity. One common reason you might be forced to use single-user mode is to correct problems with a corrupt filesystem that the system cannot handle automatically.

If you wish to boot directly into single-user mode, you may specify it at boot time with the kernel's command line through your boot loader. For instance, if you were using LILO, at the `LILO:` boot prompt, you would specify your kernel's image name and `1` or `single` for single-user mode. These arguments are not interpreted as kernel arguments but are instead passed along to the *init* process. For example, if your kernel image is named `linux`, these commands would take the system to single-user mode, bypassing the default: ·

```
LILO: linux single
```

or:

```
LILO: linux 1
```

To switch into single-user mode from another runlevel, you can simply issue a runlevel change command with *init*:

```
# init 1
```

If others are using resources on the system, they will be unpleasantly surprised, so be sure to give users plenty of warning before doing this.

Overview of the /etc directory tree and the init process

By themselves, the runlevels listed in Table 14-1 don't mean much. It's what the *init* process does as a result of a runlevel specification or change that affects the system. The actions of *init* for each runlevel are derived from Unix System V-style initialization and are specified in a series of directories and script files under */etc*.

When a Linux system starts, a number of scripts in */etc* are used to initially configure the system and switch among runlevels. System initialization techniques differ among Linux distributions. (The examples here are typical of a Red Hat Linux system. Any LSB-compliant distribution should be similar.)

rc.sysinit or /etc/init.d/rcS

On Red Hat systems, *rc.sysinit* is a monolithic system initialization script. The Debian *rcS* script does the same job but by running several small scripts placed in two different directories. This file is a script launched by *init* at boot time. It handles some essential chores to ready the system for use, such as mounting filesystems.

rc.local

Not used on Debian. On Red Hat and many other distributions, this file is a script that is called after all other *init* scripts. It contains local customizations affecting system startup and provides an alternative to modifying the other init files. Many administrators prefer to avoid changing *rc.sysint* because those changes will be lost during a system upgrade. The contents of *rc.local* are not lost in an upgrade.

rc

This file is a script that is used to change between runlevels.

The job of starting and stopping system services such as web servers is handled by the files and symbolic links in */etc/init.d* and by a series of runlevel-specific directories, *rc0.d* through *rc6.d*:

init.d

This directory contains individual startup/shutdown scripts for each service on the system. For example, the script */etc/init.d/httpd* is a Bourne shell script that safely starts or stops the Apache web server. These scripts have a standard basic form and take a single argument. Valid arguments include at least the words start and stop. Additional arguments are sometimes accepted by the script; examples are restart, status, and sometimes reload (to ask the service to reconfigure itself without exiting). Administrators can use these scripts directly to start and stop services. For example, to restart Apache, an administrator could issue commands like these:

```
# /etc/init.d/httpd stop
# /etc/init.d/httpd start
```

or simply:

```
# /etc/init.d/httpd restart
```

Either form would completely shut down and start up the web server. To ask Apache to remain running but reread its configuration file, you might enter:

```
# /etc/init.d/httpd reload
```

This has the effect of sending the SIGHUP signal to the running httpd process, instructing it to initialize. Signals, such as SIGHUP, are covered in Chapter 3, "Objective 6: Configure Communications Devices."

If you add a new service (a daemon, intended to always run in the background), one of these initialization files may be installed automatically for you. In other cases, you may need to create one yourself or, as a last resort, place startup commands in the *rc.local* file.

Directories rc0.d through rc6.d

The initialization scripts in */etc/init.d* are not directly executed by the init process. Instead, each of the directories */etc/rc0.d* through *rc6.d* contain symbolic (soft) links to the scripts in directory *init.d*. (These symbolic links could also be files, but using script files in each of the directories would be an administrative headache, since changes to any of the startup scripts would mean identical edits to multiple files.) When the init process enters runlevel *n*, it examines all of the links in the associated *rcn.d* directory. These links are given special names in the form of [K|S]Nname, described as follows:

K *and* S *prefixes*

The K and S prefixes mean kill and start, respectively. A runlevel implies a state in which certain services are running and all others are not. The S prefix is used for all services that are to be running (started) for the runlevel. The K prefix is used for all other services, which should not be running.

N

Sequence number. This part of the link name is a two-digit integer (with a leading zero, if necessary). It specifies the relative order for services to be started or stopped. The lowest number is the first link executed by init, and the largest number is the last. There are no hard-and-fast rules for choosing these numbers, but it is important when adding a new service to be sure that it starts *after* any other required services are already running. If two services have an identical start order number, the order is indeterminate but probably alphabetical.

name

By convention, the name of the script being linked is used as the last part of the link name. *init* does not use this name, but excluding it makes things difficult for human readers.

As an example, when *init* enters the default runlevel (3 for the sake of this example) at boot time, all of the links with the S prefix in */etc/rc3.d* will be executed in the order given by their sequence number (*S10network*, *S12syslog*, and so on). They will be run with the single argument start to launch their respective services. After the last of the scripts is executed, the requirements for runlevel 3 are satisfied.

Setting the default runlevel

To determine the default runlevel at boot time, *init* reads the configuration file */etc/inittab* looking for a line containing the word *initdefault*, which will look like this:

```
id:n:initdefault:
```

In the preceding, *n* is a valid runlevel number, such as 3. This number is used as the default runlevel by *init*. The S scripts in the corresponding */etc/rcN.d* directory are executed to start their respective services. If you change the default runlevel for your system, it will most likely be to switch between the standard text login runlevel and the GUI login runlevel. In any case, never change the default runlevel to 0 or 6, or your system will not boot to a usable state.

Determining your system's runlevel

From time to time, you may be unsure just what runlevel your system is in. For example, you may have logged into a Linux system from a remote location and not know how it was booted or maintained. You may also need to know what runlevel your system was in prior to its current runlevel—perhaps wondering if the system was last in single-user mode for maintenance.

To determine this information, use the *runlevel* command. When executed, *runlevel* displays the previous and current runlevel as integers, separated by a space, on standard output. If no runlevel change has occurred since the system was booted, the previous runlevel is displayed as the letter N. For a system that was in runlevel 3 and is now in runlevel 5, the output is:

```
# runlevel
3 5
```

For a system with a default runlevel of 5 that has just completed booting, the output would be:

```
# runlevel
N 5
```

runlevel does not alter the system runlevel. To do this, use the *init* command (or the historical alias *telinit*).

Changing Runlevels with init and telinit

The *init* process is the grandfather of all processes. If used as a command on a running system, *init* sends signals to the executing *init* process, instructing it to change to a specified runlevel. You must be logged in as the superuser to use the *init* command.

init

Syntax

```
init n
```

Description

The number of the runlevel, *n*, can be changed to an integer from 1 through 6.

The numeric arguments instruct *init* to switch to the specified runlevel. *init* also supports a few alphabetical options such as *S* and *s*, which are equivalent to runlevel 1, and *q*, which is used to tell *init* to reread its configuration file, */etc/inittab*.

Examples

Shut down immediately:

```
# init 0
```

Reboot immediately:

```
# init 6
```

Go to single-user mode immediately:

```
# init 1
```

or:

```
# init s
```

The *telinit* command may be used in place of *init*. *telinit* is simply a link to *init*, and the two may be used interchangeably.

Generally, you will use a runlevel change for the following reasons:

- To shut down the system using runlevel 0.
- To go to single-user mode using runlevel 1.
- To reboot the system using runlevel 6.
- To switch between text-based and X11 GUI login modes, usually runlevels 3 and 5, respectively.

On the Exam

Remember that *init* and *telinit* can be used interchangeably.

System Shutdown with shutdown

When *shutdown* is initiated, all users who are logged into terminal sessions are notified that the system is going down. In addition, further logins are blocked to prevent new users from entering the system as it is being shut down.

shutdown

Syntax

```
shutdown [options] time [warning_message]
```

Description

The *shutdown* command brings the system down in a secure, organized fashion. By default, *shutdown* takes the system to single-user mode. Options can be used to either halt or reboot instead. The command uses *init* with an appropriate runlevel argument to affect the system change.

The mandatory *time* argument tells the shutdown command when to initiate the shutdown procedure. It can be a time of day in the form *hh:mm*, or it can be in the form *+n*, where *n* is a number of minutes to wait. *time* can also be the word now, in which case the shutdown proceeds immediately. If the *time* specified is more than 15 minutes away, *shutdown* waits until 15 minutes remain before shutdown before making its first announcement.

If *warning message* (a text string) is provided, it is used in the system's announcements to end users. No quoting is necessary for *warning message* unless the message includes special characters such as * or &.

Frequently used options

-f

 Fast boot; this skips filesystem checks on the next boot.

-h

 Halt after shutdown.

-k

 Don't really shut down, but send the warning messages anyway.

-r

 Reboot after shutdown.

-F

 Force filesystem checks on the next boot.

Examples

To reboot immediately:

```
# shutdown -r now
```

To reboot in five minutes with a maintenance message:

```
# shutdown -r +5 System maintenance is required
```

To halt the system just before midnight tonight:

```
# shutdown -h 23:59
```

The two most common uses of shutdown by individuals are:

```
# shutdown -h now
```

and

```
# shutdown -r now
```

These initiate for immediate halts and reboots, respectively. Although it's not really a bug, the *shutdown* manpage notes that omission of the required *time* argument yields unusual results. If you do forget the *time* argument, *shutdown* will probably exit without an error message. This might lead you to believe that a shutdown is starting, so it's important to be sure of your syntax when using *shutdown*.

On the Exam

Make certain that you are aware of the differences between system shutdown using *init* (and its link *telinit*) and *shutdown*.

15

Printing (Topic 1.107)

As long as the paperless office remains a myth, printing will be an important aspect of the computing experience. While printing may not be something you deal with on a daily basis, as a system administrator it will inevitably be an important part of your job.

This Topic covers the setup, administration, and use of *lpr*, *lpd*, and related utilities. Although they are not covered in the current LPI Objectives, this chapter also includes an introduction to other printing systems that may be used on Linux systems.

This chapter includes three Objectives (numbered 2 through 4, because of changes during test development):

Objective 2: Manage Printers and Print Queues
> An LPIC-1 candidate should be able to manage print queues and user print jobs. This Objective includes monitoring print servers and user print queues and troubleshooting general printing problems. Weight: 1.

Objective 3: Print Files
> This Objective states that a candidate should be able to manage print queues and manipulate print jobs. This includes adding and removing jobs from configured printer queues and converting text files to postscript for printing. Weight: 1.

Objective 4: Install and Configure Local and Remote Printers
> Candidates should be able to install a printer daemon and print filters. This Objective includes making local and remote printers accessible for Linux systems, including postscript and Samba printers. Weight: 1.

An Overview of Printing

There are several implementations of printing available for Linux systems, but they all have a basic architecture in common. In every printing system, a central daemon receives print jobs, via either a user command (such as *lpr*) or the network. The print job is then processed as necessary and either sent to a local printer or another printing daemon.

Historically, there have been two competing printing implementations on Unix systems, one invented for BSD Unix, and another for System V (SysV) Unix. While the implementations are similar, they have completely different commands. The BSD printing commands include *lpd*, *lpr*, *lprm*, and *lpc*. The System V printing commands include *lp*, *enable*, *disable*, *cancel*, *lpstat*, and *lpadmin*. Table 15-1 compares the commands used by the two printing systems.

Table 15-1. BSD versus SysV printing

Description	BSD command	System V command
Printing daemon	*lpd*	*lpsched*
Print files	*lpr*	*lp*
List print queues	*lpq*	*lpstat -o*
Remove files from a queue	*lprm*	*cancel*
Enable a queue	*lpc enable*	*enable*
Disable a queue	*lpc disable*	*disable*
Move a job to another queue	*lpc move*	*lpmove*

On System V–based systems, there is a command, *lpadmin*, used to configure print queues. There is no equivalent to it on BSD-based systems, other than to simply edit */etc/printcap*. Other than that one command, there is a one-to-one relationship between BSD and System V printing commands. However, the internal details, such as files used, vary considerably.

Older Linux distributions tended to use a port of the BSD *lpd* code (and related commands). Due to various security issues with the BSD code (mostly the over-use of *root*), current distributions have largely dropped the BSD code in favor of either LPRng or Common UNIX Printing System (CUPS).

LPRng is a complete rewrite of the BSD utilities. It is designed to be portable and secure. Unlike the BSD utilities, the client programs do not need to run setuid. The server (still called *lpd*) is a complete implementation of the RFC 1179 Line Printer Daemon Protocol. It also includes *lp* and *lpstat* commands for System V compatibility.

While LPRng is a complete rewrite, configuration is still mostly the same as for the BSD utilities. It still uses */etc/printcap* (described in "Linux Printing Overview" later in this chapter). It also has two additional configuration files: */etc/lpd.conf*, which is used to control details of LPRng's *lpd*, and */etc/lpd.perms*, which is used to configure access controls for *lpd*.

LPRng is available from *http://www.lprng.com*.

CUPS is a more recent printing system that was initially designed to support Internet Printing Protocol (IPP) but has evolved into drop-in replacement for both the BSD and System V utilities, including client replacements for both and RFC 1179 (*lpd* protocol) support. It also includes support for SMB and JetDirect printing.

While it retains backward compatibility with older printing systems, the internal details of CUPS are significantly different. The server component *cupsd* handles queueing, but it also includes a web server for configuration and management. Nearly everything can be configured through the web interface or the included *lpadmin*. The various configuration files in the */etc/cups* directory rarely need to be edited by hand.

CUPS is available from *http://www.cups.org*.

Objective 2: Manage Printers and Print Queues

Printing documents is a slow and error-prone process. Printers accept data in small amounts; they run out of paper, jam, and go offline for other reasons. Printers also must accept requests from multiple system users. As a result, by design, the end user is isolated from printing functions on most computer systems. This isolation comes in the form of a *print queue*, which holds print requests until the printer is ready for them. It also manages the order in which print jobs are processed.

Linux systems typically use a family of printing utilities developed for BSD Unix. This Objective describes printer management using the *lpd* daemon. The companion commands *lpr*, *lpq*, and *lprm* are SUID programs, which run with privileges of the superuser. This is necessary to allow their use by all users, because they manipulate files in the protected print spooling directories. *lpr* is covered in the Objective 3 section. Filters and */etc/printcap* are covered in the Objective 4 section.

Linux Printing Overview

On Linux, the default printing system is derived from the BSD Unix printing system. It consists of the following elements:

lpd

> The *lpd* daemon is started at boot time and runs constantly, listening for print requests directed at multiple printers. When a job is submitted to a print queue, *lpd* forks a copy of itself to handle jobs on that queue. The copy exits when the queue is emptied. Thus, during idle periods, one *lpd* process will be running on your system. When printing is active, one additional *lpd* process will be running for each active queue.

/etc/printcap

> The *printcap* (printer capabilities) file contains printer names, parameters, and rules; it is used by *lpd* when spooling print jobs. See Objective 4 for additional information on the */etc/printcap* file.

lpr

> The *lpr* (line print) program submits both files and information piped to its standard input to print queues.

lpq

> The *lpq* program queries and displays the status and contents of print queues.

lprm

> *lprm* removes print jobs from print queues.

lpc

> The superuser administers print queues with *lpc* (line printer control).

Filters

> When a printer lacks the ability to directly render a print job, software filters are used to transform the original data into something the printer can handle. A common example is the conversion from PostScript to PCL for laser printers without native PostScript capability.

Spool directories

> The *lpd* daemon uses */var/spool/lpd* for the spooling of data awaiting printing. This directory contains a subdirectory for each printer configured on the system (both local and remote). For example, the default locally attached printer on most Linux systems is simply called *lp* (line printer), and all of its control files and queued jobs are stored in directory */var/spool/lpd/lp*.

Print jobs

> Each submitted print request is spooled to a queue and assigned a unique number. The numbered print jobs can be examined and manipulated as needed.

Managing Print Queues

As a system administrator, you'll be asked to manage and manipulate printer queues more often than you'd like. On Linux, the *lpq*, *lprm*, and *lpc* commands are your tools.

lpq

Syntax

```
lpq [options] [users] [job#s]
```

Description

Query a print queue. If numeric *job#s* are included, only those jobs are listed. If *users* are listed, only jobs submitted by those users are listed.

Options

-l

> Long output format. This option results in a multiline display for each print job.

-P *name*

> This specifies the print queue *name*. In the absence of -P, the default printer is queried.

Example 1

Examine active jobs:

```
$ lpq
lp is ready and printing
Rank    Owner    Job  Files                  Total Size
active  root     193  filter                 9443 bytes
1st     root     194  resume.txt             11024 bytes
2nd     root     196  (standard input)       18998 bytes
```

Here, *filter* is currently being printed. *resume.txt* is up next, followed by the 18,998 bytes of data piped into *lpr*'s standard input.

Example 2

Examine queue lp, which turns out to be empty:

```
$ lpq -Plp
no entries
```

Example 3

Examine those same jobs using the long format:

```
$ lpq -l
lp is ready and printing
root: active                          [job 193AsJRzIt]
        filter                        9443 bytes
root: 1st                             [job 194AMj9lo9]
        resume.txt                    11024 bytes
root: 2nd                             [job 196A6rUGu5]
        (standard input)              18998 bytes
```

Example 4

Examine jobs owned by *bsmith*:

```
$ lpq bsmith
Rank    Owner    Job  Files                  Total Size
7th     bsmith   202  .bash_history          1263 bytes
9th     bsmith   204  .bash_profile          5676 bytes
```

Using the job numbers reported by *lpq*, any user may remove her own print jobs from the queue, or the superuser may remove any job.

---

lprm

Syntax

```
lprm [-Pname] [users] [job#s]
lprm -
```

Description

Remove jobs from a print queue. In the first form, remove jobs from queue *name* or from the default queue if -P is omitted. If *users* or *jobs* are specified, only those jobs will be removed. In the second form, all of a normal user's jobs will be omitted; for the superuser, the queue will be emptied.

Example 1

As a normal user, remove all of your print jobs:

```
$ lprm -
```

Example 2

As the superuser, remove all jobs from queue *ps*:

```
# lprm -Pps -
```

You may occasionally be surprised to see a no entries response from lpq, despite observing that the printer is dutifully printing a document. In such cases, the spool has probably been emptied into the printer's buffer memory, and the result is that the job is no longer under the control of the printing system. To kill such jobs, you need to use the printer's controls to stop and delete the job from memory.

Managing print queues with lpc

Printer control on Linux includes the oversight of three distinct and independently controlled activities managed by the *lpd* daemon:

Job queuing
    Turn new print jobs on and off.

Printing
    Turn on and off the transfer of data to your printer.

lpd *child processes*
    Force the per-queue *lpd* subprocesses to exit and restart.

lpc can be used in either interactive or command-line form. If *lpc* is entered without any options, it enters interactive mode and displays its own prompt where lpc commands may then be entered. For example:

```
# lpc
lpc> help
Commands may be abbreviated.  Commands are:
abort   enable  disable help   restart status  topq   ?
clean   exit    down    quit   start   stop    up
lpc>
```

If valid commands are included on the command line, *lpc* responds identically but returns control to the terminal:

```
# lpc help
Commands may be abbreviated.  Commands are:
abort   enable  disable help   restart status  topq   ?
clean   exit    down    quit   start   stop    up
#
```

For the discussion that follows, *lpc* commands are shown as entered on the command line, but results in interactive mode are identical.

lpc

Syntax

```
lpc
lpc [command]
```

Description

In the first form, enter interactive mode and accept *lpc* commands. In the second form, submit *command* for processing directly from the command line. *lpc* has no command-line options. Instead, it has commands (see Table 15-2), which are separated here into two groups: those that affect print queues and those that don't. Most of the commands require a single argument: either the word all (meaning all printers) or a specific printer name.

Table 15-2. Commands for lpc

Command	Description
abort {all|*printer*}	This command works like *stop* but terminates printing immediately, even in the middle of a job. The job is retained for reprint when the printer is again *started*.
disable {all|*printer*} enable {all|*printer*}	These two commands control the queuing of new print jobs. With a queue disabled but printing started, printing continues but new jobs are rejected.
down {all|*printer*} [*message*]	*disable*, *stop*, and *store* the free-form *message* for display by *lpr*, informing the user why the printer is unavailable.
exit or quit	Terminate *lpc*'s interactive mode.
help	Display help information on commands, as shown earlier.
restart {all|*printer*}	Kill and restart child *lpd*, or start one when none was previously running.
start {all|*printer*} stop {all|*printer*}	These two commands control printing and the child *lpd* processes. When a *stop* command is issued, the current print job is allowed to complete. Then the child daemon is stopped and further printing is disabled. *start* enables printing and starts the child *lpd* if jobs are pending. The print queues remain active.
status [all|*printer*]	Display queue status.
topq *name jobs*	Place *jobs* at the top of queue *name*, behind any active jobs.
up {all|*printer*}	*enable* and *start*.

Example 1

Use the status command to display current printing activity:

```
# lpc status
lp:
        queuing is enabled
        printing is enabled
        2 entries in spool area
        lp is ready and printing
```

Example 2

Suppose user *jdean* has submitted two important print jobs, 206 and 207, and he needs job 207 to be moved to the top of the queue, followed immediately by 206 (see the emphasized lines in the *lpq* output). First, examine the existing jobs:

```
# lpq
Rank    Owner    Job  Files              Total Size
active  root     203  filter             9443 bytes
1st     root     204  status             25 bytes
2nd     root     205  (standard input)   6827 bytes
3rd     jdean    206  (standard input)   403 bytes
4th     jdean    207  cert1.txt          4865 bytes
```

Now modify the position of print jobs 206 and 207:

```
# lpc topq lp 207 206
lp:
        moved cfA206AlIwYoh
        moved cfA207Ad6utse
```

Finally, verify the results:

```
# lpq
Rank    Owner    Job  Files              Total Size
1st     jdean    207  cert1.txt          4865 bytes
2nd     jdean    206  (standard input)   403 bytes
3rd     root     203  filter             9443 bytes
4th     root     204  status             25 bytes
5th     root     205  (standard input)   6827 bytes
```

With this reconfiguration, printing continues with jobs 207 and 206 first, and then reverts to jobs 203 through 205.

Example 3

Disable and enable print queue lp, to allow current printing to complete while rejecting new jobs:

```
# lpc disable lp
lp:
        queuing disabled
# lpc enable lp
lp:
        queuing enabled
```

Example 4

Stop and restart printing on the printer attached to queue lp, but allow new jobs to be queued for future printing:

```
# lpc stop lp
lp:
        printing disabled
# lpc start lp
lp:
        printing enabled
        daemon started
```

If no jobs are pending, a child *lpd* will not start immediately in response to *start*, though the daemon started message is still displayed. Note also that when a child *lpd* process is stopped, its subprocesses (such as filters) are also stopped.

Example 5

Abandon all printing activity on the print queue *lp*. Note that a printer with data in its print buffer may continue to print even after an abort:

```
# lpc abort lp
lp:
printing disabled
daemon (pid 2012) killed
```

Objective 3: Print Files

The ability to manage your printers and print queues isn't very helpful until you actually need to print files. LPI 102 covers the `lpr` command to send jobs to the *lpd* daemon for printing. You can also use a combination of `lpr` with *mpage* to manipulate your print jobs to print multiple pages to a single sheet of paper.

lpr

Syntax

```
lpr [options] [files]
```

Description

Send *files* or standard input to a print queue. A copy of the input source is placed in the spool directory under */var/spool/lpr* until the print job is complete.

Frequently used options

-#*number*
> Send *number* copies of the print job to the printer.

-*s*
> Instead of copying a file to the print spooling area, make a symbolic link to the file instead, thereby eliminating transfer time and storage requirements in */var/spool/ lpr* for very large files.

-P*name*
> Specify the print queue *name*. In the absence of -P, the default printer is queried.

Example 1

Print the file */etc/lilo.conf* on the default print queue:

```
# lpr /etc/lilo.conf
```

Example 2

Print a manpage by piping to `lpr`'s standard input:

```
# man -t 5 printcap | lpr
```

Example 3

Disable a print queue:

```
# lpc disable lp
```

Then attempt to print three copies of a file to the disabled queue as superuser:

```
# lpr -#3 /etc/lilo.conf
```

Success, despite the disabled printer queue. Now try as a regular user:

```
$ lpr -#3 ~/resume.txt
lpr: Printer queue is disabled
```

As expected, normal users can't print to the disabled queue.

On the Exam

You must be familiar with *lpr* and its use with both files and standard input. Also remember that *lpr* doesn't send data to the printer, but to *lpd*, which handles sending it to the printer.

---

mpage

Syntax

```
mpage [options] [files]
```

Description

The *mpage* command reads plain text (or PostScript) files and manipulates the text size to fit multiple print pages on single sheets of paper. This tool requires a PostScript printer to print the results.

Frequently used options

-#number (1, 2, 4, or 8)
> Prints *number* of normal pages per sheet. *mpage* supports printing 1, 2, 4, or 8 pages per sheet.

Objective 4: Install and Configure Local and Remote Printers

If you've been able to run the commands listed in Objectives 2 and 3, you already have the printing system installed on your system. However, if you don't have the package, you can get the source code from *ibiblio.org* (*ftp://ibiblio.org/pub/linux/system/printing*), along with the other software mentioned later in this Objective. You should be able to build the software simply using *make* followed by *make install*.

The printing system implemented by the *lpd* suite is primitive by today's standards. It provides for queuing, administrative control, and some handling of special file formats but doesn't directly address the recent trend away from character-oriented printers to more programmable machines. Fortunately, the software is modular, making its foundation easy to build upon, making it sufficient for most printing situations.

/etc/printcap

The printing process on Linux systems is governed by the printer capability file */etc/printcap*. This text file defines all of the system's available print queues and their characteristics. The file is parsed by *lpd*, which ignores blank lines and comments beginning with a pound sign (#). Each printer definition in the file comprises one logical line, which is often broken up among multiple physical lines in the file using the \ line-continuation character. The definition itself is made up of fields delimited by colons. The first field, which begins in the first column of the file, holds the system name for the printer, such as lp. This field may contain aliases for the printer name separated by vertical bars. The rest of the fields in the definition hold mnemonics providing control flags and printer parameters. A basic *printcap* file defining a single printer is shown in Example 15-1.

Example 15-1. A basic /etc/printcap file

```
# A basic /etc/printcap
#
lp|ljet:\
        :sd=/var/spool/lpd/lp:\
        :mx#0:\
        :sh:\
        :lp=/dev/lp0:\
        :if=/var/spool/lpd/lp/filter:
        :lf=/var/spool/lpd/lp/log:
```

In this example, printer lp is defined with the alias ljet. Either name could be used to print with this printer, using *lpr -Plp* or *lpr -Pljet*. lp is the default printer unless the user overrides it by placing a different name in the PRINTER environment variable. Note that the name of the printer has a trailing colon, followed by the line-continuation character. The subsequent lines contain printer attributes inside colon pairs. Some of the frequently used attributes are:

if=*input_filter*
> Input filter (see the following section, "Filters").

lp=*printer_device*
> Local printer device, such as */dev/lp0*.

lf=*log_file*
> Error message log file.

mx=*max_size*
> Maximum size of a print job in blocks. A maximum size of #0 indicates no limit.

sd=*spool_directory*

Spool directory under */var/spool/lpd*.

sh

Suppress header pages for a single printer definition.

Both locally attached and remote printers will have queues defined in */etc/printcap*.

On the Exam

Familiarize yourself with the */etc/printcap* file and the attribute variables. Remember that a single printer definition can have multiple names and that multiple printer definitions can refer to the same hardware.

Filters

The printing process involves the rendering of various data formats by a single hardware device. Considering the wide range of possible formats (plain text, HTML, PostScript, troff, T$_E$X, and graphics files such as JPEG and TIFF, just to name a few), affordable printers can't be expected to natively handle them all. Instead, Linux systems use a two-step transformation process:

1. Raw input data is translated by a filter program into a standard Page Description Language (PDL), which is a form of PostScript for Linux. PostScript data is not printed itself but is interpreted as a program to be executed by a PostScript interpreter. PostScript can handle images, fonts, and complex page layout.

2. The PostScript program is sent to the Ghostscript utility (*gs*) from Aladdin Enterprises. (A GPL'd version of *gs* is offered for free by Aladdin, which makes it appropriate for inclusion in Linux distributions.) Ghostscript is a PostScript interpreter that contains a number of specific printer drivers. As a result, it can translate PostScript into a printer-specific format and send it to the printer.

This translation process and its intermediate data formats are depicted in Figure 15-1.

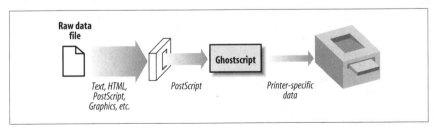

Figure 15-1. Print data translation steps

Each print queue found in */etc/printcap* can use a different input filter, as directed by the if=*filter* specification.

This data translation process sometimes isn't necessary. For example, plain text can be printed directly by most printers, making the translation to PostScript and subsequent Ghostscript invocation unnecessary for basic output. Many printers, particularly laser printers, have a built-in PostScript interpreter, making Ghostscript unnecessary. These situations are detected and controlled by the filter program.

A filter can be very simple. For example, you may have implemented a filter yourself by using a utility like *pr* to add a margin to a plain text print job before piping it into *lpr*. In practice, filters are conceptually similar, but are more complex and capable than this and usually handle multiple input formats. They do this by looking at the *magic number* at the beginning of the data file to be printed. (See the *file* command's manpage for more information on *magic* and *magic numbers*.) As a result, the filters are referred to as *magic filters*. Two such filters are *APSfilter* and *magicfilter*. Your familiarity with both filters is required for Exam 102.

APSfilter

This popular filter program accepts files in the PostScript, TEX DVI, ASCII, PCL, GIF, TIFF, Sun Raster files, FIG, PNM (pbmplus), HTML, and PDF formats. As mentioned earlier, *APSfilter* and the other software discussed here can be found at *ibiblio.org*. After downloading *APSfilter*, the compressed tarfile should be unpacked in */usr/lib*. Then, simply invoke *cd apsfilter* and run the installer, *./SETUP*. This interactive program presents a menu-based installation, where you direct such things as the Ghostscript printer driver selection, the choice of printer interface (such as */dev/lp0*), the default print resolution, the use of color, and the output paper format. It then creates new printer entries in */etc/printcap*, as well as creates new printer spool directories, and sets file permissions and ownership. It also compiles a few utilities necessary for the proper use of the filter. Once *APSfilter* is installed, your */etc/printcap* will look something like that shown in Example 15-2. (SETUP makes a backup copy of */etc/printcap* called */etc/printcap.orig* before creating its new *printcap* file.)

Example 15-2. The APSfilter /etc/printcap description

```
# apsfilter setup Tue Mar 21 02:38:48 EST 2000
#
ascii|lp1|ljet3d-letter-ascii-mono|ljet3d ascii mono:\
        :lp=/dev/lp0:\
        :sd=/var/spool/lpd/ljet3d-letter-ascii-mono:\
        :lf=/var/spool/lpd/ljet3d-letter-ascii-mono/log:\
        :af=/var/spool/lpd/ljet3d-letter-ascii-mono/acct:\
        :if=/usr/lib/apsfilter/filter/\
aps-ljet3d-letter-ascii-mono:\
        :mx#0:\
        :sh:
#
lp|lp2|ljet3d-letter-auto-mono|ljet3d auto mono:\
        :lp=/dev/lp0:\
        :sd=/var/spool/lpd/ljet3d-letter-auto-mono:\
```

Example 15-2. The APSfilter /etc/printcap description (continued)

```
        :lf=/var/spool/lpd/ljet3d-letter-auto-mono/log:\
        :af=/var/spool/lpd/ljet3d-letter-auto-mono/acct:\
        :if=/usr/lib/apsfilter/filter/\
aps-ljet3d-letter-auto-mono:\
        :mx#0:\
        :sh:
#
raw|lp3|ljet3d-letter-raw|ljet3d auto raw:\
        :lp=/dev/lp0:\
        :sd=/var/spool/lpd/ljet3d-raw:\
        :lf=/var/spool/lpd/ljet3d-raw/log:\
        :af=/var/spool/lpd/ljet3d-raw/acct:\
        :if=/usr/lib/apsfilter/filter/\
aps-ljet3d-letter-raw:\
        :mx#0:\
        :sh:
```

As you can see, the installation creates three printer definitions, each with multiple aliases and each using the same output device. This allows some degree of control over the filter, because the selection of the queue implies specific print parameters. The first definition (ascii) is intended to allow the user to force the printing of plain text even if the data is a PostScript program. The second entry (lp, the default) is the standard magic *APSfilter*, which tries to identify the data type itself. The last definition allows users to force *APSfilter* to send raw data directly to the printer with no intervention. This can be useful, for example, if you wish to print a PostScript file's programming instructions. *APSfilter* also configures logging and accounting for each printer queue. Finally, the setup routine optionally prints a graphical test page to verify your installation.

After *APSfilter* is installed, you must restart lpd to enable the new print queues:

> # **lpc restart all**

or:

> # **/etc/init.d/lpd stop**
> # **/etc/init.d/lpd start**

APSfilter allows for some controls in */etc/apsfilterrc* (and the user file *~/.apsfilterrc*). Examples of these controls are configuration for Ghostscript features, special control sequences for printers, and configuration for the use of a particular filter method. Although this file is beyond the scope of LPIC Level 1 Objectives, you should be familiar with it and its purpose.

On the Exam

You should install APSfilter to become familiar with the software and its setup.

---

magicfilter

Another filter you may wish to try is *magicfilter*, which can also be obtained from *ibiblio.org*. Unlike *APSfilter*, which is implemented as scripts, *magicfilter* is compiled from C and comes with a traditional *configure*; *make*; *make install* procedure. (See Chapter 4, "Objective 3: Make and Install Programs from Source," for additional information on how to install software.) Building and installing *magicfilter* is straightforward and shouldn't cause any difficulty. However, the installation does not automatically create print queues in */etc/printcap*, although you can easily define one by setting the input filter to */usr/local/bin/magicfilter*, as shown in Example 15-3.

Example 15-3. The magicfilter print queue

```
lp|lpmagic:\
        :sd=/var/spool/lpd/lp:\
        :mx#0:\
        :sh:\
        :lp=/dev/lp0:\
        :if=/usr/local/bin/magicfilter:
```

Multiple filters

When a filter is installed, it is placed in a directory from where it can be called as needed. The printer definitions in */etc/printcap* put the filter into service. Because you can create as many printer definitions as you like, it is possible to have multiple filters in place at the same time.

On the Exam

You should have a working knowledge of the printing process, the role of filters, the role of Ghostscript, and where PostScript data is used. Also remember that PostScript is rendered directly on some printers, eliminating the need for Ghostscript.

Remote lpd and Samba Printers

Configuring your system to use a remote Linux printer (or other *lpd* device, such as a network-attached printer) can be as simple as adding a local printer. Two additional configuration variables are added to the printer definition in */etc/printcap* to specify the remote host and the queue name on that host. For example:

```
rlp:\
        :sd=/var/spool/lpd/rlp:\
        :rm=lphost:\
        :rp=rlp:\
        :mx#0:\
        :sh:\
        :if=/usr/local/bin/magicfilter:
```

Here, this local print queue will send jobs to printer rlp residing on *lphost*. Since remote printers still have local queues, you must create the spool directory, in this example, */var/spool/lpd/rlp*.

Configuring a remote printer that's on a Windows network is also straightforward. (The Windows printer must be properly shared.) First, a local spool directory is created as usual, for example, */var/spool/lpd/winpr*. Next, an */etc/printcap* entry is added that looks something like this:

```
winpr:\
        :sd=/var/spool/lpd/winpr:\
        :mx#0:\
        :sh:\
        :if=/usr/bin/smbprint:
```

The input filter for this printer is *smbprint*, a utility from the Samba software suite. Finally, a *.config* file is created in the spool directory, which contains:

- The NetBIOS name of the Windows machine with the printer
- The service name that represents the printer
- The password used to access that service

The service name and password are set in the Sharing dialog box on the Windows machine. The *.config* file might look similar to the following:

```
server=WINBOX
service=WINPR
password=""
```

After restarting *lpd*, you should be able to print text documents to the Windows printer.

On the Exam

Remember the *rm* and *rp* printer configuration variables for remote *lpd* printers. For Samba printing on Windows clients, remember to use the *smbprint* input filter and to create the *.config* file in the local spool directory.

16

Documentation (Topic 1.108)

As a system administrator, your ability to navigate through daily computing tasks depends on your access to documentation. It is appropriate then that the LPI has made Linux documentation a part of Exam 102. There are three Objectives for this Topic:

Objective 1: Use and Manage Local System Documentation
This Objective covers two primary areas of documentation on Linux systems: the *man* (manual) facility and files stored in */usr/share/doc*. Weight: 4.

Objective 2: Find Linux Documentation on the Internet
Just as Linux itself is available via the Internet, a variety of documentation is also available. Weight: 3.

Objective 5: Notify Users on System-related Issues
As a system administrator, you'll regularly have to take responsibility to interact with users and keep them informed of scheduled downtimes, system upgrades, or new features. Such information is easily provided systemwide through the use of */etc/motd* and */etc/issue*. Weight: 1.

Objective 1: Use and Manage Local System Documentation

Each Linux system is configured by default with extensive documentation from developers, authors, and Linux community members. With these documentation projects combined, your Linux distribution offers a comprehensive body of knowledge to enhance your skills as a sysadmin.

Text Files and Paging

At a fundamental level, documents stored electronically may be encoded in a variety of formats. For example, most word processors use proprietary file formats to store characters, text formatting, and printing control languages. While these relatively modern applications can be found on your Linux system, most of the documents and configuration files for both the operating system and system tools are in plain text.

In the context of Linux systems, *plain text* means files or streams of both printable characters and control characters. Each is represented using a standard encoding scheme, such as the American Standard Code for Information Interchange (ASCII) or one of its relatives. Text files are most conveniently viewed using a *paging* program.

Paging programs

A paging program displays contents of a text file one "page" at a time. Paging programs have the advantage of speed and simplicity over text editors (such as *vi*) because only pieces of the text files are loaded into a buffer at a time, instead of the entire file. In addition, since paging programs cannot edit file contents directly, unless you tell them to invoke an editor, there isn't a chance of accidentally changing a file.

The two paging applications commonly used on Linux are *more* and *less*. The *more* tool is named because it gives you "one more screen." Humorously, the *less* command is so known because "less is more."

more is the older of the two Unix paging systems and has limited capabilities, though *more* has been beefed up on Linux systems compared to their original Unix versions. The standard Unix *more* simply presents you with the text document one screen at a time, progressing forward through the screens with the spacebar. This functionality is shadowed by *less*'s ability to move both forward and backward through a file, either line by line or a full screen at a time utilizing cursor keys and page up and page down keys, as well as standard *vi* movement keystrokes such as j, k, G, and so on. While both *more* and *less* on Linux have the ability for multidirectional movement and advanced searching capability, *less* has *more* movement options and supports *more* keyboard functions.

As a sysadmin, you will have the most exposure to these programs while reviewing manpages and system documentation.

Manpages

Traditional computer manuals covered everything from physical maintenance to programming libraries. While the books were convenient, many users didn't always want to dig through printed documentation or carry it around. So, as space became available, the *man* (*manual*) command was created to put the books on the system, allowing users immediate access to the information they needed in a searchable, quick-reference format.

There is a *manpage* for most commands on your system. There are also manpages for important files, library functions, shells, languages, devices, and other features. *man* is to your system what a dictionary is to your written language. That is, nearly everything is defined in detail, but you probably need to know in advance just what you're looking for.

man

Syntax

    man [options] [section] name

Description

Format and display system manual pages from *section* on the topic of *name*. If *section* is omitted, the first manpage found is displayed.

Frequently used options

-a

> Normally, *man* exits after displaying a single manpage. The *-a* option instructs *man* to display all manpages that match *name*, in a sequential fashion.

-d

> Display debugging information.

-w

> Print the locations of manpages instead of displaying them.

Example 1

View a manpage for *mkfifo*:

    $ man mkfifo
    ...

Results for the first manpage found are scrolled on the screen.

Example 2

Determine what manpages are available for *mkfifo*:

    $ man -wa mkfifo
    /usr/share/man/man1/mkfifo.1
    /usr/share/man/man3/mkfifo.3

This shows that two manpages are available, one in section 1 (*mkfifo.1*) of the manual and another in section 3 (*mkfifo.3*). See the next section for a description of manpage sections.

Example 3

Display the *mkfifo* manpage from manual section 3:

    $ man 3 mkfifo

Manual sections

Manpages are grouped into *sections*, and there are times when you should know the appropriate section in which to search for an item. For example, if you were interested in the *mkfifo* C-language function rather than the command, you must tell the *man* program to search the section on library functions (in this case, section 3, *Linux Programmer's Manual*):

    $ man 3 mkfifo

An alternative would be to have the *man* program search all manual sections:

```
$ man -a mkfifo
```

The first example returns the *mkfifo(3)* manpage regarding the library function. The second returns pages for both the command and the function. In this case, the pages are delivered separately; terminating the pager on the first manpage with Ctrl-C causes the second to be displayed.

Manual sections are detailed in Table 16-1.

Table 16-1. Man sections

Section	Description
1	User programs
2	System calls
3	Library calls
4	Special files (usually found in */dev*)
5	File formats
6	Games
7	Miscellaneous
8	System administration

Some systems might also have sections 9, *n*, and others, but only sections 1 through 8 are defined by the FHS.

The order in which *man* searches the sections for manpages is controlled by the MANSECT environment variable. MANSECT contains a colon-separated list of section numbers. If it is not set, *man* (as of Version 1.5k) behaves as if it were set to 1:8:2:3:4:5:6:7:9:tcl:n:l:p:o.

Manpage format

Most manpages are presented in a concise format with information grouped under well-known standard headings such as those shown in Table 16-2. Other manpage headings depend on the context of the individual manpage.

Table 16-2. Standard manpage headings

Heading	Description
Name	The name of the item, along with a description
Synopsis	A complete description of syntax or usage
Description	A brief description of the item
Options	Detailed information on each command-line option (for commands)
Return values	Information on function return values (for programming references)
See also	A list of related items that may be helpful
Bugs	Descriptions of unusual program behavior or known defects

Table 16-2. Standard manpage headings (continued)

Heading	Description
Files	A list of important files related to the item, such as configuration files
Copying or copyright	A description of how the item is to be distributed or protected
Authors	A list of those who are responsible for the item

man mechanics

System manpages are stored in */usr/share/man* and elsewhere. At any time, the manual pages available to the *man* command are contained within directories configured in your man configuration file, */etc/man.config*. This file contains directives to the *man*, telling it where to search for pages (the MANPATH directive), the paging program to use (PAGER), and many others. This file essentially controls how *man* works on your system. To observe this, use the debug (*-d*) option to *man* to watch as it constructs a *manpath* (a directory search list) and prepares to display your selection:

```
$ man -d mkfifo
```

Information in /usr/share/doc

Manpages are particularly useful when you know what you're looking for, or at least have some good leads on how to find it. However, they are not tutorial in nature, nor do they often describe overall concepts. Fortunately, individuals in the Linux world not only contribute their programming skills, but many also generate excellent tutorial documents to assist others with features, procedures, or common problems. Many of these documents end up as HOWTO guides, FAQs (lists of Frequently Asked Questions), *README* files, or even exhaustive user manuals. These documents are often part of the source distribution of a particular program and, while valuable, don't fit elsewhere on the Linux system and are deposited in */usr/share/doc*. Most of these files are ASCII text, which can be viewed with a pager, such as *less*, or with your favorite text editor. Some documents may be written in HTML for use with your web browser. Some text files may also be compressed with the *gzip* program and thus have the *.gz* extension.

 /usr/share/doc is not required by the FHS, so its contents and layout are distribution-specific.

Info Pages

The Free Software Foundation (*http://www.fsf.org*) has moved much of the documentation for the GNU project to a documentation format called *info*. Info pages are part of a system called *Texinfo*, which uses a single source file to display information on screen and on paper. Texinfo is hypertext and creates a browserlike interface on a terminal or terminal window (Emacs users will recognize the menu system as the editor's online help). For GNU software, Texinfo is the definitive documentation mechanism. Texinfo can be viewed by running the *info* command. For example, the texinfo document on *mkfifo* can be displayed using the following command:

```
$ info mkfifo
```

The result will be a display similar to the example in Figure 16-1.

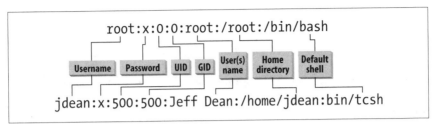

Figure 16-1. Info display in a terminal window

Basic navigation commands for the info system are listed in Table 16-3.

Table 16-3. Info commands

Command	Description
Tab	Move among hypertext links.
Enter	Follow hypertext links.
d	Return to the top (directory node) of the menu.
?	List all info commands.
p and n	Move to previous and next pages, respectively.
u	Move up one level in the texinfo hierarchy.
q	Terminate the system.
h	Show a primer for first-time users.
/string	Enter a string.
/pattern	Search forward for *pattern*, which can be a regular expression.

 Many Linux distributions also include the info viewer *pinfo*, which works much like the text-based web browser *lynx*.

Manpages and other types of system documentation are packaged and installed by default with most Linux distributions. For example, this means that both the manpage and executable program for *wc* are contained in the *coreutils* (or *textutils* on older distributions) package. Other documentation, such as Linux Documentation Project (LDP) guides and HOWTOs, may be contained in standalone packages, depending on the distribution.

Objective 2: Find Linux Documentation on the Internet

No doubt you've heard media reports regarding the genesis of Linux from a bunch of hackers. It is well-known that coders around the world are contributing to the Linux code base. Rarely mentioned, however, are the many dedicated writers working in the public domain to make sure that Linux is as well-understood as it is stable. Most of the people who contribute to the LDP do so on their own time, providing information learned from their own experiences. In most cases, the people who write for the LDP provide their names and email addresses so you can contact them with questions that remain unanswered. These writers are partially responsible for the widespread growth of Linux, because they make it understandable to individuals through documentation efforts not usually seen with commercial software.

The Linux Documentation Project

Most of the documentation in */usr/share/doc* and elsewhere on a Linux system is part of an organized approach to system documentation. The LDP is a loosely knit team of writers, proofreaders, and editors who work together to create the definitive set of documentation for Linux. The main web site can be found at *http://www.tldp.org* and at many mirror sites throughout the world.

The LDP contains a collection of freely contributed documents. Like Linux, all of the LDP's content may be freely distributed, copied, and even published for a fee without royalties to authors or to the LDP. Documents that are contributed to the LDP can be licensed a variety of ways. The LDP offers its own licensing terms, but authors aren't tied to using it. Some have opted to write their own license, while others have published their work under the GNU Public License (GPL) or the GNU Free Documentation License (GFDL).

The scope of the LDP is broad, ranging from online documents such as manpages to complete books in the form of reference guides. Some of the documents have software-style version numbers to assist with keeping up-to-date. Some of the more commonly used LDP reference guides include:

- Installation and Getting Started Guide
- The Linux Users' Guide
- The Linux System Administrators' Guide
- The Linux Network Administrators' Guide
- The Linux Programmer's Guide
- The Linux Kernel
- The Linux Kernel Hackers' Guide
- The Linux Kernel Module Programming Guide

Some of these LDP guides have been published in traditional book form, with mixed success. Any publisher can produce its own edition of the text, but since content must be identical, competing publishers can find themselves in a discounting exercise. This, coupled with frequent and unadvertised modifications, makes printed versions of LDP documents a speculative business venture at best.

Usenet Newsgroups

Usenet newsgroups can be thought of as a worldwide bulletin board service, with topics beyond your imagination (some of which probably belong beyond your imagination!). Unlike the older traditional proprietary bulletin board services you may remember from the early online days, Usenet is a distributed system where messages are posted to a user's local *news server* in a *newsgroup*. The message is then copied among thousands of news servers worldwide that also serve that same newsgroup. Some newsgroups are moderated by a responsible party to keep the content from getting out of hand. Many are not monitored at all and are a free-for-all of opinions, ideas, and occasional off-topic color.

You can access Usenet content through your ISP's news server, if one is offered, or you may use a web-based news-reading service, such as Google Groups (*http://groups.google.com*). Regardless of the method you choose, the content is the same. Messages posted to newsgroups are stored on your news server and not on a remote origin server. This fact sometimes leads ISPs and corporations to abandon news services altogether, due to the sheer volume of information that gets relayed on a daily basis.

If you use a Usenet news server, you will read messages with a *news reader* application. Many mail programs and web browsers contain news readers that communicate with Usenet news servers. Standalone GUI- and text-based news readers are also available. Since Usenet messages are plain text, they can be viewed by any paging or editing program. However, many news readers optionally group messages by thread, which makes following a particular discussion easy. Another benefit of using a news reader is that they manage *read* and *unread* message status, mark messages for later review, and so on.

A search for *Linux* in the growing list of newsgroups yields hundreds of individual groups, far too many for any single individual to keep up with. There are groups specific to development, to distributions, and to hardware platforms. There are Linux advocacy groups (both pro and con) and security groups. Perhaps the most popular are those under the *comp.os* hierarchy, which are moderated by a person who filters incoming messages before sending them out to subscribers. Some Linux-related newsgroups you should follow include:

comp.os.linux
:   A general discussion on Linux

comp.os.linux.advocacy
:   A less technical discussion of Linux, mainly by enthusiastic supporters

comp.os.linux.development
:   A Linux-related software development discussion

comp.os.linux.announce
:   Announcements from vendors, programmers, and so on

comp.os.linux.hardware
:   A discussion on hardware issues specific to Linux

comp.os.linux.answers
:   A Q&A forum

comp.os.linux.networking
Internetworking discussion, with such topics as TCP/IP, the Internet, and the like

comp.os.linux.x
A discussion on the X Window System

Subscribing to one or more of these groups for at least a few weeks will give you a good feel for the type of communication that goes on and how useful they may be to you.

Newsgroup archives

Given the explosive growth of the Usenet service, many people turn to newsgroup archives on the Internet rather than watch specific groups on a daily basis. Many groups serve hundreds of messages a day, so unless the topic is very close to your daily activity (or heart), monitoring a busy group can become a full-time job. For example, unless you are a kernel developer or are debugging specific kernel problems, watching *redhat.kernel.general* won't be of much interest to you. Archives offer information as you need it.

You'll find a searchable archive of Usenet postings that can be helpful when you need to find recent or historical comments on a particular topic at *http://groups. google.com*.

Newsgroup archives provide you with an alternate view of Usenet threaded topics. Rather than posting a request for information and waiting for a response, searching an archive may yield immediate answers found in communications that have already occurred. An archive can free you from reading the headers to messages that are ultimately of no interest to you.

Contributing to Usenet

Depending on your level of expertise on the topic you're reading, you will inevitably come across a user question that you can answer with authority. Such a question is an opportunity for you to help someone. Think of the time needed to construct a helpful response as the payment for all the tips and assistance you yourself have received from other Usenet users over time.

Mailing Lists

Usenet provides an organized set of communications channels on specific topics. Often, however, a system administrator or an organization will want to set up a limited group of users with basic messaging capabilities. Without universal demand or failing to make the case for a legitimate new Usenet group, a *mailing list* is often constructed using list-processing software.

A mailing list is an email autoresponder with a known list of mail recipients. Any inbound mail to the list server from among the known list members will be mirrored to each of the other recipients on the list. This service keeps list subscribers tuned into their topic but increases email volume, and subscriptions to a few active mailing lists can fill your inbox daily.

On the other hand, a mailing list is proactive, and email received may be more likely to be read than Usenet newsgroup information. Usenet messages are easily missed simply because recipients are not paying attention. Mailing lists can be found on many web sites, where instructions for joining the lists are available. For example, the LDP maintains a general-discussion mailing list that you can join by sending email to *discuss-subscribe@en.tldp.org*. This list is for the discussion of LDP issues, document proposals, and other commentary. Your local Linux User's Group (LUG) probably also has a mailing list to keep members up-to-date on events, meetings, and opinions.

Vendor Web Sites and Other Resources

It is impossible to list the ever-increasing number of Linux-related sites on the Internet. Each distribution and many major projects have their own sites, as do groups such as the Free Software Foundation. Table 16-4 lists some of the most popular, grouped into categories, in case you've missed them.

Table 16-4. Some Linux-related web sites

Category	Web sites
Certification	*http://www.lpi.org*
Documentation	*http://www.tldp.org*
	http://linux.oreilly.com
News	*http://linux.oreillynet.com*
	http://www.lwn.net
	http://www.linuxtoday.com
Open source	*http://freshmeat.net*
	http://www.gnu.org
	http://www.kernel.org
Search engines	*http://www.google.com/linux*
Training	*http://www.lintraining.com*

Of course, it's impossible to create a static list of resources that will fulfill your ever-changing needs. If standard and familiar sources don't offer what you're looking for, don't hesitate to use a search engine. A targeted search on a high-quality search site can be surprisingly fruitful.

Objective 5: Notify Users on System-related Issues

A key, but difficult to test, skill for Linux sysadmins is the ability to communicate with your system users. Rather than require a face-to-face visit with you to test your communication skills, LPI covers only the system-related resources to help you relay information to your system users.

There are a variety of methods to relay information to your users. For general communication or notices, you may opt to simply send a broadcast email to all users on your system. For the LPI exams, however, you are simply expected to make use of the */etc/issue* and */etc/motd* files on your server, which notify shell users.

/etc/issue

The *letc/issue* file is responsible for the text that appears after a login at the system console. The text that appears when you log in remotely is controlled by *letc/issue.net*.

Both issue files are completely text based and can contain anything from a customized system introduction to basic system information or specialized system notifications. The information within these files can be escape sequences to generate relevant system information such as the current date, time, number of system users, kernel release, and even operating system version. Some common options are listed in Table 16-5.

Table 16-5. Common escape characters

Character	Description
\d	Insert the current date.
\m	Insert the architecture identifier of the machine, e.g., i686
\n	Insert the node name of the machine, also known as the hostname.
\o	Insert the domain name of the system.
\r	Insert the release number of the kernel, e.g., 2.4.20.
\s	Insert the system name, the name of the operating system.
\t	Insert the current time.
\u	Insert the number of current users logged in.
v	Insert the version of the OS.
\U	Insert the string "*n* users" where *n* is the number of current users logged in.

Example

The following is a simple example of an *letc/issue* file. The same content may be used within *letc/issue.net*.

```
$ cat /etc/issue
Red Hat Linux release 9 (Shrike)
Kernel \r on an \m
```

The result of this *letc/issue* looks like this:

```
Red Hat Linux release 9 (Shrike)
Kernel 2.4.20-18.9 on an i686
```

/etc/motd

The *letc/motd* is intended to be used as the *message of the day*. Its development was designed to get messages to system users using less disk space than required by sending mass email. The format of *letc/motd*, like *letc/issue*, is text based.

17

Shells, Scripting, Programming, and Compiling (Topic 1.109)

Depending upon the computing environments you're used to, the concepts of shells and shell programs (usually called *scripts*) may be a little foreign. On Linux systems, the shell is a full programming environment that can be scripted or used interactively.

This chapter covers Topic 1.109 and its two Objectives:

Objective 1: Customize and Use the Shell Environment
This Objective covers your shell and basic scripting concepts, including environment variables, functions, and script files that control the login environment. Weight: 5.

Objective 2: Customize or Write Simple Scripts
Customization of the many scripts found on a Linux system is important for its management and automation. Topics for this Objective include shell syntax, checking the status of executed programs, and issues surrounding the properties of script files. Weight: 3.

It is important for Linux administrators to become comfortable with at least one shell and its programming language. This can be an area of some concern to those used to graphics-only environments, where the use of a command interpreter is not a daily activity. As you'll see, becoming adept at working with your favorite shell will empower you and will allow you to let your computer carry a larger share of your daily responsibilities.

Objective 1: Customize and Use the Shell Environment

This Objective could be considered a brief "getting started with shells" overview because it details many of the basic concepts necessary to utilize the shell environment on Linux. These concepts are fundamental and very important for system administrators working on Linux and Unix systems. If you're new to shells and shell scripting, take heart. You can think of it as a combination of computer interaction (conversation) and computer programming (automation). It is nothing more than that, but the result is far more than this simplicity implies. If you're an old hand with shell programming, you may want to skip ahead to brush up on some of the particulars necessary for Exam 102.

An Overview of Shells

A shell is a fundamental and important part of your Linux computing environment. Shells are user programs not unlike other text-based programs and utilities. They offer a rich customizable interface to your system. Some of the main items provided by your shell are:

An interactive textual user interface to the operating system
>In this role, the shell is a command interpreter and display portal to the system. It offers you a communications channel to the kernel and is often thought of as the "shell around the kernel." That's where the name *shell* originates and is a good metaphor for conceptualizing how shells fit into the overall Linux picture.

An operating environment
>Shells set up an *environment* for the execution of other programs, which affects the way some of them behave. This environment consists of any number of *environment variables*, each of which describes one particular environment property by defining a *name=value* pair. Other features such as *aliases* enhance your operating environment by offering shorthand notations for commonly used commands.

A facility for launching and managing commands and programs
>Shells are used not only by users but also by the system to launch programs and support those programs with an operating environment.

A programming language
>Shells offer their own programming languages. At its simplest, this feature allows user commands to be assembled into useful sequences. At the other end of the spectrum, complete programs can be written in shell languages, with loop control, variables, and all of the capabilities of Linux's rich set of operating system commands.

All of the shells share some common concepts:

- They are all distinct from the kernel and run as user programs.
- Each shell can be customized by tuning the shell's operating environment.
- Shells are run for both interactive use by end users and noninteractive use by the system.
- A shell can be run from within another shell, enabling you to try a shell other than your default shell. To do this, you simply start the other shell from the command line of your current shell. In fact, this happens constantly on your system as scripts are executed and programs are launched. The new shell does not replace the shell that launched it. Instead, the new shell is a process running with the original shell as a parent process. When you terminate the child shell, you go back to the original one.

- Shells use a series of *configuration files* in order to establish their operating environment.
- Shells pass on environment variables to child processes.

The Bash Shell

bash is a free implementation of the standard Unix shell *sh* from the GNU Project. As the *bash* home page (*http://www.gnu.org/software/bash*) says:

> Bash is an *sh*-compatible shell that incorporates useful features from the Korn shell (*ksh*) and C shell (*csh*). It is intended to conform to the IEEE POSIX P1003.2/ISO 9945.2 Shell and Tools standard. It offers functional improvements over sh for both programming and interactive use.

While there are a number of shells available to choose from on a Linux system, *bash* is very popular and powerful, and it is the default shell for new accounts. Exam 102 concentrates on its use and configuration. The next few sections deal with common shell concepts, but the examples are specific to *bash*.

Shell and environment variables

Many programs running under Linux require information about you and your personal preferences to operate sensibly. While you could instruct each program you run with important details it needs to proceed, much of the information you'd convey would be redundant because you'd be telling every command you enter the same ancillary information at each invocation. For example, you'd need to tell your paging program about the size and nature of your terminal or terminal window each time you use it. You would also need to give fully qualified directory names for the programs you run.

Rather than force users to include so much detail to issue commands, the shell handles much of this information for you automatically. You've already seen that the shell creates an operating environment for you. That environment is made up of a series of *variables*, each of which has a value that is used by programs and other shells. The two types of variables used by most shells are:

Environment variables
> These variables can be thought of as *global variables* because they are passed on to all processes started by the shell, including other shells. This means that child processes inherit the environment. By convention, environment variables are given uppercase names. *bash* doesn't require the case convention. It is intended for clarity to humans. However, variable names are case-sensitive. Your shell maintains many environment variables, including the following examples:

> PATH
>> A list of directories through which the shell looks for executable programs as you enter them on the command line. All of the directories that contain programs that you'll want to execute are stored together in the PATH environment variable. Your shell looks through this list in sequence, from left to right, searching for each command you enter. Your PATH may differ from the PATHs of other users on your system

because you may use programs found in different locations or you may have a local directory with your own custom programs that need to be available. The PATH variable can become quite long as more and more directories are added.

HOME
> Your home directory, such as */home/bsmith*.

USERNAME
> Your username.

TERM
> The type of terminal or terminal window you are running. This variable is likely to have a value such as xterm or xterm-color. If you are running on a physical VT100 (or compatible) terminal, TERM is set to vt100.

Shell variables
> These variables can be thought of as *local* because they are specific only to the current shell. Child processes do not inherit them. Some shell variables are automatically set by the shell and are available for use in shell scripts. By convention, shell variables are given lowercase names.

To create a new *bash* shell variable, simply enter a *name=value* pair on the command line:

```
# PI=3.14
```

To see that this value is now assigned to the local variable PI, use the *echo* command to display its contents:

```
# echo $PI
3.14
```

The dollar sign preceding the variable name indicates that the name will be replaced with the variable's value. Without the dollar sign, *echo* would just return the text that was typed, which in this case is the variable name PI. At this point, PI is a local variable and is not available to child shells or programs. To make it available to other shells or programs, the variable must be exported to the environment:

```
# export PI
```

Aliases

Among the features missing from *sh* was the ability to easily make new commands or modify existing commands. *bash* has the ability to set an alias for commonly used commands or sequences of commands. For example, if you habitually call for the older pager *more* but actually prefer *less*, an alias can be handy to get the desired behavior, regardless of the command you use:

```
$ alias more='less'
```

This has the effect of intercepting any command entries for *more*, substituting *less*. The revised command is passed along to the shell's command interpreter.

Another common use for an alias is to modify a command slightly so that its default behavior is more to your liking. Many people, particularly when operating with superuser privileges, will use this alias:

```
$ alias cp='cp -i'
```

With this alias in effect, the use of the cp (copy) command becomes safer, because with the -i option always enforced by the alias, cp prompts you for approval before overwriting a file of the same name. Additional options you enter on the command line are appended to the end of the new command, such that cp -p becomes cp -i -p and so on.

If the righthand side of the aliased command is bigger than a single word or if it contains multiple commands (separated by semicolons, *bash*'s command terminator), you probably need to enclose it in single quotation marks to get your point across. This is because you need to prevent the shell in which you're working (your current *bash* process) from interpreting file globbing or other characters that might be part of your alias value. For example, suppose you wished to use a single alias to pair two simple commands:

```
$ alias lsps=ls -l; ps
```

Your current *bash* process will interpret this command not as a single alias but as two separate commands. First the alias *lsps* will be created for *ls -l*, and then a *ps* command will be added for immediate execution. What you really want is:

```
$ alias lsps='ls -l; ps'
```

Now, entering the command *lsps* will be aliased to *ls -l; ps*, and will correctly generate *ls* output immediately followed by *ps* output, as this example shows:

```
$ lsps
total 1253
drwx------  5 root  root   1024 May 27 17:15 dir1
drwxr-xr-x  3 root  root   1024 May 27 22:41 dir2
-rw-r--r--  1 root  root  23344 May 27 22:44 file1
drwxr-xr-x  2 root  root  12288 May 25 16:13 dir3
  PID TTY          TIME CMD
  892 ttyp0    00:00:00 bash
 1388 ttyp0    00:00:00 ps
```

Admittedly, this isn't a very useful command, but it is built upon in the next section.

After adding aliases, it may become easy to confuse which commands are aliases or native. To list the aliases defined for your current shell, simply enter the *alias* command by itself. This results in a listing of all the aliases currently in place:

```
$ alias
alias cp='cp -i'
alias lsps='ls -l;ps'
alias mv='mv -i'
alias rm='rm -i'
```

Note that aliases are local to your shell and are not passed down to programs or to other shells. You'll see how to ensure that your aliases are always available in the next section, "Configuration files."

Aliases are mainly used for simple command replacement. The shell inserts your aliased text in place of your alias name before interpreting the command. Aliases don't offer logical constructs and are limited to a few simple variable replacements. Aliases can also get messy when the use of complicated quoting is necessary, usually to prevent the shell from interpreting characters in your alias.

Functions

In addition to aliases, *bash* also offers *functions*. They work in much the same way as aliases, in that some function name of your choosing is assigned to a more complex construction. However, in this case that construction is a small program rather than a simple command substitution. Functions have a simple syntax:

[*function*] *name* ( ) { *command-list*; }

This declaration defines a function called *name*. *function* is optional, and the parentheses after *name* are required if *function* is omitted. The body of the function is the *command-list* between the curly brackets ({ and }). This list is a series of commands, separated by semicolons or by newlines. The series of commands is executed whenever *name* is specified as a command. The simple lsps alias shown earlier could be implemented as a function like this:

```
$ lsps ( ) { ls -l; ps; }
```

Using this new function as a command yields exactly the same result the alias did. However, if you implement this command as a function, parameters can be added to the command. Here is a new version of the same function, this time entered on multiple lines (which eliminates the need for semicolons within the function):

```
$ lsps ( ) {
> ls -l $1
> ps -aux | grep `/bin/basename $1`
> }
```

The > characters come from *bash* during interactive entry, indicating that *bash* is awaiting additional function commands or the } character, which terminates the function definition. This new function allows us to enter a single *argument* to the function, which is inserted everywhere $1 is found in the function. These arguments are called *positional parameters* because each one's number denotes its position in the argument list. This example uses only one positional parameter; there can be many, and the number of parameters is stored for your use in a special variable $# .

The command implemented in the previous example function now returns a directory listing and process status for any program given as an argument. For example, if the Apache web server is running, the command:

```
$ lsps /usr/sbin/httpd
```

yields a directory listing for */usr/sbin/httpd* and also displays all currently running processes that match httpd:

```
-rwxr-xr-x  1 root root 165740 Apr  7 17:17 /usr/sbin/httpd
root    3802 0.0  3.8  2384 1192 ?    S 16:34 0:00 httpd
nobody 3810 0.0  4.2  2556 1292 ?    S 16:34 0:00 httpd
nobody 3811 0.0  4.2  2556 1292 ?    S 16:34 0:00 httpd
```

```
nobody  3812  0.0   4.2   2556  1292  ?       S  16:34  0:00  httpd
nobody  3813  0.0   4.2   2556  1292  ?       S  16:34  0:00  httpd
nobody  3814  0.0   4.2   2556  1292  ?       S  16:34  0:00  httpd
root    3872  0.0   1.4   1152  432   ttyp0  S  16:45  0:00  grep httpd
```

Configuration files

It's a good assumption that every Linux user will want to define a few aliases, functions, and environment variables to suit her needs. However, it's undesirable to manually enter them upon each login or for each new invocation of *bash*. To set up these things automatically, *bash* uses a number of configuration files to set its operating environment when it starts. Some of these files are used only upon initial login, while others are executed for each instance of *bash* you start, including at login time. Some of these configuration files are systemwide files for all users to use, while others reside in your home directory for your use alone.

bash configuration files important to Exam 102 are listed in Table 17-1.

Table 17-1. bash configuration files

File	Description
/etc/profile	This is the systemwide initialization file executed during login. It usually contains environment variables, including an initial PATH, and startup programs.
/etc/bashrc	This is another systemwide initialization file that may be executed by a user's .bashrc for each bash shell launched. It usually contains functions and aliases.
~/.bash_profile	If this file exists, it is executed automatically after /etc/profile during login.
~/.bash_login	If .bash_profile doesn't exist, this file is executed automatically during login.
~/.profile	If neither .bash_profile nor .bash_login exists, this file is executed automatically during login. Note that this is the original Bourne shell configuration file.
~/.bashrc	This file is executed automatically when bash starts. This includes login, as well as subsequent interactive and noninteractive invocations of bash.
~/.bash_logout	This file is executed automatically during logout.
~/.inputrc	This file contains optional key bindings and variables that affect how bash responds to keystrokes. By default, bash is configured to respond like the Emacs editor.

The syntax ~/ refers to *bash*'s "home directory." While this shortcut may not represent much of a savings in typing, some Linux configurations may place users' directories in various and sometimes nonobvious places in the filesystem. Using the tilde syntax reduces the need for you to know exactly where a user's home directory is located.

In practice, users will generally (and often unknowingly) use the systemwide */etc/profile* configuration file to start. In addition, they'll often have three personal files in their home directory: *~/.bash_profile*, *~/.bashrc*, and *~/.bash_logout*. The local files are optional, and *bash* does not mind if one or all of them are not available in your directory.

Each of these configuration files consists entirely of plain text. They are typically simple, often containing just a few commands to be executed in sequence to

Shells, Scripts, Programming

prepare the shell environment for the user. Since they are evaluated by *bash* as lines of program code, they are said to be *sourced*, or interpreted, when *bash* executes them.

Like most programming languages, shell programs allow the use of comments. Most shells including *bash* consider everything immediately following the hash mark (#) on a single line to be a comment. An important exception is the $# *variable*, which has nothing to do with comments but contains the number of positional parameters passed to a function. Comments can span an entire line or share a line by following program code. All of your shell scripts and configuration files should use comments liberally.

Files sourced at login time are created mainly to establish default settings. These settings include such things as where to search for programs requested by the user (the PATH) and creation of shortcut names for commonly used tasks (aliases and functions). After login, files sourced by each subsequent shell invocation won't explicitly need to do these things again because they *inherit* the environment established by the login shell. Regardless, it isn't unusual to see a user's *.bashrc* file filled with all of their personal customizations. It also doesn't hurt anything, provided the *.bashrc* file is small and quick to execute.

While it is not necessary to have detailed knowledge of every item in your shell configuration files, Exam 102 requires that you understand them and that you can edit them to modify their behavior and your resulting operating environment. The following examples are typical of those found on Linux systems and are annotated with comments. Example 17-1 shows a typical Linux systemwide *profile*. This file is executed by every user's *bash* process at login time. A few environment variables and other parameters are set in it.

Example 17-1. An example systemwide Bash profile

```
# /etc/profile
# Systemwide environment and startup programs
# Functions and aliases go in systemwide /etc/bashrc
# PATH was already set, this is an extension
PATH="$PATH:/usr/X11R6/bin"
# Set a default prompt string
PS1="[\u@\h \W]\\$ "
# Set an upper limit for "core" files
ulimit -c 1000000
# Set a default umask, used to set default file permissions
if [ `id -gn` = `id -un` -a `id -u` -gt 14 ]; then
    umask 002
else
    umask 022
fi
# Set up some shell variables
USER=`id -un`
LOGNAME=$USER
MAIL="/var/spool/mail/$USER"
HOSTNAME=`/bin/hostname`
HISTSIZE=1000
HISTFILESIZE=1000
```

Example 17-1. An example systemwide Bash profile (continued)

```
INPUTRC=/etc/inputrc
# Make all these into environment variables
export PATH PS1 HOSTNAME HISTSIZE HISTFILESIZE
   USER LOGNAME MAIL INPUTRC
# Execute a series of other files
for i in /etc/profile.d/*.sh ; do
   if [ -x $i ]; then
      . $i
   fi
done
unset I       # Clean up the variable used above
```

Example 17-2 shows a systemwide *.bashrc* file. This file is not sourced by default when *bash* starts. Instead, it is optionally sourced by users' local *.bashrc* files.

Example 17-2. An example systemwide .bashrc file

```
# /etc/bashrc
alias more='less'              # prefer the "less" pager
alias lsps='ls -l;ps'          # a dubious command
```

Example 17-3 shows an example user's local *.bash_profile*. Note that this file sources the systemwide */etc/bashrc*, then goes on to local customizations.

Example 17-3. An example user .bash_profile file

```
# .bash_profile
# Get the aliases and functions from the system administrator
if [ -f ~/.bashrc ]; then
   . ~/.bashrc
fi
# User-specific environment and startup programs
PATH=$PATH:$HOME/bin  # Add my binaries directory to the path
EDITOR=emacs          # Set my preferred editor to Emacs
VISUAL=emacs          # Set my preferred editor to Emacs
PAGER=less            # Set my preferred pager to less
# Make my variables part of the environment
export PATH EDITOR VISUAL PAGER
```

Example 17-4 shows an individual's *.bashrc* file. Like the *.bash_profile* earlier, this file also sources the systemwide */etc/bashrc*.

Example 17-4. An example user's .bashrc file

```
# .bashrc
# User-specific aliases and functions
# Source global definitions
if [ -f /etc/bashrc ]; then
   . /etc/bashrc
fi
alias rm='rm -i'              # Add a safety net to rm
alias cp='cp -i'              # Add a safety net to cp
alias mv='mv -i'              # Add a safety net to mv
```

Example 17-4. An example user's .bashrc file (continued)

```
lsps( ) {                            # Define a personal function
    ls -l $1
    ps -aux | grep `/bin/basename $1`
}
```

Example 17-5 shows a short, simple, and not uncommon *.bash_logout* file. Probably the most likely command to find in a logout file is the *clear* command. Including a *clear* in your logout file is a nice way of being certain that whatever you were doing just before you logging out won't linger on the screen for the next user to ponder. This file is intended to execute commands for a logout from a text session, such as a system console or terminal. In a GUI environment where logout and login are handled by a GUI program, *.bash_logout* may not be of much value.

Example 17-5. A simple .bash_logout file

```
# .bash_logout
# This file is executed when a user logs out of the system
/usr/bin/clear          # Clear the screen
/usr/games/fortune      # Print a random adage
```

On the Exam

Make certain that you understand the difference between execution at login and execution at shell invocation, as well as which of the startup files serves each of those purposes.

.inputrc

Among the many enhancements added to *bash* is the ability to perform as if your history of commands is the buffer of an editor. That is, your command history is available to you, and you may cut, paste, and even search among command lines entered previously. This powerful capability can significantly reduce typing and increase accuracy. By default, *bash* is configured to emulate the Emacs editor, but a *vi* editing interface is also available.

The portion of *bash* that handles this function, and in fact handles all of the line input during interactive use, is known as *readline*. Readline may be customized by putting commands into an initialization file, which by default is in your home directory and called *.inputrc*. For example, to configure *bash* to use *vi*-style editing keys, add this line to *.inputrc*:

```
set editing-mode vi
```

You may also set the INPUTRC variable to the name of another file if you prefer. On your system, this variable may be set to */etc/initrc* by default, which would override any settings you put into a local *.initrc*. To use your own file, you must first explicitly place unset INPUTRC in your *.bash_profile*.

The default editing facilities enabled in *bash* are extensive and are beyond the scope of this section and Exam 102. However, you need to understand the concepts of adding your own custom key bindings to the *.inputrc* file and how they can help automate common keystrokes unique to your daily routine for the test.

For example, suppose you often use *top* to watch your system's activity (*top* is a useful process-monitoring utility that is described in Chapter 3):

```
$ top -Ssd1
```

If you do this often enough, you'll get tired of typing the command over and over and will eventually want an alias for it. To create the alias, simply alias this command to top:

```
$ alias top='/usr/bin/top -Ssd1'
```

Better yet, you can use *.inputrc* to create a key binding that will enter it for you. Here's how the *.inputrc* file would look if you were to bind your top command to the key sequence Ctrl-t:

```
# my .inputrc file
Control-t: "top -Ssd1 \C-m"
```

The lefthand side of the second line indicates the key combination you wish to use (Ctrl-t). The righthand side indicates what you wish to bind to that key sequence. In this case, *bash* outputs *top -Ssd1* and a carriage return, denoted here by \C-m (Ctrl-m), when Ctrl-t is pressed.

Through modifications of your local configuration files, you can customize your environment and automate many of your daily tasks. You may also override systemwide settings in your personal files simply by setting variables, aliases, and functions.

On the Exam

You won't need to have detailed knowledge of this key-binding syntax, but be aware of the *.inputrc* file and the kinds of things it enables *bash* to do.

Objective 2: Customize or Write Simple Scripts

You've seen how the use of *bash* configuration files, aliases, functions, variables, and key bindings can customize and make interaction with your Linux system efficient. The next step in your relationship with the shell is to use its natural programming capability, or *scripting language*. The scripting language of the original Bourne shell is found throughout a Linux system, and *bash* is fully compatible with it. This section covers essential *bash* scripting language concepts as required for Exam 102.

In order to have a full appreciation of shell scripting on Linux, it's important to look at your Linux system as a collection of unique and powerful tools. Each of the commands available on your Linux system, along with those you create yourself, has some special capability. Bringing these capabilities together to solve problems is among the basic philosophies of the Unix world.

Script Files

Just as the configuration files discussed in the last section are plain text files, so are the scripts for your shell. In addition, unlike compiled languages such as C or Pascal, no compilation of a shell program is necessary before it is executed. You can use any editor to create script files, and you'll find that many scripts you write are portable from Linux to other Unix systems.

Creating a simple bash script

The simplest scripts are those that simply string together some basic commands and perhaps do something useful with the output. Of course, this can be done with a simple alias or function, but eventually you'll have a requirement that exceeds a one-line request, and a shell script is the natural solution. Aliases and functions have already been used to create a rudimentary new command, lsps. Now let's look at a shell script (Example 17-6) that accomplishes the same thing.

Example 17-6. The lsps script

```
# A basic lsps command script for bash
ls -l $1
ps -aux | grep `/bin/basename $1`
```

As you can see, the commands used in this simple script are identical to those used in the alias and in the function created earlier. To make use of this new file, instruct your currently running *bash* shell to source it, giving it an option for the $1 positional parameter:

```
$ source ./lsps /usr/sbin/httpd
```

If you have */usr/sbin/httpd* running, you should receive output similar to that found previously for the alias. By replacing the word source with a single dot, you can create an alternate shorthand notation to tell *bash* to source a file, as follows:

```
$ . ./lsps /usr/sbin/httpd
```

Another way to invoke a script is to start a new invocation of *bash* and tell that process to source the file. To do this, simply start *bash* and pass the script name and argument to it:

```
$ /bin/bash ./lsps /usr/sbin/httpd
```

This last example gives us the same result; however, it is significantly different from the alias, the function, or the sourcing of the *lsps* file. In this particular case, a new invocation of *bash* was started to execute the commands in the script. This is important, because the environment in which the commands are running is distinct from the environment in which the user is typing. This is described in more detail later in this section.

 The ./ syntax indicates that the file you're referring to is in the current working directory. To avoid specifying ./ for users other than the superuser, put the directory . in the PATH. The PATH of the superuser should not include the current working directory, as a security precaution against Trojan horse–style attacks.

Thus far, a shell script has been created and invoked in a variety of ways, but it hasn't been made into a command. A script really becomes useful when it can be called by name like any other command.

Executable files

On a Linux system, programs are said to be executable if they have content that can be run by the processor (native execution) or by another program such as a shell (interpreted execution). However, in order to be eligible for execution when called at the command line, the files must have attributes that indicate to the shell that they are executable. To make a file executable, it must have at least one of its *executable bits* set. To turn the example script from a plain text file to an executable program, that bit must be set using the *chmod* command:

```
$ chmod a+x lsps
```

Once this is done, the script is executable by its owner, group members, and everyone else on the system. At this point, running the new command from the *bash* prompt yields the familiar output:

```
$ ./lsps /usr/sbin/httpd
```

When *lsps* is called by name, the commands in the script are interpreted and executed by the *bash* shell. However, this isn't ultimately what is desired. In many cases, users will be running some other shell interactively but will still want to program in *bash*. Programmers also use other scripting languages such as Perl. To have the scripts interpreted correctly, the system must be told which program should interpret the commands in the scripts.

She-bang!

Many kinds of script files are found on a Linux system, and each interpreted language comes with a unique and specific command structure. There needs to be a way to tell Linux which interpreter to use. This is accomplished by using a special line at the top of the script naming the appropriate interpreter. Linux examines this line and launches the specified interpreter program, which then reads the rest of the file. The special line must begin with #!, a construct often called *she-bang*. For *bash*, the she-bang line is:

```
#!/bin/bash
```

This command explicitly states that the program named *bash* can be found in the */bin* directory and designates *bash* to be the interpreter for the script. You'll also see other types of lines on script files, including:

`#!/bin/sh`
    The Bourne shell

`#!/bin/csh`
    The C-shell

`#!/bin/tcsh`
    The enhanced C-shell

`#!/bin/sed`
    The stream editor

`#!/usr/bin/awk`
    The awk programming language

`#!/usr/bin/perl`
    The Perl programming language

Each of these lines specifies a unique command interpreter for the script lines that follow. (*bash* is fully backward-compatible with *sh*; *sh* is just a link to *bash* on Linux systems.)

On the Exam

An incorrectly stated she-bang line can cause the wrong interpreter to attempt to execute commands in a script.

The shell script's environment

When running a script with `#!/bin/bash`, a new invocation of *bash* with its own environment is started to execute the script's commands as the parent shell waits. Exported variables in the parent shell are copied into the child's environment; the child shell executes the appropriate shell configuration files (such as *.bash_profile*). Because configuration files will be run, additional shell variables may be set and environment variables may be overwritten. If you are depending upon a variable in your shell script, be sure that it is either set by the shell configuration files or exported into the environment for your use, but not both.

Another important concept regarding your shell's environment is *one-way inheritance*. Although your current shell's environment is passed *into* a shell script, that environment is *not passed back* to the original shell when your program terminates. This means that changes made to variables during the execution of your script are not preserved when the script exits. Instead, the values in the parent shell's variables are the same as they were before the script executed. This is a basic Unix construct; inheritance goes from parent process to child process, and not the other way around.

On the Exam

It is important to remember how variables are set, how they are inherited, and that they are inherited only from parent process to child process.

Location, ownership, and permissions

The ability to run any executable program, including a script, under Linux depends in part upon its location in the filesystem. Either the user must explicitly specify the location of the file to run or it must be located in a directory known by the shell to contain executables. Such directories are listed in the PATH environment variable. For example, the shells on a Linux system (including *bash*) are located in */bin*. This directory is usually in the PATH, because you're likely to run programs that are stored there. When you create shell programs or other utilities of your own, you may want to keep them together and add the location to your own PATH. If you maintain your own *bin* directory, you might add the following line to your *.bash_profile*:

```
PATH=$PATH:$HOME/bin
```

This statement modifies your path to include your */home/bin* directory. If you add personal scripts and programs to this directory, *bash* finds them automatically.

Execute permissions (covered in Chapter 6, "Objective 5: Use File Permissions to Control Access to Files") also affect your ability to run a script. Since scripts are just text files, execute permission must be granted to them before they are considered executable, as shown earlier.

You may wish to limit access to the file from other users using:

```
$ chmod 700 ~/bin/lsps
```

This prevents anyone but the owner from making changes to the script.

The issue of file ownership is dovetailed with making a script executable. By default, you own all of the files you create. However, if you are the system administrator, you'll often be working as the superuser and will be creating files with username *root* as well. It is important to assign the correct ownership and permission to scripts to ensure that they are secured.

SUID and GUID rights

On rare occasions, it may become necessary to allow a user to run a program under the name of a different user. This is usually associated with programs run by nonprivileged users who need special privileges to execute correctly. Linux offers two such rights: SUID and SGID.

When an executable file is granted the SUID right, processes created to execute it are owned by the user who owns the file instead of the user who launched the program. This is a security enhancement, in that the delegation of a privileged task or ability does not imply that the superuser password must be widely known. On the other hand, any process whose file is owned by *root* and which has the SUID set will run as *root* for everyone. This could represent an opportunity to break the security of a system if the file itself is easy to attack (as a script is). For this reason, Linux systems will ignore SUID and SGID attributes for script files. Setting SUID and SGID attributes is detailed in Chapter 6, "Objective 5: Use File Permissions to Control Access to Files."

On the Exam

Be sure to think through any questions that require you to determine a user's right to execute a file. Consider location, ownership, execute permissions, and SUID/SGID rights together. Also, watch for new scripts that haven't been granted any execute privileges.

Basic Bash Scripts

Now that some of the requirements for creating and using executable scripts are established, some of the features that make them so powerful can be introduced. This section contains basic information needed to customize and create new *bash* scripts.

Return values

As shell scripts execute, it is important to confirm that their constituent commands complete successfully. Most commands offer a *return value* to the shell when they terminate. This value is a simple integer and has meaning specific to the program you're using. Almost all programs return the value when they are successful and return a nonzero value when a problem is encountered. The value is stored in the special *bash* variable $?, which can be tested in your scripts to check for successful command execution. This variable is reset for every command executed by the shell, so you must test it immediately after execution of the command you're verifying. As a simple example, try using the *cat* program on a nonexistent file:

```
$ cat bogus_file
cat: bogus_file: No such file or directory
```

Then immediately examine the status variable twice:

```
$ echo $?
1
$ echo $?
```

The first *echo* yielded 1 (failure) because the *cat* program failed to find the file you specified. The second *echo* yielded 0 (success) because the first *echo* command succeeded. A good script makes use of these status flags to exit gracefully in case of errors.

If it sounds backward to equate zero with success and nonzero with failure, consider how these results are used in practice:

Error detection
> Scripts that check for errors include if-then code to evaluate a command's return status:
>
> ```
> command
> if (failure_returned) ; then
>    ...error recovery code...
> fi
> ```
>
> In a *bash* script, failure_returned is simply the $? variable, which contains the result of the command's execution.

Error classification
> Since commands can fail for multiple reasons, many return more than one failure code. For example, *grep* returns 0 if matches are found and 1 if no matches are found; it returns 2 if there is a problem with the search pattern or input files. Scripts may need to respond differently to various error conditions.

On the Exam

Make certain you understand the meaning of return values in general and that they are stored in the $? variable.

File tests

During the execution of a shell script, specific information about a file—such as whether it exists, is writable, is a directory or a file, and so on, may sometimes be required. In *bash*, the built-in command *test* performs this function. (There is also a standalone executable version of *test* available in */usr/bin* for non-*bash* shells.) *test* has two general forms:

test *expression*
> In this form, *test* and an *expression* are explicitly stated.

[*expression*]
> In this form, *test* isn't mentioned; instead, the *expression* is enclosed inside brackets.

The *expression* can be formed to look for such things as empty files, the existence of files, the existence of directories, equality of strings, and others. (See the more complete list with their operators in the later section, "Abbreviated Bash command reference.")

When used in a script's if or while statement, the brackets ([and]) may appear to be grouping the test logically. In reality, [is simply another form of the test command, which requires the trailing]. A side effect of this bit of trickery is that the spaces around [and] are mandatory, a detail that is sure to get you into trouble eventually.

Command substitution

bash offers a handy ability to do *command substitution*. This feature allows you to replace $(*command*) with the result of *command*, usually in a script. That is, wherever $(*command*) is found, its output is substituted prior to interpretation by the shell. For example, to set a variable to the number of lines in your *.bashrc* file, you could use *wc -l*:

```
$ RCSIZE=$(wc -l ~/.bashrc)
```

Another form of command substitution encloses *command* in *backquotes* (`):

```
$ RCSIZE=`wc -l ~/.bashrc`
```

The result is the same, except that the backquote syntax allows the backslash character to escape the dollar symbol ($), the backquote (`), and another backslash (\). The $(*command*) syntax avoids this nuance by treating all characters between the parentheses literally.

Mailing from scripts

The scripts you write will often be rummaging around your system at night when you're asleep or at least while you're not watching. Since you're too busy to check on every script's progress, a script will sometimes need to send some mail to you or another administrator. This is particularly important when something big goes wrong or when something important depends on the script's outcome. Sending mail is as simple as piping into the mail command:

```
echo "Backup failure 5" | mail -s "Backup failed" root
```

The -s option indicates that a quoted subject for the email follows. The recipient could be yourself, *root*, or if your system is configured correctly, any Internet email address. If you need to send a log file, redirect the input of mail from that file:

```
mail -s "subject" recipient < log_file
```

Sending email from scripts is easy and makes tracking status easier than reviewing log files every day. On the downside, having an inbox full of "success" messages can be a nuisance too, so many scripts are written so that mail is sent only in response to an important event, such as a fatal error.

Abbreviated Bash command reference

This section lists some of the important *bash* built-in commands used when writing scripts. Please note that not all of the *bash* commands are listed here; for a complete overview of the *bash* shell, see *Learning the bash Shell*, Cameron Newham (O'Reilly).

break

Syntax
```
break [n]
```

Description
Exit from the innermost (most deeply nested) for, while, or until loop or from the *n* innermost levels of the loop.

---

case

Syntax
```
case string in
    pattern1)
        commands1
        ;;
    pattern2)
        commands2
        ;;
    ...
esac
```

Description
Choose *string* from among a series of possible patterns. These patterns use the same form as file globs (wildcards). If *string* matches pattern *pattern1*, perform the subsequent *commands1*. If string matches *pattern2*, perform *commands2*. Proceed down the list of patterns until one is found. To catch all remaining strings, use *) at the end.

---

continue

Syntax
```
continue [n]
```

Description
Skip remaining commands in a for, while, or until loop, resuming with the next iteration of the loop (or skipping *n* loops).

---

echo

Syntax
```
echo [options] [string]
```

Description
Write *string* to standard output, terminated by a newline. If no *string* is supplied, echo only a newline.

Frequently used options

-e

 Enable interpretation of escape characters

-n

 Suppress the trailing newline in the output

Useful special characters

\a

 Sound an audible alert

\b

 Insert a backspace

\c

 Suppress the trailing newline (same as -n)

\f

 Form feed

---

exit

Syntax

```
exit [n]
```

Description

Exit a shell script with status n. The value for n can be 0 (success) or nonzero (failure). If n is not given, the exit status is that of the most recent command.

Example

```
if ! test -f somefile
then
    echo "Error: Missing file somefile"
    exit 1
fi
```

---

for

Syntax

```
for x in list
do
    commands
done
```

Description

Assign each word in *list* to *x* in turn and execute *commands*. If *list* is omitted, it is assumed that positional parameters from the command line, which are stored in $@, are to be used.

```
for filename in bigfile* ; do
  echo "Compressing $filename"
  gzip $filename
done
```

function

Syntax

```
function name
{
    commands
}
```

Description

Define function *name*. Positional parameters ($1, $2, ...) can be used within *commands*.

Example

```
# function myfunc
{
  echo "parameter is $1"
}
# myfunc 1
parameter is 1
# myfunc two
parameter is two
```

getopts

Syntax

```
getopts string name [args]
```

Description

Process command-line arguments (or *args*, if specified) and check for legal options. The *getopts* command is used in shell script loops and is intended to ensure standard syntax for command-line options. The *string* contains the option letters to be recognized by *getopts* when running the script. Valid options are processed in turn and stored in the shell variable *name*. If an option letter is followed by a colon, the option must be followed by one or more arguments when the command is entered by the user.

if

Syntax

```
if expression1
then
```

```
    commands1
elif expression2
then
    commands2
else
    commands
fi
```

Description

The if command is used to define a conditional statement. There are three possible formats for using the if command:

```
if-then-fi
if-then-else-fi
if-then-elif-then-...fi
```

kill

Syntax

```
kill [options] IDs
```

Description

Send signals to each specified process or job ID, which you must own unless you are a privileged user. The default signal sent with the *kill* command is TERM, instructing processes to shut down.

Options

-l

List the signal names.

-s signal or -signal

Specify the signal number or name.

read

Syntax

```
read [options] variable1 [variable2...]
```

Description

Read one line of standard input, and assign each word to the corresponding variable, with all remaining words assigned to the last variable.

Example

```
echo -n "Enter last-name, age, height, and weight > "
read lastname everythingelse
echo $lastname
echo $everythingelse
```

The name entered is placed in variable $lastname; all of the other values, including the spaces between them, are placed in $everythingelse.

return

Syntax

```
return [n]
```

Description

This command is used inside a function definition to exit the function with status *n*. If *n* is omitted, the exit status of the previously executed command is returned.

shift

Syntax

```
shift [n]
```

Description

Shift positional parameters down *n* elements. If *n* is omitted, the default is 1, so $2 becomes $1, $3 becomes $2, and so on.

source

Syntax

```
source file [arguments]
. file [arguments]
```

Description

Read and execute lines in *file*. The *file* does not need to be executable but must be in a directory listed in PATH. The dot syntax is equivalent to stating source.

test

Syntax

```
test expression
[ expression ]
```

Description

Evaluate the conditional expression and return a status of 0 (true) or 1 (false). The first form explicitly calls out the *test* command. The second form implies the *test* command. The spaces around *expression* are required in the second form. *expression* is constructed using options.

Frequently used options

-d *file*
> True if *file* exists and is a directory

-e file
> True if *file* exists

-f file
> True if *file* exists and is a regular file

-L file
> True if *file* exists and is a symbolic link

-n string
> True if the length of *string* is nonzero

-r file
> True if *file* exists and is readable

-s file
> True if *file* exists and has a size greater than zero

-w file
> True if *file* exists and is writable

-x file
> True if *file* exists and is executable

-z string
> True if the length of *string* is zero

file1 -ot file2
> True if *file1* is older than *file2*

string1 = string2
> True if the strings are equal

string1 != string2
> True if the strings are not equal

Example

To determine if a file exists and is readable, use the *-r* option:

```
if test -r file
then
    echo "file exists"
fi
```

Using the [ ] form instead, the same test looks like this:

```
if [ -r file ]
then
    echo "file exists"
fi
```

until

Syntax

```
until
    test-commands
do
    commands
done
```

Description

Execute *test-commands* (usually a *test* command) and if the exit status is nonzero (that is, the test fails), perform commands and repeat. Opposite of while.

while

Syntax

```
while
    test-commands
do
    commands
done
```

Description

Execute *test-commands* (usually a *test* command) and if the exit status is zero, perform *commands*; repeat. Opposite of until.

Example

Example 17-7 shows a typical script from a Linux system. This example is */etc/rc.d/init.d/sendmail*, which is the script that starts and stops sendmail. This script demonstrates many of the built-in commands referenced in the last section.

Example 17-7. Sample sendmail startup script

```
#!/bin/sh
#
# sendmail    This shell script takes care of starting
#             and stopping sendmail.
#
# chkconfig: 2345 80 30
# description: Sendmail is a Mail Transport Agent, which
#              is the program that moves mail from one
#              machine to another.
# processname: sendmail
# config: /etc/sendmail.cf
# pidfile: /var/run/sendmail.pid
# Source function library.
. /etc/rc.d/init.d/functions
# Source networking configuration.
. /etc/sysconfig/network
# Source sendmail configuration.
if [ -f /etc/sysconfig/sendmail ] ; then
  . /etc/sysconfig/sendmail
else
  DAEMON=yes
  QUEUE=1h
fi
# Check that networking is up.
[ ${NETWORKING} = "no" ] && exit 0
[ -f /usr/sbin/sendmail ] || exit 0
# See how we were called.
```

Example 17-7. Sample sendmail startup script (continued)

```
case "$1" in
  start)
  # Start daemons.
  echo -n "Starting sendmail: "
  /usr/bin/newaliases > /dev/null 2>&1
  for i in virtusertable access domaintable mailertable ; do
    if [ -f /etc/mail/$i ] ; then
      makemap hash /etc/mail/$i < /etc/mail/$i
    fi
  done
  daemon /usr/sbin/sendmail $([ "$DAEMON" = yes ] \
    && echo -bd) $([ -n "$QUEUE" ] && echo -q$QUEUE)
  echo
  touch /var/lock/subsys/sendmail
  ;;
  stop)
  # Stop daemons.
  echo -n "Shutting down sendmail: "
  killproc sendmail
  echo
  rm -f /var/lock/subsys/sendmail
  ;;
  restart)
  $0 stop
  $0 start
  ;;
  status)
  status sendmail
  ;;
  *)
  echo "Usage: sendmail {start|stop|restart|status}"
  exit 1
esac
exit 0
```

On the Exam

You should be familiar with a script's general structure, as well as the use of she-bang, test, if statements and their syntax (including the trailing fi), return values, exit values, and so on.

18

Administrative Tasks
(Topic 1.111)

As a system administrator in a multiuser environment, much of your activity is related to users and their system accounts, the automation of routine tasks, and system backup. This chapter covers these administrative aspects of Linux as required for Exam 102. This chapter has six Objectives:

Objective 1: Manage Users and Group Accounts and Related System Files
Candidates should be able to add, remove, suspend, and change user accounts. Tasks include to add and remove groups, to change user/group info in password/group databases. This Objective also includes creating special purpose and limited accounts. Weight: 4.

Objective 2: Tune the User Environment and System Environment Variables
Candidates should be able to modify global and user profiles. This includes setting environment variables, maintaining *skel* directories for new user accounts, and setting a command search path to the proper directory. Weight: 3.

Objective 3: Configure and Use System Log Files to Meet Administrative and Security Needs
Candidates should be able to configure system logs. This Objective includes managing the type and level of information logged, manually scanning log files for notable activity, monitoring log files, arranging for automatic rotation and archiving of logs, and tracking down problems noted in logs. Weight: 3.

Objective 4: Automate System Administration Tasks by Scheduling Jobs to Run in the Future
Candidates should be able to use *cron* or *anacron* to run jobs at regular intervals and to use at to run jobs at a specific time. Tasks include managing cron and at jobs and configuring user access to cron and at services. Weight: 4.

Objective 5: Maintain an Effective Data Backup Strategy
Candidates should be able to plan a backup strategy and back up filesystems automatically to various media. Tasks include dumping a raw device to a file or vice versa, performing partial and manual backups, verifying the integrity of backup files, and partially or fully restoring backups. Weight: 3.

Objective 6: Maintain System Time
Candidates should be able to properly maintain the system time and synchronize the clock over NTP. Tasks include setting the system date and time, setting the BIOS clock to the correct time in UTC, configuring the correct time zone for the system, and configuring the system to correct clock drift to match NTP clock. Weight: 4.

Objective 1: Manage Users and Group Accounts and Related System Files

Whether on a corporate server or personal desktop machine, managing user accounts is an important aspect of running a Linux system. The *root*, or superuser, account is established when you first install Linux. Unlike single-user systems (such as MS-DOS), multiuser systems require the notion of an *owner* for files, processes, and other system objects. A owner may be a human system user or a system service, such as a web server. Each of these owners is differentiated from others by a unique *user account*, which is assigned to it by the system administrator.

User Accounts and the Password File

When a new user account is added to a Linux system, an entry is added to a list of users in the *password file*, which is stored in */etc/passwd*. This file gets its name from its original use, which was to store user information including an encrypted form of the user's password. The password file is in plain text and is readable by everyone on the system. Each line in the password file contains information for a single user account, with fields separated by colons as illustrated in Figure 18-1.

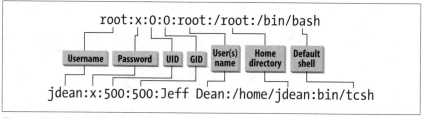

Figure 18-1. Sample lines from a password file

Each line in the file contains information for a single system account and contains the following pieces of information in colon-separated fields:

Username

The first field on a line is a unique *username* for the person or service using the account.

Password

Each username has an associated *password*. The password stored in this field is in a hashed (unreadable and unrecoverable) form. Despite the hash, for security reasons, most systems now store user passwords in a separate /etc/ shadow file that has restricted permissions. If the password is not included, its field is filled by the letter x, which indicates that the shadow password system is in use.

User ID

Each username requires a unique *user identifier*, or UID. The UID is simply a nonnegative integer. The *root* account is assigned the UID of 0, which gives it global privilege on the system. By convention, the UID values from 0 to 99 are reserved for administrative use; those over 99 are for regular system users. It's not unusual for new system accounts to start at 500.

Group ID

Each username has a default *group identifier*, or GID. The GID is also a nonnegative integer. Groups are a way of allowing users to share files through mutual group membership. Group numbers and their associated names are specified in the /etc/group file. The GID stored for each user in /etc/passwd is its default group ID, though a user may belong to many groups.

Full name (or other comment)

The user's full name or other information is stored as plain text. This field may contain spaces.

Home directory

The *home directory* is the default directory in the filesystem for the user's account. If a new account is meant for a person, a home directory will probably be created in the filesystem with standard configuration files that the user may then personalize. The full path to that home directory is listed here.

Default shell

This field specifies the default shell for the user or service, which is the shell that runs when the user logs in or opens a shell window. In most cases, the shell will be /bin/bash, but it can be any shell, or even another executable program. (Nonshell entries may be seen in the case of some services that should own files but never log in interactively. You may see the shell field filled with /bin/false, a small program that does nothing but yield an error and terminate. This ensures that a service account is secured from login.)

Looking back at Figure 18-1, the first line shows the definition of the *root* account with UID and GID of 0, a name of *root*, a home directory of /root, and a default shell of /bin/bash. The second line shows a standard user account for Jeff Dean, with UID and GID of 500. The home directory is /home/jdean and the default shell is /bin/tcsh.

Administrative
Tasks

Groups and the Group File

In addition to ownership by individual system users, filesystem objects have separate ownership settings for groups of users. This *group ownership* allows an additional level of user-specific access control beyond that of a file's individual owner. Groups are similar to users in their administration and are defined in the file */etc/group*. Like the *passwd* file, the *group* file contains colon-separated fields:

Group name
> Each group must have a unique name.

Group password
> Just as user accounts have passwords, groups can have passwords for their membership. If the password field is empty, the group does not require a password.

Group ID
> Each group requires a unique GID. Like a UID, a GID is a nonnegative integer.

Group member list
> The last field is a list of group members by username, separated by commas.

Together, these pieces of information define a group; colons separate the fields. Here are a few sample lines from a group file:

```
root:x:0:root
pppusers:x:230:jdean,jdoe
finance:x:300:jdean,jdoe,bsmith
jdean:x:500:
jdoe:x:501:
bsmith:x:502:
```

In this example, both *jdean* and *jdoe* are members of the *pppusers* group (GID 230), and *jdean*, *jdoe*, and *bsmith* are all members of the *finance* group (GID 300). The remaining groups, *root*, *jdean*, *jdoe*, and *bsmith* are single-user groups. These groups are not intended for multiple users and do not contain additional members. For security purposes, it is common to create new users with their own personal single-user group. Doing this enhances security because new files and directories will not have group privileges for other users. (Although the GID of these single-user groups may match the UID of the user for which they're created, there is no direct relationship between the UID and GID.)

The Shadow Password and Shadow Group Systems

Encrypted passwords must be secure from all users on the system, while leaving the remainder of the information in */etc/passwd* world-readable. To do this, the encrypted password is moved to a new file that *shadows* the password file line for line. The file is aptly called */etc/shadow* and is generally said to contain *shadow passwords*. Here are a couple of example lines from a shadow file:

```
root:$1$oxEaSzzdXZESTGTU:10927:0:99999:7:-1:-1:134538444
jdean:$1$IviLopPn461z47J:10927:0:99999:7:::11688:134538412
```

The first two fields contain the username and the encrypted passwords. The remaining fields contain optional additional information on password aging information.

Group passwords and shadow groups

Just as user accounts listed in */etc/passwd* are protected by encrypted passwords, groups listed in */etc/group* can also be protected by passwords. A group password can be used to allow access to a group by a user account that is not actually a member of the group. Account users can use the *newgrp* command to change their default group and enter the group password. If the password is correct, the account is granted the group privileges, just as a group member would be.

The group definition file, like the password file, is readable by everyone on the system. If group passwords are stored there, a dictionary attack could be made against them. To protect against such attacks, passwords in */etc/group* can be shadowed. The protected passwords are stored in */etc/gshadow*, which is readable only by *root*. Here are a few sample lines from a *gshadow* file:

```
root:::root
pppusers:!::
finance:0cf7ipLtpSBGg::
jdean:!::
jdoe:!::
bsmith:!::
```

In this example, the groups *pppusers*, *jdean*, *jdoe*, and *bsmith* do not have group passwords as indicated by the ! in the password field. The *finance* group is the only one with a password, which is hashed.

On the Exam

A major contrast between *passwd/group* and *shadow/gshadow* is the permissions on the files. The standard files are readable by everyone on the system, but the shadow files are readable only by *root*, which protects encrypted passwords from theft and possible cracking.

User and Group Management Commands

Although possible, it is rarely necessary (or advised) to manipulate the account and group definition files manually with a text editor. Instead, a family of convenient administrative commands is available for managing accounts, groups, password shadowing, group shadowing, and password aging. Password aging (rules governing change intervals and automated expiration of passwords) is not an explicit Objective for the LPIC Level 1 Exams.

useradd

Syntax

```
useradd [options] user
```

Description

Create the account *user* on the system. Both system defaults and specified *options* define how the account is configured. All system account files are updated as required. An initial password must subsequently be set for new users using the `passwd` command. It is the user's responsibility to go back and change that password when he first logs in to the system.

Frequently used options

-c comment
    Define the comment field, probably the user's name.

-d homedir
    Use *homedir* as the user's home directory.

-m
    Create and populate the home directory.

-s shell
    Use *shell* as the default for the account.

-D
    List (and optionally change) system default values.

Examples

Add a new user, *bsmith*, with all default settings:

```
# useradd bsmith
```

Add a new user, *jdoe*, with a name, default home directory, and the *tcsh* shell:

```
# useradd -mc "Jane Doe" -s /bin/tcsh jdoe
```

usermod

Syntax

```
usermod [options] user
```

Description

Modify an existing user account. The *usermod* command accepts many of the same options *useradd* does.

Frequently used options

-L
    Lock the password, disabling the account.

-U
    Unlock the user's password, enabling the user to once again log in to the system.

Examples

Change *jdoe*'s name in the comment field:

```
# usermod -c "Jane Deer-Doe" jdoe
```

Lock the password for *bsmith*:

```
# usermod -L bsmith
```

userdel

Syntax

```
userdel [-r] user
```

Description

Delete an existing user account. When combined with the *-r* option, the user's home directory is deleted. Note that completely deleting accounts may lead to confusion when files owned by the deleted user remain in other system directories. For this reason, it is common to disable an account rather than delete it. Accounts can be disabled using the chage, usermod, and passwd commands.

Example

Delete the user *bsmith*, including the home directory:

```
# userdel -r bsmith
```

groupadd

Syntax

```
groupadd group
```

Description

Add *group* to the system. In the rare case that a group password is desired on *group*, it must be added using the *gpasswd* command after the group is created.

groupmod

Syntax

```
groupmod [option] group
```

Description

Modify the parameters of *group*.

Option

-n name
> Change the name of group to *name*.

groupdel

Syntax

```
groupdel group
```

Description

Delete *group* from the system. Deleting groups can lead to the same confusion in the filesystem as described previously for deleting a user (see *userdel*).

passwd

Syntax

```
passwd [options] username
```

Description

Interactively set the password for *username*. The password cannot be entered on the command line.

Option

-l

Available only to the superuser, this option locks the password for the account.

gpasswd

Syntax

```
gpasswd groupname
```

Description

Interactively set the group password for *groupname*. The password cannot be entered on the command line.

Additional shadow password management commands

The shadow password utilities include a few commands for converting to and from the shadow system, as well as a command to display and adjust password aging settings for users.

pwconv

Syntax

```
pwconv
```

Description

Convert a standard password file to a password and shadow password combination, enabling shadow passwords on the system.

pwunconv

Syntax

```
pwunconv
```

Description

Revert from a shadow password configuration to a standard password file.

grpconv

Syntax

```
grpconv
```

Description

Convert a standard group file to a group and shadow group combination, enabling shadow groups on the system. Shadow passwords are rarely necessary.

grpunconv

Syntax

```
grpunconv
```

Description

Revert from a shadow group configuration to a standard group file.

Objective 2: Tune the User Environment and System Environment Variables

When you create a new user account on your Linux system, some basic setup information is necessary for the user to initially become productive. When the user logs into the system, she will need:

- A minimal set of environment variables, including a PATH that is meaningful for your system
- Basic configuration files in her home directory

The amount of default information you provide can range from minimal to extremely detailed. In general, you'll want to provide the setup information that will allow the user to begin working without extensive personal customization.

Systemwide Startup Scripts

When the *bash* shell starts, it looks for a number of configuration script files, including */etc/profile*. Commands in this file are executed at login time and contain global startup information and settings for all users. Example 18-1 contains an example profile.

Example 18-1. Sample /etc/profile

```
PATH="$PATH:/usr/X11R6/bin"
PS1="[\u@\h \W]\\$ "
ulimit -c 1000000
if [ `id -gn` = `id -un` -a `id -u` -gt 14 ]; then
        umask 002
else
        umask 022
fi
USER=`id -un`
LOGNAME=$USER
MAIL="/var/spool/mail/$USER"
HOSTNAME=`/bin/hostname`
HISTSIZE=1000
HISTFILESIZE=1000
INPUTRC=/etc/inputrc
PATH="$PATH:/usr/local/bin"
export PATH PS1 HOSTNAME HISTSIZE HISTFILESIZE
USER LOGNAME MAIL INPUTRC
```

The syntax for *bash* programming is in Chapter 17. However, you can see that this file does basic shell setup for the user, including the assignment of a number of environment variables. As an example of a common local customization, note the line containing PATH= adds an additional directory to those already listed in the PATH environment variable. In this case, the system administrator expects that most users will need to run programs stored in */usr/X11R6/bin*. Making this modification once in */etc/profile* eliminates the need for individuals to make it in their personal *bash* profiles.

Functions and aliases are not inherited by new shells, and commands in */etc/profile* are executed only at login time. For these reasons, the definition of functions and aliases typically is not done in */etc/profile*, but instead either in each individual user's *.bashrc*, or a central location such as */etc/bashrc* that is called by the user's *.bashrc*. Commands in the *.bashrc* file are executed each time a new shell starts; their effects will apply to all new shells.

Setting the Home Directory for New Accounts

When creating a new account, usually you'll want to create a default home directory for the user of the account. On Linux systems, the home directory is most likely something like */home/username*, but you can define it in any way you like.

When you create a new home directory, it is a courtesy to the new user to initially populate the directory with useful files. These might include startup files for the user's shell, for his desktop, or for X Window applications. To facilitate the automated population of new user directories, an example home directory is created in a skeleton directory */etc/skel*. This directory should contain all of the files and subdirectories that all new users will need. Example 18-2 shows the contents of an example */etc/skel* directory.

Example 18-2. Sample skeleton (/etc/skel) directory

```
-rw-r--r--  1 root    root       24 Jun 24       .bash_logout
-rw-r--r--  1 root    root      191 Apr  9 07:59 .bash_profile
-rw-r--r--  1 root    root      124 Apr  9 07:59 .bashrc
-rw-r--r--  1 root    root      854 Aug 28  2002 .emacs
drwxr-xr-x  3 root    root     4096 Aug 12  2002 .kde
```

This example */etc/skel* directory contains:

- Three configuration files for the shell (*.bash_logout*, *.bash_profile*, and *.bashrc*)
- A configuration file for the Emacs editor (*.emacs*)
- A directory for KDE (*.kde*)

The specifics of this example are not important, but illustrate that a number of default files can be included in a new user's account setup. Additions could include default files for other desktop environments such as GNOME as well as startup files for other shells.

When a new account is created with a home directory, the entire contents of */etc/skel* are copied recursively (that is, including subdirectories) to the new home directory location. The home directory and its entire contents are then set to the new account's UID and GID, making the new user owner of her initial files. She is then free to modify these files and directories as necessary.

As the system administrator, you may add, modify, and delete files in */etc/skel* as needed for your environment.

Administrative Tasks

Objective 3: Configure and Use System Log Files to Meet Administrative and Security Needs

Many events occur on your Linux system that should be logged for administrative purposes. Linux uses the *syslogd* system to display and record messages describing these events. This system allows finely controlled logging of messages from the kernel as well as processes running on your system and remote systems. Messages can be placed on the console display, in log files, and on the text screens of users logged in to the system.

Configuring syslogd

The behavior of *syslogd* is controlled by its configuration file, */etc/syslog.conf*. This text file contains lines indicating what is to be logged and where. Each line contains directives in this form:

    facility.level action

The directives are defined as follows:

facility
> This represents the creator of the message (that is, the kernel or a process) and is one of the following: auth (the facility security is equivalent to auth, but its use is deprecated), authpriv, cron, daemon, kern, lpr, mail, mark (the mark facility is meant for *syslogd*'s internal use only), news, syslog, user, uucp, or local0 through local7. The use of these facility designators allows you to control the destination of messages based on their origin. Facilities local0 through local7 are for any use you may wish to assign to them in your own programs and scripts. It's possible that your distribution has assigned one or more of the local facilities already. Check your configuration before using a local facility.

level
> Specifies a severity threshold beyond which messages are logged, and is one of the following (from lowest to highest severity): debug, info, notice, warning (or warn), err (or error), crit, alert, or emerg (or panic). (warn, error, and panic are all deprecated, but you may see them on older systems.) There is also a special level called none that will disable a facility. The level defines the amount of detail recorded in the log file. A single period separates the facility from the level, and together they comprise the *message selector*. The asterisk (*) can be used to describe all facilities or all levels.

action
> The *action* directive is arguably misnamed. It represents the destination for messages that correspond to a given selector (*facility.level*). The action can be a filename (including the full pathname), a hostname preceded by the @ sign, or a comma-separated list of users or an asterisk (this means all logged-in users will be included).

For example, if you wanted to create a separate log file for activity reported by the scripts you write, you might include a line like this in */etc/syslog.conf*:

```
# Define a new log file for the local5 facility
local5.*                              /var/log/local5
```

You could then use the logger utility to write messages to the facility from your shell script (*syslogd* must be restarted or signaled to reinitialize before the new log file is created.):

```
$ logger -p local5.info "Script terminated normally"
```

The message "Script terminated normally" would be placed into */var/log/local5*, along with a timestamp and the hostname that sent the message. Example 18-3 contains an example */etc/syslog.conf* file.

Example 18-3. Sample /etc/syslog.conf file

```
# Log everything except mail & authpriv of level info
# or higher to messages.
*.info;mail.none;authpriv.none    /var/log/messages
# The authpriv file has restricted access.
authpriv.*                        /var/log/secure
# Log all the mail messages in one place.
mail.*                            /var/log/maillog
# Everybody gets emergency messages.
*.emerg                           *
# Save boot messages also to boot.log
local7.*                          /var/log/boot.log
```

On the Exam

If you're not yet familiar with *syslogd*, spend some time with it, modifying */etc/syslog.conf* and directing messages to various files. An understanding of syslogd is critical because so many programs depend on it.

If you examine this *syslog.conf* file, you'll see that nearly all system messages are sent to the */var/log/messages* file via the *.info message selector. In this case, the asterisk directs *syslogd* to send messages from all facilities except mail and authpriv, which are excluded using the special none level. The */var/log/messages* file is the default system message destination, and you will consult it frequently for information on processes running (or failing to run) and other events on your system. In this example, the low severity level of info is used for the *messages* file, which logs all but debugging messages. On heavily loaded servers, this may result in an unwieldy file size due to message volume. Depending upon your available disk space, you may choose to save less information by raising the level for the *messages* file.

Log File Rotation

Most distributions will install a default syslog configuration for you, including logging to *messages* and other log files in */var/log*. To prevent any of these files from growing unattended to extreme sizes, a log file rotation scheme should be installed as well. The *cron* system issues commands on a regular basis (usually once per day) to establish new log files; the old files are renamed with numeric suffixes (see "Objective 4: Automate System Administration Tasks by Scheduling Jobs to Run in the Future" later in this chapter for more on cron). With this kind of rotation, yesterday's */var/log/messages* file becomes today's *messages.1*, and a new *messages* file is created. The rotation is configured with a maximum number of files to keep, and the oldest log files are deleted when the rotation is run.

The utility that establishes the rotation is *logrotate*. This privileged command is configured using one or more files, which are specified as arguments to the *logrotate* command. These configuration files can contain directives to include other files as well. The default configuration file is */etc/logrotate.conf*. Example 18-4 depicts an example *logrotate.conf* file.

Example 18-4. Sample /etc/logrotate.conf file

```
# global options
# rotate log files weekly
weekly
# keep 4 weeks worth of backlogs
rotate 4
# send errors to root
errors root
# create new (empty) log files after rotating old ones
create
# compress log files
compress
# specific files
/var/log/wtmp {
    monthly
    create 0664 root utmp
    rotate 1
}
/var/log/messages {
    postrotate
        /usr/bin/killall -HUP syslogd
    endscript
}
```

This example specifies rotations for two files, */var/log/wtmp* and */var/log/messages*. Your configuration will be much more complete, automatically rotating all log files on your system. A complete understanding of *logrotate* configuration is not necessary for LPIC Level 1 Exams, but you must be familiar with the concepts involved. See the logrotate manpages for more information.

Examining Log Files

You can learn a lot about the activity of your system by reviewing the log files it creates. At times, it will be necessary to debug problems using logged information. Since most of the log files are plain text, it is very easy to review their contents with tools such as *tail*, *less*, and *grep*.

Syslog stores the messages it creates with the following information, separated by (but also including) spaces:

- Date/time
- Origin hostname
- Message sender (such as kernel, sendmail, or a username)
- Message text

Typical messages will look like this:

```
Aug  3 18:45:16 moya kernel: Partition check:
Aug  3 18:45:16 moya kernel:  sda: sda1 sda2 sda3 < sda5 sda6 sda7 sda8 sda9
sda10 > sda4
Aug  3 18:45:16 moya kernel: SCSI device sdb: 195369520 512-byte hdwr
sectors (100029 MB)
Aug  3 18:45:16 moya kernel:  sdb: sdb1
Aug  3 18:45:16 moya kernel: Journalled Block Device driver loaded
Aug  3 18:45:16 moya kernel: kjournald starting.  Commit interval 5 seconds
Aug  3 18:45:16 moya kernel: EXT3-fs: mounted filesystem with ordered data
mode.
Aug  3 18:45:16 moya kernel: Freeing unused kernel memory: 116k freed
Aug  3 18:45:16 moya kernel: Adding Swap: 1044216k swap-space (priority -1)
```

In this case, *moya* is the hostname, and the messages are coming from the kernel. At any time, you can review the entire contents of your log files using *less*:

```
# less /var/log/messages
```

You can then page through the file. This is a good way to become familiar with the types of messages you'll see on your system. To actively monitor the output to your messages file, you could use *tail*:

```
# tail -f /var/log/messages
```

This might be useful, for example, to watch system activity as an Internet connection is established via modem. To look specifically for messages regarding your mouse, you might use *grep*:

```
# grep '[Mm]ouse' /var/log/messages
Dec  8 00:15:28 smp kernel: Detected PS/2 Mouse Port.
Dec  8 10:55:02 smp gpm: Shutting down gpm mouse services:
```

Often, if you are using *grep* to look for a particular item you expect to find in */var/log/messages*, you will need to search all of the rotated files with a wildcard. For example, to look for all messages from *sendmail*, you may issue a command like this:

```
# grep 'sendmail:' /var/log/messages*
```

When you note problems in log files, look at the hostname and sender of the message first, then the message text. In many cases, you will be able to determine what is wrong from the message. Sometimes the messages are only clues, so a broader review of your logs may be necessary. In this case, it may be helpful to temporarily turn on more messaging by using the debug level in */etc/syslog.conf* to help yield additional information that can lead you to the problem.

Objective 4: Automate System Administration Tasks by Scheduling Jobs to Run in the Future

There is a surprising amount of housekeeping that must be done to keep a complex operating system such as Linux running smoothly. Log file rotation, cleanup of temporary files and directories, system database rebuilds, backups, and other tasks should be done routinely. Clearly such mundane things should be automated by the system, freeing weary system administrators for more interesting work. Fortunately, any system task that can be accomplished without real-time human intervention can be automated on Linux using the cron and at facilities. Both have the ability to execute system commands, which may start any executable program or script, at selectable times. Further, *cron* and *at* can execute these commands on behalf of any authorized system user. *cron* is intended mainly for regularly scheduled recurring activities, and *at* is most useful for scheduling single commands for execution in the future.

Using cron

The cron facility consists of two programs (There is no individual program called *cron*, which is the overall name given to the facility. If you execute *man cron*, however, you will see the manpage for *crond*.):

crond
> This is the *cron* daemon. This is the process that executes your instructions. It starts at system initialization time and runs in the background thereafter.

crontab
> This is the *cron* table manipulation program. This program gives you access to your *cron* table or *crontab* file. Each authorized user may have his own *crontab* file to run commands and processes on a regular basis.

The *cron* daemon wakes up every minute and examines all *crontab* files, executing any commands scheduled for that time.

User crontab files

To use the *cron* facility, users do not need to interact directly with the *crond* daemon. Instead, each system user has access to the *cron* facility through her *crontab* file. These files are stored together in a single directory (usually */var/spool/cron*) and are created and maintained using the *crontab* utility.

---

crontab

Syntax
    crontab [*options*]

Description
View or edit *crontab* files.

Frequently used options

-e

> Interactively edit the *crontab* file. Unless otherwise specified in either the EDITOR or VISUAL environment variables, the editor is vi.

-l

> Display the contents of the *crontab* file.

-r

> Remove the *crontab* file.

-u user

> Operate on *user*'s *crontab* file instead of your own. Only *root* can edit or delete the *crontab* files of other users.

Examples

Display the *crontab* file for user *jdoe*:

```
# crontab -l -u jdoe
```

Edit your own *crontab* file:

```
$ crontab -e
```

crontab files use a flexible format to specify times for command execution. Each line contains six fields:

```
minute  hour  day  month  dayofweek   command
```

These fields are specified as follows:

- Minute (0 through 59)
- Hour (0 through 23)
- Day of the month (1 through 31)
- Month (1 through 12 or jan through dec)
- Day of the week (0 through 7—where 0 or 7 is Sunday—or sun through sat)
- Command (any valid command, including spaces and standard Bourne shell syntax)

For example, to execute *myprogram* once per day at 6:15 a.m., use this *crontab* entry:

```
# run myprogram at 6:15am
15 6 * * *   myprogram
```

Lines that begin with the pound sign (#) are comment lines and are ignored by crond. Comments must begin on a new line and may not appear within commands. The asterisks in this *crontab* are placeholders and match any date or time for the field where they're found. Here, they indicate that *myprogram* should execute at 6:15 a.m. on all days of the month, every month, all days of the week.

Each of the time specifications may be single, list (1,3,5), or range (1-5 or wed-fri) entries or combinations thereof. To modify the previous example to execute at 6:15 and 18:15 on the 1st and 15th of the month, use:

```
# run myprogram at 6:15am and 6:15pm on the 1st and 15th
15 6,18 1,15 * *   myprogram
```

As you can see, the time specifications are very flexible.

Because the *cron* daemon evaluates each *crontab* entry when it wakes up each minute, it is not necessary to restart or reinitialize *crond* when *crontab* entries are changed or new files are created.

System crontab files

In addition to *crontab* files owned by individual users, *crond* also looks for the system *crontab* files */etc/crontab* and files in the directory */etc/cron.d*. The format for these system *crontabs* differs slightly from user *crontabs*. System *crontabs* have an additional field for a username between the time specifications and the command. For example:

```
# /etc/crontab
# run myprogram at 6:15am as root
15 6 * * *   root   myprogram
```

In this example, myprogram will be executed by *cron* as the *root* user.

System *crontab* files located in */etc/cron.d* are of the same form as */etc/crontab*, including the extra user field. These files are usually associated with some package or service that includes a system *crontab*. Allowing a collection of files in */etc/cron.d* allows software installation and upgrade procedures to keep the *cron* configuration up-to-date on an individual package basis. In most cases, however, you won't need to change the *crontab* files in */etc/cron.d*.

On the Exam

Memorize the sequence of time/date fields used in *crontab* files.

On most Linux distributions, */etc/crontab* contains some standard content to enable the execution of programs and scripts on the minute, hour, week, and month. These arrangements allow you to simply drop executable files into the appropriate directory (such as */etc/cron.hourly*), where they are executed automatically. This eliminates cron configuration altogether for many tasks and avoids cluttering the root *crontab* file with common commands.

Using at

The *cron* system is intended for the execution of commands on a regular, periodic schedule. When you need to simply delay execution of a command or a group of commands to some other time in the future, you should use *at*. The *at* facility accepts commands from standard input or from a file.

---

at

Syntax

```
at [-f file] time
at [options]
```

Description

In the first form, enter commands to the *at* queue for execution at *time*. *at* allows fairly complex time specifications. It accepts times of the form *HH:MM* to run a job at a specific time of day. (If that time is already past, the next day is assumed.) You may also specify midnight, noon, or teatime (4 p.m.), and you suffix a time of day with AM or PM for running in the morning or evening. You can also say what day the job will be run by giving a date in month-day form, with the year being optional, or by giving a date in *MMDDYY, MM/DD/YY*, or *DD.MM.YY* form. The date specification must follow the time-of-day specification. You can also give times like now + *count time-units*, where *time-units* can be minutes, hours, days, or weeks; you can tell at to run the job today by suffixing the time with today, and you can tell it to run the job tomorrow by suffixing the time with tomorrow.

If -f *file* is given, commands are taken from the *file*; otherwise, *at* will prompt the user for commands.

In the second form, list or delete jobs from the *at* queue.

Frequently used options

-d *job1* [, *job2*, ...]
    Delete jobs from the *at* queue by number (same as the *atrm* command).

-l
    List items in the *at* queue (same as the *atq* command).

Example 1

Run myprogram once at 6:15 p.m. tomorrow:

```
$ at 6:15pm tomorrow
at> myprogram
at> ^D
```

In the previous code listing, ^D indicates that the user typed Ctrl-D on the keyboard, sending the end-of-file character to terminate the at command.

Example 2

Run commands that are listed in the file *command_list* at 9 p.m. two days from now:

```
$ at -f command_list 9pm + 2 days
```

List items in the at queue (*root* sees all users' entries):

```
$ at -l
```

Remove job number 5 from the *at* queue:

```
$ at -d 5
```

Using *at* to schedule jobs for delayed execution, such as while you're asleep or on vacation, is simple and doesn't require creation of a recurring *cron* entry.

Controlling User Access to cron and at

In most cases, it is safe to allow users to use the *cron* and *at* facilities. However, if your circumstances dictate that one or more users should be prohibited from using these services, two simple authorization files exist for each:

- *cron.allow, cron.deny*
- *at.allow, at.deny*

These files are simply lists of account names. If the *allow* file exists, only those users listed in the *allow* file may use the service. If the *allow* file does not exist but the *deny* file does, only those users not listed in the *deny* file may use the service. For *cron*, if neither file exists, all users have access to *cron*. For *at*, if neither file exists, only *root* has access to *at*. An empty *at.deny* file allows access to all users and is the default.

Objective 5: Maintain an Effective Data Backup Strategy

Regardless of how careful we are or how robust our hardware might be, it is highly likely that sometimes data will be lost. Though fatal system problems are rare, accidentally deleted files or mistakes using *mv* or *cp* are common. Routine system backup is essential to avoid losing precious data.

There are many reasons to routinely back up your systems:

- Protection against disk failures
- Protection against accidental file deletion and corruption
- Protection against disasters, such as fire, water, or vandalism
- Retention of historical data
- Creation of multiple copies of data, with one or more copies stored at off-site locations for redundancy

All of these reasons for creating a backup strategy could be summarized as insurance. Far too much time and effort goes into a computer system to allow random incidents to force repeated work.

Backup Concepts and Strategies

Most backup strategies involve copying data between at least two locations. At a prescribed time, data is transferred from a source medium (such as a hard disk) to some form of backup medium. Backup media are usually removable and include tapes, floppy disks, Zip disks, and so on. These media are relatively inexpensive, compact, and easy to store off-site. On the other hand, they are slow relative to hard disk drives.

Backup types

Backups are usually run in one of three general forms:

Full backup
 A full, or complete, backup saves all of the files on your system. Depending on circumstances, "all files" may mean all files on the system, all files on a physical disk, all files on a single partition, or all files that cannot be recovered from original installation media. Depending on the size of the drive being backed up, a full backup can take hours to complete.

Differential backup

Save only files that have been modified or created since the last full backup. Compared to full backups, differentials are relatively fast because of the reduced number of files written to the backup media. A typical differential scheme would include full backup media plus the latest differential media. Intermediate differential media are superseded by the latest and can be recycled.

Incremental backup

Save only files that have been modified or created since the last backup, including the last incremental backup. These backups are also relatively fast. A typical incremental backup would include full backup media plus the entire series of subsequent incremental media. All incremental media are required to reconstruct changes to the filesystem since the last full backup.

Typically, a full backup is coupled with a series of *either* differential backups *or* incremental backups, but not both. For example, a full backup could be run once per week with six daily differential backups on the remaining days. Using this scheme, a restoration is possible from the full backup media and the most recent differential backup media. Using incremental backups in the same scenario, the full backup media and *all* incremental backup media would be required to restore the system. The choice between the two is related mainly to the trade-off between media consumption (incremental backup requires more media) versus backup time (differential backup takes longer, particularly on heavily used systems).

For large organizations that require retention of historical data, a backup scheme longer than a week is created. Incremental or differential backup media are retained for a few weeks, after which the tapes are reformatted and reused. Full backup media are retained for an extended period, perhaps permanently. At the very least, one full backup from each month should be retained for a year or more.

A backup scheme such as this is called a *media rotation scheme*, because media are continually written, retained for a defined period, and then reused. The media themselves are said to belong to a media pool, which defines the monthly full, the weekly full, and differential or incremental media assignments, as well as when media can be reused. When media with full backups are removed from the pool for long-term storage, new media join the pool, keeping the size of the pool constant. Media may also be removed from the pool if your organization chooses to limit the number of uses media are allowed, assuming that reliability goes down as the number of passes through a tape mechanism increases.

Your organization's data storage requirements dictate the complexity of your backup scheme. On systems in which many people frequently update mission-critical data, a conservative and detailed backup scheme is essential. For casual-use systems, such as desktop PCs, only a basic backup scheme is needed, if at all.

Backup verification

To be effective, backup media must be capable of yielding a successful restoration of files. To ensure this, a backup scheme must also include some kind of backup verification in which recently written backup media are tested for successful restore operations. This could take the form of a comparison of files after the backup, an automated restoration of a select group of files on a periodic basis, or even a random audit of media on a recurring basis. However the verification is performed, it must prove that the media, tape drives, and programming will deliver a restored system. Proof that your backups are solid and reliable ensures that they will be useful in case of data loss.

Device Files

Before discussing actual backup procedures, a word on so-called device files is necessary. When performing backup operations to tape and other removable media, you must specify the device using its device file. These files are stored in /dev and are understood by the kernel to stimulate the use of device drivers that control the device. Archiving programs that use the device files need no knowledge of how to make the device work. Here are some typical device files you may find on Linux systems:

/dev/st0
> First SCSI tape drive

/dev/ft0
> First floppy-controller tape drive, such as Travan drives

/dev/fd0
> First floppy disk drive

/dev/hdd
> The slave device on the second IDE controller in a system, which could be an ATAPI Zip or other removable disk

These names are just examples. The names on your system will be hardware- and distribution-specific.

Did I Rewind That Tape?

When using tape drives, the kernel driver for devices such as /dev/st0 and /dev/ft0 automatically sends a rewind command after any operation. However, there may be times when rewinding the tape is not desirable. Since the archive program has no knowledge of how to send special instructions to the device, a *nonrewinding device file* exists that instructs the driver to omit the rewind instruction. These files have a leading *n* added to the filename. For example, the nonrewinding device file for /dev/st0 is /dev/nst0. When using nonrewinding devices, the tape is left at the location just after the last operation by the archive program. This allows the addition of more archives to the same tape.

Using tar and mt

The tar (*tape archive*) program is used to recursively read files and directories and then write them onto a tape or into a file. Along with the data goes detailed information on the files and directories copied, including modification times, owners, modes, and so on. This makes tar much better for archiving than simply making a copy, because the restored data has all of the properties of the original.

The *tar* utility stores and extracts files from an archive file known as a tarfile, (conventionally named with a *.tar* extension). Since tape drives and other storage devices in Linux are viewed by the system as files, one type of tarfile is a device file, such as */dev/st0* (SCSI tape drive 0). However, nothing prevents using regular files with tar. This is common practice and a convenient way to distribute complete directory hierarchies as a single file.

During restoration of files from a tape with multiple archives, the need arises to position the tape to the archive that holds the necessary files. To accomplish this control, use the *mt* command. (The name comes from "*magnetic tape.*") The *mt* command uses a set of simple instructions that directs the tape drive to perform a particular action.

tar

Syntax
    tar [options] files

Description
Archive or restore files. *tar* recursively creates archives of files and directories, including file properties. It requires at least one basic mode option to specify the operational mode.

Most tar options will work with or without a leading -.

Basic mode options
-c
> Create a new tarfile.

-t
> List the contents of a tarfile.

-x
> Extract files from a tarfile.

Frequently used options
-f tarfile
> Unless tar is using standard I/O, use the *-f* option with *tar* to specify the tarfile. This might be simply a regular file or it may be a device such as */dev/st0*.

-v
> Verbose mode. By default, tar runs silently. When *-v* is specified, *tar* reports each file as it is transferred.

-w
> Interactive mode. In this mode, *tar* asks for confirmation before archiving or restoring files. This option is useful only for small archives.

-z
> Enable compression. When using *-z*, data is filtered through the *gzip* compression program prior to being written to the tarfile, saving additional space. The

savings can be substantial, at times better than an order of magnitude depending on the data being compressed. An archive created using the -z option *must* also be listed and extracted with -z; *tar* will not recognize a compressed file as a valid archive without the -z option. Tarfiles created with this option often have the *.tar. gz* or *.tgz* file extension.

-N *date*

Store only files newer than the *date* specified. This option can be used to construct an incremental or differential backup scheme.

-V *label*

Adds a `label` to the tar archive. A label is handy if you find an unmarked tape or poorly named tar file.

Don't forget quotes around `label` if it includes spaces or special characters.

Example 1

Create an archive on SCSI tape of the */etc* directory, reporting progress:

```
# tar cvf /dev/st0 /etc
tar: Removing leading `/' from absolute path names
in the archive
etc/
etc/hosts
etc/csh.cshrc
etc/exports
etc/group
etc/host.conf
etc/hosts.allow
etc/hosts.deny
etc/motd
...
```

Note the message indicating that tar will strip the leading slash from */etc* for the filenames in the archive. This is done to protect the filesystem from accidental restores to */etc* from this archive, which could be disastrous.

Example 2

List the contents of the *tar* archive on SCSI tape 0:

```
# tar tf /dev/st0
...
```

Example 3

Extract the entire contents of the *tar* archive on SCSI tape 0, reporting progress:

```
# tar xvf /dev/st0
...
```

Example 4

Extract only the */etc/hosts* file:

```
# tar xvf /dev/st0 etc/hosts
etc/hosts
```

Note that the leading slash is omitted in the file specification (*etc/hosts*), to match the archive with the stripped slash as noted earlier.

Example 5

Create a compressed archive of *root*'s home directory on a floppy:

```
# tar cvzf /dev/fd0 -V "root home dir" /root
tar: Removing leading `/' from absolute path names
in the archive
root/
root/lost+found/
root/.Xdefaults
root/.bash_logout
root/.bash_profile
root/.bashrc
root/.cshrc
root/.tcshrc
...
tar (grandchild): Cannot write to /dev/fd0: No space
left on device
tar (grandchild): Error is not recoverable: exiting now
```

As you can see from reading the error messages, there isn't enough room on the floppy, despite compression. In this case, try storing the archive to an ATAPI Zip drive:

```
# tar cvzf /dev/hdd -V "root home dir" /root
...
```

As mentioned earlier, tape drives have more than one device file. A tape drive's nonrewinding device file allows you to write to the tape without sending a rewind instruction. This allows you to use *tar* again on the same tape, writing another archive to the medium. The number of archives written is limited only by the available space on the tape.

Often multiple archives are written on a single tape to accomplish a backup strategy for multiple computers, multiple disks, or some other situation in which segmenting the backup makes sense. One thing to keep in mind when constructing backups to large media such as tape is the reliability of the medium itself. If an error occurs while *tar* is reading the tape during a restore operation, it may become confused and give up. This may prevent a restore of anything located beyond the bad section of tape. Segmenting the backup into pieces may enable you to position the tape beyond the bad section to the next archive, where tar would work again. In this way, a segmented backup could help shield you from possible media errors.

See the *tar* info or manpage for full details.

---

mt

Syntax

```
mt [-h] [-f device_file] operation [count]
```

Description

Control a tape drive. The tape drive is instructed to perform the specified operation once, unless *count* is specified.

Frequently used options

-h

> Print usage information, including operation names, and exit.

-f device_file

> Specify the device file; if omitted, the default is used, as defined in the header file */usr/include/sys/mtio.h*. The typical default is */dev/tape*.

Backup Operations

Using *tar* or *mt* interactively for routine system backups can become tedious. It is common practice to create backup scripts called by *cron* to execute the backups for you. This leaves the administrator or operator with the duty of providing correct media and examining logs. This section describes a basic backup configuration using *tar*, *mt*, and *cron*.

What should I back up?

It's impossible to describe exactly what to back up on your system. If you have enough time and media, complete backups of everything are safest. However, much of the data on a Linux system, such as commands, libraries, and manpages, don't change routinely and probably won't need to be saved often. Making a full backup of the entire system makes sense after you have installed and configured your system. Once you've created a backup of your system, there are some directories that you should routinely back up:

/etc

> Most of the system configuration files for a Linux system are stored in */etc*, which should be backed up regularly.

/home

> User files are stored in */home*. On multiuser systems, */home* can be quite large.

/var/log

> If you have security or operational concerns, it may be wise to save log files stored in */var/log*.

/var/spool/mail

> If you use email hosted locally, the mail files are stored in */var/spool/mail* and should be retained.

/var/spool/at and /var/spool/cron

> Users' *at* and *crontab* files are stored in */var/spool/at* and */var/spool/cron*, respectively. These directories should be retained if these services are available to your users.

Of course, this list is just a start, as each system will have different backup requirements.

An example backup script

```sh
#!/bin/sh

# Options can be passed in either with the TAROPTIONS
# environment variable or as options on the command line.
TAROPTIONS=${TAROPTIONS:-""}

# Uncomment this block if you want tar to be verbose
# when this script is run interactively.
#if [ -t ]; then
#    TAROPTIONS="$TAROPTIONS --verbose"
#fi

TAROPTIONS="$TAROPTIONS $*"

# The tape device can be passed in the TARGET
# environment variable.  The default is /dev/st0.
TARGET=${TARGET:-"/dev/st0"}

die () {
    message="$@"
    echo "$message" >&2
    exit 1
}

exitmessage () {
    status=$?

    if [ $status -ne 0 ]; then
        echo "tar returned with exit value $status." >&2
    elif [ -t 0 -a -t 2 ]; then
        echo "tar completed successfully." >&2
    fi

    echo "Finished `date`."

    exit $status
}

trap exitmessage EXIT

label="`hostname` `date '+%A %x'`"

echo $label

echo "Started `date`."

cd / || die "Failed to change to root directory"

# This is a good time to turn compression on.
# Unfortunately, that's somewhat specific to
# particular tape drive models.
# mt -f $TARGET compression on
```

Administrative
Tasks

```
mt -f $TARGET rewind || die "Failed to rewind tape"

tar -V "$label" -lcf $TARGET --totals $TAROPTIONS \
        .           \
        ./boot      \
        ./usr       \
        ./var       \
        ./opt       \
        ./home      \
        --exclude=.journal              \
        --exclude=lost+found            \
        --exclude=./dev/gpmctl          \
        --exclude=./dev/log

# The last few lines give examples of things you
# might not want backed up or cause problems when
# they are backed up (like the /dev entries listed).
```

Verifying tar archives

Keeping tape drives clean and using fresh media lay a solid foundation for reliable backups. In addition to those preventive measures, you'll want to routinely verify your backups to ensure that everything ran smoothly. Verification is important on many levels. Clearly, it is important to ensure that the data is correctly recorded. Beyond that, you should also verify that the tape drives and the backup commands function correctly during restoration. Proper file restoration techniques should be established and tested during normal operations, before tragedy strikes and places your operation into an emergency situation.

You can verify the contents of a *tar* archive by simply listing its contents. For example, suppose a backup has been made of the */etc* directory using the following command:

```
# tar cvzf /dev/st0 /etc
```

After the backup is complete, the tape drive rewinds. The archive can then be verified immediately by reviewing the contents with the *-t* option:

```
# tar tf /dev/st0
```

This command lists the contents of the archive so that you can verify the contents of the tarfile. Additionally, any errors that may prevent tar from reading the tape are displayed at this time. If there are multiple archives on the tape, they can be verified in sequence using the nonrewinding device file:

```
# tar tf /dev/nst0
# mt -f /dev/nst0 fsf 1
# tar tf /dev/nst0
# mt -f /dev/st0 rewind
```

While this verification tells you that the tapes are readable, it does not tell you that the data being read is identical to that in the filesystem. If your backup device supports them, the tar utility contains two options, *verify* and *compare*, that may be useful to you. However, comparisons of files on the backup media against the live filesystem may yield confusing results if your files are changing constantly. In this situation, it may be necessary to select for comparison specific files that you are certain will not change after they are backed up. You would probably restore those files to a temporary directory and compare them manually, outside of tar. If it is necessary to compare an entire archive, be aware that doing so doubles the time required to complete the combined backup and verify operation.

File restoration

Restoring files from a *tar* archive is simple. However, you must exercise caution regarding exactly where you place the restored files in the filesystem. In some cases, you may be restoring only one or two files, which may be safely written to their original locations if you're sure the versions on tape are the ones you need. However, restoring entire directories to their original locations on a running system can be disastrous, resulting in changes being made to the system without warning as files are overwritten. For this reason, it is common practice to restore files to a different location and move those files you need into the directories where you want them.

Reusing a previous example, suppose a backup has been made of the */etc* directory:

```
# tar cvzf /dev/st0 /etc
```

To restore the */etc/hosts* file from this archive, the following commands can be used:

```
# cd /tmp
# tar xzf /dev/st0 etc/hosts
```

The first command puts our restore operation out of harm's way by switching to the */tmp* directory. (The directory selected could be anywhere, such as a home directory or scratch partition.) The second command extracts the specified file from the archive. Note that the file to extract is specified without the leading slash. This file specification will match the one originally written to the medium by *tar*, which strips the slash to prevent overwriting the files upon restore. *tar* will search the archive for the specified file, create the *etc* directory under */tmp*, and then create the final file: */tmp/etc/hosts*. This file should then be examined by the system administrator and moved to the appropriate place in the filesystem only after its contents have been verified.

To restore the entire */etc* directory, simply specify that directory:

```
# tar xzf /dev/st0 etc
```

To restore the *.bash_profile* file for user *jdean* from a second archive on the same tape, use mt before using tar:

```
# cd /tmp
# mt -f /dev/nst0 fsf 1
# tar xzf /dev/st0 /home/jdean/.bash_profile
```

In this example, the nonrewinding tape device file is used with *mt* to skip forward over the first archive. This leaves the tape positioned before the second archive, where it is ready for tar to perform its extraction.

Objective 6: Maintain System Time

An accurate system clock is important on a Linux system for a variety of reasons. Timestamps are used for logs. Programs such as *make* and *anacron* require accurate modification times on files. The time is used in mail and news headers.

Luckily, there are many ways to keep the time on an Internet-connected Linux system correct. The most popular of these is to use the Network Time Protocol (NTP) and the NTP software package from *http://www.ntp.org*.

NTP Concepts

The NTP is used to set and synchronize the internal clocks of network-connected systems. When properly configured, systems running the NTP daemon can be synchronized within a few milliseconds (or better), even over relatively slow WAN connections.

The NTP daemon also supports synchronization with an external time source, such as a GPS receiver. Systems directly connected to an external time source (and properly configured) are the most accurate, so they are designated *stratum 1* servers. Systems synchronizing to stratum 1 servers are designated *stratum 2* and so on down to stratum 15.

 The NTP software package has support for cryptographic key-based authentication, although setting this up is outside the scope of the LPI Level 1 Exams and will not be covered here.

The NTP Software Package Components

The NTP software package consists of several programs, including the NTP daemon and a number of programs used to configure and query NTP servers. The more commonly used programs from the package are listed here.

---

ntpd

Syntax

```
ntpd [options]
```

Description

ntpd is the heart of the NTP software package. It performs the following functions:

- Synchronizes the PC clock with remote NTP servers
- Allows synchronization from other NTP clients
- Adjusts (slews) the rate of the kernel's clock tick so that it tends to keep the correct time
- Reads time synchronization data from hardware time sources such as GPS receivers

Frequently used options

-c file
> This option tells *ntpd* to use *file* as its configuration file instead of the default */etc/ntpd.conf*.

-g
> This option will let *ntpd* start on a system with a clock that is off by more than the panic threshold (1,000 seconds by default).

-n
> Normally *ntpd* runs as a daemon, in the background. This option disables that behavior.

-q
> This option tells *ntpd* to exit after setting the time once.

-N
> When this option is specified, *ntpd* attempts to run at the highest priority possible.

-P priority
> When this option is specified, *ntpd* attempts to run with a nice value of *priority*.

ntpd is configured using the file */etc/ntp.conf*. The file is fully documented in a series of files linked to from the *ntpd* documentation, found in the software distribution or at *http://www.eecis.udel.edu/~mills/ntp/html/ntpd.html*.

The most important configuration options are restrict, which is used to implement access controls, and server, which is used to direct *ntpd* to an NTP server. Another often-used configuration option (not mentioned in the sample *ntp.conf* in Example 18-5) is peer, which is used much like server, but implies that the system is both a client and a server. A peer is usually a system that is nearby on the network, but uses different time sources than the local system.

Example 18-5. Sample /etc/ntp.conf

```
# Prohibit general access to this service.
restrict default ignore

# Permit all access over the loopback interface.  This could
# be tightened as well, but to do so would affect some of
# the administrative functions.
restrict 127.0.0.1

# -- CLIENT NETWORK -------
# Permit systems on this network to synchronize with this
# time service.  Do not permit those systems to modify the
```

Example 18-5. Sample /etc/ntp.conf (continued)

```
# configuration of this service.  Also, do not use those
# systems as peers for synchronization.
restrict 192.168.1.0 mask 255.255.255.0 notrust nomodify notrap

# --- OUR TIMESERVERS -----
# Permit time synchronization with our time source, but do not
# permit the source to query or modify the service on this system.

# time.nist.gov
restrict 192.43.244.18 mask 255.255.255.255 nomodify notrap noquery
server 192.43.244.18

# time-b.nist.gov
restrict 129.6.15.29 mask 255.255.255.255 nomodify notrap noquery
server 129.6.15.29

# --- GENERAL CONFIGURATION ---
#
# Undisciplined Local Clock. This is a fake driver intended for backup
# and when no outside source of synchronized time is available.
#
server      127.127.1.0        # local clock
fudge       127.127.1.0 stratum 10

#
# Drift file.  Put this in a directory which the daemon can write to.
# No symbolic links allowed, either, since the daemon updates the file
# by creating a temporary in the same directory and then renaming
# it to the file.
#
driftfile /etc/ntp/drift
broadcastdelay        0.008
```

Example

Normally *ntpd* slowly adjusts the time of the system to the correct time. To use it to force the system time to the right time (for example, when occasionally setting the correct time from *cron*), use the following:

```
# ntpd -g -n -q
```

---

ntpdate

Syntax

```
ntpdate [options] server [server [...]]
```

Description

ntpdate is used to set the time of the local system to match a remote NTP host.

Note that the authors intend to drop *ntpdate* in the future since *ntpd* can perform essentially the same function when used with the *-q* option.

Frequently used options

-b

> Using this option, the system time is set instead of being slowly adjusted, no matter how far off the local time is.

-d

> This option enables debugging mode. *ntpdate* goes through the motions and prints debugging information, but does not actually set the local clock.

-p n

> Use this option to specify the number of samples (where *n* is from 1 to 8) to get from each server. The default is 4.

-q

> This option causes *ntpdate* to query the servers listed on the command line without actually setting the clock.

-s

> This option causes all output from *ntpdate* to be logged via syslog instead of being printed to stdout.

-t n

> This option sets the timeout for a response from any server to *n* seconds. *n* may be fractional. It will be rounded to the nearest 0.2 second. The default value is 1 second.

-u

> Normally *ntpdate* uses a privileged port (123) as the source port for outgoing packets. Some firewalls block outgoing packets from privileged ports, so with this option, *ntpdate* uses an unprivileged port (1024 or higher).

-v

> This option makes *ntpdate* more verbose.

-B

> Using this option, the system time is slowly adjusted to the proper time even if the local time is off by more than 128 ms. Normally the time is forcibly set if it is off by more than 128 ms.
>
> If the time is off by very much, it can take a very long time to set it with this option.

Example

Quietly sync the local clock with two stratum 1 NTP servers:

```
# ntpdate -s time.nist.gov time-b.nist.gov
```

ntpq

Syntax

```
ntpq [options] [host]
```

Description

ntpq is the standard NTP query program. It is used to send NTP control messages to *host* (or *localhost* if no *host* is specified), which can be used to check the status of *ntpd* on *host* or change its configuration.

The commands that can be used with *ntpq* are documented in the NTP software documentation included with the distribution and at *http://www.eecis.udel.edu/~mills/ntp/html/ntpq.html.*

Frequently used options

-c command

> Execute *command* as if it were given interactively.

-i

> Enter interactive mode. This is the default.

-n

> Suppress reverse DNS lookups. Addresses are printed instead of hostnames.

-p

> Query the server for a list of peers. This is equivalent to the *peers* interactive command or *-c peers* on the command line.

Example

Print the list of peers known to the server by IP address:

> # **ntpq -p -n**

or

> # **ntpq -c peers -n**

or

```
# ntpq -n
ntpq> peers
remote           refid        st t when poll reach delay  offset jitter
==============================================================================
127.127.1.0      127.127.1.0  10 l 7    64   377   0.000  0.000  0.004
+10.100.187.194  172.30.191.1  2 u 72   1024 377   0.536  47.092 2.088
*10.100.187.222  172.16.123.163 2 u 35 1024 377   0.736  3.394  8.806
+192.168.0.100   10.100.187.222 3 u 90 1024 377   0.928  31.727 2.412
ntpq>
```

ntpdc

Syntax

> ntpdc [*options*] [*host*]

Description

ntpdc is much like *ntpq*, except that it supports some extended commands. For this reason, it is likely to work only when talking to *ntpd* from the same version of the NTP software package.

For the most part, the command-line options it supports are the same as those of *ntpq*. Full documentation for *ntpdc* can be found in the NTP software distribution or at *http://www.eecis.udel.edu/~mills/ntp/html/ntpdc.html.*

ntptrace

Syntax

```
ntptrace [options] server [server [...]]
```

Description

Frequently used options

-*n*

Turn off reverse DNS lookups.

-*r n*

This option sets the number of attempts to contact a host to *n*. The default is 5.

-*t n*

Set the time between retries to *n* seconds. The default is 2.

-*v*

Make ntptrace output much more verbose information about the hosts it contacts.

Examples

To see where the local system is synchronizing its lock to, run *ntptrace* with no options:

```
$ /usr/sbin/ntptrace
localhost: stratum 4, offset 0.000109, synch distance 0.16133
ntp1.example.net: stratum 3, offset 0.004605, synch distance 0.06682
ntp-1.example.edu: stratum 2, offset 0.001702, synch distance 0.01241
stratum1.example.edu:        *Timeout*
```

In this example, the stratum 1 server is not directly accessible.

ntptrace can also be used on any arbitrary NTP server, assuming it is accessible. In this example, we query two publicly accessible stratum 2 NTP servers:

```
$ /usr/sbin/ntptrace ntp0.cornell.edu
cudns.cit.cornell.edu: stratum 2, offset -0.004214, synch distance 0.03455
dtc-truetime.ntp.aol.com: stratum 1, offset -0.005957, synch distance 0.
00000, refid 'ACTS'
$ /usr/sbin/ntptrace ntp-2.mcs.anl.gov
mcs.anl.gov: stratum 2, offset -0.004515, synch distance 0.06354
clepsydra.dec.com: stratum 1, offset 0.002045, synch distance 0.00107, refid
'GPS'
```

19

Networking Fundamentals (Topic 1.112)

While it is not necessary for you to be a networking expert to pass the LPIC Level 1 Exams, you must be familiar with networking, network-related vocabulary, and basic Linux networking configuration. This chapter introduces fundamental networking, troubleshooting, and dial-up concepts specifically included in the exams. However, it is not a complete introductory treatment, and you are encouraged to review additional material for more depth. This chapter covers these three Objectives:

Objective 1: Fundamentals of TCP/IP
Candidates should demonstrate a proper understanding of network fundamentals. This Objective includes the understanding of IP addresses, network masks, and what they mean (i.e., determine a network and broadcast address for a host based on its subnet mask in *dotted quad* or abbreviated notation or determine the network address, broadcast address, and netmask when given an IP address and number of bits). It also covers the understanding of the network classes and classless subnets (CIDR) and the reserved addresses for private network use. It includes the understanding of the function and application of a default route. It also includes the understanding of basic Internet protocols (IP, ICMP, TCP, UDP) and the more common TCP and UDP ports (20, 21, 23, 25, 53, 80, 110, 119, 139, 143, 161). Weight: 4.

Objective 3: TCP/IP Configuration and Troubleshooting
Candidates should be able to view, change, and verify configuration settings and operational status for various network interfaces. This Objective includes manual and automatic configuration of interfaces and routing tables. This especially means to add, start, stop, restart, delete, or reconfigure network interfaces. It also means to change, view, or configure the routing table and to correct an improperly set default route manually. Candidates should be able to configure Linux as a DHCP client and a TCP/IP host and to debug problems associated with the network configuration. Weight: 7.

Candidates should understand the basics of the PPP protocol and be able to configure and use PPP for outbound connections. This Objective includes the definition of the chat sequence to connect (given a login example) and the setup commands to be run automatically when a PPP connection is made. It also includes initialization and termination of a PPP connection, with a modem, ISDN, or ADSL, and setting PPP to automatically reconnect if disconnected. Weight: 3.

What follows is not a complete treatment of TCP/IP, but rather a refresher of its core concepts as they apply to Exam 102. If you're interested in more in-depth coverage of TCP/IP, check out *TCP/IP Network Administration,* Craig Hunt (O'Reilly).

Objective 1: Fundamentals of TCP/IP

The TCP/IP suite of protocols was adopted as a military standard in 1983 and has since become the world standard for network communications on the Internet and on many LANs, replacing proprietary protocols in many cases. This section covers TCP/IP basics cited by the LPI Objectives.

Addressing and Masks

The early specification of the IP recognized that it would be necessary to divide one's given allotment of IP addresses into manageable subnetworks. Such division allows for distributed management, added security (fewer hosts can potentially snoop network traffic), and the use of multiple networking technologies (Ethernet, Token Ring, ATM, etc.). IP also enables convenient partitioning of the physical portions of a network across physical and geographical boundaries. To provide the capability to locally define networks, IP addresses are considered as having two distinct parts: the part that specifies a *subnet* and the one that specifies a network interface. (Remember that IP addresses are assigned to network interfaces, not host computers, which can have multiple interfaces. For this discussion, however, we assume a one-to-one relationship between hosts and interfaces.) The boundary between the network and host portions of an IP address is delineated by a *subnet mask*, required by the TCP/IP configuration of any network interface. Like the IP address, the subnet mask is simply a 32-bit number specified in four 8-bit segments using *dotted quad* decimal notation. The familiar class A, B, and C networks have these subnet masks:

Class A: 255.0.0.0 (binary 11111111.00000000.00000000.00000000)
  8-bit network address and 24-bit host address

Class B: 255.255.0.0 (binary 11111111.11111111.00000000.00000000)
  16-bit network address and 16-bit host address

Class C: 255.255.255.0 (binary 11111111.11111111.11111111.00000000)
  24-bit network address and 8-bit host address

When logically AND'd with an IP address, the bits set to 0 in the subnet mask obscure the host portion of the address. The remaining bits represent the network address. For example, a host on a class C network might have an IP address of 192.168.1.127. Applying the class C subnet mask 255.255.255.0, the network address of the subnet would be 192.168.1.0, and the host address would be 127, as depicted in Figure 19-1.

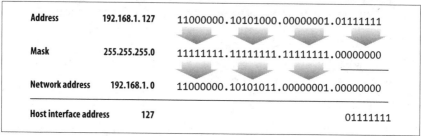

Address	192.168.1. 127	11000000.10101000.00000001.01111111
Mask	255.255.255.0	11111111.11111111.11111111.00000000
Network address	192.168.1. 0	11000000.10101011.00000001.00000000
Host interface address	127	01111111

Figure 19-1. Host interface address calculation

While it is typical to use the predefined classes (A, B, and C), the boundary can be moved left or right in the IP address, allowing for fewer or more subnets, respectively. For example, if a single additional bit were added to the class C subnet mask, its IP address would be:

255.255.255.128 (binary 11111111.11111111.11111111.10000000)
  25-bit network address and 7-bit host address

With such a subnet defined on an existing class C network such as 192.168.1.0, the 256-bit range is split into two subnets, each with 7 host bits. The first of the two subnets begins at 192.168.1.0 (the subnet address) and continues through 192.168.1.127 (the subnet broadcast address). The second subnet runs from 192. 168.1.128 through 192.168.1.255. Each of the two subnets can accommodate 126 hosts. To extend this example, consider two additional bits:

255.255.255.192 (binary 11111111.11111111.11111111.11000000)
  26-bit network address and 6-bit host address

When applied to a class C network, four subnets are created, each with 6 host bits. Just as before, the first subnet begins at 192.168.1.0 but continues only through 192.168.1.63. The next subnet runs from 192.168.1.64 through 192.168. 1.127 and so on. Each of the four subnets can accommodate 62 hosts. Table 19-1 shows more detail on class C subnets, considering only the host portion of the address.

Table 19-1. Class C IP subnet detail

Subnet mask	Number of subnets	Network address	Broadcast address	Minimum IP address	Maximum IP address	Number of hosts	Total hosts
128	2	0	127	1	126	126	
		128	255	129	254	126	252
192	4	0	63	1	62	62	
		64	127	65	126	62	
		128	191	129	190	62	

Table 19-1. Class C IP subnet detail (continued)

Subnet mask	Number of subnets	Network address	Broadcast address	Minimum IP address	Maximum IP address	Number of hosts	Total hosts
		192	255	193	254	62	248
224	8	0	31	1	30	30	
		32	63	33	62	30	
		64	95	65	94	30	
		96	127	97	126	30	
		128	159	129	158	30	
		160	191	161	190	30	
		192	223	193	222	30	
		224	255	225	254	30	240

On the Exam

Be prepared to define network and host addresses when provided an IP address and a subnet mask. Practice with a few subnet sizes within at least one classification (A, B, or C). Also, because the use of decimal notation can cloud human interpretation of IP addresses and masks, be ready to do binary-to-decimal conversion on address numbers.

As you can see, as the number of subnets increases, the total number of hosts that can be deployed within the original class C address range reduces. This is due to the loss of both broadcast addresses and network addresses to the additional subnets.

Protocols

TCP/IP is a suite of protocols, including the TCP, IP, User Datagram Protocol (UDP), and Internet Control Message Protocol (ICMP), among others. Some protocols use *handshaking* (the exchange of control information among communicating systems) to establish and maintain a connection. Such a protocol is said to be connection-oriented and reliable, because the protocol itself is responsible for handling transmission errors, lost packets, and packet arrival order. A protocol that does not exchange control information is said to be connectionless and unreliable. In this context, "unreliable" simply means that the protocol doesn't handle transmission problems itself; they must be corrected in the application or system libraries. Connectionless protocols are simpler and have less overhead than connection-oriented protocols. TCP/IP is a *stack* of protocols, because protocols are built in a hierarchy of *layers*. Low-level protocols are used by higher-level protocols on adjacent layers of the protocol stack:

TCP

TCP is a connection-oriented transport agent used by applications to establish a network connection. TCP transports information across networks by handshaking and retransmitting information as needed in response to errors on the network. TCP guarantees packet arrival and provides for the correct ordering of received packets. TCP is used by many network services, including FTP, Telnet, and SMTP. By using TCP, these applications don't need to establish their own error-checking mechanisms, thus making their design simpler and easier to manage.

IP

IP can be thought of as the fundamental building block of the Internet. IP, which is connectionless, defines datagrams (the basic unit of transmission), establishes the addressing scheme (the IP address), and provides for the routing of datagrams between networks. IP is said to provide a *datagram delivery service*. Other higher-level protocols use IP as an underlying carrier.

UDP

UDP is a connectionless transport agent. It provides application programs direct access to IP, allowing them to exchange information with a minimum of protocol overhead. On the other hand, because UDP offers no assurance that packets arrive at destinations as intended, software must manage transmission errors and other problems such as missing and incorrectly ordered packets. UDP is used by applications such as DNS and NFS.

ICMP

ICMP is a connectionless transport agent that is used to exchange control information among networked systems. It uses IP datagrams for the following control, error-reporting, and informational functions:

Flow control
>Sometimes inbound traffic becomes too heavy for a receiving system to process. In such cases, the receiving system can send a message via ICMP to the source instructing it to temporarily stop sending datagrams.

Detecting unreachable destinations
>Various parts of network infrastructure are capable of detecting that a network destination is unreachable. In this case, ICMP messages are sent to the requesting system.

Redirecting routes
>ICMP is used among network components to instruct a sender to use a different gateway.

Checking remote hosts
>Hosts can transmit echo messages via ICMP to verify that a remote system's Internet Protocol is functioning. If so, the original message is returned. This is implemented in the ping command.

PPP

PPP is used for TCP/IP dial-up network access via modem. The configuration and use of PPP is described later in Objective 4.

TCP/IP Services

When an inbound network request is made, such as that from a web browser or FTP client, it is sent to the IP address of the server. In addition, the request carries inside it a *port number* (or just *port*), which is a 16-bit value placed near the beginning of a network packet. The port number defines the type of server software that should respond to the request. For example, by default, web browsers send requests encoded for port 80. Web servers "listen" to port 80 and respond to incoming requests. The encoded port can be considered part of the address of a request. While the IP address specifies a particular interface (or host), the port specifies a specific service available on that host. Many port numbers are predefined, and the list is expanded as needed to accommodate new technologies. The official list of port number assignments is managed by the Internet Assigned Numbers Authority (IANA). The ports known by your system are listed in */etc/services*.

Port numbers 1 through 1023 are often referred to as *privileged ports* because the services that use them often run with superuser authority. Many of these, such as ports used for FTP (21), Telnet (23), and HTTP (80), are often referred to as *well-known ports* because they are standards. Port numbers from 1024 through 65535 (the maximum) are *unprivileged ports* and can be used by applications run by ordinary system users.

During the initial contact, the client includes a local (randomly selected) unprivileged port on the client machine for the server to use when responding to the request. Client-to-server communications use the well-known port and the server-to-client communications use the randomly selected port. This Objective requires you to be familiar with the privileged port numbers detailed in Table 19-2.

Table 19-2. Common privileged port numbers

Port number	Assigned use	Description
20 21	FTP data FTP control	When an FTP session is opened, the binary or ASCII data flows to the server using port 20, while control information flows on port 21. During use, both ports are managed by an FTP daemon, such as *vftpd*.
23	Telnet server	Inbound Telnet requests are sent to server port 23 and processed by *telnetd*.
25	SMTP server	This port is used by mail transfer agents (MTAs), such as Sendmail.
53	DNS server	Used by the Domain Name System (DNS) server, *named*.
67	BOOTP/DHCP server	Hands out IP addresses to workstations dynamically.
68	BOOTP/DHCP client	The client side for BOOTP/DHCP.
80	HTTP server	Web servers, such as Apache (*httpd*), usually listen in on this port.

Table 19-2. *Common privileged port numbers (continued)*

Port number	Assigned use	Description
110	POP3	The Post Office Protocol (POP) is used by mail client programs to transfer mail from a server.
119	NNTP server	This port is used by news servers for Usenet news.
139	NetBIOS	Reserved for Microsoft's LAN Manager.
143	IMAP	An alternate to POP3, Internet Message Access Protocol (IMAP) is another type of mail protocol.
161	SNMP	Agents running on monitored systems use this port for access to the Simple Network Management Protocol (SNMP).

This list is a tiny fraction of the many well-known ports, but it may be necessary for you to know those in the list both by name and by number.

On the Exam

You should commit the list of ports in Table 19-2 to memory so you can recognize a type of network connection solely by its port number. Your exam is likely to have at least one question on how a specific port is used.

TCP/IP Utilities

The following popular applications, while not strictly a part of TCP/IP, are usually provided along with a TCP/IP implementation.

---

dig

Syntax

```
dig hostname
```

Description

dig obtains information from DNS servers. Note that additional command-line arguments and options are available for dig but are beyond the scope of Exam 102.

Example

```
$ dig redhat.com
; <<>> DiG 8.2 <<>> redhat.com any
;; res options: init recurs defnam dnsrch
;; got answer:
;; ->>HEADER<<- opcode: QUERY, status: NOERROR, id: 6
;; flags: qr rd ra; QUERY: 1, ANSWER: 6, AUTHORITY: 4,
;; ADDITIONAL: 5 QUERY SECTION:
;;      redhat.com, type = ANY, class = IN
;; ANSWER SECTION:
```

```
redhat.com.              22h36m45s IN NS  ns.redhat.com.
redhat.com.              22h36m45s IN NS  ns2.redhat.com.
redhat.com.              22h36m45s IN NS  ns3.redhat.com.
redhat.com.              22h36m45s IN NS  speedy.redhat.com.
redhat.com.              23h48m10s IN MX  10 mail.redhat.com.
redhat.com.              23h48m10s IN A   207.175.42.154
;; AUTHORITY SECTION:
redhat.com.              22h36m45s IN NS  ns.redhat.com.
redhat.com.              22h36m45s IN NS  ns2.redhat.com.
redhat.com.              22h36m45s IN NS  ns3.redhat.com.
redhat.com.              22h36m45s IN NS  speedy.redhat.com.
;; ADDITIONAL SECTION:
ns.redhat.com.           1d23h48m10s IN A  207.175.42.153
ns2.redhat.com.          1d23h48m10s IN A  208.178.165.229
ns3.redhat.com.          1d23h48m10s IN A  206.132.41.213
speedy.redhat.com.       23h48m10s IN A   199.183.24.251
mail.redhat.com.         23h48m10s IN A   199.183.24.239
;; Total query time: 81 msec
;; FROM: smp to SERVER: default -- 209.195.201.3
;; WHEN: Wed Apr  5 03:15:03 2000
;; MSG SIZE  sent: 28  rcvd: 275
```

ftp

Syntax

```
ftp [options] host
...interactive commands...
```

Description

Establish an interactive FTP connection with *host* to transfer binary or text files. FTP creates an interactive dialog and allows for two-way file transfer. The dialog includes username/password authentication, user commands, and server responses.

Frequently used options

-i

Turn off interactive prompting during multiple file transfers (also see the prompt command in the nest list).

-v

Set verbose mode; display server responses and transfer statistics.

Frequently used commands

ascii, binary

Establish the transfer mode for files. ASCII mode is provided to correctly transfer text among computer architectures where character encoding differs.

get file

Receive a single *file* from the server.

mget files

Receive multiple *files* from the server. *files* can be specified using normal file glob patterns.

ls [files]

> Obtain a directory listing from the server, optionally listing *files*.

put file

> Send a single *file* to the server.

mput files

> Send multiple *files* to the server.

prompt

> Toggle on and off interactive prompting during *mget* and *mput* (also see the *-i* option in the previous list).

pwd

> Print the working remote directory.

quit, exit

> Cleanly terminate the FTP session.

Example 1

Get a file from machine *smp*:

```
$ ftp -v smp
Connected to smp.
220 smp FTP server (Version wu-2.4.2-VR17(1)
Mon Apr 19 09:21:53 EDT 1999) ready.
Name (smp:root): jdean
331 Password required for jdean.
Password:<password here>
230 User jdean logged in.
Remote system type is UNIX.
Using binary mode to transfer files.
ftp> ls myfile
200 PORT command successful.
150 Opening ASCII mode data connection for /bin/ls.
-rw-r--r--   1 jdean     jdean          29 Jan 24 01:28 myfile
226 Transfer complete.
ftp> binary
200 Type set to I.
ftp> get myfile
local: myfile remote: myfile
200 PORT command successful.
150 Opening BINARY mode data connection for myfile
(29 bytes).
226 Transfer complete.
29 bytes received in 0.000176 secs (1.6e+02 Kbytes/sec)
ftp> quit
221-You have transferred 29 bytes in 1 files.
221-Total traffic for this session was 773 bytes in 3 transfers.
221-Thank you for using the FTP service on smp.
221 Goodbye.
```

Example 2

Many FTP servers are set up to receive requests from nonauthenticated users. Such public access is said to be anonymous. Anonymous FTP is established just like any other FTP connection, except that anonymous is used as the username. An email address is commonly used as a password to let the system owner know who is transferring files:

```
# ftp -v smp
Connected to smp.
220 smp FTP server (Version wu-2.4.2-VR17(1)
Mon Apr 19 09:21:53 EDT 1999) ready.
Name (smp:root): anonymous
331 Guest login ok, send your complete e-mail address as password.
Password: me@mydomain.com
230 Guest login ok, access restrictions apply.
Remote system type is UNIX.
Using binary mode to transfer files.
ftp> <commands follow...>
```

ping

Syntax

```
ping hostname
```

Description

The *ping* command is used to send an ICMP echo request to a host and report on how long it takes to receive a corresponding ICMP echo reply. Much as sonar systems send a pulse (or "ping") to a target and measure transit time, *ping* sends a network packet to test the availability of a network node. This technique is often used as a basic debugging technique when network problems arise.

Frequently used options

-c count
    Send and receive *count* packets.

-q
    Quiet output. Display only summary lines when ping starts and finishes.

Example

Ping a remote host and terminate using **Ctrl-C** after five packets are transmitted:

```
$ ping lpi.org
PING lpi.org (209.167.177.93) from 192.168.1.30 :
  56(84) bytes of data.
64 bytes from new.lpi.org (209.167.177.93):
  icmp_seq=0 ttl=240 time=51.959 msec
64 bytes from new.lpi.org (209.167.177.93):
  icmp_seq=1 ttl=240 time=60.967 msec
64 bytes from new.lpi.org (209.167.177.93):
  icmp_seq=2 ttl=240 time=47.173 msec
64 bytes from new.lpi.org (209.167.177.93):
  icmp_seq=3 ttl=240 time=46.887 msec
64 bytes from new.lpi.org (209.167.177.93):
  icmp_seq=4 ttl=240 time=46.836 msec
--- lpi.org ping statistics ---
5 packets transmitted, 5 packets received, 0% packet loss
round-trip min/avg/max/mdev = 46.836/50.764/60.967/5.460 ms
```

telnet

Syntax

```
telnet [host] [port]
```

Description

Establish a connection to a *host* (either a system name or IP address) using *port*. If a specific port is omitted, the default port of 23 is assumed. If *host* is omitted, *telnet* goes into an interactive mode similar to FTP.

traceroute

Syntax

```
traceroute hostname
```

Description

Attempt to display the route over which packets must travel to reach a destination *hostname*. It is included here because it is mentioned in this Objective, but Objective 3 also requires *traceroute*. See Objective 3 for full information.

whois

Syntax

```
whois target[@server]
fwhois target[@server]
```

Description

Query the *whois* database for *target*. Such a database contains information on domain names, assigned IP addresses, and people associated with them.

The version of *whois* provided with Linux is a link to *fwhois*. *target* is a domain name or user *handle*. *server* is a valid *whois* server, which defaults to *rs.internic.net*. The information returned includes contact information, domain names, IP addresses, and DNS servers. Note that many web sites are available for *whois* searches as well, particularly for checking on domain name availability.

Example

```
$ fwhois linuxdoc.org@whois.networksolutions.com
Registrant:
Linux Documentation Project (LINUXDOC-DOM)
    4428 NE 74th Ave.
    Portland, OR 97218
    US
    Domain Name: LINUXDOC.ORG
    Administrative Contact, Technical Contact, Zone Contact:
```

```
Account, Hostmaster  (AH243-ORG)
    hostmaster@LINUXPORTS.COM
Command Prompt Software
4428 NE 74th Ave.
Portland, OR 97218
US
(503)493-1611
```
Billing Contact:
```
Account, Hostmaster  (AH243-ORG)
    hostmaster@LINUXPORTS.COM
Command Prompt Software
4428 NE 74th Ave.
Portland, OR 97218
US
(503)493-1611
```
Record last updated on 15-Feb-2000
Record created on 20-Feb-1999
Database last updated on 5-Apr-2000 12:51:28 EDT
Domain servers in listed order:
```
NS1.OPENDOCS.ORG          209.102.107.110
NS1.INETARENA.COM         206.129.216.1
NS.UNC.EDU                152.2.21.1
```

Objective 3: TCP/IP Configuration and Troubleshooting

Linux distributions offer various automation and startup techniques for networks, but most of the essential commands and concepts are not distribution-dependent. The exam tests fundamental concepts and their relationships to one another as well as to system problems. This Objective covers the configuration of TCP/IP on common network interfaces such as Ethernet.

Network Interfaces

A computer must contain at least one *network interface* to be considered part of a network. The network interface provides a communications link between the computer and external network hardware. This could mean typical network adapters such as Ethernet or Token Ring, PPP dial-up connections, parallel ports, wireless, or other networking forms.

Configuration files

The following files contain important information about your system's network configuration:

/etc/hosts
> This file contains simple mappings between IP addresses and names and is used for name resolution. For very small private networks, */etc/hosts* may be sufficient for basic name resolution. For example, this file associates the local address 192.168.1.30 with the system *smp* and also with *smp.mydomain.com*:

```
127.0.0.1       localhost       localhost.localdomain
192.168.1.1     gate
192.168.1.30    smp smp.mydomain.com
```

/etc/nsswitch.conf

This file controls the sources used by various system library lookup functions, such as name resolution. It allows the administrator to configure the use of traditional local files (*/etc/hosts*, */etc/passwd*), an NIS server, or DNS. *nsswitch.conf* directly affects network configuration (among other things) by controlling how hostnames and other network parameters are resolved. For example, this fragment shows that local files are used for password, shadow password, group, and hostname resolution; for hostnames, DNS is used if a search of local files doesn't yield a result:

```
passwd:    files nisplus nis
shadow:    files nisplus nis
group:     files nisplus nis
hosts:     files dns nisplus nis
```

For more information, view the manpage with *man 5 nsswitch*. The *nsswitch.conf* file supersedes *host.conf*.

/etc/host.conf

This file controls name resolution sources for pre-*glibc2* systems. It should contain:

```
order hosts,bind
multi on
```

This configuration has the resolver checking */etc/hosts* first for name resolution, then DNS. `multi on` enables multiple IP addresses for hosts. Newer Linux system libraries use */etc/nsswitch.conf* instead of */etc/host.conf*.

/etc/resolv.conf

This file controls the client-side portions of the DNS system, which is implemented in system library functions used by all programs to resolve system names. In particular, */etc/resolv.conf* specifies the IP addresses of DNS servers. For example:

```
nameserver 192.168.1.5
nameserver 192.168.250.2
```

Additional parameters are also available. For more information, view the manpage with *man 5 resolver*.

/etc/networks

Like */etc/hosts*, this file sets up equivalence between addresses and names, but here the addresses represent entire networks (and thus must be valid network addresses, ending in 0). The result is that you can use a symbolic name to refer to a network just as you would a specific host. This may be convenient (though not required) in NFS or routing configuration, for example, and will be shown in commands such as `netstat`. For example:

```
loopback    127.0.0.0
mylan       192.168.1.0
```

It's not unusual for */etc/networks* to be left blank.

On the Exam

Be familiar with all the files listed in this section; each contains specific information important for network setup. Watch for questions on */etc/host.conf*, which is not used in newer *glibc2* libraries.

Configuration commands

The commands listed in this section are used to establish, monitor, and troubleshoot a network configuration under Linux.

---

host

Syntax

```
host [options] name [server]
```

Description

Look up the system with IP address or *name* on the DNS *server*.

Frequently used options

-l

> List the entire domain, dumping all hosts registered on the DNS server (this can be very long).

-v

> Set verbose mode to view output.

Example 1

```
$ host oreilly.com
oreilly.com has address 208.201.239.37
oreilly.com has address 208.201.239.36
```

Example 2

```
$ host -v oreilly.com
Trying null domain
rcode = 0 (Success), ancount=1
The following answer is not authoritative:
The following answer is not verified as authentic by the server:
oreilly.com      17397 IN        A       204.148.40.5
For authoritative answers, see:
oreilly.com      168597 IN       NS      AUTHO3.NS.UU.NET
oreilly.com      168597 IN       NS      NS.oreilly.com
Additional information:
AUTHO3.NS.UU.NET         168838 IN       A       198.6.1.83
NS.oreilly.com  168597 IN        A       204.148.40.4 $
```

See also the *nslookup* command in the section "DNS query utilities" in Chapter 20.

---

hostname, domainname, dnsdomainname

Syntax

```
hostname [localname]
domainname [nisname]
dnsdomainname
```

Description

Set or display the current host, domain, or node name of the system. This is a single program with links defining additional names. When called as *hostname*, the system's hostname is displayed. If *localname* is provided, the hostname is set. *domainname* displays or sets the NIS domain name. *dnsdomainname* displays the current DNS domain name but does not set it. See *man 1 hostname* for full information.

ifconfig

Syntax

```
ifconfig interface parameters
```

Description

Configure network interfaces. *ifconfig* is used to create and configure network interfaces and their parameters, usually at boot time. Without parameters, the interface and its configuration are displayed. If *interface* is also omitted, a list of all active interfaces and their configurations is displayed.

Frequently used parameters

address
> The interface's IP address.

netmask *mask*
> The interface's subnet mask.

up
> Activate an interface (implied if *address* is specified).

down
> Shut down the interface.

Example 1

Display all interfaces:

```
# ifconfig
eth0      Link encap:Ethernet  HWaddr 00:A0:24:D3:C7:21
          inet addr:192.168.1.30  Bcast:192.168.1.255  Mask:255.255.255.0
          UP BROADCAST RUNNING MULTICAST  MTU:1500  Metric:1
          RX packets:1521805 errors:37 dropped:0 overruns:0 frame:37
          TX packets:715468 errors:0 dropped:0 overruns:0 carrier:0
          collisions:1955 txqueuelen:100
          Interrupt:10 Base address:0xef00
lo        Link encap:Local Loopback
          inet addr:127.0.0.1  Mask:255.0.0.0
```

```
        UP LOOPBACK RUNNING  MTU:3924  Metric:1
        RX packets:366567 errors:0 dropped:0 overruns:0 frame:0
        TX packets:366567 errors:0 dropped:0 overruns:0 carrier:0
        collisions:0 txqueuelen:0
```

Example 2

Shut down *eth0*:

```
# ifconfig eth0 down
# ifconfig eth0
eth0      Link encap:Ethernet   HWaddr 00:A0:24:D3:C7:21
          inet addr:192.168.1.30  Bcast:192.168.1.255  Mask:255.255.255.0
          BROADCAST MULTICAST  MTU:1500  Metric:1
          RX packets:1521901 errors:37 dropped:0 overruns:0 frame:37
          TX packets:715476 errors:0 dropped:0 overruns:0 carrier:0
          collisions:1955 txqueuelen:100
          Interrupt:10 Base address:0xef00
```

Note in the emphasized line the lack of the UP indicator, which is present in Example 1. The missing UP indicates that the interface is down.

Example 3

Configure *eth0* from scratch:

```
# ifconfig eth0 192.168.1.100 netmask 255.255.255.0 broadcast 192.168.1.255
```

---

netstat

Syntax

```
netstat [options]
```

Description

Depending on options, *netstat* displays network connections, routing tables, interface statistics, masquerade connections, netlink messages, and multicast memberships. Much of this is beyond the scope of the LPIC Level 1 Exams, but you must be aware of the command and its basic use.

Frequently used options

-c

Continuous operation. This option yields a *netstat* display every second until interrupted with **Ctrl-C**.

-i

Display a list of interfaces.

-n

Numeric mode. Display addresses instead of host, port, and usernames.

-p

Programs mode. Display the PID and process name.

-r

Routing mode. Display the routing table in the format of the *route* command.

-v

Verbose mode.

Example

Display the interfaces table and statistics (the example output is truncated):

```
# netstat -i
Kernel Interface table
Iface MTU  Met   RX-OK RX-ERR RX-DRP RX-OVR  TX-OK
eth0  1500 0   1518801    37      0      0   713297
lo    3924 0    365816     0      0      0   365816
```

ping

Syntax

```
ping [options] destination
```

Description

Send an ICMP ECHO_REQUEST datagram to *destination*, expecting an ICMP ECHO_
RESPONSE. *ping* is frequently used to test basic network connectivity. See "Objective 1:
Fundamentals of TCP/IP" for a more complete description.

route

Syntax

```
route [options]
route add [options and keywords] target
route del [options and keywords] target
```

Description

In the first form, display the IP routing table. In the second and third forms, respectively, add or delete routes to *target* from the table. *target* can be a numeric IP
address, a resolvable name, or the keyword default. The route program is typically
used to establish static routes to specific networks or hosts (such as the default
gateway) after an interface is configured. On systems acting as routers, a potentially
complex routing scheme can be established initially, but this is beyond the scope of
the LPIC Level 1 Exams.

Frequently used options and keywords

-h

Display a usage message.

-n

Numeric mode; don't resolve hostnames.

-v

Verbose output.

-C

Display the kernel routing cache.

-F
> Display the kernel routing table (the default behavior without *add* or *delete* keywords).

-host
> Specify that *target* is a single host. Mutually exclusive with *-net*.

-net
> Specify that *target* is a network. Mutually exclusive with *-host*.

gw gateway
> IP packets for *target* are routed through the gateway, which must be reachable.

netmask mask
> Specify the *mask* of the route to be added. Often, the netmask is not required because it can be determined to be class A, B, or C, depending on the *target* address.

When used to display routes, the following routing table columns are printed:

Destination
> The destination network or host.

Gateway
> The gateway address. If no gateway is set for the route, an asterisk (*) is displayed by default.

Genmask
> The netmask for the destination. 255.255.255.255 is used for a host and 0.0.0.0 is used for the default route.

Route status flags
> | ! | Reject route. |
> | D | Dynamically installed by daemon or redirect. |
> | G | Use gateway. |
> | H | Target is a host. |
> | M | Modified from routing daemon or redirect. |
> | R | Reinstate route for dynamic routing. |
> | U | Route is up. |

Metric
> The distance in hops to the target.

Ref
> Number of references to this route. This is displayed for compatibility with other route commands but is not used in the Linux kernel.

Use
> A count of lookups for the route. Depending on the use of *-F* and *-C*, the Use is either route cache misses (*-F*) or hits (*-C*).

Iface
> The interface to which packets for this route are sent.

Example 1

Display the current routing table for a workstation:

```
# route
Kernel IP routing table
```

```
Destination  Gateway  Genmask          Flags Met Ref Use Iface
192.168.1.30 *        255.255.255.255  UH    0   0   0 eth0
192.168.1.0  *        255.255.255.0    U     0   0   0 eth0
10.0.0.0     -        255.0.0.0        !     0   -   0 -
127.0.0.0    *        255.0.0.0        U     0   0   0 lo
default      gate     0.0.0.0          UG    0   0   0 eth0
```

In this example, the route to the local host 192.168.1.30 uses interface *eth0*. Note the mask 255.255.255.255 is used for host routes. The route to the local subnet 192.168.1.0 (with corresponding class C mask 255.255.255.0) is also through *eth0*. The route to 10.0.0.0 is rejected as indicated by the ! flag. The class A loopback network route uses device *lo*. The last route shows the *default gateway* route, which is used when no others match. This default uses *eth0* to send data to router *gate*. The mask 0.0.0.0 is used for the default route.

Example 2

Display the current routing cache; the Metric (M) and Reference (R) columns are abbreviated here:

```
# route -C
Kernel IP routing cache
Source         Destination    Gateway        Flg M R Use Iface
smp            192.168.1.255  192.168.1.255  bl  0 0   1 eth0
192.168.1.102  192.168.1.255  192.168.1.255  ibl 0 0   0 lo
192.168.1.102  smp            smp            il  0 0   1 lo
192.168.1.50   smp            smp            il  0 0 224 lo
smp            192.168.1.102  192.168.1.102      0 1   0 eth0
smp            ns1.mynet.com  gate               0 0   2 eth0
smp            192.168.1.50   192.168.1.50       0 1   0 eth0
localhost      localhost      localhost      l   0 0  15 lo
ns1.mynet.com  smp            smp            l   0 0   6 lo
smp            ns1.mynet.com  gate               0 0   6 eth0
```

Example 3

Add the default gateway 192.168.1.1 via *eth0*:

```
# route add default gw 192.168.1.1 eth0
```

---

traceroute

Syntax

```
traceroute [options] destination
```

Description

Display the route that packets take to reach *destination*, showing intermediate gateways (routers). There isn't a direct method to use to make this determination, so *traceroute* uses a trick to obtain as much information as it can. By using the time-to-live field in the IP header, *traceroute* stimulates error responses from gateways. The time-to-live field specifies the maximum number of gateway hops until the packet should expire. That number is decremented at each gateway hop, with the result that all packets will die at some point and not roam the Internet. To get the first gateway in the route, *traceroute* sets the time-to-live parameter to 1. The first gateway in the route

to *destination* decrements the counter, and finding a result, reports an ICMP TIME_
EXCEEDED message back to the sending host. The second gateway is identified by setting
the initial time-to-live value to 2 and so on. This continues until a PORT_UNREACHABLE
message is returned, indicating that the host has been contacted. To account for the
potential for multiple gateways at any one hop count, each probe is sent three times.

The display consists of lines showing each gateway, numbered for the initial time-to-
live value. If no response is seen from a particular gateway, an asterisk is printed. This
happens for gateways that don't return "time exceeded" messages, or do return them
but set a very low time-to-live on the response. Transit times for each probe are also
printed.

Frequently used options

-f ttl
> Set the initial probe's time-to-live value to *ttl*, instead of 1.

-n

> Display numeric addresses instead of names.

-v

> Use verbose mode.

-w secs
> Set the timeout on returned ICMP packets to *secs*, instead of 5.

Example

```
# traceroute www.lpi.org
traceroute to www.lpi.org (209.167.177.93),
  30 hops max, 40 byte packets
 1  gate (192.168.1.1)
        3.181 ms  1.200 ms  1.104 ms
 2  209.125.145.1 (209.125.135.1)
        16.041 ms  15.149 ms  14.747 ms
 3  a1-9-1-0-1.a01.phl1.us.io.net (137.94.47.1)
        84.132 ms  133.937 ms  77.865 ms
 4  ge-6-0.r01.phlapa01.us.io.net (126.250.29.17)
        22.450 ms  16.114 ms  16.051 ms
 5  p4-6-0-0.r01.nycmny01.us.bb.verio.net (129.250.3.126)
        18.043 ms  18.485 ms  18.175 ms
 6  nyc1.uunet.verio.net (129.250.9.62)
        19.735 ms  21.135 ms  19.212 ms
 7  105.ATM3-0.XR1.NYC1.ALTER.NET (146.188.177.154)
        20.237 ms  18.515 ms  18.712 ms
 8  295.ATM6-0.XR1.NYC4.ALTER.NET (146.188.178.90)
        26.855 ms  29.540 ms  35.908 ms
 9  189.ATM8-0-0.GW5.NYC4.ALTER.NET (146.188.179.225)
        36.541 ms  36.127 ms  30.849 ms
10  224.ATM1-0-0.BB1.TOR2.UUNET.CA.ALTER.NET (137.39.75.26)
        58.823 ms  68.675 ms  62.522 ms
11  f0-0-0.bb2.tor2.uunet.ca (205.150.242.110)
        336.310 ms  174.557 ms  394.909 ms
12  209.167.167.118 (209.167.167.118)
        56.027 ms  58.555 ms  56.289 ms
13  209.167.177.90 (209.167.177.90)
        59.349 ms  57.409 ms  57.993 ms
```

```
14  new.lpi.org (209.167.177.93)
      57.021 ms  56.162 ms  58.809 ms
```

In this example, there are 13 hops to *www.lpi.org*, reached with a time-to-live value of 14. All three probes of all time-to-live counts are successful.

On the Exam

While the creation of complete network management scripts from scratch is beyond the scope of the LPIC Level 1 Exams, you must be familiar with these commands individually, their functions, how they are used, as well as why they are used. For example, you must be familiar with *route* and its use in establishing routes to the loopback device, the localhost, the gateway machine, and the creation of the default gateway route. A general understanding of the routing table display is also required. Questions may ask you to determine the cause of a network problem based on the routing configuration (such as a missing default route).

Common manual network interface tasks

Network interfaces are established in the kernel at boot time through the probing of Ethernet hardware. As a result, these interfaces always exist unless the hardware or kernel module is removed. Other types of interfaces, such as PPP, are created by user programs. These interfaces are transient and exist only when they are in use.

To list interface parameters, use *ifconfig* with the interface name:

```
# ifconfig eth0
eth0      Link encap:Ethernet  HWaddr 00:A0:24:D3:C7:21
          inet addr:192.168.1.30  Bcast:192.168.1.255  Mask:255.255.255.0
          UP BROADCAST MULTICAST  MTU:1500  Metric:1
          RX packets:1857128 errors:46 dropped:0 overruns:0 frame:46
          TX packets:871709 errors:0 dropped:0 overruns:0 carrier:0
          collisions:2557 txqueuelen:100
          Interrupt:10 Base address:0xef00
```

If you run *ifconfig* without any parameters, it displays all active interfaces, including the loopback interface *lo* and perhaps a PPP interface if a modem is dialed into a service provider.

To shut down a network interface that is currently running, simply use *ifconfig* with the down keyword:

```
# ifconfig eth0 down
```

When the interface goes down, any routes associated with it are removed from the routing table. For a typical system with a single Ethernet interface, this means that the routes to both the interface and the default gateway will be lost. Therefore, to start a previously configured network interface, *ifconfig* is used with up followed by the necessary route commands. For example:

```
# ifconfig eth0 up
# route add -host 192.168.1.30 eth0
# route add default gw 192.168.1.1 eth0
```

To reconfigure interface parameters, follow those same procedures and include the changes. For example, to change to a different IP address, the address is specified when bringing up the interface and adding the interface route:

```
# ifconfig eth0 down
# ifconfig eth0 192.168.1.60 up
# route add -host 192.168.1.60 eth0
# route add default gw 192.168.1.1 eth0
```

Your distribution probably supplies scripts to handle some of these chores. For example, Red Hat systems come with scripts such as *ifup*, which handle all the details necessary to get an interface and its routes up and running.

On the Exam

Be prepared to answer questions on the use of *ifconfig* and *route* for basic interface manipulation. Also remember that scripts that use these commands, both manually and automatically, are usually available at boot time.

DHCP

The Dynamic Host Configuration Protocol (DHCP) is a protocol extension of the BOOTP protocol, which provides automated IP address assignment (among other things) to client systems on a network. It handles IP address allocation in one of three ways:

Dynamic allocation
In this scheme, a DHCP server maintains a preset list of IP addresses designated by the system administrator. IP addresses are assigned as clients request an address from the available addresses in the pool. The address can be used, or *leased*, for a limited period of time. The client must continually renegotiate the lease with the server to maintain use of the address beyond the allotted period. When the lease expires, the IP address is placed back into the pool for use by other requesting clients and a new IP address is assigned.

Manual allocation
The system administrator may wish to designate specific IP addresses to specific network interfaces (for example, to an Ethernet MAC address) while still using DHCP to deliver the address to the client. This allows the convenience of automated address setup and assures the same address each time.

Automatic allocation

This method assigns a permanent address to a client. Typically DHCP is used to assign a temporary address (either dynamically or statically assigned) to a client, but a DHCP server can allow an infinite lease time.

DHCP can be configured to assign not only the IP address to the client but also such things as name servers, gateways, and architecture-specific parameters. Here's an overview of how it works:

1. A DHCP client sends a broadcast message to the network to discover a DHCP server.

2. One or more DHCP servers respond to the request via their own broadcast messages, offering an IP address to the client.

3. The client chooses one of the servers and broadcasts an acknowledgment, requesting the chosen server's identity.

4. The selected server logs the connection with the client and responds with an acknowledgment and possibly additional information. All of the other servers do nothing because the client declined their offer.

Subnets and relays

Because DHCP communications are initiated using broadcasts, they are normally confined to a single subnet. To accommodate DHCP clients and servers separated by one or more routers, a DHCP *relay* system can be established on subnets without DHCP servers. A relay system listens for DHCP client broadcasts, forwards them to a DHCP server on another subnet, and returns DHCP traffic back to the client. This configuration can centralize DHCP management in a large routed environment.

Leases

As already mentioned, when a client receives a dynamically assigned IP address from a DHCP server, the address is said to be *leased* for a finite duration. The length of a DHCP lease is configurable by the system administrator and typically lasts for one or more days. Shorter leases allow for faster turnover of addresses and are useful when the number of available addresses is small or when many transient systems (such as laptops) are being served. Longer leases reduce DHCP activity, thus reducing broadcast traffic on the network.

When a lease expires without being renegotiated by the client, it as assumed that the client system is unavailable, and the address is put back into the free pool of addresses. A lease may also be terminated by a client that no longer needs the IP address, in which case it is *released*. When this occurs, the DHCP server immediately places the IP address back in the free pool.

dhcpd

The DHCP server process is called *dhcpd*. It is typically started at boot time and listens for incoming DHCP request broadcasts. *dhcpd* can serve multiple subnets via multiple interfaces, serving a different pool of IP addresses to each.

dhcpd is configured using the text configuration file */etc/dhcpd.conf*, which contains one or more subnet declarations. These are text lines of the following form:

```
subnet network-address netmask subnet-mask {
  parameter...
  parameter...
  ...
}
```

Each subnet declaration encloses parameters for each subnet between curly braces. Parameters include one or more ranges of IP addresses to serve, lease times, and optional items such as gateways (routers), DNS servers, and so forth. Each parameter line is terminated with a semicolon. For example:

```
subnet 192.168.1.0 netmask 255.255.255.0 {
  range 192.168.1.200 192.168.1.204;
  default-lease-time 600;
  option subnet-mask 255.255.255.0;
  option broadcast-address 192.168.1.255;
  option routers 192.168.1.1;
  option domain-name-servers 192.168.1.25;
}
```

In this example, the private class C network 192.168.1.0 is served five IP addresses, 200 through 204. The default DHCP lease is 600 seconds (10 minutes). Options are also set for the subnet mask, broadcast address, router (or gateway), and DNS server. For full information on *dhcpd.conf*, see its manpage.

The preceding option lines are not required to create a minimal DHCP setup that simply serves IP addresses. Details on the daemon follow.

dhcpd

Syntax

```
dhcpd [options] [interface [...]]
```

Description

Launch the DHCP server daemon. *dhcpd* requires that both its configuration file */etc/dhcpd.conf* and its lease log file (which by default is */var/state/dhcp/dhcpd.leases*, although many distributions use */var/lib/dhcp/dhcpd.leases*) exist. The daemon puts itself in the background and returns control to the calling shell.

Frequently used options

-cf config-file
　　Use *config-file* instead of the default */etc/dhcpd.conf*.

-lf lease-file
　　Use *lease-file* instead of the default to store lease information.

-q
　　Use quiet mode. This option suppresses the default copyright message, keeping log files a little cleaner.

interface

By default, *dhcpd* will attempt to listen for requests on every network interface that is configured up. It can be limited to specific network interfaces by including one or more interface names on the command line.

A full and detailed description of the configuration file syntax can be found in the *dhcpd.conf* manpage. When *dhcpd* runs, it sends output, including information on each transaction, to *syslogd*. For example, this series of four log entries in */var/log/messages* shows a successful exchange between *dhcpd* and a requesting DHCP client:

```
Apr 24 02:27:00 rh62 dhcpd: DHCPDISCOVER
    from 00:60:97:93:f6:8a via eth0
Apr 24 02:27:00 rh62 dhcpd: DHCPOFFER
    on 192.168.1.200 to 00:60:97:93:f6:8a via eth0
Apr 24 02:27:01 rh62 dhcpd: DHCPREQUEST
    for 192.168.1.200 from 00:60:97:93:f6:8a via eth0
Apr 24 02:27:01 rh62 dhcpd: DHCPACK
on 192.168.1.200 to 00:60:97:93:f6:8a via eth0
```

Objective 4: Configure Linux as a PPP Client

The Point-to-Point Protocol (PPP) is a method of constructing a network connection between two systems using a serial interface. Usually, this interface is a pair of modems connected by a telephone call over a switched voice network. However, PPP isn't specifically tied to the use of modems and can also work with a direct serial connection using a *null modem* cable (sometimes known as a *crossover* cable. When PPP is implemented on a Linux system, it creates a new network interface, usually *ppp0*, which is configured for use with TCP/IP and an IP address.

To use PPP, your kernel must be compiled with PPP support. Most distributions include PPP support in the kernels they install, but if yours doesn't or if you build your own kernels, you must select PPP Support under Network Device Support in your kernel configuration (see Chapter 13 for information on compiling kernels).

Clients and Servers

PPP is a peer-to-peer protocol, in which there is no technical difference between the two systems sharing a PPP link. When used for dial-up communications, however, it is convenient to think of the system making the call as a PPP client and the system being called as a PPP server. Linux can do both jobs simultaneously if multiple serial interfaces are available, but this section covers only the client-side configuration as required by Exam 102.

Serial ports and modems

The only hardware required to create a PPP dial-up connection is a serial interface and a modem. These may be separate devices, including an external modem device cabled to an internal serial interface. Internal modems implement both the port and the modem hardware on a single board, reducing costs. Serial ports are a standard item on most small computers and communicate using RS-232, an old standard for serial communications with terminals, modems, and other devices. On Linux, serial ports are accessed via device files, usually */dev/ttyS0*, */dev/ttyS1*, and so on. (The standard serial devices are referred to as *COM1:* and *COM2:* in MS-DOS and Windows. On older Linux systems, you may see devices named */dev/cuan*. These older names were deprecated several years ago.) In addition, a link for a default modem device, */dev/modem*, is often made to point to the serial port where a modem is attached. For example:

```
crw-------  1 root tty   Apr 25 18:28 /dev/ttyS0
crw-------  1 root tty   May  5 1998 /dev/ttyS1
lrwxrwxrwx  1 root root  Dec  7 23:04 /dev/modem -> ttyS0
```

Each byte of information to be sent through a serial interface is sent bit by bit at a periodic rate known as the *baud rate*. In the early days of modems, data was transmitted over the phone at the same baud rate as it was encoded by the serial port. However, modern modems compress data before transmitting it and can accommodate higher data rates from host systems. As a result, the serial port typically runs at its fastest speed, allowing the modem to independently set a line speed after negotiating with the server's modem. By keeping the data rate between computer and modem high, the modem has a constant stream of data ready for transmission, maximizing throughput.

Built into each serial interface is a data buffer capable of holding a finite amount of information. When serial data enters the buffer faster than it can be removed, a data overrun occurs unless the data flow is stopped through the use of a *flow control* signal. For example, when a system is sending data into a modem through a serial interface, the modem must send a stop signal when it has no more room in its buffer and later send a start signal when the buffer again has free space. The result is that, while the modem sends a constant stream to the other modem, the serial interface is running bursts of data managed by flow controls. In simple cases such as terminals, two flow control characters named XON and XOFF are transmitted in the serial data stream and are interpreted as controls to hardware. However, PPP uses the entire serial byte and is less efficient if control characters are allowed, so another means known as *ready-to-send* (RTS) and *clear-to-send* (CTS) is used for flow control. These signals are included in standard serial cables and allow *hardware flow control* between devices.

PPP overview

PPP connections are established through these general steps:

1. A serial connection is created with a remote PPP server. This involves setting local serial port parameters, setting local modem parameters, and instructing the modem to dial the telephone number of the PPP server. After the modem on the other end answers, the two modems negotiate the best possible link speed, depending on their capabilities and the quality of the telephone line.

2. User account authentication information is supplied to the PPP server. More than one method exists for this task, but in many cases, the PPP server simply

provides clear text login and password prompts, and the client responds in the same way.

3. PPP is started on the client. Many servers automatically initiate PPP upon successful authentication, while others offer a sort of command-line interface where PPP can be started with a command.

4. The PPP server selects an IP address from a pool of addresses reserved for PPP connections and provides it to the client in plain text. The server then initiates a binary data stream to link the PPP client and server software.

5. The PPP client software uses the temporarily assigned IP address to configure the new interface and its required routes. (Additional information beyond the IP address can be provided to clients using DHCP. Examples include the default gateway and DNS servers.) It then joins the server in establishing the PPP binary data stream.

Chat scripts

Most of this process requires a dialog between the calling computer and its modem and subsequently the PPP server, including the interpretation of responses. For example, it's common to begin the entire process by instructing the modem to reset itself, ensuring that settings from previous communications sessions don't affect the current session. After the reset instruction is completed, the modem responds with OK on a line by itself. It would be impractical to proceed if the reset command fails, so the modem's response must be tested, and further modem commands presented only if the appropriate responses are received. This command/response dialog function is implemented using the *chat* utility, intended specifically for use with modems. *chat* executes a script that contains lines of text to send to the modem as well as fragments of what to expect from the modem itself. The chat scripts also allow for default actions to typical modem responses, such as the ability to abort a call attempt if the modem reports a busy signal. Here is a typical chat script for a simple dial-up configuration:

```
ABORT BUSY
ABORT ERROR
ABORT 'NO CARRIER'
ABORT 'NO DIALTONE'
ABORT 'Invalid Login'
ABORT 'Login incorrect'
'' ATZ
OK ATDT8005551212
CONNECT ''
ogin: jdoe
ssword: jdoepasswd
TIMEOUT 5
> ppp
```

In this chat script, the first six lines use the ABORT keyword to provide strings that *chat* should consider to be fatal errors, terminating the call attempt. Any of the modem or server responses BUSY, ERROR, NO CARRIER, NO DIALTONE, Invalid Login, and Login incorrect will cause the script to terminate.

Each subsequent line of this example is constructed using two items: an *expected response*, followed by a *send string*. Here, the first response is simply no response at all, indicated by the empty quotes, "". This causes *chat* to issue a send string consisting of the modem reset sequence ATZ without expecting any input. chat then waits for the next expected response, which should be an *OK* from the modem indicating a successful reset. After verifying that, the modem dials as a result of the ATDT command, and *chat* waits to receive a CONNECT response from the modem. If the modem returns BUSY instead of CONNECT, *chat* terminates as a result of the ABORT string at the top of the file. When CONNECT is received, *chat* simply sends a carriage return, indicated in the script by another set of empty quotes, to stimulate the PPP server to prompt for authentication (some PPP servers require this stimulation, others don't). Because this will be the first text from the server, it's possible that the first character could be garbled, so only the fragment ogin: is used to look for the login: prompt. In response, a username (jdoe) is sent, and then the user is prompted for a password. After successful authentication, this particular PPP server requires PPP to be started using the *ppp* command at the > prompt.

Note that strings with spaces or no characters are delimited with quotes and that a depiction of carriage returns isn't required. Neither must separate lines be used for each expect/send pair. This example could also look like this:

```
ABORT BUSY ABORT ERROR ABORT 'NO CARRIER'
ABORT 'NO DIALTONE' ABORT 'Invalid Login'
ABORT 'Login incorrect'
'' ATZ OK ATDT8005551212 CONNECT ''
ogin: jdoe ssword: jdoepasswd
TIMEOUT 5
> ppp
```

It's important that *chat* is given send/expect commands in pairs. Creating the file with separate lines for each pair makes for easy comprehension, but it isn't really necessary. Regardless of the chat script format, here's what the conversation looks like from chat's point of view:

```
ATZ
OK
ATDT8005551212
CONNECT 31200/ARQ/V34/LAPM/V42BIS
User Access Verification
login:jdoe
Password:<jdoepasswd>
mxusw5>ppp
Entering PPP mode.
Async interface address is unnumbered (Loopback0)
Your IP address is 192.168.50.211. MTU is 1500 bytes
```

The PPP daemon

In addition to the kernel support mentioned at the beginning of this Objective, the PPP daemon (*pppd*) is required to run PPP on Linux. When used by a client computer to establish a dial-up connection, *pppd* does not start at boot time and remain active as do many other daemons. Instead, it runs as directed by users or automatically when a network connection is required. *pppd* has a large number of available options, but only a general understanding is necessary for Exam 102.

pppd

Syntax

```
pppd [device] [speed] [options]
```

Description

Start the PPP daemon on *device* with serial interface rate *speed*. The *speed* parameter is almost always set to the maximum speed of the serial interface (115,200 bits per second) to allow the modem to keep data compression running at full capacity.

Frequently used options

asyncap *map*

> This option can be used to eliminate bits of the serial byte from use by *pppd*, preserving control characters. Each bit in *map* is excluded. If *map* is set to 0, all 8 bits will be used. Any other setting will cause performance degradation to some degree. The default is to escape all control characters, so this option should be used if possible.

connect *script-command*

> This option calls the script that handles the modem setup and authentication, usually chat. *script-command* is a complete command string that initiates the modem dialup sequence, including *chat*, its parameters, and the chat script. Since it includes the *chat* command, options, and a script, the entire *script-command* should be quoted so that *pppd* does not attempt to interpret it as options.

crtscts

> This option instructs *pppd* to set the serial port to use hardware flow control (CTS/RTS).

debug

> This option turns on debugging. Information is logged to *syslogd* and also to the calling terminal, unless *pppd* detached (see the nodetach option).

defaultroute

> By setting this option, *pppd* creates a default route in the routing table for the new PPP device. This is a typical need for a dial-up system without network access. Note, however, that a networked system that already has a default route to its network interface would then have two default routes, which doesn't make sense. In this case, the administrator must determine how best to configure the routing for PPP connections.

ipparam *name*

> If this option is included, *name* is included as the sixth argument to */etc/ppp/ip-up*, a script that handles a few logging and network details after the PPP link is established.

lock

> This instructs *pppd* to establish a lock file to claim exclusive access to the device.

nodetach

> This option prevents *pppd* from putting itself in the background, instead remaining attached to the calling terminal. This is helpful for interactive use and debugging.

persist

> In situations in which you want PPP to be constantly available (such as with dedicated modem links or direct system-to-system cable links), use the persist option. *pppd* attempts to reestablish a terminated PPP connection. This can protect your PPP link from modem power failure, line degradation, or line interruption. Note that this capability is specifically mentioned in Objective 4 and is likely to appear on Exam 102. (It is likely that your distribution's automated PPP scripts are capable of reestablishing terminated PPP links without the persist option. This can be achieved with the use of a while loop.)

On the Exam

You should have a firm understanding of *pppd* and the nature and form of its options. In particular, be familiar with the *persist* option.

Manual PPP connection

Here's a simple one-command example of a manual PPP connection, using the chat script presented earlier. In the *pppd* command, each option appears on a separate line for clarity, though this is not required in practice:

```
# /usr/sbin/pppd /dev/ttyS0 115200 \
    nodetach \
    lock \
    debug \
    crtscts \
    asyncmap 00000000
    connect "/usr/sbin/chat -vf \
        /etc/sysconfig/network-scripts/chat-ppp0"
```

pppd first calls the chat script, the results of which can be found in */var/log/ messages* (chat logs output as a result of the -v option, as passed to pppd in the quoted chat command.):

```
kernel: PPP: version 2.3.3 (demand dialing)
kernel: PPP line discipline registered.
```

```
kernel: registered device ppp0
pppd[1291]: pppd 2.3.7 started by root, uid 0
chat[1295]: abort on (BUSY)
chat[1295]: abort on (ERROR)
chat[1295]: abort on (NO CARRIER)
chat[1295]: abort on (NO DIALTONE)
chat[1295]: abort on (Invalid Login)
chat[1295]: abort on (Login incorrect)
chat[1295]: send (ATZ^M)
chat[1295]: expect (OK)
chat[1295]: ATZ^M^M
chat[1295]: OK
chat[1295]:  -- got it
chat[1295]: send (ATDT8005551212^M)
chat[1295]: expect (CONNECT)
chat[1295]: ^M
chat[1295]: ATDT8005551212^M^M
chat[1295]: CONNECT
chat[1295]:  -- got it
chat[1295]: send (^M)
chat[1295]: expect (ogin:)
chat[1295]:  31200/ARQ/V34/LAPM/V42BIS^M
chat[1295]: ^M
chat[1295]: ^M
chat[1295]: User Access Verification^M
chat[1295]: ^M
chat[1295]: login:
chat[1295]:  -- got it
chat[1295]: send (jdow^M)
chat[1295]: expect (ssword:)
chat[1295]: jdoe^M
chat[1295]: Password:
chat[1295]:  -- got it
chat[1295]: send (<jdoepasswd>^M)
chat[1295]: timeout set to 5 seconds
chat[1295]: expect (>)
chat[1295]: ^M
chat[1295]: ^M
chat[1295]: ^M
chat[1295]: mxusw5>
chat[1295]:  -- got it
chat[1295]: send (ppp^M)
pppd[1291]: Serial connection established.
pppd[1291]: Using interface ppp0
pppd[1291]: Connect: ppp0 <--> /dev/modem
pppd[1291]: local  IP address 192.168.100.202
pppd[1291]: remote IP address 192.168.100.1
```

The calling terminal, remaining attached to *pppd* due to the nodetach option, shows debugging information:

```
Serial connection established.
Using interface ppp0
Connect: ppp0 <--> /dev/ttyS0
sent [LCP ConfReq id=0x1 <asyncmap 0x0>
```

```
        <magic 0x5f6ecfaa> <pcomp> <accomp>]
    rcvd [LCP ConfReq id=0x46 <asyncmap 0xa0000>
        <magic 0x77161be5> <pcomp> <accomp>]
    sent [LCP ConfAck id=0x46 <asyncmap 0xa0000>
        <magic 0x77161be5> <pcomp> <accomp>]
    rcvd [IPCP ConfReq id=0x3e <addr 192.168.100.1>]
    sent [LCP ConfReq id=0x1 <asyncmap 0x0>
        <magic 0x5f6ecfaa> <pcomp> <accomp>]
    rcvd [LCP ConfReq id=0x47 <asyncmap 0xa0000>
        <magic 0x7716279c> <pcomp> <accomp>]
    sent [LCP ConfAck id=0x47 <asyncmap 0xa0000>
        <magic 0x7716279c> <pcomp> <accomp>]
    rcvd [LCP ConfAck id=0x1 <asyncmap 0x0>
        <magic 0x5f6ecfaa> <pcomp> <accomp>]
    sent [IPCP ConfReq id=0x1 <addr 192.168.1.30>
    rcvd [IPCP ConfReq id=0x3f <addr 192.168.100.1>]
    sent [IPCP ConfAck id=0x3f <addr 192.168.100.1>]
    rcvd [IPCP ConfRej id=0x1 <compress VJ 0f 01>]
    sent [IPCP ConfReq id=0x2 <addr 192.168.1.30>]
    rcvd [IPCP ConfNak id=0x2 <addr 192.168.100.96>]
    sent [IPCP ConfReq id=0x3 <addr 192.168.100.96>]
    rcvd [IPCP ConfAck id=0x3 <addr 192.168.100.96>]
    local  IP address 192.168.1.220
    remote IP address 192.168.1.1
    Script /etc/ppp/ip-up started; pid = 3759
    Script /etc/ppp/ip-up finished (pid 3759), status = 0x0
```

At this point, the PPP connection is up and these two new routes should appear in the routing table:

- A route to the new *ppp0* interface
- A default route through the new *ppp0* interface

For example (here, the Met and Ref columns, mentioned earlier, are deleted for clarity):

```
# route
Kernel IP routing table
Destination    Gateway        Genmask          Flags Use Iface
192.168.100.1  *              255.255.255.255  UH      0 ppp0
192.168.1.30   *              255.255.255.255  UH      0 eth0
192.168.1.0    *              255.255.255.0    U       0 eth0
127.0.0.0      *              255.0.0.0        U       0 lo
default        192.168.100.1  0.0.0.0          UG      0 ppp0
```

When your dial-up session is complete, you can terminate pppd easily by entering Ctrl-C on the calling terminal:

```
^C
pppd[1291]: Terminating on signal 2.
pppd[1291]: Connection terminated.
pppd[1291]: Connect time 5.9 minutes.
pppd[1291]: Sent 22350 bytes, received 34553266 bytes.
pppd[1291]: Exit.
```

When *pppd* is running in the background, terminate a PPP link by sending a SIGINT or SIGTERM signal to the running pppd.

Authentication protocols

In the examples presented in this Objective, authentication with the PPP server is handled by means of a clear text username/password dialog and implemented using *chat*. This is a common setup, but three additional authentication techniques also exist. All of them embed the authentication information into the PPP data stream instead of using a clear text dialog prior to initiating PPP. These methods maintain authentication information, or *secrets*, in a file.

PAP

> The Password Authentication Protocol (PAP) is initiated by the connecting client, which sends a username/password pair. Secret information is stored in */etc/ppp/pap-secrets*.

CHAP

> The Challenge Handshake Authentication Protocol (CHAP) is initiated by the server, which sends a *challenge*. The challenge data contains the server's name, and the client must respond with its name plus a new value derived from the challenge information and the stored authentication information. For CHAP, this information is stored in */etc/ppp/chap-secrets*. CHAP may also include additional challenges over the life of the PPP connection.

MSCHAP

> This is a Microsoft-specific variant of CHAP implemented on Windows NT systems using RAS. It is supported by *pppd*, although special provisions are required. See the *Linux PPP HOWTO* for more information if you're dialing into a Windows NT RAS server using MSCHAP.

The authentication information stored in the *secrets* files for PAP and CHAP has a common format but is beyond the scope of Exam 102.

On the Exam

Be aware that PAP, CHAP, and MSCHAP exist and may be required for some dial-up situations.

PPP over ISDN

Objective 4 makes casual mention of initiating ISDN connections using PPP over ISDN technology, but ISDN devices are beyond the scope of both LPIC Level 1 Exams. That said, getting PPP running on an existing ISDN setup using supported hardware is very similar to a modem connection. Most ISDN terminal adapters supported by Linux behave much like modems, so the same connection methods may be employed. A chat script sets up the terminal adapter and instructs it to dial (probably with a special dial string that implies the ISDN BRI phone numbers), and *pppd* continues as usual. However, ISDN connections will likely require the use of one of the authentication protocols already mentioned. If PAP is used, the corresponding *pap-secrets* file is necessary.

Too many variables

Unfortunately, many of the elements involved in a dial-up PPP connection lack specific standards:

- Modems from various manufacturers may require unique settings to be made prior to dialing the PPP server. This means that setup strings included in chat scripts may be hardware-specific. *The Linux Modem HOWTO* contains information on modem requirements.

- Authentication and PPP startup schemes vary among ISPs and other PPP servers. Therefore, the configuration of a dial-up interface depends on the server's requirements. Specific information from the PPP server provider is necessary.

- PPP automation techniques vary among Linux distributions. While *pppd* comes with a default configuration style, there's no guarantee that your distribution will fully utilize it. This is particularly true for systems that include custom configuration tools that may use special configuration files and scripts.

On the Exam

PPP setup can be confusing, particularly when your Linux distribution adds additional complexity to make dial-up carefree. Be sure that you've been able to establish a PPP session with a server through both automated configuration and manual methods. You'll also need to understand how and why chat is used, how expect/send strings are constructed, how to get debugging information from *pppd*, and the routing implications of PPP (the default route). You don't need to memorize all of *pppd*'s many options or understand each script associated with automated startup of pppd, as these are beyond the scope of Exam 102. Non-chat authentication schemes and the setup of PPP servers are also beyond the scope of this exam.

20

Networking Services (Topic 1.113)

Much of the success of Linux can be attributed to bundled networking services, such as the Apache web server, Sendmail, NFS and Windows file sharing, and others. This chapter covers these six Objectives on networking services:

Objective 1: Configure and Manage inetd, xinetd, and Related Services
Candidates should be able to configure which services are available through *inetd* or *xinetd*, use *tcpwrappers* to allow or deny services on a host-by-host basis; manually start, stop, and restart Internet services; configure basic network services including *telnet* and *ftp*. Candidates should also be able to set a service to run as another user instead of the default in *inetd.conf*. Weight: 4.

Objective 2: Operate and Perform Basic Configuration of Mail Transfer Agent (MTA)
Candidates should be able to modify simple parameters in Sendmail configuration files (including the "smart host" parameter, if necessary), create mail aliases, manage the mail queue, start and stop Sendmail, configure mail forwarding and perform basic troubleshooting of Sendmail. This Objective includes checking for and closing open relays on the mail server. It does not include advanced custom configuration of Sendmail. Weight: 4.

Objective 3: Operate and Perform Basic Configuration of Apache
Candidates should be able to modify simple parameters in Apache configuration files; start, stop, and restart *httpd*; and arrange for automatic restarting of *httpd* upon boot. This objectives does not include advanced custom configuration of Apache. Weight: 4.

Objective 4: Properly Manage the NFS and Samba Daemons
A candidate should know how to mount remote filesystems using NFS; configure NFS for exporting local filesystems; start, stop, and restart the NFS server; install and configure Samba using the included GUI tools or direct edit of the */etc/smb.conf* file. (This deliberately excludes advanced NT domain

issues but includes simple sharing of home directories and printers, as well as correctly setting the *nmbd* as a WINS client.) Weight: 4.

Objective 5: Set Up and Configure Basic DNS Services
> Candidates should be able to configure hostname lookups and troubleshoot problems with local caching-only name servers. This requires an understanding of the domain registration and DNS translation process and an understanding of the key differences in configuration files for Bind 4 and Bind 8. Weight: 4.

Objective 7: Set Up Secure Shell (OpenSSH)
> The candidate should be able to obtain and configure OpenSSH. This Objective includes basic OpenSSH installation and troubleshooting, as well as configuring sshd to start at system boot. Weight: 4.

For systems deployed as servers, even in a small department, these Objectives cover some of most important system administration concepts to be performed for Linux.

Objective 1: Configure and Manage inetd, xinetd, and Related Services

To reduce the number of daemons necessary to service requests, the *Internet superdaemon*, or *inetd*, was created. Instead of running individual daemons for each service, *inetd* runs as a single service listening to all of the desired port numbers. When an inbound request is received, it is handed off to the actual daemon for processing. With this scheme, the real daemons are still used as before, but they run only when needed and are started by *inetd*, freeing resources for other tasks. In addition, using *inetd* greatly simplifies the code of the various daemons. Instead of listening for connections and everything else required to be a proper network daemon, daemons run by *inetd* need to read only from stdin and write only to stdout.

Many Linux distributions have started shipping *xinetd* as a replacement for *inetd*. The following information applies to only the original *inetd*. *xinetd* configuration is significantly different. Both are discussed in this chapter. For more information on *xinetd*, see *http://www.xinetd.org*.

The inetd Configuration File

inetd is usually started during system initialization and continues to run indefinitely (or until the process is stopped). When started (and later in response to signal SIGHUP), *inetd* reads its configuration file from */etc/inetd.conf*, which is nothing more than a plain text file that defines the services managed by *inetd*. (Commented lines begin with #.) Example 20-1 shows portions of an *inetd.conf*, with lines wrapped to fit the page (your *inetd.conf* will be different and should be configured with your security requirements in mind; more on this later).

Example 20-1. Sample inetd.conf file

```
# /etc/inetd.conf
# Internet server configuration database
# See inetd(8) for further information.
# <service_name> <socket_type> <proto> <flags> <user>  <server_path>        <args>
#
ftp      stream  tcp    nowait  root    /user/sbin/tcpd  /user/sbin/in.ftpd
telnet   stream  tcp    nowait  root    /usr/sbin/tcpd   /usr/sbin/in.telnetd
#
pop-2    stream  tcp    nowait  root    /usr/sbin/tcpd   ipop2d
pop-3    stream  tcp    nowait  root    /usr/sbin/tcpd   ipop3d
imap     stream  tcp    nowait  root    /usr/sbin/tcpd   imapd
#
finger   stream  tcp    nowait  nobody  /usr/sbin/tcpd   /usr/sbin/in-fingerd
ident    stream  tcp    nowait  nobody  /usr/sbin/identd identd -I
#
tftp     dgram   udp    wait    nobody  /usr/sbin/tcpd   /usr/sbin/in.tftpd /boot
bootps   dgram   udp    wait    root    /usr/sbin/bootpd bootpd -i -t 120
```

Each noncommented line in *inetd.conf* must contain each of the following fields:

service_name
> This is the name of a service as defined in */etc/services*.

socket_type
> This entry specifies one of a few types of communications the service will use. It's usually stream or dgram.

proto
> This field specifies the service's protocol from among those in */etc/protocols*. For most services, it will be either tcp or udp, which correspond to the stream and dgram socket types.

flags
> The wait/nowait (.max) flag is used only for datagram services, where it helps to control the handling of inbound requests and is typically set to wait. It should be set to nowait for others. You can limit the number of server instances spawned by *inetd* within any 60-second interval by appending a dot and the maximum number (.*max*). For example, to limit the service to 20 instances, use .20 after the nowait flag:
>
> nowait.20
>
> The default maximum is 40 instances (.40).

user[.group]
> This entry specifies the username (and optionally the group name) under which the service should execute, allowing them to be run with fewer permissions than root. A typical entry is the user nobody.

server_path
> This field is the full path to the executable daemon of the server program. When TCP wrappers is used, this entry specifies *tcpd*, as shown in Example 20-1.

args
> This last entry on the line may consist of multiple fields. It contains the name of the server daemon and all arguments that are to be passed to it. The daemon name is actually the first argument, or `argv[0]` from a programming point of view.

In many Linux installations, a majority of the lines in *inetd.conf* are commented out to increase security. The fewer services a system offers, the more likely it is to stand up to an attack. You should review your file to be certain that only necessary services are offered.

TCP Wrappers with inetd

Running services from *inetd* offers another convenience. Instead of launching the target daemons directly, *inetd* is usually configured to use the TCP wrappers access control facility. TCP wrappers, or *tcpd*, allows the administrator to define restrictions on the origin of inbound requests.

tcpd can be used to control access to *inetd*-managed services by IP address or by domain name. For each inbound connection to a service protected by TCP wrappers, *tcpd* consults two files that define access:

/etc/hosts.allow
> If a rule in this file is met, access to the service is allowed.

/etc/hosts.deny
> If a rule in this file is met, access to the service is denied.

Rules in these files can be constructed to match all services or alternatively to match specific services. If no match occurs in the two files, access to the service (or services) is allowed. It is common to specify particular rules in the *hosts.allow* file and provide a blanket denial in the *hosts.deny* file, thereby limiting access to clients you specifically allow.

The language in the control files consists of a service list, followed by a colon, followed by a list of hosts. Hosts may be specified by name or by IP address. For example, to deny access to all services except inbound *ftp* from the local domain, these two simple files could be used:

hosts.allow
> This entry allows FTP access to clients in the local domain:
>
> ```
> ftp: LOCAL
> ```

hosts.deny
> This entry denies access to all services from all clients:
>
> ```
> ALL: ALL
> ```

The *hosts.deny* file is consulted after *hosts.allow*, enabling the administrator to define specific allow rules that will be matched prior to deny rules or a blanket denial.

Starting and Stopping inetd Services

If *inetd* is not running, all of the services it manages are disabled. Likewise, if *inetd* is reconfigured, any changes to individual managed services take effect at the same time. To cause inetd to reread its configuration file, simply send it SIGHUP:

```
$ killall -HUP inetd
```

All *inetd* services that are commented out or missing from */etc/inetd.conf* will be disabled. However, a number of other services on Linux systems are managed through other means—typically through the runlevel system and the series of scripts and links in */etc/rc.d*. See Chapter 5 for details on starting and stopping services such as Apache (*httpd*).

On the Exam

You must be generally familiar with the content and function of *inetd.conf*, *hosts.allow*, and *hosts.deny*. Memorizing configuration details is not necessary, but be prepared for questions on available services and the effect of TCP wrappers rules in the *hosts.allow* and *hosts.deny* files. Be sure you understand what happens to services that are commented out of *inetd.conf* and that inetd must be signaled to reread the control file after any changes.

---

xinetd Configuration

The format of *inetd.conf* allows for only a specific number of options. Since *xinetd* offers many more options for services than *inetd*, it requires a different configuration file. Fortunately, the format of *xinetd.conf* (as shown in Example 20-2) is much more flexible, allowing you to mix and match a large number of options.

Example 20-2. Sample /etc/xinetd.conf

```
service discard
{
        socket_type     = stream
        protocol        = tcp
        wait            = no
        user            = root
        type            = INTERNAL
        id              = discard-stream
}

service discard
{
        socket_type     = dgram
        protocol        = udp
        wait            = yes
        user            = root
        type            = INTERNAL
```

Example 20-2. Sample /etc/xinetd.conf (continued)

```
        id              = discard-dgram
}

service telnet
{
        socket_type     = stream
        protocol        = tcp
        wait            = no
        user            = root
        server          = /usr/sbin/in.telnetd
        log_on_failure  += USERID
        disable         = yes
}
```

This example turns on the *discard* service (both TCP and UDP varieties). It also includes an entry for a *telnet* daemon, although that service is disabled.

Frequently used xinetd.conf options

These options can all be used in a service definition in *xinetd.conf*:

bind
interface
> This option can be used to listen on a specific IP address. For example, to allow connections to *localhost* only, use the following:

>   bind = 127.0.0.1

disable
enabled
> These options can be used to disable a service. Either of the following will disable a service:

>   disable = yes
>   enabled = no

> Setting disable = no or enabled = yes is not required to enable a service.

id
> This option can be used to set a unique ID for a service. By default, the ID is set to the service name, but in cases in which there is more than one entry for a service (for example, when there are entries for TCP and UDP versions of a service), unique IDs must be set for each service.

instances
> This option can be used to limit the number of simultaneous connections to a service.

> By default, the number of connections is not limited. This can also be forced by specifying instances = UNLIMITED.

log_on_failure
log_on_success
> These options can be used to control the information that is logged for failed or successful connections, respectively. For example, to specify that the result

of an *ident* query be logged for a failed connection (due to whatever access controls are in place for a service) in addition to whatever information is logged by default, you could add the following to a service definition:

```
log_on_failure += USERID
```

For both options, HOST and USERID can be specified. For log_on_failure, ATTEMPT can also be specified, but that is implied by either of the other items. For log_on_success, DURATION (the amount of time the service was connected), EXIT (notes the exit value and any signals received), PID (process ID of the program run for this connection), and TRAFFIC (the amount of data transferred in redirected connections) can be specified. You can specify a list of these items, separated by spaces.

no_access
only_from

These two options can be used to limit access to a service. IP addresses can be specified in CIDR notation (such as 192.168.1.0/24). Trailing zeros are considered wildcards, so the following are equivalent:

```
only_from = 192.168.1.0
only_from = 192.168.1.0/24
```

Hostnames, domain names (in the form *.example.com*), and network names (as specified in */etc/networks*) can also be specified.

If both of these options are specified, the rule that matches an address most closely applies. For example, the following would limit connections to any address in 192.168.1.0/24 *except* 192.168.1.42:

```
only_from = 192.168.1.0/24
no_access = 192.168.1.42
```

By default, connections are allowed from anywhere.

per_source

This option limits the number of connections for any one source address. This keeps one user from using all available connections when using the instances option.

port

This option allows you to provide a port number when you configure a service not listed in */etc/services*. Normally it is not necessary.

protocol

This option is used to specify the protocol for a given service. This could be any of the protocols listed in */etc/protocols*, but it will usually be either tcp or udp. The default is the default protocol for the service (as specified in */etc/services*).

redirect

This option tells *xinetd* to redirect connections to this port to another host and port. This can be used only for TCP services.

The following example would redirect connections to the local system's port
443 (*https*) to port 22 on 10.0.0.2:

```
service https
{
        protocol    = tcp
        redirect    = 10.0.0.2 22
        user        = root
        wait        = no
}
```

server

This option is used to specify the program to run for a service. For example,
the *imap* service might run *imapd* as follows:

```
server = /usr/sbin/imapd
```

server_args

This option is used to pass options to the server (previously specified with
the server option). For example, using rsync as a daemon requires passing
the *--daemon* option.

```
server      = /usr/bin/rsync
server_args = --daemon
```

user

This option is used to specify the user that the server program runs as. The
username must be valid (listed in */etc/passwd*).

wait

This option is used to specify whether *xinetd* should wait for a connection to
end before accepting another. Generally, this will be set to yes for udp services
and no for tcp services.

There are many more options. For a full list, see the *xinetd.conf* manpage.

Modular configuration

xinetd can be configured to scan a directory for configuration files. Some distributions use this feature to break *xinetd.conf* into separate files for each service.
Here's an example *xinetd.conf* implementing this:

```
#
# Simple configuration file for xinetd
#
# Some defaults, and include /etc/xinetd.d

defaults
{
        instances         = 60
        log_type          = SYSLOG authpriv
        log_on_success    = HOST PID
        log_on_failure    = HOST
        cps               = 25 30
}

includedir /etc/xinetd.d
```

The includedir /etc/xinetd.d directive tells *xinetd* to look at every file in */etc/ xinetd.d* for configuration. *xinetd* skips filenames containing a dot (.) or ending with a tilde (~) as a crude but effective way of avoiding backup files.

Each of these configuration files could include a service definition for a single service, which greatly simplifies packaging. For example, a distribution might include the following */etc/xinetd.d/rsync* with its *rsync* package to make it simple to turn on the *rsync* daemon:

```
service rsync
{
        disable = yes
        socket_type    = stream
        wait           = no
        user           = root
        server         = /usr/bin/rsync
        server_args    = --daemon
        log_on_failure += USERID
}
```

The system administrator could then enable the *rsync* daemon by deleting (or commenting out) the disable = yes line in that file. (On distributions that include the *chkconfig* command, *chkconfig rsync on* would have the same effect.)

Objective 2: Operate and Perform Basic Configuration of Mail Transfer Agent (MTA)

The Sendmail MTA is responsible for handling a large portion of email sent on the Internet and inside enterprises. It has broad capabilities to handle mail routing and can perform complex rewriting of email addresses. Unfortunately, *sendmail*'s configuration file can also appear to be somewhat cryptic to administrators, and detailed configuration of *sendmail* has become known as somewhat of an art.

Configuration details of *sendmail* are nontrivial and beyond the scope of the LPIC Level 1 Exams but is covered in depth at Level 2. However, a basic *sendmail* configuration for a system in an established domain is relatively simple to implement and is covered in Exam 102.

Configuring sendmail

The *sendmail* configuration file is */etc/sendmail.cf*. (Be aware that on some systems some or all of *sendmail*'s configuration files could be in an alternate location, such as */etc/mail*.) This text file contains information to control the processing of mail on your system, and it is read at every invocation of *sendmail*. Each line in the file defines a configuration command, which begins with a short one- or two-letter command definition. The file can also contain comments beginning with #. To simplify a basic setup, example *sendmail.cf* files exist in most installations.

The smart host parameter

To enable mail transfer inside an established organization, you may need to configure *sendmail* to transfer messages to a *smart host*, most likely the main mail-processing system in your domain. For example, if your enterprise's mail is handled by *mail.example.com*, you can configure your Linux systems to transfer all mail to that computer for further processing. To make this change, simply use the DS directive in *sendmail.cf*:

```
DSmail.example.com
```

Mail Aliases

Even on simple *sendmail* installations, it is useful to configure some of your system users to have their mail redirected to another user. For example, artificial users such as *nobody* shouldn't receive mail, so forwarding any mail received for that username to an administrator may help with problem solving. This forwarding is accomplished using *mail aliases*. A mail alias is simply mapping from a username to one or more recipients in this form:

```
sysadmin:      jdean, bsmith
```

Aliases are defined in */etc/aliases*. Local mail intended for *sysadmin* is received by both *jdean* and *bsmith* on the local system, as shown in Example 20-3.

Example 20-3. A typical /etc/aliases file

```
# Basic system aliases -- these MUST be present.
MAILER-DAEMON:  postmaster
postmaster:     root
# General redirections for pseudo accounts.
bin:            root
daemon:         root
games:          root
ingres:         root
nobody:         root
system:         root
toor:           root
uucp:           root
# Well-known aliases.
manager:        root
dumper:         root
operator:       root
webmaster:      root
abuse:          root
spam:           root
# Trap decode to catch security attacks
decode:         root
# Person who should get root's mail
root:           jdean
# Departmental accounts
sales:          bsmith
support:        jdoe
```

sendmail doesn't actually read the text aliases file, since it's not uncommon to find many aliases defined there. Instead, it reads a compiled database file, */etc/aliases.db*, built from */etc/aliases*. Therefore, the database must be updated after any change is made to aliases, using the *newaliases* command. *newaliases* has no options and must be run as root.

Forwarding mail from your account to another account

In addition to permanently established mail aliases, individual users have the capability to create their own mail aliases on an as-needed basis by using a *.forward* file in the home directory. Mail is sent to the alias by simply putting an email address on a line by itself in *.forward*.

On the Exam

Remember, the */etc/aliases* and *.forward* files define mail aliases, and the *newaliases* command must be executed after changing the */etc/aliases* file to re-create the alias database.

Queued Mail

If *sendmail* cannot deliver mail immediately, such as on a system using an intermittent dial-up connection, mail is queued for later processing. To see the mail queue, use the *mailq* command, like this:

```
$ mailq
Mail Queue (2 requests)
--Q-ID-- --Size-- -Priority- ---Q-Time--- -Sender/Recipient
WAA12372    3427      30043 Jul  4  2:19 bsmith
                 (host map: lookup (mydom.com): deferred)
                                      jdean@mydom.com
WAA12384     313      30055 Jul  8 22:40 jdoe
                 (host map: lookup (yourdom.com): deferred)
                                      you@yourdom.com
```

The first line printed for each message shows the internal identifier used on the local host for the message, the size of the message in bytes, the date and time the message was accepted into the queue, and the sender of the message. The second line shows the error message that caused this mail to be retained in the queue. Subsequent lines show message recipients. In this example, two outbound messages are queued because the DNS host lookups did not succeed.

On the Exam

Be aware that mail could be queued by sendmail and that mailq displays a list of those messages.

Starting and Stopping sendmail

sendmail is typically managed through the runlevel system. See "Objective 2: Change Runlevels and Shut Down or Reboot System" in Chapter 14 for details on starting and stopping services.

Objective 3: Operate and Perform Basic Configuration of Apache

Apache is a phenomenal open source success story. Despite the availability of commercial web servers, Apache continues to be the most popular web server on the Internet. It is also widely deployed inside corporate networks for managing internal communications.

Because it is so popular and likely to be found on just about every Linux server, understanding the basics of Apache administration is required for Exam 102.

Configuring Apache

Apache is configured with the file *httpd.conf* located in */etc/httpd/conf*, */etc/apache*, or possibly another location, depending on your distribution or how Apache is installed.

Configuration is managed through *configuration directives*, one per line, in *httpd.conf*. The file can also contain comments, which begin with a #. Directives are in the form:

```
DirectiveName [argument-list]
```

For example, the DocumentRoot directive, which tells Apache where the top of the HTML tree is located, might look like this:

```
DocumentRoot /home/httpd/html
```

Here are some basic Apache configuration directives:

ServerType

 This option was removed in Apache 2.0.

This directive can be either *standalone* or *inetd*. If you prefer to have *inetd* listen for inbound HTTP requests, set this to *inetd* and configure *inetd.conf* as needed. Running *httpd* from *inetd* has a major negative impact on performance, so it is almost never a good idea.

Port

 This option was removed in Apache 2.0.

This parameter defines the port to which Apache listens. The default HTTP
port is 80.

User *and* Group

These two parameters determine the name and group, respectively, that
Apache executes under. Typical examples are nobody, www, and httpd.

ServerAdmin

This directive specifies the email address of the administrator, such as
root@localhost.

DocumentRoot

This directive tells Apache where to find the top of the HTML tree, such as
/home/httpd/html.

UserDir

System users may use a standard personal subdirectory for their own HTML
documents. This directive determines the name of that directory. It is often set
to *public_html*. Files for user *jdean* in the directory */home/jdean/public_html*
would be accessed using a URL of *http://localhost/~jdean*.

Of course, there are many more, and additional syntax is used when necessary. In
httpd.conf, groups can be delineated by keywords that look like HTML. Directives
in such a group affect only a subset of the content served by Apache. For example,
the following group of directives controls CGI execution in */home/httpd/cgi-bin*:

```
<Directory /home/httpd/cgi-bin>
AllowOverride None
Options ExecCGI
</Directory>
```

On the Exam

The LPI exam Objectives don't specify particular Apache configuration directives, but you should be prepared to interpret various configuration examples
and have knowledge of the three configuration files and their likely locations.

Starting and Stopping Apache

Typically, Apache is managed through the runlevel system and the series of scripts
and links in */etc/init.d* and */etc/rcn.d*. See Chapter 5 for information on starting and
stopping services such as Apache.

Objective 4: Properly Manage the NFS and Samba Daemons

Networked file and printer sharing is among the fundamental services offered by Linux and other operating systems. For years, the standard file sharing protocol for Unix has been the NFS. Originally developed by Sun Microsystems, NFS has been implemented on many operating systems and is available in both commercial and free software implementations.

NFS

Any Linux system may act as both an NFS server and an NFS client. Clients use mount to attach remote filesystems from NFS servers to their local filesystem. Once mounted, the directory hierarchy mounted on the client appears to users as a local filesystem.

Exporting (sharing) local filesystems using NFS

To share a part of your system's filesystem, you must add a specification to */etc/exports*. Each line in this file describes a shared filesystem resource. The format of the file is:

> directory   system(options) system(options) ...

 The syntax of */etc/exports* on Linux differs significantly from the same file on systems using a Sun-derived NFS implementation.

directory is a local filesystem directory, such as */home*. Each of the space-separated *systems* describes clients by name or address, and the associated *options* control access. If the system name is omitted, no restriction is placed on which clients can connect. Typical options are:

ro
> Export with read-only attribute.

rw
> Export with read/write attribute, the default.

no_root_squash
> Allow access by user ID 0, *root*. Normally *root* on the client is mapped to the unprivileged user ID 65534 on the server. This option turns off that feature.

Example 20-4 shows three shared directories from an */etc/exports* file.

Example 20-4. Sample /etc/exports file

```
/               orion(rw,no_root_squash)
/usr            *.example.com(ro) orion(rw)
/pub            (ro,insecure,all_squash)
/pub/private    factory*.example.com(noaccess)
```

In this example, the entire filesystem (*/*) is shared with the system *orion* in read/write mode, and *root* access is accepted. The */usr* directory is shared as read-only (ro) to all systems in *example.com* and read/write (rw) to *orion*. The */pub* directory is shared as read-only (ro) to any system, but *factory*.example.com* systems cannot look into */pub/private* because the noaccess option is used.

For new or revised entries to be incorporated in the NFS configuration, NFS daemons must be reconfigured or restarted.

On the Exam

Detailed configuration of NFS exports is beyond the scope LPIC Level 1 Exams, but you must understand the contents of */etc/exports* and how to incorporate them into a running system.

Mounting remote NFS filesystems

Mounting an NFS volume requires the use of a local mount point, a directory in the filesystem over which the remote directory hierarchy will be placed. Once the directory exists, *mount* is used to create the NFS connection from the local client to the remote server. The syntax is similar to that used for local filesystems, with the addition of the NFS server name or address. For example, if *server1* is offering its */home* directory via NFS, it could be mounted locally as follows:

```
# mkdir /mnt/server1
# mount -t nfs server1:/home /mnt/server1
```

In this example, the *mount* command uses the -*t* option to specify mount type nfs. The second argument specifies the data source by concatenating the name of the NFS server (*server1*) with its exported directory (*/home*). The final argument is the directory name that will serve as the local mount point (*/mnt/server1*). After successfully mounting, */mnt/server1* appears to be a local filesystem.

This configuration could be incorporated into */etc/fstab* for automated mounting at boot time with a line like this:

```
server1:/home   /mnt/server1   nfs  defaults  0  0
```

In this example, defaults indicates that the filesystem should be mounted using the default options (see the manpage for *mount* for defaults). The two zeros indicate that the filesystem should not be backed up using *dump* and that it should not have a filesystem check at boot time.

Starting and stopping NFS

NFS consists of multiple daemons, which are typically managed through the runlevel system and the series of scripts and links in */etc/init.d* and */etc/rcn.d*. See Chapter 14, "Objective 2: Change Runlevels and Shut Down or Reboot System," for details on starting and stopping services such as the NFS family.

Samba and the SMB and NMB Daemons

Another extremely popular sharing mechanism is that used on Microsoft and IBM systems, called Server Message Block (SMB). It is implemented as free software as a suite of programs collectively known as Samba, which runs on a variety of operating systems including Linux. Samba consists of two daemons:

smbd
> This daemon handles file and printer sharing, as well as authentication.

nmbd
> This daemon implements the Windows Internet Name Service (WINS), which maps Windows system names to IP addresses.

On the Exam

It is the goal of the Samba team to eventually implement all of the services found on Windows servers, including Windows NT/2000 Domain Controller functionality. The LPI Exam deliberately avoids specifics in this area, leaving only basic Samba configuration for the test.

Getting started

Your Linux distribution probably came with a recent version of Samba. If you already have Samba installed, setting up a basic configuration is easy. To check whether Samba is already installed on your system, issue the following command on the command line:

```
# smbd -h
```

If Samba is installed on your system, you should see a message similar to:

```
Usage: smbd [-D] [-p port] [-d debuglevel] [-l log basename]
   [-s services file]
Version 2.0.3
   -D              become a daemon
   -p port         listen on the specified port
   -d debuglevel   set the debuglevel
   -l log basename. Basename for log/debug files
   -s services file. Filename of services file
   -P              passive only
   -a              append to log file (default)
   -o              overwrite log file, don't append
   -i scope        NetBIOS scope to use (default none)
```

If not, you can get source or binary distributions for Samba at *http://www.samba.org*.

To begin using Samba, you must create its configuration file, *smb.conf*. Depending on how you acquired Samba, the default location for this file may be */etc* or */usr/local/samba*. A basic *smb.conf* set up is shown in Example 20-5.

Example 20-5. Sample /etc/smb.conf file

```
[global]
workgroup = HOME
server string = LINUX
encrypt passwords = Yes
log file = /var/log/samba/log.%m
max log size = 50
socket options = TCP_NODELAY
printcap name = /etc/printcap
dns proxy = No
socket address = 192.168.1.30
wins support = no
wins server = 192.168.1.202
hosts allow = 192.168.1. 127.
[myshare]
path = /home/myshare
guest ok = yes
comment = My Shared Data
writeable = yes
[homes]
   comment = Home Directories
   browseable = no
   writable = yes
[printers]
   comment = All Printers
   printing = BSD
   print command = /usr/bin/lpr -r  %s
   path = /var/spool/samba
   guest ok = yes
   printable = yes
```

This example configuration allows Samba to participate in an SMB workgroup called HOME with a system name of LINUX. Hosts on the private network 192.168.1 as well as the loopback network (127.) are allowed to access shared resources. The default sections of Samba's /etc/smb.conf file are as follows:

[global]
   The global section defines items applying to the entire system, such as the workgroup and system names.

[homes]
   A section that defines users' home directories to be shared.

[printers]
   This section shares all of the printers located in /etc/printcap (provided that a BSD-style printer setup is in use).

Samba also has the following custom share section:

[myshare]
   This defines a shared directory myshare. The name myshare will appear as shared resources to clients. Users' home directories do not need to be explicitly shared if [homes] is used.

To use Samba, only the workgroup, server string, and a shared service such as [myshare] need to be configured.

See Samba's manpage for more detailed information on the *smb.conf* file.

WINS and browsing

Windows networks allow users to view available shared resources through *browsing*, a process by which one machine acts as a *browser* and is updated with information from other machines on the network. Client machines can then obtain lists of resources on the entire network from that single browser machine. Samba's *nmbd* daemon implements WINS. To use Samba as a WINS client, you can specify the address of the WINS server on your network using the wins server directive, as shown in Example 20-5. Samba can also act as a WINS server itself, although this is beyond the scope of the LPIC Level 1 Exams.

On the Exam

You should be generally familiar with the *smb.conf* file and with the concepts of shared directories, shared printers, WINS, and SWAT. You don't need to worry about creating custom Samba configurations for Exam 102.

Using SWAT

Samba v2.0 and later comes with a web-based configuration tool called the Samba Web Administration Tool (SWAT). To use SWAT with *inetd*, use a line similar to this in */etc/inetd.conf*:

```
swat    stream  tcp nowait.400    root /usr/sbin/swat swat
```

You can also run the *swat* daemon manually. In either case, you must list its port, 901, in */etc/services*. Once *swat* is configured, you can point your browser to *http://localhost:901* and log in using the root password; *swat* offers a convenient series of forms that you can fill in using the browser to configure Samba. When you commit changes, the *smb.conf* file is updated for your system.

Objective 5: Set Up and Configure Basic DNS Services

The DNS is the distributed database of name-to-IP-address translations. Technically, it isn't necessary to use host and domain names such as *www.lpi.org*, because it's the actual IP address that the computer requires to establish communications. DNS was created to allow the use of more convenient global domain names instead. For example, when a user enters a DNS name as part of a URL in a browser, the name portion is sent to a DNS server to be resolved into an IP address. Once the address is found, it is used to rewrite the URL and directly fetch the web page.

The server daemon that implements DNS is *named*, the *name daemon*, which is part of the Berkeley Internet Name Daemon package (BIND). It is *named*'s job to respond to requests from the resolver and return an IP address.

The Resolver

The code that resolves names to IP addresses using DNS for client programs is implemented in system libraries collectively called the *resolver*. The resolver uses one of several means to determine an IP address from a hostname or domain name:

Static local files

> The local file */etc/hosts* can contain name-to-address mapping for a few systems on a network. However, for large enterprises, using static local files to manage IP address resolution is problematic due to the frequent changes required in the data. Updating all of the client systems would be impractical. This resolution method is sometimes referred to as the *files* method.

Network Information Service (NIS)

> Some private networks use a shared information service that can include address resolution. This is NIS, or a later version of it called NIS+, and is referred to as the nis method of resolution. Both services are beyond the scope of the LPIC Level 1 Exams.

Domain Name Service (DNS)

> Because addresses and domains on the public Internet change frequently and are so numerous, static local files can't handle resolution far outside the enterprise. As already mentioned, DNS is a distributed database. That is, small portions of the DNS are managed by local authorities that are responsible only for their particular slice of the system. As you'd expect, using DNS for name resolution is called the dns method.

In most cases, */etc/hosts* will be used for name resolution of the local host and perhaps a few other nearby systems. DNS, perhaps together with NIS in enterprise environments, will handle everything else.

/etc/hosts and the other files used to configure the resolver are described in the "Configuration files" section of Chapter 19, but here's a quick recap:

/etc/hosts

> This file lists statically defined name-to-address translations.

/etc/nsswitch.conf (or /etc/host.conf on older Linux systems)

> The "name service switch" file (*nsswitch.conf*) defines the order of name server methods to be used in succession by the resolver (it can also control

other things such as passwords, but those don't apply here). Typically, this single entry is used to control name resolution:

```
hosts:  files dns
```

This entry instructs the resolver to resolve names using */etc/hosts* first and, if a match isn't found, to make a DNS query.

/etc/resolv.conf
This file lists the IP addresses of name servers:

```
nameserver 127.0.0.1
nameserver 192.168.1.5
nameserver 192.168.250.2
```

On the Exam

Be sure that you understand how */etc/nsswitch* controls the resolution order, that */etc/resolv.conf* identifies DNS servers by address, and that */etc/hosts* is for local, statically resolved addresses. Also remember that older versions of Linux used */etc/host.conf* to configure the resolution order instead of */etc/nsswitch.conf*.

When the resolver determines that a DNS query is required, it sends a request containing a domain name to one of the DNS servers listed in */etc/resolv.conf*. The DNS server uses its own records to find the domain or may resort to escalating to other DNS servers if the information isn't readily available. When a result is found by the DNS servers, the IP address corresponding to the requested name is returned to the originating client.

Domain registration

Domain names are assigned through a registration process with one of the domain name registrars available on the Internet (*http://www.internic.net/regist.html*). Originally, a single authority managed domain names. As commercial uses for domain names spread, additional entities sought the ability to charge for the service of domain registration, and today there are a number of qualified registrars (a search for *domain registrar* on one of the popular search engines will yield a daunting list). Once a domain name is registered, it is listed in a worldwide database along with contact information for the owners or their agents. The name servers that contain DNS information for the domain can go along with this record.

Most registrants offer a domain name search service, so you can test desired domain names for availability. If the domain name you're seeking is available, you can provide payment information to a registrant and purchase rights to use the name, usually for one or two years.

Using named as a local caching-only name server

named is often configured to serve DNS requests even when it does not have local information for a domain. Instead, it is used for its caching ability. When a client program requests an address resolution from the local *named*, the daemon first checks its local cache. If it doesn't find the domain there, it goes to other DNS servers as usual. If the cache does contain the domain, it is returned immediately to the client from the cache, which speeds the resolution process.

Some Linux distributions come with a caching-only *named* configuration preinstalled. If this isn't the case for you, simply follow the brief instructions in Section 3 of the *DNS HOWTO* available from *http://www.tldp.org*. Part of the configuration includes setting your local system as the default DNS server in */etc/resolv.conf*:

```
nameserver 127.0.0.1
```

You can test the configuration using the nslookup utility:

```
# nslookup
Default Server:  localhost
Address:  127.0.0.1
> lpi.org
Server:  localhost
Address:  127.0.0.1
Name:    lpi.org
Address:  209.167.177.93
> lpi.org
Server:  localhost
Address:  127.0.0.1
Non-authoritative answer:
Name:    lpi.org
Address:  209.167.177.93
> exit
```

In this example, *nslookup* attaches to the default server *localhost* (127.0.0.1). In the first query for *lpi.org*, the local *named* must find the address from external DNS servers. However, the result is found in the cache on the second try, as indicated by the Non-authoritative answer response. If this behavior isn't seen, there may be a problem with the *named* configuration in */etc/named.conf*.

Some debugging information can be found in */var/log/messages*. For example, the bold line in this short excerpt shows an error in the configuration file:

```
smp named[216]: starting.  named
smp named[216]: cache zone "" (IN) loaded (serial 0)
smp named[216]: Zone "0.0.127.in-addr.arpa"
  (file named.local): No default TTL
  set using SOA minimum instead
smp named[216]: master zone "0.0.127.in-addr.arpa"
  (IN) loaded (serial 1997022700)
smp named[216]: /etc/named.conf:18: can't redefine
channel 'default_syslog'
smp named[216]: listening on [127.0.0.1].53 (lo)
smp named[216]: listening on [192.168.1.30].53 (eth0)
smp named[216]: Forwarding source address is [0.0.0.0].1855
smp named[216]: Ready to answer queries.
```

Note that configuration of a caching-only name server is beyond the scope of the LPIC Level 1 Exams but is a useful exercise in understanding the configuration of named.

DNS query utilities

A few tools exist to verify the operation of DNS name resolution. Here's a brief synopsis of *nslookup* and *host*, both specifically mentioned in this Objective. The host utility does not offer interactive mode but uses a syntax similar to nslookup.

nslookup

Syntax

```
nslookup [host [dnsserver]]
```

Description

Look up *host*, optionally specifying a particular *dnsserver*. *nslookup* can be used in either interactive or noninteractive modes. If *host* is provided on the command line, noninteractive mode is used. In interactive mode, a number of commands are available to control *nslookup* (the *ls* command to *nslookup* is used in the example). See the manpage for more details.

Noninteractive example

In this example, *nslookup* provides immediate results because *host*, in this case *oreillynet.com*, is provided on the command line:

```
# nslookup oreillynet.com 192.168.1.2
Server:  ns1.mydomain.com
Address:  192.168.1.2
Non-authoritative answer:
Name:    oreillynet.com
Address:  208.201.239.36
```

Interactive example

Here, *nslookup* is used interactively with DNS server 192.168.1.2 to find records from *yourdomain.com*:

```
# nslookup
Default Server:  localhost
Address:  127.0.0.1
> server 192.168.1.2
Default Server:  ns1.mydomain.com
Address:  192.168.1.2
> ls -a yourdomain.com
[ns1.mydomain.com]
$ORIGIN yourdomain.com.
ipass              2D IN CNAME    snoopy
smtp               2D IN CNAME    charlie
mail               2D IN CNAME    charlie
pop                2D IN CNAME    lucy
yourdomain         2D IN CNAME    charlie
```

```
ww2                          2D IN CNAME     linus
www                          2D IN CNAME     sally
> exit
```

---

host

Syntax

```
host [options] host [dnsserver]
```

Description

Look up *host*, optionally specifying a particular *dnsserver*.

Frequently used options

-d

Enable debugging, showing network transactions in detail.

-v

Use verbose mode. Results are displayed in the official domain master file format.

Example

```
# host -v oreillynet.com
Trying null domain
rcode = 0 (Success), ancount=1
The following answer is not authoritative:
oreillynet.com  1991 IN A      208.201.239.36
For authoritative answers, see:
oreillynet.com  167591 IN      NS      NS1.SONIC.NET
oreillynet.com  167591 IN      NS      NS.SONGLINE.COM
Additional information:
NS1.SONIC.NET    167591 IN      A       208.201.224.11
NS.SONGLINE.COM 167591 IN      A       208.201.239.31
```

BIND Version 4 versus Version 8 configuration files

It's likely that a Linux administrator will maintain or install systems running BIND v4.x as well as the newer v8.x. This LPI Objective requires an understanding of the differences between the configuration files for these two BIND versions. Under BIND v4, the configuration file was called */etc/named.boot*. Example 20-6 shows a trivial BIND v4 configuration file.

Example 20-6. BIND v4 named.boot file

```
directory                       /var/named
cache   .                       root.hints
primary 0.0.127.IN-ADDR.ARPA    127.0.0.zone
primary localhost               localhost.zone
```

In BIND v8, the configuration file was renamed */etc/named.conf*. Example 20-7 shows the equivalent configuration in the BIND v8 format.

Example 20-7. BIND v8 named.conf file

```
options {
        directory "/var/named";
};
zone "." {
        type hint;
        file "root.hints";
};
zone "0.0.127.IN-ADDR.ARPA" {
        type master;
        file "127.0.0.zone";
};
zone "localhost" {
        type master;
        file "localhost.zone";
};
```

As you can see, the information contained in the files is largely the same, but the v8 format contains a more formal structure. For those upgrading to Version 8, the Perl script *named-bootconf.pl* is included in the v8 package to upgrade *named.boot* to *named.conf*.

On the Exam

You should be generally familiar with the structural differences between the configuration files for BIND v4 and v8. However, detailed *named* configuration is beyond the scope of the LPIC Level 1 Exams.

Objective 7: Set Up Secure Shell (OpenSSH)

This section explains how to acquire, compile, install, and configure OpenSSH for Linux, so that you can use it in place of *telnet*, *rsh*, and *rlogin*. For more information about using *ssh*, see Chapter 40, Objective 4: Secure Shell and *SSH, The Secure Shell: The Definitive Guide* (O'Reilly).

In the unlikely event that your Linux distribution does not include OpenSSH, it is available at *http://www.openssh.com/portable.html* and at many mirror sites around the world. It is a simple matter to compile and install OpenSSH if you have *gcc*, *make*, and the necessary libraries and header files installed. The OpenSSH build uses *autoconf* (the usual *configure*, *make*, and so on) like most other open source projects. See Chapter 4 for more information on building software in general, and see the *INSTALL* file in the top level of the source tree, or *ftp://ftp.openbsd.org/pub/OpenBSD/OpenSSH/portable/INSTALL* for more information on building OpenSSH specifically (such as what libraries are required and what options can be passed to *configure*).

To enable login from remote systems using OpenSSH, you must start *sshd*, which may be done simply by issuing the following command:

```
# sshd
```

Note that you do not need to put this command in the background, as it handles this detail itself. Once the *sshd* daemon is running, you may connect from another SSH-equipped system:

```
# ssh mysecurehost
```

The default configuration should be adequate for basic use of SSH.

On the Exam

SSH is an involved and highly configurable piece of software, and detailed knowledge of its setup is not required. However, SSH is an important part of the security landscape. Be aware that all communications using SSH are encrypted using public/private key encryption, which means that plain text passwords are unlikely to be compromised.

21

Security (Topic 1.114)

As with any multiuser-networked operating system, a secure environment is essential to system stability. This Topic covers basic Linux security administration. The following three Objectives are included:

Objective 1: Perform Security Administration Tasks
Candidates should know how to review system configuration to ensure host security in accordance with local security policies. This Objective includes how to configure TCP wrappers, find files with SUID/SGID bits set, verify packages, set or change user passwords and password aging information, and update binaries as recommended by CERT, BUGTRAQ, and/or the distribution's security alerts. Includes basic knowledge of ipchains and iptables. Weight: 4.

Objective 2: Set Up Host Security
Candidates should know how to set up a basic level of host security. Tasks include syslog configuration, shadowed passwords, setup of a mail alias for root's mail, and turning of all network services not in use. Weight: 3.

Objective 3: Set Up User-level Security
An LPIC candidate should be able to configure user-level security. Tasks include limits on user logins, processes, and memory usage. Weight: 1.

Objective 1: Perform Security Administration Tasks

A good security policy includes such things as securing inbound network requests, verifying the authenticity of software packages to assure they are not hostile, and managing local security resources. This Objective details some of the most common of these activities that a system administrator performs.

TCP Wrappers

As a Linux system operates in a networked environment, it is constantly "listening" for inbound requests from the network. Many requests come into Linux on the same network interface, but they are differentiated from one another by their *port address*, a unique numeric designator used by network protocols. Each type of service listens on a different port. Established port numbers and their corresponding services are listed in */etc/services*. Here are some lines from that file:

```
ftp       21/tcp
ssh       22/tcp
telnet    23/tcp
smtp      25/tcp    mail
domain    53/tcp
domain    53/udp
http      80/tcp    www www-http
```

The first column lists the names of various services. The second column lists the port numbers assigned to the services and the protocol (TCP or UDP) used by the service. The optional third column and any other columns list alternative names for this service. For example, *http* might be referred to as *www*. Both refer to port 80.

On the attack

As the Internet has grown, the frequency of computer break-in attempts has kept pace. To gain entry to an unsuspecting host system, some intruders configure their systems to appear to target servers (that is, your servers) as trusted hosts. This could include a forged IP address or hostname, or the exploitation of aspects of the TCP protocol. Such attacks are carried out against multiple ports, sometimes in a *port scan* in which multiple ports at a single IP address are attacked in succession.

In response to these threats, the *TCP wrapper* concept was created. The "wrappers" name comes from the idea that the services are "wrapped" in a protective layer. TCP wrappers consist of a single program, *tcpd*, which is run by *inetd* in place of actual services like *ftpd* or *telnetd*, among others.

 While *inetd* is not used on many modern Linux systems, the functionality of *tcpd* has been incorporated into many programs through the use of *libwrap*, the library version of tcpd.

tcpd performs the following functions:

- Responds to network requests and does security tests on the information provided in the connection message
- Consults local configuration files (*/etc/host.allow* and */etc/host.deny*) to restrict access
- Provides detailed logging via the authpriv facility of *syslogd* for connection requests

If a connection is approved, *tcpd* steps aside and allows the connection to be received by the true service. You could consider *tcpd* to be a gatekeeper of sorts, asking for identification at the door, and once satisfied, getting out of the way and allowing entry. By doing so, *tcpd* does not impact subsequent performance of the network connection. However, this aspect of *tcpd* prevents its use for services that handle multiple clients at one time, such has NFS and *httpd*. Instead, services protected by *tcpd* include single-client programs such as *telnet* and *ftp*.

Configuring inetd and tcpd

Chapter 20, "Objective 1: Perform Security Administration Tasks," examines *inetd* and its configuration file, */etc/inetd.conf*. Without *tcpd*, a typical service configuration looks like this:

```
telnet  stream  tcp  nowait  root  /usr/sbin/in.telnetd   in.telnetd
```

In this example, */usr/sbin/in.telnetd* is the executable program that is called when a Telnet client tries to attach to the system on the Telnet port (23). With this configuration, *in.telnetd* responds directly and immediately to inbound requests. To enable the use of TCP wrappers for *in.telnetd*, it is specified that *tcpd* be called instead. Making this change yields this revised *inetd.conf* line:

```
telnet  stream  tcp  nowait  root  /usr/sbin/tcpd   in.telnetd
```

Now, */usr/sbin/tcpd* is called in response to an inbound Telnet connection.

tcpd interacts with only the initial network connection. It does not interact with the client process (remote Telnet), the client user (the remote person initiating the Telnet session), or the server process (the local *in.telnetd*). Since it is autonomous, tcpd has these properties:

Application independence
> The same small *tcpd* program can be used on many different network services. This simplicity makes *tcpd* easy to install, configure, and upgrade.

Invisible from outside
> Anyone trying to gain access has no direct evidence that *tcpd* is in use.

tcpd access control

tcpd provides a method of limiting access from external sources both by name and by address. After receiving a network request, *tcpd* first does its IP address and hostname checks. If those pass, *tcpd* then consults two control files, named *hosts.allow* and *hosts.deny*, for access control information. These are text files that contain rules (one per line) against which incoming network connections are tested:

/etc/hosts.allow
> *tcpd* consults this file first. When an incoming network request matches one of these rules, *tcpd* immediately grants access by passing the network connection over to the server daemon. If none of the rules are matched, the next file is consulted.

/etc/hosts.deny
> This file is consulted second. If a network request matches one of these rules, *tcpd* denies access to the service.

If no matches are made in either of the files, then the connection is allowed. This implies that missing *hosts.allow* and *hosts.deny* files means that no access control is implemented.

The form of the rules in these two files is simple:

```
service_list : foreign_host_list
```

The service list is made up of space-separated program names, such as *in.telnetd* and *in.ftpd*. The foreign host list can contain special codes, which can be used on both sides of the colon:

ALL

This is the universal wildcard, which always matches all requests. When used on the left side of a rule, ALL indicates every service protected by *tcpd*. On the right side, it means all possible hosts.

EXCEPT

In the context of:

```
list1 EXCEPT list2
```

This operator matches anything that matches list1 unless it also matches list2.

KNOWN

This matches any host whose name and address are known, such as after a successful DNS lookup. Dependent on DNS servers.

LOCAL

This wildcard matches any host whose name does not contain a dot character.

PARANOID

This wildcard matches a host whose name and address do not match (when forward and reverse DNS lookups don't match). If *tcpd* is compiled with the -DPARANOID option, connections in this category are dropped prior to testing against the rules in the control files.

UNKNOWN

Opposite of KNOWN. When a DNS lookup for a host fails, this wildcard matches. This could happen for valid reasons, such as a DNS server failure, so use this one with caution.

To enable access from systems in domain *otherdom.com*, except its web server, and to allow access from systems in network 192.168.100.0, you could put the following rules in */etc/hosts.allow*:

```
ALL: .otherdom.com EXCEPT www.otherdom.com
ALL: 192.168.100.
```

Note that the leading and trailing dots are significant. .otherdom.com matches any system in that domain, such as *ftp.otherdom.com* and *lab1.otherdom.com*. The address rule with 192.168.100. matches all of the addresses on that network, including 192.168.100.1, 192.168.100.2, 192.168.100.100, and so on.

DNS is not completely reliable, so relying on it for access control should be avoided if at all possible. Use IP addresses whenever you can.

To reject everything else, put the following in */etc/hosts.deny*:

```
ALL: ALL
```

This rule denies ALL services from ALL machines anywhere. Remember that matches found in *hosts.allow* cause the search to stop.

On the Exam

Remember that *hosts.allow* is evaluated prior to *hosts.deny*. This means that if a match occurs in *hosts.allow*, the connection succeeds and any potential matches from *hosts.deny* are ignored. Also remember that, in the absence of control, access is permitted.

Keep in mind that services that are not in use may have control settings. A configuration in */etc/hosts.allow* or */etc/hosts.deny* does not imply that listed services are actually running on the system. Evaluate the complete setup of *inetd.conf*, *hosts.allow*, and *hosts.deny* when answering questions about tcpd.

---

tcpd logging

When *tcpd* is enabled, it logs to the *authpriv* facility in *syslogd*. (syslog and its configuration are described in Chapter 18, "Objective 3: Configure and Use System Log Files to Meet Administrative and Security Needs.") Check your */etc/syslog.conf* file to confirm where this facility will be logged on your system. For example, this */etc/syslog.conf* configuration line puts all authpriv messages in */var/log/secure*:

```
authpriv.*    /var/log/secure
```

Most system service daemons will do some logging on their own. For example, *in.telnetd* writes the following line to *authpriv* as the result of a Telnet connection:

```
Feb  8 17:50:04 smp login: LOGIN ON 0 BY jdean FROM 192.168.1.50
```

When *tcpd* is listening to the Telnet port in place of *in.telnetd*, it logs the request first, does its verifications, and then passes the connection on to *in.telnetd*, which then starts a *login* process as before. In this case, */var/log/secure* looks like this:

```
Feb  8 17:53:03 smp in.telnetd[1400]: connect from 192.168.1.50
Feb  8 17:53:07 smp login: LOGIN ON 0 BY jdean FROM 192.168.1.50
```

The first line was logged by *tcpd*. It indicates that a connection was received from 192.168.1.50 bound for the *in.telnetd* daemon. The smp on these example lines is the name of the host making the log entries. As you can see, the tcpd report precedes the login report.

Finding Executable SUID Files

The SUID capability of the Linux ext2 filesystem was covered in Chapter 6, "Objective 5: Use File Permissions to Control Access to Files." In that section, the SUID property was described as both a security enhancement and a security risk. It can be considered an enhancement because it allows administrators to grant superuser privileges to specific, trusted programs that may be executed by anyone on the system. The example given is *passwd*, which needs special access to manipulate the shadow password file (*/etc/shadow*). Without using the SUID property, everyone on the system would need administrative rights to change his own password, which is clearly undesirable. It is also mentioned that an SUID capability that is granted unwisely can be a security risk, and all applications of SUID must be considered carefully. The reason for this concern is that the potential exists for an attacker to exploit the superuser privilege on an SUID file. For example, if the attacker is able to somehow overwrite the contents of *passwd*, she could effectively gain superuser access to the system by running a *passwd* of her own design that changes passwords, adds new accounts, or something else shady.

For systems on corporate networks and on the Internet, it is common to minimize the number of SUID files on the system and to regularly monitor the known list of programs for changes. In the event that a new SUID program is found that was not legitimately created or if an attribute of a known file changes, it could be a warning that system security has been compromised.

The *find* command can perform the searches for attributes such as SUID (see the "Applying commands recursively through a directory tree" section in Chapter 5 for details on *find*). In this example, a *find* command that searches the entire filesystem for files that have the SUID bit set is constructed; it avoids the */proc* filesystem (kernel information) to prevent permission problems. The example generates verbose output similar to *ls -l* to log detailed information about the SUID files found:

```
# find / \
>    -path '/proc' -prune \
>    -or \
>    -perm -u+s \
>    -ls
```

The first line calls the find program and indicates that the search should begin at the root directory /. The second line specifies a *-path* directive to match */proc* utilizing the *-prune* modifier. This eliminates (or *prunes*) the */proc* directory from the search. The next line joins the *-path* directive to the *-perm* (permissions) directive with a logical *-or*, skipping execution of the *-perm* directive when *-path* matches /proc. The *-perm* directive uses a permission mode of *-u+s*, which indicates "match SUID." The next line with the *-ls* prints each match with a format similar to *ls -l*.

The result of this command is a listing of files on your system with the SUID property; the following is just a snippet of what that output would look like:

```
32773 72  -rwsr-xr-x  1 root   root   68508 Feb 24  2003 /bin/mount
32823 28  -rwsr-xr-x  1 root   root   28628 Jan 24  2003 /bin/ping
32866 100 -rwsr-xr-x  1 root   root   95564 Feb 18  2003 /bin/su
33199 32  -rwsr-xr-x  1 root   root   30816 Feb 24  2003 /bin/umount
```

As you can see, the s bit is set on the user of the file, indicating SUID. Keeping this complete list in a file can be useful, because you'll want to check your system periodically for changes.

Verifying Packages

Package management systems provide a convenient method of managing software on Linux systems. The RPM not only can install package files but also can provide for the verification of package files and software installed on your system.

Checking installed packages

If an intruder were able to penetrate your system, it is likely that he would attempt to modify or replace executable files to grant himself special abilities. To check for such files, the verification option of the package manager can be used to check installed files. With RPM, it is possible to verify the installed files contained in a specific package like this:

```
# rpm -V apache
S.5....T c /etc/httpd/conf/httpd.conf
.......T c /etc/httpd/conf/srm.conf
missing     /home/httpd/html/index.html
missing     /home/httpd/html/poweredby.gif
```

In this example, *rpm* is reporting that four files do not match the original installed configuration. None is an executable file, and all are easy to explain, so no intruder is suspected here. If an executable file does turn up in the list, you may wish to investigate. For example:

```
# rpm -V XFree86-I128
S.5....T   /usr/X11R6/bin/XF86_I128
```

This shows that the file XF86_I128 is not the same as the one originally installed. Unless you know why the file has changed, corrective action may be necessary to maintain security. In this case, the file in question is an X Server binary that was intentionally upgraded to a newer version than that supplied in the original package. Again, this is an expected result.

The output from *rpm -V* consists of an eight-character string, an optional c (indicating that the file is a configuration file), and the filename. Each column in the result string contains a dot when an attribute has not changed. The output codes listed in Table 21-1 can replace dots to indicate discrepancies.

Table 21-1. RPM verification codes

Dot Code	Description
5	The MD5 checksum, a sort of "fingerprint" for the file, is different.
S	The file size has changed.
L	Symlink attributes have changed.
T	The file's modification time (or *mtime*) has changed.
D	Device file has changed.
U	The file's user/owner has changed.

Table 21-1. RPM verification codes (continued)

Dot Code	Description
G	The file's group has changed.
M	The file's mode (permissions and file type) has changed.
?	Unknown or unexpected result.

It can be helpful to monitor all of the packages on your system and track changes to the resulting list on a regular basis. To check all installed packages, use the a verification option as follows:

```
# rpm -Va
S.5....T c /etc/exports
S.5....T c /etc/hosts.deny
S.5....T c /etc/printcap
S.5....T c /etc/services
.M......   /root
S.5....T c /usr/share/applnk/Multimedia/aktion.kdelnk
S.5....T c /etc/info-dir
..5....T c /etc/mime.types
S.5....T c /etc/httpd/conf/httpd.conf
.......T c /etc/httpd/conf/srm.conf
missing    /home/httpd/html/index.html
missing    /home/httpd/html/poweredby.gif
S.5....T c /etc/named.conf
S.5....T c /var/named/named.local
.M......   /dev/hdc
.M......   /dev/log
.M?....T   /dev/printer
.M......   /dev/pts
......G.   /dev/tty0
(... list continues ... )
```

This list will be large. As your system is configured, upgraded, and modified, you're likely to change many of the files from their original configurations. The important part is being able to explain changes that occur, particularly on executable files.

Checking packages prior to installation

From time to time, you may obtain precompiled software from various sources to add to your system. This may include updated versions of software you already have or new software you don't yet have. It's always best to obtain package files from a trusted source, such as the manufacturer or a well-known distributor. However, as an added safeguard. you may wish to verify that the packages you obtain have not been tampered with or otherwise corrupted. To check an RPM file, use the --checksig option:

```
# rpm --checksig --nopgp fileutils-4.0-1.i386.rpm
fileutils-4.0-1.i386.rpm: size md5 OK
```

The size md5 OK status indicates that size and md5 checksum tests passed for the .rpm file. This means that the size of the file and its checksum matched expected

---

values. (A checksum is a calculated value based on the contents of a file (or other piece of information) used as a sort of "fingerprint.") A NOT OK status could indicate a problem. In this example, the *--nopgp* option is also used to ignore PGP signatures, which may be necessary for you unless you have PGP installed and configured on your system.

SGID Workgroups

This Objective requires an understanding of the SGID mode bit and its application to a directory. When SGID is set on a directory, new files created within that directory are assigned the same group ownership as the directory itself. This is explored in detail in Chapter 6, "Objective 5: Use File Permissions to Control Access to Files." If you're currently preparing for Exam 102, be sure to refer back to Part I for a refresher on SGID.

Password Management

When a user calls saying she's forgotten her password, you need to use the superuser account to create a new one for her:

```
# passwd bsmith
Changing password for user bsmith
New UNIX password:(new password)
Retype new UNIX password:(new password again)
passwd: all authentication tokens updated successfully
```

Resist the temptation to use an easily guessed password, even if you expect the user to change it immediately.

Linux offers you the ability to set expiration dates on passwords. This is done to limit their lifetime, which presumably enhances security by forcing password changes. If a password has been discovered or broken, the password change will eventually correct the security lapse. The *chage* command configures password aging parameters on a per-user basis when using password aging. The following parameters are defined:

Minimum password age
    The minimum number of days between password changes.

Maximum password age
    The maximum number of days between password changes. The user is forced to change his password before using the account after this number of days has elapsed without a password change.

Last password change
    The date on which the password was last changed.

Password expiration warning
    The number of days' warning that are issued in advance of a password expiration.

Password inactive

The number of days of inactivity the system allows before locking a password. This is an automated way of avoiding stale but valid user accounts.

Account expiration date

The date on which an account expires.

chage

Syntax

```
chage user
chage [options] user
```

Description

In the first form without options, *chage* is interactive. In the second form, *chage* may be used with parameters specified via options on the command line.

Options

-d lastday

lastday is the number of days between the last password change and January 1, 1970. As an administrator, you may need to modify this value. *lastday* may also be specified as a date in */MM/DD/YY* format.

-m mindays

mindays is the minimum number of days between password changes. This prevents a user from making multiple password changes at one time.

-l

List a user's password settings.

-E expiredate

expiredate is a date on which an account will no longer be accessible. Like *lastday*, it is stored as the number of days since January 1, 1970, and may be specified as a date in */MM/DD/YY* format.

-I inactive

inactive is the number of days of inactivity allowed after a password expires before an account is locked. A value of disables the *inactive* feature.

-M maxdays

maxdays is the maximum number of days that a password remains valid. This forces users to change their passwords periodically.

-W warndays

warndays is the number of days before a password expires that the user is warned of the upcoming expiration.

Examples

User *bsmith* is to be provided with a password that cannot be changed more than once every 2 days, that must be changed at least every six months (180 days), that retains its default 7-day warning interval, that is set to lock after three weeks' of inactivity, and that expires altogether at the end of 2007. The following interactive session with chage makes these settings:

```
# chage bsmith
Changing the aging information for bsmith
Enter the new value, or press return for the default
        Minimum Password Age [0]: 2
        Maximum Password Age [99999]: 180
        Last Password Change (MM/DD/YY) [02/10/07]:<return>
        Password Expiration Warning [7]: <return>
        Password Inactive [0]: 21
        Account Expiration Date (MM/DD/YY)
            [12/31/69]: 12/31/2007
```

This creates the same settings using the command line:

```
# chage -m 2 -M 180 -I 21 -E 12/31/2007 bsmith
```

If you wish to set these parameters for groups of users or everyone on the system, you could create a simple shell script to loop over all users in *letc/passwd* and run the chage command with options.

The information on password aging is stored in either the *letc/passwd* file or, if shadow passwords are enabled, in the *letc/shadow* file.

Objective 2: Set Up Host Security

Once a Linux system is installed and working, you may need to do nothing more to it. However, if you have specific security needs or just want to be cautious, you'll want to implement additional security measures on your system.

Shadow Passwords

The shadow password system enhances system security by removing encrypted passwords from the publicly available *letc/passwd* file and moving them to the secured *letc/shadow* file. This prevents users from running password-cracking programs against all of the encrypted passwords on your system.

Shadow passwords are covered in the section "The Shadow Password and Shadow Group Systems" in Chapter 18, which describes user management. In order to secure a system, it is a good idea to implement shadow passwords if they aren't already. You can check this by looking for *letc/shadow* and verifying that the user list matches the one in *letc/passwd*. If shadow passwords are not enabled, you may enable them by entering the *pwconv* command with no arguments. In the unlikely event that you use group passwords, you should also enable group shadowing with grpconv.

inetd Minimalism

As mentioned in the "Objective 1: Configure and Manage inetd, xinetd, and Related Services" section in Chapter 20, *inetd* and *letc/inetd.conf* (its configuration file) handle access to many system services. Despite the use of TCP wrappers on these services, the best security can be achieved by simply not offering services that aren't explicitly needed. Do this by removing or commenting out lines in *inetd.conf* for services that are unnecessary. For example, to eliminate the *talk* and *finger* servers from your system, comment their configuration lines:

```
#talk   dgram udp wait    root /usr/sbin/tcpd in.talkd
#ntalk  dgram udp wait    root /usr/sbin/tcpd in.ntalkd
#finger stream tcp nowait root /usr/sbin/tcpd in.fingerd
```

After making this change, you must instruct *inetd* to reconfigure itself. For example:

```
# finger root@localhost
[localhost]
Login: root                         Name: root
Directory: /root                    Shell: /bin/bash
On since Sat Feb 12 00:11 (EST) on tty1
     2 hours 48 minutes idle  (messages off)
On since Sat Feb 12 01:11 (EST) on ttyp1 (messages off)
No mail.
No Plan.
# vi /etc/inetd.conf
# killall -HUP inetd
# finger root@localhost
[localhost]
finger: connect: Connection refused
```

In this example, *finger* is first demonstrated to work. Then *inetd* is edited to disable *fingerd*, *inetd* is reconfigured, and *finger* stops working.

Logging and Superuser Mail

The *syslog* system is a constant companion to the security-conscious system administrator. Its logs are necessary to review security breaches and to trace possible perpetrators. The configuration of syslogd is described in Chapter 18, "Objective 3: Configure and Use System Log Files to Meet Administrative and Security Needs."

Some system responses to security problems can come in the form of email to the *root* user. You may wish to log in as *root* regularly to check its mail, but you can make such checking passive by instructing Sendmail to forward *root*'s mail to administrators. To do so, add a line like this to */etc/aliases*:

```
root: jdoe, bsmith
```

Then execute the newaliases command to recompile the aliases database:

```
# newaliases
```

Now all email for *root* goes to both *jdoe* and *bsmith* (but not *root*), who will presumably act on important messages.

Watching for Security Announcements

Another important function of system administration is to keep on top of any new bugs and exploits in the software on your system. There are countless sites on the Web you can watch to find announcements about such things, but two stand out and could be mentioned on Exam 102:

CERT

In 1988, a small Computer Emergency Response Team formed at the Software Engineering Institute (SEI), a research and development center operated by Carnegie Mellon University. The Defense Advanced Research Projects Agency (DARPA) originally funded its work. It is now known as the CERT Coordination Center (CERT/CC), and *CERT* no longer officially stands for anything. Funding comes from a mix of federal, civil, and private sources.

CERT/CC is made up of network security experts who provide 24-hour technical assistance for responding to computer security incidents. It also analyzes product vulnerabilities, publishes technical documents, and presents security-related training courses. CERT/CC may be found at *http://www.cert.org*. Specifically, security advisories may be found at *http://www.cert.org/advisories*.

A periodic visit to the CERT/CC site can keep you informed of developments in computer security and on problems found with various software packages.

BUGTRAQ

In 1993, a mailing list was created to publicly disclose demonstrated bugs in popular software, with the intent of forcing responsible parties to fix the problems quickly. The list has grown into a respected resource on security topics and has thousands of subscribers. To subscribe to the BUGTRAQ list, follow the instructions in the BUGTRAQ section of *http://www.securityfocus.com*. Archives of BUGTRAQ are also available there.

Attention to these and other resources can help you keep your system up-to-date. You'll be aware of problems found in software you're using, and since updates are almost always produced quickly in response to these notifications, you can upgrade, patch, or replace software as needed to keep your systems secure.

Objective 3: Set Up User-level Security

Even after you've taken the precautions listed earlier, the potential for valid users of your system to cause problems by consuming resources still exists. Such a problem could be accidental, but if it happens intentionally, it is called a denial of service (DoS) attack. For example, a user could create processes that replicate themselves and never exit. Eventually your system would grind to a halt because of thousands of processes, each trying to create more clones. You could also have a user begin allocating memory until the system cannot cope with the requests. In either case, you'd probably need to restart the system, if it responds at all. Clearly, prevention is more desirable for everyone.

You can prevent these scenarios without undue restrictions on users by using *ulimit*. This is a *bash* built-in command that sets maximums on various system resources for users. To enforce limits on users, include `ulimit` commands in */etc/profile*.

---

ulimit

Syntax

```
ulimit [options] [limit]
```

Description

The *bash* built-in *ulimit* provides control over resources available to the shell and its child processes. For each resource, two limits may be set: a *hard* limit and a *soft* limit. Hard limits can be changed only by the superuser; soft limits may be increased by users up to the value of the hard limit. Hard and soft limits are specified with the special -H and -S options, respectively. Other options specify specific limits. If an option is provided with a *limit* value, the corresponding limit is set. If *limit* is not provided, the current limit is displayed. *limit* is either the special word *unlimited* or a numeric value.

Options

-a

> Display all current limits. This option does not accept a *limit* value.

-f

> The maximum size of files created by the shell. This is the default resource if options are not specified.

-u

> The maximum number of processes available to a single user.

-v

> The maximum amount of virtual memory available to the shell.

-H

> Specify the hard limit. Unless -H is specified, the soft limit is assumed.

-S

> Explicitly specify the soft limit. This is the default.

Example 1

Display all limits for an account:

```
$ ulimit -a
core file size (blocks)    1000000
data seg size (kbytes)     unlimited
file size (blocks)         unlimited
max memory size (kbytes)   unlimited
stack size (kbytes)        8192
cpu time (seconds)         unlimited
max user processes         256
pipe size (512 bytes)      8
open files                 1024
virtual memory (kbytes)    2105343
```

Example 2

Set the maximum number of processes to 128:

```
$ ulimit -Hu 128
```

Example 3

Set the maximum working number of processes to 128 but allow the user to raise her limit as high as 150:

```
$ ulimit -Su 128
$ ulimit -Hu 150
```

22

Exam 102 Review Questions and Exercises

This section presents review questions to highlight important concepts and hands-on exercises that you can use to gain experience with the Topics covered on the LPI's Exam 102. The exercises can be particularly useful if you're not accustomed to routine Linux administration and should help you better prepare for the exam. To complete the exercises, you need a working Linux system that is not in production use. You might also find it useful to have a pen and paper handy to write down your responses as you work your way through the review questions and exercises.

Kernel (Topic 1.105)

Review Questions

1. What is the procedure for removing and installing modules in the running kernel? Why is this procedure necessary?

2. Describe the differences between the *insmod* and *modprobe* commands.

3. Which file stores optional parameters used by kernel modules?

4. Describe the nature of a monolithic kernel and the consequences and/or advantages of using one.

5. Name the major steps required to configure, build, and install a custom kernel and its modules.

Exercises

1. Using the procedures found in Chapter 13, as well as the kernel HOWTO, configure, build, and install a custom kernel and modules. Boot the new kernel. Does your system behave normally? Are you able to boot both your original kernel and the new one?

2. Using *lsmod*, examine the modules loaded in your running kernel.

    a. Try removing a noncritical module, for example, *rmmod sound*. Did the command fail because the module was in use?

    b. Try inserting a module, for example, *modprobe fat*, followed by *lsmod*. Did the module get inserted correctly? Remove it with *rmmod fat*. Was the removal successful?

    c. What is logged in */var/log/messages* during these changes?

Boot, Initialization, Shutdown, and Runlevels (Topic 1.106)

Review Questions

1. Name and briefly describe the two parts of LILO. Which part has a configuration file and what is that file called?

2. What are the ramifications relating to new hardware when running a monolithic kernel?

3. Which three runlevels are well-defined across Linux distributions, and what actions do they perform?

4. Describe a situation that would imply the need to switch to single-user mode.

5. How can you shut down and halt a Linux system immediately using *shutdown?*

Exercises

Exercise 1.106-1. Boot

1. Examine the contents of */etc/lilo.conf*. How many kernel images or operating systems are configured for load by LILO? Explain the options you find in the file.

2. Install the boot loader by executing *lilo*. What happened?

3. Boot your system and manually specify the root filesystem using the root= keyword at the LILO prompt. What happens if you specify the wrong partition?

4. Use *dmesg* and *less* to examine boot-time messages. Compare what you find to the latest boot messages found in */var/log/messages*.

5. Boot your system and use the *single* or *1* option to boot directly into single-user mode.

Exercise 1.106-2. Runlevels

1. After booting to single-user mode, switch to your normal runlevel using *init n*.

    a. Does the system come up as expected?

    b. Enter *init 1* to go back to single-user mode. What daemons are still running?

2. Familiarize yourself with the contents of a few of the scripts in */etc/init.d* (your system directories may vary).

3. Look in *rc0.d* through *rc6.d* for links to the scripts you examined. How are the scripts used? In which runlevels is the corresponding service active?

4. Shut down your system with *init 0*.

5. Shut down your system with *shutdown -h now*.

Printing (Topic 1.107)

Review Questions

1. What does *lpd* do to handle incoming print jobs destined for empty print queues?

2. Describe the kinds of information included in */etc/printcap*.

3. What is the function of a print filter?

4. What does the *-P* option specify to the print commands?

5. When is it useful to pipe into the standard input of *lpr* instead of simply using a filename as an argument?

6. How is the Ghostscript program used in printing to a non-PostScript printer?

7. What filter is used on a Linux system to print to remote printers on Windows clients?

Exercises

1. On a system with an existing printer, examine */etc/printcap*. Which print filter is used for the printer? Which queue or queues are directed at the printer?

2. Check the printer status with *lpq -P printer* and *lpc status*. Print to the queue using *lpr -P printer file*.

3. Examine */var/spool/lpd* for the spool directory of your print queue. Examine the files you find there.

Documentation (Topic 1.108)

Review Questions

1. Describe the PAGER environment variable.

   a. How does it affect the *man* facility?

   b. If PAGER is not set, how does *man* display output?

   c. Does this environment variable affect the *info* facility?

2. In response to your query on a library function, *man* returns a page on an identically named user command. Why does this happen?

   a. How do you display the page for the function and not the command?

   b. How do you display both?

3. Name the program that displays GNU texinfo pages.

Exercises

Exercise 1.108-1. man and /usr/doc

1. Run a *man* inquiry as follows:

   ```
   $ man -a -Pless mkfifo
   ```

   There are both an *mkfifo* command and an *mkfifo* function. You'll be looking at the *mkfifo* command from section 1 of the manual. Note MKFIFO(1) at the top of the page.

   Press q to terminate the pager program. The pager is then invoked again and displays the *mkfifo* function from section 3 of the manual. Note MKFIFO(3) at the top of the page.

   Run the *man* command again, using the *-Pmore* option as follows:

   ```
   $ man -a -Pmore mkfifo
   ```

   a. What differences do you see in the output?

   b. What does the *-P* option do?

2. Run another *man* inquiry as follows:

   ```
   $ man -d ln
   ```

   a. What output do you get from *man*?

   b. What is the *-d* option?

   c. Did you see information on the *ln* command?

   Now examine the *man* configuration file:

   ```
   $ less /etc/man.config
   ```

   Notice how the contents of this file coincide with the result you received from the *-d* option.

Exercise 1.108-4. Acting as a Linux helpdesk

Suppose you are a help desk technician in a mixed-systems office, and you are relatively new to Linux. A user calls your help desk with a general question about Linux system shutdown. He indicates that he's heard from Unix gurus that using the *halt* command could be unsafe. He also reports getting frustrated with Windows NT users who use the Ctrl-Alt-Delete key combination on his system console, which causes his Linux server to reboot. He asks for specific information on:

- How to safely shut down Linux
- How to allow nonsuperusers the ability to shut down cleanly
- How to disable the Ctrl-Alt-Delete shutdown

Let's further assume you don't know how to answer these questions and that you have access to system documentation. Complete the following steps:

1. Use the *man* facility to investigate the *halt* command. Based on what you find there, answer the following:

   a. In what section of the manual is *halt* located? Why?

   b. Determine if it is "safe" to use *halt* to shut down Linux. What caused the Unix gurus to instruct the caller that using *halt* was not safe?

c. Determine if it would still be safe if the user uses the -*n* option to *halt*.

d. Is it appropriate to use *halt* on a multiuser system to which others are logged in?

e. Use *man* on the other commands referred to by the *halt* manpage in the *SEE ALSO* section.

2. Evaluate the other commands:

a. Which commands can be used to shut down the system in place of *halt*?

b. Which commands would be the most appropriate for shutting down a multiuser system?

3. From what you see in the manpages:

a. Where is the Ctrl-Alt-Delete system shutdown configured?

b. Explain how to disable it.

c. Do you need to reboot to enable the change? If so, why?

d. How can you configure the system to allow specified nonsuperusers to shut down cleanly?

e. If you use the *info* command, are you provided with additional information?

4. After successfully following your instructions, the user calls again. This time he is puzzled by error messages that are produced when his users attempt a clean shutdown from multiuser mode using the *shutdown* command without arguments.

a. Reevaluate the manpages in question. Are there any clues to common problems? (Hint: see *BUGS*.)

b. State the typical *shutdown* command to issue from multiuser mode.

Exam 102
Review

Shells, Scripting, Programming, and Compiling (Topic 1.109)

Review Questions

1. What characteristic of a *bash* variable changes when the variable is exported?

2. Describe the concept of shell aliases.

3. When is a shell function more suitable than a shell alias?

4. Describe the function of */etc/profile*.

5. What must the author of a new script file do to the file's mode?

6. How does the shell determine what interpreter to execute when starting a script?

7. How can a shell script use return values of the commands it executes?

Exercises

1. Using *bash*, enter the *export* command and the *set* command. Which set of variables is a subset of the other? What is the difference between the variables reported by *export* and those reported by *set*? Finally, enter *which export*. Where is the *export* command located?

2. Examine */etc/profile*. How is the default umask set? What customizations are done in the file for system users?

3. Create a simple *bash* script using the #!/bin/bash syntax, set the executable mode bits, and execute the shell. If it runs correctly, add errors to see the diagnostic messages. Have the script report both exported and nonexported variables. Verify that the nonexported variables do not survive the startup of the new shell.

Administrative Tasks (Topic 1.111)

Review questions

1. Why is it considered insecure to store encrypted passwords in */etc/passwd*?
   a. What is the alternative?
   b. When the alternative is implemented, what happens to the password field in */etc/passwd*?

2. What would happen to a user account if the default shell were changed to */bin/false*?

3. When a new account is created with *useradd -m*, what files are used to populate the new home directory?

4. Compare and contrast the execution of */etc/profile* and */etc/bashrc*.

5. What is the complete filename for the file where most syslog messages are sent?

6. Describe the three syslog parameters: *facility*, *level*, and *action*.

7. Compare and contrast *cron* and *at*.

8. Is there a *cron* command?

9. State the format of a *crontab* file, describing each of the six fields.

10. What does an asterisk mean in *crontab* fields 1 through 5?

11. Compare and contrast the differential and incremental backup methods.

12. Why is *mt* usually used along with *tar* to implement simple backup schemes?
    a. What special measures must be taken with regard to device names when using *mt* for multiple-volume *tar* backups?

Exercises

Exercise 1.111-1. User accounts

1. Examine the */etc/passwd* file on your system.
    a. Is this the only means of user authentication on your system?
    b. Are shadow passwords in use?
2. Repeat the first exercise for groups.
3. If you have an expendable system available, experiment with implementing shadow passwords.
4. Add a user with *useradd*, including a new home directory populated with files from */etc/skel*.
5. Add a group with *groupadd*.
6. Use *usermod* to add your new user to the new group.
7. Set the new user's password using *passwd*.
8. Log into the new account, and use *newgrp* to change to the new group.
9. Delete the new group and user (including home directory) using *groupdel* and *userdel*.

Exercise 1.111-2. User environment and variables

1. Examine the contents of */etc/skel*. How similar are they to your own home directory?
2. Review the contents of */etc/profile* and */etc/bashrc*.

Exercise 1.111-3. Syslog and log files

1. Add the local5 facility to your configuration as described in Chapter 18. Use *logger* to write to your new log file, and verify its contents. Compare your log entries with those in */var/log/messages*.
2. Examine */etc/logrotate.conf*. What happens after */var/log/messages* is rotated?

Exercise 1.111-4. cron and at

1. Add an entry in your personal *crontab* file to perform a task, such as sending you an email message. Confirm that the action occurs as expected. Experiment with the five time specifiers.
2. Schedule a command in the future with *at*. How is *at* different from *cron*?

Exercise 1.111-5. Backup

1. Imagine that you have recently been made responsible for an important production system. No formalized backup procedures are in place. Backup operations that are run are not cataloged and media are scattered. Now imagine that after a holiday weekend the system has crashed due to a power failure. Upon restart, the system has severe disk errors requiring manual *fsck*. After repairs are complete, the system is again usable, but users complain about missing, truncated, or corrupt files. If a formalized backup procedure had been in place, would the outcome have been different?

2. If you have a tape drive available, experiment with *tar*, creating small tarfiles on a tape.

   a. Using the nonrewinding tape device, create multiple archives on the tape, and use *mt* to position among them.

   b. Verify that the various archives you create are accessible to *tar*.

Networking Fundamentals (Topic 1.112)

Review Questions

1. Describe how the subnet mask affects the maximum number of hosts that can be put on a TCP/IP network.

2. Name the three default address classes and the subnet masks associated with them.

3. The UDP protocol is said to be connectionless. Describe this concept and its consequences on applications that use UDP.

4. What user command is frequently used to send ICMP messages to remote hosts to verify those hosts' functionality?

5. Describe the contents and use of */etc/hosts*.

6. In what configuration file are DNS servers listed? What is intended if the local loopback address is included there on a workstation?

7. Name two modes of the *netstat* command and the program's output in each case.

8. Describe why the *route* command is needed for a single interface on a nonrouting workstation.

9. How does *traceroute* determine the identities of intermediate gateways?

10. Describe the advantages and consequences of implementing DHCP.

11. What utility is used to configure and dial a modem prior to the creation of a PPP connection?

12. What are the four authentication modes commonly used during PPP negotiations?

Exercises

1. Examine your system's TCP/IP configuration using *ifconfig eth0* or a similar command for your network interface. Are you using DHCP? What type of subnet are you running with? Is it a class A, B, or C address? Are you using a private address? Experiment with taking the interface offline using *ifconfig eth0 down* and *ifconfig eth0 up*.

2. Examine the contents of */etc/services*.

3. Use the *dig* command to locate information from DNS servers about a domain name.

4. Examine your */etc/hosts* file. How much name resolution is accomplished in this file manually?

5. Examine your */etc/resolv.conf* file. How many DNS servers do you have available?

6. Execute *netstat -r*. How many routes are reported? What are the routes to the local network and interface for?

7. Use *traceroute* to examine the route to a favorite web site.

8. Using a standard modem (not a Winmodem), use *minicom* to connect to the modem and verify that it responds to the AT command.

9. Execute a manual PPP connection as described in Chapter 19. Does your modem successfully connect to your ISP? Examine */var/log/messages* for information on the PPP session.

Networking Services (Topic 1.113)

Review Questions

1. Describe the function of *inetd* and how it is configured.

2. Describe the TCP wrappers security tool and how it can enhance security on a networked system.

3. Describe the use of mail aliases and how to enable new aliases.

4. What files are used to configure the Apache web server?

5. How does the administrator share a directory using NFS?

6. How does the administrator mount a directory shared by a remote NFS server?

7. What is the function of *nmbd*?

8. Which file is used to configure *smbd*?

9. Describe the function and location of the *resolver*.

10. Name two programs that can be used to do queries against an NFS server.

11. Describe in general terms the main difference between BIND v4 and BIND v8 configuration files.

Exercises

1. Examine your *xinetd.d* directory. Are *telnetd* and *ftpd* enabled? If so, is TCP wrappers (*tcpd*) configured for them?

2. Enable TCP wrappers and place ALL:ALL in */etc/hosts.deny*, then attempt a Telnet session. Is the inbound request ignored as expected?

3. Familiarize yourself with */etc/sendmail.cf* and */etc/aliases*. Run *newaliases*.

4. Familiarize yourself with Apache configuration files in */etc/httpd/html/*.conf* (or your directory location).

5. Examine your */etc/exports* file, if it exists. Are you sharing NFS volumes?

6. Examine your */etc/smb.conf* file. Are you sharing Samba printers or volumes?

7. Examine your resolver configuration in */etc/resolv.conf*, */etc/hosts.conf*, and */etc/nsswitch.conf*. Is the local */etc/hosts* file consulted prior to DNS servers?

8. By examining */etc/named.conf* and noting format details, determine what general release of BIND you are using.

Security (Topic 1.114)

Review Questions

1. What daemon is associated with the control files */etc/hosts.allow* and */etc/hosts.deny*.

2. In general terms, describe a method to locate setuid programs in the local file-system. Why might an administrator do this routinely?

3. What is the function of the *md5sum* utility?

4. Why might a user run *ssh* instead of *telnet*?

5. Describe shadow passwords and the file where the passwords are stored.

Exercises

1. Use *find* as described in Chapter 21 to locate setuid files. Is the list larger than you expected? Are the entries on your list justifiably setuid programs?

2. Use the *md5sum* utility on a binary program file and examine its output.

Exam 102 Practice Test

Exam 102 consists of approximately 72 questions. Most are multiple-choice single-answer, a few are multiple-choice multiple-answer, and the remainder are fill-in questions. No notes or other materials are permitted, and you have 90 minutes to complete the exam. The answers are provided at the end of this chapter.

Questions

1. What section of the online user's manual and command reference holds administrative (not user) commands? Select one.

   a. Section 1

   b. Section 2

   c. Section 8

   d. Section n

   e. Section s

2. In the *bash* shell, entering the !! command has the same effect as which one of the following?

   a. Ctrl-P and Enter

   b. Ctrl-N and Enter

   c. Ctrl-U and Enter

   d. !-2

   e. !2

3. Name the command that displays pages from the online user's manual and command reference.

4. Which of the following commands displays the comments from a *bash* script? Select all that apply.

    a. *find "^#" /etc/rc.d/rc.local*

    b. *sed '/^#/ !d' /etc/rc.d/init.d/httpd*

    c. *grep ^# /etc/rc.d/init.d/httpd*

    d. *grep ^# /etc/passwd*

    e. *locate "^#" /etc/skel/.bashrc*

5. Which one of the following answers creates an environment variable VAR1, present in the environment of a bash child process?

    a. *VAR1="fail" ; export VAR1*

    b. *VAR1="fail" \ export VAR1*

    c. *VAR1="fail"*

    d. *set VAR1="fail" ; enable VAR1*

    e. *export VAR1 \ VAR1="fail"*

6. Name the full path and name of the file that holds most of the information on system user groups.

7. Which one of the following outcomes results from the following command?

    `# chmod g+s /home/software`

    a. The SUID bit will be set for */home/software*.

    b. The SGID bit will be set for */home/software*, preventing access by those not a member of the *software* group.

    c. The SGID bit will be set for */home/software*, to keep group membership of the directory consistent for all files created.

    d. The sticky bit will be set for */home/software*.

    e. The sticky bit will be applied to all files in */home/software*.

8. Consider the following script, stored in a file with proper modes for execution:

```
#!/bin/bash
for $v1 in a1 a2
do
echo $v1
done
```

Which one of the following best represents the output produced on a terminal by this script?

    a. `in`

       `a1`

       `a2`

    b. `a1`

       `a2`

    c. `$v1`

       `$v1`

       `$v1`

d. No output is produced, but the script executes correctly.

e. No output is produced, because the script has an error.

9. Which one of the following commands verbosely extracts files from a tar archive on a magnetic tape device?

 a. *tar cvf /dev/st0*

 b. *tar cvf /dev/ttyS0*

 c. *tar xvf /dev/st0*

 d. *tar xvf /dev/ttyS0*

 e. *tar rvf /dev/st0*

10. Alex wants to protect himself from inadvertently overwriting files when copying them, so he wants to alias cp to prevent overwrite. How should he go about this? Select one.

 a. Put alias cp='cp -i' in *~/.bashrc*.

 b. Put alias cp='cp -i' in *~/.bash_profile*.

 c. Put alias cp='cp -p' in *~/.bashrc*.

 d. Put alias cp='cp -p' in *~/.bash_profile*.

 e. Put alias cp = 'cp -I' in *~/.bashrc*.

11. Monica consults the */etc/passwd* file expecting to find encrypted passwords for all of the users on her system. She sees the following:

```
jdoe:x:500:500::/home/jdoe:/bin/bash
bsmith:x:501:501::/home/bsmith:/bin/tcsh
```

Which of the following is true? Select one.

 a. Accounts *jdoe* and *bsmith* have no passwords.

 b. Accounts *jdoe* and *bsmith* are disabled.

 c. The passwords are in */etc/passwd-*.

 d. The passwords are in */etc/shadow*.

 e. The passwords are in */etc/shadow-*.

12. What variable holds the list of directories searched by the shell to find executable programs?

13. Where does *The Linux System Administrators' Guide* originate? Select one.

 a. Red Hat Software, Inc.

 b. O'Reilly Media, Inc.

 c. The Free Software Foundation

 d. The Linux Documentation Project

 e. Usenet newsgroup *comp.os.linux*

14. Which one of these files determines how messages are stored using syslogd?

 a. */etc/sysconfig/logger.conf*

 b. */etc/syslog.conf*

 c. */etc/syslogd.conf*

 d. */etc/conf.syslog*

 e. */etc/conf.syslogd*

15. How many hosts can exist on a subnet with mask 255.255.255.128? Select one.

  a. 512

  b. 256

  c. 128

  d. 127

  e. 126

16. When running a text-mode FTP client, which command retrieves multiple files? Select one.

  a. *get *.txt*

  b. *retrieve *.txt*

  c. *mget *.txt*

  d. *mretrieve *.txt*

  e. *get -m *.txt*

17. For an Internet workstation with a single network interface, what routes must be added to interface *eth0* after it is initialized? Select one.

  a. None

  b. Interface

  c. Interface and default gateway

  d. Interface, local network, and default gateway

18. On a Linux server, what service is most likely "listening" on port 25? Select one.

  a. Apache

  b. News

  c. Sendmail

  d. Samba

  e. FTP

19. Which one of these protocols is used as a datagram delivery service by the remaining three? Select one.

  a. TCP

  b. IP

  c. UDP

  d. ICMP

20. Which command will display information about Ethernet interface *eth0*? Select one.

  a. *cat /proc/eth/0*

  b. *ifconfig eth0*

  c. *ipconfig eth0*

  d. *ipconfig /dev/eth0*

  e. *cat /etc/eth0.conf*

21. When is the PPP interface *ppp0* created? Select one.

    a. At boot time by the kernel

    b. At installation time by *mknod*

    c. At dial-up time by the chatscript

    d. At dial-up time by *pppd*

    e. When the modem powers up

22. What program is run on a client machine to request an IP address from a DHCP server? Select one.

    a. *dhcpd*

    b. *inetd*

    c. *pump*

    d. *dhcp_client*

    e. *bootp*

23. What does the *printcap* entry sd indicate? Select one.

    a. The system default printer

    b. A printer's spool directory

    c. A device file for the printer

    d. A location where errors are stored

    e. The printer driver

24. Where is TCP wrappers configured and where is it enabled?

    a. Configured in *tcpd.conf*, enabled in *tcpd.conf*

    b. Configured in *inetd.conf*, enabled in *inetd.conf*

    c. Configured in *hosts.deny* and *hosts.allow*, enabled in *inetd.conf*

    d. Configured in *inetd.conf*, enabled in *hosts.deny* and *hosts.allow*

25. Which of the following is a valid entry in */etc/fstab* for a remote NFS mount from server *fs1*? Select one.

    a. `fs1:/proc /mnt/fs1 nfs defaults 9 9`

    b. `/mnt/fs1 fs1:/proc nfs defaults 0 0`

    c. `fs1:/home /mnt/fs1 nfs defaults 0 0`

    d. `/mnt/fs1 fs1:/home nfs defaults 0 0`

    e. `/home:fs1 /mnt/fs1 nfs defaults 0 0`

26. Which network protocol is used by Telnet and FTP? Select one.

    a. ICMP

    b. UDP

    c. TCP

    d. DHCP

    e. PPP

27. Which of the following programs will display DNS information for a host? Choose all that apply.

   a. *host*

   b. *nslookup*

   c. *nsstat*

   d. *dig*

   e. *ping*

28. Consider the following entry in */etc/exports*:

   ```
   /home        pickle(rw,no_root_squash)
   ```

   How is this entry handled by the NFS daemon? Select one.

   a. Directory */home* is shared to everyone, without requiring passwords.

   b. Directory */home* is shared to everyone, requiring passwords.

   c. Directory *pickle* is mounted on */home*.

   d. Root is not allowed access to the shared directory.

   e. The mount attempt will fail.

29. From the user's point of view, which answer describes the appearance of an NFS mounted directory? Select one.

   a. A new device in */dev*.

   b. A new local volume accessed using a volume letter, such as D:.

   c. A new local volume accessed using the NFS server's name.

   d. Part of the local filesystem, accessed using ordinary pathnames.

   e. Part of the NFS server's filesystem, accessed using the NFS server's name.

30. Which of the following statements regarding the ICMP protocol is not true? Select one.

   a. ICMP is connectionless.

   b. ICMP provides network flow control.

   c. ICMP is also known as UDP.

   d. ICMP is used by *ping*.

31. What is CHAP? Select one.

   a. The PPP chat script.

   b. An authentication protocol using clear text.

   c. An authentication protocol embedded in the PPP data stream.

   d. The *pppd* configuration utility.

   e. A modem communications protocol.

32. What server daemon resolves domain names to IP addresses for requesting hosts?

33. During the two-way communication that takes place during a chat script used to start PPP, what is chat communicating with? Select one.

    a. The *pppd* daemon

    b. The PPP server

    c. The kernel

    d. The modem

    e. The *syslogd* daemon

34. What function does a print filter serve? Select one.

    a. It collates output from multiple users.

    b. It translates various data formats into a page description language.

    c. It rejects print requests from unauthorized users.

    d. It rejects print requests from unauthorized hosts.

    e. It analyzes print data and directs print requests to the appropriate lpd.

35. Consider the following excerpt from file */etc/resolv.conf* of a Linux workstation:

```
nameserver 127.0.0.1
nameserver 192.168.1.5
nameserver 192.168.250.2
```

What can be said about this configuration? Select one.

    a. Two DNS servers on the public network are being used for resolution.

    b. One DNS server on the local network is being used for resolution.

    c. The configuration contains errors that will prevent the resolver from functioning.

    d. A caching-only name server is running.

    e. The resolver library will consult nameserver 192.168.250.2 first.

36. Which of the following is true regarding BIND v4 and BIND v8 configuration files? Select one.

    a. The information is largely the same, but the syntax is different.

    b. The syntax is largely the same, but the information is different.

    c. The two BIND versions use the same configuration file.

    d. BIND v4 uses a binary configuration file instead of text.

    e. BIND v8 uses a binary configuration file instead of text.

37. What file is used to configure Sendmail? Include the entire path.

38. Name the file that contains simple mappings between IP addresses and system names.

39. What is the meaning and location of the following kernel configuration file excerpt? Select one.

```
options opl3 io=0x388
```

    a. Kernel option opl3 is set to use I/O port 0x388; */usr/src/linux/.config*.

    b. Kernel module option opl3 is set to use I/O port 0x388; */usr/src/linux/.config*.

c. Kernel module opl3 is set to use I/O port 0x388; */usr/src/linux/.config*.

d. Kernel option opl3 is set to use I/O port 0x388; */usr/src/linux/.config*.

e. Kernel module opl3 is set to use I/O port 0x388; */etc/conf.modules* or */etc/modules.conf*.

40. What program can be used to interactively change the behavior of a print queue? Select one.

    a. *lpd*

    b. *lpr*

    c. *lpq*

    d. *lprm*

    e. *lpc*

41. Which of the following represents a valid sequence of commands to compile and install a new kernel? Select one.

    a. *make modules_install; make modules; make bzImage; make clean; make dep*

    b. *make dep; make clean; make bzImage; make config; make modules; make modules_install*

    c. *make config; make dep; make clean; make bzImage; make modules; make modules_install*

    d. *make config; make bzImage; make dep; make clean; make modules; make modules_install*

    e. *make dep; make clean; make bzImage; make modules; make modules_install; make config*

42. What program will display a list of each hop across the network to a specified destination? Select one.

    a. *tracert*

    b. *rttrace*

    c. *traceroute*

    d. *routetrace*

    e. *init*

43. Which file holds configuration information used during the process of kernel compilation? Select one.

    a. */usr/src/linux/config*

    b. */usr/src/linux/.config*

    c. */usr/src/linux/kernel.conf*

    d. */etc/kernel.conf*

    e. */etc/sysconfig/kernel.conf*

44. After a PPP connection is established and authenticated, what needs to be done before the interface can be used? Select one.

    a. Add a route to *ppp0*.

    b. Enable *ppp0*.

c. ifup *ppp0*.

d. Run *pppd*.

e. Turn on the modem.

45. Which of the following is not the name of an Apache configuration file? Select one.

    a. *httpd.conf*

    b. *html.conf*

    c. *srm.conf*

    d. *access.conf*

46. Which statement is true regarding the configuration of a printer on a remote Windows machine? Select one.

    a. It can be configured like a TCP/IP network-attached printer.

    b. The input filter must be set to smbprint.

    c. The Windows printer must contain PostScript capability.

    d. The rp directive must be used in the *printcap* file.

    e. Linux can't print to Windows printers.

47. What types of files are located in the directory tree specified by the Apache DocumentRoot configuration directive? Select one.

    a. Apache documentation files.

    b. Apache configuration files.

    c. Web site HTML files.

    d. Web site configuration files.

    e. Apache startup and shutdown commands.

48. Which of the following commands will display a listing of files contained in a tar archive tape in */dev/st0* ? Select one.

    a. *tar cf /dev/st0*

    b. *tar xf /dev/st0*

    c. *tar tf /dev/st0*

    d. *tar -zf /dev/st0*

    e. *tar -zcvf /dev/st0*

49. What is the systemwide *bash* configuration file called? Include the entire path.

50. How can a nonprivileged user configure *sendmail* to forward mail to another account? Select one.

    a. She can add a new entry in */etc/aliases*.

    b. She can create a *.forward* file containing the new address.

    c. She can create an *.alias* file containing the new address.

    d. She can create a *sendmail.cf* file containing the new address.

    e. She cannot forward mail without assistance from the administrator.

51. How does a process indicate to the controlling shell that it has exited with an error condition? Select one.

   a. It prints an error message to stderr.

   b. It prints an error message to stdout.

   c. It sets an exit code with a zero value.

   d. It sets an exit code with a nonzero value.

   e. It causes a segmentation fault.

52. Consider the following trivial script called *myscript*:

    ```
    #!/bin/bash
    echo "Hello"
    echo $myvar
    ```

   Also consider this command sequence and result:

    ```
    # set myvar='World'
    # ./myscript
    Hello
    ```

   The script ran without error but didn't echo *World*. Why not? Select one.

   a. The syntax of the set command is incorrect.

   b. The script executes in a new shell, and myvar wasn't exported.

   c. The #!/bin/bash syntax is incorrect.

   d. The $myvar syntax is incorrect.

   e. The script is sourced by the current shell, and myvar is available only to new shells.

53. What does this short configuration file excerpt tell the Samba daemon? Select one.

    ```
    [home]
      path = /home
      guest ok = yes
      writable = yes
    ```

   a. The location of the Samba software is rooted at */home*.

   b. A printer called home uses */home* as a spool directory.

   c. A share called home is located on */home* and is writable by authenticated users.

   d. A share called home is located on */home* and is writable by anyone.

   e. A share called home on remote system *guest* will be mounted at */home*.

54. How can the *finger* daemon be enabled? Select one.

   a. Uncomment the *in.fingerd* line in */etc/inetd.conf*.

   b. Use cron to run *fingerd* once per minute.

   c. Include *fingerd* in the TCP wrappers configuration.

   d. Remove *fingerd* from *hosts.deny*.

   e. Add *fingerd* to *hosts.allow*.

Answers

1. c. Section 8 holds administrative commands such as *fsck* and *mkfs*.

2. a. The !! command history expansion executes the previous command. Entering the Ctrl-P keystroke uses the Emacs key-binding bash to move up one line in the history; pressing Enter executes that command.

3. The *man* command displays manpages.

4. b and c. *find* and *locate* do not search the contents of files. */etc/passwd* is not a script.

5. a. The variable must be set and exported. The semicolon separates the two commands.

6. */etc/group*.

7. c. The g indicates that we're operating on the group privilege, and the +s indicates that we should add the "set id" bit, which means that the SGID property will be applied.

8. e. The script has an error and will not produce the expected output. In a for statement, the loop variable does not have the dollar sign. Changing line 2 to for *v1* in a1 a2 will correct the error and produce the output in answer B.

9. c. *tar* should be used with the extraction option x and a tape device, such as SCSI tape */dev/st0*.

10. a. *cp* should be aliased to the interactive mode with the -i option in *.bashrc*. *.bash_profile* normally doesn't include aliases.

11. d. The shadow password system has been implemented, placing all passwords in */etc/shadow* as denoted by the x following the username.

12. PATH.

13. d. *The Linux System Administrators' Guide* is a free publication of the Linux Documentation Project (LDP) and is available online at *http://www.tldp.org*.

14. b. */etc/syslog.conf* is the configuration file for the syslog daemon *syslogd*.

15. e. With the top bit of the last byte set in the subnet mask (.128), there are 7 bits left. 2^7 is 128, less the network address and broadcast address, leaving 126 addresses for hosts.

16. c. FTP clients use *mget* with wildcards.

17. d. Routes to the interface and the network are required to exchange information on the local LAN. To act as an Internet workstation (i.e., using Netscape), a default gateway is also necessary.

18. c. As defined in */etc/services*, port 25 is the SMTP port, often monitored by *sendmail*.

19. b. IP is the underlying datagram protocol.

20. b. The *ifconfig* command is used to configure and display interface information. *ipconfig* is a Windows utility.

21. d. PPP interfaces are not persistent. Instead, they are initialized when needed.

22. c. The DHCP client is called *pump*, after the lady's shoe of the same name. That's an extension from a *boot* because DHCP is a descendant from *bootp*.

23. b. The spool directory directive looks like this:

```
sd=/var/spool/lpd/lp
```

24. c. The *hosts.deny* and *hosts.allow* files contain configuration information for TCP wrappers. The files won't be used, however, unless *tcpd* is included in *inetd.conf*.

25. c. Answer a attempts to mount the */proc* filesystem. Answers b, d, and e have incorrect syntax.

26. c. Both Telnet and FTP are connection-oriented and use TCP for reliable connections.

27. a, b, and d.

28. b. Read/write access is available to everyone, including root.

29. d. NFS-mounted directories seamlessly blend into the local filesystem, requiring no special syntax for access.

30. c. While both ICMP and UDP are connectionless, they are different protocols.

31. c. CHAP is one of the PPP authentication techniques that embeds its information inside the PPP stream. It is an alternative to clear text passwords.

32. The DNS daemon is *named*. It is included in a package called BIND.

33. d. The intent of the chat script is to prepare the modem with appropriate settings to establish a PPP connection.

34. b. A print server translates formats, such as PostScript to PCL.

35. d. The presence of the *localhost* address 127.0.0.1 indicates that *named* is running. Since the system is a workstation, it's safe to assume that it is not serving DNS to a wider community.

36. a. BIND v8 has a newer, more modular format, but the information is about the same.

37. */etc/sendmail.cf*.

38. */etc/hosts*.

39. e. options lines in */etc/modules.conf* or */etc/conf.modules* configure kernel modules.

40. e. *lpc* is the line printer control program.

41. c. Answer a is wrong because it installs modules before compiling them. Answers b and e are wrong because they build the kernel after configuring. Answer d is backward.

42. c. *tracert* is a Windows utility with the same function as traceroute.

43. b.

44. a. Just as with any interface, routes must be added before communications can occur.

45. b. Apache uses *httpd.conf*, *srm.conf*, and *access.conf*. Some implementations may roll all of these files into a single *httpd.conf*.

46. b. The *smbprint* filter is provided by the Samba package for printing to Windows printers.

47. c.

48. c. t is the option to list the contents of an archive.

49. The file is */etc/profile*.

50. b. The *.forward* file is placed in the home directory containing a single line with the target email address.

51. d. Zero exit values usually indicate success.

52. b. Instead of using set, the command should have been:

```
# export myvar='World'
```

This gives the myvar variable to the new shell.

53. d.

54. a. For security purposes, *fingerd* is usually disabled using a comment in */etc/inetd.conf*.

24

Exam 102 Highlighter's Index

Kernel (Topic 1.105)

Objective 1: Manage/Query Kernel and Kernel Modules at Runtime

- The Linux kernel is modular, and device driver software is inserted into the running kernel as needed.
- Module files are *objects*, stored under */lib/modules*.
- Kernel modules can be managed using:

  insmod
  > Insert a module into the kernel.

  lsmod
  > List modules.

  modinfo
  > Get information about a module.

  modprobe
  > Insert modules along with their prerequisites.

  rmmod
  > Remove a module from the kernel.

- Modules are configured in */etc/conf.modules* or */etc/modules.conf*.
- *modprobe* determines module dependencies using a file called *modules.dep*. This file is usually created at boot time using *depmod*.

Objective 2: Reconfigure, Build, and Install a Custom Kernel and Kernel Modules

- To build a kernel, you need the compiler, assembler, linker, *make*, kernel source, and kernel headers.

- These are typical kernel compilation steps, done in */usr/src/linux*:

  a. Make a configuration using *make oldconfig* (existing setup), *make config* (basic interactive text program), *make menuconfig* (interactive text menu program), or *make xconfig* (graphical program). Each method creates the *.config* file containing kernel options.

  b. Modify EXTRAVERSION in Makefile, if desired.

  c. Build dependencies using *make dep*.

  d. Clean old results with *make clean*.

  e. Create the kernel with *make bzImage*.

  f. Create modules with *make modules*.

  g. Install the modules with *make modules_install*.

  h. Copy the new image to */boot*.

  i. Update */etc/lilo.conf* for the new image.

  j. Update the boot loader by running the lilo command.

Boot, Initialization, Shutdown, and Runlevels (Topic 1.106)

Objective 1: Boot the System

LILO, the Linux loader

- LILO is a utility designed to load a Linux kernel (or another operating system) into memory and launch it. It has two parts:

  The boot loader
  A two-stage program intended to find and load a kernel. The first stage resides in the disk boot sector and is started by the system BIOS. It locates and launches a second, larger stage residing elsewhere on disk.

  The lilo command
  The map installer, used to install and configure the LILO boot loader. It reads */etc/lilo.conf* and writes a corresponding map file.

- The */etc/lilo.conf* file contains options and kernel image information. Popular directives are:

  boot
  The name of the hard disk partition that contains the boot sector.

  image
  Refers to a specific kernel file.

install
> The file installed as the new boot sector.

label
> Provides a label, or name, for each image.

map
> Directory where the *map* file is located.

prompt
> Prompts the user for input (such as kernel parameters or runlevels) before booting and without a keystroke from the user.

read-only
> The root filesystem should initially be mounted read-only.

root
> Used following each image, this specifies the device that should be mounted as *root*.

timeout
> The amount of time, in tenths of a second, the system waits for user input.

Kernel parameters and module configuration

- LILO can pass kernel parameters using *name=value* pairs.
- Linux kernels are modular, with portions of kernel functionality compiled as modules to be used as needed.
- Parameters to modules can be specified in */etc/conf.modules*.

Boot-time messages

- The kernel gives detailed status information as it boots. This information can also be found in system logs such as */var/log/messages* and from the *dmesg* command.

Objective 2: Change Runlevels and Shut Down or Reboot System

- Runlevels specify how a system is used by controlling which services are running.
- Runlevels are numbered through 6, as well as with a few single characters.
- Runlevel 0 implies system shutdown.
- Runlevel 6 implies system reboot.
- The intermediate runlevels differ in meaning among distributions.
- Runlevel 1 (also s or S) is usually single-user (maintenance) mode.
- Runlevels 2 through 5 usually define some kind of multiuser state, including an X login screen.

Single-user mode

- Runlevel 1 is a bare-bones operating environment intended for maintenance. Remote logins are disabled, networking is disabled, and most daemons are shut down.
- Single-user mode can be entered with the single, or simply 1, parameter at the LILO prompt.
- Switching to single-user mode is done using init 1.

The /etc/rc.d directory

- The /etc/rc.d file contains initialization scripts and links controlling the boot process for many Linux distributions:

  rc.sysinit
  > The startup script launched by init at boot time

  rc.local
  > A script for local startup customizations, started automatically after the system is running

  rc
  > A script used to change runlevels

  init.d
  > The directory containing scripts to start and stop system services

  rc0.d through rc6.d
  > Links to scripts in init.d

- Names of the links are [K|S][nn][init.d_name]:
  - K and S prefixes mean kill and start, respectively.
  - nn is a sequence number controlling startup or shutdown order.
  - init.d_name is the name of the script being linked.

Default runlevel, determining runlevel, changing runlevels

- The default runlevel is located in /etc/inittab on the line containing initdefault:

  id:n:initdefault:
  > n is a valid runlevel number such as 3.

- Runlevel is determined by the runlevel command, which displays the previous and current runlevels. An N for previous runlevel indicates that the runlevel has not changed since startup.
- Runlevels can be changed using init:

  init n
  > Change to runlevel n.

- System shutdown can also be initiated using shutdown:

  shutdown time
  > Bring the system down in a secure, organized fashion. time is mandatory, in the form of hh:mm, now, or +n for n minutes.

Printing (Topic 1.107)

Objective 2: Manage Printers and Print Queues

- Printers are assigned to queues, which are managed by *lpd*, the print daemon. *lpd* listens for inbound print requests, forking a copy of itself for each active print queue.
- *lpr* submits jobs to print queues.
- *lpq* queries and displays queue status.
- *lprm* allows jobs to be removed from print queues.
- *lpc* allows root to administer queues; it has both interactive and command-line forms.
- Filters translate data formats into a printer definition language.
- Spool directories hold spooled job data.

Objective 3: Print Files

- Files are printed with the *lpr* command:
  ```
  # lpr /etc/lilo.conf
  # man -t 5 myfile.txt | lpr -Pqueue2
  ```

Objective 4: Install and Configure Local and Remote Printers

/etc/printcap

- New printer definitions are added to */etc/printcap*:
  ```
  lp|ljet:\
          :sd=/var/spool/lpd/lp:\
          :mx#0:\
          :sh:\
          :lp=/dev/lp0:\
          :if=/var/spool/lpd/lp/filter:\
          :lf=/var/spool/lpd/lp/log:
  ```

  The lines in this example are defined as follows:

  lp|ljet:\
  > This parameter defines two alternate names for the printer, *lp* or *ljet*.

  sd=*spool_directory*
  > This parameter specifies the spool directory, under */var/spool/lpd*.

  mx=*max_size*
  > The maximum size of a print job in blocks. Setting this to #0 indicates no limit.

  sh
  > Suppress header pages. Placing this attribute in *printcap* sets it, eliminating the headers.

`lp=`*printer_device*
  The local printer device, such as a parallel port.

`if=`*input_filter*
  The input filter to be used. See "Filters" in Chapter 15 for additional information.

`lf=`*log_file*
  The file where error messages are logged.

Filters

- APSfilter is implemented as executable scripts. Installation configures */etc/printcap* automatically. Multiple queues may be defined to give the user access to specific printer capabilities.

- Magicfilter is a binary program; installation does not automatically create print queues.

Remote queues and Samba printers

- Printing on a remote system or network printer is done through a local queue. */etc/printcap* for the local queue looks something like this:

```
rlp:\
        :sd=/var/spool/lpd/rlp:\
        :rm=lphost:\
        :rp=rlp:\
        :mx#0:\
        :sh:\
        :if=/usr/local/bin/magicfilter:
```

- Printing to Windows printers is similar and uses the `smbprint` filter:

```
winpr:\
        :sd=/var/spool/lpd/winpr:\
        :mx#0:\
        :sh:\
        :if=/usr/bin/smbprint:
```

Documentation (Topic 1.108)

Objective 1: Use and Manage Local System Documentation

Text and paging

- In the context of Linux systems, *plain text* means files or streams of both printable characters and control characters, using a standard encoding scheme such as ASCII.

- Differentiating text from nontext isn't obvious, but the *file* command examines a file given as its argument and offers a response that indicates the file type.

- A *pager* is a program intended to offer a quick and simple interface for viewing text files, one screen at a time.
- *more* is a popular pager available on most Unix systems.
- *less* is a full-featured text pager, which emulates *more* and offers significant advantages. Common less commands are listed in Table 24-1.

Table 24-1. Common less commands

less command	Description
Space	Scroll forward one screen.
D	Scroll forward one-half screen.
Return	Scroll forward one line.
B	Scroll backward one screen.
U	Scroll backward one-half screen.
Y	Scroll backward one line.
g	Go to the beginning of the text (could be slow with large amounts of text).
G	Go to the end of the text (could be slow with large amounts of text).
/pattern	Search forward for *pattern*, which can be a regular expression.
?pattern	Search backward for *pattern*, which can be a regular expression.
H	Display a help screen.
:n	Display next file from command line (two-character command).
:p	Display previous file from command line (two-character command).

- A pager such as *less* is used by the *man* facility.

The man facility

- A manpage exists for most commands and is viewed using *man*:

  man [section] command
  > Format and display manpages from the manual *section* based on the topic of *command* using a pager.

- Manpages are usually found in the */usr/man* directory, but they can also be found elsewhere in the filesystem. The manpage location can be found in */etc/man.config*, along with the paging program to use and other information about the manpages.

/usr/doc

- Many documents for Linux systems are available in */usr/doc*. Included here are package-related documents, FAQs, HOWTOs, and so on.

The info facility

- The Free Software Foundation provides the *info* documentation format.
- GNU software comes with *info* documentation.

- The documentation is viewed with the *info* command, which displays a full-screen editor-like paging system. Common *info* commands are listed in Table 16-3.

Objective 2: Find Linux Documentation on the Internet

Linux Documentation Project

- A loosely knit team of writers, proofreaders, and editors who work together to create the definitive set of documentation for Linux. The Linux Documentation Project can be found online at *http://www.tldp.org*.
- The LDP has a wide range of documents, from complete books to personal accounts of problem-solving techniques.

Other sources

- Many Usenet newsgroups, such as *comp.os.linux*, *comp.os.linux.advocacy*, *comp.os.linux.development*, and others, are dedicated to Linux.
- Mailing lists offered by many Linux groups serve to keep members informed through email distribution of information.

Objective 5: Notify Users on System-related Issues

/etc/issue

- The */etc/issue* file is responsible for the text that appears after a login at the system console.

/etc/issue.net

- The */etc/issue.net* contains the text that appears when you log in remotely with Telnet.

/etc/motd

- The */etc/motd* file is intended to be used as the *message of the day*. Its content is shown after a successful system login.

Shells, Scripting, Programming, and Compiling

Objective 1: Customize and Use the Shell Environment

- A shell presents an interactive Textual User Interface, an operating environment, a facility for launching programs, and a programming language.
- Shells can generally be divided into those derived from the Bourne shell, *sh* (including *bash*), and the C-shells, such as *tcsh*.
- Shells are distinct from the kernel and run as user programs.
- Shells can be customized by manipulating variables.

- Shells use configuration files at startup.
- Shells pass environment variables to child processes, including other shells.

bash

- *bash* is a descendant of *sh*.
- Shell variables are known only to the local shell and are not passed on to other processes.
- Environment variables are passed on to other processes.
- A shell variable is made an environment variable when it is *exported*.
- This sets a shell variable:

    # PI=3.14

- This turns it into an environment variable:

    # export PI

- This definition does both at the same time:

    # export PI=3.14

- Shell aliases conveniently create new commands or modify existing commands:

    # alias more='less'

- Functions are defined for and called in scripts. This line creates a function named lsps:

    # lsps ( ) { ls -l; ps; }

- *bash* configuration files control the shell's behavior. Table 17-1 contains a list of these files.

Objective 2: Customize or Write Simple Scripts

- Scripts are executable text files containing commands.
- Scripts must have appropriate execution bits set in the mode.
- Some scripts define the interpreter using the #!/bin/bash syntax on the first line.

Environment

- A script that starts using #!/bin/bash operates in a new invocation of the shell. This shell first executes standard system and user startup scripts. It also inherits exported variables from the parent shell.
- Like binary programs, scripts can offer a return value after execution.
- Scripts use file tests to examine and check for specific information on files.
- Scripts can use *command substitution* to utilize the result of an external command.
- Scripts often send email to notify administrators of errors or status.
- Refer to Chapter 17 for details on bash commands.

Administrative Tasks (Topic 1.111)

Objective 1: Manage Users and Group Accounts and Related System Files

passwd and group

- User account information is stored in */etc/passwd*.
- Each line in */etc/passwd* contains a username, password, UID, GID, user's name, home directory, and default shell.
- Group information is stored in */etc/group*.
- Each line in */etc/group* contains a group name, group password, GID, and group member list.
- *passwd* and *group* are world-readable.

Shadow files

- To prevent users from obtaining encrypted passwords from *passwd* and *group*, shadow files are implemented.
- Encrypted passwords are moved to a new file, which is readable only by *root*.
- The shadow file for */etc/passwd* is */etc/shadow*.
- The shadow file for */etc/group* is */etc/gshadow*.

User and group management commands

The following commands are commonly used for manual user and group management:

useradd user
> Create the account *user*.

usermod user
> Modify the *user* account.

userdel user
> Delete the *user* account.

groupadd group
> Add *group*.

groupmod group
> Modify the parameters of *group*.

groupdel group
> Delete *group*.

passwd username
> Interactively set the password for *username*.

gpasswd groupname
> Interactively set the password for *groupname*.

pwconv
> Convert a standard password file to a shadow configuration.

pwunconv
> Revert from a shadow password configuration.

grpconv
> Convert a standard group file to a shadow configuration.

grpunconv
> Revert from a shadow group configuration.

chage user
> Modify password aging and expiration settings for *user*.

Objective 2: Tune the User Environment and System Environment Variables

Configuration scripts

- The *bash* shell uses systemwide configuration scripts—such as */etc/profile* and */etc/bashrc*—when it starts.
- Commands in */etc/profile* are executed at login time.
- Commands in */etc/bashrc* are executed for each invocation of bash.
- Changes to these systemwide files affect all users on the system.

New account home directories

- New user directories are populated automatically by copying */etc/skel* and its contents.
- The system administrator may add, modify, and delete files in */etc/skel* as needed for the local environment.

Objective 3: Configure and Use System Log Files to Meet Administrative and Security Needs

Syslog

- The syslog system displays and records messages describing system events.
- Messages can be placed on the console, in log files, and on the text screens of users.
- Syslog is configured by */etc/syslog.conf* in the form *facility.level action*:

  facility
  > The creator of the message, selected from among `auth`, `authpriv`, `cron`, `daemon`, `kern`, `lpr`, `mail`, `mark`, `news`, `syslog`, `user`, or `local0` through `local7`.

level
> Specifies a severity threshold beyond which messages are logged and is one of (from lowest to highest severity) debug, info, notice, warning, err, crit, alert, or emerg. The special level *none* disables a facility.

action
> The destination for messages that correspond to a given selector. It can be a filename, *@hostname*, a comma-separated list of users, or an asterisk, meaning all logged-in users.

- Together, *facility.levels* comprise the *message selector*.
- Most syslog messages go to */var/log/messages*.

Log file rotation

- Most system log files are rotated to expire old information and prevent disks from filling.
- *logrotate* accomplishes log rotation and is configured using */etc/logrotate.conf*.

Examining log files

- Files in */var/log* (such as *messages*)and elsewhere can be examined using utilities such as *tail*, *less*, and *grep*.
- Information in *syslogd* log files includes date, time, origin hostname, message sender, and descriptive text.
- To debug problems using log file information, first look at the hostname and sender, then at the message text.

Objective 4: Automate System Administration Tasks by Scheduling Jobs to Run in the Future

- Both *cron* and *at* can be used to schedule jobs in the future.
- Scheduled jobs can be any executable program or script.

Using cron

- The *cron* facility consists of *crond*, the *cron* daemon, and *crontab* files containing job-scheduling information.
- *cron* is intended for the execution of commands on a periodic basis.
- *crond* examines all *crontab* files every minute.
- Each system user has access to *cron* through a personal *crontab* file.
- The *crontab* command, shown here, allows the *crontab* file to be edited and viewed:

```
crontab
```
> View, or with -e, edit *crontab* files.

- Entries in the *crontab* file are in the form of:

minute hour day month dayofweek command

- Asterisks in any of the time fields match all possible values.
- In addition to personal *crontab* files, the system has its own *crontab* files: */etc/crontab* as well as files in */etc/cron.d.*

Using at

- The *at* facility, shown here, is for setting up one-time future command execution:

    at time
    > Enter an interactive session with *at*, where commands may be entered. *time* is of the form *hh:mm, midnight, noon,* and so on.

User access

- Access to *cron* can be controlled using lists of users in *cron.allow* and *cron.deny*.
- Access to *at* can be controlled using lists of users in *at.allow* and *at.deny*.

Objective 5: Maintain an Effective Data Backup Strategy

- System backup provides protection against disk failures, accidental file deletion, accidental file corruption, and disasters.
- System backup provides access to historical data.
- Full backups save all files.
- Differential backups save files modified or created since the last full backup.
- Incremental backups save files modified or created since the last full or incremental backup.
- A full backup will be coupled with either differential or incremental backups, but not both.
- Backup media are rotated to assure high-quality backups.
- Backup media must be verified to assure data integrity.
- Backup is often performed using tar and mt, as follows:

    tar files
    > Archive or restore files recursively, to tape or to a tarfile.

    mt operation
    > Control a tape drive, including skipping over multiple archives on tape, rewinding, and ejecting. *operations* include fsf, bsf, rewind, and offline (see the manpage for a complete list).

- Backup should include everything necessary to restore a system to operation in the event of a disaster. Examples include */etc, /home, /var/log,* and */var/spool,* though individual requirements vary.

Objective 6: Maintain System Time

- See "Objective 6: Maintain System Time" in Chapter 18.

Networking Fundamentals (Topic 1.112)

Objective 1: Fundamentals of TCP/IP

Addressing and masks

- An address mask separates the network portion from the host portion of the 32-bit IP address.
- Class A addresses have 8 bits of network address and 24 bits of host address.
- Class B addresses have 16 bits of network address and 16 bits of host address.
- Class C addresses have 24 bits of network address and 8 bits of host address.
- Subnets can be defined using the defined "class" schemes or using a locally defined split of network/host bits.
- The all-zero and all-ones addresses are reserved on all subnets for the network and broadcast addresses, respectively. This implies that the maximum number of hosts on a network with n bits in the host portion of the address is $2^n - 2$. For example, a class C network has 8 bits in the host portion. Therefore, it can have a maximum of $2^8 - 2 = 254$ hosts.

Protocols

TCP/IP is a name representing a larger suite of network protocols. Some network protocols maintain a constant connection while others do not.

IP
: The Internet Protocol is the fundamental building block of the Internet. It is used by other protocols.

ICMP
: This connectionless messaging protocol uses IP. It is used for flow control, detection of unreachable destinations, redirecting routes, and checking remote hosts (the ping utility).

UDP
: The User Datagram Protocol is a connectionless transport agent. It is used by applications such as DNS and NFS.

TCP
: The Tranmission Control Protocol is a connection-oriented transport agent. It is used by applications such as FTP and Telnet.

PPP
: The Point-to-Point Protocol is used over serial lines, including modems.

TCP/IP services

- Inbound network requests to a host include a *port number*. Common port numbers are listed in Table 19-2 in Chapter 19.

- Ports are assigned to specific programs. Definitions are stored in */etc/services*.

- Ports 1–1023 are privileged ports, owned by superuser processes.

TCP/IP utilities

- *ftp* implements the File Transfer Protocol client for the exchange of files to and from remote hosts.

- The *telnet* client program implements a Telnet session to a remote host.

- *ping* sends ICMP echo requests to a remote host to verify functionality.

- *dig* obtains information from DNS servers.

- *traceroute* attempts to display the route over which packets must travel to a remote host.

- *fwhois* queries a *whois* database to determine the owner of a domain or IP address.

Objective 3: TCP/IP Configuration and Troubleshooting

Network interfaces

- Interfaces are configured through a number of configuration files.

- */etc/hostname* contains the assigned hostname for the system.

- */etc/hosts* contains static mappings between IP addresses and names.

- */etc/nsswitch.conf* directs system library functions to specific name server methods such as local files, DNS, and NIS.

- */etc/host.conf* controls name resolution for older libraries.

- */etc/host.conf* is only rarely used and is replaced by */etc/nsswitch.conf*.

- */etc/resolv.conf* contains information to direct the resolver to DNS servers.

- */etc/networks* sets up equivalence between addresses and names for entire networks.

- The *host* command returns DNS information.

- The *hostname*, *domainname*, and *dnsdomainname* commands set or display the current host, domain, or node name.

- The *ifconfig* command configures network interfaces. It is used to create and configure interface parameters, usually at boot time. Parameters include the IP address and subnet mask.

- The *netstat* command displays network connections, routing tables, interface statistics, masquerade connections, and multicast memberships.

- The *route* command displays the routing table and can add or delete routes from the table.

DHCP

- DHCP is the Dynamic Host Configuration Protocol. It is used to assign an IP address and other information to a client system.
- The DHCP server is *dhcpd*.
- A DHCP server offers an address for a finite amount of time known as a *lease*.

Objective 4: Configure Linux as a PPP Client

- PPP is used to make a network connection over a serial interface. This could be a direct cable or modem connection.
- PPP is a peer protocol; there are no clients or servers.
- *pppd* is the PPP daemon, called when a PPP interface is needed. It uses a chat script to send configuration commands to a modem prior to dialing.
- Basic authentication for PPP can be done in clear text via the chat script. However, the PAP, CHAP, and MSCHAP methods encode their authentication information into the PPP data stream.

Networking Services (Topic 1.113)

Objective 1: Configure and Manage inetd, xinetd, and Related Services

- *inetd* is the Internet superdaemon; it listens on multiple inbound ports and launches the appropriate child daemon to service the requests.
- *inetd* uses TCP wrappers (*tcpd*) to add access security to services.
- *inetd* is configured in */etc/inetd.conf*.
- You can eliminate an inbound service managed by *inetd* simply by commenting out its declaration in */etc/inetd.conf* and restarting or signaling inetd.
- TCP wrappers allow the administrator to define access rules for hosts. The configuration files are */etc/hosts.allow* and */etc/hosts.deny*.

Objective 2: Operate and Perform Basic Configuration of Mail Transfer Agent (MTA)

- Sendmail is a Mail Transfer Agent (MTA).
- Sendmail is configured in */etc/sendmail.cf*. This file is generally regarded as difficult to configure.
- The "smart host" parameter is used to configure a local Sendmail daemon to transfer mail to a site's official mail system.
- */etc/aliases* is a file that stores aliases for inbound mail addresses; it can redirect mail to one or more users.
- Whenever */etc/aliases* is modified, *newaliases* must be executed.

- Each user can forward his own mail using a *.forward* file, containing the forwarding email address, in his home directory.

- Outbound mail that is trapped due to a network or other problem will remain queued; it can be examined using the *mailq* command.

Objective 3: Operate and Perform Basic Configuration of Apache

- Apache is configured using *httpd.conf*, *srm.conf*, and *access.conf*. On some installations, these may all be combined into *httpd.conf*.

- The configuration files contain configuration directives, one per line, consisting of a keyword and an argument list. For example:

      DocumentRoot /home/httpd/html

  sets the root directory for HTML files on the system.

- Apache is typically started at boot time using the system's startup methods.

Objective 4: Properly Manage the NFS and Samba Daemons

NFS

- Traditional Unix file sharing is done with NFS, originally developed by Sun Microsystems.

- NFS is a client/server package, and any system can hold both roles simultaneously.

- Exporting (sharing) a local filesystem with NFS is done by including a line in the */etc/exports* file, consisting of a directory and list of allowed systems, along with NFS options. For example:

      /usr   (ro) orion.mydomain.com(rw)
      /home   *.mydomain.com(rw)

- Remote NFS filesystems are mounted using the *mount* command:

      # mount -t nfs server1:/home /mnt/server1

- NFS is typically started at boot time using the system's startup methods.

Samba

- The Samba suite implements Server Message Block (SMB) protocols used on Microsoft and IBM LANs.

- *smbd* handles file and printer sharing and authentication.

- *nmbd* implements the WINS service.

- Samba is configured in */etc/smb.conf*. The file consists of sections, each with a series of *keyword = value* pairs.

- Samba 2.0 and later comes with a web-based configuration tool called SWAT; it is usually configured to be monitored by inetd.

Objective 5: Set Up and Configure Basic DNS Services

- DNS is the distributed database of name-to-IP-address translations.

The resolver

- The resolver is a library used by networked applications when a domain name needs to be translated into an IP address.
- The resolver uses local files, NIS, and DNS to resolve hostnames as directed by */etc/resolv.conf*.

Domain registration

- Domain names are assigned through a registration process with one of the *domain name registrars* on the Internet.
- The DNS server daemon is *named*, part of the BIND package.
- *named* can be configured to speed up a local system by acting as a nonauthoritative caching-only name server.
- *named* is configured using */etc/named.conf*.
- The *nslookup*, *host*, and *dig* utilities can be used to retrieve information from DNS servers.
- BIND Version 4 and Version 8 have significantly different configuration file formats, although the information contained in the files is similar.

Objective 7: Set Up Secure Shell (OpenSSH)

- See "Objective 4: Secure Shell (SSH)" in Chapter 40.

Security (Topic 1.114)

Objective 1: Perform Security Administration Tasks

TCP wrappers

- Configuring TCP wrappers (*tcpd*) using */etc/hosts.allow* and */etc/hosts.deny* can enhance security for daemons controlled by *inetd*.
- *tcpd* is often configured to deny access to all systems for all services (a blanket deny), then specific systems are specified for legitimate access to services (limited allow).
- *tcpd* logs using syslog, commonly to */var/log/secure*.

Finding executable SUID files

- *find* can perform searches for file attributes such as SUID using the *-perm* option.

Verifying packages

- RPM packages are verified using the Verify mode, enabled using the -V (capital) option.

- The output for each package contains a string of eight characters that are set to dots when the attribute has not changed. The columns represent each of eight different attributes: MD5 checksum, file size, symlink attributes, the file's mtime, device file change, user/owner change, group change, and mode change.

SGID workgroups

- The SGID bit can be applied to directories to enforce a policy whereby new files created within the directory are assigned the same group ownership as the directory itself.

The Secure Shell

- The Secure Shell, or SSH, can be used as an alternative to Telnet for secure communications.

- SSH can also protect FTP and other data streams, including X sessions.

- The Secure Shell daemon is sshd.

Objective 2: Set Up Host Security

Shadow passwords

- Enabling the use of *shadow passwords* can enhance local security by making encrypted passwords harder to steal.

- The use of shadow passwords causes the removal of password information from the publicly readable *passwd* file and places it in *shadow*, readable only by root.

- A similar system is implemented for shadow groups, using the *gshadow* file.

Objective 3: Set Up User-level Security

- Limits can be placed on users by using the ulimit command in the *bash* shell. This command allows enforcement of limitations on soft and hard limits on processes and memory usage.

General Linux Exam 201

Part 3 covers the Topics and Objectives for the LPI's General Linux Certification for Exam 201 and includes the following. sections:

25

Linux Kernel

This Topic is dedicated to all things kernel. In Chapter 13 of this book we covered Level 1 kernel topics for Exam 102. On the 201 exam, LPI covers more advanced kernel-related topics, including the various components of a Linux kernel, advanced kernel compiling, patching a kernel, and creating custom kernels.

This Topic on the Linux kernel has four Objectives:

Objective 1: Kernel Components
Candidates should be able to utilize kernel components that are necessary to specific hardware, hardware drivers, and system resources and requirements. This Objective includes implementing different types of kernel images and identifying stable and development kernels and patches, as well as using kernel modules. Weight: 1.

Objective 2: Compiling a Kernel
Candidates should be able to properly compile a kernel to include or disable specific features of the Linux kernel as necessary. This Objective includes compiling and recompiling the Linux kernel as needed, implementing updates and noting changes in a new kernel, creating a system initrd image, and installing new kernels. Weight: 1.

Objective 3: Patching a Kernel
Candidates should be able to properly patch a kernel for various purposes including to implement kernel updates, to implement bug fixes, and to add support for new hardware. This Objective also includes being able to properly remove kernel patches from existing production kernels. Weight: 2.

Objective 4: Customizing a Kernel
Candidates should be able to customize a kernel for specific system requirements by patching, compiling, and editing configuration files as required. This Objective includes being able to assess requirements for a kernel compile versus a kernel patch as well as build and configure kernel modules. Weight: 1.

Objective 1: Kernel Components

A quick look at the contents of a kernel source directory and you get a good idea of the various pieces required to make your kernel function. If that doesn't give you any ideas, a glance through the documentation available should satisfy your curiosity. As discussed in Chapter 13 for Exam 102, the Linux kernel manages all aspects of your computer, virtual memory, the device drivers, networking code, and so on. The kernel also runs applications, but in a separate space outside the kernel. Applications and services are executed in *user space*.

There are very large books out there covering the nitty-gritty details of the development of the Linux kernel, but these topics are outside of the scope of a sysadmin, thus are not covered in the LPI Level 2 Exams. Essentially what LPI is looking for is for you to understand the applications for various types of kernel images, demonstrate proficient use of the various branches of kernel development, and efficiently implement kernel *patches*.

Kernel Image Formats

Let's review a couple of fundamentals. Two types of kernel image formats can be used on Intel platforms: *zImage* and *bzImage*. The difference between them is the way they bootstrap and how large the kernel can be, not the compression algorithm as one might think. Both use *gzip* for compression.

zImage
> This is the old boot image format for Intel, which works on all known PC hardware. The bootstrap and the unpacked kernel are loaded into the good old, 8086-era 640 KB of low memory. The allowed kernel size is 520 KB. If your kernel excedes this size, you either have to switch to *bzImage* or put more of the kernel into modules. The boot image builder will tell you when this is the case.

bzImage
> The *b* in this format stands for *big*. The *bzImage* kernel image is not restricted to 520 KB or even 640 KB. *bzImage* is now the preferred boot image. Though there are some reports of boot failures using this boot image type, these problems are being pursued because the kernel developers want the format to work on all Intel hardware.

Different Kernel Trees

Your dad used to tell you that money didn't grow on trees, but kernels do. Kernel development trees aren't too dissimilar from your family tree. It all began in Finland when two offspring were born: *stable* and *development*. Traditionally, each branch of the family tree maintains its family naming schemes, but don't forget that this practice is simply for superficial version tracking and has no effect on the kernel itself. John Doe will still be the same person, even if he changed his name to John Buck.

To refresh your memory from your 102 exams, official kernels are numbered with a decimal-delimited number in the format *major.minor.patchlevel*, such as

2.6.15. The *minor* value has traditionally distinguished a stable kernel from a developoment one: an even number indicates a stable kernel, whereas an odd number indicates a development kernel. But 2.6 is on a path of constant development, however, and there is no 2.7, so the stable/development distinction is no longer as meaningful.

Choosing an appropriate kernel

For some kinds of support situations, such as with a Red Hat Enterprise Linux on which you want to run applications such as Oracle, you may not be able to choose your kernel—you have to use a Red Hat–issued kernel. Oracle, for one, is very picky about this.

Other than that, there is really no rule to follow when choosing a kernel tree to use. Common sense should tell you if you're running a production server, stable kernel code will be the best choice. However, support for new hardware and other features may not be in your stable versions, forcing you to choose the development kernel. For instance, in the 2.2 stable kernels, USB was supported by only the 2.3 development kernel. If you wanted to use a USB device on your Linux machine, you had to either run the development kernel or apply a *patch* (if available)—a package of source code that alters the kernel.

Hardware support

In your career as a Linux administrator, you may easily get in a situation in which some new machine has hardware components that are not supported by your custom kernels, or even by your distributions' kernels. Red Hat kernels usually include support for anything you can think of, but some other distributions have separate kernels that support specific hardware. If you buy some very racy new hardware, you may find that there is no support in any kernels and that you either have to develop it yourself or wait a month while someone else does it. And then you may have to get a special patch and apply it yourself, as described later in this chapter.

In most other situations, a distribution's kernel will either just work or will work if you construct a suitable initrd image for the kernel to load the needed drivers.

If you're compiling custom kernels, it is important to know all your hardware: which IDE chipsets, SCSI controllers, Ethernet cards, and so on you have. Your kernel must have support for your boot disk system, either inside the kernel or in the initrd image. Otherwise, the kernel will not be able even to boot and mount the root filesystem. To get on the network, it must either have support for your Ethernet cards, either in the kernel or as a module that is loaded during the init process (described in the section "Objective 1: Customizing System Startup and Boot Processes" in Chapter 26).

For you to identify these components, it is a good idea to boot a distribution kernel and scrutinize its boot log. On Red Hat and Debian systems, this is saved in */var/log/dmesg*. In the */proc/pci* pseudofile, or with the *lspci* command, you can find the complete list of PCI hardware in the machine. It is also a good idea to have the vendor's documentation of the hardware, because it may contain the names of chipsets and components.

One of the challenges in all this is that most hardware has two or three different names. It may have a "trade name" such as Intel Ethernet Express Pro 100, behind which there is a chipset name or part name, and even a code name or pet name given by the engineers that constructed it. Any of these three names may be found in the vendor documentation, and any of them may also be used in the Linux kernel. It will be your job to match all these names and produce a viable kernel for your hardware. Luckily, it's not as hard as we just made it sound. But there *are* a lot of different chips and hardware in a modern PC.

Patches

Kernel patches are found in both the stable and the development kernel trees. But there are also third-party patch repositories that implement some specific features that the kernel maintainers do not want or that are not mature enough to be in the stable or even development trees. Patches are minor updates or fixes that can be applied to your specific kernel, but without the need to get a whole new kernel. Depending on the nature of the patch, you may or may not need to fully recompile your existing kernel. If the patch just contains new modules or fixes existing modules, you don't generally need to. If it modifies something in the kernel proper, the whole kernel should be recompiled from scratch.

While there's nothing magical about the filenames, kernel patches are typically named with *patch-* prepended to the kernel version, such as *patch-2.4.20.bz2*. We'll discuss kernel patching more in the third section of this chapter.

Kernel modules

The Linux kernel supports loading (and unloading) modules. These modules may support different hardware, filesystems, network stacks, and anything else the kernel needs in different situations. The mass of supported *things* in the Linux kernel is quite astounding. Modules are a way to mitigate the overabundance of features and bring down the kernel image's size.

When you build kernels, you may choose to build some features as a module. When a feature is needed, it must be loaded either manually by a script or automatically. When a module is loaded, it may depend on other modules, so it cannot be loaded until those other modules are loaded. Luckily, the module-loading mechanism can search recursively for dependencies and load whatever is needed.

After a kernel is built and the modules installed in their directory hierarchy at */lib/ modules*, their interdependencies are found with the *depmod* command, an example of which is:

```
depmod -ae -F /boot/System.map-2.4.18 2.4.18
```

If any modules lack functions they need, you may see a message such as this:

```
depmod: *** Unresolved symbols in /lib/modules/2.4.18/kernel/drivers/scsi/
pcmcia/fdomain_cs.o
depmod:          isa_readb
depmod:          isa_memcpy_fromio
```

Such a message[*] is probably due to a programming error. If you have any programming and C skills, it may be possible for you to resolve the problem. Otherwise this kernel is not usable for you. The message may also appear if you have built the same kernel version several times with different options and modules. In that case, the module that the kernel is trying to load may be from an old compilation and installation and is not supposed to be present any more. If you recognize that this is, indeed, the case, you can just remove the module, and thus the problem.

You can put anything you like into a module, even parts of the kernel that are needed to boot the machine. A mechanism known as *initrd* can be used to load modules very early in the boot process. An initrd RAM disk image can be loaded with the help of the system's BIOS. A bit later, before the kernel needs to access disks or networks, the modules needed to boot are loaded into the kernel. Therefore, support for SCSI drivers, LVM, filesystems, and anything else can be included in this initrd image to get the machine booting. initrd is discussed more later in this chapter.

Other issues you need to know about relating to kernel module loading and unloading are covered in Chapter 13.

Objective 2: Compiling a Kernel

Regardless of the Linux distribution you choose, no two kernels are the same. The creators of your distribution had total freedom to customize the kernel, and so do you. Choosing and making these customizations are discussed in the next section, which covers patching. The current section explains how to apply the customizations, for which you must be able to *compile* your kernel.

Kernel Configuration Tools

The first step in compiling (or recompiling) a kernel involves the *make* tool. One set of commands provided with this tool allows you to select and deselect the exact options you want to include and modularize for the new kernel. These configuration settings are stored in a file named *.config*. Historically, this file was saved within your kernel source to */usr/src/linux* or */usr/src/linux-kernel-version*, but this is no longer the case. Older applications (based on the standard library called *libc*) required */usr/src/linux*, but the introduction of a new library, *glibc*, eliminated that dependency. For the purposes of our examples, however, we will continue to show */usr/src/linux*∗.

> This book, following LPI program objectives, will assume that kernels are built from the vanilla kernel source available at *http://www.kernel.org*. Many major distributions, however, on their web sites, offer new kernel sources that incorporate the distributions' own patches.

---

[*] This is not a real problem in 2.4.18; it had to be provoked artificially for the sake of an example.

When you configure a kernel using any of the tools described in this section, you are presented with at least 30 sets of configuration options. These options range from configuration tool preferences to hardware support and even development tools. For an introduction to the meaning of some kernel options, check *Understanding the Linux Kernel* and *Understanding Linux Network Internals* (both from O'Reilly).

There are three methods of using *make* to configure your kernel: *make config*, *make menuconfig*, and *make xconfig*. Each of these methods creates a file with the *.config* extension that is used when making the *zImage* or *bzImage* of the kernel.

 To successfully use *make*, be sure you have all the appropriate packages or applications installed: All methods of make require the *glibc-devel*, *gcc* or *egcs*, *make*, *kernel-headers*, *kernel-source*, *bin86*, and *cpp* packages. If you opt to use the *make menuconfig* option, you must also have the *ncurses* and *ncurses-devel* packages installed. If you opt for the *make xconfig* option, you must have X Window support.

All *make* commands used to build and install the kernel must be issued in the top-level directory where you placed the kernel sources.

make config

The first method, *make config*, is a text-based tool that you step through to configure kernel options one by one. It is no longer recommended because the kernel provies so many options, and the interface involves simply stepping one by one through them tediously. However, *make config* is a standard tool and is provided with all Linux distributions.

When you enter *make config*, you are prompted line by line to include support for a specific item. Following each question, you are given up to four options: y for yes, n for no, m for modularize, and ? (question mark) for help. Entering the ? option gives you details about the particular item and what the recommended settings are.

The possible settings for a particular item are noted after each question, with the default option capitalized. For instance, the first question, `Prompt for development and/or incomplete code/drivers (CONFIG_EXPERIMENTAL) [Y/n/?]` has a default answer of y for yes. So you can accept the default by pressing the Enter key. The following displays the interface used in *make config*. (The first few lines are commands issued by *make* before the prompts start.)

```
rm -f include/asm
( cd include ; ln -sf asm-i386 asm)
/bin/sh scripts/Configure arch/i386/config.in
#
# Using defaults found in .config
#
*
* Code maturity level options
*
```

```
Prompt for development and/or incomplete code/drivers
(CONFIG_EXPERIMENTAL) [Y/n/?] Enter key pressed
*
* Loadable module support
*
Enable loadable module support (CONFIG_MODULES) [Y/n/?] Enter key pressed
  Set version information on all module symbols (CONFIG_MODVERSIONS) [Y/n/?]
Enter key pressed
  Kernel module loader (CONFIG_KMOD) [Y/n/?] Enter key pressed
*
* Processor type and features
*
Processor family (386, 486, 586/K5/5x86/6x86/6x86MX, Pentium-Classic,
Pentium-MMX, Pentium-Pro/Celeron/Pentium-II, Pentium-III/
Celeron(Coppermine), Pentium-4, K6/K6-II/K6-III, Athlon/Duron/K7, Elan,
Crusoe, Winchip-C6, Winchip-2, Winchip-2A/Winchip-3, CyrixIII/C3) [Pentium-
III/Celeron(Coppermine)] Enter key pressed
    defined CONFIG_MK7
Toshiba Laptop support (CONFIG_TOSHIBA) [N/y/m/?] Enter key pressed
Dell laptop support (CONFIG_I8K) [N/y/m/?] n
/dev/cpu/microcode - Intel IA32 CPU microcode support (CONFIG_MICROCODE) [M/
n/y/?] Enter key pressed
/dev/cpu/*/msr - Model-specific register support (CONFIG_X86_MSR) [M/n/y/?]
Enter key pressed
/dev/cpu/*/cpuid - CPU information support (CONFIG_X86_CPUID) [M/n/y/?]
Enter key pressed
High Memory Support (off, 4GB, 64GB) [off] Enter key pressed
  defined CONFIG_NOHIGHMEM
Math emulation (CONFIG_MATH_EMULATION) [N/y/?] Enter key pressed
MTRR (Memory Type Range Register) support (CONFIG_MTRR) [Y/n/?] Enter key
pressed
Symmetric multi-processing support (CONFIG_SMP) [N/y/?] Enter key pressed
...
```

make menuconfig

The second type of *make* method is *make menuconfig*. It gives you a graphical
menu-based display without requiring you to use the X Window System. When
you use *make menuconfig*, you are presented with a directory tree menu system.
Following each selection, you are presented with the available options. To include
an option, use the y key; to exclude it, use the n key; and to include it as a module,
use the m key. Letters that are highlighted are considered *hotkeys* and allow you to
quickly maneuver through the menu options. To exit a window, select the Exit
option, or press the Esc key twice.

make xconfig

The third type of *make* method is *make xconfig*. This method is very popular
among new Linux users and users who are accustomed to graphical interface
tools. The *make xconfig* tool requires X Window System support. When starting
make xconfig, you are presented with a window with buttons for each class of
configuration. Pressing a configuration button, you are prompted, in a tree style,

the options available. You can then select, deselect, or modularize each option by pressing the corresponding button next to the item. One of the benefits of using this configuration method over the standard *make config* method is the backward mobility of the configuration. This means that if you change your mind, or make a mistake, you can move back and change the option in *make xconfig*; you can't do this with *make config*. Figure 13-2 in Chapter 13 shows the graphical user interface used with the *make xconfig* method.

Compiling and Installing a Custom Kernel

When compiling and installing a kernel, you use various *make* options. There are as many as 11 options, which we will describe in this section, that you can use when compiling and installing your kernel from start to finish. Follow these steps to compile and install a new kernel:

1. You must first configure your kernel as discussed in the "Kernel Configuration Tools" section earlier in this chapter. Several options are available. First, to compile your kernel, you must be in the directory with your kernel source files, such as */usr/src/linux* directory. Next, if you plan to configure your kernel completely from scratch, enter make mrproper. Doing so removes your current *.config* file and allows you to set up all new options for your kernel without knowing your current default configuration. If you wish to see your current default options, skip the *make mrproper* step. To configure your kernel, use your choice of *make config, make menuconfig*, or *make xconfig*, as discussed earlier in this chapter.

2. Next, you must do some general kernel housekeeping. This means that you need to clean up any unneeded or temporary files from the kernel source tree. To clean the source tree, run *make clean*.

3. In 2.4 kernels, build dependency tables between the various features and modules you have chosen so that they can be built in the correct order and without building unused features and modules. To build these tables, run *make dep*. This step should not be performed for 2.6 kernels, because the build process generates dependency information automatically.

4. Create the kernel image using *make bzImage* (or *make zImage* if your hardware requires this older image type; the rest of this text assumes you use *bzImage*). This command compiles a kernel image and places it in the file *arch/i386/boot/bzImage*. After the image is created, copy the *bzImage* to the */boot* directory. In the */boot* directory, you may wish to rename the image to something like *vmlinuz-kernel-version*, e.g., *vmlinuz-2.4.18*. You should also copy the file *System.map* to */boot/System.map-2.4.18*, which enables such things as module loading and the symbolic display of kernel routines by the *top* program.

5. Compile your modules. If you made a completely monolithic kernel, skip ahead to Step 7. Otherwise, run *make modules* to compile all of your selected modules.

6. Install your compiled modules by running *make modules_install*. When you install the modules with this *make* option, *make* installs them to */lib/modules*.

With the postconfiguration make options such as *make clean, make dep, make bzImage, make modules*, and *make modules_install*, you don't have to invoke each make command one at a time. You can string them together to run automatically without user intervention by simply running:

```
# make clean dep bzImage modules install modules_install
```

7. Create the RAM disk image (if required). The RAM disk image is used to preload block device modules (such as SCSI drivers to access SCSI hard drives) that are required during a boot to access the root filesystem. To create this RAM disk image, use the *mkinitrd* command, which is covered in more depth later in this chapter.

8. Lastly, you need to set up your boot loader for your new kernel. If you're using LILO, do this by editing the */etc/lilo.conf* file. Simply add an additional boot image section to */etc/lilo.conf* or change the current boot image section to reflect your new kernel image name and initrd image (if necessary).

For instance, if you just compiled kernel 2.4.18, named the image */boot/vmlinuz-2.4.18*, and created an initrd image named */boot/initrd-2.4.18*, your new boot image section of */etc/lilo.conf* should look like this:

```
boot=/dev/hda
map=/boot/map
install=/boot/boot.b
delay=20
timeout=240
root=/dev/hda3
read-only
image=/boot/vmlinuz-2.4.18
        label=2.4.18
        initrd=/boot/initrd-2.4.18
```

 After you have edited your */etc/lilo.conf* file, be sure to install the new configuration by running */sbin/lilo* or all changes to the file will be ignored.

If you use GRUB instead of LILO, the GRUB configuration file needs to be updated, although no command needs to be run for it to take effect on the next boot. A *grub.conf* that is analogous to the one shown previously should look like the following listing. GRUB's filenames are relative to the top of your boot partition; that is why the pathnames look different from those in the *lilo.conf* file shown earlier.

```
timeout=240
splashimage=(hd0,0)/grub/splash.xpm.gz

title Linux 2.4.18
        kernel (hd0,0)/vmlinuz-2.4.18 root=/dev/hda3
        initrd (hd0,0)/initrd-2.4.18
```

Using initrd

initrd is a contraction of "initial ram disk." This initrd image is used by the kernel to load drivers before it starts booting. The purpose of this is to let users build modularized kernels that do not contain support for all 40 different SCSI controllers (for example) and still are able to boot from any SCSI hardware. In this case, the initrd image would contain the needed SCSI drivers and any other drivers needed to get the kernel off the ground.

An initrd image is typically constructed automatically by the *mkinitrd* command. This command differs substantially among distributions.

mkinitrd on Red Hat/Fedora

 To be able to build and use initrd images on Red Hat, you need support for two things in your kernel: RAM disks and *loop devices*. Loop devices lets the kernel mount a file as if it were a device.

Red Hat and Fedora systems check various files for things that are likely to be needed to boot the machine. In */etc/modules.conf*, they look for a line reading alias `scsi_hostadapter` that defines which SCSI module is needed to boot. They check for LVM (Logical Volume Manager) configurations and include the LVM drivers if they find anything, in case the boot depends on LVM. They look for md configurations to see whether it's necessary to include RAID drivers. Then they check all these module dependencies and include the whole bunch in the initrd image. This is all done automatically in a script; your job is restricted to running the right command. The most likely options are shown:

--preload module
>   Name a module you want loaded before the others.

--omit-scsi-modules
>   Skip the check for SCSI modules. You can use this if you know that SCSI is not needed to boot your system. Instead, the module will be loaded after the root filesystem is mounted.

--omit-raid-modules
>   Skip the check for whether MD modules are needed.

--omit-lvm-modules
>   Skip the check for LVM modules.

--with=module
>   Include a specific module.

-v
>   Be verbose.

An example follows. It shows how to make an initrd for the 2.4.18 kernel mentioned earlier in the file */boot/initrd-2.4.18*. If the kernel has any EXTRAVERSION parts (described later), these must also be included in the version given and should be included in the filename as well.

```
# mkinitrd -v /boot/initrd-2.4.18 2.4.18
Looking for deps of module ide-disk
Looking for deps of module lvm-mod
Looking for deps of module ext2
Using modules:
Using loopback device /dev/loop0
/sbin/nash -> /var/tmp/initrd.c19229/bin/nash
/sbin/insmod.static -> /var/tmp/initrd.c19229/bin/insmod
# ls -l /boot/initrd-2.4.18
-rw-r--r--   1 root     root         101224 jan 11 13:01 /boot/initrd-2.4.18
```

mkinitrd in Debian

 To be able to use an initrd image on Debian, you need support for *cramfs* (Compressed ROM filesystem) in your kernel.

The Debian *mkinitrd* command has fewer options and more customization files, making it harder to customize for a one-time generation, but easier in the long run because the files remain around for the next time. The general behavior is described in */etc/mkinitrd/mkinitrd.conf*, and any modules you may want included are listed in */etc/mkinitrd/modules*. As usual with Debian, the files are heavily documented and are thus largely self-explanatory. A default *mkinitrd.conf* follows:

```
# /etc/mkinitrd/mkinitrd.conf:
#  Configuration file for mkinitrd(8).  See mkinitrd.conf(5).
#
# This file is meant to be parsed as a shell script.

# What modules to install.
MODULES=most

# The length (in seconds) of the startup delay during which linuxrc may be
# interrupted.
DELAY=0

# If this is set to probe, mkinitrd will try to figure out what's needed to
# mount the root filesystem.  This is equivalent to the old PROBE=on
setting.
ROOT=probe

# This controls the permission of the resulting initrd image.
UMASK=022

# Command to generate the initrd image.
MKIMAGE='mkcramfs %s %s > /dev/null'
```

With these defaults, *mkinitrd* is largely self-configuring. Generating an image analogous to the image made for Red Hat in the previous section is as simple as the following command. Note that, instead of the kernel version demanded by Red

Linux Kernel

Hat's *mkinitrd*, this one wants the name of the kernel's module directory where it will find the modules it should use.

```
# mkinitrd -o /boot/initrd-2.4.18 /lib/modules/2.4.18
# ls -ld /boot/initrd-2.4.18
-rw-r--r--    1 root     root        811008 Jan 11 13:32 /boot/initrd-2.4.18
```

Updating Your Kernel

Updating your kernel involves applying a patch or getting a complete source tree in a tarfile. The updated Linux kernels are best found at *http://www.kernel.org*. There you will also find the change logs for each patch level of the kernel. *kernel. org* stores compressed files in both bz2 and gzip formats. bz2 is compressed and decompressed by *bzip2*. gzip is compressed by the more familiar *gzip*. We will use bz2 for the rest of this chapter.

If you are looking to upgrade from 2.6.15.5 to 2.6.15.6, as an example, you will need to retrieve *patch-2.6.15.6.bz2* for just the patch or *linux-2.6.15.6.tar.bz2* for the complete source code. It is also a good idea to retrieve *ChangeLog-2.6.15.6*, which contains the developers' descriptions of what has changed in this release. In this file you may find important information about fixed bugs, including security, new features, and perhaps features that were removed.

If you fetched the full source tree, you just have to unpack it, configure it, and install it as described earlier in this chapter. If you fetched the patch, use the patching process described in the next objective.

Objective 3: Patching a Kernel

When you start patching and customizing kernels, it becomes vital to make it obvious which source tree contains which patches and exactly what special functionality is in the currently running kernel. You should use directory names and other means to actively indicate these things.

Applying the Patch

Once your desired patch has been located and fetched, you can start building a new kernel with it. In the following example, you will install a new kernel patch to take your kernel from 2.4.23 to 2.4.24. After fetching it, a good place to store it is */usr/src/patch-2.4.24.bz2*.

1. Copy your unpatched source tree to a tree that you're going to patch. Choose a target directory name that reflects the capabilities of the patched kernel. If this is going to be a symmetric multiprocessing (SMP) kernel, *linux-2.4.24-SMP* might be most appropriate:

    ```
    cp -a linux-2.4.23 linux-2.4.24-SMP
    ```

2. Inspect your patch, using *bzmore* for a bz2 file, to see what path it operates on. This one starts modifying *linux-2.4.24/Makefile*. The directory name does not match the one you've chosen earlier, and this must be corrected in the next two steps. The top of the patch file is shown here:

```
# diff -urN linux-2.4.23/Makefile linux-2.4.24/Makefile
--- linux-2.4.23/Makefile        2003-11-28 10:26:21.000000000 -0800
+++ linux-2.4.24/Makefile        2004-01-05 05:53:56.000000000 -0800
@@ -1,6 +1,6 @@
 VERSION = 2
 PATCHLEVEL = 4
```

3. Change to the top-level of the source tree:

```
# cd linux-2.4.24-SMP
```

4. Apply the patch:

```
# bzip2 -dc ../patch-2.4.24.bz2 | patch -p1
patching file Makefile
patching file arch/cris/drivers/ds1302.c
patching file arch/cris/drivers/pcf8563.c
patching file arch/m68k/bvme6000/rtc.c
...
```

The *-p1* option to *patch* instructs it to remove one level of path from the front of the filenames in the patch. In this case, it removes the leading *linux-2.4.24* and leaves *Makefile*, which is the correct path considering the directory you're standing in. Thus, the option corrects for the directory name mismatch in the path. *patch* reads patch files from its standard input, so it must always be fed by a pipe or an input redirect (the < shell metacharacter).

5. Now you must reconcile any rejected chunks in the patch. Any rejected chunks are saved into *.rej* files, which are clearly shown in the run. In case the output from *patch* is overwhelming, the files can easily be found with a find command such as *find . -name '*.rej'*.

These rejected patch chunks must be applied by hand. By this we mean that you must take out your favorite editor and look at the *.rej* file alongside the file it failed to patch. If a patch to *orinoco.c* failed, the corresponding reject file is *orinoco.c.rej*. Such a file is shown next:

```
***************
*** 4160,4168 ****
          /* Setup / override net_device fields */
          dev->init = orinoco_init;
          dev->hard_start_xmit = orinoco_xmit;
- #ifdef SET_MAC_ADDRESS
-             dev->set_mac_address = orinoco_set_mac_address;
- #endif        /* SET_MAC_ADDRESS */
          dev->tx_timeout = orinoco_tx_timeout;
          dev->watchdog_timeo = HZ; /* 1 second timeout */
          dev->get_stats = orinoco_get_stats;
--- 3947,3952 ----
          /* Setup / override net_device fields */
          dev->init = orinoco_init;
          dev->hard_start_xmit = orinoco_xmit;
          dev->tx_timeout = orinoco_tx_timeout;
          dev->watchdog_timeo = HZ; /* 1 second timeout */
          dev->get_stats = orinoco_get_stats;
```

The lines marked with a hyphen should be removed from *orinoco.c*. Any lines marked with a plus sign are to be inserted. The numbers on top are the

Linux Kernel

approximate line numbers; these can be *very* approximate, especially if you're applying a third-party patch.

Reasons for patches being rejected could be that the line numbers are too far off or that the lines cannot be matched exactly. As a human, you can do more intelligent string matching and line searching than *patch* can do.

6. If you are going to give this patched kernel a special name reflecting its special capabilities, edit the top-level *Makefile*. If you're going to build an SMP kernel, for example, you can add that as follows. If you're simply applying a kernel patch, the patch updates the SUBLEVEL itself.

```
VERSION = 2
PATCHLEVEL = 4
SUBLEVEL = 24
EXTRAVERSION = -SMP
```

Note that the directory the modules will be installed in will be named */lib/modules/2.4.24-SMP* and that the *System.map* file must be called */boot/System.map-2.4.24-SMP* after this. The *uname -r* will also show the version to be 2.4.24-SMP.

7. Update the kernel configuration. The easiest way is to run *make oldconfig*, which will reapply the configuration already in the source tree and ask you about any new kernel options. If you prefer, you can instead use your favorite of the *config*, *menuconfig* or *xconfig* methods.

8. Now build and install the kernel through the *make* commands discussed earlier.

Removing a Patch

You should not ordinarily need to remove a patch, because you should have backups of your kernel source without the patches you apply. But sometimes the kernel sources just take too much space, and sometimes you have worked, say, three different patches into the kernel and then want to reverse just one. Removing the 2.4.24 patch applied earlier is a simple matter of running patch in reverse with *-R* as shown in the following listing:

```
# bzip2 -dc ../patch-2.4.24.bz2 | patch -p1 -R
patching file Makefile
patching file arch/cris/drivers/ds1302.c
patching file arch/cris/drivers/pcf8563.c
patching file arch/m68k/bvme6000/rtc.c
...
```

When reversing a patch, you may also get rejects, so check for them and resolve them. It is also worth mentioning that *patch* understands enough of what it does that it may well deduce that you meant to use *-R*, as shown in the following command:

```
# bzip2 -dc ../patch-2.4.24.bz2 | patch -p1
patching file MakefileReversed (or previously applied) patch detected!
Assume -R? [n]
```

In that case, if you know that patch is right, just answer y. If you ever get this message while *applying* a patch, you should take a look at the patch before answering either way. It may be that the patch producer reversed the order of the old and new files on his command line and produced a reversed patch. It may also be that the patch includes a patch you have already applied. Then it will look as if the patch is reversed because patch material is already present in your sources. But the patch is *not* reversed, it only has redundant parts that will fail to apply. It is usually very easy to see if a patch is reversed. If you look at the first few lines of the following patch, they should give clues:

```
Index: linux-2.4.23/arch/alpha/defconfig
=====================================================================
--- linux-2.4.23.orig/arch/alpha/defconfig      2003-12-15 15:06:57.
853807752 +0
100
+++ linux-2.4.23/arch/alpha/defconfig   2003-12-15 15:06:58.497669693 +0100
@@ -1,6 +1,9 @@
 #
```

The first filename given, marked ---, has a path that contains .orig, a good clue that this is the original source file. The second line, marked +++, has nothing specific in its path and thus seems likely to be the modified tree. The old file is supposed to be first and the modified second, so this patch is probably not reversed.

Objective 4: Customizing a Kernel

You can apply oodles of different customizations to your kernel. The simplest customization is, of course, to just tweak options in one of the configuration interfaces. Beyond the ordinary kernel maintenance patches, there are many third-party patches. Some of these are written by the main kernel hackers and some by others around the world. Some of the most popular patches relate to performance and security enhancements. Here, we'll discuss the Access Control List (ACL) patches as an advanced example.

If you need very detailed access permissions on files and/or directories, the ACL patches may meet your requirements. There are patches for this at *http://acl.best-bits.at*. This site documents a number of different things that you need to sort through and relate to. Select which patches you need, find out which user space packages or patches you need to support the extensions, and download the needed files.

ea-version.diff.gz
　　Patch for extended attributes

acl-version.diff.gz
　　Patch for access control lists

The ACL patch is a bit more far-reaching that your ordinary kernel patch. For ACLs to work properly, all filesystem utilities such as *cp* and *mv*, and a whole lot of other commands need to know about ACLs and be able to manipulate them as well as the files. We will not go into that in this book, but briefly, the process combines software compilation (discussed in Chapter 4) and patching as illustrated earlier.

In an environment that requires high uptimes, your smartest move may be to test patches on noncritical machines for quite some time before you apply them to critical equipment. You should also be careful about how much you mix and match patches and kernels. The procedure is as follows:

1. Apply the patches:

```
# cd /usr/src/linux
# zcat ea-"version".diff.gz | patch -p1
# zcat acl-"version".diff.gz | patch -p1
```

2. Edit your *.config* file to look like this:

```
CONFIG_FS_POSIX_ACL=y
CONFIG_EXT3_FS_XATTR=y
CONFIG_EXT3_FS_XATTR_SHARING=y
CONFIG_EXT3_FS_XATTR_USER=y
CONFIG_EXT3_FS_POSIX_ACL=y
CONFIG_EXT2_FS_XATTR=y
CONFIG_EXT2_FS_XATTR_SHARING=y
CONFIG_EXT2_FS_XATTR_USER=y
CONFIG_EXT2_FS_POSIX_ACL=y
```

Alternatively, use *make config* or one of its alternatives to set up the kernel.

3. Proceed with kernel compilation and installation.

After a reboot, the system will be ready to deal with extended file attributes and access control lists.

26

System Startup

This Topic focuses on the system boot processes and recovery procedures. LPI's Level 1 Objectives covered general booting material such as *runlevels*, the *init* utility, and how the system boots. At Level 2, LPICs are expected to be able to customize a system's startup procedures and recover a system when it is not booting properly.

This Topic contains two Objectives:

Objective 1: Customizing System Startup and Boot Processes
  Candidates should be able to edit appropriate system startup scripts to customize standard system runlevels and boot processes. This Objective includes interacting with runlevels and creating custom initrd images as needed. Weight: 2.

Objective 2: System Recovery
  Candidates should be able to properly manipulate a Linux system both during the boot process and during recovery mode. This objective includes using both the *init* utility and *init=* kernel options. Weight: 3.

Objective 1: Customizing System Startup and Boot Processes

In Chapter 14, we discussed boot procedures for a Linux system. Specifically, we covered boot-time kernel parameters, boot initialization scripts, and how to change system runlevels. The 201 exam takes this subject a step further and addresses how to customize your system's startup procedures.

When the kernel has mounted the root filesystem, it executes */sbin/init*. This program's first task is to read */etc/inittab*, which defines everything done thereafter.

/etc/inittab

The */etc/inittab* file describes what processes are started at boot time and during normal operation. This file is well-documented. For the examples in this section, we'll use a typical *inittab* file from a Red Hat system. After some initial comments, the file might contain:

```
# Default runlevel. The runlevels used by RHS are:
#   0 - halt (Do NOT set initdefault to this)
#   1 - Single user mode
#   2 - Multiuser, without NFS (The same as 3, with no  networking)
#   3 - Full multiuser mode
#   4 - unused
#   5 - X11
#   6 - reboot (Do NOT set initdefault to this)
#
id:3:initdefault:
```

The comments explain when the various runlevels are used on this machine. The first noncomment line is the one tagged id:, which defines the default runlevel for this system. As explained in the listing, this is multiuser mode with no X Window System. On a Debian system, the default runlevel is 2. Debian specifies only that 2–5 are multiuser. In virtually all distributions, runlevel 0 is used to halt the system, 1 to run it in single-user mode, and 6 to reboot.

After your system is booted into a particular runlevel, you can change to another runlevel using the *init* or *telinit* commands. By issuing *init 6* at the root prompt, you can command the system to reboot. Issuing *init 1* commands the system to boot into single-user mode. These commands can be issued only by root.

The *inittab* file continues:

```
# System initialization.
si::sysinit:/etc/rc.d/rc.sysinit

l0:0:wait:/etc/rc.d/rc 0
l1:1:wait:/etc/rc.d/rc 1
l2:2:wait:/etc/rc.d/rc 2
l3:3:wait:/etc/rc.d/rc 3
l4:4:wait:/etc/rc.d/rc 4
l5:5:wait:/etc/rc.d/rc 5
l6:6:wait:/etc/rc.d/rc 6
```

The si line defines that the script */etc/rc.d/rc.sysinit* is to run first (because there are no other lines before it). It is run on all runlevels, because the second parameter on the line is empty (::). Debian also uses the *sysinit* script, but runs */etc/init. d/rcS* instead. This in turn runs the contents of the */etc/rcs.d* directory and then the */etc/rc.boot* directory. Red Hat's script is monolithic.

The six lines following, labeled l0 through l6, execute the */etc/rc.d/rc* script with an argument corresponding to the runlevel. This script runs the contents of the corresponding */etc/rcrunlevel.d* directory as explained in Chapter 14.

The next section sets specific commands and options. In particular, it maps the Ctrl+Alt+Delete key sequence, which automatically reboots the system. You can disable or change that option here. This section also has some options regarding SmartUPS settings. If the system is connected to a UPS with serial feedback that instructs the system when the UPS will run out of power, the system can automatically shut itself down with this entry. Debian systems have one additional action here for powerfailnow.

```
# Trap CTRL-ALT-DELETE
ca::ctrlaltdel:/sbin/shutdown -t3 -r now

# When our UPS tells us power has failed, assume we have a few
# minutes of power left.  Schedule a shutdown for 2 minutes from
# now. This does, of course, assume you have power installed and
# your UPS connected and working correctly.
pf::powerfail:/sbin/shutdown -f -h +2"Power Failure;System Shutting Down"

# If power was restored before the shutdown kicked in, cancel it.
pr:12345:powerokwait:/sbin/shutdown -c"Power Restored;Shutdown Cancelled"
```

The next section of the /etc/inittab file sets up your virtual consoles. The setup shown here is the default on Red Hat, and allows up to six virtual consoles. To add additional virtual consoles, duplicate the lines and then change the first field as well as the tty field to represent the appropriate number of your virtual console.

```
# Run gettys in standard runlevels
1:2345:respawn:/sbin/mingetty tty1
2:2345:respawn:/sbin/mingetty tty2
3:2345:respawn:/sbin/mingetty tty3
4:2345:respawn:/sbin/mingetty tty4
5:2345:respawn:/sbin/mingetty tty5
6:2345:respawn:/sbin/mingetty tty6
```

System Initialization Scripts

System initialization scripts, most of which are found under the /etc/init.d directory, are used to boot the system and start daemons and services. The scripts you are looking for are in /etc/rc0.d through /etc/rc6.d (runlevel directories), as well as the all-important initial script, which is named /etc/rc.d/rc.sysinit in Red Hat and /etc/init.d/rcS in Debian.

System initialization

On Debian, the /etc/init.d/rcS script is the first startup script. On Red Hat, the corresponding script is /etc/rc.d/rc.sysinit. They do a lot of chores that you might never have thought were needed and are an education to read. Because the Red Hat script is monolithic (indeed, currently more than 800 lines), it is perhaps easiest to read.

One of the most important tasks the script performs is to check all the local filesystems. If a problem is found, the script drops into a *sulogin* shell to let the administrator intervene and fix the problem. For some kinds of filesystem problems, the machine is now rebooted.

If there is a *quota* executable and quotas are configured, the *rc.sysinit* script enables the quotas. The following are some excerpts from the Red Hat *rc.sysinit* script. The excerpts include the information related to filesystem checking and quotas. If you have a Red Hat system, take a glance at your */etc/rc.sysinit* file for a complete tour.

```
# Start up swapping.  action "Activating swap partitions"
swapon -a -e

# Check filesystems
if [ -z "$fastboot" ]; then
        STRING=$"Checking filesystems"
        echo $STRING
        initlog -c "fsck -T -R -A -a $fsckoptions"
        rc=$?
        if [ "$rc" = "0" ]; then
                success "$STRING"
                echo
        elif [ "$rc" = "1" ]; then
                passed "$STRING"
                echo
        fi

        # A return of 2 or higher means there were serious problems.
        if [ $rc -gt 1 ]; then
                if [ "$BOOTUP" = "graphical" ]; then
                    chvt 1
                fi

                failure "$STRING"
                echo
                echo
                echo $"*** An error occurred during the file system check."
                echo $"*** Dropping you to a shell; the system will reboot"
                echo $"*** when you leave the shell."

                str=$"(Repair filesystem)"
                PS1="$str \# # "; export PS1
                sulogin

                echo $"Unmounting file systems"
                umount -a
                mount -n -o remount,ro /
                echo $"Automatic reboot in progress."
                reboot -f
        elif [ "$rc" = "1" -a -x /sbin/quotacheck ]; then
                _RUN_QUOTACHECK=1
        fi
fi

# Mount all other filesystems (except for NFS and /proc, which is already
# mounted). Contrary to standard usage,
# filesystems are NOT unmounted in single user mode.
```

```
action $"Mounting local filesystems: " mount -a -t nonfs,smbfs,ncpfs -O no_
netdev

# check remaining quotas other than root
if [ X"$_RUN_QUOTACHECK" = X1 -a -x /sbin/quotacheck ]; then
        if [ -x /sbin/convertquota ]; then
            # try to convert old quotas
            for mountpt in `awk '$4 ~ /quota/{print $2}' /etc/mtab` ; do
                if [ -f "$mountpt/quota.user" ]; then
                    action $"Converting old user quota files: " \
                    /sbin/convertquota -u $mountpt && \
                        rm -f $mountpt/quota.user
                fi
                if [ -f "$mountpt/quota.group" ]; then
                    action $"Converting old group quota files: " \
                    /sbin/convertquota -g $mountpt && \
                        rm -f $mountpt/quota.group
                fi
            done
        fi
        action $"Checking local filesystem quotas: " /sbin/quotacheck -aRnug
fi

if [ -x /sbin/quotaon ]; then
    action $"Enabling local filesystem quotas: " /sbin/quotaon -aug
fi

# Configure machine if necessary.
if [ -f /.unconfigured ]; then
    if [ "$BOOTUP" = "graphical" ]; then
        chvt 1
    fi

    if [ -x /usr/bin/passwd ]; then
        /usr/bin/passwd root
    fi
    if [ -x /usr/sbin/netconfig ]; then
        /usr/sbin/netconfig
    fi
    if [ -x /usr/sbin/timeconfig ]; then
        /usr/sbin/timeconfig
    fi
    if [ -x /usr/sbin/kbdconfig ]; then
        /usr/sbin/kbdconfig
    fi
    if [ -x /usr/sbin/authconfig ]; then
        /usr/sbin/authconfig --nostart
fi
    if [ -x /usr/sbin/ntsysv ]; then
        /usr/sbin/ntsysv --level 35
    fi

    # Reread in network configuration data.
    if [ -f /etc/sysconfig/network ]; then
        . /etc/sysconfig/network
```

```
            # Reset the hostname.
            action $"Resetting hostname ${HOSTNAME}: " hostname ${HOSTNAME}
    fi

    rm -f /.unconfigured
fi

# Clean out /.
rm -f /fastboot /fsckoptions /forcefsck /.autofsck /halt /poweroff
```

One weakness of the single-user runlevel is that, as you can see from the lines just quoted, all the filesystems are mounted and the operating system itself is almost completely initialized. If you're experiencing bad filesystem or hardware problems, this script may never complete. The only way to avoid this problem is to not run init when booting. This is dealt with in more detail in "Objective 2: System Recovery" later in this chapter.

Runlevel directories

The system run-level directories on Red Hat are named *etc/rc0.d* through *etc/rc6.d*. These directories don't actually contain real files or scripts. Instead, they contain links to scripts that are located in the *etc/init.d* directory.

 Due to some silly antics during an earlier release, Red Hat still stores the *rc* scripts in */etc/rc.d/init.d* and */etc/rc.d/rcn.d*. But now at least the system provides symbolic links from the more standard paths of */etc/init.d* and */etc/rcn.d*.

The links in the *rcn.d* directories run through after the system has completed the system initialization script. Each directory contains symbolic links to real scripts. Here is a list of some of the files in a typical */etc/rc0.d* directory:

```
lrwxrwxrwx 1 root root 14 Dec 10 10:27 K00cups -> ../init.d/cups*
lrwxrwxrwx 1 root root 18 Dec 23 01:07 K05keytable -> ../init.d /keytable*
lrwxrwxrwx 1 root root 16 Sep 17  2001 K08autofs -> ../init.d/autofs*
lrwxrwxrwx 1 root root 16 Dec 23 00:59 K10psacct -> ../init.d/psacct*
lrwxrwxrwx 1 root root 14 Aug 29  2002 K10wine -> ../init.d/wine*
lrwxrwxrwx 1 root root 13 Sep 17  2001 K10xfs -> ../init.d/xfs*
lrwxrwxrwx 1 root root 16 Sep 17  2001 K12mysqld -> ../init.d/mysqld*
lrwxrwxrwx 1 root root 13 Sep 17  2001 K15gpm -> ../init.d/gpm*
lrwxrwxrwx 1 root root 15 Dec 23 01:03 K15httpd -> ../init.d/httpd*
lrwxrwxrwx 1 root root 15 Sep 17  2001 K15sound -> ../init.d/sound*
```

Every symbolic link in each of the *rcn.d* directories is named with an initial S or K. S indicates that the service is to be started; K indicates that it should be stopped. Following the S or K is a two-digit number that indicates the order in which the scripts are to be run. For example, 10 gets run before 15. In the *rc0.d* directory just shown, for instance, CUPS starts first and sound support starts last.

Customizing Runlevels

As you can see, quite a lot of a system's behavior is determined through what is in the system startup scripts.

Whenever you add a service to your system, a script should be deposited in */etc/init.d* and links to it from the right runlevel directories should be made. In Red Hat and some other distributions, the *chkconfig* is used for this. On Debian and many others, you can use *update-rc.d*. Once a script to start and stop services is in */etc/init.d*, symbolic links to it can be made in the individual runlevel directories, so that the script runs at the proper runlevels.

Customizing runlevels on Red Hat

As said in the previous section, Red Hat and some related distributions use the helper utility chkconfig to make this easy.

chkconfig

Syntax

```
chkconfig --list [service]
chkconfig --add service
chkconfig --del service
chkconfig [--level levels] service [on|off|reset]
```

Description

chkconfig lets you very simply make the appropriate entries in the appropriate runlevel directories or remove them. Thereby it enables or disables the startup of the service during system boot.

Frequently used options

chkconfig --list [service]
> If no service is given, list the status of all services. If the name of a service is given, only that service is shown.

chkconfig --add service
> Add a new service rc file to the */etc/init.d* directory, then initialize all the right runlevels with links to the service rc script. After this, the service will be started when booting.

chkconfig --del service

chkconfig service off
> Disable the startup of the service during boot. Note that this does not stop a running service. To do that, invoke /etc/init.d/servicestop.

chkconfig service on
> Enable starting the service during boot. Note that this does not start the service *now*. To start it now, run /etc/init.d/servicestart.

Examples

Add a service called foo and manipulate it.

```
# chkconfig --add foo
# chkconfig --list foo
foo              0:off   1:off   2:on    3:on    4:on    5:on    6:off#
chkconfig foo off
# chkconfig --list foo
foo              0:off   1:off   2:off   3:off   4:off   5:off   6:off
```

Runlevel files

chkconfig can manipulate only *rc* files that have the correct comment lines. Two lines are needed:

```
# chkconfig: 345 99 01
# description: Starts the foo service to contribute toward world foo-ness
```

The chkconfig: line has three parameters: the runlevels the service should run at and the sequence numbers the S and K files should have. When a service is started last, it should be stopped first; that is why the start sequence number in the previous example is 99 and the stop sequence number is 01. The description is for human consumption. You will find other such labels used in some of these scripts. They are not documented.

Customizing runlevels on Debian

Debian and a number of other distributions use the script update-rc.d to manipulate the runlevels.

---

update-rc.d

Syntax

```
update-rc.d [-n] [-f] service remove
update-rc.d [-n] service defaults [nn | nn-start nn-stop]
update-rc.d [-n] service start|stop nn runlevel runlevel ...
                        [ start|stop nn runlevel runlevel ...]
```

Description

update-rc.d is used to manage init script links. Once a service *rc* script is present in */etc/init.d*, it can be manipulated by this command. The command enables or disables the startup of the service during system boot.

Frequently used options

update-rc.dz *service* defaults *nn*

> Adds the service to the startup of all runlevels at sequence number *nn*.

update-rc.d *service*start *nn* 2 3 4 5 . stop *mm* 2 3 4 5 .

> Adds start links with sequence number *nn* at runlevels 2 through 5 and stop links with sequence number *mm* at the same runlevels. Note the important use of a period (.) in this command; it's required when you want to make multiple settings in a single command line.

update-rc.d -f *service* remove

> Remove the service from the startup of any runlevels it is present in. The *-f* option is needed if the service script is present in */etc/init.d*. If it is not present, the *-f* can be left out.

Examples

```
# update-rc.d foo defaults 99
 Adding system startup for /etc/init.d/foo ...
   /etc/rc0.d/K99foo -> ../init.d/foo
   /etc/rc1.d/K99foo -> ../init.d/foo
   /etc/rc6.d/K99foo -> ../init.d/foo
   /etc/rc2.d/S99foo -> ../init.d/foo
   /etc/rc3.d/S99foo -> ../init.d/foo
   /etc/rc4.d/S99foo -> ../init.d/foo
   /etc/rc5.d/S99foo -> ../init.d/foo
# update-rc.d -f foo remove
update-rc.d: /etc/init.d/foo exists during rc.d purge (continuing)
 Removing any system startup links for /etc/init.d/foo ...
   /etc/rc0.d/K99foo
   /etc/rc1.d/K99foo
   /etc/rc2.d/S99foo
   /etc/rc3.d/S99foo
   /etc/rc4.d/S99foo
   /etc/rc5.d/S99foo
   /etc/rc6.d/K99foo
# update-rc.d foo stop 99 0 1 6 . start 99 2 3 4 5 .
 Adding system startup for /etc/init.d/foo ...
   /etc/rc2.d/K01foo -> ../init.d/foo
   /etc/rc3.d/K01foo -> ../init.d/foo
   /etc/rc4.d/K01foo -> ../init.d/foo
   /etc/rc5.d/K01foo -> ../init.d/foo
   /etc/rc2.d/S99foo -> ../init.d/foo
   /etc/rc3.d/S99foo -> ../init.d/foo
   /etc/rc4.d/S99foo -> ../init.d/foo
   /etc/rc5.d/S99foo -> ../init.d/foo
```

The first command shown is almost certainly not what you want. Also note that the policy in Debian is to enter start scripts at all runlevels where a service is to run and to add stop scripts at all other levels, but with the same sequence number. Thus, the list of runlevels for the stop and start links shown in the third command are complementary.

Customizing initrd Images

Chapter 25 discussed how to generate initrd images to enable booting all sorts of hardware with a skinny kernel that contains next to no hardware support. The initrd is not just a ram disk containing some modules, but a standalone root file-system. The modules in it are loaded by a script or executable on the disk. If they are loaded by a script, it must have an interpreter. The following documentation of the initrd boot process is found in *Documentation/initrd.txt* in any kernel source tree. We won't include a customization example here, but we'll attempt to explain how initrd boots and what the environments look like on Red Hat and Debian.

1. The boot loader loads the kernel and the initrd.

2. The kernel converts initrd into a "normal" RAM disk and frees the memory used by initrd.

3. The initrd is mounted read/write as root.

4. The /linuxrc file is executed. This file can be any valid executable, including shell scripts; it is run with UID 0 and can do basically everything init can do.

5. /linuxrc mounts the real root filesystem.

6. /linuxrc places the root filesystem at the root directory using the *pivot_root* command.

7. The usual boot sequence (the invocation of /sbin/init) is performed on the root filesystem.

8. The initrd filesystem is removed.

By studying your distribution's *mkinitrd* script, you can see how the /linuxrc script works and how you can customize it. Additionally, the documentation present in *Documentation/initrd.txt* is very detailed and extensive. Your most likely reasons to customize an initrd in this way are to support something that is too new to be supported by the *mkinitrd* script or to construct a universal rescue floppy that autodetects the root filesystem and other interesting things on the computer it boots on.

As you can see from the list of steps just enumerated, the key filename in the boot process is /linuxrc. If you take a copy of the *mkinitrd* script to customize and look in it for /linuxrc, you will be able to deduce how the bootstrap works. In both Debian and Red Hat, /linuxrc is a script.

initrd and /linuxrc on Debian

In Debian, the /linuxrc script interpreter is either *dash* or, more likely, *ash*. As you can see in the manpage for the interpreter, it offers a pretty complete set of built-in commands. (It is not, however, the standard command interpreter for the system, as the manpage claims—that honor goes to *bash*.) And in the *mkinitrd* script, you will find which other external commands are available. When /linuxrc starts, it reads configuration data from /linuxrc.conf, which was written by mkinitrd. And then the Debian people have thrown in a twist. The /linuxrc file does not execute *pivot_root* as it should. Instead, when the kernel sees that /linuxrc has terminated, it executes /sbin/init, which is the script that does the real work. One of the things it does is to execute the contents of the /scripts directory in shell sorting order. After that, the real root filesystem is mounted, *pivot_root* is executed, and the real *init* command is executed.

The supported way to modify this process is to put your scripts into /etc/mkinitrd/ scripts. They will then be executed in order. This solution requires no changes in the system tools. The alternatives are to change the template /linuxrc, the /sbin/init script it installs, or the /linuxrc.conf file. All these options are fairly straightforward, as long as you recall your limited range of commands until the root filesystem is mounted.

Debian offers the following external commands in addition to the regular shell built-ins listed in the *ash* manpage:

/sbin/init
  The special Debian initrd version of *init*, from the *initrd-tools* package

/sbin/modprobe
  The familiar *modprobe* command

/sbin/insmod
  The familiar *insmod* command

/bin/echo
  The familiar *echo* command

/bin/mount
  The familiar *mount* command

/bin/umount
  The familiar *umount* command

/bin/pivot_root
  The magical command that rotates away the initrd root filesystem and replaces it with the real one

/bin/cat
  The familiar *cat* command

/bin/mknod
  The familiar *mknod* command

/usr/sbin/chroot
  The familiar *chroot* command

In addition, there is a custom-built */dev* directory that matches your hardware pretty well. To support the executables, */lib* and */usr/lib* are filled with shared libraries. */lib/modules* contains a complement of kernel modules that fits your setup. Altogether, Debian offers a pretty rich starting point.

initrd and /linuxrc on Red Hat

Red Hat generates the */linuxrc* file dynamically, line by line. Customizing it thus becomes a question of generating the lines you need in the place you need. In the Red Hat initrd environment, customization is probably not as easy as in Debian. Few tools are provided. The shell used by Red Hat is */bin/nash*, which is linked statically. It has the commands needed in an initrd environment built in, but it has very little in the way of general shell syntax. Therefore, the filesystem contains practically nothing to support it; just the following files:

/bin/insmod
  A statically linked version of *insmod*.

/bin/modprobe
  Actually a symbolic link to nash, which exits without doing anything when started as *modprobe*.

/bin/vgchange

The *vg** commands are installed only if you use LVM. These help support for an LVM root disk.

/bin/vgscan

See previous entry.

/bin/vgwrapper

See previous entry.

/dev and */lib/modules* have contents suitable for your setup. Red Hat does not need a real modprobe because the *mkinitrd* script analyzes the module dependencies at build time and makes sure that they are loaded in the correct order. Altogether this environment is very sparse. To customize the Red Hat initrd could turn out to be a great deal of work. But it does support booting off LVM-managed USB disks.

Objective 2: System Recovery

Unfortunately, things don't always go well when working on a system. The most frequent system recovery happens automatically. Filesystems are fixed when booting, and while it takes some time, it's fully automatic most of the time. All other problems are infrequent.

One occasional problem is that one of the runlevel scripts cannot complete and causes the whole boot sequence to halt. This is easy to fix: just boot in single-user mode as described in Chapter 14, and edit the script. A harder problem is if the system initialization script or init somehow fails and foils the boot. Coping with this is described later in "init or the System Initialization Fails."

Filesystem Damage

Sometimes a filesystem is damaged in a way that the boot process does not want to fix automatically; in this case, it drops into a root password prompt with a display like the following (this is from Red Hat):

```
*** An error occurred during the file system check."
*** Dropping you to a shell; the system will reboot"
*** when you leave the shell."

Give root password for maintenance(or type Control-D for normal startup):
password
(Repair filesystem) 1 #
```

After entering the password, you can fix the filesystem manually. Fixing a filesystem manually requires running fsck *device*. Answer y to all the questions. Answering anything but y to all the questions requires quite some knowledge of how your filesystem works. Very few have such knowledge, and so the questions are cunningly posed in such a manner that answering y to all of them is the safest option. It may seem a bit silly to force you to answer y so many times, but at least it forces you to notice a bad error condition and enables you to follow the boot process after the repair is done.

init or the System Initialization Fails

If there is a failure during *init*, the system initialization script (*/etc/rc.sysinit* or */etc/init.d/rcS*, as the case may be) or a script that is executed as part of the single-user runlevel, the machine will fail to reach even single-user mode. You must take unusual measures to put your system in a state where you can fix it.

Bypassing init

The first step is to try to bypass *init*. In your boot loader, GRUB or LILO, you must enter the parameter init=/bin/bash or another interpreter. Instead of executing */sbin/init* to perform system initialization, *bash* will be started and it is then your job to initialize the system. This enables you to correct error conditions, debug scripts, or even get the machine networked and to fetch files or perform backups.

After the kernel is done initializing, you will pretty quickly be dropped into a root shell with a regular root prompt (#). You do not not have any virtual consoles now, nor any mouse support or cut-and-paste. Furthermore, you do not have a real tty or job control (and *bash* may complain about those things). Because you don't have a tty, some software will refuse to work. The lack of job control is very important, because interrupting with Ctrl-C and Ctrl-Z does not work. If you start a command that for some reason does not terminate, you will not be able to terminate it yourself; all you can do is reboot the system and make sure not to repeat the mistake (which could be as simple as trying to ping another system— the *ping* by default does not stop). All in all, the environment is quite hard to use.

Commands that may not complete should be started in the background by ending the command in & (ampersand). But this does not work well for interactive programs, because they will not be able to read input.

Working in the shell environment

The first thing to do when you have the prompt, if you are sure the root filesystem is sound, is to mount it read/write. If you are uncertain of its soundness, you should run *fsck -f /* on it first. The command to mount it is *mount -o remount,rw /*. If your */etc/fstab* file is damaged, you may have to add the device name: *fsck -f device* and *mount -o remount,rwdevice*.

Once your root filesystem is mounted, you can do almost whatever you want to troubleshoot and fix your system. Most things, however, will involve software from */usr* and files in */var* and */tmp*. Additionally, */proc* usually gets into the picture pretty quickly. All of these can be mounted with a simple *mount -av*, if your *fstab* is intact. You may want to *fsck* everything first, through *fsck -A -a*.

A lot of work will involve looking at and editing files. The software to do this invariably resides in */usr*, and if your */usr* is unavailable you need to get creative. Both *cat* and *dd* are in */bin*. *cat* can be used to list entire files, and the Linux console can be paged up and down with the key combinations Shift-Page up and Shift-Page down. *dd* with parameters *skip=n* and *count=m* can be used to read a file starting at the *n*th block for *m* blocks. When all is lost, the *cat* command is your hardcore editor. You can use *cat >/etc/fstab* to rewrite your *fstab* file. But if your system is this damaged, it may be easier to use a rescue CD, as discussed later in this chapter.

Your general tactic should be to try to find the (hopefully) single problem that stops your boot from working smoothly. You can run each of the scripts of the startup process by hand and watch them work, and note any errors without risking them scrolling beyond the top of your screen. Once you get the system initialization script and the scripts in *etc/rc1.d* working, you can do a single-user boot. In a single-user environment you will regain virtual consoles and job control; it will be much more comfortable to work in.

Once in single-user mode, if there are more problems, you can again run each single script in the default runlevel directory *etc/rcn.d* in the correct sequence. If the scripts appear to work one by one, you can stop them again and use init*n* to get init to run the runlevel scripts in the ordinary manner. The init command is discussed extensively in Chapter 14.

Booting from a Rescue CD

It is particularly hard to restore your system to working order if your disk bootstrap is damaged or if your system has serious damage—in particular, a very damaged root filesystem in which files in *etc* are corrupted or lost (*etc/fstab* and *etc/inittab* are particularly important to booting). The best solution then is a rescue disk or your distribution's boot disks.

Using your distribution's installation or rescue CDs to boot can be immensely helpful. Red Hat's installation CD has a distinct rescue boot mode. Both the Debian and Red Hat CD installation procedures fork a shell on a virtual console, so that when the first dialog appears on the main screen you can switch virtual consoles and find a root shell on one of them. Both CD environments are complete enough that you can do a good deal of troubleshooting. If you need a more complete environment, there are many dedicated rescue disks on the Internet that provide everything but the kitchen sink.

Restoring the bootstrap

There is a fairly simple workaround for damage to your disk bootstrap program, GRUB or LILO. Mount the root filesystem and then reinstall the boot loader. You can easily reinstall your bootstrap as described in Chapter 4 without any exotic options.

The following command sequence assumes that */dev/hda* is your boot disk and that */mnt* is where you mounted your root filesystem. Some boot and rescue disks use */mnt* for their own purposes. By the way, if your bootstrap program is damaged, did you put something bad in the configuration file? Perhaps you should review it.

```
# chroot /mnt /bin/bash# mount /boot# lilo -v
    or
# grub-install /dev/hda
```

Exploring the damaged system

The *chroot* command in the previous example is also useful for doing other things to explore your damaged disks. Such exploration is easier if you have a correct *mtab* file. On a lot of rescue environments, */etc/mtab* is linked to */proc/mounts*. In any case, the *mtab* file is usually correct in the rescue environment. Not so in the chroot environment. If you do the following, your *mtab* will be correct and a lot of important commands such as *df* will work right. *mount -a* can mount all your disks into the chroot environment. This is a good thing, because sometimes the problem that stops you from booting normally turns out to be a disk chock full of stuff; it needs a good cleaning before you can boot.

```
# chroot /mnt /bin/bash
# mount /proc
# cat /proc/mounts /etc/mtab
# fsck -A -a# mount -av
...
# df -k
...
```

Loss of key files

There are some things you can't recover from without doing some sort of reinstallation. Among these are missing binaries and shared libraries. A good many of the files in */etc* can easily be copied from other machines or written by hand. Booting a rescue CD, going into the chroot environment, and getting the network up by running the network initialization script are quite easy. You can then use a file copy command such as *ftp* or *scp*, or even a package update command such as *apt-get*, to copy the needed files from another machine or an FTP site. If the system is too badly damaged, it will be hard or impossible to execute programs on it. For such as a situation, both *dpkg* and *rpm* support options (*--root=/mnt* and *--root /mnt*, respectively) that let you install packages without doing the chroot first. But the easiest recovery solution is perhaps to make a tarfile of the damaged files from a similar healthy machine and get them onto the patient by FTP, floppy, USB memory stick, or some other mechanism and then untar the tarfile on top of the damaged filesystem.

Rescue initrd

Considering the usefulness of rescue disks for some kinds of system recovery scenarios and the completeness of Debian's initrd environment, it's not that far-fetched to imagine a rescue initrd. In fact, in Debian it's as simple as setting DELAY in */etc/mkinitrd/mkinitrd.conf* to a nonzero value and pressing the Enter key when booting at the Waiting for $DELAY seconds, press ENTER to obtain a shell prompt. The boot process will drop you into *ash* with the full Debian environment described earlier at your disposal. This is a bit harder to do in Red Hat.

The exam won't ask about this.

27

Filesystem

This Topic has significant overlap with Chapter 6, which covered LPIC Level 1 Topic 104, Devices, Linux Filesystems, and the File Hierarchy Standard. For that reason, this section will reiterate some content regarding filesystem management, such as creating, mounting, and maintaining filesystems. While an LPIC-1 is expected to be proficient at each of these tasks in isolation, an LPIC-2 must be able to utilize these skills in a production environment, streamlining filesystem tasks and maintaining live productive server environments.

This Topic contains three Objectives:

Objective 1: Operating the Linux Filesystem
Candidates should be able to properly configure and navigate the standard Linux filesystem. This Objective includes configuring and mounting various filesystem types. Also included is manipulating filesystems to adjust for disk space requirements or device additions. Weight: 3.

Objective 2: Maintaining a Linux Filesystem
Candidates should be able to properly maintain a Linux filesystem using system utilities. This objective includes manipulating a standard *ext2* filesystem. Weight: 4.

Objective 3: Creating and Configuring Filesystem Options
Candidates should be able to configure the automounting of filesystems. This Objective includes configuring automount for network and device filesystems. Also included is creating non-ext2 filesystems for devices such as CD-ROMs. Weight: 3.

Objective 1: Operating the Linux Filesystem

If you've been through the Level 1 program already (or simply are already familiar with the first parts of this book), you should understand the basics behind operating your Linux filesystem pretty well. The first of the following subsections reviews some utilities covered in Level 1 Topic 104.

Part of life is planning for, setting up, and living with things for some period of time, while being ready (when requirements change) to cope and alter the setup to fit the new situation without destroying what you already have. Working as a senior Linux administrator, you will likely be responsible for a number of production servers or at the very least some company's very important production server. For that reason, you don't have much room for trial and error; you need to know how things should be and what needs to be changed without fiddling around for days. The Level 2 Exams will expect you to be able to create filesystems on production servers, add swap partitions as needed, protect filesystem data integrity, and deal with changing demands.

Level 1 Review

You've covered the bases on *mount* and *umount* as well as the */etc/fstab* file in Chapter 6, but if you're a little rusty, here's a recap.

mount

Syntax

```
mount [options] device
mount [options] directory
mount [options] device directory
```

Description

Used to mount filesystems onto the filesystem hierarchy. The first and second forms consult */etc/fstab* and mount the filesystem located on *device* or attached to *directory*, respectively. The third form ignores */etc/fstab* and mounts the filesystem on *device* at mount point *directory*.

Command-line options

-*a*
> Mount all of the partitions specified in */etc/fstab*, except those with the noauto option.

-*h*
> Display help on the *mount* command.

-*o*mount_options
> Specify mount options on the command line. The following list applies to any filesystem:

async
> All I/O to the filesystem should be done asynchronously.

atime
> Update inode access time for each access. This is the default.

auto
> Can be mounted with the -*a* option.

defaults
> Use default options: rw, suid, dev, exec, auto, nouser, and async.

noatime

Do not update inode access times on this filesystem. This option might be useful, for instance, for faster access on the news spool to speed up news servers.

noauto

Can be mounted only explicitly (i.e., the *-a* option will not cause the filesystem to be mounted).

noexec

Do not allow execution of any binaries on the mounted filesystem. This option might be useful for a server that has file systems containing binaries for architectures other than its own.

nosuid

Do not allow set-user-identifier or set-group-identifier bits to take effect. Increases security.

remount

Attempt to remount an already-mounted file system. This is commonly used to change the mount flags for a file system, especially to make a read-only file system writable. It does not change device or mount point.

ro

Mount the file system read-only.

sync

All I/O to the file system should be done synchronously. All changes are physically written to the device at the time you issue the command. Recommended for removable devices.

user

Allow an ordinary user to mount the file system. The name of the mounting user is written to the *mtab* file so that she can unmount the file system again. This option implies the options noexec, nosuid, and nodev (unless overridden by subsequent options, as in the option line user, exec, dev, suid).

users

Allow every user to mount and unmount the file system. This option implies the options noexec, nosuid, and nodev (unless overridden by subsequent options, as in the option line users, exec, dev, suid).

-r

Mount the filesystem read-only.

-tfstype

Specify that the filesystem to be mounted is of type *fstype*. This option is typically used interactively, when no entry for the mount exists in */etc/fstab*.

-v

Set verbose mode.

-w

Mount the filesystem in read/write mode.

umount

Syntax

```
umount [options] device
umount [options] directory
```

Description

Unmount the filesystem on *device* or mounted on *directory*.

-a
> Unmounts all of the filesystems described in */etc/mtab*.

-t fstype
> Unmounts only filesystems of type *fstype*.

/etc/fstab

The */etc/fstab* is a plain text file and consists of lines with six fields:

- Device
- Mount point
- Filesystem type
- Mount options
- Dump frequency
- Pass number for *fsck*

Example 27-1 shows some of the items that are typically mounted.

Example 27-1. Sample /etc/fstab file

```
/dev/sda1     /            ext2    defaults         1 1
/dev/sda5     /boot        ext2    defaults         1 2
/dev/sda9     /home        ext2    defaults         1 2
/dev/sda6     /root        ext2    defaults         1 2
/dev/sda10    /tmp         ext2    defaults         1 2
/dev/sda8     /usr         ext2    defaults         1 2
/dev/sda7     /var         ext2    defaults         1 2
/dev/sda11    swap         swap    defaults         0 0
/dev/fd0      /mnt/floppy  ext2    noauto,users     0 0
/dev/hdc      /mnt/cdrom   iso9660 noauto,ro,users  0 0
/dev/hdd      /mnt/zip     vfat    noauto,users     0 0
fs1:/share    /fs1         nfs     defaults         0 0
```

Additional Filesystem Management Files

While */etc/fstab* is the most important file when it comes to manipulating your filesystems, two additional files are important too: */etc/mtab* and */proc/mounts*. These two files contain the same information, and */etc/mtab* could be dropped had it not been that Linux should work even if the */proc* filesystem is not present. Some distributions and live CDs (which let you boot a Linux system from a CD instead of installing it on your hard disk) do drop *mtab* and symbolically link it to */proc/mounts*.

The information these files contain is the list of filesystems mounted on the system. Sometimes, such as after a system crash, the *mtab* file won't be accurate, but the system initialization scripts assiduously rebuild it from scratch. The kernel maintains the *mounts* file, and it will be quite accurate, but perhaps not 100% helpful.

Examples 27-2 and 27-3 show the files' formats for a single system.

Example 27-2. /etc/mtab example

```
/dev/hda2 / ext3 rw 0 0
none /proc proc rw 0 0
usbdevfs /proc/bus/usb usbdevfs rw 0 0
/dev/hda1 /boot ext3 rw 0 0
/dev/hdb1 /home ext3 rw 0 0
none /dev/shm tmpfs rw 0 0
none /dev/pts devpts rw,gid=5,mode=620 0 0
automount(pid1017) /misc autofs rw,fd=5,pgrp=1017,minproto=2,maxproto=3 0 0
automount(pid1019) /homes autofs rw,fd=5,pgrp=1019,minproto=2,maxproto=3 0 0
none /proc/sys/fs/binfmt_misc binfmt_misc rw 0 0
```

Example 27-3. /proc/mounts example

```
rootfs / rootfs rw 0 0
/dev/root / ext3 rw 0 0
/proc /proc proc rw 0 0
usbdevfs /proc/bus/usb usbdevfs rw 0 0
/dev/hda1 /boot ext3 rw 0 0
/dev/hdb1 /home ext3 rw 0 0
none /dev/shm tmpfs rw 0 0
none /dev/pts devpts rw 0 0
automount(pid1017) /misc autofs rw 0 0
automount(pid1019) /homes autofs rw 0 0
none /proc/sys/fs/binfmt_misc binfmt_misc rw 0 0
```

If you compare these two examples, you'll see that the information for the root filesystem in *mounts* is generic and that there are two / filesystems mounted. *mtab*, in contrast, specifies the device. With regard to the oddities in the *mounts* file, if you recall the use of initrd scripts in Chapter 26, you should recognize that this is due to the use of initrd, which requires two root filesystems and assigns odd device names in the initrd environment.

Managing Swap

Setting up swap is usually done once in a machine's life, when Linux is installed. However, it may turn out that the applications you run require a lot more memory and a lot more swap to be able to run effectively, or at all. If so, you will need to have spare disk space, or new disks, and then add swap space as needed. After a new swap partition is created, issue *mkswap* to create a swap signature on it, which enables it for swap use. After that you should update */etc/fstab* appropriately, and if you don't wish to reboot, issue *swapon* to activate the partition. If for some reason you need to stop using a swap partition, *swapoff* can do it for you.

Unix has used advanced caching techniques to speed up filesystem operations for a long time. To ensure that the files on disk were updated, a process called *update* ran the *sync* command every 30 seconds. This would flush all cached writes to disk at once. Flushing everything every 30 seconds is quite crude, so at some time in the history of Linux this process was moved into the kernel and refined. The Linux program known as *update* got a new alias, *bdflush*. The 2.4 kernel carried out flushing through a pair of threads. *bdflush* looked for dirty buffers to write to disk. *kupdated* worked like the old *update* process, but flushed individual buffers instead of flushing all of them. In the 2.6 kernel, the functions are combined once again in a set of *pdflush* threads.

Data buffers are flushed 30 seconds after the kernel is done with them, and meta data buffers are flushed after 5 seconds. Some filesystems that have very strong data consistency requirements make sure their data is flushed according to a stricter schedule.

The *sync* command is still there, but you will very seldom need it. It will still flush all buffers at once, and on a active system with a lot of memory it can take a while to complete. If your disks are set up right, the system will be far from frozen, so only the *sync* command will hang.

Since it takes up to 30 seconds to flush things, it is always a good idea to either wait 30 seconds after all activity has ceased before you reboot a system or to call *sync*. You will still see old Unix hands do a repeated *sync; sync; sync; reboot* just to make sure everything is on disk before the reboot commences.

mkswap

Syntax

```
mkswap [-c] [-vn] [-f] device [ size ]
```

Description

Create a Linux swap area on a device, such as a hard drive, or in a file. The *device* is usually a disk partition but can also be a file. You can also specify *size*, but it's not recommended. When size is omitted, *mkswap* simply uses the entire partition or file specified.

Frequently Used Options

-c

Check the device for bad blocks before creating the swap area. This is in fact an infrequently used option; it's a waste of time to run it. Modern disks remap bad sectors, whereas old disks just got read errors on bad sectors.

-f

Force execution of the *mkswap* command with its options regardless of errors and warnings. Also infrequently used, unless you know that an error in /etc/mtab is confusing *mkswap*.

-vn

> Specifies the version of swap style. *-v0* creates the old swap style, whereas *-v1* creates the new one. If no *-v* argument is supplied, *mkswap* uses the new style *unless* you're running a pre-2.2 kernel. If you need to run a pre-2.2 kernel, you *must* specify *-v0*.

swapon

Syntax

swapon [*options*]

Description

The *swapon* command enables devices and files to be used for swap. *swapon* is required after creating a swap partition with *mkswap*.

Frequently used options

--a

> Enable all devices marked as swap in */etc/fstab*. Using *-e* with *-a* skips defined swap devices that do not exist.

h

> Display help for *swapon*.

-s

> Display a swap usage summary.

swapoff

Syntax

swapoff *options*

Description

Disable swap devices.

Frequently used options

-a

> Disable all devices marked as swap in */etc/fstab*. Using *-e* with *-a* skips defined swap devices that do not exist.

Linux Partitioning Scheme

Chapter 6 presented a lot of important directories. In this chapter, we'll rehash that information with a view toward when some of these different directories should be made separate filesystems.

/ (root)

Everything needed to boot a Linux system must reside on this filesystem: */dev*, */bin*, */sbin*, */etc*, and */lib*. You can certainly have many other things in this partition, but they are optional. The root filesystem can run anything from 100 MB and up; 700 MB is quite large if the other large filesystems are separated. The one imperative is to keep this filesystem from being 100% full. If it is filled, the machine will quite probably fail to boot if you try to reboot it. Separating out the logs (mostly in */var*) to a separate partition is one of the smartest things you can do to prevent this problem.

/boot

Quite a few PC BIOS can't boot anything that resides beyond the 1024th cylinder of your boot disk, which allows 64 MB of data. The */boot* partition needs to house only some kernels, so 64 MB should be plenty. Realistic usage is in the order of 10–20 MB. Due to the kernel's small space needs, it can equally well be stored in the root partition, as long as the kernel is entirely within the 1024th cylinder of the boot disk.

/usr

The main bulk of the software in a Linux distribution goes here. A pretty full installation seems to be around 4 GB these days, but there have been dramatic increases in the past. If you plan for the system to exist for a long time without being reinstalled and repartitioned, you should make this partition at least 8 GB. If you are going to build your kernels yourself, you may want to make the partition even larger. The kernel source usually resides in */usr/src*, and a full, compiled, 2.4 kernel tree is about 250 MB, so the megabytes can add up pretty quickly if you patch the kernels, keep backups, and keep a couple of versions around.

/home

Users are very inconsiderate. They won't understand if you yell at them because they filled your root filesystem so that the machine won't boot. Keeping the user home directories in a separate partition is a big favor to yourself and them. But remember that a *.mozilla* directory alone can be 200 MB because Mozilla caches web objects and mail.

/var

This is where the logs live and where download commands such as *apt-get* cache packages. On an active system, the logs can be pretty big. Make this partition at least 2 GB; anything up to 8 GB or even beyond can be useful. For example, the complete set of Fedora Core 1 RPMs is about 1.8 GB, and if you want to *yum update* a heavily loaded system, you need enough space to store all the packages. */var/tmp* is often used to offload things such as the contents of CDs to install software or data waiting to be burned to CDs.

/opt

This is the standard location for installing applications, the kind that run your business or whatever. Look at the installation requirements for each application; 8 GB goes a long way.

/usr/local

This is the standard location to install OS add-ons that are not managed by the OS package system. Separating them out can keep them from crowding out the OS from */usr*. But because a Linux distribution these days contains almost anything you can think of, there is not much call for */usr/local*, and a few hundred megabytes are usually enough.

/tmp

Some kinds of work require a lot of temporary space; */tmp* is the default place to store it. Some software will take direction from the TMP or TEMP environment variables to store temporary files somewhere else. If you want to ensure that excessive use of */tmp* does not affect any other parts of your system, you can put it on a separate partition. A few hundred megabytes usually suffice. If you have a lot of memory or the speed of temporary file operations is of importance, consider mounting */tmp* as *tmpfs*, which makes it memory-resident instead of confined to a slow disk. The complete *fstab* line to do this is:

```
swap            /tmp            tmpfs   rw,mode=1777                0 2
```

Objective 2: Maintaining a Linux Filesystem

This Objective has major overlaps with Chapter 6, Objective 2. You may wish to review the section "Maintain the Integrity of Filesystems" there. Here we'll just touch on the fine points of some *tune2fs* settings, when and how to force *fsck* to save your system, and how to resize filesystems.

Fortunately, Linux filesystems require very little maintenance. For example, Linux's allocation strategies lead to very little disk fragmentation, so defragmentation tools, while they exist, are not used much. Fragmentation does increase, though, if the disk becomes excessively full, so monitoring free space is a very good idea. Maintenance tasks are mostly restricted to watching *fsck* do its work automatically after a crash.

tune2fs

It's important, despite the availability nowadays of journaling (see the next Objective) and RAID, to run *fsck* on all filesystems from time to time. The two parameters for controlling how often a *fsck* of a filesystem is forced are: -i and -c. The default for a filesystem is shown when it is created:

```
This filesystem will be automatically checked every 29 mounts or
180 days, whichever comes first.  Use tune2fs -c or -i to override.
```

If you find that your disk systems are very reliable and experience very few corruption problems, you can increase the period between forced filesystem checks. To change the number of mounts between checks (the filesystem typically gets mounted once for each boot), use the -c option. It is relatively important that the number be odd, and even better if it's prime. The reason for this is that you do not want to wait while all your filesystems are being *fsck*'ed at the same time after, say, 24 reboots. If you use different odd numbers for -c on all your disks, they will tend to be checked at different times. The time between checks is already quite high, so you may not want to use the -i to change it. But if you do, the value is taken to be days, which you can change to weeks or months by postfixing the value with w or m, respectively.

If you ever run into errors in an *ext2* filesystem, the kernel can take three different actions based on this, regulated by the value in the *-e* option:

continue
> Just ignore the error. A read or write error should be reported to any application.

remount-ro
> Remount the filesystem read only. This prevents escalating or dominoing failures because the filesystem cannot be updated. If the error is due to filesystem inconsistency, more corruption may otherwise result. Applications will fail with write errors subsequent to this remounting, but the data already on disk is secured.

panic
> Cause a kernel panic and halt the system. This is a very obvious failure mode that forces action by the user, whereas the two previous failure modes are more subtle and the problems might go unnoticed.

Choose the *-e* option best suited to your needs. If data consistency is of the utmost importance, one of the two l ast options should be chosen. In any case, the filesystem will be marked as unclean and will be checked on next reboot.

dumpe2fs

We must admit to never having used *dumpe2fs*. Furthermore, upon reviewing the manpage, we haven't found any use for anyone without a university major in filesystem design. The one option that could be understood by a mere senior system administrator with a decade of experience but without a special interest in filesystems is:

```
# /sbin/dumpe2fs -h /dev/Disk2/test
dumpe2fs 1.34 (25-Jul-2003)
Filesystem volume name:   <none>
Last mounted on:          <not available>
...
Filesystem features:      filetype sparse_super
...
Filesystem state:         clean
Errors behavior:          Continue
...
Reserved block count:     10240
Free blocks:              197429
Free inodes:              51181
First block:              1
...
Filesystem created:       Sat Jan 24 22:14:19 2004
Last mount time:          Sat Jan 24 22:14:37 2004
Last write time:          Sat Jan 24 22:14:59 2004
Mount count:              1
Maximum mount count:      34
```

```
Last checked:            Sat Jan 24 22:14:19 2004
Check interval:          15552000 (6 months)
Next check after:        Thu Jul 22 23:14:19 2004
Reserved blocks uid:     0 (user root)
Reserved blocks gid:     0 (group root)
First inode:             11
Inode size:              128
Default directory hash:  tea
Directory Hash Seed:     b5824b65-c864-4ee5-82f1-39aaae3fb572
```

But this is identical to the output of *tune2fs -l*. In any case, it supplies information about the filesystem features. The filetype feature is standard and tells you that file types are stored in directory entries. sparse_super indicates that a long space is left between superblock backups, saving some space. If the filesystem were larger than 2 GB, large_files would be set as well, and the filesystem would support files larger than 2 GB. The free blocks and inodes information are the same as displayed by *df*. The mount counts and next check information were discussed in the previous *tune2fs* section.

debugfs

Sometimes called *debuge2fs*. Also a very intricate tool. But it has one very good feature, which helps you undelete files. *Helps* is a very important word here. First of all, it can help only on *ext2* filesystems; on *ext3* it does not work at all. Secondly, a real filesystem always has a lot of deleted files, so you have to work hard to find the right one. Finally, you can only hope that the file's blocks have not been reused since you deleted it. Following is an ideal situation with only one deleted file:

```
# debugfs -w /dev/Disk2/test
debugfs 1.34 (25-Jul-2003)
debugfs: lsdel
 Inode  Owner  Mode   Size    Blocks    Time deleted
    12      0 100644 261117  256/ 256 Sat Jan 24 22:14:55 2004
1 deleted inodes found.
debugfs: undelete <12> undeleted-file
debugfs: ^D
# mount -t ext2 /dev/Disk2/test /mnt
# cd /mnt
# file undeleted-file
undeleted-file: RPM v4 bin i386 maildrop-1.3.4-1.7.0
# mv undeleted-file maildrop-1.3.4-1.7.0.i386.rpm
```

The *lsdel* and *undel* commands in *debugfs* are undocumented in both Debian and Red Hat. The way this process works is that you find a file with a likely size and deletion date with *lsdel*. In the first column of that line is the inode number of that file. This inode number is then given to *undel* along with a filename. Note that the <> around the inode number are required. Prior experience has shown that this command sometimes will fail, and sometimes work, and that a *fsck* after an undelete can be a good idea.

badblocks and e2fsck

Luckily, the *badblocks* command is very seldom needed these days. All modern disks do bad block remapping, meaning that if they detect a bad block a spare block is substituted. Very neat and nice for system administrators. Sometime in the childhood of Linux, IDE disks could not do such things. Because the disks were small and expensive, a bad block scan was an economic thing to do.

Today disks are huge, and they all do bad block remapping, so `badblocks` is by and large useless because it takes too long to scan the disk.

There is one situation in which *badblocks* can potentially be handy. When a disk is failing, it will usually get an exponential increase in bad blocks, and after a short while it will run out of spare blocks, whereupon you will get into trouble with your filesystems on that disk.

You *may* manage to save the filesystem by running `badblocks` on it and then passing the list of bad blocks to *e2fsck* to get the filesystem working enough for a backup. Bad block scanning will take a very, very, very long time on a big device. The process is as follows:

```
# badblocks -c 4096 -n -v -v -b 1024 -o /tmp/hdc1-badblocks /dev/hdc1...
# e2fsck -l /tmp/hdc1-badblocks /dev/hdc1...
```

The *-n* does a nondestructive read/write test. The *-v -v* ensure that you get progress reports. The *-b* is important, because if *badblocks* gets the wrong block size, the badblocks file will be useless. The filesystem block size is 1024 by default, but large filesystems use 4096. You can derive the right parameter by entering *tune2fs -l* or *dumpe2fs -h*. The *-c 4096* is how many blocks should be checked at a time. The manpage warns about using this, but 4096 blocks of 1024 bytes at once uses only about 14 MB of memory. Most modern systems can handle that well enough.

All in all, and due to the number of hours it takes *badblock* to scan a modern disk with any interesting size, it seems more likely that a disk with exponential bad blocks will fail totally before the scan is completed.

fsck

Sometimes you will see strange behavior from a filesystem. Files that just disappear. File sizes that are all wrong. File permissions being odd or impossible. You should then know that it's time for a filesystem check, even if Linux thinks that the filesystem is clean and it's a long time until a forced check is due. How to do a file check was discussed in Chapter 26, but briefly summarized, you boot the machine in single-user mode, unmount the filesystem in question, and run *fsck -f* on it. *fsck* will look up the partition in */etc/fstab* and supply the filesystem type itself. If you know the filesystem to be an *ext2* or *ext3* filesystem, you can run *e2fsck -f* or *fsck.ext2 -f* directly.

mke2fs

This command does not handle filesystem maintenance as such. But there are some things you might want to consider to make maintenance easier or the filesystem more suitable or flexible for future needs. Mostly, some of the command's sizing options are interesting:

-O sparse_super

> Enable (first option) or disable (second option) sparse superblocks. On very large disks (which includes most modern disks), it is pointless to have super block backups as often as administrators used to have with small disks. *mke2fs* does a very good job of guessing what you need here.

-J size=100

> Set the size of the *ext3* journal. On some fast systems that do an unusual volume of I/O, you may find that the default journal size is too small. The journal must be between 1024 and 102,400 blocks. The size value is in megabytes.

-N number-of-inodes

> In filesystems that are going to have *a lot* of small files, such as a news spool, or the index disk of some backup systems, you need more than the usual number of inodes. One inode is used per file. Round the number up generously. For all normal filesystem uses, the default is generous.

Filesystem Resizing

An *ext2* filesystem can be resized. This can be very handy, but is of limited value if your disk does not have free space that you can add to the partition on which the filesystem resides. In Objective 3 of Chapter 28 we'll discuss LVM, which lets you easily resize data volumes. If you don't use LVM, you can use parted (Partition EDitor) to resize, move, and copy partitions and the filesystems they contain.

To enlarge a partition, you must first create free space elsewhere on the same disk. If you don't have any, find one or more underutilized partitions and make them smaller. Then move the partitions that are between the free space and the partition you want to enlarge so that the free space becomes adjacent to the partition you want to enlarge. You're now free to enlarge it.

Several cautions apply to the use of *parted*:

- *parted*, unfortunately, has been known to corrupt partition tables and ruin filesystems. Before using it, as before any major operation on your system, back up your data and feel relieved if you don't have to restore it later.
- The filesystems containing the partitions you are working on need to be unmounted when you work on them.
- You should go down to single-user mode if you're doing large operations.

If you are just resizing an existing filesystem, you'll find it simpler to use *resize2fs*, described later.

parted

Syntax

```
parted [ device [ command [ options ] ] ]
```

Description

parted can be used to edit partition tables. For human consumption, it is best to use it interactively. But scripts, or very knowledgeable humans, may give the options directly on the command line.

Some useful commands

move partition N start end
> Move the partition numbered *N* to the given start and end points. This can resize the partition at the same time.

resize partition N start end
> Resize the partition numbered *N* to fit within the new start and end. Making a filesystem smaller can be quite time consuming, because files that are stored past the new end of the filesystem must be moved.

resize2fs

Syntax

```
resize2fs [-f] device_name [ size ]
```

Description

Resize the ext2 filesystem present on the partition named by *device_name*. If the size is omitted, the filesystem is resized to fill the whole partition. *size* should be given in units of filesystem blocks, or if it is postfixed by s, K, M, or G, it is in 512-byte sectors, kilobytes, megabytes, or gigabytes, respectively. The *-f* option forces resizing.

Example

```
resize2fs /dev/hda7 5G
```

fsck

fsck is normally run automatically as needed. Under certain circumstances, you may want to make sure it runs because, for example, you see things that makes you believe the filesystem is corrupt. It could be files disappearing, files that have 0 or small sizes but appear huge if you read them with *less* or *cat*, or anything else that makes you feel that the filesystem is not acting sanely.

The commands and techniques discussed for system recovery will be useful here. If any filesystem except your root filesystem seems messed up, simply take the machine down to single-user mode, unmount the problematic partition, and run *fsck -f* on it. If it is the root filesystem that seems insane, you will need to reboot with the kernel option `init=/bin/bash` and, instead of mounting the root filesystem, run *fsck -f* on it.

After fixing the filesystem, reboot. The system should come up sanely and without any strangeness in the filesystems.

Self-Monitoring, Analysis, and Reporting Technology System (SMART)

This system is built into most modern ATA and SCSI hard disks. SMART provides an efficient and cheap solution for monitoring potential failures in your hard disk devices. A hard disks is a very delicate device, so it is well worthwhile having any potential warning that it is about to crash.

 SMART doesn't substitute for the always-recommended practice to get all your critical data stored, updated, and tested in your backup media.

SMART implementation in Linux is very mature, and there are good tools to manage it. To start using this great benefit of modern disks, you must check these prerequisites:

- The hard disk must be SMART compliant.
- Your operating system must read SMART commands.
- You must install software capable of managing and showing SMART alert messages.

Assuming you don't have problems with the first and second items, you can use *smartmontools (http://smartmontools.sourceforge.net)* to fulfill the last one. This suite contain two binaries, *smartd* and *smartctl*, along with corresponding initialization scripts.

smartd runs as a daemon working in the background and monitors the hard disk. *smartctl* is a utility that controls and monitors SMART. *smartctl* is designed to perform SMART tasks such as printing the SMART self-test and error logs, enabling and disabling SMART automatic testing, and initiating device self-tests. Assuming that */dev/hda* is the first hard disk installed in your system, you can display the status as follows:

```
# /etc/init.d/smartd start
 * Starting S.M.A.R.T. monitoring daemon...
[ ok ]
# smartctl -i /dev/hda
smartctl version 5.30 Copyright (C) 2002-4 Bruce Allen
Home page is http://smartmontools.sourceforge.net/

=== START OF INFORMATION SECTION ===
Device Model:     WDC WD400BB-00FRA0
Serial Number:    WD-WMAJF1340215
Firmware Version: 77.07W77
Device is:        In smartctl database [for details use: -P show]
```

```
ATA Version is:    6
ATA Standard is:  Exact ATA specification draft version not indicated
Local Time is:    Tue Jul 26 20:23:21 2005 BRT
SMART support is: Available - device has SMART capability.
SMART support is: Enabled
```

If the command shows:

```
SMART support is: Disabled
```

just turn it on using:

```
# smartctl -s on /dev/hda
```

You can customize *etc/smartd.conf* to monitor the temperature and error rates of disks, among other interesting things, but details are outside the scope of this objective.

Objective 3: Creating and Configuring Filesystem Options

In Chapter 6 we covered mounting various types of filesystems, but up to this point we have discussed creating only *ext2* filesystems. In this objective, LPI expects you to be able to create other types of filesystems, such as ISO9660 filesystems for CD-ROMs. In addition, you should be able to set up automounting for network and device filesystems.

Automounting Filesystems

An automounter is a system that automatically mounts disks on demand. It can mount any kind of filesystem that mount can mount, as long as there is no interactive authentication. The handiest property of an automounter is that it is dynamic. If you make an update of the configuration, it's ready to mount at once.

Linux supports an automounter called *autofs* that is inspired by a Solaris utility of the same name. autofs is configured by two kinds of files.

The master map (usually */etc/auto.master*) defines which mount points should be governed by *autofs*. Each mount point again has an automount map associated with it. The maps are usually stored in files called */etc/auto.mount_point*. *autofs* can store the maps in NIS and LDAP as well as in flat files. We'll concentrate here on flat files. Consider the following */etc/auto.master* file:

```
# Format of this file:
# mountpoint map options
# For details of the format look at autofs(8).
/misc   /etc/auto.misc  --timeout=15
/home   /etc/auto.home
```

The contents of */etc/auto.misc* are:

```
usbdisk      -fstype=vfat,umask=0,dotsOK=yes :/dev/sda1
cdrom        -fstype=iso9660              :/dev/cdrom
```

This will mount a USB memory stick or disk that appears as */dev/sda1* and the CD-ROM. All the user has to do is insert the CD and issue *cd /misc/cdrom*; there is no need for a *mount* command. Due to the *--timeout=15* option, the mount will disappear after 15 seconds of disuse. Quite convenient on end user machines.

How this works is that when a user attempts to access */misc/something*, or anything underneath it, *something* is looked up in the automount map, and if it comes up with a match, the indicated device is mounted with the indicated options. The syntax of the file is fairly trivial, looking generally like this:

```
key              [options]           location
```

The first column contains lookup keys, the directory names specified by users. The rest of each line is the matching value. Any mount options must come first and be prefixed by a hyphen (-).

After looking up `cdrom` in our previous example, we use `-fstype=iso9660 :/dev/cdrom`. The *-fstype* option is passed to *mount* as the filesystem type (*mount -tfstype*), while the other options are mount options (*mount -ooptions*). All the same mount options that were discussed in Chapter 6 can go here.

Any string containing a : specifies the thing to mount. If the colon is a prefix, as in the previous example, it's a local device. If something precedes the colon, the device is (by default) NFS-mounted. You can mount SMB/CIFS mounts by specifying something like this:

```
windows         -fstype=smbfs            ://windows/c
```

In a real environment, the main use of *autofs* is for NFS mounts. Home directories are a favorite example. The contents of */etc/auto.home* could be:

```
janl        -rw,intr,hard        server:/server/bighome/&
killroy     -rw,intr,hard        server:/server/bighome/&
*           -rw,intr,hard        server:/server/homes/&
```

Here you see that */home/janl* is mounted from *server:/server/bighome/janl*. You may recognize the use of the ampersand (&) from *sed*; it means to put the string that was matched (i.e., the whole key) in the place of the ampersand. This comes in very handy with the wildcard mount. Whenever a home directory other than *janl* or *killroy* is requested, it matches the last line and therefore mounts the corresponding directory from *server:/server/homes*. For instance, requesting */home/silug* results in an attempt to mount *server:/server/homes/silug*. The options shown are pretty common for NFS mounts.

autofs becomes more useful once you add a way to distribute the map files, whether by copying them from a master to all takers with FTP or by using NIS or LDAP.

Other Filesystems

The Objective vaguely calls for knowledge of "other" filesystems. Earlier chapters have concentrated on *ext2*, Linux's vintage filesystem, while mentioning *ext3* in passing. *ext3* is an extension to *ext2* that adds metadata journaling (or logging, if you will). If a system crashes, the log enables playback of the filesystem events (file creation, deletion, etc.) that happened up to that point from the log. This enables quick recovery after crashes, rather than having to do a full multipass scan of the filesystem to discover inconsistencies caused by the crash. Thus, the log playback guarantees consistency: some recent changes may be lost, but the files and directories are not corrupted.

Among the "other" filesystems on Linux are ReiserFS, JFS, and XFS. ReiserFS originated from independent development on Linux. JFS comes from IBM and is used in both OS/2 and AIX. XFS was made by SGI for use with IRIX. All of these are journaling filesystems but otherwise support a wide array of different goals and features. IBM and SGI have been porting JFS and XFS to Linux on their own initiatives. They started before *ext3* was really stable.

Of these journaling filesystems, only *ext3* (and to some degree, ReiserFS) see widespread use. While both ReiserFS and JFS are included in the kernel sources, many distributions do not offer to make them during installation. The most marginal of these filesystems seems to be XFS: it is not included in kernel sources and its utilities are not included in most distributions.

For now we'll concentrate on making and tweaking *ext3* filesystems. *ext3* requires both a pretty recent kernel and updated *ext2* utilities. Reiserfs, JFS, and XFS all need additional utility packages installed.

Please read the following warnings carefully: each one offers some sound advice!

If you use a journaling filesystem, it is quite important *not* to muck about with caching and flushing. A disk drive that does write caching (and most do, because their benchmarks are much nicer) also often do write reordering. But a journaling filesystem depends on the journal entries being written in the correct order. If the disk reorders them, the journal becomes corrupt. The problem becomes even worse if you use RAID, because different stripes of the same data become inconsistent. Experiments (*http://www.sr5tech.com/ write_back_cache_experiments.htm*) have shown that there is about a 10% chance of filesystem corruption on a large filesystem after an uncontrolled shutdown.

The 2.6 kernels contain "write barriers" in appropriate places to prevent such corruption. For earlier kernels, the very best cure is having a UPS and shutting down systems in an orderly manner before the power disappears. This is smart in any case, but more important if you have a lot of storage.

On a risky system that runs an old kernel and has no UPS, consider disabling write back caches on your drives. If you have IDE drives, a simple hdparm -W0 /dev/hda (and similar commands for other disks) suffices. With SCSI and RAID, there may be BIOS settings to do the job, or you may need to locate a package called *xscsi* to manipulate the drive mode pages directly. The price for this is considerably higher latency for disk writes, and this may kill the performance of some system/software combinations.

Filesystem

Using ext3

Since *ext3* is an extension of *ext2*, making an *ext3* filesystem is done by invoking *mke2fs* with the *-j* option.

```
# mke2fs -j -L test /dev/sda1
mke2fs 1.34 (25-Jul-2003)
Filesystem label=test
OS type: Linux
Block size=1024 (log=0)
Fragment size=1024 (log=0)
51200 inodes, 204800 blocks
10240 blocks (5.00%) reserved for the super user
First data block=1
25 block groups
8192 blocks per group, 8192 fragments per group
2048 inodes per group
Superblock backups stored on blocks:
        8193, 24577, 40961, 57345, 73729

Writing inode tables: done
Creating journal (4096 blocks): done
Writing superblocks and filesystem accounting information: done

This filesystem will be automatically checked every 36 mounts or
180 days, whichever comes first.  Use tune2fs -c or -i to override.
```

The *-j* option is all that is needed. You now have an *ext3* filesystem. *ext3* has the nice property that after it is *fsck*ed it's a valid *ext2* filesystem as well. Thus, you may access *ext3* disks on systems that support only *ext2*, providing that you make sure they are *fsck*ed. Conversely, a plain *ext2* filesystem can very easily be upgraded to an *ext3* filesystem; all you need to do is add the journal like this:

```
# tune2fs -j /dev/sda1
tune2fs 1.34 (25-Jul-2003)
Creating journal inode: done
This filesystem will be automatically checked every 29 mounts or
180 days, whichever comes first.  Use tune2fs -c or -i to override.
```

After you upgrade a filesystem to *ext3*, change its */etc/fstab* entry to match.

vfat filesystems

There is one more group of filesystems that deserves mention: the Microsoft DOS/Windows FAT filesystems and their variants. Under Linux, these are accessed through the *vfat* filesystem type. *vfat* is not used much on enterprise Linux systems, but it is used a lot on desktop systems for devices such as USB memory sticks or disks, MP3 players, camera memory cards, and so on.

vfat really encompasses a class of different FAT filesystems with support for differently sized devices and short or long filenames. *vfat* can also be used for NTFS partitions on modern derivatives of Windows NT. Linux can create, mount, read, and write reliably to all these. The support for checking them is not complete, though it should be good enough for most jobs. Simply use *mount -t vfat* to mount them, *mkfs.vfat* to create them, and *fsck.vfat* to check them. The last two commands come from a package called *dosfstools* in both Debian and Red Hat.

Linux also offers an *ntfs* filesystem, but it's experimental and not offered by default in many distributions. Luckily, it's not needed either. *vfat* can be used with partitions considered to be NTFS partitions on Windows. Linux's *ntfs* is also less desirable because it doesn't reliably support writes, which *vfat* does.

ISO9660 Filesystems

ISO9660 filesystems are quite a bit different from the filesystem types mentioned before; hence we offer a whole section about them. As a sysadmin, you must be comfortable creating ISO9660 for applications that write to CDs or DVDs. When writing to CD media, you don't simply save files to them as you would a floppy drive. Even non-Linux operating systems require some type of program to simulate that behavior transparently to the user. Instead, you have to create a filesystem to be written, or *burned*, to CD-writable media. This filesystem is the ISO9660 filesystem, called ISO for short.

Standards with an ISO prefix, such as ISO9660, are defined by the International Organization for Standardization. While you may find references to ISO being an acronym for this organization, it is actually intended to refer to a pun on the Greek prefix "iso-" which means "same."

Creating ISO9660 images

Before you start burning CD-ROMs, you must first create your image, or ISO. This is a job done in two steps. First, you create a directory hierarchy containing all the files you want the CD to contain. Ensure that it's no larger than the maximum size supported by the CD-R (or CD-RW or even DVD) medium you're going to burn on. After that, use *mkisofs* to generate an ISO image (sometimes called a CD image). This image can in turn be burned onto a CD.

mkisofs

Syntax

```
mkisofs options [-o filename ] path [ path... ]
```

Description

Generate an ISO9660 filesystem image for burning onto CD media. The original ISO9660 standard is quite rudimentary; for example, it supports only filenames in DOS 8.3 style. Therefore, it has many mutations, and *mkisofs* has options to support a lot of them. Most of them are obsolete or irrelevant to us.

Two mutations that are still interesting are: Rock Ridge and Joliet. The Rock Ridge extensions support filenames with up to 30 characters, UID/GID file permissions, and POSIX symbolic links and devices. Joliet is the Windows CD-ROM filesystem. *mkisofs* can generate both, and Linux understands both natively (but support for Joliet requires a kernel option).

Interesting options

-J

>Generate Joliet extensions. These are understood by Windows starting with Windows 95 and NT. Filenames are Unicode encoded and can be up to 64 characters long. Joliet alone should be used for CDs intended for Windows only.

-r -ldots -l

>These options allow Unix-style filenames. The *-r* option activates Rock Ridge extensions, mostly interesting because of the long filenames. It also defaults the UID/GID/permission settings in a way that is appropriate for a CD-ROM. The *-r* option is absolutely necessary if you want to create a CD that contains Linux executables and scripts. Omitting it removes the executable bits from all files so that they will not be executable any more. The *-ldots* allows filenames to start with a period (.), which is otherwise forbidden. The *-l* option allows 31-character names in the basic ISO9660 directories on the image. There is space for this in the directory entries, but the ordinary filename standard for ISO9660 is 8.3. Both *-ldots* and *-l* are violations of the standard, but CD-ROM images burned with seem to work on all known systems.

-T

>This creates *TRANS.TBL* files in each directory of the image. The literature says that "some" systems use these to support long filenames with special characters. These files are very often seen on old Linux CD-ROM distributions.

-o filename

>Write the image to the named file.

Example

Generate an ISO image named */var/tmp/image.iso* from the files in */var/tmp/backup*:

```
$ mkisofs -T -r -ldots -l -J -o /var/tmp/image.iso /var/tmp/backup
Warning: creating filesystem that does not conform to ISO-9660.
  6.74% done, estimate finish Wed Jan 21 14:53:06 2004
 13.46% done, estimate finish Wed Jan 21 14:53:06 2004
 20.21% done, estimate finish Wed Jan 21 14:53:06 2004
 26.93% done, estimate finish Wed Jan 21 14:53:06 2004
 33.67% done, estimate finish Wed Jan 21 14:53:06 2004
 40.39% done, estimate finish Wed Jan 21 14:53:06 2004
 47.14% done, estimate finish Wed Jan 21 14:53:06 2004
 53.86% done, estimate finish Wed Jan 21 14:53:06 2004
 60.60% done, estimate finish Wed Jan 21 14:53:06 2004
 67.32% done, estimate finish Wed Jan 21 14:53:06 2004
 74.07% done, estimate finish Wed Jan 21 14:53:06 2004
 80.79% done, estimate finish Wed Jan 21 14:53:06 2004
 87.53% done, estimate finish Wed Jan 21 14:53:06 2004
 94.25% done, estimate finish Wed Jan 21 14:53:06 2004
Total translation table size: 459
Total rockridge attributes bytes: 429
Total directory bytes: 0
Path table size(bytes): 10
Max brk space used 21ac4
74269 extents written (145 Mb)
```

Despite the warning about nonconformance with ISO9660, the image should be compatible with all modern operating systems.

Burning CD-ROMs

Burning a CD is, in a mechanical sense, quite complicated. The CD burner must be fed with data quickly enough to keep the disk rotating at just the right speed while the laser moves in a precise spiral. With older burners, if the data does not arrive soon enough, the whole burning will fail and you will have a new coaster. New burners support different kinds of BurnProof and BurnFree technologies, meaning that the CD drive has precise enough control of speed, the angular position of the disk, and the spiral position of the laser that when a data under-run occurs, it can resume the burn when data arrives. Nonetheless, CD burning is considerably more complex than writing to a disk, and special software is needed. Linux provides *cdrecord* and sometimes *dvdrecord*. We will concentrate on the former.

Burning with IDE CD burners. This applies to all except a few CD burners that are SCSI units.

In the beginning, all CD burners were SCSI units and *cdrecord* understood only SCSI CD burners. At some point, IDE CD burners appeared. To allow use of these with *cdrecord*, the *ide-scsi* kernel module was extended so that the kernel could show IDE burners as SCSI devices to *cdrecord* and then translate the SCSI commands to IDE commands. Before you can burn anything, this module must be installed, which means first of all that your kernel must be configured with it. We'll assume it is compiled as a module. On Red Hat, the lines shown next should be entered directly into */etc/modules*. On Debian, put them in */etc/modules. d/local* (for example) and run *modules-update* afterwards.

```
alias scd0 sr_mod
pre-install sg  modprobe ide-scsi
pre-install sr_mod modprobe ide-scsi
pre-install ide-scsi modprobe ide-cd
```

These lines set up the system so that if the SCSI CD device or the SCSI "generic" driver is loaded, the *ide-scsi* module will be loaded first.

In your boot loader, add the option hdc=ide-scsi on the kernel command line. For LILO, insert append="hdc=ide-scsi" to the *lilo.conf*, while in GRUB simply type the option into each kernel command line. The hdc assumes that your CD-burner is the master of the second IDE bus; if it's something else, change the device name appropriately. Now reboot; you should be all set to burn CDs.

Using cdrecord. In most cases *cdrecord* needs quite a long command, but fortunately it's not hard to figure out which options you need.

cdrecord

Syntax

```
cdrecord -scanbus
cdrecord [ general_options ] dev=device image_file
```

Description

Burn an audio or data CD according to the relevant standards. We will restrict ourselves to data CDs. The device refers to a *bus, target, lun* tuple rather than a Unix-style device name. This tuple identifies the burner device. The appropriate tuple is found using the *-scanbus* form of the command. See the examples that come later in this section.

Interesting options

-v

> Verbose output. Use one *-v* to track the burning process.

-dummy

> Only pretend to burn. This will go through all the motions of burning, but the laser will be off. If your burner does not support BurnFree or some such feature, you can use this to verify that your system can feed data fast enough to avoid data underruns. Combine the option with *-v* to get information about the data feeding process.

driveropts=burnfree

> Enables the burning mode that tolerates data underruns.

speed=speed

> Set the burning speed. This is quite often autodetected. But if your drive does not tolerate underruns, you can reduce the speed so that data is fed to it fast enough to prevent them.

dev=device

> Specify which device to burn to.

Examples

First locate your CD burner device.

```
# cdrecord -scanbus
Cdrecord-Clone 2.01a19 (i686-redhat-linux-gnu) Copyright (C) 1995-2003 Jorg
Schilling
Linux sg driver version: 3.1.25
Using libscg version 'schily-0.7'
cdrecord: Warning: using inofficial libscg transport code version (schily -
Red Hat-scsi-linux-sg.c-1.75-RH '@(#)scsi-linux-sg.c     1.75 02/10/21
Copyright 1997 J. Schilling').
scsibus0:
        0,0,0   0) 'PLEXTOR ' 'DVDR   PX-708A ' '1.02' Removable CD-ROM
        0,1,0   1) *
        0,2,0   2) *
        0,3,0   3) *
        0,4,0   4) *
        0,5,0   5) *
```

```
         0,6,0    6) *
         0,7,0    7) *
```
The output indicates that you want to use dev=0,0,0. To test burn a CD:

```
# cdrecord -v -dummy driveropts=burnfree dev=0,0,0 /var/tmp/image.iso
Cdrecord-Clone 2.01a19 (i686-redhat-linux-gnu) Copyright (C) 1995-2003 Jorg
Schilling
TOC Type: 1 = CD-ROM
scsidev: '0,0,0'
scsibus: 0 target: 0 lun: 0
Linux sg driver version: 3.1.25
Using libscg version 'schily-0.7'
cdrecord: Warning: using inofficial libscg transport code version (schily -
Red Hat-scsi-linux-sg.c-1.75-RH '@(#)scsi-linux-sg.c      1.75 02/10/21
Copyright 1997 J. Schilling').
Driveropts: 'burnfree'

... [ verbiage about drive and media capabilities deleted for brevity ]

Driver flags   : MMC-3 SWABAUDIO BURNFREE VARIREC FORCESPEED SINGLESESSION
HIDECDR

...

Power-Rec write speed:     40x (recommended)
Starting to write CD/DVD at speed 40 in dummy TAO mode for single session.
Last chance to quit, starting dummy write    0 seconds. Operation starts.
Waiting for reader process to fill input buffer ... input buffer ready.
BURN-Free is OFF.
Turning BURN-Free on
Starting new track at sector: 0
Track 01:  145 of  145 MB written (fifo 100%) [buf  97%]  27.9x.
Track 01: Total bytes read/written: 152102912/152102912 (74269 sectors).
Writing  time:   52.236s
Average write speed  19.0x.
Min drive buffer fill was 97%
Fixating...
WARNING: Some drives don't like fixation in dummy mode.
Fixating time:    0.000s
Last selected write speed: 40x
Max media write speed:     40x
Last actual write speed:   26x
BURN-Free was never needed.
cdrecord: fifo had 2396 puts and 2396 gets.
cdrecord: fifo was 0 times empty and 1388 times full, min fill was 93%.
```

An altogether successful dummy burning. If your drive can't tolerate underruns, look closely at the last line detailing fifo filling: 93% is quite acceptable; 50% should be more worrying and perhaps a clue to reduce the writing speed.

CD miscellany. A CD, burned or obtained commercially, can be accessed as a block device with ordinary Linux commands. To verify a burned CD, simply use the *cmp* to check it against your original input directory, as shown below. If there is no output, you're fine.

```
$ cmp /dev/cdrom /var/tmp/image.iso
```

If you want to burn a copy of a data CD, you can simply copy the image from the CD to disk with *dd*. For example:

```
$ dd bs=2k if=/dev/cdrom of=/var/tmp/cd-image.iso
56942+0 records in
56942+0 records out
```

After the operation is done, you can turn around and burn new CDs with the image (if you have the necessary legal rights to copy it, of course). This is also a great way to back up CDs and to have them available for use quickly without running around finding the disk, inserting it in the right computer, and so on.

ISO filesystems on CDs are easy to mount. This is discussed in Chapter 6. The complete command to mount an ISO CD is:

```
# mount -t iso9660 -o ro /dev/cdrom /mnt/cdrom
```

If loop devices are supported by your kernel, you can mount the image file directly with this command:

```
# mount -t iso9660 -o loop,ro /var/tmp/image.iso /mnt/cdrom
```

You can also use the *losetup* command to easly manage loop devices.

losetup

Syntax

```
losetup [ [-e|-E] encryption ] [-o offset] [-p pfd] loop_device file
losetup [-d] loop_device
```

Description

losetup is used to associate loop devices with regular files or block devices, to detach loop devices, and to query the status of a loop device. If only the *loop_device* argument is given, the status of the corresponding loop device is shown.

Interesting options

-e encryption
> Enable data encryption with the specified name.

-d
> Detach the file or device associated with the specified loop device.

Examples

You can use this example to encrypt (painfully) a file.

```
# dd if=/dev/zero of=/file bs=1k count=100# losetup -e des /dev/loop0 /file
Init (up to 16 hex digits):
# mkfs -t ext2 /dev/loop0 100
# mount -t ext2 /dev/loop0 /mnt
```

dd

On the face of it, *dd* may seem like an odd program, but it's widely useful because it is very good at copying data from devices to files and vice versa. In the ISO9660 section earlier in this chapter, you've already seen *dd* used to copy a CD image from the CD to a disk file. *dd* can be used with almost any Linux tool to facilitate I/O with block devices. (Moving data between files and character devices can be done with just *cat*.)

For example, if you want to move a filesystem from one device to another and the receiving device is at least as big as the originating one, just enter something such as:

```
# dd bs=1k if=/dev/from of=/dev/too
```

If you combine *dd* with *rsh* or *ssh*, a filesystem can be transferred from system to system over the network—just not very efficiently, because the free blocks will also be transferred. Add *gzip -1 -c* to the pipeline before the network copy command, and all the blocks containing zeros will be transfered much faster.

When operating on block devices, the block size can be very important. One point to remember is that larger blocks are faster. When writing to and from disks, *bs=8k* can help immensely. When operating on tar files, you should always use *bs=10k*, because tar uses a block size of 10 KB by default.

The *dd* command can copy raw data and disk images to and from such devices as floppies and tape drives. A common use is to create boot floppies:

```
dd if=kernel_image.iso of=/dev/fd0
```

Similarly, *dd* can copy the entire contents of a floppy, even one formatted with a "foreign" OS, to the hard drive as an image file.

28

Hardware (Topic 2.204)

This Topic supplements the Level 1 Topic 101, Hardware and Architecture. In Chapter 3, we discussed hardware subjects such as BIOS, modem and sound cards, SCSI devices, PC expansion cards, modems, and USB devices. For Level 2, you're expected to implement software RAID solutions, configure specialized hardware, customize software drivers and kernel configurations, and install PCMCIA hardware devices.

This Topic contains four Objectives:

Objective 1: Configuring RAID
Candidates should be able to configure and implement software RAID. This Objective includes using *mkraid* tools and configuring RAID 0, 1, and 5. Weight: 2.

Objective 2: Adding New Hardware
Candidates should be able to configure internal and external devices for a system including new hard disks, dumb terminal devices, serial UPS devices, multiport serial cards, and LCD panels. Weight: 3.

Objective 3: Software and Kernel Configuration
Candidates should be able to configure kernel options to support various hardware devices including UDMA drives and IDE CD burners. This Objective includes using LVM to manage hard disk drives and partitions as well as software tools to interact with hard disk settings. Weight: 2.

Objective 4: Configuring PCMCIA Devices
Candidates should be able to configure a Linux installation to include PCMCIA support. This objective includes configuring PCMCIA devices, such as Ethernet adapters, to autodetect when inserted. Weight: 1.

Objective 1: Configuring RAID

A RAID is a Redundant Array of Independent Disks. Sometimes it is more lovingly referred to as a Redundant Array of Inexpensive Disks, recalling RAID's roots in the search to create large disk storage from cheap, smaller-capacity hardware. While RAID is still used to maximize the use of inexpensive disks today, it is also used to achieve faster access speeds and data security.

RAID makes multiple hard disk drives look like one drive to the user's filesystem. There are multiple types of RAID, which are indicated by the level number. They achieve their effects through various combinations of mirroring and striping. *Mirroring* data refers to having identical copies of data in separate locations (disks). *Striping* data refers to distributing data across multiple disks, which involves more than a simple copy. RAID level 5 (referred to as RAID 5) is the most common form of RAID. RAID 5 uses striping with parity across your RAID array. RAID 1 is used to mirror identical copies of data between disk pairs. RAID 0 is used for simply striping data across the disks in your array.

Currently, the LPIC Level 2 Exams cover the software RAID tools *mkraid*, *raidstop*, and *raidstart*. These utilities use the */etc/raidtab* configuration file.

The mkraid Tools

The *mkraid* tools are included in almost every major Linux distribution. */etc/raidtab* is the default configuration file for the raid tools. It defines how RAID devices are configured on a system.

mkraid

Syntax

```
mkraid [-cvfu] /dev/md?
```

Description

This command sets up a set of block devices into a single RAID array. It looks in its configuration file for the md devices mentioned on the command line and initializes those arrays. *mkraid* works for all types of RAID arrays (RAID1, RAID4, RAID5, LINEAR and RAID0).

Options

-c, --configfile filename
> Use *filename* as the configuration file (*/etc/raidtab* is used by default).

-f, --force
> Initialize the constituent devices even if they appear to have data on them already.

-o, --upgrade
> Upgrade older arrays to the current kernel's RAID version, without destroying data. Although the utility detects various pitfalls, such as mixed-up disks and inconsistent superblocks, this option should be used with care.

-V, --version
> Display a short version message, then exit.

raidstart

Syntax

raidstart [*options*] *raiddevice*

Description

Activate an existing md device.

Options
-a, --all
> Apply the command to all of the configurations specified in the configuration file.

-c, --configfile filename
> Use filename as the configuration file (*/etc/raidtab* is used by default).

-h, --help
> Display a short usage message, then exit.

-V, --version
> Display a short version message, then exit.

raidstop

Syntax

raidstop [*options*] *raiddevice*

Description

Turn off an md device and unconfigure it.

Options
-a, --all
> Apply the command to all of the configurations specified in the configuration file.

-c, --configfile filename
> Use filename as the configuration file (*/etc/raidtab* is used by default).

-h, --help
> Display a short usage message, then exit.

-V, --version
> Display a short version message, then exit.

How to Create RAID 1 (Mirroring)

This procedure prepares one or more devices for redundancy. Firs,t set up the */etc/raidtab* file to describe your configuration:

```
raiddev /dev/md0
        raid-level      1
        nr-raid-disks   2
```

```
nr-spare-disks    0
persistent-superblock 1
device            /dev/sdb1
raid-disk         0
device            /dev/sdb2
raid-disk         1
```

Now issue the following command to construct the mirror:

```
mkraid /dev/md0
```

Wait for whole process to finish. Check the estimated time (which depends on device sizes) and progression by looking inside of */proc/mdstat* file. The process will happen online and the filesystem can be mounted.

Objective 2: Adding New Hardware

Configuring specialized hardware has become easier and easier, even since the development of LPI's Level 2 Exams. Items such as LCD panels and serial UPS devices used to not be as common in our homes and offices, but today they are considered standard equipment.

When you prepared for Level 1, you became familiar with a number of the tools you must utilize when adding new hardware to your systems. For the Level 2 exams, you must be prepared to understand when to use them and the most efficient methods for installing your new devices.

Reporting Your Hardware

Before you tackle adding any new hardware devices to your system, it's useful to be able to obtain information about the hardware you have installed. Some useful tools to report this information include *lsmod*, *lsdev*, and *lspci*.

lsmod

Syntax

```
lsmod [options]
```

Description

The *lsmod* command displays all the information available about currently loaded modules. Reviewing your loaded modules is often the first step in identifying possible problems, such as driver conflicts (quite frequently found with USB device drivers). This information can also be found in */proc/modules*. *lsmod* has only two options, neither of them affecting its operation.

Options
-h, --help
Display help information.

-V, --version
Display the version.

The output of *lsmod* is a series of columns identifying the module name, its size, its use number, and its status. A sample of *lsmod* output looks like this:

```
Module              Size  Used by    Not tainted
vfat                12844  0  (autoclean)
fat                 38328  0  (autoclean) [vfat]
nfs                 79960  0  (autoclean)
ide-scsi            11984  0  (autoclean)
ide-cd              35196  0  (autoclean)
cdrom               33440  0  (autoclean) [ide-cd]
tuner               11680  1  (autoclean)
tvaudio             14940  0  (autoclean) (unused)
bttv                73568  0  (autoclean)
videodev             8192  2  (autoclean) [bttv]
radeon             114244 28
agpgart             46752  3
parport_pc          18756  1  (autoclean)
lp                   8868  0  (autoclean)
parport             36480  1  (autoclean) [parport_pc lp]
```

lsdev

Syntax

lsdev

Description

The *lsdev* command displays information about your system's hardware, such as interrupt addresses and I/O ports. The command is useful for obtaining information prior to installing devices that may have hardware addressing conflicts, such as ISA devices. This command uses DMA files in */proc* to also report I/O addresses and IRQ and DMA channel information. There are no options for *lsdev*.

The output of *lsdev* is very simple, similar to *lsmod*. It lists information in four columns: device name, DMA address, IRQ address, and I/O ports. The following is some sample output from *lsdev*:

```
Device          DMA   IRQ   I/O Ports
------------------------------------------------
ATI                         c800-c8ff
bttv                  10
Creative                    e800-e81f ec00-ec07
dma                         0080-008f
dma1                        0000-001f
dma2                        00c0-00df
e100                        e000-e03f
EMU10K1               11    e800-e81f
fpu                         00f0-00ff
ide0                  14    01f0-01f7 03f6-03f6 fc00-fc07
ide1                  15    0170-0177 0376-0376 fc08-fc0f
Intel                       e000-e03f
keyboard               1    0060-006f
ohci1394              12
PCI                         0cf8-0cff c000-cfff
```

lspci

Syntax

lspci [*options*]

Description

The *lspci* command displays information about your system's PCI buses and your installed PCI devices.This information is found primarily within */proc*.

Options

-t

Show a treelike diagram containing all buses, bridges, devices, and connections between them.

-vv

Very verbose mode.

Objective 3: Software and Kernel Configuration

In the Level 1 Exams, you were prepared to compile kernels and install software to be used with your hardware, including using various hardware-specific tools. For this objective, you are expected to use these tools and kernel options for special hard drive applications, such as Logical Volume Manager (LVM).

hdparm

This command can find a lot of information about your hard drives beyond the more familiar *fdisk* output. Specifically, *hdparm* can provide this type of information:

```
# hdparm /dev/hda

/dev/hda:
 multcount    = 16 (on)
 IO_support   =  0 (default 16-bit)
 unmaskirq    =  0 (off)
 using_dma    =  1 (on)
 keepsettings =  0 (off)
 readonly     =  0 (off)
 readahead    =  8 (on)
 geometry     = 9729/255/63, sectors = 156301488, start = 0
# hdparm -i /dev/hda

/dev/hda:

 Model=ST380013AS, FwRev=3.05, SerialNo=3JV2WAWB
 Config={ HardSect NotMFM HdSw>15uSec Fixed DTR>10Mbs RotSpdTol>.5% }
 RawCHS=16383/16/63, TrkSize=0, SectSize=0, ECCbytes=4
```

```
BuffType=unknown, BuffSize=8192kB, MaxMultSect=16, MultSect=16
CurCHS=16383/16/63, CurSects=16514064, LBA=yes, LBAsects=156301488
IORDY=on/off, tPIO={min:240,w/IORDY:120}, tDMA={min:120,rec:120}
PIO modes:  pio0 pio1 pio2 pio3 pio4
DMA modes:  mdma0 mdma1 mdma2
UDMA modes: udma0 udma1 *udma2
AdvancedPM=no WriteCache=enabled
Drive conforms to: ATA/ATAPI-6 T13 1410D revision 2:

* signifies the current active mode
```

All this can be useful to troubleshoot and/or tune IDE disks. The most important thing for I/O performance is not to use PIO (programmed I/O) modes. To use PIO, the kernel must run in a loop, fetching 1 byte at a time from the disk. This is how IDE disks used to work originally, but it's not at all effective, and even the fastest Pentium 4 gets bogged down with this kind of I/O.

The next line, DMA modes, lists the original DMA modes supported by IDE disks. These are quite a bit faster, and you will probably find that CD-ROMs and DVD drives support only these modes. UDMA modes are "Ultra" DMA, which is very fast DMA. In general, you want to be the furthest down and to the right on these three lines. But beware: the BIOS and drives usually default these to the fastest mode that is commonly supported. If you set one of these the wrong way, you may well end up breaking things and massively corrupting the filesystem. The one thing that's quite safe to do is enable using_dma.

In the first listing, you can see that using_dma is already on. In the second listing, you can see that udma2 is the active DMA mode. Since this is the highest mode the drive supports, you can't do much better.

Using DMA is the default in all recent kernels, including the ones used in distributions. If you roll your own kernels, you should make sure that you configure it correctly. In 2.4 kernel configurations, there is a top-level selection called "ATA/IDE/MDM/RLL support." Select it, enable "ATA/IDE/MFM/RLL support," and then select "IDE, ATA and ATAPI Block devices." Here you will need to find and enable support for the IDE chipset or chipsets you have. Then, under "PCI IDE chipset support," you will find "Use PCI DMA by default when available." This should be safe to enable, In fact, it would have been the default were there not some systems using an old chipset called VIA VP2.

hdparm

Syntax

hdparm [*flags*] [*device*]

Description

The hdparm command configures Linux ATA/IDE driver hard disk ioctls. It can both view and set hard disk parameters. There are many options available.

Frequently used options

-a
> Get or set the sector count for filesystem read-ahead. *-a* disables or enables the read-ahead feature. The default is on.

-Bnum
> Set APM (Advanced Power Management) features. A low *num* value sets higher power management, whereas a high *num* value delivers better performance. The *num* range is 0 to 255; 255 disables APM on the drive.

-c [num]
> Query or enable IDE 32-bit I/O support. *num* can be 0, 1, or 3; 0 disables 32-bit I/O support, 1 enables support, and 3 enables support with a special sync sequence.

-d [0|1]
> Get or set the using_dma flag.

-g
> Display drive geometry.

-i
> Display identification information.

-k
> Get or set the keep_settings_over_reset flag.

-mnum
> Get or set the sector count for multiple sector I/O. A *num* value of 0 disables this feature. Most drives support 2, 4, 8, 16, or 32 sectors. Your drive manufacturer will often recommend the optimal setting.

-r [0|1]
> Get (1) or set (0) the read-only flag.

-S
> Set the standby (spindown) timeout.

-u [0|1]
> Get (1) or set (0) the interrupt-unmask flag.

-v
> Display all settings, except *-i*.

-y
> Force an IDE drive to immediately go into low power consumption mode.

-z
> Force a kernel reread of the partition table.

---

tune2fs

tune2fs was a subject on the Level 1 Exams and was also mentioned in the previous chapter. When it comes to how ext2 and ext3 filesystems interact with the kernel, there are a couple of options worth mentioning.

-e error_behavior

This parameter decides how the kernel should react when it finds errors in the specific filesystem that *tune2fs* is applied to. The possible behaviors are as follows (repeated from Chapter 27).

continue

Just ignore the error. A read or write error should be reported to any application that tries to access that part of the filesystem.

remount-ro

Remount the filesystem read only. This prevents escalating or dominoing failures that could otherwise result when a filesystem that cannot be written is remounted. After you set this option, applications that subsequently try to write to the filesystem will fail with write errors, but the data already on disk is secure.

panic

Cause a kernel panic and halt the system. This is a very obvious failure mode that is certain to get noticed. In the two previous failure modes, errors are more subtle and the problems might not be noticed right away.

-m reserved_block_percentage

When a filesystem begins to fill up, a normal user will be barred from filling the filesystem completely up. The reason for this is that a completely full filesystem will suffer bad fragmentation, which should be avoided for performance reasons. Also, if the root filesystem is 100% full, the machine may become unbootable. A full disk also usually means that users with home directories on that partition may find it impossible to log in.

Only the root user is allowed to exceed this limit. The margin of free disk allows the boot process to work and the root user to log in. But if the root user fills up the disk, you're in trouble.

Now that disks are becoming huge, the default percentage of 5% may be overly large, and something more like 1% may be suitable for some filesystems.

-u user

Change the user that can use reserved blocks. The user is stored as a numerical UID.

-g group

Set a group that can use reserved blocks. This is stored as a numerical GID in the filesystem.

-O [^]mount_option ...

Set the filesystem's mount options. This is supported only by kernels from 2.4.20 on. Any values given at mount time, or in */etc/fstab*, will override these options. An option prefixed with ^ is cleared instead of set. Many options can be given, separated by commas.

-s [0|1]

Enable or disable the sparse superblock feature. On huge filesystems, enabling this can save quite a bit of space because fewer backup superblocks are used, freeing up space. After setting or resetting this feature, you must run *e2fsck* on the filesystem to make it valid again.

Supporting IDE CD Burners

As mentioned in Chapter 27, when CD burners first appeared on the market, they were all SCSI. The standard Linux tool to burn CDs, *cdrecord*, was written to support SCSI burners. Later, cheaper IDE burners appeared. Rather than fixing cdrecord to understand IDE burning, the SCSI-IDE translation module was made to bridge the gap. This is important for CD burning in 2.4 kernels; it is no longer needed in 2.6.

This module is available in all stock distribution kernels now; CD burners are very common hardware these days. But if you roll your own 2.4 kernel, enable it like this: In the kernel configuration, select and enable "SCSI support," then enable support for SCSI CD-ROMs and SCSI generic. Back at the main level, select "ATA/IDE/MFM/RLL support," then "IDE, ATA and ATAPI Block devices." Finally, find and enable "SCSI emulation support."

After building this kernel, configure the modules in */etc/modules* (Red Hat/Fedora) or */etc/modules.d/local* (Debian) as described in the section "Burning with IDE CD burners" in Chapter 27. This procedure sets up the system so that it loads the *ide-scsi* module before loading the SCSI CD device module or the SCSI "generic" driver. As described in the same section, put the option hdc=ide-scsi onto the kernel command line in your boot loader. If you now reboot, you should be all set to burn CDs.

Logical Volume Manager (LVM)

Logical volume management is one of the most powerful disk management techniques available on Linux. It allows you to free yourself from having to think about physical volumes and, instead, think about the volumes you need in a logical fashion. Almost. It is very seductive, but you should keep in mind that disks do fail, and if you do not plan for this in your LVM management, you may lose a lot of data. What LVM does allow you to forget about entirely is all the messing about with partitions that people traditionally do when finding space for user data and system files. LVM volumes can be resized at will, so if your filesystem can be resized (and most can) you gain a great degree of freedom in managing your disk resources.

The basic way to set up LVM is to set aside some disks or disk partitions. The sequence of utilities used is as follows:

1. Put the disks or partitions under LVM management by using *pvcreate*. This puts the physical volume under LVM control.

2. Once you have one or more physical volumes, run *vgcreate* to create a volume group, combining one or more of the physical disks into one large virtual disk.

3. On this volume group, you can create one or more logical volumes using lvcreate. These logical volumes can be used for filesystems, for swap, or directly by applications such as databases.

Each of these building blocks has programs to display their properties, called *pvdisplay*, *vgdisplay*, and *lvdisplay*. There are multiple other commands to change different properties of LVM objects. And most of them have a lot of options, most of which you will never use or miss. Because there are so many commands, we'll go through them by task instead of by command and show only typical option usage. The following is ordered more or less as follows: creating, displaying, changing, and destroying LVM objects.

Initializing a disk or partition

You can initialize either a whole disk or a partition for LVM use as follows:

```
# pvcreate /dev/hdc
pvcreate -- physical volume "/dev/hdc" successfully created
```

If you're initializing a whole disk that has a partition table on it, *pvcreate* will back off, and not even *--force* will talk it into initializing it. You must destroy the partition table, as shown in the following procedure. The procedure is *very* dangerous because there are no sanity checks. Only you can stop yourself from doing something wrong, such as destroying the contents of a disk, with the dd command.

```
# pvcreate /dev/hdc
pvcreate -- device "/dev/hdc" has a partition table


pvcreate [-d|--debug] [-f[f]|--force [--force]] [-h|--help]
        [-s|--size PhysicalVolumeSize[kKmMgGtT]] [-y|--yes] [-v|--verbose]
        [--version] PhysicalVolume [PhysicalVolume...]
# dd if=/dev/zero of=/dev/hdc bs=1k count=1
1+0 records in
1+0 records out
# blockdev --rereadpt /dev/hdc# pvcreate /dev/hdc
pvcreate -- physical volume "/dev/hdc" successfully created
```

 When booting, the partition check will print hdc: unknown partition table. This is nothing to worry about, because there is no partition table on a disk that is all devoted to LVM.

When you create a physical volume in a partition, the partition needs to be the right type. You can find out the type though *fdisk* (which is normally used to change partitions, but can also be used just to view information about them):

```
# pvcreate /dev/hdc1
pvcreate -- invalid partition type 0x83 for "/dev/hdc1" (must be 0x8e)
# fdisk /dev/hdc
...Command (m for help): t
Partition number (1-4): 1
Hex code (type L to list codes): 8e
Changed system type of partition 1 to 8e (Linux LVM)
Command (m for help): w
The partition table has been altered!

Calling ioctl() to re-read partition table.
Syncing disks.
# pvcreate /dev/hdc1
pvcreate -- physical volume "/dev/hdc1" successfully created
```

Creating a volume group

A volume group occupies one or more physical volumes. A volume group, in turn, contains one or more logical volumes. A logical volume can contain several physical volumes, but it becomes more vulnerable that way, because two disks fail twice as often as one disk. Therefore, although it is seductive to pool all your physical disks into one volume group, it may also cause a lot of trouble if a disk fails.

You can create a volume group called Disk2 on */dev/hdc* this way:

```
# vgcreate Disk2 /dev/hdc
vgcreate -- INFO: using default physical extent size 4 MB
vgcreate -- INFO: maximum logical volume size is 255.99 Gigabyte
vgcreate -- doing automatic backup of volume group "Disk2"
vgcreate -- volume group "Disk2" successfully created and activated
```

A "physical extent" can be likened to a partition. When managing volume group space, LVM allocates space in units of extents.

Making a logical volume

Logical volumes can be used for filesystems, swap, or perhaps databases that want disk devices without file systems. To create a logical volume named accounting on Disk2, enter:

```
# lvcreate -L5G -n accounting Disk2
lvcreate -- doing automatic backup of "Disk2"
lvcreate -- logical volume "/dev/Disk2/accounting" successfully created
```

The size number can be postfixed by K, M, G, or T, meaning kilobytes, megabytes, gigabytes, or terabytes, respectively. The default, if no unit is given, is megabytes. If the volume is going to be used for database use and speed is important, you may want to ensure that it is allocated contiguously in one block by supplying -C y on the command line. Note that this may make it harder to resize the volume later if there are other logical volumes in the volume group and they use space around the volume you want to resize.

Instead of the -L option, you can use the -l option and give the size of the logical volume in logical extents, which are usually the same size as physical extents. If you obtain the number of available physical extents in a volume group with *vgdisplay* (discussed later), this makes it easier to specify such things as making the volume half the size of the volume group or filling the whole volume group.

Now the volume is ready to be used as if it were a disk device. As the last line of the previous output shows, the path of the device is in the form */dev/volume_ group/logical_volume*.

Displaying physical volume properties

Perhaps the most interesting property of a physical volume is how many free physical extents it contains. The following *pvdisplay* output shows that the PE size of the device is 4 MB, and that 23,497 PEs are free. There is a lot of space, and if you

want to move the contents through the *pvmove* command (shown later), there is
little to move.

```
# pvdisplay /dev/hdc
--- Physical volume ---
PV Name               /dev/hdc
VG Name               Disk2
PV Size               111.79 GB [234441648 secs] / NOT usable 4.25 MB [LVM:
239 KB]
PV#                   1
PV Status             available
Allocatable           yes
Cur LV                3
PE Size (KByte)       4096
Total PE              28617
Free PE               23497
Allocated PE          5120
PV UUID               BSN7hI-u8DU-vT4g-WUdv-aaYZ-ECNK-5f65vm
```

Displaying volume group properties

The *vgdisplay* command shows all available volume groups on the system. The
following display shows several interesting parameters: the maximum logical
volume size (MAX LV), how many logical volumes it houses (Cur LV), the number of
physical volumes it consists of (Cur PV), and how many physical extents you still
have at your disposal (Free PE).

If invoked with the -v option, *vgdisplay* also lists all the logical volumes and physical volumes associated with each disk group.

```
# vgdisplay -v Disk2
--- Volume group ---
VG Name               Disk2
VG Access             read/write
VG Status             available/resizable
VG #                  2
MAX LV                256
Cur LV                1
Open LV               0
MAX LV Size           255.99 GB
Max PV                256
Cur PV                1
Act PV                1
VG Size               111.79 GB
PE Size               4 MB
Total PE              28617
Alloc PE / Size       1280 / 5 GB
Free  PE / Size       27337 / 106.79 GB
VG UUID               K7L9Gz-foUx-gw7W-5Iy9-Sfoo-8d4C-EtZqQT

--- Logical volume ---
LV Name               /dev/Disk2/accounting
VG Name               Disk2
LV Write Access       read/write
```

```
LV Status              available
LV #                   1
# open                 0
LV Size                5 GB
Current LE             1280
Allocated LE           1280
Allocation             next free
Read ahead sectors     1024
Block device           58:7


--- Physical volumes ---
PV Name (#)            /dev/hdc (1)
PV Status             available / allocatable
Total PE / Free PE    28617 / 27337
```

Displaying logical volume properties

The default *lvdisplay* displays exactly the same information as *vgdisplay -v*. With the *-v* option, however, *lvdisplay* shows something you can't get through *vgdisplay*: which physical volumes the logical volume occupies and some additional, less interesting I/O statistics.

```
# lvdisplay -v /dev/Disk2/accounting
--- Logical volume ---
LV Name                /dev/Disk2/accounting
VG Name                Disk2
LV Write Access        read/write
LV Status              available
LV #                   1
# open                 0
LV Size                5 GB
Current LE             1280
Allocated LE           1280
Allocation             next free
Read ahead sectors     1024
Block device           58:7


    --- Distribution of logical volume on 1 physical volume  ---
    PV Name                PE on PV      reads     writes
    /dev/hdc               1280          1         82369


    --- logical volume i/o statistic ---
    1 reads   82369 writes


    --- Logical extents ---
    LE    PV                       PE      reads     writes
    00000 /dev/hdc                 00000   1         2086
    00001 /dev/hdc                 00001   0         0
...
    01278 /dev/hdc                 01278   0         0
    01279 /dev/hdc                 01279   0         64
```

Listing disks and volume groups

The *pvscan* command scans your system's disks to find physical volumes. It also shows the available volume groups as a side effect, as well as the free and occupied space in them.

```
# pvscan
pvscan -- reading all physical volumes (this may take a while...)
pvscan -- inactive PV "/dev/hdc"   is in no VG  [111.79 GB]
pvscan -- ACTIVE   PV "/dev/hda11" of VG "Disk0" [43.77 GB / 584 MB free]
pvscan -- ACTIVE   PV "/dev/hdb"   of VG "Disk1" [232.88 GB / 0 free]
pvscan -- total: 3 [388.45 GB]/in use:2 [276.66 GB]/in no VG: 1 [111.79 GB]
```

Adding disks to a volume group

To add */dev/hdd* (previously formatted as a physical volume using *pvcreate*) to Disk2, enter:

```
# vgextend Disk2 /dev/hdd
vgextend -- INFO: maximum logical volume size is 255.99 Gigabyte
vgextend -- doing automatic backup of volume group "Disk2"
vgextend -- volume group "Disk2" successfully extended
```

Removing a disk from a volume group

If the physical disk has one or more logical volumes, their contents must be moved before it is removed from its volume group. The move is done with *pvmove*, as shown in the following example:

```
# pvmove /dev/hdc
pvmove -- moving physical extents in active volume group "Disk2"
pvmove -- WARNING: moving of active logical volumes may cause data
loss!pvmove -- do you want to continue? [y/n] y
pvmove -- 249 extents of physical volume "/dev/hdc" successfully moved
# vgreduce dev /dev/hdc
vgreduce -- doing automatic backup of volume group "Disk2"
vgreduce -- volume group "Disk2" successfully reduced by physical volume:
vgreduce -- /dev/hdc
```

If the destination is not specified as a parameter, the data in */dev/hdc* will be moved to free extents on other physical volumes. It is recommended that you make a backup of your data before doing this. Once the physical volume is clear, it can be removed from the volume group with *vgreduce*, and then the disk can be removed safely.

If you have a new disk in the system where you want to move the data from the old disk, add the new disk to the volume group and enter *pmove olddisk newdisk*.

Expanding a logical volume

Expanding a volume with *lvextend* is quite easy, providing one of the major advantages of LVM. No preparation is needed, so long as you have enough space to perform the expansion. After the logical volume has been expanded, the filesystem on it can be enlarged or the application using it can be told of the change. Note that not all software using disk partitions directly is capable of taking advantage of a resized partition. You may want to just create a new logical volume for these applications and add in the application. An ext2 (or ext3) filesystem is resized with *resize2fs*, which is capable of finding the size of the underlying device itself.

```
# lvextend -L +5G /dev/Disk2/accounting
lvextend -- extending logical volume "/dev/Disk2/accounting" to 10 GB
lvextend -- doing automatic backup of volume group "Disk2"
lvextend -- logical volume "/dev/Disk2/accounting" successfully extended
# resize2fs /dev/Disk2/accounting
resize2fs 1.34 (25-Jul-2003)
Resizing the filesystem on /dev/Disk2/accounting to 2621440 (4k) blocks.
The filesystem on /dev/Disk2/accounting is now 2621440 blocks long.
```

The *-L* option to *lvextend* accepts, as its parameter, either the absolute size or size changes prefixed with + or -. Units of K, M, G, and T can be used, just as with *lvcreate*.

Shrinking a logical volume

Shrinking a logical volume is just like expanding it, except that the application or filesystem must use less space before you can shrink the volume. Even fewer applications support shrinking their disk usage than growing it. The trick with shrinking a logical volume is to shrink it no more than its contents, because otherwise you will destroy some of the contents. In the case of an ext2 filesystem, it can be convenient to take a two-step approach: first shrink the filesystem a tad too much, then shrink the logical volume, and then resize the filesystem again, letting *resize2fs* figure out the right size. So, to shrink the accounting filesystem from 5 GB to 4 GB, run something like this:

```
# resize2fs /dev/Disk2/accounting 3993M
resize2fs 1.34 (25-Jul-2003)
Resizing the filesystem on /dev/Disk2/accounting to 1022208 (4k) blocks.
The filesystem on /dev/Disk2/accounting is now 1022208 blocks long.
# lvreduce -L -1G /dev/Disk2/accounting
lvreduce -- WARNING: reducing active logical volume to 4 GB
lvreduce -- THIS MAY DESTROY YOUR DATA (filesystem etc.)
lvreduce -- do you really want to reduce "/dev/Disk2/accounting"? [y/n]: y
lvreduce -- doing automatic backup of volume group "Disk2"
lvreduce -- logical volume "/dev/Disk2/accounting" successfully reduced
# resize2fs /dev/Disk2/accounting
resize2fs 1.34 (25-Jul-2003)
Resizing the filesystem on /dev/Disk2/accounting to 1048576 (4k) blocks.
The filesystem on /dev/Disk2/accounting is now 1048576 blocks long.
```

Removing a logical volume

Of course, you should be sure that there is no data you want on the volume before removing it. Then enter a command such as:

```
# lvremove /dev/Disk2/accounting
lvremove -- do you really want to remove "/dev/Disk2/accounting"? [y/n]: y
lvremove -- doing automatic backup of volume group "Disk2"
lvremove -- logical volume "/dev/Disk2/accounting" successfully removed
```

Removing a volume group

Once a volume group has no logical volumes left, removing the volume group is a two-step process. First deactivate the group with *vgchange*, then remove it with *vgremove*:

```
# vgchange -a n Disk2
vgchange -- volume group "Disk2" successfully deactivated
# vgremove Disk2
vgremove -- volume group "Disk2" successfully removed
```

The -*a* option to vgchange changes the availability of a volume group. Use n to make it unavailable and y to make it available again.

Removing a physical volume

Actually, this section has a trick subject. There is no way to remove a physical volume. Once *pvscan* shows the volume to be "inactive" or *pvdisplay* alleges that the volume is a "new physical volume," the disk or partition may be reused for whatever purpose.

```
# pvscan
pvscan -- reading all physical volumes (this may take a while...)
pvscan -- inactive PV "/dev/hdc"   is in no VG  [111.79 GB]
pvscan -- ACTIVE   PV "/dev/hda11" of VG "Disk0" [43.77 GB / 584 MB free]
pvscan -- ACTIVE   PV "/dev/hdb"   of VG "Disk1" [232.88 GB / 0 free]
pvscan -- total:3 [388.45 GB]/in use: 2 [276.66 GB]/in no VG: 1 [111.79 GB]
# pvdisplay /dev/hdc
pvdisplay -- "/dev/hdc" is a new physical volume of 111.79 GB
```

Starting and stopping LVM

If you are in a recovery or troubleshooting situation and LVM needs to be manipulated by hand, there are two commands. *vgscan* shows you the status of the logical volumes on the system, and *vgchange* changes their status:

```
# vgscan
vgscan -- reading all physical volumes (this may take a while...)
vgscan -- found inactive volume group "Disk2"
vgscan -- found inactive volume group "Disk0"
vgscan -- found inactive volume group "Disk1"
vgscan -- "/etc/lvmtab" and "/etc/lvmtab.d" successfully created
vgscan -- WARNING: This program does not do a VGDA backup of your volume
groups
# vgchange -ay
vgchange -- volume group "Disk0" successfully activated
vgchange -- volume group "Disk1" successfully activated
vgchange -- volume group "Disk2" successfully activated
```

Stopping LVM is even easier:

```
# vgchange -an
vgchange -- volume group "Disk0" successfully deactivated
vgchange -- volume group "Disk1" successfully deactivated
vgchange -- volume group "Disk2" successfully deactivated
```

LVM snapshots

LVM supports a very useful feature called *snapshots*. With this, you can freeze a volume while it's being used and then, for example, make a backup of the frozen copy. This should get you a consistent backup image.

If you back up a partition while it's being used—unless you use special tools—the backup will in many cases be unusable. Most filesystem backup tools have no problems with the filesystem itself, but if the accounting software continues to write onto its files while they are being backed up, the backup will probably be useless. Most software needs to be shut down during backups for this reason. An LVM snapshot is a good and fast alternative:

```
# lvcreate -L100M -s -n accbackup /dev/Disk2/accounting
lvcreate -- WARNING: the snapshot will be automatically disabled once it
gets full
lvcreate -- INFO: using default snapshot chunk size of 64 KB for "/dev/
Disk2/accbackup"
lvcreate -- doing automatic backup of "Disk2"
lvcreate -- logical volume "/dev/Disk2/accbackup" successfully created

    ... do backup of /dev/Disk2/accbackup ...
# lvremove /dev/Disk2/accbackup
lvremove -- do you really want to remove "/dev/Disk2/accbackup"? [y/n]: y
lvremove -- doing automatic backup of volume group "Disk2"
lvremove -- logical volume "/dev/Disk2/accbackup" successfully removed
```

The snapshot stays unchanged because, even while the original is being updated, LVM backs up the unchanged data, a strategy called "copy on write." This has two implications. First, it means that if there are few changes to the original, the snapshot will use very little space. Second, making a snapshot is very fast—but as long as you keep the snapshot around, there is a extra read/write operation every time a block is updated. The previous command creates a reserve of 100 MB for all changes made during the snapshot, and if more space is needed for the changed data, the snapshot will be deactivated.

A snapshot can be regarded as a backup. If you make a snapshot every night, you can have several days of backups online and accessible at all times. The snapshot is read-only and can't be made read/write, so you must copy the whole snapshot to a fresh volume before it's usable as a ordinary filesystem.

Runtime Kernel Configuration

Changing a system's properties without having to reboot it, or even take down services, is one of the holy grails of system administration. Linux has many short-comings in this area, but the kernel itself is fairly reconfigurable. Not only does runtime kernel module loading and unloading allow you to change properties and hardware support in a system, but the Linux kernel has two ways of changing quite a few configuration parameters. The */proc/sys* files and *sysctl* command are different interfaces that let you manipulate these parameters. Both require *procfs* support in the kernel.

If you have a look at /proc/sys, you might find, depending on your hardware and kernel options, 300 or more different files that tune the kernel in some way. If you take one of the filenames found there, say, *fs/file-max*, you can transform it into a variable name for *sysctl* by simply exchanging the slashes with dots. Thus, *fs/file-max* becomes *fs.file-max*. If you do a long listing (*ls -l*) of *fs/file-max*, you'll see it has read/write permissions for root, which means that it can be changed. Most of the files in /proc/sys are writable. A small demonstration of the interfaces follows:

```
# cd /proc/sys# sysctl fs.file-max
fs.file-max = 92000
# cat fs/file-max
92000
# echo 92100 > fs/file-max
# cat fs/file-max
92100
# sysctl -w fs.file-max=92000
fs.file-max = 92000
```

The filesystem limits in particular are self-tuning. They grow as the system needs them to. Other parameters that you yourself need to tune will be mentioned in relevant documentation. For example, if you configure a firewall's parameters, such as net.ipv4.ip_forward and net.ipv4.conf.default.rp_filter, the *iptables* documentation lists the parameters and discusses the appropriate settings. If you struggle with a specific problem that the kernel seems to be imposing on you, you can find what can be changed through:

```
# find /proc/sys -type f -perm -0600 -print
/proc/sys/abi/fake_utsname
/proc/sys/abi/trace
...
```

sysctl

Syntax

```
sysctl [-n] [-e] variable ...
sysctl [-n] [-e] -w variable=value ...
sysctl [-n] [-e] -p [ filename ]
```

Description

The *sysctl* command displays and changes kernel parameters. The variables available are the same as found in /proc/sys and vary depending on kernel configuration, the modules loaded, and the hardware on the system.

The first syntax is used to show a kernel parameter. Several parameter names can be given on the command line. The second form changes the given parameters. The third form loads a file with settings. If no filename is given, the default is /etc/sysctl.conf, and this file is loaded on boot by most distributions.

Examples

The following is a default /etc/sysctl.conf file from a Red Hat Fedora Core system.

```
# Controls IP packet forwarding
net.ipv4.ip_forward = 0
```

```
# Controls source route verification
net.ipv4.conf.default.rp_filter = 1

# Controls the System Request debugging functionality of the kernel
kernel.sysrq = 0

# Controls whether core dumps will append the PID to the core filename.
# Useful for debugging multithreaded applications.
kernel.core_uses_pid = 1
```

The commands to get and set kernel.core_uses_pid are as follows:

```
# sysctl -w kernel.core_uses_pid=1
kernel.core_uses_pid = 1
# sysctl kernel.core_uses_pid
kernel.core_uses_pid = 1
```

Note that the syntax in the file is different from the command line. In the file, there must be spaces around the equals sign, whereas on the command line there must be none.

Objective 4: Configuring PCMCIA Devices

PCMCIA devices have historically been handled fairly well by Linux. For the most part, they will just work as long as your system has the right drivers. If you have a problem, follow the troubleshooting steps given in this section.

PCMCIA hardware is detected when the OS boots. PCMCIA devices are manufactured to relatively strict standards and generally run into few problems. On Red Hat systems, PCMCIA is supported by a module called *kernel-pcmcia-cs*. Debian-based systems use the *pcmcia-cs* module. Your PCMCIA devices often require a package called *hotplug*. This package is responsible for providing a daemon that can:

- Recognize card insertions and removals as events to be acted upon
- Load and unload drivers whenever an event is recorded
- Allow hot swapping of cards
- Provide the necessary modules for proper recognition of PCMCIA cards

The *cardmgr* process is watching your PCMCIA/PC-CARD slots. If it sees a 32-bit PC-CARD, the process ignores it. Instead, the kernel hotplug system picks up the insertion event and handles the card. Both *cardmgr* and *hotplug* will load the kernel driver module appropriate for the inserted card and then configure it according to the administrative settings. When the card is removed, the driver is taken down and unloaded. Unlike with Windows, you can safely remove cards without telling the operating oystem about it first. But sometimes you may want to. For example, if the device is a network card, you may want to release the DHCP lease before removing the card so that you can get the same IP number back when returning (this will depend on the DHCP server policy). Also, it isn't a good idea to remove a PCMCIA hard disk device while it is in operation.

When it comes to a 32-bit PC-CARD, there is little to configure. They are in reality PCI cards, and like other PCI cards they're automatically configured. PCMCIA devices, on the other hand are more closely related to the old ISA bus, and there are many things to handle. The rest of this chapter assumes that card services are installed and start on boot.

PCMCIA configuration files

Several configuration files govern *cardmgr*. When a PCMCIA card card is first inserted, its identification is read and looked up in */etc/pcmcia/config*. This causes the correct module or modules to be loaded and a script corresponding to the device class to be run to do setup work. The scripts are stored in */etc/pcmcia*. The classes found in the *config* file are currently network, isdn, cdrom, ftl, serial, parport, ide, iccc, and teles. Not all these have scripts. The scripts further consult files called */etc/pcmcia/*.opts* to fetch user/administrator settings, such as IP numbers for network cards.

/etc/pcmcia/config

This file contains the card database, which maps card identifiers to drivers. A card's identification can be shown by *cardctl* as shown here:

```
# cardctl ident
Socket 0:
  product info: "3Com", "Megahertz 589E", "TP/BNC LAN PC Card", "005"
  manfid: 0x0101, 0x0589
  function: 6 (network)
Socket 1:
  product info: "Lucent Technologies", "WaveLAN/IEEE", "Version 01.01", ""
  manfid: 0x0156, 0x0002
  function: 6 (network)
```

Based on this, you can look the card up in the *config* file. If you search for the first two strings, you will find this:

```
card "Lucent Technologies WaveLAN/IEEE Adapter"
  version "Lucent Technologies", "WaveLAN/IEEE"
  bind "orinoco_cs"
```

The bind "orinoco_cs" tells *cardmgr* to bind the card to the drivers defined for orinoco_cs. This is defined earlier in the file:

```
device "orinoco_cs"
  class "network" module "hermes", "orinoco", "orinoco_cs"
```

This shows that the card is a network card and lists the relevant driver modules. *cardmgr* will load these in sequence, with appropriate options. Then the */etc/pcmcia/network* script will run to initialize the device.

If you have a PCMCIA card that you know to be supported by some existing driver but that is not listed in the file, insert the card, check its identification, and write in a card section corresponding to the card. If needed, also write in a device section enumerating the drivers, if this is not already present. After changing the file, you must restart *cardmgr*, because it reads the file only once, at startup.

/etc/pcmcia/config.opts

This file is actually included from *etc/pcmcia/config*, but as with the other *.opts* files, it is a local configuration file. It should be installed only the first time the packages are installed, not when they are overwritten. The most important configuration options here are toward the top. On some machines, the defaults in the file do not match the actual hardware and will need tweaking.

```
...
# System resources available for PCMCIA devices

include port 0x100-0x4ff, port 0x800-0x8ff, port 0xc00-0xcff
include memory 0xc0000-0xfffff
include memory 0xa0000000-0xa0ffffff, memory 0x60000000-0x60ffffff

# High port numbers do not always work...
# include port 0x1000-0x17ff

# Extra port range for IBM Token Ring
include port 0xa00-0xaff

# Resources we should not use, even if they appear to be available

# First built-in serial port
exclude irq 4
# Second built-in serial port
#exclude irq 3
# First built-in parallel port
exclude irq 7
...
# Examples of options for loadable modules

# To fix sluggish network with IBM Ethernet adapter...
#module "pcnet_cs" opts "mem_speed=600"
...
```

If your host has an extra parallel port to support an extra printer, you should also exclude the IRQ this hardware is using. Because of hardware conflicts, a few PCMCIA adapters work better if the port ranges and memory ranges are adjusted.

/etc/pcmcia/network.opts

Network configuration options are fetched from this script by *etc/pcmcia/network*, which does the actual setup work. On Red Hat and systems derived from that distribution, this file is not used, because the system gets network parameters from its own configuration system instead. If you look in the *etc/pcmcia/network* script, it should be clear whether this file is included or not. The usual setup here is that the script tests the current "scheme" and the card hardware address and sets things according to those values. Schemes can be set with *cardctl scheme name*, where *name* is something like home or work. That way you easily have different configurations for the same network card when you are at home and at work. About 20 different options can be set in this file, some of them quite uninteresting. A very abbreviated excerpt is reproduced here to illustrate what can be done:

```
# The address format is "scheme,socket,instance,hwaddr".
...
case "$ADDRESS" in
*,*,*,00:10:5A:FB:F0:D2)
...
    # Use DHCP (via /sbin/dhcpcd, /sbin/dhclient, or /sbin/pump)? [y/n]
    DHCP="y"
    # If you need to explicitly specify a hostname for DHCP requests
    DHCP_HOSTNAME="lorbanery"
    # Host's IP address, netmask, network address, broadcast address
    IPADDR=""
    NETMASK="255.255.255.0"
    NETWORK="10.10.10.0"
    BROADCAST="10.10.10.255"
    # Gateway address for static routing
    GATEWAY="10.10.10.1"
    # Things to add to /etc/resolv.conf for this interface
    DOMAIN=""
    SEARCH=""
    DNS_1=""
    DNS_2=""
    DNS_3=""
...
```

In Debian, this file can be managed by the *pcnetconfig* command. In Red Hat, the corresponding files are */etc/sysconfig/network-scripts/ifcfg-**, one for each interface. These can be managed with Red Hat's *netconfig* command.

/etc/pcmcia/*.opts

The other class scripts and the attendant **.opts* scripts are patterned along the same lines. They are all well-commented, and the **.opts* files contain at least one complete example, which is also often used as the default configuration. There are too many options and details in these scripts to repeat here or to test on a exam. If you insert a card and the drivers are loaded but it seems not to work, you should visit and customize these files to fix it.

PCMCIA commands

As shown in the previous sections, two commands that manage PCMCIA cards are *cardmgr* and *cardctl*.

cardmgr

Syntax

cardmgr [-q] [-d]

Description

cardmgr does its work as a daemon. When invoked, it goes into the background. When it detects the insertion or removal of a PCMCIA card, it installs or removes the corresponding drivers according to the driver database in */etc/pcmcia/config*.

The *-q* (quiet) option stops *cardmgr* from beeping when cards are inserted and removed. The *-d* option causes *cardmgr* to use *modprobe* to load modules instead of insmod.

In Red Hat you can set the default options in */etc/sysconfig/pcmcia*; on Debian the filename is */etc/pcmcia.conf*. Use the CARDMGR_OPTS variable.

cardctl

Syntax

cardctl *scheme* [*name*]
cardctl *command* [*socket*]

Description

cardctl checks and manipulates PCMCIA cards. The first form is used to set the desired configuration scheme, which some distributions support. The second form takes one of several commands, the most likely of which are:

ident
> Identify the card in the given socket. If no socket is given, all cards are identified.

eject
> Shut down the driver and cut power to the socket.

insert
> Enable power to the socket and perform the insertion procedure.

Examples

Change the scheme to work:

    cardctl scheme work

Check the identification of the card in PCMCIA slot number 1:

    cardctl ident 1

PCMCIA Troubleshooting

Here are some steps to take when your PCMCIA devices don't work as expected.

Steps for troubleshooting PCMCIA devices

While the system is running, try the following:

1. Use the *cardmgr* and *cardctl* commands, as described earlier, to determine manufacturer information. This information will help you determine whether you are using the correct drivers.

2. Issue the *cardinfo* command, which shows you all of the PCMCIA slots that exist. The command provides a graphical utility that provides information about each of your system's PCMCIA slots. It shows whether the device has been suspended, whether it is receiving power, whether it is compatible with the system, and whether the device is write-protected. If not run as root, *cardinfo* will only report information. Run as root, *cardinfo* allows you to suspend, resume, and eject devices, when those operations are supported.

3. Review and, when necessary, edit the */etc/pcmcia/config* file: This file contains the drivers that configure the card. Uncomment sections relevant to your card (e.g., orinoco_cs).

4. Verify that you have the proper drivers installed.

5. Determine that the proper devices are supported. You may need to install the Atmel or package, which in turn installs the */etc/pcmcia/atmel.conf* file. You may even need to update this file after it is installed. Such additions and edits allow the system to recognize additional devices that have different firmware. Other packages may need to be installed, depending upon your card. For example, to support Linksys cards, you may need to install the WPC11 package.

6. After you have made the necessary changes, restart PCMCIA through */etc/init.d/pcmcia restart*.

7. Use the *iwconfig*, *ifup*, or *ifconfig* command to configure the system.

8. Review the */var/log/messages* and */var/log/syslog* files for information (e.g., *tail -f /var/log/messages*). If you discover a message that reads something similar to "unsupported card in socket 0," you need to map the right driver to the correct device in the */etc/pcmcia/config* file.

9. Manually load possible modules. The modules that you can install using the *modprobe* command include *pcmcia_core*, *yenta_socket*, and *ds*. In some cases, you will have to install the *i82092* or *i82365* modules.

10. Beware the probe feature: if can cause problems when PCMCIA card modules are loaded. To isolate this problem, modify the modprobe command with the following argument:

    ```
    PCMCIA_CORE_OPTS="probe_io=0 setup_delay=10"
    ```

Boot problems

At times, a system will hang during the boot process when PCMCIA devices are scanned. This problem is sometimes caused by conflicts with the ACPI subsystem. To resolve such problems quickly, boot the system to LILO or GRUB, and then enter the following at the boot prompt:

```
NOPCMCIA=yes
```

You can also enter interactive mode to load PCMCIA modules one at a time at boot time. This will help you isolate the problem and create a fix.

Common PCMCIA errors

Several types of errors occur in regard to PCMCIA cards:

The system does not respond to card insertion. ACPI is often the culprit. Reboot the system and pass the following parameter at boot time: `pci=noacpi`.

The system responds to the card, but fails to recognize it as valid. If the system fails to respond at all, it's generally because no driver is assigned, or a driver mismatch has occurred. Use the command *cardctl ident* to determine the nature of the card. Review the card's information and settings. You can then edit the */etc/pcmcia/config* file (and related files) to resolve the problem. Look in */lib/modules/kernel-version* to see what modules you may have missed.

The driver does not load. In such cases, your system will recognize the card, but it will not function. The */var/log/messages* file will contain entries related to this problem. It means you are using the wrong driver for the card. It is also possible that the PCI card containing the PCMCIA interface is experiencing an IRQ conflict. If you suspect this is the case (and such cases are rare), use the *lspci* command to determine what IRQ and I/O port is used. Devices can share IRQs, but not I/O ports.

Improper configuration. Fix the configuration with the *getcfg* command.

Kernel upgrades

When upgrading the kernel, make sure that you select the "Network device support" and "Pocket and portable adapters" portions of the kernel configuration menu. These ensure that PCMCIA support is enabled.

You may find that your PCMCIA card no longer works after upgrading your kernel. This might be because you have forgotten to install the modules for that kernel. Before taking any further action, upgrade your kernel modules to see if this resolves the problem.

29

File and Service Sharing (Topic 2.209)

This Topic covers software that is used to share files and services between systems. Samba is used to share files and services between Linux and Microsoft Windows systems. NFS, the Network File System, is used to share files between systems running NFS clients (typically other Linux- or Unix-based systems).

This Topic contains only two Objectives:

Objective 1: Configuring a Samba Server
> The candidate should be able to set up a Samba server for various clients. This Objective includes setting up a login script for Samba clients and setting up an *nmbd* WINS server. Also included is to change the workgroup in which a server participates, define a shared directory in *smb.conf*, define a shared printer in *smb.conf*, use *nmblookup* to test WINS server functionality, and use the *smbmount* command to mount an SMB share on a Linux client. Weight: 5.

Objective 2: Configuring an NFS Server
> The candidate should be able to create an exports file and specify filesystems to be exported. This Objective includes editing exports file entries to restrict access to certain hosts, subnets, or netgroups. Also included is to specify mount options in the exports file, configure user ID mapping, mount an NFS filesystem on a client, use mount options to specify soft or hard and background retries, signal handling, locking, and block size. The candidate should also be able to configure TCP wrappers to secure NFS. Weight: 3.

Objective 1: Configuring a Samba Server

Samba is the name given to the software that implements the Server Message Block (SMB) protocol on Unix systems. SMB is the name commonly used to refer to the numerous services and protocols that are involved in implementing file and print sharing between computers running Microsoft Windows. Because file and print sharing in the Windows world includes many additional features (Kerberos authentication, WINS server integration, NetBIOS name lookups, domain and workgroup membership, and browser elections, just to name a few), Samba is a relatively complex piece of software. However, configuring it is not difficult, as long as you understand some basics of how the software works and what exactly needs to be done.

Because of all the functionality that is involved and because the Samba team is always trying to play catch-up with the moving target of Microsoft Windows releases, Samba is in active development. Samba 2.0 was released in January 1999 and was a major milestone in the world of Windows-to-Unix file and print integration. Samba 2.0 brought basic emulation of the Windows Primary Domain Controller (PDC), which gave administrators the ability to replace many of their existing Windows NT–based primary domain controllers with Linux systems running Samba. Samba 3.0 was released in September, 2003 and includes such new features as Kerberos 5 and LDAP integration, full Unicode support, trust relationships with other Windows-based PDCs, and support for Windows NT access control lists. For the purposes of this chapter, we will not be going into the Samba configuration required for many of these advanced network configurations. We will focus on:

- Configuring Samba to act as a Windows PDC and handle domain logins from a Windows PC
- Configuring Samba to serve directories and printers to Windows PCs
- Accessing a resource shared on a Windows PC from a Linux workstation

Samba most likely came as a default package with your Linux distribution. Many distributions ship it in three packages named *samba-common*, *samba-server*, and *samba-client*. If you're planning on using Samba only as a server, allowing Windows PCs to access directories on your Linux server, you don't need the *samba-client* package. For the purposes of this chapter, we will assume all Samba components are installed. If your vendor does not offer Samba as a package or you'd rather go the source route and compile it yourself, you can download the latest version of the Samba source from a mirror listed at *http://www.samba.org*.

The Samba packages include many files, the most important of which are described in Table 29-1.

Table 29-1. Key Samba files

Filename	Description
/etc/samba/smb.conf	Default configuration file for Samba
/usr/bin/smbpasswd	Creates or modifies a Windows user
/usr/bin/testparm	Checks the syntax of */etc/samba/smb.conf*
/usr/bin/smbstatus	Lists connection information and open files
/usr/sbin/smbd	Samba server
/usr/sbin/nmbd	NetBIOS name server
/usr/bin/smbmount	Mounts a Windows share from Linux

Basic Configuration File

The Samba configuration file, /etc/samba/smb.conf, is similar to most other Linux configuration files in that it is a plain ASCII file that can be edited with any text editor. The other features it shares with most other Linux configuration files is its relatively free-form syntax and the huge number of options that are available. Fortunately, the manual page for this file is very well done, explaining all available options and giving many good examples. The manual page can be accessed by typing *man smb.conf* from the command line.

The *smb.conf* file is broken down into two sections: the global section and the shares section (in Windows terminology, every directory shared to other systems is called a *share*). The global section defines settings that apply to the Samba server itself or are valid across all shares. This section is defined by the [global] directive, and all settings are in the format *variable = value*. Let's look at a global section from a default installation of Samba:

```
[global]
       workgroup = WORKGROUP
       server string = My File Server
       printcap name = /etc/printcap
       printing = lprng
       load printers = yes
       security = user
       encrypt passwords = yes
       smb passwd file = /etc/samba/smbpasswd
       domain logons = yes
       logon script = login.bat
```

This is, of course, not a complete list of options available in the global section, but it is enough to get you started. The workgroup variable defines the Windows workgroup that this Samba server will belong to. Think of workgroups as an informal association of Windows PCs. There are no authentication or membership details. Membership in a workgroup simply means that your computer will show up in a Windows browse list with other workgroup members.

The server string variable can be any text that describes your server. The next three lines all deal with how Samba interacts with the underlying printing subsystem. If printing is already correctly configured on your Linux server, Samba can interact with it without much configuration. The only important variable is printing, which tells Samba what kind of printing subsystem your version of Linux uses. Popular choices are lprng and CUPS.

The security variable is one of the most important variables in the *smb.conf* file, and the one that generates the most confusion in people new to Samba. The options for this variable are share, user, and domain.

Share-level security means that Windows users connecting to shared resources on the Linux server do not necessarily have to be valid Linux users. This situation is common when you want to set up a "guest" share or some other kind of no-privilege or anonymous access.

User-level security is the most common (and is the default in Samba 2.2 and later) and requires that Windows users connecting to the Samba server successfully authenticate themselves against the server. This can be done in a number of ways, but the point is that the Windows user identifies who he is, and Samba decides what access level to apply to him.

Finally, domain-level security assumes that the Samba server is a member of an existing Windows domain (much different from the aforementioned Windows workgroup). If domain-level security is in place, every attempted connection to the Samba server by a Windows PC prompts the Samba server to pass the authentication of the Windows user to the primary domain controller for that domain. In this way, Samba is still requiring authentication to access the shared resources but is acting as a gateway for that authentication process.

If your Samba server is acting as a file server for a relatively small set of users, security = user is probably the correct choice for you.

Windows Passwords

The encrypt passwords variable brings to light an important configuration issue with Samba and one that often confuses people new to Samba. With the advent of Windows 95OSR2 in 1996, Microsoft defaulted to encrypting the passwords that were exchanged between Windows systems when they authenticated to access shared resources. Before this date, these passwords were sent in plain text over the network, which posed serious security risks. In order to understand how this affected Samba, we must first understand how the standard Linux login process works.

Each Linux user has an entry in the *letc/passwd* file that defines important details about her user account, such as UID, GID, home directory, and shell. The user's entry in *letc/shadow* contains the user's encrypted password. This password is encrypted with a one-way hash for security reasons. When a user logs into a Linux system, the password she provides is encrypted with the standard encryption libraries, and the resulting encrypted string is compared with the encrypted string in *letc/shadow*. If they match, the user is authenticated and allowed into the system. There is no easy way to derive a user's password from the encrypted string in *letc/shadow*; the encryption algorithm is one-way only.

Windows (starting with Windows95OSR2) uses a similar scheme to store encrypted passwords. When one Windows machine authenticates against another in order to access shared resources, it's the encrypted password that is sent over the network. In order for Samba to communicate with Windows machines in this way, it has to be able to authenticate Windows users using the given encrypted password.

Now, you may be thinking that this should be easy, because we know that Linux users already have an encrypted password in *letc/shadow* on the Linux server. So Samba should just be able to compare the proffered Windows encrypted password with the string in *letc/shadow* and authenticate a Windows user, right? Unfortunately, that is not the case. Windows and Linux use different password encryption algorithms, so although the password might be the same for a Linux user and a Windows user, the encrypted string will not be. This means that if your Samba server is using user-level access to share resources with Windows systems running Windows 95OSR2 or later, you must maintain a list of Windows users and their encrypted Windows passwords on your Linux server, in addition to the list of users you already have in */etc/shadow*. Because this has been a default of Microsoft Windows for so long, `encrypt passwords = yes` is the default in the *smb.conf* file. The `smb passwd file` variable defines where this list of Windows users and their passwords resides, and it defaults to */etc/samba/smbpasswd*.

An example line for user *joe* from */etc/shadow* is:

```
joe:$1$xDTY3.yX$19R4lCBFrOfDrOSQds1NAO:13159:0:99999:7:::
```

An example line for the sane user from */etc/samba/smbpasswd* is:

```
joe:504:2D09ECB6715E94F6D9243782117C7417:3ADBA9C02F6A67701B419BFFF31A21F2:
[U          ]:LCT-43C571F8:
```

While normal Linux user accounts are maintained through commands such as *useradd* and *passwd*, the */etc/samba/smbpasswd* entries are maintained by the program *smbpasswd*. Some common options to *smbpasswd* are:

-a

Add a user.

-x

Delete a user.

-d

Disable a user.

-e

Enable a user.

Acting as a PDC

If you want your Samba server to act as a primary domain controller for Windows PCs, set `domain logons = yes`. The primary advantages of having your Windows PCs be a part of a domain managed by your Samba server are more client-level security options, more logging options, the ability to maintain client PCs through login scripts, and the ability to implement domain policies on client machines.

On Windows machines running Windows95OSR2, Windows 98, or Windows ME, joining a domain is as simple as configuring the domain name on the Windows client and authenticating against the Samba server with a valid username and password. On clients running Windows NT, 2000, XP, or 2003, there is another step involved. You must first create a machine account for each workstation that will be a member of the domain. This is accomplished by running *smbpasswd* with the *-m* and *-a* options. Machine accounts look like normal accounts in the */etc/passwd* file, but the username must be the same as the computer name of the Windows client. The smbpasswd program will automatically add a $ character to the end of the username, identifying it as a special machine account. No actual password is required for these accounts; they just must be present in the password database in order for these Windows machines to connect to your domain.

If your Samba server is operating as a domain controller, you must configure a netlogon share. This can be any physical directory on your Linux server. A netlogon section in *smb.conf* looks something like this:

```
[netlogon]
    comment = Network Logon Service
    path = /home/netlogon
    guest ok = yes
    writable = no
```

This section creates a sharename called netlogon that offers the physical directory */home/netlogon* as a Samba share. Guests are allowed to connect, and the share is read-only. The netlogon share is a default share on Windows domain controllers, and Windows PCs that belong to a domain will expect to find it. Two important files that belong in the *netlogon* directory are the login script and the group policy file.

Login Settings

Login scripts are simply Windows batch files that run every time a user logs into a Windows PC that is a member of a domain. The most common use for a login script is to restore drive mapping to network resources. Here is a sample login script, called *login.cmd*, that maps the user's home directory to H: and the share public to P::

```
net use h: /home
net use p: \\server\public
```

You do not have to include a sharename when specifying */home* because the server can figure out what the users' home directories are via their usernames.

Windows ships with a program called the Group Policy Editor that can be used to specify registry settings that are applied to each workstation every time a user logs into the domain. Use the Group Policy Editor to create a policy file, name it *config.pol*, and save it to the netlogon share to ensure that it is executed on every client when a user authenticates against the domain.

Shares

Once you have a global section defined and some user accounts created with *smbpasswd*, you're ready to define some resources to share.

We've already seen the basic setup for a share with the netlogon share. Other shares are configured the same way. All share sections in *smb.conf* start with [*sharename*] followed by any options you want to enable for the share. The only required option is path, which indicates what directory on your Linux server you're actually assigning to this share. Here is a share section example from the default *smb.conf* file:

```
[public]
    comment = Public Stuff
    path = /home/samba
    public = yes
    read only = yes
    write list = @staff
```

Most of these options are relatively self-explanatory, and the *smb.conf* manual page goes into great detail on every available option. The comment directive defines a line of text that will appear next to each folder in the network browse view on a Windows PC. The path directive defines the directory that is being shared. The public directive is a synonym for guest ok, meaning that guest users can connect to this share. The read only directive means that this share is not writable by default by users on remote systems, and write list defines a Linux group that does have write access to this share (in this case, any user in the *staff* group).

Startup

Like most other Linux server applications, any change to the configuration file requires a restart of Samba before the change will take effect. Samba is restarted the standard way:

```
# /etc/init.d/smb restart
```

This will restart the two Samba processes, *smbd* and *nmbd*. *smbd* is the main daemon that shares directories from the Linux system, while *nmbd* is the NetBIOS name server. This server provides name service for NetBIOS clients over TCP/IP. The NetBIOS name service is similar to the DNS service, which translates hostnames to IP addresses. *nmbd* translates Windows machine names to IP addresses. This ability is usually handled by Windows machines that run WINS (Windows Internet Name Service). If you want your Samba server to act as a WINS server, you must enable the global option wins support = yes. Then you must configure each Windows client to register with the WINS service. Once this is done, you will be able to browse for available Windows PCs using NetBIOS over TCP/IP and do IP address–to–Windows machine name mapping.

Use the Linux command *nmblookup* to query a WINS server and return the IP address of a given Windows machine name. Here is an example:

```
# nmblookup client1
querying client1 on 192.168.1.255
192.168.1.10 client1<00>
```

This tells us that *client1* has the IP address 192.168.1.10. The subnet with a broadcast address of 192.168.1.255 was searched in order to return this information.

There is a special share section that is unique among shares: the [printers] share. If this section is included in *smb.conf*, Windows clients can spool print jobs to any printer defined on your Linux server. Here is a sample [printers] share:

```
[printers]
    comment = All Printers
    path = /var/spool/samba
    browseable = no
    guest ok = no
    writable = no
    printable = yes
```

This section looks very similar to the other share sections we've seen, with the exception of the *printable* directive. This defines this share as a special printer share, and the directory */var/spool/samba* becomes the local Linux directory to which Windows print jobs are spooled. You can assign the same level of security to the printers share as you would any other share. As long as your underlying Linux printing subsystem is set up correctly, this is all you need to do to enable Windows clients to print to your Linux printers.

Troubleshooting

Now that we've seen how to perform a basic Samba setup, allowing Windows machines to connect to shared Linux resources, we must address the next stage of any server setup: troubleshooting. The Samba suite includes a number of useful tools that allow you to identify possible problems with your Samba configuration.

The *testparm* program parses your *smb.conf* file and notifies you of any syntax errors or other potential mistakes. It's a good idea to get into the habit of running *testparm* after you make any change to *smb.conf*, but before you restart Samba.

The *smbstatus* program with a -V option gives you an overview of a currently running *smbd* process, including the version of Samba that is running, the username and machine name of all currently connected clients, and a list of all resources that are currently in use.

Samba also has extensive logging capability. By default, Samba logs everything to the directory */var/log/samba*. The *smbd.log* and *nmbd.log* files contain events specific to those services. By default, every connecting client machine gets its own log in */var/log/samba*, named after the Windows machine name. These logs are useful for identifying when certain machines attempted connections and if any errors occurred during the communication process. Samba's log level can be increased in the global section of *smb.conf* to high enough levels that every action performed by any Samba service is logged. This is very useful for debugging any connection issues that may arise.

We have so far talked mostly about using the Samba suite to enable a Linux computer to act as a server for Windows PCs. However, Samba also gives us the ability to have a Linux computer act as a client on a Windows network, accessing shared Windows resources. In order to access these resources, they must be mounted into the Linux filesystem, just like any other shared network resource. The command to accomplish this is *smbmount*.

For example, if I wish to mount the shared directory *public* that is shared from the Windows server named *server1* on my Linux machine, I would type this command as *root*:

```
# smbmount //server1/public /mnt/public -o username=adamh,password=mypassword
```

This command assumes that the directory */mnt/public* exists on the local Linux system and that the user *adamh* with password mypassword is a valid user account on the Windows machine *server1*. If the authentication is successful, I will be able to change to the directory */mnt/public* and see the files that reside in the *public* directory on *server1*. The manpage for *smbmount* contains other command-line options that are useful in this context, such as Kerberos settings for connecting to an Active Directory share and specifying the UID and GID that will "own" the mount point.

Samba is a very powerful tool, and a useful one, especially in today's heterogeneous networks. This basic overview should give you enough information to get started using it.

Objective 2: Configuring an NFS Server

The Network File System (NFS) is the standard method for sharing files between Unix (and Unix-like) systems. Linux can be both an NFS server (offering its directories to other systems) and an NFS client (offering its own users access to directories on other systems).

The NFS Server

The NFS server can be installed by default during your distribution's installation process, but if NFS was not installed, you can install it from your distribution's installation media or FTP site. In addition to the NFS packages, you will need the following daemons and utilities.

Portmap
> The NFS server system must be running the portmap daemon, a server for the RPC service directory.

The NFS-related RPC daemons
> These are typically started automatically at boot time through */etc/init.d/nfs start* and consist of:

rpc.nfsd
> Handles file serving

rpc.statd and rpc.lockd
> Handle lock management

rpc.rpquotad
> Manages quotas

rpc.mountd
> Checks mount requests and hands out access handles

Configuring NFS Server Exports

The server uses */etc/exports* to configure NFS filesystems that it offers to remote systems. The format of the file entries is typically:

> **/path/to/export** [**host**](**options**)

The first field, */path/to/export*, is the path that you want to make available via NFS. An example would be */mnt/cdrom*. The second field, *host*, is the hostname, specified by name or IP address (with an optional netmask), to which you want the filesystem to be made available. If nothing is supplied for *host*, the filesystem is exported to everyone. The last field, *options*, is a comma-separated list of export options. Some standard examples are ro for read-only and rw for read/write.

The following is an example of an */etc/exports* file:

```
/mnt/cdrom            (ro)
/tmp                  (rw)
/home                 192.168.0.0/255.255.255.0(rw)
```

The first line exports */mnt/cdrom* read-only to the world. The second line exports */tmp* read-write to the world. The third line exports */home* read/write to only the 192.168.0.0 network.

Be very careful to not have any spaces between the host specification and the export options. The following are very different:

```
host (options)
host(options)
```

For more information about the format and options of */etc/exports*, view the *exports* manpage (*man 5 exports*).

Directories can also be exported based on hostname, wildcarded domain name (**.example.com*), or NIS netgroups. If you use NIS, you can use *@netgroup* to specify the hosts defined in the given netgroup.

To initially add all your entries in */etc/exports* to the list of exported filesystems (assuming *mountd* is already running), run *exportfs -av*. The *-a* option tells *exportfs* to add the entries and the *-v* option to print the output verbosely.

After you make any change to */etc/exports*, you must update the NFS server using *exportfs -rv*. This command reexports all directories in */etc/exports*, syncing the server's list of exports (maintained by *mountd* in */var/lib/nfs/xtab*) with */etc/exports*.

To remove a filesystem from *mountd*'s list of exportable filesystems, use *exportfs -u*. More information about *exportfs* may be found in the *exportfs*(8) manpage.

NFS Server Security

NFS was ingenious when it was created, but it has been plagued by many security problems. Therefore, the Linux implementation has integrated TCP wrappers support. TCP wrappers is a somewhat paranoid IP access control mechanism that is more fully documented in Chapter 40. Suffice it to say here that all hosts that should be able to access your NFS server must be allowed to do so. To secure your NFS server, put a statement like the following in your */etc/hosts.deny* file:

```
portmap,lockd,mountd,rquotad,statd: ALL
```

This disables access to all the NFS-related services altogether. To reenable NFS for your legitimate clients, put lines like the following in your */etc/hosts.allow* file:

```
portmap,lockd,mountd,rquotad,statd: 192.168.0.0/255.255.0.0
```

This means that, even if your */etc/exports* file exports your */mnt/cdrom* and */tmp* directories to the world, no one outside the 192.168.0.0/255.255.0.0 network will be able to contact the servers.

This mechanism does not allow netgroups to be used, but it does allow hostnames and domains (*.example.com*).

Even though the portmapper is, strictly speaking, not an NFS service, it too has been subject to security problems and access to it should also be restricted.

The */etc/hosts.allow* and */etc/hosts.deny* files also apply to your NFS client. It should be secured in the same way.

A server may not want to trust the remote *root* users. Trusting a remote *root* user would mean that the remote root can read *all* files, create device files with unhealthy permissions, and create setuid root scripts on the server. All these are bad things unless you are sure that the clients are all as secure as the server. Otherwise, add root_squash to the export option list in order to deny *root* access—or, more accurately, to change the UID of *root* requests to the *nobody* user before they go to the filesystem. The opposite of root_squash is no_root_squash. If you trust no one on the client, but still want them to have some access, you can use all_squash to squash all users down to nobodies. There are also the two options anonuid=*n* and anongid=*n*, which control exactly which account the squash options apply to. They used to be useful for PC/NFS, but that is obsolete now. They are perhaps useful if you want to share a public disk, such as an FTP server disk. If the FTP server user has UID 95 and GID 95, you can export *relatively* safely to the world through:

```
/home/ftp          (ro,all_squash,anonuid=95,anongid=95)
```

The NFS Client

The NFS client software on Linux consists of several parts: *portmap*, *rpc.statd*, and *rpc.lockd*. Commands such as *mount*, *showmount*, and *rpcinfo* are the tools you use.

The NFS client requires a specific set of kernel modules: nfs, lockd, and sunrpc. These kernel modules will be automatically loaded by the kernel module loader when you mount a remote filesystem.

The NFS client (as well as the server) require the system to be running the portmapper, the *portmap* daemon. To start it, run */etc/init.d/portmap start* (or on some systems, */etc/rc.d/init.d/portmap start*).

The utility required to get access to an NFS filesystem is *mount*. It is used to mount remote NFS filesystems as well as local filesystems. Generally, *mount* is used like this:

```
mount -o options remotehost:/remote/path /local/path
```

Table 29-2 lists the most common mount options used on NFS.

Table 29-2. NFS mount options

Mount option	Description
bg	When this is specified, if a mount times out, it will be backgrounded so as to not block the boot process and to give the user his command prompt back. That is the theory anyway; it has never worked on Linux for us.
hard	If a timeout occurs, send a "Server not responding" message to the console and continue to retry. (This is the default behavior.)

Table 29-2. NFS mount options (continued)

Mount option	Description
intr	For a hard mount that has timed out, allow I/O to be interrupted with a signal to the calling program. (The default is to not allow I/O on a hard mount to be interrupted.) This allows users that get hung due to NFS server downtime to free themselves from the lockup by pressing Ctrl-C.
nolock	Disable locking on this mount.
rsize=*num*	Read *num* bytes at a time (instead of the default 1024 bytes); 8192 should be used in most cases.
soft	If a timeout occurs, return an I/O error to the calling program. There is a definite risk that the program does not handle this error correctly and that the file will be incomplete or corrupted without warning.
wsize=*num*	Write *num* bytes at a time (instead of the default 1024 bytes); 8192 should be used in most cases.

When mounting NFS shares, always include the options hard,intr. It is absolutely reckless to use soft. A good example *mount* command for mounting the filesystem */export* on the NFS server *linux.example.com* with an 8-K block size on */mnt/nfs* is the following:

```
mount -o rsize=8192,wsize=8192,hard,intr linux.example.com:/export /mnt/nfs
```

NFS Tools

In addition to using the *mount* command to mount NFS filesystems, a few other useful NFS tools can help you use and administer them. In particular, the *showmount* and *rpcinfo* commands are regularly used.

nfsstat

Syntax

nfsstat [*options*]

Description

Display NFS server and client statistics. This command displays the number of times each RPC procedure in the NFS servers and clients have been called. This is mostly uninteresting, although the counters can be used to graph loads and in some situations to do troubleshooting. By default, the command displays both server and client statistics and both NFS and RPC statistics.

Options

-c

Show client-side statistics only, not server-side statistics

-n

Show NFS statistics only, not RPC statistics

-r

Show RPC statistics only, not NFS statistics

-s

Show server-side statistics only, not client-side statistics

rpcinfo

Syntax

```
rpcinfo -p [host]
rpcinfo -n [portnum] [-t | -tu] [host] program [version]
```

Description

Show RPC services for host.

Options

-p [host]

> Probe the portmapper on *host* and list registered RPC programs. If no *host* is specified, the system's hostname is used.

-n [portnum]

> Use *portnum* as the port number for the *-t* or *-u* option instead of the port number supplied by portmapper.

-t [host] program [version]

-u [host] program [version]

> Make an RPC call to *program* on *host* and report the response. The *version* of the service can optionally be specified. If the *-t* option is used, the call is done by TCP, whereas the *-u* option does it by UDP. This can be used as a RPC ping command. Thus, the following command pings the NFS service, all versions:
>
> ```
> # rpcinfo -u fileserver nfs
> program 100003 version 2 ready and waiting
> program 100003 version 3 ready and waiting
> ```

---

showmount

Syntax

```
showmount [options] host
```

Description

Show export mount information for *host*.

Options

-a, all

> List the client hostname and the mounted directory in *host:dir* format.

-d, directories

> List only the directories mounted by a client.

-e, exports

> Show the NFS server's export list.

--no-headers

> Suppress the descriptive headings from the output.

30

System Maintenance (Topic 2.211)

This Topic is a small part of the 201 exams, but it's key for all system administrators. It represents an advance in sophistication over several topics in the Level 1 exams:

- In Exam 102, you learned to configure system logs for your server. For Exam 201, you are expected to implement these custom system logs on a central logging server for your network.

- In Exam 101, you prepared to use package management for either RPM or Debian systems. Exam 201 requires you to build your own system packages for either RPM or Debian systems.

- The Level 1 Exams also discussed methods for creating your system backups. This 201 Topic expects you to implement backup storage plans for mission-critical data.

This Topic contains three Objectives:

Objective 1: System Logging
The candidate should be able to configure *syslogd* to act as a central network log server. This Objective also includes configuring *syslogd* to send log output to a central log server, logging remote connections, and using *grep* and other text utilities to automate log analysis. Weight: 1.

Objective 2: Packaging Software
The candidate should be able to build a package. This objective includes building (or rebuilding) both RPM- and deb-packaged software. Weight: 1.

Objective 3: Backup Operations
The candidate should be able to create an off-site backup storage plan. Weight: 2.

Objective 1: System Logging

System logging on Linux (and Unix) is done via the syslog service. One of the strong points of this service is that it can log over a network, so you can set up a central logging server. Events from many systems are then logged in chronological order and important messages can be checked in one place instead of on each of your hosts.

The weak point about using syslog over a network is that there is no security. Your central syslog server has no way to authenticate who sent a given message. In addition, messages are sent by UDP, which means that a message can be lost. UDP further weakens security, because it is easily the victim of IP spoofing. On top of that, the message is transported in plain text.

In other words, your remote logging is about as secure as your network. You can trust your central syslog as far as you can trust *all* the users that have access to your network. If you need more security than this, you should look at alternative syslog implementations, such as syslog-ng (see *http://www.balabit.hu/products/syslog-ng/* for more information).

Setting Up a syslog Server

The default configuration of the Linux system log daemon, *syslogd*, is secure because it does not listen on the network. To enable network listening, you have to customize your syslog init script, and *syslogd* must be started with the *-r* option.

In Debian, write directly into */etc/init.d/sysklogd* to insert the *-r* into the SYSLOGD variable. On Red Hat and many other distributions, edit */etc/sysconfig/syslog*, and change the SYSLOGD_OPTIONS variable. After changing the initialization script, restart the service. On Red Hat, the *rc* filename is */etc/init.d/syslog*.

You can verify that *syslogd* listens on the network by running the following command. It should produce at least one line exactly like the one shown. The 0. 0.0.0:514 means that your *syslogd* listens to the "any" interface at port 514.

```
$ netstat -an | grep 514
udp       0      0 0.0.0.0:514              0.0.0.0:*
```

You can restrict which hosts your *syslogd* will log from by specifying the *-l* option and a colon-separated list of *simple hostnames* (not FQDNs). An informed enemy can defeat this check trivially due to the inherent insecurity of UDP. You should have this in the back of your head before trusting logged data.

You should increase the security using some firewall rules such as these:

```
iptables -P INPUT DROP
iptables -A INPUT -p udp --dport 514 -j ACCEPT
```

On a host dedicated to being a log server, these commands restrict it to accepting only packets addressed to the 514 UDP port and dropping all other incoming traffic.

Setting Up syslog Clients

Setting up a client for your central syslog server is a simple matter of adding one line, similar to the following, to your */etc/syslogd.conf* file. This line logs messages from all syslog facilities with priority debug and higher to the host *roke.langfeldt. net*.

```
*.debug                    @roke.langfeldt.net
```

Both *facility* and *priority* are syslog concepts. Recognized facilities are authpriv, cron, daemon, kern, lpr, mail, mark, news, security or auth, syslog, user, uucp, and local0 through local7. An asterix (*) is allowed as a wildcard to cover all facilities.

Priorities are a hierarchy, at the bottom of which is debug. When you specify a priority, all priorities from that level up are sent to the log destination. Recognized priorities in ascending order are info, notice, warning or warn, err or error, crit, alert, and emerg or panic.

The syntax of the *syslogd.conf* file is quite rich and flexible. You can also have it both ways: logging remotely does not exclude logging locally.

With your configuration file prepared, restart the syslog service on the client by using the initialization script or by just typing:

```
kill -HUP `cat /var/run/syslogd.pid`
```

which forces the daemon to reread the configuration file. If you now look at */var/ log/messages* (on most distributions), you should see the same message as is logged on the client at restart:

```
...
Jan 12 12:30:00 roke CROND[3580]: (root) CMD (   /sbin/rmmod -as)
Jan 12 12:37:45 roke -- MARK --
Jan 12 12:37:47 10.0.0.5 syslogd 1.4.1: restart.
```

The restart message shows that communication is established. If no message is received, check your setup and firewalls. You can send messages from the command line with the *logger* program. It lets you specify the priority and the prefix or label on the message. The following command:

```
$ logger -p notice -t logspam 'hello world'
```

results in a log message such as the following on the server:

```
Jan 12 12:59:51 10.0.0.5 logspam: hello world
```

Using the Central Logs

The great thing about central logs is that they are much easier to manage than logs scattered about individual hosts, and it becomes very simple to search for interesting events in them.

Exactly what constitutes an interesting event is for you to decide. Some syslog analysis packages on the Net offer good ideas of many different kinds of interesting events; these packages might make the job a whole lot easier for you.

For the sake of example, we'll assume that all log lines containing the strings error and warning are interesting. The *grep* command can be used to extract lines matching a pattern (regular expression) from a file or stream. The straightforward approach to a log extraction command is something like this:

```
# grep -i warning /var/log/messages# grep -i error /var/log/messages
```

As you add new strings to search, for this will tend to become tedious, because each command has to read through the whole file. A good alternative is to use egrep with a more complex regular expression:

```
# egrep -i '(warning|error)' /var/log/messages
```

This at least will make only one pass of the logs. But the command line will become unruly as you add strings. As luck would have it, someone has already thought about this and all the commands of the *grep* family accept a *-ffile* option. This causes them to read the regular expressions in from a file, which is much neater and easier to maintain. Just put the things you're interested in into */etc/interesting-in-logs* and the command line to invoke the search stays simple.

Another problem in searching for short and simple patterns is that you usually get back a lot of log messages you just know will never turn out to be interesting. On an IDE system that runs *smartd*, for example, you will get a lot of messages saying Raw_Read_Error_Rate changed, which is probably not very interesting and which certainly can be worrisome for someone who does not understand what's going on. They can be removed by a negative *grep* command such as *grep -v Raw_Read_Error_Rate*. This negative search expression should be as specific as possible, so as to not eliminate error messages that really are important. Thinking you know about all your problems can be quite a bit worse than knowing that you don't know about them. Here, too, you will quickly run into the problem of too many strings to remove. The solution again is the *-f* option.

A complete example command therefore is:

```
# grep -f /etc/interesting-in-logs /var/log/messages | \
>    grep -v -f /etc/interesting-in-logs-not
```

Remember that Linux also creates several other log files, such as the security or auth log files that contains events about logins, failed logins, and other security-related issues. A failed login, for example, results in "Failed password   for" messages. Occasional failed logins are to be expected because users mistype their names and passwords, but repeated messages of that sort can indicate an attack. So let's consider how to tell when you're being inundated with failed login attempts.

The full message looks like this:

```
Jan 12 08:07:07 roke sshd[1935]: Failed password for root from 10.0.0.5 port
37370 ssh2
```

If you remove the timestamp and the process ID at the beginning of the message, as well as the port number on the end, you get lines that can be counted and presented as a failed logins summary. The *cut* command was introduced in Chapter 5, in the section "Process Text Streams Using Text-Processing Filters," and is suited for this task.

```
# grep 'Failed password' secure | cut -d' ' -f 4,6-11
roke Failed password for root from 10.0.0.5
roke Failed password for root from 10.0.0.5
roke Failed password for janl from 10.0.0.5
roke Failed password for janl from 10.0.0.5
```

If you add some more plumbing to this, you get a summary that's easily readable:

```
# grep 'Failed password' secure | cut -d' ' -f 4,6-11 | sort | uniq -c | \
    sort -n
      2 roke Failed password for janl from 10.0.0.5
      2 roke Failed password for root from 10.0.0.5
```

And this may well be the sort of activity summary that can alert you to security problems. This illustrates another great thing about a central logging server: as long as an intruder does not compromise the server itself, your logs are out of reach for an intruder on one of your other hosts, and she cannot modify the logs to hide her activities. For this reason, a central log server is even better if it is well secured.

Objective 2: Packaging Software

Many package formats are used on Linux. The two main ones are Debian's deb format and Red Hat's RPM format. Debian has a package called *alien* that is able to assimilate and transform foreign package formats, specifically RPM, so they can be installed. The *alien* tool can be used to exchange *.rpm*, *.tgz*, and *.deb* package formats.

The general methodology when building a package is to set down a build process for the source that is as close as possible to what someone would do by hand, but then to pack the files into their own directory hierarchy that contains only the files that belong in the package. The contents of the hierarchy are then packaged. A lot of the magical things happen in the build process to put files into this dummy hierarchy in such a way that they will still work when the user installs them in the / and */usr* directory hierachies.

Building RPM Packages

Building RPM packages from an SRPM (source RPM) package is pretty straightforward. First, of course, you must find and download the source package. These are typically stored in *src.rpm* files.

There are two ways of building an RPM source package. If the package is satisfactory to you and you only want to recompile it for your system (for example, because you use SUSE while the binary package was built for Red Hat), you can simply enter:

```
rpmbuild --rebuild package.src.rpm
```

This builds a binary package from the source package and places the result in the *RPMS* directory discussed later.

The other way of building a source RPM package involves installing it with the ordinary *rpm* command. This is what you should do if you want to modify a package. When you use *rpm -ivh* to install a source package, the contents are distributed among different directories under */usr/src/redhat* on Red Hat and Fedora systems or under something similar, such as */usr/src/RPM*, in other RPM-based distributions. The directories are:

BUILD
> Used for the build process. If you need to troubleshoot a build process, its leftovers are here.

RPMS
> Where finished packages are placed. There are subdirectories for the different available architectures such as *athlon*, *i386*, *i486*, and so on. These are ready-to-install binary packages.

SOURCES
> Contains untouched source files and the patches needed for them.

SPECS
> Contains package build recipes. These are comparatively small text files that specify the complete build process for a package.

SRPMS
> Where finished source packages are placed. These are source packages that are ready for rebuilding into binary packages.

When you are done with a specific package, remove the build tree and accompanying files. If you build any significant number of packages, the amount of space used can grow quite a bit.

Once the package is installed, change to the *SPECS* directory. There you should find a file called *package.spec*. This is the build recipe for the package. The contents of this will be explained in the next section. To build a package, enter:

```
rpmbuild --bb package.spec
```

Once the package is built, the resulting files are dropped into the *SRPMS* and appropriate *RPMS* subdirectories. The exact locations are printed at the end of the build process, such as:

```
...
Wrote: /usr/src/redhat/SRPMS/gzip-1.3.3-11.src.rpm
Wrote: /usr/src/redhat/RPMS/i386/gzip-1.3.3-11.i386.rpm
...
```

rpmbuild

Syntax
```
rpmbuild {-ba|-bb|-bp|-bc|-bi|-bl|-bs} [rpmbuild-options] specfile
rpmbuild {-ta|-tb|-tp|-tc|-ti|-tl|-ts} [rpmbuild-options] tarbal
rpmbuild {--rebuild|--recompile} sourcepkg
```

Description

rpmbuild builds RPM binary or source packages based on *.spec* files, tarballs containing a *.spec* file, or a source RPM package. The *-b?* options build from *.spec*, and the *-t* files from tarfiles that have been compressed through *gzip* or *bzip2*.

Frequently used options

-ba, -ta
> Build binary and source packages (*a*=all).

-bb, -tb
> Build binary packages.

-bs, -ts
> Build source package.

--target {arch-vendor-os|arch}
> For packages that understand this option, it sets the compilation target. The most likely use is to specify an optimization, such as *--target i686*.

--recompile
> Build binary packages directly from a source RPM.

Modifying RPM Packages

You are already familiar with a typical build process from Chapter 4. The process for a particular package is laid out in a spec file in the package's source RPM package; by altering the spec file you can change subsequent builds. We'll show a typical spec file here, using the Fedora Core 1 *gzip* package as an example. Modifying a package is quite simple, but there is a bit of magical syntax in the spec file.

> A good, if somewhat dated, introduction to the RPM format is available in the book *Maximum RPM*. It is still available in print and also available on the Web at *http://www.rpm.org/max-rpm*.

The *gzip* spec file begins:

```
1 Summary: The GNU data compression program.
2 Name: gzip
3 Version: 1.3.3
4 Release: 11
5 License: GPL
6 Group: Applications/File
7 Source: ftp://alpha.gnu.org/gnu/gzip/gzip-%{version}.tar.gz
```

The opening lines offer various formalities. Name, Version, and Release, are important; the others less so.

```
 8 Patch0: gzip-1.3-openbsd-owl-tmp.diff
 9 Patch1: gzip-1.2.4-zforce.patch
10 Patch2: gzip-1.2.4a-dirinfo.patch
11 Patch3: gzip-1.3-stderr.patch
```

```
12 Patch4: gzip-1.3.1-zgreppipe.patch
13 Patch5: gzip-1.3-rsync.patch
14 Patch6: gzip-1.3.3-window-size.patch
```

The preceding lines enumerate the patches in the package. They are referred to by number rather than name later in the file when the time comes to apply them.

```
15 URL: http://www.gzip.org/
16 Prereq: /sbin/install-info
17 Requires: mktemp less
18 Buildroot: %{_tmppath}/gzip-%{version}-root
```

The URL tag is not very important, but the Prereq and Requires tags are. They define the prerequisites for installing the package. Requires is now a synonym for Prereq. They used to be different, Prereq specifying components that had to be installed before the package itself was installed and Requires specifying components that were needed only for the execution of the package after installation.

```
20 %description
21 The gzip package contains the popular GNU gzip data compression
22 program. Gzipped files have a .gz extension.
23
24 Gzip should be installed on your Red Hat Linux system, because it is a
25 very commonly used data compression program.
26
```

Some descriptive paragraphs. These should try to include recommendations about when the package may be needed or useful. This section is ended by the next % section heading, which in this spec file is:

```
27 %prep
28 %setup -q
29 %patch0 -p1
30 %patch1 -p1
31 #patch2 -p1
32 %patch3 -p1
33 %patch4 -p1 -b .nixi
34 %patch5 -p1 -b .rsync
35 %patch6 -p1 -b .window-size
36
```

These steps prepare the source for compilation. Note that patch number 2 is commented out. All the lines shown in this section are macros.

%setup -q unpacks the source. Each *%patchn* line applies the numbered patch, giving the options specified, such as *-p1*, to the *patch* command.

```
37 %build
38 export DEFS="-DNO_ASM"
39 export CPPFLAGS="-DHAVE_LSTAT"
40 %configure  --bindir=/bin
41
42 make
43 make gzip.info
44
```

These are all the steps needed to build the package. Not too bad. %configure is a macro that invokes a GNU-style configure script with all the right options for placement, optimization, and so on. The environment variables set before invoking the macro modify the behavior of the script.

```
45 %install
46 rm -rf ${RPM_BUILD_ROOT}
47 %makeinstall  bindir=${RPM_BUILD_ROOT}/bin
48 mkdir -p ${RPM_BUILD_ROOT}%{_bindir}
49 ln -sf ../../bin/gzip ${RPM_BUILD_ROOT}%{_bindir}/gzip
50 ln -sf ../../bin/gunzip ${RPM_BUILD_ROOT}%{_bindir}/gunzip
51
52 for i in zcmp zegrep zforce zless znew gzexe zdiff zfgrep zgrep zmore
   ; do
53    mv ${RPM_BUILD_ROOT}/bin/$i ${RPM_BUILD_ROOT}%{_bindir}/$i
54 done
55
56 gzip -9nf ${RPM_BUILD_ROOT}%{_infodir}/gzip.info*
57
58
59 cat > ${RPM_BUILD_ROOT}%{_bindir}/zless <<EOF
60 #!/bin/sh
61 /bin/zcat "\$@" | /usr/bin/less
62 EOF
63 chmod 755 ${RPM_BUILD_ROOT}%{_bindir}/zless
64
65 # we don't ship it, so let's remove it from ${RPM_BUILD_ROOT}
66 rm -f ${RPM_BUILD_ROOT}%{_infodir}/dir
67
```

While the build process wasn't too complex, the install process on the preceding lines is quite a mouthful. On line 46, the target directory for the installation is emptied of any old contents. Line 47 is another macro, this one calling make install with the right options for a GNU-style *Makefile* and overriding the directory where the binaries should be installed. Lines 49–66 are devoted to symlinking, moving, compressing, creating the *zless* command, and then removing one file we don't want distributed, the *dir* file that should already exist on the host where the installation is taking place.

```
68 %clean
69 rm -rf ${RPM_BUILD_ROOT}
70
```

The preceding lines remove some of the leftovers after the build process.

```
71 %post
72 /sbin/install-info %{_infodir}/gzip.info.gz %{_infodir}/dir
73
```

%post is a postinstall script used when installing the binary package. This script modifies the *dir* on the install subject to include the *gzip* info pages.

```
74 %preun
75 if [ $1 = 0 ]; then
76   /sbin/install-info --delete %{_infodir}/gzip.info.gz %{_infodir}/dir
77 fi
78
```

The %preun, or preuninstall script is run right before uninstalling the binary package. If a package installs services, this is a good place to stop the service so that it's not left running after the software is installed.

```
79 %files
80 %defattr(-,root,root)
81 %doc NEWS README AUTHORS ChangeLog THANKS TODO
82 /bin/*
83 %{_bindir}/*
84 %{_mandir}/*/*
85 %{_infodir}/gzip.info*
86
```

The file list enumerates all the files that are to be packaged. The list should be complete and exhaustive if some file is forgotten, *rpmbuild* will complain. If the file is not needed, remove it in the build step. Otherwise, make sure it gets on the list. The files installed here are enumerated in lines 82 through 85. Line 80 sets the default attributes: the permissions, owner, and group of the files installed. The permissions is an octal number such as you would use with *chmod*. Line 81 declares which files are documentation, so that they can be specially handled when needed.

```
87 %changelog
88 * Tue Oct 28 2003 Jeff Johnson <jbj@redhat.com> 1.3.3-11
89 - rebuilt.
90

        ...

241
242 * Tue Apr 22 1997 Marc Ewing <marc@redhat.com>
243 - (Entry added for Marc by Erik) fixed gzexe to use /bin/gzip
```

The final section is simply documentation for the build itself.

After all that verbiage, it's good to know that you don't need a deep understanding of it all to modify a package. Modifying a package mostly consists of adding a patch, removing a patch, or perhaps adding or removing an option from a build or install command. How this is done should be obvious from the preceding example and comments. If you ever find old packages that you want to compile for your newer installation, they may contain things that are now obsolete, or they may fail to enumerate some file in the %files section. In most cases, this can be dealt with by intuition, web searches, or looking through the documentation files in the RPM package itself.

Building Deb Packages

Debian source packages are documented, among other places, in *http://www.tldp. org/HOWTO/Debian-Binary-Package-Building-HOWTO* and *http://www.debian. org/doc/maint-guide*.

Debian packages are usually fetched and installed by *apt-get*. Sources can be fetched using *apt-get source package*. The Debian repository system tells *apt-get* what is needed. It fetches the files and creates a source directory, named after the package and suitable to build from, with the help of *dpkg-source*. If you make any unfortunate changes in the source directories, they can be regenerated with *dpkg-source -x package.dsc*.

During the build process, the package files are generated and are available in the directory above the source directory. The build process shows this step like this:

```
dpkg-deb: building package `gzip' in `../gzip_1.3.2-3woody1_i386.deb'.
```

These packages can be installed normally with *dpkg* or uploaded to a Debian repository. If you maintain more than a few Debian packages for more than a few machines, it will probably save time if you build a private package repository to use with *apt-get*.

Signing the package

Debian requires that packages are signed with *gpg*. Because you probably do not have the package maintainers' cryptography keys, you need your own. If you do not already have one, you can easily create one, as illustrated here:

```
$ gpg --gen-key
pg (GnuPG) 1.2.1; Copyright (C) 2002 Free Software Foundation, Inc.
This program comes with ABSOLUTELY NO WARRANTY.
This is free software, and you are welcome to redistribute it
under certain conditions. See the file COPYING for details.

gpg: keyring `/home/joe/.gnupg/secring.gpg' created
gpg: keyring `/home/joe/.gnupg/pubring.gpg' created
Please select what kind of key you want:
   (1) DSA and ElGamal (default)
   (2) DSA (sign only)
   (5) RSA (sign only)Your selection? 5What keysize do you want? (1024) 2048
Requested keysize is 2048 bits
Please specify how long the key should be valid.
        0 = key does not expire
      <n>  = key expires in n days
      <n>w = key expires in n weeks
      <n>m = key expires in n months
      <n>y = key expires in n yearsKey is valid for? (0) 3y
Key expires at Fri Jan 12 00:23:00 2007 CETIs this correct (y/n)? y

You need a User-ID to identify your key; the software constructs the user id
from Real Name, Comment and Email Address in this form:
    "Heinrich Heine (Der Dichter) <heinrichh@duesseldorf.de>"
Real name: Joe Doe
Email address: joe@example.com
Comment: <nothing>
You selected this USER-ID:
    "Joe Doe <joe@example.com>"
Change (N)ame, (C)omment, (E)mail or (O)kay/(Q)uit? o
You need a Passphrase to protect your secret key.
Enter passphrase: <passphrase>
Repeat passphrase: <passphrase>

We need to generate a lot of random bytes. It is a good idea to perform
some other action (type on the keyboard, move the mouse, utilize the
disks) during the prime generation; this gives the random number
```

```
generator a better chance to gain enough entropy.
..+++++
+++++
public and secret key created and signed.
key marked as ultimately trusted.

pub   2048R/97DAFDB2 2004-01-12 Joe Doe <joe@example.com>
      Key fingerprint = 85B2 0933 AC51 430B 3A38  D673 3437 9CAC 97DA FDB2
```

Note that this key cannot be used for encryption. You may want to use
the command "--edit-key" to generate a secondary key for this purpose.

Building the package

There are two main commands for building packages. *dpkg-buildpackage* and *debuild*. You may find cases where one works and the other does not.

dpkg-buildpackage

Syntax

```
dpkg-buildpackage [options]
```

Description

This command is roughly the same as running the following shell commands, except that *dpkg-buildpackage* also signs the package files and does a whole lot of other things to check the package.

```
# debian/rules build# debian/rules binary
```

Frequently used options

-r/usr/bin/fakeroot

> If you run the build as a user, use this option to fake being root for the Debian build scripts.

-ksigning-address

> Sign the package with this key, instead of any key that may be specified in the package.

Example

To build a package while not being root, signing with the key belonging to Joe Doe, enter:

```
dpkg-buildpackage -kjoe@example.com -r/usr/bin/fakeroot
```

debuild

Syntax

```
debuild [options]
```

Description

debuild is a fully automatic script that generates Debian package files in a form that is ready for upload to a repository. It detects when to use *fakeroot*, but that option may also be specified on the command line. The command takes *dpkg-buildpackage* options, so to sign the package with your own key, use *-k*.

Frequently used options

-rootcmd=/usr/bin/fakeroot
> If you run the build as a user, use this option to fake being root for the Debian build scripts.

-ksigning-address
> Sign the package with this key, instead of any key that may be specified in the package.

Modifying Deb Packages

The Debian build process is controlled by two files inside the source directory: *debian/control* and *debian/rules*. The *control* file defines formalities such as the package name, version, and dependencies, in addition to documenting the package. As explained in the previous sections on the *dpkg-buildpackage* command, the *rules* file controls building.

control

In this section we'll take a look at the *control* file in the package for gzip.

```
Source: gzip
Section: base
Priority: required
Maintainer: Bdale Garbee <bdale@gag.com>
Build-Depends: debhelper, automake, autoconf (>= 2.52)
Standards-Version: 3.5.6.0

Package: gzip
Architecture: any
Pre-Depends: ${shlibs:Depends}
Depends: debianutils (>= 1.6)
Essential: yes
Description: The GNU compression utility.
 This is the standard GNU file compression utility, which is also the
default
 compression tool for Debian.  It typically operates on files with names
 ending in '.gz'.
 .
 This package can also decompress '.Z' files created with 'compress'.
```

The file has two main sections, one for the source package and one for the binary package that will be built from it. Building the package requires more than just having it installed, as illustrated by comparing Build-Depends: and Depends:. The one bit of magic here is the value of the Pre-Depends: field. ${shlibs:Depends} will cause the building helper *dh_shlibdeps* to find shared library dependencies and *dh_gencontrol* to fill in the binary package control file with the actual values. *debhelper* is a package that assists in the build process of this package.

rules

The *rules* file usually starts out as a automatically generated template file that does all the right things.

```
1  #!/usr/bin/make -f
2  #       Debian rules file for gzip, requires the debhelper package.
3  #       Crafted by Bdale Garbee, bdale@gag.com, 5 November 2000
4
```

The *rules* file is a *Makefile*.

```
5  # Comment this to turn off debhelper verbose mode.
6  export DH_VERBOSE=1
7
8  # This is the debhelper compatibility version to use.
9  export DH_COMPAT=3
10
11 CFLAGS="-g -O2 -Wall"
12
```

The DH_ variables modify the behavior of the *debhelper* programs. They are documented in the *debhelper* manpage, and we will skip them here as they are outside our scope. CFLAGS is the standard *Makefile* variable that stores options for the C compiler.

```
13 configure: configure-stamp
14 configure-stamp:
15         dh_testdir
16         CFLAGS=$(CFLAGS) ./configure \
17                 --prefix=/usr \
18                 --infodir=`pwd`/debian/gzip/usr/share/info \
19                 --mandir=`pwd`/debian/gzip/usr/share/man
20         touch configure-stamp
21
```

Note the infodir and mandir settings and the difference between them and the prefix setting in the configure command. The prefix must be correct so that the program will find itself and its libraries after it is installed. After the configuration is done, the file *configure-stamp* is created to mark the event. The *dh_* programs called during the different steps in this process are *debhelper* programs that do various bits of setup and work. We'll just take them for granted in this book.

```
22 build: configure-stamp build-stamp
23 build-stamp:
24         dh_testdir
25         $(MAKE)
26         touch build-stamp
27
28 clean:
29         dh_testdir
30         dh_testroot
31         -rm -f build-stamp configure-stamp
```

```
32          make distclean || exit 0
33          dh_clean
34
```

Not much to say, because the operations are commonplace and are mostly stored in *dh_* programs. The setup was done in the configure target.

```
35   install: build
36           dh_testdir
37           dh_testroot
38           dh_clean -k
39           dh_installdirs
40
41           make install prefix=debian/gzip/usr bindir=debian/gzip/bin \
42                   scriptdir=debian/gzip/usr/bin
43           ln debian/gzip/bin/gzip debian/gzip/bin/uncompress
44
```

The *make install* command overrides a lot of variables to ensure that the files end up in the packaging directory hierarchy. The *ln* was added by the package maintainer to make sure there is an *uncompress* program in the package.

```
45   binary-indep:   build install
46
47   binary-arch:    build install
48         dh_testdir
49         dh_testroot
50         dh_installdocs README* TODO
51         dh_installmanpages
52         dh_installinfo gzip.info
53         dh_installchangelogs
54         dh_link
55         dh_strip
56         dh_compress
57         ln -s gunzip.1.gz debian/gzip/usr/share/man/man1/uncompress.1.gz
58         ln -s zgrep.1.gz debian/gzip/usr/share/man/man1/zegrep.1.gz
59         ln -s zgrep.1.gz debian/gzip/usr/share/man/man1/zfgrep.1.gz
60         dh_fixperms
61         # You may want to make some executables suid here.
62         dh_makeshlibs
63         dh_installdeb
64         dh_shlibdeps
65         dh_gencontrol
66         dh_md5sums
67         dh_builddeb
68
69   binary: binary-indep binary-arch
```

This is the whole build process. As you see, the maintainer has put some ln commands here too. Other than those, the commands just follow a templated schema to build the package.

```
70   .PHONY: build clean binary-indep binary-arch binary install configure
71
```

This just tells make that the enumerated targets are phony—that is, that they do not refer to files that are meant to be built. The line is not important unless somebody is ornery enough to actually create a file with the name of one of the targets.

Objective 3: Backup Operations

This Objective is restricted to creating an off-site backup plan. Offsite backups could be considered backup backups. They can be used if the main backup burns or breaks in some way, but the main use of off-site backup is to perform disaster recovery (e.g., to get a backup site running if the primary production site collapses in an earthquake, floods, or becomes inoperational or unavailable in some other way).

The important question as a senior administrator is: what will I do if my production machine room burns down? If the answer is satisfactory to yourself and your management, you're fine. It's likely that your company would be out of business if it lacked computers for too long. If your current plans cannot cope with a disaster, it may well be the senior system administrator's job to point this out to management and help plan for disaster recovery. To prepare for the worst, one of the first and easiest things to do is create an off-site backup scheme. This at least enables you to install software and databases when you get hardware to install it on.

You should consider three classifications of threats for disaster and recovery planning:

Natural
Hurricane, tornado, flood, and fire

Human
Operator error, sabotage, implant of malicious code, and terrorist attacks

Environmental
Equipment failure, software error, telecommunications network outage, and electric power failure

After studying and defining the initial potential threats, you need to mantain an analysis risk review cycle, because the environment is dynamic, as are the risks.

You should consider the following criteria when selecting an off-site storage plan:

Geographic area
Distance from the organization and the probability of the storage site being affected by the same disaster as the organization

Accessibility
Length of time necessary to retrieve the data from storage and the storage facility's operating hours

Security
Security capabilities of the storage facility and employee confidentiality, which must meet the data's sensitivity and security requirements

Environment
>   Structural and environmental conditions of the storage facility (i.e., tempera-ture, humidity, fire prevention, and power management controls)

Cost
>   Cost of shipping, operational fees, and disaster response/recovery services

All these list items can directly affect your backup method.

 It is important also to retrieve media on a regular basis from off-site storage and test them to ensure that the backups are being per-formed correctly.

There are many ways to do off-site backups: everything from guards or couriers collecting tapes and storing them in a huge hole in a mountain to the more dot-com way of doing it: "Just rsync the whole thing over the Internet and we will put it on tapes for you."

Because it's likely that your data is sensitive in some manner and you're not going to give it away to strangers, it is probably a good idea to practice some "due dili-gence" on the storage company. This can be anything from asking some simple questions to see whether they're security-conscious to detailed questionnaires and site visits or even a periodic security evaluation done by a professional auditor. If your company is large enough to have an audit department, they *might* have input on what to look for, though data security audits are very different from auditing ledgers and accounts.

An off-site backup plan should often support a company disaster recovery plan. This should be defined by the business side of the company. It may also provide the business case you need to justify the cost involved.

To create an off-site backup plan, you need to answer all the same questions as with normal backups, the most important of which is: exactly what are you protecting yourselves against and what do you need to get back when restoring?

Once that has been determined, it's merely a question of setting up any addi-tional backup schedules of full, incremental, cumulative, or whatever backups reflect the stated needs.

31

System Customization and Automation (Topic 2.213)

This LPI Objective covers the writing of scripts and focuses on the Bash shell and Perl because they provide a balance among ease of use, popularity, and expressive power.

It is very important for senior sysadmins to be efficient with their time and their systems. For this reason, admins typically automate tasks by implementing system scripts. Recording and rerunning a common procedure can also prevent errors that come about in manual procedures because an administrator happens to mistype or forget a step.

This Topic contains only one Objective:

Objective 1: Automating Tasks Using Scripts
The candidate should be able to write simple Perl scripts that make use of modules when appropriate, use the Perl taint mode to secure data, and install Perl modules from CPAN. This Objective includes using *sed* and *awk* in scripts and using scripts to check for process execution and to generate alerts by email or pager if a process dies. Candidates should be able to write and schedule automatic execution of scripts to parse logs for alerts and email them to administrators, synchronize files across machines using *rsync*, monitor files for changes and generate email alerts, and write a script that notifies administrators when specified users log in or out. Weight: 3.

Objective 1: Automating Tasks Using Scripts

Scripting is one of the oldest and most powerful tools in the Unix environment. Understanding scripts is also one of the most useful administrator skills when it comes to analyzing system problems, because setting down a procedure in a script, and testing it, forces the administrator to decide exactly what should be done.

The most common scripting languages in Linux are Perl and the Unix shells *sh* and *bash*. Perl is a complete scripting environment in itself. On most Linux installations, *sh* and *bash* are the same interpreter, but this is not the case on Unix in general. *sh* and *bash* adhere to the old toolbox philosophy of Unix: lots of little programs that do one task well. Among the subordinate tools they invoke are *sed* and *awk*.

Thus, using *sed* and *awk* is considered an integral part of shell scripting. One thing to note about Bash and shell scripting in general is that in an unfriendly environment it is quite easy for an intruder to subvert the scripts and turn them to their own uses.

To take this exam, you should *already* know scripting on the level described in the Objective so that you understand all the examples shown here. This book will not teach you to program. Scripting is complex enough that there are whole books devoted to the subject. We will only scratch the surface. The scripts shown in this chapter illustrate system administration tasks more than they help you learn programming.

Shell scripting is best suited for checking things and then executing something in response. For text processing and scripting that require more than 10 to 100 lines of *bash*, you will most often find Perl to be a better tool.

Learning Shell and Perl Programming

There are a plethora of excellent books on both these subjects. *Learning Perl* is a good text for a non-programmer to learn Perl from. *Programming Perl* is a good reference and introduction for programmers. For Bash scripting, take a look at *Learning the Bash Shell*. (All three books are published by O'Reilly.)

On your system, you will find that Perl has about 30 manpages divided into subject areas, with much basic and tutorial material. Bash has a gigantic manpage and built-in help for all its commands showing all options and syntax.

Scripting with Bash and Friends

Bash is the standard shell on Linux. One reference for it is the manpage; the info page (invoked at the command line through *info bash*) is probably even better. You'll learn much from reading other people's scripts, because there are quite a few clever tricks you can use.

Unix and Linux scripts start with a magic line such as:

```
#!/bin/bash
```

When the first 2 bytes of an executable file are #! Unix and Linux know that the file is a script and should be interpreted by a program. The name of the program follows. In our case it is /bin/bash, the standard path to Bash on Linux. You may include exactly one word, or cluster, of arguments as well—for example -xv to trace script execution.

Variables

When a script is invoked with arguments or options, these are stored in numbered variables $1, $2, $3, and so on. In $0 you will find the command name under which the script was started. The complete list of arguments can also be referred to as "$@", with the quotes. The often seen, older form $* should not be used because it does not preserve quoting and word separation. A short example of a script displaying its arguments:

```
#!/bin/bash
echo $0 $1 $2 $3 $4
echo $@
```

And the output from one sample invocation:

```
$ ./arg.sh 1st 2nd 3rd 4th
./arg.sh 1st 2nd 3th 4th
1st 2nd 3th 4th
```

User variables in shell scripts are, by tradition, in all uppercase characters. They are always referenced with a leading dollar sign but always assigned without the dollar sign. Thus, an assignment and a reference look like this:

```
#!/bin/bash
FOO="hello world"
echo "$FOO"
```

As shown in this example, it is a good idea to use double quotes (") a lot in shell scripts. In the case of the assignment, double quotes are also required; otherwise, FOO would be only hello, and world would be assumed to be a command to execute.

Checking process status and sending alerts

Suppose you want to write and run a script that checks whether your web server is running. In Linux, if the command you want to check is in your PATH, check it with the pidof command:

```
#!/bin/bash
if pidof httpd >/dev/null; then
    echo We have Apache servers
else
    echo There is no Apache server
fi
```

Because *pidof* prints pids, and you don't want to see those in this particular setting, the >/dev/null redirects the output to the special file */dev/null*, where it will disappear.

It's probably not very helpful to just print something in a window if you want to learn that an Apache server is not running. An email is far better. On most systems you will find the executable */usr/sbin/sendmail*, even if the systems have another MTA such as Exim or Postfix instead of Sendmail, and using this executable directly is the safest way of sending email from scripts:

```
#!/bin/bash
if pidof apache >/dev/null; then
```

```
    :; # That's OK then
else
    /usr/sbin/sendmail -t <<EOM
To: admin@example.com
Subject: Apache is not running

Apache is not running on $(uname -n)

Regards,
    The Apache posse
.
EOM
fi
```

When using *sendmail*, you should not start any lines with From because that is the envelope From header used to separate mails in standard mail spool files. Also, avoid lines containing only a single dot (.) because mail programs use such lines to denote the last line in the input.

You will often find scripts using *mail* (or *mailx* or *Mail*) to send email. This is, in general, insecure, because they tend to interpret ~ (tilde) as a command character, and if someone tricks your script into outputing a ~ sequence, he can easily compromise your system. Also, the options to these commands vary among Unixes and even among Linuxes.

There are two other things to note in the sample script shown earlier. The <<EOM construct causes the shell to set up *sendmail*'s standard input to read from the next line up to (but not including) the line that consists only of EOM. The $(uname -n) construct executes the parenthesized command and inserts its output instead. The old way of writing this is `uname -n` (i.e., a command quoted in single back-quote or backticks). The newer $( ) notation has more structured logic for quoting, which handles several levels of quoting without causing insanity.

Sending pager or SMS alerts is not supported by Linux out of the box. You need to use an Internet email-to-pager or email-to-SMS gateway or install some combination of software and hardware locally that is capable of sending out such an alert.

 It is, of course, also perfectly possible to use *ps* with suitable options in combination with *grep* or *awk* to determine whether a specific process is alive, e.g.: *ps -ef | grep apache*. A thorny problem with that approach, for example, is that the *grep* command tends to find itself, because it obviously contains the string apache. This can be especially bad if the pipe continues and ends in a kill command that then kills the *grep* command before it found all the Apache processes. Using some regular expression mangling such as: *ps -ef | grep ap[a]che* avoids showing the unwanted grep command.

Monitoring users and using awk

 Monitoring users may be subject to legal restrictions where you live and work.

User logging is done in two system files. These are most easily read in a shell script by the commands *w*, *who*, and *last*. If you want to monitor the use of the root account, look at the output of *w*:

```
$ w
 15:44:48  up 9 days,  3:44, 14 users,  load average: 0,00, 0,00, 0,00
USER      TTY      FROM              LOGIN@   IDLE   JCPU   PCPU  WHAT
annen     pts/10   10.0.0.2          Sun 5pm  1:43m  16:10  0.01s -bash
janl      pts/9    selidor.langfeld  3:34pm   0.00s  0.01s  0.01s w
```

This is helpful, but contains an oddity that can make parsing with *awk* difficult. *awk* tends to work by extracting fields separated by spaces. In the *w*, as one often sees in Unix utilities, the login time here is not always a single string of characters. If a login took place long enough ago, the date is printed with a space in the middle. If you count the fields of the output, such as *awk* does, the results are corrupted. You could use the *cut* command, but that is not in this Objective.

If we look at the output of *who*, on the other hand, we see it has a fixed number and syntax of fields:

```
annen     pts/10   Jan  4 17:21 (10.0.0.2)
janl      pts/9    Jan  5 15:34 (selidor.langfeldt.net)
```

User auditing and report generation can be done efficiently with *last*:

```
# last root
root     pts/6    pargo.un-bc.petr Tue Jul 19 16:57   still logged in
root     pts/4    nbctr36591.bc.ep Tue Jul 12 11:20 - 11:26  (00:06)
root     vc/1                      Wed Jul  6 10:13 - down   (2+08:46)
root     vc/1                      Wed Jul  6 10:01 - 10:02  (00:00)
root     pts/1    pargo.un-bc.petr Thu Jun 30 15:58 - 16:53  (00:55)
root     pts/1    pargo.un-bc.petr Thu Jun 30 14:59 - 15:51  (00:51)
root     pts/6    cherne.un-bc.pet Tue Jun 21 01:39   still logged in
root     pts/6    cherne.un-bc.pet Tue Jun 21 01:03 - 01:39  (00:35)
root     pts/11   10.185.4.14      Fri Jun 17 09:31 - 10:16  (00:44)
root     pts/11                    Thu Jun 16 19:40 - 19:40  (00:00)
root     pts/6    pargo.un-bc.petr Thu Jun 16 10:28 - 11:05  (00:36)
root     pts/6    pargo.un-bc.petr Thu Jun 16 10:23 - 10:23  (00:00)
```

awk is a quite complete programming language in itself, and you may well find yourself starting a script with #!/usr/bin/awk -f sometime. It was made to process files and produce some kind of report, much like Perl, but is not as powerful. There are a few things particularly handy to know about *awk*, and most of them are in the following example:

```
#!/bin/bash

who | awk '
BEGIN    { root=0; users=0; }
```

```
               { FROM="localy"; users++; }
/^root.*\)$/  { FROM="from "$6; }
/^root/ { print "Root is logged in at "$3" "$4" "$5" "FROM; root++; }
END     { print "Root was logged in "root" times. ";
          print "A total of "users" users seen."; }
'
```

This yields:

```
Root is logged in at Jan 5 16:02 locally
Root was logged in 1 times.
A total of 2 users seen.
```

The basic form of directives in an *awk* program is:

```
pattern { statements; }
```

Usually, *pattern* begins and ends with slash characters (/) and represents a regular expression that *awk* is supposed to search for in each line. *awk* goes line by line through the input in order and checks each line for each pattern, executing the *statements* each time a pattern matches a line.

If the pattern is BEGIN, the statements are executed at startup. Here the variables root and user are assigned starting values. That is actually superfluous in this script, because *awk* assumes that new variables start with values of zero or empty strings, but it served to illustrate the use of BEGIN.

Likewise, if the pattern is END, the statements are executed at the end of the program.

If the pattern is skipped, such as on the second line of the *awk* script, the statements are executed once for each line. Here the variable FROM is set, and the variable *users* is incremented. users++ is C-style notation for users = users + 1.

> *awk* has language elements for conditional execution, loops, and functions for searching, substitution and all sorts of other things. If you want to learn any more about *awk* for the test, study how to use its if statement and substring matching and substitution.

Advanced Regular Expressions

The regular expressions used in the Level 1 LPI Exam are not the whole story. There are two more levels. *awk* and *sed* (as well as *egrep*) implement a more advanced syntax, while remaining mostly compatible with the simpler ones. Look in the info pages for *sed* and *awk* for an explanation of these. The standard for these are determined by the POSIX Unix standards.

Perl takes *sed* and *awk* regular expressions up several steps. Perl is fairly POSIX-compatible, but extends the syntax significantly. Please refer to the *perlre* manpage for further material.

The only frequently used option to *awk* is *-F*; it is used to specify the field separator. In most cases, the default is good, but sometimes it helps a lot, as when processing a passwd file where *-F:* indicates that fields are separated by colons. Another inportant option is *-f* `file`, which causes *awk* to take the named file as input patterns and statements to execute.

Detecting changes

The previously shown scripts detect everything that matches in the input files, whenever they were added to those files. When checking system logs and doing other system monitoring, it's more useful to detect changes and then look at what changed. Two programs help do this: *cmp*, which just checks whether files are the same, and *diff*, which compares and reports differences between two text files (or directories of text files). *cmp* is faster if you simply want to see whether two files are different and is more appropriate for binary files. *diff* does complex computations to find out what changed and report it in an intelligent manner.

Both *cmp* and *diff* need a file showing how things *were* and another file that shows how things *are*. If you have a directory hierarchy (for example, an incoming hierarchy on an FTP server) that you want to monitor for changes, you may use something like this shell function:

```
lslrdir=/var/lslR

ifupdated () {
        dir=$1; shift || exit 1
        cd $dir || exit 1
        # Make a slashless name to obtain a suitable filename
        name=$lslrdir/$(echo $dir | tr '/' '-')-ls-lR
        rm -f $name.new
        # Create a new snapshot
        /bin/ls -lR >$name.new || exit 1
        # Compare with old snapshot
        cmp $name $name.new >/dev/null || {
                rm -f $name || exit 1
                mv $name.new $name
                eval "$2"
        }
}
```

The script could be invoked in a manner such as:

```
ifupdated /var/ftp/incoming /usr/local/bin/processincoming
```

With an understanding of shell $ variables and the commands being invoked, you should be able to understand how the script does its job, which is to detect whether any files have been added, deleted, or altered in */var/ftp/incoming* and to execute */usr/local/bin/process* incoming if any have.

One useful feature shown in the script is how to check for errors: a nonzero status from each command leads to the execution of the exit 1 command after the || double bar. Thus, the script exits in case of error, which is a crude way of handling the error, but better than continuing and potentially making things worse.

In order to monitor users, you might create a snapshot with *w*, *who*, or even *last*. Using *diff*, you can see which users have appeared since the most recent execution.

```
$ who >who.txt...5 minutes pass...$ who >who.txt.new$ diff who.txt who.txt.new
0a1
> root     vc/1        Jan  5 16:02
```

The lines matching the regular expression /^>/ are new. Any lines matching /^</ have disappeared. It's therefore quite easy to look for interesting new users and report on them with something like the *awk* script shown earlier.

Monitoring files can be a different problem. If a file is huge, it may not be practical to copy it and then *cmp* the new and old versions. If so, it may be suitable to use a checksumming program. On Linux, *md5sum* is present everywhere and used by a lot of software to detect changes in files. The downside with it is that it's computationally heavy. In contrast, two similar commands, *cksum* and *sum*, which should be part of all Linux installations, are fast. If you want to monitor system files throughout your machines to see if your security has been broken, there are better tools. Check, for example, aide, which is very configurable and is used by some as an intrusion detection system (IDS) tool. There is also a module in CPAN (described later) called *mon*, which underpins many kinds of monitoring.

Log munging with sed

Let's say you have an email server and want to see who the top recipients of email are. The log format of the postfix MTA is like this:

```
pickup[13422]: 7B11119: uid=0 from=<root>
cleanup[13538]: 7B11119: message-id=<20040105113325.7B11119@lorbanery.
langfeldt.net>
qmgr[13423]: 7B11119: from=<root@langfeldt.net>, size=753, nrcpt=1 (queue
active)
smtp[13540]: 7B11119: to=<janl@linpro.no>, relay=smtp.chello.no[213.46.243.
2], delay=27, status=sent (250 Message received:\
   20040105113347.CIQY15111.amsfep12-int.chello.nl@lorbanery.langfeldt.net)
smtpd[13541]: connect from head.linpro.no[80.232.36.1]
smtpd[13541]: TLS connection established from head.linpro.no[80.232.36.1]:
TLSv1 with cipher EDH-RSA-DES-CBC3-SHA (168/168 bits)
smtpd[13541]: C4B3D19: client=head.linpro.no[80.232.36.1]
cleanup[13542]: C4B3D19: message-id=<E1AdT1l-0005sS-00@sc8-sf-web1.
sourceforge.net>
smtpd[13541]: disconnect from head.linpro.no[80.232.36.1]
qmgr[13423]: C4B3D19: from=<janl@linpro.no>, size=6009, nrcpt=1 (queue
active)
smtp[13544]: C4B3D19: to=<janl@langfeldt.net>, relay=10.0.0.4[10.0.0.4],
delay=8, status=sent (250 OK id=1AdT3l-0000Bp-00)
```

The interesting bits here are the lines that start with smtp. No other lines are interesting, including the lines containing smtpd, so they must be avoided. The sed regular expression for removing nonmatching lines is /smtp\[/!d, which means "delete all lines except those containing smtp." This yields:

```
$ sed -e '/smtp\[/!d' mail.log
smtp[13540]: 7B11119: to=<janl@linpro.no>, relay=smtp.chello.no[213.46.243.
2], delay=27, status=sent (250 Message \
```

received: 20040105113347.CIQY15111.amsfep12-int.chello.nl@lorbanery.
langfeldt.net)
...

Next, you have to pick out the part of the line with the email address. This can be done by removing the other parts. Start by removing the front part with s/^.*to=<//, yielding:

```
$ sed -e '/smtp\[/!d' -e 's/^.*to=<//' mail.log
janl@linpro.no>, relay=smtp.chello.no[213.46.243.2], delay=27, status=sent
(250 Message received: \
    20040105113347.CIQY15111.amsfep12-int.chello.nl@lorbanery.langfeldt.net)
...
```

Now remove the end of the line with s/>,.*$. This yields:

```
$ sed -e '/smtp\[/!d' -e 's/^.*to=<//' -e 's/>,.*$//'  mail.log
janl@linpro.no
...
```

Now you want to make sure all addresses are cased the same, and do some plumbing to get the count of individual different addresses:

```
$ sed -e '/smtp\[/!d' -e 's/^.*to=<//' -e 's/>,.*$//' mail.log |> /
  tr '[A-Z]' '[a-z]' | sort | uniq -c | sort -nr
    330 janl@langfeldt.net
      2 andyo@oreilly.com
      1 yngve@linpro.no
      1 steve@kspei.com
      1 nicolai@langfeldt.net
      1 machine-registration@counter.li.org
      1 janl@linpro.no
      1 ftp-drift@uio.no
```

The sed expression got a bit ugly. Another property of the email addresses is that they're bracketed in <...>. If you replace the complete line by the bracketed contents, that would have the same effect as the longer command shown before:

```
$ sed -e '/smtp\[/!d' -e 's/^.*<\([^>]*\)>.*$/\1/' mail.log |> /
  tr '[A-Z]' '[a-z]' | sort | uniq -c | sort -nr
    330 janl@langfeldt.net
      2 andyo@oreilly.com
      1 yngve@linpro.no
      1 steve@kspei.com
      1 nicolai@langfeldt.net
      1 machine-registration@counter.li.org
      1 janl@linpro.no
      1 ftp-drift@uio.no
```

Not that the command is a lot prettier. Here the \(...\) marks a subexpression. The string matching the first subexpression is placed in \1. So the \1 in the replacement text refers to the email address on the line. Here it replaces the whole line. You may refer to up to nine subexpressions with the \n syntax.

Scripting with Perl

It has been said that Perl, rather than being a Swiss Army knife, is a Swiss Army chain saw. Perl is a very powerful file-processing tool and a complete programming language with object-oriented features besides. Perl has always been at the forefront of advanced support for regular expressions, which makes it a tool for easy log processing.

Since Perl Version 5 arrived on the scene, the second big thing about Perl is the Comprehensive Perl Archive Network (CPAN), where you will find a Perl module and related documentation for almost any conceivable use ready to download and install.

Using CPAN

Recent Perl versions come with a module called CPAN that provides a complete interface to retrieving and installing more modules from CPAN. The first time the CPAN module is run, it wants all manner of configuration, but answering its questions is far from rocket science. Most questions can usually be answered by accepting the defaults. But if you are behind an authenticated proxy, you should configure your proxy settings before running the CPAN module, because all the -MCPAN requests are done over the Internet. Use the following shell commands to export these two environment variables:

```
$ export ftp_proxy=http://user:password@proxy_addr:port
$ export http_proxy=http://user:password@proxy_addr:port
```

Once configured, CPAN is ready to use. If you're looking for a module to support making DNS requests in Perl, for instance, try:

```
# perl -MCPAN -e shell

cpan shell -- CPAN exploration and modules installation (v1.76)
ReadLine support enabledcpan> i /DNS/
CPAN: Storable loaded ok
Going to read /root/.cpan/Metadata
  Database was generated on Fri, 26 Sep 2003 22:50:31 GMT
CPAN: LWP::UserAgent loaded ok
Fetching with LWP:
  ftp://ftp.uninett.no/pub/languages/perl/CPAN/authors/01mailrc.txt.gz
Going to read /root/.cpan/sources/authors/01mailrc.txt.gz
CPAN: Compress::Zlib loaded ok
Fetching with LWP:ftp://ftp.uninett.no/pub/languages/perl/CPAN/modules/
02packages.details.txt.gz
Going to read /root/.cpan/sources/modules/02packages.details.txt.gz
  Database was generated on Mon, 05 Jan 2004 22:51:56 GMT
Fetching with LWP:
  ftp://ftp.uninett.no/pub/languages/perl/CPAN/modules/03modlist.data.gz
Going to read /root/.cpan/sources/modules/03modlist.data.gz
Going to write /root/.cpan/Metadata
Distribution    A/AN/ANARION/DNS-TinyDNS-0.20.1.tar.gz
...
Module          Tie::DNS        (D/DI/DIEDERICH/Tie-DNS-0.41.tar.gz)
131 items found
```

A bit overwhelming perhaps. As you may deduce from the use of slashes in the search expression, you have Perl's full regular expression syntax at your service. A better way to search is to use *http://search.cpan.org*. It lets you search and browse by various parameters (author, category, etc.), select interesting modules, and look at the documentation to see if they meet your needs. Somewhere in there you will find a module called Net::DNS. Now you can install it as follows:

```
cpan> install Net::DNS
Running install for module Net::DNS
Running make for C/CR/CREIN/Net-DNS-0.44.tar.gz
Fetching with LWP:
  ftp://ftp.uninett.no/pub/languages/perl/CPAN/authors/id/C/CR/CREIN/Net-
DNS-0.44.tar.gz
...
Warning: prerequisite Digest::HMAC_MD5 1 not found.
Writing Makefile for Net::DNS
---- Unsatisfied dependencies detected during [C/CR/CREIN/Net-DNS-0.44.tar.
gz] -----
    Digest::HMAC_MD5Shall I follow them and prepend them to the queue
...
Warning: prerequisite Digest::SHA1 1 not found.
Writing Makefile for Digest::HMAC
---- Unsatisfied dependencies detected during [G/GA/GAAS/Digest-HMAC-1.01.
tar.gz] -----
    Digest::SHA1Shall I follow them and prepend them to the queue
...
Writing /usr/lib/perl5/site_perl/5.8.0/powerpc-linux/auto/Net/DNS/.packlist
Appending installation info to /usr/lib/perl5/5.8.0/powerpc-linux/perllocal.
pod
    /usr/bin/make install  -- OK
```

The shell does everything needed. It fetches the package, along with the packages it depends on—recursively—and it unpacks, processes, tests, and installs each package.

A straightforward and noninteractive way to install modules can be done with the Perl *-e* option:

```
# perl -MCPAN -e 'install SSH::Bundle'
```

Thus, Perl packages have a way to detect dependencies, just as the Linux package managers do. They are detected during installation, whereupon the CPAN shell stops and asks whether you want to get the package (if so configured). After you say yes (as you generally should), CPAN goes and fetches and installs the package.

Two things are known to go wrong in the CPAN shell. Sometimes it stumbles when following dependencies and fails to install something properly. Then you must break the process and install these packages manually. It may be as simple as just issuing another install command in the CPAN shell. More rarely, CPAN will start fetching and installing a new Perl for you. You almost never want that. Your Perl package is usually under the control of a Linux package system, which should be managing your Perl executable, not the CPAN shell.

A corollary problem arises because all this CPAN downloading takes place outside your distribution's package system. When you upgrade your Linux distribution later, it will know nothing about what CPAN installed and will not reinstall the CPAN modules. You will have to reinstall them yourself, with or without the aid of the CPAN shell.

 For deb and RPM packages, there are ways to download CPAN modules within the package system, but this is probably a win for you only if you manage more than a handful of computers that need the same packages. For RPM, you will find scripts such as *cpanflute* or *cpan2rpm*, and deb provides *dh-make-perl*. But this still does not solve the problem of upgrading Perl. You now have to make the upgraded Perl modules yourself when upgrading a distribution.

Log watching with Perl

There are plenty of log-watching scripts out there; just do a web search for them. The purpose of these is to watch system logs for interesting events and extract or even summarize them into a web page or an email. But you can also do simple log extractions easily with *awk* or Perl. For security purposes, it makes sense to look for things in */var/log/auth.log*. This can be done quite simply with a *grep* command, but it would quickly turn ugly as you add things to watch for. There are just a huge number of things that might be interesting to know: all kinds of errors and warnings of course, but also login failures. In other logs, one should look for symptoms of hardware failure—for example, excessive messages about anything having to do with hda or sda if you have SCSI. A very simple log watcher would go like this:

```
#!/usr/bin/perl -w

use strict;

open(LOG,"</var/log/auth.log") or die;

while (<LOG>) {
    /failure/ && do { print; next; };
    /error/   && do { print; next; };
    /warning/ && do { print; next; };
}
```

If you're more in a tool-maker mind frame, you can find CPAN modules that make it trivial to read configuration files. All you have to do then is write an engine to watch the logs based on an external configuration file.

Fetching and processing web logs

It is fairly common to keep external web servers out in a firewall DMZ, semi-unavailable. They are also usually hardened and have next to no software installed. And they are probably not the place you want to publish access statistics. Therefore, you need to transfer the log files into your internal network and generate the statistics there.

For the sake of speed, web servers do not resolve the client IP address to its DNS name. This makes the statistics a bit less useful. Statistics tool such as webalizer may do DNS resolving, but they are typically as slow as molasses at it because they send one DNS query at a time. Even sending 10 DNS queries at a time does not help much with logs of many tens or hundred thousands of lines. With the Net::DNS module in Perl, you can do much better: it supports completely asynchronous name resolultion without any forking or other complications.

Getting logs from a secure machine these days mostly requires scp or rsync over ssh. For example, one of these commands copies the file:

```
$ scp -c blowfish www.linux.no:/var/log/apache/www.linux.no-access_log* .
$ rsync -avPe 'ssh -c blowfish' \
>     www.linux.no:/var/log/apache/www.linux.no-access_log* .
```

The *ssh* suite is covered more in Chapter 40. *rsync* is discussed later in this chapter.

After copying the log file, it's time to resolve it with Perl and Net::DNS. Here is a script to do that:

```perl
#!/usr/bin/perl -w

# logdoc - log-doctor
#    modify http logs for log processing/statistical purposes
#
# Written by Nicolai Langfeldt, Linpro AS.  Distribute under same terms as
# Perl itself.  Based on a script in the Net::DNS distribution.

use strict;
use IO::Select;
use Net::DNS;
use Getopt::Std;

my $default_timeout = 15; # Seconds

# Fallback to this if no nameservers are configured.
my $default_nameserver = "127.0.0.1";

#----------------------------------------------------------------------------
---
# Get the timeout or use a reasonable default.
#----------------------------------------------------------------------------
---

my $progname = $0;
$progname =~ s!.*/!!;

my %opt;
getopts("t:", \%opt);

# The thing with zcat handles gz log files.
my @files=map { $_="zcat $_ |" if /\.gz$/; $_; } @ARGV;
```

```perl
my $timeout = defined($opt{"t"}) ? $opt{"t"} : $default_timeout;
die "$progname: invalid timeout: $timeout\n" if $timeout < 0;

#---------------------------------------------------------------------------
---
# Create a socket pointing at the default nameserver.
#---------------------------------------------------------------------------
---

my $res = Net::DNS::Resolver->new;
my $ns = $res->nameservers ? ($res->nameservers)[0] : $default_nameserver;
warn "Using $ns as nameserver\n";
my $sock = IO::Socket::INET->new(PeerAddr => $ns,
                                 PeerPort => "dns(53)",
        Proto    => "udp");
die "couldn't create socket: $!" unless $sock;

my $sel = IO::Select->new;
$sel->add($sock);

#---------------------------------------------------------------------------
---
# Read IP addresses and send queries.
#---------------------------------------------------------------------------
---

my %cache=();
my $pending = 0;
my $max=0;

my ($fwip, $rest, $ip, @a, @line, $url);

# This loop resolves.

@ARGV=@files;

warn "Resolving names\n";

while(<>) {
  chomp;
  ($fwip,$rest)=split(' ',$_,2);

  @a=split('\.',$fwip);

  $ip = join(".",,reverse(@a),"in-addr.arpa");

  next if exists($cache{$ip}); # Already know it
  $cache{$ip}=['unresolved'];  # Insert place holder

  my $packet = Net::DNS::Packet->new($ip, "PTR");
  $sock->send($packet->data) or die "send: $ip: $!";

  ++$pending;
  $max = $pending if $pending>$max;
```

```perl
  # Collect answers received until now.
  while ($sel->can_read(0)) { accept_answer(); }
}

warn "Waiting for outstanding answers, Pending: $pending, maxpending: $max\
n";

while ($pending > 0 && $sel->can_read($timeout)) {
  accept_answer();
}

#----------------------------------------------------------------------------
---
# Output resolved log files
#----------------------------------------------------------------------------
---

@ARGV=@files;

warn "Rewriting logs\n";

while (<>) {
    chomp;

    @line=split(' ',$_,11);
    $line[0] = getname($line[0]);
    $url = $line[6];

    # Skip some lines
    next if
$#line < 9 or # Bogus REQUEST prolly
$line[8] eq '"-"' or #
$line[8] ne '200' or # Only 200s are interesting
$url eq '408' or # Bogus REQUEST
$url eq '/' or   # Results in redirect, not interesting
# Different unintersting files and directories
index($url,'.gif')>=0 or
index($url,'.swf')>=0 or
index($url,'.css')>=0 or
index($url,'.js')>=0 or
index($url,'/share/')>=0 or
index($url,'/usage/')>=0 or
index($url,'/cgi-bin/')>=0;

    print join(' ',@line),"\n";
}

sub getname {
  # Resolve names from the cache, resolving CNAMEs as we go
  my($from)=shift;
  my $type;
  my $i=0;
  # print "Looking for $from\n";
  do {
```

```
    return $from
      if (!exists($cache{$from}) or
   $cache{$from}[0] eq 'unresolved' or
   $i++>10);

     ($type,$from)=@{$cache{$from}};

   } while $type != 'PTR';
   return $from;
}

# Accept DNS query answers off the wire.

sub accept_answer {
  --$pending;
  my $buf = "";
  $sock->recv($buf, 512) or die "recv: $!";
  next unless $buf;

  my $ans = Net::DNS::Packet->new(\$buf);
  next unless $ans;

  foreach my $rr ($ans->answer) {
    if ($rr->type eq 'PTR') {
      $cache{$rr->name}=['PTR',$rr->ptrdname];
    } elsif ($rr->type eq 'CNAME') {
      my $cname = $rr->cname;
      $cache{$rr->name}=['CNAME',$cname];
      my $packet = Net::DNS::Packet->new($cname, "PTR");
      $sock->send($packet->data) or die "send: $cname: $!";
      ++$pending;
    } else {
      die "What do I do with a ",$rr->type,"record?\n";
    }
  }
}
```

After this processing, your logs are ready for *webalizer* or whatever log processor you favor. The whole point here is that there are Perl modules for almost anything you can imagine: from math and string manipulation to generating HTML, XML, and MIME mail with attachments to full-blown web servers and web proxies. You will also find modules not only to interface with almost any database, but also to perform SQL queries on flat text files and to write Excel spreadsheets so anyone in the organization can easily generate usage reports. Or the monitor module mentioned earlier in this chapter. You name it, look for it on CPAN first. Perl is an ideal tool to automate and accelerate any of the numerous tasks a sysadmin has and shell scripting can't quite manage.

Using Perl to add new disks attached to an HBA controller

This example shows how Perl can provide solutions to many kind of daily tasks. The example detects new external disks (SAN storage) attached to the system without requiring a reboot. Without automated help like this, you could certainly pass a few hours handling the task.

```perl
#!/usr/bin/perl -w

use IO::File;

sub catch_zap {
    my $signame = shift;
        our $shucks++;
            die "Somebody sent me a SIG$signame!";
            }
            $shucks = 0;
            $SIG{INT} = 'catch_zap';
            $SIG{INT} = \&catch_zap;
            $SIG{QUIT} = \&catch_zap;

print "Disk Probe 1.0 for Emulex HBA's\n";
print "Probing...\n";

my @lun = 0..255;
my @id = 0.15;
my %seen;
my $scsi_path = '/proc/scsi/scsi';
my $host = 0;
my $target = 0;
my $part = 0;

system "echo `/usr/sbin/lpfc/dfc << !
set board $host
lip
exit
!` > /dev/null";

$input = IO::File->new("> $scsi_path")
    or die "Couldn't open $scsi_path for writing: $!\n";

for (my $i = 0; $i <= 15; $i++) {
foreach (@lun) {
                print $input "scsi add-single-device 1 0 $i $_\n";
        }
}

$input->close();

print "...done!\n";
```

First, we set the script to work with file handles using the IO::File module previously installed through CPAN:

```perl
use IO::File;
```

It's recomended to add error handling code. Just to put all in order in case.

```perl
sub catch_zap {
    my $signame = shift;
```

```
    our $shucks++;
        die "Somebody sent me a SIG$signame!";
        }
        $shucks = 0;
        $SIG{INT} = 'catch_zap';
        $SIG{INT} = \&catch_zap;
        $SIG{QUIT} = \&catch_zap;
```

Next, declare some variables:

```
my @lun = 0..255;
my @id = 0.15;
my %seen;
my $scsi_path = '/proc/scsi/scsi';
my $host = 0;
my $target = 0;
my $part = 0;
```

You will be able to interact with external programs if needed:

```
system "echo `/usr/sbin/lpfc/dfc << !
set board $host
lip
exit
!` > /dev/null";
```

The next lines illustrate some file handling: creating a file, appending output to it, and closing it. Looping constructs (for and foreach) save a lot of time.

```
$input = IO::File->new("> $scsi_path")
    or die "Couldn't open $scsi_path for writing: $!\n";

for (my $i = 0; $i <= 15; $i++) {
foreach (@lun) {
            print $input "scsi add-single-device 1 0 $i $_\n";
        }
}

$input->close();
```

Perl is very flexible and modular, providing easy methods to create automated system procedures.

Perl in adverse environments

Perl scripts (or any software at all) that execute within *sudo*, that are SUID root, or that execute in environments such as web servers should be extra careful with what they do.

A little careless programming and suddenly the script is a cracker's best friend. An adversary can change a script's behavior in two ways: by changing the execution environment and by changing the input. To help avoid careless mistakes, Perl has a mode of operation that helps you be careful about your execution environment and inputs. If a script starts with a *-T* option Perl, will do extra bookkeeping to track which data is tainted by the user and which data is not. Thus, this silly little script may look innocent:

```
#!/usr/bin/perl -wT
use strict;
system("date");
```

but when run it reveals:

```
$ ./taint.pl
Insecure $ENV{PATH} while running with -T switch at ./taint.pl line 5.
```

This is because the PATH variable, which is used by the system call, was inherited from the environment of the user. The user may have inserted a malevolent *date* program earlier in the PATH than the system command *date*, and suddenly the easy little SUID-root script is used to break root on your machine. The fix for this is to set the PATH yourself: $ENV{PATH}='/usr/bin:/bin';. More generally, you need either to not use tainted data or to untaint it by scrubbing it. The scrubbing procedure should remove any unsafe characters or constructions from the input so that it is in fact safe to pass it on.

For example, if a CGI script takes a date as an argument and then simply passes that to system("cal $date") and if the web user inputs a $date containing 2 2004; rm -rf /, you're out of luck and quite big parts of your web server will be wiped out, if not the whole system. A date for cal should probably be allowed to contain only the characters [0-9] or something like that. If it has other characters, they should be removed at the very least or, perhaps better, be logged as an abuse attempt. Security in Perl scripts is explained extensively in the manpage perlsec.

Advancing Your Perl Skills

After you learn Perl from any of the great number of tutorial texts suited for anyone from programming beginners to senior programmers, a good book to have on the shelf is *The Perl Cookbook* (O'Reilly). It has hundreds of examples and solutions for Perl programmers to use and learn from.

Synchronizing Files Across Machines

There are many tools to copy files among machines. Among the more pedestrian ones are *rcp* and *scp*. Toward the high end is *rdist*, which is very nice for synchronizing client machines from a master machine. But *rsync* is the steamroller among these.

rsync is, along with the SSH suite, one of the new utilities that have gained almost universal acceptance in the Unix world. It is used to synchronize files and/or directories over a network connection. It also works locally. The downside of *rsync* is a quite high startup penalty when you want to synchronize a large amount of files or data. On the other hand, it has a checksum algorithm that helps it uncover how files have changed since the last run and transfer only the difference. Especially over slow lines, this is a boon, but whenever you transfer nontrivial amounts of data, *rsync* should be faster than a complete copy with any of the other candidates.

rsync has its own client/server protocol. To employ that, you need to set up a server, and we're not going to do that in this book. The alternative is to let *rsync* tunnel over *rsh*. This is quite efficient, but it's as insecure as the *rsh* protocol itself. For the more security-conscious, using *ssh* is a good alternative. But the SSH protocol encrypts all its traffic, and encryption can be quite slow. If you use the blowfish encryption algorithm instead of the default one, things will be a bit faster. The example in the Perl scripting section is a good example of this:

```
$ rsync -avPe 'ssh -c blowfish' \
> www.linux.no:/var/log/apache/www.linux.no-access_log* .
```

This form of the command is like *rcp* except that it supports *user@* in front of hostnames as *scp* does. The most common options to *rsync* are:

-a, --archive
> Equivalent to *-rlptgoD*. It mimics the *-a* option of the Linux *cp* command, attempting to preserve all important attributes of the files and directories copied. The *-r* means that the command is also recursive, able to copy entire directories with all their subdirectories. The *-l* copies symlinks as symlinks, *-p* preserves permissions, *-t* preserves timestamps, *-go* preserves file group and owner, and *-D* copies device files as device files. The *-goD* options are valid only if you are *root* on the target system.

-H, --hard-links
> If you ever mirror Linux distributions, you probably want this to preserve hard links. There are often quite a lot of them.

-P
> Shorthand for *--partial* and *--progress*. This keeps partially transferred files so the copy can be restarted later without transferring the whole file again. Progress enables progress reporting. It's more meaningful if it is combined with *-v*.

-v, --verbose
> Increase the amount of information printed while working. Using just one instance of this option is useful to give you a count while rsync prepares its worklist, and then the names of transferred files as it progresses.

-S, --sparse
> If you use rsync to make backups of operating system disks, you will find that this option helps your disk usage. Executables and libraries often contain less data than they declare as their size, and this option keeps them that way.

-x, --one-file-system
> This is handy for backups, if you want to restrict them to one partition at a time.

-e COMMAND, --rsh=COMMAND
> Replace *rsh* with something else, such as *ssh*.

--rsync-path=PATH
> If the *rsync* on the opposite side is not in the default PATH of the account you are using on that side, you will need to specify the full path with this option.

`--delete`

By default, rsync does not delete target-side files that have disappeared from the originating site. *--delete* makes sure that files that have disappeared from the originating side are also deleted on the target side.

-z, --compress

Compress file data. Good if you have more CPU capacity than bandwidth.

Scheduled execution

Linux offers two systems to schedule program execution: *cron* and *at*. Both are present on most systems and considered standard, but they have quite different uses.

cron

The way to execute something periodically is through *cron*. *cron* is run by a system daemon named *crond*, and its operation is driven by *crontab* files. Each user can have a *crontab* file (unless the system administrator disables user access to *cron*), and the system provides a number of its own files to do routine, behind-the-scenes maintenance such as cleaning up old logfiles so disks don't become filled.

There are two formats for *crontab* files in a standard Linux system. One is found in normal users' files, as well as in */etc/crontab* and related system *crontab* files. It goes like this:

```
minute hour day-of-month month day-of-week command
```

The five first fields are numbers, although the Linux version of *cron* allows three-letter names in the fourth (month) and fifth (day-of-week) fields. The *command* field is a shell command.

The other format is found in the files in */etc/cron.d*. The format has an additional field before the command field—the username of the user the command should run as. The files in the */etc/cron.d* directory can have any user's *cron* commands. But only *root* should be allowed to put files into that directory.

Additionally you will find on most Linux systems a battery of directories in */etc* called *cron.hourly*, *cron.daily*, *cron.weekly*, and *cron.monthly*. The contents of these are normally run out of */etc/crontab*, but the exact details, including when they are run, differ from distribution to distribution and among versions. If you look in these directories, you may also find references to *anacron*. This is asynchronous companion to *cron* and is very useful for laptops and other systems that are not on 24/7. It is also outside our scope.

Normal users have their crontabs stored in */var/spool/cron/crontabs*. Users invoke the *crontab* command to view and edit the files there and to include the commands they want to run regularly. The *crontab* files should not be manipulated any other way. In this directory, *root* is a normal user, but on Linux systems *root* almost never has files in */var/spool/cron/crontabs*. There are too many other places that are easier for *root* to use.

As system administrator, it's most often best to use /etc/crontab and drop files into the different directories under /etc. As a user, you can use the crontab command only to replace, list, remove, and edit your crontab. Be sure to use the -1 option to list crontabs; otherwise, you may just replace your crontab with an empty one.

Any jobs that monitor Apache or the use of the root account should, of course, be run quite often—if not every minute, then every five minutes. If you put something like the following in /etc/cron.d/watchapache, you'll run the desired script every five minutes:

```
*/5 * * * *    root    /usr/local/sbin/monitor-apache
```

This can quickly turn into a nuisance, of course. Getting a page, SMS, or email every five minutes can be a bit rough, not to mention expensive. The program should perhaps send an alert only every hour after initially reporting a problem. It can also be restricted to working hours, if the hour field (the second field) is changed to 8-17. Then it will run for only those nine hours of the day.

cron requires hours to be specified in European or "military" time, 0–23; AM and PM are not allowed. The n/m syntax gives an increment value of m, not a division by m. Thus, 4/5 means starting at the fourth minute, then every five minutes (or hour or day and so on). */5 means starting at the 0th minute. You can also enumerate like this: 0,5,10,15,20,... but that's both boring and error-prone. It is what is required on many other Unix cron systems, though.

If a cron job produces output, the cron daemon catches this and emails the cron-job owner. This also happens if the job sets its exit status to a nonzero value. This is nice for debugging but not for regular use. The subject line of cron mail is generic, so it is hard to determine what is wrong. If, for example, an Apache checking script just prints something instead of mailing it with a good subject line, it will look like all the other cron mails you receive.

One thing regularly goes wrong with cron jobs. The PATH and other environment variables read by crond may be different from those you use with your interactive shell. So executing a well-tested script in cron may well fail. To fix this, you need to set PATH and any other environment variables explicitly in the script. Running printenv inside the script may help you figure this out. Some people use absolute pathnames for commands in crontab files so that it doesn't matter what their PATH is, but this is cumbersome.

One other thing that theoretically goes wrong in a well-tested script but is much rarer and more obscure: signal and session handling in cron are a bit different than in a shell. So if a job uses signals, it may fail in odd ways. There is no easy advice to handle that.

 Linux crontab files can optionally contain variables such as MAILTO. While that is not an objective in this Topic, it's good to know at work.

Using at

at is very useful for one-off execution of jobs, mostly the kinds of jobs you want done later but can't be bothered to remember or because you're not going to be there at the time.

To use *at*, you need first to make sure the *atd* daemon is running. This is the process that runs all the jobs queued by the *at* command.

```
# /etc/init.d/atd start
# pgrep -fl atd
5486 /usr/sbin/atd
```

If you've gotten a huge 300-page PDF file that you want to print, but not during hours, so as not to hold up the printer for 20–30 minutes when your coworkers want to use it, you can employ at. First, convert the file to PostScript or some other format your print-spooling system likes, then do something like this:

```
$ at 23:00
warning: commands will be executed using /bin/shat
> lpr DNS-HOWTO.psat
> <EOT>
job 2 at 2004-01-05 23:00
```

Two things of note: as the output says, it will execute the script with */bin/sh*. In Linux, that's usually the same as *bash*. Second, use Ctrl-D (the end-of-file character in your shell) to end the input. This is shown as <EOT> in the shell. A period (.) will not work, as it does for some other utilities. With the returned job number, you can list the job: at *-c 2* (be prepared to be amazed at the output) and remove it with *atrm 2*. To find your job numbers later, use *atq*. To experiment with *at*, use at *now*, which runs your commands at once. *at* also understands English times with AM and PM—e.g., 11PM.

---

at

Syntax

```
at [-V] [-q queue] [-f file] [-mldbv] TIME at -c job [job...]
```

Description

Queue, delete, and list *at* jobs for later execution.

Options

-m

    Send mail to the user when the job has completed.

-c

    List detailed information about the queued job.

-l

    List jobs.

-d

    Delete jobs.

32

Troubleshooting
(Topic 2.214)

This Topic is the largest section forExam 201. This Topic's breadth is expansive and requires that you're fluent in almost every Topic area from both Levels 1 and 2. For this Topic, you are expected to troubleshoot your systems from boot stages and system recovery to system resources and the system's shell configuration. This chapter will not cover any network-related troubleshooting, as that is covered in Topic 2.205, Network Troubleshooting.

This Topic contains six Objectives:

Objective 1: Creating Recovery Disks
   Candidates should be able to create boot disks for system entrance and recovery disks for system repair. Weight: 1.

Objective 2: Identifying Boot Stages
   Candidates should be able to determine, from bootup text, the four stages of the boot sequence and distinguish between each. Weight: 1.

Objective 3: Troubleshooting Bootloaders
   Candidates should be able to determine specific stage failures and corrective techniques. Weight: 1.

Objective 4: General Troubleshooting
   Candidates should be able to recognize and identify boot loader- and kernel-specific stages and utilize kernel boot messages to diagnose kernel errors. This Objective includes being able to identify and correct common hardware issues and be able to determine if a problem is in hardware or software. Weight: 1.

Objective 5: Troubleshooting System Resources
   Candidates should be able to identify, diagnose, and repair local system issues when using software from the command line. Weight: 1.

Objective 6: Troubleshooting Environment Configurations
Candidates should be able to identify, diagnose, and repair local system issues when using software from the command line. Weight: 1.

Objective 1: Creating Recovery Disks

If the boot floppy is not included with your installation media, you can create it by using *dd*. To do so, first mount the CD-ROM. Next, type the command:

```
dd if=/mnt/cdrom/images/boot.img of=/dev/fd0
```

replacing */mnt/cdrom* with the mount directory of your CD-ROM. You may also need to replace */dev/fd0* with the appropriate mount point of your floppy.

If you have only a Windows machine available, the *dd* command won't do you any good. In that case, use the *rawrite.exe* command to do the same job.

Some distributions provide utilities to create boot disks after the fact. On Red Hat–based systems, there is *mkbootdisk*. You must supply the kernel version for which you want to crate a boot disk. For example, if you have kernel versions 2.6. 9-1.667, 2.6.9-1.667smp, and 2.4.1 installed on your system, you can create a boot disk for the second kernel with the following command:

```
mkbootdisk 2.6.9-1.667smp
```

This command prompts you to insert a floppy disk (use *--noprompt* if you do not wish to be asked) into device */dev/fd0* (change it with the *--device* option). The command will then write a boot sector, kernel images, and initial ramdisk to the device.

Debian has a similar command, *mkboot*, but unlike *mkbootdisk*, you supply the filename of the kernel that you want to boot, such as:

```
mkboot vmlinux
```

A boot disk itself is not sufficient to boot the system. After loading the boot loader and then the kernel, the boot disk will look for the root partition on the hard drive (pulled from */etc/fstab* when you created the boot disk). This means if there is something wrong with your hard drive or root partitions, you will still not be able to boot your system. In those cases, you will need a rescue disk such as the first CD of a Red Hat installation or a self-contained Linux system such as Knoppix.

If you need to make a custom boot disk, refer to the Bootdisk HOWTO located at *http://www.tldp.org/HOWTO/Bootdisk-HOWTO*.

Objective 2: Identifying Boot Stages

Chapter 14 covered the boot process of a Linux system. This section discusses how to identify which step of the boot process has caused a problem.

Typically, a failure at any given stage of the boot process looks like the following:

Failure to read and load the boot sector
A failure at this stage occurs after the BIOS screen disappears and before any part of the operating system is run. A failure here means that the boot sector

was not found or did not load. Typically, you will see a blank screen with just a flashing prompt or a message similar to "No operating system found.". Possible problems include:

- The boot sector is trashed and must be reinstalled.
- The partition listed as the active partition has no boot sector.
- The wrong partition has been marked as "active."

Failure to load the boot loader
What you see will depend on which boot loader you have.

If you're using LILO, the LILO prompt itself will lead you to the problem (see the next section). If you're using GRUB, an error may appear, followed by the initial GRUB screen.

Failure to load the kernel
This can have several causes, including a bad hard drive sector, inability to find a particular kernel module, or inability to find the root device. Typically, any of these errors will result in a "kernel panic." At this point, you need to review the on-screen data to determine where the problem lies.

Failure to run the init daemon and enter a specific run level
If you get past the kernel load, the next step is running the init daemon (which almost always succeeds). Problems here are usually configuration errors in */etc/inittab* such as setting the default run level to 0 (which halts the system) or 6 (which reboots the system).

Failure to start the processes in said run level
Failures at this level are usually in the applications themselves. For example, the Apache *httpd* daemon may fail to start because of a misconfigured *httpd. conf* file.

If a network process, such as Sendmail, takes several minutes to start up, it is almost invariably caused by a problem with name resolution.

Failure to present a login prompt
Depending on how your system is configured, this problem basically means the login program (such as *gd*, *getty*, *kdm*, or *xdm*) can't run for some reason.

Objective 3: Troubleshooting Boot Loaders

In this section we cover the problems you might come across in the boot stages. Both LILO and GRUB are covered, because you'll need both for the test.

One of the most common installation problems outside of hardware support relates to LILO, the LInux LOader. Occasionally, a disk sector is bad and LILO doesn't install to it properly. Other times, it doesn't work because it was misconfigured.

One of the best ways to troubleshoot your LILO problems is to watch the output of LILO itself. Watch for your LILO prompt. If you don't see any part of the LILO prompt, LILO didn't load. Otherwise, the characters in the prompt tell you how far LILO got:

L

> The first-stage boot loader is loaded and started.

LI

> The second-stage boot loader is loaded.

LIL

> The second-stage boot loader is started.

LIL?

> The second-stage boot loader was loaded at an incorrect address.

LIL-

> The descriptor table is corrupt.

LILO

> All of LILO has been loaded correctly.

A very common problem LILO users run into is forgetting to rerun */sbin/lilo* whenever a change is made to */etc/lilo.conf*. This problem, along with the cryptic error messages of LILO, was a major factor in the design of GRUB.

GRUB, the GRand Unified Bootloader, is a user-friendly replacement for LILO. GRUB boots in three stages: Stage 1, Stage 1.5, and Stage 2.

Stage 1 errors are typically errors in reading Stage 1.5 or Stage 2 from the disk. Pressing Ctrl-Alt-Del will reboot the system.

A Stage 2 error prints an error message and continues or waits for the user to fix the problem. There are 34 error messages, listed in detail in Chapter 14 of the GRUB manual, which can be found at *http://www.gnu.org/software/grub/manual/ html_node/Stage2-errors.html#Stage2-errors*.

A Stage 1.5 error prints an error number corresponding to one of the 34 error messages from Stage 2.

Objective 4: General Troubleshooting

Troubleshooting is one of the most difficult but satisfying administration tasks. Few things feel better for a professional administrator than being posed with a problem and finding a solution for it. Successful troubleshooting requires an in-depth knowledge of the system being shot at and a few rules of conduct. In this section we'll go over a few tips on how to troubleshoot and suggest places for you to look for information.

The first rule of troubleshooting is: don't jump to conclusions! Just because someone says "foo stopped working," don't start adjusting the parameters for whatever "foo" is without gathering more information. Initial problem descriptions (*especially* from nontechnical users) are notoriously misleading.

This leads to rule number two: get a complete and accurate description of the problem. Foo may have very well stopped working, but it could be a side effect of bar being misconfigured.

Rule number three: reproduce the problem. It's very difficult to shoot at a problem you can't see. The hardest problems are intermittent, but luckily, most aren't. Most intermittent problems show a pattern over time.

So, you've followed the Three Rules of Troubleshooting. Where do you look to gather more information?

If you suspect hardware problems, *dmesg* and its associated log file */var/log/dmesg* are a good place to start. *dmesg* shows you the *kernel ring buffer*, the buffer that the kernel writes messages to. (It's called a "ring" buffer because old messages disappear over time to make room for new ones.) We'll use these messages to troubleshoot a specific problem in the following example.

A partial listing of *dmesg* on my machine looks like this:

```
Linux version 2.6.9-1.667 (bhcompile@tweety.build.redhat.com) (gcc version
3.4.2 20041017 (Re
d Hat 3.4.2-6.fc3)) #1 Tue Nov 2 14:41:25 EST 2004
BIOS-provided physical RAM map:
 BIOS-e820: 0000000000000000 - 00000000000a0000 (usable)
 BIOS-e820: 00000000000f0000 - 0000000000100000 (reserved)
 BIOS-e820: 0000000000100000 - 000000005fe88c00 (usable)
 BIOS-e820: 000000005fe88c00 - 000000005fe8ac00 (ACPI NVS)
 BIOS-e820: 000000005fe8ac00 - 000000005fe8cc00 (ACPI data)
 BIOS-e820: 000000005fe8cc00 - 0000000060000000 (reserved)
 BIOS-e820: 00000000e0000000 - 00000000f0000000 (reserved)
 BIOS-e820: 00000000fec00000 - 00000000fed00400 (reserved)
 BIOS-e820: 00000000fed20000 - 00000000feda0000 (reserved)
 BIOS-e820: 00000000fee00000 - 00000000fef00000 (reserved)
 BIOS-e820: 00000000ffb00000 - 0000000100000000 (reserved)
0MB HIGHMEM available.
1534MB LOWMEM available.
zapping low mappings.
On node 0 totalpages: 39284
```

Not much there that's useful to an everyday system administrator. But if we keep scrolling down, we'll see:

```
Probing IDE interface ide0...
hda: GCR-8483B, ATAPI CD/DVD-ROM drive
hdb: PHILIPS DVD+/-RW DVD8631, ATAPI CD/DVD-ROM drive
Using cfq io scheduler
ide0 at 0x1f0-0x1f7,0x3f6 on irq 14
Probing IDE interface ide1...
ide1: Wait for ready failed before probe !
Probing IDE interface ide2...
```

Hmmm, I might have problems with my IDE bus. Looking even further...

```
hda: command error: status=0x51 { DriveReady SeekComplete Error }
hda: command error: error=0x54
ide: failed opcode was 100
end_request: I/O error, dev hda, sector 1309952
hda: command error: status=0x51 { DriveReady SeekComplete Error }
hda: command error: error=0x54
ide: failed opcode was 100
```

I seem to have problems with my /dev/hda device. Maybe that explains why I haven't been able to read CDs in my CD-ROM drive!

If too many kernel messages are sent, the kernel ring buffer will overflow and you won't see the initial boot message. In that case, take a look at /var/log/dmesg, which gets written over at each boot.

If you attach a new USB device to your system and you're not sure which device it was assigned, dmesg shows you the device:

```
# dmesg | tail
scsi4 : SCSI emulation for USB Mass Storage devices
   Vendor: SanDisk   Model: Cruzer Mini     Rev: 0.1
   Type:   Direct-Access                    ANSI SCSI revision: 02
SCSI device sdd: 501759 512-byte hdwr sectors (257 MB)
sdd: Write Protect is off
sdd: Mode Sense: 03 00 00 00
sdd: assuming drive cache: write through
 sdd: sdd1
Attached scsi removable disk sdd at scsi4, channel 0, id 0, lun 0
USB Mass Storage device found at 5
```

The USB stick I just plugged into my computer is assigned to /dev/sdd and has one partition.

Other hardware information can be found in the /proc subdirectory. Unlike other directories, /proc is not really part of the filesystem; it is an interface to the running kernel. Most of what is in /proc is read-only, but some entries can be written to. This lets you change some parameters of the running kernel.

If you don't want to go searching through /proc for hardware information, the command lsdev will gather up information from /proc/dma, /proc/interrupts, and /proc/ioports and present the data in a combined format. Similarly, lspci will list the data for the PCI buses on your system and the devices connected to them.

If the hardware seems correct (or you can't find anything wrong with the hardware), the issue may be related to the kernel modules. You can list the currently loaded modules with lsmod, insert a new module with insmod, or remove a running module with rmmod. If somebody says a feature is not working, and you know that feature requires support in the kernel, one fruitful source of information is to find out what modules that feature depends on, and to issue lsmod to see whether those modules have been loaded. (Of course, the same feature could be compiled in, in which case lsmod would not show the modules even though the functionality is there.)

Here is a partial listing of the output of lsmod:

```
Module              Size  Used by
vfat               17217  0
fat                55005  1 vfat
parport_pc         30981  1
lp                 16713  0
parport            38793  2 parport_pc,lp
```

There is some danger with using the insmod and rmmod commands. Many modules rely on other modules, so inserting or removing modules that rely on modules that aren't present can cause instabilities or even outright crashes. In the previous sample output, we see the *fat* module (a popular module supporting Windows filesystems) is used by the *vfat* module and that the *parport* module is used by two other modules: *parport_pc* and *lp*. If we were to remove the *fat* module without first removing the *vfat* module, unpredictable things most likely will happen. Depending on the module you insert or remove, the results may be nothing more serious than losing your audio capabilities—but in other cases, it could crash the system.

This is why the *modprobe* command was written; *modprobe* is designed to replace *lsmod*, *insmod* and *rmmod* and to act more intelligently. The following table shows the equivalent *modprobe* commands.

Table 32-1. Equivalent modprobe commands

Command	Is equivalent to
lsmod	*modprobe -l*
insmod	*modprobe -a*
rmmod	*modprobe -r*

As an example of how *modprobe* is more intelligent than the three **mod* commands, *rmmod* removes a module without regard to the presence of other modules, whereas *modprobe* will remove the entire stack of modules. In the example previously mentioned, the command *modprobe -r fat* would have removed the *vfat* module before the *fat* module, reducing the possibility of crashes (assuming that removing the *fat* module is a good thing in the first place!). Conversely, the command *modprobe -a vfat* inserts the *fat* module first, then inserts the *vfat* module.

The *modprobe* command relies on an updated *modules.dep* file located in the modules directory. *modules.dep* is updated by the *depmod* command. The modules directory can be found at */lib/modules/`uname -r`*.

If a problem lies with system applications such as the web server or email server, the first place to look is in the */var/log* directory. Most applications that use the *syslog* logging facility send their logging information to */var/log* unless configured differently in */etc/syslog.conf*. A good idea when you start troubleshooting is to look at */var/log/messages*. From there, the software in question may have specific log files (such as */var/log/maillog* for Postfix) or a subdirectory (such as */var/log/ httpd* for Apache) to search for further log information.

Sometimes executing the program itself is necessary to debug the problem. This is often the case when the program segfaults or crashes with no error messages or log information. The programs *strace* and *ltrace* will execute a given command name and display the system or library calls, respectively, that the command makes. These commands show us precisely what the command is doing and where it fails. While there are many useful options for *strace* and *ltrace*, two of the most useful are *-f* to follow forking children and *-o trace.out* to write the voluminous output to the file *trace.out*.

Trouble-shooting

Objective 5: Troubleshooting System Resources

Sometimes the problems we need to troubleshoot aren't with hardware or with specific applications; the problems are with the system itself. A console message of a garbled terminal console or a wrong user home directory means there is something wrong with the system and not with an application per se.

Environment Variables and Shells

Many applications use variables to modify their behavior. Some variables have local scope (meaning they are visible only in the current instance of the shell), while others have global scope (meaning they are visible in the current shell and in child shells). These latter variables are called environment variables. A local variable can be made an environment variable via the *export* command.

To view your current variables and their settings, issue the *set* or *env* command.

Some common variables are shown in table Table 32-2.

Table 32-2. Common Variables Environment

Variable	Purpose
EDITOR	Determines which editor is invoked by programs requiring user interaction
LANG	Determines which language to use (e.g., en_US.UTF-8, en_US, etc.)
PAGER	Determines which program to use to page through files (e.g., *more*, *less*, etc.)
PATH	Colon-separated list of directories to search for executable file names
PS1	Character(s) to use for the command prompt
SHELL	Current shell
TERM	Determines which terminal type is in use (e.g., *vt100*, *linux*, etc.)
UID	Current user ID
USER	Current username

While *bash* is the most popular login shell on most Linux systems, there are quite a few other shells in use. The file */etc/shells* lists the installed shells:

/bin/sh
/bin/bash
/sbin/nologin
/bin/ash
/bin/bsh
/bin/ksh
/usr/bin/ksh
/usr/bin/pdksh
/bin/tcsh
/bin/csh
/bin/zsh

Technically, */sbin/nologin* is not a shell; it is used to stop users from being able to log in (*/bin/false* is used on some systems for the same purpose). Why would you not want a user to log in? Not all users are people; many applications set up a user account that does not need to log in but is required to run the application; one example is the user *apache* that runs the *httpd* daemon.

Shell Environment

Even if your users log in graphically and never see a command line, they are still running inside of a shell. The shell is configured via environment variables set in configuration files. There are two types of configuration files: global and local. Generally, when the shell starts, it will read a global configuration file and then read a local configuration file. Normally the settings in the local configuration file override the settings from the global configuration file.

The global configuration that most shells read is */etc/profile*. Variables set here apply to every user on the system, although each user can override them; PATH and HOSTNAME are often set in */etc/profile*. Since many kinds of shells will be reading */etc/profile*, the syntax of the commands has to be Bourne shell–specific, e.g. you should never put a *zsh*-style command in */etc/profile* because it will cause an error when the *bash* shell attempts to read */etc/profile*.

After the global configuration file is read, the local (usually shell-specific) configuration files are read. The local files are located in the user's home directory. We will discuss the *bash*-related configuration files since it is the most popular shell on Linux systems.

bash can be invoked in several different ways: as a login shell, an interactive nonlogin shell, a noninteractive shell, or a Bourne shell. How it is invoked determines which files get read. If *bash* is invoked as a login shell (e.g., the login command launches it), *bash* reads the following files in order: *~/.bash_profile*, *~/.bash_login*, and *~/.profile*. If *bash* is launched as an interactive, non-login shell (e.g., from the command line or from a application such as KDE *konsole* or Gnome Terminal), *bash* reads just the *~/.bashrc* file. If *bash* is run non-interactively (e.g., to run a script), *bash* reads the environment variable $BASH_ENV to determine which file to read. Finally, if *bash* is run as *sh*, it reads the filename listed in the *$ENV* variable, if it is defined. Of course, this being Linux, there are multiple command-line options to *bash* that change each of these behaviors. Fortunately, they are not on the test.

So when the user complains that the terminal is acting "funny," you need to keep in mind which shell she is using, how the shell was invoked, and which configuration files, if any, are being read.

Editors

Many editors are available in the Linux/Unix world. However, this world falls into two general camps when it comes to editors: you are either a *vi* user or an Emacs user.

vi is a difficult editor to get used to, especially if you're used to dealing with modern-day word processors. It has been around longer than Emacs, and it shows. Since it was invented in the days before arrow keys, 64 MB of RAM, and other pleasantries, *vi* requires very little in the way of system resources, doesn't require arrow keys to navigate, and lets you edit very efficiently. There are clones of *vi*, such as popular VI Improved (*http://www.vim.org*), that add many nice features such as block copy/edit and integrated help, but you still need to know how to edit using basic *vi*.

Emacs, on the other hand, is a large, resource-hungry editor that can do the most amazing things. Through its built-in ELISP programming language, Emacs can be coerced into doing things such as fetching and reading newsgroups and running games. While you can do just about anything you want within *vi*, you generally invoke more complex functions by running external programs within the editor.

Whichever one you choose is based on what you like, but as a system administrator, you must be comfortable with *vi*. *vi* is ubiquitous; it is installed on every Unix/Linux machine and even system rescue disks. Since *vi* has been around for so long, it can run on machines with few resources, it can run from a floppy, and during system recovery sessions, it will be the only editor available to you.

Kernel Parameters

One of the more interesting features of Linux is that you can modify the running kernel not only by adding and removing modules, but also by changing the parameters of the kernel itself. Of course, you can't change everything about the kernel, but you can change a number of parameters. Examples range as far as whether the system uses IP Forwarding, the minimum and maximum speed of your RAID drives, and whether to ignore ARP requests.

Assume our Linux box is set up as a router with two network interface cards and that it has stopped routing packets for reasons unknown to us. One of the requirements for a Linux router is the ability to forward packets from one NIC to another. This ability is turned off by default. How would we troubleshoot this?

There are two ways of doing this research: via the */proc* filesystem or the *sysctl* command. The *sysctl* command is a front-end for */proc*. You must have procfs compiled in your kernel for this to work.

Most of the entries in */proc* are read-only, but a few are read/write. Even though the entries look like files, the only way to read them is by cat-ing the "file":

```
# cat /proc/sys/net/ipv4/ip_forward
0
```

This shows us that IP Forwarding is turned off. We can turn it on by writing to the "file":

```
# echo "1" > /proc/sys/net/ipv4/ip_forward
# cat /proc/sys/net/ipv4/ip_forward
1
```

The value is good only until the next reboot, so to keep this setting, you would place the echo command in *rc.local* and it will get run at every reboot.

How did we know to change the entry /proc/sys/net/ipv4/ip_forward? How you know which */proc* entries are writable? One way is to traverse the entire */proc* directory looking for files with write permissions.

An easier way to do all this is via the *sysctl* command. Typing *sysctl -a* or *sysctl -A* lists all of the changeable entries:

```
# sysctl -a | more
sunrpc.tcp_slot_table_entries = 16
sunrpc.udp_slot_table_entries = 16
sunrpc.nlm_debug = 0
sunrpc.nfsd_debug = 0
sunrpc.nfs_debug = 0
sunrpc.rpc_debug = 0
dev.parport.parport0.devices.lp.timeslice = 200
dev.parport.parport0.devices.active = none
dev.parport.parport0.modes = PCSPP,TRISTATE
dev.parport.parport0.dma = -1
--More--
```

If you go far enough down the list, you'll see the ip_forward entry we modified earlier:

```
net.ipv4.ip_forward = 1
```

Using *sysctl* to change or view the value, you would issue:

```
# sysctl net.ipv4.ip_forward=0
# sysctl net.ipv4.ip_forward
net.ipv4.ip_forward = 0
```

Just as in the previous method, the value set with *sysctl* is good only until the next boot. If you want to make the change permanent, place the key = value line in the file */etc/sysctl.conf*.

Objective 6: Troubleshooting Environment Configurations

In this section, we'll cover items not covered in previous sections.

Authorization Problems

Authorization problems are usually related to the */etc/passwd*, */etc/shadow*, and/or */etc/group* files. Modern Linux systems offer other security systems that may be involved—notably Pluggable Authentication Modules (PAM) and SELinux, a series of patches made by the National Security Agency—but those are special cases and haven't shown up on the tests (yet!).

Generally speaking, problems related to these files are caused by hand-editing the files instead of using the system tools to modify them.

crontab Problems

The programs *cron* and *at* deal with scheduling jobs: *cron* continually reruns jobs according to schedules in the config files; *at* will execute a job just once at some future time.

Every user has a *crontab* file. They are located in */var/spool/cron* on Red Hat– and Debian-based systems, On some systems, *root*'s *crontab* file is considered personal to *root* and runs whatever *root* wants to schedule, while on other systems, *root*'s *crontab* file is considered the system *crontab* file and is used to schedule system jobs.

There is also a global */etc/crontab* on Red Hat systems that is used to schedule system jobs. This *crontab* file simply runs scripts (not other *crontab* files!) located in the directories */etc/cron.daily*, */etc/cron.hourly*, */etc/cron.weekly*, and */etc/cron. monthly*. The directory */etc/cron.d* contains *crontab* files (not scripts!) that are run by *cron*. There is a difference between the user *crontab* files and the files in */etc/ cron.d*: the */etc/cron.d* files require a user argument; otherwise, they will not work.

Most problems with *cron* are not *cron* problems but rather permission or configuration problems. Permission problems occur when the user doesn't have permission to run a program or a script, so check the permissions, especially if the user wrote the script.

The configuration problem can occur because the environment that *cron* runs under is not the same as the user's environment. The cron environment is rather sparse, containing SHELL (set to */bin/sh*—see the discussion earlier in this chapter about how that affects the login files checked), LOGNAME (which may not be changed), HOME, and MAILTO. Other variables will have to be set in the *crontab* file or the scripts being executed.

Finally, if the file */etc/cron.allow* exists and the user is not listed in the file, the user will not be allowed to use *cron*. Similary, if the file */etc/cron.deny* exists and the user is listed there, the user will not be allowed to use *cron*.

Init Problems

init has been called "the mother of all processes" since every process on a Linux box can be traced back to *init*. Few things go wrong with *init*. Anything that does is usually a misconfiguration in the */etc/inittab* file or related to the program that *init* is attemtping to run.

The configuration of */etc/inittab* is pretty straightforward. The lines are of the form:

> `id:run-levels:action:process`

where the fields are:

id
> A unique one-to-four character string

run-levels
> The runlevels that the process will run in

action
> The action *init* should take with the process (see the manpage for all of the options)

process
> The actual process to run

One common problem manifests itself by the following message appearing repeatedly on the console:

```
init: 'ID "SV" respawning too fast : disabled for 5 minutes'
```

This means there is a problem with the process associated with ID SV. The process might be segfaulting or even not exist on the machine. If you debug the process, you'll fix the "init problem."

Logging Problems

Most system applications send log messages to a file via the *syslog* facilty, which is controlled by */etc/syslog.conf*. The format of the configuration file is straightforward:

```
message_types                          log_destinations
```

Types of messages are listed by *facility.priority* (check the manpage or the section "Objective 1: System Logging" in Chapter 30 for a complete listing), and the log destination can be a file, a named pipe, a remote machine, the terminal, specific users, or everyone logged on.

Logging errors are generally a problem with the configuration in */etc/syslog.conf* or, more likely, with the program sending the messages to be logged.

When debugging syslog problems, remember that syslog may not write the log entry immediately. There may be a lag of several seconds between the time syslog writes the log, the system flushes the file to disk, and you see the changes.

33

LPI Exam 201 Review
Questions and Exercises

This chapter is designed to help you learn more about the concepts, best practices, and commands tested by the LPI 201 Exam. It is organized according to the LPI Objective Topics (e.g., Networking Configuration, DNS, Network Client Management). Even advanced Linux users will find these activities useful, because they are all based on the LPI's Objectives. The things you read about in this chapter might help remind you how to do tasks that you may not have had to do in a while.

It is best if you use a live, nonproduction Linux system to conduct these exercises. This way, you can apply your knowledge, but still not worry too much if your experiments cause the system to become unstable or to no longer be as secure as before.

Linux Kernel (Topic 2.201)

Review Questions

1. You find that the *make modules* command fails repeatedly when trying to compile a new kernel. What can you do to solve this problem?

2. You need to know the CPU type on a system before updating the kernel. Which of the files in the */proc* directory can tell you what CPU you are using?

3. You want to learn more about the PCI-based hardware in a typical Intel-based computer so that you can update the kernel. What command can you use?

4. The older computer you are using does not support the *make bzImage* command. What commands can you execute if you want to create a smaller kernel?

5. You have just compiled a new kernel, but it will not boot. You intend on booting a kernel on the second partition of the first hard drive. Currently, the GRUB configuration file reads as follows:

```
title Test Kernel (2.6.0)
            root (hd0,2)
            kernel /boot/bzImage-2.6.1 ro root=LABEL=/
            initrd /boot/initrd-2.6.1.img
```

What change needs to be made?

6. When building and installing modules during the process of creating a new kernel, when do you need to be *root*?

Answers

1. Use the *make mrproper* command, then *make clean*. If these two commands do not solve the problem, you are using the wrong configuration file for your CPU type. Go to the */usr/src/linux/configs/kernelname* directory and copy the correct file.

2. */proc/cpuinfo*.

3. */bin/lspci -vv*.

4. Any of the following: *make zImage, make zdisk*, or *make zlilo*.

5. Change *root (hd0,2)* to read *root (hd0,1)*. GRUB uses a zero-based counting system, so the second partition of the system is indicated by a 1, not a 2.

6. Only when installing the modules.

Exercise

Following is an exercise for creating a custom 2.6 kernel. It contains many separate steps.

1. Make sure that you know your hardware. Use the *lspci* command with the *-vv* option to determine the type of hardware that you have. Then view the output of the */proc/cpuinfo* command to find the type of CPU your system is using.

2. Verify that you have all of the software components installed that will help you build and install a kernel. Components vary between the 2.4 series and 2. 6 series of kernels. Components and utilities include:

> *procps*
> *module-init-tools*
> *reiserfsprogs*
> *jfsutils*
> *binutils*
> *pcmcia-cs*
> *util-linux*
> *module-init-tools*
> *quota-tools*
> *nfs-utils*
> *Gnu C*

Gnu make
e2fsprogs
xfsprogs
oprofile

3. Once you have verified you have these components and utilities, you can obtain the source files from *http:www.kernel.org* or from your system's distribution repositories. For example, you can obtain the kernel files on a Red Hat or Fedora system using RPM. Novell SUSE systems provide Yast (or RPM, if you wish), and you can use *apt* or Synaptic for Debian-based systems.

   At this stage, you can also patch the kernel, if you wish. Once you have finished patching, you can configure the kernel. During this stage of the process, you have to determine whether you want a static kernel or a modular kernel. Most systems default to modular kernels.

4. Once you have made this decision, find the *Makefile* and edit it to contain unique information for your kernel. Change the *EXTRAVERSION = -1* portion of the *Makefile* to a unique value.

5. Then back up the hidden *.config* file that is in the *../linux* file of your source tree. Do this by copying the *.config* file to another location. Then type *make mrproper* to begin with a fresh installation.

6. Now you are ready to use the *make* command to create a 2.6 kernel. You have a choice between the *make config, make oldconfig, make menuconfig,* and *make xconfig* commands. The *make config* command does not provide a menu. Rather, it runs a program that asks you a long series of questions that you have to answer. *make oldconfig* reads the existing file and makes the changes you have indicated. Use *make oldconfig* only if you have made minor changes. The *make menuconfig* command presents an *ncurses*-based menu that is considerably more user-friendly than the list of questions presented by the *make config* command. Finally, the *make xconfig* command is the most user-friendly, but may not be available on your system.

7. Choose the options that are best for your system. You will see that the choices are grouped into several sections (e.g., General Setup, Loadable Module Support, Device Drivers). Go through each option and choose the features you want. When you are finished configuring your options, save them and exit the program.

8. You are now ready to build the kernel. Type the following:

   ```
   make bzImage
   ```

9. If you have chosen to build a modular kernel (the most common choice), you must then build the modules:

   ```
   make modules
   ```

10. Now, become *root* and install the modules:

   ```
   su root
   make modules_install
   ```

11. Exit *root*.

12. Now you need to create an initial ramdisk image, so that the system can boot the hard drive and begin initialization. If, for example, you are creating a kernel named *2.6.10-5-686*, issue the following command to create the accompanying ramdisk image:

```
mkinitrd /boot/2.6.10-5-686
```

13. Now copy the new kernel and *system.map* file you have created to the */boot* directory. Following is an example:

```
$ cp arch/i686/boot/bzImage /boot/bzImageYOUR_KERNEL_VERSION
$ cp System.map /boot/System.map-YOUR_KERNEL_VERSION
$ ln -s /boot/System.map-YOUR_KERNEL_VERSION /boot/System.map
```

Notice how the final command creates a symbolic link from your new *system. map* file to the */boot/System.map* file.

14. After you are finished, edit your boot loader. If you are using GRUB, edit the */boot/grub/menu.lst* file or possibly the */etc/grub.conf* file, which is usually a symbolic link to the */boot/grub/menu.lst* file. If, for example, you have created a new kernel named *2.6.10-5-686*, create the following entry for GRUB:

```
title         New, kernel 2.6.10-5-686
root          (hd0,1)
kernel        /boot/vmlinuz-2.6.10-5-686 root=/dev/hda2 ro quiet
splash
initrd        /boot/initrd.img-2.6.10-5-686
savedefault
boot
```

You do not have to run any command to enable this file; GRUB will read the *menu.lst* or *grub.conf* file automatically at boot time. If you experience any problems, you can edit the configuration file on the fly at boot time, as described later in this chapter.

Alternatively, if you are using LILO to use the same kernel, alter your */etc/lilo. conf* file as follows:

```
boot=/dev/hda
          map=/boot/map
          install=/boot/boot.b
          default=new-2.6.10-5-686
          keytable=/boot/us.klt
          lba32
          prompt
          timeout=50
          message=/boot/message
          menu-scheme=wb:bw:wb:bw
          image=/boot/vmlinuz
              label=linux
              root=/dev/hda3
              append=" ide1=autotune ide0=autotune"
              read-only

          image=/boot/vmlinuz-2.6.10-5-686
              label=test-2.6.10-5-686
              root=/dev/hda1
              read-only
```

Then run the *lilo* command to update the boot sequence.

System Startup (Topic 2.202)

Review Questions

1. Why are the files under the */etc/init.d* directory executable?

2. Some systems, such as Red Hat, do not place startup scripts in the */etc/init.d* directory. Where do Red Hat and others put these scripts?

3. What is the result of the following entry in the */etc/inittab* file?

   ```
   ca:12345:ctrlaltdel:/sbin/shutdown -t1 -a -r now
   ```

4. You find scripts named *K11anacron* and *S15bind9* in the */etc/rc2.d* directory. Which script will run first when the system starts up?

5. You wish to run the *fsck* command on a partition named */dev/hda1*. What command should you run first?

6. What is the result of the following command?

   ```
   fsck -a /dev/hda3
   ```

Answers

1. Because these files are run by the *init* program and are used to start system daemons

2. In the */etc/rc.d/init.d* directory

3. It traps the hardware-based command that normally shuts the system down, and runs the Linux *shutdown* command. As a result, system shutdown is more orderly and causes fewer problems.

4. *K11anacron*, because *K* scripts are run first. Then *S* scripts are run. Alphabetical order is followed. So *K11anacron* would run before *K11bind*, for example.

5. *umount /dev/hda1*

6. The command runs *fsck* on an IDE device and automatically repairs any problems found.

Exercises

1. Review the contents of the */etc/inittab* file. Consider adding the following line that adds a new *getty* command (standard text-based login) for runlevels 2, 3, 4, and 5 on *tty12*:

   ```
   12:2345:respawn:/sbin/getty 38400 tty12
   ```

2. Review the contents of the scripts at your particular runlevel. In some systems (Red Hat and Fedora), you can find these scripts in the subdirectories of the */etc/rc.d* directory. In other systems, you will find the files in the */etc/rcN.d* directory, where *N* is the number of the runlevel. For example, an Ubuntu system is Debian based and defaults to runlevel 2. Therefore, the scripts that run at the default runlevel are in the */etc/rc2.d* directory. Review the scripts in this directory to see what is run. Notice that there are *K* scripts and *S* scripts. The *K* scripts are run before the *S* scripts. Scripts are run first in numerical, then in alphabetical, order. Determine the order in which scripts are run.

3. Practice using the following commands as *root*:

```
init 0
init 6
init 2
init 5
```

Write down the results of each command for your particular system or systems.

4. Review the contents of the */etc/mkinitrd/mkinitrd.conf* file. Note the default settings for the initrd image that would be created. They are usually 022. The DELAY option is usually set to 0 by default. You would increase this value if you wished to give the system a chance to rest before running initialization scripts.

5. As *root*, type *init 1*. Notice what you have to do to enter maintenance mode. After you type the *root* password, you will see that you can edit files, make necessary changes, and run programs such as *fsck* (as long as you have unmounted the partition). You are now the *root* user.

6. If you are using GRUB, reboot your system and then select the default boot option when the GRUB menu screen appears. Press e. You will see that you can now edit the boot parameters for this particular session. Press the Escape key to go back to the main menu.

7. If you are using GRUB, reboot your system again. Once you see the GRUB menu screen, press c. You will be sent to a GRUB prompt, where you can create your own boot sequence. Press the Escape key to return to the menu and boot your system.

8. If you are using GRUB, execute the following commands to store Stage 1 and Stage 2 on a floppy disk:

   a. Insert a floppy disk.

   b. Change to the GRUB directory:

   ```
   cd /boot/grub/
   ```

   c. Copy the Stage 1 files and Stage 2 files to the floppy disk using the *dd* command:

   ```
   dd if=stage1 of=/dev/fd0 bs=512 count=1
   dd if=stage2 of=/dev/fd0 bs=512 seek=1
   ```

   These commands create a valid boot floppy disk for your drive.

9. If you do not have a floppy disk drive and want to create a GRUB boot CD, you need to use the file named *stage2_eltorito*. This is a special Stage 2 file required by CD-ROM drives. You do not need to use the Stage 1 or Stage 2 files. The *stage2_eltorito* file is often located in the */usr/lib/grub/i386-pc/* or */lib/grub/i386-pc* directory. The steps you take to create a bootable CD-ROM follow.

   a. Create a directory structure to store the ISO image you are going to create. This structure must be stored onto the CD-ROM as */boot/grub*:

   ```
   mkdir -p iso/boot/grub
   ```

   b. Copy the */usr/lib/grub/i386-pc/stage2_eltorito* file to the directory you have just created:

   ```
   cp /usr/lib/grub/i386-pc/stage2_eltorito ~/iso/boot/grub/
   ```

c. Use the *mkisofs* command to create an ISO image:

```
mkisofs -R -b boot/grub/stage2_eltorito -no-emul-boot -boot-load-
size 4 -boot-info-table -o grub.iso iso
```

This command tells *mkisofs* to create Rock Ridge protocol files and also specifies the path of the boot image used.

d. You can then use any application you wish to burn the ISO image (*grub.iso*) onto the CD-ROM.

10. If you are using LILO, add password protection to it using the instructions given in this book. Be sure to make a backup copy of your original *lilo.conf* file before making any changes to it. Once you are finished making your changes, be sure to install them as *lilo.conf* and then run *lilo* to make sure your changes are recognized.

Filesystem (Topic 2.203)

Review Questions

1. What is the difference between the */etc/fstab* and the */etc/mtab* files?

2. What is the meaning of the sixth field in the */etc/fstab* file?

3. Where would the following line appear, and what does it accomplish?

```
cdrom    -fstype=iso9660,ro,sync,nodev,nosuid    :/dev/cdrom
```

4. What type of information is found in the */proc/mounts* file?

5. For a device named */dev/sda1*, you wish to learn the last mount time, the maximum count of boot times that have occurred between checks by *fsck*, and the maximum mount counts. You know that some of the output may not be understood by the *dumpe2fs* command. What *dumpe2fs* option would you use to get this command to report all findings?

6. What command flushes all data and writes it to disk?

7. How can you see that an attempted copy using the *dd* command failed?

8. You have tried to use the *swapon* command on a partition named */dev/hda3*. This partition has the following entry in */etc/fstab*:

```
/dev/hda3        /              ext3    defaults,noauto,errors=remount-ro 0
```

What information in this line can help you identify the most likely problem?

Answers

1. The */etc/fstab* file shows the filesystems that will be mounted. The */etc/mtab* file lists the filesystems that are mounted. In other words, */etc/fstab* controls the behavior of the system, whereas */etc/mtab* reflects the results.

2. The sixth field of */etc/fstab* determines the order that partitions (that is, filesystems) are checked when a system boots.

3. The entry is part of the *autofs* configuration file. The entry automatically mounts the */dev/cdrom* drive as a read-only device when a disk is inserted. SUID files are not mounted, and neither are device files. The filesystem type is *iso9660*, which is standard for CD-ROM devices.

4. The filesystems that are currently mounted and active.

5. *dumpe2fs -f /dev/sda1*.

6. *sync*.

7. The failed *dd* command issues an error code greater than 0 to standard error. An error message such as "No space left on device" may also be displayed.

8. The *noauto* option precludes the use of the */dev/hda3* device as a swap file.

Exercises

1. Use the *cat* command to view the contents of the */proc/mounts* file. What do this file's contents have in common with the contents of the */etc/mtab* file?

2. Review the */etc/fstab* file and take note of the syntax. Be able to identify the following:
   - The filesystem used
   - The mount point
   - The filesystem type
   - The options: be able to describe each one
   - The dump value
   - The pass number

   Familiarize yourself with each of the fields and their possible values.

3. Use the *less* command to read the contents of the */etc/mtab* file. Then use the *badblocks* command to look for problems on one of the Linux filesystems. Make sure that you unmount the partition first. For example, if you wanted to read the */dev/hda3* partition, you would issue the following commands:

   ```
   umount /dev/hda3
   badblocks -o bad.txt /dev/hda3
   ```

   The *bad.txt* file will contain a list of all bad blocks on the partition.

4. Try out the *dd* command to copy the contents of a partition into a single file. Make sure that you have a large amount of disk space in the destination directory. Suppose you have a partition named */dev/hda3* that is 500 MB. You could write it to a single image (using a different partition) as follows:

   ```
   dd if=/dev/hda3 of=hda3.img
   ```

   The following copies the contents of *bootdisk.img* to a floppy disk:

   ```
   dd if=bootdisk.img of=/dev/fd0
   ```

5. It is also important to know the options to *dd*. For instance, you can increase the block size to make writing faster and more efficient. Or you can specify the block size to copy only the data that you need. For example, to copy the boot sector from the */dev/hda* device, you could tell *dd* to perform this operation once on the first 512 bytes:

   ```
   dd if=/boot/grub/stage1 of=/dev/fd0 bs=512 count=1
   ```

6. You can then tell *dd* to write the second stage onto the same floppy. This time, you will use the seek option, which tells *dd* to skip over the first 512

bytes, as specified in the *bs* option, and continue writing on byte 513 of the floppy:

```
dd if=/boot/grub/stage2 of=/dev/fd0 bs=512 seek=1
```

Continue experimenting with the *dd* command, but be careful: a simple mistake can destroy all data on your drive or partition.

7. On a system that has sufficient unused space, create a new 500-MB partition. Use the *fsck* command and create a type 82 partition. Next, use the *mkswap* command to make this space a swap file, for instance:

```
mkswap -c /dev/hdb2
```

Now use the *swapon* command to activate the partition so that it can be used as RAM:

```
swapon /dev/hdb2
```

Issue the *swapoff* command for the */dev/hdb2* partition. Use *fdisk* to re-create the partition. Then, use the *mke2fs -j* command to create an *ext3* partition on it. Copy data to this new partition. If you want to keep it, update the */etc/fstab* file to automatically mount it. If you wish, you can recreate the swap space and then update */etc/fstab* to automatically mount it with the following line:

```
/dev/hdb2       none        swap    sw          0      0
```

Hardware (Topic 2.204)

Review Questions

1. You have just updated the */etc/raidtab* file. What command should you run to create the RAID array?

2. What file can you read to determine which USB devices have been recognized on your system?

3. What three things can you do with the *modprobe* command?

4. You have just added a new device but do not know the interrupt that this device is using. What file in the */proc* directory can you query?

5. A coworker has just added a new CD/DVD-RW drive via USB. You wish to verify its speed. What command allows you to do this?

Answers

1. *mkraid.*

2. */proc/bus/usb/devices.*

3. You can add modules, delete modules, and list the modules that can be run on the system.

4. */proc/interrupts.*

5. *syctl -a.*

Exercises

1. View the */proc/interrupts* file and compare it to the output of the *lspci -vv* command. Notice that you can get the same IRQ information from both. However, the *lspci -vv* command gives you much more information about the devices themselves, as long as they are PCI based.

2. Use the *hdparm* command to read the parameters on your devices. For example, if you have an IDE drive as your first disk, issue the following command as *root*:

   ```
   hdparm /dev/hda
   ```

   Review the output. Is DMA turned on or off? Be careful when enabling or disabling any settings. Enable features using *hdparm* only if you are sure your hard disk supports them. Similarly, disabling features might severely impact disk performance. If you wish, use the *sysctl* command to discover the speed of your CD-ROM. Then use *hdparm*'s -E option to specify a lower speed. Return the speed back to its default using the -E option again.

3. As *root*, use the *tune2fs* command to list the filesystem parameters for your first hard drive:

   ```
   tune2fs -l /dev/hda
   ```

4. Use the -c option to specify how many times the system must be mounted before *fsck* is automatically run. Use the -C option to tell the filesystem how many times the drive has been mounted. Be careful when adjusting any other parameters, as doing so may cause you to lose data.

5. Use the *sysctl* command to view the settings for the following devices:
   - Ethernet card (wireless or standard)
   - CD-ROM drive
   - Whether or not the system is configured to ignore all ICMP packets
   - The kernel version and release

6. If the *setserial* command is installed, use it to determine the default settings for your serial devices. Then adjust those settings.

7. If you have *Xfree86* installed, use the following options to the *XFree86* command:
   - *-version*
   - *-scanpci*

   Then toggle between resolutions, if your X server supports them. Pressing Ctrl-Alt-Minus (using the minus key on the keyboard) lowers the resolution. Pressing Ctrl-Alt-Plus (using the plus key on the keyboard) increases the resolution. If multiple resolutions do not exist, use *XF86config* to create them.

File and Service Sharing (Topic 2.209)

Review Questions

1. You have verified that the *smbd* daemon is running, but remote users cannot seem to see your Samba shares. What other daemon needs to be running?

2. What is the purpose of the *root_squash* and *ro=hostname.domainname.com* options in the */etc/exports* file?

3. An administrator has just updated the */etc/exports* command. The NFS daemon is running. What NFS command should be executed, and what separate daemon should be running, so that remote users can access the share?

4. What is the purpose of the following entries in an NFS configuration file?

   ```
   uid    0-60      -     # switch to nobody
   uid    61-80     41    # map 61-80 into 41-60
   ```

5. You have configured a Linux system as a client in an older WINS network. The name of the Linux client is *jerry*. You wish to determine whether the WINS server is properly resolving your client's IP address. The name of the WINS server is *win1.garcia.com*. What command would you issue?

6. You wish to mount a remote Samba share using the *smbmount* command. You have already set up the */usr/local/zeppelin* directory as the mount point. The hostname of the remote system is *jimmy*. The name of the remote share is *page*. The username is *robert*. You want to specify the password when prompted. What does the command look like?

7. You wish to use the *smbclient* command to mount a remote directory. This command will be in a script, so you want to specify the username and password. The remote hostname is *pink*, and the share name is *floyd*. The username is *david* and the password is *gilmour*. What would the command look like?

Answers

1. The Samba NetBIOS name server, called *nmbd*.

2. The *root_squash* parameter forces the *root* user to have the same permissions as the *nobody* account. It helps ensure that remote users cannot overwrite essential system configuration files and other important files in the mounted directory.

3. The *exportfs -a* command must be executed and the *portmapper* daemon must be running.

4. The entries map remote users to local user accounts, to help ensure that user IDs are properly processed.

5. *nmblookup -U win1.garcia.com -R jerry*.

6. *smbmount //jimmy/page /usr/local/zeppelin -U=robert*.

7. *smbclient //pink/floyd -U david%gilmour*.

Exercises

1. Install NFS. Then configure the */etc/exports* file to share a single directory read-only. Use the *exportfs -a* command to inform NFS of your changes. You may also have to verify that the *portmapper* is working properly. Use the *nfsstat* command to verify the status of the NFS shares on your server.

2. Now use the *mount* command on a remote system to mount the directory you have just shared via NFS. Then unmount the directory. Reexport the directory on the server so that users can write to it. You may have to adjust the permissions using *chmod*, as well as change the contents of the */etc/exports* file. Use the *showmount* command to verify that NFS mounts for the client are working properly.

3. Once you have NFS working, verify that your NFS system is capable of conducting soft and hard retries. After making changes to your NFS server, restart the server. Then unplug the system from the network. Plug the system back in. What kind of error messages did the client receive?

4. Configure user ID mapping for your NFS server. Verify that the mapping is working correctly by using the *nfsstat* command.

5. Configure access control for your NFS server. Make sure that only a specific system can access your shares.

6. Install Samba using the appropriate packaging utility for your system. Source files, should you wish to install them by tarball, are available at *http:www. samba.org*. Then edit the */etc/samba/smb.conf* to:

    • Enable user-level security.

    • Encrypt passwords sent between systems. This enables Samba to communicate with Windows systems.

    • Specify the homes share, which allows all home directories to be shared to users that specify the proper username and password.

7. Use the *smbpasswd -a* command to create a user database, then add users that you wish to access resources.

8. Start Samba (both *nmbd* and *smbd*).

9. Mount a directory using the *smbclient* command. If you have a Windows system available, use the Windows browser to open your share. Be sure to either log on with the username your Linux server recognizes or specify the correct login credentials. If you encounter any problems, use the *smbstatus* and *nmblookup* commands to verify that your Samba system is working properly.

10. Once you have configured Samba to work correctly, configure it as a WINS server. Be careful that you do not specify the WINS server as a WINS client. Also, make sure that there is only one WINS server on the network.

11. Configure your Samba server so that it has access control. Edit the *samba. conf* file so that the Samba server responds only to certain systems.

12. Install a printer on the system. Now configure the *samba.conf* file so that the printer is shared. Use either a Linux or Windows system to access the printer share.

13. Use the *smbmount* command on a remote system to mount the Samba share you have created.

14. Use the *smbtestparm* command to verify current settings. See if there is anything that you would like to change or whether you can find any unexpected settings.

System Maintenance (Topic 2.211)

Review Questions

1. You want a central logging server to accept log entries from several remote systems. What option in the *syslogd* or *sysklogd* file would you enter to enable the logging daemon to accept remote log entries?

2. What is the format of an entry in the */etc/syslogd* file?

3. You wish to configure the */etc/hosts* file so that remote logging always works, even if the DNS server fails. Which should be specified first when creating a host entry: the host's IP address or the host's name?

4. What is the syntax of a log entry in the */var/log/messages* file?

5. What command builds a Debian package?

6. What is the command used to build an RPM package?

Answers

1. The option is *-r*.

2. facility/priority.

3. The host's IP address is entered first.

4. The date, the time, the hostname, the daemon that prompted the log entry, and the message from the daemon.

5. The *-b* option tells *dpkg* to build a package. This option specifies the name of the directory that contains the files necessary for building the package. Finally, you specify the name of the package that you are building:

    dpkg -b **file_system_tree_directory name_of_package.deb**

6. Use the *-ba* option to tell the RPM facility to build binary and source packages. The command also specifies the spec filename, not the name of the built package.

    rpm -ba **spec_file_name-1.0.spec**

Exercises

1. Go onto the Internet and read about the construction of an RPM spec file. When it comes to understanding a spec file, be able to identify the purpose of the following:

    Header
    Describes the contents of the RPM, including the name of the RPM, the version, the release date, and the URL of the source file.

Preparation

Gathers all of the files that will be used during the installation process.

Build

Used to build the software once it has been gathered together. This section does not install files. An optional section, used mostly when dealing with source RPMs.

Installation

Contains the commands necessary for actually installing the application or service.

System cleaning

Macros that ensure that the spec file is built in a clean environment.

Pre- and postinstallation scripts

Where you can place instructions for scripts that run before and after the RPM is installed.

Changelog

Describes the changes that have been made to an RPM.

You can then build the RPM using the following command:

```
rpm -ba foobar-1.0.spec
```

2. Study the components of the files necessary for creating a Debian package. Use the *dpkg* command to view the contents of a Debian package. For example, to read the file named *xpdf*, you might issue the following command:

```
dpkg -c xpdf-reader_3.00-11ubuntu3.7_i386.deb
```

You could, of course pipe the output into the *less* command, if the file listing goes off the screen.

3. Study the */var/log/messages* file and make sure you understand each field of the log entry. Make sure that you can tell the difference between locally generated log files and those that are generated from remote systems.

4. Use the *tail* command to view the last 10 lines of the */var/log/messages* file. Notice that many log facilities send messages to this file. You can create custom logs that contain less information. Open the */etc/syslog.conf* file using a text editor and create entries that send critical (crit) messages for the following facilities:

- Daemon
- Mail
- News

Make sure you restart *syslogd* after you have made your changes.

5. Edit the */etc/syslog.conf* file and configure *syslogd* to send logs to a remote system. You will have to configure the remote system to accept log files. This is accomplished by using the -r option in the *syslogd* configuration file (e.g., */etc/rc.d/init.d/syslogd* in Red Hat/Fedora systems and */etc/init.d/ sysklogd* in Debian-based systems). Consider creating custom logs that will be sent to a remote system.

6. Create a preliminary backup storage plan. When doing so, consider the following issues:

   - Backup method (differential versus incremental).

   - Medium to use (e.g., tape, CD/DVD).

   - Proper storage of backups. Consider ways to store an entire set of tapes remotely, as well as to verify all backups to make sure data has not been corrupted during backup.

   Study the difference between differential and incremental backups. For what situation or situations is each method most suited? What are the drawbacks for each method?

7. Sometimes, it is advisable to edit the */etc/hosts* file and create entries for essential systems. For example, if you have a central logging server, enter the hostname and IP address for that server. This way, your system will be able to log to the central server even if DNS goes down.

System Customization and Automation (Topic 2.213)

Review Questions

1. What is the function of the third field in a *crontab* entry?

2. Consider the following command:

   ```
   at 4:00 9/13/08 -f command_file
   ```

   What is another way to specify this time?

3. You wish to use the *rsync* command to copy the local directory of */home/james/backup* directory to the */usr/remote/backup* directory of the remote system named *sandi*. What would this command look like?

Answers

1. The day of the month.

2. *at teatime 9/13/08 -f command_file.*

3. *rsync -avz /home/james/backup/ sandi:/usr/remote/backup.*

Exercises

1. Create a user-based *crontab* using the *crontab -e* command. If you cannot think of any particular command to use, have the command list your home directory and then print the current date. Use the *mail* command to verify that the script has worked. If the script doesn't work, edit it until you specify the correct commands.

2. View the scripts in the */etc/cron.hourly*, */etc/cron.d/daily*, */etc/cron.weekly*, and */etc/cron.monthly* directories. Notice that some scripts are quite simple, whereas others are more ambitious.

3. Create a script in the */etc/cron.hourly* directory. Use the *mail* command to verify that the script has worked.

4. Use the *at* command to have a command take place one hour from the current time. Issue the *atq* command to view the status of the command.

5. Consider the following use of *awk*:

```
sudo kill `ps auxww | grep ethereal | egrep -v grep | awk '{print $2}'`
```

Study how *awk* is used in this particular command. Then go on to the Internet and review additional examples of *awk* usage.

6. Consider the following *rsync* command:

```
rsync -avz james:/home/sandi/essential/ /backup/sandi
```

7. This command copies all of the contents of the */home/sandi/essential* on the remote system named *james* to the */backup/sandi* directory of the local system. Be able to explain each option used in this command. The -*a* option enables archiving, which preserves all permissions, symbolic links, and other file elements. The next part of the command specifies the remote system name and the directory on the remote system, including a trailing slash. The final part of the command specifies the destination where the directory is copied.

Troubleshooting (Topic 2.214)

Review Questions

1. What is the last stage of the boot process?

2. You wish to configure your system to stop replying to all ICMP packets. What file in the */etc/ directory* can you edit to accomplish this?

3. You have been provided with a directory that contains all of the necessary files and libraries to run the *passwd* command in a *chroot* environment. This directory is called */usr/local/chrootenv*. What command would you form to run the *passwd* command in a *chroot* environment?

4. You wish to run the *passwd* command in a *chroot* environment. However, the command fails in this environment. You suspect a problem with the libraries that the command requires. What can you do to learn more about the libraries used by the *passwd* command?

5. Your system currently does not create home directories for each user by default whenever you use the *useradd* command. What file can you alter to change this default behavior?

6. You have been using the *dmesg* command and examining the output, a cumbersome procedure, to find out which kernel the system is currently using. Which command would give this information?

Answers

1. Initializing and setting up daemons.

2. */etc/sysctl.conf*.

3. *chroot /usr/local/chrootenv passwd*.

4. Use the *ldd* command:

```
ldd /usr/bin/passwd
```

5. */etc/login.defs*.

6. *uname -a*.

Exercises

1. Study the LDP Bootdisk HOWTO at *http://www.ibiblio.org/pub/Linux/docs/ HOWTO/Bootdisk-HOWTO*. Make sure that you understand the boot process, how to create bootable CDs, and how to troubleshoot problems.

2. Boot your system and review the boot process. Notice when the four different stages occur.

3. View the contents of the */etc/login.defs* file. Notice that this file allows you to customize various login settings. Change the FAIL_DELAY value to 10. Notice the USERGROUPS_ENAB entry. In many systems, this value is set to yes, which means that each time a user is deleted, the group will be deleted, as well. Also, review the FAILLOG_ENAB and LOG_OK_LOGINS entries.

4. As a normal user, try to view the contents of the */etc/shadow* file. You will not be able to. List the file's permissions. As *root*, view the contents of the */etc/ shadow* file. Notice that you can view it now. Make sure you understand each field of the file.

5. Many systems default to allowing the *rm* command to delete files without warning. If your system does not have this setting already, add the following alias to the *~/.bashrc* file (or to the pertinent file for your shell):

   ```
   alias rm='rm -i'
   ```

   Once you have made this change, either log out and log back in or issue the following command (both periods are necessary):

   ```
   . .bashrc
   ```

   Now, when you use *rm* to delete a file, you will be asked to confirm your choice.

6. View the contents of the */etc/ld.so.conf* file. Consider that making a change in the dynamic linking libraries involves simply opening this file in a text editor to add a path to the valid library, then running the *ldconfig* command to update the links. Using the *-v* option to *ldconfig* helps you see the changes made.

7. Use the *strings* command to view the contents of various files on the system. Start small by viewing the */bin/ls* command. Then, view other files to learn the text strings that they contain.

8. Use the *lsof* command with *grep* to discover the following:

   a. All open TCP connections

   b. All open UDP connections

   c. All processes associated with the bash shell (or whatever shell you are using

   d. All regular processes (REG)

   You may also want to pipe the output through the *less* command so that you can view the content more easily. This exercise will require you not only to

---

understand how to use *lsof*, *grep*, and *less*, but to understand each field in the output of the *lsof* command. You will see that the command is listed and then its PID, the user, its file descriptor (name), its type (regular file, FIFO, etc.), the device being used, its size in memory, and the node or filename being used.

9. View the */etc/bashrc* or */etc/bash.bashrc* file. Notice the settings, and see how this file is also used to configure the look and feel of the prompt. Make any changes you like, but create a backup file just in case.

10. Make sure that you can ping your system. Use the *cat* command to view the contents of the */proc/sys/net/ipv4/icmp_echo_ignore_all* file. It should read 0.

11. Suppose that you want to configure your system to ignore all pings. You can do this by editing the */etc/sysctl.conf* file or by manually changing the value of the */proc/sys/net/ipv4/proc/sys/net/ipv4/icmp_echo_ignore_all* file to 1. As *root*, open the */etc/sysctl.conf* file and the following entry:

```
net/ipv4/icmp_echo_ignore_all=1
```

Close the file, making sure to save your changes. Then, issue the following command to process the */etc/sysctl.conf* file:

```
sysctl -p /etc/sysctl.conf
```

Use the *cat* command to view the contents of the */proc/sys/net/ipv4/icmp_echo_ignore_all* file. It will now read 1. You can use the following command to change the value back to 0:

```
echo 0 > /proc/sys/net/ipv4/icmp_echo_ignore_all
```

34

Exam 201 Practice Test

The 201 exam is comprised of roughly 54 questions. You have 90 minutes to answer these questions correctly. Most of the exam questions are multiple choice with one correct answer. The second most common item type is multiple choice with multiple answers. Remaining questions require you to fill in the blank, which can sometimes be daunting. No notes are allowed, and you are monitored in a secure, high-stakes exam environment. For more information about the LPI 201 exam and all of LPI's exam policies, go to *http://www.lpi.org*.

This chapter gives you some questions designed to help you learn about the LPI 201 Objectives. These questions are designed to help you prepare for the questions in the actual exam. Once you become familiar with these questions, work on a live system to truly learn the concepts and practices discussed, these questions. While the questions are certainly useful, you will find that applying your knowledge is the best way to prepare for the LPI 201 exam.

Questions

1. You have just finished creating a custom kernel. Which of the following is a valid next step for creating the kernel image?

    a. *make dep*

    b. *make bzimage*

    c. *make kernel*

    d. *make image*

2. Which of the following is a common name of a kernel image?

    a. *vmlinuz-2.6.10-5-686*

    b. *minix_stage1_5*

    c. *System.map-2.6.10-5-386*

    d. *initrd.img-2.6.10-5-686*

3. Which of the following is the final stage of a kernel update?

    a. Compile dependencies.

    b. Create a RAM disk image.

    c. Configure the boot loader (e.g., GRUB).

    d. Copy the *bzImage* file to the kernel name in the */boot* directory.

4. What is the name of the file in GRUB that you need to edit in order to change the kernel that will be booted by default?

    a. *boot.conf*

    b. *grub.conf*

    c. *img.conf*

    d. *vmlinux.conf*

5. Which of the following do you have to accomplish before you can use an initrd image on your Debian system?

    a. Install all necessary modules for initrd.

    b. Switch from LILO to GRUB.

    c. Compile *cramfs* support into the kernel.

    d. Create a monolithic kernel.

6. Which of the following commands allows you to easily inspect a compressed kernel patch?

    a. *less*

    b. *bzip2*

    c. *bzmore*

    d. *source*

7. You discover that you need to remove two levels of path from a patch in order to proceed with patching a kernel. Which of the following commands will work on a file named *patch-2.6.14.4.bz2*?

    a. *bzip2 -dc patch-2.6.14.4.bz2 | patch -p2*

    b. *patch -dc | bzip2 -dc patch-2.6.14.4.bz2*

    c. *bzip2 -dc patch-2.6.14.4.bz2 | make -p2*

    d. *patch -dc patch-2.6.14.4.bz2 | bzImage -m2*

8. Consider the following entry in */etc/inittab*:

```
23:respawn:/sbin/getty 38400 tty2
```

You wish to add another entry to start a terminal (tty) that operates at runlevels 2, 3, 4, and 5 on *tty1*. Which of the following is the correct inittab entry?

    a. `0 2345:respawn:/sbin/tty01 38400 getty`

    b. `/sbin/getty 38400 tty1 :1:2345`

    c. `0:2,3,4,5:respawn:/sbin/getty 38400 tty0`

    d. `1:2345:respawn:/sbin/getty 38400 tty1`

9. What is the name of the first startup script in a Debian-based system?

    a. /boot/grub.conf

    b. /etc/init.d/rc1

    c. /etc/init.d/rcS

    d. /etc/rc.sysinit/init

10. Of the following options, which require *root* privileges? (Choose two.)

    a. Using the *make modules install* command

    b. Running the *make xconfig* command

    c. Editing the boot loader file (e.g., *grub.conf* or *lilo.conf*)

    d. Editing the *Makefile* that comes with the kernel

11. You have decided to have Sendmail start automatically on levels 3 and 5 of your Linux system. Which one of the following commands makes this change?

    a. *init sendmail 35*

    b. *init 35 sendmail --on*

    c. *chkconfig 35 sendmail on*

    d. *chkconfig --level 35 sendmail on*

12. Write in the command that allows you to adjust the system so that a file-system check is run every 200 boots.

13. You have just issued the following command:

```
mkisofs -T -r -L -l -J -o /var/tmp/image.iso /home/james/backup/
```

Which of the following describe the results of this command? (Choose two.)

    a. *mkisofs* will generate a warning that it is creating a filesystem that is not ISO9660-compatible.

    b. The command will fail because you are not creating a filesystem that is ISO9660-compatible.

    c. *mkisofs* will generate the image in such a way that non-*root* users can mount it on any Linux system.

    d. The command will create a filesystem that allows long filenames and Unix-style symbolic links.

14. You have just added a SCSI disk to a production system. The new drive is recognized as */dev/sdb*. You wish to create the ReiserFS file system on the entire disk. Which of the following commands will do this? (Choose two.)

    a. *mke2fs -j -L Disk_2 /dev/sdb*

    b. *mkfs.reiserfs --label Disk_2 /dev/sdb*

    c. *mkreiserfs --label Disk_2 /dev/sdb*

    d. *mke2fs -j -L Disk_2 /dev/sdb1*

15. You wish to learn about the last time boot information was written to the /dev/hda2 partition on your Linux system. Which of the following commands do this? (Choose two.)

    a. *tune2fs -l /dev/hda2*

    b. *fsck -l /dev/hda2*

    c. *fdisk -l /dev/hda2*

    d. *dumpe2fs -h /dev/hda2*

16. You have been asked to transfer the contents of a smaller hard disk (*/dev/hdb*) to a larger hard disk (*/dev/hdc*). Which of the following commands allows you to do this most efficiently?

    a. *cp -s /dev/hdb /dev/hdc*

    b. *dd if=/dev/hdb of=/dev/hdc*

    c. *dd bs=8k if=/dev/hdb of=/dev/hdc*

    d. *dd bs=1k if=/dev/hdb of=/dev/hdd ln -s /dev/hdb /dev/hdd*

17. Consider the following */etc/raidtab* file:

```
raiddev /dev/md0
raid-level 1
nr-raid-disks 2
chunk-size 64k
persistent-superblock 1
nr-spare-disks 0
device /dev/hda2
raid-disk 0
device /dev/hdc2
raid-disk 1
```

    Which of the following commands is necessary to activate this configuration?

    a. *mdadm /etc/md0*

    b. *mkraid /etc/md0*

    c. *mdadm /dev/md0*

    d. *mkraid /dev/md0*

18. A developer has called you and asked you to troubleshoot a device driver for a PCI card your company has decided to support. He needs to know the IRQ that the device uses, as well as the latency statistics. Which of the following commands should you issue in order to give him the information he needs?

    a. *lspci -p*

    b. *setserial*

    c. *lspci -vv*

    d. *lsdev -C /dev/*

19. You are having problems attaching a USB hard drive to your system. You wish to determine the data transfer capabilities of the device, as well as the potential connection speed of the USB controller. Write in the application that will help you determine this information in the space.

20. You suspect that a hard drive's Direct Memory Access (DMA) ability is creating problems for you as you troubleshoot problems on the system. Which of the following commands disables direct memory access on your system?

    a. *hdparm -d1 /dev/hda*

    b. *sysctl dma=disable /dev/hda*

    c. *hdparm -d0 /dev/hda*

    d. *sysctl disable=dma /dev/hda*

21. A PCMCIA device on a laptop sometimes renders the system unstable if it is ejected without warning. Which of the following commands informs the system that the card is going to be shut down?

    a. *sudo cardctl suspend*

    b. *sudo cardctl eject*

    c. *sudo cardctl config*

    d. *sudo cardctl reset*

22. You wish to temporarily prohibit a user with the account name *james* from using a system's Samba account. However, you still want to allow this user to log on to the system using the X Window System and SSH. Which of the following solutions will accomplish this goal most efficiently?

    a. Edit the */etc/passwd* file as *root* using a text editor and comment out the *james* account's username.

    b. Enter *sudo smbpasswd -x james*.

    c. Become *root*, edit the */etc/samba/smbusers* file, and comment out the *james* account's username.

    d. Enter *sudo smbpasswd -d james*.

23. Which of the following is the suggested back-end database for a Samba server that does not require LDAP or built-in database replication?

    a. *mysqlsam*

    b. *xmlsam*

    c. *shadow*

    d. *tdbsam*

24. Consider the following alternative entries in */etc/exports*:

```
/home/james/     james.stangernet.com(rw)
/home/james/     james.stangernet.com (rw)
```

What is the result of these two entries?

    a. The top entry shares the */home/james* directory with read and write permissions to any user from the *james.stangernet.com* DNS domain. The bottom entry shares the */home/james* directory with read-only permissions to any user in the *james.stangernet.com* domain, but gives read and write permissions to all other users anywhere.

b. The top entry will be ignored because it has improper syntax. The bottom entry shares the */home/james* directory with anyone in the *james. stangernet.com* DNS domain with read and write permissions. No one else will have access.

c. The top entry shares the */home/james* directory with read-only permissions to all users, except for the *james.stangernet.com* domain. The bottom entry shares the */home/james* directory with read-only permissions to the *james.stangernet.com* domain, but with read and write permissions to all other users.

d. The top entry shares the */home/james* directory with anyone in the *james. stangernet.com* DNS domain with read and write access. The bottom entry will be ignored, because it is not formatted properly.

25. What user account does NFS change *root*-owned files to, and why?

a. To the *nfs* account, to avoid allowing users to overwrite files essential to the operation of the NFS daemon

b. To the *sys* account, to avoid allowing users to overwrite files created by the *root* user

c. To the first non-*root* account listed in the */etc/passwd* file, to avoid overwriting essential system files

d. To *nfsnobody*, to avoid allowing users to upload programs that have the setuid bit set to *root*

26. Which of the following files contain real-time information that will help you troubleshoot NFS? (Choose two.)

a. */proc/fs/exports*

b. */etc/fstab*

c. */etc/exports*

d. */proc/fs/nfsd*

27. Complete the following line to configure syslog so that it sends log messages to a remote host named *backup.stangernet.com*:

`*.info;mail.none;authpriv.none;cron.none _____ .`

28. Which of the following lines sends all emergency messages to the file named */var/log/crit.log*?

a. `/var/log/crit.log emerg.*`

b. `*.emerg var/log/crit.log`

c. `/var/log/crit.log /dev/console:0:/var/log/crit.log`

d. `emerg.* /var/log/crit.log`

29. You have downloaded OpenOffice.org. You have just untarred the tarball and have discovered that it contains all RPM files. You intend to use OpenOffice.org on a Debian-based system, however. You are currently in the directory that contains the RPM files. Which of the following commands converts the RPM files to a package format that Debian can use?

a. *alien* *

b. *sudo alien* *

c. *dpkg -c *.rpm*

d. *alias -c **

30. Consider the following code:

```
%files
%attr(0755, root, bin) /usr/bin/file
%attr(0644, root, bin) /usr/local/man/man2/manpage.1
```

What type of file is this code from?

a. A Debian file

b. A typical *Makefile*

c. The */etc/manpath.config* file

d. An RPM spec file

31. You need to install an update to Perl but are not sure of the exact name of the Perl module, due to poor documentation. You need to navigate the update options in an interactive shell. Which of the following is the correct command to begin interactive mode?

a. *perl -e 'use interactive;'*

b. *perl -a -s=/bin/bash*

c. *perl -MCPAN -e shell*

d. *perl --update*

32. You need to execute a script named *backup* three hours from now, but do not plan on being in front of your system, or at a terminal where you can access your system. Which of the following commands allows you to execute this script?

a. *at now + 3 hours <backup*

b. *crontab -e < 0 3 * * * backup*

c. *at now + 3 >backup*

d. *echo "0 3 * * * backup" >> /etc/crontab*

33. You have downloaded an ISO image and have burned it to a CD several times. However, the CD never seems to work properly. You suspect a problem with the ISO image you have downloaded. Which of the following commands can you issue to verify that this ISO image is valid?

a. *sudo mount -o loop -t iso9660 /home/james/image.iso*

b. *sudo mount -t loop -o iso9660 /home/james/image.iso /mnt/iso*

c. *sudo mount -o loop -t iso9660 /home/james/image.iso /mnt/iso*

d. *sudo mount -loop -t iso9660 /home/james/image.iso /mnt/iso*

34. List the *rdev* option that allows you to specify */dev/hda5* as the swap device. (Note: There is more than one way to do this.)

35. Consider the following line in */etc/fstab*:

```
/dev/hda5          /                    ext3    defaults -ro 0       1
```

What option would you add to this partition so that no files could be executed on it?

    a. exec=0

    b. noauto

    c. e0

    d. noexec

36. Which of the following lists the four standard boot stages in the correct order?

    a. The boot loader starts, the kernel loads, hardware initialization, service/daemon startup

    b. The boot loader starts, service/daemon startup, hardware initialization, the kernel loads

    c. Hardware initialization, the boot loader starts, the kernel loads, service/daemon startup

    d. The boot loader starts, hardware initialization, the kernel loads, service/daemon startup

37. An older Linux system fails at boot time, displaying the following letters:

    LIL

    Which of the following is the most plausible explanation for the error?

    a. The second stage boot loader has loaded at an invalid address.

    b. The second stage boot loader cannot start, but can find the descriptor table.

    c. The second stage boot loader was able to start, but the descriptor table has not been found.

    d. The second stage has been able to start, but the LILO boot loader has detected a problem with the map installer.

38. You are trying to share a drive using NFS but are experiencing problems. You have tried restarting the portmapper. You have verified network connectivity and that the */etc/exports* file is formatted properly. You have properly used *root* privileges. Which of the following steps can help you determine the exact point where *nfsd* and the portmapper encounter problems?

    a. Use the following command: *tail -f /var/log/messages.*

    b. Precede your commands with the *strace* command.

    c. Restart the system to restart the networking scripts.

    d. Verify that the *nmbd* daemon is running properly.

39. Which of the following is the most plausible reason for a "Too many levels of symbolic links" error message?

    a. The symbolic links to the */boot/vmlinuz-2.6.10-5-686* file have become corrupt.

    b. A symbolic link still exists, but the file it refers to has been deleted.

    c. A series of symbolic links has led to a infinite loop.

    d. A symbolic link has been made to a symbolic link.

40. A command keeps failing, no matter what changes you make to its configuration file. You suspect that the command makes a call to a missing dynamic library. Which of the following can help you confirm your suspicions most effectively?

    a. *ltrace*

    b. *strace*

    c. *paratrace*

    d. *mtrace*

41. You have received a binary file from a coworker. You are not sure if the file is the correct one. You would like to quickly inspect its plaintext contents. Which of the following commands will help you view the human-readable contents of the file?

    a. *cat*

    b. *strings*

    c. *less*

    d. *mtrace*

42. Which of the following files contains instructions concerning the mail directory for each user?

    a. */etc/sysctl.conf*

    b. */etc/bashrc*

    c. */etc/login.defs*

    d. */etc/sysconf.conf*

43. The size of the kernel ring buffer has been set to 17384, which is 1000 more than the default. You wish to use the *dmesg* command to read the entire buffer. Write in the command that you would issue.

44. You wish to mail the results of a *cron* job to a remote account named *james.stangernet.com*. The message is supposed to be sent every 20 minutes. You have created the following script:

```
*/20 * * * * /bin/security_program | mailx -s "Security report"
user@gmail.com
```

However, the *gmail.com* account keeps bouncing the email. Which of the following can help you solve this problem?

    a. Use the *mail* program instead of *mailx*.

    b. Change the subject line of the *mailx* command. No spaces can be included.

    c. Fix the *crontab* file to have messages sent every 20 minutes, rather than every 20 days.

    d. Configure the system sending the message to rewrite the message headers so that they belong to a valid DNS domain.

45. A user has just gotten married. She complains that her old name appears in the From field whenever she sends email using the *mail* command. Which of the following will likely solve this problem?

a. Create an alias in the */etc/aliases* file to map the user's account name to her real name.

b. Edit the */etc/passwd* file and change the fourth field of the user's new name.

c. Edit the */etc/mail.conf* file to reflect the user's new name.

d. Create an alias in the user's *.bashrc* file that maps the user's old name to the user's new name.

46. A user cannot currently log in. You check the */etc/shadow* file and notice that an asterisk appears in the second field of that user's entry. Which of the following should you do to solve this problem?

a. Edit the */etc/shadow* file using a text editor and enter a default password.

b. Use the *passwd* command to create a new password for the user.

c. Use the *shadowconfig* command to create a new shadow file, because the existing file is corrupt.

d. Edit the */etc/shadow* file to remove the asterisk.

47. You need to use the *lsof* command to determine which program has caused a system to hang for an unacceptably long time when it boots. You wish to direct *lsof* to avoid making any calls to the kernel that would cause the kernel to block the function of the *lsof* command. Write in the *lsof* command and option.

48. You wish to determine whether a problem exists with the boot process of a system's second IDE hard drive. Which of the following commands helps you read kernel messages concerning the second drive?

a. *lsof | grep hdb*

b. *dmesg | grep hdb*

c. *strings /dev/hdb*

d. *modprobe -l | grep hdb*

49. You cannot get a Samba server to run. You view the */etc/samba.smb.conf* file and notice that the following lines have been uncommented:

```
wins support = yes
wins server = 192.168.2.33
```

From these lines, you can tell that the problem is:

a. Your Samba server is trying to access a nonfunctioning WINS server.

b. The WINS server is using a private IP address.

c. The wins support entry should read wins support = 1.

d. The Samba server is configured to be both a WINS client and a WINS server.

50. A new application has been installed on a Linux web server to ensure more correct tracking of user visits. This application has required the installation of several new shared libraries. A system administrator has issued the following command:

```
ldconfig -NX
```

However, the new application still complains that the libraries are not to be found. Which of the following will solve the problem?

   a. Reinstall the libraries after running *ldconfig -NX*.

   b. Specify the correct location of the libraries as an argument to *ldconfig -NX*

   c. Run *ldconfig* without arguments.

   d. Download the latest libraries from the developer.

51. Which of the following commands measures the transfer rate of the first SCSI drive on a system?

   a. *hdparm -Tt /dev/sda*

   b. *lsof -t /dev/sda*

   c. *hdparm -X /dev/sda*

   d. *lsof -X /dev/sd1*

52. A coworker has installed a new IDE optical device on a Linux server. The drive has been recognized as device */dev/hdc*. You wish to verify its drive speed and whether DMA is enabled. Which of the following commands allows you to do this?

   a. *cat /proc/ide/hdc/settings*

   b. *lsof | grep hdc*

   c. *cat /etc/mtab*

   d. *sysctl -a*

53. You have just downloaded the latest Linux kernel. Which of the following is a step you should take before running *make xconfig*?

   a. Type *oldconfig -p*

   b. Type *make restore*

   c. Type *make oldconfig*

   d. Type *mrproper*

54. You wish to run *fsck* even though the system thinks that the filesystem is clean. You also want *fsck* to automatically repair any problems, should they be encountered. What *fsck* options would you choose? (Choose two.)

   a. *-y*

   b. *-f*

   c. *-n*

   d. *-r*

Answers

1. b. Once you have configured a custom kernel by using the *make* command (e. g., *make config* or *make xconfig*), you then create the image. You can do this by using the *make bzimage* command. After this step, you would then compile modules.

2. a. It is possible to give any name you wish to a kernel image. However, the standard pattern is to use the following syntax: *vmlinuz*, kernel number, architecture. For example: *vmlinuz-2.6.10-5-686.*

3. c. When finishing a kernel update, the final step is updating the boot loader. Otherwise, you have a new kernel, but no way to boot it.

4. b. The *grub.conf* file contains the values you need to edit in order to boot a new kernel.

5. c. *cramfs* allows systems to create RAM disks. Creation of RAM disks is especially important at boot time. The *initrd* command uses *cramfs* to create a disk at boot time in order to make the process more stable. Without *cramfs* in Debian systems, it would not be possible to create an initrd image, and the system may fail to boot.

6. c. The *bzmore* application is specially designed to view files that have been compressed using *bzip2*. It is also possible to use *bzless*. Not only can you use *bzmore* or *bzless* to view files, but you can also use these commands to decompress a file to standard output, then back into a file.

7. a. Make sure that you understand the options to the patch command. It is not enough to know that the patch command exists.

8. d. Make sure that you understand entries in */etc/inittab*. This includes how to edit existing lines so that terminals are available at additional runlevels. Knowing the *inittab* file well includes knowing the ramifications of seemingly trivial errors.

9. c. The first startup script for Debian-based systems (including Knoppix and Ubuntu) is */etc/init.d/rcS*. But the */etc/init.d/rcS* script is not the first process; the script is run by the first process, which is *init*. Nevertheless, it is important to know that if the */etc/init.d/rcS* script encounters a problem, it will begin a sequence of additional problems. Thus, it is often a good idea to troubleshoot problems as early as possible. The */etc/init.d/rcS* script may be a good place to start.

10. a and c. The *make modules install* command installs the modules, and editing the boot loader allows you to boot the kernel you have just created. These steps are the only ones in the question that require root access.

11. d. The *chkconfig* command is one of many that allow you to modify the runlevel scripts. You can use *chkconfig* to list or change runlevel settings. To change run level settings, use the *--level* option, and then finish the command with either *on* or *off*. In this question, you want Sendmail to run automatically at run levels 3 and 5, so you use the *on* option.

12. The correct entry is:

```
tune2fs -c 200
```

The *tune2fs* command can be used not only to specify the maximum number of mounts before *fsck* is used, but also to change the mount count (i.e., the number of mounts the system thinks has already occurred), as shown in the following example:

```
sudo tune2fs -C 199 /dev/hda2
```

This command tells the system that the mount count is now 199. If you have set the system to run *fsck* at 200, the system will run *fsck* upon the next boot.

13. a and d. The command found in the question is quite standard. However, the command will generate a warning. This is because the *-r* option enables Rock Ridge extensions, which allow Unix-style symbolic links. Rock Ridge is an extension to the ISO9660 standard, and thus the warning. Similarly, the Joliet filesystem can generate warning messages because it is a Microsoft-inspired extension to ISO9660. Joliet allows the preservation of long file-names, which can get truncated during the CD burning process.

14. b and c. The *mkfs.reiserfs* and *mkreiserfs* commands are essentially the same. You can also use the *mkfs* command with the proper options to create various file systems, including *ext2*, *ext3*, *reiserfs*, *vfat*, *vfat32*, and *ntfs*.

15. a and d. The *tune2fs* and *dumpe2fs* commands allow you to determine the last time boot information has been written to a hard drive. For *tune2fs*, you must use the *-l* option and specify the partition (e.g., */dev/hda2*). If using *dumpe2fs*, you need to specify the *-e* option and the partition.

16. c. When using *dd* on files and interdrive transfers, specifying the block size makes a significant difference. The *dd* command is more efficent when you specify 8-KB blocks (e.g., *bs=8k*), because writing in larger blocks increases speed.

17. d The *mkraid* command is used to process instructions in files outside the */etc* directory, in this case */etc/md0*.

18. c. The *lspci* command allows you to scan the PCI bus of a computer. The *-v* option puts *lspci* into verbose mode. The *-vv* option provides especially verbose information, which allows you to obtain not only IRQ information, but also the latencies of all listed PCI devices.

19. The *usbview* command provides an X Window System graphical interface that allows you to determine the data transfer capabilities of the device, the potential connection speed of the USB controller, and much other information. The interface updates in real time, so you can see how the system reacts when you plug in and remove devices.

20. c. If you wish to disable DMA on a particular device, issue the *hdparm -d0* command against it. If you wish to enable DMA on this device, issue the command:

```
hdparm -d1 /dev/hda
```

21. b. The *cardctl* command can be used to inform the system that a PCMCIA card is going to be ejected. In order to use the *cardctl* command in this way, you need to run it as *root*.

22. d. You can use the *smbpasswd* command to add users, change passwords, and disable users. You must run the command as *root* in order to add users, change passwords of other users, and disable users.

23. d. The *tdbsam* option in Samba is recommended if you are going to use a standalone server that does not require LDAP or built-in database replication.

24. a. NFS entries are very specific. One space can mean the difference between a secure system that offers expected services and a system that provides all access to any user on the network. In this case, a simple space between the FQDN and the permissions (*rw*) means that all users outside of the *james.stangernet.com* domain get full access to the NFS share, and members of the

james.stangernet.com get read-only access. It is possible in this case that such permissions are the exact opposite of what was intended.

25. d. Modern NFS systems automatically set files owned by *root* to the *nfsnobody* account. This step avoids the possibility of a user uploading an application that has the setuid bit set to *root*.

26. d. The */proc/fs/exports* and */proc/fs/nfsd* files both provide real-time information concerning NFS shares. The */etc/fstab* file contains configuration information for *mount*. It does not reflect real-time information. Similarly, the */etc/exports* file contains configuration information for NFS; it does not report real-time NFS share information.

27. The correct answer is *@backup.stangernet.com*. syslog has the ability to log to remote systems. You must use the ampersand (@) to inform syslog that you are going to log to a remote system.

28. b. If you want to have all emergency messages from all services/daemons sent to a specific file, specify the wildcard (*), the .emerg syslog facility, and then the destination. Make sure that you understand each of the syslog facilities and their respective priority levels.

29. b. The *alien* command must be run as *root*. You do not have to use *alien* in any particular sequence when converting files. If you have a directory full of RPM files, for example, you can simply convert them using the wildcard (*).

30. d. The information given in the sample for this question comes from an RPM spec file. A spec file is essential when creating an RPM file.

31. c, The *perl -MCPAN -e shell* command allows you to enter interactive mode, where you can update, remove, and otherwise manage Perl modules.

32. a. The *at* command allows you to plan a one-time execution of a command in the future. For repeated command execution, use the *cron* or *anacron* facility. The *at* command is also capable of reading from standard input. Make sure that you understand the many ways you can specify time for the *at* command. For this question, the *now* + time syntax was used.

33. c. In order to mount an ISO, you need to specify the -o loop option and argument. You also need to be *root*. Finally, you need to specify the mount type, which in this case is iso9660.

34. You could specify either *rdev -s /dev/hda5* or *rdev -swapdev /dev/hda5*. Remember, with Linux you can usually accomplish a goal in more than one way.

35. d. The noexec option allows you to mount a partition in such a way that it forbids files to be executed on it.

36. a. Make sure you understand the boot sequence in Linux systems: The boot loader starts, the kernel loads, hardware initialization, service/daemon startup.

37. c. The LIL error message indicates that the second stage boot loader was able to start, but the descriptor table has not been found. Make sure that you understand common LILO and GRUB error messages, as well as the boot sequence for Linux systems.

38. b. The *strace* command can help you identify exactly which calls are made by an application or daemon, and when. Finding out this information can help you identify the cause of a particular failure and resolve the problem.

39. c. The error message that reads "Too many levels of symbolic links" almost always indicates an infinite loop.

40. a. The *ltrace* command is much like the *strace* command. However, *ltrace* is designed to look for calls to dynamic libraries and therefore may be able to provide more specific information than *strace*.

41. b. The *strings* command allows you to view plain text within a binary file. Using *strings*, you can learn more about the nature of a file, including notes and instructions that the programmer plans to send to standard output.

42. c. The */etc/login.defs* file contains many different instructions, including where mailbox information resides. Make sure that you are familiar with both the syntax of this file and its general purpose.

43. The *-s* option of the *dmesg* command allows you to specify the size of the buffer you wish to read when it comes to reading kernel messages. In this case, *dmesg -s17384* allows you to read all of the contents of the buffer, as this particular system has had its buffer size changed.

44. d. No matter whether you are using Sendmail, Postfix, or another MTA, remote systems may reject your emails if the sending system does not use a recognized DNS domain. Email administrators rewrite email message headers and other information to solve this problem. If the email uses a valid DNS domain, the message will be received. For example, the */etc/mail/generic-stable* file can help you rewrite addresses so that they are not rejected. If applications such as Mozilla Thunderbird are used, you may not need to rewrite headers, because Thunderbird, Outlook Express, and other graphical mail programs allow you to specify email and DNS information more readily than the *mailx* and *mail* commands.

45. b. One of the ways you can solve this problem is by editing the */etc/passwd* file and changing the name in the fourth field of the user's entry. You can also rewrite headers using *genericstable* in Sendmail.

46. b. Using the *passwd* command for the specific user will solve the problem. No additional editing of the */etc/shadow* file is necessary.

47. The answer is *lsof -b*. This option is sometimes necessary, because certain kernel calls may cause *lsof* to hang or report incorrect information.

48. b. Simply using *dmesg* with the *grep* command will help you identify the nature of the problem, as long as the kernel logger has recorded it.

49. d. A Samba server cannot be configured to be a WINS client and server at the same time.

50. c. Using *ldconfig* without arguments reads all necessary files and configures all dynamic libraries. The *-X* option tells *ldconfig* not to update links. The *-N* option tells *ldconfig* to omit updating the cache. If you specify both options, libraries will not be updated.

51. a. The *hdparm -Tt* command reads transfer rates for a hard drive.

52. a and d. The *sysctl -a* option allows you to display all values for a particular device. The information contained in the */proc/ide/hdc/settings* file provides information about various settings, including the drive speed and DMA information. The information in this file is not as comprehensive as the output of the *sysctl -a* command, however.

53. d. The *make mrproper* command erases any *.config* files and allows you to begin a clean kernel-compilation session.

54. a and b. The -*y* and -*f* options allow you to accomplish the goal, because the -*y* option tells *fsck* to automatically solve problems, while the -*f* option tells *fsck* to conduct a check, even though *fsck* thinks that no problems exist on the partition.,

IV

General Linux Exam 202

Part IV covers the Topics and Objectives for the LPI's General Linux Certification for Exam 202 and includes the following chapters:

- Chapter 35, *Networking Configuration (Topic 2.205)*
- Chapter 36, *Mail and News (Topic 2.206)*
- Chapter 37, *DNS (Topic 2.207)*
- Chapter 38, *Web Services (Apache and Squid, Topic 2.208)*
- Chapter 39, *Network Client Management (Topic 2.210)*
- Chapter 40, *System Security (Topic 2.212)*y
- Chapter 41, *Network Troubleshooting (Topic 214)*
- Chapter 42, *Exam 202 Review Questions and Exercises*
- Chapter 43, *Exam 202 Practice Test*

35

Networking Configuration (Topic 2.205)

Under the broad term "Networking Configuration," the LPI Level 2 tests group some advanced topics that administrators should have under their belts, such as Virtual Private Networks (VPNs), configuring multiple IP addresses, and dial-up and ISDN access. You should already know TCP/IP fundamentals and basic network interface configuration issues discussed in Level 1. Chapter 19 of this book is especially relevant, and as always, real experience with networking is valuable preparation for the tests. LPI organizes the topic of networking into two objectives:

Objective 1, Basic Networking Configuration
The candidate should be able to configure network devices to connect to a local network and a wide area network. This objective includes being able to communicate between various subnets within a single network, configure dialup access using *mgetty*, configure dial-up access using a modem or ISDN, configure authentication protocols such as PAP and CHAP, and configure TCP/IP logging. Weight: 5.

Objective 2, Advanced Network Configuration and Troubleshooting
The candidate should be able to configure a network device to implement various network authentication schemes. This Objective includes configuring a multihomed network device, configuring a virtual private network (VPN), and resolving networking and communication problems. Weight: 3.

Notice that Objective 1 is weighted quite heavily. This is to be expected. Computers wouldn't be much good these days if they weren't network aware, and the same goes for Linux administrators. So we recommend you spend a considerable amount of time understanding the commands and protocols discussed in this chapter before trying to bring systems onto a production network. Your boss, your end users, and your career will thank you.

Objective 1: Basic Networking Configuration

Notice how this Objective doesn't sound much more advanced than the Level 1 networking Objectives. Don't be deceived. While the tasks may seem simple when put into black and white, the LPI Level 2 Exam tends to assume that you've run into problems in your previous work and have learned to troubleshoot networking issues. So, instead of simply thinking to yourself "Yes, I know the *route* command or the *ifconfig* command," think to yourself, "How are these commands commonly used in a production environment?" Think of the commands in context.

Network Configuration Utilities, and What Lies Beneath

Quite a few configuration tools exist for configuring a network card on a Linux system to be a part of an IP network. Those tools vary widely between the Linux distributions and sometimes between the different versions of the same distribution as well, but they generally do the same thing. For instance, a tool called *netconfig* exists in both Red Hat/Fedora and Slackware but is not the exact same utility. Fedora also has a *curses*-based tool called *system-config-network-tui* that lets you configure the network connection on network interface cards, ISDN adapters, and modems. The Novell/SuSE systems wanted administrators to use YAST/Yast2 (YAST is text based, Yast2 is GUI based) to configure networking. Ubuntu Linux (*www.ubuntu.org*) currently contains a configuration tool called the Network Administration Tool as part of the Gnome Desktop Environment.

This author never uses graphical or screen-based, distribution-specific tools for configuration—not to look like the biggest alpha-geek in the room but because the tools often don't get the configuration right. All the fancy networking applets and applications do is create or alter system network configuration files, which are in simple text formats and have traditionally been created by hand. I find I usually end up having to open my trusty text editor and fix the configuration files the old-fashioned way anyway, so I may as well start out with the pure files.

Because the LPI Exam was put together by experts in the field, they, too, have found that the best way to configure a system is to go in and start editing text files. So let's get down to it and discuss the text files that your networking subsystem uses.

Common Network Configuration Files

Because network interface cards (NICs), with the exception of modems and ISDN adapters, are usually activated at boot time, Linux distributions include configurations for the cards in system files. Depending upon the system you use, you will find one of the following:

- A file called */etc/network/interfaces*
- A series of files in the */etc/sysconfig/network-scripts* directory

The /etc/network/interfaces file

This is found in Debian-based distributions, including such popular variants as Ubuntu and Knoppix. It contains *ifconfig* parameters, such as broadcast and netmask addresses, and can optionally specify commands to be run before or after a network card is brought up or down.

A sample */etc/network/interfaces* file is:

```
auto lo
iface lo inet loopback

auto eth0
iface eth0 inet static
        address 192.168.0.20
        netmask 255.255.254.0
        broadcast 192.168.1.255
        gateway 192.168.0.1
```

The file must contain at least two entries for a network-aware system: one for the loopback interface (*lo*) and one for another interface (in this case, *eth0*). To comment out an entry, simply put a # character at the start of the line.

The syntax is relatively simple. The iface entry simply defines an interface (*eth0*). The entry contains the word static, which means the interface is configured manually, not using DHCP. If you wished this interface to use DHCP, you would change the line to read as follows:

```
iface eth0 inet dhcp
```

The four lines below the iface line correspond to typical *ifconfig* options. If you change the interface to use DHCP, this invalidates the *ifconfig* options, but you do not need to comment the lines out. Once your system reads dhcp in the configuration file, it ignores any other information in the file for that particular interface.

The line before the iface entry, auto eth0, means this particular interface will be activated automatically at boot time.

My particular system is a laptop that (luckily enough) supports both my standard Ethernet card (*eth0*), and my Atheros wireless A-G card (*ath0*). Don't get flustered in the LPI Exam if an interface isn't called *eth0* or *eth1*. You will find that the underlying principles covered will remain the same, even if some names are different. Following is an example of the information I use to configure my wireless card:

```
auto ath0
iface ath0 inet static
        address 192.168.40.40
        netmask 255.255.255.0
        network 192.168.40.0
        broadcast 192.168.40.255
        gateway 192.168.40.1
        # wireless-* options are implemented by the wireless-tools package
        wireless-mode managed
        wireless-essid JAMESSTANGER
        wireless-key1 ee453fq449g0fg354wghgj12b4
```

```
      # dns-* options are implemented by the resolvconf package, if
installed
      dns-nameservers 192.168.40.4
      wireless-key ee453fq449g0fg354wghgj12b4
```

This example shows that Debian systems can contain the access point's Secure Set Identifier (SSID), as well as all necessary Wireless Equivalent Privacy (WEP) information. (WEP is an outmoded protocol and is no longer considered to be secure, but some wireless cards have not yet adopted the better WPA security.) Also, many Linux systems do not yet support WPA.

The /etc/sysconfig/network-scripts directory

Red Hat and Fedora systems store their interface configuration files in a directory named */etc/sysconfig/network-scripts/*, where each network interface has a separate file. For example, the directory in the old Red Hat system that I use as a router contains at least the files listed in Table 35-1.

Table 35-1. Sample network configuration files in /etc/sysconfig/network-scripts

Filename	Purpose
ifcfg-lo	Configures the loopback interface
ifcfg-eth0	Configures the first Ethernet interface
Ifcfg-eth1	Configures the second Ethernet interface
Ifcfg-eth2	In case the router had even a third Ethernet interface
ifup	Used to activate any interface you specify
ifdown	Dectivates any interface you specify
ifup-ppp	Used to activate Point-to-Point Protocol (PPP) dial-up connections
ifdown-ppp	Used to deactivate PPP connections
ifup-ipv6	Activates IPv6 on an interface
ifdown-ipv6	Deactivates an IPv6 interface
ifup-isdn	Activates an ISDN connection
ifdown-isdn	Deactivates an ISDN connection

An example of a simple */etc/sysconfig/network-scripts/ifcfg-eth0* file follows:

```
DEVICE=eth0
ONBOOT=yes
BOOTPROTO=static
IPADDR=172.22.1.45
NETMASK=255.255.255.0
GATEWAY=172.22.1.1
```

The syntax for this file is quite simple; standard configuration options are specified as KEYWORD=value pairs. One detail worth noting is the BOOTPROTO entry. static means that the *eth0* interface uses a manually entered IP address. To use DHCP, change the value to dhcp. If, for some reason, you wish your system to use the old *bootp* protocol, you can also specify bootp. The ONBOOT entry simply specifies whether you wish the device to be activated at boot time. If you do not wish to activate the device, set the value to no.

However, tools and runlevel scripts are all wrappers around the two main network interface configuration tools *ifconfig* and *route*. A Linux system administrator must know by heart how to use those commands. *ifconfig* takes several parameters; the IP address itself is essential.

Using ifconfig

When the IP address is configured from DHCP, you won't usually need to use *ifconfig* directly. But it's important to know how to check interfaces and bring them up if the system hasn't done so automatically.

The *ifconfig* command may be used on any kind of network interface, not only physical Ethernet or Token Ring network cards. PPP (dial-up) interfaces, loopback interfaces, and VPN tunnel endpoints may all be configured with *ifconfig*. Even though *ifconfig* defaults to the IP (Version 4) address type, it is also used when configuring other address families such as IPX, IPv6, and AppleTalk. Here is the basic syntax of the command:

    ifconfig [*interface*] [*option*] [*address*]

The *interface* is a device name, such as the familiar *lo* or *eth0*. The network card represented by the device must have been detected by the kernel before it can be configured by *ifconfig*. The *address* is the IP address to and from which traffic will go through the interface.

Following are the most frequently used options. Note that the *-a* option contains a hyphen (because it applies to the command in general) whereas the other options (which apply to the interface) do not.

-a
> Lists all interfaces, including down and unconfigured ones.

up
> Enables the interface.

down
> Disables the interface. After being disabled, the interface keeps any configured addresses, so if you enable the interface later, it still is associated with the addresses.

hw class address
> Reports *address* as the hardware address of the specified class (described in the text).

netmask netmask
> Sets the netmask on the given interface.

Virtual interfaces

ifconfig can configure virtual interfaces "on top of" the regular interface. For instance, based on the *eth0* interface, you could activate the virtual interfaces *eth0:0* and *eth0:1*. This kind of configuration is often found on web servers hosting lots of web sites and domains (when SSL certificates are in use, the IP address involved must belong to one and only one hostname) or on shell servers offering hostnames to be used on IRC and similar services.

To use virtual interfaces on a 2.2.x kernel (or earlier), support for interface aliasing must be explicitly enabled.

Following is an example of how to configure one interface to use multiple IP addresses:

```
ifconfig eth0:1 192.168.40.41 netmask 255.255.255.0
```

The resulting output of *ifconfig* is:

```
eth0      Link encap:Ethernet  HWaddr 00:0B:5D:71:FE:D1
          inet addr:192.168.40.40  Bcast:255.255.255.0  Mask:255.255.255.0
          UP BROADCAST RUNNING MULTICAST  MTU:1500  Metric:1
          RX packets:140371 errors:0 dropped:0 overruns:0 frame:0
          TX packets:105052 errors:0 dropped:0 overruns:0 carrier:0
          collisions:7218 txqueuelen:1000
          RX bytes:93678761 (89.3 MiB)  TX bytes:14520288 (13.8 MiB)
          Interrupt:19

eth0:1    Link encap:Ethernet  HWaddr 00:0B:5D:71:FE:D1
          inet addr:192.168.40.41  Bcast:192.168.40.255  Mask:255.255.255.0
          UP BROADCAST RUNNING MULTICAST  MTU:1500  Metric:1
          Interrupt:19
```

Other common uses for ifconfig

You can also use the *ifconfig* command to:

- Activate or deactivate an interface. This can also be done through the *ifup* and *ifdown* commands.
- Set the subnet mask: useful when a system has been placed onto a different subnet, but retains the same IP address.
- Set the broadcast address. If you have to change the subnet mask, you may have to change the broadcast address, as well.
- Create a custom MAC address (also known as the Ethernet address).

The last task in the list is useful in some situations in which the ISP allows only a particular MAC address to participate on the network. For example, many broadband users have had to register an NIC with their ISP, but have then had to swap out their NIC or change the entire system. The *ifconfig* command allows systems with a 2.4 kernel or newer to "spoof" a MAC address. To do this, the device driver for the NIC must also support this feature.

To create a custom MAC address, you need to specify the hardware class. The most common class is ether, which stands for Ethernet. Additional classes include ax25, ARCnet, and netrom, but for the LPI test, you need to know only about the ether class.

An example follows of how to use *ifconfig* to configure a system with the custom MAC address 1:02:03:04:05:06:

```
ifconfig eth0 192.168.40.40 netmask 255.255.255.0 broadcast 192.168.40.255 \
    hw ether 1:02:03:04:05:06
```

Examples

Here are some examples of how *ifconfig* is used in a production environment.

The following command sets the IP address of the *eth0* NIC to 192.168.45.12. Because no *netmask* is specified, the command uses the default (class C) broadcast address and network mask that apply to addresses in the 192.x.x.x range.

```
ifconfig eth0 192.168.45.12
```

The following command explicitly specifies the IP address, network mask, and broadcast address:

```
ifconfig eth0 172.20.16.34 netmask 255.255.255.128 broadcast 172.20.16.127
```

The following deactivates the interface. Obviously, this is not a command you should use when doing administration remotely on your system.

```
ifconfig eth0 down
```

The following activates a virtual network interface card based on the *eth0* interface, which must have been configured previously. The virtual address does not inherit any netmask or broadcast properties from the main interface; defaults are used. *ifconfig* will not protest if you configure virtual interfaces with different network properties from the main interface, but you may experience erratic or inconsistent behavior.

```
ifconfig eth0:0 192.168.45.13
```

The following sequence of commands sets an IP address on a network interface card, then disables and enables the network card. After each command affecting the interface, another command displays the state of the interface. Note that the IP address is still there when the interface is down and that the interface is explicitly shown as UP when it is enabled.

```
# ifconfig eth0 10.20.30.4
# ifconfig eth0
eth0      Link encap:Ethernet  HWaddr 00:60:97:16:4A:EF
          inet addr:10.20.30.4  Bcast:10.255.255.255  Mask:255.0.0.0
          UP BROADCAST MULTICAST  MTU:1500  Metric:1
          ...
# ifconfig eth0 down
# ifconfig eth0
eth0      Link encap:Ethernet  HWaddr 00:60:97:16:4A:EF
          inet addr:10.20.30.4  Bcast:10.255.255.255  Mask:255.0.0.0
          BROADCAST MULTICAST  MTU:1500  Metric:1
          ...
# ifconfig eth0 up
# ifconfig eth0
eth0      Link encap:Ethernet  HWaddr 00:60:97:16:4A:EF
          inet addr:10.20.30.4  Bcast:10.255.255.255  Mask:255.0.0.0
          UP BROADCAST MULTICAST  MTU:1500  Metric:1
          ...
```

The route Command

The *route* command is capable of setting up complicated routing arrangements, but most sites use it simply to set up the default gateway. You can use the command to set or delete static routes, as well as to view the kernel routing table. Complicated routing arrangements nowadays are done through routing protocols rather than manual configuration, although there are advanced manual techniques you don't need to know for the LPI test.

Each host uses its default gateway to access resources outside the locally defined network, such as the rest of the Internet. The host at the IP address you set to be the default gateway is usually a router or routing firewall. This gateway must have an IP address within your network. Quite often, the gateway is located at the first usable IP address in a network.

Syntax and frequently used options

The syntax for the *route* command is:

```
route [ add | delete ] [ -net | -host ] [address] \
      [netmask netmask] [gw address] [interface]
```

Each command can add a route to either an external network (*-net*) or a particular host (*-host*). A *gw* gateway address can be specified without either a *-net* or a *-host* argument, in which case the command specifies a default gateway to use for traffic from this host.

Common Uses

If your Linux system receives its IP address from a DHCP server, your system automatically sets the default route and other network parameters. You won't usually need to manually configure the default gateway using *route*. However, the LPI Exam expects you to be able to manually connect a Linux system to a network.

The following example sets the default gateway, assuming that 192.168.40.1 is the address of the hub on your local area network that accepts traffic from your host:

```
route add default gw 192.168.40.1
```

The keyword *default* is a built-in alias for the IP address 0.0.0.0, which means "any host." This command uses the defaults for the network and netmask (0.0.0.0), and is therefore equivalent to:

```
route add -net 0.0.0.0 netmask 0.0.0.0 gw 192.168.40.1
```

The default netmask of 0.0.0.0, similar to the 0.0.0.0 IP address, may be translated as "any host in any IP network." Any other routes you specify are consulted first; if the address of your destination can't be reached through those explicit routes, the system uses the default gateway.

During the exam, you'll likely be given a readout from the *route* command. Make sure that you can read it and interpret it. Here is an example:

```
james@james:~ $ route -n
Kernel IP routing table
Destination     Gateway       Genmask          Flags Metric Ref    Use
Iface
localnet             *        255.255.255.0    U     0      0        0 ath0
localnet             *        255.255.255.0    U     0      0        0 eth0
default       192.168.40.1    0.0.0.0          UG    0      0        0 eth0
james@james:~ $
```

The keyword localnet means that *ath0* and *eth0* are local interfaces. The keyword default refers to the default gateway. The other basic elements you should understand are the flags; U means the route is up (usable) while G means the address represents a gateway.

In this example, the default gateway used by both *eth0* and *ath0* is 192.168.4.1. The zeros in the first column of the final entry indicate the default gateway for these interfaces. Note that the destination IP address (0.0.0.0), the netmask (0.0.0.0), and the gateway address (192.168.40.1) are what was configured in the earlier *route* command.

The previous command included the -n option, which has the *route* command specify numerical addresses instead of hostnames. Using this option guarantees that you receive all interface-specific information, even if a name resolution problem occurs.

If you enter the command without the *-n* option, you see output such as:

```
james@james:~ $ route
Kernel IP routing table
Destination     Gateway       Genmask          Flags Metric Ref    Use
Iface
localnet             *        255.255.255.0    U    , 0     0        0 ath0
localnet             *        255.255.255.0    U     0      0        0 eth0
default       192.168.40.1    0.0.0.0          UG    0      0        0 eth0
james@james:~ $
```

The -C option causes *route* to display the complete routing cache stored on the local system; this shows how traffic has been sent to and received from other systems recently.

To add an explicit host routing entry for the host 172.25.50.33, which will be reached through a different gateway from the default one, enter:

```
route add -host 172.25.50.33 gw 192.168.45.2
```

To add a network to the routing table, routing traffic to it through the gateway found at address 192.168.45.3, enter:

```
route add -net 10.0.0.0 netmask 255.0.0.0 gw 192.168.45.3
```

To delete the default route, use either of the following commands:

```
route del default gw 192.168.45.1
route del -net 0.0.0.0 netmask 0.0.0.0 gw 192.168.45.1
```

Networking
Configuration

Finally, when it comes to using the route command in a production environment, remember the following:

If a DNS problem occurs, the output of the route command might hang.
There might be other reasons for the output to hang, but name resolution is the most common. This is why, on many commands shown in this chapter for troubleshooting, it is sometimes useful to use the -*n* option. The attempt to contact a DNS server for name resolution might cause the output to hang if the network is not functioning properly.

The netstat -r and netstat -nr commands give output similar to route and route -n commands, respectively.
However, the *route* command allows you to add and delete routing table information, whereas the *netstat* command allows you to only review settings.

ARP and Related Commands

The Internet Protocol (IP) is a Layer 3 protocol, and the NIC in the Linux system is a Layer 2 device. On a local network, the nodes know each other only by the unique 6-byte MAC (Media Access Control) address programmed into each NIC.

Because of this, devices that use IP require a protocol to map between the two layers. That protocol is the Address Resolution Protocol (ARP). ARP creates a mapping between a given IP address and the MAC address of the NIC where the IP address is configured. ARP does not map the other way—i.e., from MAC address to IP address. That is the task of the Reverse Address Resolution Protocol (RARP).

When two IP-enabled nodes need to communicate, the kernel on the originating node hands the IP packet to the NIC and says, "This is a packet for the IP address aaa.bbb.ccc.ddd; please find the recipient." The NIC then broadcasts a request to find out which network interface card (if any) has the aaa.bbb.ccc.ddd address configured on its Layer 3. This request is called an ARP request.

Perhaps the best way to understand ARP is to view it in action. Below is a *tcpdump* session that shows an ARP request and the resulting reply. This capture is of a *ping* packet that was sent from a system with the IP address of 192.168.0.20 to a system with an IP address of 192.168.1.18; *ping* uses an ICMP request and reply.

```
06:10:03.003044 arp who-has 192.168.1.18 tell 192.168.0.20
06:10:03.003092 arp reply 192.168.1.18 is-at 00:c0:f0:30:1d:5e
06:10:03.796840 IP 192.168.0.20 > 192.168.1.18: icmp 64: echo request seq 1
06:10:03.796992 IP 192.168.1.18 > 192.168.0.20: icmp 64: echo reply seq 1
```

In other words, the ARP request and reply had to execute successfully before the *ping* ICMP messages could be sent.

ARP entries are cached on the hosts in the network for a period of time, which is defined by the */proc/sys/net/ipv4/neigh/eth0/gc_stale_time* file (assuming that the system's network interface is *eth0*). By default, ARP entries are considered stale after 60 seconds.

The *arp* command shows the ARP cache. A typical display, run from the 192.168.0.20 system, might be:

```
# arp
Address                HWtype  HWaddress            Flags  Mask
Iface
192.168.0.1            ether   08:00:20:77:2B:CB    C      eth0
192.168.1.101          ether   00:30:1B:B0:9F:A1    C      eth0
192.168.1.203          ether   00:08:74:04:0A:D8    C      eth0
192.168.1.18           ether   00:C0:F0:30:1D:5E    C      eth0
```

arp command syntax

Following is the synax and description for the *arp* command:

arp [*options*] [*hostname*]

Frequently used options include:

-d hostname
    Remove *hostname* from ARP cache.

-f file
    Statically map hostnames to MAC addresses based on entries in a file. The file format is exactly like the parameters to the *-s* option: a hostname and MAC address separated by whitespace, followed by any other applicable parameters.

-n
    Do not resolve hostnames.

-s hostname MAC_address
    Statically map *hostname* to *MAC_address*. This option is often used for proxy ARP configurations, in which one system may respond to ARP requests on behalf of another. When used for proxy ARP, the parameter *pub* must be added:

    arp -s *hostname MAC_adress* pub
    If you are temporarily adding an ARP entry that should be flushed after the regular ARP timeout (60 seconds), add the parameter *temp* to the entry.

Example #1

This example performs some basic ARP manipulation.

Add a temporary ARP entry to a host's ARP cache:

```
# arp -s 192.168.0.45 00:02:03:F6:7C:4B temp
# arp -n
Address                HWtype  HWaddress            Flags  Mask
Iface
192.168.0.45           ether   00:02:03:F6:7C:4B    C
eth1
192.168.0.20           ether   00:01:02:F7:7C:4B    C
eth1
```

Add a static ARP entry to a host's ARP cache:

```
# arp -s 192.168.0.45 00:02:03:F6:7C:4B
# arp -n
Address                  HWtype  HWaddress           Flags Mask      Iface
192.168.0.45             ether   00:02:03:F6:7C:4B   CM              eth1
192.168.0.20             ether   00:01:02:F7:7C:4B   C               eth1
```

Remove a static ARP entry from a host's cache:

```
# arp -d 192.168.0.45
# arp -n
Address                  HWtype  HWaddress           Flags Mask      Iface
192.168.0.20             ether   00:01:02:F7:7C:4B   C               eth1
```

Example #2

This shows how ARP works behind the scenes.

Here, a connection to a nonexistent host is attempted:

```
# ping 192.168.1.54
PING 192.168.1.54 (192.168.1.54) 56(84) bytes of data.

--- 192.168.1.54 ping statistics ---
4 packets transmitted, 0 received, 100% packet loss, time 1999ms
```

Running *tcpdump* on any host in the network shows ARP requests with no answers:

```
15:34:43.103544 arp who-has 192.168.1.54 tell 192.168.1.18
15:34:44.103292 arp who-has 192.168.1.54 tell 192.168.1.18
15:34:45.102982 arp who-has 192.168.1.54 tell 192.168.1.18
15:34:46.103620 arp who-has 192.168.1.54 tell 192.168.1.18
...
```

The ARP cache lists the host, but has no corresponding MAC address:

```
# arp
Address                  HWtype  HWaddress           Flags Mask      Iface
192.168.1.54                     (incomplete)                        eth1
192.168.0.20             ether   00:01:02:F7:7C:4B   C               eth1
```

The arpwatch Command

Now that you understand how the *arp* command works, it is important to understand that you can use ARP to help secure your systems. The *arpwatch* package is a set of tools that allows your system to monitor ARP mappings on a network. You may need to install the package manually.

Many applications, including *ettercap* (*http://ettercap.sourceforge.net*), can engage in *ARP spoofing* in order to appear to be a different system on your local area network. As you have seen earlier in this chapter, an administrator can also use the *ifconfig* command on some systems to engage in manual ARP spoofing. ARP spoofing can be a prelude to many attacks, including connection hijacking and traffic sniffing.

The most useful conditions for running *arpwatch* are when the local area network is connected by a hub or a switch on which monitoring has been enabled. If a system is connected to a standard switch, the switch will not pass ARP traffic and all you can monitor is the traffic between the switch and the system running *arpwatch*. Similarly, any remote system you want to monitor must be connected to a hub on your network or to a switch on which monitoring has been enabled.

The purpose of *arpwatch* is to keep an eye on hosts that add themselves to your network and hosts that suddenly change IP address and MAC address mappings.

Once installed, *arpwatch* runs as a daemon, keeping track of and reporting any changed or new mappings. When a new node appears in the network, *arpwatch* sends a message to a defined email address to report information on the new host. By default, this email address is the root account. The message is usually sent via the system's email daemon. Sometimes, the messages are also logged to the */var/log/messages* or */var/log/syslog* file. You can customize *arpwatch* behavior by editing the */etc/arpwatch.conf* file.

arpwatch reports the following problems:

- Flip-flops, in which the MAC address has changed from one IP address to another
- A new MAC address

arpwatch is a very useful tool, both as a daemon and as a standalone application, when you are running a network to which no new computers should be connected without the system administrator knowing it.

arpwatch

Syntax

    arpwatch [*options*]

Description

Report unusual events related to the ARP cache.

Frequently used options

-f file
> Specifies which file to use for storing the IP/MAC mappings.

-i interface
> Specifies the interface on which to listen for ARP changes.

-m email_address
> Sets the email address to which *arpwatch* should report changes.

-n [network/netmask]
> Defines additional IP networks to watch. This is used when two or more different IP networks share the same physical infrastructure.

Sample arpwatch results

Once running, *arpwatch* keeps track of new systems that come on the network. New systems generate a "new station" email message, as shown in Figure 35-1.

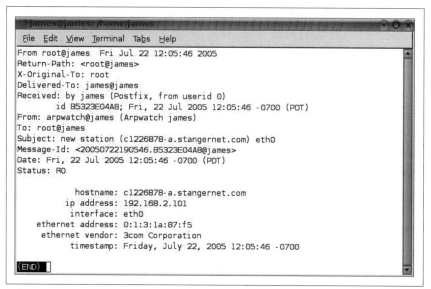

Figure 35-1. Viewing an arpwatch "new station" message

Notice in the example that the IP address and MAC address are given, along with the remote host's name name, the remote host's interface name (in this case, *eth0*), and the NIC's vendor.

Figure 35-2 shows an example of a series of flip-flops brought on by the use of *ettercap* on a switched network.

The warning shown turned up while sniffing all the packets going between all the local network hosts and a network router with IP address 192.168.2.1. The first entry, for instance, states that a flip-flop has occurred where the system with the IP address of 192.168.2.1 had the original MAC address 00:60:97:75:0E:96, but now has the MAC address 0:b:5d:91:fe:d1. In this case, *arpwatch* has just discovered a MAC address spoofing attack.

If you look at further entries in Figure 35-2, you will see that several more flip-flops have occurred for the same system. This implies active ARP spoofing from an application. It also suggests that someone on the network is sniffing connections.

Dial-up Connections

Discussing dial-up access has become somewhat controversial in LPI circles. Why? Broadband connections have become more available in many places of the world. More developed countries boast multimegabit connections. I live about 10 miles out of Olympia, Washington, a small town in the Pacific Northwest of the

```
root@jacob:~
File  Edit  View  Terminal  Tabs  Help
[root@jacob root]# tail -f /var/log/messages
Jul 22 11:30:08 jacob arpwatch: flip flop 192.168.2.1 0:80:5f:fe:14:c1 (0:b:5d:7
1:fe:d1)
Jul 22 11:30:08 jacob arpwatch: flip flop 192.168.2.104 0:13:10:22:57:f5 (0:b:5d
:71:fe:d1)
Jul 22 11:30:12 jacob arpwatch: flip flop 192.168.2.104 0:b:5d:71:fe:d1 (0:13:10
:22:57:f5)
Jul 22 11:30:12 jacob arpwatch: flip flop 192.168.2.1 0:b:5d:71:fe:d1 (0:80:5f:f
e:14:c1)
Jul 22 11:31:02 jacob arpwatch: flip flop 192.168.2.104 0:13:10:22:57:f5 (0:b:5d
:71:fe:d1)
Jul 22 11:31:05 jacob arpwatch: flip flop 192.168.2.104 0:b:5d:71:fe:d1 (0:13:10
:22:57:f5)
Jul 22 11:31:57 jacob arpwatch: flip flop 192.168.2.104 0:13:10:22:57:f5 (0:b:5d
:71:fe:d1)
Jul 22 11:31:58 jacob arpwatch: flip flop 192.168.2.1 0:80:5f:fe:14:c1 (0:b:5d:7
1:fe:d1)
Jul 22 11:31:58 jacob arpwatch: flip flop 192.168.2.104 0:b:5d:71:fe:d1 (0:13:10
:22:57:f5)
Jul 22 11:31:58 jacob arpwatch: flip flop 192.168.2.1 0:b:5d:71:fe:d1 (0:80:5f:f
e:14:c1)
```

Figure 35-2. Flip-flop warnings generated by arpwatch in the /var/log/messages file

United States. Even though I live fairly far away from a pretty small town, I regularly enjoy an inexpensive 2.5-MBps downstream connection. A few people who enjoy this widespread form of bandwidth have approached me and fellow colleagues at LPI and rather forcefully challenged us as to why the LPI even bothers talking about dial-up connections anymore. The reason is simple: most of the world still uses dial-up. The LPI Exams are published worldwide, and the LPI exams reflect how Linux is used.

Chances are, LPIC 2–certified professionals will at some time find themselves in a dial-up–only environment. Personally, I would be embarrassed if someone handed me a telephone line, and I had to say, "Sorry—I need an RJ-45. I can't network any other way." As someone who has been associated with the LPI for some time, I would be embarrassed if someone who is LPIC Level 2–certified couldn't use his system properly in a dial-up environment.

So, let's talk about what you need to know to configure a Linux system for dial-up access.

Connecting with dial-up is quite different from connecting to a LAN. A dial-up connection uses the Point-to-Point Protocol (PPP), which effectively runs on a direct link between the user's computer and the ISP. Each side runs a daemon called *pppd*. When connecting to an ISP through a modem or an ISDN adapter, you need to configure some of the files in */etc/ppp*.

Different tools exist to configure dial-up connections: Debian systems offer *pppconfig*, Slackware systems offer *pppsetup*, and Fedora systems offer *system-config-network-tui* (or *system-config-network-gui* for an X interface). On Red Hat systems, the different configuration tools are called *redhat-config* instead of Fedora's *system-config*.

PPP is a Layer 2 protocol for connection over synchronous and asynchronous circuits. Often, connections over analog devices such as modems are asynchrounous, while connections over digital devices such as ISDN adapters are synchronous. Some cable modem and DSL providers also use PPP over Ethernet (for which the PPP frames are encapsulated in Ethernet frames); this protocol is called PPPoE.

Another protocol, Link Control Protocol (LCP), is provided by PPP. This protocol knows how to handle situations such as varying packet sizes and network misconfigurations and is responsible for establishing and terminating the connection. PPP also provides the Network Control Protocol (NCP), which enables the transport of Layer 3 protocols such as IP and IPX. A separate protocol, Password Authentication Protocol (PAP) or the newer Challenge Handshake Authentication Protocol (CHAP), negotiates and sets up the session between the two endpoints.

Connecting with a modem

Some distributions include the tools *pon* (PPP on) and *poff* (PPP off) to connect to and disconnect from an ISP. A somewhat easier solution is to use the more intelligent *wvdial* utility, configured through *wvdialconf*.

For various purposes, you can set up processes to run automatically after taking a PPP line up or down. For instance, a home user with a dial-up connection being enabled at irregular intervals may want to send any outgoing emails and check for any incoming whenever she first comes online. You can add commands and the names of scripts to the files */etc/ppp/ip-up* and */etc/ppp/ip-down* to run these scripts and commands when the line goes up or down, respectively. On Fedora systems, the user is encouraged to use the files *ip-up.local* and *ip-down.local* instead.

While the regular *pon* command starts the *pppd* service before dialing the ISP, *wvdial* connects to the ISP and performs a few basic checks before starting the *pppd* service.

The following configuration was done on a Debian Linux system, but the files should be the same on most distributions. The system is set up according to the following information received from the ISP, which here we'll simply call *provider*:

    User name: foo
    Password: bar
    Phone number to dial: 22334455

First, you need to create a file named after the ISP, in this case */etc/ppp/peers/provider*. There should be one file for each ISP you connet to in the */etc/ppp/peers* directory. These files hold information on which serial interface the modem is connected to (*/dev/ttyS2*), the modem speed (115,200 baud), and the username for lookup in the */etc/ppp/chap-secrets* file used by CHAP. Each provider-specific file also tells the system how to configure its network; usually the system receives an IP address from the provider and is told to use the dial-up PPP link as its default route. Furthermore, the file tells *pppd* to run the *chat* program when connecting. The *chat* program consults a chat script (a file containing strings that each side is supposed to send) to handle authentication and PPP configuration when connected to the ISP's modem.

Configuration files

Some examples follow of files used in dial-up connections. First view the */etc/ppp/peers/provider* file:

```
hide-password
noauth
connect "/usr/sbin/chat -v -f /etc/chatscripts/provider"
debug
/dev/ttyS2
115200
defaultroute
noipdefault
user "foo"
ipparam provider
```

The */etc/chatscripts/provider* file should be created to match the */etc/peers/provider* script file. Because the authentication process changes between ISPs, these scripts need to be specific to each provider. The chat program deals with the authentication process when dialing in to an ISP.

An example follows of the */etc/chatscripts/provider* file:

```
ABORT BUSY
ABORT 'NO CARRIER'
ABORT VOICE
ABORT 'NO DIALTONE'
ABORT 'NO DIAL TONE'
ABORT 'NO ANSWER'
ABORT DELAYED
'' ATZ
OK-AT-OK "ATDT22334455"
CONNECT \d\c
```

The different situations that can abort a dial-up are listed in this file. Among the possible reasons for terminating a dial-up attempt are a busy phone line and the lack of a dial tone. The ATZ command is a key command in the Hayes modem control language, which tells the modem to reset. Following that line is the Hayes command for dialing the number to the ISP.

Usernames and passwords for dial-up connections are stored in the file */etc/ppp/chap-secrets* when using CHAP authentication. If the ISP prefers PAP authentication, the file to edit is */etc/ppp/pap-secrets*. The file format is the same for both CHAP and PAP.

A sample */etc/ppp/chap-secrets* file follows. It contains only one noncomment line, whose fields reflect the information shown earlier, given by the ISP:

```
# Secrets for authentication using CHAP
# client       server  secret          IP addresses
"foo"          *       "bar"
```

Because this file contains no IP address, the system we connect to defines our IP address.

The LPI Exam does not ask you how to use an easy-to-configure application such as *pptp-config* (*http://www.freshmeat.net*). It will ask you how to use the command-line application and files discussed previously.

pon

pon is a script that eases the somewhat complex argument list *pppd* often needs to establish a dial-up connection. *pon* connects to the profile of the provider you give on its command line. The program itself does not produce much output, but *pppd* (called by *pon*) creates some entries in the message log, especially when *pppd* is in debug mode. Following is the syntax for the command:

> pon *provider*

The message log tells us that *pon* successfully established both the dial-up connection and the PPP link:

```
Apr 24 18:22:18 foo pppd[1078]: pppd 2.4.2 started by root, uid 0
Apr 24 18:22:19 foo chat[1079]: abort on (BUSY)
Apr 24 18:22:19 foo chat[1079]: abort on (NO CARRIER)
Apr 24 18:22:19 foo chat[1079]: abort on (VOICE)
Apr 24 18:22:19 foo chat[1079]: abort on (NO DIALTONE)
Apr 24 18:22:19 foo chat[1079]: abort on (NO DIAL TONE)
Apr 24 18:22:19 foo chat[1079]: abort on (NO ANSWER)
Apr 24 18:22:19 foo chat[1079]: abort on (DELAYED)
Apr 24 18:22:19 foo chat[1079]: send (ATZ^M)
Apr 24 18:22:19 foo chat[1079]: expect (OK)
Apr 24 18:22:20 foo chat[1079]: ATZ^M^M
Apr 24 18:22:20 foo chat[1079]: OK
Apr 24 18:22:20 foo chat[1079]:  -- got it
Apr 24 18:22:20 foo chat[1079]: send (ATDT22334455^M)
Apr 24 18:22:20 foo chat[1079]: expect (CONNECT)
Apr 24 18:22:20 foo chat[1079]: ^M
Apr 24 18:22:38 foo chat[1079]: ATDT22334455^M^M
Apr 24 18:22:38 foo chat[1079]: CONNECT
Apr 24 18:22:38 foo chat[1079]:  -- got it
Apr 24 18:22:38 foo chat[1079]: send (\d)
Apr 24 18:22:39 foo pppd[1078]: Serial connection established.
Apr 24 18:22:39 foo pppd[1078]: Using interface ppp0
Apr 24 18:22:39 foo pppd[1078]: Connect: ppp0 <--> /dev/ttyS2
Apr 24 18:22:40 foo pppd[1078]: Remote message: login ok.  welcome to
PowerTech Internet.
Apr 24 18:22:40 foo pppd[1078]: PAP authentication succeeded
Apr 24 18:22:40 foo kernel: PPP BSD Compression module registered
Apr 24 18:22:41 foo kernel: PPP Deflate Compression module registered
Apr 24 18:22:41 foo pppd[1078]: local  IP address 195.159.185.53
Apr 24 18:22:41 foo pppd[1078]: remote IP address 195.159.0.36
Apr 24 18:22:41 foo pppd[1078]: primary   DNS address 195.159.0.100
Apr 24 18:22:41 foo pppd[1078]: secondary DNS address 195.159.0.200
```

The rather long preceding log example shows that the connecting process begins by starting *pppd* and then calling the *chat* program. *chat* talks to the modem, first sending all the ABORT conditions, then sending a modem reset (ATZ). The modem responds by saying OK. Then the modem is told to call the ISP's phone number, expecting a CONNECT from the modem. Upon receiving the CONNECT, *pppd* resumes control and starts the PPP negotiation. Two kernel modules are loaded in the process, the PPP BSD Compression module and the PPP Deflate Compression module. Finally, the IP addresses of the Point-to-Point Protocol connection are set.

Checking a dial-up network connection

You can make sure your system really has an IP connection to the remote system by running *ifconfig* and *route*:

```
# ifconfig ppp0
ppp0      Link encap:Point-to-Point Protocol
          inet addr:195.159.185.53  P-t-P:195.159.0.36  Mask:255.255.255.255
          UP POINTOPOINT RUNNING NOARP MULTICAST  MTU:1500  Metric:1
          RX packets:14 errors:0 dropped:0 overruns:0 frame:0
          TX packets:14 errors:0 dropped:0 overruns:0 carrier:0
          collisions:0 txqueuelen:3
          RX bytes:2251 (2.1 KiB)  TX bytes:390 (390.0 b)
# route -n
Kernel IP routing table
Destination     Gateway         Genmask         Flags Metric Ref    Use Iface
195.159.0.36    0.0.0.0         255.255.255.255 UH    0      0        0 ppp0
0.0.0.0         195.159.0.36    0.0.0.0         UG    0      0        0 ppp0
```

The poff command

The syntax for using *poff* is:

```
poff [options] [provider]
```

The *poff* command tears down the PPP connection to the named provider. If more than one ISP is connected, *poff* needs to know which ISP to disconnect. The most frequently used options are:

-a

> Stop all running PPP connections. If the *provider* argument is given, it is ignored.

-c

> Cause *pppd* to renegotiate compression, which is often useful when servers offer multiple compression protocols.

-r

> Cause the connection to be redialed after it is dropped.

The wvdial command

wvdial is a *curses*-based PPP dialer designed to replace the combinations of *pppd* configuration files and chat scripts. *wvdial* is built to handle most dial-up situations, and can try PPP commands to enable the connection if the ISP does not automatically enable one.

The syntax for the command is:

```
wvdial [options] [section]
```

The most frequently used options are:

--chat

Run *pppd* and use *wvdial* just to establish the connection, instead of the default behavior of establishing a connection and then starting *pppd*.

--config [configfile]

Use a different configuration file from the default */etc/wvdial.conf*.

--no-syslog

Suppress the debug information normally sent to syslog. Useful only if used with the *--chat* option.

Configuring wvdial: wvdialconf

The *wvdialconf* command creates the *wvdial* configuration file. This file is usually located at */etc/wvdial.conf*. Invoke *wvdialconf* as follows:

```
wvdialconf config_file
```

You can name the file anything you wish, though */etc/wvdial.conf* is the standard name and location.

wvdialconf examples

Following is the successful execution of *wvdialconf*:

```
# wvdialconf /etc/wvdial.conf
Scanning your serial ports for a modem.

Port Scan<*1>: Scanning ttyS2 first, /dev/modem is a link to it.
ttyS2<*1>: ATQ0 V1 E1 -- OK
ttyS2<*1>: ATQ0 V1 E1 Z -- OK
ttyS2<*1>: ATQ0 V1 E1 S0=0 -- OK
ttyS2<*1>: ATQ0 V1 E1 S0=0 &C1 -- OK
ttyS2<*1>: ATQ0 V1 E1 S0=0 &C1 &D2 -- OK
ttyS2<*1>: ATQ0 V1 E1 S0=0 &C1 &D2 +FCLASS=0 -- OK
ttyS2<*1>: Modem Identifier: ATI -- 3361
ttyS2<*1>: Speed 4800: AT -- OK
ttyS2<*1>: Speed 9600: AT -- OK
ttyS2<*1>: Speed 19200: AT -- OK
ttyS2<*1>: Speed 38400: AT -- OK
ttyS2<*1>: Speed 57600: AT -- OK
ttyS2<*1>: Speed 115200: AT -- OK
ttyS2<*1>: Max speed is 115200; that should be safe.
ttyS2<*1>: ATQ0 V1 E1 S0=0 &C1 &D2 +FCLASS=0 -- OK

Found a modem on /dev/ttyS2, using link /dev/modem in config.
Modem configuration written to /etc/wvdial.conf.
ttyS2<Info>: Speed 115200; init "ATQ0 V1 E1 S0=0 &C1 &D2 +FCLASS=0"
```

You can then edit the */etc/wvdial.conf* file and supply the ISP login details.

wvdialconf may fail to create a configuration file and complain that no modem can be found. If this is the case, make sure that you have attached the external modem to your serial port and turned it on. If you are using an internal modem, verify that you are not using a Winmodem, which is a low-cost modem that relies on software and the CPU to function properly. Many times, your Linux system does not have the necessary drivers to use a Winmodem device.

Sample /etc/wvdial.conf file

An example follows of a standard *wvdial.conf* file, including the parameters that the user has to enter manually:

```
[Dialer Defaults]
Modem = /dev/ttyS2
Baud = 115200
Init1 = ATZ
Init2 = ATQ0 V1 E1 S0=0 &C1 &D2 +FCLASS=0
ISDN = 0
Modem Type = Analog Modem
Phone = 22334455
Username = foo
Password = bar
```

With this file, run the *wvdial* program to establish the PPP link:

```
# wvdial
--> WvDial: Internet dialer version 1.53
--> Initializing modem.
--> Sending: ATZ
ATZ
OK
--> Sending: ATQ0 V1 E1 S0=0 &C1 &D2 +FCLASS=0
ATQ0 V1 E1 S0=0 &C1 &D2 +FCLASS=0
OK
--> Modem initialized.
--> Sending: ATDT22334455
--> Waiting for carrier.
ATDT22334455
CONNECT 115200
--> Carrier detected.  Starting PPP immediately.
--> Starting pppd at Sat Apr 24 19:42:12 2004
--> pid of pppd: 1961
```

Check with *ifconfig* and *route -n* to assure yourself that the PPP connection is now up and running.

ISDN connections

Connecting to a remote network via an ISDN adapter is more of a black box on Linux. Most distributions supply utilities to set up the ISDN link. To configure an ISDN connection manually, the programs *isdnctrl* and *ipppd* are essential. First of all, however, the ISDN adapter must be recognized by the Linux system. This part may require some work. On my system, an old ISDN adapter that uses the *hisax* module is installed. If I enter:

```
modprobe hisax type=3 protocol=2 io=0x180 irq=9
```

The kernel responds with these entries in the message log:

```
Apr 25 15:02:19 foo kernel: isapnp: Scanning for PnP cards...
Apr 25 15:02:19 foo kernel: isapnp: No Plug & Play device found
Apr 25 15:02:20 foo kernel: HiSax: Linux Driver for passive ISDN cards
Apr 25 15:02:20 foo kernel: HiSax: Version 3.5 (module)
Apr 25 15:02:20 foo kernel: HiSax: Layer1 Revision 1.1.4.1
Apr 25 15:02:20 foo kernel: HiSax: Layer2 Revision 1.1.4.1
Apr 25 15:02:20 foo kernel: HiSax: TeiMgr Revision 1.1.4.1
Apr 25 15:02:20 foo kernel: HiSax: Layer3 Revision 1.1.4.1
Apr 25 15:02:20 foo kernel: HiSax: LinkLayer Revision 1.1.4.1
Apr 25 15:02:20 foo kernel: HiSax: Certification not verified
Apr 25 15:02:20 foo kernel: HiSax: Total 1 card defined
Apr 25 15:02:20 foo kernel: HiSax: Card 1 Protocol EDSS1 Id=HiSax (0)
Apr 25 15:02:20 foo kernel: HiSax: Teles IO driver Rev. 1.1.4.1
Apr 25 15:02:20 foo kernel: HiSax: Teles 16.3 config irq:9 isac:0x980
cfg:0xD80
Apr 25 15:02:20 foo kernel: HiSax: hscx A:0x180  hscx B:0x580
Apr 25 15:02:20 foo kernel: Teles3: ISAC version (0): 2086/2186 V1.1
Apr 25 15:02:20 foo kernel: Teles3: HSCX version A: V2.1  B: V2.1
Apr 25 15:02:20 foo kernel: Teles 16.3: IRQ 9 count 0
Apr 25 15:02:20 foo kernel: Teles 16.3: IRQ 9 count 3
Apr 25 15:02:20 foo kernel: HiSax: DSS1 Rev. 1.1.4.1
Apr 25 15:02:20 foo kernel: HiSax: 2 channels added
Apr 25 15:02:20 foo kernel: HiSax: MAX_WAITING_CALLS added
```

The kernel responds this way because I have told the *hisax* module that I have a Teles 16.3 card, also known as a type=3 card. I also have told the card that I am using the DSS1 protocol for the ISDN D channel, which is known as type 2 in this situation. Finally, the I/O address is 0x180, and I am using IRQ 9 for the card.

The ipppd daemon

The ISDN Point-to-Point Protocol Daemon, *ipppd*, is a modified version of *pppd*, designed to provide synchronous PPP connections over ISDN devices. The syntax is:

```
ipppd [options] [device]
```

Some options override defaults by disabling features; these options start with hyphens. The most frequently used options are:

-bsdcomp
    Disable compression. Used when the ISP does not support compression.

defaultroute
    Indicates that when the PPP connection is established, it should be the host's default route. If a default route already exists on the system, no action is taken.

-detach
    Does not fork and become a background process. Useful when debugging.

device
> Defines the device to connect to.

mru number
> Sets the Maximum Receive Unit to *number*. The default is 1500.

noipdefault
> Lets the ISP decide the address on the local end of the PPP link.

> > `user username`

> Specifies the username to be used when dialing the ISP. The username must have a corresponding entry in */etc/ppp/pap-secrets*.

The isdnctrl command

The ISDN control command, *isdncrtl*, is used to create and delete ISDN network interfaces. It helps create the parameters and phone numbers for dial-in and dial-out. You can also use *isdncrtl* to list the current parameters of an already configured network interface.

The syntax for the command is:

> `isdnctrl action device`

Following are the most often used options:

addif device
> Lets *isdncrtl* control the named device.

addphone device `out number`
> Links the device to the number that goes to the ISP dial-in ISDN pool.

dialmode device [off|manual|auto]
> Defines how the device should react to outgoing and incoming connection requests. If set to off, no connection is possible. If set to manual, an outgoing connection can be established only by issuing the command *isdnctrl dial device*. If set to auto, the device will establish a connection when IP traffic is about to leave the system (or the local network, if your system is configured as an ISDN router).

eaz device number
> Adds the dialing system's ISDN number.

encap device `syncppp`
> Configures the device to encapsulate the IP traffic using synchronous PPP.

huptimeout device `120`
> Set the idle timeout on the device to 120 seconds. When no IP traffic runs through the ISDN adapter for 120 seconds, it will tear down the connection.

l2_prot device `hdlc`
> Indicate that HDLC is the Layer 2 protocol when using ISDN.

l3_prot device `trans`
> Indicate that trans is the Layer 3 protocol when using ISDN. This command is not really necessary, as trans is the default.

pppbind device number

> Link the ISDN device to the PPP device */dev/ipppnumber*. This works only for synchronous PPP. The last value must be a number.

secure device on

> This is not used when dialing out. When configuring a dial-in service, this may be set to allow specific phone numbers to use the dial-in service.

Using isdnctrl

Running the *isdnctrl* command with real-life parameters results in output such as the following:

```
# isdnctrl addif ippp0
ippp0 added
# isdnctrl addphone ippp0 out 21405060
# isdnctrl eaz ippp0 33129027
EAZ/MSN for ippp0 is 33129027
# isdnctrl huptimeout ippp0 120
Hangup-Timeout for ippp0 is 120 sec.
# isdnctrl secure ippp0 on
Security for ippp0 is on
# isdnctrl l2_prot ippp0 hdlc
Layer-2-Protocol for ippp0 is hdlc
# isdnctrl l3_prot ippp0 trans
Layer-3-Protocol for ippp0 is trans
# isdnctrl encap ippp0 syncppp
Encapsulation for ippp0 is syncppp
# isdnctrl pppbind ippp0 0
ippp0 bound to 0
# isdnctrl dialmode ippp0 auto
```

The ISDN adapter has now been configured to know each detail needed to establish a remote ISDN connection. To link the system's PPP stack into the ISDN system, the ISDN Point-to-Point Protocol Daemon (*ipppd*) must run:

```
# ipppd user foo defaultroute noipdefault -detach mru 1524 \
  -bsdcomp /dev/ippp0 &
```

This command creates the following log output:

```
Apr 25 15:57:12 foo ipppd[599]: Found 1 device:
Apr 25 15:57:12 foo ipppd[599]: ipppd i2.2.12 (isdn4linux version of pppd by
MH) started
Apr 25 15:57:12 foo ipppd[599]: init_unit: 0
Apr 25 15:57:12 foo kernel: ippp, open, slot: 0, minor: 0, state: 0000
Apr 25 15:57:12 foo kernel: ippp_ccp: allocated reset data structure
c3966000
Apr 25 15:57:12 foo ipppd[599]: Connect[0]: /dev/ippp0, fd: 7
```

Because we set the dial mode to auto (by issuing the command *isdnctrl dialmode ippp0 auto*), the connection will be established on demand and taken down after a specified number of seconds of idle time. This is how to manually activate the ISDN PPP connection:

```
# isdnctrl dial ippp0
Dialing of ippp0 triggered
```

Your ISDN connection has now been created. To manually hang up the PPP connection, enter:

```
# isdnctrl hangup ippp0
  ippp0 hung up
```

Multihomed systems

Computers with more than one network connection are often referred to as *multi-homed*. Examples of such network connections may be two (or more) Ethernet NICs used to connect a small or home office to a cable or DSL modem. In some situations, you may use one Ethernet NIC for connecting to the LAN and an ISDN adapter to provide Internet access, although this is rare in many countries. No matter what configuration you choose, multihomed systems are increasingly popular. There may be a variety of reasons to use a multihomed host. Most often, however, this configuration is used when a Linux system serves as a router (and usually a firewall as well).

IP routing configuration

When configuring a router, one detail must not be forgotten: enable IP routing. This is done by setting the value of */proc/sys/net/ipv4/ip_forward* to 1 (one). The system configuration files to enable this routing are */etc/network/options* in Debian (set ip_forward=yes) and */etc/sysctl.conf* in Fedora (set net.ipv4.ip_forward = 1). When this is enabled, you have a router running. If the nodes on your networks (on both or all sides of the multihomed Linux system) set your system's IP address as their default gateway, they will reach each other, being routed by the Linux host.

The following is a simple way to enable IP forwarding from a command line:

```
# sudo echo "1" > /proc/sys/net/ipv4/ip_forward
```

You can alternatively configure the */etc/network/options* file, changing the ip_forward=no value to ip_forward=yes. You have to be *root* to accomplish either of these tasks. In a safe and peaceful network environment, this is all that is needed. If you are not in that situation, adding a firewall using *iptables* is recommended, even on dial-up links. Configuring firewalls is covered by Chapter 40.

IP forwarding versus firewalling and Network Address Translation (NAT)

Simply enabling IP forwarding does not create a firewall, nor does it allow you to route private IP addresses to the Internet. Three ranges of IP addresses have been set aside for private networks. These IP addresses are automatically dropped by all Internet routers. Internal routers for your network will pass these IP addresses, however.

The private IP address ranges are:

- The entire 10.0.0.0 IP address block, with the subnet mask of 255.0.0
- All IP addresses between 172.16.0.0 and 172.31.255.255,with the subnet mask of 255.240.0.0
- All IP addresses between 192.168.0.0 and 192.168.255.255, with the subnet mask of 255.255.0.0

In order to route these IP addresses on to the Internet, you need to engage in Network Address Translation. The *iptables* or *ipchains* command allows you to do this. *iptables* is preferred in modern versions of Linux. These commands also allow you to control the packets that pass between multihomed systems, thereby making your router a firewall. See Chapter 40 for more information about using *iptables* to enable NAT and firewalling.

Objective 2: Advanced Network Configuration and Troubleshooting

For this Objective, make sure that you focus on troubleshooting, not just knowing the names of commands. By *troubleshooting*, we mean being able to:

- Use the applications and configuration files discussed earlier in the chapter
- Review configuration files for simple problems (e.g., misspellings and mis-entered lines)
- Review log files for problems
- Generally keep your cool when faced with balky systems

Although the LPI Exams don't really test you on the last item, we assume that many people reading this book are using it to learn essential Linux skills, as the LPI Exam examines real-world knowledge.

This section contains scenarios that help you learn more about the depth of troubleshooting skills you will need. We'll cover practical uses of *netstat*, *tcpdump*, *ethereal* (and the associated *tethereal* application), *lsof*, and *netcat* (*nc*). It is also important for you to understand *ping* and the utilities shown earlier in this chapter in a troubleshooting situation. But we'll start with one of the most basic utilities in networking.

Simple Connectivity Example: Telnet

Suppose an employee reports that the intranet web server is unavailable. What do you do? Open up a web browser? That won't provide much more informaiton than the employee already told you. Instead, try Telnet. Don't get incredulous—Telnet is a terrific troubleshooting tool.

Depending on your location, you can use Telnet to log in to the system and check the process list to see if the web server is running. If it is, issue the command *telnet localhost 80* while still on the web server host, specifying that you want to talk to port 80 (HTTP) on the server. A sample session looks like this:

```
# telnet localhost 80
Trying 127.0.0.1...
Connected to localhost.
Escape character is '^]'.
HEAD / HTTP/1.0

HTTP/1.1 302 Found
Date: Mon, 26 Jul 2005 13:14:44 GMT
```

```
Server: Apache/1.3.29 (Debian GNU/Linux) PHP/4.1.2 mod_ssl/2.8.16 OpenSSL/0.
9.7c
X-Powered-By: PHP/4.1.2
Location: http://intranet.company.test/
Connection: close
Content-Type: text/html; charset=iso-8859-1

Connection closed by foreign host.
```

The typical HTTP response from the web server tells you it can respond to requests properly on port 80. But this test bypasses any possible network problem, because you're on the same host as the web server when you run Telnet.

Now run the Telnet command from another host:

```
# telnet intranet.company.test 80
```

The outcome of this test determines what you do next: success will suggest you query the employee more carefully to find out why his particular request failed, while failure suggests you look at the components of your network that permit communication, including DNS and the web server configuration itself.

Simple as it may be, Telnet may be one of your most valuable tools when troubleshooting networks. We would never willingly use Telnet to configure a remote system, but it is very useful for troubleshooting. *netcat* is much more capable, of course. However, *netcat* is not always available, while Telnet usually is. You would not use SSH when troubleshooting, because it will try to encrypt the connection, causing the connection to fail.

The ability to speak directly to the service's listening port at a low level using Telnet or *netcat* is often invaluable, because client software such as a browser works at too high a level. It does not give an administrator the required level of control over situations. The great strength of using Linux is that you can break down troubleshooting into network connectivity, DNS resolution, and so on, using various tools. It is vital that you use command-line tools, because they provide the most information. A Telnet test to see whether the remote service is listening gives a quite clear answer to whether this is a network problem or a client/server application problem.

Using tcpdump

tcpdump is another extremely useful tool. Contrary to its name, it does a good deal more than display information from the TCP headers of packets; it actually understands a wide range of protocols. So you can use *tcpdump* to read packet captures created by various applications (e.g., *ethereal* and Snort).

tcpdump is text based; it does not have a fancy GUI or even an *ncurses* interface. The independence from the X Window System is a blessing, because many times you will be asked to monitor traffic from a host that does not have X running.

Some still might think that *tcpdump*'s lack of a fancy GUI indicates the tool is unsophisticated. They would be mistaken. *tcpdump* is quite sophisticated. It can sniff traffic on many types of networks, including 802.1Q VLANs. It can sniff on standard hub-based networks as well as switched-based networks. There is one

Networking
Configuration

overriding factor regarding *tcpdump*: you need to use the right options and syntax. Otherwise, you will be lost.

The reason your choice of options is so important is that a production network provides *tcpdump* with far too much information. That is the main difficulty in using *tcpdump*. You need to tell it to be selective.

The syntax for *tcpdump* is:

```
tcpdump [options] [expression]
```

Some of the most commonly used options are:

-c count
> Capture *count* packets, then stop.

-D
> List the devices (interfaces) that are configured on the system. If you are lucky, the device will have an accompanying description that will help you know whether the interface can capture packets.

-i interface
> Listen to *interface*. If set to any, *tcpdump* listens to all interfaces.

-q
> Quiet operation: show less information on each capture. (The manpages refer to *-q* as "quick" as well.)

-r file
> Read a previously written *tcpdump* file.

-s 0
> Set the "snaplength" to 0. *tcpdump* thus reads the whole packet instead of just the first 68 bytes, which is the default.

-t
> Suppress timestamp entries.

-v, -vv, -vvv
> Print a lot of information; the more *vs* in the option, the more verbose the output.

-w file
> Write the displayed information to *file*. This file may later be analyzed at your leisure using either *tcpdump* in read mode (with the *-r file* option) or *ethereal*.

tcpdump expressions

It is not enough to know *tcpdump*'s options; the volume of traffic displayed makes it unlikely you will find what you need to know unless you also use *expressions*. The ones given here are quite useful. Make sure that you understand them before you take the exam.

`not port ssh`
> Filter out any SSH traffic. Extremely useful if you run *tcpdump* from a shell on a remote host, so you won't see your own login connection.

It is more accurate to say that the not port ssh command suppresses traffic that uses port 22. The SSH protocol uses this port by default. If, for some reason, some other application was using that port, you would not view that traffic, either.

ip proto \\icmp
> Specify that only ICMP traffic is to be monitored.

dst 192.168.0.1
> Monitor only network traffic destined for host 192.168.0.1.

src 192.168.0.1
> Monitor only for network traffic originating from host 192.168.0.1.

host 192.168.0.1
> Monitor only network traffic involving host 192.168.0.1, both ways.

host 192.168.0.1 and host 192.168.0.2
> Monitor only traffic between these two hosts, both ways.

src 192.168.0.1 and dst 192.168.0.2
> Monitor only traffic from 192.168.0.1 to 192.168.0.2, not vice versa.

As these sample expressions show, you can manipulate the options by using familiar Boolean operations, expressed as words or punctuation: not (!), and (&&), or (||).

Some examples of how you can use *tcpdump* to monitor network traffic follow.

Example #1

In this example, you will view all network traffic on the second Ethernet interface (*eth1*) of the host having the IP address of 192.168.45.1, with the exception of SSH traffic:

```
tcpdump -i eth1 -v -vv -vvv -s0 not port ssh and host 192.168.45.1
```

This command might be useful if you are on a host on a local area network and want to see everything traveling to and from a hub.

Example #2

The following example captures all network traffic on interface *eth0* destined to port 80 on the host 192.168.0.20 and writes the raw data to the file */tmp/web*:

```
tcpdump -i eth0 -w /tmp/web -s0 dst 192.168.0.20 and dst port 80
```

This command actually doesn't need to specify the interface, because *tcpdump* defaults to the *eth0* interface.

Example #3

In this example, the expression captures a brief view of the handshake that occurs when an email client contacts a POP-3 daemon residing on host 192.168.0.20:

```
# tcpdump -t -n -q host 192.168.0.20 and host 192.168.1.18 and port 110
tcpdump: listening on eth0
```

```
192.168.1.18.1035 > 192.168.0.20.110: tcp 0 (DF) [tos 0x10]
192.168.0.20.110 > 192.168.1.18.1035: tcp 0 (DF)
192.168.1.18.1035 > 192.168.0.20.110: tcp 0 (DF) [tos 0x10]
192.168.0.20.110 > 192.168.1.18.1035: tcp 113 (DF)
192.168.1.18.1035 > 192.168.0.20.110: tcp 0 (DF) [tos 0x10]
192.168.1.18.1035 > 192.168.0.20.110: tcp 14 (DF) [tos 0x10]
192.168.0.20.110 > 192.168.1.18.1035: tcp 0 (DF)
192.168.0.20.110 > 192.168.1.18.1035: tcp 36 (DF)
```

tcpdump captures the packets in "quiet mode," meaning it provides only an over-view showing the IP addresses involved as well as source and destination ports. As the example shows, the source port is an arbitrary port above 1023 on the client IP. The output is useful for debugging.

Example #4

For this final example, we have set an improper static route to the client IP address on the destination POP-3 server. The result of this misconfiguration is that all of the return packets are lost. The *tcpdump* output shows that the client tries to initiate a connection, but cannot get a response from the POP-3 server:

```
# tcpdump -t -n -q host 192.168.0.20 and host 192.168.1.18 and port 110
tcpdump: listening on eth0
192.168.1.18.1037 > 192.168.0.20.110: tcp 0 (DF)
192.168.1.18.1037 > 192.168.0.20.110: tcp 0 (DF)
192.168.1.18.1037 > 192.168.0.20.110: tcp 0 (DF)
192.168.1.18.1037 > 192.168.0.20.110: tcp 0 (DF)
192.168.1.18.1037 > 192.168.0.20.110: tcp 0 (DF)
```

tcpdump output such as this is usually caused either by asymmetric routing—where the return packets leave the host on another interface from the one that received traffic—or when a service has broken down but still keeps listening to the TCP port.

Make sure that you are familiar with how to exclude packets, as well as how to "drill down" into the packets that you have captured using *tcpdump*. Not only will you find it easier to pass the exam, but you will also be a better networker.

ethereal and tethereal

Although *tcpdump* is versatile and powerful, *ethereal* has much to offer it as well; it is an excellent GUI-based packet sniffer. You can use *ethereal*, as you can *tcpdump*, to obtain a detailed analysis of network traffic. It may be used in interac-tive mode to capture network activity on the fly or in file mode to analyze an input file captured earlier. *ethereal* is capable of reading various packet capture files, including those created by *tcpdump*. A text-only version called *tethereal* is usually installed along with *ethereal*.

The syntax for *ethereal* and *tethereal* is:

```
etheral [options] [file]
tetheral [options] [file]
```

A couple of frequently used options, which are the same as the corresponding *tcpdump* options, are:

-c count
> Capture only *count* packets.

-s snaplength
> Set the amount of each packet read. Set to 0 to ensure the entire packet is captured.

tethereal's output from a simple ping packet (ICMP request) looks like this:

```
# tethereal -V -r /tmp/ping
Frame 1 (98 bytes on wire, 96 bytes captured)
    Arrival Time: Apr 26, 2004 06:20:32.926621000
    Time delta from previous packet: 0.000000000 seconds
    Time since reference or first frame: 0.000000000 seconds
    Frame Number: 1
    Packet Length: 98 bytes
    Capture Length: 96 bytes
Ethernet II, Src: 00:c0:f0:30:1d:5e, Dst: 00:01:02:f7:7c:4b
    Destination: 00:01:02:f7:7c:4b (3com_f7:7c:4b)
    Source: 00:c0:f0:30:1d:5e (Kingston_30:1d:5e)
    Type: IP (0x0800)
Internet Protocol, Src Addr: 192.168.1.18 (192.168.1.18), Dst Addr: 192.168.
0.20 (192.168.0.20)
    Version: 4
    Header length: 20 bytes
    Differentiated Services Field: 0x00 (DSCP 0x00: Default; ECN: 0x00)
        0000 00.. = Differentiated Services Codepoint: Default (0x00)
        .... ..0. = ECN-Capable Transport (ECT): 0
        .... ...0 = ECN-CE: 0
    Total Length: 84
    Identification: 0x0000 (0)
    Flags: 0x04
        0... = Reserved bit: Not set
        .1.. = Don't fragment: Set
        ..0. = More fragments: Not set
    Fragment offset: 0
    Time to live: 64
    Protocol: ICMP (0x01)
    Header checksum: 0xb832 (correct)
    Source: 192.168.1.18 (192.168.1.18)
    Destination: 192.168.0.20 (192.168.0.20)
Internet Control Message Protocol
    Type: 8 (Echo (ping) request)
    Code: 0
    Checksum: 0xb958
    Identifier: 0x3507
    Sequence number: 0x0000
    Data (54 bytes)

0000  4b aa 8c 40 3b b2 0b 00 08 09 0a 0b 0c 0d 0e 0f   K..@;...........
0010  10 11 12 13 14 15 16 17 18 19 1a 1b 1c 1d 1e 1f   ................
0020  20 21 22 23 24 25 26 27 28 29 2a 2b 2c 2d 2e 2f    !"#$%&'()*+,-./
0030  30 31 32 33 34 35                                 012345
```

As the output shows, every network layer and protocol involved are analyzed.

Figure 35-3 shows an example of *ethereal* viewing packets on an Ubuntu system.

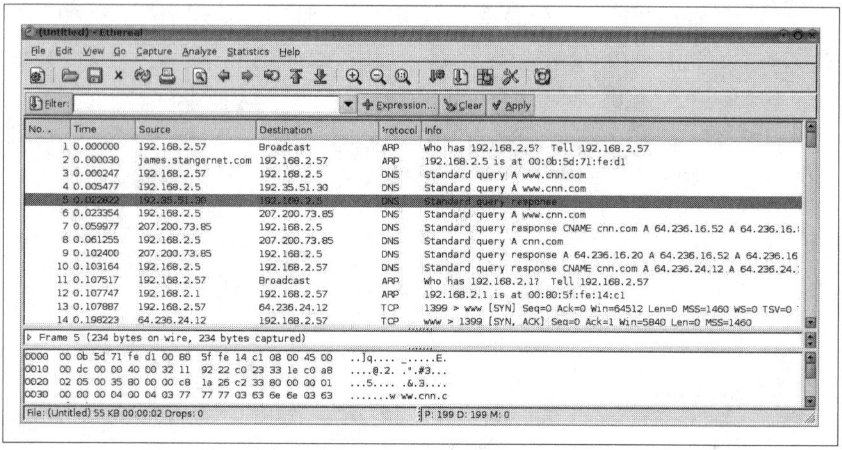

Figure 35-3. ethereal in action

The *ethereal* layout makes it much easier to view the important details of packets than the output of either *tcpdump* or *tethereal*. *ethereal* also provides fairly effective ways to measure network traffic volumes. You can filter packets either during a packet capture, using expressions, or after the capture.

The lsof command

The *lsof* command lists all open files on your system. Because Linux systems treat everything, including open network sockets, as files, *lsof* is useful when troubleshooting network connections. By using a few of its options, as well as piping it through *grep*, you can determine the origin of network connections, as well as find open ports on your system.

The syntax for using *lsof* is:

    lsof [options]

Some of the most frequently used options include:

-i

> List IP sockets. Accepts parameters that can restrict the sockets listed, such as *-i tcp*, *-i udp*, or *-i 192.168.1.1*.

-n

> Do not resolve hostnames; can make *lsof* run faster.

-P

> Do not resolve port names; can make *lsof* run faster

All the examples in this section include the *-i* option, because we want to see only sockets and not other open files on the system. Some examples further restrict the types of sockets viewed to a particular protocol.

Example #1

This example tells *lsof* to report only open network files (i.e., sockets) and to ignore hostnames:

```
# lsof -i -n
COMMAND     PID    USER  FD    TYPE DEVICE SIZE NODE NAME
dhclient    1047   root  5u    IPv4  2068       UDP  *:bootpc
portmap     1113   rpc   3u    IPv4  2183       UDP  *:sunrpc
portmap     1113   rpc   4u    IPv4  2187       TCP  *:sunrpc (LISTEN)
rpc.statd   1132 rpcuser 4u    IPv4  2217       UDP  *:1024
rpc.statd   1132 rpcuser 5u    IPv4  2207       UDP  *:884
rpc.statd   1132 rpcuser 6u    IPv4  2220       TCP  *:1024 (LISTEN)
cupsd       1267   root  0u    IPv4  2487       TCP  127.0.0.1:ipp (LISTEN)
cupsd       1267   root  2u    IPv4  2488       UDP  *:ipp
sshd        1470   root  3u    IPv6  2567       TCP  *:ssh (LISTEN)
xinetd      1483   root  5u    IPv4  2605       TCP  127.0.0.1:1025 (LISTEN)
sendmail    1501   root  4u    IPv4  2650       TCP  127.0.0.1:smtp (LISTEN)
```

Example #2

This example further restricts the listing to TCP-based connections:

```
# lsof -i tcp -n
COMMAND     PID    USER  FD    TYPE DEVICE SIZE NODE NAME
portmap     1113   rpc   4u    IPv4  2187       TCP  *:sunrpc (LISTEN)
rpc.statd   1132 rpcuser 6u    IPv4  2220       TCP  *:1024 (LISTEN)
cupsd       1267   root  0u    IPv4  2487       TCP  127.0.0.1:ipp (LISTEN)
sshd        1470   root  3u    IPv6  2567       TCP  *:ssh (LISTEN)
xinetd      1483   root  5u    IPv4  2605       TCP  127.0.0.1:1025 (LISTEN)
sendmail    1501   root  4u    IPv4  2650       TCP  127.0.0.1:smtp (LISTEN)
```

Example #3

This example lists only UDP-based connections:

```
# lsof -i udp -n
COMMAND     PID    USER  FD    TYPE DEVICE SIZE NODE NAME
dhclient    1047   root  5u    IPv4  2068       UDP  *:bootpc
portmap     1113   rpc   3u    IPv4  2183       UDP  *:sunrpc
rpc.statd   1132 rpcuser 4u    IPv4  2217       UDP  *:1024
rpc.statd   1132 rpcuser 5u    IPv4  2207       UDP  *:884
cupsd       1267   root  2u    IPv4  2488       UDP  *:ipp
```

Example #4

In this example and the next, notice how you can use *grep* to isolate the port used by the network socket:

```
# lsof -i -n -P | grep sendmail
sendmail    1501   root  4u    IPv4  2650       TCP  127.0.0.1:25 (LISTEN)
```

This example uses the -P option, which tells *lsof* not to convert port numbers to names. As a result, you see (in the right-most column, just after the colon) that *sendmail* is running on port 25, the standard SMTP port.

Example #5

In this example, notice that the +*P* option is used, so that the name of the protocol instead of the port number is listed:

```
# lsof -i -n +P | grep sendmail
sendmail 1501    root    4u IPv4    2650      TCP 127.0.0.1:smtp (LISTEN)
```

Notice now that you see smtp in the port field. The +*P* option is the default.

One possible use of *lsof* is in combination with the *fuser* command—for example, to kill certain processes associated with suspicious network connections or to stop malfunctioning network processes.

The netstat command

netstat, like *lsof*, can find standard ports open on your system, as well as ports opened by applications such as *netcat*. *netstat* can help you determine TCP- and UDP-based connections and let you view your system's routing table.

netstat's syntax is:

```
netstat [options]
```

Frequently used options include:

-a
> List all sockets.

-e
> Extended mode. Use twice for more details.

--inet
> List only IP connections.

-l
> Show only listening sockets.

-n
> Do not resolve IP addresses to hostnames.

-p
> Show the process ID (PID) and name of the program holding the socket.

-r
> Show the host's routing table (similar to the *route* command).

Example #1

List only open IP-based network connections and show the PID, as well as the program and username that opened the file:

```
# netstat -apne --inet
```

This command also places output into extended view (-*e* option). This offers more information, including the network socket's inode and the associated user.

Example #2

You can also list all of the ports that are currently listening:

```
# netstat -le --inet
```

Example #3

To view the system's routing table and ignore name resolution, enter:

```
# netstat -nre
```

netcat (nc)

netcat allows you to establish, analyze, and read connections between systems. It is a very useful program, and you should count it as one of the more useful weapons in your troubleshooting arsenal. You can also use *netcat* to open ports on your local system, which has various uses. For example, you can place your system behind the firewall and run *netcat* on your system to open up a port (e.g., port 80). You can then conduct a penetration test using a system outside of the firewall to see whether the firewall is properly blocking packets to internal systems. Conveniently enough, you can use *netcat* to simulate both the client and the server in this case.

netcat is installed by default on many systems. If it is not installed, obtain it by using your packaging tool (e.g., *rpm*, YaST, *dpkg*, *apt*, or Synaptic) or download the source code from *http://netcat.sourceforge.net*.

The syntax is:

```
nc [options] hostname [ports]
nc -l -p port [options] [hostname] [ports]
```

On many Linux systems, *nc* is the actual binary and the *netcat* file is a symbolic link to it.

netcat is capable of connecting to and listening on any port. It can use both TCP and UDP. Because *netcat* is able to both listen and send, it may be used for file transfers between systems. Many systems are not configured with Samba, FTP, or SSH; *netcat* acts as a useful, quick, adhoc file transfer solution in these cases.

Finally, you can also use *netcat* to analyze the protocol of a network client by directing the client to a listening *netcat* process. You can then view the connection's state to determine how the host handles connections.

Example #1

When you start *netcat* with host and port arguments, the service running on the given host and port are contacted. Whatever you enter into *netcat* will be sent to the service, and any response will be shown to you. Following is a simple example.

First, tell *netcat* to read port 80 on your own system:

```
$ nc localhost 80
```

Once you connect, *netcat* will keep the connection persistent. You may be tempted to think that the connection has "hung," but that is not the case. *netcat* is simply keeping it open, which allows you to then formulate a request. In this case, because you have opened a connection to your web server, create a simple HTTP request, imitating a basic web client:

```
HEAD / HTTP/1.0
```

The web server will then issue a response, similar to that shown here:

```
HTTP/1.1 302 Found
Date: Mon, 26 Jul 2005 04:27:12 GMT
Server: Apache/1.3.29 (Debian GNU/Linux) PHP/4.1.2 mod_ssl/2.8.16 OpenSSL/0.
9.7c
X-Powered-By: PHP/4.1.2
Location: http://www.company.test/
Connection: close
Content-Type: text/html; charset=iso-8859-1
```

What you see will vary, depending on how verbose your version of the Apache server is and the nature of the request you type. Notice in the preceding example how the web server has returned quite a bit of information. Legitimate uses of this information include determining the exact configuration of the web server. Illegitimate uses of this tool include trying to determine a server's configuration so that an intruder can attack its weaknesses.

Example #2

In this example, *netcat* transfers files from one host to another. Suppose that host A is the one receiving the file. The following command on host A allows *netcat* to listen to traffic on an arbitrarily chosen port and receive a file:

```
# nc -l -p 1234 | tar xvfp -
```

 In order for *netcat* to obtain a network socket, you have to run it with *root* privileges.

Now that host A is listening and ready to receive, you can send a file from host B using *netcat* on that system:

```
# tar cfp - /some/dir | nc -w 3 hostA 1234
```

Example #3

You can also use other applications instead of *tar*: for example, *dd* or *cat*. In the following example, *netcat* writes a complete backup of the */dev/hda1* partition to a file on a remote host. On host A, the receiving end, enter:

```
# nc -l -p 1234 | dd of=backup_hda1
```

On host B, the host containing the *hda1* device to be copied, issue the following command:

```
# dd if=/dev/hda1 | nc -w 3 hostA 1234
```

You now know how to use the tools referred to in the LPI 202 Exam. You also understand the advanced networking concepts and troubleshooting tools assumed in the exam. Now, find a "live" Linux system and experiment with what you have found. Once you do that, you will be ready to pass this portion of the exam.

36

Mail and News
(Topic 2.206)

This chapter covers the running and administration of mail and news services. The four LPI Exam Objectives are as follows. We deliberately cover them in this chapter out of order, because Sendmail configuration must be understood before some of the others.

Objective 2: Using Sendmail
Candidates should be able to manage a Sendmail configuration, including email aliases, mail quotas, and virtual mail domains. This Objective includes configuring internal mail relays and monitoring SMTP servers. Key files, terms, and utilities include */etc/aliases*, *sendmail.cw*, *virtusertable*, and *genericstable*. Weight: 4.

Objective 3: Managing Mail Traffic
Candidates should be able to implement client mail management software to filter, sort, and monitor incoming user mail. This objective includes using software such as Procmail on both server and client side. Weight: 3.

Objective 1: Configuring Mailing Lists
Install and maintain mailing lists using Majordomo. Monitor Majordomo problems by viewing Majordomo logs. Weight: 1.

Objective 4: Serving News
Candidates should be able to install and configure news servers using INN. This Objective includes customizing and monitoring served newsgroups. Weight: 1.

Objective 2: Using Sendmail

First, it's important to understand Sendmail's function in regard to email. To do this, it is necessary to learn some terminology. Sendmail is a Message Transfer Agent (MTA)—the oldest one in existence. The MTA has two jobs: to ensure that mail messages are transferred between entities and to place those messages in a destination directory. The MTA can also authenticate parties, but this is just part of its function of transferring messages between users or hosts.

In contrast, a POP or IMAP server is called a Message Delivery Agent (MDA). The MDA's job is responsible for providing mechanisms that allow users to retrieve their messages. Both the MTA and MDA are usually server-based functions. The tool that you use to send and receive email is called a Message User Agent (MUA). The MUA is most often a client-side tool, though with web-based mail, the MUA's function becomes complicated to some extent, because the ability to send and receive email is more evenly split between the web browser and a server.

Sendmail is an old MTA; it has has been in constant use for decades. It is the subject of one of the largest O'Reilly books, the well-known "bat book," so called because it has a bat on its cover. This section in no way is meant to replace that remarkable achievement. However, this section will help you get a handle on how much you need to learn about Sendmail in order to pass the LPI Level 2 Exam. But before we move on with the specifics of Sendmail configuration, it is important to understand that other MTAs also exist. Table 36-1 lists the most popular MTAs used with Linux servers.

Table 36-1. Common MTAs

MTA	Available at	Description
Sendmail	*http://www.sendmail.org*	The traditional MTA. This chapter's examples are based on Sendmail from the Sendmail Consortium.
Postfix	*http://www.postfix.org*	A common Sendmail replacement, considered more lightweight.
Qmail	*http://www.qmail.org*	Often used to replace Sendmail as the network MTA.
Exim	*http://www.exim.org*	A relatively new replacement, the default MTA in the Debian distribution.

Not only is the configuration of MTAs an important skill to enable mail service, but many other services also demand an MTA and interact with it. For example, mailing list servers such as Majordomo (discussed later in this chapter) use an MTA.

Sendmail Configuration

A properly configured email server doesn't need constant attention. When everything's configured properly, few things can go wrong. And when something does go wrong, the protocol used by Sendmail and other Internet MTAs, the Simple Mail Transfer Protocol (SMTP), tends to keep messages buffered until the systems are up again.

In this chapter you will be guided through the configuration and securing of your Sendmail server. The examples are based on a fairly new version of Sendmail, 8. 12.10. As Sendmail has had its share of security issues, you are strongly encouraged to upgrade your *Sendmail* software to a recent version. If your Linux distribution is not very new, check your distribution's web site for erratas and upgrades. Also, antispam features are better supported in recent versions of Sendmail.

The Continuing Importance of Sendmail

Some controversy exists in LPI circles concerning the Sendmail Objective. "Why cover Sendmail when so many have gone over to Qmail or Postfix?" people often ask. The answer is relatively simple: tradition.

Yes, Sendmail has a long, storied history of buffer overflows and security problems. Its longevity has helped contribute to code bloat and needless difficulty in configuration. Yes, other daemons have been written "from scratch" with security in mind, whereas Sendmail was put together in ragtag fashion for years. But again, Sendmail is used by most of the corporations and organizations hiring people. Sendmail also underwent a complete rewrite some years ago. Even though configuring Sendmail often requires the administrator to know its history and a good many other associated protocols (e.g., DNS), it remains the de facto standard.

Nearly 75% of all email worldwide is still handled by Sendmail. This means that regardless of your preference or passion, you are likely to come across a Sendmail installation in your career as a Linux professional.

Increasingly, Sendmail is being replaced by other MTAs by major Linux distributions. One day, LPI will find in its review of small and medium enterprises that the balance has tipped toward newer MTAs. When it does, you can rest assured that the Objective will change, too.

Also, even though most Linux distributions offer other default MTAs, they still require you to know the same concepts and principles. Many of the practices are the same, too. So, if you know Sendmail, you'll be able to quickly learn other MTAs as well.

Building and editing configuration files: the m4 utility

The Sendmail configuration file, usually stored in */etc/mail/sendmail.cf*, is designed to be easily understood by the mail server software. Unfortunately, email servers don't read files as humans do, and Sendmail has achieved a well-deserved reputation for being difficult to configure.

To remedy this, the creators of Sendmail decided to create a more human-readable set of macros to help configure the daemon. If you learn the basics of the Unix m4 macro language for which the macros are written and adapt the macros to your needs in a plain text file, you can use the *m4* utility to convert your macro file into a valid *sendmail.cf* file.

 The *m4* utility is often not installed, even if Sendmail is the MTA used on the server. Use your package management utility (such as *apt-get*, *rpm*, or YaST) to install it.

Sendmail often ships with sample *m4*-based macro files. The default file is usually called *sendmail.mc*, but you may come across *.mc* files with different names as well. Some distributions ship with many sample *.mc* files, each designed to suit different purposes. All you have to do customize these *.mc* files to meet your own needs.

Many might be tempted to simply bypass using *m4* and an *.mc* file and simply edit the *sendmail.cf* file directly. This is a mistake, because any changes you make directly to this file will be overwritten if you or an application later generates the *sendmail.cf* file from the macro file. And don't think that you or another person won't do that later on. For this reason, the recommended method is to edit only the macro file.

Additional configuration files

The *sendmail.cf* file is not the only file that is used to configure Sendmail. Various additional files exist in the */etc/mail* directory.

 Sendmail maintains much of its configuration information in a binary database format for the sake of efficiency. Therefore, after editing this information in various text files, you must convert them to a database format by running the *makemap* command and then restart Sendmail. For instance, to convert the */etc/mail/access* file to Sendmail's database format, you would change to the */etc/mail* directory and issue the following command:

```
makemap hash access > access
```

Make sure that you understand the purpose of the following files:

access
> Used to allow or deny access to systems and users. Starting with Version 8.9, Sendmail does not relay by default, so you can either use this file to override antirelaying settings in the *sendmail.cf* file or reconfigure the *sendmail.cf* file. To create the new access map, enter:
>
> ```
> makemap hash access < access
> ```

local-host-names
> Allows you to inform Sendmail about the hostname of the computer.

virtusertable
> Used to map incoming email to a local account. Using *virtusertable*, you can make sure that a message sent to one account (e.g., *sales@oreilly.com*) is actually sent to two users (e.g., *james@oreilly.com* and *sandi@oreilly.com*). Or, if you wish to set up a "catchall" email address to route mail with mistyped addresses, you can use the *virtusertable* file to which to route these messages to a particular user. To create the requisite binary file, issue the following command to read the source file that contains the *virtusertable* instructions:
>
> ```
> makemap hash /etc/mail/virtusertable < sourcefile
> ```

Older Sendmail systems might expect you to use dbm rather than hash in the previous command. You can give the source file any name you wish.

genericstable

Used for outbound mail. Allows you to rewrite local usernames (e.g., *james@albion.stangernet.com*) so that they appear to have originated from a different host or domain. Mail can even appear to originate from a different username. To create the requisite binary file, run the following command so that the *genericstable* file is read to create the *genericstable.db* file:

```
makemap -r hash genericstable.db < genericstable
```

Messages are rewritten only if they originate from your system. Incoming messages are not affected.

genericsdomain

Tells your system which addresses are considered local and which are considered remote. Populate the file by using the following command:

```
hostname -long
```

Place the results of this command into the *genericsdomain* file.

mailertable

Can route email from remote systems. Seen by some as a better way to route messages than using *virtusertable*, because it is faster and more capable. Often used to configure a Sendmail system to act as a backup email system, or *MX host*.

domaintable

Can be used, for example, if a company or organization needs to make a transition from an old domain name to a new one To create the actual binary file, issue the following command:

```
makemap hash /etc/mail/domaintable < /etc/mail/domaintable.txt
```

aliases

Used to redirect mail for local recipients. You can use the file to make sure that mail sent to the root account, for example, is mailed to your standard user account. The syntax for each line of the file is:

```
original_account: user
```

where *user* is the account that will receive email sent to *original_account*. The *aliases* file must be processed into an *aliases.db* database that Sendmail can read using the following command:

```
makemap hash /etc/mail/aliases.db < /etc/mail/aliases
```

The *aliases* file works only for mail sent to local accounts (email addresses whose domains are local to your MTA's system). It is not used to change address information for outbound user accounts.

The */etc/mail* directory does not have to contain all of the preceding files. The *aliases* file, for example, is usually found right off of the */etc* directory. The other files need to be present only if the *sendmail.cf* file is configured to use these features. You will have to create these files yourself and use the *m4* configuration files to configure the *sendmail.cf* file to refer to the files. You will learn more about the files relevant to the LPI Exam in later sections.

Restarting Sendmail. If you change any of the preceding files, you need to restart Sendmail. You can restart it in various ways, including any of the following:

```
kill -HUP `cat /var/run/sendmail.pid`
killall -HUP sendmail
/etc/rc.d/init.d/sendmail restart
/etc/init.d/sendmail restart
```

or the following two-step procedure, using the PID of the *sendmail* process found through the *ps* command:

```
ps aux | grep sendmail
kill pid
```

The most universal method is to use the *kill* or *killall* command.

Securing Sendmail

One of the first steps you can take to secure Sendmail is to disable it altogether on hosts that don't need it. For example, you likely do not need Sendmail to process mail from other hosts if you are going to use it for internal mail (i.e., mail sent between users on the same system).

In an environment in which only a few MTAs handle email routing, the MTA daemon should be disabled on all the other hosts. Disabling the daemon still lets the system send email, but not receive it from remote hosts. When installing, most distributions specifically ask if you want to enable the Sendmail daemon. Fedora and RedHat, however, have traditionally enabled the Sendmail daemon automatically after installation without consulting the administrator. On those distributions and versions, unless the host is an email-routing MTA, disable the listening Sendmail daemon by entering:

```
root@james mail# chkconfig --level 123456 sendmail off
```

Then verify that the service is disabled:

```
root@james mail# chkconfig --list sendmail
sendmail        0:off   1:off   2:off   3:off   4:off   5:off   6:off
```

On a more general level, MTA software needs to be given two pieces of information to be considered secure:

- Which IP addresses or IP networks/subnetworks may use the mail server as a relay—that is, use the server to send email to anyone chosen by the originator. Without this restriction, your mail server will be used for unauthorized mail relaying. In other words, your Sendmail server can become a spam factory.

- Which domains your mail server should accept email for. This simply means whom you're serving with your email server.

Defining a trusted network

No one wants to receive spam. Furthermore, you don't want to be an unwitting party that promotes spam. If you fail to configure Sendmail correctly, your mail server may very well be a so-called "open relay" that can be abused by spammers.

Several public lists of open relays exist on the Internet, and most MTA software can easily be configured to reject incoming email if the originating mail server is blacklisted. If your mail server gets into one of these lists, you may face a difficult process getting off the list again. You may even have to pay to be removed from some of these lists. Table 36-2 describes a few of the open relay blacklists at the time of writing.

Table 36-2. Popular relay blacklists (RBLs)

Blacklist	URL
Open Relay Database	*http://www.ordb.org*
Spamhaus	*http://www.spamhaus.org*
Blitzed	*http://www.blitzed.org*
Composite Blocking List	*http://cbl.abuseat.org*
Distributed Server Blocking List	*http://www.dsbl.org*

The /etc/mail/access file

As discussed earlier, newer versions of Sendmail do not relay by default. Also, newer versions of Sendmail default to allowing only the local host to send email. If you want to allow your users to send email from their desktop computers via your Sendmail server, you will need to add the IP addresses of those computers to Sendmail's list of allowed senders. At the same time, this file is used when someone from the outside tries to send to you and therefore can be useful to stop spammers from reaching your users.

Earlier you learned that you can use the */etc/mail/access* file to list the IP addresses, domains, and email addresses that can use the server. The input file that you write lists IP addresses, domains, and email addresses on the left side and the action to take on the right side. Table 36-3 describes the actions and results described in the input to the *access* file.

Table 36-3. Actions in access database

Action	Result
OK	Unconditionally accept the email for local delivery. Sendmail's default behavior is to OK all mail destined for the host. The explicit OK action is often used when other Sendmail rules would reject the email because of spam control or if the domain does not resolve.
RELAY	Accept the email for relaying through this Sendmail server. RELAY is also an OK to bypass other checks (spam control, etc).
REJECT	Reject the incoming email with a generic rejection message.
DISCARD	Silently discard the message. Only sender addresses or domains may be discarded, not IP addresses or networks.

The codes in Table 36-3 are all case-sensitive. Following is an example of what you can put in the input file:

```
# This guy is a known spammer.
nasty.spammer@random-mail.com    DISCARD
# Drop all mail from this DNS domain. If the host trying to send mail
```

```
# resolves into a host within the DNS domain, the mail is rejected.
spam-r-us.net                    DISCARD

# A friend of ours has an IP address that resolves to the
# spam-r-us.net domain but we'd still like to receive his email.
10.45.34.203                     OK
# Our local network is 1.2.3.0 - 1.2.3.255. Sendmail does not accept
# CIDR notation (1.2.3.0/24) so you need to operate on the traditional
# network boundaries.
1.2.3                            RELAY
# Another known mail server may use your mail server for relaying:
172.20.45.23
```

Remember, once you make changes to the access file, you need to use the *makemap* command to re-create the *access* binary file.

Testing Sendmail configuration

If you'd like to check that your Sendmail server actually does what you configured it to do, you may run Sendmail in test mode. This starts Sendmail with a special interactive session, much like a terminal session. To enter test mode, first become *root*, as Sendmail sometimes requires this privilege. You can then use the -*b* and -*t* options to the *sendmail* command. A test mode session might look something like the following:

```
root@james # sendmail -bt
ADDRESS TEST MODE (ruleset 3 NOT automatically invoked)
Enter <ruleset>; <address>
```

You would then enter the following to look up relay settings:

```
/map access 1.2.3
map_lookup: access (1.2.3) returns RELAY (0)
```

Notice in the preceding command that you precede everything you type with a forward slash. Now, issue a command that determines what happens when mail comes from the *random-mail.com* domain:

```
/map access nasty.spammer@random-mail.com
map_lookup: access (nasty.spammer@random-mail.com) returns DISCARD (0)
```

Notice that the email is discarded.

Using this testing mode is much easier than configuring an email client and sending email messagess to the SMTP server. To quit the session, enter the following:

```
/quit
```

Defining accepted email domains: local-host-names and sendmail.cw

When setting up an email server, you probably know which domains it is supposed to handle. If the hostname of your server does not happen to be the exact name of the email domain, you need to add the domain to the file */etc/mail/local-host-names*. This file defines local mail addresses for the host. If you run an old version of Sendmail, the filename is */etc/mail/sendmail.cw*. The format of this file is easy: one domain per line:

```
somedomain.com
someotherdomain.com
differentdomain.com
```

The */etc/mail/local-host-names* file is a plain text file and does not need to be turned into a hash by *makemap*. However, you must force Sendmail to reread the file in order for the changes to apply. You can do this either by restarting Sendmail or, less disruptively, by sending it a SIGHUP signal as with many other daemons. You may then want to check that Sendmail has read and accepted the virtual domains. Enter test mode and check its configuration as follows:

```
root @james mail# sendmail -bt
ADDRESS TEST MODE (ruleset 3 is NOT automatically invoked)
Enter <ruleset> <address>
```

Then enter:

$=w

You should see:

```
[192.168.1.18]
system
localhost.localdomain
localhost
someotherdomain.com
[127.0.0.1]
somedomain.com
differentdomain.com
```

Then quit the session:

/quit

You can see in the sample output that some other domains appear in this list besides those in */etc/mail/local-host-names*. This is because Sendmail, in accordance with the RFCs governing email, accepts mail for the host itself. It thus includes the host's IP addresses (in square brackets) and the hostnames that are associated with these IP addresses either in the */etc/hosts* file or by DNS lookup.

When your mail server accepts multiple domains, be aware that you cannot have users with the same name in the different domains. For example, email to *tom@somedomain.com* and *tom@someotherdomain.com* will actually end up in the same person's inbox. If these two addresses happen to be read by the same person, this is OK. Otherwise, you need to configure your Sendmail server to understand and properly process virtual user accounts. This will be explained in detail later.

Delivering Email

A mail server works differently when it delivers mail to a remote server (SMTP delivery) and when it delivers mail to users on its own system (local delivery). SMTP delivery relies on either DNS information (the usual behavior) or on local transport mechanisms (normally used in company networks using the smart host facility). Local delivery happens when either a local user (found in the */etc/passwd* file) or a virtual user exists on the system. In these cases, the MTA leaves mail in an inbox file or set of files located on the local system.

 When users check their email from separate computers, this last part is not actually regarded as delivery, but retrieval, as it is the user's initiative to actively fetch the email. The MTA's job was done when it delivered the mail to a local mailbox. Retrieving the email does not involve the MTA at all; it is taken care of by other software, normally POP or IMAP server software that reads from the local mailbox when the user logs in.

SMTP delivery based on DNS lookup

You must know on the exam exactly how Sendmail uses DNS. An example will help you learn more about the process. Suppose you send an email to *john. smith@somedomain.com*. The email address consists of two parts: the local user part and the domain part. The local user part is what comes before the @ at sign, and the domain part is what comes after. Notice that no server name is given, just the domain name. This would seem to be incomplete information, but thanks to DNS, Sendmail can get the job done.

When delivering based on DNS, Sendmail (or any MTA, for that matter) asks a nearby DNS server for the server responsible for receiving the messages that it wants to deliver. In our case, it asks, "Which mail server should accept messages for *somedomain.com*?" Sendmail really does not care much at this point about the destination directory or even the user. Right now, it's interested in finding the server responsible for receiving messages for the whole domain. Usually, other MTAs don't know the answer. DNS does know, as long as a valid MX (standing for Mail eXchange) record exists in the DNS zone of the destination domain.

More technically, when the MTA wants to know where to send email for a domain, it does the equivalent of the following command:

```
dig MX somedomain.com
```

From a DNS zone, an MX record returned for the zone looks something like this:

```
somedomain.com.     1800    IN      MX      10 mail1.somedomain.com.
somedomain.com.     1800    IN      MX      20 mail2.somedomain.com.
```

This output shows that *somedomain.com* has two MTAs running, *mail1.somedomain.com* and *mail2.somedomain.com*. These might be running Sendmail, or they might not. But they must be MTAs.

The numbers immediately in front of the mail server names (e.g., 10 for *mail1. somedomain.com*) indicate priorities. Lower numbers mean higher priorities, so *mail1.somedomain.com* has a higher priority than *mail2.somedomain.com*. As a result, if *mail1.somedomain.com* is unreachable for the moment, email messages will be sent to *mail2.somedomain.com*.

The first number given in the example (e.g., 1800) is the Time To Live (TTL) value associated with the IN entry. Many zones will list the TTL entry at the start of the output, rather than inline with the actual DNS entries.

In the preceding scenario, *mail1* is called the *primary server*, and *mail2* (along with any other nonprimary servers) is called a *secondary server* or *secondary MX*. Secondary mail servers check the DNS MX information when trying to deliver mail, so that if your mail server has suffered a major failure and will be permanently down, you could establish a new primary mail server, change the DNS information, and be up and running again.

When you send an email message, your outgoing mail server will know what to do with the priority numbers. If a primary mail server is unavailable, it automatically tries the second best mail server, the third, and so on. If no mail servers are available at all (which is quite possible in the case of a major power failure or other disaster), the company may have made arrangements so that another company or its ISP will be listed as one of the servers. If not, the sender MTA will just wait for some time and then try to send the email again, working its way through the MX priority list. The RFCs recommend that an MTA wait four days before giving up. Most MTAs send a warning to the original sender after about five hours, saying that the email is not yet delivered but that the MTA will continue to try for a given time.

It is perfectly acceptable to have more than one server with the same priority level. Thanks to the retry mechanisms of SMTP, the sender MTA will try again if one of the same-priority MXs is down, and this time perhaps it will reach one of the running servers.

Let's take a look at the MXs currently set up for the *cisco.com* domain:

```
cisco.com.        86400   IN      MX      20 sj-inbound-1.cisco.com.
cisco.com.        86400   IN      MX      20 sj-inbound-2.cisco.com.
cisco.com.        86400   IN      MX      20 sj-inbound-3.cisco.com.
cisco.com.        86400   IN      MX      20 sj-inbound-4.cisco.com.
cisco.com.        86400   IN      MX      30 proxy9.cisco.com.
cisco.com.        86400   IN      MX      50 proxy6.cisco.com.
cisco.com.        86400   IN      MX      10 sj-inbound-0.cisco.com.
cisco.com.        86400   IN      MX      20 proxy5.cisco.com.
```

As the output shows, there is only one primary MX (with a priority of 10) but no fewer than five MXs with the next-level priority of 20. If the primary MX is unavailable, the sender MTA will attempt delivery to one of the priority-20 mail servers, chosen at random.

SMTP delivery using DNS lookups is the default behavior of all MTAs. The default configuration in */etc/mail/sendmail.cf*, which defines DNS delivery, is usually quite sufficient.

 An MX record cannot point to a CNAME entry. It usually points to an A entry (for IPv4) or a AAAA entry for IPv6. You will not need to know in-depth IPv6 concepts for the LPIC 2 Exam, however.

SMTP delivery via a smart host. A smart host is another mail server to which your MTA may forward all messages for further processing. Sending through a smart host uses most of the same mechanisms as with DNS. We may compare smart host delivery to what happens when a secondary MX tries to deliver a message to the primary MX: if the primary MX is up, the server sends the mail; if not, it just waits. The previously mentioned maximum wait period also applies to smart host configurations.

The principal difference between DNS-based and smart host–based delivery is that in a smart host configuration, the email's final destination mail server (at least as far as your MTA is concerned—it could be a gateway to other systems, but that's not important here) is statically coded into the mail server's configuration, not dynamically determined through DNS mechanisms.

Smart host configurations are usually found within larger networks where different servers should use only one server for further processing. All your other servers should be configured to use your main MTA. In this case, you do not need to set up MX records on your internal DNS servers (if you even have any).

In another scenario, on which the following example is based, you tighten your firewall so that only your properly configured mail server may handle outgoing email by forwarding it to an external MTA on a so-called "bastion host." Configuring Sendmail on a bastion host will be discussed later.

On your internal Sendmail server, you need to change only one configuration directive. In your *sendmail.mc* file, find or create a line specifying your smart host as either an IP address or a server name, as shown in the following examples:

```
define(`SMART_HOST',`[172.20.45.23]')
define(`SMART_HOST',` external-mailserver.company.com')
```

IP addresses are distinguished by being enclosed in square brackets. You can choose whichever line you prefer; they have the same effect.

 Both of the SMART_HOST directives in the *sendmail.mc* file illustrate an important element of the file's syntax: you must use a backquote (`` ` ``) to start a value and an apostrophe (') to end it. This syntax is required by the *m4* processor used to transform *sendmail.mc* to *sendmail.cf*.

After changing and saving the *sendmail.mc* file, run the *m4* processor to apply the changes to the *sendmail.cf* file. As explained earlier, most distributions supply a *Makefile* that runs *m4* to convert *sendmail.mc* to *sendmail.cf*, so typing a *make* command in the */etc/mail* directory will generate the *sendmail.cf* file correctly.

Manual Entries

If you want to get your hands dirty by editing in the *sendmail.cf* file, the directive you must find (or set) is DS. An example is:

```
DS[172.20.45.23]
```

You can also add the following entry to achieve the same effect:

```
DS external-mailserver.company.com
```

Once you have made either of the preceding changes, you need to restart the Sendmail daemon (and all the daemon's children, if any). As described earlier, there are many ways to restart Sendmail, but make sure that you understand both of the following commands:

```
/etc/init.d/sendmail reload
killall -HUP sendmail
```

To confirm that you have made a change, check your message log. Following are sanitized examples from an Ubuntu and Red Hat system, respectively:

```
Apr 24 12:45:18 foo sm-mta[7679]: restarting /usr/sbin/sendmail due to
signal
Apr 24 12:45:18 foo sm-mta[7692]: starting daemon (8.12.11):
SMTP+queueing@00:10:00
```

These lines show that the Sendmail daemon has started and is now ready to queue processes. The following example shows Sendmail restarting in a Red Hat system:

```
Apr 24 12:52:28 foo sendmail: sendmail -HUP succeeded
```

After restarting, Sendmail delivers every email message not destined for a local user account through your external mail server and out onto the LAN, WAN, or Internet.

 On Red Hat/Fedora systems, the */etc/init.d/sendmail* script understands the *reload* argument even though it is not documented.

Local Delivery

An email address has two parts: the local user part and the domain part. Local delivery is defined as an instance when your mail server receives an email in which the domain part matches its own domain or list of domains. As mentioned earlier, the accepted domains are listed in the */etc/mail/local-host-names* file, for newer systems. In older systems, this information is listed in */etc/mail/sendmail.cw*.

This file is one of the first checkpoints on an email's path to final delivery, so if you want Sendmail to accept mail for your domain, you will need to edit this file so that it contains the appropriate domain names. Because the file may contain more than one domain, your mail server may even accept mail for your company and for your privately owned email domain at the same time.

Traditionally, a match between an email address and a user account is found by reading the MTA server system's */etc/passwd* file. As a result, *john.smith@somedomain.com* will be delivered to the user account named *john*.

By using an *aliases* file, you can have mail to the address *customer-support@ispcompany.com* simultaneously distributed to the accounts *tom*, *dick*, and *harry*. You will learn more about the *aliases* file later.

When running more than one email domain on the same server, you will most likely run into the following problem: an account named *tom* is found in more than one of your domains. The result could be chaos, because the MTA would try to deliver the email messages to multiple people.

The solution to this problem is the concept of virtual users, described in the following section.

Using virtusertable

In Sendmail, the concept of the *virtual user* allows you to configure Sendmail so that nonlocal email can be properly routed. You create virtual users with the file named */etc/mail/virtusertable*. Here are some examples of the format used:

```
# Tom, Dick and Harry all have local user accounts.
# Tom's system user account is tjohnson, Dick's is dsmith,
# and Harry's is hflynn.
tom@somedomain.com              tjohnson
dick@somedomain.com             dsmith
harry@somedomain.com            hflynn

# Harry is the guy that gets all wrongly addressed email
# within the @somedomain.com address space
@somedomain.com                 hflynn

# Here is the other Tom; he has a different user account.
tom@someotherdomain.com         tgoldman
@someotherdomain.com            tgoldman

# Now, a third guy named Tom -- but he's reading his mail somewhere else.
tom@differentdomain.com         tom@acme-company.com
@differentdomain.com            error:nouser Sorry, no such user.
```

Beginning at the top, you see three email addresses all belonging to *@somedomain.com*. Below those, you see a so-called *catchall rule*: if someone mistypes an email address to *@somedomain.com*, the email is forwarded to Harry (*hflynn*) instead of being returned to sender with a "no such user" error message.

Then you see the second Tom who has an email account on your server. The second Tom and the previous Tom have different local user accounts, so this does not introduce a problem. The email domain *someotherdomain.com* has a catch-all rule as well.

Then a third Tom enters the scene. Even though your mail server handles his email address, *tom@differentdomain.com*, he also has another email account at work, (*@acme-company.com*) and he likes to read all his mail there. After his entry is a *@differentcompany.com* catchall resulting in an error message. If someone misspells the local part of the email address, the email message is returned and the sender is notified.

Once you have created a *virtusertable* entry such as this one, you need to use the *makemap* command as follows to create a database file that Sendmail can read:

```
makemap hash virtusertable < virtusertable
```

Catchall Rules

When operating with virtual domains, you should have a catchall rule for each domain. If not, Sendmail will try to find a local user that will match the local part of the (wrong) email address. If *someotherdomain.com* did not have a catchall rule, an email sent to the nonexistent virtual address *mick@someotherdomain.com* could end up at a local user named *mick* even though he has nothing to do with *someotherdomain.com*.

Checking Virtual Users

Once you have created virtual users, check them by by entering Sendmail's test mode. Test mode is an interactive shell run by Sendmail that allows you confirm your settings. If you have the following */etc/mail/local-host-names* file:

```
somedomain.com
someotherdomain.com
differentdomain.com
```

the following example of an interactive session confirms your virtual users and virtual user mappings:

```
# sendmail -bt
ADDRESS TEST MODE (ruleset 3 NOT automatically invoked)
Enter <ruleset> <address>
/map virtuser tom@somedomain.com
map_lookup: virtuser (tom@somedomain.com) returns tjohnson (0)
/map virtuser tom@someotherdomain.com
map_lookup: virtuser (tom@someotherdomain.com) returns tgoldman (0)
/map virtuser tom@differentdomain.com
map_lookup: virtuser (tom@differentdomain.com) returns tom@acme-company.com
(0)
/quit
```

Email Aliases

Aliasing is different from using and mapping virtual users. On your mail server, a file named */etc/mail/aliases* (or simply */etc/aliases*) exists. On each line you will see the alias and the real address, separated by a colon and a tab. What is called the real address may be a new alias or an email address somewhere else. Consider this */etc/mail/aliases* file:

```
MAILER-DAEMON:  postmaster
postmaster:     root
john.smith:     jsmith
jack.smith:     jack@acme-company.com
custsupp:       tom,dick,harry
```

Whenever changes are made to the *aliases* file, you must run the *newaliases* command to convert the contents of the text file into a database format that Sendmail will recognize. Once you do this, Sendmail will recognize your changes.

The contents of the aliases file

The MAILER-DAEMON address shown in the preceding example is used as a sender address whenever the mail server needs to communicate with someone, such as when receiving an email message to a nonexistent user. Quite a few people actually respond to this automated message asking what to do.

The postmaster address is an address required by the email RFCs. All email domains must have a *postmaster* account, which should be processed regularly.

The entry of john.smith is an alias for the person using the user account *jsmith*. John's brother, Jack, also has an email account here, but he reads his email at work, so his entry forwards *jack.smith*'s email to *jack@acme-company.com*.

The fourth entry is somewhat more complex. The alias custsupp is translated into three different local user accounts, separated by commas. It is important to note that forwarding to more than one address is allowed only in the *aliases* file, not the *virtusertable* file. If you want all your customers to contact your team (Tom, Dick, and Harry) via the common email account *customer-support@isp.com*, you need to include one entry in the *virtusertable* file:

```
# /etc/mail/virtusertable
customer-support@isp.com       custsupp
```

and one in the *aliases* file:

```
# /etc/mail/aliases
custsupp:                      tom,dick,harry
```

To verify that Sendmail got your aliases correct, enter test mode again:

```
# sendmail -bt
ADDRESS TEST MODE (ruleset 3 NOT automatically invoked)
Enter <ruleset> <address>
/map aliases postmaster
map_lookup: aliases (postmaster) returns root (0)
/quit
```

Reversing virtual user accounts

If you or your users run scheduled jobs that report results by sending an email message or if someone uses an email client installed on the mail server (e.g., Pine, Mutt, or Gnus), the email will show the local username as the sender address. Suppose John Smith, with *jsmith* as his user account name, doesn't want *jsmith@somedomain.com* to be exposed. Rather, he wants his aliased address *john.smith@somedomain.com* to appear to recipients instead.

This request is actually quite easy to fulfill with Sendmail, as long as you have a relatively new version (e.g., Sendmail 8.10). However, this feature may not be enabled in your configuration. To enable it, use the *m4* utility. As long as you have a fairly new version of the software, it is a simple task involving the creation of a *genericstable* file.

If you have the following lines in your *sendmail.mc* file, reverse aliasing is already enabled. If not, you need to add them. Remember the backtick and apostrophe (`` ` ` ``). Otherwise, your entry will result in an error when *m4* runs.

```
FEATURE(`genericstable', `hash -o /etc/mail/genericstable.db')dnl
GENERICS_DOMAIN_FILE(`/etc/mail/generics-domains')dnl
```

After adding these lines, you need to build the *sendmail.cf* file again. It's a good idea to back up your existing *sendmail.cf* file and perhaps build the new one in a different directory:

```
m4 sendmail.mc > sendmail.cf
```

Then copy the new file to the appropriate directory (e.g., */etc/mail*) and reload Sendmail.

The genericstable file

For the *genericstable* file, you need to include the domains that you will map from; under normal circumstances this is the fully qualified name of the host. The */etc/mail/genericstable* file will be a mirror of the *virtusertable* file, so that the local account is on the left side and the alias is on the right side. Following is a *genericstable* file that matches the *virtusertable* we created earlier:

```
# Tom, Dick, and Harry all have local user accounts
tjohnson                    tom@somedomain.com
dsmith                      dick@somedomain.com
hflynn                      harry@somedomain.com
# the other tom
tgoldman                    tom@someotherdomain.com
```

The *genericstable* file must be converted to a database file so that Sendmail can read it. To do this, as usual, enter a *makemap* command:

```
# makemap hash genericstable < genericstable
```

The Sendmail test mode command for verifying the reverse virtual user mapping is:

```
/map generic [username]
```

used as follows:

```
# sendmail -bt
ADDRESS TEST MODE (ruleset 3 NOT automatically invoked)
Enter <ruleset> <address>
/map generics tjohnson
map_lookup: generics (tjohnson) returns tom@somedomain.com (0)
/quit
```

On the Exam

You are expected to know the difference between the *virtusertable* and the *genericstable* files. Be able to explain each file's function. Make sure that you know how each file is formatted as well.

Bastion Host Sendmail Server

A bastion host is a system that can be accessed from a public network, such as the Internet. It is often advisable to offer such an external server to handle all incoming email. Sometimes, this server will also process outgoing mail, if you are concerned about forwarding viruses, worms, and other problems. Your bastion host Sendmail server may also perform spam filtering and/or virus control to help keep viruses outside of your network.

A bastion host must be configured with the following concerns in mind: First, it must provide provide necessary email services, exactly as defined by the organization you are working for. This seems like an obvious concern, but always make sure that your solution provides all necessary services, as long as the requested service does not cause a security problem in and of itself. Second, your Sendmail bastion server must be configured so that it can withstand attacks. As soon as it goes live, your system will be a target of all kinds of attacks and exploit attempts. While it is not possible to anticipate all attacks, it is best to research ways to "lock down" your system as much as possible.

Locking down the server

First, the bastion host should be protected behind some kind of firewall. Preferably, this firewall should be a separate unit. Using a local solution, such as *iptables*, is also a good idea, but it is no substitute for a separate firewall. When configuring your firewall solutions, consider the following rules:

- Two firewall stances exist: open by default, and closed by default. Firewalls that are open by default allow any traffic. You must then create rules that block the ports, IP addresses, and traffic types that you wish to block. Firewalls that are closed by default will not allow any traffic at all, unless you explicitly allow the port, IP address, and traffic type. Generally, closed by default is preferable, though there is no hard and fast rule.

- Find the most secure way to allow incoming and outgoing email. By definition, a Sendmail bastion host should be running Sendmail (e.g., port 25). However, many administrators also enable POP-3 (port 110) and IMAP (port 143). Remember, also, that SMTP, POP-3, and IMAP servers all open up ports above 1024 to communicate with clients and other servers. Create rules accordingly.

- Also available are SSL-enabled SMTP (port 25, but some firewalls may reject encrypted packets), POP-3 (995), and IMAP (993). Enable these ports only if you are using them.

Next, "harden" the operating system itself. The topic of operating system hardening is the subject of entire books. Following is a brief list of hardening steps that will help you not only pass the LPI Exam, but also protect your live servers:

Disable all unnecessary services.
    If you are creating a Sendmail bastion host, this server should be offering only the SMTP service or an SSL-enabled SMTP service. Still, many people need to administer their servers remotely, so they use SSH on their systems. Additional services, such as a web server and—according to purists—POP and IMAP servers should be disabled.

Configure all running services for security.

If you must provide additional services on your bastion host, secure them as much as possible. If you plan on using SSH or VNC to administer the systems remotely, use firewall rules and internal configuration files (e.g., */etc/ssh/sshd_config*) to allow connections only from certain IP addresses, for example. Although it is possible to spoof IP addresses, such steps will help reduce the likelihood of successful attacks. Additional configuration options exist for almost any service. Use them. If you are using SSH, for example, use public-key encryption for authentication. This sounds like a basic idea, but you will be surprised at how few people actually do.

In this brief discussion, you have learned about how important it is to lock down the operating system. The Sendmail daemon needs special attention as well.

Configuring Sendmail for a bastion host

First, the Sendmail server needs to be secured from unauthorized relaying. Second, if you have internal mail servers, this server must act as a smart host for them. Under normal circumstances, only one or two IP addresses should be allowed to use this server as a smart host relay.

Third, you need to tell the external MTA where it should forward your company's email and which domains your server handles. This is done in the file */etc/mail/mailertable*. The format should be familiar; what to look for is on the left side and what to do with it is on the right side. If we continue using our three domains from before, the file will appear as follows:

```
somedomain.com          smtp:[192.168.200.3]
someotherdomain.com     smtp:[192.168.200.3]
differentdomain.com     smtp:[192.168.200.3]
```

In this example, your internal mail server has, as you probably guessed, the IP address 192.168.200.3.

Remember to convert the file to the Sendmail-readable database format with the following command:

```
makemap hash mailertable < mailertable
```

Or you can use the update scripts supplied in the */etc/mail* directory.

You may want to check the *mailertable* configuration as well:

```
# sendmail -bt
ADDRESS TEST MODE (ruleset 3 NOT automatically invoked)
Enter <ruleset> <address>
/map mailertable somedomain.com
map_lookup: mailertable (somedomain.com) returns smtp:[192.168.200.3] (0)
/quit
```

Managing Mail Traffic

You have already learned about how to verify Sendmail's configuration through the *-bt* options, a key skill in managing mail traffic. Additional considerations include:

Monitoring mail

It is not enough to know how Sendmail works to pass the LPI exam. You also need to know how to review incoming and outgoing mail by reading log files.

Filtering and sorting mail

You must know how to identify content in email messages and then filter and sort mail accordingly. You will need to know how to identify the content of the Subject, From, and To fields, as well as the content of the message body, and then configure your system to process the messages accordingly. There are many ways to filter and sort mail. This chapter focuses on Procmail.

A brief discussion follows on each of these topics.

Monitoring Mail

The most common ways to monitor Sendmail messages are:

Checking the Sendmail log

The */var/log/maillog* file, on many systems that use Sendmail, contains messages specific to Sendmail, as determined by the *sendmail.cf* file. Sendmail uses the syslog facility to generate messages. Specifically, the mail syslog level is often used to send messages to the *maillog* file.

Reviewing the /var/log/messages file

Depending upon the system, some or all Sendmail messages are sent to the */var/log/messages* file.

Each Sendmail log entry has the following format:

```
date, host, sendmail_function[pid]: <qid>: occurrence=message
```

Table 36-4 contains a brief discussion of each field in the mail log.

Table 36-4. Sendmail log

Entry	Description
date	The month, day, and time (according to system time) of the event. No year is given.
host	The host that generated the message. Useful for remote logging. If it is a local message, the host is often given as the hostname or as localhost.localdomain if the hostname has not been configured.
sendmail_function	The particular Sendmail process that generated the message.
pid	The process ID that generated the message.
qid	The ID number of the message in the queue or process assigned by Sendmail.
occurrence=message	The occurrence and associated message.

Various occurrences exist. Following are some of the more common:

Relay

Shows the system that received and sent the relayed message, in *username@domainname* format and with a *domainname* of localhost when the messages is relayed by the local system.

Delay

The total amount of time the message was delayed. Specifically, the difference between when the message was received and when it was delivered. The format for messages delayed less than a day is *HH*:*MM*:*SS*. For messages longer than a day, the format is *days*+*HH*:*MM*:*SS*.

Nrcpts

The number of recipients, after aliasing.

From

The sender of the message, in the format *from=address*. The sender value can be a user-based email address, a message from the postmaster, or a Sendmail-specific value if the message has bounced.

Pri

The priority of the message assigned by Sendmail. The message priority decreases after each resend, but the priority value given in this message is the initial one.

Size

The size of the message, in bytes.

Additional entries exist, but these are the most important ones for the LPI Exam. For example, the following entry shows that a relay has occurred for the root account on the local system:

```
jacob sendmail[15232]: jBKOllQKO15232: from=root, size=0, class=0, nrcpts=0,
relay=root@localhost
```

Log Configuration

Try opening */etc/syslog.conf* and review the settings. You do not have to use the default settings on your system. You can, for example, set syslog to send all mail messages to a remote system, which is particularly useful if you have a Sendmail bastion host or if you want a backup log for security reasons. This *syslog.conf* entry sends all mail messages to the system *jacob.stangernet.com*:

```
mail.*    @jacob.stangernet.com
```

In many cases, you may want the `mail.alert` syslog level of logging, which will relate all alert-level Sendmail information. These messages include when Sendmail starts or restarts, as well as conditions that are considered fatal including failed processes and messages that are not sent due to a system failure:

```
mail.alert        @jacob.stangernet.com
```

Objective 3: Managing Mail Traffic

Filtering and sorting mail can be accomplished in many ways on a Linux system. Solutions include:

SpamAssassin (*http://spamassassin.apache.org*)
MIMEdefang (*http://www.mimedefang.org*)
Procmail (*http://www.procmail.org*)

Procmail is one of the older solutions but is explicitly covered by the LPI Exam. Therefore, it warrants the discussion in this section.

Filtering and Sorting Techniques

Before you learn more about Procmail, it is important to understand the basics of how mail is filtered and sorted. Filtering mail requires the application to read messages and determine the parameters given in Table 36-5.

Table 36-5. Filtering techniques

Parameter	Description
The From field	Information concerning the host and user who sent the message
The To field	Information concerning the host and user intended to receive the message
The Subject field	The field that endusers enter to describe the message
Message body contents	Can include text as well as indicators of the document format (e.g., ASCII or HTML)

Once the filtering parameters are determined, messages can be sorted and processed in many ways, including:

- Forwarding the message to a remote host
- Issuing an autoreply, a useful option for messages indicating a prolonged absence (e.g., a vacation)
- Storing the message into a custom directory
- Deleting the message, often by sending the file to the */dev/null* file

You will need to know how to identify the contents of Subject, From, and To fields, as well as the content of the message body, then configure your system to filter and sort the messages accordingly. As mentioned earlier, this chapter focuses on doing these things with Procmail, which is the filtering system on the LPI test.

Using Procmail

Procmail is an MDA that allows clients to filter mail and customize delivery. Using rule sets called *recipes*, you can configure Procmail to receive, sort, and react to all mail you receive.

Procmail files

Table 36-6 provides a quick list of the binary files and configuration files used in Procmail. Familiarize yourself with each of these files for the LPI Exam.

Table 36-6. Procmail files

File	Description
/usr/bin/procmail	The binary for the Procmail service.
~/.procmailrc	The configuration file located in each user's home directory. Can contain recipes.
~/.procmail	The directory that contains user-specific procmail files. Such files can include the log files (such as a file named *log*) that can inform you about problems, and recipe files (a file you use to create a notification message when you are on vacation). This directory can also be named *.Procmail* or *Procmail*, a nonhidden directory. It can also contain dedicated files that specify recipes.

Table 36-6. Procmail files (continued)

File	Description
/etc/procmailrc	The systemwide Procmail configuration file. User-based .procmailrc files (if present) take precedence, unless they are overridden by the /etc/procmail file.
.forward	Determines which messages will be forwarded to another account.

 The locations of some of these files may vary from one distribution to another. Some of the directory names may have changed, also, because it is possible to specify custom values in the /etc/procmailrc file.

Creating recipes in Procmail

To configure Procmail, you must enter instructions called *recipes*. You can place a recipe either in the *.procmailrc* file or in a dedicated files, usually in the *.procmail* directory. If you create a dedicated file, you must refer to it in the *.procmailrc* file.

The syntax for creating a recipe is comprised of three parts:

```
beginning
condition
action
```

The *beginning* is a special character sequence, usually :0 on a line by itself, that informs *Procmail* that a recipe begins immediately below. The *condition* specifies text matches or other conditions that the mail message must meet before it is processed. There can be multiple conditions in this section. The final *action* section contains processing directives that specify what actions to take (e.g., forwarding or deleting the mail) once the conditions have been met.

On the Exam

Make sure that you know how to create and read a simple Procmail recipe.

Table 36-7 contains a list of common Procmail parameters used to create recipes.

Table 36-7. Procmail parameters

Parameter	Description
#	Starts a comment. Using comments is highly recommended for troubleshooting.
:0	Informs Procmail that a recipe is beginning. Specifying :0 c makes a copy of the matching message, meaning that the message will go on to appear in your inbox as well as be processed by the recipe.
*	Specifies a new condition. Placed at the front of a line in a recipe.
.*	Specifies the "everything" wildcard. This is never used at the start of a line and therefore can be distinguished from the previous item. For example, Subject:.*Kenya.* in a *condition* matches any message with *Kenya* in the Subject field.

Table 36-7. Procmail parameters (continued)

Parameter	Description
^	Instructs Procmail to look for the character or parameter that follows at the beginning of a line
!	In an action, forwards the message to the address you specify. For example, the following line: ! *andy@oreilly.com* sends the message to the user named *andy* at the *oreilly.com* domain.
Whc: filename. lock	Specifies a lock file for the particular message. Useful to avoid race conditions, where another Procmail process might be running the same recipe.

Sample Procmail recipes. Several recipe examples follow. The first is a rather simple example that deletes email sent from an objectionable user:

```
:0
 * ^From: knownspammer@mail.badspammers.com
/dev/null
```

The same thing can be done to an entire domain, by specifying all users in that domain in the condition:

```
:0
* ^From: .*@badspammers.com
/dev/null
```

The following example matches any email with the character sequence beegees in the Subject field and deletes it:

```
# Spam filter
:0
* ^Subject:.*beegees
/dev/null
```

Notice how the ^ character is used to denote the Subject field; a field name is always at the beginning of a line in the email header. The colon (:) is treated as a simple character, appearing like any other character in a line.

This third simple example shows how to forward an email message from a specific user email account:

```
:0
 * ^From: elvis@heaven.com
 ! elvisfan@comcast.net
```

The following example shows how to automatically reply to almost all messages sent to the current user. The only exceptions are those messages sent by email daemons and those that might cause an infinite loop because they appear to originate from the current user. The recipe contains a few additional parameters that will be explained after the example:

```
:0 Whc: autoresponder.lock
      * $^To:.*\<$\LOGNAME\>
      * !^FROM_DAEMON
      * !^X-Loop: username@udel.edu
           | formail -rD 8192 out.cache
             :0 ehc
```

```
              | (formail -rA"Precedence: junk" A"X-Loop: your@own.mail.
 address" ;
                       echo "I am currently out of the office."; \
                       echo "I will return Thursday, September 13th."; \
                       echo "-- "; cat $HOME/.signature_line.txt \
                       ) | $SENDMAIL -oi -t
```

The recipe has two parts. The first part uses the standard Procmail commands to
process the message, negating certain conditions with *! to exclude messages that
shouldn't be responded to. The *formail* command in this first part creates a file
called *out.cache* that contains all mails sent. The *-r* option to *formail* strips unnecessary headers from the mail message, while the *-D* option limits the length of the
message, to save on system resources and network bandwidth.

The second part of the message begins at the :0 ehc line. This line directs the
recipe to reply to messages even if they are not found in the *out.cache* file. The
directive portion of the message contains the actual autoresponder message,
complete with an email signature file. The backslashes are necessary for line
continuation. The *-oi* option to Sendmail causes Sendmail not to send a message
created from standard input, even if a single period is at the end. The *-t* option
removes all recipients from the message headers.

It is possible to create very sophisticated sorting and filtering recipes using Procmail. The information in this section should help you pursue the knowledge you
need to pass the LPI Exam. For more information, go to the Procmail web page at
http://www.procmail.org. The following URL contains many suggestions compiled
by the Procmail project:

> *http://pm-doc.sourceforge.net/pm-tips-body.html#procmail_flags*

It is an outstanding example of how open source projects are capable of documenting all features of an application.

Monitoring and troubleshooting Procmail

It is not enough to know how to create and use recipes. You must also be able to
determine the cause of problems. This section includes examples of ways to
monitor and troubleshoot Procmail.

As usual, start by consulting the log files. In many systems, the log file is placed
off of the *~/.procmail* directory. You can use the *tail* command with the *-f* option
to view new log entries:

```
tail -f $HOME/.procmail/pmlog
```

You may have to change the name of the log file to monitor, however. Look in the
/etc/procmailrc or *~/.procmailrc* file to determine whether a log file is being generated. If you wish to view more than the last 10 lines, use the *-n* command:

```
tail -n 20 -f ~/.procmail/pmlog
```

You can also view the */var/log/messages* file to determine whether errors have
occurred. Finally, consider the following when troubleshooting a *Procmail*
problem:

- Make sure variables are correct.
- Make sure that directories are correct.
- Check filenames (e.g., *rc.away* rather than *rc.vacation*).

To test your settings, set Procmail's VERBOSE variable, create a file of recipes and another file of test mail messages, and run the *procmail* command in a manner such as:

```
% procmail $HOME/pm/procmail_test.rc < $HOME/tmp/my_test_mail.txt
```

Objective 1: Configuring Mailing Lists

As with MTAs, mailing list servers are a very large topic. Fortunately, the LPI focuses just on the Majordomo mailing list server, found at *http://www.greatcircle.com/majordomo*. Even more fortunate for us, the LPI assigns a relatively small value to this topic.

Still, it is essential for you to know how to install and configure the revised version of Majordomo, called Majordomo 2, for various reasons. First, mailing lists are still very popular and are expected in many environments. You should know how to provide them.

Majordomo is essentially an add-on application to an MTA. It can be used with any MTA (such as Sendmail or Qmail) to manage lists of email applications. You can configure Majordomo to receive commands from potential users, who then direct Majordomo to add them to a list or drop them from a list. Majordomo does not deliver mail; that's the job of the MTA. Majordomo essentially acts as a mediator between users, the MTA, and the MDA.

Users generate postings often based on a particular discussion, which is often called a *thread*. This thread can be made public or private, depending upon the wishes of the administrator. The Majordomo administrator can configure Majordomo using various means, including a command-line interface, a web interface, or even by sending email messages to the Majordomo server.

Majordomo servers often have a moderator. This person can be the same person as the administrator, but does not have to be. The moderator is responsible for determining the content posted on the site. The moderator can also add and remove users.

Majordomo provides the following services, if properly configured:

User addition and deletion
> Users can petition to join a list simply by sending an email to the server. The user will be automatically added. The server will then send the user a confirmation message that the user must reply to in order to be added to the list. For more secure situations, Majordomo can be configured to defer the user request and forward the join message to the Majordomo administrator, who can decide whether to add that user.

List moderation
> Many times, lists are completely open and unedited. Any user is welcome to post to it at any time. However, organizations and businesses might require

moderated lists for various reasons. Messages, in these cases, are sent first to the moderator, who can then edit or drop various messages. The moderator can also drop users as necessary.

Message digests

Users often do not want to read each individual message on a thread. They would prefer receiving the entire thread after a period of time (e.g., a day or a week). Recipients will receive one large email, rather than a series of short emails.

Subscription confirmation

Whenever a user requests to be added to a list, a confirmation message is sent out to that user's email address. This step is necessary to avoid a malicious user subscribing a person to a list who does not want to belong to it. When a user unsubscribes from a list, a confirmation is also sent. The user will often have to confirm the unsubscribe request, to avoid a malicious user spoofing an unsubscribe command.

Instruction and reminder messages

Majordomo servers can be configured to send instruction messages to end users. Such messages can include instructions on how to unsubscribe. They can also include information concerning the expected content of messages sent to the Majordomo server. Also, Majordomo servers can be configured to send out reminder messages at specified times (usually the first day of the month) to remind users about their participation in the list.

Configuring Majordomo

The steps for configuring Majordomo are not particularly difficult. It is important, though, to understand Majordomo's essential components. Table 36-8 contains a list of essential Majordomo files.

Table 36-8. Majordomo configuration files, commands, and resources

Resource	Description
majordomo.cf	The Majordomo configuration file. Usually found in the */etc* directory.
create	Used to create a list name.
Archive directory	Location where list server configuration files are kept.
List server file	A file with the same name as the list. This file contains configuration information for the specific mailing list group.

When using Majordomo, two types of passwords exist:

Administrative

Required of a user who has the privileges to change the characteristics of an entire group (e.g., to enable moderation or to enable user-based passwords for submissions).

User

A user might be required to issue a password in order to change preferences (e.g., to request summary messages of group postings, called digests).

It is important to not confuse these two passwords. Following are the steps to take when preparing Majordomo.

Preparing Sendmail

The first step to take when configuring Majordomo is to set an alias for the Majordomo administrator. To do this, edit the */etc/aliases* file so that it has the following lines. This chapter assumes that you are using Sendmail, but you can use any MTA you wish:

```
majordomo-owner: domo_admin_account_name
owner-majordomo: domo_admin_account_name
majordomo:       "|/usr/local/majordomo-1.94.5/wrapper majordomo"
```

where *domo_admin_account_name* is the username of the person you wish to administer Majordomo. Now, when users send an email to the moderator account at *majordomo-owner@yourdomain.com*, those messages will go to the user account of the person administering the system. The third line has Sendmail use the Majordomo aliases file, to ensure proper routing of local messages.

 Pay close attention to the aliases file. You will have to update it regularly to include additional entries specific to the names of the groups you wish to add.

The next step to take is to edit the *sendmail.cf* file (often located in the */etc/mail* directory). This file needs to have the following changes made to it:

1. Add the following line:

   ```
   OA/usr/local/majordomo-1.94.5/majordomo.aliases
   ```

   This line creates a second alias file, which is necessary for Majordomo to process mail. Once you have done this, restart Sendmail.

2. Configure Sendmail to make Majordomo a trusted user, by adding the following line to the *sendmail.cf* file:

   ```
   Tmajordomo
   ```

   This line allows Majordomo to properly masquerade users as it resends files.

3. Determine whether Sendmail is using the *smrsh* environment. If so, you have to create a symbolic link from the */etc/smrsh* directory to the the Majordomo wrapper program (which often resides in the */usr/local/majordomo-1.94.5* directory). In this case, enter:

   ```
   ln -s /usr/local/majordomo-1.94.5/wrapper /etc/smrsh/wrapper
   ```

4. Verify that Sendmail security measures (those that concern forwarding and some spam-specific settings) do not conflict with Majordomo. If they do, you will experience possibly hours of frustration trying to figure out why a perfectly configured Majordomo list server isn't working.

Installing Majordomo

Once you have created the proper Sendmail environment, you can install Majordomo. You have various options available to you. Debian-based systems can use *apt-get*, *dpkg*, and Synaptic. Red Hat and other systems can use various RPM handlers, while Novell systems can use YaST or RPM. The source tarballs are available at *http://www.greatcircle.com/majordomo*.

Once you have installed Majordomo, you can begin configuring lists.

Creating Majordomo lists

To configure a Majordomo list, you simply need to create a new file that will be populated to specify users who wish to subscribe to the list. To create the file, issue the following command as *root*:

```
touch /usr/local/majordomo-1.94.5/lists/telecaster
```

Then, still as *root*, add the proper alias to */etc/aliases*:

```
owner-telecaster:     domo_admin_account_name
telecaster-request:   "|/usr/local/majordomo-1.94.5/wrapper request-answer
  telecaster"
telecaster-approval: domo_admin_account_name
```

You have just added a list. Users can now send messages to your list server to subscribe to the list. Notice that you had to add aliases for requests, approval, and the list owner. Failure to add these aliases will cause these group entries to behave improperly or not work at all.

Using the create command. Actually, you do not have to edit the files in the previous section manually. You can use the *create* command, which takes the following syntax:

```
create listname password
```

where *password* is the administrative password used to administer Majordomo. Thus, to add the group named *telecaster*, you would issue the following command:

```
create telecaster password
```

Customizing the list. Once a list has been created, you can view it using a command such as *less* or edit it using a text editor, using a web configuration interface, or via email messages. By editing the configuration file, you can do the following:

- Enable or disable moderation
- Require users to provide passwords for a moderated list
- Set the administrator password for the moderator
- Enable or disable message digesting

To add moderation to the Majordomo list, for example, add the following to the list's configuration file:

```
moderate = yes
```

Once you have enabled moderation in the configuration file, use the *newconfig* command to enable digesting for a particular list using the following syntax:

```
newconfig list_name-digest password
```

To create digests for the *telecaster* Majordomo group, you would issue the following command:

```
newconfig telecaster-digest password
```

End users can then ask for digests using the following syntax:

```
subscribe [listname]-digest
```

For example, if users wish to receive a digest for the *telecaster* list, they would place the following in the body of their email messages:

```
subscribe telecaster-digest
```

The LPI Objectives do not discuss further configuration of the Majordomo list server.

Testing the Implementation and Monitoring Problems

Just like with network troubleshooting, you should start small when testing your Majordomo implementation. First, see if the server is providing all of the lists you have configured. To do this, enter the following command:

```
echo lists | mail majordomo
```

This command should send a list of the server's working Majordomo lists to your email account. You can use a similar command to receive help messages from your Majordomo server:

```
echo help | mail majordomo
```

The preceding command helps you confirm that your Majordomo installation is working as expected.

You can subscribe yourself to the list by sending an email message to the Majordomo server with the following line in the body (not the subject line) of the message:

```
subscribe telecaster
```

Review the subscribe reply for any problems, and send another message to confirm that you have subscribed to this list.

Once you are fully subscribed, send a few test messages from separate user accounts and client systems to determine whether the server is processing messages from all subscribers and systems. You can then unsubscribe from the list by placing the following in the body of an email message:

```
unsubscribe telecaster
```

Review the unsubscribe reply for any problems, and confirm the fact that you have unsubscribed.

To test the contents of the information file you are using, send an email to the Majordomo server with the following contents in the body:

```
info listname
```

The server will then send you a copy of the list's information page. If you wish to obtain a list of current users of a list, place the following in the body of an email message and send it to the Majordomo server:

    who *your_list_name*

where *your_list_name* is the name of the group (e.g., *telecaster*).

Finally, consider the following tips and tricks:

- Check the configuration file for any potential problems. Several years ago, several RPM-based versions of Majordomo contained the following line in the *majordomo.cf* file:

        $whereami = `hostname`

- The `hostname` parameter stopped Majordomo from issuing messages. A simple change of the file to specify the correct hostname directly resolved the problem. This and other "problems" in the configuration file can cause an otherwise perfect server to fail.

- Review the */var/log/messages* file and any log files related to Majordomo that reside in the */var/log* directory. You will find that Majordomo's messages are relatively clear.

- Verify that permissions are correct. Many times, directories and files should be marked executable, but are not. Keep that in mind when reading Majordomo's error messages.

- Check for problems in the alias file.

- Review your MTA settings to ensure that they are not causing the problem.

- Use the *strace* command when sending messages to the Majordomo server. It may help you understand why the problem is happening.

- Check for firewall settings that may be blocking messages.

Objective 4: Serving News

Knowledge about how to configure a news server is required for the LPI Level 2 Exams. However, news servers receive even less emphasis than mailing lists. The LPI specifically mentions the InterNet News service (INN), which is offered by the Internet Systems Consortium (ISC) at *http://www.isc.org*. INN is currently in its second version, INN 2. Following is the essential information you need to know about this topic.

Overview

The INN daemon uses the Network News Transfer Protocol (NNTP), which operates on TCP port 143 by default. The protocol was first outlined in RFC 977. The name of the INN program that serves news is *innd*, the INN daemon. You can read more about INN at *http://www.isc.org/index.pl?/sw/inn*.

News servers can operate locally, meaning that they can provide access to messages posted by users on the LAN. It is also possible to connect an NNTP server to a newsfeed, which makes it possible for the server to receive messages from all of the Usenet newsgroups on the Internet. Thousands of newsgroups exist. They are organized hierarchically. Top-level discussion categories include:

alt
> By far the largest group, which includes an extremely wide variety of topics, from *alt.fan.letterman* to *alt.os.linux* to *alt.music.led-zeppelin*.

comp
> This category includes such computing-related groups as *comp.lang.c*, *comp.lang.java*, and *comp.software.testing*. The *comp.os.linux* series of groups is especially relevant to readers of this book.

humanities
> Groups in this category include *humanities.lit.authors* and *humanities.classics*.

sci
> Includes *sci.physics* and other science-related entries.

This type of access, though, often requires the ISP to pay a fee, and some ISPs have begun closing down newsgroup and Usenet access. As a result, many INN administrators use local-only configuration, which does not support Internet-based Usenet submissions.

In order to create your own NNTP group, you need an NNTP daemon such as *innd*. Table 36-9 describes some of the files and directories used by *innd*.

Table 36-9. Files and directories used by innd

File	Description
innd	The INN daemon.
ctlinnd	Used to add and delete groups, allow and disallow NNTP clients, enable or reject remote newsfeeds, and determine the status of a news server. Also used to cancel postings to a list, as well as to stop and start INN.
/etc/news/inn.conf	The primary INN configuration file.
/etc/news/readers.conf	Used to control which users and hosts access the INN server.
/etc/news/newsfeeds	Determines how postings on your system are distributed on the server and to other peers.
/etc/news/incoming.conf	Contains the names of the hosts that are allowed to connect to your system and provide it with newsgroup postings. Controls what you receive from upstream servers.
/etc/news/expire.ctl	Used to determine when articles posted on your INN server expire.
/etc/news/control.ctl	Determines how INN handles control messages sent from upstream INN servers. Control messages can include notifications of new groups.
/etc/news/innwatch.ctl	Determines what INN does to monitor its performance.
/var/log/news	A directory containing all of the INN log files, including *err.log* (critical errors), *news.notice* (daemon startup and shutdown), and *errlog* (errors relating to the posting of messages).

NNTP is designed to create a decentralized communications system. It is possible for an INN server to participate in downstream feeds, which means that it receives newsgroup lists and commands from other servers. An INN server can also be an upstream server, which means that it feeds information to other servers that reside beneath it. As decentralized as NNTP is, it is important to understand that a failure of an upstream server can cause your INN server to not receive updated information.

NNTP clients include:

Lynx (*http://lynx.isc.org*)
trn (*http://trn.sourceforge.net*)
Mozilla Mail (*http://www.mozilla.org*)
Netscape Mail (*http:/www.netscape.com*)
newsx (*http://www.kvaleberg.com/newsx.html*)
Outlook and Outlook Express (*http://www.microsoft.com*)

Installing INN

You can install INN in various ways. Many precompiled packages do not have certain useful features compiled into the binaries. If this is the case, search carefully for configuration files that may override such limitations. If you cannot find these, then you will most likely have to configure from source. You can obtain the source file from the ISC.

Configuring INN

Once you have installed INN, you can add users using the *ctlinnd* command. The syntax for adding users is as follows:

```
ctlinnd newgroup new_group_name rest group_creator
```

The *newgroup* command informs *ctlinnd* that you are creating a new group. You then specify the new group name and then the *rest* value, which indicates whether you wish to allow users to access this group. Specify y to allow access or n to disallow access. You then specify the name of the creator.

For example, supposing you wished to create a local INN group named *research*. You would issue the following command:

```
ctlinnd newgroup research y james
```

Once you issue the command, users can access the research NNTP user group on this server. In some cases, you may want to specify n as the *rest* value, because you may want to further configure INN before you actually start serving users.

The *readers.conf* file determines how INN handles control messages sent out to control news servers across the Internet. Two configuration groups exist for the *readers.conf* file:

auth
    Determines the users and hosts that are allowed to authenticate with the server

access
    Determines the newsgroups that authorized users can access

As you configure the *readers.conf* file, remember that you have to create entries for each group. Following is an example of a very simple *readers.conf* entry that opens full access to all groups on the server:

```
auth "pub" {
        hosts: *
        default: ""
}

        newsgroups: *
access "full" {
}
```

The auth entry in this example contains two subheadings: hosts and default. The hosts entry specifies the hosts that are allowed to authenticate with the system. In this case, the wildcard * is used. Therefore, any host can access the server. The value for default has empty quotation marks as its value, which means that any user can access INN on the host, because no name is given for the default username.

 In most Linux systems, INN does not allow remote access by default.

Each time you make a change to these configuration files, stop and restart *innd*. You can do this in various ways, though the most universal method is to use the *ctlinnd* command. To stop INN, issue the following command:

```
ctlinnd throttle reason
```

where *reason* is a particular reason for shutting down the server. To start INN again, issue the following command:

```
ctlinnd go reason
```

where *reason* is the exact same word you used when you shut down INN. If you do not specify a reason, you will still be able to start the server again, but the *reason* option allows you to restart only those processes that will be affected by your change.

In some systems, you will find scripts in the */etc/init.d* or */etc/rc.d/init.d* directories that allow you to stop and restart INN. Remember, though, that the LPI test generally looks for the most universal solutions, not those that are specific to a particular distribution.

Customizing newsgroups

The following example is a more ambitious entry in *readers.conf*:

```
auth "public" {
    hosts: "*"
    default: ""
}

auth "localnet" {
    hosts: "10.45.99.0/24"
    default: ""
}
```

```
auth "localhost" {
    hosts: "localhost, 127.0.0.1, stdin"
    default: ""
}

auth "useraccounts" {
    auth: "ckpasswd -f /etc/news/nntp_passwd"
}
```

These entries make it possible to use the *ckpasswd* application, which ships with INN. This application can check passwords found in a password file, in this case, *nntp_passwd*. The *nntp_passwd* file is generated using the *htpasswd* command, as follows:

```
htpasswd -c /etc/news/nntp_passwd username
```

where *username* is the first INN user you wish to create in the file. You can then add more users with commands such as the following:

```
htpasswd /etc/news/nntp_passwd sandi
```

You can create as many users as you wish using the *htpasswd* command.

 You also use the *htpasswd* command to change the passwords of users you have already created.

You are not finished editing the */etc/news/readers.conf* file yet, however. Remember, you must add the access section. This section is something like the following:

```
access "users" {
    users: "sandi,james,jamey,jacob,joseph,joel"
    newsgroups: "*"
    access: RP
}

access "localhost" {
    users: ""
    newsgroups: "*"
    access: RPA
}

access "localnet" {
    users: ""
    newsgroups: "*"
    access: RP
}

access "public" {
    users: ""
    newsgroups: "research.*,alt.comp.research"
    access: RP
}
```

Now, clients accessing your INN server will have to authenticate in order to access your resources. INN will use the *ckpasswd* command to read the */etc/news/ nntp_passwd* file and then authenticate users.

Authentication occurs in cleartext, meaning that any usernames and passwords used can be easily obtained off the network using a packet sniffer such as *tcpdump* or *ethereal*. To thwart password sniffing attacks, it is possible to configure INN to use SSL. Configuring INN for SSL is beyond the scope of the LPI Level 2 Exams, but all you need to do is use the *openssl* command or the *CA.pl* Perl script (which relies on *openssl*) to generate a certificate. You then configure INN to recognize the certificate. The result is SSL protection for your server.

Configuring downstream and upstream clients

To configure downstream access, edit the */etc/news/newsfeeds* file. Entries in this file will receive updates from your server and will become peers. Following is an example of a *newsfeed* entry that forwards Usenet articles through the *innfeed* application that INN uses to update other servers, but does not forward local articles:

```
news.uu.net/uunet\
        :*,!junk,!control*/!research\
        :Tm:innfeed!
```

Given this entry, any internal newsfeed whose name contains research will not be forwarded.

As you read earlier, the */etc/news/incoming.conf* file allows you to determine which systems can connect to yours and provide newsgroup articles. Consider the following entry:

```
peer goodsys.nntp.com {
        hostname: "nntp.com, nntp.com"
    }
```

This allows the *nntp.com* and *nntp.com* systems to provide articles to your system in a newsfeed.

Monitoring newsgroups

When it comes to monitoring INN, consider reviewing log files and configuring the */etc/news/innwatch.ctl* file. Table 36-10 explains the contents of the different log files.

Table 36-10. INN log files

File	Description
errlog	Contains entries relating to processing of messages, including the processing of message digests.
news	For problems relating to mail postings.
news.crit	Records critical errors, such as when essential services fail and when connections are no longer available.
news.err	Reports errors in configuration files.

Table 36-10. INN log files (continued)

File	Description
news.notice	Describes the connections to the INN daemon. Includes local and remote connections. The hostname, time of day, and associated actions are all reported. Includes information concerning received and rejected messages, as well as when the server is stopped and started.
rc.news	Records server stops and restarts.

Using innwatch

News servers can quickly occupy large amounts of disk space and system resources, if many users are configured to use them. After all, more than 14,000 Usenet groups exist. The creators of INN realized that robust management had to rely on more than simply viewing log files. So you can use the *innwatch* command to actively monitor the network host's load average and the amount of free disk space on the host.

If *innwatch* finds that INN is using too many resources, *innwatch* will reduce INN's draw on system resources to the point where it will shut the news server down. *innwatch* reports what it finds in the *innwatch.status* log file.

The */etc/news/innwatch.ctl* file determines the level of supervision performed by the *innwatch* command. Using this file, you can determine how often *innwatch* runs, as well as the system resources it checks.

Conclusion

You now have received a detailed review of what you need to know in regard to Sendmail, Procmail, Majordomo, and INN. You will find that the best thing to do now is to install these daemons and become familiar with the workings of each program. The LPI Exams are designed to test applied knowledge, and the only way you can be sure to do well is to work as closely with the applications and daemons as possible.

37

DNS (Topic 2.207)

This Topic is dedicated to Domain Name System (DNS) servers. DNS is the service responsible for managing the conversion of host and domain names to and from their corresponding IP addresses. The server that does this on Linux and Unix is usually called *named* (pronounced "name-dee," because it stands for "name daemon"). This server is a part of the Berkeley Internet Name Domain (BIND) package used on more than 85% of all DNS servers in the world.

This Topic contains 3 Objectives:

Objective 1: Basic DNS Server Configuration
The candidate should be able to configure BIND to function as a caching-only DNS server. This Objective includes the ability to convert a BIND 4.9 *named.boot* file to the BIND 8.x *named.conf* format and reload the service using *kill* or *ndc*. This Objective also includes configuring logging and options such as directory location for zone files. Weight: 2.

Objective 2: Create and Maintain DNS Zones
The candidate should be able to create a zone file for a forward or reverse zone or root-level server. This Objective includes setting appropriate values for the SOA resource record, NS records, and MX records. Also included are adding hosts with A resource records and adding the zone to the */etc/named. conf* file using the zone statement with appropriate type, file, and masters values. A candidate should also be able to delegate a zone to another DNS server. Weight: 3.

Objective 3: Securing a DNS Server
The candidate should be able to configure BIND to run as a nonroot user and configure BIND to run in a chroot jail. This objective includes configuring DNSSEC statements such as keys to prevent domain spoofing. Also included is the ability to split DNS configuration using the forwarders statement, and specifying a nonstandard version number string in response to queries. Weight: 3.

Objective 1: Basic DNS Server Configuration

The main configuration file for BIND 8.x is */etc/named.conf*. In it you can specify options such as the default directory for *named* files and specify the zones for the *named* entries you are hosting. You generally host two types of *named* files. The first is the database (db) entry for each domain you host. These db entries are typically named either *db.domain.com* or *domain.com.db*, depending on the naming scheme you use. The db entries are the forward DNS entries for your domain. The second type of named file you host is the reverse DNS file, denoted typically by *db. x.x.x.in-addr.arpa*, where *x.x.x* is the subnet you are hosting with its elements reversed. For example, if you host the 208.201.239 subnet, you would have a *db. 239.201.208.in-addr.arpa* reverse DNS file.

It is common for your ISP to manage the reverse DNS on the IP addresses that they have assigned to you, so *in-addr.arpa* entries may not always be necessary.

named.conf

The */etc/named.conf* file is the main configuration file for named. Within the *named.conf* file, you will specify options such as the default directory for named entries and zone entries for individual named files. The following is a sample */etc/ named.conf* file:

```
options {
        directory "/var/named";
};

zone "." {
        type hint;
        file "named.ca"'
};

zone "1.168.192.in-addr.arpa" {
        type master;
        file "db.1.168.192.in-addr.arpa";
};

zone "example.com" {
        type master;
        file "db.example.com";
};

zone "example.net" {
        type slave;
        file "db.example.net";
        masters {
                192.168.0.100;
        };
};
```

The preceding sample */etc/named.conf* has five different types of entries. The first two entries are mandatory configuration options for BIND. The first entry specifies BIND options. In this example, the directory option sets where all named files will be placed. By default, this option is set to */var/named*. Many DNS administrators are accustomed to keeping named files under */etc/named* and therefore change this directory option.

The second entry is a default zone entry to specify what file can be used as a "hint" for where to find root name servers. By default, BIND 8 uses */var/named/named.ca*. This second entry is required, and it is not recommended to edit this entry or file unless necessary.

The third entry in the example is a reverse DNS zone entry. The zone specified is `1.168.192.in-addr.arpa`. The reverse DNS is a primary DNS record, so the type entry is set to `master`. The file with the reverse DNS information is in */var/named/db.1.168.192.in-addr.arpa*, so the `file` option is set to `db.1.168.192.in-addr.arpa`.

The fourth entry in the example is a primary DNS zone entry. The zone specified is `example.com`. Because the entry is a primary DNS entry, the type is set to `master`. The file for the entry is found in */var/named/db.example.com*, so the `file` option is set to `db.example.com`.

The fifth entry in the example is a sample secondary DNS zone entry. The zone specified in the example is `example.net`. Because the entry is a secondary DNS entry, the type is set to `slave`. The file for this secondary entry is found in */var/named/db.example.net*, so the `file` option is set to `db.example.net`. Because this entry is a secondary DNS entry, you must provide the primary DNS server information where the DNS information is retrieved from. In this entry's case, the primary DNS server is 192.168.0.100, so the `masters` option is set to `192.168.0.100`.

Primary DNS

After you have a domain registered with the DNS server you specify as the primary DNS server, you will need to set up your named files by following these steps:

1. Add the corresponding zone to */etc/named.conf*. As a primary entry, your zone entry in */etc/named.conf* will look like this:

```
zone "example.com" {
        type master;
        file "db.example.com";
};
```

2. Edit *db.example.com*. Create a file under */var/named* named *db.example.com*. Add any necessary token entries and change the file serial number to reflect the current date.

   The serial number (by standard convention) should be 10 characters. The first four (1999) reflect the year, the next two (08) reflect the current month; the next two (01) reflect the current day, and the last two (01) reflect the number of times you changed that file that day (for instance, if this is the first time you made a change, the digits would be 01, the second 02, the third 03, and so on). It is important that you update the serial number upon every change, because this tells named that changes have been made to a zone.

3. Set your primary and secondary DNS servers. Add any hosts for this domain with appropriate tokens and so forth. Note that the hostname always ends

with a period (.); one of the most common errors made by DNS administrators is to leave off the trailing period. Your *db.example.com* should look something like this:

```
@           IN      SOA     ns.example.com.  root.example.com. (
                            1999080101     ; serial
                            10800   ; refresh (3 hours)
                            3600    ; retry (1 hour)
                           604800 ; expire (7 days)
                            86400 ) ; minimum (1 day)
            IN      NS              ns1.example.com.
            IN      NS              ns2.example.net.
            IN      A               192.168.0.212
www         IN      A               192.168.0.212
ftp         IN      CNAME           www
node2       IN      A               192.168.0.2
router      IN      A               192.168.0.254
ns1         IN      A
                    192.168.0.10
```

4. Set up reverse DNS. Create the *db.0.168.192.in-addr.arpa* file under */var/named*. Set up any and all reverse entries for each node, as specified in the forward DNS file. (Remember to change your file serial number accordingly!) Your reverse DNS file should look something like this:

```
@           IN      SOA     ns.example.com.  root.example.com. (
                    1999080101      ; serial
                            10800    ; refresh (3 hours)
                            3600     ; retry (1 hour)
                    604800   ; expire (7 days)
                    86400 ) ; minimum (1 day)
    IN      NS      ns1.example.com.
    2               IN      PTR     node2.example.com.
    10              IN      PTR     ns1.example.com.
    254             IN      PTR     router.example.com.
```

5. Verify changes and restart named. Verify that your IPs, hosts, and serial number information are correct. Then restart named by running */etc/rc.d/init.d/named restart*. To verify that you have your domain running properly, use *nslookup* (discussed in the "DNS Tools" section of this chapter) by running *nslookup www.example.comserver_IP_address* and *nslookup 192.168.0.212server_IP_address*. Specifying the DNS server's IP address in the command allows you to see exactly what information your server is delivering, helping to avoid caching or misconfiguration issues. You should also run *nslookup* without the server IP address argument, to help detect such issues. The command should return the appropriate IP address and domain information, if DNS is set up properly.

Secondary and Tertiary DNS

When a domain is registered, it must be registered with not only a primary DNS server, but also a secondary DNS server. If the primary server is down, the secondary server will take over. For even more failover support, a tertiary DNS server can be set up.

Setting up secondary DNS for a domain is even simpler than setting up primary DNS. Essentially, you have to do only Steps 1 and 5 from the previous list that describes setting up primary DNS. There is a difference, however, from Step 1 for primary DNS. The following steps explain how to set up secondary DNS.

1. Add the zone to */etc/named.conf*. As a secondary entry, your type is slave. With a slave entry you have to specify the master (used to pull the DNS information for the domain from), which in this example is 192.168.2.50. As a secondary entry, your zone entry in */etc/named.conf* will look like this:

```
zone "example.com" {
        type slave;
        file "db.example.com";
        masters {
                192.168.2.50;
        };
};
```

2. Verify changes and restart named. Verify that your IPs and host information are correct. Then, restart named by running */etc/rc.d/init.d/named restart*.

Objective 2: Create and Maintain DNS Zones

DNS zone files are used to resolve domain names to the domain's assigned IP addresses. These files, by default, are found under the */var/named* directory and are typically named *db.domain.com* or *domain.com.db*. In these examples, we will use *db.example.com*. The following is a sample forward DNS file for a master (primary) record:

```
@           IN      SOA     ns.example.com.  root.example.com. (
                            1999080101    ; serial
                            10800   ; refresh (3 hours)
                            3600    ; retry (1 hour)
                            604800 ; expire (7 days)
                            86400 ) ; minimum (1 day)


            IN      NS          ns1.example.com.
            IN      NS          ns2.example.com.


            IN      MX          0    mail.example.com.
            IN      A           192.168.0.212
localhost   IN      A           127.0.0.1
www         IN      A           192.168.0.212
ns1         IN      A           192.168.0.10
ns2         IN      A           192.168.0.11
ftp         IN      CNAME       www
mail        IN      CNAME       www
irc         IN      CNAME       irc.example.net.
```

The first section is the SOA (start of a zone authority) entry. The SOA entry contains the domain of the originating host, the domain address of the maintainer, the file serial number, and various time parameters (refresh, retry, expire, and minimum time to live).

The second section of the preceding sample */var/named/db.example.com* specifies the domain's primary and secondary DNS servers. These are denoted by the NS tokens. The first NS entry is the primary DNS server, and the second NS entry specifies the secondary DNS server. You can also add tertiary and further DNS servers with the same NS entries.

The third section includes other references, options, and settings for the domain entry. The A tokens point to host addresses. For example, the A token in this example sets the domain *example.com* to 192.168.0.212. Another A token sets *www.example.com* to 192.168.0.212 as well. An additional token used in this example section is CNAME (canonical name). The CNAME token points an alias to the appropriate IP address or domain. In the above example, *ftp.example.com* points to the same address as *www*, which was already defined as 192.168.0.212. Also, *mail.example.com* is directed to *www*. There is also a CNAME pointer for *irc.example.com* that redirects the request to an Internet Relay Chat (IRC) server, located in this example at *irc.example.net*.

The MX (mail exchange) token points to the mail exchange server for the domain. When the mail server program, such as Postfix, processes an email message, it first looks for this record of the destination address. If you want reliable mail delivery, you should specify an additional MX record pointing to another mail server. While mail shouldn't be dropped if the single mail server is unavailable for a while, it will be delayed.

```
MX 30 mailserver
MX 60 mailserver.backup.com
MX 90 mailserver.localdomain.org
```

The relative priority of an MX server is determined by the preference number (the second field) in the DNS MX record. The smallest preference number has the highest priority and is the first server to be tried.

The lower preference number is the higher priority!

Table 37-1 summarizes the types of heads you need to know in zone files.

Table 37-1. Common registry types used in zone files

Type	Description
SOA	Start of authority
NS	Authorized name server
A	Host address
CNAME	Canonical name
MX	Mail server exchange
PTR	Reverse name pointer

Forward DNS Zones

Forwarding is very useful in many situations. It simply forwards all DNS queries or just specific zones to other DNS servers, caching the results and speeding up future name resolutions.

It's possible to create DNS forwarding using the `forwarders` parameter at a global level or per-zone basis in a zone section of the *named.conf* file.

The following example forwards all queries to two other nameservers (10.163. 200.103 and 10.163.200.104):

```
options {
  directory "/var/named";
  forwarders {10.163.200.103; 10.163.200.104;};
};
```

A server can also be used as a forward-only DNS server that forwards all name server work. Just add the `forward only` parameter to the file:

```
options {
  directory "/var/named";
  forwarders {10.163.200.103; 10.163.200.104;};
  forward only;
};
```

The following example shows a zone-specific forwarding parameter:

```
zone "example.com" IN {
  type forward;
  forwarders {10.163.200.103; 10.163.200.104;};
};
```

This way, all nameserver queries from *example.com* will be handled by another DNS server.

Reverse DNS Files

Reverse DNS files are used to resolve IP addresses to their assigned hostnames. Reverse DNS is set up per subnet, meaning all 192.168.0.*n* addresses would have a single reverse DNS file defined, as would 192.168.1.*n*, 192.168.2.*n*, and so on (where *n* is equal to all nodes from 0 through 255).

Reverse DNS files are named by the subnet address (in reverse order) followed by the *in-addr.arpa* filename. For instance, the reverse DNS file for the 192.168.100.*n* subnet would be *db.100.168.192.in-addr.arpa*, and the reverse DNS file for the 205.23.12.*n* subnet would be *db.12.23.205.in-addr.arpa*.

Although the subnet and *in-addr.arpa* filenames are always used, many administrators replace the *db.* with *rev.*, simply for clarification (for instance, *rev.12.23. 205.in-addr.arpa* or *12.23.205.in-addr.arpa.rev*). Regardless of which naming convention you use, simply keep the same naming convention throughout your environment, and make sure all appropriate references (such as in */etc/named. conf*) match.

The following is an example of the reverse DNS file *db.0.168.192.in-addr.arpa*.
You will notice that it looks similar to the forward DNS files, with the same SOA
head entry, but uses different tokens in the body of the file.

```
@       IN      SOA     ns.example.com. root.example.com. (
                        199080101    ; serial
                        10800   ; refresh (3 hours)
                        3600    ; retry (1 hour)
                        604800 ; expire (7 days)
                        86400 ); minimum (1 day)
        IN      NS      ns.example.com.
1       IN      PTR     gateway.example.com.
2       IN      PTR     boss.example.com.
3       IN      PTR     node3.example.com.
;4      IN      PTR     node4.example.com.
212     IN      PTR     www.example.com.
254     IN      PTR     router.example.com.
```

In this example, the first six lines are identical to the forward DNS files. The first
six lines of the file are the SOA entry information, which includes the host information, the file serial number, and various time settings. The remaining body of
the example differs greatly from the forward DNS file, however. The remaining
entries use the PTR (pointer) token. The PTR token resolves the specific node on
a subnet to a domain name. The first column of PTR entries in the example specifies the node number on the subnet. For instance, 1 refers to 192.168.0.1, 2 refers
to 192.168.0.2, and so forth. You'll notice that nodes that aren't assigned are
either not listed, or the ones that are disabled are commented out. (For instance,
the entry for 4 is commented out with the semicolon at the beginning of the line.)
Therefore, the entry for 1 will resolve 192.168.0.1 to *gateway.example.com*, the
entry for 212 will resolve 192.168.0.212 to *www.example.com*, and so forth.

DNS Tools

A variety of DNS tools are available to help you utilize and test the DNS service.
The ones you should know are listed in Table 37-2. DNS tools should be installed
on every Linux workstation, not just DNS servers. Tools such as *dig* and *nslookup*
are a great help even for regular users who want to look up an IP address or
domain using a name server.

    nslookup has been deprecated in favor of *dig*.

Table 37-2. DNS tools

Tool	Simple usage	Description
dig	*dig @nameserver domain*	Queries *nameserver* for domain name packet information
dnsquery	*dnsquery -n nameserver host*	Queries domain *nameserver* for host using `resolver`
host	*host domain*	Looks up the host for a domain name
nslookup	*nslookup record* [*server*] or *nslookup* `ipaddress`	Queries Internet name servers for IP address and domain information

dig

Syntax

```
dig [@nameserver] domain
```

Description

dig is a powerful tool that can be used to retrieve detailed information from DNS name servers.

Frequently used options

server
> Specifies the name server to query.

query-type
> Specifies the registry type that you are querying. If omitted, the default is *a*. Available types include:

a
> Network address

any
> Any (all) information about the specified domain

mx
> Mail exchanger for the domain

ns
> Name servers for the domain

soa
> Zone of authority record

hinfo
> Host information

axfr
> Zone transfer

txt
> Arbitrary text

-x
> Specifies a reverse name resolution

+debug
> Useful for name resolution troubleshooting

Example

You can make simple name resolution tests using different types of records. This is how to query an SOA record:

```
# dig @nameserver.petro.org.br. petro.org.br. soa

;; global options:  printcmd
;; Got answer:
;; ->>HEADER<<- opcode: QUERY, status: NOERROR, id: 52650
;; flags: qr aa rd ra; QUERY: 1, ANSWER: 1, AUTHORITY: 13, ADDITIONAL: 6
```

```
;; QUESTION SECTION:
;petro.org.br.                    IN      SOA

;; ANSWER SECTION:
petro.org.br. 3600    IN      SOA      nameserver.petro.org.br. admin.petro.
org.br. 177 900 600 86400 3600

;; AUTHORITY SECTION:
petro.org.br. 3600    IN      NS       nameserver.petro.org.br.
petro.org.br. 3600    IN      NS       nameserver02.petro.org.br.

;; ADDITIONAL SECTION:
1        IN      PTR      gateway.petro.org.br.
2        IN      PTR      boss.petro.org.br.
3        IN      PTR      node3.petro.org.br.
212      IN      PTR      www.petro.org.br.
254      IN      PTR      router.petro.org.br.

;; Query time: 1 msec
;; SERVER: 164.85.216.64#53(nameserver)
;; WHEN: Tue Mar 21 19:27:48 2006
;; MSG SIZE  rcvd: 512
```

And how to look for the MX records:

 # dig petro.org.br mx

```
; <<>> DiG 9.2.2-P1 <<>> petro.org.br mx
;; global options:  printcmd
;; Got answer:
;; ->>HEADER<<- opcode: QUERY, status: NXDOMAIN, id: 4842
;; flags: qr aa rd ra; QUERY: 1, ANSWER: 0, AUTHORITY: 1, ADDITIONAL: 0

;; QUESTION SECTION:
;petro.org.br.INMX

;; AUTHORITY SECTION:
org.br.900INSOAa.dns.br. hostmaster.registro.br. 2006032712 1800 900 604800 900

;; Query time: 152 msec
;; SERVER: 172.24.1.20#53(172.24.1.20)
;; WHEN: Mon Mar 27 15:55:42 2006
;; MSG SIZE  rcvd: 92
```

Objective 3: Securing a DNS Server

As with any computer sitting on the Internet, you need to secure your DNS server.
Here are a few reasons:

- Losing your DNS server can mean losing access to your web server and email
  server because, without DNS, no one can find them, effectively creating a
  Denial of Service (DOS) scenario.

- An attacker who breaks into your DNS server can get information about your internal network, including the IP addresses of other servers, client machines, switches, and so on.

- By poisoning the data in your DNS server or manipulating your DNS information, an attacker can cause people attempting to connect to your servers to be rerouted to the attackers' servers. Imagine what would happen if your clients typed their credit card information into a server they thought was yours and wasn't.

Some of the things you can do to secure your DNS servers are:

- Have redundant servers. If one goes down, you'll have a backup.

- Use one or more dedicated servers for DNS. There should be no users logging in or any other services on the system that can be used to attack it.

- Restrict zone transfers so they can take place only between your DNS servers.

- Use TSIGs (transaction signatures) to encrypt zone transfers between DNS servers.

- Do not allow recursive queries to an Internet-facing nameserver. These servers should serve only name information that they are explicitly told about.

- Recursive queries should be allowed only from your internal network.

- Run BIND in a chroot jail and/or as a user with the minimum privileges necessary.

- Keep backups of your zone files in a separate environment, and monitor the information served by your DNS servers.

Depending on your setup, there are other things you may be able to do. Also, as with any other program, bug and security fixes for BIND are frequently publicized, so keep abreast of BIND developments.

Let's look at some of the items just listed, one by one.

Dedicated Servers

Ideally, your DNS server should run only DNS. If you have your DNS server running on a computer with SMTP and POP (email), user accounts, a dozen web sites, and so on, you have many attack vectors open. A bare-bones computer that has only port 53 open is much more difficult to break into than one that has open ports for Telnet, HTTP, SMTP, POP, and IMAP. You should also have separate internal and external DNS servers. The internal servers should respond to queries only from internal addresses. You do that with a command such as the following (the IP address is a typical internal subnet address):

```
allow-query {192.168.1.0/24;};
```

You can chain multiple subnets together using semicolons (;).

If the internal servers need to resolve an address from outside the network, you can have them forward the query to the external server with:

```
forwarders {200.200.1.17; 200.200.1.18;};
```

Restricting Zone Transfers

If an attacker can do a zone transfer (and anyone who has access to *nslookup* or *dig* can do a zone transfer!), she can get a pretty good idea of how your network is laid out. Knowing how your network is laid out lets her know where to attack.

Be sure that only your servers can do a zone transfer by putting a line like the following in your */etc/named.conf* files on each server:

```
options { allow-transfer {10.10.10.5;192.168.1.12;};}
```

where the 10.10.10.5 and 192.168.1.12 addresses are examples; substitute the addresses of your other DNS servers. Another good idea is to use TSIGs (discussed next).

Using Transaction Signatures (TSIG)

Transaction signatures, or TSIGs, were introduced in BIND 8.2 and more fully fleshed out in BIND 9. TSIGs encode the data whenever a zone transfer occurs. In BIND 9, TSIGs can also be used for dynamic updating of zone records.

The process of using TSIGs is not complicated, but can be difficult to trouble-shoot. One of the most important things to keep in mind is that the clocks on the DNS servers *must be synchronized*. The best and easiest way to do this is by using the Network Time Protocol (NTP). Additionally, all of your DNS servers should use the same NTP server.

Here is the process for a server running BIND:

1. Generate the MD5 key using *dnssec-keygen*. It is customary to name the key after the two servers involved:

   ```
   # dnssec-keygen -b 128 -a HMAC-MD5 -n ZONE server1-server2
   ```

   This will create two files, *Kserver1-server2.+157+55659.key* and *Kserver1-server2.+157+55659.private*, where the 157 represents the algorithm used (HMAC-MD5 in our case) and 55659 represents the footprint of the file. In the next step, we will use the value in the Key line of the second output file:

   ```
   # cat Kserver1-server2.+157+55659.private
   Private-key-format: v1.2
   Algorithm: 157 (HMAC_MD5)
   Key: 6tIpAOE/nTW677RqaBQLFQ==
   ```

2. Create an entry on both servers. You can do it right in */etc/named.conf* as follows:

   ```
   key server1-server2 {
     algorithm hmac-md5;
     secret "6tIpAOE/nTW677RqaBQLFQ==";
   }
   ```

   Better yet, create the entry in a separate file, say */etc/named.key*, and include it in */etc/named.conf* like this:

   ```
   include "/etc/named.key";
   ```

   In either case, make sure the permissions on the files are as restrictive as possible (through a *chmod 400* on the file).

3. Use an ACL for each server and tell BIND which keys to use:

```
acl "myservers" { server1, server2; };
server server2 {
  transfer-format
  keys {server1-server2;};
}
```

4. Restart both servers and check for errors in the log files.

Recursive Queries

Your DNS servers should do recursive queries only from your network. Not only will this allow for better performance, but it can help prevent a DOS scenario known as DNS cache poisoning.

All DNS servers cache the replies to their queries. Some are (mis)configured to cache all replies, even if they didn't send out a query. If an attacker sends a reply that says "*www.oreilly.com* is at 192.168.1.1" and the receiving DNS server accepts the reply and places it in the cache, the cache has been poisoned.

In BIND, recursive queries are the default, so be sure to turn them off on your external servers with:

```
recursion no;
```

If you don't have separate external and internal servers (or you just don't want to turn off recursion), you can restrict recursive queries to specific subnets with a section such as:

```
allow-recursion {192.168.1.0/24; 10.10.0.0/16;};
```

Running BIND in a chroot Jail/Reduced Privileges

Restricting which system resources BIND can access will make your server harder to break into and, if someone does break in, make it harder for her to do damage.

The classic way of doing this is to run BIND in a chroot jail. The process is quite involved, so we won't get into details here. The basic process is:

1. Create a chroot environment that contains all the files and directories that BIND will need to run.

2. Put BIND in the jail.

3. Run BIND.

The new *-uusername* and *-tdirectory* features of Bind 9 make it easier to run BIND in a chroot jail. Once the command-line options are read, BIND will chroot itself in the *directory* directory as the user *username*. This has the disadvantage that, for a short time during program startup, BIND is not chrooted. Also, some people think the chroot code in BIND needs more testing. On the other hand, it is much easier to use than a chroot jail.

 If you're going to use the *-u* and *-t* options, do not run BIND as the *root* user (*-u root*), because on most Linux systems, *root* can break out of a chroot jail.

38

Web Services (Apache and Squid, Topic 2.208)

Virtually every organization runs a web server, either for internal use—to hold documents for the organization's employees—or to serve content to the public at large. The Objectives on this part of the test cover basic configuration of a secure Apache web server. They also cover Squid, a popular open source (*http://www. opensource.org*) caching server. Despite the name of the section, the LPIC tests do not cover Web Services of the SOAP variety, which implement applications over the Web. Only basic web configuration is covered.

Objective 1: Implementing a Web Server
   Candidates should be able to install and configure a web server. This objective includes monitoring the server's load and performance, restricting client user access, configuring support for scripting languages as modules, and setting up client user authentication. Also included is configuring server options to restrict usage of resources.

Objective 2: Maintaining a Web Server
   Candidates should be able to configure a web server to use virtual hosts and the Secure Sockets Layer (SSL) and to customize file access.

Objective 3: Implementing a Proxy Server
   Candidates should be able to install and configure a proxy server, including access policies, authentication and resources usage.

Installing Apache

Like the majority of open source software, Apache gives you two choices when it comes to installation: you can download the source and compile it yourself, or you can install a binary package. The binary packages are precompiled versions of Apache that come either from your software vendor (as is the case with most Linux distributions) or directly from the Apache Foundation itself (see *http:// www.apache.org/dist/httpd/binaries*). Your first decision is therefore whether to choose a binary or a source distribution.

A source distribution has a number of advantages. First and foremost, it allows you to configure exactly what you want compiled into Apache and what you don't want. The configuration options before the actual compilation give you the ability to add or remove dozens of modules distributed with Apache. Another good reason for going with a source installation is that you may have third-party modules in source that must be compiled against the Apache source tree. If this is the case, you have to use the Apache source code in order to compile these modules.

The biggest disadvantage of a source installation (other than the potential complexity of the installation itself, if you are not familiar with such things) is package management. The easiest way to maintain a Unix-based system is to utilize the built-in package management tools to install, upgrade, and remove software for your operating system. If you install any package from source, you're bypassing the package management system. The onus then lies on you to ensure that the package you've installed is upgraded and documented correctly. Too many times have systems been migrated, only for users to discover that a certain compiled package was not included in the migration because the sysadmin failed to document its existence and didn't include it in the migration.

So although you may be in specific situations in which you need to maintain a source install of Apache, in general it is recommended to go with your vendor's binary package, for maintainability's sake. Because binary installation is usually trivial—especially when covered by package management—this chapter documents only the source installation.

Apache Installation from Source

The procedure for installing Apache from source follows the standard *./configure, make, make install* routine that should be familiar to most Linux users. The first decision you must make when compiling Apache is which version you will use. At the time of this writing, there are two major versions of Apache supported: Version 2.2.0 and Version 1.3.34. Version 1.3.34 is the latest version of the Apache source that started life as a fork of the original web server, NCSA's *httpd*. The 2.0 Apache source was a major rewrite of Apache from the ground up, sharing little code with the 1.3 branch. The Apache Foundation recommends that all users use the latest version in the 2.0 branch, although the 1.3 branch is still maintained for legacy purposes. This section will focus on compiling Apache 2.2. 0, although the procedure given here will work with Apache 1.3 as well.

The Apache source code can be downloaded from *http://httpd.apache.org*. Select the Download from a mirror link and you will see a link to the latest source code. The file will be either *httpd-2.2.0.tar.gz* or *httpd-2.2.0.tar.bz*, representing the two popular compression methods used in the Unix world, *gzip* and *bzip2*. If you're unsure of which to get, download *httpd-2.2.0.tar.gz*, as *gunzip* has been around longer and is more likely to be installed. Once you have downloaded the file, go to a shell prompt as the root user and type:

```
# tar -xvzf httpd-2.2.0.tar.gz
```

This will extract the contents of the archive into the directory *httpd-2.2.0*. Change to this directory and run the *configure --help* command to view the compile-time options:

```
# cd httpd-2.2.0
# ./configure --help | more

`configure' configures this package to adapt to many kinds of systems.

Usage: ./configure [OPTION]... [VAR=VALUE]...

To assign environment variables (e.g., CC, CFLAGS...), specify them as
VAR=VALUE.  See below for descriptions of some of the useful variables.

Defaults for the options are specified in brackets.

Configuration:
  -h, --help              display this help and exit
      --help=short        display options specific to this package
      --help=recursive    display the short help of all the included
packages
  -V, --version           display version information and exit
...
Some influential environment variables:
  CC          C compiler command
  CFLAGS      C compiler flags
  LDFLAGS     linker flags, e.g. -L<lib dir> if you have libraries in a
              nonstandard directory <lib dir>
  CPPFLAGS    C/C++ preprocessor flags, e.g. -I<include dir> if you have
              headers in a nonstandard directory <include dir>
  CPP         C preprocessor

Use these variables to override the choices made by `configure' or to help
it to find libraries and programs with nonstandard names/locations.
```

The output was drastically shortened here; there are many compile-time options for Apache. For complete documentation on all of the options, visit *http://httpd. apache.org/docs/2.2/programs/configure.html*. We will touch here on some of the more important options that you probably want to enable.

The majority of the Apache compile-time options deal with *modules*. Modules are parts of the Apache source code that can be either compiled directly into the *httpd* binary or compiled as a separate, shared object file. Apache refers to these as DSOs, or Dynamically Shared Objects. The advantages of compiling options as DSOs are that they can be dynamically loaded or unloaded from memory when they are not needed and that third-party modules compiled as DSOs do not necessarily have to be upgraded when Apache itself is upgraded. Modules can be enabled individually or enabled in one configure option as either built-ins or DSOs. Here are some common configure options:

--prefix=pref

Specifies where you want Apache installed. Common options are */opt/apache* and */var/opt/apache*. If not specified, defaults to */usr/local/apache*.

--enable-so

Enable the loading of DSOs in Apache. Without this option enabled, all your modules will have to compiled directly into the binary.

--enable-headers

Allows you to manipulate HTTP headers in your Apache configuration.

--enable-proxy

Turns Apache into a proxy server. It is not a full-featured proxy server and lacks the sophistication of a package like Squid (discussed later in this chapter), but it does work.

--enable-ssl

Allows Apache to handle connections encrypted with SSL, the Secure Sockets Layer. Recommended if you will serve web pages with sensitive information or if you require authentication (username/password).

--enable-http

Required if you want Apache to speak the HTTP protocol (as you probably do).

--enable-dav

Enables the WebDAV module, which allows you to use special client software to edit web pages directly through Apache. For example, with the WebDAV client built into Microsoft Windows, you can connect to a WebDAV-enabled Apache server and map a drive to the web server, editing HTML pages as if they were on a local drive.

--enable-cgi

Enables the execution of Common Gateway Interface scripts. These are often written in scripting languages such as Perl or a shell.

--enable-rewrite

Enables the Apache rewrite engine. This gives you the ability to apply regular expression based rules to redirect HTTP requests. This is a very powerful module and is quite useful.

Now that we've discussed some common options, we're ready to run the configure script:

```
# ./configure –prefix=/opt/apache --enable-so –enable-headers --enable-proxy
   --enable-ssl --enable-http --enable-dav --enable-cgi --enable-rewrite
```

This configure line will enable all of the modules previously listed and, when we run the *make* command, will cause all the modules to be compiled directly into the Apache binary. If we want to compile them all as DSOs instead, our configure line looks like this:

```
# ./configure –prefix=/opt/apache –enable-so –enable-http \
   –enable-mods-shared="headers proxy ssl dav cgi rewrite"
```

Note that so and http cannot be compiled as DSOs. Now that our configure command is complete and without errors (we hope), we are ready to compile Apache. The configure command has created a *Makefile* in the current directory. This file contains all of the instructions that are necessary to build Apache from source. The *make* command reads this file and follow the instructions. Note that the *make* command is not shipped with Apache; it comes with your Linux distribution as part of the program development tools.

```
# make
```

Depending upon the speed of your system, this process can take some time. Be sure to pay attention to any warnings or errors that are output. If the *make* command generates a fatal error, it is probably because a module you enabled requires certain software that is not available on your system. If this is case, either install that software and run *make* again, or rerun the configure command, removing the offending option.

Assuming the *make* command completed with no errors, you are now ready to complete the final step and install Apache onto your system:

```
# make install
```

In our case, this will create the directory */opt/apache* and copy everything necessary to it.

Once the *make install* command is complete, change to the */opt/apache/bin* directory and verify that you have a binary file called *httpd* there:

```
# cd /opt/apache/bin
# file httpd
httpd: ELF 32-bit LSB executable, Intel 80386, version 1 (SYSV), for GNU/
Linux 2.2.5, dynamically linked (uses shared libs), not stripped
```

This is the actual Apache binary. It has some command-line options that give you more information:

```
# ./httpd -h
Usage: ./httpd [-D name] [-d directory] [-f file]
               [-C "directive"] [-c "directive"]
               [-k start|restart|graceful|graceful-stop|stop]
               [-v] [-V] [-h] [-l] [-L] [-t] [-S]
Options:
  -D name            : define a name for use in <IfDefine name> directives
  -d directory       : specify an alternate initial ServerRoot
  -f file            : specify an alternate ServerConfigFile
  -C "directive"     : process directive before reading config files
  -c "directive"     : process directive after reading config files
  -e level           : show startup errors of level (see LogLevel)
  -E file            : log startup errors to file
  -v                 : show version number
  -V                 : show compile settings
  -h                 : list available command line options (this page)
  -l                 : list compiled in modules
  -L                 : list available configuration directives
  -t -D DUMP_VHOSTS  : show parsed settings (currently only vhost settings)
  -S                 : a synonym for -t -D DUMP_VHOSTS
  -t -D DUMP_MODULES : show all loaded modules
  -M                 : a synonym for -t -D DUMP_MODULES
  -t                 : run syntax check for config files
```

These options are particularly useful if you find yourself maintaining an Apache installation that you yourself did not compile.

Now change to the *opt/apache/modules* directory to see the DSOs that we compiled:

```
# cd /opt/apache/modules
# ls -1
httpd.exp
mod_dav.so
mod_proxy_ajp.so
mod_proxy_connect.so
mod_proxy_http.so
mod_rewrite.so
mod_cgi.so
mod_headers.so
mod_proxy_balancer.so
mod_proxy_ftp.so
mod_proxy.so
mod_ssl.so
```

Here we see all of the options that we compiled as modules. We see from the *file* command that these are shared objects, ready to be loaded into memory:

```
# file mod_cgi.so
mod_cgi.so: ELF 32-bit LSB shared object, Intel 80386, version 1 (SYSV), not
stripped
```

Now that we've verified that we've compiled Apache the way we want, it's time to do a test run. As noted before, the file *opt/apache/bin/httpd* is the actual Apache binary, so you can start the web server simply by running this command:

```
# /opt/apache/bin/httpd
```

The process will fork to the background and return you to a shell prompt. However, this is not the recommended way to manage the Apache process. Most Linux systems will provide you with a standard set of shell scripts that you can use to start and stop processes on your system. These shell scripts are usually called from the various runlevels, which means they start processes when the system boots and stops them when it shuts down. The advantage to this approach is that although you may have software on your system from many different sources, written in many different ways, the controlling shell scripts allow you to manage each process as if it were written in the same format. The shell scripts all take the same arguments, hiding the various command-line intricacies of the individual processes. While these scripts are usually provided by your Linux distribution, a very similar script ships with the Apache source code. It is */opt/apache/bin/apachectl* and it takes three arguments: *start*, *stop* and *restart*. This is the preferred way to manage your Apache process.

```
# /opt/apache/bin/apachectl start
```

If all goes well, you will be immediately returned to a prompt. How do you know whether the web server is running? There are three easy ways to figure that out: verify the process exists, check the log file, and look for open network ports.

To verify the Apache process exists, we use the *ps* command. The following set of options is valid on most Linux systems:

```
# ps -aux | grep http
root      21640  0.3  0.6  7756  3232 ?    Ss   21:58   0:00 /opt/apache/bin/
httpd -k start
daemon    21641  0.0  0.6  7756  3264 ?    S    21:58   0:00 /opt/apache/bin/
httpd -k start
daemon    21642  0.0  0.6  7756  3260 ?    S    21:58   0:00 /opt/apache/bin/
httpd -k start
daemon    21643  0.0  0.6  7756  3260 ?    S    21:58   0:00 /opt/apache/bin/
httpd -k start
daemon    21644  0.0  0.6  7756  3260 ?    S    21:58   0:00 /opt/apache/bin/
httpd -k start
daemon    21645  0.0  0.6  7756  3260 ?    S    21:58   0:00 /opt/apache/bin/
httpd -k start
```

We see from this output that there are six copies of the *httpd* binary currently running.

To check the log files, change to the directory */opt/apache/logs* and run the *tail* command on *error_log*, which is where Apache not only logs its errors, but also records every time it is stopped, started, or restarted.

```
# cd /opt/apache/logs
# tail error_log
[Tue Jan 03 21:58:18 2006] [notice] Apache/2.2.0 (Unix) mod_ssl/2.2.0
OpenSSL/0.9.7f DAV/2 configured -- resuming normal operations
```

Finally, we can verify that Apache is listening on a network port. By default, Apache listens on TCP port 80, which is the default port used for HTTP communication. To verify this, we use the *netstat* command:

```
# netstat -anp | grep -i httpd
tcp       0      0 :::80       :::*   LISTEN     21640/httpd
```

This tells us that the *httpd* binary (process ID # 21640) is listening on TCP port 80.

Success! We have successfully installed and started the Apache web server! Now, how do we configure it to do our bidding?

Configuring Apache

The Apache web server is controlled by configuration files that live in the directory */opt/apache/conf*. The main configuration file is *httpd.conf*, and like most configuration files for Unix services, it is a plain text file that can be edited by your favorite text editor. The configuration file is broken down into three main sections:

Global section
    This contains configuration options that apply to every host on the server.

Main section
    The configuration options here apply to any virtual host that is accessed and does not have its own section.

Virtual host section

Each virtual host that is hosted on the server gets its own configuration section.

You may be asking "What is a virtual host?" While the Apache web server is perfectly capable of serving the web pages for a single web site (such as *www. example.com*), its real strength lies in its ability to serve pages for many different web sites, all from the same machine. Each of these web sites is called a virtual host, because it appears that each of them has Apache all to itself. This allows companies or ISPs to host many (often thousands) of web sites on a single Apache installation. Virtual host syntax will be covered later in the chapter.

The global configuration section gives directives that affect the entire Apache installation, including any virtual hosts. Let's look at one of the simplest Apache *httpd.conf* files you'll ever see, Example 38-1. It's all global directives; we're not defining any virtual hosts. This is a complete *httpd.conf* file and is probably sufficient if you're just using Apache in a testing environment.

Example 38-1. Apache configuration file

```
ServerRoot "/opt/apache"
Listen 80
LoadModule headers_module modules/mod_headers.so
LoadModule proxy_module modules/mod_proxy.so
LoadModule proxy_connect_module modules/mod_proxy_connect.so
LoadModule proxy_ftp_module modules/mod_proxy_ftp.so
LoadModule proxy_http_module modules/mod_proxy_http.so
LoadModule proxy_ajp_module modules/mod_proxy_ajp.so
LoadModule proxy_balancer_module modules/mod_proxy_balancer.so
LoadModule ssl_module modules/mod_ssl.so
LoadModule dav_module modules/mod_dav.so
LoadModule cgi_module modules/mod_cgi.so
LoadModule rewrite_module modules/mod_rewrite.so
User daemon
Group daemon
ServerAdmin you@example.com
DocumentRoot "/opt/apache/htdocs"
<Directory "/opt/apache/htdocs">
    Options Indexes FollowSymLinks
    AllowOverride None
    Order allow,deny
    Allow from all
</Directory>
DirectoryIndex index.html
ErrorLog logs/error_log
LogLevel warn
LogFormat "%h %l %u %t \"%r\" %>s %b \"%{Referer}i\" \"%{User-Agent}i\"" combined
CustomLog logs/access_log combined
ScriptAlias /cgi-bin/ "/opt/apache/cgi-bin/"
DefaultType text/plain
TypesConfig conf/mime.types
AddHandler cgi-script .cgi
```

Most of these lines are pretty self-explanatory. ServerRoot defines where you installed Apache; all directory paths given after this directive can be given relative to this root. Listen 80 tells Apache what TCP port to listen for connections on. The LoadModule lines ensure that the modules we compiled as DSOs get loaded into memory every time Apache starts. The User and Group directives dictate the security context under which the Apache binary will run. The ServerAdmin directive indicates the email address that is shown to web browsers when an error is encountered, and the DocumentRoot directive tells Apache where to look for pages to serve.

The <Directory> line indicates the start of a container object. Anything between the <Directory /opt/apache/htdocs> and </Directory> tags applies only to the directory */opt/apache/htdocs*. As you can see, we're turning on some options and dictating who can request content from this directory (in this case, anyone). The Options directive is a complicated one and can be a potential security risk. For more information, visit the Apache documentation at *http://httpd.apache.org/docs/2.2/mod/core.html#options*. For our simple example here, Indexes and FollowSymLinks are two pretty safe and popular options.

DirectoryIndex defines what files Apache should look for when a directory is requested instead of a file. For example, if our site is *www.example.com* and our index page is */opt/apache/htdocs/index.html*, we want to make sure that when someone requests either *http://www.example.com* or *http://www.example.com/index.html* they see the same resource. So the line:

```
DirectoryIndex index.html
```

handles this for us. You can add additional filenames here if you want Apache to search for them (in order) every time it serves files out of a directory. A common global option would be:

```
DirectoryIndex index.html index.htm index.php
```

to try and catch most of the different ways people would name their index files.

The next three lines deal with how and where Apache saves log files. All errors will go to the file defined in the ErrorLog directive. All regular traffic will be logged to the file defined in the CustomLog directive, using the filter indicated, which is combined in this case. As you can see from the LogFormat directive, you have complete control over the formatting of your log files. However, because it's very common to use third-party tools to parse your Apache log files and generate reports for you, you probably want to stick with a standard format that these tools are expecting. The different standards for log file formatting are defined at *http://httpd.apache.org/docs/2.2/logs.html#accesslog*.

Finally, the last four lines deal with how Apache handles certain "special" content. The ScriptAlias directive tells Apache that when a file is requested from this directory, instead of sending the file directly to the requestor's web browser, the file is executed and the output is sent to the web browser. This is the most common way to allow public users to execute programs on your server. These programs are known as Common Gateway Interface (CGI) scripts. They are often written in scripting languages, such as Perl or Python, but they can also be written in C, Ruby, or any other language that you can run on your server.

The `Default Type` and `Types Config` lines tell Apache what to do with certain files. Unlike operating systems such as Microsoft Windows, where file types are usually determined by filename extensions, Apache relies on MIME types to determine the content of a file. These configuration lines tell Apache where to find the MIME types definition file and what the default MIME type should be for files that it serves. Finally, the `AddHandler` line allows you to have CGI programs anywhere in your web directory structure, not just limited to the *cgi-bin* directory. As long as your CGI program has a name that ends in *.cgi*, Apache will execute it and send the results to the web browser.

The main section of the Apache configuration file is used to define default settings for requests that come in that do not match a virtual host. If you are running Apache without any virtual hosts (so it's serving content for only one domain name) this is the only other section you'll need. All your configuration options for that one domain will go here. If you have virtual host containers later, however, this section will be used only when no virtual host matches the request.

To understand that a little better, we need to discuss the difference between name-based and IP-based virtual hosts. Years ago, when the Web was young, if you wanted to host multiple web sites on one system, you had to have a unique IP address for every domain you wanted to host. For example, if you were hosting the domains *www.example1.com* and *www.example2.com*, the IP addresses for them might be 192.168.1.1 and 192.168.2.1, respectively. If that were the case, your virtual host containers might look something like this:

```
<VirtualHost 192.168.1.1>
DocumentRoot /opt/apache/www.example1.com
ServerName www.example1.com
</VirtualHost>

<VirtualHost 192.168.2.1>
DocumentRoot /opt/apache/www.example2.com
ServerName www.example2.com
</VirtualHost>
```

For every web request that came in on 192.168.1.1, Apache would serve files out of the */opt/apache/www.example1.com* directory. For every web request that came in on 192.168.2.1, Apache would serve files out of the */opt/apache/www.example2. com* directory.

This works fine, but the problem is that IP addresses are becoming harder and harder to come by. The solution is instead to use name-based virtual hosts, which allow multiple domain names to resolve to the same IP address, while still allowing Apache to figure out what domain is being requested and serve web pages from the appropriate place. A name-based virtual host setup looks like this:

```
NameVirtualHost *:80
<VirtualHost *:80>
ServerName www.example1.com
ServerAlias example1.com
DocumentRoot /opt/apache/www.example1.com
</VirtualHost>
```

```
<VirtualHost *:80>
ServerName www.example2.com
ServerAlias example2.com
DocumentRoot /opt/apache/www.example2.com
</VirtualHost>
```

Notice that the first directive is `NameVirtualHost`. This tells Apache to expect name-based virtual hosts. We also tell Apache here to expect name-based requests coming in on port 80 (as specified by *:80). This is not required if your implementation of Apache is going to listen only on port 80 (if that's the case, you can just put `NameVirtualHost *`), but it's good practice anyway, because web servers often listen on additional ports.

In this case it's assumed that *www.example1.com* and *www.example2.com* both resolve to the same IP address. When a request comes in, Apache will look in the HTTP headers to determine what virtual host is being requested and will search the `ServerName` and `ServerAlias` directives to find a match. If a match is found, content is served from the corresponding `DocumentRoot`. If no match is found, the default virtual host is used.

Name-based virtual hosts treat the different sections of the configuration file in a special way you need to understand. In an IP-based setup, if there is no virtual host match (which means that a request came in on an IP address that was not defined in a virtual host container), the main section is used. However, with name-based virtual hosts, if no match is found, the first defined `VirtualHost` container becomes the default. Essentially, therefore, named-based virtual hosting overrides the main section of the Apache config file. Even if that section is there, the directives will never be honored.

You can put any directive in a `VirtualHost` container that you would normally put in the main section. Here is a better example of what a VirtualHost container would often contain:

```
<VirtualHost *:80>
ServerName www.example1.com
ServerAlias example1.com
CustomLog /opt/apache/logs/www.example1.com.log combined
DocumentRoot /opt/apache/www.example1.com/
ScriptAlias /cgi-bin/ /opt/apache/www.example1.com/cgi-bin/
Alias /image/    /opt/apache/image/
Options FollowSymLinks
ErrorDocument 404 /404.htm
</VirtualHost>
```

In this example, we're defining a custom log file, a unique script alias, and a unique error document for this virtual host.

Access Control

It's common to use the Apache configuration to restrict access to certain directories. The two components of this process are the configuration directives and the username and password source.

Apache has the ability to query many different sources to get authentication information. It's very common to have Apache query your existing LDAP or MySQL database if you already have user account information stored there. You can even have Apache query your Microsoft Windows Active Directory server for authentication information. Setting up this kind of advanced authentication is beyond the scope of this book. However, simple authentication with a manually maintained file of usernames and passwords is easy to do and is sufficient for most situations.

The standard authentication mode for Apache is called basic authentication. Basic authentication reads a file created by the *htpasswd* program that ships with Apache. This program allows you to create and maintain a file containing usernames and passwords that Apache can use to enforce authentication on directories.

Here is an example of creating an authentication file with *htpasswd*:

```
# /opt/apache/bin/htpasswd -c /opt/apache/password.list demouser
New password:
Re-type new password:
Adding password for user demouser
```

Note that the password you type at the prompt is not echoed back to the screen. We can now look at the contents of this file:

```
# cat /opt/apache/password.list
demouser:RRm8uBOYINC.s
```

It contains our username (*demouser*), a colon as a delimeter, and the encrypted version of the password we typed.

Now that we have this file in place, we can add security to one of our virtual hosts. Let's say that we want to allow all users to access the top level of *www.example1.com* without a password, but the subdirectory */protected* will require a username and password and will restrict access to the *demouser* user listed in the file we just created (of course, we can add more users later). Here is our new VirtualHost container to accomplish this:

```
<VirtualHost *:80>
ServerName www.example1.com
ServerAlias example1.com
CustomLog /opt/apache/logs/www.example1.com.log combined
DocumentRoot /opt/apache/www.example1.com/
ScriptAlias /cgi-bin/ /opt/apache/www.example1.com/cgi-bin/
Alias /image/    /opt/apache/image/
Options FollowSymLinks
ErrorDocument 404 /404.htm
<Directory /opt/apache/www.example1.com/protected>
AuthName "Authorized Users Only"
AuthType Basic
AuthUserFile /opt/apache/password.list
require valid-user
</Directory>
</VirtualHost>
```

After we add this directory container to the Apache config file at */opt/apache/conf/httpd.conf*, we must restart Apache (*/opt/apache/bin/apachectl restart*). Like most other Unix services, the Apache server reads its config file only at startup, so any change to the config file will go into effect only when Apache restarts.

Now when we go to *www.example1.com/protected* in our web browser, we get a pop-up box that is entitled Authorized Users Only and asks for our username and password. If our authentication as *demouser* is successful, we will be shown the content. If not, we'll be asked three times (this behavior is client-specific) before finally being shown an error page stating that our authentication failed.

Third-Party Modules

As stated earlier, the existence of third-party modules is one of the reasons that the Apache web server has remained so popular. In this section, we will look at configuring three of the most popular third-party modules: *mod_php*, *mod_perl*, and *mod_ssl*.

mod_php

The *mod_php* module integrates the PHP (Pre-Hypertext Processing) scripting language into Apache. Like most other web scripting languages, PHP works in this manner:

1. A PHP file is requested by a web client.
2. Apache loads the PHP script into memory and passes it to the PHP parsing engine.
3. The PHP parsing engine parses the script, generating HTML code.
4. The resulting HTML code is passed to the web browser via HTTP and is displayed to the end user.

This is the same model that is used for CGI scripts, but in this case the parser is not a separate program that Apache calls; it will be built into Apache itself.

Like the Apache web server, you have the choice of installing either the binary version or the source version of PHP. If you're using a binary version of Apache that accompanies your distribution, chances are good that the distribution also has a version of *mod_php* that will work with your version of Apache. If you're using a source installation of Apache, as we are in our examples, you'll need to download the source code for PHP and compile it.

You can get the latest version of PHP from *http://www.php.net*. As of this writing, the latest version is 5.1.1. Download the file *php-5.1.1.tar.bz2* from a mirror listed on the *php.net* site and save it to a directory on your hard drive. The procedure for compiling PHP is very similar to the procedure for compiling Apache: we will run *./configure* with options, then run *make*, and finally run *make install*.

The first step is to uncompress the PHP source code and run *./configure –help* to see all the compile-time options available.

```
# tar xjf php-5.1.1.tar.bz2
# cd php-5.1.1
# ./configure -help
```

There are too many compile-time options to list them all here. You can find detailed instructions on each configure option at *http://www.php.net/manual/en/configure.php*. A couple of important configuration options are described here:

--with-apxs

> Enable the building of PHP as a DSO instead of directly into the Apache binary. This is the recommended way to build PHP for the reasons stated earlier, primarily so that you can upgrade PHP independently of Apache if you compile it as a DSO.

--with-mysql

> Enable PHP to connect to a MySQL database. One of the more popular platforms for running web applications has been dubbed LAMP (for Linux/Apache/Mysql/PHP). The tight integration with the popular MySQL database makes PHP a smart choice when you're looking to develop database-driven dynamic web sites. MySQL installation is not covered in this chapter.

Although there are many more options, these two will get you off and running with a basic PHP installation that you can become familiar with.

```
# ./configure --with-apxs=/opt/apache/bin/apxs --with-mysql
```

If this command generates any errors, check your settings and try again. It's common to see errors when you're attempting to compile PHP with modules for which you don't have the necessary libraries installed. For example, if you try to enable LDAP support in PHP with the *--with-ldap* flag, but you don't have any LDAP libraries or headers installed on your system, the *configure* script will detect this and fail.

Assuming the *configure* command completes successfully, you will now have a *Makefile* that will be read by the *make* command.

```
# make
# make install
```

The **make install** command not only copies all of the necessary PHP files onto your system, but also modifies your Apache *httpd.conf* file to load the PHP module. This line is added to */opt/apache/conf/httpd.conf*:

```
LoadModule php5_module        modules/libphp5.so
```

In order for Apache to know how to identify PHP scripts, you also need to add this line to the global section of your Apache *httpd.conf* file:

```
AddType application/x-httpd-php .php .phtml
```

This tells Apache that any file ending in *.php* or *.phtml* will be assigned the MIME type application/x-httpd-php, which will be in turn handled by the PHP interpreter.

Now we're ready to restart Apache and verify that PHP is working.

```
# /opt/apache/bin/apachectl stop
# /opt/apache/bin/apachectl start
```

Since we're loading a new module, it's not sufficient just to tell Apache to reread its configuration file (which is what the restart option does). We actually need to stop it and then start it again.

The easiest way to verify our PHP installation is to create a simple PHP script and try to view it in our web browser. Save this text file in */opt/apache/www.example1. com/test.php*:

```
<?php
phpinfo( );
?>
```

Now go to *http://www.example1.com/test.php* in your browser. You should see a long table with a blue background that says PHP Version 5.1.1 at the top. You can scroll down this page to see all the different PHP settings that are currently set. Congratulations! You have a working installation of Apache and PHP!

mod_perl

Installing the *mod_perl* module is not much different than installing the *mod_php* module. *mod_perl* allows you to run Perl scripts from your web server using a Perl interpreter that is integrated into Apache.

Do you need *mod_perl* in order to run Perl scripts on your web server? No. You can just as easily configure Apache to run Perl scripts as CGI programs, calling your system's Perl interpreter every time a web request is made for a Perl script. However, this can potentially place a very high load on your web server, because every time a Perl script is requested, the web server must load the complete Perl interpreter in memory, pass the script to the interpreter, and then unload the interpreter from memory. It's much more efficient to keep the interpreter in memory all the time, which is what *mod_perl* provides. It also gives you much tighter integration with Apache itself, including the ability to extend the functionality of the web server with Perl code.

Download the latest version of *mod_perl* from *http://perl.apache.org*. As of this writing, the latest version is 2.0.2. Uncompress the file and go through the normal compile routine. The syntax is slightly different since this is a Perl package, but the concept is the same.

```
# tar xvf mod_perl-2.0-current.tar.gz
# cd mod_perl-2.0.2
# perl Makefile.PL MP_APXS=/opt/apache/bin/apxs
# make
# make install
```

We are compiling *mod_perl* as an Apache DSO, just as we did for PHP. After the *make install* is complete, we need to add this line to our Apache *httpd.conf* file:

```
LoadModule perl_module modules/mod_perl.so
```

Now we can stop and start Apache and verify that *mod_perl* is successfully loaded. In addition to the test script like the one we used earlier for PHP, you can also get information on the currently active modules by looking in the *error_log* after you restart Apache. Every time Apache starts, it writes a line to the *error_log* showing what version it is and what modules are loaded, along with their versions. After stopping and starting Apache, look in the *error_log* and you should see a line that reads something like this:

```
[Wed Jan 04 14:39:18 2006] [notice] Apache/2.2.0 (Unix) mod_ssl/2.2.0
OpenSSL/0.9.7f DAV/2 PHP/5.1.1 mod_perl/2.0.2 Perl/v5.8.6 configured --
resuming normal operations
```

This tells us all of the modules that are configured. We see that we're using *mod_perl* 2.0.2 which was compiled against Perl Version 5.8.6.

mod_ssl

mod_ssl allows Apache to encrypt HTTP connections with the Secure Sockets Layer encryption libraries. SSL was originally developed by Netscape and has become the de facto standard for secure, encrypted communication over the World Wide Web.

mod_ssl is an Apache module that allows Apache to interface with the *openssl* libraries, which are open source implementations of SSL.

Apache versions before 2.0 required that *mod_ssl* be downloaded and installed separately, similarly to what we did for *mod_php* and *mod_perl*. You can get the latest code from *http://www.modssl.org*. As of this writing, the latest version is 2.8. 25 for Apache 1.3.34. Apache 2.0 and above have *mod_ssl* built in, so there is no extra compilation process; all you need to do is configure it.

In order to understand the process of encrypting your web traffic with *mod_ssl*, we need to go into the basics of certificate-based cryptography. SSL provides us with two basic pieces of connection security: authentication and encryption.

The authentication piece works like this: when your web browser connects to an SSL-enabled web site (usually by using the *https://* protocol in your browser, which tells your browser to attempt to connect to the web server on TCP port 443 instead of port 80 and to expect an encrypted connection), the web server presents the web browser with a certificate. This certificate has detailed information about the web site, including the official fully qualified domain name, contact information, and the Certificate Authority that is vouching for the identity of this web site. Because this is still the authentication phase, we are concerned with proving that this web site really is who it claims to be. And because there is no easy way to trust this company, we instead look to a third party that we do trust in order to vouch for this company.

This is where the Certificate Authority (CA) comes into play. All of the major web browsers include a list of trusted Certificate Authorities. If a web site presents a certificate that has been signed by one of these trusted CAs, the browser accepts the certificate and the encrypted communication can begin. If the certificate was not signed by a trusted CA, the web browser will usually pop up a window warning the end user of this situation and asking if they'd like to proceed. (A lot of CAs are recognized by some popular web browsers but not others, so the warning box can often pop up for legitimate sites.) If the end user agrees to trust the CA that signed the certificate, an encrypted connection is made. If not, the connection is aborted.

Examples of trusted CAs are Verisign, Thawte Consulting, and GeoTrust, to name a few. In order to get a signed certificate from one of these companies, you create a certificate request and then send it to one of these companies. For a fee, they will sign the certificate and send you back a file you can use to handle the authentication piece on your web server. Let's go through the process of creating a certificate signing request and submitting it to a CA.

In order to accomplish this task, you must have the *openssl* program installed on your system. As of this writing, the latest version is 0.9.7. This should have come from your vendor in a standard package.

1. Create an RSA private key for your web server. This will be used during the encryption phase.

   ```
   # openssl genrsa -des3 -out server.key 1024
   ```

   You will be asked for a passphrase during this process. You cannot create the key without giving a passphrase. The passphrase will be required every time you attempt to use this key. As you can imagine, this can be a little problematic, because Apache reads this key every time it restarts. If you left this passphrase in place, you would have to give the password every time you restarted Apache, which is unworkable if Apache is restarting from an unattended script. So the recommended second step is to remove this passphrase. You *must* understand the security implications of this! After you remove this passphrase, anyone who gets hold of the *server.key* file can masquerade as your web server over SSL connections. So keep the file safe from prying eyes.

   To remove the passphrase, first make a copy of the key:

   ```
   # cp server.key server.key.passphrase
   ```

   Then, remove the passphrase:

   ```
   # openssl rsa -in server.key.passphrase -out server.key
   ```

   The *server.key* file now has no passphrase.

2. Create a certificate signing request (CSR) using your newly created RSA key. This file will be sent to a trusted CA for signing.

   ```
   # openssl req -new -key server.key -out server.csr
   ```

   You will be asked a series of questions about your organization. It is important to answer these questions correctly, as this information will be incorporated into your certificate and will be viewable by all web users visiting your site. In particular, make sure you use the correct fully qualified domain name by which your encrypted site will be referred. SSL certificates are specific to fully qualified domain names, so even though *www.example1. com* and *example1.com* give you the same content, you'll have to either decide on one to be your SSL site or buy a separate certificate for each.

3. Send the CSR to a trusted Certificate Authority.

   Most CAs have web forms that you can use to submit your CSR. After they collect their fee from you (usually anywhere from $150 to $900), you will receive a signed certificate via email. Once you receive this email, store the certificate in a file called *server.crt*.

4. Configure Apache.

   Now that you have an RSA private key and a signed certificate from a trusted CA, you're ready to set up Apache to handle encrypted SSL connections. You need to make changes to two places in the Apache configuration file. In the global section, enable Apache's SSL functionality and set some global variables. Then create a specific virtual host section for SSL connections. There are other ways to accomplish this with Apache, including running two copies of Apache, one listening on port 80 to serve unencrypted pages and the other listening on port 443 to serve encrypted pages, but the virtual host option is much more elegant and easier to maintain. Here are the lines required in the global section of Apache's *httpd.conf* file:

```
# SSL Global Options
Listen 443
SSLPassPhraseDialog  builtin
SSLSessionCache          dbm:/opt/apache/logs/ssl_scache
SSLSessionCacheTimeout  300
SSLMutex  file:/opt/apache/logs/ssl_mutex
SSLRandomSeed startup builtin
SSLRandomSeed connect builtin
```

More information on what SSL options are available can be found at *http:// httpd.apache.org/docs/2.2/mod/mod_ssl.html*.

The easiest way to set up Apache to handle SSL connections is to create a VirtualHost container that handles all traffic coming in on port 443. Adding onto our example Apache *httpd.conf* from before for *www.example1.com*, we can create a container for SSL connections to *www.example1.com* that looks like this:

```
<VirtualHost *:443>
DocumentRoot "/opt/apache/www.example1.com"
ScriptAlias /cgi-bin /opt/apache/cgi-bin
ServerName www.example1.com
ServerAdmin webmaster@example1.com
ErrorLog /opt/apache/logs/ssl_error_log
CustomLog /opt/apache/logs/ssl_access_log combined
Options FollowSymLinks
SSLEngine on
SSLCipherSuite
ALL:!ADH:!EXPORT56:RC4+RSA:+HIGH:+MEDIUM:+LOW:+SSLv2:+EXP:+eNULL
SSLCertificateFile /opt/apache/ssl/server.crt
SSLCertificateKeyFile /opt/apache/ssl/server.key
</VirtualHost>
```

The SSLCipherSuite line lists all of the SSL encryption methods that you will support. This is a pretty standard list; consult the *mod_ssl* documentation for more encryption options.

Once you've restarted Apache, you are ready to serve pages over an encrypted connection. When you point a browser to *https://www.example1.com*, you'll have an SSL-secured web connection.

But what if you just want to set up an internal SSL site and don't want to have to pay a fee to a trusted CA? Can you still have an SSL-secured site? The answer is yes. Just because your web browser has a short list of Certificate Authorities it inherently trusts doesn't mean you can't sign your own certificate. Use this command to create a self-signed certificate file:

```
# openssl req -new -x509 -nodes -sha1 -days 365 -key server.key \
  -out server.crt
```

Copy the resulting *server.crt* file to */opt/apache/ssl* and restart Apache. Now when you point your web browser to *https://www.example1.com*, you'll probably get a box that looks something like Figure 38-1.

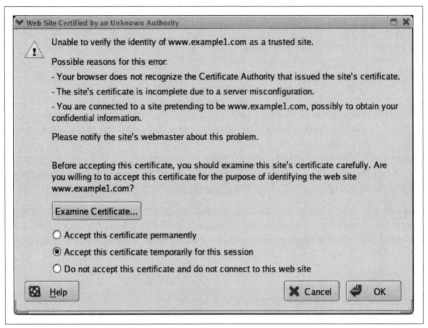

Figure 38-1. Browser accepting certificate from web server

As you can see, the default option is to accept this certificate temporarily for this session. If you select Accept this certificate permanently, you are telling the browser to accept this certificate from now on, even though it is not from a trusted CA. Clicking on Examine Certificate shows us Figure 38-2.

You can see that this certificate contains the information we entered when we signed the certificate ourselves. So why use a trusted CA at all and pay the money when you can sign your own certificates? There are two reasons:

- End users don't like to see this error box. It makes them nervous, and they may abort the connection.

- Even though the rest of the world doesn't necessarily trust you, they probably trust one of the companies on the short list of trusted Certificate Authorities. So you're basically paying these companies to vouch for you.

SSL support has become a very common option for Apache users, as security issues become more important on the Web. We encourage anyone who operates a web site that takes personal information (even usernames and passwords) to consider the benefits of SSL encryption.

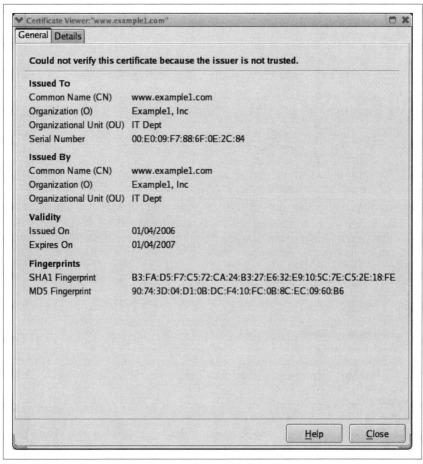

Figure 38-2. Certificate from web server displayed

mod_rewrite

The *mod_rewrite* module was mentioned during our initial compilation of Apache. *mod_rewrite* allows you to apply regular expression patterns to HTTP requests and manipulate them as you see fit. This gives you the ability to redirect incoming requests, directing users to different pages or replacing content on the fly. *mod_rewrite* is one of the most powerful Apache modules and is widely used by webmasters wanting more control over the content and layout of their site.

The complete documentation for *mod_rewrite* can be found at *http://httpd.apache. org/docs/1.3/mod/mod_rewrite.html*. Let's look at a few examples to see how *mod_ rewrite* works.

In this example, we'll use our standard web site *www.example1.com*. Let's say our company just purchased another company called *example2.com*. We are now hosting web sites for both companies, but we want to redirect people who try to go to *example2.com* to *example1.com*. This is easy to do with a VirtualHost container, as we have seen before. We could just make sure our `VirtualHost` container looked something like this:

```
<VirtualHost *:80>
ServerName www.example1.com
ServerAlias example1.com www.example2.com example2.com
DocumentRoot /opt/apache/www.example1.com
CustomLog /opt/apache/logs/www.example1.com.log combined
</VirtualHost>
```

Now, any request that comes in for any of these four web sites (*www.example1. com*, *example1.com*, *www.example2.com*, or *example2.com*) will display the content that lives in */opt/apache/www.example1.com*. However, we have two problems with this setup. First, if someone accesses this site with *www.example2. com*, the URL in his web browser stays *www.example2.com* throughout his visit to the site. Since we now own this company, we want to change that automatically to *www.example1.com*. Also, we may want to know how many people come into our site through *www.example1.com* and how many come in through *www. example2.com*. Since we have only one log file in this situation, we won't see a breakdown of traffic between the domains.

A better solution would be to use *mod_rewrite*. We set up a separate `VirtualHost` container for *www.example2.com* and use *mod_rewrite* to redirect traffic to *www. example1.com*:

```
<VirtualHost *:80>
ServerName www.example2.com
ServerAlias example2.com
DocumentRoot /opt/apache/www.example1.com
CustomLog /opt/apache/logs/www.example2.com.log combined
RewriteEngine On
RewriteRule ^(.+) http://www.example1.com [R]
</VirtualHost>
```

The `ServerName` and `ServerAlias` lines ensure that requests coming in for these domains are handled by this `VirtualHost` container (assuming we removed *www. example2.com* and *example2.com* from the *example1.com* `VirtualHost` container). The `DocumentRoot` can essentially be any valid directory, because we're not actually going to serve any content from it. The `CustomLog` will be a specific log for this `VirtualHost` so we know how many requests are coming in for *www.example2. com*. The `RewriteEngine   On` line tells Apache to turn on the rewrite rule–processing engine for this `VirtualHost`. This is a necessary step, because the rewrite engine does incur some overhead, and you don't want Apache wasting memory on it if you're not going to use it. Finally, the `RewriteRule` line does the actual work for us. The format of the `RewriteRule` syntax is:

```
RewriteRule pattern substitution [options]
```

The pattern can be any valid regular expression that will be applied to the requested URL. The substitution is what the URL is replaced with. The options are ways to modify the behavior of `RewriteRule` and are not always required. In our example, we want to redirect every request for *www.example2.com* to *www.example1.com*. We also want to ensure that if someone had bookmarked a deep-linked page of *www.example2.com* (for example, *www.example2.com/products/1/a/product.html*), she is redirected to the home page of *www.example1.com*. Since we want our initial regular expression to catch everything, we use a catchall regular expression:

```
^(.+)
```

The ^ character indicates the start of a line. The parentheses enclose the rest of our regular expression. The period (.) matches any single character, and the plus sign (+) is a modifier for the period, meaning one or more instances of the preceding character. So this regular expression essentially means "match anything."

The substitution section is what we are going to replace the URL with. In this case, we want to replace every URL with our home page of *www.example1.com*. The only option we're using in this case is the R option, which forces an external redirect. When you're redirecting from one domain to another, you need to use this R option so Apache prepends the *http://* to your rewrite destination. This option is not required if you're simply redirecting to another file in the same DocumentRoot.

Another, more complicated example takes advantage of the RewriteCond expression to query more than one variable before rewriting occurs. RewriteCond is also used to query something other than the URL before a rewrite. In this example, we've done some site redesign, but we don't want to break any bookmarks that web users may already have for our site. In the past, people accessed our pages through a CGI script, so requests looked like this:

```
http://www.example1.com/cgi-bin/go.cgi?page1
```

and

```
http://www.example1.com/cgi-bin/go.cgi?page2
```

We have changed our web layout, so the URLs should now be:

```
http://www.example1.com/page1.html
```

and

```
http://www.example1.com/page2.html
```

How can we handle this with *mod_rewrite* so the old URLs still work?

```
<VirtualHost *:80>
ServerName www.example1.com
ServerAlias example1.com
DocumentRoot /opt/apache/www.example1.com
CustomLog /opt/apache/logs/www.example1.com.log combined
RewriteEngine On
RewriteCond %{QUERY_STRING} ^page.+
RewriteRule ^(.+) /%{QUERY_STRING}.html
</VirtualHost>
```

In our RewriteCond line, we're looking at the value of the environment variable QUERY_STRING. The complete list of variables that you can query can be found in the *mod_rewrite* instructions at *http://httpd.apache.org/docs/1.3/mod/mod_rewrite.html* and includes variables such as HTTP_USER_AGENT, REMOTE_USER, and REMOTE_HOST. In this case, we're interested in performing a rewrite only if our QUERY_STRING variable matches the regular expression:

    ^page.+

Again, this is similar to our last regular expression. The ^ means the start of the line, and the .+ means "match anything," so we will perform a rewrite only if our query string starts with page and has anything else after it. If that is the case, the RewriteRule will be executed. It says "replace any URL with /%{QUERY_STRING}. html." So a URL of the form *http://www.example1.com/cgi-bin/go.cgi?page1* would be redirected to *http://www.example1.com/page1.html*.

Be sure to watch the Apache log files when you are troubleshooting your *mod_rewrite* rules. The *error_log* file in particular will give you a good idea of exactly what is going on if Apache is not behaving as you think it should.

Apache performance tuning

So far, we have looked at how to install and configure the Apache web server. We have touched on many different options, including DSO, SSL, *mod_php*, and *mod_rewrite*. This final Apache section deals with performance tuning.

The Apache web server process follows the common Unix parent/child model. When you start the Apache web server, you are starting a *parent* process. This parent process will spawn a number of *children* to handle incoming HTTP requests. If the number of web requests exceeds the number of children currently available, Apache will spawn more, up to a specified limit. As you can imagine, the spawning of new children while HTTP requests are pending not only places overhead on the web server itself, but can adversely affect the web browsing experience, as web surfers sit and wait for the web server to honor their request. There are a number of options that you can set in the global *httpd.conf* section to maximize the performance of your Apache install:

StartServers
> This option tells Apache how many children to spawn when it initially starts up. You want to ensure that this number is a few more than the average number of connections you see on your web site. If your web site averages 10 simultaneous HTTP requests at all times, it's probably a good idea to set StartServers to at least 15.

MinSpareServers
> This option sets how many idle child processes should be kept around. Idle children are useful when traffic spikes. You don't want to be in a situation in which your web surfers have to wait for Apache to spawn new children to handle their requests. Making this value between 5 and 20 (depending upon how busy your site is) ensures that your site handles spikes in traffic gracefully.

MaxSpareServers
> This option sets the maximum number of idle children. This is useful to save memory on your web server. If you have a sudden spike in traffic that causes 50 children to spawn, but then traffic goes back down to 5 connections, you don't want 45 idle children taking up memory and doing nothing. This value needs to be higher than MinSpareServers. It's usually a good idea to set this between 5 and 10 values higher than MinSpareServers.

```
MaxClients
```
This option sets how many simultaneous HTTP requests your server can handle. If this value is reached, no new HTTP requests will be handled, resulting in an error on the web browser end. The purpose of this option is to prevent Apache from attempting to handle so many requests that it consumes all the resources on the server itself. By default, Apache won't let you set this higher than 256, but that limit can be extended by modifying the code before you compile Apache.

Performance tuning can be a challenge. Careful monitoring of your Apache installation is essential in order to identify what the correct values should be for the parameters listed in this section. For more information on Apache monitoring, the *mod_status* module can be very useful. You can read its documentation at *http://httpd.apache.org/docs/1.3/mod/mod_status.html*.

Squid: History and Overview

Squid is a caching proxy server. It normally sits "between" a web surfer and a web server. The surfer requests a web page from the proxy server. The proxy server either makes the request for the surfer to the web server (a *proxy request*) or serves the client the page directly if it's already saved in the proxy server's disk cache. Because the proxy server is between the client and the server, a number of options are available, including logging, filtering, and other access control. Squid can do all of these things and more.

Squid was originally based on the Harvest project, which is an ARPA-funded set of tools for building a standards-compliant web crawler. Squid is currently maintained by open source programmers around the world and is licensed under the GNU General Public License. For more information on Harvest, visit *http://webharvest.sourceforge.net/ng*, and for more information on Squid, visit the Squid home page at *http://www.squid-cache.org*.

You can choose to install Squid from either source or a binary included with your distribution. As of this writing, the latest recommended version of Squid is 2.5STABLE12. Unlike Apache, Squid does not have nearly as many compile-time options that you might be interested in. A binary Squid package from your Linux distribution usually works fine. If, however, you are interested in discovering exactly what compile-time options are available to you, you can read about them in the Squid documentation at *http://squid-docs.sourceforge.net/latest/html/x220.html*.

If you've installed a Squid package from your Linux distribution, the files are probably laid out in your filesystem like this:

/etc/squid
    Squid configuration directory and home to the main configuration file, named *Squid.conf* or *squid.conf*

/usr/lib/squid
    Programs that Squid uses to communicate with external authentication sources

/usr/sbin/squid
> The Squid binary itself

/usr/share/doc/squid-2.5/
> Squid documentation

/usr/share/squid
> Locale-specific errors and icons

/var/log/squid
> Squid log directory

/var/spool/squid
> Home of the Squid disk cache

We will go through some basic options in the *Squid.conf* file. By default, a relatively sane set of options is chosen already. If you just want to use Squid as a basic caching proxy server, with no access control, you need to change only a few defaults. For more advanced configurations, greater tweaking of the configuration file is required.

http_port option

The default port on which Squid listens for connections is TCP port 3128. This can be anything you want, but you must make sure that each of your clients is configured to talk to Squid on this port. For example, in the Firefox web browser, select Edit → Preferences → Connection Settings. Then, assuming your Squid server is named *squidserver*, you set the proxy options shown in Figure 38-3. These settings will cause your Firefox browser to make all requests through *squidserver* at port 3128.

cache_dir option

This option dictates not only where Squid stores its cache, but also what kind of storage system is used, how much disk Squid is allowed to use, and how the directory structure is set up. The format is:

```
cache_dir storage_type directory-name megabytes L1 L2 [options]
```

The default storage type is ufs, which is the original Squid storage setup. There are other options available, but they are really necessary only if you have some specific problem with ufs. For most purposes, ufs is sufficient.

The default amount of space used is 100 MB, which you almost certainly want to change. For any reasonably sized disk cache (and considering that hard drives have never been cheaper), you probably want to allocate at least a couple of gigabytes to Squid. Squid won't be able to work effectively as a cache if it doesn't have enough disk space.

L1 sets how many top level subdirectories are created in the cache_dir directory (the default is 16) and L2 sets how many second-level subdirectories are created (the default is 256).

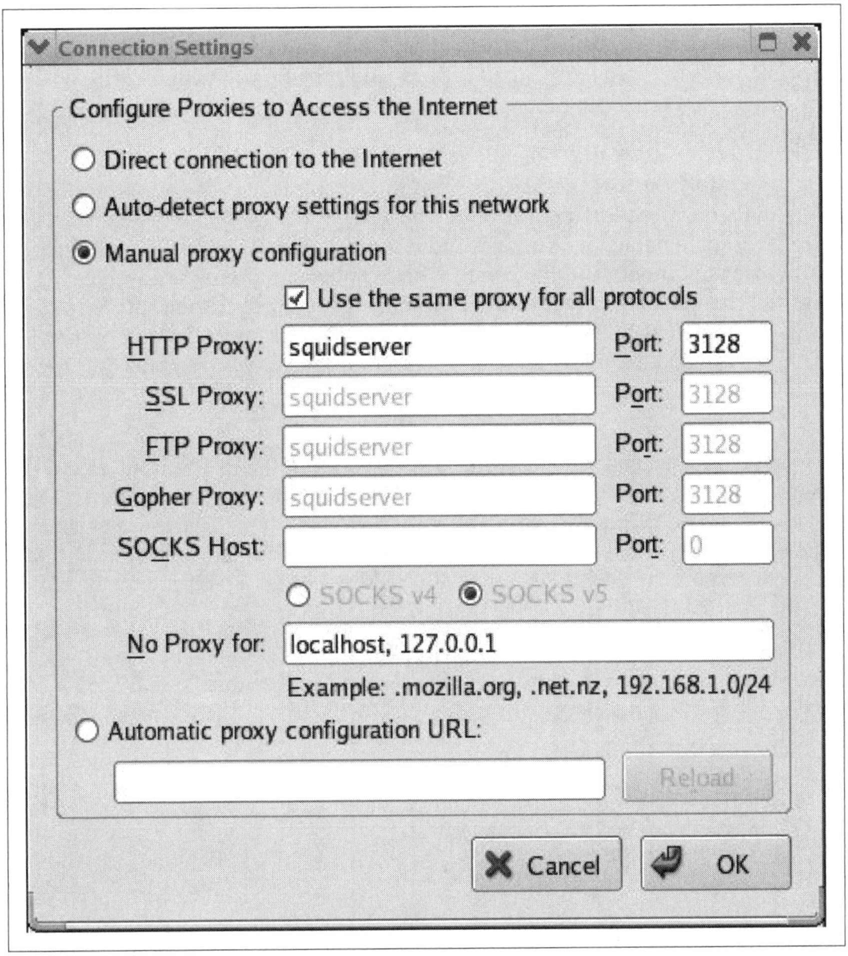

Figure 38-3. Setting proxy options in Firefox to use Squid proxy

So a standard line would look like this:

```
cache_dir ufs /var/spool/squid 10000 16 256
```

This sets a ufs cache directory at */var/spool/squid* and allocates 10 GB to it.

cache_mem option

This option lets you designate how much memory Squid can use. The more memory, the more responsive your cache is. If Squid hits this limit, it will start swapping to the disk, which decreases performance dramatically.

cache_access_log option

This option lets you designate a logfile that will keep a record of every request processed by Squid. The format of the logfile is configurable (you can even make it look like a standard Apache logfile), but it is recommended that you leave the format in the default Squid format. There are a number of good third-party reporting tools that can parse Squid log files and provide you with reports.

acl option

This is probably the most complex part of the Squid setup process. Access control lists allow you to determine not only who gets to use your proxy server (via IP address, domain name, or username and password) but also what sites they get to visit. Once you understand the concept, the implementation is relatively straightforward. The most important thing to remember is that, by default, the *Squid.conf* file is configured with ACL lines that will deny access to everything except the localhost. In order to allow anyone to use your cache, you're going to have to create some ACLs and allow them access.

In our test office environment, let's say that you have a Linux box with two network cards installed. One network card is connected to a DSL router, and the other one to a switch. Also connected to this switch are 10 office computers. You want to set up Squid on this system to cache web requests for the office to save on bandwidth. You also want to log all access, require authentication, and block access to certain web sites. The external IP address of the DSL router is dynamic, and the internal IP address is 192.168.1.1/255.255.255.0.

Here is an example *Squid.conf* file for this setup. This offers some default access control (all intranet users can access the cache) and enables cache access and logging.

```
http_port 192.168.1.1:3128
cache_mem 128M
cache_access_log /var/log/squid/access.log
cache_dir ufs /var/spool/squid 1000 16 256
acl all src 0.0.0.0/0.0.0.0
acl manager proto cache_object
acl localhost src 127.0.0.1/255.255.255.255
acl to_localhost dst 127.0.0.0/8
acl intranet src 192.168.1.0/24
acl SSL_ports port 443 563
acl Safe_ports port 80           # http
acl Safe_ports port 21           # ftp
acl Safe_ports port 443 563      # https, snews
acl Safe_ports port 70           # gopher
acl Safe_ports port 210          # wais
acl Safe_ports port 1025-65535   # unregistered ports
acl Safe_ports port 280          # http-mgmt
acl Safe_ports port 488          # gss-http
acl Safe_ports port 591          # filemaker
acl Safe_ports port 777          # multiling http
acl CONNECT method CONNECT
http_access allow manager localhost
http_access deny manager
http_access deny !Safe_ports
http_access deny CONNECT !SSL_ports
http_access allow localhost
```

```
http_access allow intranet
http_access deny all
```

The three key lines related to ACLs in the file are:

```
acl intranet src 192.168.1.0/24
http_access allow intranet
http_access deny all
```

The first ACL line defines an access control list named `intranet` that includes all systems with a source IP address in the range 192.168.1.0 through 192.168.1.255. This defines all of our internal office machines. The next line applies that ACL to a directive, in this case the `http_access` directive. This allows any system that matches the `intranet` ACL to have HTTP access to the cache. Finally, the last line denies access to any system not already explicitly allowed. This is usually good practice when setting up an ACL list, whether it's for a proxy cache, a firewall, or a router. Always have a "default deny" rule at the end, forcing you to explicitly allow anything that you want to provide access to. If your default policy is to allow, it's too easy to make a mistake in your configuration and let more through than you intend.

Now that we have a working configuration, let's add some settings to it. The first thing you might want to do is to restrict access to certain web sites. Whatever your company Internet access policy is, there are probably some web sites that you don't want your employees visiting. This is easy to implement in Squid, using an ACL. Here is an example ACL that defines some potentially nondesirable web sites:

```
acl blocked_sites dstdomain .espn.com espn.go.com .hotmail.com
```

Now that you've defined the ACL, apply it to the `http_access` directive:

```
http_access deny blocked_sites
```

Directives are processed in order, so you must ensure that your `http_access deny all` directive is *last*; otherwise, it will stop processing and override any following `allow` directives.

After you've added these two lines to your *Squid.conf* file, restart Squid and attempt to access *www.espn.com*. You should see a screen like Figure 38-4.

Also, you should see a line like this in your Squid *access.log*:

```
1136490718.221    870 192.168.1.33 TCP_DENIED/403 1419 GET http://www.espn.
com/ - NONE/- text/html
```

You can add as many domains as you wish to a directive like this. You can also filter on IP address and strings in URLs.

Squid Authentication

Now that we know how to set up our cache and allow (and deny) access to it, the next step is to consider authentication. The major advantages to requiring authentication to your cache are logging and access restriction. With authentication required, every HTTP request from evey user will be logged with a timestamp and the username. You can then easily run a report on this logfile to find out what

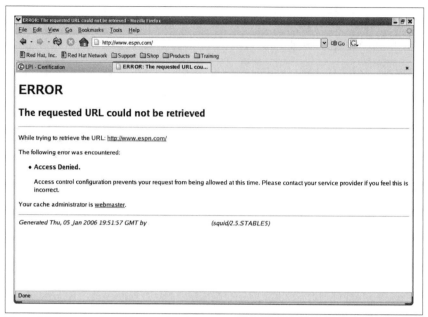

Figure 38-4. Access denied by Squid on host basis

web sites users are visiting. Squid supports many different kinds of external authentication (similarly to Apache). You can have Squid authenticate against your LDAP server, your RADIUS server, or your Microsoft Windows Active Directory server. For our purposes, we're going to demonstrate how to configure Squid to authenticate against a standard Apache authentication file created with the *htpasswd* program.

First, you must ensure that the *ncsa_auth* command came with your version of Squid. If you have a binary package from your vendor, *ncsa_auth* is probably in either */usr/sbin* or */usr/lib/squid*. If you compiled Squid from source, you have to go back to the Squid source tree and follow these steps:

```
# cd auth_modules/NCSA
# make
# make install
```

The next step is to create an authentication file with the *htpasswd* program. We already have *htpasswd* on our system at */opt/apache/bin/htpasswd* from our Apache install, so we can run this command:

```
# /opt/apache/bin/htpasswd -c /opt/squidusers.htpasswd demouser
```

Enter the password twice for *demouser* and we have our authentication file. Now we configure Squid to require all users to authenticate against this file. First we add these two lines:

```
auth_param basic program /usr/sbin/ncsa_auth /opt/squidusers.htpasswd
acl passwd proxy_auth REQUIRED
```

The auth_param line defines the program that will be used to read our password file. The ACL line creates an ACL called passwd that requires authentication. Finally, we modify our *http_access* line to look like this:

```
http_access allow intranet passwd
```

This provides access to the intranet ACL as long as the passwd ACL is satisfied. After restarting Squid, we try to go to *www.google.com* and we get a username and password dialog box. If we are unable to authenticate here, we'll see a screen that looks like Figure 38-5.

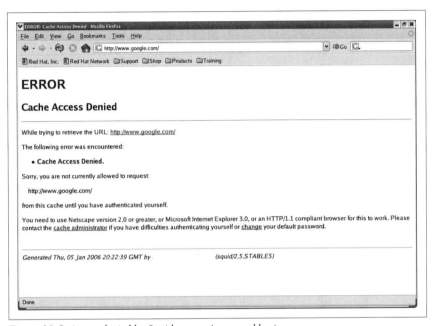

Figure 38-5. Access denied by Squid on user/password basis

Once we successfully authenticate, we don't need to reauthenticate until we restart our web browser. The Squid *access.log* file now has a line that looks like this:

```
1136492351.742    162 192.168.1.33 TCP_MISS/200 1642 GET http://www.google.
com/ demouser DIRECT/64.233.167.147 text/html
```

As you can see, the username *demouser* is now logged with every request.

Squid as Web Accelerator

In addition to the proxying aspects of Squid, it can also be used as a web accelerator. This is very similar in concept to Squid as a proxy server, but in this case, Squid is "closer" to the web server that is being queried. Squid sits "in front" of the web server, and when a request is made from any web browser for content that is on the web server, that request is handled by Squid. If Squid has the requested content in the cache, it is served directly to the client. If the content is not in the cache, Squid gets the content from the web server and then serves it to the client. This is useful in a number of situations:

If the original web server is too slow to handle all the requests
Because this setup puts less load on the web server itself (and more on Squid), performance increases.

If the original web server is on a slow line, which can't handle all of the traffic
If the Squid system is on a faster line, requests can come into Squid, and Squid will query the web server over the slow line only when a request cannot be fulfilled from the cache.

Let's look at an example configuration that would allow a Squid system to sit "in front" of a web server and handle incoming requests for it. Assume the Squid system has two network cards, one connected to a DSL router with an IP address of 1.1.1.1/255.255.255.0 and one connected to a switch with an IP address of 192.168.1.1/255.255.255.0. The web server we want to handle requests for is connected to the same switch and has an IP address of 192.168.1.2/255.255.255.0. It's running Apache, which is listening on port 80. Here is our example *Squid.conf*:

```
http_port 80
# forward incoming requests to 192.168.1.2, port 80
httpd_accel_host 192.168.1.2
acl acceleratedHost dst 192.168.1.2/255.255.255.255
httpd_accel_port 80
acl acceleratedPort port 80
httpd_accel_with_proxy on
acl all src 0.0.0.0/0.0.0.0
acl intranet src 192.168.1.0/255.255.255.0
# Allow requests when they are to the accelerated machine AND to the
# right port
http_access allow acceleratedHost acceleratedPort
http_access allow intranet
http_access deny all
```

Let's look at what each of these lines does:

http_port
Tells Squid to listen for requests on TCP port 80, because that is the default port over which web browsers will attempt to communicate

httpd_accel_host
What internal web server we are handling requests for

acl accelerated Host
Create an ACL that identifies our internal web server

httpd_accel_port
What port our internal web server is listening on

acl acceleratedPort
Create an ACL for the internal web server port

acl all
Define the catchall ACL, referred to in a later http_access statement

`acl intranet`
Define the local intranet ACL, referred to in a later `http_access` statement

`http_access allow acceleratedHost acceleratedPort`
Allow requests for our internal web server

`http_access allow intranet`
Allow proxy requests from the intranet

`http_access deny all`
Deny everything else

This configuration has the added bonus of allowing the Squid system to act as a proxy server for the internal network, as well as a web accelerator for the web site.

Once we are satisfied that this configuration works, we need to ensure that the DNS entry for our web site points to the Squid system, since it will be handling all of the incoming web requests.

Squid is a powerful tool and can make your web surfing much more efficient and easier to manage. For more information, be sure to visit the official Squid web site at *http://www.squid-cache.org*. You might also be interested in some of the Squid add-on tools. These tools include log file parsers and web site blacklists, to name a few. You can find a good list at *http://en.wikipedia.org/wiki/Squid_cache*.

39

Network Client Management
(Topic 2.210)

This Topic focuses on the tools required for network client management. This includes client network addressing, password management, and login authentication.

This Topic contains four Objectives:

Objective 1: DHCP Configuration
> The candidate should be able to configure a DHCP server and set default options, create a subnet, and create a dynamically allocated range. This Objective includes adding a static host, setting options for a single host, and adding *bootp* hosts. Also included is configuration of a DHCP relay agent and reloading the DHCP server after making changes. Weight: 2.

Objective 2: NIS Configuration
> The candidate should be able to configure an NIS server and create NIS maps for major configuration files. This Objective includes configuring a system as an NIS client, setting up an NIS slave server, and configuring ability to search local files, DNS, NIS, and so on, in *nsswitch.conf*. Weight: 1.

Objective 3: LDAP Configuration
> The candidate should be able to configure an LDAP server. This Objective includes configuring a directory hierarchy and adding group, hosts, services, and other data to the hierarchy. Also included is importing items from LDIF files and adding items with management tools, as well as adding users to the directory and changing passwords. Weight: 2.

Objective 4: PAM Authentication
> The candidate should be able to configure PAM to support authentication via traditional */etc/passwd*, shadow passwords, NIS, or LDAP. Weight: 2.

Objective 1: DHCP Configuration

DHCP is a superset of *bootp* and a replacement for that earlier protocol; both are used to assign IP addresses to clients on a network. DHCP is used for dynamic hosts that can move, connect, and disconnect from networks. DHCP can dynamically assign IP addresses from preassigned IP ranges in */etc/dhcpd.config* and set up static IP addresses based on the network interface card's Media Access Controller (MAC) address. DHCP can even restrict access by accepting requests only from specified MAC addresses.

Setting Up a DHCP Server

To set up a DHCP server, first ensure you have your DHCP package installed. Also read the README file, because it's full of useful information. Next, follow these steps:

1. Configure your */etc/dhcpd.conf* file (an example for setting random IPs for clients is in the next section).

2. Start the DHCP server in debug mode (*/usr/sbin/dhcpd -d -f*) to verify that DHCP is working properly.

3. To start the server for actual use, enter */etc/init.d/dhcpd start* or just */usr/bin/ dhcpd*, sending it into the background as a daemon.

Configuring DHCP options

The DHCP protocol has a vast number of options that it can pass to clients to configure them correctly. Some of the most important are shown in the following example:

```
default-lease-time 21600;
max-lease-time 43200;
option subnet-mask 255.255.255.0;
option broadcast-address 192.168.1.255;
option routers 192.168.1.254;
option domain-name-servers 192.168.1.1, 192.168.1.2;
option domain-name "example.com";
option ntp-servers 192.168.1.1;
```

Most of these should be self-explanatory. The lease times are how long the client can hold on to the IP address it is given without reconfirming with the server, in seconds. With the default-lease-time set to 21600, the client is instructed to contact the DHCP server at least every 6 hours. If it has not been in touch within 43,200 seconds, 12 hours, it should consider itself to be out of a lease.

Configuring dhcpd for random IP assignment

To set up DHCP to assign random IP addresses to DHCP clients on the network, you will need to configure the */etc/dhcpd.conf* file, which is the main configuration file for DHCP. The following listing contains sample settings for the */etc/ dhcpd.conf* that will allow DHCP to randomly assign IP addresses on your network between 192.168.1.10 and 192.168.1.100, as well as in the range 192. 168.1.150 through 192.168.1.200:

```
subnet 192.168.1.0 netmask 255.255.255.0 {
        range 192.168.1.10 192.168.1.100;
        range 192.168.1.150 192.168.1.200;
}
```

If you want to change the options for one subnet while leaving the global options unchanged for other subnets—for example, because one subnet is served by a different router—simply supply the options inside the subnet stanza.

With the options and subnet declarations shown, you have a working DHCP configuration. Remember to reload *dhcpd*, such as by running */etc/init.d/dhcp reload* (or *restart*, depending on the distribution).

Fixed addresses in dhcpd

Sometimes you want hosts to get the same address all the time. One trick to accomplish this is to set the lease time in the dynamic range very high (a month, perhaps). That way, a host needs to be off the net more than a month to not receive the same address.

A surer way to keep a host at a desired fixed address is to use static address assignment. This is done based on the Ethernet NIC's MAC address. In *dhcpd.conf*, insert something like this:

```
host roke {
        hardware ethernet 00:60:1D:1f:1e:ef;
        fixed-address 192.168.1.9;
}
```

When a client comes along that has an Ethernet address matching this, it will receive a lease on the 192.168.1.9 address. The address must be outside the dynamic ranges.

This host stanza is also how options are set for single hosts. Simply supply options for the host within the stanza.

bootp support

As noted earlier, *bootp* is the predecessor of DHCP. The ISC DHCP server can also support *bootp*, which is handy to support some Unix machines and network components. Each host that needs *bootp* must be listed explicitly. A declaration might look like the following.

```
host bootproke {
        hardware ethernet 08:00:2b:4c:59:23;
        fixed-address 192.168.1.105;
        filename "/tftpboot/bootproke.boot";
}
```

dhcpd.leases

This file is a log of all the leases the *dhcpd* server has given out. It includes only addresses in the dynamic ranges, and every time a dynamic lease is given, details about it are written to the end of this file. The most likely location for this file is */var/lib/dhcp/dhcpd.leases*. If you're installing DHCP service for the first time on this server, you need to make the initial lease database by just creating an empty file like this: *touch /var/lib/dhcp/dhcpd.leases*. An example entry is shown here:

```
lease 192.168.1.17 {
        starts 5 2004/01/02 10:53:18;
        ends 5 2004/01/02 20:13:57;
        hardware ethernet 00:02:2d:5e:74:8c;
        client-hostname "lookfar.langfeldt.net";
}
```

Using DHCP Clients

On Linux there are three DHCP clients, but *dhclient* and *pump* are the most common. Both are available on Debian and Red Hat systems. People are not in agreement about which of them works best, but this author has never been failed by *pump*. Both distributions' scripts should work with both clients. Using the DHCP client directly can be quite helpful in troubleshooting.

Using pump

The *pump* package comes with a usable default configuration that you will seldom want to override. The most likely reasons to change it are to stop it from modifying your DNS setup or overriding the settings given by the DHCP server. The standard configuration is in */etc/pump.conf* and looks like this:

```
domainsearch "example.com"

script /sbin/pump.script

device eth0 {
        nodns
}
```

The first line just overrides the domain list that pump would use to update */etc/resolv.conf*. The nodns keyword for *eth0* stops *pump* from changing the *resolv.conf* at all—at least based on DHCP answers received on *eth0*. Answers to *eth1* can still do it.

To get a DHCP lease for *eth0*, issue *dhcp -i eth0*. To check the status of your DHCP lease, enter:

```
# pump --status
Device eth0
        IP: 172.22.12.88
        Netmask: 255.255.252.0
        Broadcast: 172.22.15.255
        Network: 172.22.12.0
        Boot server 172.22.12.10
```

```
Next server 172.22.12.10
Gateway: 127.22.12.1
Domain: example.com
Nameservers: 172.22.12.5 172.22.12.1
Renewal time: Tue Jan 15 04:53:49 2004
Expiration time: Wed Jan 16 01:53:49 2004
```

Other important operations are -r (release lease) and -R (renew lease).

Using dhclient

dhclient can act pretty much on its own, but it is extremely configurable, and it may have more functions than you ever dreamed of—certainly too many for us to get into here. If it is started without a configuration, it finds all your network interfaces and sends out DHCP requests on all of them. Once it has received a lease and configured an interface, it goes into the background. In the background it will maintain your leases and keep your interface configured. Depending on the packager, it may or may not update your DNS configuration and configure your network based on options in the DHCP protocol. To release your lease, run the client again with -r. The background *dhclient* process will exit.

As with *pump*, you will most likely not need a configuration file. But if you do, you can set up something like the preceding *pump* configuration very simply as shown here:

```
supersede domain-name "example.com";
prepend domain-name-servers 127.0.0.1;
```

Configuring Red Hat as a DHCP client

To configure your Red Hat host to be a DHCP client, use the intuitive *neat* command. Red Hat works with either *dhclient* or *pump*.

To make sure you are connected to the DHCP server, run *ifconfig*. The eth0 section of the output should have an inet addr: entry with your DHCP-assigned network address.

Alternatively, change your interface network script */etc/sysconfig/network-scripts/ifcfg-eth0* from:

```
DEVICE=eth1
ONBOOT=yes
BOOTPROTO=none
HWADDR=00:0B:6A:10:49:5A
NETMASK=255.255.255.0
USERCTL=no
PEERDNS=yes
GATEWAY=10.163.45.254
TYPE=Ethernet
IPADDR=10.163.45.210
```

to the following, editing it to fit your needs:

```
DEVICE=eth1
ONBOOT=yes
BOOTPROTO=dhcp
HWADDR=00:0B:6A:10:49:5A
```

After that you need to reload your configuration to validate the modifications using the script provided: */etc/init.d/network reload*.

Configuring Debian as a DHCP client

You can configure a Debian host's networking during installation. After installation, the simplest way to do it is to edit */etc/network/interfaces* directly. If you want *eth0* to be managed by a DHCP client, simply make sure that the iface line, shown in the following example, is in the configuration. The auto line makes sure that the card is taken up when booting.

```
auto eth0
iface eth0 inet dhcp
```

DHCP Relay

Since DHCP uses Ethernet broadcast to get in touch with the DHCP server, it cannot get in touch with a server on another subnet, because broadcasts are not routed. In a large network, it's not very practical to put a DHCP server on each subnet, so instead you can use *DHCP relay*. This is most often done by routers. Cisco routers, for example, offer *ip helper-address* to set the address to relay DHCP requests to. If your routers do not support relaying, any Unix or Linux host can do the job. To relay all requests seen on *eth0* to the DHCP server at 192. 168.1.5, relaying can be started as follows. It will then catch all requests and relay them to the server, the server will answer back to the relay agent, and the relay agent will send the answer back to the requester.

```
# dhcrelay -i eth0 192.168.1.5
Internet Software Consortium DHCP Relay Agent V3.0pl2
Copyright 1997-2000 Internet Software Consortium.
All rights reserved.
For info, please visit http://www.isc.org/products/DHCP
Listening on LPF/eth0/00:03:93:ce:2f:c0
Sending on   LPF/eth0/00:03:93:ce:2f:c0
Sending on   Socket/fallback
```

Objective 2: NIS Configuration

NIS is Sun's Network Information Service. It was formerly known as Yellow Pages, but after a trademark dispute with British Telecom, Sun changed the name to Network Information Service. The history of Yellow Pages is why many NIS-related commands begin with *yp*.

NIS is a simple directory service whose main purpose is to allow remote authentication for systems on local network systems. NIS allows information such as *passwd* and group files, sendmail aliases, automount maps, and hosts files to be kept on a central server. Each system in the NIS domain runs the NIS client, *ypbind*, to find a server and retrieve the appropriate maps from it.

NIS uses a master/slave server configuration that resembles DNS. The master NIS server holds the NIS map files. Changes to the maps are then pushed to any slave servers. While an NIS domain can operate with only one server, it is best to have at least one slave server for redundancy.

You must run the RPC portmapper (*/usr/sbin/portmap*) to run NIS. The RPC port-mapper servers convert the RPC program numbering to TCP/IP or UDP/IP protocol port numbers.

Most Linux distributions ship with NIS Version 2. NIS Version 3 is known as NIS+ and is not in widespread use.

Before setting up servers or clients, you must decide on a domain name for your NIS setup. The domain is used to ensure that you're talking to the right NIS servers. This domain name has nothing to do with DNS, your DNS domain name, or your hostnames. Most directory administrators use the same domain in NIS as in DNS to simplify network administration, but the NIS domain could be completely different from the DNS domain. The command *domainname* or *ypdo-mainname* are usually links to the *hostname* binary and can be used to set the NIS domain. This has nothing to do with the *hostname* command.

NIS Master Server

You should have at least two NIS servers, one master and one slave. If one of them fails, the clients using it will switch to the other automatically. To set up a server, start by installing the NIS and/or YP packages in your distribution. On the server side, you have the tools shown in Table 39-1:

Table 39-1. NIS server-side tools

Tool	Description
ypserv	The NIS server program
yppasswdd	Server that handles the NIS password changes
yppush	Notifies the slave servers when changes are made to master databases
ypinit	Installs and builds an NIS database

Sometimes some of these have an *rpc.* prefix in their filenames. After having the server tools installed, you must configure and initialize them. Do the following to get a master server:

1. All planned NIS servers, masters, and slaves must be present in your */etc/hosts* file. Following the IP address, place the fully qualified domain name, which is the hostname including the DNS domain, then the bare name and any aliases, like this:

   ```
   10.0.0.5roke.example.com roke mailserver nisserver
   ```

2. Configure your domain name. On Debian, simply put the name in the */etc/ defaultdomain* file. On Red Hat you must set the NISDOMAIN variable to your domain name in */etc/sysconfig/network*.

3. Set the correct networks in */etc/ypserv.securenets*. If your internal network uses the 10.0.0.0/255.255.255.0 subnet, for instance, the file should look something like this:

   ```
   # Always allow access for localhost

   255.0.0.0      127.0.0.0
   ```

```
# This line gives access to ourselves
255.255.255.010.0.0.0
```

4. Start the master server processes. On Debian, you simply set NISSERVER=master in */etc/default/nis* and start the needed services with */etc/init. d/nis start*. On Red Hat you must start all the master server services one by one, using the scripts installed in */etc/init.d*:

   ```
   # ypserv start
   # yppasswdd start
   # ypxfrd start
   # ypbind start
   ```

   You can execute *ypserv -d* to run the process in the foreground and stream debug messages to console output. If you type *ypserv* without the *-d* option, the process will run in the background and just report errors (access violations, *dbm* failures) using the syslog facility.

5. Initialize the server maps or databases. Before doing this, you need an */etc/ networks* file, even if it's empty. Then you can do the initialization of the master server:

   ```
   /usr/lib/yp/ypinit -m
   ```

   This populates the databases from the contents of your master server system files. The work is done in */var/yp/Makefile*. By customizing this file, you can change the location of the master files. Most often people change the location of the master *passwd* and *groups* files. If you do that, you should take a look at the *yppasswdd* manpage to tell that command where the master files are.

   If you run *ypcat passwd* now, you should get a listing of all or some of the entries from your */etc/passwd* file.

6. Now you have to set up the master as a client as well.

NIS Client

The tools provided for manipulating clients arelisted in Table 39-2.

Table 39-2. NIS client-side tools

Tool	Description
ypwhich	Returns the name of the NIS server used by the NIS client
ypcat	Prints the values of all keys in the specified NIS map
yppoll	Returns the version and master server of the specified NIS map
ypmatch	Prints the values of specified keys from an NIS map
ypdomainname	Prints or sets the name of the NIS domain
yppasswd	Changes passwords in the NIS server

yppasswd is needed because the standard *passwd* command can change only passwords in */etc/passwd* and */etc/shadow*, but that is not very well-suited for a network information service. You need a special command that is aware of NIS to update the password on the master server.

Setting up an NIS client is simple. The following steps cover the process:

1. Set the NIS domain name. On Debian, */etc/defaultdomain* should contain the domain name. On Red Hat, set NISDOMAIN in */etc/sysconfig/network*.

2. Start *ypbind*. On Debian, set NISSERVER=false in */etc/default/nis* (unless you're on your master server, of course) and then run */etc/init.d/nis start*. On Red Hat, simply run */etc/init.d/ypbind start*. If your server is not on the same IP subnet, you must customize */etc/yp.conf* and set the server name there.

3. Customize */etc/nsswitch.conf*. All the name services that should get information from NIS should have nis somewhere on the line. This includes the *whole* of the NIS map contents. On the passwd, group, and shadow lines, you should always put file in front of nis.

   NIS offers an access control method based on users and groups. The entries for passwd, group, and shadow accept a special compat option, which enables you to use a + in the corresponding files. This is described later.

4. When you now enter getent passwd, you should see the contents of your local *passwd* file as well as the contents of the NIS *passwd* file.

After *ypbind* is running, you can see what NIS server it has bound itself to with *ypwhich*. *ypcatmap* lists the contents of the specified map. *ypmatchkeymap* lists just the specified entry of the specified map.

compat

When compat is listed as the passwd, shadow, and group source in *nsswitch.conf*, you can use a special syntax in the files. We'll use the password file as an example, but the same goes in the other files, save for the number of colons.

To allow access to the system to the users *janl* and *killroy*, the two first lines in the followng example do the job. The third line illustrates group access, allowing an NIS netgroup called *ftpusers* in as FTP users only. Note that even if *janl* and *killroy* are members of this netgroup, they still get full access, because they are listed in the password file before the netgroup line. The last line includes all the other users in NIS but sets their password to * and shell to */etc/nologin*, barring them from using the system.

```
+janl::::::
+killroy::::::
+@ftpusers::::::/etc/ftponly
+:*:::::/etc/nologin
```

Most often, only the last form is used in group files. But it is easier and faster to just put groups: files, nis in *nsswitch.conf*.

NIS slave server

Once a host is an NIS client, it can be set up as a slave by performing these steps:

1. Ensure that your slave server is listed in the master's */etc/hosts* file and vice versa.

2. Configure the slave's */etc/ypserv.securenets* file.

3. The master must know that it has slaves. On the master, set NOPUSH to false in /var/yp/Makefile.

4. On the master, run /usr/lib/yp/ypinit -m again. Add your slave when it asks for it.

5. Back on the slave, start the slave server processes. On Debian, set NISSERVER=slave in /etc/default/nis and run /etc/init.d/nis stop;/etc/init.d/nis restart (using restart because it's already started as a client). On Red Hat, start the server process with: /etc/init.d/ypserv start.

6. Initialize the slave server by running /usr/lib/yp/ypinit -s master-server.

7. Run ypcat -h localhost passwd to verify that the slave works correctly.

8. Because NIS servers do not autosynchronize, you need to configure synchronization on the master. Put the following in /etc/cron.d/nis to ensure that it updates the slaves regularly:

```
10 *     * * *    root  /usr/lib/yp/ypxfr_1perhour >/dev/null 2>&1
20 6,18 * * *     root  /usr/lib/yp/ypxfr_2perday  >/dev/null 2>&1
40 5     * * *    root  /usr/lib/yp/ypxfr_1perday  >/dev/null 2>&1
```

The hourly job transfers the passwd, shadow, and group maps. The twice daily job transfers hosts, netgroups, and the networks maps. The once daily file just transfers the protocols, RPC, and services maps. Of course, there is nothing wrong with running these more often, but they always transfer the complete maps, so on large sites with thousands of entries in the maps and multiple slave servers, they're going to take some time.

These map transfer scripts and cron times should be modified to meet your needs, such as including new maps and excluding old ones, as in this example:

```
[root@pirarucu yp]# cat ypxfr_1perhour
#! /bin/sh

YPBINDIR=/usr/lib/yp

MAPS_TO_GET="passwd.byname passwd.byuid shadow.byname publickey.byname
hosts.byname hosts.byaddr netgroup netgroup.byuser netgroup.byhost
group.byname group.bygid protocols.byname protocols.bynumber
networks.byname networks.byaddr rpc.byname rpc.bynumber services.byname
ypservers auto.home seismic_users"

for map in $MAPS_TO_GET
do
  echo "Syncing map: $map ..."
  $YPBINDIR/ypxfr -c -s ep.bc.nismaster.gov.br -d ep.bc.nisslave.gov.br
$map
done
```

Don't forget to make all the NIS processes start when the system boots.

NIS Maps and Tools

Map lookups and nicknames

During the previous setup, you may have noticed that NIS does not have a *passwd* file, but it does have *passwd.byname* and *passwd.byuid*. If you look in */var/yp/domain_name*, where *domain_name* is the NIS domain name, you'll see the map names that NIS has as shown in a listing like this:

```
# ls /var/yp/nismaster.gov.br
group.bygid    netgroup.byhost   protocols.byname     services.byservicename
group.byname   netgroup.byuser   protocols.bynumber   shadow.byname
hosts.byaddr   netid.byname      rpc.byname           ypservers
hosts.byname   passwd.byname     rpc.bynumber
netgroup       passwd.byuid      services.byname
```

These files are provided for the standard Unix and Linux system calls that do name resolution, such as *getpwnam* and *getpwuid*. When getting information from files, these functions have to iterate through the whole */etc/passwd* file to find the given name or UID. In NIS, instead, they do a lookup into the map indexed by the username or the UID, namely *passwd.byname* and *passwd.byuid*. The same goes for the lookup functions for the other system files that are in NIS. The following example demonstrates a lookup by name and UID in the NIS passwd files.

```
# ypmatch killroy passwd.byname
killroy:x:1002:100::/home/killroy:/bin/bash
# ypmatch 1002 passwd.byuid
killroy:x:1002:100::/home/killroy:/bin/bash
```

To obtain the complete NIS passwd file, one can iterate through the whole map, and any of the maps will do. That is what *ypcat* does. To make using NIS a bit more like the system files, there are map aliases so that you can refer to the databases by the name you're used to. passwd is a alias for passwd.byname, and so on for all the other maps. Table 39-3 shows these aliases, or nicknames.

Table 39-3. NIS map aliases

Alias	Map name
aliases	*mail.aliases*
ethers	*ethers.byname*
group	*group.byname*
hosts	*hosts.byname*
networks	*networks.byaddr*
passwd	*passwd.byname*
protocols	*protocols.bynumber*
services	*services.byname*

Check the map nickname translation table with the command *ypwhich -k*.

Keeping maps up to date

If you ever suspect that your NIS maps are out of sync, you can do what the master server does: poll their versions to compare them:

```
# yppoll -h localhost passwd.byname
Domain example.com is supported.
Map passwd.byname has order number 1076234245. [Sun Feb  8 10:57:25 2004]
The master server is debian.example.com.
# yppoll -h roke passwd.byname
Domain example.com is supported.
Map passwd.byname has order number 1076234245. [Sun Feb  8 10:57:25 2004]
The master server is debian.example.com.
```

These maps are the same. But if the slave is not up-to-date and you want to force updating just one map on one or more servers, use *yppush*. On the master, enter something like this:

```
# yppush -h roke passwd.byname
```

If you do not include the *-h* option, the map will be pushed to all the slaves. You can also enter several *-h* options to push it to several named slaves.

Netgroups

Netgroups have been mentioned before in this chapter and also in relation to NFS. They are most useful as a mechanism to support access control for machines (in the password file as shown earlier) and for restricting NFS shares to certain hosts. The general format is as follows:

```
netgroup  (host,user,domain) | netgroup [ , ... ]
```

The actual use may be clearer from the following example:

```
nfsservers      (server1,,), (server2,,)
nfsclients      (client1,,), (client2,,), nfsservers
serverusers     (,user1,), (,user2,)
```

If you use compat for passwd: in */etc/nsswitch.conf*, you can now enter +@serverusers::::::: at the end of the */etc/passwd* to allow the NIS users *user1* and *user2* access. You may need to put the equivalent entries in your */etc/shadow* file as well.

On NFS servers you can use *@netgroup* syntax in */etc/exports* instead of host-names. For instance:

```
/var/export @nfsservers(rw,no_root_squash) @nfsclients(rw,root_squash)
```

If you try to use *ypcat* on the netgroup map, it won't tell you much, because the netgroup names are only stored as keys and won't be shown. Add the *-k* option to se the keys as well, as shown here:

```
# ypcat -k netgroup
nfsservers (server1,,), (server2,,)
serverusers (,user1,), (,user2,)
nfsclients (client1,,), (client2,,), nfsservers
```

RPC calls

The utility *rpcinfo* can be used to detect and debug a variety of failures. Just type *rpcinfo -p hostname* to check how the things are going in your NIS server. Here's an output of a functional NIS server:

```
# rpcinfo -p localhost
   program vers proto   port
    100000    2   tcp    111  portmapper
    100000    2   udp    111  portmapper
    390011    4   tcp  32772
    390008    1   tcp  32776
    100004    2   udp    852  ypserv
    100004    2   tcp    855  ypserv
    100007    2   udp    725  ypbind
    100007    2   tcp    728  ypbind
    100011    1   udp    840  rquotad
    100011    1   tcp    857  rquotad
    100003    2   udp   2049  nfs
    100003    2   tcp   2049  nfs
    100021    1   udp  33745  nlockmgr
    100021    4   tcp  36331  nlockmgr
    100005    1   udp    853  mountd
    100005    1   tcp    865  mountd
    100005    2   udp    853  mountd
    100024    1   udp  32768  status
    100024    1   tcp  32769  status
```

The output from *rpcinfo* shows the RPC program and version numbers, the protocols supported, the IP port used by the RPC server, and the name of the service. If *rpcinfo* times out while attempting to reach the remote machine and reports an error, check whether the portmapper service is alive.

```
# /etc/init.d/portmap status
portmap (pid 2124) is running...
```

Objective 3: LDAP Configuration

LDAP is an open standard protocol for accessing directory information services. The LDAP protocol runs over TCP protocols and other Internet transport protocols. LDAP can be used to access either standalone directory services or X.500 directories. The hardest part about LDAP is its X.500 heritage. X.500 was part of the now failed OSI network protocol suite. There are many good reasons for the OSI suite failing, and one of them is complexity. The suite was designed by a committee, and the old joke "a camel is a horse designed by a committee" is not without justification. From X.500, the IETF (Internet Engineering Task Force) derived and specified LDAP (Lightweight Directory Access Protocol).

LDAP provides the same kind of services as DNS and NIS. When it is combined with SSL (Secure Sockets Layer) and some tricks, it should also be quite secure—unlike DNS and NIS.

LDAP directory service is based on a client/server model, quite similar to NIS. One (or more) LDAP servers contain the data used to make up the LDAP directory tree or backend database. An LDAP client connects to the LDAP server to make a request. The server responds to the request with either an answer or a pointer to where the client can get an answer to its request. One of the biggest benefits of LDAP over NIS is that LDAP servers synchronize in increments that can be pushed immediately to slave servers, whereas NIS synchronizations transfer all the data every time.

The LDAP implementation used on Linux is OpenLDAP. The OpenLDAP project is a collaborative effort to provide an open source LDAP suite of applications and tools. Like Netscape's Directory Server, OpenLDAP is based on the original University of Michigan LDAP server project.

Most LDAPs mirror DNS in how they are structured. At *example.com*, they store their LDAP data under dc=example,dc=com. The dc attribute is a domain component, referring directly to a part of a DNS domain. As in DNS, the order is significant, and the names are hierarchical with the rightmost element being the top of the tree (the start of the tree, because like all trees in computing, the LDAP tree grows from the top down).

Setting Up OpenLDAP Server

The OpenLDAP package provides the server *slapd*, which is complete in itself. There is also an X.500 gateway called *ldapd*. OpenLDAP accomplishes replication with *slurpd*.

slapd
> This is the standalone LDAP daemon. It listens for LDAP connections on default port 389 (636 for SSL).

slurpd
> This propagates changes from one LDAP database to another using a master/slave topology. OpenLDAP multimaster replication support is under development.

The configuration file that sets up LDAP server behavior is */etc/openldap/sldap.conf*. The following example file is a good start:

```
include      %SYSCONFDIR%/schema/core.schema

pidfile      %LOCALSTATEDIR%/run/slapd.pid
argsfile     %LOCALSTATEDIR%/run/slapd.args

# Load dynamic backend modules:
# modulepath    %MODULEDIR%
# moduleload    back_bdb.la
# moduleload    back_ldap.la
# moduleload    back_ldbm.la
# moduleload    back_passwd.la
# moduleload    back_shell.la

# Sample security restrictions
#     Require integrity protection (prevent hijacking)
#     Require 112-bit (3DES or better) encryption for updates
```

```
#     Require 63-bit encryption for simple bind
# security ssf=1 update_ssf=112 simple_bind=64

# Sample access control policy:
#     Root DSE: allow anyone to read it
#     Subschema (sub)entry DSE: allow anyone to read it
#     Other DSEs:
#         Allow self-write access
#         Allow authenticated users read access
#         Allow anonymous users to authenticate
#     Directives needed to implement policy:
# access to dn.base="" by * read
# access to dn.base="cn=Subschema" by * read
# access to *
#     by self write
#     by users read
#     by anonymous auth
#
# if no access controls are present, the default policy
# allows anyone and everyone to read anything but restricts
# updates to rootdn.  (e.g., "access to * by * read")
#
# rootdn can always read and write EVERYTHING!


#######################################################################
# BDB database definitions
#######################################################################

database    bdb
suffix       "dc=my-domain,dc=com"
rootdn       "cn=Manager,dc=my-domain,dc=com"
# Clear text passwords, especially for the rootdn, should
# be avoided.  See slappasswd(8) and slapd.conf(5) for details.
# Use of strong authentication encouraged.
rootpw       secret
# The database directory MUST exist prior to running slapd AND
# should only be accessible by the slapd and slap tools.
# Mode 700 recommended.
directory    %LOCALSTATEDIR%/openldap-data
# Indices to maintain
index     objectClass     eq
```

Here is the same file customized for a particular installation:

```
include        /etc/openldap/schema/core.schema
include        /etc/openldap/schema/cosine.schema
include        /etc/openldap/schema/inetorgperson.schema
include        /etc/openldap/schema/nis.schema
include        /etc/openldap/schema/openldap.schema
include        /etc/openldap/schema/solaris.schema

pidfile        /var/lib/run/slapd.pid
argsfile       /var/lib/run/slapd.args
```

```
database        bdb
suffix          "dc=company,dc=com"
rootdn          "cn=Manager,dc=company,dc=com"
rootpw          {SSHA}qBhyzgbrdg2HFEA4oy9SOVfxLfVlZCuaa
directory       /var/lib/openldap-data
index   objectClass     eq
```

And the following command validates the customized configuration:

 # slaptest
```
config file testing succeeded
```

The following list describes the directives in the file:

include
> Specifies that *slapd* should read additional configuration information from the given file.

pidfile
> Specifies the file that will contain the *slapd* server's process ID if it is not running in the foreground.

argsfile
> Specifies the file that will contain the *slapd* daemon parameters.

database
> Specifies which database backend to use to store directory information. Currently, the types listed in Table 39-4 are supported:

Table 39-4. Databse backends supported by OpenLDAP

Type	Description
bdb	Berkeley DB transactional backend
dnssrv	DNS SRV backend
ldap	LDAP Proxy backend
ldbm	Lightweight DBM backend
meta	Meta directory backend
monitor	Monitor backend
passwd	Provides read-only access to passwd
perl	Perl programmable backend
shell	Shell (external program) backend
sql	SQL programmable backend

suffix
> Specifies the DN suffix of queries that will be passed to the backend database.

rootdn
> Specifies the directory administrator's username.

> The user specified in rootdn can read and write everything.

`rootpw`

Specifies the hash of the password for the `rootdn` user.

 Never use an empty or clear password here.

A strong hash can be generated using *slappasswd* with the CRYPT, MD5, SMD5, SSHA, or SHA schemes. The default, and strongest, scheme is SSHA.

```
# slappasswd -h {SSHA}
New password:
Re-enter new password:
{SSHA}qBhyzgbrdg2HFEA4oy9S0VfxLfVlZCuaa
```

`directory`

Specifies the database files. Typical contacts are:

```
# ls -l /var/lib/openldap-data
total 548
-rw-------  1 root root   8192 Dec 29  2004 __db.001
-rw-------  1 root root 270336 Dec 29  2004 __db.002
-rw-------  1 root root  98304 Dec 29  2004 __db.003
-rw-------  1 root root 368640 Dec 29  2004 __db.004
-rw-------  1 root root  24576 Dec 29  2004 __db.005
-rw-------  1 root root   8192 Feb 17 19:26 dn2id.bdb
-rw-------  1 root root  32768 Feb 17 19:26 id2entry.bdb
-rw-------  1 root root 118789 Feb 17 19:26 log.0000000001
-rw-------  1 root root   8192 Mar 10  2005 objectClass.bdb
```

 All these files should be backed up frequently.

`index`

Specifies the indexes to maintain for the given attribute.

With the file in place, start the *slapd* daemon in debug mode to check whether things are working properly:

```
# /usr/lib/openldap/slapd -4 -d10 -f /etc/openldap/slapd.conf
@(#) $OpenLDAP: slapd 2.2.26 (Feb 16 2006 16:42:31) $
bdb_db_init: Initializing BDB database
slapd starting
daemon: added 6r
daemon: select: listen=6 active_threads=0 tvp=NULL
```

Create organizational units using the *ldapadd* command and an LDIF file like the following:

```
dn: dc=example,dc=com
objectClass: dcObject
objectClass: organization
dc: example
```

```
o: Corporation
description: Corporation

dn: cn=Manager,dc=example,dc=com
objectClass: organizationalRole
cn: Manager
description: Directory Manager
```

Commit your entries to the directory tree:

```
ldapadd -f file.ldif -x -D "cn=Manager,dc=example,dc=com" -w password
```

Setting Up Client Tools

Setting up an LDAP client requires several steps, which we'll lay out in this section. Some of the tools available to LDAP clients include:

ldapmodify
> Opens a connection to an LDAP server, binds to it, and modifies or adds entries.

ldapadd
> Adds an entry. Implemented as a hard link to the *ldapmodify* tool.

ldapdelete
> Deletes one or more entries in a database.

ldappasswd
> Changes the password of an LDAP entry.

ldapsearch
> A powerful LDAP search tool.

ldapwhoami
> Implements the LDAP "Who Am I?" extended operation.

First, enter the information in the LADP client configuration file needed to be retrieved by these tools. This file should be world-readable, but not world-writable.

```
BASE dc=example, dc=com
URI ldap://ldap.example.com ldap://ldap-master.example.com:666
```

Now verify the entries added to the directory server:

```
ldapsearch -x -b 'dc=example,dc=com' '(objectclass=*)'
```

This will retrieve every entry in the directory.

Objective 4: PAM Authentication

PAM is the Pluggable Authentication Modules system. It enables the addition of a number of advanced security features across the whole Linux system without the need to recode individual services. All security conscious programs (such as *login*, *su*, and *ftp*) are configured by PAM to do a variety of authentication and security checks.

When a service such as *login* is used, PAM will check its configuration files to determine how to authenticate the user. For instance, PAM may authenticate by checking *shadow passwords*, Kerberos, Winbind, Samba, and so on. After the method of authentication is determined, PAM returns an answer to the service to indicate whether the user was authenticated.

PAM Configuration

All the PAM configuration files are located in */etc/pam.d*. Every application or service that can use PAM has a file entry in */etc/pam.d* as well. Some of the most common entries that can be found under */etc/pam.d* include chfn, chsh, halt, linuxconf, login, passwd, ppp, reboot, rexec, rlogin, rsh, shutdown, su, xdm, and xscreensaver. If installed, you may even find KDE, Samba, and SSH here as well. Looking at these files, you will see four columns of information: module-type, control-flag, module-path, and arguments. Take a look at the following example of the login entry under */etc/pam.d*:

```
#%PAM-1.0
auth       required    /lib/security/pam_securetty.so
auth       required    /lib/secuirty/pam_pwdb.so       shadow nullok
auth       required    /lib/security/pam_nologin.so
account    required    /lib/security/pam_pwdb.so
password   required    /lib/security/pam_cracklib.so
password   required    /lib/security/pam_pwdb.so nullok use_authtok
session    required    /lib/security/pam_pwdb.so
session    optional    /lib/security/pam_console.so
```

The following subsections describe each field.

module-type

There are currently four types of modules that you will find under the module-type column in your PAM configuration files, shown inTable 39-5.

Table 39-5. Module types

Module	Description
auth	This module type provides two ways of authenticating the user. First, it establishes that the user is indeed who the user claims to be. It does this by instructing the application to prompt the user for a password. The module can then grant group membership (independent of */etc/groups*) or other privileges through its credential granting properties.
account	This module restricts authentication-based account management. It is typically used to restrict or permit access to a service based on the time of day, the maximum number of users, or even the location of the user (for instance, allowing user *root* to log in only from the console).
session	This module performs duties that need to be done for the user before she can be given access. Services that are affected by this include the logging of information about a user, mounting directories, and so on.
password	This module is required for updating the authentication token associated with each user. There is typically one module for each challenge or response, based on the authentication (auth) module type.

control-flag

The control-flag column is used to indicate how the PAM library reacts to the success or failure of the module with which it is associated. The four flags that are used to specify the module actions are shown in Table 39-6.

Table 39-6. Control flags

Flag	Description
optional	This flag marks the module as not being critical to the success or failure of the user's application for service. In fact, Linux-PAM will ignore such a module when determining whether the module stack succeeds or fails.
required	This indicates that the success of the module is required for the *module-type* facility to succeed. But if this module fails, the failure will not be apparent to the user until all the modules of the same module type have been executed.
requisite	This is similar to required, but if this module fails, control is immediately returned to the application. This flag is useful to protect against the possibility of a user being allowed to enter a password over an unsafe medium.
sufficient	This indicates that the Linux-PAM library is satisfied that this module type has succeeded in its purpose. If no previous module has failed, no more stacked modules of this type are invoked. If this module fails, the result is not deemed fatal to the application.

module-path and arguments

The module-path is the pathname to the dynamically loadable module. The default directory containing the module defaults to */lib/security*, unless another path is mentioned. Typically, the full path */lib/security* is listed regardless.

The argument column of each entry lists arguments that are passed to the module when the module is invoked. Typically, these arguments are optional and are specific to each given module. If an argument is invalid, the module ignores it. If such an error is made, the module is required to write the error to syslog, the system log daemon. The five generic arguments that are often used and understood by most modules are shown in Table 39-7.

Table 39-7. Arguments

Argument	Description
debug	Use the syslog call to log debugging information to the system log files.
no_warn	Instruct the module not to give warning messages to the application.
try_first_pass	The module should attempt authentication with the previously typed password from the preceding auth module. If that does not work, the user is prompted for a password.
use_first_pass	The module should not prompt the user for a password. Instead, it should obtain the previously typed password from the preceding auth module. If that does not work, the user will not be authenticated.
use_mapped_pass	Instructs the module to take the clear text authentication token entered by a previous module and use it to generate an encrypted (or decrypted) key to safely store or retrieve the authentication token required for the module.
	The use_mapped_pass argument is not currently supported by any of the modules in the Linux-PAM distribution because of possible consequences associated with U.S. encryption restrictions. Developers within the United States (or their own country) may implement it freely within their country.

A special argument listed in the example for auth was shadow. This refers to support for shadow passwords, which is supported by *pam_pwdb.so*. Shadow passwords utilize several methods to increase system security. They make system password files more difficult to break into for system password information, by replacing the password field of */etc/passwd* (with an x) and creating the file */etc/shadow*, readable only by *root*, to contain the password hash.

LDAP Client Authentication Using PAM

One of the best uses of LDAP is to centralize your authentication information base. It makes user administration easier and smarter. The authentication method should be changed in the PAM mechanism, and you need to change the way to search the tree where the user's information (password, UID, GID, home, shell) is placed. Multiple client platforms—Solaris, Linux, AIX, and so on—can use an LDAP server for authentication

 The following examples require a fully functional OpenLDAP server, a posix account object already created in your directory, and properly working client-side queries.

Packages for LDAP and PAM

Two packages are needed to get LDAP auhentication working:

nss_ldap
> Used by *nsswitch.conf* to retrieve information from LDAP servers

pam_ldap
> The PAM module that can be used to take advantage of LDAP in many PAM-aware applications

Both are available under GPL license at the maintainer's site, *www.padl.com*. The configuration, compilation, and installation process is simple and can be determined from the site's documentation.

Debian, Red Hat, and many other distributions make available precompiled *nss_ldap* and *pam_ldap* packages.

Configuring nss_ldap and nsswitch.conf

With the packages installed, change the *nsswitch.conf* file to the following:

```
passwd:        files ldap
group:         files ldap
shadow:        files ldap
```

To test whether *nss_ldap* is retrieving LDAP information, try:

```
# getent passwd
...(you should see the /etc/passwd accounts here)
cxp7:x:2645:347:JACQUELINE:/u/cxp7:/bin/bash
do26:x:1130:672:CARLOS:/u/do26:/bin/bash
ima3:x:548:224:PIERRE:/u/ima3:/bin/bash
...
```

Configuring pam_ldap and /etc/pam.d files

Now change the */etc/pam.d/login* file:

```
auth     required     pam_securetty.so
auth     required     pam_nologin.so
auth     sufficient   pam_ldap.so
auth     required     pam_unix_auth.so try_first_pass

account  sufficient   pam_ldap.so
account  required     pam_unix_acct.so

password required     pam_ldap.so

session  sufficient   pam_ldap.so
session  required     pam_unix_session.so
```

For users who log in using Gnome Display Manager, the file */etc/pam.d/gdm* has to be modified:

```
auth     sufficient   pam_ldap.so
auth     required     pam_nologin.so
auth     required     pam_env.so
auth     required     pam_unix_auth.so

account  sufficient   pam_ldap.so
account  required     pam_unix_acct.so

password required     pam_ldap.so

session  sufficient   pam_ldap.so
session  required     pam_unix_session.so
```

There are many configurable files under */etc/pam.d*. It's possible to authenticate FTP, *su*, SSH, and lots of other stuff over LDAP. This is outside the scope of LPI, however.

40

System Security (Topic 2.212)

This Topic focuses on the methods used to secure Linux servers and workstations. The breadth of system security topics would require an entire exam to fully test, so LPI focuses only on routers, FTP servers, using OpenSSH, TCP wrappers, and *ipchains/iptables*.

This Topic contains five Objectives (numbered 2 through 6 instead of 1 through 5, because of changes during test development):

Objective 2: Configuring a Router
   The LPIC-2 candidate should be able to configure *ipchains* and *iptables* to perform IP masquerading and state the significance of network address translation (NAT) and private network addresses in protecting a network. This objective includes configuring port redirection, listing filtering rules, and writing rules that accept or block datagrams based upon source or destination protocol, port, and address. Also included are saving and reloading filtering configurations, using settings in */proc/sys/net/ipv4* to respond to DOS attacks, using */proc/sys/net/ipv4/ip_forward* to turn IP forwarding on and off, and using tools such as PortSentry to block port scans and vulnerability probes. Weight: 2.

Objective 3: Securing FTP Servers
   The candidate should be able to configure an anonymous download FTP server. This Objective includes configuring an FTP server to allow anonymous uploads, listing additional precautions to be taken if anonymous uploads are permitted, configuring guest users and groups with chroot jail, and configuring *ftpaccess* to deny access to named users or groups. Weight: 2.

Objective 4: Secure Shell (SSH)
   The candidate should be able to configure *sshd* to allow or deny root logins, and to enable or disable X forwarding. This Objective includes generating server keys, generating a user's public/private key pair, adding a public key to a user's *authorized_keys* file, and configuring *ssh-agent* for all users.

Candidates should also be able to configure port forwarding to tunnel an application protocol over *ssh*, configure *ssh* to support the SSH protocol Versions 1 and 2, disable nonroot logins during system maintenance, configure trusted clients for SSH logins without a password, and make multiple connections from multiple hosts to guard against loss of connection to remote host following configuration changes. Weight: 2.

Objective 5: TCP wrappers

The candidate should be able to configure TCP wrappers to allow connections to specified servers from only certain hosts or subnets. Weight: 1.

Objective 6: Security Tasks

The candidate should be able to install and configure Kerberos and perform basic security auditing of source code. This objective includes arranging to receive security alerts from Bugtraq, CERT, CIAC, or other sources. It also includes being able to test for open mail relays and anonymous FTP servers and installing and configuring an intrusion detection system such as Snort or Tripwire. Candidates should also be able to update the IDS configuration as new vulnerabilities are discovered and apply security patches and bug fixes. Weight: 3.

Objective 2: Configuring a Router

This Objective is perhaps a bit misnamed. It might better be called "configuring a firewall," which is what all the activities listed in this Objective turn out to be. (A router usually contains firewall software, though, and effectively does firewall-like work while it filters traffic.)

To be able to set up a good firewall, you'll have to study a book or two on firewalls; this section of the book is only an overview of key tasks. First we'll get the Linux box to do routing, then protect the network it routes with firewall rules and NAT.

The Example Networks

For this objective, we'll use a quite simple example throughout. The small company Example Incorporated (motto: "Set an example") has a cheap SDSL subscription with one fixed IP address and a very simple internal network on which they house one web server, a file and network server, and some clients. A network diagram is shown in Figure 40-1.

When working with a firewall and doing routing, it's quite important to have a network diagram. It helps you check that you got all the directions, routings, filters, and so on straight. It's also very good to have when you are called in at odd hours to fix an urgent problem, because someone may well be working to a deadline and need you to fix a broken Internet connection as quickly as possible.

Before establishing a firewall/router, as well as all the time afterward, you should keep a written list of what the configuration should be like, so as to have something to compare your configurations and rulesets with if things seem to be broken. You can then follow the flow of a web connection through the rulesets

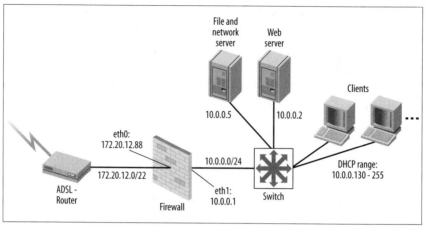

Figure 40-1. Network diagram for example network

rule by rule, checking that all the needed rules are there and that no rule that has no business in the firewall rules got in there by accident. Keep records somewhat along these lines:

Outside the firewall

- Firewall outside interface: *eth0*, address 172.20.12.88.
- Network: 172.20.12.0/255.255.252.0 (/22)
- Default router: 172.20.12.1
- Name servers: 62.179.100.29, 62.179.100.30, 213.46.243.88

Inside the firewall

- Firewall inside interface: *eth1*, address 10.0.0.1
- Network: 10.0.0.0/255.255.255.0 (/24)
- Web server: 10.0.0.2
- File server: 10.0.0.5
- DHCP range: 10.0.0.130–10.0.0.200

Outgoing traffic
   Allow all outgoing traffic

Incoming traffic
   Deny all incoming traffic, except:

- TCP port 80 (Web): Forward to web server
- TCP port 22 (*ssh*): Forward to file server
- TCP port 443 (IMAPS, IMAP over SSL): Forward to file server

Getting Routing Working

This is the first thing to do before setting up a firewall on your Linux machine. If you start filtering traffic before you even start routing, you won't know whether the routing works, and then you can't be sure whether it's the routing or the firewall ruleset biting you when traffic fails to flow. For routine, you need two working network interfaces, with networks on both. The networks should be minimally configured. There should also be a routing table making it possible for the firewall to reach both the outside network and the inside network. Keep in mind that there is no security yet, so make sure there are no production hosts connected to the router or the Internet. Use only hosts that you are confident are secure and that do not contain sensitive data.

You should be able to verify your hardware and network software as follows:

```
# ifconfig
eth0      Link encap:Ethernet  HWaddr 00:10:5A:FB:F0:D2
          inet addr:172.20.12.88  Bcast:80.111.71.255  Mask:255.255.252.0
          UP BROADCAST RUNNING MULTICAST  MTU:1500  Metric:1
          RX packets:4408974 errors:3 dropped:0 overruns:3 frame:3
          TX packets:3558877 errors:0 dropped:0 overruns:0 carrier:0
          collisions:248 txqueuelen:100
          RX bytes:1628403600 (1.5 GiB)  TX bytes:293411709 (279.8 MiB)
          Interrupt:3 Base address:0x300

eth1      Link encap:Ethernet  HWaddr 00:02:2D:49:D7:05
          inet addr:10.0.0.1  Bcast:10.0.0.255  Mask:255.255.255.0
          UP BROADCAST RUNNING MULTICAST  MTU:1500  Metric:1
          RX packets:3823262 errors:0 dropped:0 overruns:0 frame:0
          TX packets:4693316 errors:78 dropped:0 overruns:0 carrier:0
          collisions:0 txqueuelen:100
          RX bytes:265557294 (253.2 MiB)  TX bytes:2232883546 (2.0 GiB)
          Interrupt:5 Base address:0x100
...
# netstat -rn
Kernel IP routing table
Destination     Gateway         Genmask         Flags   MSS Window  irtt
Iface
10.0.0.0        0.0.0.0         255.255.255.0   U       40 0        0
eth1
172.20.12.0     0.0.0.0         255.255.252.0   U       40 0        0
eth0
0.0.0.0         172.20.12.1     0.0.0.0         UG      40 0        0
eth0
```

If you compare this to the network diagram, it should match neatly.

If you now execute the following command, your router will start routing. But since you use a private address space on the inside, the outside will not know how to send traffic back to you, so it won't be working for any practical purposes. Still, if you use *tcpdump* on the outside interface, you should see packets from the inside leave the interface on their way into the world. It won't start working for real until you have NAT configured later in this objective.

```
echo 1 > /proc/sys/net/ipv4/ip_forward
```

Firewall Rulesets

With Linux 2.2 kernels, firewalls were set up with ipchains. This is pretty much obsolete by now, as 2.4 and 2.6 kernels dominate the Linux world, and these kernels use iptables. Many things are about the same with these firewall implementations, but there are also significant differences that concern even a novice firewall administrator.

ipchains versus iptables

At the user level, the main differences between ipchains and iptables is the way packets are processed when they're routed from an input interface to an output interface. The flow of traffic in ipchains is shown in Figure 40-2, whereas the flow for iptables is shown in Figure 40-3.

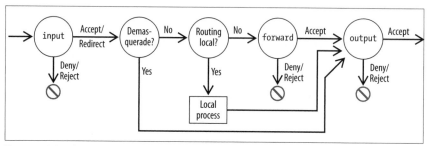

Figure 40-2. Chains and traffic flow in ipchains

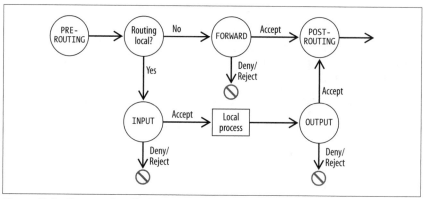

Figure 40-3. Chains and traffic flow in iptables

Considering ipchains first, you can see from Figure 40-2 that a packet from the inside network destined for the Internet will hit the input chain first. Here it will be accepted or denied. It then hits the packet router, which sees that the packet is not for local delivery and finds that the packet's destination fits the default routing, which leads it to *eth0*. The packet then passes the forward chain, unless it's rejected there, before it is sent to the output chain, where it again is checked and passed or dropped.

If the packet was destined for the local host, it gets to the receiving process directly from the packet router. When a process on the host wants to send traffic, it is checked against the output chain. Note that traffic to and from local processes do not pass the forward chain; only packets in transit do. In our example, the forward chain would contain a rule to masquerade outgoing traffic—in other words, make it look as if all outgoing traffic comes from the firewall. This is because the firewall has a public IP address, so the return traffic will find its way back to the firewall, and then the demasquerade mechanism will translate the addresses back to the original, internal addresses and pass the traffic directly to the firewall's output chain. In other words, with masquerading, the return traffic bypasses the forward filter.

It is worth noting that ipchains does not support stateful packet processing. In other words, you can't say: "Let all related traffic pass" or "Let the return traffic for all established connections pass." This valuable feature was developed for iptables.

As Figure 40-3 shows, *iptables* packet processing is quite a bit simpler than ipchains. The PREROUTING and POSTROUTING tables are the first and last tables to touch traffic, and they process all traffic. They are used for address translation. For example, changing the destination (port forwarding) of an incoming packet is done in PREROUTING, while different kinds of NAT are usually done in POSTROUTING. The destination of the packet when it hits the router determines its later fate: either local delivery through the INPUT chain or forwarding through the FORWARD chain. Any traffic originated locally is sent through the OUTPUT chain.

Given *iptables* supports stateful packet processing, as mentioned earlier, and that there are protocol agents that understand FTP and other complex protocols, so you can support them easily, there is not much reason to keep using *ipchains*.

Antispoofing

Attacks done by spoofing, or forging, the source addresses of packets to get past security mechanisms crop up in many contexts. For example, quite some time ago a security problem involving NFS was discovered. A security exploit was published that managed to alter NFS exported files by sending just one UDP packet to an NFS server. No answer was needed back; this one packet just had to be sent and accepted. NFS relies on IP authentication, but forging a source address is not hard, so the attack was quite deadly. There are many interesting new and old ways to use spoofing, and you should do your best to stop it at your firewall. On Linux, a shell loop like the following enables antispoof checking on all interfaces:

```
for f in /proc/sys/net/ipv4/conf/*/rp_filter; do
    echo 1 > $f
done
```

When this value is set, Linux checks the source address of packets against the routing table. Referring back to our example network, the checks work like this: a packet arriving at *eth1* is supposed to be on the internal network and therefore can have only source addresses in the 10.0.0.0/255.255.255.0 subnet. A packet arriving at *eth0*, which has the default or "any" routing, can have any source address *except* those allowed on the other interfaces on the machine. This mechanism is unchanged since at least Linux 2.2. If this is not correct in your network, however, this antispoof mechanism cannot be used and you will have to write explicit rules against spoofing yourself.

Using ipchains

The older Linux firewalling system used *ipchains* for packet filtering and *ipmasqadm* for masquerading.

ipchains

The general syntax for *ipchains* is:

```
ipchains main_option chain [specification] [ -j target ]
```

A variety of subcommands can be issued within *ipchains*. Table 40-1 lists the six most common options, their usage, and descriptions of what the options do. For a complete list, view the *ipchains* (5) manpage.

Table 40-1. Options for ipchains

Main option	Usage	Description
-A	*ipchains* -A *chain rule*	Append a rule specification to end of specified chain. This is what you usually want.
-D	*ipchains* -D *chain rule*	Delete a rule from specified chain.
-n -L	*ipchains* -n -L [*chain*]	List all rules in selected chain. If no chain is specified, all rules are listed. The -n option stops *ipchains* from trying to resolve IP numbers and ports to names, which usually slows it down a lot.
-F	*ipchains* -F *chain*	Flush all rules from selected chain.
-P	*ipchains* -P *chain target*	Set the policy of the specified chain to the given target.
-h	*ipchains* -h	Print a help message.

Rule specifications are required when you add (-A) or delete (-D) a rule. Several parameters can be used for rule specifications. Five popular rule specifications are:

-p

Specifies a protocol. The protocol can be tcp, udp, icmp, or all.

-s

Specifies the source address. The source can be name of host or network, or an IP address.

-j

Specifies a target to a rule, meaning what to do if a packet matches.

-i

Specifies the interface the packet source came from.

-y

The packet is a SYN packet generated as part of an opening TCP handshake. SYN+ACK will not match this.

When specifying your rule, you can specify several types of targets. The target is what happens when your rule specifications are matched. The most common target values are explained in Table 40-2.

Table 40-2. ipchains targets

Target	Description
ACCEPT	Allow packet through.
DENY	Drop packet without attempted to notify the sender.
REJECT	Similar to DENY, but send an ICMP message back to sender stating that the packet was dropped.
MASQ	Used only in forward chains (or user-defined chains). Requires CONFIG_IP_MASQUERADE to be compiled in the Linux kernel. Packets are masqueraded as if they originated from local host. (Reverse packets are also demasqueraded automatically, bypassing the forwarding chain.) Masquerading is described in more detail later in "ipmasqadm."

Then there is one special usage to masquerade the inside network:

```
ipchains -P forward DENY
ipchains -A forward -s 10.0.0.0/24 -j MASQ
```

Because masquerading bypasses the forward chain, you can close that chain entirely. But if you have any public addresses on the inside network that are not masqueraded, you must set the forward policy to ACCEPT or insert detailed rules to forward the traffic from those systems.

ipmasqadm

ipmasqadm allows port forwarding of different kinds. Only one kind is interesting to us here. The command to do port forwarding looks like this:

```
ipmaswadm portfw -a -P tcp -L local_address local_port \
  -R remote_address remote_port
```

The local address must be the firewall's own address, and the port must be the port the traffic is addressed to on the firewall. The traffic will be forwarded to the remote address and port.

Sample ipchains setup

The following is a complete script matching our example setup. The comments in the file should be enough to let you understand it. The one extra syntax issue worth noting is that an exclamation point (!) reverses the effect of the following clause. For instance, because -y means "match a TCP SYN packet, ! -y means "match any packet that is not a TCP SYN packet."

```
#!/bin/sh

# Useful variables
ALL="0.0.0.0/0"# Anything

# OUTSIDE INTERFACE
OUTIF=eth0
OUTIFA=172.20.12.1# Outside interface address
OUTNA=80.11.68.0# Outside network address
OUTNM=255.255.252.0# Outside netmask
OUTNET="$OUTNA/$OUTNM"# Outside subnet
```

```
# INSIDE INTERFACE
INIF=eth
INIFA=10.0.0.1                    # Inside interface address
INNA=10.0.0.0                     # Inside network address
INNM=255.255.255.0               # Inside netmask
INET="$INNA/$INNM"# All addresses on the inside

WEBSERV=10.0.0.2
FILESERV=10.0.0.5

# Enable antispoofing.
for f in /proc/sys/net/ipv4/conf/*/rp_filter; do
    echo 1 > $f
done

# Flush ipchains rules.
ipchains -F

# Default Policies
ipchains -P input REJECT
ipchains -P forward REJECT
ipchains -P output ACCEPT

# Masquerade the internal network; all outgoing traffic will get the
# firewall's address.
ipchains -A forward -s 10.0.0.0/24 -j MASQ

# All TCP traffic from the inside is acceptable.
ipchains -A input -p TCP -s $INET -j ACCEPT

# Web is always allowed and forwarded to the web server.
ipchains -A input -p TCP -d $ALL 80 -j ACCEPT
ipmasqadm portfw -a -P tcp -L $OUTIFA 80 -R $WEBSERV 80

# And SSH is always allowed and forwarded to the file server.
ipchains -A input -p TCP -d $ALL 22 -j ACCEPT
ipmasqadm portfw -a -P tcp -L $OUTIFA 22 -R $FILESERV 22

# IMAPS is always allowed and forwarded to the file server.
ipchains -A input -p TCP -d $ALL 443 -j ACCEPT
ipmasqadm portfw -a -P tcp -L $OUTIFA 443 -R $FILESERV 443

# Let ICMP through to enable ping, path mtu discovery,
# ECN, and other good things.
ipchains -A input -p ICMP -j ACCEPT

# Accept DNS answers from the outside.
ipchains -A input -p UDP -s $ALL 53 -j ACCEPT
ipchains -A input -p TCP -s $ALL 53 -j ACCEPT

# Put these at the end:  Incoming TCP SYN is not allowed except
# on connections opened earlier.
ipchains -A input -i $OUTIF -p TCP -d $DMZNET -y -j DENY
ipchains -A input -i $OUTIF -p TCP -d $INET -y -j DENY
```

```
# But we must allow incoming TCP non-SYN, because that is the return
# traffic from outgoing traffic.
ipchains -A input -p TCP -d $DMZNET ! -y -j ACCEPT
ipchains -A input -p TCP -d $INET ! -y -j ACCEPT

# Rules set, we can enable forwarding in the kernel.
echo "1" > /proc/sys/net/ipv4/ip_forward
```

The hardest part about using *ipchains* is remembering that openings for traffic in one direction are not enough, as the comments on the closing rules say. Due to the lack of state in the system, you actually have to let in all traffic that comes knocking on the outside interface, because it includes return traffic from outgoing connections. The only packets that can be barred are incoming SYN packets. This at least stops outsiders from starting new TCP connections, except at the ports opened previously: 22, 80, and 443, along with 53 for DNS.

 These commands just illustrate some of the possibilities and typical uses for *ipchains*. Don't just copy the ruleset and configure it on a real firewall. It would not be very secure or easy to work with. It would not be secure because there are many more things that should be blocked. Nor would it be easy to work with, because you want more logging to help you find out where this or that packet ended up when debugging the rules.

Using iptables

While people usually refer to the Linux's firewall code by the name of the command used to manipulate the rules, such as *ipchains* and *iptables*, the more proper name for the *iptables* implementation is Netfilter; that refers to the firewalling subsystem the kernel developers work on.

The iptables command

The *iptables* command is a lot like the *ipchains* command, which is not too surprising because the same person wrote both. The general format is:

```
iptables -main_option chain [specification] [ -j target ]
```

The main options are the same as *ipchains*: -A, -D, -n -L, -F, -P and -h.

The specifications are pretty much the same, but long alternatives are now present, which can make reading the rules much easier. Furthermore, built-in chain names are in all uppercase.

-p, --protocol
> Specifies the protocol. The protocol can be tcp, udp, icmp, or all.

-s, --source
> Specifies the source address. It can be a hostname or network or an IP address.

-d, --destination
> Specifies the destination address. It can be a hostname or network or an IP address.

-j, --jump
> Specifies what to do if the specification matches the packet being processed.

-i, --in-interface
> Specifies the interface the packet came from. This is allowed only in the INPUT, FORWARDING, and PREROUTING tables.

-o, --out-interface
> Specifies the interface the packet will be sent out from. This is allowed only in OUTPUT, FORWARDING, and POSTROUTING tables.

--dport, --destination-port
> Specifies the destination port of the packet.

-m state, --state state
> The *-m* option ties into a module. Here we discuss only the state module, which keeps connection state. When you select this, rules can specify connection states such as ESTABLISHED, INVALID, or RELATED or a comma-separated list of such states.

The rule targets in *iptables* will be familiar: ACCEPT, DROP, DENY, and MASQUERADE. DENY is used instead of REJECT. An additional target used for port forwarding is DNAT. A rule that uses DNAT takes an additional option that specifies the address to redirect to and optionally the port, if that too is to be changed. An example use of DNAT is:

```
iptables -t nat -A PREROUTING ... --jump DNAT --to address[:port ]
```

Example netfilter configuration

As with the *ipchains* example, you should be able to understand what the following script does from the previous explanation:

```
#!/bin/sh

IN_IF=eth1
OUT_IF=eth0

modprobe ip_conntrack


# Establish antispoofing
for f in /proc/sys/net/ipv4/conf/*/rp_filter; do
    echo 1 > $f
done

IN_NET=10.0.0.0/24
IN_NW=10.0.0.0
IN_BC=10.0.0.255
ANY=0/0

FILESERV=10.0.0.5
WEBSERV=10.0.0.2

# NEW connections to the inside network that should be accepted
```

```
iptables -N new_net
iptables -A new_net -p tcp --dport imaps --destination $FILESERV \
                       --jump ACCEPT
iptables -A new_net -p tcp --dport ssh   --destination $FILESERV \
                                                --jump ACCEPT
iptables -A new_net -p tcp --dport 80    --destination $WEBSERV \
                                                --jump ACCEPT

iptables -A new_net --jump RETURN


# INPUT traffic is for the firewall
iptables -A INPUT -m state --state INVALID              --jump DROP
iptables -A INPUT -m state --state ESTABLISHED,RELATED --jump ACCEPT
# We basically trust our loopback-interface
iptables -A INPUT -i lo  --jump ACCEPT
# Not much that is acceptable :-)
iptables -A INPUT --jump DROP


# Packets to and from the network
iptables -A FORWARD -m state --state INVALID --jump DROP
iptables -A FORWARD -m state --state ESTABLISHED,RELATED --jump ACCEPT
# Accept all traffic from the inside interface
iptables -A FORWARD -i $IN_IF -m state --state NEW        --jump ACCEPT
# Traffic from the outside interface is checked by new_net
iptables -A FORWARD -i $OUT_IF -m state --state NEW --jump new_net
# All else is junked
iptables -A FORWARD --jump DROP


iptables -A OUTPUT -m state --state INVALID --jump DROP
iptables -A OUTPUT -m state --state ESTABLISHED,RELATED  --jump ACCEPT
# Connections allowed from the firewall: all UDP, but only DNS over UDP
iptables -A OUTPUT -p tcp --jump ACCEPT
iptables -A OUTPUT -p udp --dport domain  --jump ACCEPT
# Also allow ping
iptables -A OUTPUT -p icmp --icmp-type echo-request      --jump ACCEPT
# Again: trust the loopback interface
iptables -A OUTPUT -o lo                                 --jump ACCEPT
iptables -A OUTPUT --jump DROP


# ################## NAT
# Masquerade all packets passing out from internel network

echo Masquerading
iptables -t nat -A POSTROUTING -o $OUT_IF --jump MASQUERADE


# IMAPS and SSH traffic is meant for file server
iptables -t nat -A PREROUTING -i $OUT_IF -p tcp --dport imaps \
                                        --jump DNAT --to $FILESERV
iptables -t nat -A PREROUTING -i $OUT_IF -p tcp --dport 22
                                        --jump DNAT --to $FILESERV
# Web traffic is for web server
iptables -t nat -A PREROUTING -i $OUT_IF -p tcp --dport 80 \
                                        --jump DNAT --to $WEBSERV
```

```
echo Enabeling forwarding
# Enable packet forwarding
echo 1 > /proc/sys/net/ipv4/ip_forward
echo Done
```

Things worth noting in this configuration include:

- As long as the rules regarding ESTABLISHED,RELATED are in place, all return traffic will be accepted, including the ICMP messages related to TCP connections.

- The ruleset does not need to contain a rule to accept DNS responses, because responses to outgoing DNS are accepted as part of the ESTABLISHED state.

- If connection tracking for FTP was enabled (it is not, in the rules shown), both passive and active connections would be allowed in as RELATED. The same goes for the other protocol agents available in Linux 2.4 and 2.6.

As with the earlier *ipchains* example, this ruleset is not complete. On a real firewall, you should do a lot more to protect yourself, as documented in many books and manpages.

Firewalling Miscellanea

There are a few more points to add to the firewall discussion before you go on to the next Objective.

/proc/sys/net/ipv4

Besides *ip_forward*, the kernel IP stack offers a lot of security-related tuning in the */proc/sys/net/ipv4* directory. By using *sysctl* or a simple *echo* command (see Chapter 28) to change these settings, you can do considerable benefit (or damage) to your firewall and network. Linux 2.4 has more than 50 options you can change. The complete list, with very complete descriptions, can be found in the kernel source tree, in *Documentation/networking/ip-sysctl.txt*. Some of the more useful are:

tcp_ecn
> Whether to use explicit congestion notification (ECN). This is a way to signal that there is network congestion. Unfortunately, it breaks brutally if a firewall blocks too many ICMP messages. Therefore the default is still 0, and most administrators should keep it that way.

icmp_ignore_bogus_error_responses
> Whether bogus error responses are logged. Usually they are, but that can grow tedious if some device you can't fix is sending them.

ip_dynaddr
> If your firewall uses dynamic IP, such as managed by DHCP, PPP, or diald, you should set the value in this file to 1.

tcp_syncookies
> When a system is inundated with new connections, it can either be because it is popular or because it is being attacked. An attack known as SYN flooding can cause your TCP state tables to fill up with illegitimate connections, stopping legitimate connections from getting through. If you're fairly sure this is happening and you compiled your kernel with CONFIG_SYNCOOKIES

enabled, you can enable a defense to SYN flooding by setting this to 1. It is off by default.

However, note that the syncookies defense breaks the official TCP/IP specification, disables TCP extensions, and renders some clients unable to connect at all.

To help your system cope with too many legitimate connections, look at *tcp_max_syn_backlog*, *tcp_synack_retries*, and *tcp_abort_on_overflow*.

tcp_max_syn_backlog

This sets the maximum of connections remembered while no ACK is received on them. It is 1024 on hosts with more than 128 MB memory, 128 on those with less. Increasing the value may help if you're getting connections faster than they can be completed.

tcp_synack_retries

When a SYN packet is received and a starting connection is in the SYN backlog, this is how many times a SYN+ACK will be retried as long as no corresponding ACK is received. The default of 5 causes the connection to be retried five times, which works out to 180 seconds. You may want to lower this *a bit* if your system is suffering.

tcp_abort_on_overflow

Zero (disabled) by default. If enabled, your host starts sending RST packets back to clients if a service, such as Apache, is not accepting new connections quickly enough. Doing this may disrupt your clients.

icmp_echo_ignore_broadcasts

Echo broadcasts are sometimes used in DDOS (Distributed Denial of Service) attacks, for a method known as network amplification. For obvious security reasons, all traffic from the outside that is directed to broadcast addresses within your local network should be blocked on an outer firewall (unless you are using this to find out how many hosts on your network are up).

conf/all/accept_source_route

Source routing can be used in attacks involving IP spoofing and has been considered generally harmful for more than 10 years. The default is off.

conf/all/log_martians

A Martian is a packet whose sender the router does not know how to route. A router with a default routing should never see Martians.

Saving and reloading rulesets

The *ipchains* and *iptables* packages typically include two commands, one to save the ruleset after changes and the other to restore it after a reboot. For the *iptables* commands, usage is very simple:

```
# iptables-save > firewall-rules
# iptables-restore firewall-rules
```

Many administrators prefer to write an init script that contains a commented and nicely formatted ruleset, such as the ones shown earlier in this chapter, to install a known ruleset at each boot. That way, it's easier to relate your current configuration to the documented specifications.

NAT and security

While NAT was conceived to solve the problem of running out of IP numbers, and not security, many peope consider sites more secure if internal networks are hidden and use a private IP space.

If a router has no firewall rules, the internal hosts in the network will be unreachable from the outside even if forwarding is enabled (barring tricks with spoofed source addresses and source routing). To allow access to the internal network, firewall rules have to be configured to activate port forwarding and masquerading rules. And once the firewall rules are activated, you will also have protective filtering.

Dynamic routing

In an environment that uses dynamic routing, Linux has several ways to manage it. *routed* uses a mutation of an old Xerox routing protocol, which is not very useful outside pure Unix environments in which all routers support *routed*. On the upside, *routed* is pretty automatic and requires only minimal configuration.

Another vintage dynamic routing implementation on Unix is *gated*, but neither Red Hat nor Debian supports it. If you want standards-based dynamic routing on Linux now, you should install Zebra (known as Quagga on some distributions), which supports dynamic routing protocols of every stripe: specifically, RIPv1, RIPv2, RIPng, OSPF, OSPF6, BGP4+, and BGP4-.

If you're going to run any of these routing systems, remember to make openings for their packets in the ruleset.

Objective 3: Securing FTP Servers

There is a wider variety of FTP server implementations than most like to think about. This LPI Objective is tailored for WU-FTPD, which just a few years ago was *the* standard *ftpd*. However, it is no longer included in any Red Hat or Debian distribution due to it's rather poor security record. In upcoming versions of the Level 2 LPI Exams, the only FTP daemon likely to be covered is *vsftpd* (Very Secure FTP Daemon), which is both popular and the only one included in both Debian and Red Hat.

vsftpd comes with a very good default configuration, which allows only anonymous FTP. It chroots to the *ftp* user account (which must already exist on the system) and everything just works. Unlike other software that uses *chroot*, *vsftpd* does not need a *chroot* environment to be painstakingly set up.

vsftpd reads its configuration from */etc/vsftpd.conf*. Here are some highlights:

```
# Allow anonymous FTP?
anonymous_enable=YES

# Uncomment this to allow local users to log in.
#local_enable=YES
```

These lines indicate what users to allow. The choice here is anonymous only by default. The last line can be commented out to allow regular users. For a regular user to be allowed access, his shell must be listed in */etc/shells*. However, the *ftp* user account can have a "nologin" shell and anonymous FTP; that user will still be allowed in.

```
# Uncomment this to enable any form of FTP write command.
#write_enable=YES

# Uncomment this to allow the anonymous FTP user to upload files. This
# has an effect ony if the preceding global write enable is activated. Also,
# you will obviously need to create a directory writable by the FTP user.
#anon_upload_enable=YES

# Uncomment this if you want the anonymous FTP user to be able to create
# new directories.
#anon_mkdir_write_enable=YES
```

Setting write_enable to yes gives local users permission to upload files and create directories. The anonymous user needs the two other settings as well to be able to upload files. And as the comment says, you must create a directory writable by the *ftp* user, with the right filesystem permissions.

```
# If you want, you can arrange for uploaded anonymous files to be owned by
# a different user. Note! Using "root" for uploaded files is not
# recommended!
#chown_uploads=YES
#chown_username=whoever
```

By enabling these commented-out lines, you stop the anonymous user from deleting and overwriting previously delivered files. This is often a very good idea. Be sure to use a user that has *no* other roles than being the anonymous FTP upload user. Using the *nobody* account is not quite as good, because any service or process running as *nobody* will then be able to change or delete those files.

```
# Chroot local users as well?
# chroot_local_user=YES
#
# You may specify an explicit list of local users to chroot( ) to their home
# directory. If chroot_local_user is YES, then this list becomes a list of
# users to NOT chroot( ).
# chroot_list_enable=YES
# (default follows)
#chroot_list_file=/etc/vsftpd.chroot_list
```

As long as the regular users do not need to access one another's accounts or system directories, you may as well chroot them too. As you see, you can get finer control over this by using the chroot list file.

```
# If you enable this nonanonymous logins are mapped to the guest
# account given by guest_username. The default guest user name is "ftp".
# guest_enable=YES
# guest_username=whoever
```

If this is enabled, a user will—after giving a username and correct password— have access to only the given account, not to her own account.

```
# If you set userlist_deny, then users will be allowed access only if they
# they are listed in the userlist_file.
# userlist_deny=YES
#
# If you enable userlist_enable, then any user listed in the userlist_file
# will be denied access before even being asked his password.  Denying
# at this early stage stops the user from transmitting his password
# in clear text for no purpose.
# userlist_enable=YES
#
# This is the default userlist_file:
# userlist_file=/etc/vsftpd.user_list
```

And finally, this is where you enable or deny access for specific users.

Objective 4: Secure Shell (SSH)

SSH, also known as Secure Shell, is an encrypting version of the old *rsh/rlogin/rcp* suite. The primary use for SSH is encrypted shell sessions to remote hosts, but it can also be used to copy files and to tunnel other protocols.

SSH is a server/client protocol offering *sshd* as the server and the *ssh* command as the client. The client connects to the server, they establish an encrypted session, and then the server demands authentication before finally logging in the client. For file copying in the manner of RCP, the secure replacement is the *scp* command.

In addition to simple login sessions and file copying, SSH can also provide transparent port forwarding, and as an extension of this, X authentication and forwarding. When you have an SSH session, you can start an X client on the remote machine, and the X Window System protocol will travel encrypted over your connection and display on your local machine without the need for settings such as DISPLAY=foo:0 or the *xhost* or *xauth* commands.

The implementation of SSH generally used on Linux systems is OpenSSH.

Installation and Configuration

OpenSSH may or may not be installed on your system by default. When it is installed, it generates a host key for your machine. This key will serve to authenticate your host in subsequent SSH sessions. Then you will typically want to create SSH authentication keys for your own personal account, as well as the root account. After that, you as the administrator should review the configuration of *sshd*, to see that you are comfortable with it.

The standard place for the central configuration of OpenSSH is the */etc/ssh* directory. Here you will find the server configuration in *sshd_config* and default client configuration in *ssh_config*. Here are some highlights from the server configuration as installed on Debian:

```
# What ports, IPs and protocols we listen for
Port 22
Protocol 2
```

Port 22 is the standard port for the SSH protocol. Version 2 of the protocol is the most secure, whereas Version 1 has some flaws that were hard to overcome. It is recommended to accept only Version 2 now. To support both versions, put 2, 1 on the Protocol line.

```
# Authentication:
PermitRootLogin yes

PubkeyAuthentication yes

# rhosts authentication should not be used
RhostsAuthentication no
# Don't read the user's ~/.rhosts and ~/.shosts files
IgnoreRhosts yes
# For this to work you will also need host keys in /etc/ssh_known_hosts
# (for protocol version 2)
HostbasedAuthentication no

# To disable tunneled clear text passwords, change to no here!
PasswordAuthentication yes
```

OpenSSH ignores the host operating system setting for permitting root logins on nonconsole terminals. Instead, OpenSSH has its own setting in PermitRootLogin. The PubkeyAuthentication setting allows or denies login authentication based purely on public-key cryptography. You can trust this as far as you can trust the host on which the private parts of those keys are stored (unless they are protected by passphrases, in which case you can trust them a bit further). IgnoreRhosts allows or denies the old-fashioned—and very insecure—rhosts authentication, used by the *rsh/rlogin/rcp* suite. This way of authenticating connections is not only insecure, but also made obsolete by public-key authentication. If you combine rhosts authentication with public-key authentication of the connecting host, on the other hand, it's immediately a lot more secure—but host keys cannot be protected by passphrases. That is what HostbasedAuthentication is for. It is still not recommended, but in some settings it is appropriate. PasswordAuthentication allows or denies authentication by those old-fashioned passwords. You can trust this if you can trust your users to not use silly passwords and to not jot them on Post-it notes and hang them on their screens.

```
X11Forwarding yes
```

If X11 forwarding is enabled on the server and your client requests it (using the -X option), the client and server will forward traffic from a port on the server side to your DISPLAY. The server sets the remote DISPLAY to the local port that *sshd* forwards to your local screen. To make this secure, the server will install an *xauth* authentication token that it will enforce for all new connections. This, in addition to port forwarding, which we'll return to, makes OpenSSH a very versatile remote terminal program.

Generating and Using Keys

In most cases, you will want to generate SSH keys for your own accounts and perhaps your root account. Use *ssh-keygen* for this. A reference for the needed commands is at the end of this section (the short of it is: run *ssh-keygen -t dsa* and press the Enter key at all the prompts). This key allows passwordless remote logins, as long as PubkeyAuthentication is enabled.

In ~/.ssh/id_dsa.pub you can find the public key you've generated through *ssh-keygen*. You need to transport this key to the remote machine. Because it's a public key, it does not need to be secure. On the remote machine, put the key into ~/.ssh/authorized_keys. Once the key is in that file, all users who have the private-key counterpart will be able to log in to that remote account without a password.

Sometimes it makes sense to let users log in to other machines without having to set up authentication themselves. The easiest way to do this is to create and modify all the files on one machine, as described in the following procedure, and then use *tar* and *ssh* in a pipe to transfer them to the other hosts.

1. Enable HostbasedAuthentication in */etc/ssh/sshd_config* configuration files on all hosts.

   Your client configuration is in */etc/ssh/ssh_config*. All hosts should have HostbasedAuthentication yes set there, and if they have a PreferredAuthentications statement, it should list hostbased first.

   The hosts' private keys should be readable only by *root* (otherwise the key would not be all that secret). Exactly what is needed to get SSH access to the keys depends on the version. If your SSH package includes an executable called *ssh-keysign*, it must be SUID root (it may not be installed that way, so you must make sure it is manually) and must provide the signing service that proves the host's identity in the key exchange. If the package does not contain *ssh-keysign*, make sure the *ssh* executable is SUID root through *chmod u+s /usr/bin/ssh*.

2. On each host, create */etc/ssh/shosts.equiv*. This file defines the hosts with equivalent security levels. In these files, enter the hostnames of all the hosts as they appear in reverse lookups. You can check that with the command *getent hostsip-address*. If the names you enter are not the right ones, the command will fail.

3. On each host, create */etc/ssh/ssh_known_hosts*. This file must contain the host key of all the hosts involved, under the names you used in the previous item. The easiest way to do this is to connect to all the hosts using the right names. After doing that, the user account that made the connections will have all the correct entries in his ~/.ssh/known_hosts file. Simply transfer the entries to the system file.

After the previous steps are carried out on all the hosts, all ordinary users should be able to use *ssh* back and forth between all the nodes with no other authentication. However, this is not true for the *root* user; she still needs user key or password authentication. Trusting a remote *root* is far more serious than trusting a mundane remote user.

ssh-keygen

Syntax

```
ssh-keygen [-b bits] -t type
ssh-keygen -p [ -t type ]
ssh-keygen -q -t rsa1 -f /etc/ssh/ssh_host_key -C '' -N ''
ssh-keygen -q -t rsa -f /etc/ssh/ssh_host_rsa_key -C '' -N ''
ssh-keygen -q -t dsa -f /etc/ssh/ssh_host_rsa_key -C '' -N ''
```

Description

ssh-keygen generates keys to identify hosts or users in the SSH protocol, Versions 1 and 2.

The first form creates a key. For Version 1 of the protocol, the type should be rsa1. For Version 2, it can be either rsa or dsa. The -b option sets the number of bits in the keys: 512 is the minimum while 1024 bits is the default and is considered "sufficient" today. In general, you can use as many bits as you like. During key generation, you will be asked to give a passphrase. A passphrase is different from a password in that it is a phrase, not simply a word, and is expected to be long. It is recommended that you pick a good long one.

The second form is used to change your passphrase.

The three last forms are used to generate the three different kinds of host keys. The first is for Version 1 of the protocol, the two others for Version 2. The -f option sets the output filename; if you omit the option, you will be prompted for the name. The -C option sets a comment on the key and -N sets the passphrase.

Examples

Generate a private key and then change its passphrase:

```
$ ssh-keygen -t dsa -b 2048
Generating public/private dsa key pair.Enter file in which to save the key
(/home/janl/.ssh/id_dsa): Press the Enter key
Created directory '/home/janl/.ssh'.Enter passphrase (empty for no
passphrase): passphraseEnter same passphrase again: passphrase
Your identification has been saved in /home/janl/.ssh/id_dsa.
Your public key has been saved in /home/janl/.ssh/id_dsa.pub.
The key fingerprint is:
c2:be:20:4a:17:2e:3f:b2:73:46:5c:00:ef:38:ca:03 janl@debian
$ ssh-keygen -p -t dsaEnter file in which the key is (/home/janl/.ssh/id_
dsa): Press the Enter keyEnter old passphrase: passphrase
Key has comment '/home/janl/.ssh/id_dsa'Enter new passphrase (empty for no
passphrase): passphraseEnter same passphrase again: passphrase
Your identification has been saved with the new passphrase.
```

ssh-agent

ssh-agent makes it practical to use passphrases on your private keys. The principle is to use *ssh-agent* to add your keys to a background agent on the system that will hold them in escrow. You give your passphrase only once: when you add the key. The agent will give the keys out to other processes owned by you that request the keys. You should be aware that the *root* user can also request the keys without your noticing, so you must trust the *root* user.

The process is quite simple; start the agent and then add the passphrase you used to create the key:

```
$ eval `ssh-agent`
Agent pid 11487
$ ssh-add
Enter passphrase for /home/janl/.ssh/id_dsa: passphrase
Identity added: /home/janl/.ssh/id_dsa (/home/janl/.ssh/id_dsa)
```

By default, all your keys will be added. If several of your keys have the same passphrase, they will all be added without further questions. If they have different passphrases, *ssh-add* will be prompted for them. If you include a file on the *ssh-add* command line, the key in that file will be added and the command will not prompt for keys.

ssh-agent works by setting two environment variables: SSH_AUTH_SOCK, which names the socket on which to communicate with the agent, and SSH_AGENT_PID, which makes it easy to kill the agent. That is also why the PID shows up in the previous listing. The agent emits a shell script which, when evaluated, sets those variables correctly.

Since using passphrases makes remote logins immeasurably more convenient, it may be a good idea to make it simple for your users to use passphrases by starting ssh-agent in their login scripts. It is probably not a good idea to put it in users' *.bashrc* or *.login* scripts, nor in the system */etc/profile*. A good place to put it is in the systemwide *Xsession* scripts. Exactly which script is used to start an X session depends on which distribution and which desktop people use (KDE, GNOME, classical X, their own custom session). But on Debian and Red Hat, there are standard ways to do it.

On Debian, if you put use-ssh-agent on a line by itself in */etc/X11/xdm/xdm. options*, then when you log in with the X Window System, the script */etc/X11/ Xsession.d/90xfree86-common_ssh-agent* is run. It is reproduced here for convenience:

```
STARTSSH=
SSHAGENT=/usr/bin/ssh-agent
SSHAGENTARGS=

if grep -qs ^use-ssh-agent "$OPTIONFILE"; then
  if [ -x "$SSHAGENT" -a -z "$SSH_AUTH_SOCK" -a -z "$SSH2_AUTH_SOCK" ]; then
    STARTSSH=yes
    if [ -f /usr/bin/ssh-add1 ] && cmp -s $SSHAGENT /usr/bin/ssh-agent2;
then
        # use ssh-agent2's ssh-agent1 compatibility mode
```

```
        SSHAGENTARGS=-1
      fi
    fi
  fi

  if [ -n "$STARTSSH" ]; then
    REALSTARTUP="$SSHAGENT $SSHAGENTARGS $REALSTARTUP"
  fi
```

This script first looks for the systemwide use-ssh-agent setting, then very carefully checks whether any of the *ssh-agent*-related variables are set already, because if they are set, an agent should already be running. Finally, it redefines REALSTARTUP so that the agent will be started later in the Debian scripts. The script could just as well have run eval `ssh-agent` directly. On Red Hat, you can do the same by adding the preceding script to *etc/X11/xinit/xinitrc.d*, but it should be changed to run the agent directly, and Red Hat does not set up all those environment variables. In Fedora Core 1, the agent is started automatically.

But none of these automated systems adds any keys to the agent. That means that users will still be prompted for a passphrase. Users can run *ssh-add* (perhaps in their *.bashrc* files) and enter their passphrases once into a shell terminal, each time X starts.

It may be a good idea to doctor the automated X setup further with an *ssh-add* command. If run without a terminal, *ssh-add* pops up a graphical passphrase input box.

Other ssh Tricks

OpenSSH respects TCP wrapper configurations, described in the following Objective.

sshd, like the Linux *login* program, denies logins when the file */etc/nologin* exists. When remotely maintaining hosts in a way that may disrupt user activities, you should create this file with a helpful explanation of what is happening. This will stop all nonroot logins, by whichever method, so you can do your maintenance undisturbed. The file is usually created by the *shutdown* command as well, to keep users from logging in while the machine is shutting down. The file is removed after a complete boot.

    # **cat >/etc/nologin**

If there is any reason to suspect that your maintenance work can disconnect you or break the login mechanism, you should keep multiple login sessions open while doing the work. Test logging in again before closing them. Otherwise, doing a tiny PAM change that breaks all authentication could force you to reboot the machine into single-user mode to recover.

Consider scheduling an *at* job to remove */etc/nologin* at a particular time, in the event you log yourself out. Such a job can be handy when restarting *sshd* from a remote location as well.

The only thing left in this Objective is one of the handiest features of SSH: port forwarding.

ssh port forwarding

Syntax

ssh -R|L *port:host:host_port* [*user@*]*hostname* [*command*]

Description

When the main option is *-L*, *ssh* redirects traffic from the local *port* port to the remote machine and port given by *host:host_port*. The *host* is resolved by the resolver on the host you connect to. For security reasons, it binds only to the localhost address, not to any Ethernet or other interfaces you may have.

When a program connects to the localhost port, the connection is forwarded to the remote side. A very useful application for this is forwarding local ports to your company's mail server so you can send email as if you were at the office. All you have to do then is to configure your email client to connect to the right port on localhost. This is shown by the example in the following section.

When using *-R*, the reverse happens. The *port* port of the remote host's localhost interface is bound to and connections to it will be forwarded to the local machine given by *host:host_port*.

Example

Log in to *login.example.com*. Then forward connections to localhost port 2525 to port 25 on *mail.example.com*, which would otherwise reject relaying for you. The reason for binding to port 2525 is that one needs to be *root* to bind port 25.

```
ssh -L 2525:mail.example.com:25 login.example.com
```

Objective 5: TCP Wrappers

TCP wrappers allows you to check the origin of a connection when another machine connects to your own, because you may not want to talk to that machine. Using the */etc/hosts.allow* and */etc/hosts.deny* configuration files, you can specify who can and cannot use specific services. TCP wrappers is most commonly used to protect services that are controlled by *inetd*, but other services such as SSH and the portmapper, as well as most of the NFS service suite, also respect the settings. If you use *xinetd* instead of *inetd*, there is another way to restrict access, described later in this Objective.

To activate checks by TCP wrappers of access to services, make sure that your */etc/inetd.conf* has *tcpd* in the command line, as shown here:

```
ftp  stream  tcp  nowait  root  /usr/sbin/tcpd /usr/sbin/vsftpd
```

When a connection request arrives at a service guarded by TCP wrappers, the request origin and the service name will be checked against the contents of */etc/hosts.allow* and */etc/hosts.deny*. The checking works as follows:

1. Do the service and origin have a match in */etc/hosts.allow*? If so, allow the connection to continue at once.

2. Do they have a match in */etc/hosts.deny*? If so, the connection is closed without reading any input.

3. Otherwise, the connection is allowed to continue.

/etc/hosts.allow and /etc/hosts.deny

The entries in the */etc/hosts.allow* and */etc/hosts.deny* files have the general syntax of *service*: *granted_to*, where *service* specifies the name of the service and *granted_to* specifies which hosts have permission to use the service.

Specifying services

When specifying a service to provide access to, you have the option of specifying the particular service, such as *ftpd*, or to specify all services. To specify a particular service, just insert its name. Unfortunately, some services use names you didn't quite expect. When TCP wrappers is invoked from *inetd*, the service name is always the same as the executable name. ALL matches all services.

To grant access to a service, such as *ftpd*, to everyone on your local 10.0.0.x network, you need an entry in your */etc/hosts.allow* file that looks like this:

```
vsftpd: 10.0.0.0/255.255.255.0.
```

With this entry, TCP wrappers will allow access to a *vsftpd* daemon connecting from any IP in the subnet. To grant access to all services from your network, simply put ALL as the service name.

When granting or denying access to a service to a host, you have the option of specifying a specific domain, an IP address, a range of IP addresses, or all hosts. In addition, you can use an EXCEPT argument that allows you to single out domains and IP addresses from which you want to withhold access.

To specify all services' access to a specific domain, such as *lpi.org*, use the first entry in the following example. With this entry, any host in *lpi.org* can access all available services on your machine. To specify an additional domain, such as *oreilly.com*, you can just add the second line of the example.

```
ALL: .lpi.org
ALL: .oreilly.com
```

Or put the two together:

```
ALL: .lpi.org, .oreilly.com
```

To specify permission to all services to a specific IP address such as 10.0.0.1, use ALL: 10.0.0.1. With this entry, users from 10.0.0.1 can access all services on the machine. To specify an additional IP address, separate them with commas as just shown. To specify permission to all services to all users, use ALL: ALL.

You can specify EXCEPT cases with any of the previously mentioned arrangements. For instance, ALL: ALL EXCEPT 10.0.0.5 would grant access to everyone but the host at 10.0.0.5. In addition, ALL: ALL EXCEPT .redhat.com grants access to all except anyone connecting from a system on the *redhat.com* domain. An additional use of EXCEPT is in the services specification ALL EXCEPT vsftpd: ALL. Any combination of services and hosts can be used in these files.

A sample */etc/hosts.allow* file follows:

```
#
# hosts.allow  This file describes the names of the hosts which are
#              allowed to use the local INET services, as decided
#              by the '/usr/sbin/tcpd' server.
#
vsftpd:ALL EXCEPT 10.28.2.23, 10.28.0.1
in.telnetd: .example.com
lockd: fileserver.example.com
statd: fileserver.example.com, localhost
```

The following is a reasonable */etc/hosts.deny* that bars all other access to the services granted in the allow file, and makes TCP wrappers paranoid about the rest. PARANOID makes TCP wrappers check the reverse lookup of an incoming connection based on the IP address. The name obtained is then checked in a forward lookup. If TCP wrappers gets back the same IP address as it started with, the host passes the PARANOID check.

```
ALL: PARANOID
statd: ALL
lockd: ALL
in.telnetd: ALL
vsftpd: ALL
```

By default, TCP wrappers is actually compiled to default all checks to PARANOID in such a way that it cannot be disabled. For this reason, it's very important to keep your DNS forward and reverse databases consistent.

xinetd and access control

xinetd was introduced in Chapter 20. It is used by some distributions, among them Red Hat. It has the functionality of TCP wrappers built in, with a different user interface. The *xinetd* daemon is configured in */etc/xinetd.conf* or perhaps by several files in */etc/xinetd.d*. A typical stanza for a service looks like this:

```
service rsync
{
        disable = no
        socket_type     = stream
        wait            = no
        user            = root
        server          = /usr/bin/rsync
        server_args     = --daemon --server .
        log_on_failure  += USERID
}
```

Two keywords can be added for access restrictions by host: only_from grants exclusive access to the enumerated hosts and nets, whereas no_access excludes the enumerated hosts and nets. If neither keyword is present for a service, all hosts get access. If both are present, the most specific match gets priority. Thus, given this configuration:

```
service rsync
{
```

```
        disable = no
        socket_type    = stream
        wait           = no
        user           = root
        server         = /usr/bin/rsync
        server_args    = --daemon --server .
        log_on_failure += USERID
no_access      = 10.0.0.0/16
        only_from      = 0.0.0.0/0, 10.0.0.0/24
}
```

everyone on the whole Internet gets access, excluding anyone from the 10.0.*x*.*x*
network, but the 10.0.0.*x* network on the other hand gets access. That is because
10.0.0.*x* is more specific than the others, and 10.0.0.0/16 is more specific than 0.
0.0.0/0.

These two keywords accept host specifications in many different formats:

- An IP address. Any zeros to the right in the number are treated as wildcards:
  thus, 10.1.2.0 matches the entire 10.1.2 subnet. 0.0.0.0 matches the whole
  Internet.

- An IP address with a shell style {} wildcard. This can be only on the right side
  of the IP number, but any octets to the right of it may be dropped. Thus, 10.
  1.{2,3,4} matches the three subnets 10.1.2, 10.1.3, and 10.1.4.

- A network name from */etc/networks*.

- A hostname. When *xinetd* receives a connection, a reverse lookup is performed and matched to the name. Incomplete names such as .example.com
  are allowed in the configuration and match all hosts in the *example.com*
  domain.

- An IP address with a netmask in the /*n* format: for instance, 10.0.0.0/24 for
  the 10.0.0.*x* network.

Objective 6: Security Tasks

Kerberos

There are two current versions of Kerberos, 4 and 5. But we will describe only
Version 5, which is the more stable and secure version, along with the basic
concepts and configurations, because Kerberos has a minimum weight in LPI
Objectives. To go deeper, read *Kerberos: The Definitive Guide* (O'Reilly).

Overview

Kerberos is known in Greek mythology as a very strange creature that authenticates who can pass through the gates of the underworld. But in our world,
Kerberos is an authenticating system developed at MIT. Kerberos uses encryption
technology and a trusted third party (the Kerberos in Greek mythology had three
heads) to perform secure user authentication among multiple users and application servers.

A Kerberos server can solve many authentication problems using a centralized password database and encrypting the traffic that performs authentication—passwords are never sent over the network in clear text). Thus, it centralizes authentication services with some of the highest-level security known.

Currently, a bunch of Kerberos software tools are available. MIT Kerberos is the first one and is widely supported, Heimdal is new and is developed by many people around the world, which makes the code more wide open and flexible to users outside the U.S.

 Microsoft has adopted Kerberos, including its own version with Windows domain controllers, but that isn't relevant to this Topic. Windows Kerberos servers have extensions that make them difficult to interoperate with Linux or other standard Kerberos servers.

Server installation and configuration

To use Kerberos, you'll first need to install all of its server binaries and libraries. Download it from your distribution repository or from the developers site *http://web.mit.edu/kerberos*. The package must include the tools in Table 40-3:

Table 40-3. Kerberos executables

Type	Description
kadmind.local	The administration server daemon
kdb5_util	Kerberos database maintainance utility
krb5kdc	Kerberos authentication service daemon
kpropd	Kerberos database propagation daemon

You can now set up your Kerberos Domain Controller (KDC), the central server that other hosts look to in order to perform authentication. To create your Kerberos realm, edit the */etc/krb5.conf* file. Generally, the package you installed comes with an example file that you'll find very useful and practical. Just fill in your information (realm name and kerberos server FQDN).

```
[logging]
 default = FILE:/var/log/krb5libs.log
 kdc = FILE:/var/log/krb5kdc.log
 admin_server = FILE:/var/log/kadmind.log

[libdefaults]
 default_realm = LPI.ORG.BR
 dns_lookup_realm = false
 dns_lookup_kdc = false

[realms]
 EXAMPLE.COM = {
  kdc = kerberos.lpi.org.br:88
  admin_server = kerberos.lpi.org.br:749
  default_domain = lpi.org.br
 }
```

```
[domain_realm]
 .lpi.org.br = LPI.ORG.BR
 lpi.org.br = LPI.ORG.BR

[kdc]
 profile = /var/kerberos/krb5kdc/kdc.conf

[appdefaults]
 pam = {
   debug = false
   ticket_lifetime = 36000
   renew_lifetime = 36000
   forwardable = true
   krb4_convert = false
 }
```

Issue the command to create the Kerberos database and initialize the realm:

```
# kdb5_util create -s
Loading random data
Initializing database '/var/kerberos/krb5kdc/principal' for realm 'LPI.ORG.
BR',
master key name 'K/M@LPI.ORG.BR'
Enter KDC database master key: Enter key
Re-enter KDC database master key to verify: Re-enter key
```

 You will be prompted for the database master password. Remember this password, because you need it later to administer the Kerberos server—but don't let out the password, because you will then put all your site's security in the hands of whoever finds it.

A Kerberos server must run the *krb5kdc* and *kadmin* daemons. On the KDCs, those services should be configured to start automatically on boot time.

The following commands run the servers:

```
# /etc/init.d/krb5kdc start
# /etc/init.d/kadmin start
```

You can create the principal user in Kerberos with the following command:

```
# kadmin.local
# kadmin.local:  addprinc user
WARNING: no policy specified for user@LPI.ORG.BR; defaulting to no policy
Enter password for principal "user@LPI.ORG.BR":
Re-enter password for principal "user@LPI.ORG.BR":
Principal "user@LPI.ORG.BR" created.
```

Client configuration

Basic client configuration is straightforward. Edit the file */etc/krb5.conf* as you did on the server. You must also modify the */var/Kerberos/krb5kdc/kdc.conf* file, which contains information about the encryption algorithm policy of the realm.

The configuration information for the system on which you wish to perform Kerberos authentication is the same information that you placed in the /etc/krb5.conf file on the KDC.

To obtain and cache a Kerberos ticket, enter:

```
# kinit user
Password for user@LPI.ORG.BR:
```

If nothing is returned, you are doing well. To list the tickets granted, enter:

```
# klist
Ticket cache: FILE:/tmp/krb5cc_0
Default principal: user@LPI.ORG.BR

Valid starting     Expires            Service principal
01/06/06 21:37:02  01/07/06 20:42:03  krbtgt/LPI.ORG.BR@LPI.ORG.BR
```

You can destroy tickets using this intuitive command:

```
# kdestroy
```

Now make sure that everything has been cleaned up.

```
# klist
klist: No credentials cache found (ticket cache FILE:/tmp/krb5cc_0)
```

Check the /etc/pam.d directory and use the PAM module *pam_krb5* to add Kerberos authentication in a network or local resource. Look at this example:

```
auth        required     /lib/security/pam_krb5.so use_first_pass
```

More information about PAM authentication can be found in Chapter 39.

You can use Kerberized Telnet and FTP services to test your new enviroment. Kerberos also can be used as an authentication mechanism for the Apache Web Server. The *mod_auth_kerb* Apache module provides that functionality; it can be downloaded from *http://modauthkerb.sourceforge.net*. Change the APACHE configuration file following this example:

```
<Directory "/home/httpd/htdocs/content">
    AllowOverride None
    AuthType KerberosV5
    AuthName "Kerberos Login"
    KrbAuthRealm LPI.ORG.BR
    require valid-user
</Directory>
```

It's very important to keep time synchronized on all systems. Otherwise, you could fall into a common problem:

```
# kinit user
 Password for user@LPI.ORG.BR:
 kinit(v5): Clock skew too great while getting initial credentials
```

Use *ntpdate* in your *crontab* files to update the system time frequently from a trusted source (NTP server). It should solve the problem.

Security Auditing Source Code

This is a very challenging field. There are almost no courses on the subject of writing secure software, and almost no one takes the courses that do exist. When talking about security, many people just talk about encryption, but encryption makes things more secure only if it is used properly (and it very often isn't). The rest of the program, and the environment it runs in, in must also be secure (and very often aren't). To do a real audit, you should know the programming language in question well and have extensive knowledge of how it and other languages have been exploited in the past. Linux, Unix, and the family of C languages were never designed for security, and a compendium of security pitfalls would go on forever. The task of writing secure programs falls upon the programmer, who is usually not prepared for it.

If you want to learn about secure programming, one place to start is the Linux HOWTO "Secure Programming for Linux and Unix" (*http://www.dwheeler.com/secure-programs/Secure-Programs-HOWTO*). You can also read books such as *Innocent Code* (Wiley), which deals exclusively with web application security. Following some mailing lists, such as the ones mentioned later in this chapter, will also orient you about how things go wrong in software. If you start to follow this field, you will see, as described earlier, that pitfalls are legion. And also that you quite probably should be just a little bit scared.

When a program runs as *root* and interacts with a user in any way, it is most important for it not to have weaknesses. We'll look at four of the worst offenders, two of which are quite easy to audit for.

Executing subprograms

Linux gives you many good reasons to execute a program from within a program. After all, Linux, like Unix, was built on a toolbox philosophy: many small utilities working together. Hence the long command lines that pipe data from one program to another. The subprograms may not be secure themselves, but that is another matter.

You should look out for three system calls, provided by C and mimicked by other popular languages on Linux: *system*, *popen*, and the *exec** family. The first two calls execute shells that run subprograms, while the third set replaces the current program with a new one without invoking a shell.

A shell can mainly be subverted in three ways: via the PATH, via IFS, and via insecure input. We'll return to how to check input shortly.

The PATH variable is used by shells as a list of where to look for executable programs. If the user executing the program has changed the shell to start with his *$HOME/bin* directory and has some well-chosen executables that he knows your program will execute, such as *gzip* to read compressed files, your program is broken into. He can replace *gzip* with anything he likes.

Second, if the subprogram is a shell script, the variable IFS can be changed to change the meaning of the script. The IFS variable contains the Input Field Separators—the characters recognized as word separators in a script. Ordinarily, IFS contains space, tab, and newline. If it is changed to include colon and semicolon, and perhaps single and double quotes, a script can suddenly get a very different meaning.

The fallout of this is: set the PATH and IFS variables explicitly in any programs that execute as a privileged user.

You should look out for calls in the *exec** family for the same reason. Even if the PATH is not used for the *exec* call itself, the called program will inherit the path and may call another program. And the IFS warning also applies, because surprisingly often a Linux program is a script.

Checking input

While it is true that a program should try to be as understanding of its user as possible to make it easy to use, it is also true that a program should be very critical of everything a user says. If a program gets the user to input values that are going to be used in a SQL statement and it accepts things such as quotes in the value, the user can construct an entirely different SQL statement. If you start out with something like this statement:

```
select * from employees
    where name like "$value"
```

then the user could give a carefully constructed value such as Smith%"; delete from employees where name like "%. When inserted into your SQL query, this becomes:

```
select * from employees
    where name like "Smith%"; delete from employees where name like "%"
```

which will very likely empty the employees table. This is a very brute-force and stupid example; the more subtle thing to do is to adjust the wages table. Quite a lot of faults can lead to this kind of attack, but the main one is failing to check input values in the program. The rule for input values should be that all the input that is not explicitly allowed is forbidden. When inputting names, there is no reason to accept quotes and semicolons—in fact, one should exclude any character that is not alphabetic, a space, an apostrophe, or a period, which should at least handle most Western names. (If we're talking about Unicode, this becomes a whole other headache.) If a program takes this kind of approach to all values that are input, it will become dramatically safer. In a web setting, the kind of attack used as an example here is called *SQL injection* and is wildly popular.

In a Linux setting, when subprograms are executed using *system* or *popen* as mentioned earlier, it has also been quite popular to give values such as:

```
foo; rm -rf /
```

which in a privileged program that does not check its input would cause the whole filesystem to be deleted.

The moral of this? Never trust your user, check everything, and reject or suppress anything that is even remotely fishy.

Buffer overflows

This class of insecurity has also been wildly popular with the crackers. It is another example of not checking input properly. The C/C++ languages and the libraries they use are very vulnerable to this, because many of the functions do not do bounds checking. They will gladly input 5000 characters into a 128-character buffer. Overflows are the most fun (for those who deliberately cause them) when the flaw appears in a network service, so that a remote user can gain root shell on the host just by sending some magical input to the network service. But vulnerabilities are also seen in programs that users can run when logged in to a machine.

A buffer overflow works when giving a variable a value, by also overwriting the contents of variables adjacent to it on the stack, heap, or global variable store of the program. By putting her own values into the neighboring memory areas, an intruder can subvert a program to do anything, and the most common trick is to start a root shell.

There are *many* ways to achieve a buffer overflow, all of which involve not checking the length of the data the program is handling. If you're going to copy an environment variable into a string buffer, always check the length of the value first or use the dynamic *strdup* function or one of the *strn* * functions that refuses to copy more than a set number of characters. If you're reading input from a user or the network, do not use *gets* or some other function that does not accept a length parameter. *fgets* does the same job but limits the input. And remember that return values from functions such as *gethostbyaddr* should also be considered as input; you have no way of knowing that the hostname fits in the 64-byte buffer set aside for it.

Unsafe temporary file creation

Programs that use temporary files are in danger because they most often use a common temporary area such as */tmp* or */var/tmp* in which users can leave nasty surprises beforehand to subvert the program. If it is well-known what a temporary file is named, such as */tmp/work.pid*, and the program does not create the file the right way, it can be bamboozled into overwriting critical system files. If the attacker is lucky, the victim is even a file that then lets him log in as root afterward.

Many programs use combinations of calls such as *tmpnam*, *mktemp*, and *open* to create a temporary file. The *tmpnam* function does not create a very safe name. *mktemp* creates safe names on Linux, but not on some BSD variants. Then, after obtaining a safe, or unsafe, name, one opens the file with *open* or *fopen*, but if this is not done correctly, someone may create a symbolic link with exactly that name that points to some file she wants overwritten. A temporary file in a public file area should be opened only with the flags O_CREAT and O_EXCL, which ensure that the file is new and did not previously exist, not even as a symbolic link. The *fopen* call is not suitable for this at all; the *open* call must be used. The easy way to do this in one step is to use *mkstemp*, which fashions a name and opens the file correctly. If the program needs to use standard I/O functions, it should use *fdopen* to obtain a FILE * handle from the file descriptor returned by *mkstemp* or *open*.

IDS

In a secure environment, you usually want IDS tools somewhere to help detect attempts at break-ins and most definitively to help discover a break-in once it has happened. IDSs are broadly put into two categories: network and host, depending on what they monitor. Network tools usually base themselves on firewalls and use network snooping techniques, whereas host tools monitor system activities. A third kind of IDS tool is a host resident network scanning detector. PortSentry is one such tool. It is included in Debian, but not in many other distributions, but it is easy enough to compile. It can be downloaded from *http://sourceforge.net/projects/sentrytools*.

PortSentry works by listening on a lot of likely ports—ports that are often subject to network scans. The default configuration is quite good. On a Debian system, it is stored in */etc/portsentry*. Some excerpts from *portsentry.conf* (the lines are broken to fit the page; PortSentry does not support line continuation) follow:

```
# Use these if you just want to be aware:
TCP_PORTS="1,11,15,79,111,119,143,540,635,1080,1524,2000,5742,6667, \
    12345,12346,20034,27665,31337,32771,32772,32773,32774,40421,49724,\
    54320"
UDP_PORTS="1,7,9,69,161,162,513,635,640,641,700,37444,34555,31335, \
    32770,32771,32772,32773,32774,31337,54321"
...
# iptables support for Linux
#KILL_ROUTE="/sbin/iptables -I INPUT -s $TARGET$ -j DROP"
```

PortSentry will listen to all these ports. If something connects to them, PortSentry will log it or optionally run a command. The log entry looks something like this (lines truncated):

```
portsentry[578]: attackalert: Connect from host: 172.16.73.1/172.16.73.1
    to TCP port: 32772
portsentry[578]: attackalert: Ignoring TCP response per configuration
    file setting.
portsentry[578]: attackalert: Connect from host: 172.16.73.1/172.16.73.1
    to TCP port: 79
portsentry[578]: attackalert: Host: 172.16.73.1 is already blocked. Ignoring
```

As shown in the previous configuration, PortSentry can run firewall configuration commands to block attackers entirely. If you want to do so, you should probably put rules into the FORWARD table as well as the INPUT table that the example shows. The -I option inserts the rule in the front of the table instead of appending it as -A does. This can be quite dangerous and a useful aide to a DOS attack. If someone does a spoofed scan of you by UDP, he can easily provoke PortSentry into blocking the spoofed address he's using. This could be an important address, like your DNS server, your email server, or some such. Therefore an attacker can very easily cause you major trouble, and even long downtimes. The best way to use such a tool is probably to generate real-time alerts for administrators to pursue and then *perhaps* to take action against it.

There is a considerable downside to PortSentry. If a host monitored by it is scanned, it may be a very tempting target because it appears to run a lot of services that are useful break-in tools because they have a history of weaknesses.

Furthermore, the upside may not be that big. Most recognizance tools used in network probing, such as *nmap -sS*, do not actually open a connection. They cause a half opening by sending a SYN, and when the SYN+ACK get back, they conclude that the port is open. But they never send an ACK back, so the connection never goes up and PortSentry never gets a whiff of the scan.

As stated in this chapter, IDS tools fall into two categories: host and network. Here we'll look at one tool in each category.

Tripwire

Tripwire uses file fingerprinting to detect changes in files. Information that goes into a fingerprint includes size, time, and date but, more importantly, checksums of different kinds. Tripwire was the first well-known software to do this, and when the work on these LPI Exams started, it had not yet been usurped. Its name is still held in high regard around the Internet. But the free Tripwire version is at this point very much abandonware. Originally from Purdue University, they licensed it to Tripwire Inc. in 1997, and Purdue has made no releases since Version 1.2 from August 1994, except for a patch in 1996. Version 1.x remains available in quite old releases of Red Hat, SuSE, and other Linuxes. The subsequent Version 2.x was released under GPL, and Version 2.3.1 from March 2001 is still available there, but it is not possible to compile with current versions of *gcc* without modifying the source code.

There is another tool called *aide* that is included in Debian, but not Red Hat. It does more or less the same job as Tripwire and is being maintained. This is what you should use if you want to install a fingerprinting tool now.

Still, Tripwire is documented, and a summary of the documentation follows.

Overview of Tripwire. The basic work flow in Tripwire is pretty simple. First, you create the needed site and local encryption keys on a one-time basis with *twadmin*. These are later used to encrypt and sign Tripwire files to ensure that any changes to the files by an intruder will be plainly detectable. Then the real work starts—writing a policy file. This file controls what attributes of a file are fingerprintable and the severity of the situation if it is changed. The policy file is then encrypted and signed with the *twadmin* command. Once a policy is set, you generate a database with the fingerprints of all the files as set in the policy. This is often called the *baseline* of the system and it is created with the *tripwire* command. Later *tripwire* is run in the checking or update mode to find deviations from the baseline and optionally to accept the changes as legitimate.

Tripwire uses several files. In most cases there is no need to override their locations. */etc/tripwire/tw.cfg* contains system information and file paths; a useful default is installed during the first installation. */var/lib/hostname.twd* is the fingerprint database file. Tripwire uses cryptography to make it impossible to interfere with its operation without its becoming obvious. The */etc/tripwire/site.key* key is used for files that can be used across several hosts. The */etc/tripwire/hostname-local.key* key is used on files specific to the given host. The Tripwire policy is stored in an encrypted and signed format in */etc/tripwire/tw.pol* and in plain text in */etc/tripwire/twpol.txt*. Policy files are created with *twadmin*.

Tripwire policy file format. The policy file is made up of comments and rules. Most of the examples in this section are from the *twpolicy* manpage in the GPL version of Tripwire 2.3, all written by Tripwire Inc. The general file format is like this:

```
# This is a comment.
# This is a variable assignment
mask1 = value;

# A rule line path  ->  property_mask;  # A comment can go here, too.

# A stop point
!path;
```

All lines that are not comments must end in semicolons. Each *path* is the path of a file or directory. On a rule line, it is followed by one or more whitespaces and then the separator (->) followed by more whitespace. If the path is a directory, the setting works for the directory and everything underneath. The stop points are used to exempt files or directories from scanning. A somewhat realistic example is:

```
# This demonstrates regular rule lines
# Defines Tripwire behavior for entire /bin directory tree.
/bin          -> $(ReadOnly);

# Defines Tripwire behavior for a single file.  In this case,
# Tripwire watches for all properties of hostname.hme0.
/etc/hostname  -> $(IgnoreNone) -ar;

mask1 = $(IgnoreAll) +ugp;
mask1 = $(IgnoreNone) -li;

# Scan the entire /etc directory tree using mask1, except the
# file /etc/passwd, which should be scanned using mask2.
/etc          -> $(mask1);
/etc/passwd   -> $(mask2);

# This demonstrates stop points
# The directory /etc/init.d will not be scanned.
!/etc/init.d;
!/etc/rc.d;
!/etc/mnttab;
# To summarize: scan all of /etc, but do not scan two particular files
# and one directory in the /etc hierarchy.
```

In the listing, $(ReadOnly) refers to a variable. Variables can be used anywhere on a line. The property masks decide what makes up the fingerprint of the given file or directory. The basic building blocks of property masks are single characters specifying a single property prefixed by a plus or minus to enable or disable checking of this property. A number of predefined variables define useful property masks. ReadOnly is used for files that should not change at all. Growing is good for files that should grow, logs mostly. Device is good for device files, and it stops Tripwire from trying to read them to generate checksums. IgnoreAll is a good starting point if you want to watch only a few attributes. IgnoreNone is good if you're watching all but a few attributes.

Each of the 18 attributes shown in Table 40-4 controls the recording and checking of one property of the file.

Table 40-4. Tripwire attributes

Attribute	Description
a	Access time.
b	Number of blocks allocated.
c	Creation timestamp.
d	Device number of the inode/file.
g	File group.
i	Inode number.
l	File size is growing (violated if the file is ever smaller than before, such as after a log rotation).
m	Modification time.
n	Number of links to the inode.
p	Permission bits.
r	For device files: major and major device number.
s	File size.
t	File type.
u	File owner.
C	CRC-32 checksum. Not a good idea to use this, because it is easily duped.
H	Haval hack value.
M	MD5 hash value. This is cryptologically safe and extremely hard to dupe.
S	SHA hash value. Also safe.

Rules can be given attributes in two ways:

```
/etc           -> $(ReadOnly) (attribute = value, attribute = value);

(attribute = value ... )
{
     /usr/lib -> $(ReadOnly);
}
```

The rule attributes are:

rulename=*name*
> This is used when checking/updating the database you can search in the reports for this rule name.

emailto=*email_address*
> If a file fails the fingerprinting test and the check is run with the --email-report option, the specified address will be emailed about the problem.

severity=*integer*
> Severities run from 0 to 1000000, with 0 as the default. When running a check, you can ignore files with a severity lower than a given level.

```
recurse=true|false|integer
```
Disable or limit recursion of directories. If set to false, the directory will be handled as if it were a file. If set to true, Tripwire will recurse infinitely. An integer value sets the maximum depth of recursion. Stop points override this setting.

In addition, you can put directives in the policy files. To wit:

```
@@section section name      # Updates and checks can be restricted to
                            # certain sections only.

@@ifhost hostname [ || hostname ]
   rules                    # To get different rules for different hosts.
@@else
   rukes
@@endif

@@print message             # Print message on standard output
@@error message             # Print message and exit
@@end                       # Stop processing here
```

tripwire

Syntax

```
tripwire -m i|--init    [ options ... ]
tripwire -m c|--check   [ options ... ] [ object1 ... ]
tripwire -m u|--update  [ options ... ]
tripwire -m p|--update-policy [ options ... ] policyfile.txt
tripwire -m t|--test -e|--email e-mail address
```

Description

To build a fingerprint database, use the initialization mode. Then run a check once a day, or hour, from a *crontab* file. If a reported change is legitimate, use update mode to update the fingerprints.

Database initialization

Once the policy is correct, the database can be created. Some relevant options include:

-m i, --init
    Mode selector: initialize the database.

-v, --verbose
    Be verbose.

-s, --silent, --quiet
    Be silent.

-e, --no-encryption
    Disable cryptographic signing of the database.

Checking mode

Tripwire should be run in checking mode periodically. This verifies that the files watched are OK and have not been changed. Some popular options include:

-m c, --check
    Activate checking mode.

-I, --interactive
    Open the check summary in an editor. This summary can then be edited to enable changes in the database on a file-by-file basis.

-r report, --twrfile report
    The default location for reports is */var/lib/tripwire/report/hostnamedate.twr*.

-l level|name, --severity level|name
    Check only rules with severity at or above the given level. Valid level names are low, medium, and high, corresponding to a level of 33, 66, and 100 respectively.

-R rule, --rule-name rule
    Check only the named rule. Cannot be combined with *-l*.

Database updates

If the database is not updated interactively in check mode, it can be updated wholesale or interactively with this mode. Options include:

-m u, --update
    Activate update mode.

-a, --accept-all
    Accept all changes.

-V editor, -visual editor
    Use the given editor to accept individual changes interactively.

Replace policy file

You can replace the policy file with -m p or --update-policy, but this is better done with twadmin (discussed later).

E-mail test report

This option is used to send a test report to the given address.

-m t, --test
    Activate test mode.

-e mail address, --email mail_address
    Send mail to this address.

twadmin

Syntax

```
twadmin -m F|--create-cfgfile options...  configfile.txt
twadmin -m f|--print-cfgfile [ options... ]
twadmin -m P|--create-polfile [ options... ] policyfile.txt
twadmin -m p|--print-polfile [ options... ]
twadmin -m R|--remove-encryption } [ options... ] file1 [ file2... ]
twadmin -m E|--encrypt [ options... ] file1 [ file2... ]
```

```
twadmin -m e|--examine [ options... ] file1 [ file2... ]
twadmin -m G|--generate-keys options...
```

Description

twamin administers Tripwire configuration and policy files. These are kept in an encoded format and signed with the local or site encryption keys. The keys are also generated with this utility.

General options

-v, --verbose
    Verbose output.

-s, --silent, --quiet
    Silent mode.

-Ssite_key, --site-key filesite_key
    Use the given site key for encrypting or decrypting.

-Qpass_phrase, --site-pass phrasepass_phrase
    Use together with -S to give the passphrase for encoding and signing.

-Llocal_key, -Llocal_key
    Use the given local key for encrypting or decrypting.

-Ppass_phrase, --local-passphrase pass_phrase
    Use this passphrase with the local key.

-e, --no-encryption
    Do not encrypt (or sign) the file. Usually you need to use -S, -L, or -e (or one of their long equivalents) in an operation.

-ccfgfile, --cfgfile cfgfile
    When operating on a configuration file, print or save to this filename.

-ppolfile, --polfile polfile
    When operating on a policy file, print or save to this filename.

Configuration file operations

Configuration files can be replaced or printed. Configuration files are either unencrypted or signed with the site key.

Use *-m F* or *--create-cfgfile* to create a configuration file. An input text file should be given as the last argument on the command line.

You can print the configuration file through *-m f* or *--print-cfgfile*.

Policy file operations

Policy files are encrypted and signed with the site key. They can be created or printed.

To create a policy file, use the *-m P* or *--create-polfile* option. The last thing on the command line should be the name of a text file containing the new policy file.

To print a policy file, use *-m p* or *-print-polfile*.

Encryption operations

twadmin can also be used to encrypt, decrypt, and check the encryption of files using either site or local keys.

A Tripwire file can be unencrypted with *-m R* or *--remove-encryption*. Last on the command line should be the name of the file or files to decrypt.

The reverse is accomplished with *-m E* or *--encrypt*. It too takes the name of the input file or files last on the command line.

Encrypting and signing files is useless without a way to verify the signature to see whether the file is unchanged. This is accomplished with the -m e or --examine option. Here too you should list the file or files to examine last on the command line.

Generating encryption keys

With the *-m G* or *--generate-keys* option, you can generate local or site keys as needed.

Snort

Snort is a network IDS. It listens in on network traffic, looking for specific patterns in the traffic that indicate some kind of attack or scanning. Snort is included in Debian, but not Red Hat. The Snort web page at *http://www.snort.org* has documentation and RPMs. This material is based on Snort 2.

Snort can be installed with different database backends, such as MySQL or PostgreSQL, but it can also log to flat files. In most cases you will want a database backend and a presentation frontend such as ACID. Snort has three modes of operation: sniffer (which shows packets on your terminal), packet logger (which saves packets to disk), and most interestingly, intrusion detection mode (in which it analyzes packet traffic according to different rules). We'll focus on Snort with no database backends in intrusion detection mode. Even with this restriction, a full description of Snort is unreasonable and the description here will be focused very directly on elementary use and rule writing.

The Snort configuration is in */etc/snort/snort.conf*. A distribution-specific configuration used by the *init.d* script is found in */etc/snort/snort.debian.conf* on Debian and */etc/sysconfig/snort* on Red Hat systems. What the Debian packager and the Red Hat packager considered as useful to put in there does not overlap much, but both define which interfaces should be listened on. You should review these and adjust as needed. On Debian, for example, you should define HOME_NET in the system configuration file. On Red Hat this is done in the main *snort.conf* file. All in all, the *init.d* scripts build pretty complex command lines, specifically:

```
/usr/sbin/snort -m 027 -D -S HOME_NET=[172.16.73.127/24] -c /etc/snort/ \
    snort.conf -l /var/log/snort -d -u snort -g snort -i eth0
```

on Debian, and you should either always use the scripts or never use them.

The significance of the HOME_NET definition on the command line or in the configuration file is that Snort will know who's friend and who's foe. This helps restrict the pattern matches. The *-l* option specifies the log directory. The *-u* and *-g* options tell Snort what user and group to run as when it is done with the setup work that requires root access. The *-d* option causes application data to be logged, while the *-m* option sets the file creation umask. It is the *-c* option that brings in the IDS configuration and turns Snort into a Network IDS. This default configuration is probably not enough to keep up with a full gigabit Ethernet. If you need to do that, you will find ways to do it and other tuning tips in the documentation and forums on the web site.

Once Snort is running, you can try to scan your Snort host with *nmap -sS host* (shown later) while looking at */var/log/snort/alert*. If you scan from a host that Snort regards as external, you should get a good number of alerts, some examples of which are shown here:

```
[**] [1:469:1] ICMP PING NMAP [**]
[Classification: Attempted Information Leak] [Priority: 2]
02/01-12:07:22.770254 172.16.73.1 -> 172.16.73.127
ICMP TTL:59 TOS:0x0 ID:35658 IpLen:20 DgmLen:28
Type:8  Code:0  ID:44124  Seq:60516  ECHO
[Xref => http://www.whitehats.com/info/IDS162]

[**] [117:1:1] (spp_portscan2) Portscan detected from 172.16.73.1: \
  1 targets 21 ports in 1 seconds [**]
02/01-12:07:23.073961 172.16.73.1:57705 -> 172.16.73.127:688
TCP TTL:54 TOS:0x0 ID:10591 IpLen:20 DgmLen:40
******S* Seq: 0x11BFB904  Ack: 0x0  Win: 0xC00  TcpLen: 20

[**] [1:618:4] SCAN Squid Proxy attempt [**]
[Classification: Attempted Information Leak] [Priority: 2]
02/01-12:07:23.114308 172.16.73.1:57705 -> 172.16.73.127:3128
TCP TTL:37 TOS:0x0 ID:29886 IpLen:20 DgmLen:40
******S* Seq: 0x11BFB904  Ack: 0x0  Win: 0x800  TcpLen: 20

[**] [1:1420:2] SNMP trap tcp [**]
[Classification: Attempted Information Leak] [Priority: 2]
02/01-12:07:23.136749 172.16.73.1:57705 -> 172.16.73.127:162
TCP TTL:39 TOS:0x0 ID:4837 IpLen:20 DgmLen:40
******S* Seq: 0x11BFB904  Ack: 0x0  Win: 0x1000  TcpLen: 20
[Xref => http://cve.mitre.org/cgi-bin/cvename.cgi?name=CAN-2002-0013][Xref
=> http://cve.mitre.org/cgi-bin/cvenam
e.cgi?name=CAN-2002-0012]

...
```

Configuring Snort. The main *snort.conf* file is very generic, but can take a lot of customization. Most importantly, it defines some networks (HOME_NET, EXTERNAL_NET) to help it see who it's working for. Because most Snort rules concentrate on traffic from EXTERNAL_NET to HOME_NET, it's important to define those variables in a way that lets you detect the traffic you want to. Sometimes you don't trust people on the inside either.

Next, you can enumerate DNS servers to help Snort restrict its DNS attack checking to traffic headed for the actual DNS server. This saves time. You can do the same for SMTP, HTTP, SQL, and Telnet servers. For the full list of options, see the comments in the configuration file and the documentation. On the bottom of the config file are a lot of include statements. These include the actual IDS rules that help identify specific attacks. The easiest high-level configuration of Snort is to simply include and exclude rulesets here.

Understanding Snort rules. When you come to the actual rules, there is rather a lot to learn. We'll use some examples. If you refer back to the previous alerts, you will find this message:

```
[**] [1:618:4] SCAN Squid Proxy attempt [**]
[Classification: Attempted Information Leak] [Priority: 2]
02/01-12:07:23.114308 172.16.73.1:57705 -> 172.16.73.127:3128
TCP TTL:37 TOS:0x0 ID:29886 IpLen:20 DgmLen:40
******S* Seq: 0x11BFB904  Ack: 0x0  Win: 0x800  TcpLen: 20
```

It corresponds to this rule:

```
alert tcp $EXTERNAL_NET any -> $HOME_NET 3128 \
    (msg:"SCAN Squid Proxy attempt"; flags:S,12; \
    classtype:attempted-recon; sid:618; rev:4;)
```

This rule says that all traffic from any port on EXTERNAL_NET to port 3128 on HOME_NET is a reconnaissance attempt. It does not matter whether the connection comes up. And the rule is right; because web proxies are usually for internal use only, access from the outside is suspect.

Now we'll look at two rules to detect X Window System connections going up from the outside. Each rule starts with an action. Actions can be one of:

activate
> Raise an alert and activiate a dynamic rule.

alert
> Raise an alert and log the packet.

dynamic
> This rule must be activated, but once active, it logs packets.

log
> Log the packet.

pass
> Ignore the packet.

The next field is the IP protocol. Snort can currently handle tcp, ucp, icmp, and ip.

Next is the source address and port, followed by a direction operator, -> here, and the destination address and port. The example shown earlier simply uses variables for this, but some more complex syntax is available:

any
> Any address

d.d.d.d
> Regular dotted decimal, such as 172.20.12.88

d.d.d.d/m
> Dotted decimal with network mask such as 172.20.12.0/22

[*a,a,...*]
> List of addresses and networks, such as [172.20.12.88,62.179.100.29,192.168.0.0/24]

!a

> Not the address or list; examples include !172.20.12.88 and ![172.20.12.88,192.168.0.0/24]

The ports can be specified like this:

any

> Any port.

d

> A port number, such as 22 for SSH.

d:d, :d, d:

> A port range. If the lower bound is left out, it defaults to 0. If the higher bound is left out, it defaults to 65536. Examples include 6000:6010 for X Window System ports, and :1024 for all privileged ports.

!ports

> Not the given ports.

Between the addresses comes the direction operator. It is either -> or <>. The latter string can be used to log both sides of a protocol exchange. There is no <- operator because that would cause insanity.

activate and dynamic rules are very powerful, but are being replaced by tagging. An example from the Snort documentation follows. It's worth noting that there are no dynamic rules in the default rule base.

```
activate tcp !$HOME_NET any -> $HOME_NET 143 (flags: PA; \
    content: "E8C0FFFFFF!/bin"; activates: 1; \
    msg: "IMAP buffer overflow!";)
dynamic tcp !$HOME_NET any -> $HOME_NET 143 \
    (activated_by: 1; count: 50;)
```

The activate rule detects an IMAP buffer overflow attempt (the connection has to be up for this to occur) and the dynamic rule logs the 50 following packets. This should be able to document what happened or what the attacker attempted to accomplish.

Once a combination of protocol, from address/port, and to address/port has been matched, processing continues inside the parentheses. The most useful processing commands are probably flags to match TCP flags, content to do simple packet content matching, and msg to specify the alert text.

flags

> Flags are character codes corresponding to TCP protocol bits. Most administrators have heard of the SYN and ACK bits, which are coded S and A respectively. Also available are F, R, P, U, 1, and 2 corresponding to FIN, RST, PSH, URG, reserved bit 1, and reserved bit 2. 0 means no flags. Prefixed with +, all the given flags must be present, but others are allowed (this is the default). The * prefix matches if any of the given bits is set. ! matches if none of the bits is set. The flag requirements may be followed by a flag mask, which indicates flags whose settings should be masked away before testing. Typically, the two reserved bits are masked. Thus, flags:S,12 matches packets with only the SYN flag set, ignoring the 1 and 2 flags.

content
> The content-matching capability in Snort is quite rich, and it may contain both ASCII and binary data. There are keywords to restrict searching in the payload. This is good because string searching is time consuming. An example may help here:
>
> ```
> alert tcp any any -> any 80 (content:"GET"; depth 3; nocase;)
> ```
>
> This will match any packet to port 80 that has the string GET in the first 3 bytes. Matching will be done in a case-insensitive manner. Additionally, the offset keyword tells the processor where to start looking for the string. There are quite a few other options, but these should do here. There also are numerous other ways to match content; please refer to the documentation. To match binary data, quote hexadecimal numbers with a | (pipe). An example is |DE AD BE EF| (a magic number in Unix mythology).

msg
> A message to be logged or alerted with.

reference
> A reference to an IDS attack profile database for further explanation of this rule. In the alert log, it will be shown as an expanded URL.

sid, rev
> These aid in refinding rules. For example, when an attack gets a specific rule assigned to detect it, it is also given a sid and rev, and if it is later found that this rule gives too many false positives, it can be refined. Users concerned with keeping this rule updated can easily check whether they have the latest revision of the rule and replace it with a newer one. There is no need to use these in private rules.

classtype
> Attack class types. These are enumerated in the *classification.config* file, which gives each code class type a description and a priority. One example is attempted-admin, which means "attempted administrator privilege gain" and has a high priority. There are currently more than 30 attack classes.

Miscellaneous

Scanning in general

We mentioned *nmap* earlier. It is a very effective port scanner with some useful stealth features that can help you check for poor firewall setups as well. *nmap* is very effective at doing a quick scan of many services on all hosts in a network or perhaps to look only for FTP and email servers in a net range like this:

```
# nmap -sS -P0 -p 21,25 10.0.0.0/24
...

Host lorbanery.langfeldt.net (10.0.0.1) appears to be up ... good.
Initiating SYN Stealth Scan against lorbanery.langfeldt.net (10.0.0.1) at
11:55
Adding open port 25/tcp
```

```
The SYN Stealth Scan took 2 seconds to scan 3 ports.
Interesting ports on lorbanery.langfeldt.net (10.0.0.1):
PORT    STATE    SERVICE
21/tcp  filtered ftp
25/tcp  open     smtp

...

Host roke.langfeldt.net (10.0.0.4) appears to be up ... good.
Initiating SYN Stealth Scan against roke.langfeldt.net (10.0.0.4) at 11:55
Adding open port 25/tcp
Adding open port 80/tcp
The SYN Stealth Scan took 0 seconds to scan 3 ports.
Interesting ports on roke.langfeldt.net (10.0.0.4):
PORT    STATE  SERVICE
21/tcp  closed ftp
25/tcp  open   smtp

...
```

After locating your mail and FTP servers, you can then test them manually or with simple scripts. For example, you may want to have no anonymous FTP servers on your network. It is simple enough to attempt an anonymous login.

A real problem on networks nowadays is the existence of open email relays. If you have one, it will surely be abused for spreading spam. With a list of the SMTP servers present on your network, it is also quite easy to script a test for this. You don't have to test whether the server will relay mail from a host on the company network; this may be what it is set up to do. But if you have a mail server that accepts email from the Internet, it is very practical to have a remote shell account and do such a check from there. The SMTP protocol is simple enough, and the test is to see whether the email server will accept mail to a party outside your relay domain list. The main rules are that when accepting email from the inside network, any email should be accepted. There may be local policies that restricts this, for example checking that the "From" address is valid, and that the email does not contain spam or virus. But that does not concern an open relay test. From the outside, the server should accept emails only *to* the inside domain. It should not accept email that is to someone outside and claims to be from the inside. Thus, you might run the following test from *false.linpro.no*, outside your local area network, to your mail server:

```
$ telnet mail.example.com 25
...
220 How may I help you? ESMTP
HELO false.linpro.no
250 mail.example.com
MAIL FROM:<santa@north-pole.org>
250 Ok
RCPT TO:<toothfarie@faries.org>
554 <toothfarie@faries.org>: Relay access denied
quit
221 Bye
```

```
$ telnet mail.example.com 25
...
220 How may I help you? ESMTP
HELO false.linpro.no
250 mail.example.comM
AIL FROM:<postmaster@example.com>
250 Ok
RCPT TO:<toothfarie@faries.org>
554 <toothfarie@faries.org>: Relay access denied
quit
221 Bye
```

This server is properly set up and does not seem to allow any relaying. It does not accept mail from just anyone to anyone, nor does it accept email that pretends to come from the inside.

Several automated tools for network scanning make much better use of your time than these manual methods. Nessus, for example, which is included in Debian but not in Red Hat, will scan a network range and includes a lot of very specific vulnerability tests, including anonymous FTP and mail relays. Debian, as a rule, does not update programs to the latest version when holes are discovered, but instead backports the fix and keeps the same version. So when Nessus thinks it has found an old hole-riddled version, it might in fact not have a hole after all—if the machine is kept up-to-date, that is.

Security alerts

To keep abreast of developments in the security area, you and hopefully all your colleagues—in case you're on vacation sometime—should subscribe to one or several security announce lists. These follow two different schools. CERT and CIAC follow what they consider to be responsible practices. This means that they give vendors (Unix, Linux, Windows, and others) ample (some would call it infinite) time to release fixes before CERT or CIAC publishes advisories about specific security problems. The problem with this is that it has previously taken many years to fix even the most trivial and well-known problems. This does not make for a very secure network, because a well-informed crook can get in while administrators, being busy at doing more productive things, are oblivious to the problems.

Bugtraq and Full Disclosure follow a more aggressive policy. Holding that an unknown security hole is still a security hole and nothing anyone should have to live with, they publish problems very quickly. On Bugtraq, it is preferred that people submit the problem to the vendor and let the vendor take a reasonable amount of time, perhaps a month, before the information on the problem is posted. The Full Disclosure list is less concerned with this and seeks what they see as fully open information with no compromises. That at least gets security holes fixed fast, at the cost of wider exposure for a shorter time, rather than the long time with unknown exposure that the CERT tactic gives.

So some of the different places to get security information are:

Computer Emergency Response Team (CERT)

The original network security coordination center, located at Carnegie Mellon University. They make announcements on a mailing list. See *http://www.cert.org/contact_cert/certmaillist.html* for further information. Their web site also contains updated security information, including viruses and vulnerabilities.

Computer Incident Advisory Capability (CIAC)

Operated by the U.S. Department of Energy, CIAC keeps a web site at *http://www.ciac.org/ciac/*. They release bulletins and "C-Notes" as well as links to papers, documentation, and software. Because they are devoted to keeping the DoE secure, their papers are quite likely to be relevant to practical security work you may need to do. CIAC publishes their bulletins and notes only on their web site.

Bugtraq

Hosted by SecurityFocus, this is the original full disclosure list, now somewhat more conservative. Subscribe at *http://www.securityfocus.com/archive/1*.

Full Disclosure

The Full Disclosure list should need no further introduction. See *http://www.netsys.com/cgi-bin/displaynews?a=301* to subscribe.

Red Hat

Most Linux distributions have announce lists and security pages. Red Hat's security page is at *http://www.redhat.com/security*, where you can subscribe to alerts and browse their archives.

Debian

The team keeps their security information at *http://www.debian.org/security*. You'll find information about how to keep Debian up-to-date, announce archives, and announcement subscription instructions.

Updating Linux

All your hosts, especially the Internet-exposed ones, need to be kept secure and up-to-date. The best way to keep updated about exactly what is found and what updates to install is to follow a distribution-specific alert mailing list. But a good second option is to just keep updating packages as updates are published. In Debian, this is especially simple, but there are also ways to do it in Red Hat and Fedora. Updating a package is the way fixes and patches are installed on Linux. On Solaris and other operating systems, you would install a patch or fix that modifies some installed package; not so on Linux.

Keeping Debian up-to-date. The first thing to do is put the following in your */etc/apt/sources.list* file (if you use Woody):

```
deb http://security.debian.org/ woody/updates main contrib non-free
```

If you also drop the *apt* script, which follows, into */etc/cron.daily*, you will receive a email every night after a package has received an upgrade. You will then need to do the actual upgrade yourself.

```
#!/bin/sh

apt-get --quiet=2 update

apt-get --quiet=2 --yes --print-uris dist-upgrade |
        awk '{ print $2; };'
```

And that is all there is to it.

Keeping Red Hat up-to-date. Red Hat runs a centralized service called up2date, which, unless you subscribe, can be very slow. Since most production servers in the future will run Red Hat Enterprise Linux and all these users will have premium subscriptions and priority up2date access this may gain popularity.

If you run an unlicensed desktop version of Red Hat, you may be more comfortable running YUM or *apt-rpm*. YUM is a native RPM package download manager, while *apt-rpm* is a port of the apt suite to RPM. The yum utility takes pretty much the same commands as *apt-get: update* to get new package lists, *update* or *distupgrade* to install new packages, and *install package* to install or upgrade a specific package.

41

Network Troubleshooting (Topic 214)

This chapter covers the Topic of troubleshooting for the LPI 202 Exam. This Topic has one long Objective:

Objective 7: Troubleshooting Network Issues
> Candidates should be able to identify and correct common network setup issues to include knowledge of locations for basic configuration files and commands. Key files, terms, and utilities include */sbin/ifconfig*, */sbin/route*, */bin/netstat*, */etc/network* and */etc/sysconfig/network-scripts*, system log files such as */var/log/syslog* and */var/log/messages*, */bin/ping*, */etc/resolv.conf*, */etc/hosts*, */etc/hosts.allow* and */etc/hosts.deny*, */etc/hostname* and */etc/HOST-NAME*, */sbin/hostname*, */usr/sbin/traceroute*, */usr/bin/nslookup*, */usr/bin/dig*, */bin/dmesg*, and *host*. Weight: 1.

Notice that most of the commands and concepts discussed in these sub-Objectives have been covered elsewhere in this book. Chapter 19 covers most of the commands used in this chapter, and several other chapters discuss essential networking applications and daemons (services).

So, why discuss these things again? Because there is a difference between simply knowing what a daemon or command does and actually troubleshooting it. So, this chapter won't attempt to re-discuss options to the *ifconfig* command or the syntax for the */etc/hosts.deny* files. Rather, it will focus on how to troubleshoot various services and how to use some of the commands you already know in an efficient way when problems occur.

Network Troubleshooting Essentials

One of the things that the creators of the LPI Exams knew was that you need to take a systematic approach to troubleshooting. When faced with a networking problem, inexperienced administrators often begin clicking the mouse button and pecking away at the keyboard without first clearly identifying the problem.

You need a methodology before you can begin altering files and running commands. The LPI Exam will not necessarily ask you what that method should be. However, the questions that deal with troubleshooting will often be phrased in a way that suggests a problem exists for some mysterious reason.

If you take the time to think about the situation being presented, you will find that the problem is not that mysterious and that you can make an educated guess at the correct answer. Once you are equipped with the proper perspective, you can then focus on the commands to use and the files to edit. Table 41-1 discusses essential troubleshooting steps to take when approaching a problem.

Table 41-1. Essential network troubleshooting steps

Troubleshooting step	Description
Gather all of the facts.	Carefully observe the problem. Many times, you will be presented with different ways to survey the issue. Read log files, analyze screen output, and use applications such *strace* and *ltrace* to gain a more informed perspective.
Listen to your first impressions.	If you have experience with system administration, your intuition can be useful.
Remain flexible.	Do not stubbornly stick to one idea. After a few failed attempts, consider taking a new approach to the problem, at least for a while. If this new approach does not solve the problem, return to your original idea, or take another direction.
Categorize the problem.	Try to determine if the problem is hardware- or software-related. Then, determine if the client or the server is experiencing issues. Remember to be flexible. A problem might seem to belong in one category at first, but may belong in another.
Make educated guesses.	An educated guess is not a wild stab at a solution. Form a hypothesis, then conduct experiments. Make sure that the changes you make are not harmful.
Document your impressions and attempts.	Writing down the steps you take will help you be more systematic and will help you recover from mistakes. Other administrators who come after you will appreciate it. In many cases, troubleshooting can take considerable time. Notes can help you remember exactly what steps you took, what files you reviewed and altered, and the result of each step.
Create and verify backups.	Before you alter a file to solve a problem, make sure that you store backups of the files.

Common Troubleshooting Commands

A discussion follows of commands you can use to resolve network problems.

ping

ping can do more than just determine basic connectivity. You can also use it to discover the quality of a network connection. If users are complaining about a spotty network connection, using *ping* in the right way can give you a reasonably accurate idea of how much of a problem exists.

You will not be able to determine that this is the problem by using the *ping* command in the standard way. However, if you use *ping* to generate a flood of packets, you can get a fairly accurate idea of how intermittent the connection really is. As *root*, use the *-f* option to generate a *ping* flood, as shown here:

```
root@james:~ # ping -f albion
PING albion.stangernet.com (192.168.2.57) 56(84) bytes of data.
.............................................................................
.............................................................................
.............................................................................
...............................................
--- albion.stangernet.com ping statistics ---
433 packets transmitted, 153 received, 64% packet loss, time 4833ms
rtt min/avg/max/mdev = 2.470/2.859/6.359/0.623 ms, ipg/ewma 11.189/3.012 ms
root@james:~ #
```

Notice that the output says that 64% of the packets were lost. Generally, a packet loss rate between 1% and 2% is tolerable, except by the most sensitive applications. Rates higher than even 2%, and especially 5%, are generally too high for a reliable network connection that is doing any real work (e.g., an X Window System session or a database connection).

So far, *ping* has not yet helped you determine if this system is experiencing a hardware problem or a software problem. But now that you know some sort of problem exists, you can begin hypothesizing. Steps to take might include:

1. Make sure that other systems are not experiencing the same problem. This may involve verifying that the hub or switch is working properly.

2. Send a flood of packets to additional systems to make sure that the problem does not reside on the remote system.

3. Check the physical connection on the local system, as well as to the hub or switch.

4. Make sure that the driver on the local system matches the hardware.

5. Check the NIC's subnet mask.

 Intrusion detection systems (IDS), described in Chapter 40, cannot tell the difference between an authorized, well-intended *ping* flood and one that is intended as an attack. If necessary, warn your security team that you are conducting *ping* floods before you create one.

If the system can't connect to a remote network such as the Internet, ping the router. Doing so involves more than a ping of the interface for the subnet. Ping the interface on the far side of the router. Then move to pinging hosts on the other side of the router. Understand, however, that many system administrators use access control lists to disable pinging across routers and switches.

Finally, when using *ping*, consider the following:

Use the -I option to choose the correct interface
Many systems have multiple Ethernet interfaces. You will want to make sure you are pinging the correct system.

Use the -n option if name resolution has failed
Doing so helps ensure that only IP address information is used and returned.

telnet and netcat

You have already learned that you can use *telnet* and *netcat* (*nc* on some systems) to query ports and gather information. It is important, however, to understand that you will be presented with different types of messages and errors in the context of a troubleshooting situation. Not all responses and errors are equally meaningful. But most of the responses can be quite useful. Table 41-2 provides a useful list of the most common responses.

Table 41-2. Responses to telnet and netcat queries

Response	Explanation
"Name or service not known" or "No route to host"	No system exists with that IP address or name.
"Connection refused"	Confirms that a remote system is listening. However, the port you have attempted to connect to is not open or is blocked by an *iptables* or *ipchains* rule. You nevertheless have found a live system.
"Name or service not known" or "Forward host lookup failed: Unknown host"	A DNS error indicating that no host by this name exists. This does not mean that the host does not exist at all. The name server is simply reporting that this *name* does not exist. Try connecting to this host by IP address. Possibly useful when troubleshooting DNS.
Connection hangs for a moment, then is dropped with no explanation	An application such as TCP wrappers has processed the connection, then dropped it. Useful when troubleshooting TCP wrappers configuration or in determining problems with nonworking services.
Connection seems to hang indefinitely	Usually implies that *telnet* or *netcat* has connected to a port. Note that in some cases, if you do not wait long enough, you can mistake a connection for a failed connection. Wait 4 or 5 seconds before you think that you have made a connection.

Once you have made a connection using *telnet* or *netcat*, you can then type in commands and send them to the listening port. Sometimes, that port may not respond at all. At other times, the port drops the connection immediately or returns gibberish.

In some cases, the port may allow an interactive session. SMTP, POP-3, and IMAP servers allow you to open a session and send commands. Many system administrators have memorized the necessary commands to send and receive email using nothing more than a *telnet* client or *netcat*. Following is an example of how you can use *netcat* to read e-mail from a POP-3 server:

```
# netcat mail.company.com 110
Trying 214.27.208.3...
Connected to mail.company.com.
Escape character is '^]'.
+OK (rwcrpxc59) Maillennium POP3/PROXY server #65
USER lpicprofessional
+OK
PASS passedexam1
+OK ready
LIST
+OK 1 messages (31227)
```

```
1 31227
.
```
RETR 1
```
From: certification@lpi.org
Subject: Congratulations
Congratulations upon achieving LPIC 2 status.
```
QUIT

In this sequence, *netcat* was used to connect to port 110 (the standard POP-3 port), and the user proceeded to enter a series of commands to read an email. First, the user issued the USER and PASS commands to authenticate to the remote system. Then, the LIST command was issued to see if any emails were waiting. In this particular session, one message was waiting.

To read the email message, the user simply typed RETR 1. The contents of the message were then displayed, giving good news in this case. If multiple email messages existed, the user could have typed RETR 3 to read the third message, or RETR 41 to read the 41st message. To end the session, the user typed QUIT. A session using *telnet* would use the identical POP-3 commands.

You can also communicate with web servers using *telnet* or *netcat*. Following is a simple HTTP session using *netcat*:

```
$ netcat stageserver.company.com 80
GET /
<html>
<head>
<title>Web site</title>
</head>
<body bgcolor="teal">
<p>Placeholder for Web site.</p>
</body>
</html>
$
```

First, *netcat* was used to connect to the Web server named *stageserver.company.com*. The HTTP GET / command was then used to returned the default web page that would normally be read by a standard web client. Instead of using the GET / command, you can simply type in gibberish. Many web servers, especially if they are still using default settings, will reveal the server version and other information:

```
$ netcat james 80
asdf
<!DOCTYPE HTML PUBLIC "-//IETF//DTD HTML 2.0//EN">
<html><head>
<title>501 Method Not Implemented</title>
</head><body>
<h1>Method Not Implemented</h1>
<p>asdf to /index.html not supported.<br />
</p>
<hr>
<address>Apache/2.0.53 (Ubuntu) PHP/4.3.10-10ubuntu4.3 Server at james.
stangernet.com Port 80</address>
</body></html>
$
```

Here, *netcat* was used to connect to a private web server maintained by the author at the host system *james*. In response to the gibberish entered by the user, the server issued a response that included not only the version of Apache Server, but also the server operating system and the fact that PHP is enabled. Not all daemons will respond with useful information, however.

ifconfig

The *ifconfig* command can be quite helpful during troubleshooting if you take the time to read all the information it provides. In addition to standard networking information (e.g., the IP address and subnet mask), the typical *ifconfig* output tells you the following:

- Whether or not the interface is up (the UP flag)
- If it is in broadcast and multicast mode
- The number of packets received and transmitted since last activation
- The number of errors and overruns
- The number of bytes received and transmitted
- The interrupt used, and base address

Here is an example of *ifconfig* output:

```
$ ifconfig eth0
eth0      Link encap:Ethernet  HWaddr 00:80:5F:EA:86:8F
          inet addr:24.17.140.230  Bcast:255.255.255.255  Mask:255.255.252.0
          UP BROADCAST RUNNING MULTICAST  MTU:1500  Metric:1
          RX packets:44354070 errors:0 dropped:0 overruns:0 frame:0
          TX packets:3078006 errors:0 dropped:0 overruns:0 carrier:0
          collisions:113575 txqueuelen:100
          RX bytes:1730626695 (1650.4 Mb)  TX bytes:553335663 (527.7 Mb)
          Interrupt:11 Base address:0x6100
```

The information gathered here can help you narrow down both hardware and software errors.

traceroute

Don't underestimate the usefulness of the *traceroute* command. Don't be too confident that you know everything about *traceroute*, either. For the exam, be able to identify each element of *traceroute* output. Consider the following example:

```
# traceroute 213.236.195.41
traceroute to 213.236.195.41 (213.236.195.41), 30 hops max, 38 byte packets
 1  linpro-intra-gw (80.232.36.129)  0.212 ms  0.154 ms  0.133 ms
 2  tott (80.232.38.218)  0.931 ms  0.783 ms  1.209 ms
 3  tdc-A100M-0225-hsrp.linpro.net (80.232.38.220)  1.471 ms  1.505 ms  1.
678 ms
 4  212.37.252.2 (212.37.252.2)  1.469 ms  1.834 ms  2.457 ms
 5  pos3-0.622M.osl-nyd-cr1.ip.teledanmark.no (213.236.195.41)  2.043 ms  *
2.906 ms
```

In the output, notice that each hop has three latency times shown. If you were to ping these systems, you would receive the same times. If the routing is randomized through some routing daemon, subsequent uses of *traceroute* could discover new hosts.

An asterisk represents either a lost packet or the fact that a router has been programmed not to respond to the particular type of ICMP packets *traceroute* uses within the timeout period you have specified. The default timeout period for *traceroute* is five seconds.

Sometimes, you may see the !N or !X flags in place of the latency information *traceroute* usually provides. The !N flag means that the host or network cannot be reached. The !X flag means that the administrator of the remote system has prohibited the use of ICMP, but was kind enough to configure the router to send a message informing *traceroute* about the prohibition.

netstat and route

You already know that *netstat* is useful for checking open connections, as well as viewing the routing table. We also discussed the *route* command in Chapter 19. The output of each command is slightly different, and this difference might be important in a troubleshooting situation.

Consider the following *netstat* output:

```
$ netstat -r
Kernel IP routing table
Destination    Gateway         Genmask        Flags  MSS Window  irtt
Iface
localnet       *               255.255.255.0  U      500 0       0 eth0
default        system1234.stan 0.0.0.0        UG     5000 0      0 eth0
$
```

For the sake of comparison, consider the following *route* output:

```
$ route
Kernel IP routing table
Destination    Gateway         Genmask        Flags Metric Ref    Use
Iface
localnet       *               255.255.255.0  U     0      0      0 eth0
default        system1234.stan 0.0.0.0        UG    0      0      0 eth0
$
```

The information from the two commands seems identical, but there are subtle differences. The output for *netstat* contains information for both the Maximum Segment Size (MSS) and Initial Round Trip Time (IRRT). The *route* command does not report these values by default.

The MSS value indicates the largest amount of data (in bytes) that the system can handle without fragmenting the packet. Generally, you want the MSS value to be less than the Maximum Trnsmission Unit (MTU), which is 1500 for Ethernet systems. A value of 0 means that the default is used, which is 536 bytes for Linux systems. The previous output shows that the MSS is 500, so the system is likely functioning well in this regard.

The IRRT value displays (in milliseconds) the amount of time allowed for initial TCP connections to complete. On our system there is a 0 value, which means that the system is using the default value (300 milliseconds).

The *route* command provides the routing metric and the Use field, which *netstat* does not. The Metric field indicates the distance to a destination target. It is no longer used by modern systems, though if you use a routing daemon, you may need to read this value. Knowledge of routing daemons is not required for the LPI Exams.

The Use field indicates the number of lookups for the particular route. If you use *route*'s -C option, you will see the number of times the cache has correctly looked up the route. If you use *route*'s -F option, you will see the number of misses.

Hardware Problems

One of the truisms of networking is that the majority of problems occur at the physical layer. Problems can include a failed NIC, a hub that has lost power, or bad cabling. A discussion of the relevant applications for troubleshooting physical networking issues follows.

Physical Connection Issues

Although the LPI Exam focuses mostly on local configuration issues that can be discovered and resolved by using applications such as *ifconfig* and *hostname*, it is important to understand that other devices may be causing problems.

Cabling

While relatively unusual, cables can become weakened and wires can sever. Some offices may have wiring that is routed beneath carpets that receive substantial traffic. Users may also be able to roll over the cables with their chairs. When it comes to troubleshooting such cabling problems, consider the following steps:

1. Obtain a working system and attach it to the cable in question. If the cable works, you know you have a problem with the Linux system.

2. Check for loose or broken cable connectors. If a connector is broken, the cable may be only partially inserted, causing failed or intermittent connections.

Failed networking devices

Hubs, switches, and routers are generally quite reliable, but it is possible that an intervening device, rather than the Linux system, has failed. One way to confirm your suspicion that a hub or switch has failed is to use a crossover cable and connect the affected system to another working system. A crossover cable is essentially the same thing as a standard LAN cable, but with four of the pins reversed. As a result, two systems can communicate directly with each other. If the two systems can communicate, it is likely that a hub or switch servicing the system you once suspected is experiencing a problem.

When inspecting a hub or switch, look for the following:

Whether the device has power
> Most hubs and all switches in a larger network are active devices. If they do not have power, you won't have a network connection.

Disconnected cables
> The system's cable may have been simply disconnected and needs to be reconnected.

Steadily blinking lights
> If lights are blinking steadily and continuously or remain on steadily, the device is experiencing a problem. Sometimes power surges cause devices to fail. Try powering it down and back on or simply replacing it.

Activated warning lights
> Some hubs and switches have warning lights that will indicate a problem. Look for them, then take steps to solve the problem.

Misconfigured hardware settings
> In one case, a Linux administrator noticed that a hub had a button pressed that caused one of its ports to effectively act as a straight through connection, rather than as a proper hub. Simply deselecting the button solved the problem. Look on the hub to see if there are any other improperly selected switches.

Problems with the Interface Card

If an NIC completely fails, it will fail to initialize at boot or respond to the *ifup* command. The *lspci* and *usbview* commands can help you determine whether the NIC has been recognized as valid hardware. If these commands do not show that the system recognizes the NIC, consider installing a new one. But problems can also exist elsewhere than the NIC. Make sure that you know what your system is telling you by consulting log files and reviewing screen output.

Finally, you can inspect the lights that ship with most NICs. These lights may seem to be useless, but they can help you determine whether the NIC is receiving power. If the lights are flashing randomly, it is likely that the device is receiving traffic. If you find that the lights are blinking steadily, it is likely the device has a configuration problem. If you find that one or more lights are simply staying on constantly, you likely have a hardware configuration problem. Of course, if the lights are not turned on at all, the NIC has not been recognized by your system's bus or has completely failed.

To solve such problems, make sure that the NIC is recognized by the Linux server. Consult the distribution's Hardware Compatibility List (HCL). You may find that you will have to get a new NIC.

Reviewing Screen Output

Do not simply focus on the NIC's lights or on the system's log files. Some systems are configured to report critical problems directly to the screen. In other cases, problems experienced by the NIC can cause warning messages to be printed on the screen, even though the system is not specially configured for this.

In most cases, the messages you see printed to the screen will be seen when the system boots. Messages can indicate that the system is delaying the interface's intialization or can report errors in transmission and reception.

Changes to the Kernel and /etc/modules

When a Linux system scans for PCI devices at boot time, it recognizes the devices it finds in the order that it finds them. The first card recognized becomes *eth0*, the second card recognized becomes *eth1*, and so forth. Recognition involves the act of detecting the hardware and assigning any drivers and modules. Sometimes, a seemingly innocuous change to the system can cause problems with PCI-based network devices.

In some cases, changes to the */etc/modules.conf* file can cause devices to go undetected or to be detected in a different order. In one case, an application completely unrelated to networking rewrote the */etc/modules.conf* file and inadvertently changed the order that modules were installed for a dual-NIC Linux router. The update to */etc/modules.conf* changed the order in which the NICs were recognized. With the change, the NIC that used to be recognized as *eth0* for two years was suddenly recognized as *eth1*. Because this system was a router, the *eth0* device was configured to masquerade connections, whereas the *eth1* device was not.

Normally, this would not be a problem, except that the company's ISP required all Internet-facing network interfaces to register their MAC addresses. Now the system was recognizing an unregistered card as *eth0*, and the ISP would not recognize the new *eth1* card as an Internet-addressable device. So a seemingly simple change to the */etc/modules.conf* file caused serious networking problems for the company.

Updating the kernel can also sometimes affect the order in which PCI devices are scanned, similarly to the previous example.

Finally, if for some reason a NIC's driver is loaded at a different time from previous boots, this NIC may be recognized earlier or later than before. As a result, the NIC may be assigned a different name.

Solving the problems discussed in this section is relatively trivial—once you know what caused the problems in the first place. In the first instance, simply editing the */etc/modules.conf* file and specifying the previous module installation order solved the problem. For the second problem, physically swapping the NICs would work. For the third problem, you can either swap the NICs or change the time when the drivers are assigned during the boot process. You would have to either reconfigure some boot scripts or possibly use an application such as YaST or *netconfig*.

Whatever solution you choose, it is important to understand that a seemingly unrelated change to the system can cause a ripple effect.

Checking Log Files

If you have an interface experiencing problems, you likely will be able to read about it in the */var/log/messages* or */var/log/syslog files*. You can also review *dmesg* output to view the contents of the kernel message buffer. Understand, however, that this buffer can be overwritten, resulting in incomplete information from the kernel.

This is because this buffer is a "round-robin buffer," meaning that if the kernel needs more space, it will delete log entries, starting at the beginning. It is important to understand that even though the log file can be overwritten starting at the beginning of the log file, the latest messages are stored at the end of the buffer. So, you will at least be able to read the most current messages.

Network Device Configuration Files

A network administrator can find himself spending a great deal of network troubleshooting time editing the configuration files for Ethernet NICs. You will need to know how to edit both the Debian-based configuration file and the configuration scripts found in Red Hat–based distributions.

The /etc/network/interfaces File

You should already know that you edit the the the /etc/network/interfaces to control settings for Ethernet NICs in Debian systems. Several GUI-based applications exist for editing these files, but the test focuses on editing the file manually.

The *interfaces* file is organized into stanzas. Each device (even the loopback device) receives its own stanza. A typical stanza is given below:

```
auto eth1
iface eth1 inet static
        address 10.0.0.5
        netmask 255.255.255.0
        gateway 10.0.0.1
```

The auto keyword tells the system to activate the NIC when the system boots. Usually, the system uses the /etc/init.d/networking script. The stanza shows that a system has been statically configured. If you wish to configure the system for DHCP, change static to dhcp. Once you make that change, the system will not consider the rest of the stanza and will look to the DHCP server to get its configuration information. Because this is the case, make sure that the DHCP server provides the correct subnet mask, DNS server, and default gateway information, because your system won't get that information locally.

The /etc/sysconfig/network-scripts Directory

Red Hat and many other distributions use the files in the /etc/sysconfig/network-scripts directory to configure Ethernet NICs. Each network device, even the loopback device, receives its own file. Settings for the *eth0* device are found in the *ifcfg-eth0* file, settings for the *eth1* device are found in the *ifcfg-eth1* file, and so forth.

A relatively simple entry for the second NIC in a system follows:

```
DEVICE=eth1
ONBOOT=yes
```

```
BOOTPROTO=static
IPADDR=10.0.0.4
NETMASK=255.255.255.0
GATEWAY=10.0.0.1
```

In this sample, the ONBOOT=yes entry has the system activate at boot time using the *etc/init.d/network* script. If you have a removable card, such as a USB wireless card, you would see the ONBOOT=no directive.

The BOOTPROTO directive can be either static, as shown before, or dhcp. As with Debian-based systems, if dhcp is specified, all other manual settings in this file are ignored for this NIC.

If you find that an NIC will not respond to the *ifup* or *ifconfig* commands, study the files discussed in this section carefully for problems.

PCMCIA Card Configuration

PCMCIA network cards are often configured using the *etc/pcmcia/network.opts* file, rather than any other configuration file. You can edit this file by hand or by using the *pcnetconfig* command. You will likely find that editing the file by hand is easier. Essential directives to troubleshoot in this file include those in Table 41-3. Additional settings also exist; review the file to learn more.

Table 41-3. Important PCMCIA configuration directives

Directive	Purpose
IPADDR	Sets the IP address for the NIC
NETMASK	Determines the subnet mask
NETWORK	Configures the NIC's network address
GATEWAY	Provides the default gateway
DOMAIN	Sets the DNS domain for the NIC
DHCP	Informs the NIC whether it should look for a DHCP server
PPOE	Establishes PPOE support for NICs that will be on DHCP lines

The /etc/networks File

Study the *etc/networks* file. Make sure it does not list the wrong network; if it does, simply edit the file by hand and insert the correct network. If your system belonged to the 192.168.2.0 network, the entry would be:

```
localnet 192.168.2.0
```

The /etc/nsswitch File

Make sure that the *etc/nsswitch* file is configured correctly for your situation. The system you are using may think that it should no longer look for a DNS server for name resolution or should look for an NIS server instead of its own password database to authenticate users.

Additional Configuration Files

Sometimes, systems will seem to hang for an unacceptably long period of time during a DNS lookup. It might appear that this problem is somehow related to your DNS server or to some other name resolution issue, such as resolution order.

If you are relatively sure that your DNS server is working well, that */etc/nsswitch. conf* file is configured correctly, and that your system is trying to resolve with the correct server via */etc/resolv.conf*, consider reviewing the */etc/host.conf* and */etc/ modprobe.d/aliases* files. They are discussed next.

/etc/host.conf

This file specifies your system's resolution order. If it is configured to look only for the */etc/host.conf* file and not for BIND, make sure that a line exists that reads:

```
order hosts, bind
```

You can reverse the order if you wish.

/etc/modprobe.d/aliases

This file contains instructions that affect which type of IP you are using. Most systems still use IPv4, but IPv6 is becoming more common all the time. Some Linux systems default to using IPv6 first. If your system is configured to look for an IPv6 address first, then an IPv4 address, network connections can become quite slow.

To solve the problem, edit the */etc/modprobe.d/aliases* file as *root* and uncomment or add the following lines:

```
alias net-pf-10 off
alias ipv6 off
```

These lines make sure that IPv6 lookups are turned off. You may find, after doing this, that resolution and other network activities work much faster. The reverse may be true, of course; you may find that your system is not using the IPv6 addresses you have configured. If that is the case, comment the two entries.

Regardless of the changes you make to the */etc/modprobe.d/aliases* file, you will need to run the *update-modules* command as *root* to make sure that your system recognizes your changes.

The /etc/hostname file

The */etc/hostname* file simply contains the system's hostname, as you might expect. The */bin/hostname* command reads the contents of the */etc/hostname* file at boot time.

In some systems, the name of the hostname file is */etc/HOST-NAME*.

If the name in this file conflicts with other system settings, your system may experience serious problems. This is particularly the case in older systems (e.g., circa 1999).Some applications and daemons are very rigid about reading the information in the */etc/hostname* file. Some daemons may become confused, because DNS tells them one name as the IP address, and the */etc/hostname* file tells them another. To solve the problem, simply edit the file using a text editor as *root* and provide the correct name.

Application Issues

Applications also often have configuration files that can cause connectivity problems. First, consider the fact that web browsers, email clients, and many other clients often need to be configured to use a proxy server. A connectivity problem may be as simple as making sure that the client is properly configured to use a proxy server.

Clients must sometimes be configured to work efficiently on a network. Firefox, for example, is sometimes configured to look for IPv6 addresses first and then IPv4. To make Firefox use IPv4 first, type about:config into the address bar. You will see a large, long listing of configuration settings for Firefox.

Scroll down and find the following value:

```
network.dns.disableIPv6
```

Double-click on this value to change its value to true.

You can take additional steps to optimize Firefox, but they are beyond the scope of this exam. It is important to understand, however, that when troubleshooting, application settings should also be considered.

DNS Errors

DNS errors can often cause problems for seemingly unrelated services. This is because DNS is a foundational service; a problem with DNS will likely manifest itself in other services, often in seemingly strange and unpredictable ways.

For instance, a resolver (i.e., a DNS client) first conducts a reverse DNS lookup and then a forward lookup. If a conflict exists between a reverse and a forward lookup, the network connection may fail. SSH and Kerberos servers often rely on reverse DNS lookups as one of the ways to help verify that a system is exactly what it purports to be. Thus, an improper entry in the reverse DNS lookup zone can often cause an SSH connection to fail. The error returned by the SSH client may refer to an authentication problem, when the real problem is with DNS. The same problem has also been known to affect the performance of some TCP wrappers implementations.

Sometimes, a slow DNS server can cause similar authentication problems with SSH, Kerberos, and other daemons. If this is the case, investigate why the DNS response is slow. You may find a problem with the DNS server itself. Or the network connection between your network and the DNS server may be experiencing a problem.

In the case of a seemingly random DNS client problem, use the *nslookup*, *dig*, or *host* command to discover the DNS server and then compare this information in the */etc/resolv.conf* file. If the lookup fails and you are sure that DNS is working properly, try using the search keyword in */etc/resolv.conf* and specify the domain your system is in. Even though you have specified the correct DNS server, your system may think that it belongs to a different domain. If you place the correct search entry into */etc/resolv.conf*, this might solve your connectivity issue.

 One of the simpler, but still common, frustrations is if an entry in the */etc/hosts* file conflicts with the DNS server. The DNS server will still report the name to IP address mapping from its zone file if you use the *nslookup*, *dig*, or *host* command. However, if you use any application ranging from *ping* to Firefox, it will probably read the */etc/hosts* file first. So don't just consider DNS server problems; your issue may be more local than you think.

Determining the Cause of Inaccessible Services

To confirm that a problem exists with a service, any number of commands can be used. *netstat* is very useful, but so are applications such as *nmap*, *lsof*, and *strace*. You can also inspect your system's configuration files to see whether unexpected changes have been made to your configuration.

Using netstat

While *netstat* is useful, it does not always reveal all information concerning a service. Review the following *netstat* output:

```
# netstat -a
Active Internet connections (servers and established)
Proto Recv-Q Send-Q Local Address      Foreign Address      State
tcp   0      0      0.0.0.0:6000        0.0.0.0:*            LISTEN
tcp   0      0      127.0.0.1:53        0.0.0.0:*            LISTEN
tcp   0      0      0.0.0.0:22          0.0.0.0:*            LISTEN
tcp   0      0      10.0.0.5:34386      80.232.36.131:22     ESTABLISHED
tcp   0      0      10.0.0.5:35191      80.232.36.131:993    ESTABLISHED
tcp   0      0      10.0.0.5:35190      80.232.36.131:993    ESTABLISHED
tcp   0      0      10.0.0.5:35189      80.232.36.131:993    ESTABLISHED
tcp   0      0      10.0.0.5:35188      80.232.36.131:993    ESTABLISHED
tcp   0      0      10.0.0.5:34387      10.0.0.1:22          ESTABLISHED
tcp   0      0      10.0.0.5:35193      10.0.0.4:993         ESTABLISHED
tcp   0      0      10.0.0.5:35196      10.0.0.4:993         ESTABLISHED
tcp   0      0      10.0.0.5:35187      10.0.0.4:993         ESTABLISHED
udp   0      0      0.0.0.0:32779       0.0.0.0:*
udp   0      0      127.0.0.1:53        0.0.0.0:*
```

The first connection shown indicates that this host presumably has an X server running, because X uses port 6000. The second connection shows that a DNS server is presumably listening on port 53, ready for a zone transfer. The next lines show port 22 open, so there is likely an SSH server open, as well.

Notice that we are not authoritatively saying that X, DNS, and SSH are listening on these ports. This is because *netstat* does not actually analyze the connections. Without additional arguments, *netstat* simply listens for an open port. It can also map that port to a name in the */etc/services* file, but the preceding output didn't give the names.

nmap

The *nmap* command is no better in this case. While it can provide you with a useful listing of open ports, it will not give you details about the actual service that opened that port. *nmap* can also determine the type of operating system being scanned, but it cannot inform you what actual service opened the port.

Finding Authoritative Information with lsof and strace

While you can specify extra options to *netstat* to gain additional information, using *lsof* will provide you with extensive information about the actual service listening on the port. This command actually names names, as it were, providing you with detailed information about the daemon and user that opened the port. You will also receive information such as the daemon's PID, as well as connection details and the system call information that you normally would not see.

Another invaluable command for troubleshooting network problems is the *strace* command. By running an application or daemon under *strace*, you can read exactly what the application was doing at the time of failure. From this output, you can then begin to identify the problem and formulate a solution.

Unexpected Changes to Files and Settings

Review the */etc/hosts.allow* and */etc/hosts.deny* files and make sure that they are unchanged. It is possible that a service or another administrator updated these files. One way to verify whether a system is configured to use TCP wrappers is to review the */etc/inetd.conf* file or the */etc/xinet.d* directory. Look for references to *tcpd*. If you see a reference, this daemon is protected.

You can usually tell the difference between a daemon that is simply not responding and one that is protected by TCP wrappers. If a daemon is protected by TCP wrappers, the connection will hang for a brief period of time, then fail. This short period of time reflects the amount of time it takes for *tcpd* to analyze its settings and respond to the connection. If the connection is immediately refused, the daemon is simply not responding.

Also, review the *iptables* or *ipchains* settings. Make sure that a rule has not been added by an application such as Portsentry or by another administrator. Use the *iptables -L* command, for example, to discover settings.

 Remember that *iptables* and *ipchains* settings apply to all network connections, not just those protected by TCP wrappers.

Failure to consult such files and features may cause you to take much more time solving a problem. The writers of the LPI Exams know that less experienced administrators fall into this trap.

Conclusion

In this chapter, you have learned about essential troubleshooting steps and applications. You are likely already familiar with the applications discussed. However, this chapter is more than just a review of these applications and daemons. It is meant to help you approach these applications with the goal of trying to solve problems.

Before you take the LPI Exams, take the time to consider the steps that you would take to resolve a problem. You likely will find yourself thinking less about command options and configuration files and more about how to diagnose problems, make educated guesses, and formulate solutions. While you will need to use many applications, including some discussed in this chapter, you will likely find that the key to understanding troubleshooting relies on knowing when and how to use these applications. You will also find that the LPI Exam takes this approach.

42

Exam 202 Review Questions and Exercises

This chapter is designed to help you learn more about the concepts, best practices, and commands tested in the LPI 202 Exam. Even advanced Linux users will find these activities useful, because they are all based on the LPI's Objectives. The things you read about in this chapter might help remind you about how to do tasks that you may not have had to do in a while.

It is best if you use a "live," nonproduction Linux system to conduct these exercises. This way, you can apply your knowledge, but still not worry too much if your experiments cause the system to become unstable or to no longer be as secure as before.

Networking Configuration (Topic 2.205)

Review Questions

1. You have learned that a system does not currently specify the correct default gateway. The correct default gateway address is 192.168.2.1. What commands would you issue to delete the existing gateway address and add a new one?

2. What command would you issue to assign a second IP address of 192.168.2. 55 and a netmask of 255.255.255.0 to your *eth1* card?

3. The *arpwatch* daemon has discovered several "flip-flops," implying that ARP poisoning has occurred on your network. Where can you read the alerts sent by the daemon?

4. A remote office has had to swap out a failed NIC in its Linux router. This router must work with an ISP's cable modem to allow the remote office to access the Internet. However, the ISP's cable modem recognizes only the MAC address of the failed card. What command can help you solve this problem?

5. You have tried to use *tcpdump* to capture packets and analyze them. However, *tcpdump* captures only the first few parts of the packet by default, and you want to capture and display the entire packet. You also want to save the capture into a file named *cap1.cap*. What command allows you to do this?

6. You have just used the *netstat* command, and have read the following entry:

```
tcp     0    6 64-128-206-189.ge:53208 mail1.oreilly.com:imap2 ESTABLISHED
```

What system has opened port 143?

Answers

1. Run two commands:

   ```
   # route del default gw
   # route add default gw 192.168.2.1
   ```

2. Run:

   ```
   # ifconfig eth1:1 192.168.2.55 netmask 255.255.255.0
   ```

3. *arpwatch* alerts are usually mailed to the *root* user. Use the *mail* command to read the messages.

4. Use the *ifconfig* command to specify the same MAC address as the failed NIC:

   ```
   # ifdown eth0
   # ifconfig eth0 hw ether 00:02:03:06:07:08
   # ifup eth0
   ```

5. Use the following *tcpdump* command:

   ```
   # tcpdump -vvv -s 1518 -i eth0 -w cap1.cap
   ```

6. The system named *mail1.oreilly.com* has opened port 143, because this port is the IMAP port.

Exercise

1. As *root*, experiment with the *tcpdump* command. Many examples exist in the manpage for *tcpdump*. Specifically for the LPI 202 Exam, experiment with the following command:

   ```
   # tcpdump host host1 and \( host2 or host3 \)
   ```

   The *tcpdump* command captures all packets sent between the host named *host1* and either the host named *host2* or the host named *host3*. Now, try the following command:

   ```
   # tcpdump -i eth1 not arp and not '(port ssh)' and not '(port http)'
   ```

   This command excludes ARP packets, as well as those associated with SSH and standard web traffic. You can add more ports by adding more and not phrases. Notice also that the previous command specifies an interface, in this case the second one on the system. If you are using a standard hub-based network, you will be able to sniff the packets going to and from remote systems. However, if you are on a switch-based network, *tcpdump* will capture only packets going to and from your local system.

2. Experiment with the *ifconfig* command. Use it to add a second IP address. Then ping the new address from both your local system and a remote system. Change your system's MAC address. You can also stop and start interfaces and change the system's IP address. Finally, use *ifconfig* to change your network interface's IP address. Reboot your system and see whether the change you made remains. Then, review the */etc/network/interfaces* file (for Debian-based systems) or the */etc/sysconfig/network-scripts* file (for Red Hat/ Fedora-based systems).

3. The *arp* command allows you to view and manipulate the ARP cache. View the cache by running the *arp* command without arguments, then use it to add and delete entries. Notice that if you delete an entry, then reconnect to the system, you will see that the deleted system has been added back.

4. The *netcat* command (also *nc*) has become a standard tool. It is ideal for testing to see whether local or remote ports are open. You can also use it as a primitive port scanner and even as a quick and dirty way to transfer files between systems. Use *netcat* to monitor your systems only.

5. The *arpwatch* command monitors MAC address and IP address pairings on a network. These pairings should not change often. Install and run *arpwatch* if it is not already working. Use an application such as *ettercap*, or use *ifconfig* to change a system's MAC address, then see how *arpwatch* sends the *root* account on the local system notifications that a pairing has changed. Sudden changes can be evidence that an attacker is trying to spoof connections or engage in packet sniffing on a switch-based network.

6. The *ping* command is quite standard. However, familiarize yourself with various options, including *ping -c*, *ping -a*, and *ping -f*. The *-f* option will work only when run as *root*. If you want, use *tcpdump* to collect the flood of packets sent when you use the *-f* option. Experiment also with specifying packet sizes and different time to live (TTL) settings.

7. Use *wvdialconf* and *wvdial* to configure PPP-based dial-up access for your system. Also, familiarize yourself with the chat program and the contents of a standard chat file. Examples of this file exist in this book, as well as on the Internet. Make sure that you understand the purpose of the *chap-secrets* and *pap-secrets* files.

8. Once you have configured PPP access, configure VPN access using the *pptp* command. Make sure that you clearly understand the ports used in *pptp* and how to troubleshoot connections by reviewing files such as */var/log/messages* using *tail* with the *-f* option.

9. Linux systems are extremely flexible. For example, it is possible to add a second NIC to your Linux system and use it as a router. Once you have two NICs installed and recognized, configure each with IP addresses. Then enable IP forwarding. You can do this either by changing the value of */proc/sys/net/ ipv4/ip_forward* to 1 or by editing the */etc/sysctl.conf* file. As *root*, simply add the following line:

```
net/ipv4/ip_forward=1
```

Then run the following command:

```
# sysctl -p /etc/sysctl.conf
```

Once you have done this, your system will forward packets between the two NICs. You can return your system to normal by changing the 1 value to 0 in the */proc/sys/net/ipv4/ip_forward* file.

10. The *netstat* command is deceptively simple. Familiarize yourself with all of the fields in *netstat* output. Also, become familiar with the many options to *netstat*, including *-na*, *-nr*, and *-M*.

Mail and News (Topic 2.206)

Review Questions

1. You wish to map mail from one local user account to another local user account. What file would you edit?

2. You wish to map mail from remote hosts to your hosts to different accounts on the system. What file would you use?

3. You wish to rewrite outgoing emails from the system *mail.company1.com* so that they appear to come from the *mail.company2.com* domain. What file would you use to create the proper mappings?

4. What command is used to add or remove groups in *innd*?

5. You have just installed Majordomo 2 on a system named *listserv.company. com*. The password is listserv1. What command would you issue to create a list named *operations*?

6. You are reading the following Procmail recipe:

   ```
   * ^From: .*@sales.com
   /dev/null
   ```

   What is the result of the recipe?

Answers

1. Use the */etc/aliases* file.

2. Use the *virtusertable* file.

3. Use the *genericstable* file.

4. Use the *ctlinnd* command.

5. Enter:

   ```
   # create operations listserv1
   ```

6. All email messages from *sales.com* will be redirected to the */dev/null* file and thus be deleted.

Exercises

1. Install and configure a simple Sendmail server. Configure the proper aliases according to RFC 821. Use the proper files, *m4* macros, and commands to configure the system of your choice. Do not forget to configure the MX records for the domain so that emails sent to your domain will be properly mapped to your Sendmail server. Test your configuration and settings using the commands discussed in this book and at *http://ww.sendmail.org*.

2. Once you have configured Sendmail to work in a basic manner, experiment with the server. For example, use the *genericstable* file so that emails sent from the system appear to be sent from another related domain. Do not engage in illicit activity. Simply experiment with how to rewrite headers.

3. After working on your Sendmail configuration, secure it. Shut down and remove all unnecessary services, such as web and database servers. Use the *iptables* or (if you have an older system) *ipchains* command to block unnecessary connections. If you are using SSH or VNC, lock down these services so that they use the best encryption available and accept connections only from trusted hosts.

4. Install and configure Procmail. Use recipes to forward email to another user. Then create a recipe that automatically responds and informs people that the user is on vacation.

5. Install and configure Majordomo 2. Prepare Sendmail or your alternative MTA to work well with Majordomo 2. Then, create new lists. Subscribe and unsubscribe from these lists. Customize these lists by enabling and disabling moderation, as well as enabling and disabling message digesting.

6. Experiment with the different ways to configure Majordomo 2. You can configure it either by editing the *readers.conf* file or by sending control email messages.

7. Install INN. Configure it to serve up at least two newsgroups. You will likely find that the server is configured by default to reject posts from remote hosts. Configure the system to accept remote posts. You will likely need to do this using both the *ctlinnd* command and by configuring the *readers.conf* file.

8. Once you have configured INN to accept posts from remote users, enable password protection using the *htpasswd* command. You will likely have to edit the *readers.conf* file to recognize your use of the database. Your entry will likely appear as follows:

```
auth "useraccounts" {
    auth: "ckpasswd -f /etc/news/nntp_passwd"
}
```

Now experiment with user authentication on the server, and monitor when users make posts.

9. Once you have configured user authentication, experiment with upstream and downstream feeds. Even if you do not have access to these streams, configure INN as if you did.

DNS (Topic 2.207)

Review Questions

1. You wish to use the *dig* command to query the server named *dns1.company. com* to see whether the PTR record for the system named *adam* exists. What would this command look like?

2. Consider the following text:

```
zone "." {
    type hint;
    file "/etc/bind/db.root";
};
```

What is the purpose of this entry, and what file does this entry belong in?

3. You have been given a new host to enter into the forward DNS zone. This hostname is for the Web server. The host's IP address is 192.168.2.5, and the host's name is *www.company.com*. Write in the entry you would create in the DNS server's forward zone file for this server.

4. You wish to establish a chroot jail for your DNS server. You are using BIND. Why is it necessary to copy or move directories such as the */etc/bind* directory to another, special location on the hard drive?

5. Your system ships with the BIND 8 *dnskeygen* command, rather than the BIND 9 *dnssec-keygen* command. Both have the same function. Using *dnskeygen* or its equivalent, what command would you issue to create a public-key pair with the size of 1024 bits that can be used only for authentication for the *mycompany.com* domain?

6. You are in an interactive *nslookup* session. What command would you issue to switch from the default nameserver to *dns2.company.com*?

Answers

1. Enter:

   ```
   # dig @dns1.company.com PTR adam
   ```

2. The text primes the DNS server to look for root servers. This entry belongs in the *named.conf* file.

3. Create the following entry in the DNS server's forward zone file:

   ```
   IN        A        www              192.168.2.5
   ```

4. The purpose is to provide BIND with an isolated environment. If a buffer overflow or other problem occurs, any exploit or other problem will remain local to that environment and will not be able to spread easily to the rest of the system.

5. The command is:

   ```
   # dnskeygen -H 1024 -c -h  key.mycompany.com.
   ```

6. The command is:

   ```
   > server dns2.company.com
   ```

Exercises

1. Install BIND on your system. Take some time to verify where the configuration files are. In many newer systems, the files will be located in the */etc/bind* directory. In other systems, the files will be located in both the */etc* directory and in the */var/named* subdirectories. Once you have confirmed the location of these files, verify the location of the startup script. In some systems, it will be in the */etc/rc.d/init.d* directory. In other systems, it will be in the */etc/bind*

directory. Sometimes, the startup file is called *named*. In other cases, it is called *bind9*. The names and locations of files may vary. This series of exercises will assume that all configuration files reside off of the */etc/bind* directory.

2. Using sample zone files that reside on the local system or on the Internet, review the syntax of valid DNS entries. Also review the syntax for the *named. conf* file, the top-level nameserver file, and the forward and reverse loopback zone files.

3. Configure BIND to act as a DNS server for your network. First, configure the */etc/bind/named.conf* file so that it contains references for the root servers, and so that this server knows that it is authoritative for the zone you are going to create. You will also need to add forward and reverse loopback zones, as well as references for the forward and reverse zones you are going to create. Remember the names and locations of the forward and reverse zone files. You will be creating these files in the next step.

4. As you configure *named.conf*, make sure that you are referencing all files properly and that these files exist, even if they are currently empty. Use the *touch* command to create the files, or download sample files from the Internet. The files for the forward and reverse loopback zones should already exist on your system. If your system has not already provided them, obtain hint files from *http://www.bind.org*.

5. Using a text editor, create both forward and reverse lookup zone files in the */etc/bind* directory. Make sure that these files have the same names as those indicated in the */etc/bind/named.conf* file. Populate the forward and reverse zone files with valid entries. The entries you create will include valid TTL and SOA information, valid nameserver information, and A records. Make sure as you start BIND that you review the */var/log/messages* file. Using the *tail -f* command is a good idea, as it will help you read any error messages BIND gives. You may also have to verify that the BIND service is running. One way to do this is to use the *ps aux* command and pipe the output through *grep*:

```
ps aux | grep bind
```

6. You will likely have to make several changes to the forward and reverse zone files before BIND properly initializes and begins resolving names. You will have to restart your server whenever you make a change to your zone or configuration files.

7. Once you have started BIND, configure the */etc/resolv.conf* file for your DNS server and also for your clients so that they are using your DNS server. Use the *ping* command to verify that you can access hosts by both IP address and by DNS hostname.

8. Use *nslookup* in interactive mode, as well as a one-time command, to verify that your server is properly resolving names. In some systems, *nslookup* is deprecated. You can use the *-sil* option to eliminate the warning messages. While using *nslookup*, change between DNS servers, view A and PTR records, review the SOA record for the zone, and see if you can conduct a zone transfer.

9. The *dig* command is quite sophisticated. Use the *dig* command to query your forward and reverse zone records, as well as review the SOA fields. You can also use BIND to query other DNS servers and conduct zone transfers if the DNS server allows such activity (increasingly unlikely). Make sure that you know the options that allow you to conduct multiple inquiries.

10. The *host* command is quite handy for conducting quick DNS searches. Make sure that you know the options that allow you to conduct zone transfers and specify the types of records you wish to view (e.g., SOA, CNAME, and AXFR).

11. You already have a working server. However, you can add more names. Add CNAME and MX records to your zones. When you make changes, make sure that you increment the serial number so that changes are recognized by secondary (i.e., slave) DNS servers.

12. Configure a secondary (slave) DNS server. Conduct zone transfers to verify that your configuration has worked.

13. Once you are confident that your master/primary and secondary/slave DNS servers are working properly, secure them. Use the *dnskeygen* command (or its equivalent) to create public keys for your zones. Then take the necessary steps to require authentication and encryption for all zone transfers. Then configure *named.conf* to restrict zone transfers to certain servers. Even though such settings can be rather easily fooled by attackers who know how to spoof IP addresses, you may as well lock down as many settings as possible. Also consider stopping all other daemons and dedicating this system to just providing name resolution. Even if you are simply experimenting, consider the daemons that you would shut down if you were to configure this system as a dedicated DNS server.

Web Services (Topic 2.208)

Review Questions

1. No startup script exists to start, stop, or restart your apache server. What is the most nearly universal command that you can use to start the Apache server?

2. You wish to enable *.htaccess* files on your web server to enable user-based access. Where should these files be located?

3. You have noticed that an *.htaccess* file you have created is not being recognized. You have copied it from another server, so you know it is formatted correctly What can you do to solve this problem?

4. You need to run *htpasswd* for the first time and create a database named */etc/apache2/users*. What command should you issue to create the database?

5. You wish to start the Apache server with SSL support. What command would you issue? Also, what files might need to be edited to enable SSL support?

6. You wish to create a virtual host in an older version of Apache. What file should you edit to enable virtual hosts?

7. You wish to forbid all web-based access to URLs that contain the words
   Paris and Hilton. You have created the following ACL entry in Squid:

   ```
   acl Paris1 url_regex Paris
           acl Hilton1 url_regex Hilton
           http_access deny Paris1
       http_access deny Hilton1
       http_access allow all
   ```

   However, you still notice that many users have been able to access URLs such
   as *http://naughtysite.us/paris*. Why is this the case?

Answers

1. Use the *apachectl* command:

   ```
   # apachectl start
   ```

2. It should be a hidden file in the resource you wish to restrict.

3. Edit *httpd.conf* or *apache2.conf* and enable support for *.htaccess* files. Look
   for a directive similar to the following and make sure that the directive is not
   commented out:

   ```
   AccessFileName .htaccess

   <Files ~ "^\.ht">
       Order allow,deny
       Deny from all
   </Files>
   ```

4. Issue the following command as *root*:

   ```
   # htpasswd -c /etc/apache2/users
   ```

5. Issue the following command:

   ```
   # apachectl startssl
   ```

   You may also need to edit the *http.conf* file or the *ssl.conf* and *ssl.load* files.

6. The *http.conf* file. Apache 2.0 is configured using the *apache2.conf* file.

7. Squid ACLs are case-sensitive, as is common with many Unix-based applications and daemons. The ACL given forbids only Paris and Hilton, not paris
   and hilton.

Exercises

1. Install the Apache server using any method you prefer (e.g., RPM for Red
   Hat/Fedora systems, *apt* or Synaptic for Debian-based systems). After you
   install Apache, review the location and contents of the Apache configuration
   files. Look for *httpd.conf* or the equivalent, as well as associated configuration files. Review the location of all log files, as well. If you wish, write down
   the location of the configuration and log files on a separate piece of paper.

2. Configure the Apache server so that it will serve up a basic page. You may
   have to enable certain directives, such as the user and group Apache uses. It
   is also sometimes necessary to specify the server root (e.g., where the server's
   configuration files exist) and the directory that contains all of the sites. In

some versions of Apache, all of this information is included in the *httpd.conf* file. In newer versions (Apache 2), look for the *sites-available* directory. Once you have confirmed that you have configured all the basic directives, start Apache and use either a web browser or *netcat* (*nc*) to verify connectivity. You can use a startup script or the *apachectl* or *apache2ctl* application, depending upon the version of Apache you are using.

3. Find the location of the directives that allow the use of *.htaccess* files in Apache. Make sure that the directives are not commented out. If you have to uncomment any of these directives, restart Apache Server to ensure that it recognizes the use of *.htacess* files. Now, create an *.htaccess* file that requires user-based authentication. Use the *htpasswd* or *htpasswd2* commands to create a new user database. Configure Apache to recognize this database. Test your work.

4. Now, configure Apache to use SSL. If necessary, create SSL certificates using the *openssl* command or the *CA.pl* application, which is usually available in the */usr/lib/ssl/misc* directory. The *CA.pl* application requires that Perl be installed. Once you have created the certificate, configure Apache to recognize it. Then configure a directory to require SSL-based access. Using any web browser that supports SSL, access the resource.

5. Enable PHP and Perl support. Do this by editing the *httpd.conf* file or its equivalent and uncommenting the appropriate directives. You will have to restart Apache after doing so. Download some sample scripts from the Internet. For example, O'Reilly has a web site called ONLamp.com (*http:// www.onlamp.com*) where you can obtain scripts that you can run. Make sure to put them into the *cgi-bin* directory and make them executable by the correct user.

6. Web servers often have to throttle connections and bandwidth. Apache makes this quite simple. Open the *httpd.conf* or its equivalent and look for the following settings:

StartServers
> The number of servers to start by default. The default setting is often 2; set it to a reasonable number for your system.

MaxClients
> The maximum number of clients that will be served at one time. The default is often set to 150. Set it to the number that your system can reasonably support.

MaxRequestsPerChild
> Limits the number of requests a child process can respond to. Usually set to 25. Set it to a reasonable number. The higher the number, the slower a particular process will be to serve clients if the system becomes overtaxed.

MinSpareThreads
> Determines the lowest number of threads that the server is allowed to have at one time. Limits the number of servers that can be started.

7. Review the log files that the Apache server generates. These include the access log, the referrer log, and the error logs. These are usually located off of the */var/log* directory.

8. Apache is not only a standard web server. It also sports a proxy server that is capable of caching requests, thereby speeding up access. Configure the Apache server proxy feature and then configure a web browser to use the proxy server. Review the Apache Server log files and list the files, proxy cache directory to verify that the proxy server is working.

9. Now install Squid. You can obtain Squid using your system's package manager or at *http://www.squid-cache.org*. Once you have installed Squid, familiarize yourself with the configuration files, including *squid.conf*. Review the settings in *squid.conf*, then start the service. Review the Squid log files and */var/log* messages to make sure Squid is running properly. Configure a web browser as a Squid client and access the Internet. You can also review the Squid cache directory to ensure that Squid is working.

10. Once Squid is working, enable filtering. Create an ACL that limits usage by URL to a particular text string. Also, enable user authentication. Review the access logs and other log files that Squid generates to verify that your proxy server is running as expected.

Network Client Management (Topic 2.210)

Review Questions

1. Consider the following entry in a configuration file:

```
host voip
  {
    hardware ethernet 00:13:10:22:57:f5;
    fixed-address 192.168.2.104;
  }
```

This code belongs in a configuration file of a particular service. Name the service, and explain the practical result of this file.

2. You wish to learn about the active leases on a DHCP server. What file will give you this information?

3. You have configured a portion of the *nsswitch.conf* to read as follows:

```
passwd:     nisplus files
shadow:     nisplus files
group:      nisplus files
```

What will happen during the login process once these changes take effect?

4. Consider the following entry in the */etc/nisswitch.conf* file:

```
hosts:      files nisplus dns
```

Which resource is consulted last when a host makes a name query?

5. What file can you check to verify whether NIS clients are allowed to use your NIS server?

6. When editing the *slapd.conf* file, what must you remember about lines that begin with white space at the beginning of a line?

7. You have just made a change to the */etc/pam.d/login* file. What do you need to do in order for PAM to recognize the change?

Answers

1. This file belongs to the DHCP service (*dhcpd*). The host named *voip* will always receive the address of 192.168.2.104 via the DHCP server when it boots.

2. The *dhcpd.leases* file, which is often located in the */var/lib/dhcp* directory, gives you the information you need about leases on the system.

3. Users who log in will be authenticated using NIS, rather than local files (e.g., */etc/passwd* and */etc/shadow*).

4. DNS is last.

5. The *securenets* file.

6. OpenLDAP considers the blank space the continuation of the previous line. If you do not know this, you may experience considerable configuration problems.

7. No additional step is needed. PAM will recognize the changes immediately.

Exercises

1. Configure a DHCP server. As you configure the server, create a valid range of IP addresses. Also create a reserved address so that a client always receives the same IP address. Experiment with DHCP reservations to see how they work.

2. Now install the DHCP daemon and configure your system to be a DHCP client. You will have to find the configuration files for your system. In Red Hat and Fedora systems, go to the */etc/sysconfig/network-scripts* directory and configure the appropriate file. For Debian-based systems, configure the */etc/network/interfaces* file to make the necessary changes. If your system is already a DHCP client, configure it to use a static address. Configure it to use a plausible IP address and subnet mask. Supply a default gateway, if applicable. As you work, review the */var/log/messages* file, as well as the *dhcpd.leases* file, to verify that your DHCP server is working

3. A DHCP server relay agent is necessary to forward DHCP requests and replies across subnets. DHCP requests are broadcast based and thus must be forwarded across a router. If you have configured a Linux router, install the DHCP relay agent. Then configure the appropriate settings in the *dhcrelay* file. Once you have done this, you can then use the *dhcrelay* application to start the agent.

4. Install the NIS package for your system. Once you have installed the server, familiarize yourself with the configuration files and associated applications. Pay special attention to the *ypserv.conf* file, because you will use it to configure essential settings. Also, remember that the *portmapper* daemon must also be running for NIS to work.

5. NIS allows many configuration options related to authentication. Configure PAM (e.g., the *etc/pam.conf* file or the appropriate files in the *etc/pam.d* directory) so that the *etc/passwd* and *etc/shadow* files are used.

6. Install the *slapd* LDAP server. Once you familiarize yourself with *slapd*, create a simple directory hierarchy. Verify that *slapd* is working correctly.

7. Once you have your LDAP server running, add a group and a host to it. Configure the host as an LDAP client. You can also add a user and experiment with adding a group.

8. Change the password of a user in LDAP, and verify that the information has been updated to the client. To reduce the possibility of confusion, verify that the LDAP client is properly configured before you change the password. This way, you will be able to more easily tell what has gone wrong in your configuration.

9. Remember that Linux systems can work well with other operating systems and features. After adding users and groups, experiment further with your LDAP server by importing items from an LDIF file, if one is available.

10. By default, all users must enter a password when using the *su* command to become root. If you wish, you can change this default behavior so that any user in the *wheel* group can use *su* without having to supply a password. To do this, edit the *etc/pam.d/su* file as *root*. Search for the following entry and uncomment it:

        auth   sufficient   /lib/security/pam_wheel.so trust use_uid

11. Now edit the *etc/group* file so that a standard user account is a member of the *wheel* group. Become that user, then issue the *su* command. You will become *root* without first issuing a password.

System Security (Topic 2.212)

Review Questions

1. Which file is considered first by TCP wrappers, *hosts.allow* or *hosts.deny*?

2. Why is it a good idea to store the Tripwire database on a read-only medium, such as a CD-ROM disk?

3. You have configured an internal network to use the 192.168.2.0/24 block of IP addresses. You have also configured a Linux system with two NICs and have enabled IP address forwarding. However, no users can access the Internet. You have decided not to use a proxy server. What else can you do to allow Internet access through your Linux router?

4. Consider the following line in the *etc/ssh/ssh_config* file. What does it instruct *sshd* to do?

        Protocol 2

5. You have been asked to use the *iptables* command to configure a system to automatically drop all connections from systems that attempt to access TCP ports 21 through 80 on your local system. Your supervisor wants this rule to be the first rule processed. Write in the command that will accomplish this.

6. Why do many FTP servers contain their own copies of files such as *ls*, *passwd*, and *chmod*?

7. You wish to use public-key authentication for an SSH session with a remote user. What must you first place into your *~/.ssh/authorized_keys* or *~/.ssh/authorized_keys2* file?

Answers

1. The *hosts.allow* file is considered first. Then TCP wrappers reads the contents of the *hosts.deny* file.

2. Because storing the database on a read-only medium helps make you reasonably sure that the database has not been changed.

3. Use *iptables* to enable Network Address Translation (NAT) using the MASQUERADE target.

4. It instructs *sshd* to always use Version 2 of the SSH protocol, and never to use Version 1.

5. The command is:

    ```
    # iptables -I INPUT -p tcp --dport 20:80 -j REJECT
    ```

6. Many FTP servers contain their own copies because many administrators choose to place FTP server daemon files inside of a chroot jail for added security.

7. The public key generated by the remote user.

Exercises

1. The SSH daemon is likely installed by default. If it is not, install it using your package manager or from the source files located at *http://www.openssh.org*. Familiarize yourself with the configuration files. Start *sshd*, then conduct a simple session. When you have done this, configure *sshd* to accept only clients that can use SSH Version 2, as it is by far the more secure protocol. Configure it also to forbid non-*root* logins, which is a way to keep the system secure during maintenance

2. Use SSH's port forwarding capabilities to protect an unencrypted protocol such as FTP, standard HTTP, or standard email traffic. To do this, you will need two systems that support SSH.

3. Use *tcpdump* or Ethereal to sniff SSH default transactions. Note that, by default, all transactions are encrypted. However, by default, you must still provide your username and password. Even though authentication information is strongly encrypted by SSH in most cases, it is not a good idea to allow authentication information to exist on a network connection. Use the *ssh-keygen* command to generate a key pair for your user account. Configure the necessary identification files in your *~/.ssh* directory, and exchange public keys with a remote user. Then experiment with conducting key-based authentication, as opposed to password-based authentication

4. Use the *iptables* command (or the *ipchains* command in older systems) to create and list rules. Consider enabling the following settings:

    • Block all traffic destined for local port 23 (Telnet).

    • Block all traffic destined for a remote system that you deem objectionable.

    • Log all traffic to port 80 to the */var/log/messages* file.

5. Now that you understand *iptables*, find a system with two NICs and enable both IP forwarding and masquerading. (*iptables* uses the term *masquerading* rather than Network Address Translation or NAT). To do this, simply use the nat table and enable masquerading for your public interface.

6. The networking system in Linux systems is capable of thwarting various types of attacks. You have already seen how you can use the */proc/sys/net/ipv4/icmp_echo_ignore_all* file or the */etc/sysctl.conf* file to protect a system against ICMP packets. You can also protect your system against SYN floods by changing the value of 0 to 1 in the */proc/sys/net/ipv4/tcp_syncookies* file. You can also configure the */etc/sysctl.conf* file to do this automatically. Experiment with these changes.

7. Install and configure an FTP daemon. Once it is working well, experiment with the *ftpaccess* file. Limit bandwidth and the number of connections. Also, experiment with creating settings for both anonymous users and those that supply actual usernames and passwords. Consider how using anonymous FTP is more secure than using standard FTP, which encrypts neither the initial authentication session nor the ensuing data transfer.

8. Download and install the Snort intrusion detection application, which is available via the Snort home page (*http://www.snort.org*) or via your operating system's package management application. Configure the *snort.conf* file to reflect your network. You are also given a choice of several preprocessors. Some of these preprocessors will help detect port scans. Others help detect suspicious network traffic.

9. Experiment with the preprocessors. Some will create *false positives*, in which legitimate traffic is mistaken for an attack. You will also find that actual attacks may be ignored, which in some cases can be seen as a *false negative*. Also, Snort ships with many signatures, which can help you identify and react to attacks. Your chances of receiving false positives increases with each signature you enable. It is up to you to determine the sensitivity level of your intrusion detection system.

10. Remember that Snort will not detect traffic on a switch-based network. You can configure your switch to go into monitor mode.

11. Download and install the open source version of Tripwire from the following URL: *http://sourceforge.net/projects/tripwire*. Once you have downloaded the package, install it, then configure Tripwire to protect only the most important sources. While it is best to install Tripwire on a brand-new system that has never been connected to a network, it is important to get practical experience configuring Tripwire and running reports before you take the LPI Exam.

12. Experiment with the */etc/hosts.allow* and */etc/hosts.deny* files. As *root*, edit the */etc/hosts.allow* file and enter the following:

```
ALL: .testsystem.yourdnsdomain.com EXCEPT testsystem.yourdnsdomain.com
```

Then edit the */etc/hosts.deny* file to contain the following entry:

```
ALL: ALL
```

The result of this use of */etc/hosts.allow* and */etc/hosts.deny* is that all systems from your network will be able to connect to daemons controlled by TCP wrappers, except for the host named *testsystem.yourdnsdomain.com*.

Remember that */etc/hosts.deny* is considered after */etc/hosts.allow*. So this configuration helps lock down all applications controlled by TCP wrappers. Some applications, such as Sendmail and Apache, may not use TCP wrappers. So don't let that confuse you.

Network Troubleshooting (Topic 2.214)

Review Questions

1. What is the purpose of the search keyword in the */etc/resolv.conf* file?

2. You know that your DNS server is accepting requests. However, several hosts are consistently trying to connect to the wrong email server. Clearly, these hosts are mapping the hostname to the wrong IP address. You have checked the */etc/resolv.conf* files on each of these hosts, and they list your DNS server and domain. What is the most likely cause of this problem?

3. What is the most likely location of the file that configures network interfaces in a Debian-based system?

4. What command will best help you learn what has occurred during the boot process?

5. You are currently logged in to a Linux system that has three interfaces. You wish to send a large number of *ping* packets in a short amount of time out of the third interface to a system named *jacob*. What command would you issue?

6. A DNS server is currently responding to requests very slowly. As a result, your query using the *host* command times out before the DNS server can respond. What option to the *host* command can you specify to make your system wait indefinitely for the DNS server to respond?

Answers

1. The search keyword has the resolver search the specified domain rather than the default domain. Sometimes this keyword is necessary because the host thinks that there is no default domain.

2. The */etc/hosts* file probably contains incorrect IP address information for the email server. The */etc/hosts* file overrides DNS and NIS lookups on most systems by default.

3. The file is */etc/network/interfaces*.

4. The *dmesg* command.

5. Enter:

   ```
   # ping -f -i eth2 jacob
   ```

6. Use the *-w* option.

Exercises

1. Review the format for either the */etc/network/interfaces* or the */etc/sysconfig/ network-scripts/ifcfg-eth0* file. If you are using a different network interface from *eth0*, substitute the correct number for *ifcfg-eth0*. Learn the meaning of each line.

2. Study the */etc/hosts* file. Read the manpage for it. Notice that this file can contain IPv4 and IPv6 instructions. Create an entry in your */etc/hosts* file that conflicts with your DNS server information. If your system uses a default configuration, the entry you just placed into the */etc/hosts* file will take precedence. Review the */etc/nsswitch.conf* file and confirm which resource gets precedence. Also review the */etc/host.conf* file and verify the resolution order.

3. Use the *cat* command to view the */etc/hostname* file. If this file is empty or has a different hostname from what you expected, edit the file as *root* and correct the information.

4. Issue the following command as a normal user:

   ```
   netstat -ni
   ```

   Notice that this command provides information about the interface, including the Maximum Transmission Unit (MTU), sending and receiving information, error information, and routing metrics. The output also gives several flags. These flags are listed in Table 42-1.

Table 42-1. Flags in netstat output

Flag	Meaning
B	Shows that the interface can send and receive broadcasts
R	Shows that the interface is recognized by the system
U	Shows that the interface is active
L	Indicates a loopback interface
M	Shows that the interface is capable of multicasting

5. Review your interface to determine its statistics.

6. Using the *ifconfig* command, experiment with the MTU for your system. The highest MTU for an Ethernet network is 1500. This is most often the MTU that you will see for your network adapters. Sometimes, however, you will need to change the MTU, due to network problems or nonstandard equipment.

7. For the sake of practice, change the MTU to 1300 using the following command as an example:

```
# ifconfig eth0 192.168.2.5 netmask 255.255.255.0 mtu 1300
```

8. You should, of course, substitute your own interface, IP address, and subnet mask. Notice that the *mtu* option allows you to specify any value you wish. Use the *ifconfig* command to verify that the MTU has changed. Return your system back to its standard MTU. While changing the MTU of a host is not very common, it is important to know all of the options of the *ifconfig* command.

43

Exam 202 Practice Test

As with the LPI 201 exam, the 202 exam is comprised of roughly 54 questions. You have 90 minutes to answer these questions correctly. This exam has the same format as the 201: Most of the exam questions are multiple choice, with one correct answer. The secondmost common item type is multiple choice, multiple answer. The remaining questions require you to fill in the blank. No notes are allowed, and you are monitored in a secure, high-stakes exam environment. For more information about the LPI 202 exam and all of LPI's exam policies, go to *http://www.lpi.org*.

This chapter gives you some questions designed to help you learn about the LPI 202 Objectives. These questions should help you prepare for the questions in the actual exam. Once you become familiar with these questions, work on a live system to truly learn the concepts and practices discussed here. While the questions are certainly useful, you will find that applying your knowledge is the best way to prepare for the LPI 202 exam.

Questions

1. What is the standard MTU for Ethernet interfaces?

    a. 1500

    b. 1300

    c. 500

    d. 300

2. Which of the following files would you edit to rewrite the headers of outgoing email messages so that the messages appear to originate from a completely different domain?

    a. *virtusertable*

    b. *genericstable*

c. *aliases*

d. *sendmail.cf*

3. What two programs can be destructive if run against a mounted volume?

    a. *badblocks* and *lsof*

    b. *fsck* and *lsof*

    c. *mkraid* and *badblocks*

    d. *fsck* and *badblocks*

4. You wish to mount a Samba share named *docs* on a system named *filesrv. company.com*. The username to access the share is *davis* and the password is *access1*. Which of the following commands will allow you to do this? (Choose two.)

    a. *smbmount //filesrv.company.com/docs /mnt/smb *

       -o username=davis,password=access1

    b. *smbclient -U davis%access1 //filesrv.company.com/docs*

    c. *smbclient //filesrv.company.com/docs -U davis%access1*

    d. *smbmount /mnt/smb //filesrv.company.com/docs *

       -o username=davis,password=access1

5. You have a directory named */mnt/nfs* on your system that you use for NFS mounts. Write in the command that mounts an NFS volume named */home/ james* located on a system named *bentley*.

6. You suspect that several routers on a particular WAN connection are too slow. Which of the following commands allows you to make *traceroute* wait 20 seconds for a response to a packet?

    a. *traceroute -w 20 router23.company.com*

    b. *traceroute -c 20 router23.company.com*

    c. *traceroute -i 20 router23.company.com*

    d. *traceroute -t 20 router23.company.com*

7. Your DNS server is named *dns.company.com*. Which of the following commands allows you to query another server named *dns.isp.com* for the A record information of the host *www.company.com*? (Choose two.)

    a. *dig -t A www.company.com @dns.isp.com*

    b. *host www.company.com dns.isp.com*

    c. *dig @dns.isp.com www.company.com*

    d. *host dns.isp.com www.company.com*

8. You wish to add a second IP address to your third Ethernet card. Which of the following commands does this?

    a. *ifconfig eth3:2 202.168.85.3 netmask 255.255.255.0*

    b. *ifconfig eth0:3 202.168.85.3 netmask 255.255.255.0*

    c. *ifconfig eth1 -a 2 202.168.85.3 netmask 255.255.255.0*

    d. *ifconfig eth2:1 202.168.85.3 netmask 255.255.255.0*

9. The *route* command hangs when used without any arguments. This system is on a Gigabit Ethernet network. Which of the following explanations are plausible? (Choose two.)

    a. The *route* command requires the -g argument when querying a Gigabit Ethernet network.

    b. Name resolution has failed on the network.

    c. A kernel panic has caused the NIC to be kicked off the network.

    d. The default gateway is no longer available.

10. Which of the following commands helps you begin the process of testing an SMTP server named *smtp.newcompany.com* to see whether it is an open relay?

    a. *telnet smtp.newcompany.com*

    b. *nc telnet smtp.newcompany.com*

    c. *telnet smtp.newcompany.com 25*

    d. *ssh smtp.newcompany.com 25*

11. You have been asked to run a manual integrity scan on a system using Tripwire. Which of the following commands would accomplish this?

    a. *tripwire --verify*

    b. *tripwire -s /dev/hda*

    c. *tripwire --check*

    d. *scan -now /dev/hda*

12. Which of the following organizations issue reports concerning the latest verified vulnerabilities and attacks? (Choose two.)

    a. ISO

    b. CERT

    c. Bugtraq

    d. IDS

13. Which of the following should be run each time you log out from a Kerberos session?

    a. *kdestroy*

    b. *klogout*

    c. *kinit -l user*, where *user* is the username of the person logging out

    d. *kadmin logout user*, where *user* is the username of the person logging out.

14. What two services are vital to the proper functioning of a Kerberos implementation?

    a. A fully functioning Network Time Protocol (NTP) server

    b. A fully functioning LDAP server

    c. A fully functioning Domain Name System (DNS) server

    d. A fully functioning Samba server

15. Which of the following commands creates a Kerberos database that you can then populate with principals?

   a. *kdb5_util initialize -s*

   b. *kdb5_util create -s*

   c. *kdb5_create initialize -s*

   d. *kdb5_create -s*

16. You wish to conduct a *ping* scan of systems on your network. Which of the following commands does this?

   a. *nmap -ping 192.168.2.1-254*

   b. *nmap -P 192.168.2.1-254*

   c. *nmap -sP 192.168.2.2-254*

   d. *nmap -Ps 192.168.2.1-254*

17. What term describes a situation in which an intrusion detection system (IDS) identifies legitimate traffic as an attack?

   a. An event anomaly

   b. An event horizon

   c. A false signature

   d. A false positive

18. What is the result of the following entry in the *hosts.deny* file of your Linux system?

   ```
   ALL: .company.com: DENY
   ```

   a. No incoming or outgoing connections will be possible to the *company.com* domain.

   b. Users on the Linux system will not be able to access resources on the *company.com*domain.

   c. All hosts from the *company.com* domain will be prohibited from using all services on the Linux system.

   d. All hosts from the *company.com* domain will be prohibited from using services protected by TCP wrappers.

19. Consider the following entry in *hosts.deny*:

   ```
   ALL:ALL
   ```

   Imagine also the following entry in *hosts.allow*:

   ```
   ALL: .mycompany.com
   ```

   What is the result of this combination?

   a. All attempted connections to resources protected by TCP wrappers will fail, because the *hosts.deny* file takes precedence.

   b. Only members of the *mycompany.com* domain will be able to connect to resources protected by TCP wrappers.

   c. Because the entries conflict, all people will be allowed to access all resources on the server.

   d. TCP wrappers will fail due to the conflict, and no one will be allowed to access the protected resources.

20. What does the *~/.ssh/authorized_keys* file contain?

    a. The private keys of users who wish to access your system

    b. The host keys of SSH servers that have connected to your system

    c. The public keys of users who wish to access your system

    d. The certificate of each SSH server that has connected to your system

21. You wish to use an SSH client to connect to a remote system with public key authentication. What command would you issue to create a key pair that uses Version 2 of the RSA algorithm?

    a. *ssh-keygen -a rsa*

    b. *ssh-keygen -rsa*

    c. *ssh-keygen -s rsa*

    d. `ssh-keygen -t rsa`

22. What file would you edit to change the facility or priority that SSH uses to log events?

    a. */etc/ssh/sshd_config*

    b. */var/ssh/ssh.config*

    c. *~/.ssh/ssh.config*

    d. */usr/lib/sshd/ssh_config*

23. What entry in the SSH configuration file would you add to temporarily disable non-*root* logins to an SSH server during maintenance?

    a. `Users_Deny`

    b. `DisableUsers`

    c. `DenyUsers`

    d. `Users:Deny`

24. You have enabled X11 forwarding in the SSH configuration file. You wish to tunnel X11 traffic inside of SSH to access a system named *blake.romantics. org*. Which of the following commands allows you to tunnel X11 sessions to a remote system so that they are encrypted?

    a. *ssh -t blake.romantics.org*

    b. *ssh -x 1.blake.romantics.org*

    c. *ssh -r blake.romantics.org*

    d. *ssh -f blake.romantics.org*

25. What command would you issue to remove an identity from *ssh-agent*?

    a. *ssh-remove*

    b. *ssh-add -r*

    c. *ssh-del*

    d. *ssh-add -d*

26. You wish to authenticate via public keys with a remote user. You and the remote user have just created key pairs. What must you do next?

  a. Exchange private keys and place the remote user's private key into the ~/.ssh/identity file.

  b. Each user must use the *ssh-add* and *ssh-agent* applications to place each other's public key into memory.

  c. Exchange public keys and then place the remote user's public key into the ~/.ssh/identity file.

  d. Each user must use the *ssh-add* and *ssh-agent* applications to place each other's private key into memory.

27. Each time you authenticate using public keys in SSH, you are asked for the password of your private key. What can you do to keep your private key secure but avoid having to constantly enter the password each time you use SSH?

  a. Use the *ssh-keygen -P* command to store the password in a restricted text file.

  b. Use *ssh-agent* and *ssh-add* commands to store the private key in memory.

  c. Use *ssh-askpass* and *ssh-keyscan* to store the private key password in memory.

  d. Use the *ssh-copy-id* command to store the private key in memory.

28. You are configuring a server that allows anonymous FTP access. Write in the entry that would go in the *ftpaccess* file that forbids anonymous users from uploading files.

29. You wish to forbid the root account from logging in to your FTP server. What steps would you take?

  a. Edit the *ftpusers* file and add the root account name.

  b. Edit the *ftpaccess* file and add the root account name.

  c. Edit the *ftpgroups* file and add the root account name.

  d. Edit the */etc/passwd* file and place an asterisk in front of the *ftp* account.

30. What are the names of the classes of users recognized by the WU-FTPD daemon?

  a. `anonymous, limited, and standard`

  b. `privileged, anonymous, and real`

  c. `restricted, privileged, and standard`

  d. `real, anonymous, and guest`

31. You've decided to create a chroot environment for your FTP server. Accordingly, you copied the *ls*, *rm*, *cp*, and *gzip* commands to the */chroot/ftp/bin* directory that you created. You have verified that they are executable. After starting the FTP server, you notice that you cannot use these commands during the FTP session. Which of the following steps will most likely get these commands to work?

  a. Make all of the applications SUID root.

  b. List all files you wish to have executable permissions in the *ftpaccess* file, then make sure that each file is placed into the */chroot/ftp/bin* directory.

c. Use the *ldd* command to discover the libraries the applications require, and copy the libraries to the */chroot/ftp/bin* directory.

d. Create a bash script that precedes each of the commands you wish to make executable, and place the script in the */chroot/ftp/bin* directory.

32. You wish to enable Network Address Translation (NAT) on a Linux system. What table in *iptables* would you specify to masquerade a connection?

33. What command do you have to execute to make sure changes to the */etc/syctl.conf* file are recognized?

    a. *sysctl, without any arguments*

    b. *sysctl -c /etc/sysctl.conf*

    c. *sysctl /etc/sysctl.conf*

    d. *sysctl -p /etc/sysctl.conf*

34. Which of the following commands can help a Linux system withstand a SYN flood?

    a. *echo 1 > /proc/sys/net/ipv4/tcp_abort_on_overflow*

    b. *echo 1 > /proc/sys/net/ipv4/tcp_nosyn*

    c. *echo 1 > /proc/sys/net/ipv4/tcp_syncookies*

    d. *echo 1 > /proc/sys/net/ipv4/tcp_nores*

35. How can you enable IP forwarding in a Linux system? (Choose two.)

    a. Issue *echo 1 > /proc/sys/net/ipv4/ip_forward*.

    b. Edit the */etc/network/options* file and enter the following line:

        `ip_forward=yes`

    c. Issue *echo 1 > /proc/sys/net/ipv4/ip_enable_fw*.

    d. Edit the */etc/sysctl* file and enter the following line:

        `ip_forward=yes`

36. Users have called complaining that they can no longer access resources necessary to do their jobs. You have determined that entries automatically added to the */etc/hosts.deny* file by an application are responsible. You have removed these entries manually. Which of the following applications is capable of updating the */etc/hosts.deny* file?

    a. TCP wrappers

    b. *iptables*

    c. *ipchains*

    d. Portsentry

37. Which of the following commands would you use to update an LDIF file?

    a. *moddif*

    b. *ldapadd*

    c. *ldifmod*

    d. *slapd*

38. You are adding individuals to an LDIF file. What does ou= indicate?

    a. The online utilization value for the LDIF file

    b. The object URL of the user in the LDAP scheme

    c. The organizational unit the user belongs to

    d. The owner UML, which describes users as computer-based objects

39. Which of the following applications is responsible for maintaining binding information for an NIS server?

    a. *yppoll*

    b. *yppush*

    c. *ypbind*

    d. *ypmatch*

40. You are having problems with your NIS server and suspect a problem with the portmapper. You can see that the portmapper daemon has a process ID, but you are not sure that the daemon is working properly. Which of the following applications can help you determine more information about how the portmapper daemon is functioning?

    a. *rpcinfo*

    b. *pmreport*

    c. *yppoll*

    d. *netgroup*

41. You wish to have your DHCP server provide a default gateway and DNS server to each client. The IP address of the default gateway is 192.168.2.1. The IP address of the DNS server is 10.45.45.3. Write in the option entries you would make in a subnet section of your DHCP configuration file.

42. Which of the following do you specify when configuring a *dhcrelay*? (Choose two.)

    a. The IP address of the DHCP server

    b. The MAC address of the DHCP server

    c. The interfaces that *dhcrelay* will listen on

    d. The MAC addresses of all local network interface cards

43. Which of the following applications help a news server avoid filling up a hard disk and overtaxing the CPU?

    a. *control.ctl*

    b. *sysctl*

    c. *expire.ctl*

    d. *innwatch*

44. Davis (username *davis*) wishes to create a new newsgroup named *scuba*. The password for the newsgroup is regulator1. Write in the command that he would issue to create the group.

45. What three parts is a Procmail recipe comprised of?

    a. Beginning, condition, action

    b. Header, instructions, condition

    c. Stipulation, condition, action

    d. Header, descriptor, options

46. What is the name of the file used to store a user's private key?

    a. */etc/ssh/users/identity*

    b. *~/.ssh/authorized_keys*

    c. *~/.ssh/identity*

    d. *~/.ssh/.shosts*

47. What command would you issue to enter interactive mode in Sendmail and test changes you have made to the *virtusertable* and *genericstable* files?

    a. *procmail -t*

    b. *sendmail -bt*

    c. *sendmail -rv*

    d. *mail -s test*

48. Which of the following steps allows you to deny Sendmail access to users from the *haxors1.com* DNS domain?

    a. Enter the following in the *sendmail.cf* file: TDISCARD haxors1.com.

    b. Enter the following into the */etc/mail/access* file: haxors1.comDISCARD.

    c. Enter the following into the */etc/mail/generic* file: FROM: haxors1.com REJECT.

    d. Enter the following into the */etc/mail/virtusertable* file: haxors1.com REJECT.

49. Which of the following commands captures all traffic except SSH packets between the hosts named *lewis* and *clark*?

    a. *tcpdump host lewis and clark and not -p ssh*

    b. *tcpdump host lewis and clark and not '(port ssh)'*

    c. *tcpdump host lewis and clark and not -p 22*

    d. *tcpdump host lewis and clark not '(ssh)'*

50. You are editing the main Apache configuration file. You wish to control how many servers are started at one time. Which of the following values would you change?

    a. StartServers

    b. MaxRequests

    c. MaxServers

    d. StartProcess

51. You are using *.htaccess* files to enable password protection for a web site directory. You are confident that the *.htaccess* file you are using is valid. However, the file does not seem to be recognized by the server. Which of the following changes will most likely enable the use of *.htaccess* files?

   a. Change the `Override None` directive to `Override All`.

   b. Change the `HtAccess None` directive to `HtAccessAll`.

   c. Change the `AllowOverride AuthConfig` directive to `AllowOverride HtAccess`.

   d. Change the `AllowOverride None` directive to `AllowOverride AuthConfig`.

52. You have been asked to increase the size of the cache directory for Squid from 1 GB to 3 GB. Which of the following would be the correct entry in *squid.conf*?

   a. *cache_dir /usr/local/squid/cache/ 3000000 160 800*

   b. *cache_dir /usr/local/squid/cache/ 160 800 3GB*

   c. *cache_dir /usr/local/squid/cache/ 3000 160 800*

   d. *cache_dir /usr/local/squid/cache/ 3GB 160 800*

53. Why is a DHCP server relay agent necessary in a routed network?

   a. All routers are configured to drop UDP port 1964, which is used by DHCP.

   b. DHCP servers rely on broadcasts to configure clients on the network.

   c. DHCP clients have not yet configured their default gateways.

   d. All routers are configured to drop TCP port 1964, which is used by DHCP.

54. While reviewing a *slapd.conf* file, you notice the following entry:

   ```
   database   ldbm
   ```

   What is the meaning of this entry?

   a. It identifies the database manager that *slapd* consults when authenticating users.

   b. It specifies the type of encryption used during LDAP sessions.

   c. It provides the community name (cn) for the LDAP database.

   d. It gives the organizational unit (ou) name for the LDAP database.

55. What entries would you make in the */etc/hosts.allow* and */etc/hosts.deny* files so that TCP wrappers automatically denies all services except FTP?

   a. Put `ALL:ALL` in */etc/hosts.allow*, and put `ALL:ALL, EXCEPT FTP` in */etc/hosts.deny*.

   b. Put `ALL:ALL` in */etc/hosts.deny*, and put `in.ftpd: ALL:ALLOW` in */etc/hosts.allow*.

   c. Put `ALL:ALL EXCEPT FTP` in */etc/hosts.allow*, and put nothing in */etc/hosts.deny*.

   d. Put nothing in */etc/hosts.allow*, and put `ALL: EXCEPT svc: in.ftpd` in */etc/hosts.deny*.

Answers

1. a. Ethernet networks have a maximum MTU of 1500. It is possible that you would want to adjust the MTU if conditions warranted. However, you will find that your Ethernet NIC's MTU will usually be 1500.

2. b. In Sendmail, the *genericstable* file is responsible for rewriting headers of outgoing messages.

3. d. Both the *fsck* and *badblocks* commands can be destructive if run against a mounted partition. You should unmount the drive before using either one. You may need to go into single mode to do so.

4. a and c. You can use *smbmount* and *smbclient*. To draw an analogy, *smbclient* is something like a command-line FTP client. You can use *smbclient* to access a Samba share and navigate it just as you would an FTP session. The *smbmount* command, on the other hand, is more like the standard *mount* command. You must specify a mount point, unlike *smbclient*.

5. `mount -t nfs bentley:/home/james/mnt/nfs`

6. a. The -*w* option in *traceroute* allows you to specify the wait period. *traceroute* will wait five seconds by default, then move on to the next hop.

7. b and c. You can use the *dig* command with the @ option to specify a different DNS server. With the *host* command, the second hostname given in the command specifies the name server.

8. d. When using the *ifconfig* command to specify a second IP address for a NIC, simply use a colon with no space after the interface:

    `ifconfig eth2:1 202.168.85.3 netmask 255.255.255.0`

9. b and d. Two reasons exist for a *route* command to hang: DNS service has failed, or the default gateway is down. Use the -*n* option to the *route* command to bypass name resolution issues.

10. c. The *telnet* command is very handy when it comes to troubleshooting servers. All you have to do is specify a port number after the hostname, and the *telnet* command will use that instead of the default Telnet port (TCP 23). Once *telnet* connects to the desired port, you may see messages and commands from the server. Even though you likely will not be able to control the server or view data as you would with the proper client, you will still be able to see the operations of the service in a helpful way.

11. c. The way to conduct a manual scan of the files and drives that Tripwire is configured to protect is by specifying the --*check* option to the *tripwire* command.

12. b and c. CERT (*http://www.cert.org*) and Bugtraq (*http://www.securityfocus. com/archive/1*) are dedicated to discussing vulnerabilities, attacks, and system bugs. Although attackers usually know about the bugs and exploits before CERT and Bugtraq report them, it is nevertheless useful for you to receive warnings about the latest security-related issues.

13. a. The *kdestroy* command purges the system of any credentials that could be used illicitly. It is a good idea to place this command in the logout script for your shell.

14. a and c. If you do not have an NTP server and a properly configured DNS server, your Kerberos implementation will likely fail, no matter how well you have defined your Kerberos database and principals. NTP and DNS are foundational for Kerberos because Kerberos relies heavily on both time-based calculations and hostname services.

15. b. The *kdb5_util* command has many functions. In particular, the *create -s* option allows you to create the database that will eventually hold the principals.

16. c. If you want to conduct a *ping* scan, use the *-sP* option, then specify a range using a hyphen.

17. d. The term *false positive* describes instances when intrusion detection or antivirus applications mistakenly label legitimate activity as an attack. While careful configuration helps to avoid most false positives, it is very difficult to avoid all instances.

18. d. Even if you were to block off all services using */etc/hosts.deny*, various services still might be accessible because they simply do not consult these files.

19. b. It is possible to use both the */etc/hosts.allow* and */etc/hosts.deny* files to improve security. The */etc/hosts.allow* file is consulted first. The */etc/hosts. deny* file does not negate statements in the */etc/hosts.allow* file. Thus, it is often encouraged to explicitly allow services, hosts, and networks in */etc/ hosts.allow*, then block off all other services in */etc/hosts.deny*. It is also important to understand that not all services use TCP wrappers.

20. c. The *~/.ssh/authorized_keys* file (or the *~/.ssh/authorized_keys2* file, for newer versions of SSH) contains the public keys of users that you wish to allow into your system without providing a standard password.

21. d. The *ssh-keygen -t rsa* command allows you to begin the process of creating a new key pair. This key pair will be stored in the *~/.ssh* directory by default. The files generated will be clearly marked (e.g., *id_rsa* and *id_rsa.pub*). You can also specify *ssh-keygen -t dsa* if you wish to use DSA keys instead of RSA keys. The filenames generated will be slightly different to reflect your use of DSA.

22. a. The */etc/ssh/sshd_config* file allows you to configure most aspects of SSH, including its logging. Using this file, you can also disable non-*root* access, restrict support to SSH Version 2, and enable X11 port forwarding.

23. c. If you wish to disable non-*root* access for an SSH server, use the DenyUsers directive in the */etc/ssh/sshd_config* file.

24. b. The *-x* option to *ssh* allows you to tunnel X11 through SSH, thereby encrypting all transmissions. You must first enable X11 tunneling by editing the */etc/ssh/sshd_config* file.

25. d. To remove an identity from *ssh-agent*, use the *ssh-agent -d* command. If you are using *ssh-agent* and *ssh-add*, it is wise to place *ssh-agent -d* in your shell's logout file.

26. c. You must first exchange public keys. The public keys of users you wish to allow without providing a standard password are stored in the *~/.ssh/ authorized_keys* or *~/.ssh/authorized_keys2* files.

27. b. The *ssh-agent* and *ssh-add* commands store private keys in memory. You first run *ssh-agent*, specifying a shell (e.g., *ssh-agent /bin/bash*). This shell runs until you exit it. After the shell is active, you then run *ssh-add* from within this shell to add the private key to *ssh-agent*. You will then never be asked for the private key's password until you exit the shell started under *ssh-agent*.

28. The command is:

```
upload /home/ftp * no
```

This directive goes in the *ftpaccess* file and ensures that anonymous users cannot upload files.

29. a. Any account listed in the *ftpusers* file will be prohibited from logging in to the FTP server.

30. d. The three classes of users that are allowed to log in to an FTP server are real, anonymous, and guest.

31. c. It is not enough to simply copy the executables into the correct directories when creating a chroot environment for any service. You must also copy the appropriate libraries and ensure that permissions are correct.

32. The nat table. When you wish to use *iptables* to masquerade connections (i.e., do Network Address Translation), you do not use the three default tables listed by the *iptables -L* command (e.g., INPUT, FORWARD, and ACCEPT). You use the somewhat hidden nat table, which you must specify using the *-t* option:

```
iptables -t nat -L
```

33. d. Whenever you make any changes to the */etc/sysctl.conf* file, you must use the *sysctl -p /etc/sysctl.conf* command to make sure the system recognizes the changes.

34. c. Changing the value of the */proc/sys/net/ipv4/tcp_syncookies* file to 1 helps make the Linux system more capable of handing SYN floods. You can do this by using the *echo* command or by editing the */etc/sysctl.conf* file and then running the following command:

```
sysctl -p /etc/sysctl.conf
```

35. a and b. As usual, there is more than one way to do it in Linux. You can use the *echo* command (*echo 1 > /proc/sys/net/ipv4/ip_forward*), or you can edit the */etc/network/options* file and enter the line ip_forward=yes. Both have the same effect. The first option is the most nearly universal, which you should keep in mind. The LPI Exam is vendor-neutral.

36. d. Portsentry has many capabilities, including the ability to write to the */etc/hosts.deny* file, if that feature is something you find useful.

37. b. The *ldapadd* command allows you to update an LDIF file and have your LDAP server recognize the changes.

38. c. The ou= field in an LDAP LDIF file indicates the organizational unit. The ou designation is essential, as it helps identify legitimate users.

39. c. The *ypbind* command allows you to maintain binding information for an NIS server.

40. a. The *rpcinfo* command provides information about RPC calls made to the local system, and is ideal for determining the status of the portmapper daemon. The portmapper daemon is an essential element of NIS.

41. When defining a default gateway and a DNS server in a subnet section of the *dhcp.conf* file, you simply use the option keyword followed by the required network element (e.g., routers or domain-name-servers) and then the appropriate IP address:

```
option routers 192.168.2.1;
option domain-name-servers 1.10.45.45.3;
```

42. a and c. When configuring a DHCP relay, you need to tell it which interface to listen on. It is also important to give the address of the DHCP server on the subnet, to help the relay work faster.

43. d Using *innwatch* helps you monitor your INN server. It runs in the background periodically searching for problem conditions, including full hard drives and overburdened processors.

44. The command is:

```
ctlinnd newgroup scuba y davis
```

The final argument is davis because *davis* is the user creating the newsgroup.

45. a. The three parts of a recipe are the beginning (where flags are stored), the conditions, and the action. A recipe first identifies the conditions, then specifies an action.

46. c. The *~/.ssh/identity* file (or the *id_rsa* file in some Linux systems) contains the identity SSH requires the user to define before public-key authentication will work for her account.

47. b. Although you could also send email messages, the quickest way to verify settings on Sendmail is to issue the *sendmail -bt* command and begin an interactive test shell. Once in this shell, you can send test messages and conduct queries to verify that your settings have been recognized and are having the intended effect.

48. b. Modifying the */etc/mail/access* file is the only way listed that will allow you to control access from a domain.

49. b. The single quotes around the (port ssh) statement are necessary to escape the parenthese from the shell. It is important to understand the sometimes arcane *tcpdump* options for the exam. Consider this question just the beginning.

50. a. The StartServers directive allows you to control how many servers Apace Server starts. Familiarize yourself with other directives concerning processes and threads before you take the exam.

51. d. If you want to use *.htaccess* files, you would change the AllowOverride directive to use AuthConfig, rather than None.

52. c. Specify 3000 in the cache_dir statement. Squid specifies this value in megabytes, and 3000 megabytes is 3 gigabytes. The remaining two numbers refer to the number of directories that will be generated to store the proxy cache files.

53. b. DHCP servers require broadcasts, and routers are to isolate broadcasts to a single network. So if you wish to forward DHCP broadcasts to other networks, you have to use a DHCP relay agent.

---

54. a. When you configure an LDAP server, you have to tell *slapd* what type of database to use. ldbm, which stands for LDAP Database Manager, is traditional.

55. b. It is often advisable to configure your system to block all services except those you want to explicitly allow. Using the */etc/hosts.allow* and */etc/hosts. deny* files in the way described here gives you this policy for all services that recognize TCP wrappers.

Index

Symbols

& (ampersand)
&& (Boolean and), 707
background commands, 98, 521
< > (angle brackets)
< (input redirection) operator, 87
> (right angle bracket)
> redirection operator, 87
>> redirection operator, 87
bash shell, interactive function entry, 320
\< and \>, matching word boundaries, 104
* (asterisk), 239
.info message selector, syslog.conf, 353
` (backquotes)
command quoting in bash, 609
command substitution, 332
\ (backslash)
escaping regular expression metacharacters, 104
escaping shell metacharacters, 56
^ (caret), beginning of line matching in regular expressions, 104, 787
{ } (curly braces), enclosing function body, 320
- (dash), leading dash (nice command), 102

$ (dollar sign)
$# variable, 322
$( ) notation, command quoting, 609
$? variable, 331
end of a line, matching in regular expressions, 104
user prompt, xvi
in variable names, 318, 608
! (exclamation mark), Boolean not operator, 707
(hash mark)
#! (she-bang line), 327, 480, 607
in comments, 322
/etc/modules.conf file, 266
/etc/printcap file, 298
root shell prompt, xvi
( ) parentheses, bash functions, 320
. (period)
at job input and, 628
regular expressions, matching any single character, 787
| (pipe character), 86
|| (Boolean or), 707
regular expression modifier, 240
+ (plus sign), regular expression modifier, 240, 787
? (question mark), 239
" (quotes, double)
in regular expressions, 106
in shell scripts, 608

We'd like to hear your suggestions for improving our indexes. Send email to *index@oreilly.com*.

break command, 333

breakins, detecting attempts and actual breakins, 852

broadcast address, setting with ifconfig, 684

BSD options, ps command, 91

BSD Unix, printing, 289

buffer overflows, 851

buffers, flushing, 529

bug reports, 446

Bugtraq, 447, 865

build link (kernel module), 164

burning CDs, 545–549

bus (SCSI), 16

    speed, 18

    termination, 18

bzImage kernel image, 274, 494

bzip2 utility, 34, 767

    opening compressed files, 34

C

C compiler, 269

cables, troubleshooting for hardware connections, 875

cache (DNS), poisoning, 765

caching proxy server (see Squid)

caching-only name servers, 430

canonical name (CNAME) records, 758

cardctl command, 570, 573, 574

cardinfo command, 574

cardmgr command, 569, 573, 574

CAs (Certificate Authorities), 781

    reasons to use, 784

case command, 333

cat command, 519, 521

CD burners, IDE, 559

cdrecord command, 546

cdrom (kernel) subdirectories, 259

CDs, burning, 545–549

CERT (Computer Emergency Response Team), 447, 866

    CERT/CC (CERT Coordination Center), 447

certificate-based cryptography, 781–784

    self-signed certificate, creating, 783

CGI (Common Gateway Interface) scripts, 774, 787

    execution, control by Apache, 422

    running Perl scripts on Apache as CGI scripts, 780

chage command, 444, 482

chains

    ipchains, 824

    iptables, 825

%changelog macro, 598

CHAP (Challenge Handshake Authentication Protocol), 408, 694

character classes (GNU sed), 113

character sets (regular expressions), 105, 239

chat program, 696

chat scripts, 402

checksumming programs, 613

chgrp command, 162, 246

child processes, 89

chkconfig command, 515

chmod command, 158–160, 246

    -R (recursive) option, 64

    symbolic access modes, 158

chown command, 161, 246

chroot command, 519

    exploring damaged system, 523

chroot jail, running BIND in, 765

CIAC (Computer Incident Advisory Capability), 866

ckpasswd application (INN), 750

cksum command, 613

class drivers (USB), 23

classes

    network, subnet masks, 377–379, 485

    /pcmcia/config file, 570

%clean macro, 597

clear command (.bash_logout file), 324

clear-to-send (CTS) signals, 401

client/server model, X Window System, 182, 248

    remote X clients, 198, 250

    X Server, 183–189

client-to-server communications, port numbers, 381

clock, 11

    maintaining, 370–375

cmp command, 612

CNAME (canonical name) records, 758

command history, 61, 233

    editing, 62

    substitution, 62

command line, 54

    defined, 56

    (see also commands, working on command line)

CPAN (Comprehensive Perl Archive
　　　　Network), 615–617
　　mon module, 613
　　searching and browing for
　　　　modules, 616
　　shell, 616
create command, for Majordomo
　　　　lists, 744
cron facility, 455, 483
　　at versus, 358
　　backup scripts called by, 366–368
　　controlling access to, 484
　　controlling user access to, 359
　　log file rotation, 354
　　programs, 356
　　scheduling program execution, 626
　　system administration tasks,
　　　　scheduling, 356–358
　　troubleshooting problems with, 640
crond, 356, 483
crontab files
　　formats, 626
　　problems with, 640
　　quotacheck, scheduling, 151
crontab utility, 356, 484
　　crontab command, 483
　　system crontab files, 358
　　user crontab files, 356
　　viewing or editing crontab files, 356
crossover cable, 400
cryptography
　　certificate-based, 781–784
　　　　self-signed certificate,
　　　　　creating, 783
　　encrypting web traffic with SSL, 781
　　keys for package maintainer, 599
　　public-key, 837
　　　　generating and using SSH
　　　　　keys, 837–841
　　Tripwire files, encryption, 858
C-shells, 479
CSR (certificate signing request), 782
ctlinnd command, 748
Ctrl-C, 96
Ctrl-D, using to end at job input, 628
Ctrl-Z, 96, 98
CTS (clear-to-send) signals, 401
CUPS (Common UNIX Printing
　　　　System), 289, 290
curly braces (see { }, under symbols)
current working directory, 90
　　specifying, 327

curses, PPP dialer based on, 697
cut command, 65, 234, 593

D

dash interpreter, 518
data categories, 169, 247
datagram delivery service (IP), 380
dates and times
　　attacks using malevolent date
　　　　programs, 624
　　hardware clock, configuring, 11
　　hours, specifying in cron facility, 627
　　maintaining system time, 370–375
　　NTP (Network Time Protocol), 764
　　synchronizing time on all
　　　　systems, 848
　　times for crontab command
　　　　execution, 357
db (database) entries, named files, 754
dd utility, 521
　　burning copy of data CD, 548
　　creating boot floppy, 630
　　facilitating I/O with block
　　　　devices, 549
DDoS (distributed denial of service
　　　　attacks), using echo
　　　　broadcasts, 833
.deb file extension, 41
debhelper programs, 602
Debian-based systems
　　building packages, 598
　　　　signing packages, 599
　　configuring as DHCP client, 803
　　creating boot floppy, 630
　　initrd and /linuxrc, 518
　　keeping Debian up to date, 866
　　mkinitrd command, 503
　　modifying packages, 601–604
　　NIS master server, 805
　　package management, 25, 41–47,
　　　　232
　　　　alien command, 47
　　　　apt-get command, 45–46
　　　　dpkg command, 42–45
　　　　dselect command, 46
　　pcmcia-cs module, 569
　　pcnetconfig command, 572
　　pppconfig tool, 693
　　runlevels, customizing, 515
　　　　update-rc.d command, 516
　　security information, 866

O

object files (.o), 259
Objectives, LPI exams, xiv, xv
  weights, 4
objects, Apache shared objects (see
  DSOs)
octal access modes, 154, 157, 158
octal dump, 69, 234
od command, 69, 234
offsite backups, planning, 604
  storage site, selecting, 604
OHCI (Open Host Controller
  Interface), 22
one-way inheritance, 328
open email relays, 721
  checking mail server for, 864
Open Host Controller Interface
  (OHCI), 22
OpenLDAP, 811
  setting up server, 811–815
OpenSSH, 433, 836–842
  generating and using keys, 837–841
  installing and configuring, 836
    authentication, 837
    root logins, permitting, 837
    X11 forwarding, 837
  ssh port forwarding, 842
  TCP wrappers, 841
openssl program, 782
operating environment (see
  environments)
operating systems, 258
  booting with LILO, 29
  hardening for Sendmail bastion
    host, 733
  shell user interface, 316
/opt directory, 172
/opt partition, 531
options (command), 58
options, modules.conf, 266
or operator (||), 707
order of operations, redirection and
  commands, 87
OSI network protocol suite, 810
other access mode, 245
output redirection operators, 87
ownership of files, 161–162, 246
  groups and group files, 344
  shell scripts, 329

P

package management
  Debian-based systems, 25, 41–47,
    232
    alien command, 47
    apt-get command, 45–46
    dpkg command, 42–45
    dselect command, 46
  review exercises, 204
  review questions, 203
  RPM (Red Hat Package
    Manager), 25, 47–53, 232
    rpm command, 49–53
    running rpm, 48
    verifying packages, 441–443, 490
package.spec file, 594
packages, 593–604
  build process, 593
  building deb packages, 598
    signing packages, 599
  building RPM packages, 593–595
  Debian package names, 41
  modifying deb packages, 601–604
  modifying RPM packages, 595–598
  Perl, 616
  security concerns, 441
Page Description Language (PDL), 299
pager alerts
  sending from script, 609
pagers, 305, 478
PAM (Pluggable Authentication
    Modules), 639, 815–819
  configuration, 816
    control-flag, 817
    module-path and arguments, 817
    module-type, 816
  LDAP client authentication, 818
  pam_krb5, adding Kerberos
    authentication, 848
pam_ldap package, 818
  configuring, 819
PAP (Password Authentication
    Protocol), 408, 694
parallel ports, 12
parent process, 90
parent process ID (PID), 90
parted (Partition EDitor), 536, 537

R

RAID (Redundant Array of Independent Disks)
  configuring, 551–553
  RAID 1 (mirroring), creating, 552
raidstart command, 552
raidstop command, 552
ranges (in regular expressions), 110
rawrite.exe command, 630
rc script, 282, 475, 510
rc.local script, 282, 475
rc.sysinit script, 282, 475, 510, 511–514
rcp utility, 624
rcS script, 282, 510
read comand, 336
read permission, 153, 245
readers.conf file (INN), 748
  customizing newsgroups, 749–751
readline, 324
README files, 308
read-only directive, 474
ready-to-send (RTS) signals, 401
rebooting
  init command, using, 285
  shutdown command, using, 286
  telinit command, using, 285
recipes (Procmail), 738–740
  examples, 739
records, DNS, 758
recovery
  creating recovery disks, 630
  planning, 604
  system, 520–523
    booting from rescue CD, 522
    filesystem damage, 520
    init or system initialization failure, 521
    loss of key files, 523
recursion, DNS server queries, 765
recursive commands, 63, 233
  rm -r, -R, 82
Red Hat Certified Engineer (RHCE) program, xiii
Red Hat Linux
  configuring as DHCP client, 802
  creating boot disk, 630
  dial-up connection configuration, 693
  initrd and /linuxrc file, 519
  keeping up to date, 867
  mkinitrd, 502

netconfig tool, 680
network configuration, PCMCIA devices, 571
network interface configuration files, 682
PCMCIA support, 569
runlevels, customizing, 515
security information, 866
system initialization techniques, 282
system runlevel directories, 514
Red Hat Package Manager (see RPM)
redirection, 55, 86–88, 236
  HTTP requests for Apache, 785
  shell script results, 608
redirection operators, 87, 236
Redundant Array of Independent Disks (see RAID)
regexp or regex (see regular expressions)
registrars, domain name, 429
registration, domain names, 489
regular expressions, 55, 103–114, 239–240
  awk program, 611
  egrep command
    extracting lines from system logs, 592
  examples, 110–114
    anchors, 110
    groups and ranges, 110
    modifiers, 111
    patterns, 112
    sed (stream editor), 113
  grep command, 105–107
    extracting lines from system logs, 592
  mod_rewrite Apache module, 785–788
    catch-all regular expression, 787
  Perl, 616
  sed (stream editor), 107–110
    removing nonmatching lines, 613
  syntax, 103–104
ReiserFS, 541
relay, DHCP, 803
relaying email, 721
  checking for open relays, 864
  open relays used by spammers, 721
relays, DHCP, 398
reminder messages (Majordomo), 742
remote printers, configuring, 302, 477
remote X clients, 198, 250

V

/var directory, 122, 172, 231, 247
  /lib/dpkg, 42
  /log directory, 635
  /log/dmesg, 634
  /log/messages, 280, 353, 474
    named configuration, 430
    rotation, 354
  /log/wtmp file, rotation, 354
  /named/, 755
  /spool/cron/crontabs, 626
  /spool/lpd, 291
  subdirectories, 173
/var partition, 531
  guidelines for, 27
  size of, 26
variable data, 169
variables
  cron environment, 640
  environment variables, 317
  inheritance in shell
    environment, 328
  queried with mod_rewrite, 787
  shell, 56, 318
  shell scripts, 608
verify mode, rpm, 52
versions, kernel, 269
vertical refresh frequency
    (monitors), 183
Very Secure FTP Daemon (vsftpd), 834
vfat filesystem, 244, 542
vg* commands, 520
vgchange command, 566
vgdisplay command, 559, 562
vgscan command, 566
vi editor, 55, 114–116
  commands, 240
  troubleshooting, 637
VI Improved, 638
video
  kernel subdirectories, 260
  XFree86 hardware, 183
virtual consoles, 193
virtual hosts, 773
  defining default settings for requests
    not matching, 775
virtual interfaces, configuring with
    ifconfig, 683
virtual memory partition, 27
Virtual Private Network (VPN),
    configured with ifconfig, 683

virtual users, 729
  checking, 730
  reversing accounts, 731
VirtualHost container (Apache), 776
  access control, 777
  SSL connections, handling, 783
virtusertable file (Sendmail), 719, 729,
    731
volume groups
  adding disks, 564
  creating, 561
  displaying properties, 562
  listing with pvscan, 564
  removing, 566
  removing hard disks, 564
VPN (Virtual Private Network), tunnel
    end-points configured with
    ifconfig, 683
vsftpd (Very Secure FTP Daemon), 834

W

w command, 610
wc command, 77, 234
web accelerator, Squid as, 795–797
web logs, fetching and processing with
    Perl, 617–621
web services, 766–797
  Apache
    configuring, 772–789
    installing, 766–772
    Exam 202 review, 892–895
    Squid, 789–797
web site for this book, xviii
web sites, Linux-related, 313
well-known ports, 381
WEP (Wireless Equivalent Privacy), 682
whatis command, 179, 248
which command, 176, 247
while command, 339
while loops, 60
who command, 610
whois, 386
  fwhois command, 486
wildcards, 85
  file-naming, 83–85, 235
window managers, 181, 182, 196–201,
    248, 249
  default, starting, 196
  security, 200
  X libraries, 198

About the Authors

Steven Pritchard maintains the Linux Hardware Compatibility HOWTO documentation, writes about hardware for *Linux Journal*, and provides custom workstation and server consulting and other services. He lives in Fairview Heights, Illinois.

Bruno Gomes Pessanha has been a collaborating translator for the Linux Professional Institute since 2002. He also works as a consulting analyst for a Brazilian government petroleum enterprise, covering Linux migration and initiatives and administering high-end performance projects, high availability clusters, and mission critical services. He lives in Rio de Janeiro, Brazil.

Nicolai Langfeldt is a programmer, system administrator, and systems integrator who lives in Oslo, Norway. A Linux consultant since 1994, Nicolai works for Linpro (a well-established Norwegian Linux consulting firm) and is the cofounder of Linux Norge (*http://www.linux.no*), an information portal for Linux. He has written several well-regarded HOWTOs for the Linux Documentation project and is author of *The Concise Guide to DNS and BIND* (Que).

James Stanger has been involved with Linux since 1995, and has worked closely with the Linux Professional Institute (LPI) since its inception in 1999. He is Chair of the LPI Advisory Council, where he helps the LPI coordinate input from corporations and the open source community. James has a unique understanding of LPI's certification exams, as he is an expert in both the certification industry and in Gnu/Linux, networking, and security.

Jeff Dean is a freelance author and consultant in Philadelphia, Pennsylvania. Jeff has professional experience in IT management, training delivery, and system administration of the VMS, Unix, AS/400, and Windows NT operating systems. He holds an undergraduate degree in electrical engineering from the University of Pittsburgh and a Master of Engineering with emphasis in computer design from Penn State. He is a Red Hat Certified Engineer (RHCE) and LPI Certified.

Colophon

The animal on the cover of *Linux LPI Certification in a Nutshell* is a bull. Christopher Columbus originally brought cattle to the New World from Spain. Descendants of these animals mated with English cows, and the offspring gradually evolved into the breed we know today.

The cover image is an original illustration created by Lorrie LeJeune. The cover font is Adobe ITC Garamond. The text font is Linotype Birka; the heading font is Adobe Myriad Condensed; and the code font is LucasFont's TheSans Mono Condensed.

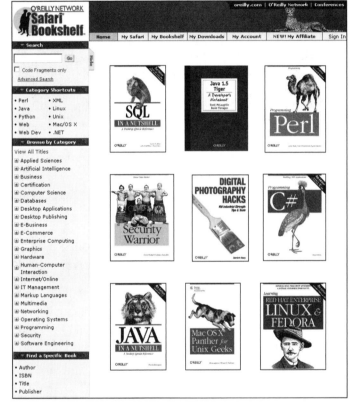

Related Titles from O'Reilly

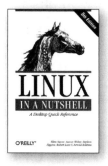

Linux

Building Embedded Linux
Systems

Building Secure Servers
with Linux

The Complete FreeBSD,
4th Edition

Even Grues Get Full

Exploring the JDS Linux
Desktop

Extreme Programming
Pocket Guide

GDB Pocket Reference

Knoppix Hacks

Knoppix Pocket Guide

Learning Red Hat Enterprise
Linux and Fedora,
4th Edition

Linux Annoyances for Geeks

Linux Cookbook

Linux Desktop Hacks

Linux Desktop Pocket Guide

Linux Device Drivers,
3rd Edition

Linux in a Nutshell,
5th Edition

Linux in a Windows World

Linux iptables Pocket
Reference

Linux Multimedia Hacks

Linux Network Administrator's
Guide, *3rd Edition*

Linux Pocket Guide

Linux Security Cookbook

Linux Server Hacks, *Volume 2*

Linux Unwired

Linux Web Server CD
Bookshelf, *Version 2.0*

LPI Linux Certification
in a Nutshell

Managing RAID on Linux

More Linux Server Hacks

OpenOffice.org Writer

Producing Open Source
Software

Programming with Qt,
2nd Edition

Root of all Evil

Running Linux, *5th Edition*

Samba Pocket Reference,
2nd Edition

Test Driving Linux

Understanding Linux
Network Intervals

Understanding the Linux
Kernel, *3rd Edition*

Understanding Open Source
& Free Software Licensing

User Friendly

Using Samba, *2nd Edition*

Version Control with
Subversion

Our books are available at most retail and online bookstores.

To order direct: 1-800-998-9938 • *order@oreilly.com* • *www.oreilly.com*

Online editions of most O'Reilly titles are available by subscription at *safari.oreilly.com*